LONG-LIVED ASSETS (Chapter 9)

Calculation of Annual Depreciation Expense

Straight-line	$\dfrac{\text{Cost} - \text{Residual value}}{\text{Useful life (in years)}}$	
Diminishing-balance	Carrying amount at beginning of year × Straight-line rate	
	Straight-line rate = 1 ÷ Useful life (in years)	
Units-of-production	$\dfrac{\text{Cost} - \text{Residual value}}{\text{Estimated total units of activity}} \times$	Units of activity during year

Notes: 1. If depreciation is calculated for partial periods, the straight-line and diminishing-balance methods must be adjusted for the relevant proportion of the year. Multiply the annual depreciation expense by the number of months expired in the year divided by 12 months.

2. The total depreciation under the diminishing-balance method is limited to cost − residual value.

Disposal of Property, Plant, and Equipment

Step 1	Update the depreciation for the appropriate portion of the year.	Depreciation Expense Accumulated Depreciation
Step 2	Calculate the carrying amount	Cost − Accumulated Depreciation
Step 3	Calculate the gain or loss	Proceeds − Carrying Amount
Step 4	Record the disposal	Cash (or Receivable) Accumulated Depreciation Loss (or credit Gain) Asset account

NOTES PAYABLE (Chapter 10)

Instalment Payment Schedule (assuming monthly payments)

Payments	Interest Period	A Cash Payment		B Interest Expense	C Reduction of Principal	D Principal Balance
Fixed Principal	Month	Variable B+C	D ×	$\dfrac{\text{Annual}}{\text{Interest Rate}} \times \frac{1}{12}$	$\dfrac{\text{Principal*}}{\text{\# of months}}$	D − C
Blended	Month	Fixed B+C	D ×	$\dfrac{\text{Annual}}{\text{Interest Rate}} \times \frac{1}{12}$	A − B	D − C

*From the prior period

BONDS (Chapter 10)

Premium	Market interest rate < Contractual interest rate
Face Value	Market interest rate = Contractual interest rate
Discount	Market interest rate > Contractual interest rate

Amortization of Bond Discount (Premium) Using Effective-Interest Method

Bond interest expense	−	Bond interest paid
Carrying amount of bonds at beginning of period × market interest rate		Face amount of bonds × contractual interest rate

SHAREHOLDER'S EQUITY (Chapter 11)

Comparison of Dividend Effects

	Cash	Share Capital	Retained Earnings	Total Shareholders' Equity	No. of Shares
Cash Dividend	Decrease	No effect	Decrease	Decrease	No effect
Stock Dividend	No effect	Increase	Decrease	No effect	Increase
Stock Split	No effect	No effect	No effect	No effect	Increase

INVESTMENTS (Chapter 12)

Comparison of Long-Term Bond Investment and Liability Journal Entries

Event	Investor	Investee
Purchase / issue of bonds	Bond Investments Cash	Cash Bonds Payable
Interest receipt / payment	Cash Bond Investments Interest Revenue	Interest Expense Bonds Payable Cash

INVESTMENTS (Chapter 12) *continued*

Valuation of Passive Investments

Investment	Valuation	Unrealized Gains/ Losses	Realized Gains/ Losses
Held-for-trading (debt or equity)	Market	Net earnings	Net earnings
Available-for-sale (debt or equity)	Market	Other comprehensive income	Net earnings
Held-to-maturity (debt)	Amortized cost		Net earnings

Comparison of Cost and Equity Methods of Accounting for Strategic Equity Investments

Event	Cost	Equity
Acquisition	Equity Investments Cash	Equity Investments Cash
Investee reports earnings	No entry	Equity Investments Investment Revenue
Investee pays dividends	Cash Dividend Revenue	Cash Equity Investments

CASH FLOW STATEMENT (Chapter 13)

Operating activities (**indirect method**)

Net earnings

Add:	Decreases in noncash current assets	$X
	Increases in noncash current liabilities	X
	Depreciation	X
	Losses on disposals of assets	X
Deduct:	Increases in noncash current assets	(X)
	Decreases in noncash current liabilities	(X)
	Gains on disposals of assets	(X)
Cash provided (used) by operating activities		$X

Operating activities (**direct method**)

Cash receipts

(Examples: from sales of goods and services to customers, from receipts of interest and dividends on loans and investments) $X

Cash payments

(Examples: to suppliers, for operating expenses, for interest, for taxes) (X)

Cash provided (used) by operating activities $X

NAME OF COMPANY Cash Flow Statement Period Ended	
Operating activities	
Note: May be prepared using the direct or indirect method as shown above	
Cash provided (used) by operating activities	$X
Investing activities	
(Examples: purchase/sale of long-term assets)	
Cash provided (used) by investing activities	X
Financing activities	
(Examples: issue/repayment of long-term liabilities, issue of shares, payment of dividends)	
Cash provided (used) by financing activities	X
Net increase (decrease) in cash	X
Cash, beginning of the period	X
Cash, end of the period	$X

IRREGULAR ITEMS (Chapter 14)

Discontinued operations	Statement of earnings (presented separately after earnings from continuing operations)
	Balance sheet (assets [net of liabilities] presented separately as current and/or noncurrent)
Changes in accounting principle	Statement of shareholders' equity (adjustment of beginning retained earnings)

Note: These items are net of income tax.

RATIO ANALYSIS

Liquidity Ratios

Chapter	Ratio	Formula	Purpose
2	Working capital	Current assets – Current liabilities	Measures short-term debt-paying ability
2	Current ratio	$\dfrac{\text{Current assets}}{\text{Current liabilities}}$	Measures short-term debt-paying ability
6	Inventory turnover	$\dfrac{\text{Cost of goods sold}}{\text{Average inventory}}$	Measures liquidity of inventory
6	Days in inventory	$\dfrac{365 \text{ days}}{\text{Inventory turnover}}$	Measures the number of days inventory is on hand
8	Receivables turnover	$\dfrac{\text{Net credit sales}}{\text{Average gross accounts receivable}}$	Measures liquidity of receivables
8	Average collection period	$\dfrac{365 \text{ days}}{\text{Receivables turnover}}$	Measures number of days receivables are outstanding
13	Cash current debt coverage ratio	$\dfrac{\text{Cash provided (used) by operating activities}}{\text{Average current liabilities}}$	Measure short-term debt-paying ability (cash basis)

Solvency Ratios

Chapter	Ratio	Formula	Purpose
2, 10	Debt to total assets	$\dfrac{\text{Total liabilities}}{\text{Total assets}}$	Measures percentage of total assets provided by creditors
2	Free cash flow	Cash provided (used) by operating activities – Net capital expenditures – Dividends paid	Measures cash available from operating activities for discretionary purposes
10	Times interest earned	$\dfrac{\text{Net earnings + Interest expense + Income tax expense (EBIT)}}{\text{Interest expense}}$	Measures ability to meet interest payments
13	Cash total debt coverage	$\dfrac{\text{Cash provided (used) by operating activities}}{\text{Average total liabilities}}$	Measures long-term debt-paying ability (cash basis)

Profitability Ratios

Chapter	Ratio	Formula	Purpose
	Corporate measures:		
5	Gross profit margin	$\dfrac{\text{Gross profit}}{\text{Net sales}}$	Measures margin between selling price and cost of goods sold
5	Profit margin	$\dfrac{\text{Net earnings}}{\text{Net sales}}$	Measures net earnings generated by each dollar of sales
9	Return on assets	$\dfrac{\text{Net earnings}}{\text{Average total assets}}$	Measures overall profitability of assets
9	Asset turnover	$\dfrac{\text{Net sales}}{\text{Average total assets}}$	Measures how efficiently assets are used to generate sales
11	Return on common shareholders' equity	$\dfrac{\text{Net earnings – Preferred dividends}}{\text{Average common shareholders' equity}}$	Measures profitability of shareholders' investment
	Investor measures:		
2, 11	Earnings per share	$\dfrac{\text{Net earnings – Preferred dividends}}{\text{Weighted average number of common shares}}$	Measures net earnings for each common share
2	Price-earnings ratio	$\dfrac{\text{Market price per share}}{\text{Earnings per share}}$	Measures relationship between market price per share and earnings per share
11	Payout ratio	$\dfrac{\text{Cash dividends}}{\text{Net earnings}}$	Measures percentage of earnings distributed as cash dividends
11	Dividend yield	$\dfrac{\text{Dividend per share}}{\text{Market price per share}}$	Measures earnings generated for the shareholder by each share, based on the market price per share

FINANCIAL STATEMENTS

Order of Preparation	Date
1. Statement of earnings	Period ended
2. Statement of comprehensive income	Period ended
3. Statement of shareholders' equity	Period ended
4. Balance sheet	End of the period
5. Cash flow statement	Period ended

Financial Statement Interrelationships

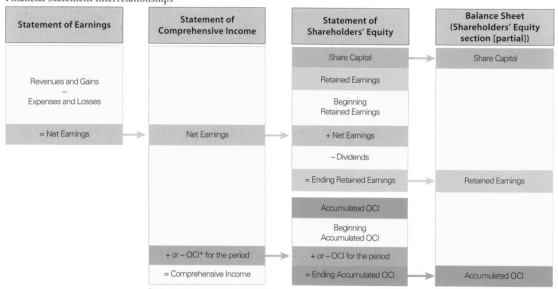

* Other Comprehensive Income (OCI)

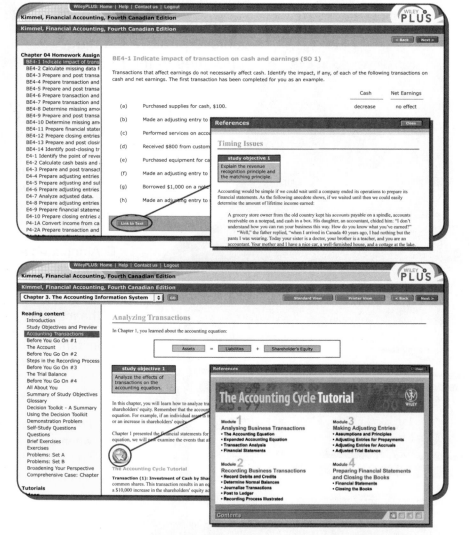

WileyPLUS **combines robust course management tools with the complete online text and all of the interactive teaching and learning resources you and your students need in one easy to use system.**

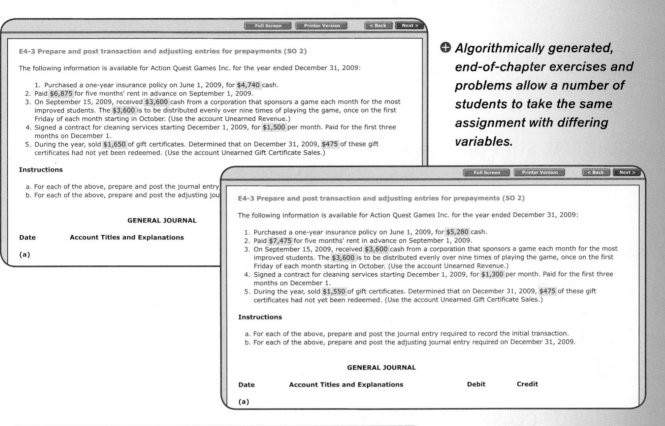

⊕ *Algorithmically generated, end-of-chapter exercises and problems allow a number of students to take the same assignment with differing variables.*

⊕ *Assessment and Homework Management tools help instructors monitor students' progress individually—or by class.*

"WileyPLUS can really help students to get a better grade. The self tests and assignments are very helpful."
— New Brunswick Accounting Student

www.wileyplus.com

Wiley is committed to making your entire *WileyPLUS* experience productive and enjoyable by providing the help, resources, and personal support you and your students need, when you need it. It's all here: *www.wileyplus.com* –

TECHNICAL SUPPORT: www.wileyplus.com/support

⊕ A fully searchable knowledge base of FAQs and help documentation, available 24/7

⊕ Live chat with a trained member of our support staff during business hours

⊕ A form to fill out and submit online to ask any question and get a quick response

FACULTY-LED TRAINING THROUGH THE WILEY FACULTY NETWORK:

Register online: www.wherefacultyconnect.com

Connect with your colleagues in a complimentary virtual seminar, with a personal mentor in your field, or at a live workshop to share best practices for teaching with technology.

1ST DAY OF CLASS...AND BEYOND!

Resources you and your students need to get started & use *WileyPLUS* from the first day forward.

⊕ 2-Minute Tutorials on how to set up and maintain your *WileyPLUS* course

⊕ User guides, links to technical support and training options

⊕ ***WileyPLUS for Dummies:*** Instructors' quick reference guide to using *WileyPLUS*

⊕ Student tutorials and instruction on how to register, buy, and use *WileyPLUS*

⊕ Visit www.wileyplus.com/first day for more information

YOUR *WileyPLUS* ACCOUNT MANAGER:

Contact your *WileyPLUS* Account Manager at www.wileyplus.com/accountmanager.
Students can access the 24-hour chat line for technical support at www.wileyplus.com/support.

SET UP YOUR *WileyPLUS* COURSE IN MINUTES!

Selected *WileyPLUS* courses with QuickStart contain pre-loaded assignments and presentations created by subject matter experts who are also experienced *WileyPLUS* users.

Interested? See and try **WileyPLUS** *in action!*
Details and Demo: ***www.wileyplus.com***

FINANCIAL ACCOUNTING

TOOLS FOR BUSINESS DECISION-MAKING

Fourth Canadian Edition

Paul D. Kimmel PhD, CPA
University of Wisconsin—Milwaukee

Jerry K. Weygandt PhD, CPA
Arthur Andersen Alumni Emeritus Professor of Accounting
University of Wisconsin—Madison

Donald E. Kieso PhD, CPA
KPMG Emeritus Professor of Accountancy
Northern Illinois University

Barbara Trenholm MBA, FCA
University of New Brunswick

John Wiley & Sons Canada, Ltd.

Dedicated to my husband, Brian Trenholm, for his assistance and support throughout the writing of this book.

Library and Archives Canada Cataloguing in Publication

Financial accounting: tools for business decision-making / Paul D. Kimmel ... [et al.]. -- 4th Canadian ed.

Includes index.
Has supplement: Study guide to accompany Financial accounting: tools for business decision-making, fourth Canadian edition.
ISBN 978-0-470-15535-6

1. Accounting--Textbooks. I. Kimmel, Paul D.

HF5635.F44 2009   657'.044   C2008-903803-7

Production Credits

Vice President & Publisher: Veronica Visentin
Acquisitions Editor: Zoë Craig
Editorial Manager: Karen Staudinger
Vice President, Publishing Services: Karen Bryan
Developmental Editor: Daleara Hirjikaka
Editorial Assistant: Tamara Capar
Marketing Manager: Aida Krneta
Design and Typesetting: OrangeSprocket Communications
Cover Design: Ian Koo
Printing and Binding: Worldcolor

Printed and bound in the United States of America
2345 WC 13 12 11 10

WILEY

John Wiley & Sons Canada, Ltd.
6045 Freemont Blvd.
Mississauga, Ontario L5R 4J3

Visit our website at: www.wiley.ca

ABOUT THE AUTHORS

Canadian Edition

Barbara Trenholm, MBA, FCA has taught accounting at the Faculty of Business Administration, University of New Brunswick, and in its international programs, since 1980. Her teaching and educational leadership is renowned. She is a recipient of the National Post/PricewaterhouseCoopers Leaders in Management Education Award, the Global Teaching Excellence Award, and the University of New Brunswick's Merit Award and Dr. Allan P. Stuart Award for Excellence in Teaching. She has been cited as one of the University of New Brunswick's most popular professors in multiple editions of the *Maclean's Guide to Canadian Universities and Colleges*. In 2003, she was named a Teaching Fellow of the University of New Brunswick.

Her experience in accounting education is widely recognized throughout Canada. She has served as chair of the Canadian Institute of Chartered Accountants Academic Research Committee, Interprovincial Education Committee, and Canadian Institute of Chartered Accountants/Canadian Academic Accounting Association Liaison Committee. She has served as a member of the Canadian Institute of Chartered Accountants Qualification Committee, International Qualifications Appraisal Board, and Education Reeingineering Task Force and the American Accounting Association's Globalization Initiatives Task Force. She has chaired and been a member of numerous other education committees at the international, national, and provincial levels of the profession.

Professor Trenholm is a member of the boards of several organizations, including Atomic Energy of Canada Limited and Plazacorp Retail Properties Ltd. She chairs the audit committee of both of these organizations. She is a member of the Institute of Corporate Directors, and a past board member of the Canadian Institute of Chartered Accountants and the Atlantic School of Chartered Accountancy. She is a past president of the New Brunswick Institute of Chartered Accountants and past co-chair of the University of New Brunswick Pension Board of Trustees.

In addition to her involvement with her profession, she has an extensive record of service in leadership roles in the university and the community. She has served as acting dean of the Faculty of Business Administration and as a member of the University Senate, in addition to chairing and serving on many university and faculty committees.

She has a number of presentations to her credit and has published articles in journals including *Accounting Horizons, International Journal of Production Economics, CAmagazine, CGA Magazine,* and *CMA Magazine*. She is also a co-author of Weygandt, Kieso, Kimmel, Trenholm, and Kinnear, *Accounting Principles*, published by John Wiley & Sons Canada, Ltd.

U.S. Edition

Paul D. Kimmel, PhD, CPA, received his bachelor's degree from the University of Minnesota and his doctorate in accounting from the University of Wisconsin. He is an Associate Professor at the University of Wisconsin—Milwaukee, and has public accounting experience with Deloitte & Touche. He was the recipient of the UWM School of Business Advisory Council Teaching Award and the Reggie Taite Excellence in Teaching Award, and is a three-time winner of the Outstanding Teaching Assistant Award at the University of Wisconsin. He is also a recipient of the Elijah Watts Sells Award for Honorary Distinction for his results on the CPA exam.

He is a member of the American Accounting Association and has published articles in *Accounting Review, Accounting Horizons, Advances in Management Accounting, Managerial Finance, Issues in Accounting Education,* and *Journal of Accounting Education*, as well as other journals. His research interests include accounting for financial instruments and innovation in accounting education. He has published papers and given numerous talks on incorporating critical thinking into accounting education, and helped prepare a catalogue of critical thinking resources for the Federated Schools of Accountancy.

Jerry J. Weygandt, PhD, CPA, is the Arthur Andersen Alumni Emeritus Professor of Accounting at the University of Wisconsin—Madison. He holds a PhD in accounting from the University of Illinois. Articles by Professor Weygandt have appeared in *Accounting Review, Journal of Accounting Research, Accounting Horizons, Journal of Accountancy,* and other academic and professional journals. Professor Weygandt is author of other accounting and financial reporting books and is a member of the American Accounting Association, the American Institute of Certified Public Accountants, and the Wisconsin Society of Certified Public Accountants. He has served on numerous committees of the American Accounting Association and as a member of the editorial board of *Accounting Review;*

he also has served as President and Secretary-Treasurer of the American Accounting Association. In addition, he has been actively involved with the American Institute of Certified Public Accountants and has been a member of the Accounting Standards Executive Committee of that organization. He has also served as a trustee of the Financial Accounting Foundation. Professor Weygandt has received the Chancellor's Award for Excellence in Teaching and the Beta Gamma Sigma Dean's Teaching Award. He is on the board of directors of M&I Bank of Southern Wisconsin. He is the recipient of the Wisconsin Institute of CPA's Outstanding Educator's Award and the Lifetime Achievement Award. In 2001 he received the American Accounting Association's Outstanding Accounting Educator Award.

Donald E. Kieso, PhD, CPA, received his bachelor's degree from Aurora University and his doctorate in accounting from the University of Illinois. He has served as chairman of the Department of Accountancy and is currently the KPMG Emeritus Professor of Accounting at Northern Illinois University. He has public accounting experience with Price Waterhouse & Co. and Arthur Andersen & Co. and research experience with the Research Division of the American Institute of Certified Public Accountants. He is a recipient of NIU's Teaching Excellence Award and four Golden Apple Teaching Awards. Professor Kieso is a member of the American Accounting Association, the American Institute of Certified Public Accountants, and the Illinois CPA Society. He has served as a member of the Board of Directors of the Illinois CPA Society, the

AACSB's Accounting Accreditation Committees, the State of Illinois Comptroller's Commission, as Secretary-Treasurer of the Federation of Schools of Accountancy, and as Secretary-Treasurer of the American Accounting Association. Professor Kieso is currently serving on the Board of Trustees and Executive Committee of Aurora University, and is a member of various other boards. From 1989 to 1993, he served as a charter member of the national Accounting Education Change Commission. He is the recipient of the Outstanding Accounting Educator Award from the Illinois CPA Society, the FSA's Joseph A. Silvoso Award of Merit, the NIU Foundation's Humanitarian Award for Service to Higher Education, the Distinguished Service Award from the Illinois CPA Society, and in 2003 an honorary doctorate from Aurora University.

The goal of this text is to introduce students to accounting in a way that demonstrates the importance of accounting to society and the relevance of accounting to their future careers. We strive to teach the students those things that they really need to know and to do it in a way that maximizes their opportunities for successful completion of the course. To accomplish these goals, the foundation of this text relies on a few key beliefs:

"It really matters."

The economic and financial crisis that we are currently facing has heightened awareness of the importance of accounting. Many of our feature stories, *Accounting Matters* boxes, and *Broadening Your Perspective* cases have been designed to reveal accounting's critical role in society. In short, it has never been more evident that accounting really matters!

"Less is more."

Our instructional objective is to provide students with an understanding of those concepts that are fundamental to the use of accounting. Most students will forget procedural details within a short period of time. On the other hand, concepts, if well taught, should be remembered for a lifetime. Concepts are especially important in a world where accounting standards are evolving.

"Don't just sit there— do something."

Students learn best when they are actively engaged. The overriding pedagogical objective of this book is to provide students with opportunities for active learning. One of the best tools for active learning is strategically placed questions. Our discussions are framed by questions and activities, often beginning with rhetorical questions and ending with *Review It* questions and *Do It* exercises. In addition, demonstration problems enable students to practise concepts and techniques covered in the chapter. Technology also offers many opportunities to enhance the learning environment. Through WileyPLUS, students can access a wide array of learning resources to support every learning style. At the book's companion website, wiley.com/canada/kimmel, we offer many opportunities for active learning.

"I'll believe it when I see it."

Students are most willing to commit time and energy to a topic when they believe that it is relevant to their future career. There is no better way to demonstrate relevance than to ground discussion in the real world. We do this in several ways. First, we use well-known companies such as Canadian Tire, iTunes, Loblaw, lululemon, Sears, and Tim Hortons to frame our discussion of accounting issues. Second, the book employs a "macro" approach in its first two chapters, teaching students how to understand and use the real financial statements of Jean Coutu and Shoppers Drug Mart, before teaching how to record transactions. Many students determine their opinion of a course during the initial weeks, and this macro approach clearly demonstrates the relevance of accounting while students are forming their first impression of the course. Finally, our *Accounting Matters* boxes and *All About You* feature specifically connect accounting to business functions such as finance, marketing, and management and show uses of accounting for students both professionally and personally, regardless of whether they are majoring in accounting.

"You need to make a decision."

All businesspeople must make decisions. Decision-making involves critical evaluation and analysis of the information at hand, and this takes practice. We have integrated important analytical tools throughout the book. After each new decision tool is presented, we summarize the key features of that tool in a *Decision Toolkit*. At the end of each chapter, we provide a comprehensive demonstration of an analysis of a real company using the decision tools presented in the chapter. The presentation of these tools throughout the book is cumulative, sequenced to take full advantage of the tools presented in earlier chapters. This sequence of decision tools culminates in a capstone analysis chapter at the end of the book.

"It's a small world."

In today's global economy, few business decisions can be made without consideration of international factors. This is especially true as we transition to International Financial Reporting Standards. To heighten student awareness of international accounting in each chapter, we have provided insight into how Canadian accounting standards have changed, or are expected to change in the near future, as Canadian GAAP converges with international GAAP. In addition, many of our *Accounting Matters* boxes and problems in the end-of-chapter material have an international focus.

Financial Accounting: Tools for Business Decision-Making, 4th Edition, provides many proven pedagogical tools to help students learn accounting concepts and apply them to decision-making in the business world. Here are a few key features.

Learning How to Use the Text

- On the book's companion website, you will find a **Learning Styles Quiz** that will help students identify their learning style. There, you will also find learning strategies and tips for different learning styles, and available resources in WileyPLUS and the textbook that relate to those learning styles.

- **The Navigator** guides students through each chapter by pulling all the learning tools together into a learning system. Throughout the chapter, the Navigator prompts students to use the learning aids and to set priorities as they study.

The Navigator

- Marginal notes in yellow boxes in Chapter 1 explain how to use the text's learning tools to help achieve success in the course.

Understanding the Context

- **Study Objectives**, listed at the beginning of each chapter, reappear in the margins and again in the Summary of Study Objectives.

- The **Accounting Matters! Feature Story** helps students understand how the chapter topic relates to the real world of accounting and business and illustrates the necessity of sound accounting as the basis of informed decisions.

- A chapter **Preview** links the Feature Story to the major topics of the chapter and provides a road map to the chapter.

- An **All About You** feature links some aspect of the chapter topic to a student's personal life, and often to some financial situation they are likely to face now or in the near future.

ALL ABOUT YOU

Your Personal Annual Report

If you have not already done so, in the not too distant future you will prepare a resumé. In some ways your resumé is like a company's annual report. Its purpose is to enable others to evaluate your past, in an effort to predict your future.

A resumé is your opportunity to create a positive first impression. It is important that it be impressive, but it should also be accurate. In order to increase their job prospects, some people are tempted to "inflate" their resumés by overstating the importance of some past accomplishments or positions.

The Association of Executive Recruiting Consultants estimates that approximately one in five resumés contain information that is not accurate. A study conducted by Infocheck, a reference checking firm in Toronto, found that of the 1,000 job applicants on whom they conducted reference checks and education verifications, 27 percent had embellished their educational backgrounds. John Challenger of Challenger Gray & Christmas, an outplacement consulting organization, says only about 15 percent of resumés are ever checked thoroughly.

A recent example of resumé fraud was committed by David Edmondson, the former chief executive officer of RadioShack Corporation. He overstated his accomplishments by claiming that he had earned a bachelor of science degree, when in fact he had not.

Some Facts

- One bad hiring decision can easily cost a minimum of $25,000 in wasted advertising, training, compensation, and revenue for

Learning the Material

- Emphasis on accounting experiences of **real companies** and business situations throughout.

- Four types of **Accounting Matters!** boxes highlight ethics, investor, management, and international perspectives. These stories provide glimpses into how real companies make decisions using accounting information and how individuals in non-accounting functions use accounting information in their decision making.

ACCOUNTING MATTERS! | Management Perspective

There are many challenges involved in taking a physical inventory for certain kinds of businesses. One of the more difficult types of inventory to count is at a salmon farm, where the inventory is swimming around in the ocean.

Salmon farms can be found in Nova Scotia, New Brunswick, and British Columbia, with the salmon kept in net cages in the ocean. An average salmon farm contains between 6 and 14 cages, and each cage contains from 50,000 to 80,000 fish. At Cooke Aquaculture Inc., headquartered in New Brunswick, salmon are initially counted when they are put in cages as smolts, or young salmon, from the hatchery. Every week, divers then go down and count the number of fish at the bottom of the cage that have died. The remainder is the company's best estimate of what is left. Other factors, such as fish escaping or predators getting some of the fish, will reduce these estimates.

After the salmon reach about 10 pounds, they are harvested. The actual number of salmon harvested is compared to the number estimated. The percentage differences are tracked and future estimates are adjusted for expected differences.

International Resources

- In each chapter, we provide insight into how Canadian accounting standards have changed, or may change in the near future, as Canadian standards converge with international accounting standards. The **International Resources** icon refers students to additional information available on the companion website.

- **Colour illustrations**, including **infographics**, create "visual anchors" that help students visualize and apply accounting concepts.

- **Review It!** questions at the end of each study objective prompt students to stop and review the key points they have just studied. One of these questions asks students to use Shoppers Drug Mart's financial statements. Answers to the Shoppers question appear at the end of the chapter.

- **Do It!** exercises appear at key breaks in the chapter narrative. These mini demonstration problems invite students to test their understanding of the just-completed section before they proceed to the next one.

- **Financial statements** appear regularly throughout the book. Those from real companies are usually identified by a logo or have the company name highlighted in red type.

A	=	L	+	SE
−1,000,000		−1,000,000		

⬇ Cash flows: −1,000,000

- **Accounting equation analyses** in the margin next to key journal entries reinforce understanding of the impact of an accounting transaction on the financial statements. They also report the cash effect of each transaction to reinforce understanding of the difference between **cash effects** and **accrual accounting**.

- **Helpful Hints**, **Alternative Terminology**, and blue-highlighted **Key Terms** help focus students on important concepts as they study the material.

- A **web** icon directs students to the companion website, where additional learning resources, such as tutorials, are available.

- **Decision tools** useful for analyzing and solving business problems are presented and then summarized in **Decision Toolkits**.

Putting It Together

At the end of each chapter are several features useful for review and reference.

- A **Summary of Study Objectives** reviews the main points of the chapter.

- The **Decision Toolkit—A Summary** presents in one place the decision tools used throughout the chapter.

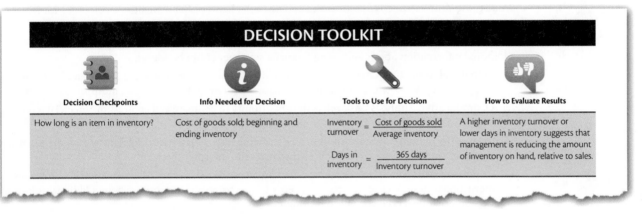

- A **Glossary** of key terms gives definitions with page references to the text. A searchable, comprehensive glossary is also available on the companion website.

- A **Demonstration Problem**, with an **Action Plan**, gives students another opportunity to study a detailed solution to a representative problem before they do homework assignments. Addtional demonstration problems are available on the companion website.

- A **Using the Decision Toolkit** problem asks students to apply the decision tools presented in the chapter to a real company, and takes them through the problem-solving steps.

- **Self-Study Questions** provide a practice test that gives students an opportunity to check their knowledge of important topics. Answers appear on the last page of each chapter. Additional self-assessment quizzes are available on the companion website.

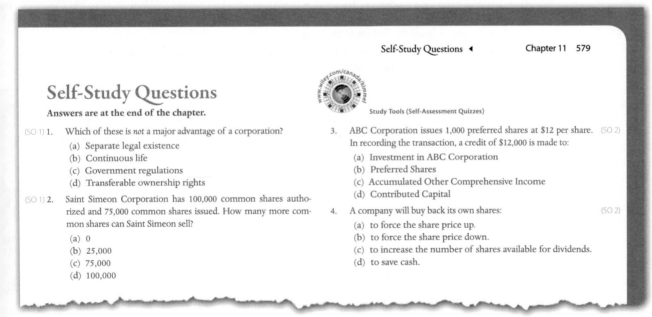

Developing Skills through Practice

Each chapter is supported by a full complement of assignment material:

- Questions, Brief Exercises, Exercises, and two sets of Problems, all keyed to the Study Objectives.
- Some of the assignment material makes use of the decision tools presented in the chapter. These are marked with the icon ⌐━◖. Also, some of this material requires students to practise their written business communications skills. These are marked with the ✐ icon.
- **Broadening Your Perspective** cases at the end of each chapter offer a wealth of resources for instructors who want to broaden the learning experience by bringing in more real-world decision-making, analysis, and critical thinking activities. An Analysis Tools icon directs students to the companion website, where additional information about analyzing financial statements can be found.

Analysis Tools

  o A **Financial Reporting Case** directs students to study various aspects of the 2007 financial statements of Shoppers Drug Mart, which are printed in Chapter 1 (in simplified form) and in Appendix A (in full).

  o A **Comparative Analysis Case** offers the opportunity to compare and contrast the financial reporting of Shoppers Drug Mart with a competitor, Jean Coutu.

  o **Interpreting Financial Statements** cases ask students to read parts of financial statements of actual companies and use the decision tools of the chapter to interpret them.

International Resources

  o A **Global Focus** case focuses on specific situations faced by actual international companies. The International Resources icon directs students to the companion website where additional information about international accounting can be found.

  o **Collaborative Learning Activities** help prepare students for the business world, where they will be working with many people, by giving students practice in solving problems with colleagues. They also allow students to learn from each other.

  o **Communication Activities** provide practice in written communication, a skill much in demand among employers.

Ethics in Accounting

  o **Ethics Cases** ask students to analyze situations, identify the ethical issues involved, and decide on an appropriate course of action. The Ethics in Accounting icon directs students to the companion website, where additional information about ethics can be found.

  o A new **"All About You" Activity** offers students an opportunity to link the accounting concepts learned in the chapter to some aspect of personal finance such as applying for a student loan, protecting themselves from identity theft, and the use of credit cards. These topics provide great opportunities for classroom discussion.

  o A **Serial Case** in every chapter traces the growth of an entrepreneurial venture, Cookie Creations. In each chapter, students apply their newly acquired accounting skills to solve the financial accounting and reporting issues faced by this small business.

- A **Comprehensive Case** (in Chapters 3, 4, 6, 9, 11, and 14) combines material of the current chapter with previous chapters so that students understand how "it all fits together."

Comprehensive Case: Chapter 4

True North Consultants Ltd. commenced operations January 1, 2009. In order to keep on top of its accounting, True North plans to record and adjust its accounts monthly. It incurred the following transactions during January:

Jan.	2	Issued $30,000 of common shares for cash.
	2	Signed a five-year lease for office space.
	31	Reviewed the accounts for any further adjustments. Office equipment will not be depreciated until the year end. The monthly adjustment is immaterial to the financial statements.

Instructions

(a) Record the above transactions.

(b) Prepare T accounts and post the general and adjusting journal entries.

(c) Prepare a trial balance as at January 31.

(d) Prepare the (1) statement of earnings, (2) statement of retained earnings, and (3) balance sheet for the month.

(e) True North closes its books annually. If True North closed its books on a monthly basis, identify which accounts would be closed.

(f) True North needs to maintain a current ratio of 2.5 to 1 in order to maintain its financial standing with its bankers. Calculate the current ratio. Has it achieved the 2.5 to 1 benchmark?

The third edition of *Financial Accounting: Tools for Business Decision-Making* was a tremendous success. Faculty and students alike praised the format and presentation of the material and the use of real-world examples. While we did not want to tamper with the distinguishing features of this text, in the spirit of continuous improvement we did feel some changes would be beneficial after consulting with both users and non-users of this text. Some of the more significant changes include the following:

- After three editions, we have changed our "comparison companies" to Shoppers Drug Mart and Jean Coutu. They were chosen because they have high name recognition with students, they operate in a single industry, and they have relatively simple financial statements. References to these companies have been included throughout the textbook, including simplified financial statements in the chapter material where appropriate, ratio analysis, Review It questions, Using the Decision Toolkit, end-of-chapter assignments, and detailed financial statements in Appendices A and B at the end of the textbook.

- This edition was subject to comprehensive updating to ensure that it continues to be relevant and fresh. Updating involved replacing numerous feature stories, Accounting Matters! boxes, and real-world examples cited in the chapter and end-of-chapter material. Those that were not replaced, were updated as required. Our textbook includes more than 240 references to real-world companies. All of the company information was updated and replaced, as necessary. In addition, more than half of the chapter-opening feature stories were replaced with new stories, two-thirds of the Accounting Matters! boxes are new, all the Review It questions relating to Shoppers Drug Mart are new, and 15 new Do It activities were added. These activities give students an opportunity to stop and actively test their understanding of the material as they read the chapter. In addition, new demonstration problems were added for appendix material where appropriate.

- This edition was thoroughly updated for changes in accounting standards that have occurred, and are expected to occur, as Canada transitions its accounting to International Financial Reporting Standards. We worked hard to find the right balance for an introductory accounting course to inform the students and prepare them for the convergence of Canadian standards with international standards, without overwhelming them with detail. In addition to references in each chapter as appropriate, many of our Accounting Matters! boxes and problems in the end-of-chapter material also have an international focus.

- An exciting new feature, All About You, was added to each chapter to help students better understand the relevance of accounting to them. This feature links some aspect of the chapter topic to a students' personal life, or to a financial situation they are likely to face. In addition, an All About You activity was added to the Broadening Your Perspective section of each chapter, offering students an opportunity to explore further aspects of this topic.

- All of the end-of-chapter material was carefully reviewed. Topical gaps were identified and additional material added as required. In total, 386 new questions, brief exercises, exercises, problems, and cases have been added to the end-of-chapter material. The remaining material was updated and revised, as required.

- In the Broadening Your Perspective section of the end-of-chapter material, we removed the Research and Financial Analysis on the Web cases, which were seldom used by instructors. We added the All About You activity mentioned above to the Broadening Your Perspective section and rewrote all of the collaborative learning activities, to better challenge students to apply their skills while working in groups.

- A new feature, a comprehensive case, was added to Chapters 3, 4, 6, 9, 11, and 14. These cases integrate and build on material from prior chapters to help students understand how topics fit together.

Key Features of Each Chapter

Chapter 1: The Purpose and Use of Financial Statements

- Feature story about Shoppers Drug Mart and how accounting aids decision-making

- Describes why accounting should matter to students, regardless of their planned career path

- Identifies the users and uses of financial accounting information and forms of business organization

- Describes the business activities—financing, investing, and operating activities—that affect companies

- Explains the content, purpose, and interrelationships of each of the financial statements

- Uses financial statements of a hypothetical company (to keep it simple), followed by those for a real company, Shoppers (to make it relevant)

- All About You feature about a student's personal annual report (resumé)

- Using the Decision Toolkit compares Jean Coutu's financial statements to Shoppers'

- *Key changes*: Deleted separate section on ethics, integrating it instead throughout the textbook where appropriate. Expanded explanation of forms of business organizations and clarified financing, investing, and operating activities

Chapter 2: Financial Statements—Framework, Presentation, and Usage

- Feature story about Nortel Networks and the importance of high-quality accounting standards

- Describes the conceptual framework of accounting

- Presents the classified balance sheet

- Applies ratio analysis to Empire and Loblaw's statement of earnings (earnings per share and price-earnings ratio), balance sheet (working capital, current ratio, and debt to total assets), and cash flow statement (free cash flow)

- All About You feature about preparing a personal balance sheet

- Using the Decision Toolkit analyzes Canadian Tire's liquidity, profitability, and solvency

- *Key changes*: Rewrote conceptual framework section to incorporate proposed standard changes. Explained why the conceptual framework is of increasing importance as accounting standards rapidly evolve. Added information about the convergence of Canadian standards with international standards, including how it will affect students

Chapter 3: The Accounting Information System

- Feature story about BeaverTails' experiences with an accounting information system

- Covers transaction analysis—emphasizes fundamentals while avoiding unnecessary detail

- Explains the first three steps in the accounting cycle, from journalizing to posting to preparation of the trial balance

- All About You feature about keeping track of personal documents and records

- Using the Decision Toolkit prepares a trial balance for lululemon athletica, and identifies on which financial statement each account would be presented

- *Key changes*: Changed equation sign format of tabular accounting equation. Added a brief discussion and illustration of the complete accounting cycle. Clarified discussion about naming accounts and added additional end-of-chapter material on this topic

Chapter 4: Accrual Accounting Concepts

- Feature story about the University of Western Ontario's application of accrual accounting

- Explains the revenue recognition and matching principles

- Emphasizes the difference between cash and accrual accounting

- Completes the accounting cycle, from adjusting entries to the closing process

- All About You feature about recording environmental clean-up costs

- Using the Decision Toolkit prepares a balance sheet and closing entries for Highliner Foods

- *Key changes*: Revised revenue recognition guidelines. Added more illustrations of subsequent journal entries, after adjusting entries recorded. Added a brief mention of reversing entries and expanded the discussion of closing entries

Chapter 5: Merchandising Operations

- Feature story about Wal-Mart's inventory control and distribution system

- Introduces merchandising concepts using perpetual inventory system (periodic inventory system presented in an appendix)

- Explains how to record purchases and sales of merchandise

- Presents multiple-step statement of earnings

- Applies ratio analysis to Wal-Mart and Carrefour (gross profit margin and profit margin)

- All About You feature about the cost of sales returns, such as textbooks

- Using the Decision Toolkit compares Wal-Mart and Costco's profitability

- *Key changes*: Expanded discussion of perpetual and periodic inventory systems, including a discussion of how to decide which system to use. Clarified the determination of cost of goods purchased in perpetual inventory system. Added a comparison of journal entries for seller and buyer. Added a demonstration problem for appendix (periodic inventory system)

Chapter 6: Reporting and Analyzing Inventory

- Feature story about Caterpillar's inventory management

- Explains how inventory quantities and ownership is determined

- Covers cost determination methods and their financial statement effects using perpetual inventory system (periodic inventory system presented in an appendix)

- Discusses effects of inventory errors on financial statements

- Outlines how to value and record inventory at the lower of cost and net realizable value

- Applies ratio analysis to Caterpillar and Komatsu (inventory turnover and days in inventory)

- All About You feature about inventory theft and loss prevention techniques

- Using the Decision Toolkit reviews Case New Holland's inventory performance

Key changes: Updated definition of internal control. Deleted discussion of manufacturing inventories. Moved perpetual inventory system to chapter, and periodic inventory system to appendix, to improve consistency with Chapter 5. Deleted LIFO, updated discussion of factors affecting choice of cost formulas, and rewrote section on lower of cost and net realizable value to incorporate new standards. Added a demonstration problem for appendix (periodic inventory system)

Chapter 7: Internal Control and Cash

- Feature story about cash control at the Granite Brewery and Ginger's Tavern
- Covers internal control activities and the limitations of internal control
- Identifies control activities over cash receipts and cash payments
- Discusses bank reconciliations in detail as a control feature
- Explains how cash is reported and managed
- All About You feature about preventing identity theft
- Using the Decision Toolkit reviews internal control issues at a local basketball association
- *Key changes*: Expanded definition of internal control to include primary components, with a focus on control activities. Discussed how cash flows through the banking system, and clarified discussion of EFT, NFS cheques, and errors. Updated bank statement format to reflect current practice at banks. Deleted detailed discussion of cash budgeting

Chapter 8: Reporting and Analyzing Receivables

- Feature story about Canadian Tire's receivables
- Presents the basics of accounts and notes receivable and bad debt estimation
- Discusses statement presentation of receivables
- Identifies various ways to manage receivables, including methods used to accelerate cash receipts
- Applies ratio analysis to Apple (receivables turnover and average collection period)
- All About You feature about credit cards
- Using the Decision Toolkit compares Dell's receivables management and liquidity to Apple's
- *Key changes*: Clarified the difference between calculating interest for short- and long-term notes receivable

Chapter 9: Reporting and Analyzing Long-Lived Assets

- Feature story about VIA Rail
- Covers the acquisition and disposition of property, plant, and equipment and intangible assets

- Reviews buy or lease decisions
- Discusses the implications of alternative depreciation and amortization methods
- Reviews the reporting of long-lived assets
- Applies ratio analysis to VIA Rail and Amtrak (return on assets and asset turnover)
- All About You feature about leasing versus buying a car
- Using the Decision Toolkit reviews and analyzes Research In Motion's long-lived assets
- *Key changes*: Updated all terminology to be consistent with IFRS. Clarified distinction between operating and capital expenditures. Moved calculation details for diminishing-balance and units-of-production depreciation methods from appendix into chapter. Updated discussion of factors affecting choice of depreciation and amortization methods, impairment losses, and disclosure requirements to reflect new standards. Briefly introduced the revaluation model and component depreciation. Expanded discussion of revising depreciation. For intangible assets, removed section on deferred charges and separated discussion of goodwill

Chapter 10: Reporting and Analyzing Liabilities

- Feature story about Plazacorp Retail Properties' liabilities
- Covers current liabilities, including operating lines of credit, notes payable, sales taxes, property taxes, payroll, and current maturities of long-term debt
- Covers long-term liabilities, including notes payable and bonds payable
- Applies effective-interest method of amortization to long-term notes and bonds
- Reviews the reporting of liabilities and discusses other analysis issues, including contingencies and off–balance sheet financing
- Applies ratio analysis to Plazacorp and Crombie REIT (debt to total assets and times interest earned)
- All About You feature about student loans
- Using the Decision Toolkit compares First Capital Realty's liquidity and solvency to Plazacorp's
- *Key changes*: Clarified operating lines of credit and bank indebtedness. Simplified method of recording property taxes. Expanded payroll discussion and added a comparison of accounts and notes payable. Expanded discussion of how to determine short- and long-term portions of a loan. Deleted straight-line method of amortization; moved effective-interest method from appendix to chapter. Netted bond premiums and discounts for recording and reporting purposes. Added present value tables to chapter, as an appendix. Deleted section adjusting debt to total assets ratio for operating lease effects

Chapter 11: Reporting and Analyzing Shareholders' Equity

- Feature story about lululemon athletica

- Discusses corporate form of organization

- Covers issues related to common and preferred shares, including reasons why companies repurchase their own shares

- Explains cash dividends, stock dividends, stock splits, and implications for analysis

- Describes the presentation of equity items in balance sheet, statement of shareholders' equity, and cash flow statement

- Applies ratio analysis to CN Railway (payout ratio and dividend yield) and to lululemon (earnings per share and return on common shareholders' equity)

- All About You feature about investing in shares

- Using the Decision Toolkit compares Limited Brand's dividend record and earnings performance to lululemon's

- *Key changes*: Added a brief discussion about market capitalization, treasury stock, and complex capital structures for earnings per share purposes. Clarified reacquisition of shares and reasons for retained earnings restrictions. Added an explanation of how dividends and stock splits affect an individual investor, as well as a corporation. Added the statement of shareholders' equity

Chapter 12: Reporting and Analyzing Investments

- Feature story about Microsoft's investment in Facebook

- Explains why companies purchase debt and equity securities as passive or strategic investments

- Describes the accounting for, and valuation of, held-for-trading, available-for-sale, and held-to-maturity securities

- Describes the accounting for strategic investments, including cost and equity methods

- Explains how investments are reported on the financial statements, including the statement of earnings, statement of comprehensive income, statement of shareholders' equity, and balance sheet

- Presents consolidation accounting for financial reporting purposes at conceptual level

- All About You feature about investing in debt (Canada Savings Bonds) versus equity securities

- Using the Decision Toolkit reviews the Royal Bank's investment portfolio

- *Key changes*: This chapter was substantially rewritten to incorporate new financial instrument material. In addition, the presentation of investments was expanded and enhanced, including interrelationships among the financial statements. The appendix was updated to integrate the investment changes in this chapter and the change to the effective-interest method of amortization

Chapter 13: Cash Flow Statement

- Feature story about Teck Resources' cash flows

- Explains the purpose and content of the cash flow statement

- Describes the preparation of the operating, investing, and financing activities of the cash flow statement. Splits the operating activities section into two parts, allowing instructor to use either the indirect approach, the direct approach, or both

- Applies ratio analysis to Teck and Freeport-McMoRan (cash current debt coverage and cash total debt coverage)

- All About You feature about where students spend their cash

- Using the Decision Toolkit calculates cash-based ratios and analyzes cash flows for Stantec

- *Key changes*: Updated chapter for proposed changes to cash equivalents. Clarified and summarized typical cash flows from each type of activity. Restructured presentation of operating activities section to include both indirect and direct methods

Chapter 14: Performance Measurement

- Feature story reviews PotashCorp's award-winning annual report

- Discusses sustainable earnings, and implications of discontinued operations and changes in accounting principles

- Demonstrates horizontal and vertical analysis for PotashCorp

- Capstone chapter, summarizing ratio analyses introduced in previous chapters

- Discusses factors that limit financial analysis, including alternative accounting principles, professional judgement, inflation, and diversification

- A comprehensive analysis of PotashCorp, compared to Agrium and their industry, is included in an appendix, to reinforce analytical tools and review how the tools relate to each other

- All About You feature about purchasing shares for dividend income

- Using the Decision Toolkit assesses the liquidity, profitability, and solvency of Goldcorp and Yamana Gold

- *Key changes*: Discontinued operations section updated for changes in standards. Extraordinary items deleted. Quality of earnings section rewritten to reflect broader limitations of financial analysis

ACKNOWLEDGEMENTS

During the course of development of the fourth Canadian edition of *Financial Accounting: Tools for Business Decision-Making*, the author benefited from the feedback from instructors and students of financial accounting across the country, including many users of the previous editions of this text. The constructive suggestions and innovative ideas helped focus this revision on meeting users' needs. In addition, the input and advice of the ancillary authors of the text and supplements provided valuable feedback throughout the development of this edition.

Reviewers

Delano Antoine, *Seneca College*
Jo Axe, *Royal Roads University*
Paul Berry, *Mount Allison University*
Margo Burtch, *Seneca College*
Peggy Coady, *Memorial University*
Judy Cumby, *Memorial University*
Angela Davis, *University of Winnipeg*
Gerry Dupont, *Carleton University*
Esther Deutsch, *Ryerson University*
Laurence Eng, *University of Regina*

Elizabeth Grasby, *University of Western Ontario*
Else Grech, *Ryerson University*
Sharon Halpern, *Seneca College*
Joanne Hinton, *University of New Brunswick*
Ian Hutchinson, *Acadia University*
Marg Johnson, *Thompson Rivers*
Rafik Kurji, *Mount Royal College*
Valorie Leonard, *Laurentian University*

John Love, *Ryerson University*
Rachelle Naherney, *Assiniboine Community College*
Rita MacDonald, *Ryerson University*
Traven Reed, *Canadore College/ Nipissing University*
Rik Smistad, *Mount Royal College*
Amanda Wallace, *Nipissing University*
Bill Waterman, *Mount Allison University*

Textbook Contributors

Sally Anderson, *Mount Royal College*—Broadening Your Perspective case contributor
Alison Arnot—feature story author
Joan Barlow, *Mount Royal College*—End-of-chapter material contributor
Judy Cumby, *Memorial University*—Chapter contributor

Joanne Hinton, *University of New Brunswick*—All About You feature and Broadening Your Perspective case contributor
Valerie Kinnear, *Mount Royal College*—Chapter contributor
Wayne Irvine, *University of Calgary*—Chapter contributor

Shari Mann, *Ryerson University*—End-of-chapter material contributor
Helen Vallee, *Kwantlen Polytechnic University*—Rapid Review contributor
Nancy Zowkewych, *Centennial College*—Broadening Your Perspective and comprehensive case contributor

Supplement Contributors

Ron Baker, *University of Guelph*—Testbank author
Vida Barker, *Centennial College*—WileyPLUS programmer
Peggy Coady, *Memorial University*—PowerPoint slides author
Robert Ducharme, *University of Waterloo*—Solutions Manual accuracy checker and online demonstration problem contributor

Gerry Dupont, *Carleton University*—Study Guide author
Cecile Laurin, *Algonquin College*—Solutions Manual author
Shari Mann, *Ryerson University*—Solutions Manual author
Annie Papazian, *Ryerson University*—Solutions Manual accuracy checker
Eckhard Schumann, *McMaster University*—online quiz contributor

Catherine Seguin, *University of Toronto*—PowerPoint slides author, supplement accuracy checker
Gallia Mina Singer, *McGill University*—WileyPLUS accuracy checker
Rik Smistad, *Mount Royal College*—Solutions Manual accuracy checker
Amanda Wallace, *Nipissing University*—Instructor's Manual author

I appreciate the exemplary support and professional commitment given me by the talented team in the Wiley Canada higher education division, including Karen Bryan, Tamara Capar, Zoë Craig, Deanna Durnford, Andrea Grzybowski, Daleara Hirjikaka, Aida Krneta, Isabelle Moreau, Karen Staudinger, Maureen Talty, Veronica Visentin, and Carolyn Wells, all of whom I worked closely with. I value the strong relationship we have developed over the life of this and prior editions of this, textbook. I also wish to specifically thank Wiley's dedicated sales managers and representatives, who continue to work tirelessly to service your needs.

It takes many people to produce a quality textbook and supplements. I would particularly like to thank Becky Tibble, typesetter; David Schwinghamer, copyeditor; Zofia Laubitz, proofreader; and Nancy Mucklow, indexer, for their assistance and creativity in improving the design and accuracy of this text.

It would not have been possible to write this text without the understanding of my employer, colleagues, students, friends, and family. Together, they provided a creative and supportive environment for my work.

We have tried our best to produce a text and supplement package that is error-free and that meets your specific needs. Suggestions and comments from users are encouraged and appreciated. Please don't hesitate to let us know of any improvements that we should consider for subsequent printings or editions.

Barbara Trenholm
trenholm@unb.ca

BRIEF CONTENTS

CONTENTS

CHAPTER 1
The Purpose and Use of Financial Statements

ACCOUNTING MATTERS!

The **Feature Story** helps you picture how the chapter relates to the real world of accounting and business. You will find references to the story throughout the chapter.

National Growth, Local Focus

In 2007, Shoppers Drug Mart became the first Canadian retailer to reach the 1,000th store mark, staking its claim as Canada's largest retail pharmacy. By 2008, that number was 1,060 and counting, as Shoppers Drug Mart operated stores in prime locations in each province (it's called Pharmaprix in Quebec) and two territories.

The 1,000th store's location in Don Mills, Ontario, is actually near the site of one of the first locations in the chain that was founded more than 40 years ago. The company's beginnings date even further back though, to 1921, when Leon Koffler opened the first two Koffler drugstores in Toronto. Mr. Koffler's son, Murray Koffler, took over the family business in 1941 at the age of 20. In 1962, the younger Koffler changed the way pharmacies operated by introducing the self-serve concept and building a network of 17 drugstores called Shoppers Drug Mart, each owned by a fellow pharmacist, or what he called an "Associate." Mr. Koffler's goal was to build a national network of pharmacies without sacrificing the personal service of a local community pharmacist.

Shoppers' associate concept combines the principles of a franchise arrangement with the benefits of a corporate infrastructure. The company licenses drugstores to individual associates, who are pharmacist-owners, allowing them to operate a retail drugstore at a specific location using the company's trademarks. The idea behind the associate concept is to combine the efforts, motivation, and onsite management skills of an independent businessperson with the larger company's marketing capabilities, purchasing scale, financial stability, and standardized operating policies and procedures. The result is a consistent retail format across Canada, adapted to meet local market needs.

In addition to changing the way pharmacies operated, Mr. Koffler created the Shoppers Life brand in 1962, a brand that still exists today, offering hundreds of health, beauty, baby, cleaning, and convenience products at Shoppers Drug Mart stores across the country. In 1972, the company expanded into Quebec with the first of its Pharmaprix stores, which now number more than 100 in the province. The company introduced the HealthWATCH system to support pharmacy customers in 1991, and the Shoppers Optimum Card reward points program arrived in 2000.

Shoppers Drug Mart completed its initial public offering in November 2001, issuing 30 million common shares at a price of $18 per share. By 2008, these shares were trading in the $50 range.

In addition to the regular and large format stores, the company owns 64 Shoppers Home Health Care stores, making it the largest Canadian retailer of home health-care products and services as well. And, in 2006, the company acquired 100 percent of MediSystem Technologies Inc., a provider of pharmaceutical products and services to long-term care facilities in Ontario and Alberta. "We view the acquisition of MediSystem as a good fit for Shoppers Drug Mart as it allows us to bolster our capacity to provide valuable pharmacy services across the entire continuum of patient care," said Glenn Murphy, Shoppers' chairman and chief executive officer at the time.

From its beginnings as a family retail business, Shoppers Drug Mart has grown steadily and strategically. The path it has taken has involved many decisions. Assessing when and where to open new stores, introducing a new franchising concept and negotiating franchise agreements, preparing for an initial public offering, deciding whether to invest in another company, or simply tracking revenues and expenses all require important financial decisions. Then there are the decisions that executives do not control, such as investors choosing whether or not to purchase Shoppers shares. To make any of these decisions, all parties rely on one key tool—accounting.

Shoppers Drug Mart Corporation: shoppersdrugmart.ca

The **Navigator** is a learning system designed to prompt you to use the learning aids in the chapter and set priorities as you study.

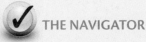

THE NAVIGATOR

☐ Read *Feature Story*

☐ Scan *Study Objectives*

☐ Read *Chapter Preview*

☐ Read text and answer *Before You Go On*

☐ Read *All About You*

☐ Review *Summary of Study Objectives*

☐ Review *Using the Decision Toolkit—A Summary*

☐ Work *Using the Decision Toolkit*

☐ Work *Demonstration Problem*

☐ Answer *Self-Study Questions*

☐ Complete Assignments

STUDY OBJECTIVES

After studying this chapter, you should be able to:

Study Objectives give you a framework for learning the specific concepts that are covered in the chapter.

Identify the users and uses of accounting.

Explain the three main types of business activity.

Describe the content and purpose of each of the financial statements.

The Navigator

PREVIEW OF CHAPTER 1

How do you start a business? How do you make it grow into a widely recognized brand name like Shoppers Drug Mart? How do you determine whether your business is making or losing money? When you need to expand your operations, where do you get money to finance the expansion—should you borrow, issue shares, or use company funds? How do you convince lenders to lend you money or investors to buy your shares? To be successful in business, countless decisions have to be made—and decisions require financial information.

The purpose of this chapter is to show you accounting's role in providing useful financial information for decision-making. The chapter is organized as follows:

THE PURPOSE AND USE OF FINANCIAL STATEMENTS

Accounting Matters!	Business Activities	Communicating with Users
▶ Users and uses of accounting ▶ Forms of business organization	▶ Financing activities ▶ Investing activities ▶ Operating activities	▶ Sierra's financial statements ▶ Shoppers Drug Mart's financial statements ▶ Elements of an annual report

The Navigator

Accounting Matters!

Accounting is the information system that identifies and records the economic events of an organization, and then communicates them to a wide variety of interested users. Why does accounting matter to these users? The world's economic systems depend on highly transparent, reliable, and accurate financial reporting. Accounting has long been labelled "the language of business." That's one of the reasons why accounting has consistently ranked as one of the top career opportunities in business.

It is also one of the reasons that so many people who do not plan on becoming accountants study accounting. For example, Wilfrid Wilkinson, President of Rotary International; Brian Cummings, a pathologist at the Grand River Hospital; Paul Massicotte, a senator and owner of Attractions Hippiques Québec Inc.; George Melville, chairman of Boston Pizza International; Paul Sobey, president and CEO of Empire Company Limited; and Barbara Stymiest, Chief Operating Officer of the Royal Bank of Canada, all have backgrounds in accounting.

Marketing offers a good example of how having an understanding of the basics of accounting can be helpful in a field that might otherwise seem unrelated to accounting. If you plan on working in marketing, you will learn the importance of being able to determine not only whether or not a sale is profitable but also whether it can eventually be collected from a customer. Marketing managers must also be able to decide on pricing strategies based on costs. Accounting is what quantifies these costs and explains why a product or service costs what it does.

On the companion website to this text, there is additional information about the potential career opportunities that are available to accountants. There are also profiles of businesspeople who use accounting information, to help you understand that, whether you plan to become an accountant or not, a working knowledge of accounting will be relevant and useful in whatever role you assume as a user of accounting information.

Users and Uses of Accounting

Users of accounting information can be divided broadly into two types: internal users and external users.

Internal Users

Internal users of accounting information plan, organize, and run companies. They work for the company. These include finance directors, marketing managers, human resource personnel, production supervisors, and company officers. In running a business, internal users must answer many important questions, as shown in Illustration 1-1.

Finance
Is there enough cash to pay the bills?

Marketing
What price should we sell iPods
for to maximize profits?

Human Resources
How many employees can we
afford to hire this year?

Production
Which product line is the most profitable?

To answer these and other questions, users need detailed accounting information on a timely basis—that is, it must be available when it is needed. For internal users, accounting provides internal reports: for example, financial comparisons of operating alternatives, projections of earnings from new sales campaigns, forecasts of cash needs for the next year, analyses of sales costs, and budgeted financial statements.

External Users

There are several types of external users of accounting information. Investors use accounting information to make decisions to buy, hold, or sell their ownership interest. Creditors, such as suppliers and bankers, use accounting information to evaluate the risks of granting credit or lending money. **Investors and creditors are the main external users of accounting information**, but there are also many other external users with a large variety of information needs and questions.

For example, labour unions want to know whether the company can pay increased wages and benefits. Customers are interested in whether a company will support its product lines and honour product warranties. Taxing authorities, such as the Canada Revenue Agency, want to know whether the company respects the tax laws. Regulatory agencies, such as provincial securities commissions, want to know whether the company is operating within prescribed rules. Finally, economic planners use accounting information to analyze and forecast economic activity.

Some questions that external users may ask about a company are shown in Illustration 1-2.

Investors
Is the company earning enough to
give me a return on my investment?

Creditors
Will the company be able to pay
its debts as they come due?

Labour Unions
Can the company afford the pay
raise we are asking for?

Customers
Will the company stay in business
long enough to service the
products I buy from it?

Ethics in Accounting

Ethical Behaviour

In order for financial information to have value to its users, whether internal or external, it must be prepared by individuals with high standards of ethical behaviour. Ethics in accounting is of the utmost importance to accountants and decision-makers who rely on the financial information they produce.

Fortunately, most individuals in business are ethical. Their actions are both legal and responsible. They consider the organization's interests when they make decisions. Accountants and other professionals have extensive rules of conduct to guide their behaviour with each other and the public. In addition, many companies today have codes of conduct that outline their commitment to ethical behaviour in their internal and external relationships.

Throughout this textbook, ethical considerations will be presented to highlight the importance of ethics in financial reporting.

⚖ ACCOUNTING MATTERS! | Ethics Perspective

In the early 2000s, the world was shocked to learn about corporate reporting scandals in big companies like Nortel Networks and Hollinger International in Canada, Enron and WorldCom in the U.S., and Parmalat in Italy. Many schemes were uncovered that falsely increased earnings or hid a company's true financial position. As a result, there were financial restatements, company restructurings and closures, lawsuits, fines, and criminal convictions. People in general started to lose confidence in financial reporting.

Because of the importance of the financial reporting system to the economy, regulators and lawmakers made a number of changes to help investors regain confidence in corporate reporting. Today, business behaviour in general, and accounting in particular, are guided by improved business practices, corporate governance, public oversight, and accountability requirements. More than ever, sound ethical behaviour is essential for these measures to be effective.

The **Accounting Matters! Perspectives** give examples of accounting situations from four different points of view—ethics, management, investor, and international.

Forms of Business Organization

If you were to decide to open your own company, one of your first decisions would be about the organizational form that your business should take. There are three forms of business organization—proprietorship, partnership, or corporation. A business owned by one person is a **proprietorship**. A business owned by more than one person is a **partnership**. A business organized as a separate legal entity owned by shareholders is a **corporation**.

Proprietorships

The proprietorship form of business organization is simple to set up and gives you control over the business. A proprietorship is usually operated by the owner.

In most cases, only a relatively small amount of money (capital) is needed to start in business as a proprietorship. The owner (the proprietor) receives any profits, suffers any losses, and is personally liable (responsible) for all debts of the business. There is no legal distinction between the business as an economic unit and the owner.

Small service businesses such as hair salons, plumbers, and mechanics are often proprietorships, as are farms and small retail stores.

Partnerships

Another possibility would be for you to join forces with other individuals to form a partnership. In most respects, a partnership is similar to a proprietorship except that there is more than one owner. Partnerships are often formed because one person does not have enough economic resources to initiate or expand the business, or because partners bring unique skills or resources to the partnership.

Although there are advantages to working with others, there are also disadvantages. Each partner generally has unlimited liability for all debts of the partnership, even if one of the other partners created the debt. This means that any of the partners can be forced to give up his or her personal assets in order to repay the partnership debt, just as can happen to an owner in a proprietorship. There are situations, however, where partnerships can be formed with limited liability for selected partners.

Partnerships are typically used to organize retail and service businesses, including the professional practices of lawyers, doctors, architects, engineers, and accountants.

Corporations

As a third alternative, you might organize as a corporation. As an investor in a corporation, you receive shares to indicate your ownership claim. Individuals can become owners of shares (shareholders) by investing relatively small amounts of money. This advantage makes it is easier for corporations to raise funds.

Buying shares in a corporation, especially a large corporation, is often more attractive than investing in a proprietorship or partnership because shares are easy to sell. Selling a proprietorship or partnership interest is much more complicated.

Successful corporations like Shoppers Drug Mart often have thousands of shareholders, and their shares are traded on organized stock exchanges, such as the Toronto Stock Exchange which is part of the TMX Group in Canada.

Many businesses start as proprietorships or partnerships and eventually incorporate. As the feature story pointed out, Shoppers Drug Mart began in 1921 with two small operator-owned pharmacies in Toronto, called Koffler Drug Stores. By 1962, the company had grown to 17 pharmacies and was renamed Shoppers Drug Mart. It subsequently became a private corporation and in 2001 became a publicly traded corporation.

There are other factors that need to be considered when deciding which organizational form to choose. These include legal liability and income taxes. If you choose a proprietorship or partnership, you are personally liable for all debts of the business, whereas corporate shareholders are not. Shareholders enjoy limited liability since they only risk losing the amount that they have invested in the company's shares. Proprietors and partners pay personal income tax on their respective share of the profits, while corporations pay income taxes as separate legal entities on any corporate profits. Corporations may also receive a more favourable tax treatment than other forms of business organization. We will discuss these issues in more depth in a later chapter.

Although the combined number of proprietorships and partnerships in Canada is more than the number of corporations, the revenue produced by corporations is far greater. Most of the largest companies in Canada—for example, Barrick Gold, Encana, General Motors of Canada, Loblaw, Magna International, Research In Motion, and the Royal Bank of Canada—are corporations. Recently, more than 50 of Canada's largest corporations each reported annual revenues of more than $7.5 billion.

Corporations such as these are publicly traded. That is, their shares are listed on Canadian stock exchanges. **Public corporations** commonly distribute their financial statements to shareholders, creditors, other interested parties, and the general public upon request. Shoppers Drug Mart is a public corporation. You can access its financial statements on its website, which is given in our feature story, as well as in Appendix A at the back of this textbook.

In addition to public corporations like Shoppers Drug Mart, there are **private corporations**. Private corporations do not issue publicly traded shares. Some of the largest private companies in Canada include Sobeys, The Jim Pattison Group, the Irving Group of Companies, and McCain Foods. Like proprietorships and partnerships, these companies almost never distribute their financial statements publicly.

Because most Canadian business is transacted by corporations, this book focuses mainly on the corporate form of organization.

BEFORE YOU GO ON...

Review It

1. Why does accounting matter to both accountants and non-accountants?
2. How can the study of accounting benefit you?
3. What are the two main types of users of accounting information? Give examples of each.
4. Why is ethics important to internal and external users?
5. What are the three forms of business organization and the advantages of each?

> **Alternative terminology** notes give synonyms that you may hear or see in the workplace.

> **Alternative Terminology**
> *Shares* are also known as *stock*.

> **Helpful hints** help clarify concepts or items that are being discussed.

> **Helpful Hint** You can usually tell if a company is a corporation by looking at its name. The words *Limited (Ltd.)*, *Incorporated (Inc.)*, or *Corporation (Corp.)* normally follow its name.

> **Review It questions** at the end of major text sections tell you to stop and review the key points you have just studied. Sometimes Review It questions appear alone; other times they are accompanied by practice exercises called Do It.

The Navigator

Business Activities

study objective 2

Explain the three main types of business activity.

All businesses are involved in three types of activity—financing, investing, and operating. For example, Shoppers Drug Mart needed financing in 2006 to expand its operations, so it borrowed money from outside sources. The cash obtained was then used to purchase MediSystem Technologies, an innovative pharmaceutical company based in Ontario and Alberta. This helped Shoppers increase its operating activities of providing pharmaceutical goods and services. Let's now look at these three types of business activity in more detail.

Financing Activities

It takes money to make money. The two primary ways of raising outside funds for corporations are (1) borrowing money and (2) issuing (selling) shares in exchange for cash.

Shoppers Drug Mart may borrow money in a variety of ways. For example, it can take out a loan at a bank or borrow money from other lenders. The persons or companies that Shoppers owes money to are its creditors, some of the primary users of accounting information. Amounts owed to creditors—in the form of debt and other obligations—are called liabilities.

Specific names are given to different types of liabilities, depending on their source. For instance, Shoppers Drug Mart may have taken funds from an operating line of credit with its bank, which results in **bank indebtedness**. It may have a short-term **note payable** to a bank for the money borrowed to purchase racks and display cabinets, for example. Shoppers may also have **long-term debt**, which can include **notes payable**, **mortgages payable**, **lease obligations**, and other types of debt securities borrowed for longer periods of time.

A corporation may also obtain financing by selling shares of ownership, or share capital, to investors. Shoppers Drug Mart first issued common shares in 2001, when it became a publicly traded corporation. **Common shares** is the term used to describe the amount paid by investors for shares of ownership in a company. Common shares are just one class or type of share capital that a company can issue.

Companies can also use cash for financing activities, such as repaying debt or repurchasing shares from investors. The claims of creditors differ from those of shareholders. If you loan money to a company, you are one of its creditors. In loaning money, you specify a repayment schedule—for example, payment at the end of each month. In addition, interest is normally added to the amount due or overdue. As a creditor, you have a legal right to be paid at the agreed time. In the event of nonpayment, you may force the company to sell its property to pay its debts. The law requires that creditor claims be paid before shareholder claims.

Shareholders have no claim to corporate resources until the claims of creditors are satisfied. If you buy a company's shares instead of loaning it money, you have no legal right to expect any payments until all of its creditors are paid. Also, once shares are issued, the company has no obligation to buy them back, whereas debt obligations must be repaid.

Many companies pay shareholders a return on their investment on a regular basis, as long as there is enough cash to cover required payments to creditors. Payments to shareholders are called dividends. Shoppers Drug Mart paid a dividend of $0.60 per share to its shareholders in 2007.

Investing Activities

After a company raises money through financing activities, it then uses that money for investing activities. Investing activities involve the purchase (or sale) of the long-lived resources—called assets—that a company needs in order to operate. Assets are resources that a company owns. Every asset is capable of providing future services or benefits that can be short- or long-lived. Investing activities generally involve long-lived assets. For example, restaurant equipment, computers, vehicles, buildings, and land are all examples of long-lived assets that result from investing activities. Together, they are referred to as **property, plant, and equipment** or "property and equipment," as Shoppers Drug Mart calls this asset category.

Cash is one of the more important assets owned by Shoppers Drug Mart, or any other business. While cash can be used for, or result from, an investing activity, it is not itself an investing activity. For example, if a company has excess cash that it does not need for a while, it might choose to invest it in debt or equity securities of other corporations or organizations. **Investments** are another example of an asset and an investing activity. Investments can be either short- or long-term.

Operating Activities

Most of a company's long-lived assets are purchased through investing activities, as described above. Other assets with shorter lives, however, generally result from operating activities—transactions which create revenues and expenses. For example, Shoppers Drug Mart sells prescription and non-prescription drugs, as well as health and beauty aids and household products. We call the amounts earned from the sale of these goods **revenues**. In accounting language, revenues are increases in economic resources—normally an increase in an asset but sometimes a decrease in a liability—that result from a business' operating activities.

Revenues come from different sources and are identified by various names, depending on the nature of the business. For instance, Shoppers Drug Mart's main source of revenue is the money it earns from the sales of prescription and other products to consumers. However, it may also earn interest revenue on excess cash held as investments. Sources of revenue that are common to many businesses are **sales revenue**, **service revenue**, and **interest revenue**.

When Shoppers Drug Mart sells prescription drugs to a customer who has a drug plan, such as Blue Cross, it does not immediately receive all of the cash for the sale. Instead, it must send a bill to Blue Cross for the amount covered by the drug plan and then wait for Blue Cross to pay Shoppers the amount owed, which Blue Cross will do sometime in the near future. This right to receive money in the future is called an **account receivable**. Accounts receivable are assets because they will result in a future benefit—cash—when the amounts owed are eventually collected. Companies also have other types of receivables, such as income tax receivable (also known as "future income tax assets") that is due from the government.

Before Shoppers Drug Mart can sell products to its customers, it must first buy prescription drugs, health-care aids, cosmetics, household items, and other goods. Items such as these that are held for future sale to customers result in an asset called **inventory** or **merchandise inventory**. Once the goods are sold, they are called expenses. More specifically, the cost of the merchandise inventory sold is an expense called **cost of goods sold**. In accounting language, **expenses** are the cost of assets that are consumed or services that are used in the process of generating revenues.

There are many kinds of expenses and they are identified by various names, depending on the type of asset consumed or service used. For example, Shoppers Drug Mart keeps track of these types of expenses: **cost of goods sold, operating expenses** (such as salaries, advertising, utilities, professional fees, rent, and other costs associated with running the business), **depreciation expense** (i.e., allocation of the cost of using property and equipment), **interest expense** (amounts of interest paid on various debts), and **income taxes** (corporate taxes paid to the government).

Alternative Terminology
Depreciation expense is also called *amortization expense*.

Shoppers Drug Mart may also have short-term liabilities that come from these expenses. This occurs, for example, when Shoppers purchases drugs on credit from pharmaceutical companies in making the goods available for sale to its customers. The obligations that Shoppers has to pay for these goods are called **accounts payable**. Shoppers also has **bank indebtedness**, created by amounts owed to the bank on an operating line of credit or demand loan. It may also have **interest payable** on the outstanding (unpaid) amounts owed to various lenders, **dividends payable** to shareholders, **salaries payable** to employees, **provincial sales taxes** and **property taxes payable** to the provincial government, and **goods and services taxes payable** to the federal government. **Income tax payable** (also known as "future income tax liabilities") is an example of another liability that is payable to the government.

To determine whether it earned a profit, Shoppers Drug Mart compares the revenues of a period with the expenses of that same period. When revenues are more than expenses, **net earnings** result. When expenses exceed revenues, a **net loss** results.

Alternative Terminology
Net earnings are also commonly known as *net income*.

To summarize, there are three types of business activities that companies engage in: (1) financing, (2) investing, and (3) operating, as shown in Illustration 1-3.

Financing Activities

Investing Activities

Operating Activities

◀ Illustration 1-3

Business activities

1. **Financing activities** include borrowing cash from lenders by issuing debt, or conversely, using cash to repay debt. Cash can also be raised from shareholders by issuing shares, or paid to shareholders by distributing dividends.
2. **Investing activities** include purchasing and disposing of long-lived assets such as property, plant, and equipment and short- or long-term investments.
3. **Operating activities** result from day-to-day operations and include revenues and expenses and related accounts such as receivables, inventory, and payables.

BEFORE YOU GO ON...

➡ **Review It**
1. What are the three types of business activities? Give an example of each.
2. What are assets, liabilities, share capital, dividends, revenues, and expenses?

➡ **Do It**
Classify each of the following items, first as a financing, investing, or operating activity, and then as an asset, liability, share capital, dividend, revenue, or expense:
   (a) An amount paid to an employee for work performed
   (b) An amount earned from providing a service
   (c) An issue of common shares
   (d) A truck that is purchased
   (e) An amount owed to a bank
   (f) Excess cash invested in a long-term investment

Action Plan
• Distinguish between financing, investing, and operating activities.
• Understand the distinction between assets, liabilities, share capital, dividends, revenues, and expenses.
• Classify each item based on its economic characteristics.

Solution
   (a) Operating activity; expense (salary expense)
   (b) Operating activity; revenue (service revenue)
   (c) Financing activity; share capital (common shares)
   (d) Investing activity; asset (truck—property, plant, and equipment)
   (e) Financing activity; liability (bank loan payable)
   (f) Investing activity; asset (investment)

The Navigator

Communicating with Users

study objective 3

Describe the content and purpose of each of the financial statements.

You will recall that we learned about internal and external users of accounting information earlier in this chapter. Users, especially external users, are interested in a company's assets, liabilities, shareholders' equity, revenues, and expenses. For external reporting purposes, it is customary to arrange this information in four different financial statements that are the backbone of financial reporting:

1. **Statement of earnings**: A statement of earnings reports revenues and expenses to show how successfully a company performed during a period of time.
2. **Statement of retained earnings**: A statement of retained earnings indicates the portion of a company's earnings that was distributed to you and the other shareholders of a company in the form of dividends, and how much was retained in the business to allow for future growth.
3. **Balance sheet**: A balance sheet presents a picture of what a company owns (its assets), what it owes (its liabilities), and its net worth (its shareholders' equity) at a specific point in time.
4. **Cash flow statement**: A cash flow statement shows where a company obtained cash during a period of time and how that cash was used.

Additional information is reported in **notes to the financial statements** that are cross-referenced to the four statements.

While the above four financial statements are the most commonly provided statements, there are other financial statements such as the statement of shareholders' equity. The statement of shareholders' equity explains the changes in *all* of the equity components, not just retained earnings. In addition, a statement of comprehensive income must be prepared when a company reports other comprehensive income from certain kinds of gains and losses. We will wait until Chapter 11 to discuss these statements.

Sierra's Financial Statements

We will now look at the financial statements of a fictitious marketing agency called Sierra Corporation to introduce you to the four primary financial statements—the statement of earnings, statement of retained earnings, balance sheet, and cash flow statement.

Statement of Earnings

The **statement of earnings** reports the success or failure of the company's operations for a period of time—annually, quarterly, or monthly. In our example, Sierra Corporation has been in operation for only the current month, the month ended October 31, 2009. To indicate that Sierra's statement of earnings reports the results of operations for a period of one month, its statement is dated "Month Ended October 31, 2009."

The statement of earnings lists the company's revenues first and then its expenses. Expenses are deducted from revenues to determine earnings before income tax. Income tax expense is usually shown separately, immediately following the earnings before income tax line. Finally, the net earnings (or net loss) are determined by deducting the income tax expense.

Why are financial statement users interested in net earnings? Investors are interested in a company's past earnings because these numbers provide information that suggests future earnings. Investors buy and sell shares based on their beliefs about the future performance of a company. If you believe that Sierra will be even more successful in the future, and that this success will translate into a higher share price, you should buy Sierra's shares.

Like investors, creditors also use the statement of earnings to predict the future. When a bank loans money to a company, it does this because it believes it will be repaid in the future. If it thought it was not going to be repaid, it would not loan the money. Thus, before making the loan, the bank's loan officer must try to predict whether the company will be profitable enough to repay it.

Note that the **issue of shares and distribution of dividends do not affect net earnings**. For example, if Sierra Corporation received $10,000 of cash from issuing new shares, this would not be reported as revenue in the statement of earnings. Rather, this transaction would increase cash and common shares in the balance sheet. If dividends of $500 were paid, it would not be regarded as a business expense, because it was not incurred to generate revenue. Instead, dividends are reported as a reduction of retained earnings in the statement of retained earnings.

A sample statement of earnings for Sierra Corporation is shown in Illustration 1-4.

◀ Illustration 1-4

Statement of earnings

SIERRA CORPORATION Statement of Earnings Month Ended October 31, 2009		
Revenues		
Service revenue		$10,600
Expenses		
Salaries expense	$6,800	
Supplies expense	1,500	
Rent expense	900	
Depreciation expense	83	
Insurance expense	50	
Interest expense	25	
Total expenses		9,358
Earnings before income tax		1,242
Income tax expense		250
Net earnings		$ 992

Every chapter presents useful information about how decision-makers use financial statements. **Decision Toolkits** summarize discussions of key decision-making contexts and techniques.

Note that cents are not included in the dollar figures recorded in financial statements, as illustrated here for Sierra Corporation. It is important to understand, however, that cents should be and are used in recording transactions in a company's internal accounting records. It is only for financial reporting purposes that financial statement amounts are normally rounded to the nearest dollar, thousand dollars, or million dollars, depending on the size of the company. External reporting condenses and simplifies information so that it is easier for the reader to understand.

It also really does not matter whether the data in the statements are listed in two columns, as they are for Sierra Corporation, or in one column. Companies use a variety of presentation formats, depending on their preference and what they think is easiest for the reader to understand.

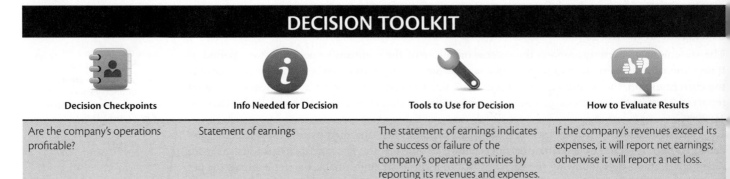

DECISION TOOLKIT

Decision Checkpoints	Info Needed for Decision	Tools to Use for Decision	How to Evaluate Results
Are the company's operations profitable?	Statement of earnings	The statement of earnings indicates the success or failure of the company's operating activities by reporting its revenues and expenses.	If the company's revenues exceed its expenses, it will report net earnings; otherwise it will report a net loss.

Statement of Retained Earnings

If Sierra is profitable, at the end of each period it must decide what portion of its earnings to pay to shareholders through dividends. In theory, it could pay all of its current period earnings, but few companies choose to do this. Why? Because they want to retain part of the earnings, or profits, in the business so that the company can expand when it chooses to. **Retained earnings** are the cumulative earnings that have been retained in the corporation. In other words, they are the earnings that have not been paid out to shareholders and have accumulated since the company's date of incorporation.

The **statement of retained earnings** shows the amounts and causes of changes in retained earnings during the period. The time period is the same as for the statement of earnings—for the year, quarter, or month. The beginning retained earnings amount is shown on the first line of the statement. Then net earnings are added and dividends (if any) are deducted to calculate the retained earnings at the end of the period. If a company has a net loss, it is deducted (rather than added) in the statement of retained earnings.

By monitoring the statement of retained earnings, financial statement users can evaluate dividend payment practices. Some investors look for companies that pay high dividends. For example, banks and such companies as Manitoba Telecom and Rothmans pay a high dividend rate. Other investors seek companies that pay no dividends and instead reinvest earnings to increase the company's growth. Examples of such companies are Indigo Books & Music, Research In Motion, and WestJet Airlines, which do not normally pay a dividend.

Illustration 1-5 presents Sierra Corporation's statement of retained earnings.

Illustration 1-5 ➡

Statement of retained earnings

SIERRA CORPORATION Statement of Retained Earnings Month Ended October 31, 2009	
Retained earnings, October 1	$ 0
Add: Net earnings	992
	992
Less: Dividends	500
Retained earnings, October 31	$492

In Chapter 11, we will learn about the statement of shareholders' equity, in which the statement of retained earnings is often included.

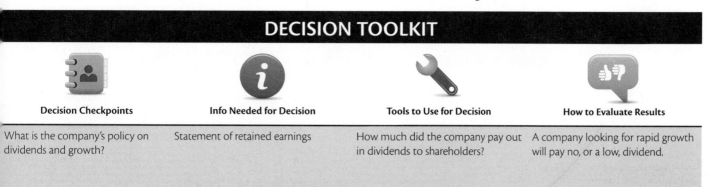

DECISION TOOLKIT

Decision Checkpoints	Info Needed for Decision	Tools to Use for Decision	How to Evaluate Results
What is the company's policy on dividends and growth?	Statement of retained earnings	How much did the company pay out in dividends to shareholders?	A company looking for rapid growth will pay no, or a low, dividend.

Balance Sheet

The **balance sheet** reports assets and claims to those assets at a specific point in time. These claims are subdivided into two categories: claims of creditors and claims of shareholders. As noted earlier, claims of creditors are called liabilities. Claims of shareholders, the owners of the company, are called **shareholders' equity**. This relationship is shown in Illustration 1-6 in a form that is known as the basic **accounting equation**.

This relationship is where the name *balance sheet* comes from. Assets must be in balance with the claims to the assets. The right-hand side of the equation—the liabilities and equity—also shows how the assets have been financed (through borrowing from creditors, investing by shareholders, or self-financing through earnings retained in the company).

As you can see from looking at Sierra's balance sheet in Illustration 1-7 on the following page, assets are listed first, followed by liabilities and shareholders' equity. Sierra's assets total $21,867 and include cash, accounts receivable, advertising supplies, prepaid insurance (insurance paid in advance but not yet used), and office equipment. Of these assets, only office equipment would be presented as an investing activity in the cash flow statement, as we will see in the next section. The other items (except for cash) are examples of assets that come from operating activities.

Sierra's liabilities total $11,375 and consist of notes payable, accounts payable, interest payable, unearned revenue (cash received in advance for which the service has not yet been provided and is therefore still owed), salaries payable, and income tax payable. Of these liabilities, only the notes payable is an example of a financing activity. The other items are examples of liabilities coming from operating activities.

Shareholders' equity consists of two parts: (1) share capital and (2) retained earnings. Share capital represents the shareholders' investments and includes all the classes of shares that a company has issued. If only one class of shares is issued, it is always common shares. We will learn about another class of shares, called preferred shares, in Chapter 11. Retained earnings are the cumulative net earnings retained in the corporation. Sierra has common shares of $10,000 and retained earnings of $492, for total shareholders' equity of $10,492.

Creditors analyze a company's balance sheet to determine the likelihood that they will be repaid. They carefully evaluate the nature of the company's assets and liabilities. For example, does the company have assets that could easily be sold, if required, to repay its debts? Do the company's assets exceed its liabilities in both the short and long terms?

Managers use the balance sheet to determine whether inventory is adequate to support future sales and whether cash on hand is sufficient for immediate cash needs. Managers also look at the relationship between total liabilities and shareholders' equity to determine whether they have the best proportion of debt and equity financing.

Alternative Terminology
The *balance sheet* is also commonly known as the *statement of financial position*.

◀ Illustration 1-6

Basic accounting equation

Illustration 1-7 ➡

Balance sheet

SIERRA CORPORATION Balance Sheet October 31, 2009	
Assets	
Cash	$15,200
Accounts receivable	200
Advertising supplies	1,000
Prepaid insurance	550
Office equipment	4,917
Total assets	$21,867
Liabilities and Shareholders' Equity	
Liabilities	
Notes payable	$ 5,000
Accounts payable	2,500
Interest payable	25
Unearned revenue	800
Salaries payable	2,800
Income tax payable	250
Total liabilities	11,375
Shareholders' equity	
Common shares	10,000
Retained earnings	492
Total shareholders' equity	10,492
Total liabilities and shareholders' equity	$21,867

Helpful Hint The balance sheet is dated at a *specific point in time*. The statement of earnings, statement of retained earnings, and cash flow statement cover a *period of time*.

DECISION TOOLKIT

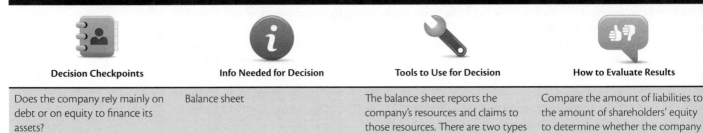

Decision Checkpoints	Info Needed for Decision	Tools to Use for Decision	How to Evaluate Results
Does the company rely mainly on debt or on equity to finance its assets?	Balance sheet	The balance sheet reports the company's resources and claims to those resources. There are two types of claims: liabilities and shareholders' equity.	Compare the amount of liabilities to the amount of shareholders' equity to determine whether the company relies more on creditors or on shareholders for its financing.

Cash Flow Statement

The main function of a **cash flow statement** is to provide financial information about the cash receipts and cash payments of a business for a specific period of time. To help investors, creditors, and others in their analysis of a company's cash position, the cash flow statement reports the effects on cash of a company's (1) operating activities, (2) investing activities, and (3) financing activities during the period of time.

Recall from earlier in the chapter that operating activities result from transactions that create revenues and expenses. Investing activities involve the purchase or sale of long-lived resources such as property, plant, and equipment that a company needs to operate, or the investment in short- or long-term securities. Financing activities involve borrowing (or repaying) long-term debt from creditors and issuing shares or distributing dividends to shareholders.

Operating activities are normally presented first in the cash flow statement, followed by either investing or financing activities. In addition, the statement shows the net increase or decrease in cash during the period, and the cash amount at the end of the period.

Users are interested in the cash flow statement because they want to know what is happening to a company's most important resource. The cash flow statement provides answers to these simple but important questions:

- Where did cash come from during the period?
- How was cash used during the period?
- What was the change in the cash balance during the period?

The cash flow statement for Sierra, in Illustration 1-8, shows that cash increased by $15,200 during the month. This increase resulted because operating activities (services to clients) increased cash by $5,700, and financing activities increased cash by $14,500. Investing activities used $5,000 of cash for the purchase of office equipment. Note that the positive numbers indicate cash inflows. Numbers in parentheses indicate cash outflows. Parentheses are often used in financial statements to indicate negative amounts.

For now, you should not worry too much about where the numbers came from. We will learn more about the preparation of cash flow statements in a later chapter.

SIERRA CORPORATION Cash Flow Statement Month Ended October 31, 2009		
Operating activities		
Cash receipts from operating activities	$11,200	
Cash payments for operating activities	(5,500)	
Cash provided by operating activities		$ 5,700
Investing activities		
Purchase of office equipment	$(5,000)	
Cash used by investing activities		(5,000)
Financing activities		
Issue of common shares	$10,000	
Issue of note payable	5,000	
Payment of dividend	(500)	
Cash provided by financing activities		14,500
Net increase in cash		15,200
Cash, October 1		0
Cash, October 31		$15,200

◄— Illustration 1-8

Cash flow statement

DECISION TOOLKIT

Decision Checkpoints	Info Needed for Decision	Tools to Use for Decision	How to Evaluate Results
Does the company generate enough cash from operating activities to fund its investing activities?	Cash flow statement	The cash flow statement shows the amount of cash provided or used by operating activities, investing activities, and financing activities.	Compare the amount of cash provided by operating activities with the amount of cash used by investing activities. Any deficiency in cash from operating activities must be made up with cash provided by financing activities.

Relationships between the Statements

Because the results on some statements are used as data for other statements, the statements are said to be interrelated (related to each other). These interrelationships are evident in Sierra's financial statements:

1. The statement of retained earnings depends on the results of the statement of earnings. Sierra reported net earnings of $992 for the period, as shown in Illustration 1-4. This amount is added to the beginning amount of retained earnings as part of the process of determining ending retained earnings in Illustration 1-5.
2. The balance sheet and statement of retained earnings are interrelated because the ending amount of $492 on the statement of retained earnings in Illustration 1-5 is reported as the retained earnings amount in the shareholders' equity section of the balance sheet in Illustration 1-7.

3. The cash flow statement and the balance sheet are also interrelated. The cash flow statement presented in Illustration 1-8 shows how the cash account changed during the period by stating the amount of cash at the beginning of the period, the sources and uses of cash during the period, and the amount of cash at the end of the period, $15,200. The ending amount of cash shown on the cash flow statement must agree with the amount of cash shown in the assets section of the balance sheet shown in Illustration 1-7.

Study these interrelationships carefully. To prepare financial statements, you must understand the sequence in which these amounts are determined and how each statement affects the next. Because each financial statement depends on information contained in another statement, financial statements must be prepared in a certain order: (1) statement of earnings; (2) statement of retained earnings; (3) balance sheet; and (4) cash flow statement.

Shoppers Drug Mart's Financial Statements

The same relationships that you observed among the financial statements of Sierra Corporation can be seen in the 2007 simplified financial statements of Shoppers Drug Mart Corporation, presented in Illustrations 1-9 through 1-12. Shoppers Drug Mart's actual financial statements are presented in Appendix A at the end of the book. In the illustrations, we have simplified the financial statements to assist your learning—but they may look complicated to you anyway. Do not be alarmed by this. By the end of the book, you will have a lot of experience in reading and understanding financial statements such as these, and they will no longer look so complicated.

Before examining them, we need to explain a few points:

1. An accounting time period that is one year in length is called a fiscal year. Shoppers Drug Mart's fiscal year ends on the Saturday nearest the end of the calendar year. Consequently, its year end does not fall on the same date each year. For example, its 2007 year end was December 29, 2007, while its 2006 year end was December 30, 2006.
2. Shoppers Drug Mart, like most companies, presents its financial statements for more than one fiscal year. Financial statements that report information for more than one period are called comparative statements. Comparative statements allow users to compare the financial position of a business at the end of one accounting period to the positions of previous periods.
3. Shoppers Drug Mart presents **consolidated** financial statements. This simply means that Shoppers' financial results include the results from the more than 1,000 associate-owned pharmacies.
4. Note that numbers are reported in thousands of dollars on Shoppers Drug Mart's financial statements—that is, the last three zeros (000) are omitted. Thus, Shoppers Drug Mart's net earnings in 2007 are $493,628,000 not $493,628.

🧑 ACCOUNTING MATTERS! | Management Perspective

Nearly 75 percent of Canadian companies use December 31 for their year end. Why does every company not use December 31 as its accounting year end? Many companies choose to end their accounting year when their inventory or operations are at a low. This is advantageous because gathering accounting information requires a lot of time and effort from managers. They would rather do it when they are not too busy operating the business. Also, inventory is easier and less costly to count when it is low. Some companies whose year ends differ from December 31 are Bombardier (January 31), Empire Company (first Saturday in May), Intrawest (June 30), CoolBrands (August 31), and Salter Street Films (October 31). Most governments use March 31 for their fiscal year end.

Statement of Earnings

A simplified version of Shoppers Drug Mart's statement of earnings is presented in Illustration 1-9. While Sierra is a service company, providing services to earn its revenue, Shoppers is a retailer as it sells products to earn its revenue. Shoppers' main source of revenue is called sales. For 2007, Shoppers Drug Mart reports sales of $8,478,382 thousand. It then subtracts a variety of expenses related to operating the business. These expenses, totalling $7,741,239 thousand, include the cost of goods sold, other operating expenses, depreciation expense (which it calls amortization expense), and interest expense.

Total expenses are deducted from revenue to determine earnings before income taxes of $737,143 thousand. After subtracting the income tax expense of $243,515 thousand, the company reports net earnings for the year ended December 29, 2007 of $493,628 thousand. This is a 17-percent increase over the results of the previous year, when net earnings of $422,491 thousand was reported.

◀ Illustration 1-9

Shoppers Drug Mart statement of earnings

SHOPPERS DRUG MART CORPORATION Statement of Earnings Year Ended December 29, 2007 (in thousands)		
	2007	2006
Revenues		
Sales	$8,478,382	$7,786,436
Expenses		
Cost of sales and other operating expenses	7,516,291	6,958,361
Amortization expense	172,075	144,549
Interest expense	52,873	49,872
Total expenses	7,741,239	7,152,782
Earnings before income taxes	737,143	633,654
Income tax expense	243,515	211,163
Net earnings	$ 493,628	$ 422,491

Statement of Retained Earnings

Shoppers Drug Mart presents information about its retained earnings in the simplified statement of retained earnings in Illustration 1-10. Find the line "Retained earnings, beginning of year," in Illustration 1-10 and you will see that retained earnings at the beginning of 2007 were $1,225,616 thousand. Note that this amount agrees with the end-of-year balance for 2006. The next figure for 2007 is net earnings of $493,628 thousand. This figure was taken from Shoppers Drug Mart's statement of earnings, presented in Illustration 1-9. Shoppers paid $138,398 thousand in dividends to its shareholders. There was a $42-thousand adjustment to retained earnings for reasons that we will learn about in Chapter 11. The 2007 ending balance of retained earnings is $1,580,888 thousand. Find this amount of retained earnings in the shareholders' equity section of Shoppers Drug Mart's 2007 balance sheet, presented in Illustration 1-11.

◀ Illustration 1-10

Shoppers Drug Mart statement of retained earnings

SHOPPERS DRUG MART CORPORATION Statement of Retained Earnings Year Ended December 29, 2007 (in thousands)		
	2007	2006
Retained earnings, beginning of year	$1,225,616	$ 941,672
Add: Net earnings	493,628	422,491
	1,719,244	1,364,163
Less: Dividends	138,398	102,952
Other	(42)	35,595
Retained earnings, end of year	$1,580,888	$1,225,616

Balance Sheet

As shown in Shoppers Drug Mart's balance sheet in Illustration 1-11, Shoppers' assets include the types of assets mentioned in this chapter: cash, accounts receivable, inventory, and property and equipment. The balance sheet also includes other types of assets that we will discuss in later chapters, such as future income taxes, prepaid expenses, goodwill, and other intangible assets.

Similarly, its liabilities include bank indebtedness, accounts payable, income taxes payable, dividends payable and long-term debt, as well as items not yet discussed, such as accrued liabilities and commercial paper, which we will learn about in later chapters. Shoppers Drug Mart's balance sheet shows that total assets increased from $4,929,014 thousand on December 30, 2006 (for the 2006 fiscal year), to $5,644,039 thousand on December 29, 2007 (for the 2007 fiscal year).

▶ The Purpose and Use of Financial Statements

You can see that Shoppers relies more on equity financing than debt. It has nearly 22 percent more total shareholders' equity than it has liabilities. As you learn more about financial statements, we will discuss how to interpret the relationships and changes in financial statement items.

Illustration 1-11 ➡

Shoppers Drug Mart balance sheet

SHOPPERS DRUG MART CORPORATION Balance Sheet December 29, 2007 (in thousands)		
	2007	2006
Assets		
Cash	$ 27,588	$ 62,865
Accounts receivable	372,306	307,779
Inventory	1,577,524	1,372,124
Future income taxes	60,089	46,407
Prepaid expenses and deposits	134,692	32,248
Property and equipment	1,126,513	907,728
Goodwill	2,245,441	2,122,162
Other intangible assets	57,930	45,249
Other assets	41,956	32,452
Total assets	$5,644,039	$4,929,014
Liabilities and Shareholders' Equity		
Liabilities		
Bank indebtedness	$ 225,152	$ 134,487
Commercial paper	543,847	503,550
Accounts payable and accrued liabilities	990,545	843,278
Income taxes payable	95,996	92,361
Dividends payable	34,686	25,797
Long-term debt	298,990	300,000
Other liabilities	357,776	305,587
Total liabilities	2,546,992	2,205,060
Shareholders' equity		
Share capital	1,506,020	1,491,264
Contributed surplus	9,892	7,074
Accumulated other comprehensive income	247	—
Retained earnings	1,580,888	1,225,616
Total shareholders' equity	3,097,047	2,723,954
Total liabilities and shareholders' equity	$5,644,039	$4,929,014

Cash Flow Statement

Shoppers Drug Mart's cash decreased by $35,277 thousand from 2006 to 2007. The reasons for the decline in cash can be determined by examining the cash flow statement in Illustration 1-12. This statement presents Shoppers' sources and uses of cash during the period.

As Shoppers is currently renovating its existing stores and adding more of them, it consequently spent considerable cash—$612,747 million—on investing activities. For example, it spent $395,526 million on new property and equipment and $139,833 for business acquisitions (of new stores). Note that the cash provided by operating activities—$565,058 million—was enough to finance a large part of Shoppers Drug Mart's growth. The remainder was financed primarily by borrowing from the bank and issuing commercial paper (notes payable). In addition, Shoppers paid $129,509 million of dividends to its shareholders. The net result of the sources and uses of cash during the year was a cash decrease of $35,277 thousand.

SHOPPERS DRUG MART CORPORATION Cash Flow Statement Year Ended December 29, 2007 (in thousands)		
	2007	2006
Operating activities		
Cash receipts from operating activities	$8,478,382	$7,786,436
Cash payments for operating activities	(7,913,324)	(7,216,620)
Cash provided by operating activities	565,058	569,816
Investing activities		
Purchase of property and equipment	(395,526)	(287,216)
Proceeds from disposition of property and equipment	18,014	3,269
Business acquisitions	(139,833)	(93,866)
Other	(95,402)	(3,570)
Cash used by investing activities	(612,747)	(381,383)
Financing activities		
Bank indebtedness	90,665	(29,359)
Commercial paper	40,800	33,700
Repayment of long-term debt	–	(27,025)
Proceeds from shares issued for stock options	13,710	10,898
Repurchase of share capital	(29)	(41,789)
Dividend payments	(129,509)	(98,498)
Other	(3,225)	1,981
Cash provided (used) by financing activities	12,412	(150,092)
Increase (decrease) in cash	(35,277)	38,341
Cash, beginning of year	62,865	24,524
Cash, end of year	$ 27,588	$ 62,865

← Illustration 1-12

Shoppers Drug Mart cash flow statement

Elements of an Annual Report

Publicly traded companies must give their shareholders an **annual report** each year. The annual report is a document that includes useful nonfinancial information about the company, as well as financial information. Nonfinancial information may include the company's mission, goals and objectives, products, and people.

Financial information normally includes a management discussion and analysis (often abbreviated as MD&A), a statement of management responsibility for the financial statements, an auditors' report, the comparative financial statements introduced in this chapter, notes to the financial statements, and a historical summary of key financial ratios and indicators. No analysis of a company's financial situation and prospects is complete without a review of each of these items.

Now is a good time to go to Appendix A, where you will find Shoppers Drug Mart's financial statements taken from its annual report. Carefully examine the format and content of each financial statement outlined earlier in Illustrations 1-9 through 1-12. What similarities can you find between the simplified financial statements shown in this chapter and the more complicated financial statements shown in the appendix?

www.wiley.com/canada/kimmel

Tutorials
(Annual Report Walkthrough)

🧑 ACCOUNTING MATTERS! | Management Perspective

A company's annual report is of interest to a wide range of users, including human resource (HR) practitioners. HR practitioners should compare their own company's profitability, corporate themes and beliefs, competitive position, and transparency with what the company's major competitors report in their annual reports. HR practitioners who are able to understand not only their own company's culture, but that of their competitors, can use this information to help their company attract and retain one of its most valuable assets—its employees.

Source: Michael Thomsett, "Why HR Should Study the Annual Report," *Canadian HR Reporter,* January 15, 2007, p. 19.

BEFORE YOU GO ON...

To answer **Review It** questions about **Shoppers Drug Mart**, our feature company, you need to use Shoppers' financial statements in Appendix A at the end of this book.

Review It

1. What are the content and purpose of each statement: the statement of earnings, statement of retained earnings, balance sheet, and cash flow statement?
2. Why does it matter in which order the financial statements are prepared?
3. The basic accounting equation is: Assets = liabilities + shareholders' equity. Replacing words with dollar amounts, what is Shoppers Drug Mart's accounting equation as at December 29, 2007? The answer to this question is at the end of the chapter.
4. What financial information, in addition to the financial statements, might you expect to find in an annual report?

Do It

CSU Corporation began operations on January 1, 2009. The following account information is available for CSU Corporation on December 31, 2009: service revenue $22,200; accounts receivable $4,000; accounts payable $2,000; rent expense $9,000; notes payable $5,000; common shares $10,000; equipment $16,000; insurance expense $1,000; supplies $1,800; supplies expense $200; cash $1,400; income tax expense $5,200; and dividends $600. Using this information, prepare a statement of earnings, statement of retained earnings, balance sheet, and cash flow statement for the year.

For the operating activities section of the cash flow statement, cash receipts from operating activities were $18,200 and cash payments for operating activities were $15,200. You will have to determine the cash receipts and cash payments for the investing and financing activities sections. Assume that all transactions for these activities were cash transactions.

Action Plan

• Classify each account into the following categories: revenues, expenses, dividends, assets, liabilities, and shareholders' equity.
• Report revenues and expenses for the period in the statement of earnings.
• Show the amounts and causes (net earnings and dividends) of the changes in retained earnings for the period in the statement of retained earnings.
• Present assets and claims to those assets (liabilities and shareholders' equity) at a specific point in time in the balance sheet.
• Show the changes in cash for the period, classified as operating, investing, or financing activities in the cash flow statement.
• Remember that the statement of earnings, statement of retained earnings, and cash flow statement cover a period of time, while the balance sheet is reported at a specific point in time.

Solution
See facing page.

The Navigator

CSU CORPORATION
Statement of Earnings
Year Ended December 31, 2009

Revenues		
Service revenue		$22,200
Expenses		
Rent expense	$9,000	
Insurance expense	1,000	
Supplies expense	200	
Total expenses		10,200
Earnings before income tax		12,000
Income tax expense		5,200
Net earnings		$ 6,800

CSU CORPORATION
Statement of Retained Earnings
Year Ended December 31, 2009

Retained earnings, January 1	$ 0
Add: Net earnings	6,800
	6,800
Less: Dividends	600
Retained earnings, December 31	$6,200

CSU CORPORATION
Balance Sheet
December 31, 2009

Assets

Cash	$ 1,400
Accounts receivable	4,000
Supplies	1,800
Equipment	16,000
Total assets	$23,200

Liabilities and Shareholders' Equity

Liabilities	
Notes payable	$ 5,000
Accounts payable	2,000
Total liabilities	7,000
Shareholders' equity	
Common shares	10,000
Retained earnings	6,200
Total shareholders' equity	16,200
Total liabilities and shareholders' equity	$23,200

CSU CORPORATION
Cash Flow Statement
Year Ended December 31, 2009

Operating activities		
Cash receipts from operating activities	$ 18,200	
Cash payments for operating activities	(15,200)	
Cash provided by operating activities		$ 3,000
Investing activities		
Purchase of equipment	$(16,000)	
Cash used by investing activities		(16,000)
Financing activities		
Issue of notes payable	$ 5,000	
Issue of common shares	10,000	
Payment of dividends	(600)	
Cash provided by financing activities		14,400
Net increase in cash		1,400
Cash, January 1		0
Cash, December 31		$ 1,400

ALL ABOUT YOU

Your Personal Annual Report

If you have not already done so, in the not too distant future you will prepare a resumé. In some ways your resumé is like a company's annual report. Its purpose is to enable others to evaluate your past, in an effort to predict your future.

A resumé is your opportunity to create a positive first impression. It is important that it be impressive, but it should also be accurate. In order to increase their job prospects, some people are tempted to "inflate" their resumés by overstating the importance of some past accomplishments or positions.

The Association of Executive Recruiting Consultants estimates that approximately one in five resumés contain information that is not accurate. A study conducted by Infocheck, a reference checking firm in Toronto, found that of the 1,000 job applicants on whom they conducted reference checks and education verifications, 27 percent had embellished their educational backgrounds. John Challenger of Challenger Gray & Christmas, an outplacement consulting organization, says only about 15 percent of resumés are ever checked thoroughly.

A recent example of resumé fraud was committed by David Edmondson, the former chief executive officer of RadioShack Corporation. He overstated his accomplishments by claiming that he had earned a bachelor of science degree, when in fact he had not.

Some Facts

- One bad hiring decision can easily cost a minimum of $25,000 in wasted advertising, training, compensation, and revenue for a regular worker—and $1 million or more for a bad CEO.
- Employers can minimize losses by checking an applicant's criminal record, worker's compensation claims history, and job qualifications on their resumé.
- A workplace can be liable if an employee's misconduct affects colleagues, clients, or the general public, resulting in expensive litigation costs.
- Without good hiring checks and procedures, an entire workforce can quickly become mediocre.

What Do You Think?

Using RadioShack as an example, what should the company have done when it learned of the falsehoods on Mr. Edmondson's resumé? Should RadioShack have fired him?

YES | RadioShack is a publicly traded company. Investors, creditors, employees, and others doing business with the company will not trust it if its leader is known to have poor integrity.

NO | Mr. Edmondson had been a RadioShack employee for 11 years. The company may want to stand behind an executive who has committed an ethical violation in the past, because the company may feel that the executive has been a good manager and that his or her operating performance is so strong that it outweighs any negative impact of the ethical violation.

Sources:

Daisy Wright, "Lying on Resumés… A Common Occurrence," *Career Professionals of Canada*, careerprocanada.ca.

Omar El Akkad, "Confronting the Fib No Easy Task for Boards," *Globe and Mail*, February 20, 2006, B12.

ISB Corporate Services, Compliance, isbcorporate.com.

The Navigator

Summary of Study Objectives

1. **Identify the users and uses of accounting.** The purpose of accounting is to provide useful information for decision-making. There are two types of user groups who use accounting information: internal users and external users. Internal users work for the business and need accounting information to plan, organize, and run operations. The primary external users are investors and creditors. Investors (present and future shareholders) use accounting information to help decide whether to buy, hold, or sell shares. Creditors (suppliers and bankers) use accounting information to evaluate the risk of granting credit or loaning money to a business.

There are three types of organizations that use accounting information: proprietorships, partnerships, and corporations. A proprietorship is a business owned by one person. A partnership is a business owned by two or more people. A corporation is a separate legal entity whose shares provide evidence of ownership.

2. **Explain the three main types of business activity.** Financing activities involve collecting the necessary funds (through debt or equity) to support the business. Investing activities involve acquiring the resources (such as property, plant, and equipment) that are needed to run the business. Operating activities involve putting the resources of the business into action to generate net earnings.

3. **Describe the content and purpose of each of the financial statements.** The statement of earnings presents the revenues and expenses of a company for a specific period of time. The statement of retained earnings summarizes the changes in retained earnings that have occurred for a specific period of time. Retained earnings are the cumulative earnings (less losses) over the company's life, less any dividends paid to shareholders. The balance sheet reports the assets, liabilities, and shareholders' equity of a business at a specific date. The cash flow statement summarizes information on the cash inflows (receipts) and outflows (payments) for a specific period of time. These statements are included in an annual report, along with nonfinancial and other financial information.

The Navigator

Glossary

Study Tools (Glossary)

Accounting The process of identifying, recording, and communicating the economic events of a business to interested users of the information. (p. 4)

Accounting equation Assets = liabilities + shareholders' equity. (p. 13)

Annual report A report prepared by management that presents financial and nonfinancial information about the company. (p. 19)

Assets The resources owned by a business. (p. 8)

Balance sheet A financial statement that reports the assets, liabilities, and shareholders' equity at a specific date. (p. 13)

Cash flow statement A financial statement that provides information about the cash inflows (receipts) and cash outflows (payments) for a specific period of time. (p. 14)

Comparative statements A presentation of the financial statements of a company for two or more years. (p. 16)

Corporation A business organized as a separate legal entity having ownership divided into transferable shares held by shareholders. (p. 6)

Dividends The distribution of retained earnings from a corporation to its shareholders, normally in the form of cash. (p. 8)

Expenses The cost of assets consumed or services used in ongoing operations to generate revenue. (p. 9)

Fiscal year An accounting period that is one year long. (p. 16)

Liabilities The debts and obligations of a business. Liabilities are claims of creditors on the assets of a business. (p. 8)

Net earnings The amount by which revenues are more than expenses. Also known as net income. (p. 9)

Net loss The amount by which expenses are more than revenues. (p. 9)

Partnership A business owned by more than one person. (p. 6)

Proprietorship A business owned by one person. (p. 6)

Retained earnings The amount of accumulated net earnings (less losses, if any), from the prior and current periods, that has been kept in the corporation for future use and not distributed to shareholders as dividends. (p. 12)

Revenues The economic resources that result from the operating activities of a business, such as the sale of a product or provision of a service. (p. 9)

Share capital Shares representing the ownership interest in a corporation. If only one class of shares exists, it is known as common shares. (p. 8)

Shareholders' equity The shareholders' claim on total assets, represented by the investments of the shareholders (share capital) and undistributed earnings (retained earnings) generated by the company. (p. 13)

Statement of earnings A financial statement that presents the revenues and expenses and resulting net earnings or net loss of a company for a specific period of time. Also known as income statement. (p. 11)

Statement of retained earnings A financial statement that summarizes the changes in retained earnings for a specific period of time. (p. 12)

DECISION TOOLKIT—A SUMMARY

Decision Checkpoints	Info Needed for Decision	Tools to Use for Decision	Info Needed for Decision
Are the company's operations profitable?	Statement of earnings	The statement of earnings indicates the success or failure of the company's operating activities by reporting its revenues and expenses.	If the company's revenues exceed its expenses, it will report net earnings; otherwise it will report a net loss.
What is the company's policy on dividends and growth?	Statement of retained earnings	How much did the company pay out in dividends to shareholders?	A company looking for rapid growth will pay no, or a low, dividend.
Does the company rely mainly on debt or on equity to finance its assets?	Balance sheet	The balance sheet reports the company's resources and claims to those resources. There are two types of claims: liabilities and shareholders' equity.	Compare the amount of liabilities to the amount of shareholders' equity to determine whether the company relies more on creditors or on shareholders for its financing.
Does the company generate enough cash from operating activities to fund its investing activities?	Cash flow statement	The cash flow statement shows the amount of cash provided or used by operating activities, investing activities, and financing activities.	Compare the amount of cash provided by operating activities with the amount of cash used by investing activities. Any deficiency in cash from operating activities must be made up with cash provided by financing activities.

Analysis Tools
(Decision Toolkit Summaries)

The Navigator

Using the Decision Toolkit cases ask you to use information from financial statements to make financial decisions. Before you study the solution, we encourage you to think about how the questions related to the decision would be answered.

Using the Decision Toolkit

The Jean Coutu Group (PJC) Inc. is the No. 2 pharmacy chain in Canada. The company dominates the Quebec market but trails Shoppers Drug Mart in overall store count. Assume that you are reviewing the financial information of each company to determine if you should invest in Shoppers Drug Mart or Jean Coutu.

Instructions

(a) What financial statements should you request from Jean Coutu?

(b) What should each of these financial statements tell you? Which financial statement will you likely be most interested in?

(c) In 2007, Jean Coutu merged with Rite Aid, the third largest U.S. drug store chain. Prior to this, Jean Coutu's fiscal year end was the Saturday closest to the end of May. In order to coincide with Rite Aid's fiscal year end, Jean Coutu changed its fiscal year end in 2008 to the Saturday closest to the end of February. Is it possible to compare the March 1, 2008, year-end financial statements to those of June 4, 2007, since they cover different periods?

(d) Shoppers Drug Mart's fiscal year end is the end of December. Jean Coutu's fiscal year end is the end of February. Will it be possible to compare financial statements of these companies in future years since they have different fiscal year ends?

(e) Simplified financial statements for Jean Coutu follow. What comparisons can you make between Shoppers Drug Mart and Jean Coutu in terms of their financial positions and results of operations?

THE JEAN COUTU GROUP (PJC) INC.
Statement of Earnings
Period Ended March 1, 2008
(in millions)

	2008	2007
Revenues		
Sales	$1,676	$13,265
Expenses		
Cost of goods sold	1,370	10,041
General and operating expenses	140	2,622
Amortization expense	12	75
Other expenses	396	96
Interest expense	5	243
Total expenses	1,923	13,077
Earnings (loss) before income taxes	(247)	188
Income tax expense	4	25
Net earnings (loss)	$ (251)	$ 163

THE JEAN COUTU GROUP (PJC) INC.
Statement of Retained Earnings
Period Ended March 1, 2008
(in millions)

	2008	2007
Retained earnings, beginning of year	$1,320	$1,188
Add: Net earnings (loss)	(251)	163
	1,069	1,351
Less: Dividends	31	31
Other	107	—
Retained earnings, end of year	$ 931	$1,320

THE JEAN COUTU GROUP (PJC) INC.
Balance Sheet
March 1, 2008
(in millions)

	2008	2007
Assets		
Cash and cash equivalents	$ —	$ 41
Accounts receivable	168	163
Inventory	155	138
Prepaid expenses and other	5	8
Investments	1,143	1,598
Property and equipment	329	319
Goodwill	35	20
Other long-term assets	114	50
Total assets	$1,949	$2,337
Liabilities and Shareholders' Equity		
Liabilities		
Accounts payable and accrued liabilities	$ 202	$ 259
Income taxes payable	63	23
Long-term debt	171	8
Other liabilities	29	29
Total liabilities	465	319
Shareholders' equity		
Share capital	715	790
Contributed surplus	17	5
Retained earnings	931	1,320
Accumulated other comprehensive income (loss)	(179)	(97)
Total shareholders' equity	1,484	2,018
Total liabilities and shareholders' equity	$1,949	$2,337

THE JEAN COUTU GROUP (PJC) INC. Cash Flow Statement Period Ended March 1, 2008 (in millions)		
	2008	2007
Operating activities		
Cash receipts from operating activities	$1,671	$13,658
Cash payments for operating activities	(1,525)	(13,466)
Cash provided by operating activities	146	192
Investing activities		
Purchase of property and equipment	(23)	(154)
Investments and business acquisition	(66)	(2)
Proceeds from disposal of the retail sales segment	(46)	2,450
Proceeds from disposal of property and equipment	1	9
Other	(9)	(3)
Cash provided (used) by investing activities	(143)	2,300
Financing activities		
Issue of long-term debt	164	5
Repayment of long-term debt	(1)	(2,541)
Proceeds from shares issued	1	2
Dividend payments	(31)	(31)
Other	(177)	(37)
Cash used by financing activities	(44)	(2,602)
Increase (decrease) in cash	(41)	(110)
Cash, beginning of year	41	151
Cash, end of year	$ 0	$ 41

Solution

(a) Before you invest, you should investigate the statement of earnings, statement of retained earnings, balance sheet, cash flow statement and the accompanying notes.

(b) You would probably be most interested in the statement of earnings because it shows past performance and this gives an indication of future performance. The statement of retained earnings shows the impact that current earnings and dividends have on the company's retained earnings. The balance sheet reveals the financial position of the company and the relationship between assets, liabilities, and shareholders' equity. Finally, the cash flow statement reveals where the company is getting and spending its cash. This is especially important for a company that wants to grow.

(c) Jean Coutu's balance sheet, which presents the financial position of the company at a specific point in time, should still be comparable. The company's other statements—statement of earnings, statement of retained earnings, and cash flow statement—are more difficult to compare because the 2008 statements contain data for a 9-month period while the 2007 statements contain data for a 12-month period. These statements are still comparable, as long as the analysis takes into consideration the differing periods of time reported for revenues, expenses, and so on.

(d) In future years (not including the current fiscal year in which Jean Coutu changed its year end), Shoppers Drug Mart's fiscal year will overlap Jean Coutu's for 10 months (March through December). If there have been no substantial changes to the economy that would affect their business during the two-month period that Jean Coutu's financial results cover but Shoppers Drug Mart's do not (or vice versa), it really does not matter when each company's fiscal year ends. It is more important that we compare what each company was able to achieve within an equivalent period of time—whether it be one year, six months, or one quarter.

  If, however, a major change does occur in the intervening period (the period where the statements do not overlap), such a change would likely reduce the usefulness of a comparison of the financial statements of the two companies.

(e) Many interesting comparisons can be made between the two companies. Jean Coutu is much smaller, about a third the size of Shoppers Drug Mart. For example, at the end of each company's most recent fiscal year, Jean Coutu has total assets of $1,949 million versus $5,644 million for Shoppers Drug Mart. Jean Coutu has a balance of $931 million of accumulated retained earnings, while Shoppers Drug Mart's retained earnings of $1,581 million are nearly 1.7 this amount.

  Jean Coutu has lower revenue—total revenues of $1,676 million versus $8,478 million for Shoppers Drug Mart —for the current fiscal year. Jean Coutu reported a net loss for its current fiscal year of $251 million, compared to Shoppers Drug Mart's net earnings of $494 million. In 2007, Jean Coutu generated cash from operating activities of $146 million, whereas Shoppers Drug Mart generated $565 million in cash from its operating activities. Recall, however, that Jean Coutu's results are only for a 9-month period, while Shoppers Drug Mart's are for a 12-month period.

  While these comparisons are useful, these basic measures are not enough to determine whether one company will be a better investment than the other. In later chapters, you will acquire more tools to help you compare the relative profitability and financial health of these, and other, companies.

The Navigator

Demonstration Problem

Jeff Andringa, a former university hockey player, quit his job and started Ice Camp Ltd., a hockey camp for kids from ages 8 to 18. Eventually he would like to open hockey camps nationwide. Jeff has asked you to help him prepare financial statements at the end of his first year of operations. He tells you the following facts about his business activities.

In order to get the business off the ground, he decided to incorporate. He sold common shares to a few close friends and bought some of the shares himself on January 1, 2009. He initially raised $25,000 through the sale of these shares. In addition, the company borrowed $10,000 from a local bank. A used bus for transporting kids was purchased for $12,000 cash. Hockey nets and other miscellaneous equipment were purchased with $1,500 cash. The company earned camp tuition of $100,000 during the year but had collected only $80,000 of this amount. Thus, at the end of the year it was still owed $20,000. The company rents time at a local rink for $50 per hour. Total rink rental costs during the year were $8,000, insurance was $10,000, salaries were $20,000, administrative expenses totalled $9,000, and income taxes amounted to $15,000—all of which were paid in cash. The company incurred $800 in interest expense on the bank loan, which it still owed at the end of the year.

The company paid dividends during the year of $5,000 cash. The balance in the corporate bank account at December 31, 2009, was $34,500 ($25,000 + $10,000 − $12,000 − $1,500 + $80,000 − $8,000 − $10,000 − $20,000 − $9,000 − $15,000 − $5,000). Cash payments for operating activities totalled $62,000 ($8,000 + $10,000 + $20,000 + $9,000 + $15,000).

Instructions

Prepare a statement of earnings, statement of retained earnings, balance sheet, and cash flow statement for the year.

Solution to Demonstration Problem

ICE CAMP LTD.
Statement of Earnings
Year Ended December 31, 2009

Revenues		
Camp tuition revenue		$100,000
Expenses		
Salaries expense	$20,000	
Insurance expense	10,000	
Administrative expense	9,000	
Rink rental expense	8,000	
Interest expense	800	
Total expenses		47,800
Earnings before income taxes		52,200
Income tax expense		15,000
Net earnings		$37,200

ICE CAMP LTD.
Statement of Retained Earnings
Year Ended December 31, 2009

Retained earnings, January 1		$ 0
Add: Net earnings		37,200
		37,200
Less: Dividends		5,000
Retained earnings, December 31		$32,200

Study Tools
(Demonstration Problems)

Demonstration Problems are a final review before you begin homework. **Action Plans** that appear in the margins give you tips about how to approach the problem, and the **Solution** provided demonstrates both the form and content of complete answers.

The **Web icon** indicates there are additional demonstration problems on the Toolkit website.

Action Plan

- On the statement of earnings, show revenues and expenses for a period of time.

- On the statement of retained earnings, show the changes in retained earnings for a period of time.

- On the balance sheet, report assets, liabilities, and shareholders' equity at a specific date.

- On the cash flow statement, report sources and uses of cash provided or used by operating, investing, and financing activities for a period of time.

ICE CAMP LTD.
Balance Sheet
December 31, 2009

Assets

Cash	$34,500
Accounts receivable	20,000
Bus	12,000
Equipment	1,500
Total assets	$68,000

Liabilities and Shareholders' Equity

Liabilities		
Bank loan payable		$10,000
Interest payable		800
Total liabilities		10,800
Shareholders' equity		
Common shares		25,000
Retained earnings		32,200
Total shareholders' equity		57,200
Total liabilities and shareholders' equity		$68,000

ICE CAMP LTD.
Cash Flow Statement
Year Ended December 31, 2009

Operating activities		
Cash receipts from operating activities	$ 80,000	
Cash payments for operating activities	(62,000)	
Cash provided by operating activities		$18,000
Investing activities		
Purchase of bus	$(12,000)	
Purchase of equipment	(1,500)	
Cash used by investing activities		(13,500)
Financing activities		
Issue of bank loan	$ 10,000	
Issue of common shares	25,000	
Dividends paid	(5,000)	
Cash provided by financing activities		30,000
Net increase in cash		34,500
Cash, January 1		0
Cash, December 31		$34,500

The Navigator

This would be a good time to return to the Student **Owner's Manual** at the beginning of the book (or look at it for the first time if you skipped it before) to read about the various types of assignment materials that appear at the end of each chapter. If you know the purpose of the different assignments, you will appreciate what each one contributes to your accounting skills and competencies.

Self-Study Questions

Answers are at the end of the chapter.

www.wiley.com/canada/kimmel

Study Tools (Self-Assessment Quizzes)

1. Which statement about users of accounting information is *incorrect*?

    (a) Management is an internal user.
    (b) The Canada Revenue Agency is an external user.
    (c) Creditors are external users.
    (d) Investors are internal users.

2. Which of the following is not one of the three forms of business organization?

    (a) Proprietorship
    (b) Entrepreneurship
    (c) Partnership
    (d) Corporation

3. In which of the following areas do corporations have an advantage over partnerships and proprietorships?

    (a) Raising funds, transfer of ownership, and reduced legal liability
    (b) Ease of organizing, raising of funds, and payment of income taxes
    (c) Transfer of ownership, reduced income taxes, and unlimited legal liability
    (d) Simple to form, no income taxes, and unlimited legal liability

4. Which is *not* one of the three primary business activities?

    (a) Financing
    (b) Operating
    (c) Planning
    (d) Investing

5. Which of the following is *not* an example of a financing activity?

    (a) Borrowing money from a bank
    (b) Repaying money to a bank
    (c) Selling goods on credit
    (d) Paying dividends

6. Operating activities include all of the following except: (SO 2)

    (a) Purchasing goods for resale
    (b) Performing services
    (c) Paying employee salaries
    (d) Purchasing a cash register

7. Net earnings will result during a time period when: (SO 2)

    (a) assets exceed liabilities.
    (b) assets exceed revenues.
    (c) expenses exceed revenues.
    (d) revenues exceed expenses.

8. Which financial statement reports assets, liabilities, and (SO 3) shareholders' equity?

    (a) Statement of earnings
    (b) Statement of retained earnings
    (c) Balance sheet
    (d) Cash flow statement

9. Financial statements must be prepared in the following (SO 3) order:

    (a) (1) Statement of earnings, (2) statement of retained earnings, (3) cash flow statement, and (4) balance sheet.
    (b) (1) Statement of retained earnings, (2) statement of earnings, (3) cash flow statement, and (4) balance sheet.
    (c) (1) Balance sheet, (2) statement of earnings, (3) statement of retained earnings, and (4) cash flow statement.
    (d) (1) Statement of earnings, (2) statement of retained earnings, (3) balance sheet, and (4) cash flow statement.

10. As at December 31, Stoneland Corporation has assets of (SO 3) $3,500 and shareholders' equity of $2,000. What are the liabilities for Stoneland Corporation as at December 31?

    (a) $1,500
    (b) $2,000
    (c) $3,500
    (d) $5,500

The Navigator

Questions

1. What is accounting?

2. "Accounting is ingrained in our society and is vital to our economic system." Do you agree? Explain.

3. Why should everyone study accounting whether they are going to be an accountant or not?

4. Distinguish between internal and external users of accounting information.

5. What kind of questions might internal users of accounting (SO 1) information want answered? External users?

6. Financial reporting is aimed mostly at two external user (SO 1) groups of accounting—investors and creditors. Distinguish between the needs of these two groups.

7. Why are ethics as important to accountants as they are to the (SO 1) decision-makers who rely on financial information?

(SO 1) 8. (a) What are the three basic forms of business organization?
        (b) Identify the advantages and disadvantages of each form.

(SO 2) 9. Distinguish between operating, investing, and financing
        activities.

(SO 2) 10. Give two examples of each kind of business activity: (a)
        operating, (b) investing, and (c) financing.

(SO 2) 11. Explain why operating activities include some assets (e.g.,
        receivables) but not others (e.g., property, plant, and
        equipment).

(SO 2) 12. Explain why accounts receivable, an asset, is classified as an
        operating activity on the cash flow statement and not as an
        investing activity.

(SO 2) 13. Explain why accounts payable, a liability, is classified as an
        operating activity on the cash flow statement and not as a
        financing activity.

(SO 2) 14. ▭ Why would a bank want to monitor the dividend
        payment practices of a corporation it lends funds to?

(SO 2) 15. Explain the following terms and give an example of each: (a)
        asset, (b) liability, (c) shareholders' equity, (d) revenues, and
        (e) expenses.

(SO 3) 16. Why is a balance sheet prepared as at a specific point in time,
        while the other financial statements cover a period of time?

(SO 3) 17. What are retained earnings? What items increase the balance
        in retained earnings? What items decrease the balance in
        retained earnings?

The financial results of real companies are included in the end of chapter
material. These company names are shown in **orange**.

▭ The **tool icon** means that an activity uses one of the decision tool
presented in the chapter.

18. (a) What is the purpose of the cash flow statement?
    (b) What are the three main categories of activities in the
         cash flow statement?

19. How are each of the following pairs of financial statements
    related?
    (a) Statement of earnings and statement of retained earnings
    (b) Statement of retained earnings and balance sheet
    (c) Balance sheet and cash flow statement

20. (a) What is the basic accounting equation?
    (b) How does the accounting equation relate to the balance
         sheet?

21. André is puzzled reading **Shoppers Drug Mart's** financial
    statements. He notices that the numbers have all been rounded
    to the nearest thousand. He thought financial statements
    were supposed to be accurate and wonders what happened to
    the rest of the money. Respond to André's concern.

22. Instead of **Shoppers Drug Mart's** year end being a fixed date,
    it varies slightly from one year to the next. Will this cause any
    problems for financial statement users?

Brief Exercises

BE1–1   The following list presents different types of evaluations made by various users of accounting
information:

1. Determining if the company respected income tax regulations
2. Determining if the company pays fair wages
3. Determining if the company can pay its obligations
4. Determining if a marketing proposal will be cost-effective
5. Determining if the company's net earnings will result in a share price increase
6. Determining if the company should use debt or equity financing

(a) In the table that follows, beside each user of accounting information, write the number of the
    evaluation above (1–6) that the user makes.

(b) Indicate if the user is internal or external. The first item has been done for you as an example.

	(a) Type of Evaluation	(b) Type of User
Investor	5	External
Marketing manager		
Creditor		
Chief financial officer		
Canada Revenue Agency		
Labour union		

BE1–2   Write the correct form of business organization—proprietorship (Prop.), partnership (Part.), or corporation (Corp.)—beside each set of characteristics.

    (a) _____   Simple to set up; founder retains control

    (b) _____   Shared control; increased skills and resources

    (c) _____   Easier to transfer ownership and raise funds; no personal liability

Identify forms of business organization.
(SO 1)

BE1–3   Classify each item by type of business activity—operating (O), investing (I), or financing (F).

    (a) _____   Cash received from customers

    (b) _____   Dividends paid to shareholders

    (c) _____   Common shares issued to investors

    (d) _____   Money borrowed from a bank

    (e) _____   An office building purchased

    (f) _____   Income taxes paid

Classify items by activity.
(SO 2)

BE1–4   For each of the following items, indicate (a) the type of business activity—operating (O), investing (I), or financing (F)—and (b) whether it increased (+), decreased (–), or had no effect (NE) on cash:

Identify business activity and effect on cash.
(SO 2)

	(a) Type of Activity	(b) Cash Effect
1. Sold goods for cash.	O	+
2. Obtained a bank loan.		
3. Purchased inventory on credit.		
4. Sold goods on account.		
5. Paid accounts payable.		
6. Paid wages in cash.		
7. Purchased a delivery truck.		

BE1–5   The **Calgary Exhibition and Stampede Limited** has the following selected accounts included in its financial statements. In each case, identify whether the item would appear on the balance sheet (BS) or statement of earnings (SE).

Determine on which financial statement items appear.
(SO 3)

    (a) _____ Accounts receivable   (h) _____ Accounts payable and accrued liabilities

    (b) _____ Inventories   (i) _____ Cash and short-term deposits

    (c) _____ Amortization expense   (j) _____ Administration, marketing, and

    (d) _____ Common shares   park services expenses

    (e) _____ Building   (k) _____ Interest expense

    (f) _____ Stampede revenue   (l) _____ Prepaid expenses

    (g) _____ Horse racing revenue

BE1–6   Indicate which statement—statement of earnings (SE), balance sheet (BS), statement of retained earnings (RE), or cash flow statement (CF)—you would examine to find each of the following items:

Determine on which financial statement items appear.
(SO 3)

    (a) _____   Revenue earned during the year

    (b) _____   Supplies on hand at the end of the year

    (c) _____   Cash received from borrowing money during the year

    (d) _____   Total debt at the end of the year

    (e) _____   Dividends paid to shareholders during the year

    (f) _____   Income tax expense for the year

BE1–7   Use the accounting equation to determine the missing amounts below:

Use accounting equation.
(SO 3)

Assets	=	Liabilities	+	Shareholders' Equity
$75,000		$45,000		(a)
(b)		$45,000		$45,000
$90,000		(c)		$50,000

Use accounting equation.
(SO 3)

BE1–8   Use the accounting equation to answer these independent questions:

(a) The shareholders' equity of Sansom Corporation is $110,000. Its total liabilities are $45,000. What is the amount of Sansom's total assets?

(b) The liabilities of Houle Corporation are $190,000. Houle's share capital is $100,000 and its retained earnings are $100,000. What is the amount of Houle's total assets?

(c) The total assets of Pitre Limited are $170,000. Its share capital is $55,000 and its retained earnings are $25,000. What is the amount of its total liabilities?

(d) The total assets of Budovitch Inc. are $450,000 and its liabilities are equal to half its total assets. What is the amount of Budovitch's shareholders' equity?

Use accounting equation.
(SO 3)

BE1–9   At the beginning of the year, Lam Ltd. had total assets of $500,000 and total liabilities of $300,000. Use this information to answer each of the following independent parts.

(a) If Lam's total assets increased by $100,000 during the year and total liabilities decreased by $50,000, what is the amount of shareholders' equity at the end of the year?

(b) During the year, Lam's total liabilities increased by $50,000. The company reported net earnings of $50,000, sold additional shares for $50,000, and paid no dividends during the year. What is the amount of total assets at the end of the year?

(c) If Lam's total assets decreased by $80,000 during the year and shareholders' equity increased by $80,000, what is the amount of total liabilities at the end of the year?

Identify assets, liabilities, and
shareholders' equity.
(SO 3)

BE1–10   Indicate whether each of these items is an asset (A), a liability (L), or shareholders' equity (SE):

(a) _____ Accounts receivable   (e) _____ Common shares

(b) _____ Salaries payable   (f) _____ Notes payable

(c) _____ Equipment   (g) _____ Retained earnings

(d) _____ Office supplies   (h) _____ Cash

Determine effect of
transactions on shareholders'
equity.
(SO 3)

BE1–11   Determine whether each transaction affects common shares (C), dividends (D), revenue (R), expenses (E), or has no effect on any of these shareholders' equity components (NE).

(a) _____ Purchase of equipment   (e) _____ Costs incurred for income tax

(b) _____ Issue of common shares   (f) _____ Amounts earned by employees

(c) _____ Services performed for cash   (g) _____ Dividends paid to shareholders

(d) _____ Services performed on account   (h) _____ Interest incurred on note payable

Exercises

Identify users and uses of
accounting information.
(SO 1)

E1–1   **Roots Canada Ltd.** is known around the world for its wide range of leather goods, clothing, and accessories.

Instructions

(a) Identify two internal users of Roots' accounting information. Write a question that each user might try to answer by using accounting information.

(b) Identify two external users of Roots' accounting information. Write a question that each user might try to answer by using accounting information.

Identify business activity and
effect on cash.
(SO 2)

E1–2   For each of the following items, indicate (a) the type of business activity—operating (O), investing (I), or financing (F)—and (b) whether the item would increase (+), decrease (–), or have no effect (NE) on cash. The first one has been completed for you as an example.

	(a) Type of Activity	(b) Cash Effect
1. Purchase of equipment for cash	Investing	–
2. Purchase of goods for resale on account		
3. Issue of long-term debt		
4. Collection of notes receivable		
5. Collection of accounts receivable		
6. Issue of common shares		

7. Sale of investments	_____	_____
8. Payment of dividends	_____	_____
9. Repayment of long-term debt	_____	_____
10. Cash sales made to customers	_____	_____

E1–3   You are employed as an accounting assistant by Multi Hills Ski Area Limited. You have been asked to classify each of the following items by type of business activity—operating, investing or financing. The first one has been done for you as an example.

Classify business activities.
(SO 2)

	Type of Activity
1. Cash receipts from customers paying for daily ski passes.	_____Operating_____
2. Payments made to purchase additional snow-making equipment.	_____
3. Payments made to repair the grooming machines.	_____
4. Receipt of funds from the bank to finance the purchase of the additional snow-making equipment.	_____
5. Issue of shares to raise funds for a planned expansion.	_____
6. Repayment of a portion of the loan from the bank (see #4).	_____
7. Payment of interest on the bank loan.	_____
8. Payment of salaries to the "lifties" (employees who operate the ski lifts).	_____
9. Receipt of a grant from the government for training a group of blind skiers.	_____

E1–4   Here is a list of terms discussed in this chapter:

Match words with descriptions.
(SO 1, 2, 3)

1. Accounts payable	6. Corporation
2. Creditor	7. Common shares
3. Financing activities	8. Accounts receivable
4. Retained earnings	9. Fiscal year
5. Dividends	10. Assets

Instructions

Match each term to the appropriate description below:

(a) _____   A company that raises money by issuing shares

(b) _____   Amounts owed to suppliers of goods

(c) _____   Resources owned by a company

(d) _____   A party that a company owes money to

(e) _____   Obtaining cash from borrowing money or issuing shares

(f) _____   An accounting period that is one year long

(g) _____   Cumulative earnings that have been retained in the company

(h) _____   The ownership interest of shareholders in the company

(i) _____   Amounts due from customers

(j) _____   Distributions of earnings to shareholders

E1–5   Indicate on which statement—statement of earnings (SE), balance sheet (BS), statement of retained earnings (RE), or cash flow statement (CF)—you would find each of the following accounts or items:

Determine on which financial statement items appear.
(SO 3)

(a) _____ Cash	(i) _____ Income tax expense
(b) _____ Advertising expense	(j) _____ Accounts receivable
(c) _____ Service revenue	(k) _____ Interest expense
(d) _____ Common shares	(l) _____ Cash collected from customers
(e) _____ Sales	(m) _____ Cash received from a sale of equipment
(f) _____ Dividends	(n) _____ Notes payable
(g) _____ Inventory	(o) _____ Equipment
(h) _____ Cash paid for income tax	(p) _____ Cash borrowed on a note payable

Use financial statement relationships to determine missing amounts.
(SO 3)

E1–6 Summaries of data from the balance sheets and statements of earnings for three corporations follow:

	Chiasson Corporation	Maxim Enterprises, Ltd.	K-Os Corporation
Beginning of year			
Total assets	$ 95,000	$125,000	$60,000
Total liabilities	80,000	(c)	25,000
Total shareholders' equity	(a)	95,000	35,000
End of year			
Total assets	160,000	180,000	(e)
Total liabilities	120,000	50,000	65,000
Total shareholders' equity	40,000	130,000	(f)
Changes during year in shareholders' equity			
Issue of shares	(b)	25,000	4,000
Dividends	24,000	(d)	30,000
Total revenues	215,000	100,000	54,000
Total expenses	175,000	85,000	40,000

Instructions
Determine the missing amounts for (a) to (f).

Classify accounts and prepare accounting equation.
(SO 3)

E1–7 The following accounts and amounts (in thousands) were taken from the January 27, 2008, balance sheet of **The Forzani Group Ltd.**, Canada's biggest sporting goods retailer:

___ Accounts payable and accrued liabilities	$279,910	___ Other assets	20,072
___ Accounts receivable	75,506	___ Other liabilities	61,122
___ Capital assets	188,621	___ Other shareholders' equity items	(8)
___ Cash	47,484	___ Prepaid expenses	14,501
___ Goodwill and other intangibles	89,335	___ Retained earnings	191,176
___ Inventory	319,445	___ Share capital	164,315
___ Long-term debt	58,449		

Instructions

(a) Classify each account as an asset (A), liability (L), or shareholders' equity (SE) item.

(b) Determine Forzani's accounting equation by calculating the amount of total assets, total liabilities, and total shareholders' equity.

Prepare balance sheet.
(SO 3)

E1–8 The following list of accounts, in alphabetical order, is for Aventura Inc. at November 30, 2009:

Accounts payable	$ 16,200	Inventory	$18,000
Accounts receivable	9,500	Land	50,000
Bank loan payable	20,000	Mortgage payable	97,500
Building	100,000	Other payables	7,800
Cash	10,000	Prepaid insurance	500
Common shares	20,000	Retained earnings	18,500
Income tax payable	2,000	Unearned revenue	6,000

Instructions
Prepare a balance sheet at November 30.

Classify accounts and prepare statement of earnings.
(SO 3)

E1–9 The following selected accounts and amounts (in thousands) were taken from the **Transat A.T. (Air Transat) Inc.** October 31, 2007, statement of earnings and balance sheet:

__L__ Accounts payable	$281,985	___ Operating expenses	$2,912,847
___ Accounts receivable	109,128	___ Other expenses	15,837
___ Amortization expense	42,973	___ Other revenues	30,251
___ Cash	166,768	___ Prepaid expenses	45,981
___ Income tax expense	35,618	___ Retained earnings	190,534
___ Interest expense	8,158	___ Revenues	3,045,917
___ Interest income	19,745	___ Share capital	156,964
___ Inventories	8,931		

Instructions

(a) For each of the above accounts, identify whether it is an asset (A), liability (L), shareholders' equity (SE), revenue (R), or expense (E). The first one has been done for you as an example.

(b) Prepare a statement of earnings for Air Transat for the year ended October 31, 2007.

E1–10   The following information is for Kon Inc. for the year ended December 31, 2009:

Retained earnings, Jan. 1	$57,000	Service revenue	$58,000
Advertising expense	1,800	Utilities expense	2,400
Dividends	7,000	Salaries expense	28,000
Rent expense	10,400	Income tax expense	6,000

Prepare statements of earnings and retained earnings.
(SO 3)

Instructions

Prepare a statement of earnings and statement of retained earnings for the year.

E1–11   Sea Surf Campground, Inc. is a public camping ground in Ocean National Park. It has the following financial information as at December 31, 2009:

Revenues—camping fees	$137,000	Dividends	$ 14,000
Revenues—general store	35,000	Notes payable	50,000
Accounts payable	8,000	Operating expenses	128,000
Cash	7,500	Supplies	2,500
Equipment	119,000	Common shares	30,000
Income tax expense	7,000	Retained earnings (Jan. 1)	18,000

Calculate net earnings and prepare statement of retained earnings and balance sheet.
(SO 3)

Instructions

(a) Determine net earnings for the year.

(b) Prepare a statement of retained earnings and balance sheet for the year.

E1–12   This information is for Van Tran Corporation for the year ended December 31, 2009:

Cash received from customers	$70,000
Cash paid for new equipment	55,000
Cash dividends paid	5,000
Cash received from lenders	25,000
Cash paid for expenses	30,000
Cash, Jan. 1	12,000

Prepare cash flow statement.
(SO 3)

Instructions

Prepare a cash flow statement for Van Tran Corporation for the year.

E1–13   ▬◖ Consider each of the following independent situations:

Interpret financial information.
(SO 3)

(a) The statement of retained earnings of Yu Corporation shows dividends of $68,000, while net earnings for the year were $75,000.

(b) The cash flow statement for Surya Corporation shows that cash provided by operating activities was $10,000; cash used by investing activities was $110,000; and cash provided by financing activities was $130,000.

(c) Naguib Ltd.'s balance sheet reports $150,000 of total liabilities and $250,000 of shareholders' equity.

Instructions

For each company, write a brief interpretation of these financial facts. For example, you might discuss the company's financial health or what seems to be its growth philosophy.

Problems: Set A

Identify users and uses of financial statements.
(SO 1)

P1–1A   Financial decisions made by users often depend on one financial statement more than the others. Consider each of the following independent, hypothetical situations:

(a) An Ontario investor is considering purchasing the common shares of Fight Fat Ltd., which operates 13 fitness centres in the Toronto area. The investor plans on holding the investment for at least three years.

(b) Comeau Ltée is considering extending credit to a new customer. The terms of the credit would require the customer to pay within 45 days of receipt of the goods.

(c) The CEO of Private Label Corporation is trying to determine whether the company is generating enough cash to increase the amount of dividends paid to investors in this, and future, years. She needs to ensure that there will still be enough cash to expand operations when needed.

(d) Laurentian Bank is considering extending a loan to a small company. The company would be required to make interest payments at the end of each month for five years, and to repay the loan at the end of the fifth year.

Instructions
For each situation, state whether the user would be most interested in the statement of earnings, balance sheet, or cash flow statement. Choose only one financial statement in each case, and briefly give reasons for your choice.

Determine forms of business organization.
(SO 1)

P1–2A   Five independent situations follow:

(a) Dawn Addington, a student looking for summer employment, has opened a vegetable stand along a busy local highway. Each morning, she buys produce from local farmers, then sells it in the afternoon as people return home from work.

(b) Joseph Counsell and Sabra Surkis each own a bike shop. They have decided to combine their businesses and try to expand their operations to include skis and snowboards. They expect that in the coming year they will need funds to expand their operations.

(c) Three chemistry professors have formed a business which uses bacteria to clean up toxic waste sites. Each has contributed an equal amount of cash and knowledge to the venture. The use of bacteria in this situation is experimental, and legal obligations could result.

(d) Abdur Rahim has run a successful but small cooperative health and organic food store for over five years. The increased sales at his store have made him believe that the time is right to open a chain of health and organic food stores across the country. Of course, this will require a substantial investment for inventory and property, plant, and equipment, as well as for employees and other resources. Abdur has no savings or personal assets.

(e) Mary Emery, Richard Goedde, and Jigme Tshering recently graduated with law degrees. They have decided to start a law practice in their home town.

Instructions
In each case, explain what form of organization the business is likely to take—proprietorship, partnership, or corporation. Give reasons for your choice.

Identify business activities
(SO 2)

P1–3A   All businesses are involved in three types of activities—operating, investing, and financing. The names and descriptions of companies in several different industries follow:

Abitibi Consolidated Inc.—manufacturer and marketer of newsprint
Ryerson Student Union—university student union
Biovail Corporation—manufacturer and distributor of pharmaceutical products
Maple Leaf Sports & Entertainment Ltd.—owner of the Toronto Maple Leafs hockey team and Raptors basketball team
Grant Thornton LLP—professional accounting and business advisory firm
WestJet Airlines Ltd.—discount airline

Instructions

(a) For each company, provide a likely example of (1) one of its operating activities, (2) one of its investing activities, and (3) one of its financing activities.

(b) Which of the activities that you identified in (a) are common to most businesses? Which activities are not?

P1–4A As a student, you have many cash inflows and outflows, each of which can be identified as operating, investing, or financing. Examples of cash flows that you might have as a student follow:

Identify business activities.
(SO 2)

1. _____ Receipt of a scholarship
2. _____ Purchase of textbooks
3. _____ Payment of tuition
4. _____ Purchase of a used car
5. _____ Purchase of a bus pass

Instructions

(a) For each of the cash flows listed above, indicate whether it is an operating, investing, or financing activity.

(b) For each of type of activity (operating, investing, and financing), provide an example of a cash inflow or outflow you encounter that is not listed above.

P1–5A The Mill Run Golf & Country Club details the following selected accounts in its financial statements:

Classify accounts.
(SO 2, 3)

	(a)	(b)		(a)	(b)
Initiation fees	___	___	Office and general expenses	___	___
Capital assets	___	___	Payables and accruals	___	___
Income—food and beverage operations	___	___	Receivables	___	___
Income—golf course operations	___	___	Long-term debt	___	___
Inventory	___	___	Wages and benefits expense	___	___

Instructions

(a) Classify each account as an asset (A), liability (L), shareholders' equity (SE), revenue (R), or expense (E) item.

(b) Classify each account as being used for operating (O), investing (I), or financing (F) activities. If you believe a particular account does not fit in any of these activities, explain why.

P1–6A Gulfstream Inc. reports the following list of accounts, in alphabetical order:

Classify accounts.
(SO 3)

	(a)	(b)		(a)	(b)
Accounts payable	___	___	Land	___	___
Accounts receivable	___	___	Mortgage payable	___	___
Building	___	___	Notes payable	___	___
Cash	___	___	Operating expenses	___	___
Common shares	___	___	Other payables	___	___
Cost of goods sold	___	___	Other revenue	___	___
Dividends paid	___	___	Preferred shares	___	___
Equipment	___	___	Prepaid insurance	___	___
Income tax expense	___	___	Retained earnings	___	___
Income tax payable	___	___	Salaries payable	___	___
Interest expense	___	___	Sales revenue	___	___
Inventory	___	___	Unearned revenue	___	___

Instructions

(a) Classify each account as an asset (A), liability (L), shareholders' equity (SE), revenue (R), or expense (E) item.

(b) Identify on which financial statement—statement of earnings (SE), statement of retained earnings (RE), or balance sheet (BS)—each account would be reported.

▸ The Purpose and Use of Financial Statements

Use accounting equation.
(SO 3)

P1–7A   Selected information is available for Tim Hortons Inc. and Starbucks Corporation for the most recent fiscal year:

	Tim Hortons (in CAD millions)	Starbucks (in USD millions)
Beginning of year		
Total assets	$1,745	$ (4)
Total liabilities	(1)	4,429
Total shareholders' equity	1,018	2,229
End of year		
Total assets	1,797	(5)
Total liabilities	795	3,060
Total shareholders' equity	(2)	(6)
Changes during year in shareholders' equity		
Issue (repurchase) of shares	13	(18)
Dividends	(3)	0
Total revenues	1,896	9,522
Total expenses	1,626	8,849
Other increases (decreases) in shareholders' equity	(246)	(616)

Instructions

(a) Use the accounting equation to calculate the missing amounts for each company.

(b) Is it possible to compare Tim Hortons to Starbucks even though Tim Hortons reports its financial results in Canadian dollars and Starbucks reports in U.S. dollars?

(c) Tim Horton's year end is December 30. Starbucks' year end is September 30. If you were to compare the two companies, how would these differing year-end dates affect your assessment?

Prepare financial statements.
(SO 3)

P1–8A   Aero Flying School Ltd. started on May 1, 2009 and reports the following assets, liabilities, and share capital on May 31, and revenues, expenses, and dividends for the month of May, its first month of operations:

Cash	$ 4,300	Advertising expense	$ 900
Accounts receivable	11,200	Rent expense	1,200
Equipment	60,300	Repair expense	700
Accounts payable	2,400	Fuel expense	3,300
Notes payable	25,000	Insurance expense	400
Service revenue	9,600	Income tax expense	600
Interest expense	100	Dividends	800
Common shares	46,800		

Instructions

Prepare a statement of earnings, statement of retained earnings, and balance sheet for the month of May.

Prepare cash flow statement.
(SO 3)

P1–9A   Selected financial statement items follow for Frenette Corporation at June 30, 2009:

Cash, July 1, 2008	$ 30,000	Cash dividends paid	$ 13,000
Inventory	55,000	Cash paid to buy equipment	26,000
Cash paid to suppliers	89,000	Equipment	40,000
Building	400,000	Revenues	200,000
Common shares	20,000	Cash received from customers	158,000
Cash paid for income tax	20,000	Bank loan payable	100,000

Instructions

Determine which of the above items should be included in a cash flow statement, and then prepare this statement for Frenette Corporation for the year ended June 30.

Use financial statement relationships to calculate missing amounts; write memo.
(SO 3)

P1–10A ◖▬▬▶ Incomplete financial statements for Wu, Inc. appear on the facing page.

Instructions

(a) Calculate the missing amounts (1) to (8). Note that you may not be able to be solve each item in numerical order.

(b) Write a memo explaining (1) the sequence for preparing and presenting the financial statements, and (2) the interrelationships between the statement of earnings, statement of retained earnings, and balance sheet.

◖▬▬▶ The **Pencil Icon** means that you have to write a detailed answer for an activity.

WU, INC.
Balance Sheet
August 31, 2009

Assets		Liabilities and Shareholders' Equity	
Cash	$ (1)	Liabilities	
Accounts receivable	20,000	Accounts payable	$19,000
Land	15,000	Shareholders' equity	
Building and equipment	45,000	Common shares	(3)
Total assets	$ (2)	Retained earnings	(4)
		Total liabilities and	
		shareholders' equity	$85,000

WU, INC.
Statement of Earnings
Year Ended August 31, 2009

Service revenue	$75,000
Operating expenses	(5)
Earnings before income tax	35,000
Income tax expense	9,000
Net earnings	$ (6)

WU, INC.
Statement of Retained Earnings
Year Ended August 31, 2009

Retained earnings, Sept. 1, 2008	$10,000
Add: Net earnings	(7)
Less: Dividends	(8)
Retained earnings, Aug. 31, 2009	$31,000

Problems: Set B

P1–1B   Financial decisions made by users often depend on one financial statement more than the others. Consider each of the following independent hypothetical situations:

Identify users and uses of financial statements.
(SO 1)

(a) The North Face Inc. is considering extending credit to a new customer. The terms of the credit would require the customer to pay within 30 days of receiving goods.

(b) An investor is considering purchasing the common shares of Music Online, Inc. The investor plans on holding the investment for at least five years.

(c) Caisse d'Économie Base Montréal is thinking about extending a loan to a small company. The company would be required to make interest payments at the end of each month for three years, and to repay the loan at the end of the third year.

(d) The CEO of Tech Toy Limited is trying to determine whether the company is generating enough cash to increase the amount of dividends paid to investors in this, and future, years. He needs to be sure that Tech Toy will still have enough cash to buy equipment when needed.

Instructions

For each situation, state whether the user would be most interested in the statement of earnings, balance sheet, or cash flow statement. Choose only one financial statement in each case, and briefly give reasons for your choice.

Determine forms of business organization.
(SO 1)

P1–2B   Five independent situations follow:

(a) Three computer science professors have formed a business to sell software to reduce and control spam e-mail. Each has contributed an equal amount of cash and knowledge to the venture. While their software looks promising, they are concerned about the legal liabilities that their business might confront.

(b) Joseph LeBlanc, a student looking for summer employment, has opened a bait shop in a small shed on a local fishing dock.

(c) Robert Steven and Tom Cheng each owned a snow board manufacturing business and have now decided to combine their businesses. They expect that in the coming year they will need funds to expand their operations.

(d) Darcy Becker, Ellen Sweet, and Meg Dwyer recently graduated with business degrees, with majors in accounting. Friends since childhood, they have decided to start an accounting and business consulting practice.

(e) Hervé Gaudet wants to rent DVD players and DVDs in airports across the country. His idea is that customers will be able to rent equipment and DVDs at one airport, watch the DVDs on their flight, and return the equipment and DVDs at their destination airport. Of course, this will require a substantial investment for equipment and DVDs, as well as employees and space in each airport.

Instructions

In each case, explain what form of organization the business is likely to take—proprietorship, partnership, or corporation. Give reasons for your choice.

Identify business activities.
(SO 2)

P1–3B   All businesses are involved in three types of activities—operating, investing, and financing. The names and descriptions of companies in several different industries follow:

Indigo Books & Music—book retailer
High Liner Foods Incorporated—processor and distributor of seafood products
Mountain Equipment Co-op—outdoor equipment retailer
Ganong Bros. Limited—maker of candy
Royal Bank—banking and financial service provider
The Gap, Inc.—casual clothing retailer

Instructions

(a) For each company, provide a likely example of (1) one of its operating activities, (2) one of its investing activities, and (3) one of its financing activities.

(b) Which of the activities that you identified in (a) are common to most businesses? Which activities are not?

Identify business activities.
(SO 2)

P1–4B   Your parents have many cash inflows and outflows, each of which can be identified as operating, investing, or financing. Examples of cash flows that your parents might have follow:

1. _____ Receipt of salary
2. _____ Payment of mortgage on family home
3. _____ Purchase of a new van
4. _____ Purchase of gas for van
5. _____ Purchase of a new kitchen stove

Instructions

(a) For each of the cash flows listed above, indicate whether it is an operating, investing, or financing activity.

(b) For each of type of activity (operating, investing, and financing), provide an example of a cash inflow or outflow you encounter that is not listed above.

Classify accounts.
(SO 2, 3)

P1–5B   The following accounts have been selected from the financial statements of Maple Leaf Foods Inc.:

	(a)	(b)			(a)	(b)
Accounts payable and accrued charges	___	___	Inventories		___	___
Accounts receivable	___	___	Long-term debt		___	___

Cash	____ ____	Property and equipment	____ ____
Common shares	____ ____	Retained earnings	____ ____
Income and other taxes payable	____ ____	Sales	____ ____
Interest expense	____ ____		

Instructions

(a) Classify each account as an asset (A), liability (L), shareholders' equity (SE), revenue (R), or expense (E) item.

(b) Classify each account as being used for operating (O), investing (I), or financing (F) activities. If you believe a particular account does not fit in any of these activities, explain why.

P1–6B Slipstream Ltd. reports the following list of accounts, in alphabetical order:

Classify accounts.
(SO 3)

	(a)	(b)		(a)	(b)
Accounts payable	____	____	Parts revenue	____	____
Accounts receivable	____	____	Preferred shares	____	____
Cash	____	____	Prepaid insurance	____	____
Common shares	____	____	Rent expense	____	____
Dividends	____	____	Repairs and maintenance expense	____	____
Equipment	____	____	Retained earnings	____	____
Income tax expense	____	____	Salaries payable	____	____
Income tax payable	____	____	Service revenue	____	____
Insurance expense	____	____	Travel expense	____	____
Interest expense	____	____	Truck	____	____
Notes payable	____	____	Truck loan payable	____	____
Other payables	____	____	Unearned revenue	____	____

Instructions

(a) Classify each account as an asset (A), liability (L), shareholders' equity (SE), revenue (R), or expense (E) item.

(b) Identify on which financial statement—statement of earnings (SE), statement of retained earnings (RE), or balance sheet (BS)—each account would be reported.

P1–7B Selected information (in millions) is available for **Sears Canada Inc.** and **Canadian Tire Corporation, Limited** for their fiscal 2007 year ends:

Use accounting equation.
(SO 3)

	Sears	Canadian Tire
Beginning of year		
Total assets	$ (1)	$5,804.6
Total liabilities	2,275.3	(4)
Total shareholders' equity	785.0	2,785.2
End of year		
Total assets	3,003.1	(5)
Total liabilities	(2)	3,648.8
Total shareholders' equity	1,093.1	(6)
Changes during year in shareholders' equity		
Issue of shares	0	0.2
Dividends	0	60.4
Total revenues	6,326.4	8,621.4
Total expenses	(3)	8,203.8
Other decreases in shareholders' equity	(0.4)	(48.7)

Instructions

(a) Use the accounting equation to calculate the missing amounts for each company.

(b) Which company has a higher proportion of debt financing at the end of 2007? Of equity financing?

(c) Sears' year end is February 2, 2008. Canadian Tire's year end is December 29, 2007. How might these differing year-end dates affect your comparison in (b)?

Prepare financial statements.
(SO 3)

P1–8B   On June 1, 2009, One Planet Cosmetics Corp. was formed. Here are the assets, liabilities, and share capital of the company at June 30, and the revenues, expenses, and dividends for the month of June:

Cash	$ 5,000	Service revenue	$10,000
Accounts receivable	4,000	Supplies expense	1,200
Cosmetic supplies	2,400	Gas and oil expense	900
Equipment	32,000	Advertising expense	500
Notes payable	14,000	Utilities expense	300
Accounts payable	1,100	Income tax expense	1,000
Common shares	26,200	Salaries expense	3,000
Dividends	1,000		

Instructions
Prepare a statement of earnings, statement of retained earnings, and balance sheet for the month of June.

Prepare cash flow statement.
(SO 3)

P1–9B   Selected financial information follows for Maison Corporation at December 31, 2009:

Cash, Jan. 1	$ 20,000	Cash paid to purchase	
Inventory	25,000	equipment	$ 25,000
Cash paid to suppliers	100,000	Equipment	40,000
Building	200,000	Revenues	100,000
Common shares	50,000	Cash received from customers	140,000
Cash dividends paid	10,000	Accounts payable	25,000

Instructions
Determine which of the above items should be included in a cash flow statement and then prepare this statement for Maison Corporation for the year ended December 31, 2009.

Use financial statement relationships to calculate missing amounts; write memo.
(SO 3)

P1–10B   ▬▬▶ Here are incomplete financial statements for Baxter, Inc.:

BAXTER, INC.
Balance Sheet
November 30, 2009

Assets		Liabilities and Shareholders' Equity	
Cash	$ 5,000	Liabilities	
Accounts receivable	10,000	Notes payable	$ 50,000
Land	(1)	Accounts payable	(3)
Building and equipment	75,000	Total liabilities	74,000
Total assets	$ (2)	Shareholders' equity	
		Common shares	(4)
		Retained earnings	(5)
		Total shareholders' equity	(6)
		Total liabilities and shareholders' equity	$110,000

BAXTER, INC.
Statement of Earnings
Year Ended November 30, 2009

Revenues	$80,000
Operating expenses	(7)
Earnings before income tax	30,000
Income tax expense	6,000
Net earnings	$ (8)

BAXTER, INC. Statement of Retained Earnings Year Ended November 30, 2009	
Retained earnings, Dec. 1, 2008	$ 12,000
Add: Net earnings	(9)
Less: Dividends	10,000
Retained earnings, Nov. 30, 2009	$ (10)

Instructions

(a) Calculate the missing amounts for (1) to (10). Note that you may not be able to be solve each item in numerical order.

(b) Write a memo explaining (1) the sequence for preparing the financial statements, and (2) the interrelationships between the statement of earnings, statement of retained earnings, and balance sheet.

BROADENING YOUR PERSPECTIVE

Financial Reporting and Analysis Cases

Financial Reporting: *Shoppers Drug Mart*

Analysis Tools

BYP1–1 Actual financial statements (rather than the simplified financial statements presented in the chapter) for Shoppers Drug Mart are presented in Appendix A at the end of this book.

Instructions

(a) Notice that the dates on Shoppers Drug Mart's financial statements are December 29, 2007, and December 30, 2006. (The company's 2005 financial statements were dated December 31.) What is Shoppers Drug Mart Corporation's fiscal year end?

(b) What were Shoppers Drug Mart's total assets as at December 29, 2007? December 30, 2006?

(c) How much cash did Shoppers Drug Mart generate from operating activities in fiscal 2007? In fiscal 2006? Was this amount enough to cover Shoppers' investing activities in either fiscal year? (Note that Shoppers presents the operating activities section of its cash flow statement differently than how this section was presented in the chapter. We will learn more about this in Chapter 13.)

(d) What were Shoppers Drug Mart's sales in fiscal 2007? In 2006? By what percentage did Shoppers' sales increase in 2007?

(e) Did Shoppers Drug Mart's net earnings change by roughly the same percentage as its sales? If not, identify the main reason for the difference.

Comparative Analysis: *Shoppers Drug Mart and Jean Coutu*

BYP1–2 The financial statements of Jean Coutu are presented in Appendix B following the financial statements for Shoppers Drug Mart in Appendix A.

Instructions

(a) Based on the information in these financial statements, determine the following for each company:

1. Shoppers Drug Mart's total assets, liabilities, and shareholders' equity at December 29, 2007, and Jean Coutu's total assets, liabilities, and shareholders' equity at March 1, 2008

2. Shoppers Drug Mart's and Jean Coutu's sales and net earnings for the most recent fiscal year

3. Shoppers Drug Mart's and Jean Coutu's increase or decrease in cash for the most recent fiscal year

(b) What conclusions about the two companies can you draw from the data you determined in (a)?

(c) Companies that operate in the same industry often have the same year end to help statement users make comparisons. Knowing that the year ends of Shoppers Drug Mart and Jean Coutu are not the same, do you have any concerns about the comparisons you made in (b)?

Interpreting Financial Statements

BYP1–3 Gildan Activewear Inc. reports the following selected information (in USD thousands) for two recent years:

	2007	2006
Statement of Earnings		
Sales	$964,429	$773,190
Cost of goods sold	655,280	521,095
Net earnings	130,020	106,829
Statement of Retained Earnings		
Dividends	0	0
Ending retained earnings	545,388	415,368
Balance Sheet		
Total assets	874,486	723,276
Total liabilities	210,836	192,711
Total shareholders' equity	663,650	530,565
Cash Flow Statement		
Cash receipts from operating activities	91,163	94,721
Cash receipts from (payments for) financing activities	23,550	(39,383)
Cash payments for investing activities	(134,689)	(96,053)
Cash, end of year	9,250	29,007

Instructions

(a) What is the probable reason that a Canadian company such as Gildan Activewear would present its financial statements in U.S. dollars rather than Canadian dollars?

(b) Did the company's sales increase faster or slower than its net earnings in 2007? What do you think is the main reason for this?

(c) Why, in your opinion, did Gildan Activewear not pay a dividend to its shareholders in 2007 or 2006?

(d) By what percentage did the company's assets increase in 2007? By what percentage did the company's liabilities increase in 2007?

(e) Why, in your opinion, did the company's cash decline by U.S. $19,757 thousand in 2007?

(f) What is the probable reason that net earnings increased in 2007 but cash decreased?

A Global Focus

www.wiley.com/canada/kimmel

International Resources

BYP1–4 Zachary Wall is thinking about expanding the product offerings in his automotive supply store. He would like to include tires. In deciding which product lines to carry, Zachary knows that it is important to consider many factors, including quality, performance rating, price, and warranty. However, he is also interested in investigating the financial health of the tire manufacturers and has obtained recent financial statements for **The Goodyear Tire & Rubber Company** ("Goodyear") and **Compagnie Générale des Établissements Michelin** ("Michelin").

As it turns out, however, Zachary is having trouble comparing the two companies' financial results. Goodyear's headquarters are in Ohio, U.S.A., and it reports its financial results in U.S. dollars. Michelin's headquarters are located in Clermont-Ferrand, France, and its financial statements are in Euros. In addition, Michelin has ordered the accounts in its balance sheet differently than Goodyear. The ordering that Goodyear uses is familiar to Zachary because Canadian companies also use that order. Zachary is not sure how to read Michelin's balance sheet: "I had no idea that there was more than one way to prepare a balance sheet. How can this be useful to people outside the company?"

Instructions

(a) Who are the external users of accounting information?

(b) Zachary understands that the purpose of accounting is to provide information for decision-making. He understands that currencies change from country to country (e.g., Canadian dollars, U.S. dollars, Euros, etc.) but he would like to know whether you think that basic decision-making also changes from country to country.

(c) Will Zachary be able to find the information he needs about the the different tires' quality, performance rating, price, and warranty in the financial statements? If not, where might he find such information?

(d) Zachary is having difficulty comparing Michelin's balance sheet to Goodyear's because of the different ordering used in each set of financial statements. Explain to Zachary how the order of these two balance sheets differs and whether he will still be able to compare the two sets of statements.

Critical Thinking Cases and Activities

Collaborative Learning Activity

BYP1–5 Financial statements aim to provide reliable information to a diverse group of users. Information must be enough for external investors to make decisions, but not so much that a company reveals its operating processes and competitive advantage.

Instructions

With the class divided into groups, answer the following questions as if you were regional sales managers for **Shoppers Drug Mart**:

(a) What information is contained in the company's financial statements that is important to the sales manager position (consider both a short-term and long-term perspective)?

(b) Identify several types of information that are not presented in these statements and that sales managers would use to carry out their responsibilities.

Communication Activity

BYP1–6 Robert Foote, the new accountant for Hill Corporation, has prepared the following balance sheet:

HILL CORPORATION Balance Sheet December 31, 2009	
Assets	
Cash	$10,500
Accounts receivable	5,000
Supplies	2,000
Equipment	20,500
Total assets	$38,000
Liabilities and Shareholders' Equity	
Liabilities	
Accounts payable	$ 5,000
Note payable	12,000
Total liabilities	17,000
Shareholders' equity	
Common shares	18,000
Retained earnings	?
Total shareholders' equity	?
Total liabilities and shareholders' equity	$?

Robert was unsure of how to determine the balance for the retained earnings account. The company also paid a $1,000 cash dividend, and while Robert knew where to record the cash (and did so correctly), he did not know where to record the dividend.

Instructions

(a) What is the correct balance for the retained earnings account at December 31?

(b) How should Robert account for the dividend?

(c) In a memo, explain to Robert (1) how the financial statements are interrelated, and (2) why the order of preparation of each financial statement matters.

Ethics Case

Ethics in Accounting

BYP1–7 Chief executive officers (CEOs) and chief financial officers (CFOs) of publicly traded companies are required to personally certify that their companies' financial statements and other financial information contain no untrue statements and do not leave out any important facts. Khan Corporation just hired a new management team, and its members say they are too new to the company to know whether the most recent financial reports are accurate or not. They refuse to sign the certification.

Instructions

(a) Who are the stakeholders in this situation?

(b) Should the CEO and CFO sign the certification? Explain why or why not.

(c) What are the CEO's and CFO's alternatives?

"All About You" Activity

BYP1–8 Every company needs to plan in order to move forward. Its top management must consider where it wants the company to be in three to five years. Like a company, you need to think about where you want to be in three to five years from now, and you need to start taking steps now in order to get there. With some forethought, you can help yourself avoid a bad situation, like the one described in the "All About You" feature in this chapter, where the resumé is based more on creative writing than facts.

Instructions

(a) Where would you like to be working in three to five years? Describe your plan for getting there by identifying specific steps that you need to take in order to get there.

(b) In order to get the job you want, you will need a resumé. Your resumé is the equivalent of a company's annual report. It needs to provide relevant and reliable information about your past and accomplishments so that employers can decide whether to "invest" in you. Do a search on the Internet to find a good resumé format. What are the basic elements of a resumé?

(c) A company's annual report provides information about the company's accomplishments. In order for investors to use the annual report, the information must be reliable; that is, users must have faith that the information is accurate and believable. How can you provide assurance that the information on your resumé is reliable?

(d) Do a search on the Internet for David Edmondson. Is Mr. Edmondson still employed by RadioShack? If not, was he fired or did he resign?

Serial Case

This **serial case** starts in this chapter and continues in each chapter of the book.

BYP1–9 Natalie Koebel spent much of her childhood learning the art of cookie-making from her grandmother. They passed many happy hours mastering every type of cookie imaginable and later devised new recipes that were both healthy and delicious. Natalie is investigating various possibilities for starting her own business as part of the requirements of the college entrepreneurship program she is taking.

A long-time friend insists that Natalie has to somehow include cookies in her business plan and, after a series of brainstorming sessions, Natalie settles on the idea of operating a cookie-making school. She will start on a part-time basis and offer her services in people's homes. Now that she has started thinking about it, the possibilities seem endless. She will offer group sessions (which will probably be more entertainment than education for the participants) and individual lessons. Natalie also decides to include children in her target market. The first difficult decision is coming up with the perfect name for her business. In the end she settles on "Cookie Creations," and she then moves on to more important issues.

Instructions

(a) What form of business organization—proprietorship, partnership, or corporation—do you recommend that Natalie use for her business? Discuss the benefits and weaknesses of each form that Natalie might consider and give your reasons for choosing the form of business organization you are recommending.

(b) Will Natalie need accounting information? If yes, what information will she need and why? How often will she need this information?

(c) Identify specific asset, liability, and equity accounts that Cookie Creations will likely use to record its business transactions.

Answers to Chapter Questions

Answer to Shoppers Drug Mart Review It Question 3

Shoppers Drug Mart's accounting equation as at December 29, 2007, is (in thousands):

Assets	=	Liabilities	+	Shareholders' equity
$5,644,039	=	$2,433,873	+	($113,119 + $3,097,047)

Answers to Self-Study Questions

. d   2. b   3. a   4. c   5. c   6. d   7. d   8. c   9. d   10. a

Remember to go back to the beginning of the chapter to check off your completed work!

←

CHAPTER 2

Financial Statements— Framework, Presentation, and Usage

ACCOUNTING MATTERS!

Getting the Numbers Right

Many investors rely on financial statements in order to make informed decisions on whether to buy or sell a company's shares. In the early 2000s, corporate reporting scandals shocked the world, with companies like Nortel and Hollinger in Canada, Enron and WorldCom in the United States, and Parmalat in Italy making big headlines. Investors learned that they could not always rely on financial statements.

The most high-profile Canadian organization deep in scandal was Brampton, Ontario–based Nortel Networks Corporation. In January 2005, Nortel released revised financial statements for 2003, 2002, and 2001, reducing its net earnings for 2003 from the previously reported U.S. $732 million, or 17 cents a share, to U.S. $434 million, or 10 cents a share.

The original results for 2003 had indicated the first profitable year in seven, triggering a jump in share price and increased investor confidence. In March 2004, however, Nortel revealed that there had been accounting irregularities, with net earnings overstated by up to 50 percent. Nortel's chief executive officer and nine senior financial officers were soon fired "with cause," and the share price began to drop.

But the telecommunications company's financial problems were not over. In March 2006, it announced that it would again restate its financial results, this time for 2003, 2004, and the first nine months of 2005, and with further adjustments to periods before 2003. These restatements were mainly due to revenue that had been recognized in prior periods but should have been deferred to future periods.

Still, the juggling of the numbers was not yet complete. March 2007 brought another announcement of restatements to the financial results for 2004, 2005, and the first nine months of 2006, with adjustments to periods before 2004. This time the cause was third-party actuarial calculation errors going back to before 2000 on liabilities for employee benefit plans and timing errors on the recognition of revenue.

The company has faced several shareholders' class action lawsuits. The RCMP and securities regulators in both Canada and the United States were also involved in investigating Nortel's financial accounting situation. The focus on the numbers had an additional consequence as it diverted attention away from the company's product. Industry analysts reported in 2005 that Nortel lagged behind in product development, running 6 to 12 months behind on product upgrades.

Nortel's board of directors then made a commitment to rebuild a finance environment based on principles of transparency and integrity, and on ensuring sound financial reporting and comprehensive disclosure.

Announced in 2006, the terms of a global settlement to the class action lawsuits saw Nortel pay U.S. $575 million in cash, issue 62,866,775 of its common shares (representing 14.5% of its equity), and contribute one-half of the amounts recovered from its own litigation against the senior officers who were fired in 2004.

Nortel reached a settlement with the Ontario Securities Commission in 2007. The Commission recognized Nortel's restructured ethics policy and establishment of a new code of conduct, its improvement of financial processes and controls, remedy of its internal control issues, improved corporate governance, and the settlement of shareholder class action lawsuits. The company also reached a settlement on all issues with the U.S. Securities Exchange Commission in 2007, agreeing to pay a civil penalty of U.S. $35 million and accepting injunctions against it for violations of certain provisions of federal securities laws.

Corporate scandals like the ones at Nortel and other companies have made it clear that high quality accounting standards are essential. Financial statements *should* provide relevant and faithfully represented information, and regulators and lawmakers have since made changes in financial reporting requirements worldwide to help ensure that the corporate scandals of the past do not happen again.

It may take years for Nortel to regain full investor confidence in its numbers—all the more reason for companies to get them right the first time around.

rtel Networks Corporation: nortel.com

THE NAVIGATOR

- [ ] Read *Feature Story*
- [ ] Scan *Study Objectives*
- [ ] Read *Chapter Preview*
- [ ] Read text and answer *Before You Go On*
- [ ] Read *All About You*
- [ ] Review *Summary of Study Objectives*
- [ ] Review *Using the Decision Toolkit—A Summary*
- [ ] Work *Using the Decision Toolkit*
- [ ] Work *Demonstration Problem*
- [ ] Answer *Self-Study Questions*
- [ ] Complete assignments

ᵗUDY OBJECTIVES

ᵗer studying this chapter, you should be able to:

Describe the conceptual framework of accounting, including the objective, qualitative characteristics, and elements of financial reporting.

Identify and apply assumptions, principles, and constraints of the conceptual framework.

Identify the sections of a classified balance sheet.

Identify and calculate ratios for analyzing a company's profitability.

Identify and calculate ratios for analyzing a company's liquidity and solvency.

✓

e Navigator

PREVIEW OF CHAPTER 2

If you are thinking of purchasing a company's shares, how can you decide what the shares are worth? If you own shares, how can you determine if it is time to buy more or time to bail out? Your decision will be influenced by a variety of considerations, and one of these should be your careful analysis of the company's financial statements.

In this chapter, we begin by looking at the conceptual framework of accounting, which provides a general guide for financial reporting. We then take a closer look at the balance sheet and introduce some useful ways of evaluating the information in the financial statements. The chapter is organized as follows:

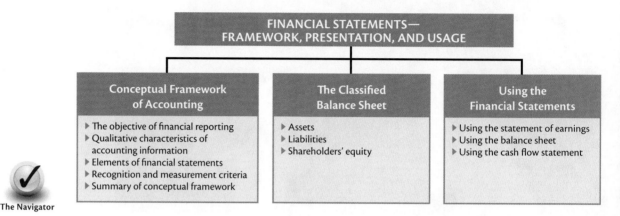

FINANCIAL STATEMENTS—
FRAMEWORK, PRESENTATION, AND USAGE

Conceptual Framework of Accounting
▸ The objective of financial reporting
▸ Qualitative characteristics of accounting information
▸ Elements of financial statements
▸ Recognition and measurement criteria
▸ Summary of conceptual framework

The Classified Balance Sheet
▸ Assets
▸ Liabilities
▸ Shareholders' equity

Using the Financial Statements
▸ Using the statement of earnings
▸ Using the balance sheet
▸ Using the cash flow statement

The Navigator

Conceptual Framework of Accounting

study objective 1

Describe the conceptual framework of accounting, including the objective, qualitative characteristics, and elements of financial reporting.

According to standard-setters, the conceptual framework of accounting is "a coherent system of inter-related objectives and fundamentals that can lead to consistent standards and that prescribes the nature, function, and limits of financial accounting statements." In other words, the conceptual framework of accounting guides decisions about what to present in financial statements, alternative ways of reporting economic events, and appropriate ways of communicating this information.

Why do we need a conceptual framework of accounting? As a foundation for accounting, the conceptual framework does the following:

1. It ensures that existing standards and practices are clear and consistent.
2. It makes it possible to respond quickly to new issues.
3. It increases the relevance, faithful representation, comparability, and understandability of financial reporting results.

A conceptual framework ensures that we have a coherent set of standards. New standards are easier to understand and are more consistent when they are built on the same foundation as existing standards. By relying on an existing framework of basic theory, it should be possible to solve new and emerging problems more quickly.

However, it is difficult, if not impossible, to create a rule for every situation. Canadian standards are therefore based mostly on general principles rather than specific rules. With the help of a conceptual framework and their professional judgement, it is hoped that accountants will be able to quickly determine an appropriate accounting treatment for each situation.

A conceptual framework also makes financial statements more relevant, objective, and easier to compare. It increases users' understanding of, and confidence in, financial reporting. This is especially important today as more and more countries are moving away from their own national sets of accounting standards and adopting instead a uniform, global set of standards.

Accounting standards can differ significantly, and do, from country to country. This lack of uniformity has arisen over time because of differences in legal systems, in processes for developing standards, in government requirements, and in economic environments. The International Accounting Standards Board (IASB) was formed to try to reduce these areas of difference and unify global standard-setting.

www.wiley.com/canada/kimmel

International Resources

In Canada, we currently have our own accounting standards. They are developed by the Accounting Standards Board (AcSB), an independent standard-setting body created by the Canadian Institute of Chartered Accountants. The Accounting Standards Oversight Council—with representation from business, finance, government, academe, the accounting and legal professions, and regulators—oversees and contributes to the activities of the AcSB. In 2006, the AcSB recommended that profit-oriented publicly traded companies in Canada move to International Financial Reporting Standards (IFRS) by 2011. In many respects, Canadian standards are already quite similar to international standards. However, there are some key differences that we will learn about in later chapters that will result in significant changes in the way Canadian companies account for, and report, their financial information.

The AcSB has already begun a convergence strategy that will ensure that all Canadian standards become the same as IFRS, or close to them, over the next few years. After 2011, Canadian standards will cease to exist for profit-oriented publicly traded companies. Not-for-profit companies and private companies will move to a simplified set of standards considered to be more suitable for their own needs. Over the next few years, there will be a mix of standards in use, including future changes that are impossible to fully capture at this point. Indeed, some of the IFRS themselves are still evolving at the time of writing.

In terms of the transition to international standards over the next few years, we can expect to see different timing and patterns of adoption. Some companies might choose to adopt IFRS earlier than 2011. Other companies may wait until January 1, 2011, to move to IFRS. We will also see a transition from U.S. standards to international standards for some Canadian companies. Canadian companies whose shares trade on a U.S. stock exchange, a situation that currently permits a Canadian company to use U.S. accounting standards, are also required to change to IFRS in 2011.

So how does this affect you as a student today? This text will teach you Canadian standards, as they will still be in place up to, and including, December 31, 2010. We will also introduce international standards, where appropriate to do so, as some companies will start using these standards soon and all Canadian companies will be using them as of January 1, 2011. More importantly, we will help you gain the critical skills throughout this text that will assist you in navigating through a changing body of knowledge.

If you feel a bit overwhelmed by what this transition to new standards will require of you as a student, remember that accounting is not the only profession that has to cope with change. Think about the medical profession, where new procedures, drugs, and treatments are available on a daily basis. If you give it a bit of thought, you can likely also identify other professions whose body of knowledge is transitory.

🌐 ACCOUNTING MATTERS! | International Perspective

More than 100 countries throughout the world have already adopted International Financial Reporting Standards. This number is expected to rise substantially in the near future as nearly every major economy has either adopted or announced a plan to converge its standards with IFRS. A number of countries, such as Canada, India, Japan, and Korea, have announced their planned move to international standards by 2011. In addition, the United States is considering the adoption of IFRS, and have prepared a "roadmap" that suggests IFRS could be phased in from 2014 to 2016 depending on the size of the company..

Christopher Cox, chairman of the U.S. Securities and Exchange Commission (SEC), said during an SEC roundtable on international financial reporting standards: "Virtually everyone—issuers, investors, and stakeholders alike—agrees that the world's cap[ital] markets would benefit from the widespread acceptance and use of high-quality global standards. Replacing the babel of competing and often contradictory standards would improve investor confidence, allow investors to draw better conclusions, and simplify the process and cut costs for issuers."

With such an unprecedented level of change in accounting standards about to occur, never before has the conceptual framework been as important as it is today to companies and other users of accounting, whose need to interpret financial data accurately always remains the same.

Along with the move to international accounting standards described above, accounting standard-setters are also currently working on a project to update and produce a common conceptual framework. The first two sections of the framework—the objective of financial reporting and the qualitative characteristics—have been issued in draft form. These proposed sections are described below, as these sections are expected to be finalized in the near future. The last two sections are still being worked on, so we will describe the conceptual framework that is currently used in Canada for the elements of financial statements and recognition and measurement criteria.

The conceptual framework of accounting has four main sections:

1. The objective of financial reporting
2. The qualitative characteristics of accounting information
3. The elements of financial statements
4. Recognition and measurement criteria (assumptions, principles, and constraints)

The Objective of Financial Reporting

The main objective of financial reporting **is to provide information that is useful to individuals who are making investment and credit decisions.** Remember that we learned in Chapter 1 that investors and creditors are the main external users of financial information. The information that these users require generally meets the needs of other users.

To help users make decisions whether to invest or lend, or allocate their resources in some other way, financial reporting should provide information about the amounts, timing, and uncertainty of future cash flows, economic resources (assets), and claims to those resources (liabilities and equity). Financial reporting should also include management's explanations about the company's financial activities, since management knows more about the company than external users do.

Qualitative Characteristics of Accounting Information

To be useful for decision-making, information should have these qualitative characteristics: **relevance, faithful representation, comparability,** and **understandability**.

Relevance

Accounting information has relevance if it will make a difference in users' decisions. Relevant information helps users make predictions about the potential effects of past, present, or future transactions or other events. It is therefore said to have **predictive value**. For example, when Shoppers Drug Mart issues financial statements, the information in them is considered relevant because it gives a basis for predicting future cash flows. As we learned in our feature story, Nortel's financial statements did *not* have predictive value as the company later had to issue revised financial statements to correct inaccuracies and irregularities.

Relevant information also helps users confirm or correct their previous expectations. It is said to have **feedback value**. When Nortel revised its financial statements, the company corrected expectations about its financial health. In most cases, financial statements are expected to *confirm* and not correct expectations.

For accounting information to be relevant, it must also be **timely**. It must be available to decision-makers before it loses its ability to influence their decisions. Nortel lost the battle with timeliness with its revised financial statements. It released its first round of revised financial statements in 2005 (for 2003, 2002, and 2001), revised its financial statements again in 2006 (for 2005, 2004, and 2003), and yet again in 2007 (for 2006, 2005, and 2004).

> **Alternative Terminology**
> *Feedback value* is also called *confirmatory value*.

Faithful Representation

For information to be useful, it must be a faithful representation of what really exists or happened. It must represent economic reality. In other words, financial reporting must present the economic substance of a transaction, not just its legal form.

Faithful representation also means that the information must be **verifiable, neutral,** and **complete**. Verifiability means that two or more people reviewing the same information and using the same methods would reach the same results or similar conclusions. Although it is critical for information to be verifiable, users must also understand that financial reporting information is often based on estimates, rather than on exact measures of transactions and events. For example, liabilities for future environmental cleanup costs must be estimated and are difficult to verify.

Neutrality means the absence of bias. That is, accounting information cannot be selected, prepared, or presented to favour one set of interested users over another. Completeness means that all the information that is needed to faithfully represent economic reality must be included. Factual, unbiased, and complete information is critical in financial reporting. These criteria were obviously not respected at Nortel, described in our feature story, which is why the company was under siege by irate shareholders.

Comparability

In accounting, there is comparability when companies with similar circumstances use the same accounting standards. Comparability enables users to identify the similarities and differences between companies. However, as we have seen in our discussion of international accounting standards earlier, comparability is sometimes difficult. For example, U.S. inventory cost flow assumptions can differ from Canadian (and international) inventory cost flow assumptions (which we will learn about in Chapter 6). As a result, it can be difficult to compare and evaluate the financial results of companies like U.S.-based Wal-Mart with those of Sears Canada. The movement to international accounting standards will help eliminate or reduce some of these differences.

Users of accounting information also want to be able to compare a company's financial results over time. For example, to compare a company's net earnings over several years, you would need to know that the same accounting standards have been used from year to year; otherwise, you might be comparing apples to oranges. Consistency means that a company uses the same accounting treatment for similar events from year to year. When a company's financial information is reported on a consistent basis, the financial statements can be used for a meaningful analysis of trends within the company.

This does not mean that a company can never change from one accounting standard to another. Companies can change accounting standards, but only if the change is required by the Accounting Standards Board, or if the change will result in more relevant information for decision-making.

Understandability

In order for information in financial statements to be useful, all users have to be able to understand it. One of the benefits of most countries moving to a common set of international accounting standards is that they are more likely to be understood by global users.

Financial statements cannot always satisfy the varied needs of all users, however. Consequently, the objective of financial reporting focuses mostly on the information needs of investors and creditors. Even within these two groups, users vary widely in the types of decisions they make and in their level of interest in the information. At one extreme is a sophisticated creditor who carefully scrutinizes all aspects of the financial information. At the other extreme is an unsophisticated investor who may only scan the text and not study the numbers.

It is therefore necessary to agree on a base level of understandability that will help both the preparer of financial information and its users. That base level is this: **The average user is assumed to have a reasonable understanding of accounting concepts and procedures, as well as of general business and economic conditions.** Users who do not have this level of understanding and ability are expected to rely on professionals who do have an appropriate level of expertise.

Understandability is greater when the information is classified, characterized, and presented clearly and concisely.

The qualitative characteristics of accounting information are summarized in Illustration 2-1.

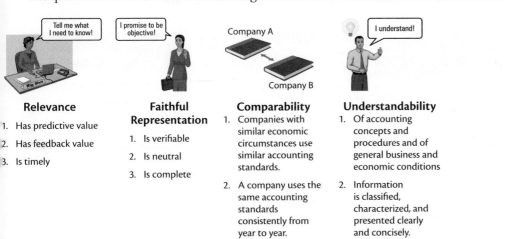

Relevance
1. Has predictive value
2. Has feedback value
3. Is timely

Faithful Representation
1. Is verifiable
2. Is neutral
3. Is complete

Comparability
1. Companies with similar economic circumstances use similar accounting standards.
2. A company uses the same accounting standards consistently from year to year.

Understandability
1. Of accounting concepts and procedures and of general business and economic conditions
2. Information is classified, characterized, and presented clearly and concisely.

◄ Illustration 2-1

Qualitative characteristics of accounting information

These qualitative characteristics are complementary concepts—that is, they work together. Nonetheless, they must be applied in a certain order. The qualitative characteristic of **relevance** should be applied first because it will help identify what specific information that would affect the decisions of investors, creditors, and other users of accounting information should be included in the financial reports.

Once relevance is applied, **faithful representation** should be applied to ensure that the economic information faithfully represents the information being described. Taken together, relevance and faithful representation make financial reporting information decision-useful.

The next qualitative characteristics are **comparability** and **understandability**. They add to the decision-usefulness of financial reporting information that is relevant and representationally faithful. They must be applied after the first two characteristics because they cannot, either individually or together, make information decision-useful if it is irrelevant or not faithfully represented.

Elements of Financial Statements

An important part of the conceptual framework is a set of definitions that describe the basic terms used in accounting. This set of definitions is referred to as the elements of financial statements. It includes such terms as **assets, liabilities, equity, revenues,** and **expenses.**

Because these elements are so important and are often interrelated, they must be precisely defined and universally applied. We learned a few definitions in Chapter 1. We will review and expand on these definitions in more detail later in this chapter.

BEFORE YOU GO ON...

Review It

1. Why do we need a conceptual framework of accounting?
2. What is the basic objective of financial information?
3. What qualitative characteristics make accounting information useful?
4. Does it matter in what order the qualitative characteristics are applied?

The Navigator

Recognition and Measurement Criteria

study objective 2

Identify and apply assumptions, principles, and constraints of the conceptual framework.

The objective of financial reporting, the qualitative characteristics of accounting information, and the elements of financial statements are very broad. Because accountants must solve practical problems, they need more detailed criteria to help them decide when items should be included in the financial statements and how they should be measured. We classify these recognition and measurement criteria as **assumptions, principles,** and **constraints**.

Assumptions create a foundation for the accounting process. Principles indicate how economic events should be reported. Constraints make it possible to relax the principles under certain circumstances. Illustration 2-2 outlines these recognition and measurement criteria.

Illustration 2-2 ➡

Recognition and measurement criteria

Assumptions	Generally Accepted Accounting Principles	Constraints
Monetary unit	Cost	Materiality
Economic entity	Full disclosure	Cost-benefit
Time period	Revenue recognition	
Going concern	Matching	

Assumptions

Four assumptions guide when to recognize (include) and how to measure economic events: the **monetary unit, economic entity, time period,** and **going concern** assumptions.

Monetary Unit Assumption The monetary unit assumption requires that only those things that can be expressed in money be included in the accounting records. This might seem so obvious that it does not need to be mentioned, but it has important implications for financial reporting. Because the exchange of money is fundamental to business transactions, it makes sense that we measure a business in terms of money. However, it also means that some important information needed by investors and creditors is not reported in the financial statements. For example, customer satisfaction is important to every business, but it is not easily quantified in dollars. It is therefore not reported in the financial statements. Similarly, the quality and integrity of management are not reported because they cannot be expressed in dollars.

The monetary unit assumption also assumes that the unit of measure remains stable over time. That is, the effects of inflation (or deflation) are assumed to be minor and are therefore ignored. The Bank of Canada's inflation policy is to keep inflation at between 1 and 3 percent. Consequently, inflation is considered to be a non-issue for accounting purposes in Canada.

It is worth noting that in some countries inflation is so significant that companies have to adjust for it in their financial reports. For example, in Zimbabwe, the annual rate of inflation is nearly 1,000 percent! In such cases, a general price-level index is typically used to adjust for the effects of inflation so that the information is comparable from year to year.

Economic Entity Assumption The economic entity assumption states that the economic activity can be identified with a particular accounting unit (e.g., a company) which is separate and distinct from the activities of the shareholders and of all other economic entities.

Suppose you are one of Shoppers Drug Mart's shareholders. The amount of cash that you have in your personal bank account and the balance you owe on your personal car loan are not reported in Shoppers Drug Mart's balance sheet. This is because, for accounting purposes, you and Shoppers' are separate accounting entities.

In addition, as we learned from the Chapter 1 feature story, Shoppers Drug Mart has a number of independent drug stores owned and operated by "Associates." Each drug store is operated by a pharmacist (called an Associate) who, through a separate corporation, has entered into a licensing agreement with Shoppers Drug Mart. Although the financial results of these companies are consolidated (combined) for reporting purposes, individual accounting records and financial statements are also produced for each specific company. In order to accurately assess the performance and financial position of each company, it has to be possible to distinguish each company's activities from the transactions of any other company, even if the companies are related.

Time Period Assumption The time period assumption states that the life of a business can be divided into artificial time periods and that useful reports covering those periods can be prepared for the business. In other words, it is assumed that the activities of a company, such as Shoppers Drug Mart, can be subdivided into months, quarters, or years for meaningful financial reporting even though the company's operations do not cease at the end of these time periods.

> **Alternative Terminology**
> The *time period* assumption is also called the *periodicity* assumption.

All companies report at least annually, at the end of their fiscal year. Publicly traded companies also report to shareholders every three months (quarterly) and prepare monthly statements for internal purposes. Reporting periods of less than one year are known as interim periods, which are essential for timely and relevant decision-making.

The shorter the time period, the more difficult it is to faithfully represent the financial results for the period. A month's results are usually harder to verify than a quarter's results, and a quarter's results are harder to verify than a year's results. This is because economic activities are seldom complete in a month, or even a quarter, and often not even within a year. Consequently, estimates and assumptions are required that artificially divide economic activity into artificial periods of time. Waiting until an economic activity is complete before recording it is not an acceptable alternative, because it would not result in timely financial information. Consequently, the time period assumption recognizes that estimates are essential for producing information that is still relevant for decision-making.

Going Concern Assumption The going concern assumption states that the business will remain in operation for the foreseeable future. Of course some businesses do fail. However, if a business has a history of profitable operations and access to financial resources, it is reasonable to assume that it will continue operating long enough to carry out its existing objectives and commitments.

The going concern assumption has important implications in accounting. It is directly related to the cost principle, which we will learn about in the next section. If a going concern is not assumed, assets should be stated at their liquidation value (the selling price less the cost of disposal), not at their cost. Classifying assets and liabilities as short- and long-term would not matter either.

The only time that the going concern assumption should not be used is when the liquidation of a business is likely. Accounting for liquidations is discussed in advanced accounting courses.

Accounting Principles

Based on the fundamental assumptions of accounting described in the previous section, the accounting profession has developed principles that describe how economic events should be recorded and reported. These are known as generally accepted accounting principles (GAAP). "Generally accepted" means that these principles are widely recognized and have authoritative support through the Canadian and provincial business corporations acts and securities legislation. Legislation is currently being updated in Canada to allow the use of international accounting standards. All companies whose shares or debt are publicly traded must follow GAAP, whether Canadian, U.S., or international depending on the jurisdiction the company is operating in. Most other companies also follow GAAP as it provides the most useful information.

We will introduce four key accounting principles in this text. We will learn about the **cost principle** and **full disclosure principle** in this chapter, and the **revenue recognition principle** and **matching principle** in Chapter 4.

Cost Principle The cost principle dictates that assets be recorded at their cost at the time of acquisition. This is generally true not only at the time when an asset is purchased, but also during the time that an asset is held. For example, if a company were to purchase land for $3 million, it would first be reported on the balance sheet at $3 million. But what would the company do if by the end of the next year the land had increased in value to $4 million? The answer is that under the cost principle the land would still be reported at $3 million. In this particular case, cost is the most **relevant** value because the land is intended for use in the business. It is not being held for resale. The land will continue to be reported at cost until either it is sold or the **going concern assumption** is no longer valid.

The cost principle is often criticized as being irrelevant, especially for predicting the value of an asset. When the asset is first recognized, its cost and fair value (what it is worth) are usually the same. Over time, however, fair value can move substantially away from the historical (i.e., original) cost value. Supporters of the cost principle counter that cost is the more **faithful representation** because it can easily be verified and is neutral. Fair value, they say, is more subjective.

Despite these limitations, accounting does revalue certain types of assets to their fair value after acquisition. The movement to international financial reporting standards is expected to result in even more of a mixed cost and market valuation model. We will learn more about this in later chapters, but for now we will concentrate on using cost to record transactions.

Full Disclosure Principle. The full disclosure principle requires that all circumstances and events which would make a difference to financial statement users be disclosed. It is important that investors be made aware of events that can affect the financial health of a company.

The full disclosure principle is respected by providing the data contained in the financial statements and the accompanying notes to the financial statements. In most cases, the first note to the financial statements is a summary of significant accounting policies. Other notes provide additional details or explanations for information given in the financial statements. Notes can also add new information about events or situations that cannot be quantified in the financial statements.

For example, as we learned in our feature story, Nortel's shareholders filed class action lawsuits against the company. Nortel included two full pages of description about these lawsuits in the notes to its financial statements, including the expected impact of the lawsuits on the business. Nortel's board of directors is committed to providing a complete and transparent disclosure of all relevant events and transactions.

Deciding how much disclosure is enough can be difficult. Accountants could disclose every financial event that occurs, or is expected to occur, so that the statements are as complete as possible. But, as we will learn in the next section, the benefits of giving this additional information may be less than the cost of making it available.

Constraints in Accounting

The goal of the generally accepted accounting principles discussed above is to provide users of financial statements with the most useful information for decision-making. If they are followed too rigidly, however, the effort to provide useful financial information may be far too costly for a company. Some constraints have therefore been agreed upon to ensure that accounting principles are applied in a reasonable way, from the perspectives of both the company and the user. **Constraints** permit a company to make changes to generally accepted accounting principles as long as the reported information is still useful. Two of these constraints are materiality and cost-benefit.

Materiality Materiality relates to a financial statement item's impact on a company's overall financial condition and operations. An item is **material** when including it, or leaving it out, is likely to influence the decision of an investor or creditor. A financial report should include all the information that is material. Information that is not material should be omitted. An item is **immaterial** if including it or not will have no impact on a decision-maker. To clutter a financial report with immaterial information could result in important information being difficult to find, thus making the report less useful to decision-makers.

If the item does not make a difference in decision-making, it does not have to be disclosed and applying GAAP may not be important. Determining if an item is material is a difficult decision; professional judgement has to be used and one has to understand the relative amount and importance of the item in each particular circumstance.

International standards do not include a quantitative definition for what is material and what is not. There are concerns that using a specific number or threshold (e.g., 10% of earnings) to determine materiality is too rules-based. You will recall that we mentioned earlier in this chapter that Canadian and international standards are deliberately based on general principles rather than specific rules.

Cost-Benefit The cost-benefit constraint ensures that the value of the information is greater than the cost of providing it. That is, the benefits of financial reporting information should justify the costs of providing and using it.

For example, to achieve completeness, which we discussed along with the qualitative characteristic of faithful representation, accountants could record or disclose every financial event that occurs and every uncertainty that exists. However, providing additional information increases costs, and the benefits of providing this information, in some cases, may be less than the costs.

As there have been more and more changes to reporting requirements, the costs of giving this information have increased. Because of these increasing costs, some critics have argued that the costs of applying GAAP to smaller or non–publicly traded companies are too high compared to the benefits. To respond to this problem, the CICA has developed a differential reporting model for smaller, private companies that allows them to use a simplified version of Canadian GAAP. As Paul Cherry, the chairman of the Accounting Standards Board recently concluded, "One size does not necessarily fit all." As mentioned earlier, the Accounting Standards Board is trying to decide what basis private companies should report on once there is international convergence of accounting standards for public companies.

Summary of Conceptual Framework

As we have seen, the conceptual framework for developing sound reporting practices starts with the objective of financial reporting. It then describes the qualitative characteristics of accounting information and the elements of the financial statements. Finally, more detailed recognition and measurement criteria are provided. These criteria exist as assumptions, principles, and constraints. The conceptual framework is summarized in Illustration 2-3. Recall, as mentioned earlier in the chapter, that the elements of financial statements and recognition and measurement criteria in the conceptual framework are currently under review by standard setters and can be expected to change at some point in the future.

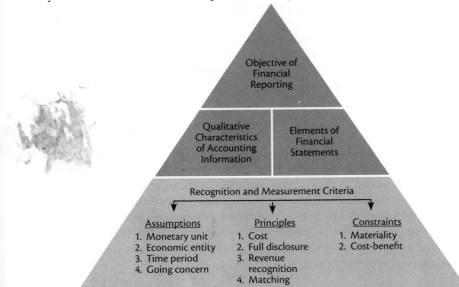

◀ Illustration 2-3

Conceptual framework

BEFORE YOU GO ON...

→ **Review It**

1. Describe the monetary unit, economic entity, time period, and going concern assumptions.
2. Describe the cost and full disclosure principles.
3. What are the materiality and cost-benefit constraints?

The Navigator

The Classified Balance Sheet

study objective 3

Identify the sections of a classified balance sheet.

In Chapter 1, we introduced the four financial statements: the balance sheet, statement of earnings, statement of retained earnings, and cash flow statement. In this section, we will look at the balance sheet in more detail and introduce standard balance sheet classifications.

The balance sheet presents a snapshot of a company's financial position—its assets, liabilities, and equities—at a point in time. To improve users' understanding of a company's financial position, companies group similar assets and similar liabilities together. This is useful because it tells the user that items in a group have similar economic characteristics. A classified balance sheet generally contains the standard classifications listed in Illustration 2-4.

Illustration 2-4 →

Standard balance sheet classifications

Assets	Liabilities and Shareholders' Equity
Current assets	Current liabilities
Long-term investments	Long-term liabilities
Property, plant, and equipment	Shareholders' equity
Intangible assets	Share capital
	Retained earnings

Alternative Terminology
The *balance sheet* is also known as the statement of *financial position*. The latter term is commonly used by international companies.

These classifications or groupings help readers determine such things as (1) whether the company has enough assets to pay its debts as they come due and (2) the claims of short- and long-term creditors on the company's total assets. A classified balance sheet also makes it easier to compare companies in the same industry, such as Shoppers Drug Mart and Jean Coutu.

The classifications shown in Illustration 2-4 are illustrated in a hypothetical balance sheet for Frenette Corporation in Illustration 2-5. The illustration explains each classification.

Assets

Assets are the resources that a company owns that will provide future economic benefits. As part of the conceptual framework project, this definition is currently being reviewed by standard setters, who want to revise and clarify the economic benefit part. For our purposes, we will continue to use the current definition.

Assets can include resources whose benefits will be realized within one year (current assets) and resources whose benefits will be realized over more than one year (noncurrent assets). Noncurrent assets are normally divided further into long-term investments; property, plant, and equipment; and intangible assets. A company may also report other assets on its balance sheet, such as noncurrent receivables, future income tax assets, and property held for sale. These are usually separately reported so that users can get a better idea of their nature.

Current Assets

Current assets are assets that are expected to be converted into cash or will be sold or used up by the business within one year of the balance sheet date. For example, accounts receivable are current assets because they will be converted to cash as the amounts are collected throughout the year. Inventory is a current asset because it will be sold and converted to cash or accounts receivable during the year. Supplies are a current asset because we expect that these will be used up by the business within the year.

Common types of current assets are (1) cash; (2) short-term investments, such as debt or equity securities; (3) receivables, such as notes receivable, accounts receivable, and interest receivable; (4) inventories; (5) supplies; and (6) prepaid expenses, such as rent and insurance.

FRENETTE CORPORATION
Balance Sheet
October 31, 2009

Assets

Current assets			
Cash		$ 6,600	
Short-term investments		2,000	
Accounts receivable		7,000	
Inventories		4,000	
Supplies		2,100	
Prepaid insurance		400	
Total current assets			$ 22,100
Long-term investments			
Equity investment		$ 5,200	
Debt investment		2,000	
Total long-term investments			7,200
Property, plant, and equipment			
Land		$40,000	
Buildings	$75,000		
Less: Accumulated depreciation	15,000	60,000	
Office equipment	$24,000		
Less: Accumulated depreciation	5,000	19,000	
Total property, plant, and equipment			119,000
Goodwill			3,100
Total assets			$151,400

Liabilities and Shareholders' Equity

Current liabilities			
Notes payable		$11,000	
Accounts payable		2,100	
Salaries payable		1,600	
Unearned revenue		900	
Interest payable		450	
Current portion of mortgage payable		1,000	
Total current liabilities			$ 17,050
Long-term liabilities			
Mortgage payable		$ 9,000	
Notes payable		1,300	
Total long-term liabilities			10,300
Total liabilities			27,350
Shareholders' equity			
Common shares		$74,000	
Retained earnings		50,050	
Total shareholders' equity			124,050
Total liabilities and shareholders' equity			$151,400

On the balance sheet, these items are normally listed in the order in which they are expected to be converted into cash—that is, in their order of liquidity. This arrangement is shown in Illustration 2-6 on the following page for Canada Post.

Illustration 2-6 ➡

Current assets section

CANADA POST Balance Sheet (partial) December 31, 2007 (in millions)	
Current assets	
Cash and cash equivalents	$ 386
Marketable securities	309
Accounts receivable	592
Income tax recoverable	10
Prepaid expenses	68
Current portion of future income tax assets	20
Total current assets	1,385

Canada Post combines cash equivalents with its cash balance above. Cash equivalents are near cash items, which include things like treasury bills and money market funds. Many companies that we will illustrate in this chapter currently use the term cash equivalents. We will learn more about cash equivalents in Chapter 7.

The International Accounting Standards Board and the Financial Accounting Standards Board are working on a project to improve the presentation of information in certain financial statements, including the balance sheet. While this project is still in its early stages, preliminary views have been issued and discussed. One of the recommendations is not combine cash equivalents with cash in the balance sheet, but rather to report cash equivalents with other short-term investments.

International Resources

Long-Term Investments

Long-term investments are generally multi-year investments in debt (e.g., loans, notes, bonds, or mortgages) and equity (e.g., shares) of other corporations. They also include investments in long-lived assets, such as real estate, if the asset is not being used in the company's operating activities. Often, long-term investments are referred to only as *investments*. If the word "investment" is used without any modifier (short- or long-term), it is assumed to be long-term.

In Illustration 2-5, Frenette Corporation reported total long-term investments of $7,200 on its balance sheet, comprising of both debt and equity investments. Research in Motion reports only long-term debt investments in the partial balance sheet shown in Illustration 2-7. In the notes to the financial statements, it describes these investments as consisting of commercial paper, corporate and government notes, corporate bonds, and asset-backed securities.

Illustration 2-7 ➡

Long-term investments section

RESEARCH IN MOTION LIMITED Balance Sheet (partial) March 1, 2008 (in USD thousands)	
Long-term investments	$738,889

Property, Plant, and Equipment

Alternative Terminology
Property, plant, and equipment are sometimes called *capital assets* or *fixed assets*.

Property, plant, and equipment are tangible assets with relatively long useful lives that are currently being used in operating the business. This category includes land, buildings, equipment, and furniture. In Illustration 2-5, Frenette Corporation reported property, plant, and equipment of $119,000.

Although the order of property, plant, and equipment items can vary among companies, these items are normally listed in the balance sheet in their order of permanency. That is, land is usually listed first as it has an indefinite life, and is followed by the asset with the next longest useful life, normally buildings, and so on.

These long-lived assets, except land, have estimated useful lives over which they are expected to generate revenues. Because property, plant, and equipment benefit future periods, their cost is matched to revenues over their estimated useful lives through a process called **depreciation**. This is considered better than simply expensing (recording as an expense) the full purchase price of the asset and matching the cost to revenues that were generated only in the year of acquisition. Land also generates revenue, but its estimated useful life is considered to be infinite as land does not usually wear out or lose its value. Consequently, the cost of land is never depreciated.

Assets that are depreciated should be reported on the balance sheet at cost less their accumulated depreciation. Accumulated depreciation shows the amount of depreciation taken so far over the *life of the asset*. It is a contra asset; that is, its balance is subtracted from the balance of the asset that it relates to. The difference between cost and accumulated depreciation is referred to as **carrying amount.** This is also commonly known as net book value. In Illustration 2-5, Frenette Corporation reported its buildings at a carrying amount of $60,000 and its office equipment at a carrying amount of $19,000.

The Forzani Group details its property, plant, and equipment—which it calls capital assets—as shown in Illustration 2-8. Forzani also uses the term *amortization* rather than *depreciation* and *net book value* rather than *carrying amount* here, as do many other companies. Note that, except for land, all of Forzani's capital assets are amortized. This includes leasehold improvements, which are long-lived additions or renovations made to leased property.

◄ Illustration 2-8

Property, plant, and equipment section

THE FORZANI GROUP LTD. Balance Sheet (partial) January 27, 2008 (in thousands)	Cost	Accumulated Amortization	Net Book Value
Capital assets			
Land	$ 3,173	$ –	$ 3,173
Buildings	20,928	4,680	16,248
Building on leased land	4,583	2,852	1,731
Furniture, fixtures, equipment, software, and automotive	217,365	149,386	67,979
Leasehold improvements	239,439	146,003	93,436
Construction in progress	6,054	–	6,054
	$491,542	$302,921	$188,621

Intangible Assets

Many companies have assets that cannot be seen but are very valuable. Intangible assets are noncurrent assets that do not have physical substance and that represent a privilege or a right granted to, or held by, a company. They include goodwill, patents, copyrights, trademarks, trade names, and licences.

Intangible assets are normally divided into two groups for accounting purposes: those with definite lives and those with indefinite lives. Similar to buildings and equipment, intangible assets with definite useful lives are amortized. Similar to land, intangible assets with indefinite lives are not amortized.

Note that while the term *depreciation* is normally used for the allocation of cost over the useful lives of property, plant, and equipment, the term *amortization* is used for the allocation of the cost of intangible assets. And, as mentioned earlier in the chapter, some companies use the term amortization for both property, plant, and equipment and intangible assets. We will learn more about intangible assets in Chapter 9.

Frenette Corporation reported goodwill of $3,100 in its intangible assets section. Goodwill is usually the largest intangible asset that appears on a company's balance sheet and is reported separately from other intangibles. It results from the acquisition of another company when the price paid for the company is higher than the fair value of the purchased company's net assets.

Illustration 2-9 shows how Shaw Communications reported its intangible assets, which consist of broadcast rights and goodwill.

◄ Illustration 2-9

Intangible assets section

SHAW COMMUNICATIONS INC. Balance Sheet (partial) August 31, 2007 (in thousands)	
Intangible assets	
Broadcast rights	$4,776,078
Goodwill	88,111
	4,864,189

Liabilities

Liabilities are obligations that result from past transactions. Similar to assets, they are also classified as current (due within one year) and noncurrent (due after more than one year).

Current Liabilities

Current liabilities are obligations that are to be paid in the coming year from current assets, or through the creation of other current liabilities. Common examples are accounts payable, accrued liabilities (we will learn about these in Chapter 4), salaries or wages payable, bank loans or notes payable, interest payable, income and sales taxes payable, unearned or deferred revenue (we will learn more about unearned revenue in Chapter 4) and current maturities of long-term debt (payments to be made in the next year on long-term liabilities). In Illustration 2-5, Frenette Corporation reported six different types of current liabilities, for a total of $17,050.

Similar to current assets, current liabilities are often listed in order of liquidity. That is, the liabilities that are expected to be paid first are listed first. However, for many companies, the items in the current liabilities section are arranged according to an internal company custom rather than a prescribed rule. The current liabilities section from the balance sheet of Canwest Global Communications is shown in Illustration 2-10.

Illustration 2-10 ➡

Current liabilities section

CANWEST GLOBAL COMMUNICATIONS CORP. Balance Sheet (partial) August 31, 2007 (in thousands)	**Canwest**
Current liabilities	
Accounts payable	$216,988
Accrued liabilities	332,728
Income taxes payable	64,967
Broadcast rights accounts payable	71,603
Deferred revenue	42,167
Future income taxes	38,153
Current portion of long-term debt	15,295
	781,901

Users of financial statements look closely at the relationship between current assets and current liabilities. This relationship is important in evaluating a company's ability to pay its current liabilities. We will talk more about this later in the chapter when we learn how to use the information in the balance sheet.

Long-Term Liabilities

Alternative Terminology
Long-term liabilities are also called *long-term debt*.

Obligations that are expected to be paid after one year are classified as long-term liabilities. Liabilities in this category include bonds payable, mortgages payable, long-term notes payable, lease liabilities, pension liabilities, and future income taxes payable. Many companies report long-term debt maturing after one year as a single amount in the balance sheet and show the details of the debt in notes that go with the financial statements. In Illustration 2-5, Frenette Corporation reported long-term liabilities of $10,300. TELUS reported long-term debt of $7,375.4 million on a recent balance sheet, as shown in Illustration 2-11.

Illustration 2-11 ➡

Long-term liabilities section

TELUS CORPORATION Balance Sheet (partial) December 31, 2007 (in millions)	**TELUS**
Long-term liabilities	
Long-term debt	$4,583.5
Other long-term liabilities	1,743.8
Future income taxes payable	1,048.1
	7,375.4

Additional detail about its debt was reported by TELUS in the notes to its financial statements. There it indicated that its long-term debt consisted of notes, commercial paper, and bonds, and it gave details about the amounts, interest rates, and maturity dates. Its other long-term liabilities comprise liabilities for pensions and other post-retirement benefits, as well as other items.

Shareholders' Equity

Shareholders' equity is divided into two parts: share capital and retained earnings. For some companies, there may also be other parts to this section, such as accumulated other comprehensive income. We will learn more about comprehensive income in Chapter 11.

Share Capital

Shareholders purchase shares in a company by investing cash (or other assets). These investments are recorded as either common or preferred shares. If preferred shares are issued in addition to common shares, the total of all classes of shares issued is classified as, or titled, **share capital**. Quite often, companies only have one class of shares and the title is simply common shares, as shown in Illustration 2-5 for Frenette Corporation.

> **Alternative Terminology**
> *Share capital* is also commonly known as *capital stock*.

Retained Earnings

The cumulative earnings that have been retained for use in a company are known as **retained earnings**. Recall from Chapter 1 that ending retained earnings is reported on the end-of-period balance sheet. The amount is determined from the statement of retained earnings, which begins with the opening retained earnings amount and then adds net earnings for the period (or deducts a net loss) and deducts any dividends paid to arrive at the ending retained earnings amount. In Illustration 2-5, Frenette Corporation reports an ending retained earnings balance of $50,050.

The share capital and retained earnings accounts are combined and reported as shareholders' equity on the balance sheet. The shareholders' equity section of Danier Leather's balance sheet is shown in Illustration 2-12. In addition to share capital and retained earnings, Danier Leather also reports contributed surplus. Contributed surplus arises from the sale of shares; we will learn more about it in Chapter 11.

DANIER LEATHER INC. Balance Sheet (partial) June 30, 2007 (in thousands) **DANIER** LEAVE ORDINARY BEHIND™	
Shareholders' equity	
Share capital	$22,044
Contributed surplus	431
Retained earnings	26,234
	48,709

◄ **Illustration 2-12**

Shareholders' equity section

The Canadian practice of classifying the balance sheet in the order of liquidity (from the most to the least liquid) is not widespread internationally. International standards permit this ordering but classify the balance sheet using a reverse-liquidity order more often. That is, noncurrent (long-term) assets are presented before current assets, noncurrent (long-term) liabilities are presented before current liabilities, and shareholders' equity is shown before liabilities. Both alternatives are permitted, so Canadian companies will not be forced to change the order of the balance sheet classifications unless they choose to.

www.wiley.com/canada/kimmel

International Resources

BEFORE YOU GO ON...

Review It

1. What are the major sections in a classified balance sheet?
2. What factor determines whether assets should be classified as current or long-term?
3. How should accounts be ordered in the (a) current assets; (b) property, plant, and equipment; and (c) current liabilities sections of the balance sheet according to Canadian practice?
4. What was Shoppers Drug Mart's largest current asset at December 29, 2007? The answer to this question is at the end of the chapter.

⟶ Do It

Ouyang Corporation recently received the following information for its December 31, 2009, balance sheet:

Accounts receivable	$11,100	Inventories	$ 7,500
Accumulated depreciation—building	3,000	Land	50,000
Accumulated depreciation—office equipment	2,000	Office equipment	10,000
Building	75,000	Supplies	300
Cash	1,800		

Prepare the assets section of Ouyang Corporation's classified balance sheet.

Action Plan

• Determine which classification (current assets or property, plant, and equipment) each account should be reported in.
• Present current assets first, listing them in order of liquidity.
• List property, plant, and equipment accounts in order of permanency.
• Subtract accumulated depreciation on the building and office equipment to determine their carrying amount.

Solution

OUYANG CORPORATION
Balance Sheet (partial)
December 31, 2009

Current assets			
Cash		$ 1,800	
Accounts receivable		11,100	
Inventories		7,500	
Supplies		300	
Total current assets			$ 20,700
Property, plant, and equipment			
Land		$50,000	
Building	$75,000		
Less: Accumulated depreciation	3,000	72,000	
Office equipment	$10,000		
Less: Accumulated depreciation	2,000	8,000	
Total property, plant, and equipment			130,000
Total assets			$150,700

The Navigator

Using the Financial Statements

In Chapter 1, we briefly discussed how the financial statements give information about a company's performance and financial position. In this chapter, we continue this discussion by showing you specific tools, such as ratio analysis, that can be used to analyze financial statements in order to make a more meaningful evaluation of a company.

Ratio analysis expresses the relationships between selected items of financial statement data. Liquidity, profitability, and solvency ratios are the three general types of ratios that are used to analyze financial statements, as shown in Illustration 2-13.

Illustration 2-13 ⟶

Ratio classifications

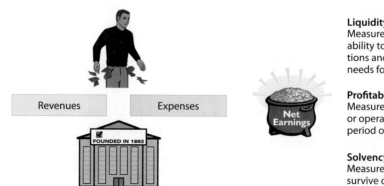

Liquidity Ratios
Measure a company's short-term ability to pay its maturing obligations and to meet unexpected needs for cash

Profitability Ratios
Measure a company's earnings or operating success for a given period of time

Solvency Ratios
Measure a company's ability to survive over a long period of time

Ratios can give clues about underlying conditions that may not be easy to see when the items of a particular ratio are examined separately. Since a single ratio by itself is not very meaningful, in this and later chapters we will use the following wherever possible:

1. **Intracompany comparisons** covering two years for the same company
2. **Intercompany comparisons** based on comparisons with a competitor in the same industry
3. **Industry average comparisons** based on average ratios for particular industries

In the following sections, we will introduce some examples of liquidity, profitability, and solvency ratios, using Empire Company Limited's statement of earnings, balance sheet, and cash flow statement. Empire Company owns Sobeys, one of Canada's top two grocery store chains. Most of Empire's revenue (97%) is generated from Sobeys, which operates more than 1,300 food and drug stores across Canada under the names Sobeys, IGA, Foodland, Price Chopper, and Lawtons Drugs. While Sobeys itself is a private company, which means that its financial statements are not publicly available, its parent company, Empire, is a public company.

To broaden our analysis to include an intercompany comparison, we will then compare Empire's ratios for these two years to those of one of its competitors, Loblaw Companies Limited. Loblaw operates more than 1,000 grocery stores across Canada under the names Loblaws, Atlantic SaveEasy, Extra Foods, Fortinos, No Frills, Provigo, Your Independent Grocer, and Zehrs Markets.

Finally, we will compare ratios for Empire and Loblaw to industry averages for the grocery industry.

Using the Statement of Earnings

Empire's statement of earnings reports how successful the company is at generating profit. It reports the revenue earned during the period and the expenses incurred during the same period. Illustration 2-14 shows Empire's statement of earnings for 2007, with comparative data for 2006.

study objective 4

Identify and calculate ratios for analyzing a company's profitability.

◀ Illustration 2-14

Empire's statement of earnings

EMPIRE COMPANY LIMITED Statement of Earnings Year Ended May 5, 2007 (in millions)		
	2007	2006
Revenue	$13,366.7	$13,063.6
Operating expenses		
Cost of sales, selling, and administrative expenses	12,724.0	12,378.2
Depreciation expense	243.9	225.8
Total costs and expenses	12,967.9	12,604.0
Operating income	398.8	459.6
Other expense (income)	8.4	(74.1)
Interest expense	60.1	83.8
Earnings before income taxes	330.3	449.9
Income tax expense	120.2	153.1
Net earnings	$ 210.1	$ 296.8

From the statement of earnings, we can see that Empire's total revenues increased slightly during the year. However, even though revenues increased by 2%, operating income and net earnings decreased by 13% and 29%, respectively. How could this happen? The answer is that the company's operating expenses increased faster than its revenues. In addition, other income declined from $74.1 million in 2006 to an other expense of $8.4 million in 2007. The explanation for this change is that in 2006 Empire sold 44 commercial properties at a one-time gain and the amount was recorded as other income.

In order to increase net earnings in the future, the company needs its revenues to increase more than its expenses, or its expenses to decline more than its revenues.

Profitability

Existing and potential investors and creditors are interested in a company's profitability. Profitability ratios measure the earnings or operating success of a company for a specific period of time. We will look at two examples of profitability ratios in this chapter: earnings per share and the price-earnings ratio.

Earnings per Share Earnings per share (EPS) measures the net earnings for each common share. Accordingly, earnings per share is reported only for common shareholders. It is calculated by dividing net earnings available to the common shareholders by the weighted average number of common shares.

Unless a company has preferred shares, the net earnings available to common shareholders will be the same as the net earnings reported on a company's statement of earnings. We will learn more about how to calculate net earnings available to common shareholders and the weighted average number of shares in Chapter 11. In Empire's case, its net earnings are equal to earnings available to common shareholders as it has no preferred shares. Its weighted average number of shares was 65.5 million in 2006 and 65.6 million in 2007.

Shareholders usually think in terms of the number of shares they own—or plan to buy or sell—so reducing net earnings to a per share amount gives a useful number for determining the investment return. Earnings per share amounts for Empire and its competitor Loblaw are calculated in Illustration 2-15.

Illustration 2-15 ➡

Earnings per share

EARNINGS PER SHARE =	NET EARNINGS AVAILABLE TO COMMON SHAREHOLDERS / WEIGHTED AVERAGE NUMBER OF COMMON SHARES	
(in millions except per share amounts)	**2007**	**2006**
Empire	$\dfrac{\$210.1}{65.6} = \$3.20$	$\dfrac{\$296.8}{65.5} = \$4.53$
Loblaw	$1.20	$(0.80)
Industry average	n/a	n/a

Note that Loblaw reported a loss per share of $0.80 in 2006, rather than a positive earnings per share as it did in 2007.

Comparisons of earnings per share are not very meaningful among companies, because of the wide variation in the number of shares and in the financing structures. This is why there is no industry average for earnings per share in Illustration 2-15. When industry averages are not available for the ratios that we calculate in this text, "n/a" (not available) appears.

ACCOUNTING MATTERS! | Investor Perspective

Profitability matters. When Wal-Mart reported better than expected results for its third quarter in 2007, its share price rose 6.1 percent. Although it is not unusual for a company's share price to be affected by earnings announcements, what was unusual was that the share prices of other companies also rose as a result of the news. In this case, investors reacted because Wal-Mart's financial health was viewed as a good indicator of the strength of the economy as a whole. Many believe that there is no better gauge of the overall health of the economy than the world's biggest retailer.

Source: John Heinzl, "As Wal-Mart Goes, So Too Does the Market," *Globe and Mail,* November 14, 2007, B14.

Price-Earnings Ratio Although we cannot compare earnings per share, we can use this amount to calculate the price-earnings (P-E) ratio, which can be compared across companies. The price-earnings ratio is a frequently quoted statistic that measures the ratio of the stock market price of each common share to its earnings per share. It is calculated by dividing the market price per share by earnings per share.

The market price of Empire shares at year end was $42.25 and $39.00, respectively, for 2007 and 2006. This price is divided by the earnings per share amounts presented in Illustration 2-15 above to determine the price-earnings ratio. The price-earnings ratios for Empire and its competitor Loblaw are presented in Illustration 2-16.

PRICE-EARNINGS RATIO = $\dfrac{\text{MARKET PRICE PER SHARE}}{\text{EARNINGS PER SHARE}}$		
	2007	**2006**
Empire	$\dfrac{\$42.25}{\$3.20} = 13.2$ times	$\dfrac{\$39.00}{\$4.53} = 8.6$ times
Loblaw	28.9 times	n/a
Industry average	35.7 times	19.1 times

The price-earnings ratio shows what investors expect of a company's future earnings. The ratio of the share price to earnings will be higher if investors think that current earnings levels will continue or increase; it will be lower if investors think that earnings will decline.

From 2006 to 2007, Empire's earnings per share decreased while its price-earnings ratio increased. This increase shows that investors were not worried about Empire's declining earnings and had confidence in the company's ability to increase its profitability in the future. In both years, Empire's price-earnings ratio was substantially below that of the industry, indicating that investors had more confidence in other companies than in Empire.

There is no price-earnings ratio available in 2006 for Loblaw. Because Loblaw's earnings per share amount was negative in 2006 (i.e., there was a loss per share), no meaningful price-earnings ratio can be calculated. In 2007, Loblaw reported a much higher price-earnings ratio than did Empire. Investors favoured Loblaw's shares over those of Empire.

DECISION TOOLKIT

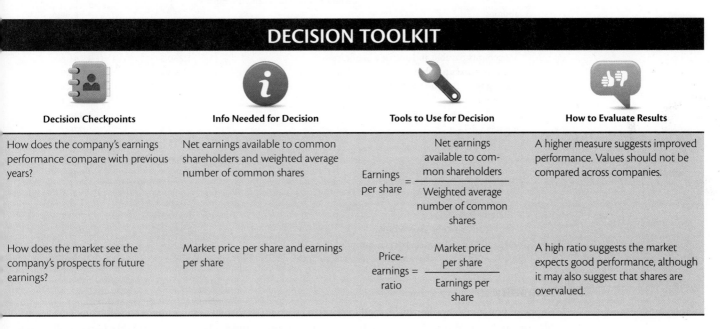

Decision Checkpoints	Info Needed for Decision	Tools to Use for Decision	How to Evaluate Results
How does the company's earnings performance compare with previous years?	Net earnings available to common shareholders and weighted average number of common shares	$\text{Earnings per share} = \dfrac{\text{Net earnings available to common shareholders}}{\text{Weighted average number of common shares}}$	A higher measure suggests improved performance. Values should not be compared across companies.
How does the market see the company's prospects for future earnings?	Market price per share and earnings per share	$\text{Price-earnings ratio} = \dfrac{\text{Market price per share}}{\text{Earnings per share}}$	A high ratio suggests the market expects good performance, although it may also suggest that shares are overvalued.

BEFORE YOU GO ON...

Review It

1. Identify three types of useful comparisons in ratio analysis.
2. Identify three types of ratios.
3. What are profitability ratios? Explain the earnings per share and the price-earnings ratio.

The Navigator

Using the Balance Sheet

study objective 5

Identify and calculate ratios for analyzing a company's liquidity and solvency.

Illustration 2-17 ➡

Empire's balance sheet

You can learn a lot about a company's financial health by evaluating the relationships between its various assets and liabilities. A simplified balance sheet for Empire is shown in Illustration 2-17.

EMPIRE COMPANY LIMITED
Balance Sheet
May 5, 2007
(in millions)

EMPIRE COMPANY LIMITED

	2007	2006
Assets		
Current assets		
Cash and cash equivalents	$ 294.9	$ 341.1
Receivables	326.8	275.4
Inventories	757.5	694.3
Income taxes receivable	3.6	
Prepaid expenses	51.4	51.5
Total current assets	1,434.2	1,362.3
Investments	332.5	517.4
Property and equipment	2,302.9	2,143.6
Goodwill	786.6	731.8
Total assets	368.7	296.4
	$5,224.9	$5,051.5
Liabilities and Shareholders' Equity		
Liabilities		
Current liabilities		
Bank indebtedness	$ 30.1	$ 98.6
Accounts payable and accrued liabilities	1,260.3	1,241.8
Income taxes payable	40.4	81.9
Long-term debt due within one year	82.5	95.4
Other liabilities	6.8	7.1
Total current liabilities	1,420.1	1,524.8
Long-term debt	829.5	728.1
Future income taxes	133.6	131.8
Other liabilities	706.3	701.6
Total liabilities	3,089.5	3,086.3
Shareholders' equity		
Common shares	196.1	195.1
Retained earnings	1,939.3	1,770.1
Total shareholders' equity	2,135.4	1,965.2
Total liabilities and shareholders' equity	$5,224.9	$5,051.5

Liquidity

Suppose you are a supplier interested in entering into an exclusive arrangement to sell fruits and vegetables on credit to Empire. You would be concerned about Empire's liquidity—its ability to pay obligations that are expected to become due within the next year. To have an idea of the company's liquidity, you would use liquidity ratios to look closely at the relationship of its current assets to its current liabilities. Liquidity ratios measure the short-term ability of a company to pay its maturing obligations and to meet unexpected needs for cash.

Working Capital One measure of liquidity is working capital, which is the difference between current assets and current liabilities. When working capital is positive, there is a greater likelihood that the company will pay its liabilities. When working capital is negative, a company may have to borrow money; otherwise, short-term creditors may not be paid, and the company may ultimately be forced into bankruptcy. Illustration 2-18 shows the calculation of working capital for Empire for 2007 and 2006, and compares it to that of Loblaw.

◄ Illustration 2-18

Working capital

WORKING CAPITAL = CURRENT ASSETS – CURRENT LIABILITIES		
(in millions)	2007	2006
Empire	$1,434.2 – $1,420.1 = $14.1	$1,326.3 – $1,524.8 = $(198.5)
Loblaw	$471.0	$675.0
Industry average	n/a	n/a

Empire reported negative working capital in 2006, which means that its current liabilities exceeded its current assets. It moved to a positive working capital balance of $14.1 million in 2007. Its working capital is still much smaller in absolute dollars than that of Loblaw.

Industry averages are not very meaningful for working capital, because working capital is expressed in absolute dollars rather than as a ratio.

Current Ratio An important liquidity ratio is the current ratio, which is calculated by dividing current assets by current liabilities. The current ratio is a more dependable indicator of liquidity than working capital. Two companies with the same amount of working capital may have significantly different current ratios. The 2007 and 2006 current ratios for Empire, Loblaw, and the industry average are shown in Illustration 2-19.

◄ Illustration 2-19

Current ratio

$$\text{CURRENT RATIO} = \frac{\text{CURRENT ASSETS}}{\text{CURRENT LIABILITIES}}$$		
(in millions)	2007	2006
Empire	$\dfrac{\$1,434.2}{\$1,420.1} = 1.0{:}1$	$\dfrac{\$1,326.3}{\$1,524.8} = 0.9{:}1$
Loblaw	1.1:1	1.2:1
Industry average	1.1:1	1.2:1

What does the ratio actually mean? The 2007 current ratio of 1:1 means that for every dollar of current liabilities, Empire has $1 of current assets. Because Empire's current assets increased in absolute dollars in 2007 at the same time as its current liabilities decreased, the current ratio increased from 2006 to 2007. However, when compared to Loblaw and the industry average, Empire's short-term liquidity is not quite as strong, although moving closer to both in 2007.

The current ratio is only one measure of liquidity. It does not take into account the **composition** of the current assets. For example, a satisfactory current ratio does not reveal that a portion of the current assets may be tied up in uncollectible accounts receivable or slow-moving inventory. The composition of the assets matters because a dollar of cash is more easily available to pay the bills than is a dollar of inventory. For example, suppose a company's cash balance declined while its merchandise inventory increased significantly. If inventory increased because the company was having difficulty selling it, then the current ratio would not fully reflect the reduction in the company's liquidity. We will look at these effects in more detail in later chapters.

Solvency

Now suppose that instead of being a short-term creditor, you are interested in either buying Empire's shares or making a long-term loan to the company. Shareholders and long-term creditors are interested in a company's long-run solvency—its ability to pay interest as it comes due and to repay the face value of debt at maturity. Solvency ratios measure a company's ability to survive over a long period of time. The debt to total assets ratio is one source of information about debt-paying ability.

Helpful Hint Some users evaluate solvency using a ratio of debt divided by shareholders' equity. The lower this ratio, the better a company's solvency.

Debt to Total Assets The debt to total assets ratio measures the percentage of assets that are financed by creditors rather than by shareholders. Financing provided by creditors is riskier than financing provided by shareholders because debt must be repaid at specific points in time, whether the company is performing well or not.

The debt to total assets ratio is calculated by dividing total debt (both current and long-term liabilities) by total assets. The higher the percentage of debt to total assets, the greater the risk that the company may be unable to pay its debts as they come due. The ratios of debt to total assets for Empire, Loblaw, and the industry average are shown in Illustration 2-20.

Illustration 2-20 ➡

Debt to total assets

DEBT TO TOTAL ASSETS = $\dfrac{\text{TOTAL LIABILITIES}}{\text{TOTAL ASSETS}}$		
(in millions)	2007	2006
Empire	$\dfrac{\$3,089.5}{\$5,224.9} = 59.1\%$	$\dfrac{\$3,086.3}{\$5,051.5} = 61.1\%$
Loblaw	59.4%	59.7%
Industry average	45.9%	47.4%

The 2007 ratio of 59.1% means that 59 cents of every dollar that Empire invested in assets was provided by its creditors. Empire's ratio is improving and, in 2007, is slightly lower than Loblaw's debt to total assets ratio of 59.4% which has stayed relatively unchanged. Both companies' debt to total assets ratios are higher than the industry average. The higher the ratio, the lower the equity "cushion" available to creditors if the company becomes insolvent (unable to pay its debts). Thus, from the creditors' point of view, a high ratio of debt to total assets is undesirable. In other words, Empire and Loblaw's solvency is less attractive to creditors, as their solvency is not as good as that of the average company in the industry.

DECISION TOOLKIT

Decision Checkpoints	Info Needed for Decision	Tools to Use for Decision	How to Evaluate Results
Can the company meet its short-term obligations?	Current assets and current liabilities	Working capital = Current assets − Current liabilities	A higher amount indicates liquidity.
		Current ratio = $\dfrac{\text{Current assets}}{\text{Current liabilities}}$	A higher ratio suggests favourable liquidity.
Can the company meet its long-term obligations?	Total debt and total assets	$\dfrac{\text{Debt to}}{\text{total assets}} = \dfrac{\text{Total liabilities}}{\text{Total assets}}$	A lower value suggests favourable solvency.

BEFORE YOU GO ON...

➡ **Review It**
1. What is liquidity? How can it be measured?
2. What is solvency? How can it be measured?

➡ **Do It**

Selected financial data for Drummond Inc. at January 31, 2009, are as follows: cash $60,000; accounts receivable $80,000; inventory $70,000; property, plant, and equipment $100,000. Current liabilities are $140,000 and long-term liabilities $50,000. (a) Calculate the current ratio and debt to total assets. (b) State whether the current and debt to total assets ratios are better or worse than the industry average. The industry average for the current ratio is 1.3:1 and the debt to total assets ratio is 65%.

Action Plan

• Use the formula for the current ratio: current assets ÷ current liabilities.

• Understand the composition of current assets (cash + receivables + inventory + prepaid expenses).

• Use the formula for debt to total assets: total liabilities ÷ total assets.

• Understand how to determine total liabilities (current liabilities + long-term liabilities) and total assets (current assets + investments + property, plant, and equipment + intangible assets).

• Understand that higher is better for profitability and liquidity ratios and lower is better for solvency ratios.

Solution

a) Current ratio: $\dfrac{\$60,000 + \$80,000 + 70,000}{\$140,000} = 1.5{:}1$

Debt to total assets: $\dfrac{\$140,000 + \$50,000}{\$60,000 + \$80,000 + \$70,000 + \$100,000} = 61\%$

(b) Both the current and debt to total assets ratios are better than the industry averages.

The Navigator

Using the Cash Flow Statement

As you learned in Chapter 1, the cash flow statement gives financial information about the sources and uses of a company's cash. Investors, creditors, and others want to know what is happening to a company's most liquid resource—its cash. In fact, it is often said that "cash is king" since a company that cannot generate cash will not survive. To help analyze cash, the cash flow statement reports the cash effects of a company's **operating activities, investing activities,** and **financing activities**. A simplified cash flow statement for Empire Company is provided in Illustration 2-21.

◀ Illustration 2-21

Empire's cash flow statement

EMPIRE COMPANY LIMITED
Cash Flow Statement
Year Ended May 5, 2007
(in millions)

EMPIRE
COMPANY LIMITED

	2007	2006
Operating activities		
Cash receipts from operating activities	$ 13,366.7	$13,063.6
Cash payments for operating activities	(12,917.3)	(12,437.0)
Cash provided by operating activities	449.4	626.6
Investing activities		
Purchase of property and equipment, net of disposals	(476.3)	(517.1)
Purchase of Sobeys shares	(48.6)	(49.5)
Sale of investments	185.4	186.5
Other	(95.9)	(92.8)
Cash used by investing activities	(435.4)	(472.9)
Financing activities		
Repayment of debt, net of issues	(10.7)	(63.6)
Payment of dividends	(39.5)	(36.7)
Other	(10.0)	6.0
Cash used by financing activities	(60.2)	(94.3)
Increase (decrease) in cash and cash equivalents	(46.2)	59.4
Cash and cash equivalents, May 6, 2006	341.1	281.7
Cash and cash equivalents, May 5, 2007	$ 294.9	$ 341.1

Different users have different reasons for being interested in the cash flow statement. If you were a creditor of Empire (either short-term or long-term), you would be interested in knowing the sources of its cash in recent years. This information would give you some indication of where it might get cash to pay you. If you had a long-term interest in Empire as a shareholder, you would look to the cash flow statement for information about the company's ability to generate cash over the long run to meet its cash needs for growth.

Companies get cash from two sources: operating activities and financing activities. In the early years of a company's life, the company usually cannot generate enough cash from operating activities to meet its investing needs, and therefore has to either issue shares or borrow money. An established company like Empire, however, will often be able to meet most of its cash needs with the cash provided by operating activities.

Empire's cash provided by operating activities declined in 2007 to $449.4 million. Empire also used a total of $435.4 million of cash for investing activities, consisting mainly of purchases of property and equipment that were offset by the sale of some investments.

Empire used a total of $60.2 million of cash for financing activities, repaying debt, and paying dividends. Empire financed most of its investing and financing activities through the cash provided by its operating activities ($449.4 million) and by reducing its cash and cash equivalents balance at the end of the year by $46.2 million. At the end of fiscal 2007, Empire's cash and cash equivalents declined from $341.1 million to $294.9 million.

Free Cash Flow

Cash provided by operating activities is often adjusted to take into account the fact that a company must invest in new assets just to maintain its current level of operations. In addition, if a company is a dividend-paying company, it must also have cash available so that it can continue paying dividends to satisfy investors. Free cash flow is a solvency-based measure that adjusts for these demands on cash and therefore helps creditors and investors understand how much discretionary cash flow a company has left from its operating activities and can use to expand operations, reduce debt, go after new opportunities, or pay additional dividends, among other alternatives.

Free cash flow is calculated by deducting net capital expenditures and dividends from cash provided by operating activities. Net capital expenditures—representing amounts paid for the acquisition of property, plant, and equipment less any recoveries from the sale of these assets—can be found in the investing activities section of the cash flow statement. Dividends paid, if any, are reported in the financing activities section of the cash flow statement.

Illustration 2-22 presents the free cash flow numbers for Empire and Loblaw. Industry measures are not available for these ratios.

Illustration 2-22 ➡

Free cash flow

FREE CASH FLOW =	CASH PROVIDED (USED) BY OPERATING ACTIVITIES	−	NET CAPITAL EXPENDITURES	−	DIVIDENDS PAID
(in millions)	2007				2006
Empire	$449.4 − $476.3 − $39.5 = $(66.4)				$626.6 − $517.1 − $36.7 = $72.8
Loblaw	$625.0				$169.0
Industry average	n/a				n/a

Empire's free cash flow declined substantially in 2007. In fact, with a negative amount of $66.4 million, it doesn't have any "free" cash flow at all. It spent more on capital expenditures than it generated from operating activities. Loblaw, on the other hand, generated sufficient cash from operating activities to cover capital expenditures and dividends and still has $625 million remaining for other uses, an increase of $456 million of free cash flow compared to 2006.

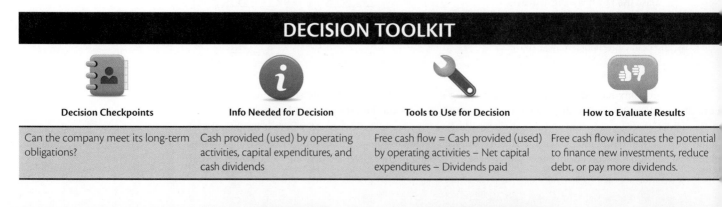

DECISION TOOLKIT

Decision Checkpoints	Info Needed for Decision	Tools to Use for Decision	How to Evaluate Results
Can the company meet its long-term obligations?	Cash provided (used) by operating activities, capital expenditures, and cash dividends	Free cash flow = Cash provided (used) by operating activities − Net capital expenditures − Dividends paid	Free cash flow indicates the potential to finance new investments, reduce debt, or pay more dividends.

ACCOUNTING MATTERS! | Investor Perspective

Amazon.com, Inc., which used to be the Earth's biggest bookstore, is now the Earth's biggest anything store. Amazon.com's website offers millions of books, DVDs, videos and CDs and MP3s (which still account for most of the company's sales), in addition to nearly anything else you might want to buy.

The company states in its annual report: "Our financial focus is on long-term, sustainable growth in free cash flow." In fact, Amazon.com considers free cash flow to be so important that it includes a reconciliation of net cash provided (used) by operating activities to free cash flow in its annual report. For the year ended December 31, 2007, its net cash provided by operating activities doubled while its free cash flow increased 143 percent, surpassing $1 billion for the first time.

BEFORE YOU GO ON...

Review It

1. What information does the cash flow statement provide that is not available in the statement of earnings or balance sheet?
2. What is the difference between cash from operating activities and free cash flow?

The Navigator

Summary of Study Objectives

1. Describe the conceptual framework of accounting, including the objective, qualitative characteristics, and elements of financial reporting. The key components of the conceptual framework are (1) the objective of financial reporting, (2) the qualitative characteristics of accounting information, (3) the elements of financial statements, and (4) recognition and measurement criteria (assumptions, principles, and constraints).

The objective of financial reporting is to provide information that is useful to individuals making investment and credit decisions. For it to be useful, information should have these qualitative characteristics: relevance, faithful representation, comparability, and understandability. The elements of financial statements include assets, liabilities, shareholders' equity, revenues, and expenses.

2. Identify and apply assumptions, principles, and constraints of the conceptual framework. Assumptions include the monetary unit assumption, economic entity assumption, time period assumption, and going concern assumption. Generally accepted accounting principles include the cost principle and full disclosure principle. The two constraints of materiality and cost-benefit can change how these principles are applied.

3. Identify the sections of a classified balance sheet. In a classified balance sheet, assets are classified as current assets; investments; property, plant, and equipment; and intangible assets. Liabilities are classified as either current or long-term. There is also a shareholders' equity section, which shows share capital and retained earnings, amongst other equity items.

4. Identify and calculate ratios for analyzing a company's profitability. Profitability ratios, such as earnings per share and the price-earnings ratio, measure a company's operating success for a specific period of time.

5. Identify and calculate ratios for analyzing a company's liquidity and solvency. Liquidity ratios, such as working capital and the current ratio, measure a company's short-term ability to pay its maturing obligations and meet unexpected needs for cash. Solvency ratios, such as debt to total assets and free cash flow, measure a company's ability to survive over a long period.

The Navigator

Your Personal Balance Sheet

By now you should be comfortable with how to prepare a company's balance sheet. Perhaps it is time to look at your personal position. Similar to a corporate balance sheet, a personal balance sheet reports what you own and what you owe.

What are the items of value that you own—your personal assets? Some of your assets are liquid—cash and items of value that can easily be converted to cash. Others, such as vehicles, real estate, and some types of investments, are less liquid. Some assets, such as investments and real estate, tend to increase in value over time, thereby increasing your personal equity. Other assets, such as vehicles and furniture, tend to fall in value, thereby decreasing your personal equity.

What are the amounts you owe—your personal liabilities? These liabilities may be either current (to be repaid within 12 months) or long-term (not to be paid until more than a year from now). Student loans, vehicle loans, credit card bills, and mortgages are all examples of liabilities.

Your personal equity is the difference between your total assets and your total liabilities. A person may have a high equity position but still have financial difficulties because of a shortage of cash. You can increase your equity in various ways, including increasing your savings, decreasing your spending, and increasing the value of investments. Your personal equity is not money that is available for use. Rather, it is an indication of your net assets (assets less liabilities) or financial position at a specific point in time.

Some Facts

- Age is the biggest single factor in determining where you stand in the race for wealth. Most of us spend our twenties launching a career and repaying student loans. We devote our thirties and a good portion of our forties to paying off mortgages and raising children. It is only in our fifties that we begin to accumulate wealth.
- Household debt in Canada, in the form of consumer credit and mortgages, continued to outpace increases in equity during 2007. The ratio of debt to equity increased by 17.9%, while the overall household debt amounted to 115.7% of personal disposable income.
- National equity in Canada reached $5.4 trillion by 2007, or $163,700 per capita.
- Nearly 80% of Canadians who have savings/investments feel that it is either very, or fairly, important to make regular contributions to their investments.
- Retirement is by far the most common reason why Canadians are currently saving or investing. Other reasons include:
  - To build an emergency fund (38%)
  - To travel or go on a vacation (37%)
  - To pay off their mortgage or other debts (23%)
  - To pay for home renovations (23%)
  - To pay for day-to-day living expenses (20%)

What Do You Think?

Should you prepare a personal balance sheet?

YES | In order to attain your financial objectives, you need to set goals early. The personal balance sheet provides a benchmark that allows you to measure your progress toward your financial goals.

NO | Your present financial position is dramatically different from what it will look like in the future. After graduation, you will have a job, or a better job, and you will not have to pay tuition.

The Navigator

Sources:

"Most Canadians Investing Regularly: 2008 Scotiabank Investment Study," CNW Group, January 17, 2008, www.newswire.ca.

Statistics Canada, "National Balance Sheet Accounts," December 14, 2007, www.statcan.ca.

Glossary

Comparability A quality for describing a company's accounting information when it can be compared to the information of another company because both companies use similar accounting standards and operate in similar circumstances. (p. 53)

Conceptual framework of accounting A coherent system of interrelated elements that guides the development and application of accounting principles. It includes the objective of financial reporting, qualitative characteristics of accounting information, elements of financial statements, and recognition and measurement criteria. (p. 50)

Consistency Use of the same accounting standards from year to year within a company. (p. 53)

Cost-benefit The constraint that the costs of obtaining and providing information should not be higher than the benefits that are gained by providing it. (p. 57)

Cost principle A generally accepted accounting principle that states that assets should be recorded at cost at the time of acquisition. (p. 56)

Current assets Cash and other resources that it is reasonable to expect will be converted into cash, or will be sold or used up by the business, within one year. (p. 58)

Current liabilities Obligations that will be paid from existing current assets or through the creation of other current liabilities, within the next year. (p. 62)

Current ratio A measure used to evaluate a company's liquidity and short-term debt-paying ability. It is calculated by dividing current assets by current liabilities. (p. 69)

Debt to total assets A measure of solvency showing the percentage of total financing that is provided by creditors. It is calculated by dividing total liabilities by total assets. (p. 70)

Earnings per share (EPS) A profitability measure of the net earnings earned by each common share. It is calculated by dividing net earnings available to common shareholders by the weighted average number of common shares. (p. 66)

Economic entity assumption An assumption that economic events can be identified with a particular accounting unit (e.g., a company) whose activities are separate and distinct from the activities of the shareholders and of all other economic entities. (p. 55)

Elements of financial statements Definitions of basic terms in accounting. (p. 54)

Faithful representation A quality for describing information that represents economic reality. It must be verifiable, neutral, and complete. (p. 52)

Free cash flow A solvency measure that indicates the amount of cash generated during the current year that is available for expansion or for the payment of additional dividends. It is calculated by deducting net capital expenditures and dividends from cash provided by operating activities. (p. 72)

Full disclosure principle A generally accepted accounting principle that states that circumstances and events which matter to financial statement users must be disclosed. (p. 56)

Generally accepted accounting principles (GAAP) A general guide, having substantial authoritative support, that describes how economic events should be recorded and reported for financial reporting purposes. (p. 56)

Going concern assumption The assumption that the business will remain in operation for the foreseeable future. (p. 55)

Intangible assets Assets of a long-lived nature that do not have physical substance but represent a privilege or a right granted to, or held by, a company. (p. 61)

Interim periods Accounting time periods that are less than a year long. (p. 55)

Liquidity ratios Measures of a company's short-term ability to pay its maturing obligations and to meet unexpected needs for cash. (p. 68)

Long-term investments Investments in debt and equity securities of other companies that are normally held for many years. Also includes long-term assets, such as land, that are not currently being used in the company's operating activities. (p. 60)

Long-term liabilities Obligations that are not expected to be paid within one year. (p. 62)

Materiality The constraint that for an item to be reported it must be likely to influence the decision of an investor or creditor. (p. 57)

Monetary unit assumption An assumption stating that only transaction data that can be expressed in terms of money should be included in the accounting records. (p. 54)

Objective of financial reporting The objective of financial reporting is to provide information that is useful to individuals making investment and credit decisions. (p. 52)

Price-earnings (P-E) ratio A profitability measure of the ratio of the market price of each common share to the earnings per share. It reflects investors' beliefs about a company's future earnings potential. (p. 66)

Profitability ratios Measures of a company's earnings or operating success for a specific period of time. (p. 65)

Property, plant, and equipment Tangible assets of a long-lived nature that are being used in the operating activities of the business. (p. 60)

Relevance A quality for describing information that makes a difference in a decision. It should have predictive and feedback value and be timely. (p. 52)

Short-term investments   Investments in debt and equity securities of other companies that are available for sale within the year. (p. 58)

Solvency ratios   Measures of a company's ability to survive over a long period of time. (p. 69)

Time period assumption   An accounting assumption that the economic life of a business can be divided into artificial time periods. (p. 55)

Understandability   A quality for describing information provided in the financial statements that is understandable for users. The average user is assumed to have a reasonable understanding of accounting concepts and procedures, as well as of general business and economic conditions. (p. 53)

Working capital   The excess of current assets over current liabilities. (p. 68)

Analysis Tools (Decision Toolkit Summaries)

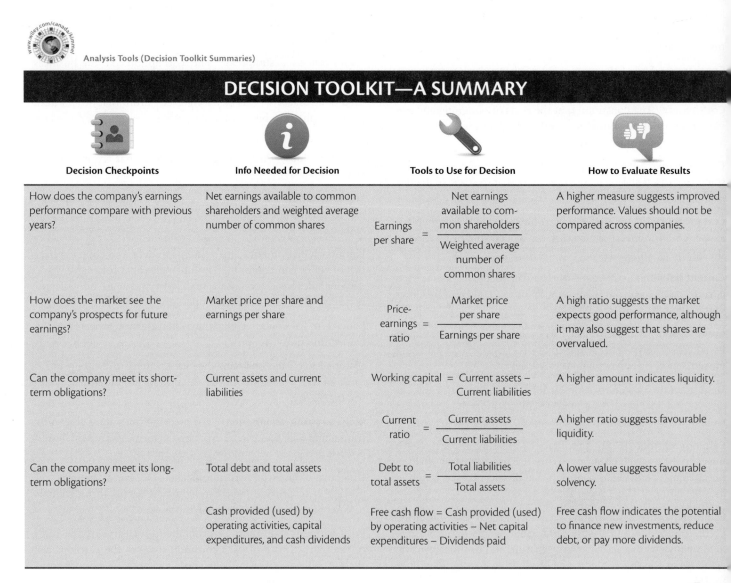

DECISION TOOLKIT—A SUMMARY

Decision Checkpoints	Info Needed for Decision	Tools to Use for Decision	How to Evaluate Results
How does the company's earnings performance compare with previous years?	Net earnings available to common shareholders and weighted average number of common shares	$\text{Earnings per share} = \dfrac{\text{Net earnings available to common shareholders}}{\text{Weighted average number of common shares}}$	A higher measure suggests improved performance. Values should not be compared across companies.
How does the market see the company's prospects for future earnings?	Market price per share and earnings per share	$\text{Price-earnings ratio} = \dfrac{\text{Market price per share}}{\text{Earnings per share}}$	A high ratio suggests the market expects good performance, although it may also suggest that shares are overvalued.
Can the company meet its short-term obligations?	Current assets and current liabilities	$\text{Working capital} = \text{Current assets} - \text{Current liabilities}$	A higher amount indicates liquidity.
		$\text{Current ratio} = \dfrac{\text{Current assets}}{\text{Current liabilities}}$	A higher ratio suggests favourable liquidity.
Can the company meet its long-term obligations?	Total debt and total assets	$\text{Debt to total assets} = \dfrac{\text{Total liabilities}}{\text{Total assets}}$	A lower value suggests favourable solvency.
	Cash provided (used) by operating activities, capital expenditures, and cash dividends	Free cash flow = Cash provided (used) by operating activities – Net capital expenditures – Dividends paid	Free cash flow indicates the potential to finance new investments, reduce debt, or pay more dividends.

The Navigator

Using the Decision Toolkit

Canadian Tire Corporation, Limited sells a wide array of products, including casual clothing and home, car, sports, and leisure products.

CANADIAN TIRE CORPORATION, LIMITED
Balance Sheet
December 29, 2007
(in millions)

	2007	2006
Assets		
Current assets	$3,116.1	$2,541.0
Long-term receivables and other assets	238.8	283.5
Goodwill	51.8	46.4
Intangible assets	52.4	52.4
Property and equipment	3,283.6	2,881.3
Total assets	$6,742.7	$5,804.6
Liabilities and Shareholders' Equity		
Liabilities		
Current liabilities	$2,109.6	$1,663.6
Long-term debt	1,341.8	1,168.4
Future income taxes	71.8	75.0
Other long-term liabilities	125.6	112.4
Total liabilities	3,648.8	3,019.4
Shareholders' equity		
Share capital	700.7	702.7
Contributed surplus	2.3	0.1
Other equity items	(50.0)	(5.7)
Retained earnings	2,440.9	2,088.1
Total shareholders' equity	3,093.9	2,785.2
Total liabilities and shareholders' equity	$6,742.7	$5,804.6

CANADIAN TIRE CORPORATION, LIMITED
Statement of Earnings
Year Ended December 29, 2007
(in millions)

	2007	2006
Operating revenue	$8,621.4	$8,269.1
Expenses		
Cost of merchandise sold and operating expenses	7,685.1	7,415.7
Interest	78.4	75.7
Depreciation	206.9	191.7
Other	30.9	30.6
Total expenses	8,001.3	7,713.7
Earnings before income taxes	620.1	555.4
Income taxes	202.5	200.8
Net earnings	$ 417.6	$ 354.6

Additional information:

• Canadian Tire's net earnings are the same as its net earnings available to common shareholders. The weighted average number of shares was 81.5 million in 2007 and 81.6 million in 2006. The share price was $73.53 at the end of the 2007 fiscal year, and $70.88 at the end of the 2006 fiscal year.

- Canadian Tire's cash provided by operating activities was $174.7 million in 2007 and $395.3 million in 2006. Net capital expenditures and dividends paid were $584.7 million and $58.8 million in 2007, respectively, and $189.1 million and $52.2 million in 2006, respectively.
- Industry averages are as follows: current ratio, 1.5:1 in 2007 and 1.5 in 2006; price-earnings ratio, 15.2 times in 2007 and 15.7 times in 2006; debt to total assets, 34.2% in 2007 and 29.6% in 2006. Industry averages are not available for earnings per share or free cash flow.

Instructions

Using the above statements and additional information, do the following:

(a) Calculate Canadian Tire's current ratio for both fiscal years. Discuss the company's liquidity generally, and compared to the industry.

(b) Calculate Canadian Tire's earnings per share and price-earnings ratio for both fiscal years. Discuss the company's profitability generally, and compared to the industry.

(c) Calculate Canadian Tire's debt to total assets and free cash flow for both fiscal years. Discuss the company's solvency generally, and compared to the industry.

Solution

(a) <u>Liquidity</u> (in millions)

Current ratio:

2007: $3,116.1 ÷ $2,109.6 = 1.5:1

2006: $2,541.0 ÷ $1,663.6 = 1.5:1

Based on the current ratio, Canadian Tire's liquidity appears strong and stable, at 1.5:1 for both years. This means that Canadian Tire had 1.5 times more current assets than current liabilities. This is also consistent with the current ratio of its industry competitors.

(b) <u>Profitability</u>

Earnings per share (in millions):

2007: $417.6 ÷ 81.5 = $5.12

2006: $354.6 ÷ 81.6 = $4.35

Price-earnings ratio:

2007: $73.53 ÷ $5.12 = 14.4 times

2006: $70.88 ÷ $4.35 = 16.3 times

Canadian Tire's profitability appears to be improving. The company's earnings per share increased in 2007. Despite this increase, its price-earnings ratio decreased in 2007, from 16.3 times to 14.4 times. This ratio is also below that of the industry average in 2007, at 15.2 times.. The declining price-earnings ratio likely reflects investors' concerns about the future profitability of the retail industry as a recession appears imminent.

(c) <u>Solvency</u> (in millions)

Debt to total assets:

2007: $3,648.8 ÷ $6,742.7 = 54.1%

2006: $3,019.4 ÷ $5,804.6 = 52.0%

Free cash flow:

2007: $174.7 − $584.7 − $58.8 = $(468.8)

2006: $395.3 − $189.1 − $52.2 = $154.0

Canadian Tire's solvency worsened slightly in 2007. Its debt to total assets ratio increased from 52.0% in 2006 to 54.1% in 2007. In addition, its reliance on debt financing is higher (worse) than that of the industry in both years.

At the same time, its free cash flow declined from a positive $154 million in 2006 to a negative $468.8 million in 2007. Its cash flow from operating activities declined at the same time its capital expenditures and dividends increased. There is no industry average for this measure.

The Navigator

Demonstration Problem

The following accounts and amounts are taken from the financial statements of the Visentin Corporation for the year ended January 31, 2009:

Accounts payable	$ 779,000
Accounts receivable	602,000
Accumulated depreciation—building	150,000
Accumulated depreciation—equipment	100,000
Depreciation expense	100,000
Building	1,000,000
Cash	85,000
Common shares	1,500,000
Cost of goods sold	5,900,000
Dividends	37,000
Equipment	250,000
Goodwill	152,000
Income tax expense	45,000
Interest expense	42,000
Land	89,000
Long-term investments	175,000
Merchandise inventory	1,485,000
Mortgage payable	383,000
Mortgage payable due within one year	125,000
Operating expenses	1,138,000
Prepaid expenses	78,000
Retained earnings, February 1, 2008	740,000
Sales	7,400,000
Short-term notes payable	1,000

Instructions

Prepare a statement of earnings, statement of retained earnings, and balance sheet using the above items.

Study Tools
(Demonstration Problems)

Action Plan

- First identify which accounts should be reported on each statement. Then determine which classification each account should be reported in (e.g., in current assets, current liabilities, or something else on the balance sheet; or in revenues, expenses, or something else on the statement of earnings).

- Prepare the statements in this order: (1) statement of earnings, (2) statement of retained earnings, and (3) balance sheet.

- The statement of earnings covers a period of time. In preparing the statement of earnings, first list revenues, and then expenses. Report income tax expense separately.

- The statement of retained earnings covers the same period of time as the statement of earnings. This statement calculates the ending retained earnings balance (which is also reported on the balance sheet) by adding net earnings (from the statement of earnings), less dividends, to the opening retained earnings amount.

- The balance sheet is prepared at a specific point in time. In preparing a classified balance sheet, list items in order of their liquidity in the current classifications and in order of their permanency in the noncurrent classifications.

Solution to Demonstration Problem

VISENTIN CORPORATION
Statement of Earnings
Year Ended January 31, 2009

Sales		$7,400,000
Expenses		
Cost of goods sold	$5,900,000	
Operating expenses	1,138,000	
Depreciation expense	100,000	
Interest expense	42,000	
Total expenses		7,180,000
Earnings before income taxes		220,000
Income tax expense		45,000
Net earnings		$ 175,000

VISENTIN CORPORATION
Statement of Retained Earnings
Year Ended January 31, 2009

Retained earnings, February 1, 2008	$740,000
Add: Net earnings	175,000
	915,000
Less: Dividends	37,000
Retained earnings, January 31, 2009	$878,000

VISENTIN CORPORATION
Balance Sheet
January 31, 2009

Assets

Current assets			
Cash		$ 85,000	
Accounts receivable		602,000	
Merchandise inventory		1,485,000	
Prepaid expenses		78,000	
Total current assets			$2,250,000
Investments			175,000
Property, plant, and equipment			
Land		$ 89,000	
Building	$1,000,000		
Less: Accumulated depreciation	(150,000)	850,000	
Equipment	$ 250,000		
Less: Accumulated depreciation	(100,000)	150,000	1,089,000
Goodwill			152,000
Total assets			$3,666,000

Liabilities and Shareholders' Equity

Liabilities			
Current liabilities			
Accounts payable		$ 779,000	
Notes payable		1,000	
Mortgage payable due within one year		125,000	
Total current liabilities			$ 905,000
Long-term liabilities			
Mortgage payable			383,000
Total liabilities			1,288,000
Shareholders' equity			
Common shares		$1,500,000	
Retained earnings		878,000	2,378,000
Total liabilities and shareholders' equity			$3,666,000

The Navigator

Self-Study Questions

Answers are at the end of the chapter.

1. Which of the following is not one of the four main sections in the conceptual framework of accounting?
   (a) The objective of financial reporting
   (b) The qualitative characteristics of accounting information
   (c) The dimensions of financial statements
   (d) Recognition and measurement criteria

2. Which of the following is not a qualitative characteristic of accounting information?
   (a) Reliability
   (b) Relevance
   (c) Faithful representation
   (d) Comparability

3. Which of the following is not an accounting assumption?
   (a) Economic entity
   (b) Monetary unit
   (c) Time period
   (d) Materiality

4. The cost principle states that:
   (a) assets should be recorded only at the time when cash is paid.
   (b) the activities of a company should be kept separate and distinct from those of its shareholders.
   (c) only transaction data that can be expressed in terms of money should be included in the accounting records.
   (d) assets should be recorded at their original cost at acquisition.

5. An item is considered material when:
   (a) it is more than $1,000.
   (b) it occurs infrequently.
   (c) not reporting it would influence or change a decision.
   (d) it affects net earnings.

6. In a classified balance sheet, assets are usually classified as: (SO 3)
   (a) current assets; long-term investments; property, plant, and equipment; and intangible assets.
   (b) current assets and current liabilities.
   (c) current assets, long-term investments, and share capital.
   (d) current assets and noncurrent assets.

7. Current assets are normally listed: (SO 3)
   (a) by importance.
   (b) by permanence.
   (c) by liquidity.
   (d) alphabetically.

8. Which of the following is not an indicator of (SO 4) profitability?
   (a) Current ratio
   (b) Earnings per share
   (c) Net earnings
   (d) Price-earnings ratio

9. Which of these measures is an evaluation of a company's (SO 5) ability to pay current liabilities?
   (a) Price-earnings ratio
   (b) Current ratio
   (c) Debt to total assets
   (d) Free cash flow

10. Which of these measures is an evaluation of a company's (SO 5) ability to survive over the long term?
    (a) Price-earnings ratio
    (b) Current ratio
    (c) Debt to total assets
    (d) Working capital

The Navigator

Questions

1. Describe the conceptual framework of accounting and explain how it helps financial reporting.

2. (a) What is the basic objective of financial reporting? (b) Explain how the movement to international financial reporting standards will better achieve this objective.

3. Identify and explain the four qualitative characteristics of accounting information.

4. The four qualitative characteristics should be applied in a certain order. Identify the order and explain why the order matters.

5. What is the difference between comparability and consistency?

6. Explain the following assumptions: (a) monetary unit, (b) economic entity, (c) time period, and (d) going concern.

7. Explain the following generally accepted accounting (SO 2) principles: (a) cost and (b) full disclosure.

8. Your roommate believes that accounting principles are the (SO 2) same around the world. Is your roommate correct? Explain.

9. Describe the two constraints that affect the presentation of (SO 2) accounting information.

10. Explain how the full disclosure principle relates to the cost- (SO 2) benefit constraint.

11. Explain how the time period assumption relates to the (SO 1, 2) qualitative characteristic of faithful representation.

12. (a) Why does it matter whether accountants assume an (SO 1, 2) economic entity will remain a going concern? (b) How does the going concern assumption support the use of the cost principle?

(SO 3) 13. What basis is used for ordering items in the balance sheet in North America? Internationally?

(SO 3) 14. (a) Distinguish between current assets and noncurrent assets. (b) Distinguish between current liabilities and long-term liabilities.

(SO 3) 15. What is the purpose of depreciation? How is accumulated depreciation reported in the property, plant, and equipment section of the balance sheet?

(SO 3) 16. (a) Distinguish between long-term investments and intangible assets. (b) Distinguish between property, plant, and equipment and intangible assets.

(SO 3) 17. Identify the two components of shareholders' equity in a corporation and indicate the purpose of each.

(SO 3) 18. Is the opening balance or ending balance of retained earnings reported in the shareholders' equity section of the balance sheet? Explain why.

(SO 4) 19. Why is it difficult to compare earnings per share among different companies?

(SO 4) 20. ⬤▬ The **Bank of Montreal** has a price-earnings ratio of 11, while **Scotiabank** has a price-earnings ratio of 12.5. Which company do investors appear to favour?

21. ⬤▬ "The current ratio should not be used as the only measure of liquidity, because it does not take into account the composition of the current assets." Explain what this statement means.

22. ⬤▬ Dong Corporation has a debt to total assets ratio of 45%, while its competitor, Du Ltd., has a debt to total assets ratio of 55%. Based on this information, which company is more solvent?

23. Name ratios that are useful in assessing (a) liquidity, (b) solvency, and (c) profitability.

24. ⬤▬ Are short-term creditors, long-term creditors, and shareholders mostly interested in the same ratios when they analyze a company? Explain.

25. ⬤▬ Explain why increases in the price-earnings ratio, the current ratio, and free cash flow are considered to be signs of improvement, but an increase in the debt to total assets ratio is considered to be a sign of deterioration in a company's financial health.

Brief Exercises

Identify items included in conceptual framework.
(SO 1)

BE2–1   Indicate which of the following items are included in the conceptual framework by writing "Yes" or "No" beside each item.

(a) The analysis of financial statement ratios
(b) The objective of financial reporting
(c) The qualitative characteristics of accounting information
(d) The elements of financial statements
(e) The rules for calculating taxable income
(f) The constraints on the application of generally accepted accounting principles

Identify qualitative characteristics of accounting information.
(SO 1)

BE2–2   Presented below is a chart showing the qualitative characteristics of accounting information. Fill in the blanks from (a) to (d).

**Qualitative Characteristics
of Accounting Information**

Relevance	Faithful Representation	Comparability	(d)
1. Predictive value	1. Verifiable	1. (c)	1. Of accounting concepts and procedures and general business and economic conditions
2. (a)	2. Neutral	2. Consistent	
3. Timely	3. (b)		2. Information is classified, characterized, and presented clearly and concisely.

BE2–3 The following are the accounting assumptions, principles, and constraints discussed in this chapter:

Identify assumption, principle, or constraint.
(SO 2)

1. Economic entity assumption
2. Going concern assumption
3. Monetary unit assumption
4. Time period assumption
5. Cost principle
6. Full disclosure principle
7. Cost-benefit constraint
8. Materiality constraint

Match the number of the most relevant assumption, principle, or constraint above to each situation that follows:

(a) _____ A company is assumed to continue its business indefinitely.

(b) _____ Assets are recorded at their cost at the time of acquisition.

(c) _____ All relevant financial information which would make a difference to users should be reported.

(d) _____ The dollar is the "measuring stick" for reporting economic events.

(e) _____ The value of the information should be greater than the cost of providing it.

(f) _____ Accounting units are separate and distinct from the activities of the shareholders and all other companies.

(g) _____ Items of insignificance that would not likely influence a decision do not have to be disclosed.

(h) _____ Financial information is reported periodically, normally each quarter.

BE2–4 The following are the major balance sheet classifications:

Classify accounts on balance sheet.
(SO 3)

1. Current assets
2. Long-term investments
3. Property, plant, and equipment
4. Intangible assets
5. Current liabilities
6. Long-term liabilities
7. Share capital
8. Retained earnings

Match each of the following accounts to its proper balance sheet classification above:

(a) _____ Accounts payable
(b) _____ Accounts receivable
(c) _____ Accumulated depreciation
(d) _____ Building
(e) _____ Cash
(f) _____ Patent
(g) _____ Dividends
(h) _____ Income tax payable
(i) _____ Land held for resale
(j) _____ Land
(k) _____ Merchandise inventory
(l) _____ Common shares
(m) _____ Supplies
(n) _____ Mortgage payable

BE2–5 A list of financial statement items for Swann Limited includes the following: accounts receivable $12,500; cash $18,400; inventory $8,000; prepaid insurance $3,900; and supplies $5,200. Prepare the current assets section of the balance sheet.

Prepare current assets section of balance sheet.
(SO 3)

BE2–6 A list of financial statement items for Shum Corporation includes the following: accumulated depreciation—building $30,000; accumulated depreciation—equipment $28,000; building $100,000; equipment $70,000; and land $75,000. Prepare the property, plant, and equipment section of the balance sheet.

Prepare property, plant, and equipment section of balance sheet.
(SO 3)

BE2–7 Hirjika Inc. reports the following current and long-term liabilities: accounts payable $22,500; income tax payable $8,400; salaries payable $3,900; notes payable (due in 90 days) $5,200; mortgage payable (due within the year) $2,500; mortgage payable (due in more than one year) $50,000. Prepare the current liabilities section of the balance sheet.

Prepare current liabilities section of balance sheet.
(SO 3)

BE2–8 For each of the following events affecting the shareholders' equity of Wu Corporation, indicate whether the event would increase share capital (+), decrease share capital (–), increase retained earnings (+), or decrease retained earnings (–). Write "NE" if there is no effect.

Identify items affecting shareholders' equity.
(SO 3)

	Share Capital	Retained Earnings
(a) Issued common shares	_____	_____
(b) Paid a cash dividend	_____	_____
(c) Reported net earnings	_____	_____
(d) Paid cash to creditors	_____	_____
(e) Reported a net loss	_____	_____
(f) Issued preferred shares	_____	_____

Calculate ratios and evaluate profitability.
(SO 4)

BE2–9 The following information is available for Leon's Furniture Limited for the year ended December 31 (in thousands, except for share price):

	2007	2006
Net earnings available to common shareholders	$58,494	$53,602
Weighted average number of common shares	70,777	70,800
Share price	$12.82	$12.46

(a) Calculate the earnings per share and the price-earnings ratio for each year. Round your answers to two decimal places.

(b) Indicate whether profitability improved or deteriorated in 2007.

Calculate ratios and evaluate liquidity.
(SO 5)

BE2–10 Indigo Books & Music Inc. reported the following selected information for its years ended March 31, 2007, and April 1, 2006 (in thousands):

	2007	2006
Total current assets	$261,523	$244,989
Total current liabilities	232,827	244,650

(a) Calculate the working capital and current ratio for 2007 and 2006. Round your answer to one decimal place, where appropriate.

(b) Was Indigo's liquidity stronger or weaker in 2007 compared to 2006?

Calculate ratios and evaluate solvency.
(SO 5)

BE2–11 Alimentation Couche-Tard Inc. reported the following selected information for December 31 of each year (in U.S. millions):

	2007	2006
Total assets	$3,043.2	$2,369.2
Total liabilities	1,897.8	1,403.2
Cash provided (used) by operating activities	403.0	401.5
Net capital expenditures	355.6	229.4
Dividends paid	19.5	8.7

(a) Calculate the debt to total assets ratio and free cash flow for 2007 and 2006. Round your answer to one decimal place, where appropriate.

(b) Was the company's solvency stronger or weaker in 2007 compared to 2006?

Exercises

Identify qualitative characteristics.
(SO 1)

E2–1 Here are some qualitative characteristics of accounting information, followed by a list of statements:

1. Predictive value	6. Comparability
2. Neutrality	7. Feedback value
3. Verifiability	8. Consistency
4. Timeliness	9. Completeness
5. Faithful representation	10. Understandability

(a) _____ Accounting information cannot be selected, prepared, or presented to favour one set of interested users over another.

(b) _____ Accounting information must be available to decision-makers before it loses its ability to influence their decisions.

(c) _____ Accounting information is prepared on the assumption that users have a reasonable understanding of accounting and general business and economic conditions.

(d) _____ Accounting information provides a basis to evaluate a previously made decision.

(e) _____ Accounting information reports the economic substance, not the legal form, of the transaction.

(f) _____ Accounting information helps users make predictions about the outcome of past, present, and future events.

(g) _____ Accounting information about one company can be evaluated by comparing it to accounting information from another company.

(h) _____ All the accounting information that is necessary to faithfully represent economic reality is included.

(i) _____ Accounting information is free of error and bias.

(j) _____ Accounting information in a company is prepared using the same principles from year to year.

Instructions

Match each qualitative characteristic to one of the statements, using the numbers 1 to 10.

E2–2   Marietta Corp. had the following reporting issues during the year:

(a) Land with a cost of $208,000 was reported at its fair value of $260,000.

(b) The president of Marietta, Deanna Durnford, purchased a truck for personal use and charged it to her expense account.

(c) Marietta wanted to make its net earnings look better, so it added two more weeks to the year, creating a 54-week year. Previous years were 52 weeks.

(d) The president wanted to make sure that the company was not accused of hiding anything from its shareholders, so she instructed the chief financial officer to disclose everything that happened during the year in the notes to the financial statements. The notes ended up being 95 pages long.

Identify assumption, principle, or constraint violated.
(SO 2)

Instructions

In each situation, identify the assumption, principle, or constraint that has been violated, if any, and explain what should have been done.

E2–3   This chapter describes qualitative characteristics of accounting information and recognition and measurement criteria, which include assumptions, generally accepted accounting principles, and constraints. The following situations are representative of one or more of these components of the conceptual framework.

Identify qualitative characteristics and recognition and measurement criteria.
(SO 1, 2)

(a) A piece of land, purchased in 1960, has been recorded and reported at its original cost.

(b) Phipp Corporation has used the straight-line method of depreciating its assets as have most other companies in the industry.

(c) An investment in shares of TELUS Corporation has been reported at its fair value.

(d) Details on the operation of the company's pension plan are disclosed in the notes to the financial statements.

(e) The value of the company's staff, appreciated by consumers, has not been included in the financial statements.

(f) The company reports its financial information each quarter.

Instructions

For each of the above situations, identify the appropriate qualitative characteristic and/or assumption, principle, or constraint.

Classify accounts on balance sheet.
(SO 3)

E2–4   The following are the major balance sheet classifications:

1. Current assets
2. Long-term investments
3. Property, plant, and equipment
4. Intangible assets

5. Current liabilities
6. Long-term liabilities
7. Share capital
8. Retained earnings

Instructions

Classify each of the following selected accounts taken from TELUS Corporation's balance sheet by writing in the number of the appropriate classification above:

(a) _____ Accounts payable and accrued liabilities

(b) _____ Accounts receivable

(c) _____ Accumulated depreciation

(d) _____ Buildings and leasehold improvements

(e) _____ Common shares

(f) _____ Current maturities of long-term debt

(g) _____ Goodwill

(h) _____ Income and other taxes receivable

(i) _____ Inventories

(j) _____ Investments

(k) _____ Land

(l) _____ Long-term debt

(m) _____ Office equipment and furniture

(n) _____ Prepaid expenses and other

(o) _____ Short-term investments

(p) _____ Spectrum licences

Prepare assets section of balance sheet.
(SO 3)

E2–5   The assets that follow were taken from Big Rock Brewery's December 31, 2007, balance sheet:

Accounts receivable	$ 1,641,777
Accumulated amortization—buildings	2,397,008
Accumulated amortization—furniture and fixtures	1,395,674
Accumulated amortization—production equipment	14,743,389
Accumulated amortization—vehicles	669,316
Buildings	11,289,633
Cash and cash equivalents	798,382
Deferred charges and other assets	226,307
Furniture and fixtures	2,127,877
Inventories	2,910,027
Land	2,516,234
Prepaid expenses and other	248,103
Production equipment	32,423,888
Vehicles	914,303

Instructions

Prepare the assets section of the balance sheet.

Prepare liabilities and equity section of balance sheet.
(SO 3)

E2–6   The liabilities and shareholders' equity items that follow were taken from Saputo Inc.'s March 31, 2007, balance sheet (in thousands):

Accounts payable	$ 343,911
Bank loans payable (short-term)	139,001
Common shares	511,737
Current portion of long-term debt	21
Income taxes payable	86,938
Long-term debt	254,012
Other reductions in shareholders' equity	63,800
Other long-term liabilities	131,466
Retained earnings	1,085,081

Instructions

Prepare the liabilities and shareholders' equity section of the balance sheet.

E2–7   These items are taken from the financial statements of Summit's Bowling Alley Ltd. at December 31, 2009:

Prepare balance sheet. (SO 3)

Cash	$ 18,040	Accumulated depreciation—	
Accounts receivable	13,780	equipment	$17,770
Accounts payable	12,300	Interest payable	2,600
Supplies	740	Mortgage payable	94,780
Prepaid insurance	390	Common shares	50,000
Investments	25,000	Retained earnings, Jan. 1	66,520
Land	64,000	Bowling revenues	64,180
Building	128,800	Operating expenses	35,600
Accumulated depreciation—		Equipment	62,400
building	45,600	Income tax expense	5,000

Instructions

(a) Calculate net earnings and the ending balance of retained earnings at December 31, 2009. It is not necessary to prepare formal statements.

(b) Prepare a balance sheet. Assume that $13,600 of the mortgage payable will be paid in 2010.

E2–8   These financial statement items are for Batra Corporation at year end, July 31, 2009:

Prepare financial statements. (SO 3)

Salaries expense	$34,700	Supplies expense	$ 900
Utilities expense	2,600	Dividends	12,000
Equipment	25,900	Depreciation expense	3,000
Accounts payable	4,220	Retained earnings, Aug. 1, 2008	17,940
Commission revenue	71,100	Rent expense	10,800
Rent revenue	18,500	Income tax expense	5,000
Common shares	10,000	Supplies	1,500
Cash	5,060	Short-term investments	30,000
Accounts receivable	17,100	Note payable (due Dec. 31, 2009)	21,800
Accumulated depreciation	6,000	Interest expense	2,000
Interest payable	1,000		

Instructions

Prepare a statement of earnings, statement of retained earnings, and balance sheet for the year.

E2–9   ⚬ The following information is available for **Cameco Corporation** for the year ended December 31 (in thousands, except share price):

Calculate ratios and evaluate profitability. (SO 4)

	2007	2006
Net earnings available for common shareholders	$416,112	$375,715
Weighted average number of common shares	351,175	351,224
Share price	$39.57	$47.20

Instructions

(a) Calculate the earnings per share and price-earnings ratio for each year. Round your answers to two decimal places.

(b) Based on your calculations above, how did the company's profitability change from 2006 to 2007?

E2–10   ⚬ **Metro Inc.** is a direct competitor of Empire and Loblaw, operating about 600 grocery stores across Canada. Metro reported the following information at September 29, 2007 (in millions):

Calculate ratios and comment on liquidity. (SO 5)

	2007	2006
Current assets	$1,054.7	$1,061.3
Current liabilities	1,069.1	1,093.9

▸ Financial Statements–Framework, Presentation, and Usage

Instructions

(a) Calculate the working capital and current ratio for each fiscal year. Round your answers to one decimal place, where appropriate.

(b) Did Metro's liquidity improve or worsen during the year?

(c) Using the data in the chapter, compare Metro's liquidity with that of Empire, Loblaw, and the industry for 2007.

Calculate ratios and comment on solvency.
(SO 5)

E2–11   The following data were taken from the April 30 financial statements of the Québec Winter Carnival:

	2007	2006
Total assets	$1,767,598	$1,635,769
Total liabilities	949,516	882,357
Cash provided by operating activities	696,966	132,920
Net capital expenditures	36,995	43,780
Dividends paid	0	0

Instructions

(a) Calculate the debt to total assets ratio and free cash flow for 2007 and 2006. Round your answers to one decimal place, where appropriate.

(b) Discuss the Carnival's solvency in 2007 versus 2006.

Problems: Set A

Discuss elements of financial statements.
(SO 1)

P2–1A   Assets and liabilities are critical elements of financial statements. Assets are defined as a resource that will provide future economic benefits. Three examples include:

1. Land owned by Shoppers Drug Mart
2. The Nike trademark
3. Accounts receivable

Liabilities are defined as obligations that result from past transactions. Three examples include:

1. Long-term bank loan
2. Accounts payable
3. Unearned service revenue

Instructions

(a) Discuss how each of the three assets listed above will provide future economic benefits.

(b) Discuss how each of the three liabilities listed above arose.

Comment on qualitative characteristics and recognition and measurement criteria.
(SO 1, 2)

P2–2A   Until January 1, 2008, no separate disclosure was required on the statement of earnings for the cost of goods sold (the cost of merchandise sold to customers). Because this disclosure was not specifically required, only about 20 percent of reporting companies disclosed their cost of goods sold separately on their statements of earnings. Most companies included it with other operating expenses in their reporting of this item, as Shoppers Drug Mart did in its statement of earnings shown in Appendix A to this textbook. Effective January 1, 2008, separate disclosure of this expense became mandatory.

Instructions

Refer to the appropriate qualitative characteristics and recognition and measurement criteria in your answers to the following questions.

(a) Why do you think that companies generally did not want to disclose their cost of goods sold?

(b) Why do you think standard setters made the disclosure of cost of goods sold mandatory?

Classify accounts.
(SO 3)

P2–3A   You are provided with the following list of accounts:

Accounts payable	Income tax expense
Accounts receivable	Income taxes payable
Accumulated depreciation—building	Interest expense
Accumulated depreciation—equipment	Inventories
Building	Land

Cash	Long-term debt
Common shares	Operating expenses
Cost of goods sold	Prepaid expenses
Current portion of long-term debt	Retained earnings, beginning of year
Depreciation expense	Sales
Dividends	Short-term investments
Equipment	Supplies
Goodwill	Wages payable

Instructions

Identify the financial statement and category for classifying each account. For example, Accounts Payable should be classified as a current liability on the balance sheet.

P2–4A The following items are from the assets section of Reitmans (Canada) Limited's February 3, 2007, balance sheet (in thousands):

Prepare assets section of balance sheet.
(SO 3)

Accounts receivable	$ 3,439
Accumulated depreciation—buildings and improvements	8,256
Accumulated depreciation—fixtures and equipment	68,799
Accumulated depreciation—leasehold improvements	66,371
Buildings and improvements	46,671
Cash and cash equivalents	188,491
Fixtures and equipment	166,739
Future income tax assets	3,407
Goodwill	42,426
Land	4,615
Leasehold improvements	152,135
Long-term equity investments	52,675
Merchandise inventories	61,834
Prepaid expenses	21,405

Instructions

(a) Identify the category in which each of the above assets should be classified.

(b) Prepare the assets section of the balance sheet.

P2–5A The following items are from the liability and shareholders' equity section of Reitmans (Canada) Limited's February 3, 2007, balance sheet (in thousands):

Prepare liabilities and equity section of balance sheet.
(SO 3)

Accounts payable and accrued items	$ 85,317
Current portion of long-term debt	1,076
Future income taxes payable (long-term)	112
Future income taxes payable (short-term)	248
Income taxes payable	40,289
Long-term debt	15,097
Other long-term liabilities	22,153
Retained earnings	411,213
Share capital	24,906

Instructions

(a) Identify the category in which each of the above items should be classified.

(b) Prepare the liabilities and equity section of the balance sheet.

(c) If you completed P2-4A, compare the total assets in P2-4A to the total liabilities and shareholders' equity in P2-5A. Do these two amounts agree?

Prepare financial statements.
(SO 3)

P2–6A   These items are taken from the December 31, 2009, financial statements of Beaulieu Limited:

Cash	$ 8,000	Retained earnings, Jan. 1	$34,000
Building	80,000	Dividends	3,500
Accumulated depreciation—		Service revenue	82,000
building	12,000	Repair expense	4,200
Accounts receivable	7,500	Depreciation expense	5,400
Prepaid insurance	250	Insurance expense	2,400
Equipment	32,000	Salaries expense	41,000
Accumulated depreciation—		Utilities expense	3,700
equipment	19,200	Income tax payable	1,750
Accounts payable	12,000	Land	50,000
Salaries payable	3,000	Mortgage payable	70,000
Common shares	20,000	Current portion of	
Income tax expense	6,000	mortgage payable	10,000
Long-term investments	20,000		

Instructions

Prepare a statement of earnings, statement of retained earnings, and balance sheet for the year.

Prepare financial statements
and discuss relationships.
(SO 3)

P2–7A   You are provided with the following information for Crusaders Inc., effective as at its January 31, 2009, year end:

Accounts payable	$ 2,000	Income tax expense	$ 2,000
Accounts receivable	8,100	Income taxes payable	250
Accumulated depreciation—		Interest expense	4,000
building	4,500	Inventories	9,700
Accumulated depreciation—		Land	60,000
equipment	4,800	Mortgage payable	55,000
Building	45,000	Operating expenses	6,000
Cash	5,700	Prepaid expenses	1,200
Common shares	20,000	Retained earnings,	
Cost of goods sold	10,000	Feb. 1, 2008	43,150
Current portion of mortgage		Sales	64,000
payable	14,500	Short-term investments	12,000
Depreciation expense	4,000	Wages expense	27,000
Dividends	2,500	Wages payable	1,000
Equipment	12,000		

Instructions

(a) Prepare a statement of earnings, statement of retained earnings, and balance sheet for the year.

(b) Explain how each financial statement is related to the others.

Calculate liquidity, profitability,
and solvency ratios.
(SO 4,5)

P2–8A   The financial statements of Fast Corporation are presented here:

FAST CORPORATION		
Balance Sheet		
December 31		
Assets		
Current assets		
Cash	$ 23,100	
Short-term investments	34,800	
Accounts receivable	86,200	
Inventory	109,750	$253,850
Property, plant, and equipment		465,300
Total assets		$ 719,150

Liabilities and Shareholders' Equity		
Current liabilities		
Accounts payable	$134,200	
Income taxes payable	10,350	$144,550
Mortgage payable		132,000
Total liabilities		276,550
Shareholders' equity		
Common shares	$100,000	
Retained earnings	342,600	442,600
Total liabilities and shareholders' equity		$719,150

FAST CORPORATION Statement of Earnings Year Ended December 31		
Sales		$712,000
Expenses		
Cost of goods sold	$420,000	
Operating expenses	144,000	
Interest expense	10,000	574,000
Earnings before income taxes		138,000
Income tax expense		41,400
Net earnings		$ 96,600

Additional information:

1. Net earnings available to common shareholders were $96,600.
2. The weighted average number of common shares was 10,000.
3. The share price at December 31 was $50.
4. Cash provided by operating activities was $82,300.
5. Net capital expenditures were $40,000.
6. Dividends paid were $15,000.

Instructions

Calculate the following values and ratios. Round your answers to two decimal places, where appropriate.

(a) Current ratio
(b) Earnings per share
(c) Price-earnings ratio
(d) Debt to total assets
(e) Free cash flow

P2–9A ⚫◯⊂ Selected financial statement data for a recent year for Belliveau Corp. and Shields Corp., two competitors, are as follows:

Calculate ratios and comment on liquidity, profitability, and solvency.
(SO 4, 5)

	Belliveau	Shields
Current assets	$180,000	$700,000
Property, plant, and equipment	705,000	800,000
Current liabilities	60,000	250,000
Long-term liabilities	215,000	200,000
Earnings per share	$ 0.28	$ 0.43
Share price	2.50	5.00
Cash provided by operating activities	$ 20,000	$185,000
Net capital expenditures	5,000	95,000
Dividends paid	10,000	25,000

Instructions

Please round your answers to one decimal place, where appropriate.

(a) Calculate the current ratio for each company. Comment on their relative liquidity.

(b) Calculate the price-earnings ratio of each company. Comment on their relative profitability.

(c) Calculate debt to total assets and free cash flow for each company. Comment on their relative solvency.

Calculate ratios and comment on liquidity, profitability, and solvency.
(SO 4, 5)

P2–10A ◼️ Condensed balance sheet and other data for Giasson Corporation are as follows:

GIASSON CORPORATION Balance Sheet December 31		
	2009	2008
Assets		
Current assets	$135,000	$128,000
Investments	50,000	40,000
Property, plant, and equipment	536,000	400,000
Total assets	$721,000	$568,000
Liabilities and Shareholders' Equity		
Current liabilities	$ 88,000	$ 75,000
Long-term liabilities	95,000	70,000
Shareholders' equity	538,000	423,000
Total liabilities and shareholders' equity	$721,000	$568,000

Additional information:

1. Net earnings available to common shareholders were $65,000 in 2009 and $84,000 in 2008.
2. The weighted average number of common shares was 76,000 in 2009 and 65,000 in 2008.
3. The share price at December 31, 2009, was $4; it was $6 at the end of 2008.
4. Cash provided by operating activities was $60,000 in 2009 and $125,000 in 2008.
5. Net capital expenditures were $100,000 in 2009 and $110,000 in 2008.
6. Dividends of $10,000 were paid in each year.

Instructions

(a) Calculate these values and ratios for 2009 and 2008. Round your answers to two decimal places, where appropriate.

1. Working capital
2. Current ratio
3. Earnings per share
4. Price-earnings ratio
5. Debt to total assets
6. Free cash flow

(b) Based on the ratios and other values that you calculated, briefly discuss Giasson's change in liquidity, profitability, and solvency.

Calculate ratios and comment on liquidity, profitability, and solvency.
(SO 4, 5)

P2–11A ◼️ Selected financial data from fiscal 2007 for two forest products companies, Canfor Corporation and Tembec Inc., are presented here (in millions, except for share price):

	Canfor	Tembec
Current assets	$1,219	$ 830
Total assets	3,508	2,655
Current liabilities	404	501
Total liabilities	1,691	2,089
Net loss available to common shareholders	$ (361)	$ (49)
Weighted average number of common shares	143	86
Share price	$ 8.73	$ 0.37
Cash provided (used) by operating activities	$ (483)	$ 26
Net capital expenditures	87	71
Dividends paid	0	0

Instructions

(a) For each company, calculate the following values and ratios. Round your answer to two decimal places, where appropriate. Where available, industry averages have been included in parentheses.

1. Current ratio (1.7:1)
2. Earnings (loss) per share (n/a)
3. Price-earnings ratio (1.1 times)
4. Debt to total assets (71.8%)
5. Free cash flow (n/a)

(b) Compare the liquidity, profitability, and solvency of the two companies and their industry.

Problems: Set B

P2–1B You are meeting with a friend of yours whom you have not spoken to for four years. The two of you have one hour to catch up on what has happened during the last four years. Therefore, you must make a decision on what needs to be covered as part of this discussion. You want to be sure to cover the important events.

Apply qualitative characteristic of relevance.
(SO 1)

Instructions

Compare the decision you must make on what to include in your discussion during your one-hour meeting to the qualitative characteristic of relevance.

P2–2B A friend of yours, Ryan Konotopsky, has come to you looking for some answers about financial statements. Ryan tells you that he is thinking about opening a movie theatre in his home town. Before doing so, he wants to find out how much he could expect to make in sales from food concessions as opposed to ticket sales. He wants to know what portion of ticket sales he could expect for children, youths, and seniors, who pay less, versus adults, who pay the highest admission rate. He also wants to know how much net earnings he would make on ticket sales versus sales at the concession stands, and he would like to know the average wage per employee.

Comment on full disclosure principle and constraints of accounting.
(SO 2)

Ryan downloaded the financial statements of Empire Company Limited, which in addition to owning Sobeys also owns Empire Theatres, the No. 2 movie exhibitor in Canada. He noticed that the company's statement of earnings reported revenues for the year ended May 5, 2007, of $13,367 million and cost of sales, selling, and administrative expenses of $12,724 million. He read through Empire's annual report and learned that Empire Theatres is just one part of the Investments and Other Operations division of the company. There are food retailing and real estate divisions as well.

Ryan is disillusioned because he cannot find many details about Empire Theatres in the financial statements. He has come to you looking for explanations.

Instructions

(a) Describe the full disclosure principle, and the two constraints in accounting.

(b) Explain what impact the full disclosure principle and these constraints have likely had on the financial reporting by Empire Company Limited.

P2–3B You are provided with the following selected balance sheet accounts for Leon's Furniture Limited:

Classify accounts.
(SO 3)

Accounts payable and accrued liabilities	Equipment
Accounts receivable	Future tax assets
Accumulated amortization	Future tax liabilities
Buildings	Income taxes payable
Building improvements	Income taxes recoverable
Cash and cash equivalents	Inventory
Common shares	Land
Computer hardware and software	Retained earnings
Customers' deposits	Short-term investments
Dividends payable	Vehicles

Instructions

Identify the balance sheet category for classifying each account. For example, Accounts Payable and Accrued Liabilities should be classified as current liabilities on the balance sheet.

Prepare assets section of balance
sheet.
(SO 3)

P2–4B   The following items are from the assets section of WestJet Airlines Ltd.'s December 31, 2007, balance sheet (in thousands):

Accounts receivable	$ 15,009
Accumulated depreciation—aircraft	288,909
Accumulated depreciation—buildings	5,825
Accumulated depreciation—ground property and equipment	81,345
Accumulated depreciation—leasehold improvements	5,112
Accumulated depreciation—spare engines and parts	13,610
Aircraft	2,273,509
Buildings	40,028
Cash and cash equivalents	653,558
Ground property and equipment	158,477
Inventory	10,202
Leasehold improvements	7,039
Other assets	105,320
Prepaid expenses and deposits	39,019
Spare engines and parts	76,862

Instructions

(a) Identify the category in which each of the above items should be classified.

(b) Prepare the assets section of the balance sheet.

Prepare liabilities and equity
section of balance sheet.
(SO 3)

P2–5B   The following items are from the liability and shareholders' equity section of WestJet Airlines Ltd.'s December 31, 2007, balance sheet (in thousands):

Accounts payable and accrued liabilities	$ 168,171
Advance ticket sales	194,929
Capital lease liabilities (long-term)	1,108
Current portion of long-term debt	173,367
Future income tax (long-term)	174,737
Long-term debt	1,256,526
Other current liabilities	54,139
Other long-term liabilities	11,337
Other shareholders' equity items	45,975
Retained earnings	455,365
Share capital	448,568

Instructions

(a) Identify the category in which each of the above items should be classified.

(b) Prepare the liabilities and equity section of the balance sheet.

(c) If you completed P2-4B, compare the total assets in P2-4B to the total liabilities and shareholders' equity in P2-5B. Do these two amounts agree?

Prepare financial statements.
(SO 3)

P2–6B   These items are taken from the financial statements of Mbong Corporation for December 31, 2009:

Retained earnings, Jan. 1	$60,000	Depreciation expense	$ 6,200
Utilities expense	2,000	Accounts receivable	14,200
Equipment	66,000	Insurance expense	2,200
Accounts payable	13,300	Salaries expense	37,000
Building	72,000	Accumulated	
Cash	5,200	depreciation—equipment	17,600
Salaries payable	3,000	Income tax expense	6,000
Common shares	34,200	Supplies	200
Dividends	5,000	Supplies expense	1,000
Service revenue	81,200	Note payable, due 2012	55,000
Prepaid insurance	3,500	Short-term investments	20,000
Repair expense	1,800	Accumulated	
Land	40,000	depreciation—building	18,000

nstructions

Prepare a statement of earnings, statement of retained earnings, and balance sheet for the year.

P2–7B   You are provided with the following information for Cheung Corporation for its April 30, 2009, year end:

Prepare financial statements and discuss relationships.
(SO 3)

Accounts payable	$ 2,875	Income tax expense	$ 2,500
Accounts receivable	7,800	Income taxes payable	500
Accumulated depreciation	9,220	Interest expense	450
Cash	10,200	Notes payable, due 2012	5,700
Common shares	10,000	Prepaid rent	750
Depreciation expense	4,610	Rent expense	9,000
Dividends	5,000	Retained earnings, May 1, 2008	19,065
Equipment	23,050	Salaries expense	19,000
Fee revenue	46,000	Short-term investments	11,000

Instructions

(a) Prepare a statement of earnings, statement of retained earnings, and balance sheet for the year.

(b) Explain how each financial statement is related to the others.

P2–8B   Here are the financial statements of Johannsen Inc.:

Calculate liquidity, profitability, and solvency ratios
(SO 4, 5)

JOHANNSEN INC.
Statement of Earnings
Year Ended December 31

Sales		$2,218,500
Expenses		
Cost of goods sold	$1,012,500	
Operating expenses	906,000	
Interest expense	98,000	2,016,500
Earnings before income taxes		202,000
Income tax expense		42,000
Net earnings		$ 160,000

JOHANNSEN INC.
Balance Sheet
December 31

Assets

Current assets		
Cash	$ 60,100	
Short-term investments	54,000	
Accounts receivable	207,800	
Inventory	125,000	$ 446,900
Property, plant, and equipment		625,300
Total assets		$1,072,200

Liabilities and Shareholders' Equity

Current liabilities		
Accounts payable	$100,000	
Income taxes payable	15,000	
Current portion of mortgage payable	27,500	$ 142,500
Mortgage payable		310,000
Total liabilities		452,500
Shareholders' equity		
Common shares	$307,630	
Retained earnings	312,070	619,700
Total liabilities and shareholders' equity		$1,072,200

Additional information:

1. Net earnings available to common shareholders were $160,000.
2. The weighted average number of shares was 20,000.
3. The share price at December 31 was $35.
4. Cash provided by operating activities was $110,800.
5. Net capital expenditures were $75,000.
6. No dividends were paid.

Instructions

Calculate the following values and ratios. Round your answers to two decimal places, where appropriate.

    (a) Current ratio

    (b) Earnings per share

    (c) Price-earnings ratio

    (d) Debt to total assets

    (e) Free cash flow

Calculate ratios and comment on liquidity, profitability, and solvency.
(SO 4, 5)

P2–9B ⚷ Selected financial statement data for a recent year for Chen Corporation and Caissie Corporation, two competitors, are as follows:

	Chen	Caissie
Current assets	$425,000	$190,000
Property, plant, and equipment	525,000	140,000
Current liabilities	166,000	95,000
Long-term liabilities	108,500	30,000
Earnings per share	$ 3.25	$ 2.30
Share price	25.00	15.00
Cash provided by operating activities	$165,000	$ 25,000
Net capital expenditures	90,000	10,000
Dividends paid	10,000	0

Instructions

Round your answers to one decimal place, where appropriate.

    (a) Calculate the current ratio for each company. Comment on their relative liquidity.

    (b) Calculate the price-earnings ratio of each company. Comment on their relative profitability.

    (c) Calculate the debt to total assets ratio and free cash flow for each company. Comment on their relative solvency.

Calculate ratios and comment on liquidity, profitability, and solvency.
(SO 4, 5)

P2–10B ⚷ Condensed balance sheet and other data for Pitka Corporation are as follows:

PITKA CORPORATION Balance Sheet December 31		
	2009	2008
Assets		
Current assets	$185,000	$155,000
Investments	75,000	60,000
Property, plant, and equipment	500,000	470,000
Total assets	$760,000	$685,000
Liabilities and Shareholders' Equity		
Current liabilities	$175,000	$130,000
Long-term liabilities	85,000	160,000
Shareholders' equity	500,000	395,000
Total liabilities and shareholders' equity	$760,000	$685,000

Additional information:

1. Net earnings available to common shareholders were $105,000 for 2009 and $94,500 for 2008.

2. The weighted average number of common shares was 30,000 in 2009 and 30,000 in 2008.

3. The share price at December 31, 2009, was $20; it was $16 at the end of 2008.

4. Cash provided by operating activities was $75,000 in 2009 and $60,000 in 2008.

5. Net capital expenditures were $30,000 in 2009 and $25,000 in 2008.

6. No dividends were paid in either year.

Instructions

(a) Calculate the following values and ratios for 2009 and 2008. Round your answers to two decimal places, where appropriate.

1. Working capital	4. Price-earnings ratio
2. Current ratio	5. Debt to total assets
3. Earnings per share	6. Free cash flow

(b) Based on the ratios and other values that you calculated, briefly discuss Pitka's change in liquidity, profitability, and solvency.

P2–11B ◯◼◖ Selected financial data for fiscal 2007 for two competitors, Le Château Inc. and H&M AB, are presented here (in millions, except share price):

Calculate ratios and comment on liquidity, profitability, and solvency.
(SO 4, 5)

	Le Château (in CAD)	H&M (in SEK)
Current assets	$107	31,045
Total assets	186	41,734
Current liabilities	61	8,834
Total liabilities	78	9,641
Net earnings available to common shareholders	$ 25	13,588
Weighted average number of common shares	6	827
Share price	$ 49	323
Cash provided by operating activities	$ 38	15,381
Net capital expenditures	28	3,522
Dividends paid	6	9,515

Instructions

(a) For each company, calculate the following values and ratios. Round your answers to two decimal places, where appropriate. Where available, industry averages are included in parentheses.

1. Current ratio (2.1:1)

2. Earnings per share (n/a)

3. Price-earnings ratio (15.5 times)

4. Debt to total assets (18.7%)

5. Free cash flow (n/a)

(b) Compare the liquidity, profitability, and solvency of the two companies and their industry.

BROADENING YOUR PERSPECTIVE

Financial Reporting and Analysis Cases

Financial Reporting: *Shoppers Drug Mart*

BYP2–1 The financial statements of Shoppers Drug Mart are presented in Appendix A at the end of this book.

Instructions

(a) What were the balances of Shoppers' total current assets and total assets at the end of fiscal 2007 and 2006?

(b) Are the current assets listed in order of liquidity or some other order? Explain.

(c) How are Shoppers' assets classified?

(d) What were the balances of Shoppers' total current liabilities and total liabilities at the end of fiscal 2007 and 2006?

(e) What portion of its assets does Shoppers finance with debt? Did this proportion change a lot between 2006 and 2007?

Comparative Analysis: *Shoppers Drug Mart and Jean Coutu*

BYP2–2 The financial statements of Jean Coutu are presented in Appendix B following the financial statements for Shoppers Drug Mart in Appendix A.

Instructions

(a) For each company, calculate or find the following ratios and values for the most recent fiscal year:
1. Working capital
2. Current ratio
3. Earnings per share
4. Price-earnings ratio (the year-end share price for Shoppers was $52.83 and $10.36 for Jean Coutu)
5. Debt to total assets
6. Free cash flow

(b) Based on your findings for question (a), discuss the relative liquidity, profitability, and solvency of the two companies.

Interpreting Financial Statements

BYP2–3 The following information (in U.S. millions) was reported by the Gap, Inc.:

	2007	2006	2005	2004	2003
Total assets	$7,838	$8,544	$8,821	$10,048	$10,713
Working capital	$1,653	$2,757	$3,297	$4,062	$4,156
Current ratio	1.7:1	2.2:1	2.7:1	2.8:1	2.6:1
Earnings per share	$1.05	$0.94	$1.26	$1.29	$1.15
Price-earnings ratio	18.3×	20.7×	13.8×	16.9×	16.2×
Debt to total assets	45.5%	39.4%	38.5%	50.8%	56.6%
Free cash flow	$1,158	$435	$799	$1,099	$1,821

Instructions

(a) Comment on the change in The Gap's liquidity. Which value seems to provide a better indication of The Gap's liquidity: working capital or the current ratio? What might explain the change in The Gap's liquidity during this period?

(b) Comment on the change in The Gap's profitability during this period. Is the change in earnings per share consistent with the change in the price-earnings ratio? Explain why these two ratios might not always move in the same direction.

(c) Comment on the change in The Gap's solvency during this period.

A Global Focus

BYP2–4 Nexen Inc., headquartered in Calgary, is a globe-trotting oil and gas and chemicals company. It has exploration and production activities in the Gulf of Mexico, the United Kingdom, the United States, West Africa, and Yemen in addition to Canada.

International Resources

One of the challenges global companies face is to make themselves attractive to investors from other countries. This is difficult to do when different accounting principles in other countries can blur the real impact of earnings. For example, in its statement of earnings for the year ended December 31, 2007, Nexen reported net earnings of $1,086 million, using Canadian GAAP. Had it reported under U.S. GAAP, its net earnings would have been $1,012 million.

Instructions

(a) Suppose you wish to compare Nexen to a U.S.-based competitor, such as Exxon Mobil. Do you believe the use of different countries' accounting principles would help your comparison or make it more difficult? Explain your reasoning.

(b) Suppose you wish to compare Nexen to a Canadian-based competitor, such as Imperial Oil. If Imperial Oil chose to use different Canadian accounting principles than Nexen, how could this affect your comparison of the financial results?

(c) Do you see any significant difference between (1) comparing statements prepared in different countries and (2) comparing statements in the same country but prepared using different accounting principles?

Critical Thinking Cases and Activities

Collaborative Learning Activity

BYP2–5 Jon Andersen invests his savings in a small portfolio of shares of publicly traded corporations. Jon has had some modest success but feels that he always "misses" the big stock picks like Amazon or Yahoo.

Jon's stock evaluation method includes comparing the price-earnings ratio of his potential investment to the industry average for that sector. Because stocks like Amazon and Yahoo did not report positive earnings in their early years, price-earnings ratio calculations were not possible (because they had losses and no earnings). Therefore, these shares were excluded from Jon's analysis.

Instructions

With the class divided into groups, answer the following questions:

(a) Can an industry average for the price-earnings ratio be a meaningful benchmark for a particular industry? Consider industries that are stable versus those that are undergoing rapid expansion and/or technological change.

(b) When companies do not report net earnings on their financial statements, management and analysts often estimate future earnings, that is, the earnings that the company expects to produce over the foreseeable future. Assess the quality of this financial information against the criteria of the conceptual framework. Can this information be relied on?

Communication Activity

BYP2–6 Two business students, John and Sally, are discussing the price-earnings ratio. They both agree that the ratio shows what the investors expect of a company's future earnings. John feels the ratio is used by investors to assess the fairness of the share price. Sally feels there are no "right" price-earnings numbers and you can therefore not say that a price-earnings per share of 15 times, for example, is either good or bad. John says that he likes to invest in technology shares because technology shares have high price-earnings and investors assume technology shares will increase in value. Sally responds by saying that she likes to invest in bank shares even though the price-earnings is normally lower than the price-earnings of technology shares. Sally explains that bank shares are safer to invest in because banks are well established.

Instructions

Write a memo to John and Sally, commenting on their concerns and explaining how investors should use the price-earnings ratio in their analysis.

Ethics Case

Ethics in Accounting

BYP2–7 When new accounting principles are issued, the required implementation date is usually 12 months or more after the date of issue, but early implementation is encouraged.

Kathy Johnston, the accountant at Redondo Corporation, discusses with Redondo's vice-president the need for early implementation of a recently issued recommendation. She says it will result in a much fairer presentation of the company's financial condition and earnings. When the vice-president determines that early implementation would decrease reported net earnings for the year, he strongly discourages Kathy from implementing the recommendation until it is required.

Instructions

(a) Who are the stakeholders in this situation?

(b) What, if any, are the ethical considerations in this situation?

(c) What could Kathy gain by supporting early implementation? Who might be affected by the decision against early implementation?

"All About You" Activity

BYP2–8 As discussed in the "All About You" feature presented in this chapter, in order to evaluate your personal financial position, you need to prepare a personal balance sheet. Assume that you have gathered the following information about your personal finances:

Amount owed on student loan (long-term)	$10,000
Balance in chequing account	1,200
Automobile	8,000
Balance on automobile loan (current)	2,400
Balance on automobile loan (long-term)	3,600
Computer and accessories	1,200
Clothes and furniture	4,000
Balance owed on credit cards	1,000

Instructions

Prepare a personal balance sheet using the format you have learned for a balance sheet for a company. For the shareholders' equity account, use Personal Equity (Deficit).

Serial Case

(*Note:* This serial case was started in Chapter 1 and will continue in each chapter.)

BYP2–9 After investigating the different forms of business organization, Natalie Koebel decides to operate her business as a corporation, Cookie Creations Ltd. She begins the process of getting her business running. While at a trade show, Natalie is introduced to Gerry Richards, operations manager of Biscuits, a national food retailer. After much discussion, Gerry asks Natalie to consider being Biscuits' major supplier of oatmeal chocolate chip cookies. He provides Natalie with the most recent copy of the financial statements of Biscuits. He expects that Natalie will need to supply Biscuits' Red Deer warehouse with approximately 1,500 dozen cookies a week. Natalie is to send Biscuits a monthly invoice and she will be paid approximately 30 days from the date the invoice is received in Biscuits' Toronto office.

Natalie is thrilled with the offer; however, she has recently read in the newspaper that Biscuits has a reputation for selling cookies and doughnuts with high amounts of sugar and fat and, as a result, consumer demand has decreased.

Instructions

Natalie has come to you for advice and asks the following questions:

(a) Explain to me the type of information each financial statement provides.

(b) I would like to be sure that Biscuits will be able to pay my invoices. What type of information can these financial statements give that will reassure me that my invoices will be paid?

(c) Will Biscuits have enough cash to meet its current liabilities? Where can I find this information?

(d) Will Biscuits be able to survive over a long period of time? Where can I find this information?

(e) Is Biscuits profitable? Where can I find this information?

(f) Does Biscuits have any debt? Is Biscuits able to pay off both its debt and the interest on it? Where can I find this information?

(g) Does Biscuits pay any dividends? Where can I find this information?

(h) Before I seriously consider this opportunity, are there other areas of concern that I should be aware of?

Answers to Chapter Questions

Answer to Shoppers Drug Mart Review It Question 4

Shoppers Drug Mart's largest current asset at December 29, 2007, is inventory ($1,577,524 thousand).

Answers to Self-Study Questions

1. c   2. a   3. d   4. d   5. c   6. a   7. c   8. a   9. b   10. c

Remember to go back to the beginning of the chapter to check off your completed work!

←

ACCOUNTING MATTERS!

Learning to Handle the Dough

For generations, grandmothers in Grant Hooker's family would make a pastry of flattened, whole wheat dough as a special treat. Now called a BeaverTail®, it became a Sunday staple with Mr. Hooker's own kids during the 1970s.

In 1978, Mr. Hooker sold the family secret to the public for the first time at a music festival near Killaloe, Ontario. The crowd loved it. The delectable dough was then served up at several Ottawa Valley agricultural fairs throughout that fall. Encouraged by the enthusiasm for his treats, Mr. Hooker, a builder by trade, trademarked the name "BeaverTails" and built his own booth in Ottawa's Byward Market in 1980 to sell them full-time. However, sales were not as swift as at the fairs.

Undaunted, Mr. Hooker secured permission to sell BeaverTails on the Rideau Canal during Ottawa's Winterlude festival. "We had lineups down the lake," he says. The whole family—Mr. Hooker's wife, Pamela, and teenaged son, Nicholas, and daughter, Lisa—pitched in, giving out free samples and letting people know the treats were for sale year-round in the Market.

Within three years, BeaverTails Canada Inc. had the contract to sell all the food on the Rideau Canal and employed 450 people. The business continued to grow. BeaverTails began franchising in 1990 and now has 120 locations across Canada.

At first, keeping track of the money was straightforward and did not require a formal accounting system. It was just a matter of staying on top of how much was owed to suppliers and staff, and in rent and utilities. Mr. Hooker, who has no formal business training, got along fine simply managing the chequebook.

But this changed with franchising. "We weren't just selling products to people for cash, putting the cash in the bank, and then writing cheques for what we owed," says Mr. Hooker. "We were into receivables; people owed us money." The company also had liabilities—in the form of an operating loan from a bank.

Mr. Hooker hired a firm to set up an accounting system for the business, an experience he describes as a "rude awakening" that cost him approximately $200,000. One of the accounting staff was negligent, writing cheques for government remittances but not sending them—out of fear the company's line of credit would not cover the cheques. Clearly, the company's accounts were not properly balanced.

"I realized how much improper accounting could cost me and how, if I didn't understand accounting, I'd have to trust somebody," Mr. Hooker says. He hired another accountant to rebuild the accounting system, working closely with him to learn how it worked.

The breakthrough point for him, he says, was understanding that "cash is a debit." Assets (from the balance sheet) and expenses (from the statement of earnings) have normal debit balances. Liabilities and shareholders' equity (from the balance sheet) and revenues (from the statement of earnings) have normal credit balances. To increase the amount in an account, an entry has to be the same sign, he adds. In other words, only debits increase debit accounts and only credits increase credit accounts.

Now that he understands the basics of the accounting system, Mr. Hooker monitors it very closely. He insists his accountant provide him with "TAMFS"—timely, accurate, monthly financial statements. "That is an absolute necessity any time a business grows to where the owner puts his trust in somebody else to handle the money," he says. A lesson this entrepreneur learned the hard way.

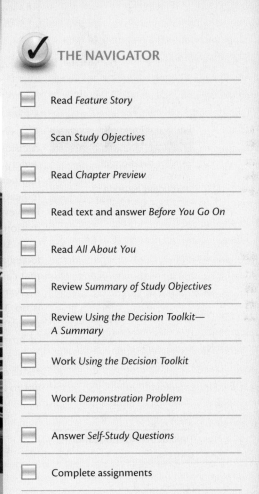

BeaverTails Canada Inc.: beavertailsinc.com

THE NAVIGATOR

- [ ] Read *Feature Story*
- [ ] Scan *Study Objectives*
- [ ] Read *Chapter Preview*
- [ ] Read text and answer *Before You Go On*
- [ ] Read *All About You*
- [ ] Review *Summary of Study Objectives*
- [ ] Review *Using the Decision Toolkit—A Summary*
- [ ] Work *Using the Decision Toolkit*
- [ ] Work *Demonstration Problem*
- [ ] Answer *Self-Study Questions*
- [ ] Complete assignments

STUDY OBJECTIVES

After studying this chapter, you should be able to:

Analyze the effects of transactions on the accounting equation.

Define debits and credits and explain how they are used to record transactions.

Identify the basic steps in the recording process.

Prepare a trial balance.

The Navigator

PREVIEW OF CHAPTER 3

As indicated in the feature story, an accounting information system that produces timely and accurate financial information is a necessity for a company like BeaverTails. The purpose of this chapter is to explain and illustrate the features of an accounting information system. The chapter is organized as follows:

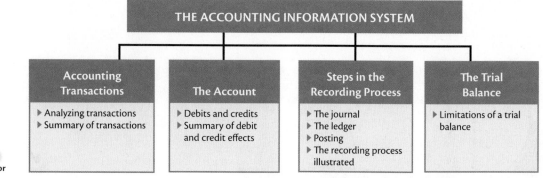

THE ACCOUNTING INFORMATION SYSTEM

Accounting Transactions	The Account	Steps in the Recording Process	The Trial Balance
▶ Analyzing transactions ▶ Summary of transactions	▶ Debits and credits ▶ Summary of debit and credit effects	▶ The journal ▶ The ledger ▶ Posting ▶ The recording process illustrated	▶ Limitations of a trial balance

The Navigator ✓

Accounting Transactions

The system of collecting and processing transaction data and communicating financial information to decision-makers is known as the **accounting information system**. Accounting information systems vary widely. Some factors that shape these systems are the type of business and its transactions, the size of the company, the amount of data, and the information that management and others need. For example, as indicated in the feature story, BeaverTails did not need a formal accounting system when it first began. However, as the business and the number and types of transactions grew, an organized accounting information system became essential.

An accounting information system begins with determining what transaction data should be collected and processed. Not all events are recorded and reported as accounting transactions. Only events that cause changes in assets, liabilities, or shareholders' equity should be recorded. For example, suppose a new employee is hired. Should this event be recorded in the company's accounting records? The answer is no. While the hiring of an employee will lead to a future accounting transaction (e.g., the payment of salary after the work has been completed), no accounting transaction has occurred at the actual time of hiring.

An **accounting transaction** occurs when assets, liabilities, or shareholders' equity items change as a result of some economic event. Illustration 3-1 summarizes the process that is used to decide whether or not to record economic events.

Illustration 3-1 ➡️

Transaction identification process

Events

Purchase a computer

Discuss product design with a potential customer

Pay rent

Criterion

Is the financial position (assets, liabilities, and shareholders' equity) of the company changed?

Yes · No · Yes

Record/Don't Record

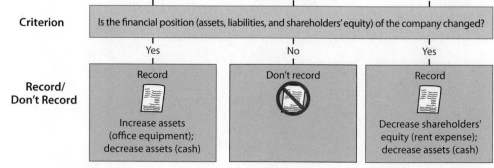

Record — Increase assets (office equipment); decrease assets (cash)

Don't record

Record — Decrease shareholders' equity (rent expense); decrease assets (cash)

ACCOUNTING MATTERS! | International Insight

In 2007, international soccer superstar David Beckham left Spain's Real Madrid to join the Los Angeles Galaxy soccer team in a bid to raise soccer's profile in America. Although his reported U.S. $250-million contract with the L.A. Galaxy creates an economic event that leads to an accounting transaction, there are other events related to this move that may not lead directly to an accounting transaction but will create additional value for the sport.

On the television program *Good Morning America*, Beckham explained: "This move ... is not about the money. It's hopefully making a difference in the U.S. with soccer... The main thing for me is to improve the soccer and improve the standard and change history really."

Source: "Beckham Looking Forward to U.S. Challenge," *ABC News*, January 12, 2007.

Tutorials
(Accounting Cycle)

Analyzing Transactions

In Chapter 1, you learned about the accounting equation:

Assets	=	Liabilities	+	Shareholders' Equity

In this chapter, you will learn how to analyze transactions for their effect on each component of the accounting equation—assets, liabilities, and shareholders' equity. Remember that the accounting equation must always balance, so each transaction will have a dual (double-sided) effect on the equation. For example, if an individual asset is increased, there must be either a corresponding decrease in another asset, an increase in a specific liability, and/or an increase in shareholders' equity.

When you analyze the accounting equation, remember that more than two items could be affected. For example, one asset could increase by $50 (the asset cash, for example), a second and different asset could increase by $150 (perhaps accounts receivable), and shareholder's equity in the form of sales revenue might have increased by $200.

Chapter 1 presented the financial statements for Sierra Corporation for its first month of operations, October 2009. To illustrate the effects of economic events on the accounting equation, we will now examine the events that affected Sierra Corporation in its first month and were ultimately reported on its financial statements in Chapter 1 in Illustrations 1-4, 1-5, 1-7, and 1-8.

Transaction (1): Investment by Shareholders. On October 1, cash of $10,000 was invested in Sierra Corporation in exchange for $10,000 of common shares. This transaction results in an equal increase in assets and shareholders' equity. There is an increase of $10,000 in the asset account Cash and an increase of $10,000 in the shareholders' equity account Common Shares. The effect of this transaction on the accounting equation is:

	Assets	=	Liabilities	+	Shareholders' Equity
	Cash	=			Common Shares
(1)	+$10,000	=			+$10,000

Notice that the two sides of the accounting equation remain equal. Note also that investments by shareholders are not recorded as revenue, but as share capital of the corporation.

Transaction (2): Issue of Note Payable. Also on October 1, Sierra borrowed $5,000 from Scotiabank by signing a note payable. It promised to repay the note, plus 6-percent interest, in three months. This transaction results in an equal increase in assets and liabilities: Cash (an asset) increases by $5,000 and Notes Payable (a liability) increases by $5,000. The specific effect of this transaction and the cumulative effect of the first two transactions are:

	Assets	=	Liabilities	+	Shareholders' Equity
Balance	Cash	=	Notes Payable	+	Common Shares
Beginning	$10,000				$10,000
(2)	+5,000		+$5,000		
Ending	$15,000	=	$5,000	+	$10,000
			$15,000		

Total assets are now $15,000 and shareholders' equity plus the new liability also total $15,000.

Transaction (3): Purchase of Office Equipment. On October 1, Sierra acquired office equipment by paying $5,000 cash to Superior Equipment Corp. This transaction results in an equal increase and decrease in Sierra's assets, although the composition of the assets changed. Office Equipment (an asset) increases by $5,000 and Cash (an asset) decreases by $5,000, as shown:

	Assets		=	Liabilities	+	Shareholders' Equity
		Office				
Balance	Cash	+ Equipment	= Notes Payable	+		Common Shares
Beginning	$15,000		$5,000			$10,000
(3)	−5,000	+$5,000				
Ending	$10,000 +	$5,000	= $5,000	+		$10,000

$15,000 $15,000

The total assets are $15,000. Liabilities plus shareholders' equity also total $15,000.

Transaction (4): Receipt of Cash in Advance from Customer. On October 2, Sierra received a $1,200 cash advance from R. Knox, a client, for advertising services that are expected to be completed before November 15. Revenue should not be recorded until the work has been performed. However, since cash was received before performing the advertising services, Sierra has a liability for the work due. We call this liability unearned service revenue.

Note that the word "unearned" indicates that this is a liability account rather than a revenue account. Although many liability accounts have the word "payable" in their title, not all do. Unearned Service Revenue is a liability account even though the word "payable" is not used.

This transaction results in an increase in Cash (an asset) of $1,200 and an increase in Unearned Service Revenue (a liability) by the same amount:

	Assets		=	Liabilities		+ Shareholders' Equity
		Office		Notes	Unearned	
Balance	Cash	+ Equipment	= Payable	+ Service Revenue	+	Common Shares
Beginning	$10,000	$5,000	$5,000			$10,000
(4)	+1,200			+$1,200		
Ending	$11,200 +	$5,000	= $5,000	$1,200	+	$10,000

$16,200 $16,200

Transaction (5): Payment of Rent. Also on October 2, Sierra Corporation paid $900 cash for its office rent for the month of October. To record this transaction, Cash is decreased by $900 and Rent Expense is increased by $900. Rent is an expense that Sierra incurs in its effort to generate revenues. Expenses decrease retained earnings, which in turn decrease shareholders' equity. You will recall from earlier chapters that shareholders' equity usually consists of common shares (or share capital) and retained earnings. Retained earnings are decreased by dividends, increased by revenues, and decreased by expenses.

We have expanded our accounting equation to show the detailed components of retained earnings. As there is not enough room to use specific account names for each individual revenue and expense account in this illustration, they will be summarized under the column headings Revenues (abbreviated as "Rev."), Expenses (abbreviated as "Exp."), and Dividends (abbreviated as "Div."). Revenue and dividend transactions will be added later in this section.

	Assets		=	Liabilities		+	Shareholders' Equity		
		Office		Notes	Unearned		Common	Retained Earnings	
Balance	Cash	+ Equipment	= Payable	+ Service Revenue	+		Shares	+ Rev. − Exp. − Div.	
Beginning	$11,200	$5,000	$5,000	$1,200			$10,000		
(5)	−900							−$900	
Ending	$10,300 +	$5,000	= $5,000 +	$1,200	+		$10,000	− $900	

$15,300 $15,300

As mentioned above, expenses reduce retained earnings and ultimately shareholders' equity. Therefore, this transaction reduces both assets and shareholders' equity by $900, keeping the equation in balance.

Transaction (6): Purchase of Insurance. On October 6, Sierra paid $600 for a one-year insurance policy effective October 1 that expires next year on September 30. This event is a transaction because one asset was exchanged for another. The asset Cash is decreased by $600. The asset Prepaid Insurance (abbreviated as "Pre. Ins.") is increased by $600 because the payment is for more than the current month. Payments of expenses that will benefit more than one accounting period are identified as prepaid expenses or prepayments. We will learn more about how to account for prepayments in the next chapter.

As shown, the balance in total assets did not change: the decrease in one asset account was in the same amount as the increase in another asset account.

			Assets			=	Liabilities			+	Shareholders' Equity				
			Pre.		Off.				Unearned		Common		Retained Earnings		
Balance	Cash	+	Ins.	+	Equip.	=	N/P	+	Serv. Rev.	+	Shares	+	Rev.	– Exp.	– Div.
Beginning	$10,300				$5,000		$5,000		$1,200		$10,000			$900	
(6)	–600		+$600												
Ending	$ 9,700	+	$600	+	$5,000	=	$5,000	+	$1,200	+	$10,000			– $900	

$15,300 $15,300

Transaction (7): Hiring of New Employees. On October 6, Sierra hired four new employees to begin work on Monday, October 12. Each employee will receive a weekly salary of $500 for a five-day (Monday–Friday) work week, payable every two weeks. Employees will receive their first pay cheques on Friday, October 23. There is no effect on the accounting equation because the assets, liabilities, and shareholders' equity of the company have not changed. An accounting transaction has not occurred. At this point, there is only an agreement that the employees will begin work on October 12. (See transaction 10 for the first payment of salaries.)

Transaction (8): Purchase of Supplies on Account. On October 9, Sierra purchased a supply of advertising materials on account from Aero Supply Corp. for $2,500. The account is due in 30 days. This transaction is referred to as a purchase "on account," or "on credit." Instead of paying cash, the company incurs a liability by promising to pay cash in the future.

Assets are increased by this transaction because supplies are a resource that will be used in providing services to customers. Liabilities are increased by the amount that is owed to Aero Supply. The asset Advertising Supplies (abbreviated as "Ad. Sup.") is increased by $2,500, and the liability Accounts Payable (abbreviated as "A/P") is increased by the same amount. The effect on the equation is:

				Assets					=			Liabilities			+	Shareholders' Equity				
			Ad.		Pre.		Off.							Unearned		Common		Retained Earnings		
Bal.	Cash	+	Sup.	+	Ins.	+	Equip.	=	N/P	+	A/P	+	Serv. Rev.	+	Shares	+	Rev.	– Exp.	– Div.		
Beg.	$9,700				$600		$5,000		$5,000				$1,200		$10,000			$900			
(8)			+$2,500								+$2,500										
End.	$9,700	+	$2,500	+	$600	+	$5,000	=	$5,000	+	$2,500	+	$1,200	+	$10,000			– $900			

$17,800 $17,800

Transaction (9): Services Performed on Account. On October 13, Sierra performed $10,000 of advertising services for Copa Ltd. Sierra sent Copa a bill for these services that asks for payment before the end of the month.

Companies often provide services "on account" or "for credit." Instead of receiving cash, the company receives a different type of asset, an account receivable. Accounts receivable represent the right to receive payment at a future date.

Revenue, however, is earned when services are performed, not when payment is received. As a result, the revenue from this transaction is recorded now when the services are performed rather than in the future when the payment will be received. As revenue increases retained earnings—a shareholders' equity account—both assets and shareholders' equity are increased by this transaction.

> ▸ The Accounting Information System

In this transaction, Accounts Receivable (abbreviated as "A/R") is increased by $10,000 and Service Revenue is increased by the same amount. The new balances in the equation are:

		Assets						=		Liabilities			+		Shareholders' Equity			
Bal.	Cash +	A/R +	Ad. Sup. +	Pre. Ins. +	Off. Equip.	=	N/P +	A/P +	Unearned Serv. Rev. +		Com. Shares +		Retained Earnings		
													Rev. −	Exp. −	Div.
Beg.	$9,700		$2,500	$600	$5,000	=	$5,000	$2,500	$1,200		$10,000			$900	
(9)		+$10,000											+$10,000		
End.	$9,700 +	$10,000 +	$2,500 +	$600 +	$5,000	=	$5,000 +	$2,500 +	$1,200	+	$10,000 +		$10,000 −	$900	
		$27,800										$27,800			

Transaction (10): Payment of Salaries. On October 23, employees are paid for having worked two weeks, earning $4,000 in salaries (4 employees × $500/week × 2 weeks). Salaries are an expense similar to rent because they are a cost of generating revenues. While the act of hiring the employees in transaction 7 did not result in an accounting transaction, the payment of the employees' salaries after they perform the work is a transaction because assets and shareholders' equity are affected. Cash is decreased by $4,000 and Salaries Expense is increased by $4,000:

		Assets					=		Liabilities			+		Shareholders' Equity			
Bal.	Cash +	A/R +	Ad. Sup. +	Pre. Ins. +	Off. Equip.	=	N/P +	A/P +	Unearned Serv. Rev. +		Com. Shares +		Retained Earnings		
													Rev. −	Exp. −	Div.
Beg.	$9,700	$10,000	$2,500	$600	$5,000	=	$5,000	$2,500	$1,200		$10,000		$10,000	$ 900	
(10)	−4,000													−4,000	
End.	$5,700 +	$10,000 +	$2,500 +	$600 +	$5,000	=	$5,000 +	$2,500 +	$1,200	+	$10,000 +		$10,000 −	$4,900	
		$23,800										$23,800			

Transaction (11): Payment of Dividend. On October 26, Sierra paid a $500 cash dividend. Dividends are a distribution of retained earnings rather than an expense. Expenses are incurred for the purpose of generating revenue and are reported on the statement of earnings. Dividends are not incurred for the purpose of generating revenue; they are reported on the statement of retained earnings as a reduction of retained earnings.

A cash dividend transaction reduces both cash (an asset) and retained earnings (shareholders' equity). Cash is decreased by $500 and Dividends (abbreviated as "Div.") are increased by $500:

		Assets					=		Liabilities			+		Shareholders' Equity			
Bal.	Cash +	A/R +	Ad. Sup. +	Pre. Ins. +	Off. Equip.	=	N/P +	A/P +	Unearned Serv. Rev. +		Com. Shares +		Retained Earnings		
													Rev. −	Exp. −	Div.
Beg.	$5,700	$10,000	$2,500	$600	$5,000	=	$5,000	$2,500	$1,200		$10,000		$10,000	$4,900	
(11)	−500														−$500
End.	$5,200 +	$10,000 +	$2,500 +	$600 +	$5,000	=	$5,000 +	$2,500 +	$1,200	+	$10,000 +		$10,000 −	$4,900 −	$500
		$23,300										$23,300			

Transaction (12): Collection of Account. On October 30, Copa paid Sierra the amount owing on its account. Recall that an account receivable and the revenue from this transaction were recorded earlier in transaction 9, when the service was provided. Revenue should not be recorded again when the cash is collected. Rather, Cash is increased by $10,000 and Accounts Receivable is decreased by $10,000. Total assets and total liabilities and shareholders' equity are unchanged, as shown:

		Assets					=		Liabilities			+		Shareholders' Equity			
Bal.	Cash +	A/R +	Ad. Sup. +	Pre. Ins. +	Off. Equip.	=	N/P +	A/P +	Unearned Serv. Rev. +		Com. Shares +		Retained Earnings		
													Rev. −	Exp. −	Div.
Beg.	$ 5,200	$10,000	$2,500	$600	$5,000	=	$5,000	$2,500	$1,200		$10,000		$10,000	$4,900	$500
(12)	+10,000	−10,000													
End.	$15,200 +	$ 0 +	$2,500 +	$600 +	$5,000	=	$5,000 +	$2,500 +	$1,200	+	$10,000 +		$10,000 −	$4,900 −	$500
		$23,300										$23,300			

Summary of Transactions

The transactions of Sierra Corporation are summarized in Illustration 3-2 to show their cumulative effect on the accounting equation. The transaction number, the specific effects of the transaction, and the final balances are indicated. Remember that event 7—the hiring of employees—did not result in a transaction, so no entry is included for that event.

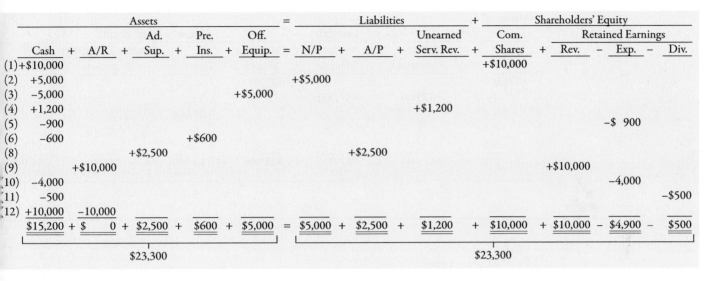

▼ Illustration 3-2

Tabular summary of transactions

	Assets						=	Liabilities			+	Shareholders' Equity			
			Ad.	Pre.	Off.					Unearned		Com.	Retained Earnings		
	Cash	+ A/R +	Sup. +	Ins. +	Equip.	=	N/P +	A/P +	Serv. Rev. +		Shares +	Rev. −	Exp. −	Div.
(1)	+$10,000										+$10,000			
(2)	+5,000						+$5,000							
(3)	−5,000				+$5,000									
(4)	+1,200								+$1,200					
(5)	−900												−$ 900	
(6)	−600			+$600										
(8)			+$2,500					+$2,500						
(9)	+10,000											+$10,000		
(10)	−4,000												−4,000	
(11)	−500													−$500
(12)	+10,000	−10,000												
	$15,200 +	$ 0 +	$2,500 +	$600 +	$5,000	=	$5,000 +	$2,500 +	$1,200	+	$10,000 +	$10,000 −	$4,900 −	$500

$23,300 = $23,300

The illustration demonstrates that (1) each transaction must be analyzed for its effect on the three main components of the accounting equation (assets, liabilities, and shareholders' equity) and (2) the two sides of the equation must always be equal.

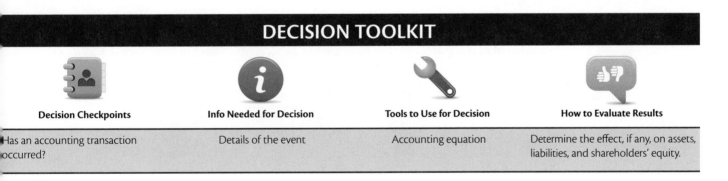

DECISION TOOLKIT

Decision Checkpoints	Info Needed for Decision	Tools to Use for Decision	How to Evaluate Results
Has an accounting transaction occurred?	Details of the event	Accounting equation	Determine the effect, if any, on assets, liabilities, and shareholders' equity.

BEFORE YOU GO ON...

Review It

1. Provide examples of two kinds of transactions: (a) economic events that should be recorded, and (b) events that should not be recorded.
2. If an asset increases, what are the three possible effects on the accounting equation? What are the possible effects if a liability increases?

Do It

Transactions by Virmari Corporation for the month of August follow:

1. Common shares were issued to shareholders for $25,000 cash.
2. Office equipment costing $7,000 was purchased on account.
3. Cash of $8,000 was received for services performed.
4. Rent was paid for the month, $850.
5. Dividends of $1,000 were paid to shareholders.

Prepare an analysis in table format (like the tabular summary in Illustration 3-2) that shows the effects of these transactions on the accounting equation.

Action Plan

- Analyze the effects of each transaction on the accounting equation.
- Keep the accounting equation in balance.

Solution

	Assets			=	Liabilities	+			Shareholders' Equity			
			Office		Accounts		Common			Retained Earnings		
	Cash	+	Equipment	=	Payable	+	Shares	+	Revenues	–	Expenses	– Dividend.
1.	+$25,000						+$25,000					
2.			+$7,000		+$7,000							
3.	+8,000								+$8,000			
4.	−850										−$850	
5.	−1,000											−$1,000
	$31,150	+	$7,000	=	$7,000	+	$25,000	+	$8,000	–	$850	– $1,000

$38,150

$38,150

The Navigator

The Account

study objective 2

Define debits and credits and explain how they are used to record transactions.

Instead of using a tabular summary like the one in Illustration 3-2 for Sierra Corporation, an accounting information system uses accounts. An **account** is an individual accounting record of increases and decreases in a specific asset, liability, or shareholders' equity item. For example, Sierra Corporation has separate accounts for cash, accounts receivable, accounts payable, service revenue, salaries expense, and so on.

In its simplest form, an account has three parts: (1) the title of the account, (2) a left or debit side, and (3) a right or credit side. Because the alignment of these parts of an account resembles the letter T, it is referred to as a **T account**. The basic form of an account is shown in Illustration 3-3.

Illustration 3-3 ➡

Basic form of T account

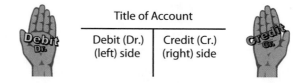

The actual account form that is used in real life looks different from the above T account. It has several other columns to make it easier to include additional information. However, because of its simplicity, the T account is used for teaching purposes and will be used throughout this textbook to explain basic accounting relationships.

Debits and Credits

The term **debit** means left, and the term **credit** means right. These terms are commonly abbreviated as Dr. for debit and Cr. for credit. Debits and credits are simply directional signals that describe where entries are made in the accounts. For example, the act of entering an amount on the left side of an account is called **debiting** the account, and making an entry on the right side is **crediting** the account. When the totals of the two sides are compared, an account will have a debit balance if the total of the debit amounts exceeds the credits. Conversely, an account will have a credit balance if the credit amounts are more than the debit amounts.

Each transaction affects two or more accounts in order to keep the accounting equation in balance. In other words, for each transaction, debits must equal credits. The equality of debits and credits is the basis for the **double-entry accounting system**, in which the dual (two-sided) effect of each transaction is recorded in appropriate accounts. This system provides a logical method for recording transactions and ensuring that amounts are recorded accurately. If every transaction is recorded with equal debits and credits, then the sum of all the debits to the accounts must equal the sum of all the credits.

The following diagram will help us understand how debit and credit effects apply to the accounting equation:

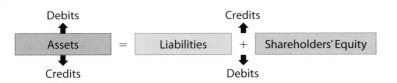

Helpful Hint Debits and credits do not always mean "increases" and "decreases." While debits do increase certain accounts (e.g., assets), they decrease other accounts (e.g., liabilities).

Beginning on the left-hand side of the accounting equation (asset accounts), we can see that increases in asset accounts are recorded by debits. The converse is also true: decreases in asset accounts are recorded by credits. If we cross to the right-hand side of the equation, it must follow (for the equation to remain balanced) that increases and decreases in liabilities and shareholders' equity are recorded *opposite from* increases and decreases in assets. Thus, increases in liabilities and shareholders' equity are recorded by credits, and decreases by debits.

We will apply debit and credit procedures to T accounts for each component of the accounting equation—assets, liabilities, and shareholders' equity—in the following sections.

Assets

If we apply the accounting equation to a T account for assets, we can see that increases in assets must be entered on the left or debit side, and decreases in assets must be entered on the right or credit side. **Asset accounts normally show debit balances.** That is, debits to a specific asset account should exceed credits to that account. It was a breakthrough for Mr. Hooker in the feature story when he learned that assets, such as cash, are normally debits.

The diagram below shows the effects that debits and credits have on asset accounts, and an asset account's normal balance:

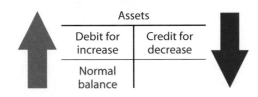

Helpful Hint The normal balance of an account is always on its increase side.

Knowing an account's normal balance may help when you are trying to identify errors. For example, a credit balance in an asset account such as Land would indicate a recording error. Occasionally, however, an abnormal balance may be correct. The Cash account, for example, will have a credit balance if a company has overdrawn its bank balance. If the Cash account has a credit balance, it is called "bank indebtedness" and reported as a current liability rather than as a current asset. We will learn more about cash and bank indebtedness in Chapter 7.

Liabilities and Shareholders' Equity

Liability and shareholders' equity accounts are increased by credits and decreased by debits. Increases are entered on the right or credit side of the T account, and decreases are entered on the left or debit side of the T account. Just as asset accounts normally show debit balances, **liability and equity accounts normally show credit balances.**

Because assets are on the opposite side of the accounting equation from liabilities and shareholders' equity, increases and decreases in assets are recorded opposite from increases and decreases in liabilities and shareholders' equity. In this way, the total amount of debits always equals the total amount of credits and the accounting equation stays in balance.

The effects that debits and credits have on liabilities and shareholders' equity, and the normal balances are as follows:

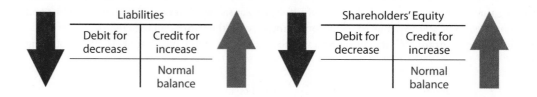

All asset and liability accounts have the same debit/credit rule procedures. That is, all asset accounts are increased by debits and decreased by credits. All liability accounts are increased by credits and decreased by debits. Shareholders' equity is different. It comprises different components and they do not all move in the same direction. You will recall that shareholders' equity normally consists of common shares (or share capital if there is more than one class of shares) and retained earnings. Retained earnings comprise revenues, expenses, and dividends. Common shares, retained earnings, and revenues all increase shareholders' equity. Dividends and expenses decrease shareholders' equity.

In the following sections, we will look at how debit and credit procedures apply to each of these equity components.

Increases in Shareholders' Equity. Common shares and retained earnings both increase shareholders' equity. Common shares are issued in exchange for the shareholders' investments. Retained earnings are the portion of shareholders' equity that has been accumulated through the profitable operation of the company. Retained earnings are divided further into revenues and expenses (which make up net earnings) and dividends. Of these, revenues increase retained earnings, which then increase shareholders' equity.

The common shares, retained earnings, and revenue accounts are increased by credits and decreased by debits. **The normal balance in these accounts is a credit balance.** This, and the effects that debits and credits have on them, are shown below:

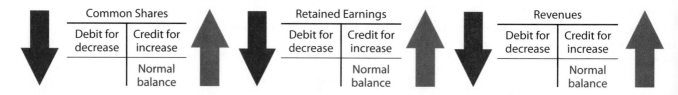

Decreases in Shareholders' Equity. Dividends and expenses both decrease retained earnings, which then decrease shareholders' equity. Since decreases in shareholders' equity are recorded by debits, it makes sense that **dividend and expense accounts would have a normal debit balance.**

As dividends are a distribution of retained earnings to shareholders, they reduce retained earnings. If retained earnings are decreased by debits, it follows that increases in the Dividends account are recorded with debits. Credits to the Dividends account are unusual, but might be used to correct a dividend that was recorded in error, for example.

Expenses, along with revenues, combine to determine net earnings. Since expenses are the negative factor in the calculation of earnings, and revenues are the positive factor, it is logical that the increase and decrease sides of expense accounts should be the reverse of revenue accounts. Thus, expense accounts are increased by debits and decreased by credits.

The normal balance in these accounts, and the effects that debits and credits have on them, are shown below:

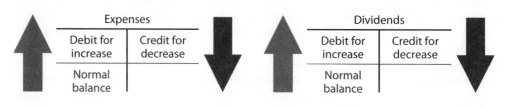

Summary of Debit and Credit Effects

Illustration 3-4 summarizes the debit and credit effects on the accounting equation. It also expands the basic accounting equation to show the types of accounts that make up shareholders' equity. Assets (on the left-hand side of the accounting equation) are increased by debits. Liabilities and shareholders' equity, on the other side of the equation, are increased by credits. Recall Mr. Hooker's comment in the feature story that increases to accounts have to be the same sign, which is a way of saying that a debit will increase a debit account and a credit will increase a credit account.

As we learned above, shareholders' equity can be further divided into two components: common shares and retained earnings. Since shareholders' equity is increased by credits, both of these accounts—common shares and retained earnings—are also increased by credits.

Retained earnings can be further subdivided into revenues, expenses (revenues and expenses combine to determine net earnings), and dividends. Since revenues increase retained earnings and shareholders' equity, increases in revenue accounts are recorded by credits. Expenses and dividends decrease retained earnings, and thus shareholders' equity. Decreases in shareholders' equity are recorded by debits. Because expenses and dividends decrease shareholders' equity, increases in each of these accounts are recorded by debits.

The debit/credit rules and effects on each type of account are summarized in Illustration 3-4. Like the basic accounting equation, the expanded equation must always be in balance (total debits must equal total credits). Study this carefully. It will help you understand the fundamentals of the double-entry accounting system.

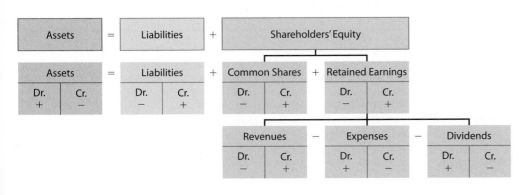

◄ Illustration 3-4

Summary of debit and credit rules for expanded accounting equation

---

BEFORE YOU GO ON...

Review It

1. What do the terms *debit* and *credit* mean?
2. What are the effects of debits and credits on assets, liabilities, and shareholders' equity?
3. What are the effects of debits and credits on revenues, expenses, and dividends?
4. What are the normal balances of asset, liability, common share, revenue, expense, and dividend accounts?
5. What are the normal balances for Shoppers Drug Mart's Accounts Receivable, Dividends Payable, Sales, and Interest Expense accounts? The answer to this question is at the end of the chapter.

Do It

Lin Limited has the following selected accounts:

1. Service Revenue
2. Dividends
3. Office Equipment
4. Accounts Receivable
5. Office Supplies
6. Unearned Service Revenue
7. Accounts Payable
8. Common Shares
9. Salaries Expense
10. Cash

(a) Indicate whether each of the above accounts is an asset, liability, or shareholders' equity account. If the account is an asset or liability, indicate its balance sheet classification. If it is a shareholders' equity account, indicate what specific type it is (e.g., common shares, revenue, expense, or dividend).

▶ The Accounting Information System

(b) Indicate whether a debit would increase or decrease each account.
(c) Identify the normal balance.

Action Plan

• Classify each account into its spot in the expanded accounting equation.
• Apply the debit and credit rules. Remember that assets are increased by debits, and liabilities and shareholders' equity are increased by credits.
• Remember that the normal balance of an account is on its increase side.

Solution

	Account	(a) Classification	(b) Debit Effect	(c) Normal Balance
1.	Service Revenue	Shareholders' equity (revenue)	Decrease	Credit
2.	Dividends	Shareholders' equity (dividends)	Increase	Debit
3.	Office Equipment	Assets (property, plant, and equipment)	Increase	Debit
4.	Accounts Receivable	Assets (current)	Increase	Debit
5.	Office Supplies	Assets (current)	Increase	Debit
6.	Unearned Service Revenue	Liabilities (current)	Decrease	Credit
7.	Accounts Payable	Liabilities (current)	Decrease	Credit
8.	Common Shares	Shareholders' equity (common shares)	Decrease	Credit
9.	Salaries Expense	Shareholders' equity (expense)	Increase	Debit
10.	Cash	Assets (current)	Increase	Debit

The Navigator

Steps in the Recording Process

study objective 3

Identify the basic steps in the recording process.

The basic steps in the recording process are:

1. Analyze each transaction for its effect on the accounts.
2. Enter the transaction information in a general journal (book of original entry).
3. Transfer the information from the general journal to the appropriate accounts in the general ledger (book of accounts).

The actual sequence of events begins with the transaction. Evidence of the transaction comes from a **source document**, such as a sales slip, cheque, bill, or cash register tape. In the early days of BeaverTails, as described in our feature story, Grant Hooker used cheques to begin the recording process.

This evidence of the transaction is analyzed to determine the effect on specific accounts. Deciding what to record is the most critical point in the accounting process. The transaction is then entered in the general journal. Finally, the journal entry is transferred to the designated accounts in the general ledger. The sequence of events in the recording process is shown in Illustration 3-5.

Illustration 3-5 ▶

The recording process

Analyze each transaction   Enter transactions in a journal   Transfer journal information to ledger accounts

The basic steps in the recording process occur repeatedly in every company, whether a manual or a computerized accounting system is used. However, the first two steps—the analysis and entering of each transaction—must be done by a person even when a computerized system is used. The basic difference between a manual and computerized system is in the last step in the recording process—transferring information (and subsequent steps that we will learn about later). In a computerized system, this step is done automatically by the computer. In order to understand how this happens, we need to first understand manual approaches to the recording process, which is what we will focus on in this chapter.

ACCOUNTING MATTERS! | Management Perspective

Organizations of all shapes and sizes use computerized accounting systems. Cathy Love, the administrator of Bryony House, a Halifax women's shelter, agrees. "We really need our computerized system to track our accounts in detail," she says. The shelter users the popular small-business electronic accounting package Simply Accounting. In addition, the shelter's fundraising activities are tracked in detail using custom donation software. The shelter's staff have found that the more easily and quickly they can get the information they need, the more time they have to do their main work with the women who come for help.

The Journal

Transactions are first recorded in chronological order (i.e., by date) in a journal and then transferred to the accounts. For this reason, the journal is referred to as the book of original entry. For each transaction, the journal shows the debit and credit effects on specific accounts. Companies may use various kinds of journals, but every company has the most basic form of journal, a **general journal**.

The general journal makes several contributions to the recording process:

1. It discloses the complete effect of a transaction in one place, including an explanation and, where applicable, identification of the source document.
2. It provides a chronological record of transactions.
3. It helps to prevent and locate errors, because the debit and credit amounts for each entry can be quickly compared.

Entering transaction data in the general journal is known as **journalizing**. To illustrate the technique of journalizing, let's look at the first transaction of Sierra Corporation. On October 1, common shares were issued in exchange for $10,000 cash. As an equation in a table, this transaction appeared in our earlier discussion as follows:

	Assets	=	Liabilities	+	Shareholders' Equity
	Cash	=			Common Shares
(1)	+$10,000	=			+$10,000

This transaction would be recorded in the general journal as follows:

GENERAL JOURNAL			
Date	Account Titles and Explanation	Debit	Credit
2009 Oct. 1	Cash	10,000	
	Common Shares		10,000
	(Issued common shares)		

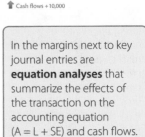

A	=	L	+	SE
+10,000				+10,000

⬆ Cash flows +10,000

In the margins next to key journal entries are **equation analyses** that summarize the effects of the transaction on the accounting equation (A = L + SE) and cash flows.

Note the following features of the journal entry:

1. The date of the transaction is entered in the Date column.
2. The account to be debited is entered first and at the left margin. The account to be credited is then entered on the next line, indented under the line above. The indentation differentiates debits from credits and decreases the chance of switching the debit and credit amounts by mistake.

3.   The amounts for the debits are recorded in the Debit (left) column, and the amounts for the credits are recorded in the Credit (right) column.
4.   A brief explanation of the transaction is given.

If a journal entry affects only two accounts—i.e., there is one debit and one credit— it is considered to be a simple journal entry. When three or more accounts are required in one journal entry, the entry is called a compound entry. Regardless of the number of accounts used in the journal entry, **the total debit and credit amounts must be equal**.

In assignments when specific account titles are given, they should be used in journalizing. When account titles are not given, you should create account titles that identify the nature and content of each account. Ambiguous or multiple account titles with similar names can lead to incorrect financial reporting. For example, a company could use any one of these account titles for recording the cost of delivery trucks: Automobiles, Delivery Trucks, or Trucks. However, if it uses more than one of these account titles, it will be harder for it to determine the total cost of its delivery trucks.

Once the company chooses the specific account title to use (say, Delivery Trucks), all future transactions related to trucks should be recorded in the Delivery Trucks account. Note that the account title itself should not contain explanations or descriptions (such as Delivery Trucks Purchased). Explanations are given as a separate part of the journal entry and should not be included in the account title.

The Ledger

The entire group of accounts that are maintained by a company is referred to as the ledger. The ledger keeps all the information about changes in specific account balances in one place.

Companies may use various kinds of ledgers, but every company has a general ledger. A general ledger contains all the asset, liability, shareholders' equity, revenue, and expense accounts. Each account has a number so that it is easier to identify. A company can use a loose-leaf binder or card file for the general ledger, with each account kept on a separate sheet or card. However, most companies today use a computerized accounting system that keeps each account in a separate file.

The general ledger is often arranged in the order in which accounts are presented in the financial statements, beginning with the balance sheet accounts. The asset accounts come first, followed by liability accounts, and then shareholders' equity accounts, including share capital, retained earnings, dividend, revenue, and expense accounts. Of course, in a computerized accounting system, the accounts can easily be rearranged in whatever order is wanted.

Most companies list their ledger accounts in a chart of accounts. The chart of accounts is the framework for the accounting database. It lists the accounts and the account numbers that identify where the accounts are in the ledger. The numbering system that is used to identify the accounts can be quite sophisticated or pretty simple. Goodyear Tire & Rubber Company, for example, uses an eight-digit numbering system. Other companies may only use two or three digits, depending on how many accounts they have. The chart of accounts usually starts with the balance sheet accounts, followed by the statement of earnings accounts. These account numbers are often referred to in both the general journal and the general ledger.

The chart of accounts for Sierra Corporation is shown in Illustration 3-6. For your information, the illustration also indicates each account's financial statement category on the right. Accounts shown in red are used in this chapter; accounts shown in black are explained in later chapters. The four-digit numbering system that is used allows lots of room for new accounts to be created as needed during the life of the business.

Illustration 3-6 ⬇

Chart of accounts

SIERRA CORPORATION—CHART OF ACCOUNTS				
Assets	Liabilities	Shareholders' Equity	Revenues	Expenses
1000 Cash	3000 Notes Payable	4000 Common Shares	5000 Service Revenue	7000 Advertising Supplies Expense
1100 Accounts Receivable	3100 Accounts Payable	4500 Retained Earnings		7100 Depreciation Expense
1500 Advertising Supplies	3200 Interest Payable	4600 Dividends		7500 Insurance Expense
1550 Prepaid Insurance	3300 Salaries Payable			7600 Interest Expense
2000 Office Equipment	3400 Unearned Service Revenue			8200 Salaries Expense
2010 Accumulated Depreciation— Office Equipment				8400 Rent Expense
				9000 Income Tax Expense

A master chart of accounts for a sample company is included in the Study Tools section of the textbook website. This will help you become familiar with many account titles that are commonly used in accounting, although the list of possibilities of account titles is endless.

Posting

The procedure of transferring journal entries to the general ledger accounts is called posting. This phase of the recording process accumulates the effects of journalized transactions in the individual accounts. Posting involves transferring information from the general journal to the general ledger. For example, the date and amount shown on the first line of a general journal entry are entered in the debit column of the appropriate account in the general ledger. The same is done for the credit side of the entry—the date and amount are entered in the credit column of the general ledger account.

Posting should be done in chronological order. That is, all the debits and credits of a journal entry should be posted before going on to the next journal entry. Posting should also be done on a timely basis—at least monthly—to ensure that the general ledger is up to date. In a computerized accounting system, posting usually occurs simultaneously after each journal entry is prepared.

The Recording Process Illustrated

The following transaction analyses show the basic steps in the recording process using the transactions for the month of October for Sierra Corporation. A basic analysis and a debit-credit analysis are done before the journalizing and posting of each transaction.

Study these transaction analyses carefully. The purpose of transaction analysis is first to identify the type of account involved and then to determine whether a debit or a credit to the account is required. You should always perform this type of analysis before preparing a journal entry. Doing this will help you understand the journal entries discussed in this chapter, as well as more complex journal entries described in later chapters.

◄ **Transaction (1)**

Investment by shareholders

Transaction	October 1: shareholders invest $10,000 cash in an advertising venture to be known as Sierra Corporation.		
Basic Analysis	The asset Cash is increased by $10,000, and the shareholders' equity account Common Shares is increased by $10,000.		
Debit-Credit Analysis	Debits increase assets: debit Cash $10,000. Credits increase shareholders' equity: credit Common Shares $10,000.		

Journal Entry	Oct. 1	Cash
		    Common Shares
		      (Issued common shares)
			10,000
			           10,000

Posting	Cash		Common Shares	
	Oct. 1 10,000			Oct. 1 10,000

◄ **Transaction (2)**

Issue of note payable

Transaction	October 1: cash of $5,000 is received by issuing a three-month, 6%, $5,000 note payable.		
Basic Analysis	The asset Cash is increased by $5,000, and the liability Notes Payable is increased by $5,000.		
Debit-Credit Analysis	Debits increase assets: debit Cash $5,000. Credits increase liabilities: credit Notes Payable $5,000.		

Journal Entry	Oct. 1	Cash
		    Notes Payable
		      (Issued three-month, 6% note payable
		        for cash)
			5,000
			           5,000

Posting	Cash		Notes Payable	
	Oct. 1 10,000 1 5,000			Oct. 1 5,000

Transaction (3) ➡

Purchase of office equipment

Transaction	October 1: used $5,000 cash to purchase office equipment.		
Basic Analysis	The asset Office Equipment is increased by $5,000; the asset Cash is decreased by $5,000.		
Debit-Credit Analysis	Debits increase assets: debit Office Equipment $5,000. Credits decrease assets: credit Cash $5,000.		

Journal Entry	Oct. 1 Office Equipment
	            Cash
	            (Purchased office equipment
	            for cash)
		5,000	5,000

Posting	Cash				Office Equipment	
	Oct. 1 1	10,000 5,000	Oct. 1	5,000	Oct. 1 5,000	

Transaction (4) ➡

Receipt of cash in advance from customer

Transaction	October 2: a $1,200 cash advance is received from R. Knox, a client, for advertising services that are expected to be completed by November 15.		
Basic Analysis	The asset Cash is increased by $1,200; the liability Unearned Service Revenue is increased by $1,200 because the service has not yet been performed.		
Debit-Credit Analysis	Debits increase assets: debit Cash $1,200. Credits increase liabilities: credit Unearned Service Revenue $1,200.		

Journal Entry	Oct. 2 Cash
	            Unearned Service Revenue
	            (Received advance from R. Knox for
	            future service)
		1,200	1,200

Posting	Cash				Unearned Service Revenue	

	Oct. 1
	    1
	    2
		10,000
		5,000
		1,200
			Oct. 1	5,000		Oct. 2 1,200

Transaction (5) ➡

Payment of rent

Transaction	October 2: rent for October is paid in cash, $900.		
Basic Analysis	The expense Rent Expense is increased by $900 because the payment is only for the current month; the asset Cash is decreased by $900.		
Debit-Credit Analysis	Debits increase expenses: debit Rent Expense $900. Credits decrease assets: credit Cash $900.		

Journal Entry	Oct. 2 Rent Expense
	            Cash
	            (Paid cash for October office rent)
		900	900

Posting	Cash				Rent Expense	

	Oct. 1
	    1
	    2
		10,000
		5,000
		1,200
			Oct. 1
			    2
				5,000
				900
					Oct. 2 900	

Transaction	October 6: $600 is paid for a one-year insurance policy that will expire next year on September 30.			

Basic Analysis: The asset Prepaid Insurance is increased by $600 because the payment extends to more than the current month; the asset Cash is decreased by $600.

Debit-Credit Analysis: Debits increase assets: debit Prepaid Insurance $600.
Credits decrease assets: credit Cash $600.

Journal Entry:

Oct. 6	Prepaid Insurance	600	
	Cash		600
	(Paid one-year insurance policy; effective October 1)		

Posting:

Cash				Prepaid Insurance	
Oct. 1	10,000	Oct. 1	5,000	Oct. 6	600
1	5,000	2	900		
2	1,200	6	600		

← **Transaction (6)**

Purchase of insurance

Transaction	October 6: hired four employees to begin work on Monday, October 12. Each employee is to receive a weekly salary of $500 for a five-day work week (Monday–Friday), payable every two weeks—first payment to be made on Friday, October 23.

Basic Analysis: An accounting transaction has not occurred. There is only an agreement that the employees will begin work on October 12. Thus, a debit-credit analysis is not needed because there is no accounting entry. (See transaction of October 23 for first entry.)

← **Transaction (7)**

Hiring of new employees

Transaction	October 9: a supply of advertising materials is purchased on account from Aero Supply for $2,500.

Basic Analysis: The asset Advertising Supplies is increased by $2,500; the liability Accounts Payable is increased by $2,500.

Debit-Credit Analysis: Debits increase assets: debit Advertising Supplies $2,500.
Credits increase liabilities: credit Accounts Payable $2,500.

Journal Entry:

Oct. 9	Advertising Supplies	2,500	
	Accounts Payable		2,500
	(Purchased supplies on account from Aero Supply)		

Posting:

Advertising Supplies		Accounts Payable	
Oct. 9	2,500	Oct. 9	2,500

← **Transaction (8)**

Purchase of supplies on account

Transaction	October 13: Copa is billed $10,000 for advertising services performed to date.

Basic Analysis: The asset Accounts Receivable is increased by $10,000. The revenue account Service Revenue is increased by $10,000. Note that revenue is recorded when the service is performed, regardless of when the cash is received.

Debit-Credit Analysis: Debits increase assets: debit Accounts Receivable $10,000.
Credits increase revenues: credit Service Revenue $10,000.

Journal Entry:

Oct. 13	Accounts Receivable	10,000	
	Service Revenue		10,000
	(Performed services on account for Copa)		

Posting:

Accounts Receivable		Service Revenue	
Oct. 13	10,000	Oct. 13	10,000

← **Transaction (9)**

Services performed on account

Transaction (10) ➡

Payment of salaries

Transaction	October 23: employee salaries of $4,000 (4 employees × $500/week × 2 weeks) are paid in cash. (See October 6 transaction.)
Basic Analysis	The expense account Salaries Expense is increased by $4,000; the asset Cash is decreased by $4,000.
Debit-Credit Analysis	Debits increase expenses: debit Salaries Expense $4,000. Credits decrease assets: credit Cash $4,000.

Journal Entry	Oct. 23	Salaries Expense	4,000	
		Cash		4,000
		(Paid salaries for Oct. 12–23)		

Posting

Cash					Salaries Expense		
Oct. 1	10,000	Oct. 1	5,000		Oct. 23	4,000	
1	5,000	2	900				
2	1,200	6	600				
		23	4,000				

Transaction (11) ➡

Payment of dividend

Transaction	October 26: Sierra paid a $500 cash dividend to shareholders.
Basic Analysis	The account Dividends is increased by $500; the asset Cash is decreased by $500.
Debit-Credit Analysis	Debits increase dividends: debit Dividends $500. Credits decrease assets: credit Cash $500.

Journal Entry	Oct. 26	Dividends	500	
		Cash		500
		(Paid cash dividend)		

Posting

Cash					Dividends		
Oct. 1	10,000	Oct. 1	5,000		Oct. 26	500	
1	5,000	2	900				
2	1,200	6	600				
		23	4,000				
		26	500				

Transaction (12) ➡

Collection of account

Transaction	October 30: received $10,000 in cash from Copa in payment of its account. (See October 13 transaction.)
Basic Analysis	The asset Cash is increased by $10,000. The asset Accounts Receivable is decreased by $10,000. Note that Service Revenue is not recorded here; it was originally recorded on October 13 when the service was performed.
Debit-Credit Analysis	Debits increase assets: debit Cash $10,000. Credits decrease assets: credit Accounts Receivable $10,000.

Journal Entry	Oct. 30	Cash	10,000	
		Accounts Receivable		10,000
		(Received cash on account from Copa)		

Posting

Cash					Accounts Receivable			
Oct. 1	10,000	Oct. 1	5,000		Oct. 13	10,000	Oct. 30	10,000
1	5,000	2	900					
2	1,200	6	600					
30	10,000	23	4,000					
		26	500					

The general journal for Sierra Corporation for the month of October is summarized below.

	SIERRA CORPORATION General Journal		
Date	Account Titles and Explanations	Debit	Credit
2009 Oct. 1	Cash	10,000	
	Common Shares		10,000
	(Issued common shares)		
1	Cash	5,000	
	Notes Payable		5,000
	(Issued three-month, 6% note payable for cash)		
1	Office Equipment	5,000	
	Cash		5,000
	(Purchased office equipment for cash)		
2	Cash	1,200	
	Unearned Service Revenue		1,200
	(Received advance from R. Knox for future service)		
2	Rent Expense	900	
	Cash		900
	(Paid cash for October office rent)		
6	Prepaid Insurance	600	
	Cash		600
	(Paid one-year insurance policy; effective October 1)		
9	Advertising Supplies	2,500	
	Accounts Payable		2,500
	(Purchased supplies on account from Aero Supply)		
13	Accounts Receivable	10,000	
	Service Revenue		10,000
	(Performed services on account for Copa)		
23	Salaries Expense	4,000	
	Cash		4,000
	(Paid salaries for Oct. 12–23)		
26	Dividends	500	
	Cash		500
	(Paid cash dividend)		
30	Cash	10,000	
	Accounts Receivable		10,000
	(Received cash on account from Copa)		

The general ledger for Sierra Corporation follows with all balances highlighted in red.

SIERRA CORPORATION
General Ledger

		Cash						Accounts Payable		
Oct.	1	10,000	Oct.	1	5,000			Oct.	9	2,500
	1	5,000		2	900			Bal.		2,500
	2	1,200		6	600					
	30	10,000		23	4,000			Unearned Service Revenue		
				26	500			Oct.	2	1,200
Bal.		15,200						Bal.		1,200

		Accounts Receivable						Common Shares		
Oct.	13	10,000	Oct.	30	10,000			Oct.	1	10,000
Bal.		0						Bal.		10,000

		Advertising Supplies					Dividends	
Oct.	9	2,500			Oct.	26	500	
Bal.		2,500			Bal.		500	

Prepaid Insurance			Service Revenue		
Oct. 6	600			Oct. 13	10,000
Bal.	600			Bal.	10,000

Office Equipment			Salaries Expense		
Oct. 1	5,000		Oct. 23	4,000	
Bal.	5,000		Bal.	4,000	

Notes Payable			Rent Expense		
		Oct. 1	5,000	Oct. 2	900	
		Bal.	5,000	Bal.	900	

The basic steps in the recording process shown in the (1) transaction analyses, (2) general journal, and (3) general ledger are the first three steps in what is called the accounting cycle, which is illustrated below. In Illustration 3-7, you can see that the cycle begins with the analysis of business transactions (step 1), followed by journalizing the transactions (step 2), and posting to general ledger accounts (step 3). The fourth step is to prepare a trial balance, which we will discuss in the next section. The remaining steps, 5 through 9, will be discussed in the next chapter.

Illustration 3-7 ➡

The accounting cycle

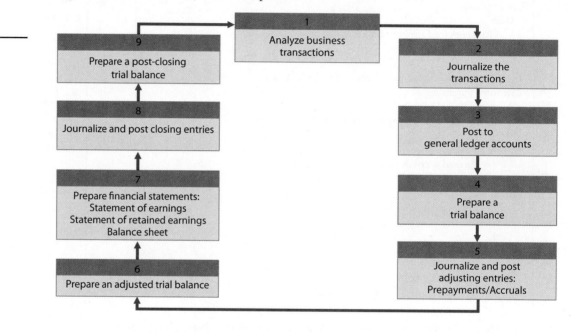

BEFORE YOU GO ON...

➡ **Review It**

1. What are the first three steps in the accounting cycle?
2. What does the general journal contribute to the recording process?
3. How does journalizing differ from posting?
4. Explain how a chart of accounts relates to the general ledger.

➡ **Do It**

The following events occurred during the first week of business of Hair It Is, Inc., a beauty salon:

May 1 Issued common shares to shareholders for $20,000 cash.
   4 Purchased $4,800 of equipment on account (to be paid in 30 days).
   5 Interviewed three people for the position of hair stylist. Will choose one and make an offer next week.
   6 Purchased supplies for $600 cash.

(a) Record these transactions in the general journal.
(b) Post the transactions to the general ledger.

Action Plan

Understand which events (the ones with economic effects) should be recorded.

Analyze the transactions. Determine which accounts are affected and whether the transaction increases or decreases the account.

Record the transactions in the general journal, which provides a chronological record of the transactions.

Post the transactions by transferring the journalized debits and credits to specific T accounts in the general ledger.

Ensure that general ledger accounts are arranged in financial statement order.

Determine the ending balance of each ledger account by netting (calculating the difference between) the total debits and credits.

Solution:

(a)

May	1	Cash	20,000		
		Common Shares		20,000	
		(Invested cash in business)			
	4	Equipment	4,800		
		Accounts Payable		4,800	
		(Purchased equipment on account)			
	5	No entry because no transaction occurred			
	6	Supplies	600		
		Cash		600	
		(Purchased supplies)			

(b)

Cash				
May 1	20,000	May 6	600	
Bal.	19,400			

Accounts Payable	
May 4	4,800

Supplies	
May 6	600

Common Shares	
May 1	20,000

Equipment	
May 4	4,800

The Navigator

The Trial Balance

A **trial balance** is a list of general ledger accounts and their balances at a specific time. A trial balance is normally prepared monthly, and at least at the end of each accounting period. For Sierra Corporation, we have assumed that its accounting period is one month.

In the trial balance, the accounts are listed in the order in which they appear in the ledger, with debit balances listed in the left column and credit balances in the right column. The totals of the two columns must be equal.

The main purpose of a trial balance is to prove (check) that the debits equal the credits after posting. That is, the sum of the debit account balances must equal the sum of the credit account balances. If the debit and credit totals do not agree, this means that an error was made in journalizing or posting. The trial balance helps uncover such errors. For example, the trial balance will not balance if a debit or credit amount is unequal in a journal entry, or if the amount is transferred incorrectly to the general ledger from a journal entry. If the trial balance does not balance, then the error must be located and corrected before proceeding.

study objective 4

Prepare a trial balance.

Ethics Note Auditors see errors and irregularities differently when they evaluate an accounting system. An error is the result of an unintentional mistake. It is therefore neither ethical nor unethical. An irregularity, on the other hand, is an intentional misstatement, which is generally viewed as unethical.

A trial balance is also useful in the preparation of financial statements, as will be explained in the next chapter. The procedure for preparing a trial balance is as follows:

1. List the account titles and their balances in the same order as the chart of accounts. Debit balances should be entered in the debit column and credit balances in the credit column.
2. Total the debit column and the credit column.
3. Ensure that the debit and credit column totals are equal (i.e., that they agree).

Illustration 3-8 presents the trial balance prepared from the general ledger of Sierra Corporation shown earlier in the chapter on pages 121–122. Accounts with zero balances, such as Accounts Receivable, are normally not included in the trial balance. Note that the total for debits, $28,700, equals the total for credits, $28,700.

Illustration 3-8 ➡

Sierra Corporation trial balance

SIERRA CORPORATION Trial Balance October 31, 2009		
	Debit	Credit
Cash	$15,200	
Advertising supplies	2,500	
Prepaid insurance	600	
Office equipment	5,000	
Notes payable		$ 5,000
Accounts payable		2,500
Unearned service revenue		1,200
Common shares		10,000
Dividends	500	
Service revenue		10,000
Salaries expense	4,000	
Rent expense	900	
	$28,700	$28,700

Limitations of a Trial Balance

Although a trial balance reveals many types of errors in the recording process, it does not prove that all transactions have been recorded or that the general ledger is correct. Errors may exist even though the trial balance columns agree. For example, the trial balance may balance even when (1) a transaction is not journalized, (2) a correct journal entry is not posted, (3) a journal entry is posted twice, (4) incorrect accounts are used in journalizing or posting, or (5) errors that cancel each other's effect are made in recording the amount of a transaction. In other words, as long as equal debits and credits are posted, even to the wrong account or in the wrong amount, the total debits will equal the total credits. Nevertheless, despite its limitations, the trial balance is a useful screen for finding errors.

👤 ACCOUNTING MATTERS! | Management Perspective

In his autobiography, Sam Walton described the accounting information system he used when Wal-Mart was just getting started. "We kept a little pigeonhole on the wall for the cash receipts and paperwork of each store. I had a blue binder ledger book for each store. ... Then once a month, [the bookkeeper] and I would close those books—enter the merchandise, enter the sales, enter the cash, balance it, and close them.

...[B]ack then, we were using the ESP method, which really sped things along when it came time to close those books. It's a pretty basic method: if you can't make your books balance, you take however much they're off by and enter it under the heading ESP, which stands for Error Some Place."

Source: Sam Walton with John Huey, *Made in America: My Story*, (New York: Bantam Books, 1993), pp. 67–68.

BEFORE YOU GO ON...

Review It

1. What is a trial balance and how is it prepared?
2. What is the main purpose of a trial balance?
3. What are the limitations of a trial balance?

Do It

Koizumi Kollections Ltd. has the following alphabetical list of accounts and balances at July 31, 2009:

Accounts payable	$33,700	Land	$ 51,000
Accounts receivable	71,200	Machinery and equipment	35,700
Building	86,500	Notes payable	49,500
Cash	3,200	Operating expenses	93,100
Common shares	99,400	Service revenue	171,100
Dividends	4,000	Unearned service revenue	3,000
Income tax expense	12,000		

Each of the above accounts has a normal balance. Prepare a trial balance, rearranging the accounts in normal ledger (financial statement) order.

Action Plan

- Reorder the accounts as they would normally appear in the general ledger—balance sheet accounts are listed first (assets, liabilities, and equity), and then statement of earnings accounts (revenues and expenses).
- Determine whether each account has a normal debit or credit balance.
- List the amounts in the appropriate debit or credit column.
- Total the trial balance columns. Total debits must equal total credits or a mistake has been made.

Solution

KOIZUMI KOLLECTIONS LTD.
Trial Balance
July 31, 2009

	Debit	Credit
Cash	$ 3,200	
Accounts receivable	71,200	
Land	51,000	
Building	86,500	
Machinery and equipment	35,700	
Accounts payable		$ 33,700
Unearned service revenue		3,000
Notes payable		49,500
Common shares		99,400
Dividends	4,000	
Service revenue		171,100
Operating expenses	93,100	
Income tax expense	12,000	
Totals	$356,700	$356,700

 The Navigator

DECISION TOOLKIT

Decision Checkpoints	Info Needed for Decision	Tools to Use for Decision	How to Evaluate Results
How do you determine that debits equal credits?	All general ledger account balances	Trial balance	List the account titles and their balances; total the debit and credit columns; and verify equality.

ALL ABOUT YOU

Keeping Track of the Documents in Your Life

In this chapter, you learned about the features of accounting information systems that help companies keep track of their important financial information. As you know, each company is an economic entity and its daily transactions create a large amount of financial information and documents. Its economic events need to be accounted for and kept separate from the activities of the company's shareholders (owners) and all other economic entities. Although you are not a company, you are an economic entity and each day you, too, are involved in a variety of economic transactions. And just as they do for companies, some of these transactions produce important financial or personal documents that you need to keep track of.

As we are all individuals, however, we vary in the way we keep track of this information. Some of us are meticulous with record keeping, while others wait for a rainy day to record or keep track of important information. Whichever style is yours, to save yourself time and grief in the future, you really should set aside time regularly to keep your financial records up to date and in order.

What are some of the documents and records in your life? Suppose you had five minutes to collect your most important possessions and flee to safety. Would you know where to find your vital personal papers? Are they in one place or scattered about your home?

Some Facts

- Some examples of your personal documents and records might include:
  - o Identification records (birth certificate, driver's licence, passport, social insurance card, health card)
  - o Bank account statements and loan information
  - o Titles, deeds, and registrations for property and vehicles owned
  - o Credit card statements and receipts
  - o Insurance policies and employer benefit statements (if you have a job with benefits)
  - o Income tax information (copies of past returns, assessment notices, and proof of tax payments)
- You can keep financial and personal records in filing cabinets, on your computer, or in a safety deposit box at a bank. Where to keep records depends on the characteristics of each record. It is more practical to keep such papers as income tax receipts and employment benefit statements at home. A safety deposit box is the safest choice for storing the original documents of such critical items as birth certificates and passports.
- On your computer, keep lists of the contents of your safety deposit box and contact information. You may want to print out a copy of this information and store it in your safety deposit box. You should also make a backup copy of items on your computer and store the backup off site.
- Signing up for direct payroll deposit as well as automatic bill payment can be a useful precaution against possible disaster. If you do this, many of your financial transactions will at least continue to occur normally while you are trying to put the rest of your life back in order.
- How long should you keep your income tax records? In general, supporting documents for taxes need to be kept for six years. Have the receipts and documentation to support your claims ready in case you are selected for review.

What Do You Think?

Do you really need to take the time to organize your financial documents?

YES | Everyone engages in financial transactions each day. For a variety of reasons (such as tax reporting or job application), we need to maintain documentation of these transactions.

NO | I lead a relatively uncomplicated life, and I can usually find the documents that I need when I need them.

The Navigator

Summary of Study Objectives

. **Analyze the effects of transactions on the accounting equation.** Each business transaction has a dual effect on the accounting equation. For example, if an individual asset is increased, here must be a corresponding decrease in another asset, or an increase in a specific liability or in shareholders' equity.

. **Define debits and credits and explain how they are used to record transactions.** The terms *debit* and *credit* mean the same thing as *left* and *right*, respectively. Assets, dividends, and expenses are increased by debits and decreased by credits. The normal balance of these accounts is a debit balance. Liabilities, common shares, retained earnings, and revenues are increased by credits and decreased by debits. The normal balance of these accounts is a credit balance.

3. **Identify the basic steps in the recording process.** The basic steps in the recording process are (a) analyzing each transaction for its effect on the accounts, (b) entering the transaction information in a general journal, and (c) posting (transferring) the information in the general journal to the appropriate accounts in the general ledger. These are also the first three steps in the accounting cycle.

4. **Prepare a trial balance.** The preparation of a trial balance is the fourth step in the accounting cycle. The trial balance is a list of accounts and their balances at a specific time. The main purpose of the trial balance is to prove the mathematical equality of debits and credits after posting. A trial balance also uncovers errors in journalizing and posting and is useful in preparing financial statements.

The Navigator

Glossary

 www.wiley.com/canada/kimmel **Study Tools (Glossary)**

Account An individual accounting record of increases and decreases in a specific asset, liability, or shareholders' equity item. (p. 110)

Accounting information system The system of collecting and processing transaction data and communicating financial information to interested parties. (p. 104)

Accounting transaction An economic event that is recorded in the financial statements because it involves an exchange that affects assets, liabilities, or shareholders' equity. (p. 104)

Chart of accounts A list of a company's accounts and account numbers, which identify where the accounts are in the general ledger. (p. 116)

Credit The right side of an account. (p. 110)

Debit The left side of an account. (p. 110)

Double-entry accounting system A system that records the dual effect of each transaction in appropriate accounts. (p. 110)

General journal The book of original entry in which transactions are recorded in chronological order. (p. 115)

General ledger The book of accounts that contains a company's asset, liability, and shareholders' equity, revenue, and expense accounts. (p. 116)

Posting The procedure of transferring journal entries to the general ledger accounts. (p. 117)

T account The basic form of an account, with a debit (left) side and a credit (right) side showing the effect of transactions on the account. (p. 110)

Trial balance A list of general ledger accounts and their balances at a specific time, usually at the end of each month. (p. 123)

www.wiley.com/canada/kimmel **Analysis Tools (Decision Toolkit Summaries)**

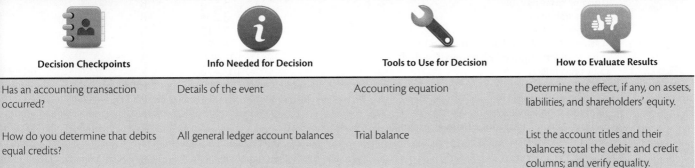

DECISION TOOLKIT—A SUMMARY

Decision Checkpoints	Info Needed for Decision	Tools to Use for Decision	How to Evaluate Results
Has an accounting transaction occurred?	Details of the event	Accounting equation	Determine the effect, if any, on assets, liabilities, and shareholders' equity.
How do you determine that debits equal credits?	All general ledger account balances	Trial balance	List the account titles and their balances; total the debit and credit columns; and verify equality.

The Navigator

Using the Decision Toolkit

lululemon athletica inc. is one of Canada's leading designers and suppliers of athletic wear. Nearly three-quarters of its stores are in Canada, with the remaining stores found in the U.S., Australia, and Japan. lululemon reports the following list of accounts, in alphabetical order. All accounts have normal balances.

LULULEMON ATHLETICA INC. List of Accounts July 31, 2007 (in USD thousands)	lululemon athletica
Accounts payable and accrued expenses	$ 16,471
Accounts receivable	3,458
Cash and cash equivalents	9,727
Cost of goods sold	49,413
Depreciation expense	3,369
Income tax expense	8,247
Income taxes payable	5,553
Intangible assets	7,204
Inventories	23,848
Long-term debt	5,713
Other additions to shareholders' equity	6,424
Other assets	10,819
Other liabilities	3,295
Other revenue	293
Prepaid expenses	1,227
Property, plant, and equipment	27,215
Sales revenue	103,470
Selling, general, and administrative expenses	34,071
Shareholders' equity, beginning of period	37,379

Instructions

(a) Prepare a trial balance for lululemon, reordering the accounts in financial statement order.

(b) In the trial balance, identify on which financial statement (FS) each account should be reported. Write "B" beside the accounts that should be shown on the balance sheet and "E" beside the ones that should be shown on the statement of earnings.

Solution

LULULEMON ATHLETICA INC. Trial Balance July 31, 2007 (in USD thousands)			lululemon athletica
	(a)		(b)
	Debit	Credit	FS
Cash and cash equivalents	$ 9,727		B
Accounts receivable	3,458		B
Inventories	23,848		B
Prepaid expenses	1,227		B
Property, plant, and equipment	27,215		B
Intangible assets	7,204		B
Other assets	10,819		B
Accounts payable and accrued expenses		$ 16,471	B
Income taxes payable		5,553	B
Other liabilities		3,295	B
Long-term debt		5,713	B
Other additions to shareholders' equity		6,424	B
Shareholders' equity, beginning of period		37,379	B
Sales revenue		103,470	E
Other revenue		293	E
Cost of goods sold	49,413		E
Depreciation expense	3,369		E
Selling, general, and administrative expenses	34,071		E
Income tax expense	8,247		E
	$178,598	$178,598	

The Navigator

Demonstration Problem

Campus Laundry Inc. opened on September 1, 2009. During the first month of operations, the following transactions occurred:

Sept 1 Shareholders invested $20,000 cash in the business.

3 Paid $1,000 cash for September rent.

4 Purchased washers and dryers for $25,000, paying $10,000 in cash and signing a six-month, 8%, $15,000 note payable.

7 Paid $1,200 for a one-year insurance policy.

11 Paid employee salaries of $2,500.

15 Performed services on account for a nearby restaurant, $6,200.

21 Paid a $700 cash dividend to shareholders.

29 Cash receipts for laundry services performed throughout the month were $5,000.

30 Paid employee salaries of $2,500.

30 Utilities of $700 and income taxes of $500 are owed at the end of the month.

Study Tools
(Demonstration Problems)

Instructions

(a) Journalize the September transactions.
(b) Open T accounts and post the transactions to the general ledger.
(c) Prepare a trial balance.
(d) Prepare a statement of earnings, statement of retained earnings, and balance sheet.

Solution to Demonstration Problem

(a)

	CAMPUS LAUNDRY INC. General Journal			
Date	Account Titles and Explanation	Debit	Credit
2009 Sept. 1	Cash	20,000	
	Common Shares		20,000
	(Issued common shares)		
3	Rent Expense	1,000	
	Cash		1,000
	(Paid September rent)		
4	Laundry Equipment	25,000	
	Cash		10,000
	Notes Payable		15,000
	(Purchased laundry equipment for cash and six-month, 8% note payable)		
7	Prepaid Insurance	1,200	
	Cash		1,200
	(Paid one-year insurance policy)		
11	Salaries Expense	2,500	
	Cash		2,500
	(Paid salaries)		
15	Accounts Receivable	6,200	
	Service Revenue		6,200
	(To record revenue for laundry services provided)		
21	Dividends	700	
	Cash		700
	(Paid a $700 cash dividend)		
29	Cash	5,000	
	Service Revenue		5,000
	(To record collection for laundry services provided)		
30	Salaries Expense	2,500	
	Cash		2,500
	(Paid salaries)		
30	Utilities Expense	700	
	Income Tax Expense	500	
	Accounts Payable		700
	Income Tax Payable		500
	(To record utilities and income taxes due in October)		

Action Plan

- Make separate journal entries for each transaction.
- In journalizing, make sure debits equal credits.
- In journalizing, use specific account titles taken from the chart of accounts and provide an appropriate explanation of the journal entry.
- Arrange the general ledger in statement order, beginning with the balance sheet accounts.
- Prepare a trial balance that lists the accounts in the same order as in the ledger.
- In the trial balance, list debit balances in the left column and credit balances in the right column. Check the accuracy of your work. Total debits must equal total credits.

(b)

CAMPUS LAUNDRY INC.
General Journal

Cash					
Sept.	1	20,000	Sept.	3	1,000
	29	5,000		4	10,000
				7	1,200
				11	2,500
				21	700
				30	2,500
Bal.		7,100			

Accounts Receivable		
Sept.	15	6,200

Prepaid Insurance		
Sept.	7	1,200

Laundry Equipment		
Sept.	4	25,000

Notes Payable		
	Sept	4	15,000

Accounts Payable		
	Sept.	30	1,200

Common Shares		
	Sept.	1	20,000

Dividends		
Sept.	21	700

Service Revenue		
	Sept.	15	6,200
		29	5,000
	Bal.		11,200

Salaries Expense		
Sept.	11	2,500
	30	2,500
Bal.		5,000

Rent Expense		
Sept.	3	1,000

Utilities Expense		
Sept.	30	700

Income Tax Expense		
Sept.	30	500

(c)

CAMPUS LAUNDRY INC.
Trial Balance
September 30, 2009

	Debit	Credit
Cash	$ 7,100	
Accounts receivable	6,200	
Prepaid insurance	1,200	
Laundry equipment	25,000	
Notes payable		$15,000
Accounts payable		1,200
Common shares		20,000
Dividends	700	
Service revenue		11,200
Salaries expense	5,000	
Rent expense	1,000	
Utilities expense	700	
Income tax expense	500	
	$47,400	$47,400

(d)

CAMPUS LAUNDRY INC.
Statement of Earnings
Month ended September 30, 2009

Revenues		
Service revenue		$11,200
Expenses		
Salaries	$5,000	
Rent	1,000	
Utilities	700	6,700
Earnings before income tax		4,500
Income tax expense		500
Net earnings		$ 4,000

CAMPUS LAUNDRY INC.
Statement of Retained Earnings
Month ended September 30, 2009

Retained earnings, Sept. 1	$ 0
Add: Net earnings	4,000
	4,000
Less: Dividends	700
Retained earnings, Sept. 30	$3,300

CAMPUS LAUNDRY INC.
Balance Sheet
September 30, 2009

Assets		
Current assets		
Cash	$ 7,100	
Accounts receivable	6,200	
Prepaid insurance	1,200	$14,500
Property, plant, and equipment		
Laundry equipment		25,000
Total assets		$39,500
Liabilities and Shareholders' Equity		
Current liabilities		
Notes payable	$15,000	
Accounts payable	1,200	$16,200
Shareholders' equity		
Common shares	$20,000	
Retained earnings	3,300	23,300
Total liabilities and shareholders' equity		$39,500

The Navigator

Self-Study Questions

Answers are at the end of the chapter.

Study Tools (Self-Assessment Quizzes)

(SO 1) **1.** When cash is received in advance of performing a service, the effects on the accounting equation are:

(a) an increase in assets and a decrease in shareholders' equity.

(b) an increase in assets and an increase in shareholders' equity.

(c) an increase in assets and an increase in liabilities.

(d) an increase in liabilities and an increase in shareholders' equity.

(SO 1) **2.** Shareholders' equity usually consists of the following:

(a) assets, revenues, and expenses.

(b) dividends payable, revenues, and expenses.

(c) liabilities, common shares, and retained earnings.

(d) common shares and retained earnings.

(SO 2) **3.** Which statement about an account is true?

(a) An account is an individual accounting record of increases and decreases in specific asset, liability, and shareholders' equity items.

(b) There are separate accounts for specific assets and liabilities but only one account for shareholders' equity items.

(c) The left side of an account is the credit (decrease) side.

(d) The right side of an account is the debit (increase) side.

(SO 2) **4.** Debits:

(a) increase both assets and liabilities.

(b) decrease both assets and liabilities.

(c) increase assets and decrease liabilities.

(d) decrease assets and increase liabilities.

(SO 2) **5.** Which accounts normally have debit balances?

(a) Assets, expenses, and revenues

(b) Assets, expenses, and retained earnings

(c) Assets, liabilities, and dividends

(d) Assets, dividends, and expenses

6. Which of these statements about a general journal is false?

(a) It is not a book of original entry.

(b) It provides a chronological record of transactions.

(c) It helps to locate errors because the debit and credit amounts for each entry can be quickly compared.

(d) It discloses the complete effect of a transaction in one place.

7. A general ledger:

(a) contains only asset and liability accounts.

(b) should show accounts in alphabetical order.

(c) is a collection of the entire group of accounts maintained by a company.

(d) provides a chronological record of transactions.

8. Posting:

(a) normally occurs before journalizing.

(b) transfers general ledger transaction data to the general journal.

(c) is an optional step in the accounting cycle.

(d) transfers general journal entries to general ledger accounts.

9. A trial balance:

(a) is a list of accounts with their balances at a specific time.

(b) proves that transactions have been correctly journalized.

(c) will not balance if a correct journal entry is posted twice.

(d) proves that all transactions have been recorded.

10. A trial balance will not balance if:

(a) a journal entry to record a cash sale is posted twice.

(b) the purchase of supplies on account is debited to Supplies and credited to Cash.

(c) a $100 cash dividend is debited to Dividends for $1,000 and credited to Cash for $100.

(d) a $450 payment on account is debited to Accounts Payable for $45 and credited to Cash for $45.

The Navigator

Questions

(SO 1) **1.** Why are some events recorded as accounting transactions but others are not?

(SO 1) **2.** Which of the following events are recorded in the accounting records? Explain your answer in each case.

(a) The company wins an award as one of the top 50 companies in Canada to work for.

(b) Supplies are purchased on account.

(c) An employee is terminated.

(d) The company pays a cash dividend to its shareholders.

(e) A local lawyer agrees to provide legal services to the company for the next year.

3. Can a business enter into a transaction that affects only the left (assets) side of the accounting equation? If yes, give an example.

4. What is the effect of each of the following transactions on the accounting equation?

(a) Paid cash for janitorial services.

(b) Purchased equipment on account.

(c) Issued common shares to investors in exchange for cash.

(d) Paid an account payable.

(e) Performed services on account.

5. Hiroshi Uehara, a fellow student, claims that the double-entry system means each transaction must be recorded twice. Is Hiroshi correct? Explain.

6. Natalie Boudreau, an introductory accounting student, believes debit balances are favourable and credit balances are unfavourable. Is Natalie correct? Discuss.

7. State the debit and credit effects and identify the normal balance for the following types of accounts: (a) assets, (b) liabilities, (c) common shares, (d) retained earnings, (e) dividends, (f) revenues, and (g) expenses.

8. For each of the following accounts, indicate (a) whether the account would have a normal debit or credit balance, and (b) the appropriate statement classification.
   1. Accounts Receivable
   2. Accounts Payable
   3. Equipment
   4. Dividends
   5. Supplies
   6. Service Revenue
   7. Unearned Service Revenue
   8. Income Tax Expense

9. Identify the two account titles that should be used to record each side of the following transactions:
   (a) Cash sales
   (b) Services performed on account
   (c) Supplies purchased on account
   (d) Collection of a customer's account
   (e) Payment of an amount owing to a supplier
   (f) Payment of a dividend to shareholders
   (g) Payment of income taxes

10. For each transaction, indicate the account that is debited and the account that is credited:
   (a) Supplies are purchased on account.
   (b) Cash is received on signing a note payable.
   (c) Employees are paid salaries in cash.
   (d) Services are performed on account.
   (e) Cash is collected on account.

11. For each account, indicate whether it generally will have debit entries only, credit entries only, or both debit and credit entries:
   (a) Cash
   (b) Accounts Receivable
   (c) Dividends
   (d) Accounts Payable
   (e) Service Revenue
   (f) Salaries Expense

12. A company received cash from a customer. It debited the Cash (SO 2) account. Name three credit accounts that the company might have used to record a cash receipt from a customer. Describe the circumstances where you would use each of these three accounts.

13. Identify and describe the first four steps in the accounting (SO 3) cycle.

14. An efficiency expert who was reviewing the steps in the (SO 3) accounting cycle suggested dropping the general journal step and recording and summarizing transactions directly into the general ledger instead. Comment on this suggestion.

15. (a) What is a general ledger? (b) In what order are accounts (SO 3) usually arranged in a general ledger?

16. What is a chart of accounts and why is it important? How (SO 3) does numbering the accounts help?

17. Arrange the following accounts in their normal order in a (SO 3) chart of accounts: common shares, prepaid insurance, cash, service revenue, dividends, unearned revenue, supplies, income tax expense.

18. Does it matter how frequently transactions are posted from (SO 3) the general journal to the general ledger? Explain.

19. (a) What is a trial balance? (b) From what source document(s) (SO 4) is it prepared?

20. Do the accounts have to be in a specific order in the trial (SO 4) balance? Explain.

21. What are the limitations of the trial balance? (SO 4)

22. ⚬━ Two students are discussing the use of a trial balance. (SO 4) They wonder whether the following errors, each considered separately, would prevent the trial balance from balancing. What would you tell the students?
   (a) The bookkeeper debited Supplies for $750 and debited Accounts Payable for $750 for the purchase of supplies on account.
   (b) Cash collected on account was debited to Cash for $1,000, and credited to Service Revenue for $1,000.
   (c) A journal entry recording the payment of dividends was posted to the general ledger as a $650 debit to Dividends and a $560 credit to Cash.

Brief Exercises

Analyze effects of transactions.
(SO 1)

BE3–1 Seven economic events follow. Using the format shown after the transactions, indicate whether the event (including its amount) increased (+), decreased (–), or had no effect (NE) on each element of the accounting equation. The first one has been done for you as an example.

1. Purchased supplies on account, $250.
2. Provided a service on account, $500.
3. Paid operating expenses, $300.
4. Issued common shares in exchange for cash, $5,000.
5. Paid a cash dividend to shareholders, $400.
6. Received $500 cash from a customer who had previously been billed for services provided, (see item 2).
7. Paid $250 on an account owed to a supplier (see item 1).

				Shareholders' Equity		
			Common		Retained Earnings	
Transaction	Assets	Liabilities	Shares	Revenues	Expenses	Dividends
1.	+$250	+$250	NE	NE	NE	NE

Indicate debit and credit effects.
(SO 2)

BE3–2 For each of the following accounts, indicate (a) the effect of a debit or credit on the account, (b) the normal balance, and (c) the statement classification for reporting the account:

1. Accounts payable
2. Advertising expense
3. Service revenue
4. Accounts receivable
5. Unearned service revenue
6. Cash
7. Dividends
8. Common shares
9. Prepaid insurance
10. Office equipment
11. Retained earnings
12. Income tax expense

Match account names with transactions.
(SO 2)

BE3–3 The list of account titles below is followed by a list of cash transactions. Write the number of the account title that should be used to record the noncash side of each transaction. The first one has been done for you as an example.

1. Accounts Receivable
2. Automotive Equipment
3. Common Shares
4. Dividends
5. Interest Expense
6. Merchandise Inventory
7. Note Payable
8. Prepaid Insurance
9. Professional Fees Expense
10. Rent Expense
11. Sales
12. Unearned Revenue
13. Wages Expense

___3___ (a) Issued common shares.
_____ (b) Repaid amount owing on note payable.
_____ (c) Paid dividend.
_____ (d) Paid for accounting services.
_____ (e) Paid insurance in advance for the next year.
_____ (f) Paid interest on a bank loan.
_____ (g) Paid rent for the current month.
_____ (h) Paid wages to employees.
_____ (i) Purchased a truck.
_____ (j) Purchased merchandise for resale.
_____ (k) Collected account due from a customer.
_____ (l) Performed services for a customer.
_____ (m) Received an advance from a customer for future services.

BE3–4   The following transactions are for Ing Corporation for the month of June. Identify the accounts to be debited and credited for each transaction.

Identify accounts to be debited and credited. (SO 2)

June   1   Issued common shares to shareholders in exchange for $5,500 cash.
       2   Purchased equipment on account for $3,000.
       3   Paid $750 to landlord for June rent.
       8   Purchased supplies for $250 cash.
      12   Billed J. Kronsoble $300 for welding work done.
      22   Received cash from J. Kronsoble for work billed on June 12.
      25   Hired an employee to start work on July 2.
      29   Paid for equipment purchased on June 2.
      30   Paid $100 for income tax.

BE3–5   Riko Corporation has the following selected transactions:

Indicate basic debit-credit analysis. (SO 2)

   1.   Issued common shares to shareholders in exchange for $5,000 cash.
   2.   Paid rent in advance for six months, $2,100.
   3.   Paid secretary's salary, $500.
   4.   Billed clients $1,200 for services provided.
   5.   Received $900 from clients for services provided.
   6.   Purchased $500 of supplies on account.
   7.   Paid supplier amount owing, $500.

For each transaction, indicate (a) the basic type of each account to be debited and credited (asset, liability, shareholders' equity); (b) the specific accounts to debit and credit (Cash, Rent Expense, Service Revenue, etc.) and (c) whether each account is increased (+) or decreased (–), and by what amount. Use the following format, in which the first one has been done for you as an example:

	Account Debited			Account Credited		
	(a)	(b)	(c)	(a)	(b)	(c)
Transaction	Basic Type	Specific Account	Effect	Basic Type	Specific Account	Effect
1.	Asset	Cash	+$5,000	Shareholders' equity	Common shares	+$5,000

BE3–6   Journalize the transactions in BE3–1.

Record transactions. (SO 3)

BE3–7   Journalize the transactions for Ing Corporation in BE3–4.

Record transactions. (SO 3)

BE3–8   Using T accounts, post the journal entries in BE3–6 to the general ledger.

Post journal entries. (SO 3)

BE3–9   Using T accounts, post the following journal entries to the general ledger.

Post journal entries. (SO 3)

GENERAL JOURNAL			
Date	Account Titles and Explanation	Debit	Credit
May 5	Accounts Receivable	3,200	
	Service Revenue		3,200
12	Cash	1,900	
	Accounts Receivable		1,900
15	Supplies	200	
	Accounts Payable		200
20	Cash	2,000	
	Service Revenue		2,000
25	Salaries Expense	2,500	
	Cash		2,500
28	Accounts Payable	200	
	Cash		200
30	Income Tax Expense	750	
	Income Tax Payable		750

Prepare trial balance.
(SO 4)

BE3–10 From the general ledger balances that follow, prepare a trial balance for Carland Inc. at June 30, 2009.

Accounts payable	$ 3,000	Income tax expense	$ 400
Accounts receivable	4,000	Investments	6,000
Accumulated depreciation	3,600	Operating expenses	5,000
Cash	4,400	Retained earnings	2,650
Common shares	20,000	Service revenue	7,600
Dividends	200	Unearned service revenue	150
Equipment	17,000		

Identify effects of posting
errors on trial balance.
(SO 4)

BE3–11 ▢ Different types of posting errors are identified in the following table. For each error, indicate (a) whether the trial balance will balance, (b) the amount of the difference if the trial balance will not balance, and (c) the trial balance column that will have the larger total. Consider each error separately. Use the following format, in which error 1 is given as an example:

Error	(a) In Balance	(b) Difference	(c) Larger Column
1. A $1,200 debit to Supplies was posted as a $2,100 debit.	No	$900	Debit
2. A $1,000 credit to Cash was posted twice as two credits to Cash.			
3. A $5,000 debit to Dividends was posted to the Common Shares account.			
4. A journal entry debiting Cash and crediting Service revenue for $2,500 was not posted.			
5. The collection of $500 cash on account was posted as a debit of $500 and a credit of $500.			
6. The payment of $1,000 on an account payable owed to the insurance company was posted as a debit to the Insurance Expense account. No credit was posted.			

Prepare corrected trial balance.
(SO 4)

BE3–12 ▢ An inexperienced bookkeeper prepared the following trial balance. She finished with a huge sigh of relief because she was able to balance it. (a) Is the trial balance correct? (b) If you believe it is wrong, prepare a correct trial balance, assuming all account balances are normal.

BOURQUE LIMITED
Trial Balance
December 31, 2009

	Debit	Credit
Cash	$10,000	
Accounts receivable	6,500	
Supplies	3,500	
Accounts payable	1,500	
Unearned revenue	2,200	
Common shares	5,000	
Retained earnings	13,500	
Dividends		$ 4,500
Service revenue		20,000
Salaries expense		9,100
Office expense		4,400
Supplies expense		1,200
Travel expense		2,000
Income tax expense		1,000
	$42,200	$42,200

Exercises

E3-1   Selected transactions follow for Green Lawn Care Ltd.:

Analyze effects of transactions.
(SO 1)

1. Issued common shares to shareholders in exchange for cash.
2. Paid monthly rent.
3. Purchased equipment on account.
4. Billed customers for services performed.
5. Paid a dividend to shareholders.
6. Received cash from customers billed in transaction 4.
7. Incurred advertising expense on account.
8. Purchased additional equipment, issuing cash and a note payable in payment.
9. Received cash from customers when service was provided.
10. Paid cash for equipment purchased in transaction 3.
11. Paid salaries to employees.

Instructions

Indicate the effect that each of the transactions had on the accounting equation: increase (+), decrease (–), or no effect (NE). Use the following format, in which the first one has been done for you as an example:

				Shareholders' Equity		
				Common	Retained Earnings		
Transaction	Assets	Liabilities	Shares	Revenues	Expenses	Dividends
1.	+	NE	+	NE	NE	NE

E3-2   Wang Computer Corporation entered into these transactions during the month of May:

Analyze effects of transactions.
(SO 1)

1. Purchased a computer on account for $10,000 from Digital Equipment.
2. Paid $1,500 for rent for the month of May.
3. Provided computer services for $3,500 on account.
4. Paid Ontario Hydro $600 cash for utilities used in May.
5. Issued common shares to Li Wang in exchange for an additional $20,000 investment in the business.
6. Paid Digital Equipment for computers purchased in transaction 1.
7. Purchased a one-year accident insurance policy for $500 cash.
8. Received $3,500 cash in payment of the account in transaction 3.
9. Paid Li Wang a $500 dividend.
10. Paid income taxes of $400 for the month.

Instructions

Indicate the effect (including its amount) that each of the transactions had on the accounting equation: increase (+), decrease (–), or no effect (NE). Use the following format, in which the first one has been done for you as an example:

			Shareholders' Equity			
			Common	Retained Earnings		
Transaction	Assets	Liabilities	Shares	Revenues	Expenses	Dividends
1.	+$10,000	+$10,000	NE	NE	NE	NE

E3-3   Data for Green Lawn Care Ltd. are presented in E3-1.

Identify account names.
(SO 2)

Instructions

Identify the account names that should be used to record each transaction. For example, in item 1, the accounts would be Cash and Common Shares.

E3-4   You are presented with the following alphabetical list of accounts, selected from the financial statements of Krispy Kreme Doughnuts, Inc.:

Identify statement classification and normal balance.
(SO 2)

Accounts payable	Income taxes payable
Accounts receivable	Interest expense
Buildings	Interest income
Cash and cash equivalents	Inventories
Common stock	Land
Deficit	Machinery and equipment
Dividends	Prepaid expenses
General and administrative expenses	Rent payable
Goodwill	Revenues

Instructions

(a) Identify the normal balance of each account.

(b) Indicate the financial statement—balance sheet, statement of earnings, or statement of retained earnings—where each account should be reported and its classification (e.g., current assets, long-term liabilities, revenues, etc.).

Identify debits, credits, and
normal balances.
(SO 2)

E3–5   Selected transactions for Decorators Mill Ltd., an interior decorating corporation in its first month of business, are as follows:

Mar.	2	Issued common shares for $20,000 cash.
	4	Purchased a used car for use in the business for $12,000 cash.
	6	Purchased supplies on account for $500.
	10	Billed customers $2,100 for services performed.
	13	Paid $225 cash to advertise the grand opening.
	25	Received $1,000 cash from customers billed on March 10.
	27	Paid $500 to the supplier for the supplies purchased on March 6.
	30	Received $700 cash from a customer for services to be performed in April.
	31	Paid dividends of $500 to shareholders.

Instructions

For each transaction indicate (a) the basic type of each account to be debited and credited (asset, liability, shareholders' equity); (b) the specific accounts to debit and credit (Cash, Rent Expense, Service Revenue, etc.) and (c) whether the specific account is increased (+) or decreased (–), and by what amount. Use the following format, in which transaction 1 is given as an example:

	Account Debited			Account Credited		
	(a)	(b)	(c)	(a)	(b)	(c)
	Basic	Specific		Basic	Specific	
Transaction	Type	Account	Effect	Type	Account	Effect
Mar. 2	Asset	Cash	+$9,000	Shareholders' equity	Common shares	+$9,000

Record transactions.
(SO 3)

E3–6   Data for Wang Computer Corporation are presented in E3–2.

Instructions

Journalize the transactions.

Record transactions.
(SO 3)

E3–7   Data for Decorators Mill Ltd. are presented in E3–5.

Instructions

Journalize the transactions.

Analyze, record, and post
transactions.
(SO 1, 3)

E3–8   Selected transactions for Basler Corporation during its first month in business follow:

Sept.	1	Issued common shares for $20,000 cash.
	4	Purchased equipment for $12,000, paying $5,000 in cash and the balance by issuing a note payable.
	10	Purchased $500 of supplies on account.
	25	Received $4,500 cash in advance for architectural services to be provided next month.
	28	Paid a $500 dividend to shareholders.
	30	Paid account owing for supplies (see September 10).
	30	Paid $35 of interest expense on the note payable (see September 4).

Instructions

   (a) Prepare a tabular equation analysis of the above transactions.

   (b) Journalize the transactions.

   (c) Using T accounts, post the transactions to the general ledger.

E3–9   The information that follows is for Aubut Real Estate Agency Corporation:

Record transactions.
(SO 3)

Oct.	1	Issued common shares in exchange for $15,000 cash.
	2	Hired an administrative assistant at an annual salary of $30,000. The assistant will start work on October 5.
	5	Purchased office furniture for $3,000, paying $500 cash and the balance on account.
	6	Sold a house and lot for F. Omana. Commission of $6,500 on the sale is due on October 31.
	9	Received a $250 cash commission for renting an apartment.
	15	Paid $700 for advertising costs for October.
	24	Paid $2,500 on account for the office furniture purchased on October 5.
	30	Paid the administrative assistant $2,500 in salary for October.
	31	Received $6,500 cash from F. Omana, owed from October 6.

Instructions

Journalize the transactions.

E3–10   The journal entries for Aubut Real Estate Agency Corporation were prepared in E3–9.

Post journal entries and prepare trial balance.
(SO 3, 4)

Instructions

   (a) Using T accounts, post the transactions to the general ledger.

   (b) Prepare a trial balance at October 31, 2009.

E3–11   Selected transactions from the general journal of Kang Inc. are presented here:

Post journal entries and prepare trial balance.
(SO 3, 4)

GENERAL JOURNAL			
Date	Account Titles and Explanation	Debit	Credit
Aug. 1	Cash	3,000	
	Common Shares		3,000
7	Cash	1,800	
	Service Revenue		1,800
11	Office Equipment	4,000	
	Cash		1,000
	Notes Payable		3,000
14	Accounts Receivable	1,450	
	Service Revenue		1,450
28	Cash	700	
	Accounts Receivable		700
30	Salary Expense	2,000	
	Cash		2,000
31	Dividends	500	
	Cash		500

Instructions

   (a) Using T accounts, post the transactions to the general ledger.

   (b) Prepare a trial balance at August 31, 2009.

Prepare trial balance from
general ledger.
(SO 4)

E3–12   Here is the general ledger for Holly Corp.:

GENERAL LEDGER						

Cash

Oct.	1	5,000	Oct.	5	400
	9	650		12	1,500
	15	5,000		16	300
	20	500		30	250
	23	2,000		30	500

Accounts Receivable

Oct.	6	800	Oct.	20	500
	20	940			

Supplies

Oct.	5	400			

Furniture

Oct.	2	2,000			

Notes Payable

			Oct.	15	5,000

Accounts Payable

Oct.	12	1,500	Oct.	2	2,000
				28	400

Common Shares

			Oct.	1	5,000
				23	2,000

Dividends

Oct.	16	300			

Service Revenue

			Oct.	6	800
				9	650
				20	940

Wages Expense

Oct.	30	500			

Rent Expense

Oct.	30	250			

Advertising Expense

Oct.	28	400			

Instructions
Prepare a trial balance at October 31, 2009.

Prepare trial balance and
financial statements.
(SO 4)

E3–13   The following is a list of accounts for Speedy Delivery Service, Inc., at July 31, 2009:

Accounts payable	$ 7,500	Interest expense	$ 3,000
Accounts receivable	13,500	Notes payable, due 2012	39,000
Accumulated depreciation	19,400	Prepaid insurance	200
Cash	7,000	Rent expense	9,000
Common shares	40,000	Repair and maintenance expense	5,700
Delivery equipment	97,000	Retained earnings	20,750
Depreciation expense	9,700	Salaries expense	25,000
Dividends	700	Salaries payable	800
Gas and oil expense	4,750	Service revenue	75,000
Income tax expense	4,500	Short-term investments	20,000
Insurance expense	2,400		

Instructions

(a) Prepare a trial balance.

(b) Prepare a statement of earnings, statement of retained earnings, and balance sheet.

Analyze errors and their effects
on trial balance.
(SO 4)

E3–14   🔧 The bookkeeper for Castle's Equipment Repair Corporation made these errors in journalizing and posting:

1. A credit posting of $400 to Accounts Receivable was omitted.
2. A debit posting of $750 for Prepaid Insurance was debited to Insurance Expense.
3. A collection on account of $100 was journalized and posted as a $100 debit to Cash and a $100 credit to Service Revenue.
4. A credit posting of $500 to Accounts Payable was made twice.
5. A cash purchase of supplies for $250 was journalized and posted as a $250 debit to Supplies and a $25 credit to Cash.
6. A debit of $465 to Advertising Expense was posted as $456.

Instructions

For each error, indicate (a) whether the trial balance will balance, (b) the amount of the difference if the trial balance will not balance, and (c) the trial balance column that will have the larger total. Consider each error separately. Use the following format, in which error 1 is given as an example:

Error	(a) In Balance	(b) Difference	(c) Larger Column
1.	No	$400	Debit

Problems: Set A

P3–1A Tony's Repair Shop Inc. was started on May 1. The following transactions were completed during the month:

Analyze transactions and calculate retained earnings. (SO 1)

1. Issued common shares for $14,000 cash.
2. Purchased equipment for $8,000, paying $2,000 cash and signing a note payable for the balance.
3. Paid May office rent, $640.
4. Purchased supplies on account, $350.
5. Received $2,100 cash from customers for repair services provided.
6. Paid dividends to shareholders, $500.
7. Provided repair services on account to customers, $1,800.
8. Paid for supplies purchased in transaction 4.
9. Paid May telephone bill, $100.
10. Paid employee salaries, $1,000.
11. Billed a customer $350 for repair services provided.
12. Collected $800 from customers for services billed in transaction 7.
13. Paid income tax, $300.

Instructions

(a) Prepare a tabular analysis of the effects of the above transactions on the expanded accounting equation.

(b) From an analysis of the retained earnings accounts (revenues, expenses, and dividends), calculate the ending balance in Retained Earnings.

P3–2A The general ledger of Corso Care Corp., a veterinary business, showed the following balances on August 31, 2009: Cash $4,500; Accounts Receivable $1,800; Supplies $350; Office Equipment $6,500; Accounts Payable $3,200; Common Shares $2,500; and Retained Earnings $7,450. During September, the following transactions occurred:

Analyze transactions and prepare financial statements. (SO 1)

Sept.	1	Paid the accounts payable owing at August 31.
	1	Paid $1,200 rent for September.
	3	Collected $1,450 of accounts receivable due from customers.
	4	Hired a part-time office assistant at $50 per day to start work the following week, on Monday, September 7.
	8	Purchased additional office equipment for $2,050, paying $700 cash and the balance on account.
	14	Billed $500 for veterinary services provided on account.
	15	Paid $300 for advertising expenses.
	18	Collected cash for services performed on account on September 14.
	25	Received $7,500 from Canadian Western Bank; the money was borrowed on a note payable.
	25	Sent a statement reminding a customer that he still owed the company money from August.
	28	Earned revenue of $4,500. A cash payment of $3,000 was received immediately and the balance is due in October.
	28	Paid part-time office assistant $750 for working fifteen days in September.
	30	Incurred utility expenses for the month on account, $175.
	30	Paid dividends to shareholders, $1,000.
	30	Paid income tax for the month, $550.

Instructions

(a) Beginning with the August 31 balances, prepare a tabular analysis of the effects of the September transactions on the accounting equation.

(b) Prepare a statement of earnings, statement of retained earnings, and balance sheet for the month.

Identify normal balance and statement classification.
(SO 2)

P3–3A   You are presented with the following list of accounts selected from the financial statements of Reitmans (Canada) Limited:

Account	(a) Normal Balance	(b) Financial Statement	(c) Classification
Accounts payable and accrued items	Credit	Balance Sheet	Current liabilities
Accounts receivable			
Buildings and improvements			
Cash and cash equivalents			
Common shares			
Cost of goods sold and selling, general, and administrative expenses			
Depreciation expense			
Dividends			
Fixtures and equipment			
Goodwill			
Income tax expense			
Income taxes payable			
Interest expense			
Investment income			
Land			
Marketable securities			
Merchandise inventories			
Prepaid expenses			
Retained earnings			
Sales			

Instructions

For each account, indicate (a) whether the normal balance is a debit or credit; (b) the financial statement where the account should be reported (e.g., balance sheet, statement of earnings, or statement of retained earnings); and (c) the appropriate classification (e.g., current assets, long-term liabilities, revenues, etc.). The first one is done for you as an example.

Identify debit and credit effects and record transactions.
(SO 2, 3)

P3–4A   You are presented with the following transactions for Kailynn Corporation for the month of January:

Jan. 2 Issued common shares for $10,000 cash.
      5 Provided services on account, $2,500.
      7 Purchased a hybrid car for $40,000 for use in the business: paid $10,000 cash and issued a note payable for the remainder.
      9 Received a $5,000 deposit from a customer for services to be provided in the future.
     12 Billed customers $20,000 for services performed during the month.
     19 Paid $500 to purchase supplies.
     20 Provided service for customers who paid in advance on January 9.
     23 Collected $5,000 owing from customers from the January 12 transaction.
     26 Received a bill for $125 for utilities, due February 26.
     29 Paid rent for the month, $1,500.
     31 Paid $4,000 of salaries to employees.
     31 Paid income tax for the month, $4,000.

Instructions

(a) For each transaction, indicate (1) the basic type of each account to be debited and credited (asset, liability, shareholders' equity); (2) the specific accounts to debit and credit (Cash, Service Revenue, etc.); and (3) whether each account is increased (+) or decreased (–), and by what amount. Use the following format, in which the first transaction is given as an example:

	Account Debited			Account Credited		
	(1)	(2)	(3)	(1)	(2)	(3)
	Basic	Specific		Basic	Specific	
Transaction	Type	Account	Effect	Type	Account	Effect
Jan. 2	Asset	Cash	+$10,000	Shareholders' equity	Common shares	+$10,000

(b) Prepare journal entries to record the above transactions.

P3–5A The Adventure Biking Park Corp. was formed on April 1. These selected events and transactions occurred during April:

Record transactions. (SO 3)

Apr.	1	Issued common shares for $50,000 cash.
	3	Purchased an out-of-use ski hill costing $320,000, paying $30,000 cash and signing a note payable for the balance. The $320,000 purchase price consisted of land, $174,000; building, $101,000; and equipment, $45,000.
	8	Purchased advertising space on account, $2,800.
	10	Paid salaries to employees, $1,800.
	13	Hired a park manager at a salary of $4,000 per month, effective May 1.
	14	Paid $5,500 for a one-year insurance policy.
	17	Paid $600 of dividends to shareholders.
	20	Received $8,600 in cash from customers for admission fees.
	30	Paid $2,800 on account for the advertising purchased on April 8.
	30	Paid $1,250 of interest on the note payable.

Instructions

Journalize the April transactions.

P3–6A During the first month of operations, these events and transactions occurred for Astromech Accounting Services Inc.:

Record and post transactions. (SO 3)

May	1	Issued common shares for $20,000 cash.
	1	Paid office rent of $950 for the month.
	4	Hired a secretary-receptionist at a salary of $2,000 per month. She started work the same day.
	4	Purchased $750 of supplies on account from Read Supply Corp.
	11	Completed an income tax assignment and billed the client $2,725 for services provided.
	12	Received $3,500 in advance on a management consulting engagement.
	15	Received $1,350 for services completed for Arnold Corp.
	20	Received $1,725 from a client for work completed and billed on May 11.
	22	Paid one-third of the balance due to Read Supply Corp.
	25	Received a $275 telephone bill for May, to be paid next month.
	29	Paid the secretary-receptionist $2,000 salary for the month.
	29	Paid the monthly income tax instalment, $300.
	29	Paid a $250 dividend.

Instructions

(a) Journalize the transactions.

(b) Using T accounts, post the journal entries prepared in (a) to the general ledger.

P3–7A On March 31, Lake Theatre Inc.'s general ledger showed Cash $6,000; Land $100,000; Buildings $80,000; Equipment $25,000; Accounts Payable $5,000; Mortgage Payable $125,000; Common Shares $50,000; and Retained Earnings $31,000. During April, the following events and transactions occurred:

Record transactions, post, and prepare trial balance. (SO 3, 4)

Apr.	2	Paid film rental fee of $800 on first movie to run during the month.
	3	Paid advertising expenses, $620.
	3	Hired Thoms Limited to operate a concession stand. Thoms agrees to pay Lake Theatre 20% of the gross concession receipts, payable monthly, for the right to operate the concession stand.
	6	Ordered two additional films at $750 each.
	11	Received $1,950 from customers for admissions.
	15	Paid $2,000 on the mortgage principal. Also paid $500 in interest on the mortgage.

17	Paid $2,800 of the accounts payable.
20	Received one of the films ordered on April 6 and was billed $750. The film will be shown in April.
25	Received $5,300 from customers for admissions.
28	Prepaid a $700 rental fee on a special film to be run in May.
30	Paid salaries, $1,900.
30	Received statement from Thoms showing gross concession receipts of $2,600 and the balance due to Lake Theatre of $520 ($2,600 × 20%) for April. Thoms paid half of the balance due and will remit the remainder on May 5.

Instructions

(a) Using T accounts, enter the beginning balances in the general ledger as at March 31.

(b) Journalize the April transactions.

(c) Post the April journal entries to the general ledger.

(d) Prepare a trial balance at April 30, 2009.

Record transactions, post, and prepare trial balance.
(SO 3, 4)

P3–8A KG Spring Skating School Inc. had the following account balances as at April 30, 2009: Cash $23,000; Equipment $2,000; Accounts Payable $500; Advance Registration Fees $17,500; Common Shares $1,000; and Retained Earnings $6,000. The following events and transactions occurred during May:

May	4	Additional registrations for the May four-week skating session received, $5,500 cash.
	4	Paid for ice time for first two weeks of the May school, $7,200.
	9	Paid accounts payable outstanding at April 30.
	11	Booked ice with the city for the July session. It will cost $14,400.
	11	Received and paid a bill for $500 for advertising of the May skating school.
	15	Paid coaches and assistant coaches, $600.
	18	Paid for ice time for second two weeks of the May school, $7,200.
	21	Received a bill for internet service for $100. This invoice is due on June 15.
	29	Last day of May session.
	29	Received advance registrations for the next four-week skating session in July, $2,200.
	29	Purchased refreshments and supplies for end-of-school test day and ribbons for skaters, $200.
	29	Purchased gifts for volunteers who helped out during May session, $300.
	29	Paid coaches and assistant coaches, $600.

Instructions

(a) Using T accounts, enter the beginning balances in the general ledger as at April 30.

(b) Journalize the May transactions.

(c) Post the May journal entries to the general ledger.

(d) Prepare a trial balance as at May 31.

Prepare trial balance and financial statements.
(SO 4)

P3–9A Bay Department Store Limited has the following alphabetical list of accounts and balances (in thousands) as at January 31, 2009:

Accounts payable	$ 92,600	Land	$ 25,000
Accounts receivable	60,400	Mortgage payable	38,300
Building	79,000	Mortgage payable due within one year	12,600
Cash	800	Merchandise inventories	148,500
Common shares	65,800	Notes payable (due 2012)	20,100
Cost of goods sold	488,400	Operating expenses	135,500
Dividends	3,700	Other assets	52,500
Equipment	21,800	Other short-term liabilities	24,400
Goodwill	15,200	Prepaid expenses	7,900
Income tax expense	24,900	Retained earnings, February 1, 2008	74,100
Interest expense	4,300	Sales	740,000

Instructions

(a) Prepare a trial balance, listing the accounts in financial statement order.

(b) Prepare a statement of earnings, statement of retained earnings, and balance sheet for the year.

P3–10A 🔑 A first year co-op student working for Insidz Corp. recorded the company's transactions for the month. He was a little unsure about the recording process, but he did the best he could. He had a few questions, however, about the following transactions:

Analyze errors and effect on trial balance. (SO 4)

1. Insidz received $255 cash from a customer on account. It was recorded as a debit to Cash of $255 and a credit to Accounts Receivable of $552.

2. A service provided for cash was posted as a debit to Cash of $2,000 and a credit to Accounts Receivable of $2,000.

3. A credit of $750 for interest earned was neither recorded nor posted. The debit was recorded and posted correctly.

4. The debit to record $1,000 of dividends paid to shareholders was posted to the Salary Expense account. The credit was posted correctly.

5. Services of $325 were provided to a customer on account. The company debited Accounts Receivable for $325 and credited Service Revenue for $325.

6. A purchase of supplies for $500 on account was recorded as a debit to Supplies and a debit to Accounts Payable.

7. Insidz received advances of $500 from customers for work to be done next month. The student debited Cash for $500 but did not credit anything as he was not sure what to credit.

8. A cash payment of $495 for salaries was recorded as a debit to Salaries Expense and a credit to Salaries Payable.

9. Insidz purchased $1,500 of equipment on account. This transaction was recorded as a $5,100 debit to Equipment and a $5,100 credit to Accounts Payable.

10. A cash payment of $850 for rent for the month was not recorded.

Instructions

(a) Indicate which of the above transactions are correct, and which are incorrect.

(b) For each error identified in (a), answer the following questions:
1. Will the trial balance be in balance?
2. Which account(s) will be incorrectly stated because of the error?
3. For each account that you identified in (2) as being incorrect, state whether it will be overstated or understated, and by how much.

P3–11A 🔑 The trial balance of Messed Up Ltd. does not balance:

Prepare corrected trial balance. (SO 4)

MESSED UP LTD.
Trial Balance
May 31, 2009

	Debit	Credit
Cash	$ 7,376	
Accounts receivable		$ 2,630
Equipment	9,200	
Accumulated depreciation		4,200
Accounts payable		4,600
Common shares		4,250
Retained earnings		4,429
Service revenue	14,340	
Salaries expense	8,150	
Advertising expense		1,132
Depreciation expense	2,100	
Income tax expense	200	
Insurance expense	600	
	$41,966	$21,241

> The Accounting Information System

Each of the listed accounts has a normal balance per the general ledger. An examination of the general journal and general ledger reveals the following errors:

1. Prepaid Insurance, Accounts Payable, and Income Tax Expense were each understated by $100.
2. A transposition error was made in Service Revenue. Based on the posting made, the correct balance in the Service Revenue account should be $14,259.
3. A debit posting to Salaries Expense of $250 was omitted.
4. A $750 dividend paid to shareholders was debited to Salaries Expense and credited to Cash.
5. A $630 purchase of supplies on account was debited to Equipment and credited to Cash.
6. A payment of $320 for advertising was debited to Advertising Expense for $32 and credited to Cash for $32.
7. A $120 collection on account was recorded as a debit to Accounts Payable and a credit to Accounts Receivable.
8. A $2,000 note payable was issued in exchange for the purchase of equipment. The transaction was neither journalized nor posted.

Instructions
Prepare a correct trial balance.

Problems: Set B

Analyze transactions and calculate retained earnings. (SO 1)

P3–1B   On April 1, Seall Travel Agency Inc. started operations. The following transactions were completed during the month:

1. Issued common shares for $12,000 cash.
2. Paid $600 cash for April office rent.
3. Purchased office equipment for $5,500, paying $2,000 cash and signing a note payable for the balance.
4. Purchased $300 of advertising in the *Halifax Herald*, on account.
5. Paid $725 for office supplies.
6. Earned $9,000 for services performed: cash of $1,000 is received from customers, and the balance of $8,000 is billed to customers on account.
7. Paid $200 in dividends to shareholders.
8. Paid *Halifax Herald* the amount due in transaction 4.
9. Paid employees' salaries, $3,200.
10. Received $6,000 cash from customers billed in transaction 6.
11. Paid the utility bill for the month, $1,000.
12. Paid $20 of interest on the note payable in transaction 3.
13. Paid income tax, $1,500.

Instructions

(a) Prepare a tabular analysis of the effects of the above transactions on the accounting equation.

(b) From an analysis of the retained earnings accounts (revenues, expenses, and dividends), calculate the ending balance in Retained Earnings.

Analyze transactions and prepare financial statements. (SO 1)

P3–2B   Ivan Izo, LLP, specializes in providing legal services. On July 31, 2009, the company's general ledger showed the following balances: Cash $4,000; Accounts Receivable $1,500; Supplies $500; Office Equipment $5,000; Accounts Payable $4,100; Common Shares $5,500; and Retained Earnings $1,400. During August the following transactions occurred:

Aug.	3	Collected $1,200 from customers for accounts receivable that were due.
	6	Paid $2,700 cash on accounts payable owing.
	7	Earned fees of $6,500: $3,000 is collected in cash and the remainder is due on account.
	12	Purchased additional office equipment for $1,200, paying $400 cash and the balance on account.
	14	Paid $3,500 in salaries, $900 for rent, and $275 in advertising expenses for the month of August.

18   Collected the balance of the fees earned on August 7.

20   Paid $500 in dividends to shareholders.

24   Billed a client $1,000 for legal services provided on account.

26   Received $2,000 from Laurentian Bank; the money was borrowed on a note payable.

27   Signed an engagement letter to provide legal services to a client in September for $4,500.

28   Received the utility bill for the month of August in the amount of $275; it is not due until September 15.

31   Paid income tax for the month, $800.

Instructions

(a) Beginning with the July 31 balances, prepare a tabular analysis of the effects of the August transactions on the accounting equation.

(b) Prepare a statement of earnings, statement of retained earnings, and balance sheet for the month.

P3–3B   You are presented with the following list of selected accounts for O'Laney's Sales Ltd.:

Identify normal balance and statement classification.
(SO 2)

Account	(a) Normal Balance	(b) Financial Statement	(c) Classification
Accounts payable	Credit	Balance Sheet	Current liabilities
Accounts receivable			
Accumulated depreciation			
Building			
Common shares			
Cost of goods sold			
Depreciation expense			
Equipment			
Income tax expense			
Income taxes payable			
Insurance expense			
Interest revenue			
Inventories			
Long-term debt			
Notes payable (due in 90 days)			
Prepaid insurance			
Retained earnings			
Salary expense			
Sales revenue			
Unearned sales revenue			

Instructions

For each account, indicate (a) whether the normal balance is a debit or credit; (b) the financial statement where the account should be reported (e.g., balance sheet or statement of earnings); and (c) the appropriate classification (e.g., current assets, long-term liabilities, revenues, etc.). The first one has been done for you as an example.

P3–4B   You are presented with the following transactions for Paddick Enterprises Ltd. for the month of February:

Identify debit and credit effects and record transactions.
(SO 2, 3)

Feb.   2   Purchased supplies on account, $600.

        3   Purchased furniture for $10,000 by signing a note that is due in three months.

        6   Earned revenue of $50,000. Of this amount, $30,000 was received in cash. The balance was on account.

       13   Paid $1,000 in dividends to shareholders.

       20   Paid the amount owing for the supplies purchased on February 2.

       23   Collected $20,000 of the amount owing from the February 6 transaction.

       24   Paid operating expenses for the month, $22,000.

       27   Recorded wages due to employees for work performed during the month, $14,000.

Instructions

(a) For each transaction, indicate (1) the basic type of account to be debited and credited (asset, liability, shareholders' equity); (2) the specific accounts to debit and credit (Cash, Service Revenue, etc.); and (3) whether each account is increased (+) or decreased (−), and by what amount. Use the following format, in which the first transaction is given as an example:

	Account Debited			Account Credited		
	(1)	(2)	(3)	(1)	(2)	(3)
Transaction	Basic Type	Specific Account	Effect	Basic Type	Specific Account	Effect
Feb. 2	Asset	Supplies	+$600	Liability equity	Accounts payable	+$600

(b) Prepare journal entries to record the above transactions.

Record transactions.
(SO 3)

P3–5B   The Bucket Club Miniature Golf and Driving Range Inc. opened on May 1. These selected events and transactions occurred during the month:

May	1	Issued common shares for $70,000 cash.
	4	Purchased Lee's Golf Land for $210,000. The price consists of land $95,000; building $70,000; and equipment $45,000. Paid cash of $50,000 and signed a mortgage payable for the balance.
	4	Purchased golf clubs and other equipment for $6,000 on account from Woods Corporation.
	5	Advertised the opening of the driving range and miniature golf course, paying advertising expenses of $1,500.
	6	Paid $2,500 for a one-year insurance policy.
	15	Paid Woods Corporation in full for equipment purchased on May 4.
	18	Received $15,800 from customers for golf fees earned.
	20	Paid dividends of $500 to shareholders.
	22	Received $14,200 from customers for golf fees earned.
	29	Paid salaries of $12,400.
	29	Paid $1,000 of interest on the mortgage payable.

Instructions
Journalize the May transactions.

Record and post transactions.
(SO 3)

P3–6B   During the first month of operations, these events and transactions occurred for Virmani Architects Inc.:

Apr.	1	Cash of $15,000 and equipment of $6,000 was invested in the company in exchange for common shares.
	1	A secretary-receptionist was hired at a monthly salary of $1,900.
	2	Paid office rent for the month, $950.
	3	Purchased architectural supplies on account from Halo Ltd., $1,750.
	10	Completed blueprints on a carport and billed the client $900.
	13	Received an $800 cash advance from a client for the design of a new home.
	20	Received $1,500 for services performed for a client.
	21	Received $500 from a client for work completed and billed on April 10.
	23	Received April's telephone bill, $135 due May 15.
	30	Paid the secretary-receptionist for the month, $1,900.
	30	Paid $1,750 to Halo Ltd. on account (see April 3 transaction).
	30	Paid a $500 dividend.

Instructions

(a) Journalize the transactions.

(b) Using T accounts, post the journal entries prepared in (a) to the general ledger.

Record transactions, post, and prepare trial balance.
(SO 3, 4)

P3–7B   The Star Theatre Inc. is unique as it shows only triple features of sequential theme movies. As at February 28, 2009, the Star's general ledger showed Cash $15,000; Land $85,000; Buildings $77,000; Equipment $20,000; Accounts Payable $12,000; Mortgage Payable $118,000; Common Shares $40,000; and Retained Earnings $27,000. During the month of March, the following events and transactions occurred:

Mar. 2 Received three *Harry Potter* movies to be shown during the first three weeks of March. The film rental was $27,000. Of that amount, $10,000 was paid in cash and the remainder will be paid on March 10.

2 Hired M. Brewer to operate the concession stand. Brewer agrees to pay Star Theatre 15% of the gross receipts for the right to operate the concession stand, payable on the last day of each month.

3 Ordered three *Shrek* movies, to be shown the last 10 days of March. The film rental cost is $300 per night.

9 Received $16,300 from customers for admissions.

10 Paid the balance due on the *Harry Potter* rental.

13 Paid the accounts payable owing at the end of February.

17 Paid advertising expenses, $950.

20 Received $16,600 from customers for admissions.

23 Received the *Shrek* movies and paid the rental fee of $3,000 ($300 × 10 nights).

25 Received $18,400 from customers for admissions.

27 Paid salaries of $4,200.

31 Received a statement from M. Brewer, showing gross concession receipts of $8,500, and the balance due to Star Theatre of $1,280 for March. Brewer paid half of the balance due and will remit the remainder on April 5.

31 Paid $1,250 of mortgage principal and $750 of interest on the mortgage.

Instructions

(a) Using T accounts, enter the beginning balances in the general ledger as at February 28.

(b) Journalize the March transactions.

(c) Post the March journal entries to the general ledger.

(d) Prepare a trial balance at March 31, 2009.

P3–8B Pamper Me Salon Inc.'s general ledger at April 30, 2009 included the following: Cash $7,000; Supplies $500; Equipment $24,000; Accounts Payable $2,100; Loan Payable $10,000; Gift Certificates Outstanding $3,000; Common Shares $5,000; and Retained Earnings $11,400. The following events and transactions occurred during May:

Record transactions, post, and prepare trial balance.
(SO 3, 4)

May 1 Paid rent for the month of May, $1,000.

5 Paid $1,100 of the account payable at April 30.

7 Issued gift certificates for $2,500 cash.

8 Received $1,200 cash from customers for services performed.

14 Paid $1,200 in salaries to employees.

15 Received $800 in cash from customers for services performed.

15 Customers receiving services worth $700 used gift certificates in payment.

20 Paid the remaining accounts payable from April 30.

22 Received $1,000 in cash from customers for services performed.

22 Purchased supplies of $700 on account. All of these were used during the month.

25 Received a bill for advertising for $500. This bill is due on June 13.

25 Received and paid a utilities bill for $400.

29 Received $700 in cash from customers for services performed.

29 Customers receiving services worth $600 used gift certificates in payment.

31 Interest of $50 was paid on the loan.

31 Paid $1,200 in salaries to employees.

Instructions

(a) Using T accounts, enter the beginning balances in the general ledger as at April 30.

(b) Journalize the May transactions.

(c) Post the May journal entries to the general ledger.

(d) Prepare a trial balance as at May 31.

▸ The Accounting Information System

P3–9B   You are presented with the following alphabetical list of accounts and balances (in thousands) for Taggar Enterprises Inc. at June 30, 2009:

Accounts payable	$ 1,500	Income tax payable	$ 500
Accounts receivable	3,000	Interest expense	1,000
Accumulated depreciation—building	4,000	Inventories	5,100
Accumulated depreciation—equipment	1,000	Land	5,000
Building	15,000	Long-term investment	4,950
Cash	1,800	Mortgage payable	13,750
Common shares	5,000	Operating expenses	3,300
Cost of goods sold	13,700	Prepaid insurance	900
Current portion of mortgage payable	1,250	Retained earnings, July 1, 2008	6,250
Equipment	3,000	Sales revenue	25,000
Income tax expense	1,500		

Instructions

(a) Prepare a trial balance, listing the accounts in financial statement order.

(b) Prepare a statement of earnings, statement of retained earnings, and balance sheet for the year.

P3–10B   The bookkeeper for Cater's Dance Studio Ltd. did the following in journalizing and posting:

1. A debit posting to the Interest Revenue account of $600 was omitted.

2. A credit of $500 for revenue received in advance was posted as a credit to the Unearned Service Revenue account.

3. A purchase of supplies on account of $540 was debited to Inventory for $540 and credited to Accounts Payable for $540.

4. A credit to the Wages Payable account for $1,200 was posted as a credit to the Cash account.

5. A debit posting of $250 to the Cash account was posted twice.

6. The debit side of the entry to record the payment of $600 for dividends was posted to the Salaries Expense account.

7. The collection of an account receivable of $250 was posted as a debit to the Cash account and a credit to the Accounts Payable account.

8. The provision of services on account was debited to Accounts Receivable and credited to Service Revenue.

9. A purchase of equipment on account for $4,600 was posted as a $6,400 debit to Equipment and a $6,400 credit to Cash.

10. Rent of $1,000 for the month was neither recorded nor posted.

Instructions

(a) Indicate which of the above transactions are correct, and which are incorrect.

(b) For each error identified in (a), answer the following questions:

1. Will the trial balance be in balance?

2. Which account(s) will be incorrectly stated because of the error?

3. For each account that you identified in (2) as being incorrect, state whether it will be overstated or understated, and by how much.

P3–11B   The trial balance of Cantpost Ltd., shown on the next page, does not balance:

Each of the listed accounts has a normal balance per the general ledger. An examination of the general journal and general ledger reveals the following errors:

1. Cash received from a customer on account was debited for $570, and Accounts Receivable was credited for the same amount. The actual collection was for $750.

2. The purchase of equipment on account for $360 was recorded as a debit to Supplies for $360 and a credit to Accounts Payable for $360.

3. Services were performed on account for a client for $890. Accounts Receivable was debited for $890 and Service Revenue was credited for $89.

4. A debit posting to Depreciation Expense of $600 was omitted.

5. A payment made by a customer on account for $206 was debited to Cash for $206 and credited to Accounts Receivable for $602.

6. A transposition (reversal of digits) error was made when copying the balance in the Salaries Expense account. The correct balance should be $4,300.

7. A payment for rent in the amount of $1,000 was neither recorded nor posted.

CANTPOST LTD. Trial Balance June 30, 2009	Debit	Credit
Cash		$ 5,170
Accounts receivable	$ 3,230	
Supplies	860	
Equipment	3,000	
Accumulated depreciation	$ 600	
Accounts payable		$ 2,665
Unearned revenue	1,200	
Common shares		8,000
Dividends	800	
Service revenue		6,440
Salaries expense	3,400	
Office expense	910	
Income tax expense	440	
	$14,440	$22,275

Instructions

Prepare a correct trial balance.

BROADENING YOUR PERSPECTIVE

Financial Reporting and Analysis Cases

Financial Reporting: *Shoppers Drug Mart*

Analysis Tools

BYP3–1 The financial statements of Shoppers Drug Mart are presented in Appendix A at the end of this book. They contain the following selected accounts:

Accounts Payable and
   Accrued Liabilities
Accounts Receivable
Amortization Expense

Property and Equipment
Interest Expense
Income Taxes Payable
Sales

Instructions

(a) What is the increase and decrease side for each account? What is the normal balance for each account?

(b) Identify the probable other account(s) in the transaction and the effect on that (those) account(s) when:

1. Accounts Payable is decreased.
2. Accounts Receivable is decreased.
3. Amortization Expense is increased.
4. Property and Equipment is increased.

5. Interest Expense is increased.
6. Income Taxes Payable is increased.
7. Sales is increased.

Comparative Analysis: *Shoppers Drug Mart and Jean Coutu*

BYP3–2 The financial statements of Jean Coutu are presented in Appendix B following the financial statements for Shoppers Drug Mart in Appendix A.

Instructions

(a) Using Shoppers' balance sheet, put the accounts and amounts provided into a trial balance format as at December 29, 2007.

(b) Using Jean Coutu's balance sheet, put the accounts and amounts provided into a trial balance format as at March 1, 2008.

Interpreting Financial Statements

BYP3–3 Japan Tobacco Inc., headquartered in Japan, and Imperial Tobacco Group PLC, headquartered in the United Kingdom, compete internationally in the tobacco industry. The assets section for each company's balance sheet follows:

International Resources

JAPAN TOBACCO INC. Balance Sheet (partial) March 31, 2007 (in JPY millions)	
Current assets	
Cash and cash equivalents	¥ 1,179,522
Short-term investments	6,167
Trade notes and accounts receivable	147,846
Inventories	417,276
Other current assets	89,997
Total current assets	1,840,808
Net property, plant, and equipment	600,436
Total investments and other assets	923,419
Total assets	¥ 3,364,663

IMPERIAL TOBACCO GROUP PLC Balance Sheet (partial) September 30, 2007 (in GBP millions)	
Non-current assets	
Intangible assets	£4,950
Property, plant, and equipment	640
Investments and other assets	665
Total non-current assets	6,255
Current assets	
Inventories	998
Trade and other receivables	1,254
Cash and cash equivalents	380
Other current assets	121
Total current assets	2,753
Total assets	£9,008

Instructions

(a) Which company presents its assets in the same order that North American companies use?

(b) Japan Tobacco and Imperial Tobacco do not present the assets sections of their balance sheets in the same order. Do you think that this difference between the two companies would affect your interpretation of each company's liquidity relative to the other? Explain.

A Global Focus

International Resources

BYP3–4 XBRL (eXtensible Business Reporting Language) is being developed by an international not-for-profit consortium of approximately 550 companies, organizations, and government agencies. It is a technical language for the consistent marking and electronic communication of business and financial data. By using XBRL, data from different companies with different accounting systems can be assembled and disseminated quickly, cheaply, and efficiently.

Currently, XBRL Canada is working on a project to help companies with the movement to IFRS. The project is being conducted with the International Accounting Standards Board and will result in a taxonomy that conforms with the IFRS being used in Canada. It will also create tools that cross-reference current Canadian GAAP and IFRS.

Instructions

(a) If financial information will be stored and shared through electronic media, does this mean that the manual accounting concepts discussed in this chapter are outdated?

(b) Why, in your opinion, are companies spending time and money converting accounting information into an XBRL format? Would this be more beneficial to large international companies or smaller regional ones?

Critical Thinking Cases and Activities

Collaborative Learning Activity

BYP3–5 A partial list of transactions for Sprucehill Enterprises Ltd. follows:

	Cash	Accounts Receivable	Prepaid Insurance	Office Equipment	Building	=	Accounts Payable	Mortgage Payable	Common Shares	Revenue	Expenses
1.				+$5,000			+$ 5,000				
2.	+$150,000								+$150,000		
3.	−90,000				+$450,000			+$360,000			
4.		+$17,500								+$17,500	
5.			+$7,200				+7,200				
6.			−1,200								−$1,200
7.	−4,100							−500			−3,600
	$ 55,900	+ $17,500	+ $6,000	+ $5,000	+ $450,000	=	$12,200 +	$359,500 +	$150,000 +	$17,500 −	$4,800

$534,400

$534,400

Instructions

With the class divided into groups, do the following:

(a) Create an appropriate description for each of the above transactions.

(b) Share your answers with another group of students. If you cannot all agree on the results, share again with a second group of students.

Communication Activity

BYP3–6 Three equestrians recently incorporated their riding business, naming it Chestnut Stables Inc. The company generates revenue from riding lessons and boarding horses. It also incurs expenses for insurance, feed, farrier (blacksmith) and veterinary services, and salaries. This is the first company that the equestrians have operated and they need your guidance on how to set up an accounting information system.

Instructions

Write a memo to the equestrians in which you outline the system of collecting and processing transaction data that is relevant for Chestnut Stables Inc. Explain and illustrate the steps in recording transactions for this type of company. Be sure to also mention the accounts that should be set up for the company.

Ethics Case

Ethics in Accounting

BYP3–7   Diego Olaya is the assistant chief accountant at Digitech Corporation. It is the end of the first quarter and Diego is hurriedly trying to prepare a trial balance so that quarterly financial statements can be prepared and released to management and the regulatory agencies. To Diego's dismay, the total credits on the trial balance exceed the debits by $1,000.

In order to meet the 4 p.m. deadline, Diego decides to force the debits and credits into balance by adding the amount of the difference to the Equipment account. He chose Equipment because it is one of the larger account balances—$250,000. Proportionally, it will be the least misstated. He wishes that he had a few more days to find the error but realizes that the financial statements are already late.

Instructions

(a) Who are the stakeholders in this situation?

(b) What ethical issues are involved?

(c) What are Diego's alternatives?

"All About You" Activity

BYP3–8   In this chapter, you learned the features of accounting information systems that companies use to keep track of their important financial information. Let's now apply these same concepts to your personal financial information.

Instructions

(a) Why is it important that you develop a system to maintain and keep your personal records up to date?

(b) How should you organize such a system for yourself?

(c) What would you do if you lost your wallet with your credit cards and identification included? (*Hint:* Visit the Service Canada website, www.servicecanada.gc.ca/en/lifeevents/wallet.shtml, and review the list that Service Canada has prepared to help you understand the process of replacing your cards and identification.)

Serial Case

(*Note:* This is a continuation of the serial case from Chapters 1 and 2.)

BYP3–9   In February 2009 after incorporating Cookie Creations Ltd., Natalie begins operations. After much deliberation, Natalie decides not to accept the Biscuits offer raised in Chapter 2 to supply oatmeal chocolate chip cookies. At this point, Natalie believes it best to focus on her cookie classes until she has more time and oven space to consider making 1,500 dozen cookies a week. The following events occur in the month of February:

Feb.   2   Natalie cashes her Canada Savings Bonds and receives $520, which she deposits in her personal bank account.

2   A bank account is opened for Cookie Creations.

5   Cookie Creations issues 500 common shares to Natalie for $500.

11   Natalie designs a brochure and a poster to advertise the company and the services available.

11   The brochures and posters are printed, at a cash cost of $95. They will be distributed as the opportunity arises.

13   Baking supplies, such as flour, sugar, butter, and chocolate chips, are purchased for $125 cash.

16   Natalie starts to gather some baking equipment to take with her when teaching the cookie classes. She has an excellent top-of-the-line food processor and mixer that originally cost her $550. Natalie decides to start using it only in her new business. She estimates that the equipment is currently worth $300 and she transfers the equipment into the business in exchange for 300 additional common shares.

18 The company needs more cash to sustain its operations. Natalie's grandmother lends the company $2,000 cash, in exchange for a one-year, 6% note payable. Interest and principal are repayable at maturity.

19 Cookie Creations purchases more baking equipment for $900 cash.

20 Natalie books her first class for February 26 for $100. One of her mother's friends needed a novel idea for her young daughter's birthday party.

23 Natalie books a second class for March 5 for $125. As a down payment, $50 cash is received in advance.

26 Natalie teaches her first class, booked on February 20, and collects the $100 cash.

27 A one-year insurance policy is purchased for $1,200.

27 Natalie teaches a group of grade one students how to make animal cookies. At the end of the class, Natalie leaves an invoice for $250 with the school principal. The principal says that he will pass it along to head office and it will be paid sometime in March.

27 A $50 invoice for use of Natalie's cell phone is received. The cell phone is used exclusively for Cookie Creations' business. The invoice is for services provided in February and is due on March 13.

Instructions:

(a) Journalize the February transactions.

(b) Using T accounts, post the journal entries to the general ledger accounts.

(c) Prepare a trial balance at February 28, 2009.

Answers to Chapter Questions

Answer to Shoppers Drug Mart Review It Question 5

Accounts Receivable (Asset-Dr.), Dividends Payable (Liability-Cr.), Sales (Revenue-Cr.), and Interest Expense (Expense-Dr.).

Answers to Self-Study Questions

1. c   2. d   3. a   4. c   5. d   6. a   7. c   8. d   9. a   10. c

Remember to go back to the beginning of the chapter to check off your completed work!

←

Comprehensive Case: Chapter 3

HomeComputerCare Inc. was organized on May 1, 2009, to provide customized support to design and maintain in-home computer networks. The company does not have any full-time employees other than the principal shareholder and manager, Gerry Windham. Instead it hires "consultants" to perform the work for the company. Initially, the company and the consultant split the revenue evenly. Consultants who stay with the company or who have special expertise increase their percentage of client revenue to as much as 70% of the total billing. This is an incentive for consultants to stay with the company and to develop their range of skills.

HomeComputerCare plans to use the following chart of accounts:

1000	Cash	4500	Retained Earnings
1100	Accounts Receivable	5000	Revenue—Client Services
1200	Office Supplies	7000	Advertising Expense
1300	Prepaid Insurance	7100	Consultant Fees Expense
1400	Prepaid Rent (security deposit)	7200	Insurance Expense
2000	Office Equipment	7300	Office Administration Expense
2100	Computer Equipment	7400	Office Rent Expense
2500	Goodwill	7500	Telephone Expense
3000	Accounts Payable	7600	Travel and Entertainment Expense
3100	Bank Loan Payable	9000	Income Tax Expense
4000	Common Shares		

The company had the following transactions in the month of May:

May 4 Issued 1,000 common shares for $10 each.

5 Borrowed $25,000 from the bank on a long-term loan.

5 Purchased office equipment for $15,000 cash.

6 Purchased computer equipment for $10,000 on account, to be used during in-home client visits.

7 Paid annual insurance policy, $3,000.

8 Purchased office supplies on account, $500.

11 Paid for an advertisement in a local paper, $250.

12 Paid for several advertising spots on the local radio station, $1,500.

13 Attended a local business fair. Paid $500 for promotional items and $250 for booth rental.

14 Took the manager of a local computer store to lunch, $75.

15 Summarized and recorded the billings to clients for the first two weeks of May. Billings totalled $7,500. These amounts are due by the 10th of the next month.

18 Calculated and recorded amounts payable to consultants for their work. Payments of $3,750 will be made to the consultants on the 18th of the next month.

19 The company shares office space with another business. Finalized the lease and paid the first month's rent of $1,500 plus a security deposit of $3,000.

20 Paid $1,000 for the company's share of the current month's office administration expenses.

21 Purchased a client list for $2,000 cash from a graduate student who had a similar business and is moving out of town (use the account Goodwill).

22 Received $1,500 from clients in settlement of their accounts billed on the 15th.

25 Summarized and recorded the billings to clients for the last two weeks of May. Billings totalled $9,000. These amounts are due by the 25th of the next month.

29 Calculated and recorded amounts payable to consultants for their work. Payments of $5,000 will be made to the consultants on the 29th of the next month.

Instructions

(a) Journalize the May transactions.

(b) Set up T accounts and post the journal entries prepared in (a).

(c) Prepare a trial balance at May 31, 2009.

(d) Prepare a (1) statement of earnings, (2) statement of retained earnings, and (3) balance sheet for the month.

(e) Will HomeComputerCare have enough money to pay its accounts payable in the next 30 days? Explain.

CHAPTER 4
Accrual Accounting Concepts

School's Out, Time to Balance the Books

At the University of Western Ontario in London, classes for most students start in September and end in April, as they do at schools across the country. Likewise, the university's fiscal year end is April 30, so the university basically closes its books at the same time as students do.

This cohesion helps the university to satisfy the revenue recognition and matching principles, where it has to apply revenues and expenses in the accounting period in which the service is performed or the expense is incurred.

However, many students at Western take intersession courses. They pay their course fees before the year end of April 30, but the courses don't start until May or later. "We get intersession fees and other fees in advance of our year end, so there is a deferral there," says Carter Scott, Western's controller. The university defers the recognition of that revenue until the following accounting period, the one when it provides the teaching services.

"Accrual accounting is considered the most appropriate method of financial reporting because revenues and expenses are recognized in the period to which they relate, regardless of whether there has been a receipt or payment of cash," Mr. Scott explains. "A more meaningful picture of financial position and operations is provided under accrual accounting than on a cash flow basis."

Western offers more than 400 different majors, minors, and specializations, through 12 faculties and three affiliated colleges. With approximately 30,000 undergraduate and graduate students, tuition fees are a major source of funding for the university, along with government grants. However, the university also takes in revenue from corporate training. For certain non-credit courses, a company may pay in advance for a customized executive program at the Richard Ivey School of Business, for example. Like other tuition amounts, this revenue is also deferred to the fiscal year in which the program is provided.

Another example of the deferral of revenue according to accrual accounting is the advance fees that students pay for residence admission to hold their spot for the coming year. The university defers recognition of this revenue until the start of the academic year in September, when the students move into the residence.

Research provides another example. Western receives more than $200 million per year in external support for projects, making research an integral part of the university's activities. "In a lot of cases, granting agencies' year ends are in March, so they send the funds in at the beginning of March," Mr. Scott points out. "For any faculty member who gets a grant, it's deferred until he starts expending it, because it's restricted for that purpose. Restricted revenues for which the related expenses have not been incurred are reported as unearned revenue on the university's balance sheet." The grant money is matched against expenses incurred over the course of the research project, which could go on for years.

Expenses, too, must be recorded in the year in which they are incurred. "Post-employment benefits, at most universities, is a very large number that you accrue for," Mr. Scott explains. Other expenses that would have to be accrued at year end include vacation pay, outstanding salary for the approximately 3,500 full-time faculty and staff members, and utility bills.

Western also has a significant amount of construction projects ongoing. The construction companies usually bill around the 15th of the month, so some of these bills will come in after the year end, Mr. Scott explains. These companies provide estimates for the university to use in its accrual process.

Recording revenues and expenses in the correct period is a challenge, but one that has to be met to reflect the various activities of a large university like Western.

the University of Western Ontario: uwo.ca

STUDY OBJECTIVES

After studying this chapter, you should be able to:

1. Explain the revenue recognition principle and the matching principle.

2. Prepare adjusting entries for prepayments.

3. Prepare adjusting entries for accruals.

4. Describe the nature and purpose of the adjusted trial balance, and prepare one.

5. Prepare closing entries and a post-closing trial balance.

THE NAVIGATOR

☑ Read *Feature Story*

☑ Scan *Study Objectives*

☑ Read *Chapter Preview*

☑ Read text and answer *Before You Go On*

☑ Read *All About You*

☑ Review *Summary of Study Objectives*

☑ Review *Using the Decision Toolkit— A Summary*

☑ Work *Using the Decision Toolkit*

☑ Work *Demonstration Problem*

☑ Answer *Self-Study Questions*

☑ Complete assignments

The Navigator

PREVIEW OF CHAPTER 4

In Chapter 3, we examined the recording process up to and including the preparation of the trial balance. Although we prepared financial statements directly from the trial balance in that chapter, additional steps are necessary to properly update the accounts before the financial statements are prepared. These steps adjust accounts for timing mismatches, like the ones described for the University of Western Ontario in the feature story.

In this chapter, we introduce you to the accrual accounting concepts that guide the recognition of revenue and the matching of expenses in the appropriate time period. We will also describe the remaining steps in the accounting cycle.

The chapter is organized as follows:

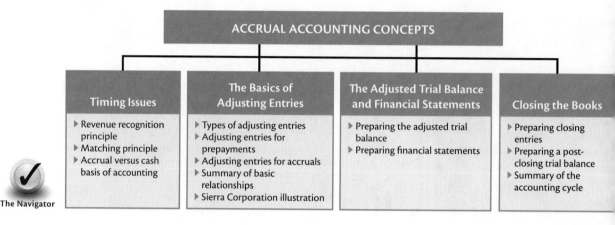

The Navigator

Timing Issues

study objective 1

Explain the revenue recognition principle and the matching principle.

Accounting would be simple if we could wait until a company ended its operations to prepare its financial statements. As the following anecdote shows, if we waited until then we could easily determine the amount of lifetime income earned:

A grocery store owner from the old country kept his accounts payable on a spindle, accounts receivable on a notepad, and cash in a box. His daughter, an accountant, chided him: "I don't understand how you can run your business this way. How do you know what you've earned?"

"Well," the father replied, "when I arrived in Canada 40 years ago, I had nothing but the pants I was wearing. Today your sister is a doctor, your brother is a teacher, and you are an accountant. Your mother and I have a nice car, a well-furnished house, and a cottage at the lake. We have a good business and everything is paid for. So, you add all that together, subtract the pants, and there's your net earnings."

Although the old grocer may be correct in his evaluation of how to calculate earnings over his lifetime, most companies need more immediate feedback about how well they are doing. For example, management needs monthly reports on financial results, large corporations present quarterly and annual financial statements to shareholders, and the Canada Revenue Agency requires all businesses to file monthly sales tax reports and annual income tax returns.

Consequently, accounting divides the economic life of a business into artificial time periods. As indicated in Chapter 2, this is known as the **time period assumption**. Accounting time periods are generally one month, one quarter (three months), or one year.

Many accounting transactions affect more than one of these arbitrary time periods. For example, we saw in the feature story that research grants received by faculty at the University of Western Ontario can span multiple years. We also saw how Western collects intersession course fees in one fiscal year but teaches the courses in the next fiscal year.

Determining the amount of revenue and expenses to report in a particular accounting period can be difficult. Generally accepted accounting principles include two principles for recognizing revenue and expenses: the revenue recognition principle and the matching principle.

We should note that the revenue recognition and matching principles as they currently exist are likely to change significantly in the future. The International Accounting Standards Board, along with U.S standard setters, are working on a joint project to develop new standards for revenue recognition. They are considering a new model of revenue recognition where revenue would be recognized based on changes in assets and liabilities (performance obligations) arising from contracts with customers. By using balance sheet elements to measure and record the earnings process, the concept of matching is anticipated to be of less importance in the future than it is today. Because these deliberations are still at an early stage and not anticipated to be completed in the near future, in this chapter we will describe the revenue recognition and matching principles in use today.

Revenue Recognition Principle

The **revenue recognition principle** states that revenue must be recognized in the accounting period in which it is earned. In a merchandising company, revenue is considered to be earned when the merchandise is sold (normally at the point of sale). In a service company, revenue is considered earned at the time the service is performed.

Revenue recognition is governed by guidelines, which sometimes require a significant amount of professional judgement to apply. In general, though, revenue is recognized when the sales or performance effort is substantially complete, the amount is determinable (measurable), and collection is reasonably assured.

To illustrate, assume a dry-cleaning business cleans clothing on June 30, but customers do not claim and pay for their clothes until the first week of July. Under the revenue recognition principle, revenue is earned in June when the service is performed, not in July when the cash is received. In this case, we know the amount owed and it is reasonable to assume that the customers will pick up the clothes and pay for their cleaning. At June 30, the dry-cleaning service would report a receivable on its balance sheet and revenue on its statement of earnings for the service performed.

DECISION TOOLKIT

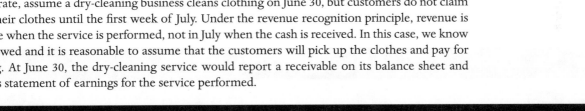

Decision Checkpoints	Info Needed for Decision	Tools to Use for Decision	How to Evaluate Results
At what point should the company record revenue?	Need to understand the nature of the company's business	Revenue should be recorded when earned. For a service company, revenue is earned when a service is performed. For a merchandising company, revenue is earned when the merchandise is sold.	Recognizing revenue too early overstates current period revenue; recognizing it too late understates current period revenue.

Matching Principle

In recognizing expenses, a simple rule is followed: "Let the expenses follow the revenues." Thus, expense recognition is tied to revenue recognition. Consider again the dry-cleaning business mentioned in the last section. Matching expenses with revenues means that the salary expense for the employee who performed the cleaning service on June 30 should be reported in the same period in which the service revenue is recognized. In the case of the University of Western Ontario, described in our feature story, matching expenses with revenues means that the salary expense and other costs of providing teaching services should be reported in the same period as the revenue from the course fees.

The critical issue in expense recognition is determining when the expense contributes to revenue. This may or may not be the same period in which the expense is paid. If the salary incurred on June 30 is not paid until July, the dry cleaner would still report salaries expense on its statement of earnings and salaries payable on its balance sheet for June.

The practice of expense recognition is referred to as the **matching principle** because it states that efforts (expenses) must be matched with accomplishments (revenues) wherever this is possible. Some expenses are easy to match with revenues. For example, the cost of goods sold can be directly matched to sales revenue in the period in which the sale occurs.

Other costs are more difficult to directly associate with revenue. For example, it is difficult to match administrative salary expense or interest expense with the revenue these help earn. Such costs are normally expensed in the period in which they are incurred. Other examples include costs that help generate revenue over multiple periods of time, such as the depreciation of equipment. The association of these types of expense with revenue is less direct than matching cost of goods sold, and we therefore have to make assumptions about how to best allocate these costs to each period. We will learn more about allocating expenses later in this chapter.

ACCOUNTING MATTERS! | Management Perspective

Canadian-born director Norman Jewison describes the film industry as a terrible business when it comes to accounting. The person behind the lens of the classic *In the Heat of the Night*, as well as *The Hurricane*, says, "When I make a film, it has to make three times its negative cost. If a picture costs $20 million, my picture has to earn $60 million before it shows any kind of profit." And that $20 million spent on the film has to be expensed over its economic life, which could be less than a year or many years, depending on the success of the film. The filmmaker also needs to estimate how much revenue will be earned from box office sales, DVD sales, television, Internet downloads, games, and toys. Properly matching expenses to revenues is no small task for those who are focused on big pictures.

Source: Mark Brown, "Live and Learn: Norman Jewison," *Canadian Business*, February 28, 2005, p. 94.

DECISION TOOLKIT

Decision Checkpoints	Info Needed for Decision	 Tools to Use for Decision	How to Evaluate Results
At what point should the company record expenses?	Need to understand the nature of the company's business	Expenses should "follow" revenues—that is, the effort (expense) should be matched with the result (revenue).	Recognizing expenses too early overstates current period expenses; recognizing them too late understates current period expenses.

Accrual versus Cash Basis of Accounting

The combined application of the revenue recognition principle and the matching principle results in accrual basis accounting. **Accrual basis accounting means that transactions that affect a company's financial statements are recorded in the periods in which the events occur, rather than when the company actually receives or pays cash.** This means recognizing revenues when they are earned rather than when cash is received. Likewise, expenses are recognized in the period in which services or goods are used or consumed to produce these revenues, rather than when cash is paid. This results in matching revenues that have been earned with the expenses incurred to earn these same revenues.

An alternative to the accrual basis is the cash basis. Under **cash basis accounting, revenue is recorded only when cash is received, and an expense is recorded only when cash is paid.** This cash basis can lead to misleading financial statements. Why? Because the cash basis fails to record revenue that has been earned if cash has not yet been received, thus violating the revenue recognition principle and giving the impression that the business is not as profitable as it was for the period. Similarly, a cash basis statement of earnings fails to match expenses with earned revenues, which violates the matching principle and could make the business look more or less profitable than it was for the period.

As Carter Scott, the controller of the University of Western Ontario in our feature story, said, "Accrual accounting is considered the most appropriate method of financial reporting because revenues and expenses are recognized in the period to which they relate, regardless of whether there has been a receipt or payment of cash. A more meaningful picture of financial position and operations is provided under accrual accounting than on a cash flow basis."

Illustration 4-1 compares accrual-based numbers and cash-based numbers, using a simple example. Suppose that you own a painting company and you paint a large building during year 1. In year 1, you incur and pay total expenses of $50,000, which includes the cost of the paint and your employees' salaries. You bill your customer $80,000 at the end of year 1, but you are not paid until year 2. On an accrual basis, you would report the revenue during the period when it is earned—year 1. The expenses would be recorded (matched) in the period in which the revenues were earned. Thus, your net earnings for year 1 would be $30,000, and no revenue or expense from this project would be reported in year 2. The $30,000 of earnings reported for year 1 provides a useful indication of the profitability of your efforts during that period.

If, instead, you were reporting on a cash basis, you would report expenses of $50,000 in year 1 and revenues of $80,000 in year 2. Net earnings for year 1 would be a loss of $50,000, while net earnings for year 2 would be $80,000. While total earnings are the same over the two-year period ($30,000), cash basis measures are not very informative about the results of your efforts during year 1 or year 2.

Illustration 4-1

Accrual versus cash basis accounting

	Year 1		Year 2	
Activity	Purchased paint, painted building, paid employees		Received payment for work done in year 1	
Accrual basis	Revenue	$ 80,000	Revenue	$ 0
	Expense	50,000	Expense	0
	Net earnings	$ 30,000	Net earnings	$ 0
Cash basis	Revenue	$ 0	Revenue	$80,000
	Expense	50,000	Expense	0
	Net loss	$(50,000)	Net earnings	$80,000

BEFORE YOU GO ON...

Review It

1. What are the revenue recognition and matching principles?
2. What are the differences between the cash and accrual bases of accounting?

Do It

During the year ended December 31, 2009, Jomerans Corp. received $125,000 cash from customers. At December 31, 2008, customers owed Jomerans $30,000 for services provided in 2008. On December 31, 2009, customers owed Jomerans $19,500 for services provided in 2009. Calculate the revenue for 2009 using (a) the cash basis of accounting, and (b) the accrual basis of accounting.

Action Plan

- For the cash basis of accounting, revenue is equal to the cash received.
- For the accrual basis of accounting, use the revenue recognition principle. Report revenue in the period in which it is earned, not when it is collected.
- Under the accrual basis of accounting, cash collected in 2009 for revenue earned in 2008 should not be included in the 2009 revenue.
- Under the accrual basis of accounting, amounts still owing at the end of 2009 for services provided in 2009 should be included in the 2009 revenue.

Solution

(a) Revenue using the cash basis of accounting   <u>$125,000</u>

(b) Cash received from customers in 2009 $125,000
     Deduct: Collection of 2008 receivables   (30,000)
     Add: Amounts owing at December 31, 2009   <u>19,500</u>
     Revenue using the accrual basis of accounting   <u>$114,500</u>

The Navigator

The Basics of Adjusting Entries

For revenues to be recorded in the period in which they are earned, and for expenses to be matched with the revenue they generate, adjusting entries are made to update accounts at the end of the accounting period. Adjusting entries make it possible to produce relevant financial information at the end of the accounting period. Thus, the balance sheet reports appropriate assets, liabilities, and shareholders' equity at the statement date, and the statement of earnings shows the proper revenues, expenses, and net earnings (or loss) for the period.

Adjusting entries are necessary because the trial balance—the first pulling together of the transaction data—may not contain complete and up-to-date data. This is true for several reasons:

1. Some events are not recorded daily, because it would not be useful or efficient to do so. Examples are the use of supplies and the earning of wages by employees.
2. Some costs are not recorded during the accounting period, because these costs expire with the passage of time rather than as a result of recurring daily transactions. Examples include rent, insurance, and depreciation.
3. Some items may be unrecorded. An example is a utility service bill that will not be received until the next accounting period. The bill, however, covers services delivered in the current accounting period.

Adjusting entries are required every time financial statements are prepared, and preparing adjusting entries is often a long and detailed process. Each account in the trial balance needs to be analyzed to see if it is complete and up to date, which requires an understanding of the company's operations and the interrelationship of accounts. To accumulate the adjustment data, a company may need to count its remaining supplies. It may also need to prepare supporting schedules of insurance policies, rental agreements, and other commitments.

Adjustment data are often not available until after the end of the period. For example, telephone and other bills will not be received until after the month end or year end. Carter Scott, in our feature story, notes that Western will not receive its construction bill until around May 15 for the month of April, which is after its year end. In such cases, the data are gathered as soon as possible after the end of the period and adjusting entries are made, but they are still dated as at the balance sheet date.

Types of Adjusting Entries

Adjusting entries can be classified as either prepayments or accruals. Each of these classes has two subcategories, as follows:

Prepayments
1. **Prepaid expenses**: Expenses paid in cash and recorded as assets before they are used or consumed
2. **Unearned revenues**: Cash received and recorded as liabilities before revenue is earned

Accruals
1. **Accrued revenues:** Revenues earned but not yet received in cash or recorded
2. **Accrued expenses:** Expenses incurred but not yet paid in cash or recorded

Specific examples and explanations of each type of adjustment are provided in the following pages. Each example is based on the October 31 trial balance of Sierra Corporation, from Chapter 3, shown again here in Illustration 4-2.

◄ Illustration 4-2

Trial balance

SIERRA CORPORATION
Trial Balance
October 31, 2009

	Debit	Credit
Cash	$15,200	
Advertising supplies	2,500	
Prepaid insurance	600	
Office equipment	5,000	
Notes payable		$ 5,000
Accounts payable		2,500
Unearned service revenue		1,200
Common shares		10,000
Dividends	500	
Service revenue		10,000
Salaries expense	4,000	
Rent expense	900	
	$28,700	$28,700

For illustration purposes, we assume that Sierra Corporation uses an accounting period of one month. Thus, monthly adjusting entries need to be made.

Adjusting Entries for Prepayments

Prepayments are either prepaid expenses or unearned revenues. Adjusting entries for prepayments record the portion of the payment that applies to the current accounting period. This means that for prepaid expenses, the adjusting entry records the expense that applies to the current period and reduces the asset account where the prepaid expense was originally recorded. This type of adjustment is necessary because the prepayment no longer has future benefit and consequently is no longer an asset—it has been used.

For unearned revenues, the adjusting entry records the revenue earned in the period and reduces the liability account where the unearned revenue was originally recorded. This type of adjustment is necessary because the unearned revenue is no longer owed and consequently is no longer a liability—the service has been provided and the revenue earned.

Prepaid Expenses

Costs that are paid for in cash before they are used are recorded as prepaid expenses. When such a cost is incurred, an asset (prepaid) account should be increased (debited)—to show the service or benefit that will be received in the future—and cash should be decreased (credited). In a few cases, the asset is purchased on account, but ultimately cash is paid.

Prepaid expenses are costs that expire either with the passage of time (e.g., insurance, rent, and depreciable assets) or through use (e.g., supplies). It is not practical to record the expiration of these costs on a daily basis. Instead, we record these expired costs when financial statements are prepared. At each statement date, adjusting entries are made for two purposes: (1) to record the expenses (expired costs) applicable to the current accounting period, and (2) to show the remaining amounts (unexpired costs) in the asset accounts.

Until prepaid expenses are adjusted, assets are overstated and expenses are understated. If expenses are understated, then net earnings and shareholders' equity will be overstated. As shown below, **an adjusting entry for prepaid expenses results in an increase (a debit) to an expense account and a decrease (a credit) to an asset account.**

study objective 2

Prepare adjusting entries for prepayments.

Helpful Hint A cost can be an asset or an expense. If the cost has future benefits (i.e., the benefits have not yet expired), it is an asset. If the cost has no future benefits (i.e., the benefits have expired), it is an expense.

Prepaid Expenses

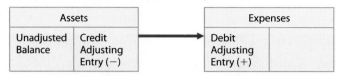

Assets			Expenses	
Unadjusted Balance	Credit Adjusting Entry (−)	→	Debit Adjusting Entry (+)	

We now look in more detail at some specific types of prepaid expenses, beginning with supplies.

Supplies. The purchase of supplies, such as paper, results in an increase (a debit) to an asset account. During the accounting period, supplies are used. Rather than record supplies expense as the supplies are used, supplies expense is recognized at the end of the accounting period. At that time, the company must count the remaining supplies. The difference between the balance in the supplies (asset) account and the actual cost of supplies on hand gives the supplies used (an expense) for that period.

Recall from Chapter 3 that Sierra Corporation purchased advertising supplies costing $2,500 on October 9. This is an example of a prepayment made on account, rather than by paying cash. The payment was recorded by increasing (debiting) the asset account Advertising Supplies and increasing (crediting) the liability account Accounts Payable. The Advertising Supplies account therefore shows a balance of $2,500 in the October 31 trial balance. A count at the close of business on October 31 reveals that $1,000 of supplies are still on hand. Thus, the cost of supplies used is $1,500 ($2,500 − $1,000).

This use of supplies decreases an asset, Advertising Supplies. It also decreases shareholders' equity by increasing an expense account, Advertising Supplies Expense. The use of supplies is recorded as follows:

A = L + SE
−1,500   −1,500
Cash flows: no effect

Oct.	31	Advertising Supplies Expense	1,500	
		Advertising Supplies		1,500
		(To record supplies used)		

After the adjusting entry is posted, the two supplies accounts are as follows in T account form:

Advertising Supplies				Advertising Supplies Expense			
Oct.	9	2,500	Oct. 31 Adj. 1,500	Oct.	31 Adj.	1,500	
Oct.	31 Bal.	1,000		Oct.	31 Bal.	1,500	

The asset account Advertising Supplies now shows a balance of $1,000, which is equal to the cost of supplies on hand at the statement date. In addition, Advertising Supplies Expense shows a balance of $1,500, which equals the cost of supplies used in October. If the adjusting entry (abbreviated in the T account above as "Adj.") is not made, October expenses will be understated and net earnings overstated by $1,500. Moreover, as the accounting equation shows, both assets and shareholders' equity will be overstated by $1,500 on the October 31 balance sheet.

Insurance. Companies purchase insurance to protect themselves from losses caused by fire, theft, and unforeseen accidents. Insurance must be paid in advance, often for one year. Insurance payments (premiums) made in advance are normally recorded in the asset account Prepaid Insurance. At the financial statement date, it is necessary to make an adjustment to increase (debit) Insurance Expense and decrease (credit) Prepaid Insurance for the cost of insurance that has expired during the period.

On October 6, Sierra Corporation paid $600 for a one-year insurance policy. Coverage began on October 1. The payment was recorded by increasing (debiting) Prepaid Insurance when it was paid. This account shows a balance of $600 in the October 31 trial balance. An analysis of the insurance policy reveals that $50 of insurance expires each month ($600 ÷ 12 mos.). The expiration of the prepaid insurance would be recorded as follows:

A = L + SE
−50   −50
Cash flows: no effect

Oct.	31	Insurance Expense	50	
		Prepaid Insurance		50
		(To record insurance expired)		

After the adjusting entry is posted, the accounts appear as follows:

Prepaid Insurance				Insurance Expense			
Oct.	6	600	Oct. 31 Adj. 50	Oct. 31 Adj.	50		
Oct. 31 Bal.		550		Oct. 31 Bal.	50		

The asset Prepaid Insurance shows a balance of $550, which represents the cost that applies to the remaining 11 months of insurance coverage (11 × $50). At the same time, the balance in Insurance Expense is equal to the insurance cost that was used in October. If this adjustment is not made, October expenses will be understated and net earnings overstated by $50. Moreover, both assets and shareholders' equity will be overstated by $50 on the October 31 balance sheet.

Depreciation. A company typically owns a variety of assets that have long lives, such as buildings and equipment. Each one is recorded as an asset, rather than as an expense, in the year it is acquired because these long-lived assets provide a service for many years. The period of service is called the useful life.

From an accounting standpoint, the acquisition of long-lived assets is essentially a long-term prepayment for services. Similar to other prepaid expenses, there is a need to recognize the cost that has been used (an expense) during the period and to report the unused cost (an asset) at the end of the period. Depreciation is the process of allocating the cost of a long-lived asset, such as property, plant and equipment, to expense over its useful life. Only assets with specified useful lives are depreciated. We call them depreciable assets. When an asset, such as land, has an unlimited useful life, it is not depreciated.

While the term *depreciation* is normally used in relation to property, plant, and equipment, the term *amortization* is used in relation to intangible assets. It means the same thing—the allocation of the cost of a long-lived asset to expense over its useful life. We will learn about amortizing intangible assets in Chapter 9. As was mentioned in earlier chapters, some companies use the term *amortization* in place of *depreciation*.

One point about depreciation is very important to understand: **Depreciation is an allocation concept, not a valuation concept.** That is, we depreciate an asset to allocate its cost to the periods over which we use it. We are not trying to record a change in the actual value of the asset. We are only trying to match expenses with the revenues they generate in each period.

Calculation of Depreciation. A common practice for calculating depreciation expense is to divide the cost of the asset by its useful life. This is known as the straight-line method of depreciation. Of course, at the time an asset is acquired, its useful life is not known with any certainty. It must therefore be estimated. In other words, depreciation is an estimate rather than a factual measurement of the cost that has expired.

Sierra Corporation purchased office equipment that cost $5,000 on October 1. If its useful life is expected to be five years, annual depreciation is $1,000 ($5,000 ÷ 5). Illustration 4-3 shows the formula to calculate depreciation expense in its simplest form.

◀ Illustration 4-3

Formula for depreciation

Of course, if you are calculating depreciation for partial periods, the annual expense amount must be adjusted for the correct portion of the year. For example, if we wish to determine the depreciation for one month, we would multiply the annual result by one-twelfth as there are 12 months in a year. Calculating depreciation will be refined and examined in more detail in Chapter 9.

For Sierra Corporation, depreciation on the office equipment is estimated to be $83 per month ($1,000 × 1/12). Accordingly, depreciation for October is recognized by this adjusting entry:

Oct. 31	Depreciation Expense	83	
	Accumulated Depreciation—Office Equipment		83
	(To record monthly depreciation)		

A	=	L	+	SE
−83				−83

Cash flows: no effect

After the adjusting entry is posted, the accounts appear as follows:

Accumulated Depreciation–Office Equipment			Depreciation Expense		
	Oct. 31 Adj.	83	Oct. 31 Adj.	83	
	Oct. 31 Bal.	83	Oct. 31 Bal.	83	

The balance in the Accumulated Depreciation account will increase by $83 each month until the asset is fully depreciated in five years. Accumulated depreciation represents the cumulative total of the depreciation expense since the asset was purchased, less any reductions when assets are sold (which we will learn about in Chapter 9).

As in the case of other prepaid expenses, if this adjusting entry is not made, total assets, shareholders' equity, and net earnings will all be overstated by $83 and depreciation expense will be understated by $83.

Helpful Hint Every contra account has increases, decreases, and normal balances that are opposite to those of the account it relates to.

Statement Presentation. As we learned in Chapter 2, a contra account is an account that is offset against (deducted from) a related account on the statement of earnings or balance sheet. Accumulated Depreciation—Office Equipment is a **contra asset account**. That means it is offset against an asset account (Office Equipment) on the balance sheet. Its normal balance is a credit—the opposite of the normal debit balance of its related account, Office Equipment.

There is a simple reason for using a separate contra account instead of decreasing (crediting) Office Equipment: using this account discloses both the original cost of the equipment and the total estimated cost that has expired to date. This also helps separate actual amounts (cost) from estimated amounts (accumulated depreciation).

In the balance sheet, Accumulated Depreciation—Office Equipment is deducted from the related asset account as follows:

Office equipment	$5,000
Less: Accumulated depreciation—office equipment	83
Carrying amount	4,917

The difference between the cost of a depreciable asset and its related accumulated depreciation is referred to as the **carrying amount** of that asset. The carrying amount is also commonly known as net book value, or simply book value. Shoppers Drug Mart, for example, uses amortization instead of depreciation and net book value instead of carrying amount in its financial statements.

In the above illustration, the carrying amount of the office equipment at the balance sheet date is $4,917. Be sure to understand that, except at acquisition, the carrying amount of the asset and its fair value (the price at which it could be sold) are two different amounts. As noted earlier, the purpose of depreciation is not to state an asset's value, but to allocate its cost over time.

Unearned Revenue

Alternative Terminology *Unearned revenues* are also called *deferred revenues*.

Cash received before revenue is earned is recorded by increasing (crediting) a liability account for **unearned revenues**. Items like rent, magazine subscriptions, and customer deposits for future service may result in unearned revenues. Airlines, such as Air Canada, treat receipts from the sale of tickets as unearned revenue until the flight service is provided. Similarly, tuition fees received by universities before the academic session begins are considered unearned revenue, as at the University of Western Ontario in our feature story.

Unearned revenues are the opposite of prepaid expenses. Indeed, unearned revenue on the books of one company is likely to be a prepayment on the books of the company that has made the advance payment. For example, if identical accounting periods are assumed, your landlord will have unearned rent revenue when you (the tenant) have prepaid rent.

When a payment is received for services that will be provided in a future accounting period, Cash should be increased (debited) and an unearned revenue account (a liability) should be increased (credited) to recognize the obligation that exists. Unearned revenues are later earned when the service is provided to the customer.

It is not practical to make daily journal entries as the revenue is earned. Instead, recognition of earned revenue is delayed until the adjustment process. At that time an adjusting entry is then made to record the revenue that has been earned during the period and to show the liability that remains at the end of the accounting period. Typically, until the adjustment is made, liabilities are overstated and revenues are understated. If revenues are understated, then net earnings and shareholders' equity are also understated. As shown below, **the adjusting entry for unearned revenues results in a decrease (debit) to a liability account and an increase (credit) to a revenue account.**

Unearned Revenues

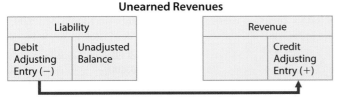

Returning to our example, we note that Sierra Corporation received $1,200 on October 2 from R. Knox for advertising services expected to be completed before the end of next month, November 30. The payment was credited to Unearned Service Revenue, and this liability account shows a balance of $1,200 in the October 31 trial balance. From an evaluation of the work performed by Sierra for Knox during October, it is determined that $400 worth of work was done in October.

The following adjusting entry is made:

Oct.	31	Unearned Service Revenue		400	
		Service Revenue			400
		(To record revenue earned)			

A	=	L	+	SE
		−400		+400

Cash flows: no effect

After the adjusting entry is posted, the accounts appear as follows:

Unearned Service Revenue						Service Revenue			
Oct.	31	Adj.	400	Oct.	2	1,200		Oct.	13	10,000
				Oct.	31	Bal.	800		31	Adj.	400
								Oct.	31	Bal.	10,400

The liability Unearned Service Revenue now shows a balance of $800, which represents the remaining advertising services expected to be performed in the future. At the same time, Service Revenue shows total revenue earned in October of $10,400. If this adjustment is not made, revenues and net earnings will be understated by $400 in the statement of earnings. Moreover, liabilities will be overstated by $400 and shareholders' equity will be understated by that amount on the October 31 balance sheet.

👤 ACCOUNTING MATTERS! | Management Perspective

Retailers and consumers both love them. A recent survey found that gift cards were second only to clothing as the most frequently given present during the holiday season. According to a Statistics Canada survey, 82 percent of Canadian retailers offer gift cards for sale.

The most successful gift card in North America is offered by Starbucks. About 96 million Starbucks cards have been used since they were launched in 2001—and customers have reloaded those cards more than 38 million times.

Retailers initially record the sale of gift cards as unearned revenue, and subsequently record the gift card purchase as a sale when it is actually redeemed for merchandise. But what about the gift cards that are never redeemed? According to the Consumers' Association of Canada, one in four gift cards is not redeemed. Electronics retailer Best Buy reported a U.S. $46-million gain in 2007 from gift cards that were unlikely to be redeemed. Gains such as this are likely to decline in future as a result of new legislation in many provinces which eliminates the use of expiry dates on gift cards.

Source: "Gift Cards: The Lure of Plastic," CBC News, December 10, 2007.

BEFORE YOU GO ON...

Review It

1. What are the four types of adjusting entries?
2. What is the effect on assets, liabilities, shareholders' equity, revenues, expenses, and net earnings if an adjusting entry for a prepaid expense is not made?
3. What was the amount of Shoppers Drug Mart's accumulated amortization and net book value of its property and equipment as at December 29, 2007? (*Hint:* These amounts are reported in the notes to the financial statements.) The answer to this question is provided at the end of this chapter.
4. What is the effect on assets, liabilities, shareholders' equity, revenues, expenses, and net earnings if an adjusting entry for unearned revenue is not made?

Do It

Hammond, Inc.'s general ledger includes these selected accounts on March 31, 2009, before adjusting entries are prepared:

	Debit	Credit
Prepaid insurance	$ 3,600	
Office supplies	2,800	
Office equipment	25,000	
Accumulated depreciation—office equipment		$9,583
Unearned service revenue		9,200

An analysis of the accounts shows the following:

1. The insurance policy is a one-year policy, effective March 1.
2. Office supplies on hand total $800.
3. The office equipment was purchased April 1, 2007, and is estimated to have a useful life of five years.
4. Half of the unearned service revenue was earned in March.

Prepare the adjusting entries for the month of March.

Action Plan
• Make sure you prepare adjustments for the appropriate time period.
• Adjusting entries for prepaid expenses require a debit to an expense account and a credit to an asset account.
• Adjusting entries for unearned revenues require a debit to a liability account and a credit to a revenue account.

Solution

1. Mar. 31	Insurance Expense		300	
	Prepaid Insurance			300
	(To record insurance expired: $3,600 ÷ 12)			
2. 31	Office Supplies Expense		2,000	
	Office Supplies			2,000
	(To record supplies used: $2,800 – $800)			
3. 31	Depreciation Expense		417	
	Accumulated Depreciation—Office Equipment			417
	(To record monthly depreciation: $25,000 ÷ 5 × 1/12)			
4. 31	Unearned Service Revenue		4,600	
	Service Revenue			4,600
	(To record revenue earned: $9,200 × 1/2)			

The Navigator

Adjusting Entries for Accruals

study objective 3

Prepare adjusting entries for accruals.

The second category of adjusting entries is **accruals**. Adjusting entries for accruals are required in order to record revenues earned, or expenses incurred, in the current accounting period. Unlike prepayments, accruals have not been recognized through daily entries and thus are not yet reflected in the accounts. Until an accrual adjustment is made, the revenue account (and the related asset account), or the expense account (and the related liability account), is understated. Thus, adjusting entries for accruals will increase both a balance sheet account and a statement of earnings account.

There are two types of adjusting entries for accruals—accrued revenues and accrued expenses. We now look at each type in more detail.

Accrued Revenues

Alternative Terminology
Accrued revenues are also called accrued receivables.

Revenues that have been earned but not yet received in cash or recorded at the statement date are **accrued revenues**. Accrued revenues may accumulate (accrue) with the passing of time, as in the case of interest revenue. Or they may result from services that have been performed but not yet billed or collected, such as fees. The former are unrecorded because, as when interest is earned, they do not involve daily transactions. The latter may be unrecorded because only a portion of the total service has been provided and the client will not be billed until the service has been completed.

An adjusting entry is required for two purposes: (1) to show the receivable that exists at the balance sheet date, and (2) to record the revenue that has been earned during the period. Until the adjustment is made, both assets and revenues are understated. Consequently, net earnings and shareholders' equity will also be understated. As shown below, **an adjusting entry for accrued revenues results in an increase (a debit) to an asset account and an increase (a credit) to a revenue account**.

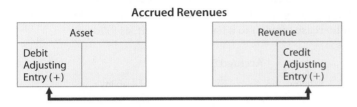

Accrued Revenues

In October, Sierra Corporation earned $200 for advertising services that were not billed to clients before October 31. Because these services have not been billed, they have not been recorded. The adjusting entry would be as follows:

Oct. 31	Accounts Receivable	200	
	Service Revenue		200
	(To accrue revenue earned but not billed or collected)		

A	=	L	+	SE
+200				+200

Cash flows: no effect

After the adjusting entry is posted, the accounts appear as follows:

Accounts Receivable					Service Revenue		
Oct. 13	10,000	Oct. 30	10,000		Oct. 13		10,000
Oct. 31 Adj.	200				31 Adj.		400
Oct. 31 Bal.	200				31 Adj.		200
					Oct. 31 Bal.		10,600

The asset Accounts Receivable shows that $200 is owed by clients at the balance sheet date. The balance of $10,600 in Service Revenue represents the total revenue earned during the month. If the adjusting entry is not made, assets and shareholders' equity on the balance sheet, and revenues and net earnings on the statement of earnings, will be understated.

In the next accounting period, cash will be collected from clients for services provided in October, as well as for services provided in November. When this occurs, the entry to record the collection should recognize that $200 of the revenue was earned in October and has already been recorded in the October 31 adjusting entry and should not be re-recorded. For example, assume that $2,500 of revenue is collected from clients on November 6. Of this amount, $2,300 relates to services provided for cash in the first week of November, and $200 is for the services provided in October. The collection of cash from clients will be recorded as follows:

Nov. 6	Cash	2,500	
	Accounts Receivable		200
	Service Revenue		2,300
	(To record collection of account and cash receipts from services provided)		

A	=	L	+	SE
+2,500				+2,300
−200				

⬆ Cash flows: +2,500

Some accountants prefer to reverse accrual entries at the beginning of a new accounting period rather than try to remember what entries had been made in the prior period. A reversing entry is made at the beginning of the next accounting period. It is the exact opposite of the adjusting entry made in the previous period. The preparation of reversing entries is an optional accounting procedure that is not a required step in the accounting cycle and will not be discussed here.

Accrued Expenses

Expenses incurred but not yet paid or recorded at the statement date are called accrued expenses. Interest, rent, salaries, property taxes, and income taxes are common examples of accrued expenses. Accrued expenses result from the same factors as accrued revenues. In fact, an accrued expense on the books of one company is an accrued revenue to another company. For example, the $200 accrual of service revenue for Sierra Corporation discussed above is an accrued expense for the client that received the service.

Adjustments for accrued expenses are necessary to (1) record the obligations that exist at the balance sheet date, and (2) recognize the expenses that apply to the current accounting period. Until the adjustment is made, both liabilities and expenses are understated. Consequently, net earnings and shareholders' equity are overstated. **An adjusting entry for accrued expenses results in an increase (debit) to an expense account and an increase (credit) to a liability account,** as follows:

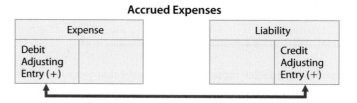

We now look in more detail at some specific types of accrued expenses, beginning with accrued interest.

Interest. Sierra Corporation signed a three-month note payable for $5,000 on October 1. The note requires interest at an annual rate of 6 percent. The amount of the interest accumulation is determined by three factors: (1) the face value, or principal amount, of the note, (2) the interest rate, which is always expressed as an annual rate, and (3) the length of time that the note is outstanding (unpaid).

Interest is sometimes due monthly, and sometimes when the principal is due. In this instance, interest is due on the $5,000 note at its due date, three months in the future. The total interest due at that time will be $75 ($5,000 × 6% × 3/12), or $25 for one month. Note that the time period is expressed as a fraction of a year.

The formula for calculating interest and how it applies to Sierra Corporation for the month of October are shown in Illustration 4-4.

Helpful Hint To make the illustration easier to understand, a simplified method of interest calculation is used. In reality, interest is calculated using the exact number of days in the interest period and year.

Illustration 4-4 ➡

Formula for calculating interest

The accrual of interest at October 31 is reflected in an adjusting entry, as follows:

A = L + SE
+25 −25
Cash flows: no effect

Oct. 31	Interest Expense	25	
	Interest Payable		25
	(To accrue interest on note payable)		

After the adjusting entry is posted, the accounts appear as follows:

Interest Expense			Interest Payable		
Oct. 31 Adj.	25			Oct. 31 Adj.	25
Oct. 31 Bal.	25			Oct. 31 Bal.	25

Interest Expense shows the interest charges for the month of October. The amount of interest owed at the statement date is shown in Interest Payable. It will not be paid until the note comes due on January 1, 2010. The Interest Payable account is used, instead of crediting Notes Payable, to disclose the two different types of obligations—interest and principal—in the accounts and statements. If this adjusting entry is not made, liabilities and interest expense will be understated and net earnings and shareholders' equity will be overstated.

Since this is a three-month note, Sierra will also need to make identical adjustments at the end of November and December to accrue for interest expense incurred in each of these months. After the three adjusting entries have been posted, the balance in Interest Payable will be $75 ($25 × 3). The following entry is made on January 1, 2010, when the note and interest are paid:

Jan.	1	Interest Payable	75	
		Note Payable	5,000	
		Cash		5,075
		(To record payment of note and interest)		

A = L + SE
  −5,075   −75
           −5,000
⬇Cash flows: −5,075

This entry does two things: (1) it eliminates the liability for Interest Payable that was recorded in the October 31, November 30, and December 31 adjusting entries; and (2) it eliminates the note payable. Notice also that the account Interest Expense is not included in this entry, because the full amount of interest incurred was accrued in previous months.

Salaries. Some types of expenses, such as employee salaries, are paid for after the services have been performed and require an accrual adjustment when financial statements are prepared. For example, at its year end the University of Western Ontario, described in our feature story, accrues vacation pay and salary for approximately 3,500 faculty and staff.

At Sierra Corporation, salaries are paid every two weeks. Sierra's four employees were last paid on October 23. The next payment of salaries will not occur until November 6. As shown on the calendar in Illustration 4-5, there are five working days that remain unpaid for October (October 26–30).

◄ Illustration 4-5

Calendar showing Sierra
Corporation's pay periods

At October 31, the salaries for these five days (Monday, October 26, through Friday, October 30) represent an accrued expense and related liability for Sierra. As the four employees each receive a salary of $500 a week for a five-day work week from Monday to Friday, or $100 a day, accrued salaries at October 31 are $2,000 (5 days × $100/day × 4 employees). This accrual increases both the expense account Salaries Expense and the liability account Salaries Payable through the following adjusting entry:

Oct.	31	Salaries Expense	2,000	
		Salaries Payable		2,000
		(To record accrued salaries)		

A = L + SE
        +2,000   −2,000
Cash flows: no effect

After this adjusting entry is posted, the accounts are as follows:

Salaries Expense			Salaries Payable		
Oct. 23	4,000			Oct. 31 Adj.	2,000
31 Adj.	2,000			Oct. 31 Bal.	2,000
Oct. 31 Bal.	6,000				

After this adjustment, the balance in Salaries Expense of $6,000 (15 days × $100/day × 4 employees) is the actual salary expense for October. The balance in Salaries Payable of $2,000 is the amount of the liability for salaries owed as at October 31. If the $2,000 adjustment for salaries is not recorded, Sierra's expenses and liabilities will be understated by $2,000. Net earnings and shareholders' equity will be overstated by $2,000.

▸ Accrual Accounting Concepts

At Sierra Corporation, salaries are payable every two weeks. Consequently, the next payday is November 6, when total salaries of $4,000 will again be paid. The payment consists of $2,000 of salaries payable at October 31 plus $2,000 of salaries expense for November (5 days × $100/day × 4 employees). Therefore, the following entry is made on November 6:

A	=	L	+	SE
−4,000		−2,000		−2,000

⬇ Cash flows: −4,000

Nov.	6	Salaries Payable (Oct. 26–30)		2,000	
		Salaries Expense (Nov. 2–6)		2,000	
		Cash			4,000
		(Paid salaries for Oct. 26–Nov. 6)			

This entry eliminates the liability for salaries payable that was recorded in the October 31 adjusting entry and records the proper amount of salaries expense for the period between Monday, November 2, and Friday, November 6.

Income Taxes.   For accounting purposes, corporate income taxes must be accrued based on the current year's estimated earnings. Sierra's monthly income tax expense is estimated to be $350. This accrual increases an expense account, Income Tax Expense, and a liability account, Income Tax Payable.   The adjusting entry is:

A	=	L	+	SE
		+350		−350

Cash flows: no effect

Oct.	31	Income Tax Expense		350	
		Income Tax Payable			350
		(To record accrued income taxes)			

After this adjusting entry is posted, the accounts are as follows:

Income Tax Expense				Income Tax Payable		
Oct.	31	Adj.	350		Oct.	31	Adj.	350
Oct.	31	Bal.	350		Oct.	31	Bal.	350

Corporations are required to pay corporate income taxes in monthly instalments. The instalment payment is normally based on the income tax that was actually payable for the prior year. If there was no prior year, as is the case with Sierra, or if there was no tax payable in the prior year, then no income tax instalment payments are required. However, the liability must still be accrued based on the current year's estimated earnings.

If the adjustment for income taxes is not recorded, Sierra's expenses and liabilities will be understated by $350 and its net earnings and shareholders' equity will be overstated by $350.

BEFORE YOU GO ON...

▸ **Review It**
1. What is the effect on assets, liabilities, shareholders' equity, revenues, expenses, and net earnings if an adjusting entry for an accrued revenue is not made?
2. What is the effect on assets, liabilities, shareholders' equity, revenues, expenses, and net earnings if an adjusting entry for an accrued expense is not made?

▸ **Do It**
Micro Computer Services Inc. began operations on August 1, 2009, and management has decided to prepare monthly financial statements. The following information is for August:
1. Revenue earned but not yet billed or recorded for August totalled $1,100.
2. On August 1, the company borrowed $30,000 from a local bank on a one-year note payable. The interest rate is 5% and interest is payable at maturity.
3. At August 31, the company owed its employees $800 in salaries that will be paid on September 1.
4. Estimated income tax payable for August totalled $275.

Prepare the adjusting entries needed at August 31.

Action Plan

Remember that accruals are entries that were not previously recorded; therefore, the adjustment pattern is different from the pattern for prepayments.

Adjusting entries for accrued revenues require a debit to a receivable account and a credit to a revenue account.

Adjusting entries for accrued expenses require a debit to an expense account and a credit to a liability account.

Recall that interest rates are always stated as an annual rate.

Solution:

1. Aug. 31	Accounts Receivable		1,100	
	Service Revenue			1,100
	(To accrue revenue earned but not billed or collected)			
2. 31	Interest Expense		125	
	Interest Payable			125
	(To record accrued interest: $\$30,000 \times 5\% \times \frac{1}{12}$)			
3. 31	Salaries Expense		800	
	Salaries Payable			800
	(To record accrued salaries)			
4. 31	Income Tax Expense		275	
	Income Tax Payable			275
	(To record accrued income taxes)			

The Navigator

Summary of Basic Relationships

The two basic types of adjusting entries—prepayments and accruals—are summarized below. Take some time to study and analyze the adjusting entries. **Be sure to note that each adjusting entry affects one balance sheet account and one statement of earnings account.**

	Type of Adjustment	Reason for Adjustment	Accounts before Adjustment	Adjusting Entry
Prepayments	Prepaid expenses	Prepaid expenses, originally recorded in asset accounts, have been used.	Assets overstated; expenses understated	Dr. Expense Cr. Asset
	Unearned revenues	Unearned revenues, initially recorded in liability accounts, have been earned.	Liabilities overstated; revenues understated	Dr. Liability Cr. Revenue
Accruals	Accrued revenues	Revenues have been earned but not yet received in cash or recorded.	Assets understated; revenues understated	Dr. Asset Cr. Revenue
	Accrued expenses	Expenses have been incurred but not yet paid or recorded.	Expenses understated; liabilities understated	Dr. Expense Cr. Liability

It is important to understand that adjusting entries never involve the Cash account (except for bank reconciliations, which we will study in Chapter 7). In the case of prepayments, cash has already been received or paid and recorded in the original journal entry. The adjusting entry simply reallocates, or adjusts, amounts between a balance sheet account (e.g., prepaid expenses or unearned revenues) and a statement of earnings account (e.g., expenses or revenues). In the case of accruals, cash will be received or paid in the future and recorded then. The adjusting entry simply records the receivable or payable and the related revenue or expense.

Sierra Corporation Illustration

The journalizing and posting of the adjusting entries described in this chapter for Sierra Corporation on October 31 are shown below and on the next page. As you review the general ledger, notice that the adjustments are highlighted in colour.

Note also that an account for retained earnings has been added in the general ledger. Because this is Sierra's first month of operations, there is no balance in the Retained Earnings account. Although accounts with a zero balance are not normally included in the trial balance, we have added it here to make it easier to prepare the statement of retained earnings in the next section. In addition, we will need to use this account again in the section on closing entries later in this chapter.

	GENERAL JOURNAL			
Date	Account Titles and Explanations		Debit	Credit
2009				
Oct. 31	Advertising Supplies Expense		1,500	
	Advertising Supplies			1,500
	(To record supplies used)			
31	Insurance Expense		50	
	Prepaid Insurance			50
	(To record insurance expired)			
31	Depreciation Expense		83	
	Accumulated Depreciation–Office Equipment			83
	(To record monthly depreciation)			
31	Unearned Service Revenue		400	
	Service Revenue			400
	(To record revenue earned)			
31	Accounts Receivable		200	
	Service Revenue			200
	(To accrue revenue earned but not billed or collected)			
31	Interest Expense		25	
	Interest Payable			25
	(To accrue interest on note payable)			
31	Salaries Expense		2,000	
	Salaries Payable			2,000
	(To record accrued salaries)			
31	Income Tax Expense		350	
	Income Tax Payable			350
	(To record accrued income taxes)			

GENERAL LEDGER	

Cash

Oct.	1	10,000	Oct.	1	5,000
	1	5,000		2	900
	2	1,200		6	600
	30	10,000		23	4,000
				26	500
Oct. 31 Bal.		15,200			

Accounts Receivable

Oct.	13	10,000	Oct.	30	10,000
	31	200			
Oct. 31 Bal.		200			

Income Tax Payable

			Oct.	31	350
			Oct.	31 Bal.	350

Common Shares

			Oct.	1	10,000
			Oct.	31 Bal.	10,000

Retained Earnings

			Oct.	1	0
			Oct.	31 Bal.	0

Advertising Supplies

Oct. 9	2,500	Oct. 31	1,500
Oct. 31 Bal.	1,000		

Prepaid Insurance

Oct. 6	600	Oct. 31	50
Oct. 31 Bal.	550		

Office Equipment

Oct. 1	5,000		
Oct. 31 Bal.	5,000		

Accumulated Depreciation–Office Equipment

		Oct. 31	83
		Oct. 31 Bal.	83

Notes Payable

		Oct. 1	5,000
		Oct. 31 Bal.	5,000

Accounts Payable

		Oct. 9	2,500
		Oct. 31 Bal.	2,500

Interest Payable

		Oct. 31	25
		Oct. 31 Bal.	25

Unearned Service Revenue

Oct. 31	400	Oct. 2	1,200
		Oct. 31 Bal.	800

Salaries Payable

		Oct. 31	2,000
		Oct. 31 Bal.	2,000

Dividends

Oct. 26	500		
Oct. 31 Bal.	500		

Service Revenue

		Oct. 13	10,000
		31	400
		31	200
		Oct. 31 Bal.	10,600

Salaries Expense

Oct. 23	4,000		
31	2,000		
Oct. 31 Bal.	6,000		

Advertising Supplies Expense

Oct. 31	1,500		
Oct. 31 Bal.	1,500		

Rent Expense

Oct. 2	900		
Oct. 31 Bal.	900		

Depreciation Expense

Oct. 31	83		
Oct. 31 Bal.	83		

Insurance Expense

Oct. 31	50		
Oct. 31 Bal.	50		

Interest Expense

Oct. 31	25		
Oct. 31 Bal.	25		

Income Tax Expense

Oct. 31	350		
Oct. 31 Bal.	350		

The Adjusted Trial Balance and Financial Statements

After all adjusting entries have been journalized and posted, another trial balance is prepared from the general ledger accounts. This trial balance is called an adjusted trial balance. It shows the balances of all accounts at the end of the accounting period, including those that have been adjusted. The purpose of an adjusted trial balance is to prove the equality of the total debit balances and the total credit balances in the ledger after all adjustments have been made. Because the accounts contain all the data that are needed for financial statements, the adjusted trial balance is the main source for the preparation of financial statements.

> **study objective 4**
>
> Describe the nature and purpose of the adjusted trial balance, and prepare one.

▸ Accrual Accounting Concepts

Preparing the Adjusted Trial Balance

The adjusted trial balance for Sierra Corporation presented in Illustration 4-6 has been prepared from the general ledger accounts shown in the previous section. Compare the adjusted trial balance to the unadjusted trial balance presented earlier in the chapter in Illustration 4-2. The amounts that are affected by the adjusting entries are highlighted in colour.

Illustration 4-6 ➡

Adjusted trial balance

	Debit	Credit
SIERRA CORPORATION		
Trial Balance		
October 31, 2009		
Cash	$15,200	
Accounts receivable	200	
Advertising supplies	1,000	
Prepaid insurance	550	
Office equipment	5,000	
Accumulated depreciation—office equipment		$ 83
Notes payable		5,000
Accounts payable		2,500
Interest payable		25
Unearned service revenue		800
Salaries payable		2,000
Income tax payable		350
Common shares		10,000
Retained earnings		0
Dividends	500	
Service revenue		10,600
Salaries expense	6,000	
Advertising supplies expense	1,500	
Rent expense	900	
Depreciation expense	83	
Insurance expense	50	
Interest expense	25	
Income tax expense	350	
	$31,358	$31,358

Preparing Financial Statements

Financial statements can be prepared directly from an adjusted trial balance. The relationships between the data in the adjusted trial balance of Sierra Corporation are presented in Illustration 4-7.

As Illustration 4-7 shows, the statement of earnings is prepared from the revenue and expense accounts. The statement of retained earnings is prepared from the Retained Earnings account, Dividends account, and the net earnings (or net loss) shown in the statement of earnings. The balance sheet is then prepared from the asset, liability, and shareholders' equity accounts. Shareholders' equity includes the ending retained earnings as reported in the statement of retained earnings.

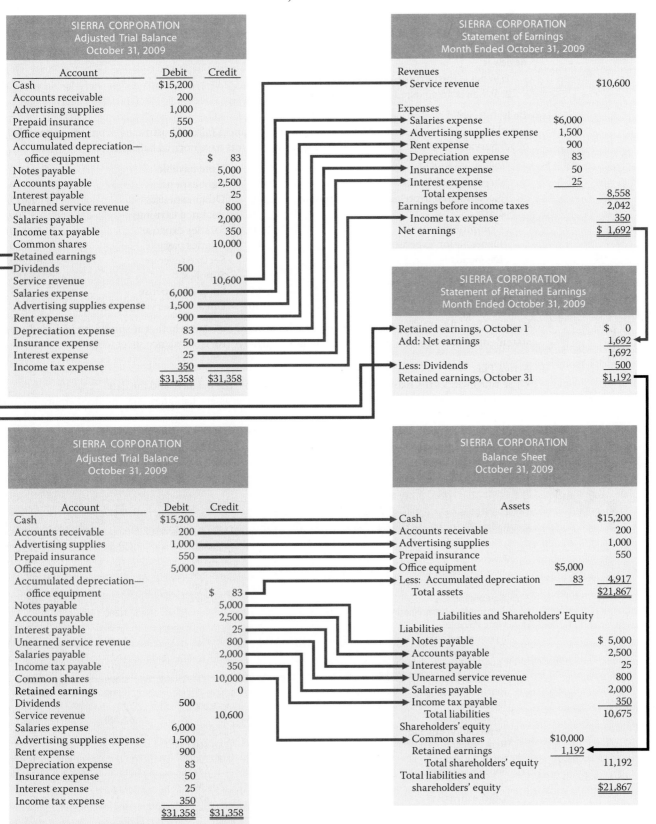

↑ Illustration 4-7

Preparation of the financial statements from the adjusted trial balance

BEFORE YOU GO ON...

➡ **Review It**
1. What is the purpose of an adjusted trial balance?
2. When is an adjusted trial balance prepared?

➡ **Do It**

Listed below, in alphabetical order, are the account balances (after adjustments) from the general ledger of KS Services Limited at December 31, 2009. All accounts have normal balances.

Accounts payable	$ 4,660	Note payable	$ 1,000
Accounts receivable	9,600	Rent expense	16,800
Accumulated depreciation—equipment	5,200	Other expenses	1,675
Cash	1,100	Retained earnings	3,700
Common shares	5,000	Salaries expense	30,700
Depreciation expense	2,600	Salaries payable	710
Dividends	1,000	Service revenue	67,200
Equipment	20,800	Supplies	180
Income tax expense	3,500	Supplies expense	475
Interest expense	50	Unearned service revenue	1,010

Prepare the adjusted trial balance. Beside each account, indicate whether it should be included on the statement of earnings (E), statement of retained earnings (RE), or balance sheet (BS).

Action Plan
• The title includes the name of the company, the type of trial balance, and the date.
• Accounts are listed in the same order as in a trial balance: assets, liabilities, shareholders' equity, revenues, and expenses.
• Apply the normal balance rules and list the account balances in the correct columns.
• Ensure that the totals of the two columns are equal.

Solution

KS SERVICES LIMITED
Adjusted Trial Balance
December 31, 2009

	Debit	Credit	Statement
Cash	$ 1,100		BS
Accounts receivable	9,600		BS
Supplies	180		BS
Equipment	20,800		BS
Accumulated depreciation—equipment		$ 5,200	BS
Note payable		1,000	BS
Accounts payable		4,660	BS
Salaries payable		710	BS
Unearned service revenue		1,010	BS
Common shares		5,000	BS
Retained earnings		3,700	RE & BS
Dividends	1,000		RE
Service revenue		67,200	E
Depreciation expense	2,600		E
Rent expense	16,800		E
Salaries expense	30,700		E
Supplies expense	475		E
Interest expense	50		E
Other expenses	1,675		E
Income tax expense	3,500		E
	$88,480	$88,480	

The Navigator

Closing the Books

In previous chapters, you learned that revenue and expense accounts and the dividends account are subdivisions of retained earnings, which is reported in the shareholders' equity section of the balance sheet. Because revenues, expenses, and dividends are only for a particular accounting period, they are considered **temporary accounts**. In contrast, all balance sheet accounts are considered **permanent accounts** because their balances are carried forward into future accounting periods. Illustration 4-8 identifies the accounts in each category.

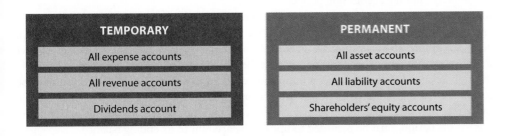

◀ Illustration 4-8

Temporary and permanent accounts

Preparing Closing Entries

At the end of the accounting period, the temporary account balances are transferred to the permanent shareholders' equity account Retained Earnings through the preparation of closing entries. **Closing entries** formally record in the general ledger the transfer of the balances in the revenue, expense, and dividends accounts to the Retained Earnings account. In Illustration 4-6, you will note that Retained Earnings has an adjusted balance of zero. Until the closing entries are made, the balance in Retained Earnings will be its balance at the beginning of the period. For Sierra, this is zero because it is Sierra's first year of operations. After closing entries are recorded and posted, the balance in Retained Earnings is the end-of-period balance. This ending account balance will now be the same as the balance reported in the statement of retained earnings and the balance sheet.

study objective 5

Prepare closing entries and a post-closing trial balance.

In addition to updating Retained Earnings to its ending balance, closing entries produce a zero balance in each temporary account. As a result, these accounts are ready to accumulate data about revenues, expenses, and dividends in the next accounting period separately from the data in the prior periods. Permanent accounts are not closed.

When closing entries are prepared, each revenue and expense account could be closed directly to Retained Earnings. This is common in computerized accounting systems where the closing process occurs automatically when it is time to start a new accounting period. However, in manual accounting systems, this practice can result in too much detail in the Retained Earnings account. Accordingly, the revenue and expense accounts are first closed to another temporary account, **Income Summary**. Only the resulting total amount (net earnings or net loss) is transferred from this account to the Retained Earnings account. Illustration 4-9 shows the closing process.

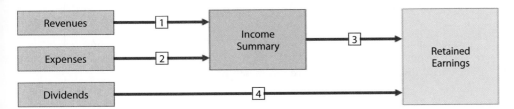

◀ Illustration 4-9

Closing process

To prepare closing entries, four steps are necessary:

1. To close revenue accounts: Debit each individual revenue account for its balance, and credit Income Summary for total revenues.
2. To close expense accounts: Debit Income Summary for total expenses, and credit each individual expense account for its balance.

3. To close Income Summary: Debit Income Summary for the balance in the account (or credit it if there is a net loss), and credit (debit) Retained Earnings.

4. To close the Dividends account: Debit Retained Earnings for the balance in the Dividends account, and credit Dividends.

Do not close Dividends to the Income Summary account along with expenses. Dividends are not expenses and do not affect net earnings.

Journalizing and posting closing entries is a required step in the accounting cycle. This step is done after financial statements have been prepared. Closing entries are generally recorded and posted only at the end of a company's annual accounting period.

Closing entries can be prepared directly from the general ledger or the adjusted trial balance. If we were to prepare closing entries for Sierra Corporation, we would likely use the adjusted trial balance presented earlier in the chapter in Illustration 4-6. In Sierra's case, all temporary accounts (Dividends, Service Revenue, and its seven different expense accounts) must be closed.

Even though Retained Earnings is not a temporary account, it will also be involved in the closing process. Remember that the Retained Earnings balance presented in the adjusted trial balance is the beginning balance, not the ending balance. This permanent account is not closed, but the net earnings (loss) and dividends for the period must be recorded to update the account to its ending balance.

Sierra's general journal (showing the closing entries) and its general ledger (showing the posting of the closing entries) follow:

	GENERAL JOURNAL		
Date	Account Titles and Explanation	Debit	Credit
	Closing Entries		
2009	(1)		
Oct. 31	Service Revenue	10,600	
	Income Summary		10,600
	(To close revenue account)		
	(2)		
31	Income Summary	8,908	
	Salaries Expense		6,000
	Advertising Supplies Expense		1,500
	Rent Expense		900
	Depreciation Expense		83
	Insurance Expense		50
	Interest Expense		25
	Income Tax Expense		350
	(To close expense accounts)		
	(3)		
31	Income Summary	1,692	
	Retained Earnings		1,692
	(To close net earnings to retained earnings)		
	(4)		
31	Retained Earnings	500	
	Dividends		500
	(To close dividends to retained earnings)		

GENERAL LEDGER

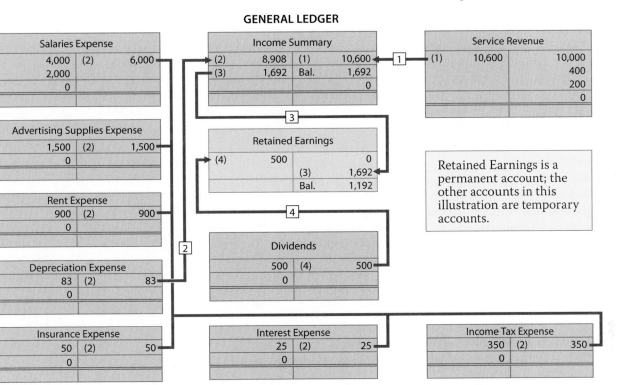

Stop and check your work after the closing entries are posted:

1. The balance in the Income Summary account, immediately before the final closing entry to transfer the balance to the Retained Earnings account, should equal the net earnings (or net loss) reported in the statement of earnings.
2. All temporary accounts (dividends, revenues, expenses, and income summary) should have zero balances.
3. The balance in the Retained Earnings account should equal the ending balance reported in the statement of retained earnings and balance sheet.

ACCOUNTING MATTERS! | Management Perspective

World-class companies can close their books in five days, while top performers can do it in three, says Scott Holland, IT practice leader at the Hackett Group, a strategic advisory firm. The Hackett Group's studies show that world-class companies spend 45 percent less time on their closing and reporting efforts than other companies *and* provide better information faster.

Mike Robins, the chief financial officer at Atomic Energy of Canada Limited (AECL), notes that AECL closes its books within three and a half days of month end. Like other top-performing companies, "AECL's ability to do a quick close gives managers sufficient time to analyze the results to make informed and timely decisions," says Mr. Robins.

Source: Galen Gruman, "Close Fast, Close Smart," CIO.com-Business Technology Leadership, February 26, 2007.

*	MARCH				*	
				1	2	3
4	5	6	7	8	9	10
11	12	13	14	15	16	17
18	19	20	21	22	23	24
25	26	27	28	29	30	31

Preparing a Post-Closing Trial Balance

After all closing entries are journalized and posted, another trial balance, called a post-closing trial balance, is prepared from the ledger. We have learned about the unadjusted and adjusted trial balances so far. The last trial balance is the **post-closing trial balance**, which lists all permanent accounts and their balances after closing entries are journalized and posted. The purpose of this trial balance is to prove the equality of the permanent account balances that are carried forward into the next accounting period. Since all temporary accounts will have zero balances, the post-closing trial balance will contain only permanent— balance sheet—accounts. Illustration 4-10 shows Sierra Corporation's post-closing trial balance.

Illustration 4-10 ➡

Post-closing trial balance

SIERRA CORPORATION Post-Closing Trial Balance October 31, 2009	Debit	Credit
Cash	$15,200	
Accounts receivable	200	
Advertising supplies	1,000	
Prepaid insurance	550	
Office equipment	5,000	
Accumulated depreciation—office equipment		$ 83
Notes payable		5,000
Accounts payable		2,500
Interest payable		25
Unearned revenue		800
Salaries payable		2,000
Income tax payable		350
Common shares		10,000
Retained earnings		1,192
	$21,950	$21,950

Summary of the Accounting Cycle

The accounting cycle was first introduced in Chapter 3, and is reproduced here in Illustration 4-11. The cycle begins with the analysis of business transactions and ends with the preparation of a post-closing trial balance. The steps are done in sequence and are repeated in each accounting period.

Steps 1 to 3 may occur daily during the accounting period, as we learned in Chapter 3. Steps 4 to 7 are done on a periodic basis, such as monthly, quarterly, or annually. Steps 8 and 9, closing entries and a post-closing trial balance, are usually prepared only at the end of a company's annual accounting period.

Illustration 4-11 ➡

Steps in the accounting cycle

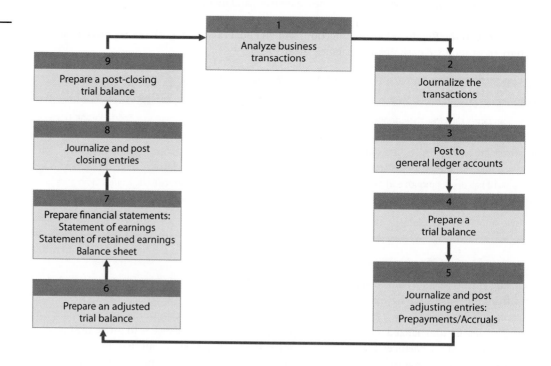

BEFORE YOU GO ON...

Review It

1. How do permanent accounts differ from temporary accounts?
2. What four different types of entries are required in closing the books?
3. After closing entries are posted, what amount on what financial statement should agree with the balance in the Retained Earnings account?
4. What are the differences between a trial balance, an adjusted trial balance, and a post-closing trial balance?

Do It

The adjusted trial balance for Nguyen Corporation shows the following selected accounts: Dividends $500; Common Shares $30,000; Retained Earnings $12,000; Service Revenue $18,000; Rent Expense $1,500; Supplies Expense $500; Salaries Expense $8,000; and Income Tax Expense $2,000. Prepare the closing entries at December 31.

Action Plan

• Debit each individual revenue account for its balance and credit the total to the Income Summary account.
• Credit each individual expense account for its balance and debit the total to the Income Summary account.
• Stop and check your work: Does the balance in the Income Summary account equal the reported net earnings (loss)?
• If there are net earnings, debit the balance in the Income Summary account and credit the amount to the Retained Earnings account (do the opposite if the result is a net loss).
• Credit the balance in the Dividends account and debit the amount to the Retained Earnings account. Do not close Dividends with the expenses.

Solution

Dec. 31	Service Revenue	18,000	
	Income Summary		18,000
	(To close revenue account)		
31	Income Summary	12,000	
	Rent Expense		1,500
	Supplies Expense		500
	Salaries Expense		8,000
	Income Tax Expense		2,000
	(To close expense accounts)		
31	Income Summary	6,000	
	Retained Earnings		6,000
	(To close income summary)		
31	Retained Earnings	500	
	Dividends		500
	(To close dividends)		

The Navigator

ALL ABOUT YOU

Are Your Electronics a Liability?

Do you have an old television or computer that needs replacing? Many people do, as growth and rapid advancements in electronics technology are major factors in the increase of e-waste. You may have outdated electronic products stored in your, or your parents', garage or basement. Consumer product manufacturers continue to focus more on performance and price than on the end-of-life management of electronic equipment.

Environment Canada reports that 158,000 tonnes of e-waste are accumulating in Canadian landfills each year, and that amount is expected to triple by 2010. Some provincial governments along with the electronics industry are developing plans to recycle or reuse this e-waste. Old televisions and computers are loaded with lead, cadmium, mercury and other toxic chemicals. If you have electronic equipment, you have a responsibility, and a probable cost, for disposing of it.

What about companies? Many have potential pollution or environmental-disposal problems. How do we fit these issues into the accounting equation? Are these costs and related liabilities something that companies should report? In the past, two arguments were made for excluding environmental costs from the financial statements of product manufacturers. First, it was argued that the manufacturing companies had no responsibility for environmental concerns and therefore the companies had no liability. Second, if there was a liability, the companies argued they could not estimate an amount.

Some Facts

- In some Canadian provinces, consumers will be able to drop off their products at collections facilities free of charge. The cost of the program will be covered by the electronics industry. The industry may charge consumers a fee when purchasing new products. These fees may range from $5 for a notebook computer up to $45 for a large television.
- A television takes 16 minutes to recycle with shredding. In that time, plants in China will have made 623 new ones.
- During the 90 seconds it takes to dismantle a television, an average of 58.4 new flat panel sets will be produced in China, the world's biggest television manufacturer.
- In 2006, Apple recycled 9.5% of the weight of all products it sold seven years earlier. Apple's forecast for 2010 is to recycle 30% of the product weight sold seven years earlier.
- In 2007, IDC Canada surveyed 231 executives at large and mid-sized Canadian organizations. The survey revealed that a high proportion of companies are planning to adopt more environmentally friendly workplace approaches over the next three to five years, as shown in the following survey summary:

	Doing it now	Planning on doing it in 3 years	Planning on doing it in 5 years
Recycling services for hardware	53%	79%	83%
Improved PC energy savings	47%	80%	82%
Telework/remote office (reducing carbon footprint)	32%	55%	61%
Energy-efficient means of powering equipment	28%	61%	68%
Smart energy-efficient office systems	23%	54%	65%

What Do You Think?

Should companies accrue environmental clean-up costs as liabilities on their financial statements?

YES | The Ontario Securities Commission says many public companies are providing poor disclosure of their environmental risks and liabilities. The Commission recommends companies should put more information about their potential environmental costs and liabilities into their financial statements, including dollar valuations where possible. Investors appear to be asking for more and improved disclosure of environmental matters.

NO | The amounts are still too difficult to estimate. Reporting inaccurate estimates on the financial statements reduces their usefulness. Instead, why not charge the costs later, when the actual environmental clean-up or disposal occurs, at which time the company knows the actual cost?

Sources:

Paul Lima, "How to Navigate the Recycling Maze," *Globe and Mail*, March 10, 2008, B9.
Grant Robertson, "The Dark Side of Booming TV Sales," *Globe and Mail*, December 28, 2007, B3.
Janet McFarland, "Clean Up Environmental Disclosure: OSC," *Globe and Mail*, February 28, 2008, B4.

The Navigator

Summary of Study Objectives

1. Explain the revenue recognition principle and the matching principle. The revenue recognition principle states that revenue must be recognized in the accounting period in which it is earned. The matching principle states that expenses must be recognized when they make their contribution to revenues.

2. Prepare adjusting entries for prepayments. Adjusting entries for prepayments are required in order to record the portion of the prepayment that applies to the expense incurred or revenue earned in the current accounting period. Prepayments are either prepaid expenses or unearned revenues. The adjusting entry for prepaid expenses results in an increase (debit) to an expense account and a decrease (credit) to an asset account. The adjusting entry for unearned revenues results in a decrease (debit) to a liability account and an increase (credit) to a revenue account.

3. Prepare adjusting entries for accruals. Adjusting entries for accruals are required in order to record the revenues and expenses that apply to the current accounting period and that have not been recognized through daily entries. Accruals are either accrued revenues or accrued expenses. The adjusting entry for accrued revenues results in an increase (debit) to an asset account and an increase (credit) to a revenue account. The adjusting entry for accrued expenses results in an increase (debit) to an expense account and an increase (credit) to a liability account.

4. Describe the nature and purpose of the adjusted trial balance, and prepare one. An adjusted trial balance is a trial balance that shows the balances of all accounts at the end of an accounting period, including those that have been adjusted. The purpose of an adjusted trial balance is to show the effects of all financial events that have occurred during the accounting period. It also facilitates the preparation of the financial statements.

5. Prepare closing entries and a post-closing trial balance. One purpose of closing entries is to update the Retained Earnings account to its end-of-period balance. A second purpose is to make all temporary accounts (dividends, revenue, and expense accounts) begin the new period with a zero balance. To accomplish this, entries are made to close each individual revenue and expense account to a temporary summary account called Income Summary. The Income Summary account is then closed to the Retained Earnings account. The Dividends account is also closed to Retained Earnings. Only temporary accounts are closed.

A post-closing trial balance lists only permanent accounts (i.e. balance sheet accounts) and the balances that are carried forward to the next accounting period. The purpose of the post-closing trial balance, as with other trial balances, is to prove the equality of total debits and total credits.

The Navigator

Study Tools (Glossary)

Glossary

Accrual basis accounting An accounting basis in which transactions that change a company's financial statements are recorded in the periods in which the events occur, rather than in the periods in which the company receives or pays cash. (p. 162)

Accrued expenses Expenses incurred but not yet paid in cash or recorded. (p. 171)

Accrued revenues Revenues earned but not yet received in cash or recorded. (p. 170)

Adjusted trial balance A list of accounts and their balances after all adjustments have been made. (p. 177)

Adjusting entries Journal entries made at the end of an accounting period because of the time period assumption and to ensure that the revenue recognition and matching principles are followed. (p. 164)

Carrying amount The difference between the cost of a depreciable asset and its accumulated depreciation. Also known as book value. (p. 168)

Cash basis accounting An accounting basis in which revenue is recorded only when cash is received, and an expense is recorded only when cash is paid. (p. 162)

Closing entries Entries at the end of an accounting period to transfer the balances of temporary accounts (revenues, expenses, and dividends) to the permanent shareholders' equity account Retained Earnings. (p. 181)

Contra asset account An account that is offset against (reduces) an asset account on the balance sheet. (p. 168)

Depreciation The process of allocating the cost of a depreciable asset (e.g., property, plant, and equipment) over its useful life. Also known as amortization. (p. 167)

Income summary A temporary account used in closing revenue and expense accounts. (p. 181)

Matching principle The principle of expense recognition that states that efforts (expenses) must be matched with accomplishments (revenues), wherever possible. (p. 161)

Permanent accounts Balance sheet accounts whose balances are carried forward to the next accounting period. (p. 181)

Post-closing trial balance A list of permanent accounts and their balances after closing entries have been journalized and posted. (p. 183)

Prepaid expenses   Expenses that are generally paid in cash and recorded as assets before they are used or consumed. (p. 165)

Revenue recognition principle   The principle that states that revenue must be recognized in the accounting period in which it is earned. (p. 161)

Straight-line method of depreciation   A depreciation method in which depreciation expense is calculated as the cost of an asset divided by its useful life. (p. 167)

Temporary accounts   Revenue, expense, and dividend accounts whose balances are transferred to Retained Earnings at the end of an accounting period. (p. 181)

Unearned revenues   Cash, or a promise to pay cash, that is received before revenue is earned and is therefore recorded as a liability until it is earned. (p. 168)

Useful life   The length of service of a depreciable asset. (p. 167)

Analysis Tools (Decision Toolkit Summaries)

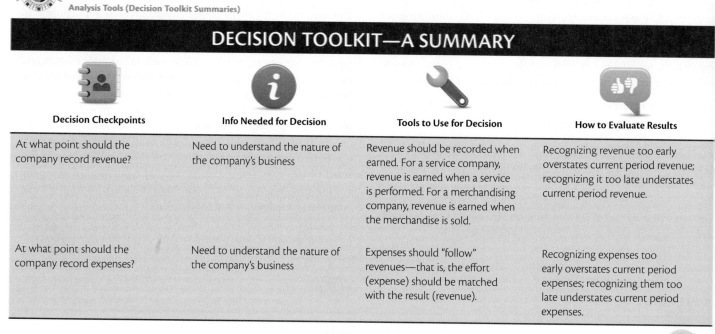

DECISION TOOLKIT—A SUMMARY

Decision Checkpoints	Info Needed for Decision	Tools to Use for Decision	How to Evaluate Results
At what point should the company record revenue?	Need to understand the nature of the company's business	Revenue should be recorded when earned. For a service company, revenue is earned when a service is performed. For a merchandising company, revenue is earned when the merchandise is sold.	Recognizing revenue too early overstates current period revenue; recognizing it too late understates current period revenue.
At what point should the company record expenses?	Need to understand the nature of the company's business	Expenses should "follow" revenues—that is, the effort (expense) should be matched with the result (revenue).	Recognizing expenses too early overstates current period expenses; recognizing them too late understates current period expenses.

The Navigator

Using the Decision Toolkit

High Liner Foods Incorporated, headquartered in Lunenburg, Nova Scotia, is the world's largest frozen seafood processing company. A simplified version of High Liner Foods' December 29, 2007, year-end adjusted trial balance follows:

HIGH LINER FOODS INCORPORATED
Adjusted Trial Balance
December 29, 2007
(in thousands)

HIGH LINER FOODS
INCORPORATED

	Debit	Credit
Cash	$ 7,064	
Accounts receivable	68,662	
Inventories	107,589	
Prepaid expenses	4,644	
Other current assets	3,716	
Land	2,193	
Buildings	38,471	
Computer and electronic equipment	7,194	
Machinery and equipment	55,073	
Accumulated depreciation — buildings		$ 13,641

Accumulated depreciation — computers and electronic equipment		4,620
Accumulated depreciation — machinery and equipment		26,432
Intangible assets and goodwill	42,762	
Other assets	7,779	
Bank loans (short-term)		61,280
Accounts payable and accrued liabilities		51,068
Income taxes payable		437
Current portion of long-term debt		603
Long-term debt		51,709
Other liabilities		4,486
Preferred shares		50,270
Common shares		59,290
Other shareholders' equity items		(18,801)
Retained earnings		36,106
Dividends	3,283	
Sales		275,391
Cost of sales	221,202	
Selling, general, and administrative expenses	38,998	
Depreciation expense	3,087	
Other expenses	1,507	
Interest expense	377	
Other revenue		738
Income tax expense	3,669	
	$617,270	$617,270

Instructions

(a) Calculate net earnings for the year and retained earnings at December 29.
(b) Prepare a classified balance sheet.
(c) Prepare the closing journal entries.

Solution

(a)

Calculation of net earnings:

Revenues		
Sales		$275,391
Other revenue		738
Total revenues		276,129
Expenses		
Cost of sales	$221,202	
Selling, general, and administrative expenses	38,998	
Depreciation expense	3,087	
Other expenses	1,507	
Interest expense	377	
Total expenses		265,171
Earnings before income taxes		10,958
Income tax expense		3,669
Net earnings		$ 7,289

Calculation of retained earnings:

Retained earnings, beginning of year	$36,106
Add: Net earnings	7,289
	43,395
Less: Dividends	3,283
Retained earnings, end of year	$40,112

(b)

HIGH LINER FOODS INCORPORATED
Balance Sheet
December 29, 2007
(in thousands)

HIGH LINER FOODS
INCORPORATED

Assets

Current assets			
Cash			$ 7,064
Accounts receivable			68,662
Inventories			107,589
Prepaid expenses			4,644
Other current assets			3,716
Total current assets			191,675
Property, plant, and equipment			
Land		$ 2,193	
Buildings	$38,471		
Accumulated depreciation—buildings	13,641	24,830	
Computers and electronic equipment	$ 7,194		
Accumulated depreciation—computers and electronic equipment	4,620	2,574	
Machinery and equipment	$55,073		
Accumulated depreciation—machinery and equipment	26,432	28,641	58,238
Intangible assets and goodwill			42,762
Other assets			7,779
Total assets			$300,454

Liabilities and Shareholders' Equity

Liabilities			
Current liabilities			
Bank loans			$ 61,280
Accounts payable and accrued liabilities			51,068
Income tax payable			437
Current portion of long-term debt			603
Total current liabilities			113,388
Long-term debt			51,709
Other long-term liabilities			4,486
Total liabilities			169,583
Shareholders' equity			
Preferred shares		$50,270	
Common shares		59,290	
Other shareholders' equity items		(18,801)	
Retained earnings		40,112	
Total shareholders' equity			130,871
Total liabilities and shareholders' equity			$300,454

(c)

Dec. 29	Sales	275,391	
	Other Revenue	738	
	Income Summary		276,129
29	Income Summary	268,840	
	Cost of Sales		221,202
	Selling, General, and Administrative Expenses		38,998
	Depreciation Expense		3,087
	Other Expenses		1,507
	Interest Expense		377
	Income Tax Expense		3,669
29	Income Summary	7,289	
	Retained Earnings		7,289
29	Retained Earnings	3,283	
	Dividends		3,283

The Navigator

Demonstration Problem

www.wiley.com/canada/kimmel

Study Tools
(Demonstration Problems)

The Green Thumb Lawn Care Corporation was incorporated on April 1. At April 30, the trial balance shows the following balances for selected accounts:

Prepaid insurance	$ 3,600
Equipment	30,000
Note payable	20,000
Unearned service revenue	4,200
Service revenue	1,800

Analysis reveals the following additional data about these accounts:

1. Prepaid insurance is the cost of a one-year insurance policy, effective April 1.
2. The equipment is expected to have a useful life of four years.
3. The note payable is dated April 1. It is a six-month, 6% note. Interest is payable on the first of each month.
4. Seven customers paid for the company's six-month, $600 lawn service package beginning in April. These customers were serviced in April.
5. Lawn services provided to other customers but not billed at April 30 totalled $1,500.
6. Income tax expense for April is estimated to be $100.

Instructions

Prepare the adjusting entries for the month of April.

Solution to Demonstration Problem

	GENERAL JOURNAL		
Date	Account Titles and Explanation	Debit	Credit
	Adjusting Entries		
Apr. 30	Insurance Expense	300	
	Prepaid Insurance		300
	(To record insurance expired: $3,600 × 1/12)		
30	Depreciation Expense	625	
	Accumulated Depreciation—Equipment		625
	(To record monthly depreciation: $30,000 ÷ 4 = $7,500 × 1/12)		
30	Interest Expense	100	
	Interest Payable		100
	(To accrue interest on note payable: $20,000 × 6% × 1/12)		
30	Unearned Service Revenue	700	
	Service Revenue		700
	(To record revenue earned: $600 ÷ 6 mos. × 7)		
30	Accounts Receivable	1,500	
	Service Revenue		1,500
	(To accrue revenue earned but not billed or collected)		
30	Income Tax Expense	100	
	Income Tax Payable		100
	(To accrue income taxes payable)		

Action Plan

- Note that adjustments are being made for only one month.
- Before determining what adjustments are necessary, look at the amounts that are currently recorded in the accounts.
- Show your calculations.
- Select account titles carefully. Use existing titles wherever appropriate.

The Navigator

Self-Study Questions

Answers are at the end of the chapter.

www.wiley.com/canada/kimmel

Study Tools (Self-Assessment Quizzes)

(SO 1) 1. Which principle or assumption states that efforts (expenses) must be recorded with accomplishments (revenues)?

    (a) Matching principle

    (b) Cost principle

    (c) Time period assumption

    (d) Revenue recognition principle

(SO 1) 2. Adjusting entries are made to ensure that:

    (a) expenses are matched to revenues in the period in which the revenue is generated.

    (b) revenues are recorded in the period in which they are earned.

    (c) balance sheet and statement of earnings accounts have correct balances at the end of an accounting period.

    (d) All of the above

(SO 2) 3. The trial balance shows Supplies $1,350 and Supplies Expense $0. If $600 of supplies are on hand at the end of the period, the adjusting entry is:

(a) Supplies		600	
Supplies Expense			600
(b) Supplies Expense		600	
Supplies			600
(c) Supplies		750	
Supplies Expense			750
(d) Supplies Expense		750	
Supplies			750

(SO 2) 4. On February 1, Magazine City received $600 in advance for ten 12-month subscriptions to *Climbing Magazine* and credited the Unearned Subscription Revenue account. What adjusting journal entry should Magazine City make on February 28?

(a) Subscription Revenue		50	
Unearned Subscription Revenue			50
(b) Unearned Subscription Revenue		50	
Subscription Revenue			50
(c) Unearned Subscription Revenue		550	
Subscription Revenue			550
(d) Cash		600	
Subscription Revenue			600

(SO 3) 5. A bank has a three-month, $6,000 note receivable, issued on January 1 at an interest rate of 4%. Interest is due at maturity. What adjusting entry should the bank make at the end of January?

(a) Note Receivable		20	
Interest Revenue			20
(b) Interest Receivable		60	
Interest Revenue			60

(c) Cash		20	
Interest Revenue			20
(d) Interest Receivable		20	
Interest Revenue			20

6. Kathy Kiska earned a salary of $400 for the last week of September and will be paid on October 1. The adjusting entry for Kathy's employer at September 30 is:

(a) Salaries Expense		400	
Salaries Payable			400
(b) Salaries Expense		400	
Cash			400
(c) Salaries Payable		400	
Cash			400

    (d) No entry is required.

7. Which statement about the adjusted trial balance is *incorrect*?

    (a) An adjusted trial balance proves the equality of the total debit balances and total credit balances in the ledger after all adjustments are made.

    (b) The adjusted trial balance is the main source for the preparation of financial statements.

    (c) The adjusted trial balance is prepared after the closing entries have been journalized and posted.

    (d) The adjusted trial balance is prepared after the adjusting entries have been journalized and posted.

8. The Retained Earnings balance in an unadjusted trial balance is $10,000. Net earnings for the period are $2,500 and dividends are $500. The Retained Earnings account balance in the adjusted trial balance will be:

    (a) $9,500.

    (b) $10,000.

    (c) $12,000.

    (d) $12,500.

9. Which account will have a zero balance after closing entries have been journalized and posted?

    (a) Service Revenue

    (b) Advertising Supplies

    (c) Unearned Revenue

    (d) Accumulated Depreciation

10. Which type of account will appear in the post-closing trial balance?

    (a) Permanent accounts

    (b) Temporary accounts

    (c) Statement of earnings accounts

    (d) Cash flow statement accounts

The Navigator

Questions

1. Why are adjusting entries needed? Include in your explanation a description of the assumption and two generally accepted accounting principles that relate to adjusting the accounts.

2. ⚷ Tony Galego, a lawyer, accepts a legal engagement in March, does the work in April, bills the client $8,000 in May, and is paid in June. If Galego's law firm prepares monthly financial statements, when should it recognize revenue from this engagement? Why?

3. ⚷ In completing the engagement in question 2, Galego incurs expenses that are specifically related to this engagement as follows: none in March, $4,500 in April, and none in May and June. How much expense should be deducted from revenues in the month(s) when the revenue is recognized? Why?

4. ⚷ The Higher Education University collects tuition in September for the fall term from registered students. The fall term runs from September to December. In what month(s) should the university recognize the revenue earned from tuition fees? Explain your reasoning.

5. How does the cash basis of accounting differ from the accrual basis of accounting? Which basis gives more useful information for decision-making? Why?

6. The name "prepaid expense" implies that this type of account is an expense account and belongs on a statement of earnings. However, these accounts actually appear on the balance sheet as assets. Explain why this is appropriate and why prepaid expense items need to be adjusted at the end of each period.

7. The name "unearned revenue" implies that this type of account is a revenue account and belongs on a statement of earnings. However, these accounts actually appear on the balance sheet as liabilities. Explain why this is appropriate and why unearned revenue items require adjustment at the end of each period.

8. "Depreciation is a process of valuation that results in the reporting of the fair value of the asset." Do you agree? Explain.

9. Explain the difference between (a) depreciation expense and accumulated depreciation, and (b) cost and carrying amount.

10. What is a contra asset account? Why do we use a contra asset account to record accumulated depreciation instead of directly reducing the depreciable asset account?

11. The trial balance of Hoi Inc. includes the balance sheet accounts listed below. Identify the accounts that might require adjustment. For each account that requires adjustment, indicate (1) the type of adjusting entry (prepaid expenses, unearned revenues, accrued revenues, or accrued expenses) and (2) the related account in the adjusting entry.

(a) Accounts Receivable
(b) Prepaid Insurance
(c) Rent Receivable
(d) Accumulated Depreciation
(e) Interest Payable
(f) Income Tax Payable
(g) Unearned Service Revenue

12. "An adjusting entry may affect more than one balance sheet or statement of earnings account." Do you agree? Why or why not? (SO 2, 3)

13. Adjusting entries for prepayments *always* include the Cash account, and adjusting entries for accruals *never* include the Cash account. Do you agree? Why or why not? (SO 2, 3)

14. Reactor Corp. has incurred utility costs for the month of December, but the utility company does not send out its bills until the 15th of the following month. Reactor does not plan on recording the utility costs until it receives the bill on January 15. Should Reactor record in December this cost that has been incurred but will only be billed and paid in January? Why or why not? If you believe that this cost should be recorded in December, identify the date of the entry and which accounts should be debited and credited. (SO 3)

15. Why is it appropriate to prepare financial statements directly from an adjusted trial balance but not from an unadjusted trial balance? (SO 4)

16. How do adjusting journal entries differ from transaction journal entries? How do closing journal entries differ from adjusting journal entries? (SO 2, 3, 5)

17. Explain how an unadjusted trial balance, adjusted trial balance, and post-closing trial balance differ. How often should each one be prepared? (SO 4, 5)

18. What items are disclosed on a post-closing trial balance? Why are the financial statements prepared using an adjusted trial balance instead of the post-closing trial balance? (SO 4, 5)

19. What are the two reasons for recording closing entries? (SO 5)

20. Why is the account Dividends not closed with the expense accounts? Why is a separate closing entry required for this account? (SO 5)

21. Identify the summary account(s) that are debited and credited in each of the four closing entries, assuming the company has (a) net earnings for the year, and (b) a net loss for the year. (SO 5)

22. Which steps in the accounting cycle may be done daily, which steps are done on a periodic basis (monthly or quarterly), and which steps are usually done only at the company's fiscal year end? (SO 5)

Brief Exercises

BE4–1   Transactions that affect earnings do not necessarily affect cash. Identify the impact, if any, of each of the following transactions on cash and net earnings. The first transaction has been completed for you as an example.

	Cash	Net Earnings
(a) Purchased supplies for cash, $100.	–$100	$0

(b) Made an adjusting entry to record use of $75 of the supplies in (a).

(c) Performed services on account, $1,000.

(d) Received $800 from customers in payment of their accounts in (c).

(e) Purchased office equipment for cash, $5,000.

(f) Made an adjusting entry to recorded depreciation of office equipment, $1,000.

(g) Borrowed $1,000 on a note payable.

(h) Made an adjusting entry to accrue interest on the note in (g), $50.

(i) Received $500 cash for services to be provided in the future.

(j) Made an adjusting entry to record utilities incurred but not yet paid, $250.

BE4–2   Data are provided for two independent situations. Calculate the missing amount for each company.

	A Ltd.	B Ltd.
Supplies on hand, beginning of year	$ 675	$ 640
Supplies purchased during the year	1,695	2,825
Supplies on hand, end of year	225	(b)
Supplies used during the year	(a)	2,715

BE4–3   Sain Advertising Ltd.'s opening trial balance on January 1 shows Advertising Supplies $750. On May 1, the company purchased additional supplies for $2,400 on credit. On December 31, there are $1,150 of advertising supplies on hand.

(a) Prepare the journal entry to record the purchase of advertising supplies on May 1.

(b) Calculate the amount of advertising supplies used during the year.

(c) Prepare the adjusting entry required at December 31.

(d) Using T accounts, enter the opening balances in the affected accounts, post the journal entries in (a) and (c), and indicate the adjusted balance in each account.

BE4–4   On January 2, 2009, Cretien Corporation purchased a delivery truck for $40,000 cash. The company uses straight-line depreciation and estimates that the truck will have a five-year useful life. The company has a December 31 year end and adjusts its accounts annually.

(a) Prepare the journal entry to record the purchase of the delivery truck on January 2, 2009.

(b) Prepare the adjusting entries required on December 31, 2009 and 2010.

(c) Indicate the balance sheet presentation of the delivery truck at December 31, 2009 and 2010.

(d) Indicate the statement of earnings presentation of the depreciation expense for the years ended December 31, 2009 and 2010.

BE4–5   On June 1, 2009, Bere Ltd. pays $6,000 to Marla Insurance Corp. for a one-year insurance policy. Both companies have fiscal years ending December 31 and adjust their accounts annually.

(a) Record the June 1, 2009 transaction on the books of (1) Bere and (2) Marla.

(b) Calculate the amount of insurance that expired during 2009 and the unexpired cost at December 31, 2009.

(c) Prepare the adjusting entry required on December 31 by (1) Bere and (2) Marla.

(d) Post the above entries and indicate the adjusted balance in each account.

BE4–6   The total payroll for Classic Auto Repairs Ltd. is $5,000 ($1,000 per day). The payroll is paid every Monday for employee salaries earned during the previous five-day work week (Monday through Friday, inclusive). Salaries were last paid on Monday, December 28. This year the company's year end, December 31, falls on a Thursday. Salaries will be paid next on Monday, January 4, at which time employees will receive pay for the five days (including the New Year's holiday). Prepare the journal entries to record each of the following:

(a) Payment of the salaries on December 28

(b) The adjustment to accrue salaries at December 31

(c) Payment of the salaries on January 4

BE4–7   On July 1, 2009, a company purchased a truck for $40,000, paying $10,000 cash and signing a 6% note payable for the remainder. The interest and principal of the note are due on January 1, 2010. Prepare the journal entries to record each of the following:

Prepare transaction and adjusting entries for interest.
(SO 3)

(a) The purchase of the truck on July 1, 2009

(b) The accrual of interest at year end, December 31, 2009, assuming interest has not previously been accrued

(c) Repayment of the interest and the note on January 1, 2010

BE4–8   Fill in the missing amounts in the following income tax schedule for the Ducharme Corporation. Assume that 2009 was the company's first year of operations.

Determine missing amounts for income taxes.
(SO 3)

	2009	2010	2011
Income tax expense	$2,600	$3,600	$ (c)
Income tax payable	(a)	500	700
Income tax paid	2,200	(b)	4,200

BE4–9   Zieborg Maintenance Corp. has a $375 monthly contract with Crispy Treat Inc. for general maintenance services. Zieborg invoices Crispy on the first of the month for services that it provided in the previous month. Crispy must then pay for these services by the 10th of the following month (i.e., the month after the month when Crispy is billed).

Prepare and post transaction and adjusting entries for accrued revenue.
(SO 3)

(a) Zieborg has a November 30 fiscal year end. Why will it need to prepare an adjusting entry on November 30?

(b) Prepare Zieborg's adjusting entry on November 30.

(c) Will Zieborg need to record a journal entry on December 1 when it invoices Crispy? Why or why not?

(d) Zieborg receives $375 from Crispy on December 9 for services provided in November. Prepare Zieborg's journal entry.

BE4–10   The unadjusted and adjusted trial balances for Miscou Island Corporation at February 28, 2009, are as follows:

Determine missing amounts.
(SO 4)

	Trial Balance Debit	Trial Balance Credit	Adjusted Trial Balance Debit	Adjusted Trial Balance Credit
Cash	$ 8,000		$ 8,000	
Accounts receivable	26,000		(d)	
Supplies	(a)		1,000	
Prepaid insurance	6,000		(e)	
Equipment	22,000		22,000	
Accumulated depreciation—equipment		$ 1,000		(h)
Accounts payable		13,000		$13,000
Salaries payable		0		2,000
Income tax payable		0		(i)
Common shares		20,000		20,000
Retained earnings		(c)		21,000
Dividends	(b)		2,000	
Fees earned		30,000		32,000
Salary expense	7,000		(f)	
Rent expense	6,000		6,000	
Depreciation expense	0		(g)	
Insurance expense	0		4,000	
Supplies expense	0		4,000	
Utilities expense	2,400		2,400	
Miscellaneous expense	600		600	
Income tax expense	0		300	
Totals	$85,000	$85,000	$93,700	$93,700

▶ Accrual Accounting Concepts

The company adjusts its accounts annually. Selected data for the year-end adjustments are as follows:

1. Revenue earned but not yet billed, $2,000
2. Salaries earned, but not yet paid, $2,000
3. Depreciation expense, $4,400
4. Insurance expired, $4,000
5. Supplies used, $4,000
6. Estimated income tax expense, $300

Determine the missing amounts.

Prepare financial statements.
(SO 4)

BE4–11 Refer to the data in BE4–10 for Miscou Island Corporation. Prepare a statement of earnings, statement of retained earnings, and balance sheet for the year.

Prepare closing entries.
(SO 5)

BE4–12 Refer to the data in BE4–10 for Miscou Island Corporation. Prepare the closing journal entries.

Prepare and post closing entries.
(SO 5)

BE4–13 The statement of earnings for Edgebrook Golf Club Ltd. for the year ended November 30 shows Green Fees Earned $160,000; Salaries Expense $90,000; Maintenance Expense $25,000; and Income Tax Expense $10,000. The statement of retained earnings shows an opening balance for Retained Earnings of $30,000 and Dividends $10,000.

(a) Prepare the closing journal entries.

(b) Using T accounts, post the closing entries and determine the ending balances.

Identify post-closing trial balance accounts.
(SO 5)

BE4–14 The following selected accounts appear in the adjusted trial balance for Atomic Energy of Canada Limited (AECL). Identify which accounts would be included in AECL's post-closing trial balance.

(a) Accounts Receivable
(b) Interest Expense
(c) Interest Revenue
(d) Inventory
(e) Depreciation Expense
(f) Accounts Payable and Accrued Liabilities
(g) Cost of Sales
(h) Operating Expenses
(i) Accumulated Depreciation
(j) Revenue from Nuclear Products and Services

Exercises

Identify point of revenue recognition.
(SO 1)

E4–1 ▪━━◖ The following independent situations require professional judgement to determine when to recognize revenue from the transactions:

(a) WestJet Airlines sells you a nonrefundable airline ticket in September for your flight home at Christmas.

(b) Leon's Furniture sells you a home theatre on a "no money down, no interest, and no payments for one year" promotional deal.

(c) The Toronto Blue Jays sell season tickets to games in the Rogers Centre on-line. Fans can purchase the tickets at any time, although the season only begins officially in April and ends in October.

(d) The RBC Financial Group loans you money in August. The loan and the interest are repayable in full in November.

(e) In August, you order a sweater from Sears using its on-line catalogue. The sweater arrives in September and you charge it to your Sears credit card. You receive and pay the Sears bill in October.

(f) You purchase a gift card in December from iTunes to give to your friend for Christmas.

Instructions
Identify when revenue should be recognized in each situation.

Calculate cash basis and accrual basis earnings.
(SO 1)

E4–2 In its first year of operations, Brisson Corp. earned $26,000 in service revenue. Of that amount, $4,000 was on account and the remainder, $22,000, was collected in cash from customers.

The company incurred operating expenses of $15,500, of which $13,750 was paid in cash. At year end, $1,750 was still owing on account. In addition, Brisson prepaid $1,000 for insurance coverage that covered the last half of the first year and the first half of the second year. Brisson expects to owe $2,100 for income taxes when it files its corporate income tax return after year end.

Instructions

(a) Calculate the first year's net earnings under the cash basis of accounting

(b) Calculate the first year's net earnings under the accrual basis of accounting.

(c) Which basis of accounting (cash or accrual) gives the most useful information for decision-makers?

E4–3 Action Quest Games Inc. initially records all prepaid costs as assets and all revenue collected in advance as liabilities. The company adjusts its accounts annually. The following information is available for the year ended December 31, 2009:

Prepare and post transaction and adjusting entries for prepayments.
(SO 2)

1. Purchased a one-year insurance policy on June 1, for $1,800 cash.

2. Paid $6,500 on September 1 for five months' rent in advance.

3. On September 15, received $3,600 cash from a corporation to sponsor a game each month for the most improved students. The amount is to be distributed evenly over nine times of playing the game, once on the first Friday of each month starting in October. (Use the account Unearned Game Revenue.)

4. Signed a contract for cleaning services starting December 1, for $1,000 per month. Paid for the first two months on December 1.

5. During the year, sold $1,500 of gift certificates. Determined that on December 31, $475 of these gift certificates had not yet been redeemed. (Use the account Unearned Gift Certificate Revenue.)

Instructions

(a) For each of the above transactions, prepare the journal entry to record the initial transaction.

(b) For each of the above transactions, prepare the adjusting journal entry that is required on December 31, 2009.

(c) Post the journal entries in questions (a) and (b) to T accounts and determine the final balance in each account. (Note: Posting to the Cash account is not required.)

E4–4 Action Quest Games Inc. owns the following long-lived assets:

Prepare adjusting entries for depreciation; calculate carrying amount.
(SO 2)

Asset	Date Purchased	Cost	Estimated Useful Life
Computer equipment	July 1, 2007	$12,000	3 years
Lighting equipment	Jan. 1, 2006	28,000	7 years
Furniture	Jan. 1, 2009	10,000	5 years

Instructions

(a) Prepare depreciation adjusting entries for Action Quest Games for the year ended December 31, 2009, assuming the company adjusts its accounts annually.

(b) For each asset, calculate its accumulated depreciation and carrying amount at December 31, 2009.

E4–5 Action Quest Games Inc. has the following information available for accruals that must be recorded for the year ended December 31, 2009. The company adjusts its accounts annually.

Prepare adjusting and subsequent entries for accruals.
(SO 3)

1. The December utility bill for $425 was unrecorded on December 31. Action Quest paid the bill on January 11, 2010.

2. Action Quest is open seven days a week and employees are paid a total of $3,500 every Monday for a seven-day (Monday–Sunday) work week. December 31, 2009, is a Thursday, so employees will have worked four days (Monday–Thursday) since their last payday. Employees will be paid next on January 4, 2010.

3. Action Quest has a 5% note payable to its bank for $45,000. Interest is payable on the first day of each month.

4. Action Quest receives a commission from Pizza Shop next door for all pizzas sold to customers using Action Quest's facility. The amount owing for December is $300, which Pizza Shop will pay on January 4, 2010.

5. Action Quest sold some equipment on November 1, 2009, in exchange for a 6%, $6,000 note receivable. The principal and interest are due on February 1, 2010.

Instructions

(a) For each situation, prepare the adjusting entry required at December 31, 2009. Round any calculations to the nearest dollar.

(b) For each situation, prepare the journal entry to record the subsequent cash transaction in 2010.

Prepare adjusting entries.
(SO 2, 3)

E4–6   On March 31, 2009, Easy Rental Agency Inc.'s trial balance included the following unadjusted account balances. The company's year-end is December 31 and it adjusts its accounts quarterly.

	Debits	Credits
Prepaid insurance	$ 3,600	
Supplies	2,800	
Equipment	21,600	
Accumulated depreciation—equipment		$ 5,400
Note payable		20,000
Unearned rent revenue		9,600
Rent revenue		30,000
Wage expense	14,000	

An analysis of the accounts shows the following:

1. The equipment, which was purchased January 1, 2008, is estimated to have a useful life of four years.

2. One-third of the unearned rent revenue is still unearned at the end of the quarter.

3. The note payable has an interest rate of 6%. Interest is paid monthly on the first of each month and was last paid March 1, 2009.

4. Supplies on hand total $850 at March 31.

5. The one-year insurance policy was purchased on January 1, 2009.

6. Income tax is estimated to be $2,200 for the quarter.

Instructions

Prepare the quarterly adjusting entries required at March 31, 2009.

Analyze adjusted data.
(SO 2, 3, 4)

E4–7   A partial adjusted trial balance follows for Nolet Ltd. The company's fiscal year end is December 31 and it makes adjustments monthly.

NOLET LTD. Adjusted Trial Balance January 31, 2009		
	Debit	Credit
Supplies	$ 700	
Prepaid insurance	2,400	
Equipment	7,680	
Accumulated depreciation—equipment		$4,880
Income tax payable		800
Unearned service revenue		750
Service revenue		2,000
Depreciation expense	80	
Insurance expense	400	
Supplies expense	950	
Income tax expense	1,800	

Instructions

(a) If $1,700 was received in January for services performed in January, what was the balance in Unearned Service Revenue at January 1?

(b) If the amount in the Depreciation Expense account is the depreciation for one month, when was the equipment purchased? Assume that there have been no purchases or sales of equipment since this original purchase.

(c) If the amount in Insurance Expense is the amount of the January 31 adjusting entry, and the original insurance premium was for one year, what was the total premium and when was the policy purchased?

(d) If the amount in Supplies Expense is the amount of the January 31 adjusting entry, and $850 of supplies were purchased in January, what was the balance in Supplies on January 1?

(e) If $2,500 of income tax was paid in January, what was the balance in Income Tax Payable at January 1?

E4–8   The unadjusted and adjusted trial balances follow for Inuit Inc. at the end of its fiscal year, August 31. The company adjusts its accounts annually.

Prepare adjusting entries from analysis of trial balances.
(SO 2, 3, 4)

INUIT INC.
Trial Balance
August 31, 2009

	Unadjusted Debit	Unadjusted Credit	Adjusted Debit	Adjusted Credit
Cash	$10,400		$10,400	
Accounts receivable	18,800		20,275	
Office supplies	2,450		900	
Prepaid insurance	3,775		2,575	
Office equipment	14,100		14,100	
Accumulated depreciation— office equipment		$ 3,525		$ 4,700
Accounts payable		5,800		5,800
Salaries payable		0		1,250
Interest payable		0		1,600
Income tax payable		0		900
Unearned service revenue		1,600		600
Note payable, 8%, due Sept. 1, 2009		20,000		20,000
Common shares		5,000		5,000
Retained earnings		5,600		5,600
Dividends	800		800	
Service revenue		40,800		43,275
Salaries expense	17,000		18,250	
Rent expense	15,000		15,000	
Interest expense	0		1,600	
Office supplies expense	0		1,550	
Insurance expense	0		1,200	
Depreciation expense	0		1,175	
Income tax expense	0	0	900	0
	$82,325	$82,325	$88,725	$88,725

Instructions

Prepare the adjusting entries that were made.

E4–9   The adjusted trial balance for Inuit Inc. is given in E4–8.

Prepare financial statements.
(SO 4)

Instructions

Prepare the statement of earnings, statement of retained earnings, and balance sheet for the year.

E4–10   The adjusted trial balance for Inuit Inc. is given in E4–8.

Prepare closing entries and post-closing trial balance.
(SO 5)

Instructions

(a) Prepare the closing entries at August 31.

(b) Prepare a post-closing trial balance.

Problems: Set A

Convert income from cash to
accrual basis.
(SO 1)

P4–1A   Your examination of the 2009 records of Northland Corp. shows the company collected $156,200 cash from customers and paid $107,800 cash for operating costs. If Northland followed the accrual basis of accounting, it would report the following year end balances:

	2009	2008
Accounts payable	$ 1,810	$ 1,640
Accounts receivable	2,900	3,200
Accumulated depreciation	17,250	15,000
Prepaid insurance	1,620	1,330
Unearned revenues	1,400	1,560
Income tax payable	9,200	8,070

Instructions

(a) Determine Northland's net earnings on a cash basis for 2009.

(b) Determine Northland's net earnings on an accrual basis for 2009.

(c) Which method do you recommend Northland use? Why?

Prepare transaction and adjusting
entries for prepayments.
(SO 2)

P4–2A   Bourque Corporation began operations on January 2. Its fiscal year end is December 31, and it prepares financial statements and adjusts its accounts annually. Selected transactions for the current year follow:

1. On January 2, purchased office supplies for $2,100 cash. A physical count at December 31 revealed that $550 of supplies were still on hand.

2. Purchased office equipment for $20,000 cash on March 1. The office equipment is estimated to have a useful life of five years.

3. Purchased a one-year, $5,040 insurance policy for cash on June 1. The policy came into effect on that date.

4. On November 15, received a $1,275 advance cash payment from three clients for services to be provided in the future. As at December 31, work had been completed for two of the clients ($425 each).

5. On December 15, the company paid $2,500 rent in advance for the next month (January).

Instructions

(a) For each of the above situations, prepare the journal entry for the original transaction.

(b) For each of the above situations, prepare any adjusting journal entry required at December 31.

Prepare adjusting and
subsequent entries for
accruals.
(SO 3)

P4–3A   Hangzhou Corporation had the following selected transactions in the month of November. The company adjusts its accounts monthly.

1. Hangzhou has a biweekly payroll of $6,000. Salaries are normally paid every second Monday for work completed for the two preceding weeks. Employees work a five-day week, Monday through Friday. Salaries were last paid Monday, November 23, and will be paid next on Monday, December 7.

2. The company has a 7%, $20,000 note payable due September 1 of the next year. Interest is payable the first of each month. It was last paid on November 1, and will be paid next on December 1.

3. At the end of November, Hangzhou has $1,000 of invoices that have not yet been sent to customers. It mails these invoices on December 1, and collects the amounts due on December 21.

4. At the end of November, the company earned $10 interest on the cash in its bank account. The bank deposited this amount in the company's bank account on November 30, but the company did not learn of the interest until it received its bank statement on December 4.

5. At the end of November, it was estimated that the company owed $1,000 of income tax. This amount was paid on December 18.

Instructions

(a) For each of the above situations, prepare the monthly adjusting journal entry required at November 30.

(b) Prepare any subsequent transaction entries that occur in the month of December.

P4–4A The following independent items for Repertory Theatre Ltd. during the year ended December 31, 2009, may require either a transaction journal entry or an adjusting journal entry, or both. The company adjusts its accounts annually.

Prepare transaction and adjusting entries. (SO 2, 3)

1. Supplies on hand amounted to $500 at the beginning of the year. During the year, additional supplies were purchased for $1,750 cash. At the end of the year, a physical count showed that supplies on hand amounted to $300.

2. The theatre owns a truck that was purchased on January 2, 2008, for $40,000. The estimated useful life of the truck is four years.

3. On June 1, the theatre borrowed $10,000 from La Caisse Populaire Desjardins at an interest rate of 6%. The principal is to be repaid in one year. The interest is paid at the beginning of each month.

4. The theatre has nine plays each season, which starts in September 2009 and ends in May 2010 (one play per month). Season tickets sell for $225. On August 21, 200 season tickets were sold for the upcoming 2009–2010 season. The Theatre credited Unearned Season Ticket Revenue for the full amount received on August 21.

5. Every Monday, the total payroll for the theatre is $3,000 for wages earned during a six-day work week (Tuesday–Sunday). This year, December 31 falls on a Thursday. Wages were last paid (and recorded) on Monday, December 28.

6. Repertory Theatre rents its facilities for $200 a month to a local seniors' choir that uses the space for rehearsals. The choir's treasurer was ill during December, and on January 4, 2010, the theatre received a cheque for both the amount owing for the month of December 2009 and the rent for the month of January 2010.

7. Upon reviewing its books on December 31, the theatre noted that a telephone bill for the month of December had not yet been received. A call to Aliant determined that the telephone bill was for $375. The bill was paid on January 12.

Instructions

(a) Prepare the journal entry to record the original transaction for items 1, 2, 3, 4, and 5.

(b) Prepare the year end adjusting entry required for items 1 through 7 on December 31.

(c) Record the subsequent cash transaction in 2010 for (1) the interest paid on January 1 (item 3), (2) payment of the payroll on January 4 (item 5), (3) receipt of the rent on January 4 (item 6), and (4) payment of the telephone bill on January 12 (item 7).

P4–5A A review of the ledger of Greenberg Corporation at November 30, 2009, produces the following unadjusted data for the preparation of annual adjusting entries:

Prepare adjusting entries. (SO 2, 3)

1. Prepaid Advertising, Nov. 30 unadjusted balance, $14,160: This balance consists of payments on two advertising contracts. The contracts provide for monthly advertising in two trade magazines, and specify that the first advertisement runs in the month following the month in which the contract is signed. In other words, if the contract is signed March 1, the first advertisement will run in the month of April. The terms of the contracts are as follows:

Contract	Signing Date	Amount	Number of Magazine Issues
A650	March 1	$ 6,240	12
B974	July 1	7,920	16
		$14,160	

2. Salaries Payable, Nov. 30 unadjusted balance, $0: There are eight salaried employees. Salaries are paid every Friday for a five-day work week (Monday–Friday). Six employees receive a salary of $750 each per week, and two employees earn $600 each per week. November 30 is a Monday.

3. Unearned Rent Revenue, Nov. 30 unadjusted balance, $303,000: The company began subleasing office space in its new building on October 1. At November 30, the company had the following rental contracts that are paid in full for the entire term of the lease:

Date	Term (in months)	Monthly Rent	Number of Leases	Rent Paid
Oct. 1	6	$4,500	5	$135,000
Nov. 1	6	7,000	4	168,000
				$303,000

4. Note Payable, Nov. 30 unadjusted balance, $85,000: This represents a one-year, 7% note issued on May 1. Interest is payable at maturity.

5. Delivery Truck, Nov. 30 unadjusted balance, $39,000: The company owns a delivery truck purchased for $39,000 on May 1, 2007. The truck has a five-year useful life.

Instructions

Prepare the adjusting journal entries at November 30, 2009.

Convert earnings from cash to accrual basis; prepare financial statements.
(SO 1, 2, 3, 4)

P4–6A The Radical Edge Ltd., a ski tuning and repair shop, opened in November 2008. The company did not record any transactions since its opening, but carefully kept track of all its cash receipts and cash payments. The following information is available at the end of the first ski season, April 30, 2009:

	Cash Receipts	Cash Payments
Issue of common shares	$10,000	
Ski and snowboard repair services	33,250	
Repair equipment		$23,520
Rent		2,275
Insurance		1,380
Advertising		460
Utility bills		950
Wages		3,600
Income tax		3,000
	$43,250	$35,185

Additional information:

1. At the end of April, customers owe The Radical Edge $720 for services they have received and not yet paid for.

2. The repair equipment was purchased at the beginning of November and has an estimated useful life of eight years.

3. On November 1, the company began renting space at a cost of $325 per month on a one-year lease. As required by the lease contract, the company paid the last month's rent in advance.

4. The insurance policy was purchased November 1 and is effective for one year.

5. At April 30, $2,120 is owed for unpaid wages.

6. At April 30, an additional $600 is owed for income taxes.

Instructions

(a) Calculate the cash balance at April 30, 2009.

(b) Prepare an accrual basis statement of earnings, statement of retained earnings, and balance sheet for the six months ended April 30, 2009.

P4–7A The following is Ortega Limo Service Ltd.'s unadjusted trial balance at its year end, December 31. The company adjusts its accounts annually.

ORTEGA LIMO SERVICE LTD. Trial Balance December 31, 2009	Debit	Credit
Cash	$ 12,400	
Accounts receivable	8,220	
Prepaid insurance	3,600	
Prepaid rent	1,150	
Supplies	2,500	
Automobiles	58,000	
Accumulated depreciation—automobiles		$ 14,500
Office furniture	16,000	
Accumulated depreciation—office furniture		4,000
Note payable		46,000
Unearned service revenue		3,600
Common shares		5,000
Retained earnings		7,600
Dividends	3,800	
Service revenue		115,600
Salaries expense	57,000	
Interest expense	2,415	
Rent expense	6,000	
Repairs expense	4,690	
Gas and oil expense	20,075	
Income tax expense	450	
	$196,300	$196,300

Additional information:

1. The insurance policy has a one-year term beginning March 1.

2. A physical count of supplies at December 31 shows $570 of supplies on hand.

3. The automobiles were purchased on January 2, 2008, and have an estimated useful life of four years.

4. The office furniture was purchased on July 2, 2005, and has an estimated useful life of 10 years.

5. Service revenue earned but not billed or recorded at December 31 is $1,750.

6. Interest on the 7% note payable is paid on the first day of each quarter (January 1, April 1, July 1, and October 1).

7. One of Ortega's customers paid in advance for a six-month contract at the rate of $600 per month. The contract began on November 1 and Ortega credited Unearned Service Revenue at the time.

8. Drivers' salaries total $230 per day. At December 31, three days of salaries are unpaid.

9. On December 28, Ortega paid $1,150 for January 2010 rent.

10. Income taxes for the year are estimated to be $850. The company has paid $450 in income tax instalments to date.

Instructions

(a) Prepare T accounts and enter the trial balance amounts.

(b) Prepare and post the adjusting journal entries required at December 31.

(c) Prepare an adjusted trial balance at December 31, 2009.

Complete accounting cycle
through to preparation of
financial statements.
(SO 2, 3, 4)

P4–8A   On August 31, 2009, the Rijo Equipment Repair Corp.'s post-closing trial balance was as follows. The company prepares its adjusting entries monthly.

RIJO EQUIPMENT REPAIR CORP.		
Post-Closing Trial Balance		
August 31, 2009		
	Debit	Credit
Cash	$ 4,880	
Accounts receivable	3,720	
Supplies	800	
Equipment	15,000	
Accumulated depreciation—equipment		$ 1,500
Accounts payable		3,100
Unearned service revenue		400
Salaries payable		700
Common shares		10,000
Retained earnings		8,700
	$24,400	$24,400

During September, the following transactions were completed:

Sept. 8   Paid employees $1,100 for salaries due, of which $400 was for September salaries payable and $700 for August.

10   Received $1,200 cash from customers in payment of accounts.

11   Received $4,400 cash for services performed in September.

17   Purchased supplies on account, $1,000.

21   Paid creditors $3,500 of accounts payable due.

22   Paid September and October rent, $1,000 ($500 per month).

22   Paid salaries, $1,100.

28   Performed services on account, $800.

29   Received $650 from customers for services to be provided in the future.

30   Paid income tax for the month, $300.

Adjustment data for the month:

1. Supplies on hand total $600.

2. Accrued salaries payable are $800.

3. The equipment has a useful life of 10 years.

4. Unearned service revenue of $400 has been earned.

Instructions

(a) Prepare T accounts, and enter the opening balances at September 1.

(b) Prepare and post the September transaction entries.

(c) Prepare a trial balance at September 30.

(d) Prepare and post the adjusting journal entries for the month.

(e) Prepare an adjusted trial balance at September 30.

(f) Prepare a statement of earnings, statement of retained earnings, and balance sheet for the month.

Prepare and post closing
entries; prepare post-closing
trial balance.
(SO 5)

P4–9A   Refer to the data for Rijo Equipment Repair Corp. in P4–8A. Assume that Rijo closes its books monthly.

Instructions

(a) Prepare the closing journal entries.

(b) Post the closing entries to the T accounts prepared in P4–8A.

(c) Prepare a post-closing trial balance at September 30.

Prepare adjusting entries and financial statements; assess financial performance.
(SO 2, 3, 4)

P4–10A ⬤━C The unadjusted and adjusted trial balances for Grant Advertising Agency Limited at its year end, December 31, 2009, follow. The company adjusts its accounts annually.

GRANT ADVERTISING AGENCY LIMITED				
Trial Balance				
December 31, 2009				
	Unadjusted		Adjusted	
	Debit	Credit	Debit	Credit
Cash	$ 11,000		$ 11,000	
Short-term investments	10,850		10,850	
Accounts receivable	18,650		19,750	
Art supplies	7,200		1,265	
Prepaid insurance	2,400		800	
Printing equipment	66,000		66,000	
Printing equipment—accumulated depreciation		$ 26,400		$ 39,600
Accounts payable		4,200		4,800
Interest payable		0		700
Note payable		10,000		10,000
Unearned advertising revenue		7,100		6,200
Salaries payable		0		1,625
Income tax payable		0		7,000
Common shares		20,000		20,000
Retained earnings		10,400		10,400
Dividends	2,000		2,000	
Advertising revenue		58,600		60,600
Salaries expense	12,000		13,625	
Insurance expense	0		1,600	
Interest expense	0		700	
Depreciation expense	0		13,200	
Art supplies expense	0		5,935	
Rent expense	6,600		7,200	
Income tax expense	0		7,000	
	$136,700	$136,700	$160,925	$160,925

Instructions

(a) Prepare the adjusting journal entries that were made for the year.

(b) Prepare a statement of earnings, statement of retained earnings, and balance sheet for the year.

(c) A friend of yours is considering investing in the company and asks you to comment on the results of operations and financial position. Is the company performing well or not? Does the financial position look healthy or weak? Use specific information from the financial statements to support your answer.

Prepare closing entries and post-closing trial balance.
(SO 5)

P4–11A   The adjusted trial balance is presented for Grant Advertising Agency Limited in P4–10A.

Instructions

(a) Prepare the closing journal entries.

(b) Prepare a post-closing trial balance at December 31.

Prepare and post adjusting
entries; prepare adjusted trial
balance and financial statements.
(SO 2, 3, 4)

P4–12A   The following is the unadjusted trial balance for Highland Cove Resort Inc. at its year end, August 31. The company adjusts its accounts annually.

HIGHLAND COVE RESORT INC. Trial Balance August 31, 2009		
	Debit	Credit
Cash	$ 19,410	
Prepaid insurance	6,360	
Supplies	3,495	
Land	35,000	
Cottages	145,000	
Accumulated depreciation—cottages		$ 43,500
Furniture	28,600	
Accumulated depreciation—furniture		11,440
Accounts payable		6,500
Unearned rent revenue		35,500
Mortgage payable		60,000
Common shares		20,000
Retained earnings		36,000
Dividends	5,000	
Rent revenue		248,500
Salaries expense	153,000	
Utilities expense	37,600	
Interest expense	3,850	
Repair expense	14,125	
Income tax expense	10,000	
	$461,440	$461,440

Additional information:

1. The one-year insurance policy was purchased on May 31 for $6,360.

2. A count of supplies on August 31 shows $690 of supplies on hand.

3. The cottages have an estimated useful life of 50 years.

4. The furniture has an estimated useful life of 10 years.

5. Customers must pay a $100 deposit if they want to book a cottage during the peak period. An analysis of these bookings indicates 355 deposits were received and credited to Unearned Rent Revenue. Only 45 of these deposits have not been earned by August 31.

6. Salaries of $840 were unpaid at August 31.

7. The August utility bill of $1,560 has not yet been recorded or paid.

8. On August 25, a local business contracted with Highland Cove to rent one of the cottages for six months, starting October 1, at a rate of $1,500 per month. An advance payment equal to two months' rent was received on August 31 and credited to Rent Revenue.

9. The mortgage interest rate is 7%. Interest has been paid to July 31; the next payment is due September 1.

10. Additional income taxes payable are estimated to be $1,000.

Instructions

(a) Prepare T accounts, and enter the trial balance amounts.

(b) Prepare and post the adjusting journal entries for the year.

(c) Prepare an adjusted trial balance at August 31.

(d) Prepare a statement of earnings, statement of retained earnings, and balance sheet for the year.

P4–13A Refer to the data for Highland Cove Resort Inc. in P4–12A.

Prepare and post closing entries; prepare post-closing trial balance.
(SO 5)

Instructions

(a) Prepare the closing journal entries.

(b) Post the closing entries to the T accounts prepared in P4–12A.

(c) Prepare a post-closing trial balance at August 31.

Problems: Set B

P4–1B Your examination of the records of Southlake Corp. shows the company collected $93,900 cash from customers and paid $54,700 cash for operating costs. If Southlake followed the accrual basis of accounting, it would report the following year end balances:

Convert income from cash to accrual basis.
(SO 1)

	2009	2008
Accounts receivable	$ 4,200	$ 2,700
Prepaid insurance	1,500	1,300
Accumulated depreciation	12,300	10,000
Accounts payable	1,500	2,250
Unearned revenues	1,400	1,500
Income tax payable	7,900	7,000

Instructions

(a) Determine Southlake's net income on a cash basis for 2009.

(b) Determine Southlake's net income on an accrual basis for 2009.

(c) Which method do you recommend Southlake use? Why?

P4–2B Ouellette Corporation began operations on January 2. Its fiscal year end is December 31, and it adjusts its accounts annually. Selected transactions during the current year follow:

Prepare transaction and adjusting entries for prepayments.
(SO 2)

1. On January 2, purchased office supplies for $4,100 cash. A physical count at December 31 revealed that $700 of supplies were still on hand.

2. Purchased a truck for $45,000 cash on April 1. The truck is estimated to have a useful life of five years.

3. Purchased a $3,780, one-year insurance policy for cash on August 1. The policy came into effect on that date.

4. Received a $1,600 advance cash payment from a client on November 9 for services to be provided in the future. As at December 31, half of these services had been completed.

5. On December 1, the company rented out excess office space for a six-month period starting on this date and received two cheques for $540 each for the first and last months' rent.

Instructions

(a) For each of the above situations, prepare the journal entry for the original transaction.

(b) For each of the above situations, prepare any adjusting entry required at December 31.

P4–3B Zheng Corporation had the following selected transactions in the month of March. The company adjusts its accounts monthly.

Prepare adjusting and subsequent entries for accruals.
(SO 3)

1. The company has an 8%, $12,000 note payable due in one year. Interest is payable the first of each month. It was last paid on March 1, and will be paid next on April 1.

2. At the end of March, the company earned $250 interest on its investments. The bank deposited this amount in Zheng's bank account on April 1.

3. Zheng has five employees who each earn $200 a day. Salaries are normally paid on Fridays for work completed Monday through Friday of the same week. Salaries were last paid Friday, March 27, and will be paid next on Friday, April 3.

4. At the end of March, the company owed the utility company $550 and the telephone company $200 for services received during the month. These bills were paid on April 10.

5. At the end of March, Zheng has earned $3,000 that it has not yet billed. It bills its clients April 1. On April 30, it collects $2,000 of this amount due.

Instructions

(a) For each of the above situations, prepare the monthly adjusting journal entry required at March 31.

(b) Prepare any subsequent transaction entries that occur in the month of April.

Prepare transaction and adjusting entries.
(SO 2, 3)

P4–4B   The following independent items for New Age Theatre Ltd. during the year ended November 30, 2009, require either a transaction journal entry or an adjusting journal entry, or both. The company adjusts its accounts annually.

1. On December 1, 2007, the theatre purchased a truck for $40,000 cash. The estimated useful life of the truck is five years.

2. On June 1, 2009, the theatre borrowed $50,000 from the Bank of Montreal at an interest rate of 6%. The principal is to be repaid in one year. The interest is payable the first of each month.

3. The theatre has eight plays each season. This year's season started October 2009 and ends in May 2010 (one play per month). Season tickets sell for $160. On October 1, 200 season tickets were sold for the 2009–2010 season. The Theatre credited Unearned Season Ticket Revenue for the full amount received on October 1.

4. Office supplies on hand amounted to $500 at the beginning of the year. On February 17, additional office supplies were purchased for cash at a cost of $1,550. At the end of the year, a physical count showed that supplies on hand amounted to $250.

5. The New Age Theatre rents its facilities for $200 a month to a local dance club which uses the space for rehearsals. On November 2, the club's treasurer accidentally sent a cheque for only $100 for the November rent. She promised to send a cheque in December for the balance when she returned from vacation. On December 4, the theatre received a cheque for the balance owing from November plus all of December's rent.

6. The total payroll is $3,500, paid every Monday for employee wages earned during the prior seven-day week (Sunday to Saturday). Wages were last paid (and recorded) on Monday, November 30.

7. Upon reviewing its books on November 30, the theatre noted that the utility bill for the month of November had not yet been received. A call to Hydro-Québec determined that the amount owed was $1,250. The bill was paid on December 10.

Instructions

(a) Prepare the journal entry to record the original transaction for items 1, 2, 3, 4, 5, and 6.

(b) Prepare the year end adjusting entry required for items 1 through 7.

(c) Record the subsequent cash transaction in December 2009 for (1) the interest paid on December 1 (item 2), (2) receipt of the rent on December 4 (item 5), (3) payment of the payroll on Monday, December 7 (item 6), and (4) payment of the utility bill on December 10 (item 7).

Prepare adjusting entries.
(SO 2, 3)

P4–5B   A review of the ledger of Come-By-Chance Corporation at December 31, 2009, produces the following unadjusted data for the preparation of annual adjusting entries:

1. Note Receivable, Dec. 31 unadjusted balance, $80,000: The note was issued on September 1, 2009, at an annual interest rate of 8%, and matures on June 1, 2010. The interest and principal are to be paid at maturity.

2. Prepaid Insurance, Dec. 31 unadjusted balance, $12,600: The company has separate insurance policies on its building and its motor vehicles. Policy B4564 on the building was purchased on July 1, 2008, for $10,800. The policy has a term of two years. Policy A2958 on the vehicles was purchased on January 1, 2009, for $4,500. This policy has a term of 18 months.

3. Buildings, Dec. 31 unadjusted balance, $290,250: The company owns two buildings. The first

was purchased on September 1, 1995, for $125,250 and has an estimated 30-year useful life. The second was purchased on May 1, 2003, for $165,000 and has an estimated 50-year useful life.

4. Unearned Subscription Revenue, Dec. 31 unadjusted balance, $51,000: The selling price of a magazine subscription is $50 for 12 monthly issues. A review of subscription contracts reveals the following:

Subscription Date	Number of Subscriptions
October 1	220
November 1	310
December 1	490
	1,020

5. Salaries Payable, Dec. 31 unadjusted balance, $0: There are nine salaried employees. Salaries are paid every Monday for the previous five-day work week (Monday to Friday). Six employees receive a salary of $625 each per week, and three employees earn $750 each per week. December 31 is a Thursday.

Instructions

(a) Prepare a calculation to show why the unadjusted balance in the Prepaid Insurance account is $13,500 and why the unadjusted balance in the Unearned Subscription Revenue account is $51,000.

(b) Prepare the adjusting journal entries at December 31, 2009.

P4–6B   During the first week of January 2009, Creative Designs Ltd. began operations. In its second year, Creative Designs approached the local bank for a $10,000 loan and was asked to submit financial statements prepared on an accrual basis. Although the company kept no formal accounting records, it did maintain a record of cash receipts and disbursements. The following information is available for the year ended December 31, 2009:

Convert earnings from cash to accrual basis; prepare financial statements.
(SO 1, 2, 3, 4)

	Cash Receipts	Cash Payments
Issue of common shares	$10,000	
Design revenue	78,800	
Equipment		$17,700
Supplies		8,400
Rent		10,000
Insurance		1,920
Advertising		3,400
Wages		29,900
Telephone		900
Dividends		5,000
	$88,800	$77,220

Additional information:

1. Design revenue earned but not yet collected amounted to $1,200.

2. The equipment was purchased at the beginning of January and has an estimated six-year useful life.

3. Supplies on hand on December 31 were $630.

4. Rent payments included a $750 per month rental fee and a $1,000 deposit that is refundable at the end of the two-year lease.

5. The insurance was paid for a one-year period expiring on January 31, 2010.

6. Wages earned for the last four days in December and to be paid in January 2010 amounted to $1,525.

7. At December 31, $4,000 is owed for income taxes.

Instructions

(a) Calculate the cash balance at December 31, 2009.

(b) Prepare an accrual basis statement of earnings, statement of retained earnings, and balance sheet for the year.

P4–7B   The following is River Tours Limited's unadjusted trial balance at its year end, November 30. The company adjusts its accounts annually.

RIVER TOURS LIMITED		
Trial Balance		
November 30, 2009		
	Debit	Credit
Cash	$ 3,000	
Accounts receivable	2,640	
Prepaid insurance	7,320	
Supplies	965	
Equipment	13,440	
Accumulated depreciation—equipment		$ 3,300
Boats	140,400	
Accumulated depreciation—boats		46,800
Accounts payable		1,985
Notes payable		54,000
Unearned revenue		14,000
Common shares		10,000
Retained earnings		15,000
Tour revenue		110,575
Salaries expense	69,560	
Interest expense	3,465	
Advertising expense	825	
Rent expense	2,175	
Fuel and maintenance expense	11,170	
Income tax expense	700	
	$255,660	$255,660

Additional information:

1. The insurance policy has a one-year term beginning April 1, 2009.

2. The equipment has an estimated useful life of 8 years. The boats have an estimated useful life of 12 years.

3. A physical count shows $240 of supplies on hand at November 30.

4. The note payable has a 7% interest rate. Interest is paid at the beginning of each month.

5. Deposits of $1,400 each were received for advance tour reservations from 10 school groups. At November 30, all of these deposits have been earned.

6. Employees are owed a total of $425 at November 30.

7. A senior citizens organization that had not made an advance deposit took a fall river tour for $1,150. This group was not billed until December for the services provided.

8. Additional advertising costs of $260 have been incurred, but the bills have not been received by November 30.

9. Income taxes payable for the year are estimated to be an additional $4,000 beyond that recorded to date.

Instructions

(a) Prepare T accounts, and enter the trial balance amounts.

(b) Prepare and post the adjusting journal entries required at November 30.

(c) Prepare an adjusted trial balance at November 30, 2009.

P4–8B   On October 31, 2009, the Alou Equipment Repair Corp.'s post-closing trial balance was as follows. The company adjusts its accounts monthly.

ALOU EQUIPMENT REPAIR CORP.
Post-Closing Trial Balance
October 31, 2009

	Debit	Credit
Cash	$ 7,790	
Accounts receivable	7,910	
Supplies	2,000	
Equipment	9,000	
Accumulated depreciation—equipment		$ 1,800
Accounts payable		2,300
Unearned service revenue		500
Salaries payable		500
Common shares		5,000
Retained earnings		16,600
	$26,700	$26,700

During November, the following transactions were completed:

Nov. 9   Paid $1,100 to employees for salaries due, of which $600 is for November salaries payable and $500 for October.
      12   Received $1,200 cash from customers in payment of accounts.
      19   Received $5,700 cash for services performed in November.
      20   Purchased supplies on account, $1,300.
      20   Paid creditors $2,300 of accounts payable due.
      23   Paid November rent, $300.
      23   Paid salaries, $1,200.
      27   Performed services on account, $1,900.
      30   Received $550 from customers for services to be provided in the future.

Adjustment data for the month:

1. Supplies on hand are valued at $1,000.

2. Accrued salaries payable are $500.

3. The equipment has an estimated useful life of five years.

4. Unearned service revenue of $400 was earned during the month.

5. Income taxes payable are estimated to be $600.

Instructions

(a) Prepare T accounts, and enter the opening balances at November 1.

(b) Prepare and post the November transaction entries.

(c) Prepare a trial balance at November 30.

(d) Prepare and post the adjusting journal entries for the month.

(e) Prepare an adjusted trial balance at November 30.

(f) Prepare a statement of earnings, statement of retained earnings, and balance sheet for the month.

P4–9B   Refer to the data for Alou Equipment Repair Corp. in P4–8B. Assume that Alou closes its books monthly.

Prepare and post closing entries; prepare post-closing trial balance.
(SO 5)

Instructions

(a) Prepare the closing journal entries.

(b) Post the closing entries to the T accounts prepared in P4–8B.

(c) Prepare a post-closing trial balance at November 30.

▶ Accrual Accounting Concepts

Prepare adjusting entries and
financial statements; assess
financial performance.
(SO 2, 3, 4)

P4–10B ◼▬ⅭThe unadjusted and adjusted trial balances of Ozaki Corp. at the end of its first quarter of operations, September 30, are as follows. The company adjusts its accounts quarterly.

OZAKI CORP.
Trial Balance
September 30, 2009

	Unadjusted		Adjusted	
	Debit	Credit	Debit	Credit
Cash	$ 3,250		$ 3,250	
Accounts receivable	6,335		8,435	
Prepaid rent	1,500		0	
Supplies	1,750		1,265	
Equipment	15,040		15,040	
Accumulated depreciation—				
equipment		$ 0		$ 750
Note payable		7,000		7,000
Accounts payable		4,250		4,460
Salaries payable		0		840
Interest payable		0		105
Income tax payable		0		1,000
Unearned commission revenue		775		550
Common shares		10,000		10,000
Dividends	700		700	
Commission revenue		20,160		22,485
Salaries expense	13,000		13,840	
Rent expense	0		1,500	
Depreciation expense	0		750	
Supplies expense	0		485	
Utilities expense	610		820	
Interest expense	0		105	
Income tax expense	0		1,000	
	$42,185	$42,185	$47,190	$47,190

Instructions

(a) Prepare the adjusting journal entries that were made for the quarter.

(b) Prepare a statement of earnings, statement of retained earnings, and balance sheet for the quarter.

(c) A friend of yours is considering investing in Ozaki Corp. and asks you to comment on the company's operations and financial position. Is the company performing well or not? Does the financial position look healthy or weak? Use specific information from the financial statements to support your answer.

Prepare closing entries and
post-closing trial balance.
(SO 5)

P4–11B   The adjusted trial balance for Ozaki Corp. is presented in P4–10B. Assume that the company closes its books quarterly.

Instructions

(a) Prepare the closing journal entries.

(b) Prepare a post-closing trial balance at September 30.

Prepare and post adjusting entries; prepare adjusted trial balance and financial statements.
(SO 2, 3, 5)

P4–12B   The following is the unadjusted trial balance for Salmon Lodge Inn Ltd. at its year end, May 31. The company adjusts its accounts monthly.

SALMON LODGE INN LTD.
Trial Balance
May 31, 2009

	Debit	Credit
Cash	$ 3,200	
Accounts receivable	5,900	
Prepaid insurance	2,275	
Supplies	2,440	
Land	53,185	
Lodge	84,000	
Accumulated depreciation—lodge		$ 8,050
Furniture and equipment	16,800	
Accumulated depreciation—furniture and equipment		6,440
Accounts payable		4,700
Unearned rent revenue		8,750
Mortgage payable		63,000
Common shares		30,000
Retained earnings		22,290
Dividends	1,000	
Rent revenue		100,160
Salaries expense	49,350	
Interest expense	4,620	
Insurance expense	1,820	
Utilities expense	13,300	
Advertising expense	500	
Income tax expense	5,000	
	$243,390	$243,390

Additional information:

1. The annual insurance policy was purchased on October 1, 2008, for $5,460.

2. A count of supplies shows $670 of supplies on hand on May 31.

3. The lodge has an estimated useful life of 20 years.

4. The furniture and equipment have an estimated useful life of five years.

5. Customers must pay a $50 deposit if they want to book a room in advance during the peak period. An analysis of these bookings indicates that 175 deposits were received and credited to Unearned Rent Revenue. By May 31, 25 of the deposits were earned.

6. On May 25, a local business contracted with Salmon Lodge Inn to rent one of its housekeeping units for four months, starting June 1, at a rate of $1,400 per month. An advance payment equal to one month's rent was paid on May 25 and credited to Rent Revenue.

7. On May 31, Salmon Lodge Inn has earned $890 of rent revenue from customers who are currently staying at the inn. The customers will only pay the amount owing when they check out in early June.

8. Salaries of $795 are unpaid at May 31.

9. The mortgage interest rate is 8%. Interest has been paid to May 1; the next payment is due June 1.

10. The May utility bill of $1,120 has not yet been recorded or paid.

11. Additional income taxes are estimated to be $500.

Instructions

(a) Prepare T accounts, and enter the trial balance amounts.

(b) Prepare and post the adjusting journal entries for the month.

(c) Prepare an adjusted trial balance at May 31.

(d) Prepare a statement of earnings, statement of retained earnings, and balance sheet for the year.

Prepare and post closing
entries; prepare post-closing
trial balance.
(SO 5)

▸ Accrual Accounting Concepts

P4–13B   Refer to the data for Salmon Lodge Inn Ltd. in P4–12B.

Instructions

(a) Prepare the closing journal entries.

(b) Post the closing entries to the T accounts prepared in P4–12B.

(c) Prepare a post-closing trial balance at May 31.

BROADENING YOUR PERSPECTIVE

www.wiley.com/canada/kimmel

Analysis Tools

Financial Reporting and Analysis Cases

Financial Reporting: *Shoppers Drug Mart*

BYP4–1   The financial statements of Shoppers Drug Mart are presented in Appendix A at the end of this book.

Instructions

(a) Does Shoppers Drug Mart report any prepayments on its balance sheet? If it does, identify each of these items as either a prepaid expense or unearned revenue. Using the statement of earnings, indicate the other account that is likely used in preparing adjusting entries for these items.

(b) Does Shoppers Drug Mart report any accruals on its balance sheet? If it does, identify each of these items as either an accrued revenue or accrued expense. Using the statement of earnings, indicate the other account that is likely used in preparing adjusting entries for these items.

(c) Reconstruct the summary closing journal entries prepared by Shoppers Drug Mart at December 29, 2007.

Comparative Analysis: *Shoppers Drug Mart and Jean Coutu*

BYP4–2 The financial statements of Jean Coutu are presented in Appendix B, after the financial statements for Shoppers Drug Mart in Appendix A.

Instructions

(a) Identify two accounts on Jean Coutu's balance sheet which show that Jean Coutu uses accrual accounting. In each case, identify the statement of earnings account that would be affected by the adjustment process.

(b) Identify two accounts on Shoppers Drug Mart's balance sheet which show that Shoppers Drug Mart uses accrual accounting. In each case, identify the statement of earnings account that would be affected by the adjustment process.

Interpreting Financial Statements

BYP4–3   Google Inc. is the most used site in the world for Internet searches. An excerpt from the notes to Google's financial statements follows:

GOOGLE INC.
Notes to the Financial Statements
December 31, 2007

Note 1. The Company and Summary of Accounting Policies—Revenue Recognition

We recognize as revenues the fees charged advertisers each time a user clicks on one of the text-based ads that are displayed next to the search results pages on our site or on the search results pages or content pages of our Google Network members' web sites and, for those advertisers who use our cost-per impression pricing, the fees charged advertisers each time an ad is displayed on our members' sites. In addition, we recognize as revenues the fees charged advertisers when ads are published in the magazines or broadcasted by the radio stations (or each time a listener responds to that ad) of our Google Network members.

We generate fees from search services on a per-query basis. Our policy is to recognize revenues from per-query search fees in the period we provide the search results.

We also generate fees from the sale and license of our Search Appliance, which includes hardware, software and 12 to 24 months of post-contract support. As the elements are not sold separately, sufficient vendor-specific objective evidence does not exist for the allocation of revenue. As a result, the entire fee is recognized ratably over the term of the post-contract support arrangement.

Instructions

(a) When does Google recognize the revenue from its advertising services? From its search services? From its sale and licence of the Search Appliance?

(b) When would Google likely incur the expenses related to its advertising, search and Search Appliance services? Explain how the matching principle does, or does not, relate to Google's revenue recognition practices.

(c) Google reports U.S. $178.1 million of unearned revenue in the current liabilities section of its balance sheet. Under what circumstances should Google record unearned revenue from its advertising services? From its search services? From the sale and licence of the Search Appliance?

A Global Focus

BYP4–4 Internet Initiative Japan Inc. (IIJ) is one of Japan's leading Internet-access and comprehensive Internet solution providers. It reported the following selected information at March 31 (in JPY millions):

	2008	2007
Cash and cash equivalents	¥11,471	¥13,555
Accounts receivable	12,255	9,676
Total revenues	66,835	57,055
Net earnings	5,177	5,410
Cash provided by operating activities	4,538	7,402

International Resources

Instructions

(a) Explain how the company's net earnings could decrease only ¥233 million (4 percent) between fiscal 2007 and 2008, while its cash provided by operating activities decreased ¥2,864 million (39 percent) during the same period.

(b) Explain how the company's cash from operating activities could be ¥4,538 million for the year ended March 31, 2008, while its cash and cash equivalents balance is ¥11,471 million at the end of this same fiscal year.

(c) For the year ended March 31, 2008, the company's revenues were ¥66,835 million. At the beginning of the year, it had ¥9,676 million of accounts receivable. At the end of the year, it had ¥12,255 million of accounts receivable. Based on these data, determine the amount of cash collected from customers during the year.

▶ Accrual Accounting Concepts

Critical Thinking Cases and Activities

Collaborative Learning Activity

BYP4–5 Air Canada sells tickets for airline flights that can vary a great deal in price and conditions. For example, at the low end of the pricing scheme, you can purchase a ticket from Fredericton to Toronto for a one-way "Tango" fare of $330. At the high end of the pricing scheme, you can purchase a ticket from Fredericton to Toronto for a one-way "Latitude" fare of $590.

Assume that Air Canada's management team is brainstorming its options for recognizing the revenue from the different categories of fares. One member of the management team says it should recognize the revenue as soon as the tickets are sold for the Tango-type fares because these tickets are non-cancellable and have a change fee. Passengers seldom change these fares. Another member of the management team states that revenue should be recognized when passengers pick up their tickets and pay for the flight. "What about when the boarding passes are collected at the gate?" a third asks. "Or when passengers arrive at their destinations?" a fourth adds.

Instructions

After the class has been divided into groups and you have been assigned one of the two fare types (Tango or Latitude), do the following:

(a) Evaluate the effect of each of the revenue recognition choices on recorded revenues, expenses, and net earnings for your assigned fare type.

(b) Determine the point at which you think Air Canada should recognize the revenue from ticket sales for your fare type. Explain why you believe your chosen point of revenue recognition is the best, referring to appropriate generally accepted accounting principles in your answer.

Communication Activity

BYP4–6 There are many people today who believe that cash is a better indicator of a company's future success than net earnings. This notion gained popularity after many reports of corporate financial scandals where management was apparently able to manipulate prepayments and accruals to influence net earnings.

Instructions

Write a memo discussing whether you believe cash is a more reliable performance measure than net earnings. Include in your memo the answers to the following questions:

(a) What is the difference between accrual-based net earnings and cash?

(b) Do you believe that it is possible for management to manipulate net earnings? If so, identify one way that management might be able to increase net earnings by manipulating prepayments or accruals.

(c) Do you believe that it is possible for management to manipulate cash? If so, identify one way that management might be able to increase cash flow.

Ethics Case

Ethics in Accounting

BYP4–7 Die Hard Corporation is a pesticide manufacturer. Its sales declined greatly this year because of new legislation that outlaws the sale of several Die Hard chemical pesticides. During the coming year, Die Hard will have environmentally safe and competitive chemicals to replace these discontinued products. Sales in the next year are expected to be much higher than those of any prior year. The decline in this year's sales and profits appears, therefore, to be a one-year aberration.

Even so, the company president believes that a large dip in the current year's profits could cause a significant drop in the market price of Die Hard's shares and make the company a takeover target. To avoid this possibility, he urges Carole Denton, the company's controller, to accrue all possible revenues and to defer as many expenses as possible when making this period's year-end adjusting entries. The president says to Carole, "We need the revenues this year, and next year can easily absorb expenses deferred from this year. We can't let our share price be hammered down!" Carole did not get around to recording the adjusting journal entries until January 17, but she dated the entries December 31 as if they were recorded then. Carole also made every effort to comply with the president's request.

Instructions

(a) Who are the stakeholders in this situation?

(b) What are the ethical considerations of the president's request and Carole's dating the adjusting entries December 31?

(c) Can Carole aggressively accrue revenues and defer expenses and still be ethical?

"All About You" Activity

BYP4–8 In the "All About You feature in this chapter, you learned how important it is that companies report or disclose information about all liabilities, including potential liabilities related to an environmental clean-up. There are many situations in which you will be asked to provide personal financial information about your own liabilities, in addition to your assets, revenue, and expenses. Sometimes you will face difficult decisions regarding what to disclose and how to disclose it. Suppose that you are putting together a loan application to purchase a home. Based on your income and assets, you qualify for the mortgage loan, but just barely.

Instructions

How would you address the following situations in reporting your financial position for the loan application?

(a) You signed a guarantee for a bank loan that a friend took out for $20,000. If your friend doesn't pay, you will have to pay. Your friend has made all of the payments so far, and it appears he will be able to pay in the future.

(b) The company where you work is not doing very well, and it has recently laid off employees. You are still employed, but it is quite possible that you will lose your job in the next few months.

Serial Case

(*Note:* This serial case started in Chapter 1 and continued in chapters 2 and 3. From the information gathered through Chapter 3, follow the instructions below using the general ledger accounts you have already prepared.)

BYP4–9 Cookie Creations is gearing up for a busy spring. During the month of March 2009, the following transactions occur:

Mar.	3	An assistant is hired at an hourly wage of $8 to help Natalie with cookie making and some administrative duties.
	5	Natalie teaches the class that was booked on February 23. You will recall that a down payment of $50 was received in February. The balance, $75, is received.
	6	A cheque in the amount of $250 is received for the amount due from the neighbourhood school for the class given on February 27.
	10	The local school board pays $625 in advance for five classes that are to be given during March and April.
	17	The cell phone invoice outstanding at the end of February is paid, $50.
	19	A deposit of $50 is received on a cookie class scheduled for early April.
	25	Additional revenue earned during the month for cookie-making classes amounts to $3,500. (Natalie has not had time to account for each class individually.) Cash of $3,000 has been collected and $500 is still outstanding. (This is in addition to the March 5 and March 10 transactions.)
	25	Additional supplies of sugar, flour, and chocolate chips purchased during the month amount to $1,250 cash.
	25	A cheque is issued to Natalie's assistant for $800. Her assistant worked approximately 100 hours from when she was hired until March 25.
	25	Natalie is paid $500 cash for her salary earned to date.
	30	A dividend of $100 is paid to the common shareholder (Natalie).

As at March 31, Cookie Creations' quarter end, the following adjusting entry data are available:

1. A count reveals that $50 worthof brochures and posters remain at the end of March.

2. Depreciation is recorded on the baking equipment purchased in February. The baking equipment has a total cost of $1,200 and a useful life of five years. (Assume that only one month's worth of depreciation is required.)

3. Interest on the note payable is accrued. You will recall that a one-year, 6% note payable wa: issued for $2,000 on February 18. (Assume that one and a half months of interest are accrued fo: February and March.)

4. One month's worth of insurance has expired. You will recall that a one-year insurance policy wa: purchased for $1,200 on February 27.

5. Natalie is unexpectedly telephoned on March 27 to give a cookie class, before month end, at the neighbourhood community centre. The community centre is invoiced in early April for $375.

6. A count reveals that $1,000 of baking supplies were used. You will recall that there were $125 of supplies on hand at the beginning of the month.

7. A cellphone invoice is received for $75. The invoice is for services provided during the month of March and is due on April 15.

8. Because the cookie-making class occurred unexpectedly on March 28 and is for such a large group of children, Natalie's assistant helps out. Her assistant worked seven hours at a rate of $8 per hour.

9. An analysis of the Unearned Revenue account reveals that two of the five classes paid for by the local school board on March 10 have still not been taught by the end of March. The $50 deposit received on March 19 for another class also remains unearned.

10. Cookie Creations calculates that it currently owes $310 of income tax.

Instructions

(a) Record the above transactions.

(b) Using T accounts, post the March transactions to the general ledger. (Use the general ledger accounts that you prepared in Chapter 3.)

(c) Prepare a trial balance at March 31.

(d) Prepare and post adjusting journal entries for the month of March.

(e) Prepare an adjusted trial balance at March 31.

(f) Prepare a statement of earnings and a statement of retained earnings for the quarter ending March 31, and a balance sheet at March 31.

Answers to Chapter Questions

Answer to Shoppers Drug Mart Review It Question 3
Accumulated amortization, $645,798 thousand and net book value, $1,126,513 thousand (see note 6 in Notes to the Consolidated Financial Statements). Note that Shoppers uses the terms *amortization* rather than *depreciation* and *net book value* rather than *carrying amount*.

Answers to Self-Study Questions
1. a   2. d   3. d   4. b   5. d   6. a   7. c   8. b   9. a   10. a

Remember to go
back to the beginning
of the chapter to
check off your
completed work!

←

Comprehensive Case: Chapter 4

True North Consultants Ltd. commenced operations on January 1, 2009. In order to keep on top of its accounting, True North plans to record and adjust its accounts monthly. It conducted the following transactions during January:

Jan. 2   Issued $30,000 of common shares for cash.

   2   Signed a five-year lease for office space.

   5   Prepaid six months of liability insurance, $900.

   5   Paid the first (January 2009) and last (December 2009) month's rent, $3,000 per month, for a total payment of $6,000.

   6   Purchased office equipment on account, $12,000.

   7   Purchased $2,000 of office supplies for cash.

   8   Visited client offices and agreed on the terms of a consulting project. True North will invoice the client, Anjou Productions, on the 15th of each month for work performed.

   9   Leased a vehicle for a four-year term. Paid the first month's lease payment of $450 and a security deposit of $3,000. Use the accounts Vehicle Lease Expense and Prepaid Vehicle Lease (long-term), respectively, to record these amounts.

   12   Negotiated a $25,000 line of credit at the bank to be used as needed to cover temporary cash overdrafts.

   13   Met with a new client, Babson Technologies. Received $5,000 cash as a retainer for future work to be performed.

   15   Invoiced Anjou Productions for $4,000 of consulting services provided on account.

   16   Paid a telecommunications bill of $475.

   19   Received an invoice for routine legal advice, $1,200. The amount is not due until February 15.

   21   Completed the first phase of the project for Babson Technologies. Recognized $3,000 of revenue from the cash retainer previously received. Issued the client an invoice marked "Paid."

   22   Received $4,000 cash from Anjou Productions in payment of the invoice issued on the 15th.

   26   Received and deposited a $500 fee for speaking at an industry conference.

   30   Prepared an adjusting entry to record $250 of office supplies used (see January 7 transaction).

   30   Prepared an adjusting entry to record the expiry of one month's liability insurance (see January 5 transaction).

   31   Reviewed the accounts for any further adjustments. Office equipment will not be depreciated until the year end. The monthly adjustment is immaterial to the financial statements.

Instructions

(a) Record the above transactions.

(b) Prepare T accounts and post the general and adjusting journal entries.

(c) Prepare a trial balance as at January 31.

(d) Prepare the (1) statement of earnings, (2) statement of retained earnings, and (3) balance sheet for the month.

(e) True North closes its books annually. If True North closed its books on a monthly basis, identify which accounts would be closed.

(f) True North needs to maintain a current ratio of 2.5 to 1 in order to maintain its financial standing with its bankers. Calculate the current ratio. Has it achieved the 2.5 to 1 benchmark?

CHAPTER 5
Merchandising Operations

ACCOUNTING MATTERS!

The Right Way to Retail

Until the twentieth century, to be labelled a "consumer" was an insult. In fact, one of the deadliest diseases in history, tuberculosis, was often referred to as "consumption." Today, however, being a consumer is central to life in the Western world. North America was the birthplace of consumerism and has led the world in its devotion to the concept ever since. And nowhere is this consumerism more evident than in the discount retail industry led by the U.S.-based giant Wal-Mart Stores, Inc.

Wal-Mart opened its first store in 1962 in Rogers, Arkansas, and grew steadily and profitably. By 1970, the company had 38 stores and sales of U.S. $44.2 million. It entered Canada in 1994 with the purchase of 122 Woolco stores. Today, Wal-Mart Canada has 278 locations employing more than 70,000 people across the country. These are among its more than 2,980 stores located in 13 countries other than the U.S., including Argentina, Brazil, Canada, China, Costa Rica, El Salvador, Guatemala, Honduras, Japan, Mexico, Nicaragua, Puerto Rico, and the United Kingdom. This international presence, added to the more than 4,000 Supercenters, Sam's Clubs, Neighborhood Markets, and Wal-Mart stores in the United States, makes Wal-Mart the number one retailer in the world, with sales of U.S. $374.5 billion in the year ended January 31, 2008.

A key contributor to Wal-Mart's success is its inventory control and distribution system. Using satellite technology, the company receives millions of updates every minute on what items customers buy and the relationship among the items sold to each person. The result is an enormous database of purchasing information that is transmitted to the accounting systems. This allows stores to keep shelves stocked with exactly what the customers want, while still keeping inventory under control.

To help track its inventory, Wal-Mart uses electronic product codes (EPCs). Similar to bar codes, which tell a retailer how many boxes it has of a specific product, EPCs go a step further, helping distinguish each box of the same product. This allows retailers to better monitor product inventory along the path from supplier to distribution centre to store.

The tags use radio frequency identification (RFID) technology, the same technology found in keyless remotes that unlock car doors. The RFID tags are passed by a special reader that receives and transmits their unique product identifier codes to an inventory control system. RFID readers installed at distribution centres automatically let Wal-Mart's operations and merchandising teams, as well as suppliers, know that a specific shipment has arrived. The readers installed at stores automatically confirm that the shipment is in the back room and individual products are then stocked as needed.

Today, nearly 1,000 Wal-Mart locations use EPC technology. According to the company website, more than 600 of Wal-Mart's suppliers also use it. An independent study done in 2005 by the University of Arkansas found that Wal-Mart's EPC use had reduced out of stock items by up to 16 percent. Stores with EPC technology were 63 percent more effective in replenishing tagged items than control stores and experienced a 10-percent reduction in manual orders, which reduced excess inventory. The technology has also shortened the time that it takes to put new items on store shelves, making the process as much as three times faster than for non-tagged products.

While EPCs are currently used to track shipments from supplier to distribution centre to store, other potential uses include monitoring product expiration dates and acting quickly on product recalls. Wal-Mart also expects to see faster returns and warranty processing in the future. For the time being, however, the main benefit to the all-important consumer is better merchandise availability.

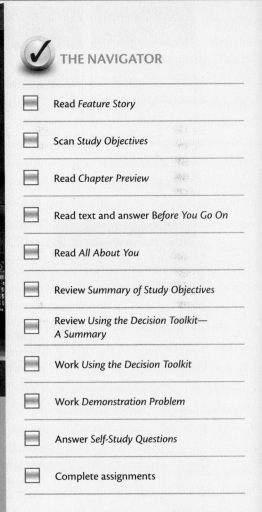

I-Mart: walmart.com

UDY OBJECTIVES

er studying this chapter, you should be able to:

Identify the differences between service and merchandising companies.

Prepare entries for purchases under a perpetual inventory system.

Prepare entries for sales under a perpetual inventory system.

Prepare a single-step and a multiple-step statement of earnings.

Calculate the gross profit margin and profit margin.

Prepare entries for purchases and sales under a periodic inventory system and calculate cost of goods sold (Appendix 5A).

✔ THE NAVIGATOR

☐ Read *Feature Story*

☐ Scan *Study Objectives*

☐ Read *Chapter Preview*

☐ Read text and answer *Before You Go On*

☐ Read *All About You*

☐ Review *Summary of Study Objectives*

☐ Review *Using the Decision Toolkit—A Summary*

☐ Work *Using the Decision Toolkit*

☐ Work *Demonstration Problem*

☐ Answer *Self-Study Questions*

☐ Complete assignments

e Navigator

PREVIEW OF CHAPTER 5

The first four chapters of this text focused mostly on service companies, like the fictional Sierra Corporation. In this and the next chapter, we turn our attention to merchandising companies. Merchandising companies such as Wal-Mart buy and sell merchandise for profit rather than perform a service. In this chapter, you will learn the basics of accounting for merchandising transactions. You will also learn how to prepare and analyze the statement of earnings for a merchandising company.

The chapter is organized as follows:

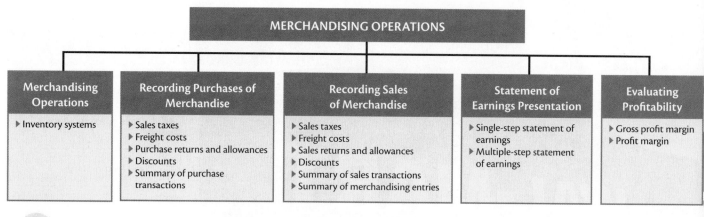

MERCHANDISING OPERATIONS				
Merchandising Operations	**Recording Purchases of Merchandise**	**Recording Sales of Merchandise**	**Statement of Earnings Presentation**	**Evaluating Profitability**
▸ Inventory systems	▸ Sales taxes ▸ Freight costs ▸ Purchase returns and allowances ▸ Discounts ▸ Summary of purchase transactions	▸ Sales taxes ▸ Freight costs ▸ Sales returns and allowances ▸ Discounts ▸ Summary of sales transactions ▸ Summary of merchandising entries	▸ Single-step statement of earnings ▸ Multiple-step statement of earnings	▸ Gross profit margin ▸ Profit margin

The Navigator

Merchandising Operations

study objective 1

Identify the differences between service and merchandising companies.

Merchandising involves purchasing products—also called merchandise inventory or just inventory—to resell to customers. Merchandising is one of the largest and most influential industries in Canada and around the world. For example, in 2007, Canada exported $465 billion of merchandise and imported $416 billion. The steps in the accounting cycle for a merchandising company are the same as the steps for a service company. However, merchandising companies need additional accounts and entries in order to record merchandising transactions.

In addition, the operating cycle—the time it takes to go from cash to cash in producing revenues—is usually longer for a merchandising company than it is for a service company. The purchase of merchandise inventory and the lapse of time until it is sold lengthen the cycle. In a service company, the company performs services for cash or on account (on credit, which eventually results in cash when the account is collected). In a merchandising company, the company first has to purchase merchandise before it can sell it for cash, or on account.

Measuring net earnings for a merchandising company is basically the same as for a service company. That is, net earnings (or loss) results when expenses are matched with revenues. In a merchandising company, the main source of revenue is the sale of merchandise, often referred to simply as sales revenue or just sales. Unlike expenses for a service company, expenses for a merchandising company are divided into two categories: (1) cost of goods sold and (2) operating expenses. Some merchandising companies may also have other revenues and expenses, which we will learn about later in the chapter.

The cost of goods sold is the total cost of the merchandise that was sold during the period. This expense is directly related to the revenue that is recognized from the sale of goods. Sales revenue less the cost of goods sold is called gross profit. For example, as mentioned in the feature story, Wal-Mart reported sales revenue of U.S. $374.5 billion for the year ended January 31, 2008. It cost Wal-Mart U.S. $286.5 billion to purchase this merchandise to sell, so the company earned a gross profit of U.S. $88 billion ($374.5 billion – $286.5 billion) on these sales.

Alternative Terminology
Gross profit is also called *gross margin*.

After gross profit is calculated, operating expenses are deducted to determine earnings before income tax. Operating expenses are expenses that are incurred in the process of earning sales revenue. The operating expenses of a merchandising company include many of the same expenses found in a service company, such as salaries, insurance, utilities, and depreciation.

Then, as is done for a service company, income tax expense is deducted from earnings before income tax to determine net earnings (loss). The earnings measurement process for a merchandising company, assuming it has no other revenues and expenses, is shown in Illustration 5-1. The items in the two blue boxes are unique to a merchandising company; they are not used by a service company.

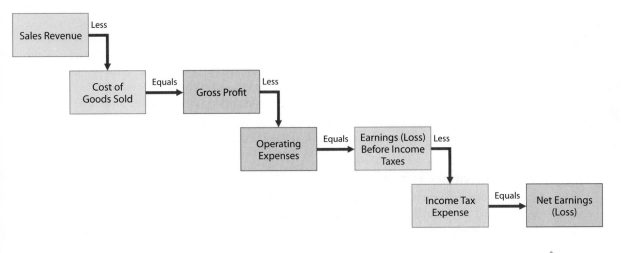

↑ Illustration 5-1

Earnings measurement process for a merchandising company

Inventory Systems

A merchandising company keeps track of its inventory to determine what is available for sale (inventory) and what has been sold (cost of goods sold). Goods available for sale are reported as merchandise inventory, a current asset on the balance sheet. Goods sold are reported as cost of goods sold expense on the statement of earnings.

One of two kinds of systems is used to account for inventory and the cost of goods sold: a **perpetual inventory system** or a **periodic inventory system**.

Perpetual Inventory System

In a perpetual inventory system, detailed records are maintained for the cost of each product that is purchased and sold. These records continuously—perpetually—show the quantity and cost of the inventory purchased, sold, and on hand. By using the sophisticated electronic inventory system described in the feature story, Wal-Mart knows the quantity, cost, and location of every item that it buys and sells.

When inventory items are purchased under a perpetual inventory system, the purchased item is recorded by debiting (increasing) the Merchandise Inventory account. Not all purchases are debited to Merchandise Inventory, however. Purchases of assets that the company will use rather than resell, such as supplies and equipment, are recorded as increases to specific asset accounts rather than as increases to the Merchandise Inventory account. For example, Wal-Mart would increase the Supplies account to record the purchase of cash register receipt paper or materials that it uses to make shelf signs.

When merchandise inventory is later sold, the cost of the goods that have just been sold (the original purchase cost of the merchandise) is obtained from the inventory records. This cost is transferred from the account Merchandise Inventory (an asset) to the account Cost of Goods Sold (an expense). Under a perpetual inventory system, the cost of goods sold and the reduction in inventory—both its quantity and cost—are recorded each time a sale occurs.

Inventory is usually the largest current asset for a merchandiser. Effective control over the merchandise on hand is an important feature of a perpetual inventory system. Since the inventory records show the quantities that should be on hand, the merchandise can be counted at any time to see whether the amount actually on hand matches the inventory records. Any shortages that are found can be investigated. For control purposes, a physical inventory count is always taken at least once a year, and ideally more often, under the perpetual inventory system. We will learn more about counting inventory in the next chapter.

A perpetual inventory system also makes it possible to monitor merchandise availability and maintain optimum inventory levels. As mentioned in the feature story, Wal-Mart was able to reduce its out of stock items by 16 percent by using electronic product codes to keep track of its inventory.

ACCOUNTING MATTERS! | Management Perspective

Thirty-five thousand cases of canned goods—enough to fill a dozen trucks—seemingly disappeared from a warehouse on the west coast recently. The company had had no prior losses of this size at any of its warehouses during its century in business.

How did 35,000 cases of canned goods disappear? It seems unlikely that this amount of inventory was simply removed. Instead, a mismanaged warehouse move, software changes, and other events conspired to make truckloads of canned goods "appear to disappear." How was the "missing" inventory discovered? By comparing the physical inventory count with the perpetual inventory records and tracing all inbound and outbound inventory movements back to the original source documents, it was finally determined that the inventory was still there, just in a different location than expected.

Source: Paul Engle, "The Case of the Missing Cases," *Industrial Engineer,* July 2007, 22.

Periodic Inventory System

In a periodic inventory system, detailed inventory records of the merchandise on hand are not kept throughout the period. As a result, **the cost of goods sold is determined only at the end of the accounting period**—that is, periodically—when a physical inventory count is done to determine the cost of the goods on hand.

In a periodic inventory system, after the cost of the goods on hand (ending inventory) at the end of the period has been determined, we can use this information to calculate the cost of the goods that were sold during the period. To determine the cost of goods sold under a periodic inventory system, the following steps are necessary:

1. Beginning inventory: Determine the cost of goods on hand at the beginning of the accounting period.
2. Cost of goods available for sale: Add the cost of goods purchased to the beginning inventory. The total is the cost of goods available for sale during the period.
3. Ending inventory: Subtract the cost of goods on hand at the end of the accounting period (ending inventory) from the cost of goods available for sale. The result is the cost of goods sold.

Illustration 5-2 gives the formula to calculate the cost of goods sold.

Illustration 5-2 ➡

Formula for cost of goods sold

This calculation is in fact also used in a perpetual inventory system. The difference, however, is that in a perpetual inventory system the cost of goods sold is calculated and recorded at the time of each sale. In a periodic inventory system, there is only one calculation of cost of goods sold: it is done to find the total cost of goods sold for the period and is done at the end of the accounting period.

How do companies decide which inventory system to use? They compare the cost of the detailed record keeping that is required for a perpetual inventory system to the benefits of having the additional information about, and control over, their inventory. In the past, only companies that sold merchandise with high unit values—such as automobiles or major home appliances—used the perpetual inventory system. Today, however, the cost of computerized perpetual inventory software and electronic scanners is much lower, to the point where many companies, selling nearly any product, are now using it.

Because the perpetual inventory system is widely used, we illustrate it in this chapter. The periodic inventory system, still used by some companies, is described in the appendix to this chapter.

BEFORE YOU GO ON...

➡ **Review It**

1. What is the operating cycle? Why is it longer for a merchandising company than for a service company?
2. How does the measurement of net earnings in a merchandising company differ from its measurement in a service company?
3. How does a perpetual inventory system differ from a periodic system?

The Navigator

Recording Purchases of Merchandise

Purchases of inventory can be made for cash or on account. Purchases are normally recorded by the buyer when the goods are received from the seller. Every purchase should be supported by a document that provides written evidence of the transaction. In larger companies, when orders are placed with a supplier, each order is documented with a purchase order.

Cash purchases should be supported by a cash register receipt indicating the items purchased and amounts paid. Cash purchases are recorded by an increase (debit) in Merchandise Inventory and a decrease (credit) in Cash.

Credit purchases should be supported by a **purchase invoice** that indicates the total purchase price and other relevant information. The buyer does not prepare a separate purchase invoice. Instead, an invoice is prepared by the seller. The original copy of the invoice goes to the buyer to be used as a purchase invoice, and a copy is kept by the seller to be used as a sales invoice. In Illustration 5-3, for example, the sales invoice prepared by PW Audio Supply, Inc. (the seller) is used as a purchase invoice by Sauk Stereo Ltd. (the buyer).

study objective 2

Prepare entries for purchases under a perpetual inventory system.

◀ Illustration 5-3

Sales/purchase invoice

						INVOICE NO. 731
			PW Audio Supply, Inc.			
			277 Wellington Street, West			
			Toronto, Ontario, M5V 3H2			
S O L D	Firm name:	Sauk Stereo Ltd.				
	Attention of:	James Hoover, Purchasing Agent				
	Address:	21 King Street West				
T O		Hamilton	Ontario		L8P 4W7	
		City	Province		Postal Code	
Date: May 4, 2009		Salesperson: Malone	Terms 2/10, n/30		FOB shipping point	
Catalogue No.		Description		Quantity	Price	Amount
X572Y9820		Printed Circuit Board		1	2,300	$2,300
A2547Z45		Production Model Circuits		5	300	1,500
IMPORTANT: ALL RETURNS MUST BE MADE WITHIN 10 DAYS					TOTAL	$3,800

The buyer, Sauk Stereo, would make the following entry to record the purchase of merchandise:

May 4	Merchandise Inventory	3,800	
	Accounts Payable		3,800
	(To record goods purchased on account from PW Audio		
	Supply per invoice #731, terms 2/10, n/30)		

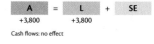

A	=	L	+	SE
+3,800		+3,800		

Cash flows: no effect

Sales Taxes

Sales taxes are collected by most merchandising and service companies on the goods they sell and the services they provide. Sales taxes in Canada include the Goods and Services Tax (GST) and the Provincial Sales Tax (PST). In 2008, the federal GST was assessed at a rate of 5% across Canada. Note that this rate is subject to change. It was 6% in 2007 and 7% before that. At the time of writing this textbook, it is expected that the GST rate will remain at 5% for the foreseeable future.

Provincial sales tax rates vary throughout the provinces and territories. In the Atlantic provinces (except for P.E.I.), GST and PST have been combined into one 13% tax called the Harmonized Sales Tax (HST).

When merchandising companies purchase goods for resale, they pay GST on the cost of the goods. However, because companies can get back any GST they pay on purchases (by offsetting it against the GST they collect from customers), this cost is not part of the cost of the merchandise. PST, on the other hand, is never paid by a merchandiser on goods it purchases for resale—it is paid only by the final consumer.

Sales taxes add much complexity to the accounting process, and not all companies and their goods and services are taxable. The accounting transactions described in this and other chapters are therefore presented without the added complication of sales taxes. That is why Invoice No. 731 in Illustration 5-3 did not include the sales taxes that would normally be added to the invoice price.

Freight Costs

The sales/purchase invoice should indicate whether the seller or the buyer must pay the cost of transporting the goods to the buyer's place of business. Freight terms state who pays the freight charges (i.e., shipping costs) and who is responsible for the risk of damage to the merchandise during transit. Freight terms can vary, but are often expressed as either FOB shipping point or FOB destination. The letters FOB mean "free on board" until the point where ownership is transferred.

FOB shipping point means that the goods are delivered to the point of shipping (normally the seller's place of business) by the seller. The buyer pays the freight costs to get the goods from the point of shipping to the destination (normally the buyer's place of business) and is responsible for any damages that may occur along the way.

FOB destination means that the goods are delivered by the seller to their destination. The seller pays the freight to get the goods from the point of shipping to their destination and is responsible for any damages that may occur along the way. Illustration 5-4 shows these shipping terms.

Illustration 5-4 ➡

Freight terms

The purchase invoice in Illustration 5-3 shown earlier indicates that the freight terms are FOB shipping point. This means that the buyer (Sauk Stereo) paid the freight charges and then increased (debited) its Merchandise Inventory account for the additional cost. Why? Recall from Chapter 2 that the cost principle dictates that assets should be stated at their cost. Consequently, the cost of inventory includes all costs of purchase and other costs that are incurred in bringing inventories to their present location and getting them ready for sale. As a result, any **freight paid by the buyer is recorded as being part of the cost of the merchandise purchased**.

Assume upon delivery of the goods on May 4, Sauk Stereo (the buyer) pays Public Carrier Co. $150 for freight charges. The entry on Sauk Stereo's books is:

May 4	Merchandise Inventory	150	
	Cash		150
	(To record payment of freight on goods purchased)		

Purchase Returns and Allowances

A purchaser may be dissatisfied with the merchandise received. The goods may be damaged or defective, of inferior quality, or might not fit the buyer's specifications. In such cases, the buyer may return the goods to the seller. The buyer will receive a cash refund if the purchase was made for cash. Credit is given if the purchase was made on account.

Alternatively, the buyer may choose to keep the merchandise if the seller is willing to give an allowance (deduction) from the purchase price. These types of transactions are known as purchase returns and allowances. In both cases, the result is a decrease in the cost of goods purchased.

Assume that Sauk Stereo returned goods costing $300 to PW Audio Supply on May 8. The entry by Sauk Stereo for the returned merchandise is:

May 8	Accounts Payable	300	
	Merchandise Inventory		300
	(To record return of goods to PW Audio Supply)		

A	=	L	+	SE
−300		−300		

Cash flows: no effect

Sauk Stereo increased Merchandise Inventory and Accounts Payable when the goods were originally purchased. Sauk Stereo therefore decreases Merchandise Inventory and Accounts Payable when it returns the goods, or when it is granted an allowance. Merchandise Inventory is credited to show the reduction in the cost of the inventory. Accounts Payable is debited to show the reduction in the amount owed by Sauk Stereo to PW Audio Supply.

Discounts

The terms of a purchase may include an offer of a quantity discount for a bulk purchase. A **quantity discount** gives a reduction in price according to the volume of the purchase. In other words, the larger the number of items purchased, the better the discount. Quantity discounts are not recorded or accounted for separately. For example, PW Audio Supply may offer a 10% price discount on orders of 25 or more items. So, if 25 printed circuit boards were ordered, the price per board would be $2,070 ($2,300 × 90%) rather than $2,300. Only the $2,070 amount would be recorded by Sauk Stereo.

Quantity discounts are not the same as a **purchase discount**, which is offered to customers for early payment of the balance due on account. A purchase discount offers advantages to both parties: the purchaser saves money, and the seller is able to shorten the operating cycle by converting accounts receivable into cash earlier.

Purchase discounts are noted on the invoice through credit terms. These terms specify the amount of the discount and the time period during which it is offered. They also indicate the date by which the purchaser is expected to pay the full invoice price. In the sales invoice in Illustration 5-3, credit terms are 2/10, n/30, which is read "two-ten, net thirty." This means that a 2% cash discount may be taken on the invoice price, less ("net of") any returns or allowances, if payment is made within 10 days of the invoice date (the discount period). Otherwise, the invoice price, less any returns or allowances, is due 30 days from the invoice date.

Not every seller offers purchase discounts, although they are common in certain industries. When the seller chooses not to offer a discount for fast payment, credit terms will specify only the maximum time period for paying the balance due. For example, the time period may be stated as n/30, meaning that the net amount must be paid in 30 days.

In contrast to quantity discounts, purchase discounts are recorded separately. When an invoice is paid within the discount period, the amount of the discount decreases the Merchandise Inventory account. By paying within the discount period, the merchandiser has reduced the cost of its inventory.

To illustrate, assume Sauk Stereo pays the balance due of $3,500 (gross invoice price of $3,800 less purchase returns and allowances of $300) on May 14, the last day of the discount period. Note that discounts are not taken on freight costs. The discount is $70 ($3,500 × 2%), and the amount of cash paid by Sauk Stereo is $3,430 ($3,500 − $70). The entry to record the May 14 payment by Sauk Stereo is:

May 14	Accounts Payable	3,500	
	Cash		3,430
	Merchandise Inventory		70
	(To record payment to PW Audio Supply within discount period)		

A	=	L	+	SE
−3,430		−3,500		
−70				

Cash flows: −3,430

A merchandising company should usually take all available purchase discounts. Passing up the discount may be viewed as paying interest for use of the money. For example, if Sauk Stereo passed up the discount, it would be paying 2% for the use of $3,500 for 20 days. This equals an annual interest rate of 36.5% (2% × 365 ÷ 20). Obviously, it would be better for Sauk Stereo to borrow at bank interest rates than to lose the discount.

Summary of Purchase Transactions

A summary of the effect of the previous purchase transactions on Merchandise Inventory is provided in the following T account (with transaction descriptions in parentheses). Sauk Stereo originally purchased $3,800 worth of inventory for resale. It paid $150 in freight charges. It then returned $300 worth of goods. Finally, it received a $70 discount off the balance owed because it paid within the discount period. This results in a balance in the Merchandise Inventory account of $3,580, as follows:

			Merchandise Inventory				
(Purchase)	May	4	3,800	May	8	300	(Purchase return)
(Freight)		4	150		14	70	(Purchase discount)
	Bal.		3,580				

The balance of $3,580 in the Merchandise Inventory account represents the **cost of the goods purchased**. Illustration 5-5 shows the calculation of cost of goods purchased as a formula:

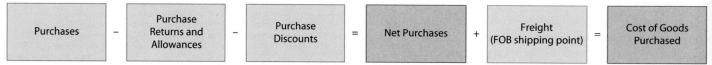

Illustration 5-5

Formula for cost of goods purchased

Purchases of merchandise for resale are debited to the Merchandise Inventory account. These amounts are reduced by any returns and allowances and discounts. The difference between purchases of merchandise, less returns and allowances and discounts, is commonly known as net purchases. Freight incurred by the buyer is debited to the Merchandise Inventory account. The total of all of these amounts (before the cost of the sales is credited to the Merchandise Inventory account which we will discuss in the next section), is known as the cost of goods purchased. Note that the purchaser only incurs freight if the shipping terms are FOB shipping point. As shown in Illustration 5-2, cost of goods purchased is an essential component in the calculation of cost of goods sold. And, as indicated earlier in the chapter, this calculation is used in both perpetual and periodic inventory systems. In a perpetual inventory system, the cost of goods sold is calculated and recorded at the point of sale; in a periodic inventory system, it is calculated only at the end of the period.

BEFORE YOU GO ON...

⟶ **Review It**

1. Who pays the freight—the seller or the buyer—when the shipping terms are (a) FOB shipping point, and (b) FOB destination?
2. Under the perpetual inventory system, what entries (if any) are made to record purchases, freight costs, purchase returns and allowances, quantity discounts, and purchase discounts?
3. Explain how cost of goods purchased is calculated.

⟶ **Do It**

On September 2, Brighthouse Corp. buys merchandise on account from Junot Inc. for $1,500, terms 2/10, n/30, FOB shipping point. The correct company pays freight charges of $75 on September 4. On September 8, Brighthouse returns $200 of the merchandise to Junot. On September 11, Brighthouse pays the total amount owing. Record the transactions on Brighthouse's books.

Action Plan

• Purchases of goods for resale are recorded in the asset account Merchandise Inventory when a perpetual inventory system is used.
• Examine freight terms to determine which company pays the freight charges. Freight charges paid by the purchaser increase the cost of the merchandise inventory.
• The Merchandise Inventory account is reduced by the cost of merchandise returned.
• Calculate purchase discounts using the net amount owing (not including freight). Reduce the Merchandise Inventory account by the amount of the purchase discount.

Solution

Brighthouse (Buyer)

Sept.	2	Merchandise Inventory	1,500	
		Accounts Payable		1,500
		(To record goods purchased on account from		
		Junot, terms 2/10, n/30)		
	4	Merchandise Inventory	75	
		Cash		75
		(To record freight paid on goods purchased)		
	8	Accounts Payable	200	
		Merchandise Inventory		200
		(To record return of goods)		
	11	Accounts Payable ($1,500 − $200)	1,300	
		Merchandise Inventory ($1,300 × 2%)		26
		Cash ($1,300 − $26)		1,274
		(To record cash payment within the discount period)		

The Navigator

Recording Sales of Merchandise

To comply with the revenue recognition principle, sales revenue is recorded when it is earned, just as service revenue is. Typically, sales revenue is earned when the goods are transferred from the seller to the buyer. At this point, the sales transaction is completed and the selling price is established.

A sale may be made for cash or credit. Every sales transaction should be supported by a business document that provides written evidence of the sale. Cash register tapes provide evidence of cash sales. A **sales invoice**, like the one that was shown in Illustration 5-3, provides support for a credit sale.

Two entries are made for each sale in a perpetual inventory system. The first entry records the sales revenue: Cash (or Accounts Receivable, if it is a credit sale) is increased by a debit and Sales is increased by a credit for the selling (invoice) price of the goods. The second entry records the cost of the merchandise sold: Cost of Goods Sold is increased by a debit and Merchandise Inventory is decreased by a credit for the cost of the goods. As a result, at all times Merchandise Inventory will show the amount of inventory that should be on hand.

To illustrate a credit sales transaction, we will use the sales invoice shown earlier in Illustration 5-3 for PW Audio Supply's sale of $3,800 of merchandise on May 4 to Sauk Stereo. Assume the merchandise cost PW Audio Supply $2,400 when it was originally purchased. The sale is recorded as follows:

study objective 3

Prepare entries for sales under a perpetual inventory system.

May	4	Accounts Receivable	3,800	
		Sales		3,800
		(To record credit sale to Sauk Stereo per invoice #731, terms		
		2/10, n/30)		
	4	Cost of Goods Sold	2,400	
		Merchandise Inventory		2,400
		(To record cost of merchandise sold on invoice #731		
		to Sauk Stereo)		

A = L + SE
+3,800   +3,800
Cash flows: no effect

A = L + SE
−2,400   −2,400
Cash flows: no effect

For internal decision-making purposes, merchandising companies may use more than one sales account. For example, PW Audio Supply may decide to keep separate sales accounts for its major product lines, rather than a single combined sales account. This enables company management to monitor sales trends more closely and respond in a more strategic way to changes in sales patterns. For example, if sales of wireless speakers are increasing while sales of powered speakers are decreasing, the company should re-evaluate both its advertising and pricing policies on each of these items to ensure that they are optimal.

On its statement of earnings presented to outside investors, a merchandising company would normally provide only a single sales figure—the sum of all of its individual sales accounts. This is done for two reasons. First, providing detail on all of its individual sales accounts would make its statement of earnings much longer. Second, companies do not want their competitors to know the details of their operating results.

Sales Taxes

Sales taxes are collected by merchandising companies on the goods that they sell. When a company collects sales taxes from selling a product or service, these sales taxes are not recorded as revenue. The sales taxes are collected for the federal and provincial governments, and must be periodically remitted to these collecting authorities. Sales taxes that are collected from selling a product or service are recorded as a liability until they are paid to the government. As stated earlier, accounting for sales taxes is complicated and is not discussed in detail in this textbook.

Freight Costs

As discussed earlier in the chapter, freight terms on the sales invoice—FOB destination and FOB shipping point—indicate who is responsible for shipping costs. If the term is FOB destination, the seller assumes the responsibility for getting the goods to their intended destination. Freight costs incurred by the seller on outgoing merchandise are an operating expense to the seller. These costs are debited to the account Freight Out or Delivery Expense. When the freight charges are paid by the seller, the seller will usually set a higher invoice price for the goods to cover the cost of shipping.

In PW Audio Supply's sale of electronic equipment to Sauk Stereo, the freight terms (FOB shipping point) indicate that Sauk Stereo (the buyer) must pay the cost of shipping the goods from the shipping point to their destination. PW Audio Supply makes no journal entry to record the cost of shipping, since this cost was incurred by the buyer and not the seller. If the freight terms had been FOB destination, PW Audio Supply would have paid the freight costs and prepared a journal entry to record the cost as an operating expense as described above.

Sales Returns and Allowances

We now look at the "flip side" of purchase returns and allowances, as these are recorded as sales returns and allowances on the books of the seller. When customers (buyers) return goods, or are given price reductions, the seller will either return cash to the buyer, or reduce the buyer's accounts receivable if the goods were originally purchased on credit.

Just as a sale requires two entries in a perpetual inventory system, so too will returns and allowances. PW Audio Supply prepares the two separate journal entries shown below to record the $300 credit for goods returned by Sauk Stereo. The first entry records an increase (debit) in Sales Returns and Allowances and a decrease (credit) in Accounts Receivable for the $300 selling price. Note that if the sales return had been on a cash sale, Cash would be credited instead of Accounts Receivable.

The second entry records an increase (debit) in Merchandise Inventory (assuming a $140 cost) and a decrease (credit) in Cost of Goods Sold. This second entry assumes that the merchandise is not damaged and is resaleable and restored to inventory. If the merchandise is not resaleable and is discarded, a second entry is generally not made. This results in the cost of damaged merchandise remaining in the Cost of Goods Sold account.

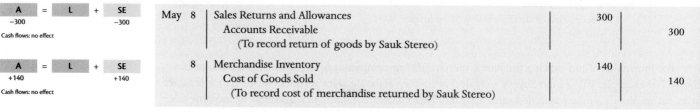

A	=	L	+	SE
−300				−300

Cash flows: no effect

A	=	L	+	SE
+140				+140

Cash flows: no effect

May 8	Sales Returns and Allowances			300	
	Accounts Receivable				300
	(To record return of goods by Sauk Stereo)				
8	Merchandise Inventory			140	
	Cost of Goods Sold				140
	(To record cost of merchandise returned by Sauk Stereo)				

A second entry is not required when the seller gives the buyer an allowance. Since the goods have not been returned, the seller cannot increase its Merchandise Inventory and the original cost of goods sold recorded is still the correct amount. Giving a customer a sales allowance does not change the cost of the goods sold; it only changes the amount of revenue earned on the sale.

Sales Returns and Allowances is a contra revenue account to Sales. The normal balance of the Sales Returns and Allowances account is a debit. A contra account is used, instead of debiting the Sales account, to disclose the amount of sales returns and allowances. A decrease (debit) recorded directly to Sales would hide the percentage of total sales that ends up being lost through sales returns and allowances. It could also distort comparisons between total sales in different accounting periods.

This information is important to management. Excessive returns and allowances suggest inferior merchandise, inefficiencies in filling orders, errors in billing customers, or mistakes in the delivery or shipment of goods. Wal-Mart carefully monitors and streamlines its returns through the use of its electronic product codes, as described in the feature story.

👥 ACCOUNTING MATTERS! | Management Perspective

Returned goods can put a dent in a company's profits. When a customer returns a product, the company has to decide whether to scrap, liquidate, refurbish, return to seller, or return to stock. Calgary-based Liquidation World Inc., the largest liquidator in Canada, has made a successful business out of giving companies an opportunity to obtain some value out of unwanted products by liquidating them. It buys its merchandise from companies in Canada, the U.S., the Caribbean, and the Far East and sells it in its outlets in Canada and the U.S. at prices 30 to 70 percent below normal. It is essentially a win-win situation for businesses and consumers: consumers get good value on a variety of quality goods, while manufacturers, wholesalers, and retailers have a place to dispose of unwanted merchandise.

Discounts

When quantity discounts and sales discounts are given on invoice prices, they affect the seller, as well as the buyer. No separate entry is made to record a **quantity discount**. Sales are recorded at the invoice price—whether it is the full retail price, a sale price, or a volume discount price.

Like a purchase discount, the seller may offer the buyer a cash discount for quick payment of the balance due. From the seller's point of view, this is called a sales discount and is offered on the invoice price less returns and allowances, if any.

Although no new account is added to record purchase discounts in a perpetual inventory system—the discount is recorded as a reduction in the Merchandise Inventory account—a new account, called Sales Discounts, is added to record sales discounts. Like the account for sales returns and allowances, Sales Discounts is a **contra revenue account** to Sales. Its normal balance is a debit. This account is used, instead of debiting Sales, to show the amount of cash discounts taken by customers.

The entry by PW Audio Supply to record the cash receipt on May 14 from Sauk Stereo within the discount period is:

May 14	Cash	3,430	
	Sales Discounts	70	
	Accounts Receivable		3,500
	(To record collection from Sauk Stereo within		
	2/10, n/30 discount period)		

A	=	L	+	SE
+3,430				−70
−3,500				

⬆ Cash flows: +3,430

Summary of Sales Transactions

A summary of the effects of the previous transactions on Sales and its contra accounts is provided in the following T accounts. PW Audio Supply sold merchandise for $3,800, and $300 of it was later returned. A sales discount of $70 was granted as the invoice was paid within the discount period. In contrast to the purchase transactions illustrated earlier in the chapter, which affected only one account, Merchandise Inventory, sales transactions are recorded in different accounts.

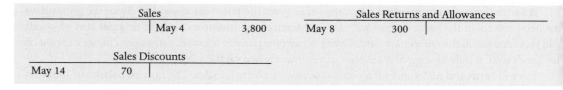

These three accounts are combined to determine net sales. Illustration 5-6 shows the calculation of net sales.

Illustration 5-6 ➡

Formula for net sales

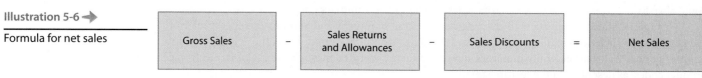

Total sales, before deducting any sales returns and allowances and sales discounts, are known as **gross sales**. Gross sales less returns and allowances and discounts are called **net sales**. Freight paid by the seller is recorded as an operating expense and not as part of net sales. Note that the seller only incurs freight if the shipping terms are FOB destination. The calculation of net sales is the same whether the company uses a perpetual or a periodic inventory system.

Summary of Merchandising Entries

In the previous two sections, we have explained the journal entries made to record purchases and sales of merchandise. The following is a summary of the entries for merchandising accounts in a perpetual inventory system:

	Transactions	Recurring Journal Entries	Debit	Credit
Purchases	Purchasing merchandise for resale.	Merchandise Inventory Cash or Accounts Payable	XX	XX
	Paying freight costs on merchandise purchased, FOB shipping point.	Merchandise Inventory Cash	XX	XX
	Receiving purchase returns or allowances from suppliers.	Cash or Accounts Payable Merchandise Inventory	XX	XX

	Paying creditors on account within discount period.	Accounts Payable
		    Merchandise Inventory
		    Cash
			XX	XX
				XX

	Paying creditors on account after discount period.	Accounts Payable Cash	XX	XX
Sales	Selling merchandise to customers.	Cash or Accounts Receivable Sales	XX	XX
		Cost of Goods Sold Merchandise Inventory	XX	XX
	Giving sales returns or allowances to customers.	Sales Returns and Allowances Cash or Accounts Receivable	XX	XX
		Merchandise Inventory Cost of Goods Sold	XX	XX
	Paying freight costs on sales, FOB destination.	Freight Out Cash	XX	XX
	Receiving payment on account from customers within discount period.	Cash Sales Discounts Accounts Receivable	XX XX	XX
	Receiving payment on account from customers after discount period.	Cash Accounts Receivable	XX	XX

BEFORE YOU GO ON...

Review It

1. Under a perpetual inventory system, what are the two entries that must be recorded for each sale and sales return?
2. What journal entries, if any, are recorded by the seller when the shipping terms are FOB destination? FOB shipping point?
3. When goods are returned or sold with a discount payment period, why is it important to use contra revenue accounts such as Sales Returns and Allowances and Sales Discounts, rather than simply reduce the Sales account?
4. Compare the entries made by the buyer and the seller for (a) sales and purchases, (b) returns and allowances, and (c) payments on account.

Do It

On September 4, Lalonde Ltée sells merchandise on account to Guerette Corp., terms 1/10, n/30, FOB shipping point. The selling price of the goods is $1,500, and the cost to Lalonde was $800. On September 8, goods with a selling price of $300 and a cost of $140 are returned for credit and restored to inventory. On September 14, Lalonde receives payment in full from Guerette. Record the transactions on the books of both companies, assuming a perpetual inventory system is used.

Action Plan

- Seller: Record two entries for the sale and return of goods: one to record the selling price and one to record the cost of the sale. Record the selling price of returns in the contra account Sales Returns and Allowances. Calculate sales discounts using the net amount owing and record the result in the contra account Sales Discounts.
- Buyer: Record purchases of inventory at cost. Reduce the Merchandise Inventory account for returned goods and purchase discounts. Calculate purchase discounts using the net amount owing.

Solution:

Lalonde Ltée (Seller)

Sept.	4	Accounts Receivable	1,500	
		Sales		1,500
		(To record credit sale to Guerette, terms 1/10, n/30)		
	4	Cost of Goods Sold	800	
		Merchandise Inventory		800
		(To record cost of goods sold to Guerette)		
	8	Sales Returns and Allowances	300	
		Accounts Receivable		300
		(To record credit granted for receipt of returned goods from Guerette)		
	8	Merchandise Inventory	140	
		Cost of Goods Sold		140
		(To record cost of goods returned from Guerette)		
	14	Cash ($1,200 − $12)	1,188	
		Sales Discounts [($1,500 − $300) × 1%]	12	
		Accounts Receivable ($1,500 − $300)		1,200
		(To record collection from Guerette within discount period)		

▸ Merchandising Operations

Guerette Corp. (Buyer)

Sept.	4	Merchandise Inventory	1,500	
		Accounts Payable		1,500
		(To record goods purchased on account from Lalonde, terms 1/10, n/30)		
	8	Accounts Payable	300	
		Merchandise Inventory		300
		(To record return of goods to Lalonde)		
	14	Accounts Payable ($1,500 – $300)	1,200	
		Merchandise Inventory [($1,500 – $300) × 1%]		12
		Cash ($1,200 – $12)		1,188
		(To record payment to Lalonde within discount period)		

The Navigator

Statement of Earnings Presentation

study objective 4

Prepare a single-step and a multiple-step statement of earnings.

Merchandisers use the classified balance sheet introduced in Chapter 2, but add a merchandise inventory account in the current assets section of the balance sheet. In addition, two forms of the statement of earnings are widely used by merchandising companies. One is the **single-step statement of earnings**. It has this name because only one step—subtracting total expenses from total revenues—is required for determining earnings before income tax. A second form of the statement of earnings is the **multiple-step statement of earnings**. This statement gets its name because it shows multiple steps in determining earnings before income tax. Canadian companies are relatively evenly split in their use of the single- and multiple-step forms to present their statement of earnings. About 49 percent of Canadian companies use the single-step form, while 51 percent use the multiple-step form.

We will look at each of these statement forms in the following sections.

Single-Step Statement of Earnings

In a single-step statement of earnings, all data are classified into two categories: (1) revenues and (2) expenses. Income tax expense is usually disclosed separately from the other expenses in a single-step statement of earnings.

Illustration 5-7 shows a condensed single-step statement of earnings for PW Audio Supply, Inc., using assumed data.

Illustration 5-7 ➡

Single-step statement of earnings

PW AUDIO SUPPLY, INC. Statement of Earnings Year Ended December 31, 2009		
Revenues		
Net sales	$460,000	
Interest revenue	3,600	$463,600
Expenses		
Cost of goods sold	$316,000	
Operating expenses	114,000	
Interest expense	1,800	
Casualty loss from vandalism	200	432,000
Earnings before income tax		31,600
Income tax expense		6,300
Net earnings		$ 25,300

The single-step statement of earnings is the form we have used in the text so far. There are two main reasons for using the single-step form: (1) a company does not realize any type of profit or earnings until total revenues exceed total expenses, so it makes sense to divide the statement into these categories; and (2) the single-step form is simple and easy to read.

Multiple-Step Statement of Earnings

The **multiple-step statement of earnings** shows several steps in determining net earnings (or loss). It is often considered more useful because it highlights the components of net earnings separately.

The multiple-step statement of earnings shows five main steps:

1. Net sales: Sales returns and allowances and sales discounts are subtracted from gross sales to determine net sales.
2. Gross profit: Cost of goods sold is subtracted from net sales to determine gross profit.
3. Earnings from operations: Operating expenses are deducted from gross profit to determine earnings from operations.
4. Non-operating activities: The results of activities that are not related to operations are added (as other revenue) or subtracted (as other expenses) to determine earnings before income tax.
5. Net earnings: Income tax expense is subtracted from earnings before income tax to determine net earnings (loss).

The first three steps involve the company's principal operating activities. The fourth step distinguishes between **operating** and **non-operating activities**, and is only necessary if the company has non-operating activities. The last step is the same step shown in a single-step statement. We will now look more closely at the components of a multiple-step statement of earnings.

Net Sales

The multiple-step statement of earnings for a merchandising company begins by presenting sales revenues. As contra revenue accounts, Sales Returns and Allowances and Sales Discounts are deducted from gross sales in the statement of earnings to arrive at net sales. The sales revenues section of the statement of earnings for PW Audio Supply, using assumed data, is as follows:

Sales revenues		
Sales		$480,000
Less: Sales returns and allowances	$12,000	
Sales discounts	8,000	20,000
Net sales		460,000

This presentation shows the key aspects of the company's main revenue-producing activities. Many companies condense this information and report only the net sales figure in their statement of earnings, as was shown in Illustration 5-7.

Gross Profit

From Illustration 5-1, you learned that the cost of goods sold is deducted from net sales to determine **gross profit**. Based on the sales data presented above (net sales of $460,000) and an assumed cost of goods sold amount of $316,000, the gross profit for PW Audio Supply is $144,000, calculated as follows:

Net sales	$460,000
Cost of goods sold	316,000
Gross profit	144,000

Earnings from Operations

Operating expenses are the next component in measuring net earnings for a merchandising company. As indicated earlier, these expenses are similar in merchandising and service companies. Earnings from operations, or the results of the company's normal operating activities, are calculated by subtracting operating expenses from gross profit.

At PW Audio Supply, operating expenses are assumed to be $114,000. Thus, its earnings from operations are $30,000, as shown below:

Gross profit	$144,000
Operating expenses	114,000
Earnings from operations	30,000

Sometimes operating expenses are subdivided into selling expenses and administrative expenses. **Selling expenses** are associated with making sales. They include advertising expenses as well as the expenses of completing the sale, such as delivery and shipping expenses. **Administrative expenses** relate to general operating activities such as management, accounting, and legal matters.

Non-Operating Activities

Non-operating activities consist of other revenues and expenses that are unrelated to the company's main operations. Examples of other revenues include interest revenue, rental revenue (if the company's main activity is not rentals), and investment revenue. Examples of other expenses include interest expense.

In addition, special gains or losses that are infrequent or unusual are normally reported in this section. Gains reported as other revenues can arise from the sale of investments or property, plant, and equipment. Losses reported as other expenses can arise from the sale of investments, sale of property, plant, and equipment, employee strikes, or writing off assets due to casualty and theft.

When a company has non-operating activities, they are presented in the statement of earnings right after "earnings from operations." The distinction between operating and non-operating activities is crucial to many external users of financial data. Earnings from operations are viewed as sustainable and therefore long-term, and non-operating activities are viewed as nonrecurring and therefore short-term.

PW Audio Supply's non-operating activities, using assumed data, are presented below. Depending on whether the non-operating activities result in a net increase (other revenues exceed other expenses) or net decrease (other expenses exceed other revenues), they are added to or deducted from the earnings from operations. The result is earnings before income tax.

Earnings from operations		$30,000
Other revenues		
Interest revenue	$3,600	
Other expenses		
Interest expense	$1,800	
Casualty loss from vandalism	200	
Total non-operating expenses	2,000	
Net non-operating revenue		1,600
Earnings before income tax		31,600

If there are no non-operating activities, earnings from operations will be the same as earnings before income tax.

Net Earnings

Net earnings is the final outcome of all the company's operating and non-operating activities. PW Audio Supply's net earnings are $25,300 after deducting its income tax expense of $6,300:

Earnings before income tax	$31,600
Income tax expense	6,300
Net earnings	$25,300

In Illustration 5-8, we bring together all the steps above in a comprehensive multiple-step statement of earnings for PW Audio Supply. Note that the net earnings in Illustrations 5-8 (multiple-step) and 5-7 (single-step) are the same. The differences between the two statements of earnings are the amount of detail displayed and the order of presentation.

PW AUDIO SUPPLY, INC.
Statement of Earnings
Year Ended December 31, 2009

Sales revenue		
Sales		$480,000
Less: Sales returns and allowances	$12,000	
Sales discounts	8,000	20,000
Net sales		460,000
Cost of goods sold		316,000
Gross profit		144,000
Operating expenses		
Salaries expense	$45,000	
Rent expense	19,000	
Utilities expense	17,000	
Advertising expense	16,000	
Depreciation expense	8,000	
Freight out	7,000	
Insurance expense	2,000	
Total operating expenses		114,000
Earnings from operations		30,000
Other revenues		
Interest revenue	$ 3,600	
Other expenses		
Interest expense	$ 1,800	
Casualty loss from vandalism	200	
	2,000	1,600
Earnings before income tax		31,600
Income tax expense		6,300
Net earnings		$ 25,300

BEFORE YOU GO ON...

Review It

1. How does a single-step statement of earnings differ from a multiple-step statement?
2. How are sales and contra revenue accounts reported in the statement of earnings?
3. How do operating activities differ from non-operating activities?
4. Does Shoppers Drug Mart use a single-step or multiple-step statement of earnings? The answer to this question is at the end of the chapter.

Do It

Abela Corporation reported the following selected information:

Cost of goods sold	$619,000
Income tax expense	11,500
Interest expense	2,000
Operating expenses	161,000
Rent revenue	18,000
Sales	910,000
Sales returns and allowances	85,000
Sales discounts	15,000

Calculate the following amounts for Abela Corporation: (a) net sales, (b) gross profit, (c) earnings from operations, (d) earnings before income tax, and (e) net earnings.

Action Plan

- Recall the formula for net sales: Sales – sales returns and allowances – sales discounts.
- Recall the formula for gross profit: Net sales – cost of goods sold.
- Separate the items into operating and non-operating (other revenues and other expenses).

▸ Merchandising Operations

- Recall the formula for earnings from operations: Gross profit – operating expenses.
- Recall the formula for earnings before income tax: Earnings from operations + other revenue – other expenses.
- Recall the formula for net earnings: Earnings before income tax – income tax expense.

Solution

(a)   Net sales: $910,000 – $85,000 – $15,000 = $810,000
(b)   Gross profit: $810,000 – $619,000 = $191,000
(c)   Earnings from operations: $191,000 – $161,000 = $30,000
(d)   Earnings before income tax: $30,000 + $18,000 – $2,000 = $46,000
(e)   Net earnings: $46,000 – $11,500 = $34,500

The Navigator

Evaluating Profitability

In Chapter 2, we learned about two profitability ratios: earnings per share and the price-earnings ratio. We add two more examples of profitability ratios in this chapter: the gross profit margin and profit margin, which take into account the impact of inventory. Inventory has a significant effect on a company's profitability because cost of goods sold is usually the largest expense on the statement of earnings.

Gross Profit Margin

study objective 5

Calculate the gross profit margin and profit margin.

When a company's gross profit is expressed as a percentage, this number is called the **gross profit margin**. It is calculated by dividing the amount of gross profit by net sales. For PW Audio Supply, the gross profit margin is 31.3% ($144,000 ÷ $460,000). The gross profit *margin* is generally considered more informative than the gross profit *amount* because the margin expresses a more meaningful relationship between gross profit and net sales. For example, a gross profit amount of $1 million may sound impressive, but if it is the result of sales of $100 million the company's gross profit margin is only 1%.

Gross profit represents the merchandising profit of a company. As operating expenses have not been deducted from gross profit, it is not a measure of the overall profit of a company. Nevertheless, the amount and trend of gross profit are closely watched by management and other interested parties. Comparisons of current gross profit with past amounts and margins, and with those in the industry, indicate the effectiveness of a company's purchasing and pricing policies. In general, a higher gross profit margin is better than a lower gross profit margin.

In the following illustration, we will calculate the gross profit margin for Wal-Mart and its next largest competitor, Carrefour, SA. As we learned earlier in this chapter, Wal-Mart is the largest retailer in the world, with operations in 13 countries outside the United States. The second largest retailer in the world, is Carrefour, headquartered in France and operating in 30 different countries. The gross profit margin for Wal-Mart, Carrefour, and the retail industry for two recent fiscal years is presented in Illustration 5-9.

Illustration 5-9 ➤

Gross profit margin

GROSS PROFIT MARGIN = $\dfrac{\text{GROSS PROFIT}}{\text{NET SALES}}$		
(in USD millions)	2007	2006
Wal-Mart	$\dfrac{\$88,011}{\$374,526} = 23.5\%$	$\dfrac{\$80,840}{\$344,992} = 23.4\%$
Carrefour	21.4%	21.4%
Industry average	34.9%	32.8%

Wal-Mart's gross profit margin remained relatively unchanged in 2007, improving marginally from 23.4% to 23.5%. Carrefour's gross profit margin, although lower than that of Wal-Mart, also did not change.

At first glance, it might seem surprising that Wal-Mart and Carrefour have a lower gross profit margin than the industry average. It is likely, however, that this can be explained by the fact that grocery products are becoming an increasingly large component of both companies' sales. Because food items generally carry a lower gross profit margin than other merchandise, food sales tend to have an unfavourable impact on the gross profit margin in comparison to many other companies in the industry.

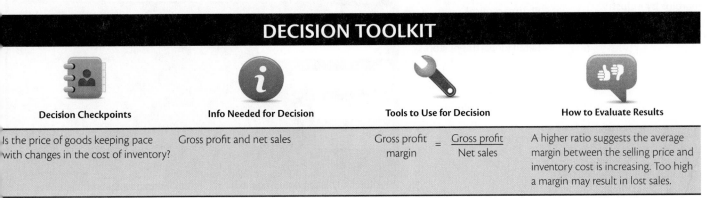

DECISION TOOLKIT

Decision Checkpoints	Info Needed for Decision	Tools to Use for Decision	How to Evaluate Results
Is the price of goods keeping pace with changes in the cost of inventory?	Gross profit and net sales	$\text{Gross profit margin} = \dfrac{\text{Gross profit}}{\text{Net sales}}$	A higher ratio suggests the average margin between the selling price and inventory cost is increasing. Too high a margin may result in lost sales.

Profit Margin

Like gross profit, net earnings is often expressed as a percentage of sales. The **profit margin** measures the percentage of each dollar of sales that results in net earnings. It is calculated by dividing net earnings by net sales for the period.

What is the difference between gross profit margin and profit margin? Gross profit margin indicates how much higher the selling price is than the cost of goods sold. Profit margin indicates how well the selling price covers all expenses (including the cost of goods sold). A company can improve its profit margin by increasing its gross profit margin or by controlling its operating expenses (and non-operating activities), or by doing both.

Profit margins for Wal-Mart and Carrefour, and the industry average, are presented in Illustration 5-10.

◄ Illustration 5-10

Profit margin

PROFIT MARGIN = $\dfrac{\text{NET EARNINGS}}{\text{NET SALES}}$		
(in USD millions)	2007	2006
Wal-Mart	$\dfrac{\$12{,}731}{\$374{,}526} = 3.4\%$	$\dfrac{\$11{,}284}{\$344{,}992} = 3.3\%$
Carrefour	3.0%	3.2%
Industry average	1.7%	2.5%

Wal-Mart generated 3.4 cents on each dollar of sales in fiscal 2007. Its profit margin remained relatively unchanged in 2007, improving marginally from 3.3% to 3.4%. Although its sales increased, its net earnings increased proportionately, so its cost of goods sold and operating expenses therefore kept the same relationship to its sales revenue.

How does Wal-Mart compare to its competitors? Its profit margin is higher than that of Carrefour, and increasing, albeit slightly, while Carrefour's is decreasing. The industry average is also decreasing, in part due to a challenging economic environment. Wal-Mart's stability in light of an increasingly competitive, and declining, industry is noteworthy.

Both the gross profit margin and profit margin are **profitability measures** that vary according to the specific industry. Businesses with a high turnover of inventory, such as food stores (e.g., Sobeys), generally experience lower gross profit and profit margins. Low-turnover businesses, such as computer services (e.g., Microsoft), have higher gross profit and profit margins. Gross profit margins and profit margins from a variety of industries are shown in Illustration 5-11.

Illustration 5-11 ➡

Gross profit and profit margins by industry

Industry	Profit Margin	Gross Profit Margin
Computer services	20%	75%
Pharmaceutical manufacturers	16%	71%
Retail (department stores)	2%	35%
Retail (grocery)	4%	26%
Metals and mining	9%	20%
Forestry and wood products	4%	20%

ACCOUNTING MATTERS! | Management Perspective

It is important for companies to pay close attention to their pricing practices, as pricing is one of the biggest drivers of profitability. A study by Marn and Rosiello found that a 1-percent increase in price, with no loss of sales volume, resulted in an 11-percent increase in profit for the average company. The authors found that the fastest and most effective way for companies to maximize their profitability was to get their pricing strategy right—a concept that has been proven over and over again in all sectors of business.

Source: Scott Miller, "Is the Price Right?" *CMA Management,* May 2007, 19.

DECISION TOOLKIT

Decision Checkpoints	Info Needed for Decision	Tools to Use for Decision	How to Evaluate Results
Is the company maintaining an adequate margin between sales and expenses?	Net earnings and net sales	Profit margin $= \dfrac{\text{Net earnings}}{\text{Net sales}}$	A higher value suggests a favourable return on each dollar of sales.

BEFORE YOU GO ON...

The Navigator

➡ **Review It**

1. Distinguish between the gross profit margin and profit margin.
2. What is the effect on the profit margin when a company makes its operations more efficient?

APPENDIX 5A — PERIODIC INVENTORY SYSTEM

As described in this chapter, there are two basic systems of accounting for inventories: (1) the perpetual inventory system and (2) the periodic inventory system. In the chapter, we focused on the characteristics of the perpetual inventory system. In this appendix, we discuss and illustrate the periodic inventory system.

> **study objective 6**
>
> Prepare entries for purchases and sales under a periodic inventory system and calculate cost of goods sold.

One key difference between the two systems is when the cost of goods sold is calculated. In a periodic inventory system, revenues from the sale of merchandise are recorded when sales are made, in the same way as in a perpetual inventory system. However, on the date of sale, the cost of the merchandise sold is not recorded. Instead, a physical inventory count is done at the end of the period to determine the cost of the merchandise on hand (the ending inventory). This figure and other information is then used to calculate the cost of the goods sold during the period.

There are other differences between the perpetual and periodic inventory systems. Under a periodic system, purchases of merchandise are recorded in the expense account Purchases rather than the asset account Merchandise Inventory. In addition, freight costs paid by the buyer, purchase returns and allowances, and purchase discounts are all recorded in separate expense and contra expense accounts. That way, amounts are known for each category.

To illustrate the recording of merchandise transactions under a periodic inventory system, we will use purchase and sale transactions between PW Audio Supply, Inc. (the seller) and Sauk Stereo Ltd. (the buyer), as illustrated for the perpetual inventory system earlier in this chapter.

Recording Purchases of Merchandise

Based on the purchase invoice (invoice No. 731 in Illustration 5-3) and receipt of the merchandise ordered from PW Audio Supply, Sauk Stereo records the $3,800 purchase on May 4 as follows:

May 4	Purchases	3,800	
	Accounts Payable		3,800
	(To record goods purchased on account from PW Audio Supply per invoice #731, terms 2/10, n/30)		

A	=	L	+	SE
		+3,800		−3,800

Cash flows: no effect

Purchases is a temporary expense account reported on the statement of earnings. Its normal balance is a debit.

Freight Costs

You will recall that the freight terms on Sauk Stereo's purchase of merchandise are FOB shipping point. When the buyer pays for the freight costs, the account Freight In is debited. Upon delivery of the goods, Sauk Stereo pays Public Carrier Co. $150 for freight charges on its purchases from PW Audio Supply. The entry on Sauk Stereo's books is as follows:

May 4	Freight In	150	
	Cash		150
	(To record payment of freight on goods purchased)		

A	=	L	+	SE
−150				−150

⬇ Cash flows: −150

Like Purchases, Freight In is a temporary expense account whose normal balance is a debit. Just as freight was part of the cost of the merchandise inventory in a perpetual inventory system, **freight is part of the cost of goods purchased** in a periodic inventory system. In accordance with the cost principle, the cost of goods purchased should include any freight charges incurred in bringing the goods to the buyer. As a result, freight in is added to net purchases to determine the cost of goods purchased.

Purchase Returns and Allowances

When $300 of merchandise is returned to PW Audio Supply, Sauk Stereo prepares the following entry to recognize the return:

May 8	Accounts Payable	300	
	Purchase Returns and Allowances		300
	(To record return of goods to PW Audio Supply)		

A	=	L	+	SE
		−300		+300

Cash flows: no effect

Purchase Returns and Allowances is a temporary account whose normal balance is a credit. It is a contra expense account whose balance is subtracted from the Purchases account.

Purchase Discounts

Recall that the invoice terms were 2/10, n/30. On May 14, Sauk Stereo pays the balance due on account to PW Audio Supply of $3,500, less the 2% cash discount allowed by PW Audio Supply for payment within 10 days. Note that freight costs are not subject to a purchase discount. Purchase discounts apply on the invoice cost of the merchandise purchased, less any returns. In this case, the purchase discount is $70, calculated as follows: ($3,800 − $300) × 2% = $70.

The payment and discount are recorded by Sauk Stereo as follows:

May 14	Accounts Payable ($3,800 − $300)	3,500	
	Cash		3,430
	Purchase Discounts ($3,500 × 2%)		70
	(To record payment to PW Audio Supply within discount period)		

Purchase Discounts is a temporary account whose normal balance is a credit. Like Purchase Returns and Allowances, it is a contra expense account subtracted from the Purchases account.

In each of the above cases, a temporary expense account was used to record purchases of merchandise instead of the Merchandise Inventory account that is used in a perpetual inventory system. The Purchases and Freight In accounts were debited rather than Merchandise Inventory in the first two entries, and Purchase Returns and Allowances and Purchase Discounts were credited in the last two entries rather than Merchandise Inventory. As we will see later in this appendix, these temporary accounts are needed for calculating the cost of goods purchased at the end of the period.

Recording Sales of Merchandise

The sale of $3,800 of merchandise to Sauk Stereo on May 4 is recorded by the seller, PW Audio Supply, as follows:

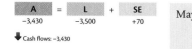

May 4	Accounts Receivable	3,800	
	Sales		3,800
	(To record credit sale to Sauk Stereo per invoice #731, terms 2/10, n/30)		

The sales entries illustrated in this section are exactly the same as those illustrated earlier in the chapter for a perpetual inventory system, with one exception. In a perpetual inventory system, two journal entries are made for each transaction. The first entry records the accounts receivable and sales revenue, as illustrated above. The second journal entry records the cost of the sale by transferring the inventory to the Cost of Goods Sold account.

In a periodic inventory system, there is only one journal entry made at the time of the sale (the entry to record the sales revenue). The cost of the sale is not recorded. Instead, the cost of goods sold is determined by calculation at the end of the period.

Freight Costs

Freight costs incurred by the seller on outgoing merchandise are an operating expense to the seller. There is no distinction in accounting for these costs between a perpetual and periodic inventory system. Under both systems, these costs are debited to the Freight Out or Delivery Expense account.

You will recall that Sauk Stereo (the buyer) paid the shipping costs in our sales illustration, so no journal entry is required by PW Audio Supply (the seller) at this point.

Sales Returns and Allowances

When Sauk Stereo returns merchandise on May 8, PW Audio Supply records the $300 sales return as follows:

May 8	Sales Returns and Allowances	300	
	Accounts Receivable		300
	(To record return of goods by Sauk Stereo)		

ust as we observed that only one entry is needed when sales are recorded in a periodic inventory system, ne entry is also all that is needed to record a return. In a perpetual inventory system, two entries are eeded to record the sales return and its cost.

ales Discounts

On May 14, PW Audio Supply receives a payment of $3,430 [($3,800 − $300) × (100% − 2%] on account rom Sauk Stereo. PW Audio Supply honours the 2% cash discount and records the payment of Sauk tereo's account receivable in full as follows:

May 14	Cash	3,430	
	Sales Discounts ($3,500 × 2%)	70	
	Accounts Receivable ($3,800 − $300)		3,500
	(To record collection from Sauk Stereo within 2/10, n/30 discount period)		

A	=	L	+	SE
+3,430				−70
−3,500				

⬆ Cash flows: +3,430

Comparison of Entries—Perpetual vs. Periodic

The periodic inventory system entries for purchases and sales are shown in Illustration 5A-1 next to those hat were illustrated earlier in the chapter under the perpetual inventory system. Having these entries ide by side should help you compare the differences. The entries that are different in the two inventory ystems are highlighted.

⬇ **Illustration 5A-1**

Comparison of entries under perpetual and periodic inventory systems

	ENTRIES ON SAUK STEREO'S BOOKS (BUYER)					
Transaction	Perpetual Inventory System			Periodic Inventory System		
May 4 Purchase of merchandise on credit	Merchandise Inventory	3,800		Purchases	3,800	
	Accounts Payable		3,800	Accounts Payable		3,800
4 Freight costs on purchases	Merchandise Inventory	150		Freight In	150	
	Cash		150	Cash		150
8 Purchase returns and allowances	Accounts Payable	300		Accounts Payable	300	
	Merchandise Inventory		300	Purchase Returns and Allowances		300
14 Payment on account with a discount	Accounts Payable	3,500		Accounts Payable	3,500	
	Cash		3,430	Cash		3,430
	Merchandise Inventory		70	Purchase Discounts		70

	ENTRIES ON PW AUDIO SUPPLY'S BOOKS (SELLER)					
Transaction	Perpetual Inventory System			Periodic Inventory System		
May 4 Sale of merchandise on credit	Accounts Receivable	3,800		Accounts Receivable	3,800	
	Sales		3,800	Sales		3,800
	Cost of Goods Sold	2,400		No entry		
	Merchandise Inventory		2,400			
8 Return of merchandise sold	Sales Returns and Allowances	300		Sales Returns and Allowances	300	
	Accounts Receivable		300	Accounts Receivable		300
	Merchandise Inventory	140		No entry		
	Cost of Goods Sold		140			
14 Cash received on account with a discount	Cash	3,430		Cash	3,430	
	Sales Disounts	70		Sales Discounts	70	
	Accounts Receivable		3,500	Accounts Receivable		3,500

Calculating Cost of Goods Sold

Calculating the cost of goods sold is different in a periodic inventory system than in a perpetual inventory ystem. When a company uses a perpetual inventory system, all transactions that affect inventory (such as purchases, freight costs, returns, and discounts) are recorded directly to the Merchandise Inventory ac-count. In addition, the cost of goods sold is calculated at the time of each sale and recorded as an increase (debit) in the Cost of Goods Sold account and a decrease (credit) in the Merchandise Inventory account.

Under a periodic inventory system, there is no running account (continuous updating) of changes in nventory. As we saw in the entries above, temporary accounts are used instead to record the cost of the goods purchased throughout the period. The balance in ending inventory, as well as the cost of goods sold for the period, is calculated at the end of the period.

▶ Merchandising Operations

To calculate the cost of goods sold in a periodic inventory, three steps are required:

1. Calculate the cost of goods purchased.
2. Determine the cost of goods on hand (ending inventory) at the end of the accounting period.
3. Calculate the cost of goods sold.

We will discuss each of these steps in the following sections.

Cost of Goods Purchased

Earlier in this appendix, we used four accounts—Purchases, Freight In, Purchase Returns and Allowances, and Purchase Discounts—to record the purchase of inventory. These four accounts combine to determine the cost of goods purchased. First, purchase returns and allowances and purchase discounts are deducted from purchases to determine **net purchases**. Second, freight in is added to net purchases to arrive at the **cost of goods purchased**.

Using assumed data for PW Audio Supply, the calculation of net purchases and the cost of goods purchased is as follows:

Purchases		$325,000
Less: Purchase returns and allowances	$10,400	
Purchase discounts	6,800	17,200
Net purchases		307,800
Add: Freight in		12,200
Cost of goods purchased		320,000

Cost of Goods on Hand

To determine the cost of the inventory on hand, PW Audio Supply must take a physical inventory. Taking a physical inventory involves these procedures:

1. Count the units on hand for each item of inventory.
2. Apply unit costs to the total units on hand for each item of inventory (we will learn more about how to do this in the next chapter).
3. Total the costs for each item of inventory to determine the total cost of goods on hand.

The total cost of goods on hand is known as the ending inventory. PW Audio Supply's physical inventory count on December 31, 2009, determines that the cost of its goods on hand, or ending inventory, is $40,000. This ending inventory amount will be used to calculate the cost of goods sold, as shown in the next section. Ending inventory is subsequently recorded in the Merchandise Inventory account as part of the closing process (not illustrated here).

Cost of Goods Sold

There are two steps in calculating the cost of goods sold:

1. Add the cost of goods purchased to the cost of goods on hand at the beginning of the period (beginning inventory). The result is the cost of goods available for sale.
2. Subtract the cost of goods on hand at the end of the period (ending inventory) from the cost of goods available for sale. The result is the cost of goods sold.

For PW Audio Supply, the cost of goods available for sale is $356,000 and the cost of goods sold is $316,000, as follows:

Inventory, Jan. 1		$ 36,000
Purchases	$325,000	
Less: Purchase returns and allowances and discounts	17,200	
Net purchases	307,800	
Add: Freight in	12,200	
Cost of goods purchased		320,000
Cost of goods available for sale		356,000
Inventory, Dec. 31		40,000
Cost of goods sold		$316,000

In summary, the cost of goods purchased is added to the beginning inventory to determine the cost of goods available for sale. Ending inventory is then deducted from the cost of goods available for sale to determine the cost of goods sold. In other words, what you have on hand at the beginning of the period, plus what you purchase during the period, gives you the total goods available for sale during the period. Subtract what you have not sold, and you are left with the amount that must have been sold.

Illustration 5A-2 presents this as a formula and inserts the relevant data for PW Audio Supply. Note that this formula was also shown in Illustration 5-2 in the main body of the chapter.

← **Illustration 5A-2**

Formula for cost of goods sold

Once cost of goods sold is calculated in a periodic inventory system, gross profit, operating expenses, and net earnings are reported in a multiple-step or single-step statement of earnings in the same way as they are in a perpetual inventory system. The only reporting difference in a multiple-step statement of earnings is that the cost of goods sold section has more detail in a periodic inventory system—the same detail shown above—than in a perpetual inventory system, where only one line is reported for the cost of goods sold.

Using the periodic inventory system does not affect the content of the balance sheet. As in the perpetual system, the ending balance of merchandise inventory is reported in the current assets section, and at the same amount.

Summary of Study Objectives

1. Identify the differences between service and merchandising companies. A service company performs services. It has service or fee revenue and operating expenses. A merchandising company sells goods. It has sales revenue, cost of goods sold, and gross profit in addition to operating expenses. Both types of company also report income tax expense.

2. Prepare entries for purchases under a perpetual inventory system. The Merchandise Inventory account is debited for all purchases of merchandise, and for freight costs if they are paid by the buyer. It is credited for purchase discounts, and purchase returns and allowances.

3. Prepare entries for sales under a perpetual inventory system. When inventory is sold, two entries are required: (1) Accounts Receivable (or Cash) is debited and Sales is credited for the selling price of the merchandise, and (2) Cost of Goods Sold is debited and Merchandise Inventory is credited for the cost of inventory items sold. Contra accounts are used to record sales returns and allowances and sales discounts. Two journal entries are also required for sales returns so that both the selling price and the cost of the returned merchandise are recorded. Freight costs paid by the seller are recorded as an operating expense.

4. Prepare a single-step and a multiple-step statement of earnings. In a single-step statement of earnings, all data (except for income tax expense) are classified under two categories—revenues or expenses—and earnings before income tax is determined in one step. Income tax expense is separated from the other expenses and reported separately after earnings before income tax to determine net earnings (loss).

A multiple-step statement of earnings shows several steps in determining net earnings. Step 1 deducts sales returns and allowances and sales discounts from gross sales to determine net sales.

Step 2 deducts the cost of goods sold from net sales to determine gross profit. Step 3 deducts operating expenses from gross profit to determine earnings from operations. Step 4 adds or deducts any non-operating items to determine earnings before income tax. Finally, step 5 deducts income tax expense to determine net earnings (loss).

5. Calculate the gross profit margin and profit margin. The gross profit margin, calculated by dividing gross profit by net sales, measures the gross profit earned for each dollar of sales. The profit margin, calculated by dividing net earnings by net sales, measures the net earnings (total profit) earned for each dollar of sales. Both are measures of profitability that are closely watched by management and other interested parties.

6. Prepare entries for purchases and sales under a periodic inventory system and calculate cost of goods sold (Appendix 5A). Unlike recording purchases in a perpetual inventory system, in a periodic system separate temporary accounts are used to record (1) purchases, (2) purchase returns and allowances, (3) purchase discounts, and (4) freight costs that are paid by the buyer. The formula for cost of goods purchased is as follows: Purchases – purchase returns and allowances – purchase discounts = net purchases; and net purchases + freight in = cost of goods purchased.

As in a perpetual inventory system, temporary accounts are used to record (1) sales, (2) sales returns and allowances, and (3) sales discounts. However, in a periodic inventory system, only one journal entry is made to record a sale of merchandise as the cost of goods sold is not recorded throughout the period as it is in a perpetual inventory system. Instead, the cost of goods sold is determined only at the end of the period.

To determine the cost of goods sold, first calculate the cost of goods purchased, as indicated above. Then, calculate the cost of goods sold as follows: Beginning inventory + cost of goods purchased = cost of goods available for sale; and cost of goods available for sale – ending inventory = cost of goods sold.

The Navigator

Do Your Sales Returns Cost Companies Money?

In this chapter, you learned that goods may be returned by the buyer to the seller for a number of reasons. Perhaps you have returned an unwanted gift. For retailers, sales returns are a big headache as they are costly and time-consuming. Sales returns take up considerable staff time with sorting and handling, while turning attention to administrative chores instead of tending to customers.

Retailers are trying to get a handle on the return issue—and pare down costs. Some have tightened their return policies; others are finding that promoting and selling more gift cards has led to fewer returns. A number of major retailers have turned to "reverse logistics" specialists for help. Hudson's Bay, Canadian Tire and Best Buy Canada, for example, ship returns to a specialist, Genco Distribution Systems. Genco manages processing centres for each of the retailers, sending most of the goods back to suppliers while the rest are sold to a host of discount dealers or given to charity. The result for companies using a specialist like Genco is cost savings.

What do you do with your textbook when you complete a university course? Do you keep the book because you may need it in a future course as reference material, do you sell the book, or do you use your university bookstore's buyback services?

Follett of Canada has been serving many Canadian colleges and universities since 1983. Its computerized inventory control system tracks all titles and updates its database of virtually every college and university textbook used in the classroom. Follett has more used textbooks than any other campus bookstore management company. The availability of used texts and a solid buyback program are important to many students. Follett will buy back textbooks that have been adopted for the upcoming term at up to 50% of the purchase price.

Some Facts

- Returns eat up about 6 percent of a retailer's sales, although the rate can almost double in the post-holiday period.
- What a third-party "reverse logistics" firm typically does with returned goods:
  - About 45 percent is returned to the supplier.
  - About 40 percent is sent to other retailers such as Winners for liquidation.
  - About 5 percent is sent back to the retailer for resale.
  - About 10 percent is sent to charities or recycled. Less than 1 percent is destroyed.
- New editions of textbooks are coming out, on average, about every three-and-a-half years.

What Do You Think?

Consider the following and decide what action you would take: Suppose you are tired of carrying a backpack full of thick, hardcover textbooks. E-texts are an alternative to regular textbooks. Would you consider purchasing an e-text instead of a hardcover textbook?

YES | You know that e-texts would have some cost and environmental benefits and in a changing field such as business, e-texts can be updated quickly. Tools are available on line for note-taking and highlighting your e-text.

NO | You spend too much time on your computer already. You like to curl up in a cozy chair and run a highlight marker over key points or make notes in the margins. To do this, you would have to print out the pages. Also, you would not be able to sell an e-text back to the bookstore.

Source:

Marina Strauss, "Retailers' Bane Proves Boon to Returns Experts," *Globe and Mail*, January 15, 2007, B1.

The Navigator

Glossary

Contra revenue account An account that is offset against (reduces) a revenue account on the statement of earnings. (p. 231)

Cost of goods available for sale The sum of beginning inventory and the cost of goods purchased. (p. 224)

Cost of goods purchased The sum of net purchases and freight in. (p. 228)

Cost of goods sold The total cost of merchandise sold during the period. In a perpetual inventory system, it is calculated and recorded for each sale. In a periodic inventory system, it is calculated at the end of the accounting period by deducting ending inventory from the cost of goods available for sale. (p. 222)

Earnings from operations The results of a company's normal operating activities. It is calculated as gross profit less operating expenses. (p. 235)

FOB (free on board) destination Freight terms indicating that the seller will pay for the shipping costs of the goods until they arrive at their destination (normally the buyer's place of business). (p. 226)

FOB (free on board) shipping point Freight terms indicating that the seller is responsible for the goods only until they reach their shipping point (normally the seller's place of business). The buyer will pay for the shipping costs of the goods from the shipping point until they arrive at their destination. (p. 226)

Gross profit Sales revenue less cost of goods sold. (p. 222)

Gross profit margin Gross profit expressed as a percentage of sales. It is calculated by dividing gross profit by net sales. (p. 238)

Gross sales Total sales before deducting any sales returns and allowances and sales discounts. (p. 232)

Multiple-step statement of earnings A statement of earnings that shows several steps to determine net earnings or net loss. (p. 235)

Net purchases Purchases less purchase returns and allowances and purchase discounts. (p. 228)

Net sales Gross sales less sales returns and allowances and sales discounts. (p. 232)

Non-operating activities Other revenues and expenses that are unrelated to the company's main operations. (p. 236)

Operating cycle The time required to go from cash to cash in producing revenues. (p. 222)

Operating expenses Expenses incurred in the process of earning sales revenue. They are deducted from gross profit to arrive at earnings from operations. (p. 222)

Periodic inventory system An inventory system in which detailed records are not maintained and the ending inventory and cost of goods sold are determined only at the end of the accounting period. (p. 224)

Perpetual inventory system A detailed inventory system in which the quantity and cost of each inventory item is maintained. The records continuously show the inventory that should be on hand and the cost of the items sold. (p. 223)

Profit margin Net earnings expressed as a percentage of net sales. It is calculated by dividing net earnings by net sales. (p. 239)

Purchase discount A price reduction, based on the invoice price less any returns and allowances, claimed by a buyer for early payment of a credit purchase. (p. 227)

Purchase returns and allowances A return of goods for cash or credit, or a deduction granted by the seller on the selling price of unsatisfactory merchandise. (p. 226)

Quantity discount A price reduction that reduces the invoice price and is given to the buyer for volume purchases. (p. 227)

Sales discount A price reduction that is based on the invoice price less any returns and allowances and is given by a seller for early payment of a credit sale. (p. 231)

Sales returns and allowances A return of goods or reduction in price of unsatisfactory merchandise. (p. 230)

Sales revenue The main source of revenue in a merchandising company. (p. 222)

Single-step statement of earnings A statement of earnings that shows only one step (revenues less expenses) in determining net earnings (or net loss). (p. 234)

 The Navigator

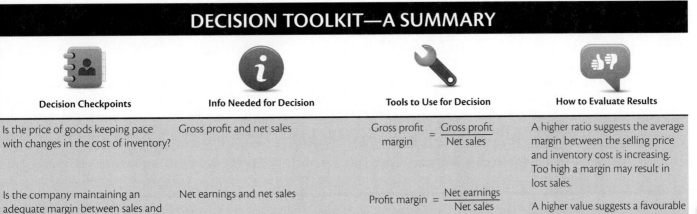

Decision Checkpoints	Info Needed for Decision	Tools to Use for Decision	How to Evaluate Results
Is the price of goods keeping pace with changes in the cost of inventory?	Gross profit and net sales	$\text{Gross profit margin} = \dfrac{\text{Gross profit}}{\text{Net sales}}$	A higher ratio suggests the average margin between the selling price and inventory cost is increasing. Too high a margin may result in lost sales.
Is the company maintaining an adequate margin between sales and expenses?	Net earnings and net sales	$\text{Profit margin} = \dfrac{\text{Net earnings}}{\text{Net sales}}$	A higher value suggests a favourable return on each dollar of sales.

 The Navigator

Analysis Tools (Decision ToolKit Summaries)

Using the Decision Toolkit

Costco Wholesale Corporation competes head to head with Wal-Mart, offering discount prices on 4,000 different products. The following financial data are available for Costco and Wal-Mart:

(in USD millions)	Costco		Wal-Mart	
	Fiscal 2007	Fiscal 2006	Fiscal 2007	Fiscal 2006
Net sales	$63,088	$58,963	$374,526	$344,992
Cost of goods sold	56,450	52,475	286,515	264,152
Net earnings	1,083	1,103	12,731	11,284

Instructions

(a) Wal-Mart is nearly six times larger than Costco. Can a comparison of the financial results of these two companies be meaningful?

(b) Wal-Mart's fiscal year end is January 31, 2008 (called "fiscal 2007" above), and Costco's fiscal year end is September 2, 2007 ("fiscal 2007"). Is it possible to compare the financial data for these two companies even though they have different fiscal year ends?

(c) Calculate the gross profit margin and profit margin for Costco and Wal-Mart for the 2007 and 2006 fiscal years.

(d) Using the ratios calculated in (c), compare Costco's profitability to Wal-Mart's.

Solution

(a) It does not matter that Wal-Mart is nearly six times larger than Costco. Ratio analysis puts both companies' financial information into the same perspective for a comparison. It is the relationship between the figures that is meaningful.

(b) Both companies' financial data cover a one-year period, with Wal-Mart's fiscal year overlapping Costco's for seven months (February 1, 2007, through September 2, 2007). If there were no substantial changes in the economy or environment during the period covered by Wal-Mart's financial results but not Costco's, or vice versa, it really does not matter when each company's fiscal year ends. It is more important that we compare what each company was able to achieve in its own operating period. If, however, a major change did occur in the intervening period (the period where the statements do not overlap), such a change should be taken into consideration in comparing the relative performance of the two companies.

(c)

(in USD millions)	Costco	
	Fiscal 2007	Fiscal 2006

Gross profit margin

$$\frac{(\$63{,}088 - \$56{,}450)}{\$63{,}088} = 10.5\% \qquad \frac{(\$58{,}963 - \$52{,}745)}{\$58{,}963} = 10.5\%$$

Profit margin

$$\frac{\$1{,}083}{\$63{,}088} = 1.7\% \qquad \frac{\$1{,}103}{\$58{,}963} = 1.9\%$$

(in USD millions)	Wal-Mart	
	Fiscal 2007	Fiscal 2006

Gross profit margin

$$\frac{(\$374{,}526 - \$286{,}515)}{\$374{,}526} = 23.5\% \qquad \frac{(\$344{,}992 - \$264{,}152)}{\$344{,}992} = 23.4\%$$

Profit margin

$$\frac{\$12{,}731}{\$374{,}526} = 3.4\% \qquad \frac{\$11{,}284}{\$344{,}992} = 3.3\%$$

(d) Costco's gross profit margin remained unchanged from 2006 to 2007, while its profit margin decreased slightly. Wal-Mart's gross profit and profit margins are relatively unchanged from 2006 to 2007, showing a slight improvement in both ratios.

Wal-Mart's gross profit margin is significantly better than Costco's. Comparing Wal-Mart's gross profit margin to Costco's, it appears that Wal-Mart has a higher mark-up on its goods. This is not surprising since Costco sells only discounted goods, which would have a lower gross profit margin, and Wal-Mart sells a mix of discounted and non-discounted goods.

Wal-Mart's profit margin is also much higher than Costco's. This could be an indication that Wal-Mart is better able to control its operating costs—which is not surprising because it has the advantage of being much larger than Costco.

The Navigator

Demonstration Problem
Perpetual Inventory System)

The adjusted trial balance at December 31, 2009, for Dykstra Inc. follows:

DYKSTRA INC.
Adjusted Trial Balance
December 31, 2009

	Debit	Credit
Cash	$ 4,500	
Accounts receivable	11,100	
Merchandise inventory	29,000	
Prepaid insurance	2,500	
Land	150,000	
Building	500,000	
Accumulated depreciation—building		$ 40,000
Equipment	95,000	
Accumulated depreciation—equipment		18,000
Notes payable		25,000
Accounts payable		10,600
Property tax payable		4,000
Mortgage payable—currently due		21,000
Mortgage payable—long-term		530,000
Common shares		70,000
Retained earnings		61,000
Dividends	10,000	
Sales		536,800
Sales returns and allowances	6,700	
Sales discounts	5,000	
Cost of goods sold	363,400	
Salaries expense	56,000	
Rent expense	24,000	
Utilities expense	18,000	
Advertising expense	12,000	
Depreciation expense	9,000	
Freight out	7,600	
Insurance expense	4,500	
Interest revenue		2,500
Interest expense	4,600	
Income tax expense	6,000	
	$1,318,900	$1,318,900

Instructions
Assuming Dykstra uses a perpetual inventory system, prepare a multiple-step statement of earnings, statement of retained earnings, and balance sheet for the year.

Solution to Demonstration Problem (Perpetual Inventory System)

DYKSTRA INC.
Statement of Retained Earnings
Year Ended December 31, 2009

Retained earnings, January 1	$61,000
Add: Net earnings	22,500
	83,500
Less: Dividends	10,000
Retained earnings, December 31	$73,500

Action Plan

- Prepare the statement of earnings in steps:

  1. Sales less sales returns and allowances and sales discounts equals net sales.

  2. Net sales less cost of goods sold equals gross profit

  3. Gross profit less operating expenses equals earnings from operations.

  4. Earnings from operations plus or minus non-operating revenue or expense items equals net earnings.

- Merchandise Inventory is a current asset in the classified balance sheet.

DYKSTRA INC.
Statement of Earnings
Year Ended December 31, 2009

Sales		$536,800
Less: Sales returns and allowances	$ 6,700	
Sales discounts	5,000	11,700
Net sales		525,100
Cost of goods sold		363,400
Gross profit		161,700
Operating expenses		
Salaries expense	$56,000	
Rent expense	24,000	
Utilities expense	18,000	
Advertising expense	12,000	
Depreciation expense	9,000	
Freight out	7,600	
Insurance expense	4,500	
Total operating expenses		131,100
Earnings from operations		30,600
Other revenues		
Interest revenue	$ 2,500	
Other expenses		
Interest expense	4,600	
Net non-operating expense		2,100
Earnings before income tax		28,500
Income tax expense		6,000
Net earnings		$ 22,500

DYKSTRA INC.
Balance Sheet
December 31, 2009

Assets

Current assets			
Cash		$ 4,500	
Accounts receivable		11,100	
Merchandise inventory		29,000	
Prepaid insurance		2,500	
Total current assets			$ 47,100
Property, plant, and equipment			
Land		$150,000	
Building	$500,000		
Less: Accumulated depreciation	40,000	460,000	
Equipment	$ 95,000		
Less: Accumulated depreciation	18,000	77,000	
Total property, plant, and equipment			687,000
Total assets			$734,100

Liabilities and Shareholders' Equity

Liabilities			
Current liabilities			
Notes payable		$ 25,000	
Accounts payable		10,600	
Property tax payable		4,000	
Mortgage payable		21,000	
Total current liabilities			$ 60,600
Long-term liabilities			
Mortgage payable			530,000
Total liabilities			590,600
Shareholders' equity			
Common shares		$ 70,000	
Retained earnings		73,500	143,500
Total liabilities and shareholders' equity			$734,100

The Navigator

Demonstration Problem
Periodic Inventory System—Appendix 5A)

The adjusted trial balance at December 31, 2009, for Dykstra Inc. follows:

	Debit	Credit
DYKSTRA INC.		
Adjusted Trial Balance		
December 31, 2009		
Cash	$ 4,500	
Accounts receivable	11,100	
Merchandise inventory, Jan. 1	25,000	
Prepaid insurance	2,500	
Land	150,000	
Building	500,000	
Accumulated depreciation—building		$ 40,000
Equipment	95,000	
Accumulated depreciation—equipment		18,000
Notes payable		25,000
Accounts payable		10,600
Property tax payable		4,000
Mortgage payable—currently due		21,000
Mortgage payable—long-term		530,000
Common shares		70,000
Retained earnings		61,000
Dividends	10,000	
Sales		536,800
Sales returns and allowances	6,700	
Sales discounts	5,000	
Purchases	370,000	
Purchase returns and allowances		15,000
Purchase discounts		5,000
Freight in	17,400	
Salaries expense	56,000	
Rent expense	24,000	
Utilities expense	18,000	
Advertising expense	12,000	
Depreciation expense	9,000	
Freight out	7,600	
Insurance expense	4,500	
Interest revenue		2,500
Interest expense	4,600	
Income tax expense	6,000	
	$1,338,900	$1,338,900

Instructions

Assuming Dykstra uses a periodic inventory system, prepare a multiple-step statement of earnings for the year. A physical inventory count on December 31 determined that ending inventory was $29,000.

Action Plan

- Remember the major subtotal headings in the statement of earnings: net sales, cost of goods sold, gross profit, earnings from operations, earnings before income tax, and net earnings.

- Recall the following formulas: purchases − purchase returns and allowances − purchase discounts = net purchases + freight in = cost of goods purchased. Beginning inventory plus cost of goods purchased = cost of goods available for sale. Cost of goods sold = cost of goods available for sale − ending inventory.

Solution to Demonstration Problem (Periodic Inventory System—Appendix 5A)

DYKSTRA INC.
Statement of Earnings
Year Ended December 31, 2009

Sales			$536,800
Less: Sales returns and allowances		$ 6,700	
Sales discounts		5,000	11,700
Net sales			525,100
Cost of goods sold			
Inventory, Jan. 1			25,000
Purchases		$370,000	
Less: Purchase returns and allowances	$15,000		
Purchase discounts	5,000	20,000	
Net purchases		350,000	
Add: Freight in		17,400	
Cost of goods purchased			367,400
Cost of goods available for sale			392,400
Inventory, Dec. 31			29,000
Total cost of goods sold			363,400
Gross profit			161,700
Operating expenses			
Salaries expense		$56,000	
Rent expense		24,000	
Utilities expense		18,000	
Advertising expense		12,000	
Depreciation expense		9,000	
Freight out		7,600	
Insurance expense		4,500	
Total operating expenses			131,100
Earnings from operations			30,600
Other revenues			
Interest revenue		$2,500	
Other expenses			
Interest expense		4,600	
Net non-operating expense			2,100
Earnings before income tax			28,500
Income tax expense			6,000
Net earnings			$ 22,500

Note that Dykstra's statement of retained earnings and balance sheet are the same as those presented in the demonstration problem using the perpetual inventory system.

The Navigator

Note: All questions, exercises, and problems below with an asterisk (*) relate to material in Appendix 5A.

Self-Study Questions

Answers are at the end of the chapter.

Study Tools (Self-Assessment Quizzes)

1. Which of the following statements about a perpetual inventory system is true?
   (a) Cost of goods sold is only determined at the end of the accounting period.
   (b) Detailed records of the cost of each inventory purchase and sale are kept continuously.
   (c) The periodic inventory system provides better control over inventories than a perpetual system.
   (d) A physical inventory count is not performed in a perpetual inventory system.

2. A $750 purchase of merchandise inventory is made on June 12, terms 2/10, n/30. On June 16, merchandise costing $50 is returned. What amount will be paid as payment in full on June 22?
   (a) $685
   (b) $686
   (c) $700
   (d) $735

3. Enrage Inc. purchased merchandise for $310 on May 12, terms 1/10, n/30, FOB shipping point. On May 12, freight costs of $12 were also paid by the company. On May 15, Enrage returned merchandise costing $10. On May 22, the company paid the amount owing, taking the purchase discount of $3. What is the ending balance in the Merchandise Inventory account related to these transactions, if Enrage uses a perpetual inventory system?
   (a) $297
   (b) $300
   (c) $309
   (d) $310

4. When goods are shipped with the freight terms FOB shipping point in a perpetual inventory system:
   (a) the buyer pays the freight costs and debits Merchandise Inventory.
   (b) the buyer pays the freight costs and debits Freight Out.
   (c) the seller pays the freight costs and debits Delivery Expense.
   (d) the seller pays the freight costs and debits Merchandise Inventory.

5. To record the sale of goods for cash in a perpetual inventory system:
   (a) only one journal entry is necessary to record the cost of goods sold and reduction of inventory.
   (b) only one journal entry is necessary to record the receipt of cash and the sales revenue.
   (c) two journal entries are necessary: one to record the receipt of cash and sales revenue, and one to record the cost of the goods sold and reduction of inventory.
   (d) two journal entries are necessary: one to record the receipt of cash and reduction of inventory, and one to record the cost of the goods sold and sales revenue.

6. Which of the following is a contra sales account that normally has a debit balance? (SO 3)
   (a) Sales
   (b) Sales Returns and Allowances
   (c) Cost of Goods Sold
   (d) Freight Out

7. Net sales are $400,000; cost of goods sold is $310,000; operating expenses are $60,000; other revenue is $10,000; and income tax expense is $8,000. What is the gross profit? (SO 4)
   (a) $30,000
   (b) $32,000
   (c) $90,000
   (d) $100,000

8. Which of the following appears on both a single-step and multiple-step statement of earnings? (SO 4)
   (a) Gross profit
   (b) Earnings from operations
   (c) Non-operating activities
   (d) Earnings before income tax

9. Which of the following would affect the gross profit margin? (SO 5)
   (a) An increase in advertising expense
   (b) A decrease in depreciation expense
   (c) An increase in cost of goods sold
   (d) A decrease in insurance expense

10. Net sales are $400,000; cost of goods sold is $310,000; operating expenses are $60,000; other revenue is $10,000; and income tax expense is $8,000. What are the gross profit margin and profit margin? (SO 5)
    (a) 7.5% and 8.0%
    (b) 8.0% and 22.5%
    (c) 22.5% and 8.0%
    (d) 25.0% and 8.0%

*11. When goods are purchased for resale by a company using a periodic inventory system: (SO 6)
    (a) purchases are debited to Merchandise Inventory.
    (b) purchases are debited to Purchases.
    (c) purchase returns are debited to Purchase Returns and Allowances.
    (d) freight costs are debited to Purchases.

*12. Beginning inventory is $60,000; purchases are $400,000; purchase returns and allowances are $25,000; freight in is $5,000; and ending inventory is $50,000. What is the cost of goods sold? (SO 6)
    (a) $380,000
    (b) $390,000
    (c) $435,000
    (d) $440,000

Questions

(SO 1) 1. How do revenues and expenses differ for a merchandising company and a service company?

(SO 1) 2. What is meant by the term "operating cycle"? Why is the normal operating cycle for a merchandising company likely to be longer than that of a service company?

(SO 1) 3. Suppose you are starting a company that sells used clothes. What factors would you consider in determining whether to use a perpetual or periodic inventory system?

(SO 1) 4. Song Yee wonders why a physical inventory count is necessary in a perpetual inventory system. After all, the accounting records show how much inventory is on hand. Explain why a physical inventory count is required in a perpetual inventory system.

(SO 1) 5. Explain when cost of goods sold is calculated in a perpetual inventory system, and when it is calculated in a periodic inventory system.

(SO 2) 6. Why are purchases of merchandise for resale not recorded in the same account as purchases of other items, such as supplies or equipment? Would it not be better to use one account to record all these purchases?

(SO 2) 7. Distinguish between FOB shipping point and FOB destination. What freight term will result in a debit to Merchandise Inventory by the buyer? A debit to Freight Out by the seller?

(SO 2) 8. What is the formula for calculating the cost of goods available for sale? The cost of goods sold?

(SO 2, 3) 9. Inventory was purchased on credit in April and paid for in May. It was sold in June. In which month(s) should the company record the revenue and expense from these transactions?

(SO 2, 3) 10. Explain why purchase returns are credited directly to the Merchandise Inventory account but sales returns are not debited directly to the Sales account.

(SO 2, 3) 11. Distinguish between a quantity discount, a purchase discount, and a sales discount. Explain how each kind of discount is recorded.

12. Distinguish between gross and net sales.

13. If merchandise is returned and restored to inventory, the Cost of Goods Sold account is credited. However, if merchandise is returned but not restored to inventory (because it is not resaleable), Cost of Goods Sold is not credited. Why not?

14. Distinguish between a single-step and a multiple-step statement of earnings for a merchandising company.

15. Identify the sections of a multiple-step statement of earnings that relate to (a) operating activities, and (b) non-operating activities.

16. Why is interest expense reported as a non-operating expense and not as an operating expense on a multiple-step statement of earnings?

17. How do the gross profit margin and profit margin differ?

18. What factors affect a company's gross profit margin— that is, what can cause the gross profit margin to increase and what can cause it to decrease?

19. Identify two types of companies that you would expect to have a high gross profit margin and two types of companies that you would expect to have a low gross profit margin.

*20. Distinguish between the journal entries made by the buyer in a periodic inventory system and a perpetual inventory system.

*21. Distinguish between the journal entries made by the seller in a periodic inventory system and a perpetual inventory system.

*22. Identify the accounts that are added to or deducted from purchases in a periodic inventory system to determine the cost of goods purchased. For each account, indicate (a) whether its balance is added or deducted and (b) what its normal balance is.

*23. How is the cost of goods sold calculated and recorded in a periodic inventory system? In a perpetual inventory system?

*24. What differences would be found on a statement of earnings prepared for a company using a periodic inventory system, compared to a company using a perpetual inventory system?

Brief Exercises

Determine missing amounts.
(SO 2)

BE5–1 The following Merchandise Inventory general ledger account is available for a company that uses the perpetual inventory system:

Merchandise Inventory			
Bal., beg. of Year 1	(a)		
Purchases	(b)	Purchase returns	1,000
Freight	500	Purchase discounts	100
		Cost of goods sold	8,000
Bal., end of Year 1	4,000		
Purchases	11,720	Purchase returns	200
Freight	600	Purchase discounts	(c)
		Cost of goods sold	(d)
Bal., end of Year 2	6,000		

Net purchases in Year 1 and Year 2 were $9,500 and $11,400, respectively. Fill in the missing amounts.

BE5–2 Prepare the journal entries to record the following purchase transactions in Xiaoyan Ltd.'s books. Xiaoyan uses a perpetual inventory system.

Jan. 2 Xiaoyan purchased $9,000 of merchandise from Feng Corp., terms n/30, FOB destination.

5 The correct company paid freight costs of $135.

6 Xiaoyan returned $1,000 of the merchandise purchased on January 2, because it was not needed.

12 Xiaoyan paid the balance owed to Feng.

BE5–3 (a) Prepare the journal entries to record the following purchase transactions in Jarek Corporation's books. Jarek uses a perpetual inventory system.

Mar. 12 Jarek purchased $12,000 of merchandise from Dalibor Inc., terms 2/10, n/30.

13 Jarek returned $2,000 of the merchandise purchased on March 12, because it was damaged.

20 Jarek paid the balance owing to Dalibor.

(b) Repeat the journal entry to record the payment of the balance owing to Dalibor, but assume that Jarek paid on March 31 rather than March 20.

BE5–4 Refer to BE5–2 and prepare the journal entries to record the following sales transactions in Feng Corp.'s books. Feng uses a perpetual inventory system.

Jan. 2 Feng sold $9,000 of merchandise to Xiaoyan Ltd., terms n/30, FOB destination. The cost of the merchandise sold was $7,200.

5 The correct company paid freight costs of $135.

6 Xiaoyan returned $1,000 of the merchandise purchased from Feng on January 2, because it was not needed. The cost of the merchandise returned was $800, and it was restored to inventory.

12 Feng received the balance due from Xiaoyan.

BE5–5 (a) Refer to BE5–3 and prepare journal entries to record the following sales transactions in Dalibor Inc.'s books. Dalibor uses a perpetual inventory system.

Mar. 12 Dalibor sold $12,000 of merchandise to Jarek Corporation, terms 2/10, n/30, FOB destination. The cost of the merchandise sold was $7,500.

13 Jarek returned $2,000 of the merchandise purchased on March 12, because it was damaged. The cost of the merchandise returned was $1,250. Dalibor examined the merchandise, decided it was no longer saleable, and discarded it.

20 Dalibor received the balance due from Jarek.

(b) Repeat the journal entry to record the receipt of the amount owing from Jarek, but assume that the balance due was received on March 31 rather than March 20.

BE5–6 The list of merchandising terms below is followed by definitions. Beside each definition, write the number of the term that it defines.

1. Purchase discount
2. Merchandise inventory
3. Purchase return
4. Quantity discount
5. FOB destination
6. FOB shipping point
7. Sales allowance
8. Contra revenue account
9. Cost of goods sold

_____ (a) Freight terms indicating that the seller will pay for the shipping costs of the goods
_____ (b) An account, such as Sales Returns and Allowances, that is offset against (deducted from) a revenue account in the statement of earnings
_____ (c) The return of unsatisfactory purchased merchandise
_____ (d) The total cost of merchandise sold during the period
_____ (e) Freight terms indicating that the buyer will pay for the shipping costs of the goods
_____ (f) A cash discount given to the buyer for volume purchases
_____ (g) The reduction in price of unsatisfactory sold merchandise
_____ (h) A cash discount given to a buyer for early payment of the balance due
_____ (i) Goods purchased for resale to customers

Determine missing amounts.
(SO 4)

BE5–7   Presented here are selected components of the multiple-step statement of earnings for three companies. Determine the missing amounts.

Company	Sales	Cost of Goods Sold	Gross Profit	Operating Expenses	Other Revenues (Expenses)	Income Tax Expense	Net Earnings
A	$ 85,000	(b)	$ 30,000	(d)	$6,000	$3,200	$12,800
B	108,000	$ 75,000	(c)	$20,000	(e)	4,300	17,200
C	(a)	200,000	100,000	60,000	(2,000)	8,000	(f)

Calculate amounts from statement of earnings.
(SO 4)

BE5–8   Saguenay Limited reports the following information: sales $550,000; sales returns and allowances $25,000; sales discounts $25,000; cost of goods sold $285,000; operating expenses $120,000; other revenues $18,000; other expenses $22,000; and income tax expense $22,000. Calculate the following: (a) net sales, (b) gross profit, (c) earnings from operations, (d) earnings before income tax, and (e) net earnings.

Identify placement of items on statement of earnings.
(SO 4)

BE5–9   Explain where each of the following items would appear on (a) a multiple-step statement of earnings and (b) a single-step statement of earnings: depreciation expense, cost of goods sold, freight out, gain on sale of equipment, income tax expense, interest expense, rent revenue, sales discounts, and sales returns and allowances.

Calculate profitability ratios and comment.
(SO 5)

BE5–10   The Forzani Group Ltd. reports sales revenue of $1,331.0 million, cost of goods sold of $852.6 million, and net earnings of $47.5 million for 2008. It reported sales revenue of $1,264.0 million, cost of goods sold of $812.4 million, and net earnings of $35.2 million for 2007. Calculate the gross profit margin and profit margin for each of 2008 and 2007. Comment on Forzani's changing profitability.

Record purchase transactions.
(SO 6)

*BE5–11   From the information in BE5–2, prepare the journal entries to record the purchase transactions on Xiaoyan Ltd.'s books, assuming a periodic inventory system is used instead of a perpetual inventory system.

Record sales transactions.
(SO 6)

*BE5–12   From the information in BE5–4, prepare the journal entries to record the sales transactions on Feng Corp.'s books, assuming a periodic inventory system is used instead of a perpetual inventory system.

Calculate amounts from statement of earnings.
(SO 6)

*BE5–13   Bassing Corp. uses a periodic inventory system and reports the following information: sales $700,000; sales returns and allowances $25,000; sales discounts $50,000; purchases $400,000; purchase returns and allowances $11,000; purchase discounts $8,000; freight in $16,000; beginning inventory $60,000; and ending inventory $90,000. Calculate (a) net sales, (b) net purchases, (c) cost of goods purchased, (d) cost of goods sold, and (e) gross profit.

Prepare cost of goods sold section.
(SO 6)

*BE5–14   Haida Corporation reported the following selected data for the year ended December 31, 2009: purchases $140,000; purchase returns and allowances $4,000; purchase discounts $13,600; freight in $6,000; freight out $10,000; beginning inventory $60,000; and ending inventory $70,000. Prepare the cost of goods sold section for Haida in a multiple-step statement of earnings.

Exercises

Record purchase transactions.
(SO 2)

E5–1   This information is for Olaf Corp.:

April 3   Purchased merchandise from DeVito Ltd. for $18,000, terms 1/10, n/30, FOB shipping point.

6   The appropriate company paid freight costs of $500 on the merchandise purchased on April 3.

7   Purchased supplies on account for $6,000.

8   Returned damaged merchandise to DeVito and was given a purchase allowance of $2,500. The merchandise was repaired by DeVito and returned to inventory for future resale.

30   Paid the amount due to DeVito in full.

Instructions

(a) Record the transactions in Olaf's books, assuming a perpetual inventory system is used.

(b) Assume that Olaf paid the balance due to DeVito on April 13 instead of April 30. Prepare the journal entry to record this payment on Olaf's books.

E5–2   Refer to the information in E5–1 for Olaf Corp. and the following additional information:

1. The cost of the merchandise sold on April 3 was $10,800.
2. The cost of the merchandise returned on April 8 was $1,500.

Instructions

(a) Record the transactions in the books of DeVito, assuming a perpetual inventory system is used.

(b) Assume that DeVito received the balance due from Olaf on April 13 instead of April 30. Prepare the journal entry to record this collection.

E5–3   The following merchandise transactions occurred in December. Both companies use a perpetual inventory system.

Dec. 3	Pippen Ltd. sold $48,000 of merchandise to Thomas Corp., terms 2/10, n/30, FOB shipping point. The cost of the merchandise sold was $32,000.
7	Shipping costs of $750 were paid by the correct company.
8	Thomas returned unwanted merchandise to Pippen. The returned merchandise has a sales price of $2,400, and a cost of $1,600. It was restored to inventory.
11	Pippen received the balance due from Thomas.

Instructions

(a) Record the above transactions in the books of Pippen Ltd.

(b) Record the above transactions in the books of Thomas Corp.

(c) Calculate the gross profit earned by Pippen on the above transactions.

E5–4   On September 1, Campus Office Supply Ltd. had an inventory of 10 calculators at a cost of $24 each. The company uses a perpetual inventory system. During September these transactions occurred:

Sept. 7	Purchased 60 calculators at $24 each from Digital Corp. on account, terms 1/10, n/30.
10	Returned two calculators to Digital for $48 credit because they did not meet specifications.
11	Sold 26 calculators for $30 each to Campus Book Store, terms 1/10, n/30.
14	Granted credit of $30 to Campus Book Store for the return of one calculator that was not ordered. The calculator was restored to inventory.
15	Paid Digital the amount owing.
18	Received payment in full from Campus Book Store.
21	Sold 30 calculators for $30 each to Student Card Shop, terms 1/10, n/30.

Instructions

(a) Record the September transactions. Round your answers to the nearest cent.

(b) Post the appropriate entries to the Merchandise Inventory and Cost of Goods Sold accounts. Determine the ending balances in both dollars and cents, and quantities.

E5–5   The following list of accounts is from the adjusted trial balance for Swirsky Corporation:

Accounts payable	Dividends	Prepaid insurance
Accounts receivable	Equipment	Property tax payable
Accumulated depreciation—building	Freight out	Salaries expense
Accumulated depreciation—equipment	Insurance expense	Salaries payable
Advertising expense	Interest expense	Sales
Building	Interest payable	Sales discounts
Cash	Land	Sales returns and allowances
Common shares	Merchandise inventory	Unearned sales revenue
Depreciation expense	Mortgage payable	Utilities expense

Instructions

For each account, identify whether it should be reported on the balance sheet, statement of retained earnings, or statement of earnings. Also specify where the account should be classified. For example, Accounts Payable would be classified under current liabilities on the balance sheet.

Prepare statement of earnings.
(SO 4)

E5–6 **Gildan Activewear Inc.** reported the following condensed data for the year ended September 30 2007 (in USD millions):

Cost of sales	$655.3
Income tax recovery	(4.8)
Interest expense	4.9
Other non-operating expenses	29.3
Sales	964.4
Selling, general, and administrative expenses	149.8

Instructions

(a) Prepare a single-step statement of earnings.

(b) Prepare a multiple-step statement of earnings.

Determine missing amounts.
(SO 4)

E5–7 You have been provided with the following information in respect of the statement of earnings of Petals Ltd. for the year ended May 30, 2008.

PETALS LTD.
Statement of Earnings
Year Ended May 30, 2008

Sales		$ (a)
Less: Sales returns and allowances	35,000	
Sales discounts	15,000	
Net sales		$400,000
Cost of goods sold		(b)
Gross profit		160,000
Operating expenses		144,000
Earnings from operations		(c)
Other revenues		
Interest revenue	$ 4,000	
Other expenses		
Interest expense	(d)	
Net non-operating expense		9,000
Earnings before income tax		(e)
Income tax expense		2,000
Net earnings		$ (f)

Instructions

Calculate the amounts that would be presented on the statement of earnings for (a) through (f) inclusive.

Determine missing amounts
and calculate profitability
ratios.
(SO 4, 5)

E5–8 Financial information is presented here for two companies:

	Young Ltd.	Rioux Ltée
Sales	$89,000	$ (f)
Sales returns and allowances	(a)	5,000
Net sales	81,000	95,000
Cost of goods sold	52,750	(g)
Gross profit	(b)	40,000
Operating expenses	18,500	(h)
Earnings from operations	(c)	18,250
Non-operating revenues	250	500
Earnings before income tax	(d)	(i)
Income tax expense	2,000	(j)
Net earnings	(e)	15,000

Instructions

(a) Calculate the missing amounts.

(b) Calculate the gross profit margin and profit margin for each company.

E5–9   ◯**C** Best Buy Co., Inc. reported the following selected information at its February year end for three fiscal years (in USD millions):

Calculate profitability ratios and comment.
(SO 5)

	2007	2006	2005
Net sales	$35,934	$30,848	$27,433
Cost of goods sold	27,165	23,122	20,938
Earnings from operations	1,999	1,644	1,442
Net earnings	1,377	1,140	984

Instructions

(a) Calculate the gross profit margin and profit margin for Best Buy for each of the three years.

(b) Recalculate the profit margin for the three years using earnings from operations instead of net earnings. Does this result in a different trend than you saw in (a)? If yes, what might be the reason for this change?

(c) Comment on whether the ratios have improved or deteriorated over the last three years.

*E5–10   Data for Olaf Corp. and DeVito Ltd. are presented in E5–1 and E5–2.

Record purchase and sales transactions.
(SO 6)

Instructions

Repeat the requirements for E5-1 and E5-2, assuming a periodic inventory system is used instead of a perpetual inventory system.

*E5–11   Duvall Ltd. and Pele Ltd. incurred the following merchandise transactions in June:

Record purchase and sales transactions.
(SO 6)

June 10   Duvall sold $10,000 of merchandise to Pele, terms 1/10, n/30, FOB shipping point. The merchandise cost Duvall $7,500 when it was originally purchased.

    11   Freight costs of $500 were paid by the appropriate company.

    12   Duvall received damaged goods returned by Pele for credit. The goods were originally sold for $500; the cost of the returned merchandise was $375. The merchandise was not returned to inventory.

    19   Duvall received full payment from Pele.

Instructions

(a) Prepare journal entries for each transaction in the books of Pele Ltd., assuming (1) a perpetual inventory system is used, and (2) a periodic inventory system is used.

(b) Prepare journal entries for each transaction for Duvall Ltd., assuming (1) a perpetual inventory system is used, and (2) a periodic inventory system is used.

*E5–12   Memories Inc. commenced operations on July 1. Memories Inc. uses a periodic inventory system. During July, Memories Inc. was involved in the following merchandise transactions:

Record purchase and sales transactions and calculate gross profit.
(SO 6)

July   2   Purchased $20,000 of merchandise from Supplies Inc. on account, terms 2/10, n/30, FOB shipping point.

    5   Paid freight costs on July 2 shipment of $500 cash.

    8   Sold merchandise for $1,000 cash.

   11   Paid Supplies Inc. for the July 2 shipment.

   15   Sold merchandise for $5,000 on account, 1/10, n/30, FOB shipping point.

   23   Received full payment for merchandise sold on July 15.

Instructions

(a) Record the above transactions in the books of Memories.

(b) Assuming that a physical inventory count on July 31 indicated that Memories had $16,500 of inventory on hand, what was the gross profit for the month of July?

*E5–13   Below are the cost of goods sold sections for the most recent two years for two companies using a periodic inventory system:

Determine missing amounts.
(SO 6)

	Company 1		Company 2	
	Year 1	Year 2	Year 1	Year 2
Beginning inventory	$ 250	$ (e)	$1,000	$ (n)
Purchases	1,500	(f)	(j)	9,550
Purchase returns and allowances	50	100	300	400
Purchase discounts	30	50	150	100
Net purchases	(a)	1,850	7,210	(o)

▸ Merchandising Operations

Freight in	110	(g)	(k)	550
Cost of goods purchased	(b)	(h)	7,900	(p)
Cost of goods available for sale	(c)	2,300	(l)	(q)
Ending inventory	(d)	400	1,450	1,250
Cost of goods sold	1,480	(i)	(m)	(r)

Instructions

Fill in the lettered blanks to complete the cost of goods sold sections.

Prepare statement of earnings.
(SO 6)

*E5–14   The following selected information is presented for Okanagan Corporation for the year ended February 28, 2009. Okanagan uses a periodic inventory system.

Accounts receivable	$ 25,000	Purchases	$200,000
Common shares	85,000	Purchase discounts	20,000
Dividends	42,000	Purchase returns and allowances	6,000
Freight in	7,500	Rent expense	20,000
Freight out	7,000	Salaries expense	60,000
Income tax expense	4,500	Sales	335,000
Insurance expense	12,000	Sales discounts	31,000
Interest expense	6,000	Sales returns and allowances	12,000
Merchandise inventory, Mar. 1, 2008	42,000	Unearned sales revenue	4,500
Merchandise inventory, Feb. 28, 2009	61,000		

Instructions

Prepare a multiple-step statement of earnings.

Problems: Set A

Identify appropriate inventory system.
(SO 1)

P5–1A   The Fashion Palace Inc. sells a variety of home decorating merchandise, including pictures, small furniture items, dishes, candles, and area rugs. The company uses a periodic inventory system and counts inventory once a year. Most customers use the option to purchase on account and many take more than a month to pay. The company does not have any specific credit terms for its regular customers.

The general manager of The Fashion Palace, Rebecca Sherstabetoff, believes the company needs a bank loan because the accounts payable have to be paid long before the accounts receivable are collected. The bank manager is willing to give The Fashion Palace a loan but wants monthly financial statements.

Rebecca has also noticed that, while some of the company's merchandise sells very quickly, other items do not. Sometimes she wonders just how long some of those older items have been in stock. She has also noticed that the company seems to run out of some merchandise items on a regular basis. And she is wondering how she is going to find someone with the time to count the inventory every month so that monthly financial statements can be prepared for the bank. She has come to you for help.

Instructions

(a) Explain to Rebecca what an operating cycle is and why the company is having problems paying its bills.

(b) Make a recommendation about what inventory system the company should use and explain why.

Record and post purchase and sales transactions.
(SO 2, 3)

P5–2A   Travel Warehouse Ltd. distributes suitcases to retail stores and extends credit terms of n/30 to all of its customers. At the end of June, Travel Warehouse's inventory consisted of 40 suitcases purchased at $30 each. It uses a perpetual inventory system. During the month of July, the following merchandising transactions occurred:

July 2 Purchased 50 suitcases on account for $30 each from Trunk Manufacturers Ltd., terms n/30.
    3 Received a $150 credit from Trunk Manufacturers after returning five suitcases because they were damaged.
    6 Sold 40 suitcases on account to Satchel World Inc. for $55 each.
    7 Issued a $275 credit for five suitcases returned by Satchel World because they were the wrong colour. The suitcases were returned to inventory.
   13 Sold 30 suitcases on account to The Going Concern, Limited for $55 each.
   16 Purchased 60 suitcases on account for $1,800 from Holiday Manufacturers, terms n/30, FOB shipping point.
   17 Paid $50 freight to Safe Truckers Inc. for merchandise purchased from Holiday Manufacturers.
   27 Received payment in full from Satchel World.

31 Paid Trunk Manufacturers the balance owing.

Instructions

(a) Record the July transactions for Travel Warehouse.

(b) Post the transactions to the Merchandise Inventory account and calculate the July 31 balance.

(c) What is the average cost of these suitcases? (Hint: Divide the ending balance in the Merchandise Inventory account calculated in (b) and divide it by the number of suitcases on hand at July 31). Why is this average amount not equal to the amount paid for each suitcase, $30?

P5–3A Presented here are selected transactions for Shaoshi Inc. during October of the current year. Shaoshi uses a perpetual inventory system.

Record purchase and sales transactions.
(SO 2, 3)

Oct. 1 Purchased merchandise on account from Micron Ltd. at a cost of $65,000, terms 1/15, n/30, FOB shipping point.

1 Freight charges of $2,000 were paid by the appropriate party on the October 1 purchase of merchandise.

5 Returned for credit $7,000 of damaged goods purchased from Micron on October 1.

8 Sold the remaining merchandise purchased from Micron to Guidant Corp. for $90,000 on account, terms 2/10, n/30, FOB destination.

8 Freight charges of $3,000 were paid by the appropriate party on the October 8 sale of merchandise.

9 Guidant returned some of the merchandise purchased on October 8 for a $4,000 credit on account. The merchandise originally cost $2,400 and was restored to inventory.

12 Purchased office supplies for $5,000 cash.

14 Paid Micron the balance owing.

15 Purchased merchandise for $7,500 cash.

16 Received the balance owing from Guidant.

20 Purchased delivery equipment on account for $45,000.

28 Sold merchandise for $30,000 on account to Deux Ltée, terms 2/10, n/30, FOB shipping point. The merchandise had a cost of $18,000.

28 Freight charges of $1,000 were paid by the appropriate party on the October 28 sale of merchandise.

Instructions

Record the October transactions.

P5–4A At the beginning of the current tennis season, on April 1, 2009, the general ledger of Kicked-Back Tennis Shop showed Cash $2,500; Merchandise Inventory $1,700; Common Shares $3,000; and Retained Earnings $1,200. Kicked-Back Tennis Shop uses a perpetual inventory system. The following transactions occurred in April:

Record, post, and prepare trial balance and partial statement of earnings.
(SO 2, 3, 4)

Apr. 2 Purchased racquets and balls from Roberts Inc. for $1,460, terms 2/10, n/30, FOB shipping point.

3 The appropriate party paid $40 freight on April 2.

7 Received credit of $35 from Roberts for a damaged racquet that was returned.

10 Paid Roberts in full.

13 Purchased tennis shoes from Niki Sports Ltd. for $460 cash.

14 Purchased supplies for $650 cash from Discount Supplies Limited.

17 Received a $55 cash refund from Niki Sports for damaged merchandise that was returned.

20 Returned $60 of the supplies purchased on April 14 and received a cash refund.

21 Sold merchandise to members for $1,800, terms n/30. The cost of the merchandise was $1,170.

27 Purchased equipment for use in the business from DomCo Ltd. for $1,800, terms n/30.

28 Granted a $50 sales allowance to a member for slightly torn tennis clothing. No merchandise was returned.

30 Received cash payments on account from members, $1,000.

Instructions

(a) Prepare T accounts and enter the opening balances.

(b) Record and post the April transactions. Round all amounts to the nearest dollar.

(c) Prepare a trial balance as at April 30, 2009.

(d) Prepare a statement of earnings through to gross profit.

Record, post, and prepare
partial financial statements.
(SO 2, 3, 4)

P5–5A   Nisson Distributing Ltd. completed the following merchandising transactions in the month of April 2009. At the beginning of April, Nisson's general ledger showed Cash $4,000; Accounts Receivable $5,000; Common Shares $5,000; and Retained Earnings $4,000. Nisson uses a perpetual inventory system.

Apr.   2   Purchased merchandise on account from Kai Supply Corp. for $8,900, terms 1/15, n/30, FOB shipping point.
      3   The appropriate party paid $100 freight on the April 2 purchase.
      6   Sold $11,600 of merchandise on account to Kananaskis Supply Ltd., terms 1/10, n/30, FOB destination. The cost of the merchandise was $7,200.
      6   The appropriate party paid $350 freight on the April 6 sale of merchandise.
      7   Issued a $580 credit for merchandise returned by Kananaskis Supply. The merchandise originally cost $360 and was returned to inventory.
      10 Paid Kai Supply in full.
      14 Purchased merchandise for $6,100 cash.
      15 Received the balance owing from Kananaskis Supply.
      16 Received a $500 refund for merchandise that was returned to the supplier in the April 14 cash purchase.
      17 Purchased merchandise from Pigeon Distributors Limited for $4,200, terms 1/10, n/30, FOB destination.
      20 The appropriate party paid $125 freight on the April 17 purchase.
      21 Received a $300 credit for merchandise returned to Pigeon Distributors.
      23 Sold merchandise for $6,400 cash. The cost of the merchandise was $5,200.
      27 Paid Pigeon Distributors in full.

Instructions

(a) Prepare T accounts and enter the opening balances.
(b) Record and post the April transactions. Round all amounts to the nearest dollar.
(c) Prepare a statement of earnings through to gross profit.
(d) Prepare the current assets section of the balance sheet.

P5–6A   The following list of accounts has been selected from the adjusted trial balance of We Make It Inc.:

Accounts payable	Goodwill	Prepaid expenses
Accounts receivable	Income tax expense	Rent revenue
Accumulated depreciation	Income tax payable	Retained earnings
Buildings	Interest expense	Sales
Cash	Inventories	Sales discounts
Common shares	Land	Sales returns and allow-
Cost of goods sold	Machinery and equipment	ances
Current portion of long-term debt	Long-term debt	Unearned sales revenue
Depreciation expense	Operating expenses	

Instructions

For each account, indicate whether it is reported on We Make It's balance sheet, multiple-step statement of earnings, or statement of retained earnings. Also specify where the account is most likely classified. For example, Accounts Payable would be classified as a current liability on the balance sheet.

Prepare single- and multiple-
step statements of earnings.
(SO 4)

P5–7A   The adjusted trial balance of Poorten Wholesale Ltd. (on the following page) contained the following accounts at November 30, the company's fiscal year end:

Instructions

(a) Prepare a single-step statement of earnings.

(b) Prepare a multiple-step statement of earnings.

(c) Compare the two statements and comment on the usefulness of each one.

POORTEN WHOLESALE LTD.
Adjusted Trial Balance
November 30, 2009

	Debit	Credit
Cash	$ 12,100	
Accounts receivable	15,700	
Merchandise inventory	45,200	
Supplies	1,500	
Notes receivable	25,000	
Land	60,000	
Building	85,000	
Accumulated depreciation—building		$ 17,000
Delivery equipment	48,000	
Accumulated depreciation—delivery equipment		24,000
Accounts payable		48,500
Unearned sales revenue		3,000
Income tax payable		5,500
Mortgage payable		51,000
Common shares		30,000
Retained earnings		90,000
Sales		750,300
Interest revenue		1,620
Sales returns and allowances	4,200	
Sales discounts	3,750	
Advertising expense	26,400	
Cost of goods sold	497,500	
Depreciation expense	10,125	
Freight out	16,700	
Income tax expense	5,500	
Insurance expense	3,420	
Interest expense	3,700	
Salaries expense	136,625	
Supplies expense	6,500	
Utilities expense	14,000	
	$1,020,920	$1,020,920

P5–8A The unadjusted trial balance of Fashion Centre Ltd. contained the following accounts at November 30, the company's fiscal year end:

Record, post, and prepare adjusted trial balance and financial statements. (SO 4)

FASHION CENTRE LTD.
Trial Balance
November 30, 2009

	Debit	Credit
Cash	$ 14,000	
Accounts receivable	30,600	
Merchandise inventory	27,500	
Supplies	1,650	
Prepaid insurance	1,800	
Investments	37,000	
Furniture and equipment	26,800	
Accumulated depreciation—furniture and equipment		$ 10,720
Leasehold improvements	42,000	
Accumulated depreciation—leasehold improvements		8,400
Accounts payable		34,400
Unearned sales revenue		3,000

Note payable		35,000
Common shares		50,000
Retained earnings		30,000
Dividends	10,000	
Sales		238,500
Sales discounts	4,520	
Sales returns and allowances	4,600	
Cost of goods sold	157,000	
Salaries expense	31,600	
Rent expense	13,850	
Miscellaneous expenses	6,100	
Income tax expense	1,000	
	$410,020	$410,020

Adjustment data:

1. The 12-month insurance policy was purchased on August 1.

2. There is $950 of supplies on hand at November 30.

3. Depreciation expense for the year is $5,360 on the furniture and equipment, and $4,200 on the leasehold improvements.

4. Salaries of $1,210 are unpaid at November 30.

5. Accrued interest expense at November 30 is $1,200.

6. Of the unearned sales revenue, $2,400 has been earned by November 30. The cost of goods sold incurred in earning this revenue is $1,475.

7. Of the note payable, $5,000 is to be paid in 2010.

8. Income tax of $1,100 is due and unpaid.

Instructions

(a) Prepare T accounts and enter the trial balance amounts.

(b) Record and post the adjusting entries, assuming the company adjusts its accounts annually.

(c) Prepare an adjusted trial balance.

(d) Prepare a multiple-step statement of earnings, statement of retained earnings, and balance sheet for the year.

Calculate missing amounts and assess profitability. (SO 4, 5)

P5–9A MacLean Corp. purchases all merchandise inventory on credit and uses a perpetual inventory system. The Accounts Payable account is used for recording merchandise inventory purchases only; all other current liabilities are accrued in separate accounts. You are provided with the following selected information for the fiscal years 2007 through 2009:

	2009	2008	2007
Statement of Earnings Data			
Net sales	$ (1)	$227,600	$219,500
Cost of goods sold	144,400	(5)	133,500
Gross profit	81,300	80,100	(9)
Operating expenses	(2)	47,000	(10)
Net earnings	$ 36,300	(6)	$ 30,000
Balance Sheet Data			
Merchandise inventory	$ (3)	$14,700	$10,000
Accounts payable	25,000	(7)	20,000
Additional Information			
Purchase of merchandise inventory on account	$141,000	(8)	$132,000
Cash payments to suppliers	(4)	161,000	127,000

Instructions

(a) Calculate the missing amounts for items (1) through (10).

(b) Calculate the gross profit margin and profit margin for each year.

(c) Sales increased between 2007 and 2008. Does this mean that profitability should also have increased in the same period? Refer to the gross profit margin to explain and support your answer.

P5–10A ⬤━ℂ The following selected information is available for AB Volvo, headquartered in Sweden, for three fiscal years (in SEK millions):

Calculate ratios and comment. (SO 5)

	2007	2006	2005
Current assets	159,160	134,388	140,485
Current liabilities	140,935	105,918	108,740
Net sales	285,405	258,835	240,559
Cost of sales	219,600	199,054	186,662
Net earnings	15,028	16,318	13,108

Instructions

(a) Calculate the current ratio, gross profit margin, and profit margin for each year. Comment on whether the ratios have improved or deteriorated over the three years.

(b) Compare the 2007 ratios to the following industry averages: current ratio 1.7:1; gross profit margin 13.6%; and profit margin (3.1)%. Are Volvo's ratios better or worse than those of its industry?

P5–11A Data for Travel Warehouse Ltd. are presented in P5–2A.

Record purchase and sales transactions. (SO 6)

Instructions

Record the July transactions, assuming a periodic inventory system is used instead of a perpetual inventory system.

P5–12A Data for Shaoshi Inc. are presented in P5–3A.

Record purchase and sales transactions. (SO 6)

Instructions

Record the October transactions, assuming a periodic inventory system is used instead of a perpetual inventory system.

P5–13A Data for Kicked-Back Tennis Shop are presented in P5–4A. Assume a physical inventory count determines inventory on hand at April 30 is $2,371.

Record, post, and prepare trial balance and partial statement of earnings. (SO 6)

Instructions

(a) Prepare T accounts and enter the opening balances.

(b) Record and post the April transactions, assuming a periodic inventory system is used instead of a perpetual inventory system.

(c) Prepare a trial balance as at April 30, 2009.

(d) Prepare a statement of earnings through to gross profit.

P5–14A ⬤━ℂ You have been provided with the following selected accounts for Sparkles Inc. for the year ended June 30, 2009:

Prepare partial statement of earnings; calculate gross profit. (SO 5, 6)

Inventory, July 1, 2008	$ 280,000	Sales discounts	$ 50,000
Purchases	3,120,000	Interest expense	10,000
Accounts receivable	330,000	Investment income	20,000
Sales	3,900,000	Accounts payable	270,000
Purchase returns and allowances	120,000	Office expense	80,000
Freight in	40,000	Freight out	60,000
Salaries expense	290,000	Cash	250,000
Land	700,000	Common shares	150,000

Sparkles conducted a physical inventory count on June 30, 2009. Inventory on hand at that date was determined to be $310,000.

Instructions

(a) Based on the information provided, prepare a multiple-step statement of earnings through to gross profit for the year.

(b) Calculate the gross profit margin. If the industry average gross profit margin is 26%, how does Sparkles' gross profit margin compare?

Prepare financial statements.
(SO 6)

*P5–15A The Goody Shop Ltd.'s adjusted trial balance amounts appear as follows on November 30, 2009, the end of its fiscal year:

Accounts payable	$ 32,310	Land	$ 85,000
Accounts receivable	13,770	Merchandise inventory	34,360
Accumulated depreciation—		Mortgage payable	106,000
building	61,200	Prepaid insurance	4,500
Accumulated depreciation—		Property tax expense	3,500
equipment	19,880	Property tax payable	3,500
Building	175,000	Purchases	634,700
Cash	8,500	Purchase discounts	16,000
Common shares	26,000	Purchase returns and allowances	3,315
Depreciation expense	14,000	Retained earnings	70,800
Dividends	5,000	Salaries expense	122,000
Equipment	57,000	Salaries payable	8,500
Freight in	5,060	Sales	889,000
Freight out	8,200	Sales discounts	15,000
Income tax expense	5,000	Sales returns and allowances	10,000
Income tax payable	1,000	Unearned sales revenue	3,000
Insurance expense	9,000	Utilities expense	19,600
Interest expense	11,315		

Additional information:

1. The Goody Shop uses a periodic inventory system.

2. A physical inventory count determined that merchandise inventory on November 30, 2009, was $37,350.

3. Of the mortgage payable, $8,000 is due in the next year.

Instructions

Prepare a statement of earnings, statement of retained earnings, and balance sheet for the year.

Problems: Set B

Identify appropriate inventory system.
(SO 1)

P5–1B   The Breeze Hair Salon Inc. commenced operations six months ago. The salon's main business is hair styling, colouring and other hair treatment services. The salon also keeps some of the product it uses on hand to sell to its customers. The resale of the products is secondary to the salon's main business.

Amounts owing for services provided (hair styling, etc.) are recognized as revenue when the service is provided. Amounts owing for products sold are recognized as revenue when the customer takes the product. Generally, all amounts owing are paid in cash or by debit or bank credit card when the service is performed or the product is sold. Debit and bank credit cards are equivalent to cash.

When the salon's accounting system was set up, a perpetual inventory system was established to track the products sold.

Staff have been complaining to Karen, the owner of the salon, that it is very time-consuming to scan each product sold. Also, given that the sale of the products makes up only a small portion of their business, the salon has only one scanner, which does not always function well. Both the staff and customers are finding the additional time it takes to scan to be frustrating, especially when the salon is busy.

Karen had a physical inventory count performed after the salon's first six months of operations. When the quantities of merchandise determined at the physical count were compared to the quantities per the perpetual system, there were a number of discrepancies.

Instructions

(a) Provide possible explanations to Karen as to why the quantities determined per the physical count did not tie into the quantities per the perpetual system.

(b) Make a recommendation about what inventory system the salon should use and explain why.

P5–2B Phantom Book Warehouse Ltd. distributes hardcover books to retail stores and extends credit terms of n/30 to all of its customers. At the end of May, Phantom's inventory consists of 240 books purchased at $6 each. Phantom uses a perpetual inventory system. During the month of June, the following merchandise transactions occurred:

Record purchase and sales transactions.
(SO 2, 3)

June 1 Purchased 160 books on account for $6 each from Reader's World Publishers, terms n/30.

     3 Sold 120 books on account to The Book Nook for $10 each.

     5 Received a $60 credit for 10 books returned to Reader's World Publishers.

     8 Sold 75 books on account to Read-A-Lot Bookstore for $10 each.

     9 Issued a $50 credit memorandum to Read-A-Lot Bookstore for the return of five damaged books. The books were determined to be no longer saleable and were destroyed.

   12 Purchased 110 books on account for $6 each from Read More Publishers, terms n/30.

   16 Sold 100 books on account to Readers Bookstore for $10 each.

   18 Granted Readers Bookstore a $150 credit for 15 returned books. These books were restored to inventory.

   26 Received payment in full from Read-A-Lot Bookstore.

   29 Paid Reader's World Publishers in full.

   30 Received payment in full from The Book Nook.

Instructions

(a) Record the June transactions for Phantom Book Warehouse.

(b) Post the transactions to the Merchandise Inventory account and calculate the June 30 balance.

(c) How many books does Phantom Book Warehouse have on hand on June 30? What is the relationship between the number of books on hand and the balance in the Merchandise Inventory account calculated in (b)?

P5–3B Presented here are selected transactions for Norlan Inc. during September of the current year. Norlan uses a perpetual inventory system.

Record purchase and sales transactions.
(SO 2, 3)

Sept. 2 Purchased delivery equipment on account for $26,000, terms n/30, FOB destination.

    3 Freight charges of $600 were paid by the appropriate party on the September 2 purchase of delivery equipment.

    4 Purchased merchandise on account from Hillary Corp. at a cost of $60,000, terms 1/10, n/30, FOB shipping point.

    4 Purchased supplies for $4,000 cash.

    7 Freight charges of $1,000 were paid by the appropriate party on the September 4 purchase of merchandise.

    8 Returned damaged goods costing $8,000 received from Hillary on September 4.

    9 Sold merchandise costing $15,000 to Fischer Limited for $20,000 on account, terms 2/10, n/30, FOB destination.

   10 Freight charges of $250 were paid by the appropriate party on the September 9 sale of merchandise.

   14 Paid Hillary the balance due.

   16 Received the balance due from Fischer.

   18 Purchased merchandise for $6,000 cash.

   22 Sold inventory costing $20,000 to Where's Waldo Inc. for $27,000 on account, terms 2/10, n/30, FOB shipping point.

   23 Freight charges of $300 were paid by the appropriate party on the September 22 sale of merchandise.

   28 Waldo returned merchandise sold for $10,000 that cost $7,500. The merchandise was restored to inventory.

Instructions

Record the September transactions.

P5–4B At the beginning of the current golf season, on April 1, 2009, the general ledger of Weir's Pro Shop showed Cash $2,500; Merchandise Inventory $3,500; Common Shares $5,000; and Retained Earnings $1,000. Weir's Pro Shop uses a perpetual inventory system. The following transactions occurred in April:

Record, post, and prepare trial balance and partial statement of earnings.
(SO 2, 3, 4)

▸ Merchandising Operations

Apr.   3   Purchased golf bags, clubs, and balls on account from Balata Corp. for $2,700, terms 1/10, n/30, FOB shipping point.

7   Freight of $80 was paid by the appropriate party on the April 3 purchase from Balata.

9   Received a $150 credit from Balata for returned merchandise.

10   Sold merchandise on account to members for $1,950, terms n/30. The merchandise had a cost of $1,200.

13   Paid Balata in full.

14   Purchased golf shoes, sweaters, and other accessories on account from Arrow Sportswear Limited for $770, terms 1/10, n/30.

17   Received a $75 credit from Arrow Sportswear for returned merchandise.

20   Made sales on account to members for $890, terms n/30. The cost of the merchandise sold was $500.

21   Paid Arrow Sportswear in full.

27   Granted a $50 sales allowance to a member for soiled clothing. No merchandise was returned.

30   Received payments on account from members, $1,250.

Instructions

(a) Prepare T accounts and enter the opening balances.

(b) Record and post the April transactions. Round all amounts to the nearest dollar.

(c) Prepare a trial balance as at April 30, 2009.

(d) Prepare a statement of earnings through to gross profit.

Record, post, and prepare partial financial statements.
(SO 2, 3, 4)

P5–5B   Eagle Hardware Store Ltd. completed the following merchandising transactions in the month of May 2009. At the beginning of May, Eagle's ledger showed Cash $2,500; Accounts Receivable $5,000; Common Shares $5,000; and Retained Earnings $2,500. Eagle Hardware uses a perpetual inventory system.

May   1   Purchased merchandise on account from Depot Wholesale Supply Ltd. for $5,800, terms 1/10, n/30, FOB shipping point.

4   Freight charges of $200 were paid by the appropriate party on the merchandise purchased on May 1.

4   Sold merchandise on account for $2,450, terms 1/10, n/30, FOB destination. The cost of the merchandise was $1,500.

5   Freight charges of $100 were paid by the appropriate party on the May 4 sale.

7   Received a $200 credit from Depot Wholesale Supply for returned merchandise.

8   Paid Depot Wholesale Supply in full.

11   Purchased supplies for $400 cash.

13   Received payment in full from customers billed for merchandise sold on account on May 4.

15   Received a cash refund of $230 from a supplier for the return of poor-quality merchandise.

18   Purchased merchandise from Harlow Distributors Inc. for $1,900, terms 1/10, n/30, FOB shipping point.

19   Freight of $250 was paid by the appropriate party on the May 18 purchase of merchandise.

22   Sold merchandise for $6,200 cash. The cost of the merchandise was $4,600.

28   Paid Harlow Distributors in full.

29   Paid a $100 cash refund to customers for returned merchandise. The cost of the returned merchandise was $70. It was restored to inventory.

Instructions

(a) Prepare T accounts and enter the opening balances.

(b) Record and post the May transactions. Round all amounts to the nearest dollar.

(c) Prepare a statement of earnings through to gross profit.

(d) Prepare the current assets section of the balance sheet.

Classify accounts.
(SO 4)

P5–6B   The following list of accounts has been selected from the financial statements of Leon's Furniture Limited:

Accounts payable and accrued liabilities	Equipment
Accounts receivable	Income tax expense
Accumulated depreciation	Income taxes payable
Advertising expense	Interest income
Buildings	Inventory
Cash and cash equivalents	Land
Common shares	Rent and property tax expense
Computer hardware and software	Retained earnings
Cost of sales	Salaries and commissions expense
Depreciation expense	Sales
Dividends	Short-term investments
Dividends payable	Vehicles

Instructions

For each account, identify whether it should be reported on the balance sheet, multiple-step statement of earnings, or statement of retained earnings. Also specify where the account should be classified. For example, Accounts Payable and Accrued Liabilities would be classified as current liabilities on the balance sheet.

P5–7B   The adjusted trial balance of Club Canada Wholesale Inc. contained the following accounts at December 31, the company's fiscal year end:

Prepare single- and multiple-step statements of earnings. (SO 4)

CLUB CANADA WHOLESALE INC.
Adjusted Trial Balance
December 31, 2009

	Debit	Credit
Cash	$ 18,875	
Accounts receivable	7,600	
Merchandise inventory	72,400	
Supplies	3,780	
Notes receivable	30,000	
Land	72,000	
Building	197,000	
Accumulated depreciation—building		$ 93,575
Equipment	83,500	
Accumulated depreciation—equipment		33,400
Accounts payable		37,500
Unearned revenue		7,550
Income tax payable		3,500
Mortgage payable		86,000
Common shares		20,000
Retained earnings		139,675
Sales		923,560
Interest revenue		1,200
Sales returns and allowances	18,050	
Sales discounts	4,615	
Cost of goods sold	712,100	
Salaries expense	69,800	
Depreciation expense	13,275	
Utilities expense	9,400	
Interest expense	8,525	
Freight out	5,900	
Insurance expense	3,640	
Income tax expense	15,500	
	$1,345,960	$1,345,960

Instructions

(a) Prepare a single-step statement of earnings.

(b) Prepare a multiple-step statement of earnings.

(c) Compare the two statements and comment on the usefulness of each one.

P5–8B   The unadjusted trial balance of Mesa Inc. at the company's fiscal year end of December 31 follows:

MESA INC. Trial Balance December 31, 2009		
	Debit	Credit
Cash	$ 12,000	
Accounts receivable	31,700	
Merchandise inventory	28,750	
Supplies	2,940	
Prepaid insurance	2,980	
Land	30,000	
Building	150,000	
Accumulated depreciation—building		$ 24,000
Equipment	45,000	
Accumulated depreciation—equipment		18,000
Accounts payable		35,600
Unearned sales revenue		4,000
Mortgage payable		147,100
Common shares		10,000
Retained earnings		31,425
Dividends	2,000	
Sales		263,770
Sales returns and allowances	2,500	
Sales discounts	3,275	
Cost of goods sold	171,225	
Salaries expense	30,950	
Utilities expense	5,100	
Interest expense	9,975	
Income tax expense	5,500	
	$533,895	$533,895

Adjustment data:

1. The 12-month insurance policy was purchased and is effective February 1, 2009.
2. There was $750 of supplies on hand on December 31.
3. Depreciation expense for the year is $6,000 for the building and $4,500 for the equipment.
4. Salaries of $940 are accrued and unpaid at December 31.
5. Accrued interest expense at December 31 is $1,000.
6. Unearned sales revenue of $975 is still unearned at December 31. On the sales that were earned, the cost of goods sold was $2,000.
7. Of the mortgage payable, $9,800 is payable next year.
8. Income tax of $500 is due and unpaid.

Instructions

(a) Prepare T accounts and enter the trial balance amounts.

(b) Record and post the adjusting entries, assuming the company adjusts its accounts annually. Round all amounts to the nearest dollar.

(c) Prepare an adjusted trial balance.

(d) Prepare a statement of earnings, statement of retained earnings, and balance sheet for the year.

P5–9B   ⦿▬ Psang Inc. purchases all merchandise inventory on credit and uses a perpetual inventory system. The Accounts Payable account is used for recording merchandise inventory purchases only; all other current liabilities are accrued in separate accounts. You are provided with the following selected information for the fiscal years 2007 through 2009:

	2009	2008	2007
Statement of Earnings Data			
Net sales	$87,000	$ (5)	$96,900
Cost of goods sold	26,500	27,000	(9)
Gross profit	(1)	61,500	69,300
Operating expenses	45,100	(6)	53,500
Net earnings	$ (2)	$14,500	$ (10)
Balance Sheet Data			
Merchandise inventory	$ (3)	$14,700	$11,000
Accounts payable	(4)	4,600	6,500
Additional Information			
Purchase of merchandise inventory on account	$22,000	$ (7)	$25,900
Cash payments to suppliers	24,000	(8)	25,000

Instructions

(a) Calculate the missing amounts for items (1) through (10).

(b) Calculate the gross profit margin and profit margin for each year.

(c) Sales declined over the three-year period 2007 to 2009. Does this mean that profitability also had to decline? Refer to the gross profit margin and profit margin to explain and support your answer.

P5–10B ⬤💳 The following selected information is available for **Danier Leather Inc.** for three fiscal years (in thousands):

Calculate ratios and comment. (SO 5)

	2007	2006	2005
Current assets	$ 56,422	$ 48,623	$ 52,455
Current liabilities	30,275	12,243	8,170
Net sales	158,099	148,351	166,350
Cost of goods sold	79,565	76,953	82,863
Net earnings (loss)	1,653	(5,503)	(185)

Instructions

(a) Calculate the current ratio, gross profit margin, and profit margin for each year. Comment on whether the ratios have improved or deteriorated over the three years.

(b) Compare the 2007 ratios to the following industry averages: current ratio 2.1:1; gross profit margin 45.7%; and profit margin 8.7%. Are Danier Leather's ratios better or worse than those of its industry?

*P5–11B Data for Phantom Book Warehouse Ltd. are presented in P5–2B.

Record purchase and sales transactions. (SO 6)

Instructions

Record the June transactions, assuming a periodic inventory system is used instead of a perpetual inventory system.

*P5–12B Data for Norlan Inc. are presented in P5–3B.

Record purchase and sales transactions. (SO 6)

Instructions

Record the September transactions, assuming a periodic inventory system is used instead of a perpetual inventory system.

*P5–13B Data for Weir's Pro Shop are presented in P5–4B. Assume a physical inventory count determines inventory on hand at April 30 is $5,092.

Record, post, and prepare trial balance and partial statement of earnings. (SO 6)

Instructions

(a) Prepare T accounts and enter the opening balances.

(b) Record and post the April transactions, assuming a periodic inventory system is used instead of a perpetual inventory system. Round all amounts to the nearest dollar.

(c) Prepare a trial balance as at April 30, 2009.

(d) Prepare a statement of earnings through to gross profit.

Prepare partial statement of earnings; calculate gross profit.
(SO 5, 6)

*P5–14B ◯▬C You have been provided with the following selected accounts for Feisty Ltd. for the year ended April 30, 2009:

Inventory, May 1, 2008	$ 630,000	Sales returns and allowances	$150,000
Purchases	6,950,000	Interest expense	30,000
Accounts receivable	780,000	Interest income	20,000
Sales	9,200,000	Accounts payable	600,000
Purchase discounts	40,000	Office expense	160,000
Freight in	120,000	Freight out	150,000
Salaries expense	650,000	Cash	160,000
Land	900,000	Common shares	200,000

Feisty conducted a physical inventory count on April 30, 2009. Inventory on hand at that date was determined to be $670,000.

Instructions

(a) Based on the information provided, prepare a multiple-step statement of earnings through to gross profit for the year.

(b) Calculate the gross profit margin. If the industry average gross profit margin is 20%, how does Feisty's gross profit margin compare?

Prepare financial statements.
(SO 6)

*P5–15B Tater Tot Ltd.'s adjusted trial balance amounts appear as follows on December 31, 2009, the end of its fiscal year:

Accounts payable	$ 86,300	Merchandise inventory	$ 40,500
Accounts receivable	44,200	Mortgage payable	155,000
Accumulated depreciation—building	51,800	Prepaid insurance	2,400
Accumulated depreciation—equipment	42,900	Property tax expense	4,800
Building	190,000	Property tax payable	4,800
Cash	17,000	Purchases	441,600
Common shares	75,000	Purchase discounts	22,500
Depreciation expense	23,400	Purchase returns and allowances	6,400
Dividends	8,000	Retained earnings	68,600
Equipment	110,000	Salaries expense	127,500
Freight in	5,600	Salaries payable	3,500
Freight out	7,500	Sales	637,000
Income tax expense	6,000	Sales discounts	15,000
Insurance expense	7,200	Sales returns and allowances	8,000
Interest expense	10,400	Unearned sales revenue	8,300
Land	75,000	Utilities expense	18,000

Additional information:

1. Tater Tots uses a periodic inventory system.

2. A physical inventory count determined that merchandise inventory on December 31, 2009, was $72,600.

3. Of the mortgage payable, $17,000 is due in the next year.

Instructions

Prepare a statement of earnings, statement of retained earnings, and balance sheet for the year.

BROADENING YOUR PERSPECTIVE

Financial Reporting and Analysis Cases

Analysis Tools

Financial Reporting: *Shoppers Drug Mart*

BYP5–1 The financial statements of Shoppers Drug Mart are presented in Appendix A at the end of this book.

Instructions

(a) Is Shoppers Drug Mart a service company or a merchandising company?

(b) Are any non-operating revenues and non-operating expenses included in Shoppers Drug Mart's statement of earnings? If so, identify the accounts included.

(c) Using "cost of goods sold and other operating expenses" in place of cost of goods sold, calculate Shoppers Drug Mart's gross profit margin for the two fiscal years presented.

(d) Calculate Shoppers Drug Mart's profit margin for the two fiscal years presented in the annual report.

(e) Comment on the trend in Shoppers Drug Mart's gross profit margin and profit margin.

Comparative Analysis: *Shoppers Drug Mart and Jean Coutu*

BYP5–2 The financial statements of Jean Coutu are presented in Appendix B following the financial statements for Shoppers Drug Mart in Appendix A.

Instructions

(a) Determine the following values for each company for each of the two most recent years presented in their financial statements:

1. Percentage change in sales
2. Percentage change in operating income
3. Gross profit margin (use "cost of goods sold and other operating expenses" in place of cost of goods sold)
4. Profit margin

(b) What conclusions about the relative profitability of the two companies can be drawn from these data?

Interpreting Financial Statements

BYP5–3 Big Rock Brewery is a western producer and marketer of premium quality beers. Information from Big Rock's statement of earnings for the current year, and the preceding year is as follows:

	2007	2006
Net sales	$36,450,872	$38,700,675
Cost of sales	14,191,579	13,773,219
Operating expenses	16,960,249	16,182,796
Income tax (recovery) expense	(168,982)	364,595

Instructions

(a) Calculate the gross profit and gross profit margin for each of the two years. Comment on any trend in this percentage.

(b) Calculate the net earnings and profit margin for each of the two years. Comment on any trend in this percentage.

(c) How well has Big Rock managed its operating expenses over the two-year period?

A Global Focus

BYP5–4 InBev, headquartered in Belgium, is the world's leading brewer. Before InBev's acquisition of Anheuser-Busch in 2008 to form Anheuser-Busch InBev, Anheuser-Busch, headquartered in the United

International Resources

States, was one of InBev's primary competitors. Below are selected financial data for InBev (in euros) and Anheuser-Busch (in U.S. dollars) for 2007, the year before the two companies combined their operations.

	InBev (in EUR millions)	Anheuser-Busch (in USD millions)
Sales	€14,430	$16,688
Cost of goods sold	5,936	10,836
Net earnings	3,048	2,115
Current assets	5,539	2,024
Total assets	28,699	17,155
Current liabilities	6,685	2,304
Total liabilities	13,789	14,003

Instructions

(a) Calculate the gross profit margin for each company. Discuss their relative profitability and ability to control their cost of goods sold.

(b) Calculate the profit margin for each company. Discuss their relative profitability and ability to control their operating expenses.

(c) Calculate the current ratio and the debt to total assets ratio for each company. Discuss their relative liquidity and solvency.

(d) Does the fact that each company is using different currencies hinder your comparison? Do you have any other concerns in relying on this comparison? Explain.

Critical Thinking Cases and Activities

Collaborative Learning Activity

BYP5–5 Chinook Auto Parts Limited is a distribution company whose mobile sales force covers large territories of automotive repair shops and automobile dealerships. The company's statement of earnings is as follows:

CHINOOK AUTO PARTS LIMITED Statement of Earnings Year Ended March 31, 2010		
Sales	$22,000,000	
Less: Sales returns	2,200,000	
Net sales		$19,800,000
Cost of goods sold		13,585,000
Gross profit		6,215,000
Operating expenses		5,500,000
Earnings before income tax		715,000

Chinook's manager is concerned that, while sales have been increasing steadily, earnings have not. Sales returns of 10% of sales are much greater than the industry average of 6.5%. Upon further investigation, it was determined that the company's process of manually recording customer order data is producing a large number of order errors. As these errors are caused by Chinook's sales staff, Chinook absorbs the handling costs of sales returns. The problem is made worse because many products have been customized and cannot be resold. The following is an estimate of the cost of these order processing errors:

Sales returns	$2,200,000	
% of products that are not resaleable	50%	
Sales value of unsaleable products	1,100,000	
Average cost as a % of sales	65%	
Cost of unsaleable products		$715,000
Operating expenses—reverse logistics		125,000
Total estimated costs		$840,000

Chinook is investigating a mobile electronic order system that would cost the company $100,000 for its first year of operations but would reduce the percentage of returned sales to a figure in line with the industry average (6.5%). To be conservative, assume that operating expenses will not change.

Instructions

With the class divided into groups, do the following:

(a) Review the calculation of the cost of order processing errors. Recalculate the estimated cost of assuming the electronic order system (with 6.5% returns) was purchased. Should the electronic order system be purchased?

(b) Consider the impact on customer relationships if Chinook continues to use its current manual order management system. Would you recommend a change in system even if the financial analysis completed in question (a) is negative?

Communication Activity

BYP5–6 Consider the following events:

Sept.	23	Dexter Maersk decides to buy a custom-made snowboard and calls the Great Canadian Snowboard Corporation to inquire about its products.
	28	Dexter asks Great Canadian Snowboard to manufacture a custom board for him.
Oct.	3	The company sends Dexter a purchase order to fill out, which he immediately completes, signs, and sends back with a required 25% down payment.
	7	Great Canadian Snowboard receives Dexter's purchase order and down payment, and begins working on the board.
Dec.	31	Great Canadian Snowboard has its fiscal year end. At this time, Dexter's board is 75% completed.
Jan.	28	The company completes the snowboard for Dexter and notifies him that he can take delivery.
Feb.	3	Dexter picks up his snowboard from the company and takes it home.
	4	Dexter tries the snowboard out and likes it so much that he carves his initials in it.
	21	Great Canadian Snowboard bills Dexter for the cost of the snowboard, less the 25% down payment.
	28	The company receives partial payment (another 25%) from Dexter.
Mar.	18	The company receives payment of the remaining amount due from Dexter.

Instructions

(a) In a memo to the president of Great Canadian Snowboard, outline the alternatives for, and recommend when, the company should record the revenue and expense related to the snowboard.

(b) If Dexter had not been required to make a down payment with his purchase order, would your answer to part (a) be different?

Ethics Case

BYP5–7 Rita Pelzer was just hired as the assistant controller of Zaz Stores Ltd., a specialty chain store company that has nine retail stores concentrated in one city. Among other things, the payment of all invoices is centralized in one of the departments Rita will manage. Her main responsibilities are to maintain the company's high credit rating by paying all bills when they are due and to take advantage of all cash discounts.

Jamie Caterino, the former assistant controller, who has been promoted to controller, is training Rita in her new duties. He instructs Rita that she is to continue the practice of preparing all cheques for the amount due less the discount and to date the cheques the last day of the discount period. "But," Jamie continues, "we always hold the cheques at least four days beyond the discount period before mailing them. That way we get another four days of interest on our money. Most of our creditors need our business and don't complain. And, if they scream about our missing the discount period, we blame it on Canada Post. We've only lost one discount out of every hundred we take that way. I think everybody does it. By the way, welcome to our team!"

Ethics in Accounting

Instructions

(a) What are the ethical considerations in this case?

(b) What stakeholders are harmed or benefited?

(c) Should Rita continue the practice started by Jamie? Does she have any choice?

"All About You" Activity

BYP5–8 In the "All About You" feature in this chapter, you learned about sales returns and how costly they are for retailers. Suppose that after you graduate with a business degree, you take a job as a manager at a bookstore called Sage Books Limited. The bookstore has expanded rapidly in order to compete with Indigo Books & Music and Amazon.com.

Instructions

(a) Sage has begun selling gift cards for its books because it believes that people who receive a gift card and purchase a book with the gift card are less likely to return their purchase than if someone had given them a book as a gift. At what point should the revenue from the gift cards be recognized? Should the revenue be recognized at the time the card is sold, or should it be recognized when the card is redeemed?

(b) Sage is ten times smaller than Indigo but would still like to compare its gross profit margin and profit margin to Indigo's. Would a comparison of the financial results of these two companies be meaningful?

(c) Sage's management is concerned with its gross profit margin. It believes it is too low. What steps can be taken to improve the gross profit margin?

Serial Case

(*Note:* This serial case was started in Chapter 1 and continued in Chapters 2 through 4. From the information gathered through Chapter 4, follow the instructions below using the general ledger accounts you have already prepared.)

BYP5–9 Cookie Creations, after experiencing a successful initial operating period, is considering other opportunities to develop business. One opportunity is the sale of deluxe European mixers. The sales manager of Mixer Deluxe has approached Cookie Creations to become the exclusive Canadian distributor of these mixers. The current cost of the European mixer is approximately $525 Canadian, and the company would sell each one for $1,050.

Natalie, struggling to do the accounting for the company, comes to you for advice on how to account for these mixers. Each appliance has a serial number and can easily be identified. Natalie asks you the following questions:

1. "Would you consider these mixers to be inventory? Or, should they be classified as supplies or equipment?"

2. "I've learned a little about keeping track of inventory using both the perpetual and periodic inventory systems. Which system do you think is better? Which one would you recommend for the type of inventory that Cookie Creations wants to sell?"

3. "How often should the company count inventory if the perpetual inventory system is used? Does it need to count inventory at all?"

4. "Should I prepare a single-step or multiple-step statement of earnings?"

In the end, Cookie Creations decides to use the perpetual inventory system. The following transactions occur during the month of April:

Apr.	6	The company buys five deluxe mixers on account from Kzinski Supply Corp. for $2,625, terms n/30, FOB shipping point.
	7	$100 freight is paid on the April 6 purchase.
	8	One of the mixers is returned to Kzinski because it was damaged during shipping. Kzinski issues a credit note to Cookie Creations for the cost of the mixer plus $20 for the cost of freight that was paid on April 7 for one mixer.
	9	The amount due from the neighbourhood community centre that was accrued at the end of March, $375, is collected.
	13	Three deluxe mixers are sold to various customers on account for $3,150, terms 1/10, n/30, FOB destination. The cost of each mixer sold is $545 ($525 cost + $20 freight).
	14	$75 of freight charges are paid for the three mixers that were sold on April 13.
	15	The cellphone bill, $75, previously accrued in the March adjusting journal entries is paid.
	16	Four deluxe mixers are purchased on account from Kzinski Supply Co. for $2,100, terms n/30, FOB shipping point.

17    $80 freight is paid on the April 16 purchase.

20   1,000 new common shares are issued for $1,000 cash.

21   Two deluxe mixers are sold for $2,100 cash. The cost of each mixer sold is $545 ($525 cost + $20 freight).

22   Amounts due from customers for the April 13 transaction are collected.

28   The assistant's wages are paid. She worked 20 hours at an hourly rate of $8 per hour in April and is also paid for amounts owing at March 31, 2009, $56.

30   Kzinski is paid all amounts due.

30    $750 of dividends are paid to shareholders.

As at April 30, the following adjusting entry data are available:

1. A count of brochures and posters reveals that none were used in April. You will recall that there were $95 of advertising supplies on hand at the beginning of the month.

2. A count of baking supplies reveals that none were used in April. You will recall that there were $1,375 of baking supplies on hand at the beginning of the month.

3. Another month's worth of depreciation needs to be recorded on the baking equipment bought in February. (Recall that the baking equipment has a total cost of $1,200 and a useful life of five years.)

4. An additional month's worth of interest on the $2,000 note payable needs to be accrued. (The interest rate is 6%.)

5. One month's worth of the $1,200 one-year insurance policy has expired.

6. The cellphone bill is received, $75. The bill is for services provided in April and is due May 15. (Recall that the cellphone is only used for business purposes.)

7. An analysis of the unearned revenue account reveals that no lessons have been taught this month because Natalie has been so busy selling mixers. As a result, there is no change to the unearned revenue account. Natalie hopes to book the outstanding lessons in May.

8. An inventory count of mixers at the end of April reveals that three mixers remain.

9. Cookie Creations estimates that it owes an additional $308 of income tax.

Instructions

Using the information that you have gathered through Chapter 4, and the new information above, do the following:

(a) Answer Natalie's questions.

(b) Record and post the April 2009 transactions.

(c) Prepare a trial balance.

(d) Record and post the adjusting journal entries required.

(e) Prepare an adjusted trial balance.

(f) Prepare a single-step statement of earnings and statement of retained earnings for the four months ending April 30.

(g) Prepare a balance sheet at April 30.

Answers to Chapter Questions

Answer to Shoppers Drug Mart Review It Question 4

Shoppers Drug Mart uses a multiple-step statement of earnings. Note that Shoppers' statement of earnings does not match cost of sales directly against revenue to determine gross profit. Instead, it combines its cost of goods sold with other operating expenses, and only reports its non-operating costs, such as interest, separate from operating income.

Answers to Self-Study Questions

1. b	2. b	3. c	4. a	5. c	6. b
7. c	8. d	9. c	10. c	*11. b	*12. b

Remember to go back to the beginning of the chapter to check off your completed work!

←

Comprehensive Case: Chapter 5

Heritage Furniture Limited reports the following information for the first two months of the year in its February 28, 2009, trial balance:

HERITAGE FURNITURE LIMITED Trial Balance February 28, 2009		
	Debit	Credit
Cash	$ 65,000	
Accounts receivable	350,000	
Merchandise inventory	2,750,000	
Supplies	7,500	
Prepaid expenses	15,000	
Store furniture and fixtures	100,000	
Accumulated depreciation—Store furniture and fixtures		$ 23,333
Office furniture and equipment	45,000	
Accumulated depreciation—Office furniture and equipment		5,250
Accounts payable		1,650,000
Customer deposits		35,000
Bank loan payable		175,000
Shareholders' loan payable		99,000
Common shares		11,000
Retained earnings		425,417
Dividends	5,000	
Sales		5,479,400
Sales returns and allowances	107,000	
Sales discounts	65,000	
Advertising and promotion expense	75,000	
Cost of goods sold	3,843,900	
Delivery expense	180,000	
Depreciation expense	3,883	
Interest expense	17,500	
Office expense	26,117	
Rent expense	10,000	
Salaries expense	205,000	
Travel expense	12,500	
Utilities expense	20,000	
	$7,903,400	$7,903,400

Heritage Furniture incurred the following transactions for the month of March. The company uses a perpetual inventory system.

March 2 Received $125,000 on account from a major customer.

3 Paid a supplier an amount owing of $200,000, taking the full discount. Terms 2/10, n/30.

4 Purchased merchandise from a supplier, $300,000, terms 2/10, n/30, FOB destination.

6 Recorded cash sales for the week, $194,750. The cost of goods sold for the same period was $126,600.

6 Returned scratched merchandise to the supplier from the March 4 purchase, $25,000.

9 Received and paid a freight invoice from the supplier's trucking company for the March 4 purchase, $16,750.

10 Sold $200,000 of merchandise on account, terms 2/10, n/30, FOB destination. The cost of goods sold was $130,000.

11 Ordered custom merchandise for a local designer totalling $50,000. Received $12,500 as a deposit.

12 Accepted returned merchandise from the sale on March 10, $20,000. The cost of the goods returned to inventory was $12,000.

13 Paid for merchandise purchased on March 4, adjusted for the returns recorded on March 6.

13 Paid bi-weekly salaries of $45,000.

16 Paid the freight company for the movement of goods related to the March 10 sale, $4,000.

18 Received full payment of merchandise sold on March 10, net of merchandise returns on March 12.

20 Recorded cash sales for the week, $165,000. The cost of goods sold for the same period was $103,950.

27 Recorded cash sales for the week, $180,000. The cost of goods sold for the same period was $115,000.

27 Paid bi-weekly salaries of $50,000.

30 Paid rent, $5,000.

31 Accrued $10,000 for utilities, $10,000 for salaries, and $9,000 for interest on the bank loan.

31 Recorded monthly depreciation on furniture and equipment. The store furniture and fixtures are depreciated over 5 years; the office furniture and equipment over 10 years.

Instructions

(a) Prepare T accounts and enter the opening balances.

(b) Record and post the March transactions.

(c) Prepare a trial balance as at March 31.

(d) Prepare a multiple-step statement of earnings, statement of retained earnings, and balance sheet for the quarter ended March 31, 2009.

CHAPTER 6
Reporting and Analyzing Inventory

How Many Dump Trucks Did You Want?

Let's talk inventory—BIG inventory. The world's largest dump truck, the Caterpillar 797B, is as tall as a three-storey building and has a 380-tonne capacity. It is manufactured by Caterpillar Inc., the world's largest manufacturer and retailer of construction and mining equipment, diesel and natural gas engines, and industrial gas turbines.

With nearly 300 operations in 40 countries, Caterpillar Inc. produces hundreds of machines for a variety of industries. Exports account for approximately 50 percent of its sales. In Canada, Caterpillar has manufacturing operations in Edmonton and Montreal, logistics operations in Guelph and Saskatoon, financial services in Calgary and Toronto, and a training and demonstration centre in Toronto.

The first 19 units of the predecessor to 797B, the Cat 797, rolled off the production line in 1998. Caterpillar sent six of these square behemoths to Fort McMurray, Alberta—no easy feat, since many highways and bridges cannot take their weight—to be tested at Syncrude Canada. Syncrude, the world's largest producer of crude oil from oil sands, evaluated the Cat 797 for long-term production capability, durability, and maintenance in an oil sands mine, one of the toughest mining environments. Used at the company's Base and Aurora mines, the trucks haul massive quantities of oil sand, ore, and dirt to the mines' extraction plants for partial processing on site. Not surprisingly, the trucks scored top marks—Syncrude had in fact been a key collaborator with Caterpillar on the development of the truck. By 2007, Syncrude had more than 40 Cat 797s.

A Cat 797B can cost millions of dollars and requires one heck of a big garage for storage. Obviously, Caterpillar needs to avoid having too much of this kind of inventory sitting around tying up its resources. Conversely, it has to have enough inventory to meet customers' demands. In short, Caterpillar is a big company that makes big products—and has big inventory challenges.

And big sales. Caterpillar has enjoyed record sales, profits, and growth for several years. Faced with unprecedented customer demand, the company generated U.S. $45 billion in sales and revenues in 2007. Its expectations for the remainder of the decade included a compound growth rate of 15 to 20 percent with top line sales of $50 billion by 2010.

While part of this success can be attributed to diversification of its products and services, effective inventory management has been key. From 1993 to 2007, Caterpillar's sales increased nearly 300 percent, while its inventory increased by only 250 percent. Items spent an average 76 days in inventory instead of 87.

To achieve this reduction in the amount of resources tied up in inventory while continuing to meet its customers' needs, Caterpillar used a two-pronged approach. First, it completed a factory modernization program in 1993, which dramatically increased its production efficiency. This reduced by 75 percent the time it takes to manufacture a part.

Second, Caterpillar vastly improved its distribution system. It now ships products to job sites in nearly 200 countries and can do so in less than 24 hours more than 99.7 percent of the time.

In fact, Caterpillar is so well known for its parts distribution expertise, it formed a wholly owned subsidiary in 1987 to market integrated supply chain solutions to other companies looking to improve customer service and their own financial performance. Caterpillar Logistics Services now includes 105 facilities and operations in 25 countries on six continents. It serves more than 65 companies in industries ranging from automotive, industrial equipment, high technology and electronics, aerospace and defence, to consumer durables.

The bottom line is that Caterpillar's inventory management and accounting practices make a crucial contribution to its own and other companies' profitability.

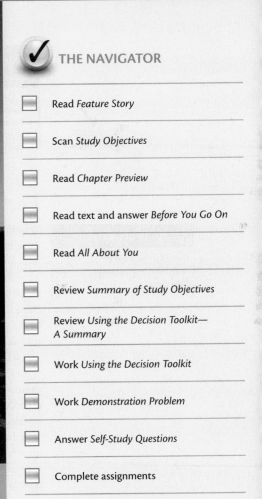

Photo credit: terpillar Inc.: cat.com

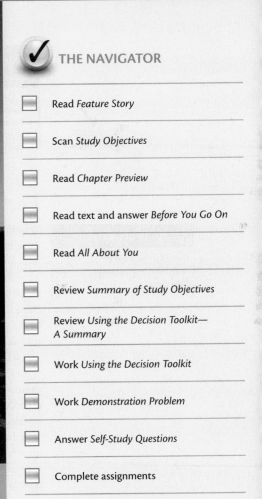

THE NAVIGATOR

- [ ] Read *Feature Story*
- [ ] Scan *Study Objectives*
- [ ] Read *Chapter Preview*
- [ ] Read text and answer *Before You Go On*
- [ ] Read *All About You*
- [ ] Review *Summary of Study Objectives*
- [ ] Review *Using the Decision Toolkit—A Summary*
- [ ] Work *Using the Decision Toolkit*
- [ ] Work *Demonstration Problem*
- [ ] Answer *Self-Study Questions*
- [ ] Complete assignments

STUDY OBJECTIVES

After studying this chapter, you should be able to:

1. Describe the steps in determining inventory quantities.

2. Apply the methods of cost determination—specific identification, FIFO, and average—under a perpetual inventory system.

3. Explain the financial statement effects of the inventory cost determination methods and of inventory errors.

4. Demonstrate the presentation and analysis of inventory.

5. Apply the inventory cost formulas—FIFO and average—under a periodic inventory system (Appendix 6A).

The Navigator

PREVIEW OF CHAPTER 6

In the previous chapter, we discussed the accounting for merchandise transactions. In this chapter, we first explain the procedures for determining inventory quantities. We then discuss the three methods for determining the cost of goods sold and the cost of inventory on hand: the specific identification method and the two cost formulas, FIFO and average. We also discuss the effects of inventory errors on a company's financial statements. We conclude by first discussing how to present inventory on the financial statements and then introducing a new liquidity measure called inventory turnover, which is used to analyze inventory.

The chapter is organized as follows:

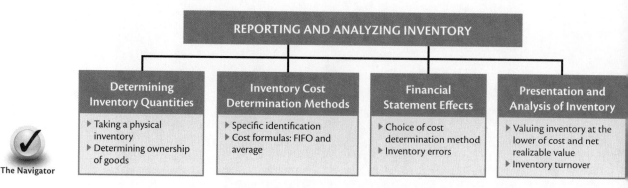

The Navigator

Determining Inventory Quantities

study objective 1

Describe the steps in determining inventory quantities.

Whether they are using a perpetual inventory system or a periodic one, all companies need to determine their inventory quantities at the end of each accounting period by physically counting their inventory (i.e., a count of all the inventory on hand).

Recall from Chapter 5 that in a perpetual inventory system the accounting records continuously—perpetually—show the quantity of inventory that *should* be on hand, not what necessarily *is* on hand. Even if the records are continuously updated, companies that use a perpetual inventory system must still take a physical inventory at year end for two purposes: (1) to check the accuracy of their perpetual inventory records and (2) to determine the amount of inventory lost due to shrinkage or theft.

If the physical inventory count does not match what is recorded in the general ledger, then any errors or losses can be determined and an adjusting entry made to correct the inventory balance. For example, assuming that a company's physical inventory count revealed less inventory on hand than was recorded in the account, an adjusting entry would be made to debit cost of goods sold (even though the inventory was not actually sold) and credit inventory.

In a periodic inventory system, inventory quantities are not updated on a continuous basis. Companies that use a periodic inventory system must therefore take a physical inventory to determine the inventory on hand at the end of each accounting period. Once the ending inventory amount is determined, this amount is then used to calculate the cost of goods sold for the period. It is not possible to determine errors or amounts lost due to shrinkage or theft in a periodic inventory system.

Determining inventory quantities involves two steps: (1) taking a physical inventory of goods on hand and (2) determining the ownership of goods.

Taking a Physical Inventory

Taking a physical inventory involves actually counting, weighing, or measuring each kind of inventory on hand. In many companies, taking an inventory is a formidable task. For example, retailers such as Shoppers Drug Mart have thousands of different inventory items. An inventory count is also generally more accurate when goods are not being sold or received during the counting. Consequently, companies often take inventory when the business is closed or when business is slow.

To make fewer errors in taking the inventory, a company should ensure that it has a good system of internal control. **Internal control** consists of all the related methods and measures adopted within an organization to help it achieve reliable financial reporting, effective and efficient operations, and compliance with relevant laws and regulations. Some internal control procedures for counting inventory include the following:

1. The counting should be done by employees who do not have responsibility for the custody or record-keeping of the inventory.
2. Each counter should establish the validity of each inventory item: this means checking that the items actually exist, how many there are of them, and what condition they are in.
3. There should be a second count by another employee or auditor. Counting should take place in teams of two.
4. Prenumbered inventory tags should be used to ensure that all inventory items are counted and that none are counted more than once.

We will learn more about internal controls in Chapter 7.

After the physical inventory is taken, the quantity of each kind of inventory is listed on inventory summary sheets. To ensure accuracy, the listing should be verified by a second employee or auditor. Unit costs are then applied to the quantities in order to determine the total cost of the inventory—this will be explained later in the chapter when we discuss the methods of inventory cost determination.

ACCOUNTING MATTERS! | Management Perspective

There are many challenges involved in taking a physical inventory for certain kinds of businesses. One of the more difficult types of inventory to count is at a salmon farm, where the inventory is swimming around in the ocean.

Salmon farms can be found in Nova Scotia, New Brunswick, and British Columbia, with the salmon kept in net cages in the ocean. An average salmon farm contains between 6 and 14 cages, and each cage contains from 50,000 to 80,000 fish. At Cooke Aquaculture Inc., headquartered in New Brunswick, salmon are initially counted when they are put in cages as smolts, or young salmon, from the hatchery. Every week, divers then go down and count the number of fish at the bottom of the cage that have died. The remainder is the company's best estimate of what is left. Other factors, such as fish escaping or predators getting some of the fish, will reduce these estimates.

After the salmon reach about 10 pounds, they are harvested. The actual number of salmon harvested is compared to the number estimated. The percentage differences are tracked and future estimates are adjusted for expected differences.

Determining Ownership of Goods

When we take a physical inventory, we need to consider the ownership of goods. To determine who owns what inventory, two questions must be answered: (1) Do all of the goods included in the count belong to the company? (2) Does the company own any goods that were not included in the count?

Goods in Transit

Goods in transit at the end of the period (on board a truck, train, ship, or plane) make determining ownership a bit more complicated. The company may have purchased goods that have not yet been received, or it may have sold goods that have not yet been delivered. To arrive at an accurate count, ownership of these goods must be determined.

The rule to follow is straightforward. **Goods in transit should be included in the inventory of the company that has legal title to the goods.** As we learned in Chapter 5, legal title, or ownership, is determined by the terms of the sale as follows:

1. **FOB (free on board) shipping point:** Legal title (ownership) of the goods passes to the buyer when the public carrier accepts the goods from the seller.
2. **FOB destination:** Legal title (ownership) of the goods remains with the seller until the goods reach the buyer.

The following table summarizes when ownership (legal title) passes while goods are in transit between either the seller's location or that of the public carrier (the shipping point) and the buyer's location (the destination). It also indicates who pays the shipping costs under each set of shipping terms.

Shipping Terms	Ownership Transfers to Buyer When Goods Passed To	Shipping Costs Paid By
FOB shipping point	Public Carrier	Buyer
FOB destination	Buyer	Seller

If the shipping terms are FOB shipping point, the buyer is responsible for paying the shipping costs and has legal title to the goods while they are in transit. If the shipping terms are FOB destination, the seller is responsible for paying the shipping costs and has legal title to the goods while they are in transit. These terms are important in determining the exact date that a purchase or sale should be recorded and what items should be included in inventory, even if the items are not physically present at the time of the inventory count.

For example, publishers normally ship textbooks to campus bookstores on FOB shipping point terms. This means that the bookstores (and ultimately the student) pay the cost of shipping. This also means that if the bookstore has a December 31 year end, it must adjust its inventory count for any textbooks still in transit for the beginning of the winter term. The bookstore also accepts the risk of damage or loss when the books are in transit.

Consigned Goods

In some lines of business, it is customary to hold goods belonging to other parties and sell them, for a fee, without ever taking ownership of the goods. These are called consigned goods. Under a consignment arrangement, the holder of the goods (called the *consignee*) does not own the goods. Ownership remains with the shipper of the goods (called the *consignor*) until the goods are actually sold to a customer. Because consigned goods are not owned by the consignee, they should not be included in the consignee's physical inventory count. Conversely, the consignor should include in its inventory any of the consignor's merchandise that is being held by the consignee.

For example, artists often display their paintings and other works of art at galleries on consignment. In such cases, the art gallery does not take ownership of the art—it still belongs to the artist. Therefore, if an inventory count is taken, any art on consignment should not be included in the art gallery's inventory. When the art sells, the gallery then takes a commission and pays the artist the remainder. Many craft stores, second-hand clothing stores, used sporting goods stores, and antique dealers sell goods on consignment to keep their inventory costs down and to avoid the risk of purchasing an item they will not be able to sell.

Other Situations

Sometimes goods are not physically on the premises because they have been taken home *on approval* by a customer. Goods on approval should be added to the physical inventory count because they still belong to the seller. The customer will either return the item or decide to buy it at some point in the future.

In other cases, goods are sold but the seller is holding them for alteration, or until they are picked up or delivered to the customer. These goods should not be included in the physical count, because legal title to ownership has passed to the customer. Damaged or unsaleable goods should also be separated from the physical count, and any loss should be recorded.

BEFORE YOU GO ON...

▸ **Review It**

1. What steps are involved in determining inventory quantities?
2. How is ownership determined for goods in transit?
3. Who has title to consigned goods?

▸ **Do It**

The Too Good To Be Threw Corporation completed its inventory count. It arrived at a total inventory amount of $200,000 after counting everything currently on hand in its warehouse. How will the following additional information affect the inventory count and cost?

1. Goods costing $15,000 and held on consignment for another company were included in the inventory.
2. Purchased goods of $10,000 were in transit (terms FOB shipping point) and not included in the count.
3. Inventory sold for $18,000 that cost $12,000 when purchased was in transit (terms FOB destination) and not included in the count.

Action Plan

- Apply the rules of ownership to goods held on consignment:
    - Goods held on consignment for another company are not included in inventory.
    - Goods held on consignment by another company are included in inventory.
- Apply the rules of ownership to goods in transit:
    - FOB shipping point: Goods sold or purchased and shipped FOB shipping point belong to the buyer.
    - FOB destination: Goods sold or purchased and shipped FOB destination belong to the seller until they reach their destination.

Solution

1. The $15,000 of goods being held on consignment should be deducted from Too Good To Be Threw's inventory count.
2. The $10,000 of goods in transit that were purchased FOB shipping point should be added to the company's inventory count.
3. The $12,000 of goods in transit that were sold FOB destination should be added to the company's inventory count.

The correct inventory cost is $207,000 ($200,000 − $15,000 + $10,000 + $12,000), and not $200,000, as originally reported.

The Navigator

Inventory Cost Determination Methods

The physical inventory count we discussed in the last section determines the quantities on hand, but does not determine their cost. Before they can be compared to the perpetual inventory records, these quantities therefore still need to have costs applied to them. How do we determine what cost to apply? And, a related question, how do we determine what cost to apply when we first record merchandise transactions in our accounting records?

The journal entries related to purchases and sales of merchandise were illustrated in Chapter 5. At that time, however, you were either told the cost of the goods sold, or it was assumed, for simplicity, that all inventory items had the same unit cost. In practice, though, a company often purchases different items of inventory at different costs on different dates and from different suppliers. The cost of acquiring inventory therefore normally does change.

Entries to record purchases of merchandise do not show the unit cost of each item of merchandise that was acquired. The account Merchandise Inventory is simply debited for the total cost paid for all the units together, and Cash or Accounts Payable is credited. The entry to record the sales price is also not directly affected by the unit cost. Cash or Accounts Receivable is debited and the Sales account is credited for the sales price of the merchandise sold, not its unit cost.

However, the unit cost is needed in order to prepare the entry to record the cost of goods sold and remove the cost of the items sold from inventory. As mentioned above, because units of the same inventory item are typically purchased at different prices, it is necessary to determine which unit costs to use in the calculation of the cost of the goods sold. One method—specific identification—uses the actual physical flow of the goods to determine cost. We will look at this method next.

Specific Identification

The specific identification method tracks the actual physical flow of the goods in a perpetual inventory system. Each item of inventory is marked, tagged, or coded with its specific unit cost so that, at any point in time, the cost of the ending inventory and the cost of the goods sold can be determined.

Assume, for example, that Jaguar Canada buys three different cars at a cost of $89,400 for an XK coupe, $94,300 for an XK convertible, and $95,200 for an XKR coupe. During the month, the two coupes are then sold at the selling price of $103,000 for the XK coupe and $108,000 for the XKR coupe. At December 31, the XK convertible is still on hand. The cost of goods sold is therefore $184,600 ($89,400 + $95,200) and the ending inventory is $94,300. This determination is possible because it was easy to track the actual physical flow of these three inventory items.

Illustration 6-1 ➡

Specific identification

Cost: $94,300

SOLD $103,000

Cost: $89,400

SOLD $108,000

Cost: $95,200

Conceptually, specific identification appears to be the ideal method for determining cost. This method matches the cost of goods sold against sales revenue and reports ending inventory at its actual cost. However, not surprisingly, it can be time-consuming and expensive to apply.

Specific identification is appropriate and required for goods that are not ordinarily interchangeable, and for goods that are produced and segregated for specific projects. It is used most often where a relatively small number of costly, easily distinguishable items (e.g., by their physical characteristics, serial numbers, or special markings) are involved. Examples include some types of jewellery, art work, pianos, and automobiles. Specific identification is also suitable for many types of special orders.

While specific identification works well when a company sells high-unit-cost items that can be clearly identified from purchase through to sale, there are also disadvantages to using this method.

For example, this method may allow management to manipulate net earnings. To see how, assume that Jaguar Canada also sells automobile parts. It has 15 fuel pumps in stock, for which it paid between $155 and $175 when they were purchased. They sell for $300. If the company wanted to maximize its net earnings just before its year end, management could choose to sell the units with the lowest cost ($155) to match against revenues ($300). Or, it could minimize net earnings by selecting the highest-cost ($175) fuel pumps to sell.

The requirement that the specific identification method only be used for goods that are not ordinarily interchangeable is an attempt to ensure that management does not use this method to manage earnings. Consequently, companies like Jaguar Canada use the specific identification method to track the cost of their automobile inventory while using another method to determine the cost of their parts inventory.

Cost Formulas: FIFO and Average

Because the specific identification method is only suitable for certain kinds of inventories, other methods of cost determination, known as cost formulas, are available to choose from. They include these two common inventory cost formulas that are used in Canada and internationally:

1. First-in, first-out (FIFO), where the cost of the first item purchased is considered to be the cost of the first item sold

2. Average, where the cost is determined using an average of the cost of the items purchased

FIFO and average are known as "cost formulas" because they assume a flow of costs that may not be the same as the actual physical flow of the goods, unlike the specific identification method.

While specific identification is normally used only in a perpetual inventory system, FIFO and average can be used in both the perpetual and periodic inventory systems. Recall from Chapter 5 that a key difference between these two inventory systems is how the cost of goods available for sale is allocated to the cost of goods sold and ending inventory.

Under a perpetual inventory system, the cost of goods available for sale (beginning inventory plus the cost of goods purchased) is allocated to the cost of goods sold as each item is sold. Under a periodic inventory system, the allocation is made only at the end of the period, with the cost of goods sold then calculated by deducting the ending inventory from the cost of goods available for sale.

For your review, Illustration 6-2 summarizes what we learned previously about the determination of cost of goods sold in these two inventory systems.

PERPETUAL INVENTORY SYSTEM		PERIODIC INVENTORY SYSTEM	
Merchandise inventory, beginning of period	$x	Merchandise inventory, beginning of period	$x
+ Cost of goods purchased (debit Merchandise Inventory and credit Cash or Accounts Payable at the time of each purchase)	X	+ Cost of goods purchased (debit Purchases and related accounts and credit Cash and Accounts Payable at the time of each purchase)	X
= Cost of goods available for sale	x	= Cost of goods available for sale	x
− Cost of goods sold (debit Cost of Goods Sold and credit Merchandise Inventory at the time of each sale)	X	− Ending inventory (counted at the end of the period)	X
= Ending inventory (perpetual record continuously updated)	$x	= Cost of goods sold (calculated at the end of the period)	$x

◀ Illustration 6-2

Determination of cost of goods sold in perpetual and periodic inventory systems

International Resources

Canadian and international accounting standards allow the use of both the perpetual and periodic inventory systems. However, the methods of cost determination are limited to specific identification, FIFO, and average. Another method, last-in, first-out (LIFO), is used by about 10 percent of the companies in the United States, including U.S.-based Caterpillar Inc., introduced in our feature story. LIFO is not permitted for use in Canada or internationally and is not discussed in this textbook.

Similar to the structure of Chapter 5, the perpetual inventory system will be used to illustrate the FIFO and average cost inventory formulas in this chapter. The chapter appendix explains how FIFO and average cost are determined in a periodic inventory system.

Perpetual System—First-In, First-Out (FIFO)

The first-in, first-out (FIFO) cost formula assumes that the earliest (oldest) goods purchased are the first ones to be sold. This does not necessarily mean that the oldest units are in fact sold first, only that the cost of the oldest units is recognized first. Although the cost formula chosen by a company does not have to match the actual physical movement of merchandise, it should correspond as closely as possible. FIFO generally does match because it is good business practice to sell the oldest units first.

To illustrate the application of FIFO in a perpetual inventory system, we will assume that Wynneck Electronics Ltd. has the following information for one of its products, the Astro Condenser:

WYNNECK ELECTRONICS LTD. Astro Condensers					
Date	Explanation	Units	Unit Cost	Total Cost	Balance in Units
Jan. 1	Beginning inventory	100	$10	$ 1,000	100
Apr. 15	Purchases	200	11	2,200	300
May 1	Sales	150			150
Aug. 24	Purchases	300	12	3,600	450
Sept. 10	Sales	400			50
Nov. 27	Purchases	400	13	5,200	450
		450		$12,000	

We note that there was inventory on hand at the beginning of the year and additional merchandise was purchased on April 15. This results, as of April 15, in 300 units available for sale at a total cost of $3,200 ($1,000 + $2,200). Of these, 100 units have a cost of $10 each and 200 units a cost of $11 each.

This information is used to start the preparation of a perpetual inventory schedule, as shown in Illustration 6-3.

	Purchases			Cost of Goods Sold			Balance		
Date	Units	Cost	Total	Units	Cost	Total	Units	Cost	Total
Jan. 1							100	$10	$1,000
Apr. 15	200	$11	$2,200				100 200	10 11	} 3,200

◀ Illustration 6-3

Perpetual inventory system—FIFO

▶ Reporting and Analyzing Inventory

On May 1, the date of the first sale, we must apply FIFO to determine whether the 150 units that were sold cost $10, $11, or a mix of both amounts. The cost must be determined on this date so that the Cost of Goods Sold account can be debited and the Merchandise Inventory account credited for the cost of this sale. Note that the sale must also be recorded on this same date, by debiting Cash or Accounts Receivable and crediting Sales. Although the sales price is required to record this entry, the above table does not include information about the sales price as this is not needed to determine the *cost* of the goods sold or the *cost* of the ending inventory.

Under FIFO, the cost of the oldest goods on hand before each sale is allocated to the cost of goods sold. Accordingly, the cost of goods sold on May 1 is assumed to consist of all 100 units of the January 1 beginning inventory and 50 units of the items purchased on April 15. This leaves 150 units of the April 15 purchase remaining in ending inventory. In Illustration 6-4, we have added this information to the inventory schedule that we first saw in Illustration 6-3.

Illustration 6-4 ➡

Perpetual inventory system—FIFO

	Purchases			Cost of Goods Sold			Balance		
Date	Units	Cost	Total	Units	Cost	Total	Units	Cost	Total
Jan. 1							100	$10	$1,000
Apr. 15	200	$11	$2,200				100	10	} 3,200
							200	11	
May 1				100	$10	} $1,550	150	11	1,650
				50	11				

After additional purchases are made on August 24, the cost of goods available for sale on this date now consists of 150 units at $11 and 300 units at $12, or 450 units costing $5,250 in total, as Illustration 6-5 shows.

Illustration 6-5 ➡

Perpetual inventory system—FIFO

	Purchases			Cost of Goods Sold			Balance		
Date	Units	Cost	Total	Units	Cost	Total	Units	Cost	Total
Jan. 1							100	$10	$1,000
Apr. 15	200	$11	$2,200				100	10	} 3,200
							200	11	
May 1				100	$10	} $1,550	150	11	1,650
				50	11				
Aug 24	300	12	3,600				150	11	} 5,250
							300	12	

On September 10, when 400 units are sold, the cost of goods sold is assumed to consist of the remaining units purchased on April 15 (150 units), and 250 of the units purchased on August 24. This leaves 50 units in ending inventory at a cost of $12 per unit, or $600 in total.

After a purchase of 400 units on November 27, the ending inventory consists of 450 units, of which 50 units cost $12 from the August 24 purchase and 400 units cost $13 from the November 27 purchase. These two transactions are shown in Illustration 6-6, completing the inventory schedule begun in Illustration 6-3.

Illustration 6-6 ➡

Perpetual inventory system—FIFO

	Purchases			Cost of Goods Sold			Balance		
Date	Units	Cost	Total	Units	Cost	Total	Units	Cost	Total
Jan. 1							100	$10	$1,000
Apr. 15	200	$11	$2,200				100	10	} 3,200
							200	11	
May 1				100	$10	} $1,550	150	11	1,650
				50	11				
Aug 24	300	12	3,600				150	11	} 5,250
							300	12	
Sept. 10				150	11	} 4,650	50	12	600
				250	12				
Nov. 27	400	13	5,200				50	12	} 5,800
							400	13	
	900		$11,000	550		$6,200			

On November 27, the total cost of goods sold is $6,200 and the ending inventory is $5,800. A useful check against calculation errors is to check whether the total of the cost of goods sold and ending inventory equals the total cost of goods available for sale of $12,000 (beginning inventory of $1,000 + purchases of $11,000). Because the cost of goods available for sale minus the cost of goods sold equals ending inventory, we can check our answers against this formula.

In summary, FIFO assumes that the first goods purchased are the first ones sold, and therefore that the last goods purchased are still in ending inventory. The cost formula always indicates the order of selling. This assumption is also evident in the phrase "last-in, still-here," which some people use in referring to this ending inventory.

Whether a periodic or perpetual inventory system is used, FIFO will always result in the same cost of goods sold and ending inventory amounts. The same costs will always be first in, and therefore first out, whether the costs are allocated throughout the accounting period as in the perpetual inventory system or at the end of the accounting period as in the periodic inventory system. The periodic inventory system using FIFO is demonstrated in detail in Appendix 6A. About 28 percent of Canadian companies use FIFO to determine the cost of their inventory, whether in a perpetual or periodic inventory system.

Perpetual Inventory System—Average

The average cost formula recognizes that it is not possible to measure a specific physical flow of inventory when the goods available for sale are homogeneous or nondistinguishable. Under this cost formula, the allocation of the cost of goods available for sale between cost of goods sold and ending inventory is made based on the weighted average unit cost of the merchandise. Using the same information provided in the FIFO section of the chapter for Wynneck Electronics, the formula and calculation of the weighted average unit cost are given in Illustration 6-7.

◂ **Illustration 6-7**

Calculation of weighted average unit cost

Note that the weighted average unit cost is not calculated by taking a simple average of the costs of each purchase, but by weighting the quantities purchased at each unit cost. This is done by dividing the cost of goods available for sale by the units available for sale at the date of each purchase. Consequently, a new average is calculated, or "moves," after each purchase. Because of this, this cost formula is commonly known as the **moving average cost formula** in a perpetual inventory system.

Use of the average cost formula by Wynneck Electronics is shown in Illustration 6-8.

	Purchases			Cost of Goods Sold			Balance		
Date	Units	Cost	Total	Units	Cost	Total	Units	Cost	Total
Jan. 1							100	$10.00	$1,000.00
Apr. 15	200	$11.00	$ 2,200.00				300	10.67	3,200.00
May 1				150	$10.67	$1,600.00	150	10.67	1,600.00
Aug. 24	300	12.00	3,600.00				450	11.56	5,200.00
Sept. 10				400	11.56	4,622.22	50	11.56	577.78
Nov. 27	400	13.00	5,200.00				450	12.84	5,777.78
	900		$11,000.00	550		$6,222.22			

◂ **Illustration 6-8**

Perpetual inventory system—average

As indicated above, **a new average is calculated each time a purchase (or purchase return) is made.** On April 15, after 200 units are purchased for $2,200, a total of 300 units costing $3,200 ($1,000 + $2,200) is on hand.

The average cost is not calculated by taking a simple average [($10 + $11) ÷ 2 = $10.50 per unit], but by weighting the quantities purchased at each unit cost. The average unit cost on April 15 is therefore $10.67 ($3,200 ÷ 300). Accordingly, the unit cost of the 150 units sold on May 1 is shown at $10.67, and the total cost of goods sold is $1,600. This unit cost is used in costing the units sold until another purchase is made, and a new unit cost must then be calculated.

On August 24, after 300 units are purchased for $3,600, a total of 450 units costing $5,200 ($1,600 + $3,600) are on hand. This results in an average cost per unit of $11.56 ($5,200 ÷ 450). This new cost is used to calculate the cost of the September 10 sale and the units still on hand after the sale.

A new unit cost will be calculated again after the November 27 purchase of 400 units for $5,200. After this purchase, there are 450 units on hand with a total cost of $5,777.78 ($577.78 + $5,200). This results in a new average cost of $12.84 ($5,777.78 ÷ 450), which will be used until another purchase is made in the following year.

As at November 27, therefore, the total cost of goods sold is $6,222.22 and the total ending inventory is $5,777.78. The total of these amounts should agree with our cost of goods available for sale, $12,000 ($6,222.22 + $5,777.78). This is a useful check, or proof, of the accuracy of your calculations.

In practice, average unit costs may be rounded to the nearest cent, or even to the nearest dollar. This illustration used the exact unit cost amounts, as would a computerized schedule, even though the unit costs have been rounded to the nearest digit for presentation in Illustration 6-8. However, it is important to remember that this is a method of allocating costs and not a method to track actual costs. Using four digits, or even cents, suggests a false level of accuracy.

In summary, this cost formula uses the average cost of the goods that are available for sale to determine the cost of goods sold and ending inventory. When a perpetual inventory system is used, the average cost is determined after each purchase because the cost of goods sold must be recorded at the time of each sale. When a periodic inventory system is used, the average cost is determined once at the end of the accounting period, as Appendix 6A will show in detail.

In contrast to FIFO, under the average cost formula, different amounts for the cost of goods sold and ending inventory will arise depending on whether a perpetual or periodic inventory system is used. About 46 percent of Canadian companies use average to determine the cost of their inventory, whether in a perpetual or periodic inventory system.

BEFORE YOU GO ON...

▶ **Review It**

1. When should the specific identification method be used to determine the cost of inventory?
2. Distinguish between the FIFO and average inventory cost formulas.
3. Which inventory method of cost determination—specific identification, FIFO, or average—can be manipulated?
4. Which method of inventory cost determination does Shoppers Drug Mart use to account for its inventories? The answer to this question is provided at the end of the chapter.

▶ **Do It**

The inventory records of Ag Implement Inc. show the following data for the month of March:

Date	Explanation	Units	Unit Cost	Total Cost
Mar. 1	Beginning inventory	4,000	$3	$12,000
10	Purchase	6,000	4	24,000
19	Sale	8,000		
22	Purchase	5,000	5	25,000
28	Sale	5,500		
		1,500		$61,000

Determine the cost of goods sold and ending inventory under a perpetual inventory system using (a) FIFO and (b) average.

Action Plan
• For FIFO, allocate the first costs to the cost of goods sold at the date of each sale. The latest costs will be allocated to the goods on hand (ending inventory).
• For average, determine the weighted average unit cost (cost of goods available for sale ÷ number of units available for sale) after each purchase. Multiply this cost by the number of units sold to determine the cost of goods sold, and by the number of units on hand to determine the cost of ending inventory.
• Prove that the cost of goods sold and ending inventory equals the cost of goods available for sale.

Solution

(a) FIFO—Perpetual

Date	Purchases			Cost of Goods Sold			Balance		
	Units	Cost	Total	Units	Cost	Total	Units	Cost	Total
Mar. 1							4,000	$3	$12,000
10	6,000	$4	$24,000				4,000 6,000	3 4	} 36,000
19				4,000 4,000	$3 4	} $28,000	2,000	4	8,000
22	5,000	5	25,000				2,000 5,000	4 5	} 33,000
28				2,000 3,500	4 5	} 25,500	1,500	5	7,500
	11,000		$49,000	13,500		$53,500			

Check: $53,500 + $7,500 = $61,000 ($12,000 + $49,000)

(b) Average—Perpetual

Date	Purchases			Cost of Goods Sold			Balance		
	Units	Cost	Total	Units	Cost	Total	Units	Cost	Total
Mar. 1							4,000	$3.00	$12,000
10	6,000	$4	$24,000				10,000	3.60	36,000
19				8,000	$3.60	$28,800	2,000	3.60	7,200
22	5,000	5	25,000				7,000	4.60	32,200
28				5,500	4.60	25,300	1,500	4.60	6,900
	11,000		$49,000	13,500		$54,100			

Check: $54,100 + $6,900 = $61,000 ($12,000 + $49,000)

The Navigator

Financial Statement Effects

Inventory affects both the balance sheet and statement of earnings since ending inventory is included as a current asset on the balance sheet and cost of goods sold is included on the statement of earnings. Cost of goods sold also affects gross profit and net earnings, which in turn, will affect retained earnings in the shareholders' equity section of the balance sheet (as well as the statement of retained earnings). Thus, the choice of cost determination method can have a significant impact on the financial statements.

Errors can also occur when a physical inventory is being taken or when the cost of the inventory is being determined. The effects of these errors on financial statements can be significant. We will address both of these topics—choice of cost determination method and errors—in the next two sections.

> **study objective 3**
>
> Explain the financial statement effects of the inventory cost determination methods and of inventory errors.

Choice of Cost Determination Method

If companies have goods that are not ordinarily interchangeable, or goods that have been produced and segregated for specific projects, they must use the specific identification method to determine the cost of their inventory. Otherwise, they can choose to use either FIFO or average.

How should a company choose between FIFO and average? It should consider the following objectives in making its choice:

1. Choose a method that corresponds as closely as possible to the physical flow of goods.

2. Report an inventory cost on the balance sheet that is close to the inventory's recent cost.

3. Use the same method for all inventories having a similar nature and usage in the company.

As we mentioned earlier in this chapter, about 28 percent of Canadian companies use FIFO. Alimentation Couche-Tard, Magna International, and Loblaw are examples of companies that use FIFO to determine the cost of their inventories. About 46 percent of Canadian companies use average. Ballard Power Systems, Canadian Tire, and Sears Canada use average to determine the cost of their inventories.

About 22 percent of Canadian companies use more than one method of inventory cost determination. Companies can use more than one method if they have different types of inventory. Finning International, for example, uses specific identification to account for its equipment inventory, FIFO to account for about two-thirds of its inventory of parts and supplies, and average to account for the rest. And a small number of companies, about 4 percent, use other methods that are not discussed in this textbook.

After a company chooses a method of determining the cost of its inventory, that method should be used consistently from one period to the next. You will recall, from Chapter 2, that **comparability** of financial statements over successive time periods is an important qualitative characteristic of accounting information. Using FIFO in one year and average in the next year would make it difficult to compare the net earnings for the two years.

This is not to say that a company can never change from one method to another. However, a change in the method of cost determination can only occur if the physical flow of inventory changes and a different method would result in a more reliable and more relevant presentation in the financial statements. We will learn more about changing accounting principles in Chapter 14. Until then, all you need to understand is that such changes are accounted for retroactively and are clearly explained, and that their effects are disclosed in the financial statements. This respects the **full disclosure principle**, introduced in Chapter 2, which requires all relevant information to be disclosed.

Statement of Earnings Effects

To understand the impact of the FIFO and average cost formulas on the statement of earnings, we will now examine their effects on Wynneck Electronics. The condensed statements of earnings in Illustration 6-9 use the amounts we determined for cost of goods sold after applying the FIFO and average cost formulas earlier in the chapter. This illustration also assumes that Wynneck had sales of $11,500, operating expenses of $2,000, and an income tax rate of 30 percent.

Illustration 6-9 ➡

Comparative effects of inventory cost formulas

WYNNECK ELECTRONICS LTD.
Condensed Statement of Earnings

	FIFO	Average
Sales	$11,500	$11,500
Cost of goods sold	6,200	6,222
Gross profit	5,300	5,278
Operating expenses	2,000	2,000
Earnings before income tax	3,300	3,278
Income tax expense (30%)	990	983
Net earnings	$ 2,310	$ 2,295

The sales and operating expense figures are the same under both FIFO and average. But the costs of goods sold amounts are both different. This difference is because of the unit costs that are allocated under each cost formula. Each dollar of difference in cost of goods sold results in a corresponding dollar difference in earnings before income tax. For Wynneck, there is a $22 difference between the FIFO and average amounts for cost of goods sold. A fixed percentage (30%) applied to determine income tax expense results in a difference in net earnings between the two formulas of $15.

In periods of changing prices, the choice of inventory cost formula can have a significant impact on earnings. In a period of inflation (rising prices), as is the case for Wynneck, FIFO produces higher net earnings because the lower unit costs of the first units purchased are matched against revenues. As Illustration 6-9 shows, FIFO reports the highest net earnings ($2,310) and average the lowest ($2,295).

This difference is not very large for Wynneck, because prices are changing slowly. The more rapidly prices change, the larger this difference will be. In periods of rising prices, there may be income tax advantages to using average. Because earnings before income tax are lower, income tax expense will also be lower.

If prices are falling, the results from the use of FIFO and average are reversed: FIFO will report the lowest net earnings and average the highest. If prices are stable, both cost formulas will report the same results.

Compared to FIFO, average will result in more recent costs being reflected in the cost of goods sold. This will better match current costs with current revenues and result in a better statement of earnings valuation. Of course, the specific identification method provides the best match of costs and revenues, as it exactly matches each cost with the revenue it generates.

You will recall that the matching principle is important in accounting. Despite its importance, however, the matching principle is not critical in the choice of an inventory cost determination method and is expected to be even less important in future years as we move to international financial reporting standards. If companies do not meet the criteria to use the specific identification method, they must choose between FIFO and average based on objectives other than matching, such as which cost formula best approximates the physical flow of goods or represents recent costs on the balance sheet, as discussed earlier in the chapter.

Balance Sheet Effects

One advantage of FIFO is that the costs allocated to ending inventory will approximate the inventory items' current (replacement) cost. For example, for Wynneck, 400 of the 450 units in the ending inventory are costed under FIFO at the higher November 27 unit cost of $13. Since management needs to replace inventory when it is sold, a valuation that approximates the replacement cost is helpful for decision-making. That is why one of the objectives in choosing an inventory cost formula is to "report an inventory cost on the balance sheet that is close to the inventory's recent cost." FIFO provides a better balance sheet valuation than does average.

By extension, therefore, one limitation of average is that in a period of inflation the costs that are allocated to ending inventory may be understated in terms of the current cost of inventory. That is, the average cost formula results in older costs being included in ending inventory. For example, the average cost of Wynneck's ending inventory, $12.84, includes the $10 unit cost of the beginning inventory as well as the cost of some of its earlier purchases. The understatement becomes greater over extended periods of inflation if the inventory includes goods that were purchased in one or more earlier accounting periods.

Although average provides a better statement of earnings valuation than does FIFO because more current costs are included in the cost of goods sold, and FIFO provides a better balance sheet valuation because more current costs are included in the ending inventory, in most cases both cost formulas result in relatively close valuations. This is especially true in the Wynneck Electronics example where prices were not changing rapidly.

While the specific identification method provides the best cost of goods sold valuation, it may not provide the best balance sheet valuation, depending on which costs remain in ending inventory. If older items purchased at a lower cost happen to remain in inventory, they do not represent the most recent costs and therefore do not represent replacement cost.

Illustration 6-10 summarizes the advantages of each of the three major cost determination methods.

Helpful Hint Specific identification provides the best statement of earnings valuation, but FIFO provides the best balance sheet valuation.

Specific Identification	FIFO	Average
• Exactly matches costs and revenues on the statement of earnings. • Tracks the actual physical flow.	• Ending inventory on the balance sheet includes the most current costs (closest to replacement cost). • Approximates the physical flow of most retailers.	• Cost of goods sold on the statement of earnings includes more current costs than FIFO. • Smooths the effects of price changes by assigning all units the same average cost.

◀ Illustration 6-10

Advantages of cost determination methods

Summary of Financial Statement Effects

The key financial statement differences that will result from using the three different cost determination methods during a period of rising prices are summarized in Illustration 6-11. These effects will be the inverse if prices are falling, and the same for all three methods if prices are constant. In all cases, it does not matter whether a company uses the perpetual or periodic inventory system.

	Specific Identification	FIFO	Average
Statement of earnings			
Cost of goods sold	Variable	Lowest	Highest
Gross profit	Variable	Highest	Lowest
Net earnings	Variable	Highest	Lowest
Balance sheet			
Cash (pre-tax)	Same	Same	Same
Ending inventory	Variable	Highest	Lowest
Retained earnings	Variable	Highest	Lowest

◀ Illustration 6-11

Summary of financial statement effects of cost determination methods

▸ Reporting and Analyzing Inventory

We have seen that both inventory on the balance sheet and net earnings on the statement of earnings are highest when FIFO is used in a period of inflation. Do not confuse this with cash flow. All three methods of cost determination—specific identification, FIFO, and average—produce exactly the same cash flow before income taxes. Sales and purchases are not affected by the method of inventory cost determination. The only thing that is affected is the allocation of the cost of goods available for sale between the cost of goods sold and ending inventory—which does not involve cash.

It is also worth remembering that all three methods will give exactly the same result over the life cycle of the business or its product. That is, the allocation between the cost of goods sold and ending inventory may vary annually, but it will produce the same cumulative results over time. Although much has been written about the impact of the choice of inventory cost determination method on a variety of performance measures, in reality there is little real economic distinction among the methods over time.

🌐 ACCOUNTING MATTERS! | International Perspective

Whatever happened to last-in, first-out (LIFO)? Until January 1, 2008, LIFO was permitted in Canada. Even though it was allowed, however, because it was not permitted for income tax purposes, few companies actually used it in Canada. The few that did were subsidiaries of U.S. companies, where the use of LIFO is permitted for income tax purposes.

Both international and Canadian standard setters have eliminated the use of the LIFO cost formula. The reasons were many, including the following two: (1) assigning the oldest (earliest) costs to ending inventory did not represent physical inventory flows reliably for most goods, and (2) because the oldest costs were assigned to ending inventory under LIFO, the cost of ending inventory did not provide a fair representation of the recent cost of inventories on hand.

Inventory Errors

Unfortunately, errors occasionally occur in accounting for inventory. In some cases, errors are caused by mistakes in counting the quantities during the physical inventory. In other cases, errors are caused by mistakes in determining or recording the cost of the inventory items. A physical inventory count should uncover these differences in a perpetual inventory system. When the physical inventory count disagrees with what is reported in the accounting records, an investigation is undertaken that will (hopefully) be able to isolate the error or problem so that a suitable action can be taken. This, after all, is one of the strengths of a perpetual inventory system.

Sometimes, though, the reason for the discrepancy cannot be determined. For example, the volume of transactions may make finding the error impractical, creating a situation where the costs outweigh the benefits. In such cases, the Merchandise Inventory and Cost of Goods Sold accounts are adjusted to agree to the count.

Recall that the Merchandise Inventory and Cost of Goods Sold accounts are affected by the following transactions:

Merchandise Inventory			Cost of Goods Sold	
Beginning inventory Cost of goods purchased	Cost of goods sold	→	Cost of goods sold	
Ending inventory				

Because both accounts are affected by inventory errors, both the statement of earnings (through cost of goods sold) and the balance sheet (through inventory) are affected. In the following sections, we will show how these statements are affected.

Statement of Earnings Effects

In Chapters 5 and 6, we learned that cost of goods available for sale (beginning inventory + cost of goods purchased) is allocated to the cost of goods sold. Consequently, if there is an error in either of these components, then the cost of goods sold will be similarly affected. That is, if the cost is wrong in beginning inventory and/or the cost of goods purchased, then the unit costs allocated to the cost of goods sold will also be in error.

The overall effects of inventory errors on the current year's statement of earnings can be determined by looking at the specific components of cost of goods sold. This is shown in Illustration 6-12.

Nature of Error	Net Sales	–	Cost of Goods Sold	=	Gross Profit	–	Operating Expenses	=	Earnings Before Income Taxes	–	Income Tax Expense	=	Net Earnings
Understate beginning inventory or cost of goods purchased	NE		U		O		NE		O		NE		O
Overstate beginning inventory or cost of goods purchased	NE		O		U		NE		U		NE		U

U = Understatement   O = Overstatement   NE = No Effect

⬆ **Illustration 6-12**

Effects of inventory errors on statement of earnings

As shown on the first line of Illustration 6-12, if beginning inventory is understated or if the cost of goods purchased is understated (assuming no offsetting errors have occurred), then cost of goods sold will also be understated. Gross profit is also affected. Because cost of goods sold is deducted from net sales, an understatement in cost of goods sold will produce an overstatement in gross profit. Assuming there are no errors in operating expenses or income tax expense, net earnings will be affected by the inventory error in the same amount and direction as gross profit.

For simplicity, we have assumed above that there is no error in calculating the income tax expense. Typically, however, if earnings before income taxes are overstated, then income tax expense will also be overstated, and vice versa if there is an understatement. We will soon add the complexity of errors in income tax expense to our discussion.

As you know, the ending inventory of one period automatically becomes the beginning inventory of the next period. Consequently, **an error in the ending inventory of the current period will have a reverse effect on net earnings of the next accounting period** if it is not found and corrected.

To illustrate, assume that ending inventory in 2008 is understated by $3,000 because of pricing errors in the inventory. The Merchandise Inventory account has been reproduced below using both the incorrect ending inventory figure ($12,000) and the correct inventory figure ($15,000).

Incorrect Inventory Amount

Merchandise Inventory			
2008			
Beg. inv.	20,000	CGS	48,000
Purchases	40,000		
End.inv.	12,000		
2009			
Purchases	68,000	CGS	57,000
End. inv.	23,000		

Correct Inventory Amount

Merchandise Inventory			
2008			
Beg. inv.	20,000	CGS	45,000
Purchases	40,000		
End. inv.	15,000		
2009			
Purchases	68,000	CGS	60,000
End. inv.	23,000		

Because of the $3,000 understatement in ending inventory at the end of 2008 ($12,000 instead of $15,000), cost of goods sold (CGS) is overstated by $3,000 ($48,000 instead of $45,000). In addition, because the inventory balance was wrong at the end of 2008, it is also wrong at the beginning of 2009. The effects of this error on the costs assigned to the goods sold continue for a second year, where cost of goods sold is now understated by $3,000 ($57,000 instead of $60,000). Assuming the ending inventory is calculated correctly at the end of the second year, 2009, this error stops now but it has had a two-year effect, as shown in Illustration 6-13.

Illustration 6-13 ➡

Effects of inventory errors on statement of earnings for two years

	2008		2009	
SAMPLE COMPANY				
Statement of Earnings				
	Incorrect	Correct	Incorrect	Correct
Sales	$80,000	$80,000	$90,000	$90,000
Cost of goods sold	48,000	45,000	57,000	60,000
Gross profit	32,000	35,000	33,000	30,000
Operating expenses	10,000	10,000	20,000	20,000
Earnings before income tax	22,000	25,000	13,000	10,000
Income tax expense (25%)	5,500	6,250	3,250	2,500
Net earnings	$16,500	$18,750	$ 9,750	$ 7,500

($2,250)
Net earnings understated

$2,250
Net earnings overstated

The combined net earnings for two years is correct because the errors cancel each other out.

In this illustration, the understatement of ending inventory results, in the same year, in an overstatement of the cost of goods sold and an understatement of gross profit, earnings before income tax, and net earnings. It also results in an understatement of the cost of goods sold in 2009 and an overstatement of gross profit, earnings before income tax, and net earnings for that year.

Note that the difference in net earnings is not $3,000, the amount of the inventory error. Instead, it is $2,250. This is because we have also introduced an error in income tax in this example. Here, we have assumed that income tax is calculated as 25% of earnings before income tax. Consequently, income tax expense is affected by any change in earnings before income tax. Income tax expense is understated by $750 in 2008 and overstated by the same amount in 2009.

Over the two years, total net earnings are correct because the errors offset each other. Notice that total earnings using incorrect data are $26,250 ($16,500 + $9,750), which is the same as the total earnings of $26,250 ($18,750 + $7,500) using correct data.

Balance Sheet Effects

The effect of ending inventory errors on the balance sheet can be calculated by using the basic accounting equation: Assets = liabilities + shareholders' equity. Errors in the ending inventory have the effects shown in Illustration 6-14.

Illustration 6-14 ➡

Effects of inventory errors on balance sheet

Ending Inventory Error	Assets	=	Liabilities	+	Shareholders' Equity
Overstated	O		NE		O
Understated	U		NE		U

U = Understatement   O = Overstatement   NE = No Effect

If there are errors in net earnings, as we discussed in the previous section, then shareholders' equity will be affected by the same amount since net earnings are closed into the Retained Earnings account, which is part of shareholders' equity. Consequently, an error in ending inventory affects both the asset account Merchandise Inventory and the shareholders' equity account Retained Earnings.

Depending on whether income tax has been paid or not, the Income Tax Payable account might also be affected. For simplicity in this chapter, we will assume that all income tax has been paid, so that the effects on assets and shareholders' equity are equal.

The effect of an error in ending inventory on the next period was shown in Illustration 6-13. Recall that if the error is not corrected, the combined total net earnings for the two periods would be correct. In the example, therefore, the assets and shareholders' equity reported on the balance sheet at the end of 2009 will be correct.

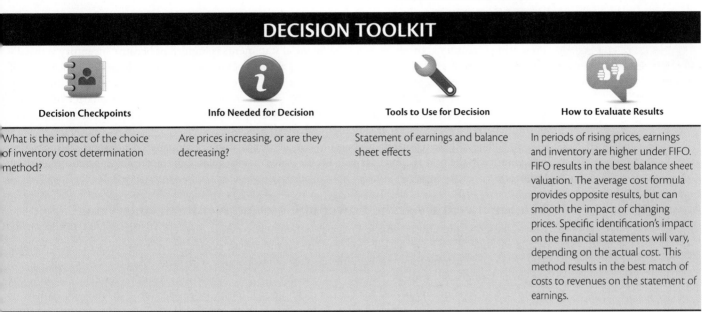

DECISION TOOLKIT

Decision Checkpoints	Info Needed for Decision	Tools to Use for Decision	How to Evaluate Results
What is the impact of the choice of inventory cost determination method?	Are prices increasing, or are they decreasing?	Statement of earnings and balance sheet effects	In periods of rising prices, earnings and inventory are higher under FIFO. FIFO results in the best balance sheet valuation. The average cost formula provides opposite results, but can smooth the impact of changing prices. Specific identification's impact on the financial statements will vary, depending on the actual cost. This method results in the best match of costs to revenues on the statement of earnings.

BEFORE YOU GO ON...

Review It

1. What factors should management consider when choosing an inventory cost determination method?
2. Identify the advantages of each of the three methods of cost determination—specific identification, FIFO, and average.
3. Which cost formula—FIFO or average—produces the higher net earnings in a period of rising prices? The higher ending inventory valuation? The higher pre-tax cash flow?
4. How do inventory errors affect the statement of earnings? How do they affect the balance sheet?

Do It

On July 31, Zhang Inc. counted $600,000 of inventory. This count did not include $90,000 of goods in transit that were purchased on July 29 on account and shipped to Zhang FOB shipping point. Zhang recorded the purchase on August 3 when the goods were received. (a) Determine the correct July 31 inventory amount. (b) Identify any accounts that are in error at July 31, and state the amount and direction (e.g., understated or overstated) of the error. You can ignore income tax effects.

Action Plan

• Use the statement of earnings relationships to determine the error's impact on statement of earnings accounts.
• Use the accounting equation to determine the error's impact on balance sheet accounts.

Solution:

a)   The inventory count should have included the goods in transit and the purchase should have been recorded in July instead of August. The correct amount of inventory on July 31 was $690,000 ($600,000 + $90,000).

b)

Statement of earnings accounts: Because these inventory items were not sold, there is no error in cost of goods sold.

Balance sheet accounts: Merchandise Inventory and Accounts Payable are both understated (U) by $90,000. The accounting equation shows the impact:

Assets	=	Liabilities	+	Shareholders' equity
U $90,000	=	U $90,000	+	no effect

The Navigator

Presentation and Analysis of Inventory

Presenting inventory appropriately on the financial statements is important because inventory is usually the largest current asset (merchandise inventory) on the balance sheet and the largest expense (cost of goods sold) on the statement of earnings. For example, Caterpillar Inc., introduced in our feature story, reported inventory of U.S. $7,204 million in 2007, which comprises more than one-quarter of its total current assets. Caterpillar's cost of goods sold of U.S. $32,626 million amounts to more than 80 percent of total operating expenses on its statement of earnings.

In addition, these reported numbers are critical for analyzing a company's effectiveness in managing its inventory. In the next sections, we will discuss issues that are related to the presentation and analysis of inventory.

Valuing Inventory at the Lower of Cost and Net Realizable Value

Before presenting inventory on the financial statements, we must first ensure that it is properly valued. While we hope that we can sell our merchandise for more than we paid for it, in some cases this is not possible. For example, inventory may become obsolete or less popular with time. The prices of seasonal goods can drop dramatically with a change in season—few people want to buy a snow blower in the summer months. And, in some industries, such as the technology industry, prices decline as technology evolves.

Suppose you are the owner of a retail store that sells computer chips. During the recent 12-month period, the price of the computer chips dropped by almost 25 percent. At the end of your fiscal year, you have some of these computer chips in inventory. Do you think your inventory should be stated at cost in accordance with the cost principle, or at its lower value?

As you probably reasoned, when this situation occurs, the cost basis of accounting is no longer followed. When the value of inventory is lower than its cost, inventory is written down to its net realizable (fair) value in the period when the loss occurs. This is called the lower of cost and net realizable value (LCNRV) rule, where value is defined as the net realizable value of the inventory. For a merchandising company, net realizable value (NRV) is the selling price, less any costs required to make the goods ready for sale.

Why is the cost principle overridden when the value of the inventory is less than its recorded amount? First, users of financial information assume that inventory can be converted into at least as much cash as the value recorded for it on the balance sheet, and hopefully more. Second, because of the matching principle, a loss in the value of the inventory should be deducted from (matched with) revenues in the period when the loss occurs, not in the period when the inventory is sold.

The lower of cost and NRV rule is applied to the inventory at the end of the accounting period after specific identification, FIFO, or average has been used to determine the cost. To apply this rule, the following steps must be followed:

1. Determine the cost of the inventory.
2. Determine the net realizable value of the inventory.
3. Compare the values determined in steps 1 and 2. Use the lower value to report inventory on the financial statements.

To illustrate, assume that at March 31, 2009, Wacky World Limited has the following lines of merchandise with costs and net realizable values as indicated. The lower of cost and NRV rule produces the following results:

	Cost	NRV	Lower of Cost and NRV
Televisions			
LCD	$ 60,000	$ 55,000	$ 55,000
Plasma	45,000	52,000	45,000
	105,000	107,000	100,000
Car video and audio equipment			
LCD media packages	48,000	45,000	45,000
GPS	15,000	14,000	14,000
	63,000	59,000	59,000
Total inventory	$168,000	$166,000	$159,000

The lower of cost and net realizable value rule should be applied to individual inventory items, rather than total inventory. In certain cases, it can be applied to groups of similar items. In the above example, we compare the cost of the LCD televisions ($60,000) to their net realizable value ($55,000) and choose the net realizable value because it is the lower of cost and NRV. In the case of plasma televisions, the cost ($45,000) is the lower of cost and NRV. This comparison would continue for the remaining items in inventory (the car video and audio equipment) until the total value using the lower of cost and NRV rule, or $159,000, has been determined.

Recording Lower of Cost and NRV

After the lower of cost and net realizable value has been determined, it must be used at the end of each accounting period to report inventory. If Wacky World uses a perpetual inventory system, an adjusting journal entry is required to write the inventory down by $9,000 ($168,000 − $159,000) as follows:

Mar. 31	Cost of Goods Sold	9,000	
	Allowance to Reduce Inventory to NRV		9,000
	(To record decline in inventory value from original cost of $168,000 to net realizable value of $159,000)		

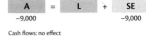

A	=	L	+	SE
−9,000				−9,000

Cash flows: no effect

The adjusting journal entry shown above does not change the value of the Inventory account. Rather it establishes a contra asset account to Inventory on the balance sheet, named Allowance to Reduce Inventory to NRV. This is called the **allowance method** of recording inventory at the lower of cost and NRV. Similar to the accumulated depreciation contra asset account, the inventory contra asset account allows us to keep estimated values (NRV) separate from the actual cost recorded in the inventory account.

Another method of recording a decline in value is also permitted. Known as the **direct method**, it debits Cost of Goods Sold for the loss and credits the Inventory account directly. Although both methods are permitted, we will use the allowance method in this textbook. This method reports the decline separately and does not distort the Inventory account as is the case in the direct method.

In both methods, a loss account is sometimes used instead of debiting Cost of Goods Sold. The end result is the same, however, as the loss account is normally closed into the Cost of Goods Sold account at the end of the period for reporting purposes. Note that a decline in the value of inventory is considered to be an overall cost of buying and selling merchandise, and should therefore not be reported as a non-operating "other expense" item.

When the circumstances that previously caused inventories to be written down below cost no longer exist, or when there is clear evidence of an increase in net realizable value because of changed economic circumstances, the amount of the write-down is reversed. This occurs, for example, when an item of inventory that is carried at net realizable value, because its selling price had declined, is still on hand in a subsequent period and its selling price has increased.

It is not usual for inventory reversals to happen. Most companies will sell their inventory at a reduced price rather than keep it in stock and hope for a recovery in value. Nonetheless, it can happen. For example, Thailand's Sahaviriya Steel Industries recently recorded a 369-million-Baht reversal of an inventory loss following a surge in commodity prices.

There are a number of ways to record a reversal of an inventory write-down. Most companies leave the allowance account on the books and adjust its balance at the end of the next accounting period to agree with the difference between cost and the lower of cost and NRV at that time. This is similar to the approach we will use to value receivables in Chapter 8.

To illustrate, assume that the total cost of Wacky World's television and car video and audio equipment inventory one year later, at March 31, 2010, was $188,000. The lower of cost and NRV was $185,000 on this same date. Consequently, an allowance account of $3,000 ($188,000 − $185,000) is now required. Because we have an allowance account with $9,000 already recorded for 2009, the allowance account is not credited for the $3,000 loss in the current period but rather debited for a $6,000 recovery of the prior period's loss.

A = L + SE
+6,000 +6,000

Cash flows: no effect

Mar. 31	Allowance to Reduce Inventory to NRV	6,000	
	Cost of Goods Sold		6,000
	(To adjust allowance account to $3,000 to reflect decline in inventory value in current period from original cost of $188,000 to net realizable value of $185,000)		

As shown in the T account below, this adjusting entry results in an ending credit balance of $3,000 in the allowance account.

Allowance to Reduce Inventory to NRV			
		Mar. 31, 2009 Adj.	9,000
Mar. 31, 2010 Adj.	6,000		
		Mar. 31, 2010 Bal.	3,000

Note that the credit to the Cost of Goods Sold account in the above journal entry is not "revenue" or a "gain." Rather, it is a recovery of the previously recognized loss. Recovering the loss up to the original cost is permitted, but **the total amount may never exceed the original cost**. Consequently, although the allowance account may be debited and credited, it will never have a debit balance at year end.

If Wacky World uses a periodic inventory system, as described in the chapter appendix, no journal entry will be needed to adjust the inventory. Wacky World would instead use $159,000 as the ending inventory amount in the cost of goods sold calculation on its 2009 statement of earnings. This will result in cost of goods sold being $9,000 ($168,000 − $159,000) higher than if cost had been used. When the accounting cycle is complete, Wacky World will update its inventory account to $159,000 through the closing entry process.

Reporting Inventory

Ending inventory is reported in the current assets section of the balance sheet. Using our Wacky World example, inventory had a cost of $168,000 at March 31, 2009, and a cost of $188,000 at March 31, 2010. The allowance account had a balance of $9,000 and $3,000, respectively, on these same dates.

The allowance to reduce inventory to its net realizable value is reported in the current assets section of Wacky World's balance sheet as a contra account to the inventory, as follows:

WACKY WORLD LIMITED Balance Sheet (partial) March 31		
	2010	2009
Current assets		
Inventory, at cost	$188,000	$168,000
Less: Allowance to reduce inventory to NRV	3,000	9,000
Inventory, at lower of cost and NRV	185,000	159,000

In the financial statements or accompanying notes, the following information related to inventory should be disclosed: (1) the total amount of inventory; (2) the cost of goods sold; (3) the method of cost determination (specific identification, FIFO, or average); (4) the basis of valuation (cost or lower of cost and net realizable value); and (5) the amount of any write-down to net realizable value or reversals of previous write-downs, including the reason why the write-down was reversed.

⊕ ACCOUNTING MATTERS! | International Perspective

Almost every country in the world applies the lower of cost and "market" rule; however, the definition of the market value can vary. The International Accounting Standards Board defines market as net realizable value, as does Canada. The U.S. allows a number of definitions of market, including net realizable value and replacement cost. Replacement cost is the amount that would be required in order to purchase the equivalent item in the normal course of business.

Another difference is that the U.S. views the write-down of inventory as permanent. Most other countries, including Canada, either require or allow the recovery of value back to the original cost if the net realizable value recovers.

Inventory Turnover

As we have seen in previous chapters, ratios are important for any analysis of a company's performance. The two ratios that we introduce in this chapter are the inventory turnover and days in inventory ratios, both of which help a company manage its inventory levels. These ratios are also important in evaluating a company's liquidity—i.e., its ability to pay obligations that are expected to come due in the next year.

In Chapter 2 we introduced the current ratio, which is also a measure of liquidity. Inventory is a significant component of the current ratio and a high level of inventory will result in a high current ratio. But if the inventory is not turning over very quickly, this may be a problem. The **inventory turnover** ratio measures the number of times, on average, that inventory is sold ("turned over") during the period. It is calculated as the cost of goods sold divided by the average inventory.

Whenever a ratio compares a balance sheet figure (e.g., inventory) to a statement of earnings figure (e.g., cost of goods sold), the balance sheet figure must be averaged. Averages for balance sheet figures are determined by adding the beginning and ending balances together and then dividing the result by two. Averages are used to ensure that the balance sheet figures (which represent end-of-period amounts) cover the same period of time as the statement of earnings figures (which represent amounts for the entire period).

A complement to the inventory turnover ratio is the **days in inventory** ratio. It converts the inventory turnover into a measure of the average age of the inventory. It is calculated as 365 days divided by the inventory turnover ratio.

A low inventory turnover ratio (high days in inventory) could mean that the company has too much of its funds in inventory. It could also mean that the company has excessive carrying costs (e.g., for interest, storage, insurance, and taxes) or that it has obsolete inventory.

A high inventory turnover ratio (low days in inventory) could mean that the company has little of its funds in inventory—in other words, that it has a minimal amount of inventory on hand at any specific time. Although having minimal funds tied up in inventory suggests efficiency, too high an inventory turnover ratio may indicate that the company is losing sales opportunities because of inventory shortages. For example, when analysts felt recently that they were seeing too many empty shelves at Loblaw, they suggested that the company had gone too far in reducing its inventory. Management should watch this ratio closely so that it achieves the best balance between too much and too little inventory.

In our feature story, we noted that effective inventory management was key to Caterpillar Inc.'s success. The following data are available for Caterpillar for three recent years (in USD millions):

	2007	2006	2005
Inventory	$ 7,204	$ 6,351	$ 5,224
Cost of goods sold	32,626	29,549	26,558

Using these data, Illustration 6-15 presents the inventory turnover and days in inventory ratios for Caterpillar and Komatsu, its primary competitor, for 2007 and 2006. U.S.-based Caterpillar Inc. is the world's largest construction equipment maker and Japan-based Komatsu Ltd. is the second largest.

Illustration 6-15 ➡

Inventory turnover and days in inventory

INVENTORY TURNOVER = $\dfrac{\text{COST OF GOODS SOLD}}{\text{AVERAGE INVENTORY}}$			
DAYS IN INVENTORY = $\dfrac{\text{365 DAYS}}{\text{INVENTORY TURNOVER}}$			

(in USD millions)		2007	2006
Caterpillar	Inventory turnover	$\dfrac{\$32,626}{(\$7,204 + \$6,351)\div 2} = 4.8$ times	$\dfrac{\$29,549}{(\$6,351 + \$5,224)\div 2} = 5.1$ times
	Days in inventory	$\dfrac{365\ \text{days}}{4.8} = 76$ days	$\dfrac{365\ \text{days}}{5.1} = 72$ days
Komatsu	Inventory turnover	3.3 times	3.4 times
	Days in inventory	111 days	107 days
Industry average	Inventory turnover	4.5 times	5.0 times
	Days in inventory	81 days	73 days

The calculations in Illustration 6-15 show that Caterpillar's inventory turnover declined slightly from 2006 to 2007. The industry average also declined during this period, although Caterpillar continues to perform better than the industry in general, in fact, increasingly so.

Caterpillar also turns its inventory over much faster than Komatsu. This suggests that Caterpillar is more efficient in its inventory management than its primary competitor. As the feature story suggested, Caterpillar's sophisticated distribution system appears to allow it to keep minimum amounts of inventory on hand, while still giving customers what they are looking for.

DECISION TOOLKIT

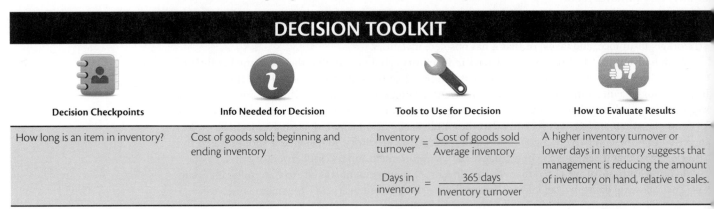

Decision Checkpoints	Info Needed for Decision	Tools to Use for Decision	How to Evaluate Results
How long is an item in inventory?	Cost of goods sold; beginning and ending inventory	$\text{Inventory turnover} = \dfrac{\text{Cost of goods sold}}{\text{Average inventory}}$ $\text{Days in inventory} = \dfrac{\text{365 days}}{\text{Inventory turnover}}$	A higher inventory turnover or lower days in inventory suggests that management is reducing the amount of inventory on hand, relative to sales.

BEFORE YOU GO ON...

➡ **Review It**

1. When should inventory be reported at its net realizable value rather than its cost?
2. Why is it correct to write inventory down to its net realizable value if this amount is less than cost, but inventory cannot be written up to net realizable value if that amount is greater than cost?
3. What is the purpose of the inventory turnover ratio? What is the relationship between the inventory turnover and days in inventory ratios?

➡ **Do It**

E-Warehouse Inc. has five HD DVD players on hand at March 31, 2009, that cost $400 each. Because of an industry switch to Blu-Ray technology, the net realizable value of the DVD players dropped to $100 per unit. (a) Prepare any journal entry required to record the decline in value of the DVD players, assuming E-Warehouse uses a perpetual inventory system. (b) Show how inventory would be reported on E-Warehouse's balance sheet at March 31, 2009.

Action Plan

- Determine the cost of the inventory.
- Determine the net realizable value of the inventory.
- Compare the cost and NRV. Use the lower value to increase the cost of goods sold and record the decline in NRV in an allowance account.
- Present the allowance account separately as a contra asset along with inventory on the balance sheet.

Solution

(a)   The cost of the inventory is $2,000 (5 × $400).
       The net realizable value of the inventory is $500 (5 × $100).

Mar. 31	Cost of Goods Sold ($2,000 – $500)	1,500	
	Allowance to Reduce Inventory to NRV		1,500
	(To record decline in inventory value from original cost of $2,000 to net realizable value of $500)		

(b)

E-WAREHOUSE INC. Balance Sheet March 31, 2009	
Current assets	
Inventory, at cost	$2,000
Less: Allowance to reduce inventory to NRV	1,500
Inventory, at lower of cost and NRV	500

The Navigator

APPENDIX 6A – INVENTORY COST FORMULAS IN PERIODIC SYSTEMS

Both of the inventory cost formulas described in the chapter for a perpetual inventory system may be used in a periodic inventory system. To show how to use FIFO and average in a periodic system, we will use the data below for Wynneck Electronics' Astro Condenser.

study objective 5

Apply the inventory cost formulas—FIFO and average—under a periodic inventory system.

	WYNNECK ELECTRONICS LTD. Astro Condensers			
Date	Explanation	Units	Unit Cost	Total Cost
Jan. 1	Beginning inventory	100	$10	$ 1,000
Apr. 15	Purchase	200	11	2,200
Aug. 24	Purchase	300	12	3,600
Nov. 27	Purchase	400	13	5,200
	Total	1,000		$12,000

These data are the same as what was shown earlier in the chapter, except that the sales information has been omitted. In the periodic inventory system, we ignore the different dates of each of the sales. Instead we make the allocation **at the end of a period** and assume that the entire pool of costs is available for allocation at that time.

Wynneck Electronics had a total of 1,000 units available for sale during the period. The total cost of these units was $12,000. A physical inventory count at the end of the year determined that 450 units remained on hand. Using these data, Illustration 6A-1 shows the formula for calculating cost of goods sold that we first learned in Chapter 5.

▶ Reporting and Analyzing Inventory

Formula for cost of goods sold

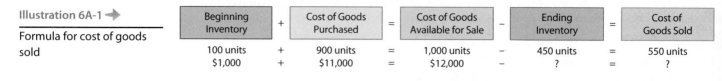

Beginning Inventory	+	Cost of Goods Purchased	=	Cost of Goods Available for Sale	−	Ending Inventory	=	Cost of Goods Sold
100 units	+	900 units	=	1,000 units	−	450 units	=	550 units
$1,000	+	$11,000	=	$12,000	−	?	=	?

If we apply this formula to the unit numbers, we can determine that 550 units must have been sold during the year. The total cost (or "pool of costs") of the 1,000 units available for sale was $12,000. We will demonstrate the allocation of this pool of costs using FIFO and average in the next sections. In a periodic inventory system, the cost formulas are applied to the ending inventory, which is then deducted from the cost of goods available for sale to calculate the cost of goods sold.

Periodic System—First-In, First-Out (FIFO)

Similar to perpetual FIFO, the cost of the oldest goods on hand is allocated to the cost of goods sold. This means that the cost of the most recent purchases is assumed to remain in ending inventory (last-in, still here). The allocation of the cost of goods available for sale at Wynneck Electronics under FIFO is shown in Illustration 6A-2.

Periodic system—FIFO

COST OF GOODS AVAILABLE FOR SALE				
Date	Explanation	Units	Unit Cost	Total Cost
Jan. 1	Beginning inventory	100	$10	$ 1,000
Apr. 15	Purchase	200	11	2,200
Aug. 24	Purchase	300	12	3,600
Nov. 27	Purchase	400	13	5,200
	Total	1,000		$12,000

STEP 1: ENDING INVENTORY				STEP 2: COST OF GOODS SOLD	
Date	Units	Unit Cost	Unit Total		
Nov. 27	400	$13	$5,200	Cost of goods available for sale	$12,000
Aug. 24	50	12	600	Less: Ending inventory	5,800
Total	450		$5,800	Cost of goods sold	$ 6,200

The cost of the ending inventory is determined by taking the unit cost of the most recent purchase and working backward until all units of inventory have been costed. In this example, the 450 units of ending inventory must be costed using the most recent purchase costs. The last purchase was 400 units at $13 on November 27. The remaining 50 units are costed at the price of the second most recent purchase, $12, on August 24.

Once the cost of the ending inventory is determined, the cost of goods sold is calculated by subtracting the cost of the units not sold (ending inventory) from the cost of all goods available for sale (the pool of costs).

The cost of goods sold can also be separately calculated or proven as shown below. To determine the cost of goods sold, simply start at the first item of beginning inventory and count forward until the total number of units sold (550) is reached. Note that of the 300 units purchased on August 24, only 250 units are assumed sold. This agrees with our calculation of the cost of the ending inventory, where 50 of these units were assumed unsold and thus included in ending inventory.

Date	Units	Unit Cost	Total Cost of Goods Sold
Jan. 1	100	$10	$1,000
Apr. 15	200	11	2,200
Aug. 24	250	12	3,000
Total	550		$6,200

Because of the potential for calculation errors, we recommend that the cost of goods sold amounts be separately calculated and proven in your assignments. The ending inventory and cost of goods total can then be compared to the cost of goods available for sale to check the accuracy of the calculations. It would be as follows for Wynneck: $5,800 + $6,200 = $12,000. You will recall that we also did a similar check of our numbers under the perpetual inventory system.

Although the calculation format may differ, the results under FIFO in a periodic inventory system are the **same as in a perpetual inventory system** (see Illustration 6-6 where, similarly, the ending inventory is $5,800 and the cost of goods sold is $6,200). Under both inventory systems, the first costs in are the ones assigned to cost of goods sold.

Periodic System—Average

The weighted average cost is calculated in the same manner as we calculated it in a perpetual inventory system: by dividing the cost of goods available for sale by the units available for sale. The key difference between the two cost formulas is that this calculation is done after each purchase in a perpetual inventory system. In a periodic inventory system, it is done only at the end of the period, as shown in Illustration 6A-3.

Cost of Goods Available for Sale	÷	Units Available for Sale	=	Weighted Average Unit Cost
$12,000	÷	1,000	=	$12

◀ Illustration 6A-3

Calculation of weighted average unit cost

The weighted average unit cost, $12 in this case, is then applied to the units on hand to determine the cost of the ending inventory. The allocation of the cost of goods available for sale at Wynneck Electronics using the average cost formula is shown in Illustration 6A-4.

◀ Illustration 6A-4

Periodic system—Average

COST OF GOODS AVAILABLE FOR SALE				
Date	Explanation	Units	Unit Cost	Total Cost
Jan. 1	Beginning inventory	100	$10	$ 1,000
Apr. 15	Purchase	200	11	2,200
Aug. 24	Purchase	300	12	3,600
Nov. 27	Purchase	400	13	5,200
	Total	1,000		$12,000

STEP 1: ENDING INVENTORY			STEP 2: COST OF GOODS SOLD	
$12,000 ÷ 1,000 = $12			Cost of goods available for sale	$12,000
Units	Unit Cost	Total Cost	Less: Ending inventory	5,400
450	$12	$5,400	Cost of goods sold	$ 6,600

We can verify the cost of goods sold under the average cost formula by multiplying the units sold by the weighted average unit cost (550 × $12 = $6,600). And, again, we can prove our calculations by ensuring that the total of the ending inventory and cost of goods sold equals the cost of goods available for sale ($5,400 + $6,600 = $12,000).

The results from applying the average cost formula under the periodic inventory system should be compared to Illustration 6-8 shown earlier in the chapter, which presents the results from applying the average cost formula under a perpetual inventory system. Notice that under a periodic inventory system the ending inventory of $5,400 and cost of goods sold of $6,600 are not the same as the values calculated under a perpetual inventory system even though the average cost formula was used for both systems. This is because in a perpetual system a new (moving) average is calculated with each purchase; in a periodic system the same weighted average is used to calculate the cost of goods sold for all the units sold during the period.

ALL ABOUT YOU

Inventory Theft—An Inside or Outside Job?

Inventory theft is a huge problem for businesses, whether it is committed by employees or customers. Findings from a recent Ipsos Reid survey indicated that the majority (87 percent) of owners of small and medium-sized retail businesses in Canada have been subject to some form of retail crime in the past 12 months. Employee theft can be reduced by running thorough background checks on prospective employees. Some people have a tendency to steal from the get-go, so it is important on a resumé to look for a lack of references, gaps in employment, or vague reasons for leaving a previous job. Human resources staff should subject potential employees to integrity tests that pose pointed questions like these: Have most people you worked with stolen at one time or another? Do you feel it is acceptable for others to steal?

One of the biggest problems in retail is that the fitting room is a private space, so it is possible to stuff bags with items that have not been purchased or for customers to put on multiple items under their regular clothing. Technology helps a retailer control the fitting room environment in a passive way without customers feeling as though they are being watched. In 2005, Le Château was the first retailer in Canada to implement a new touchscreen/barcode combination technology from Fitting Room Central, of Westmount, Quebec.

The Fitting Room Central solution offers a simple alternative that minimizes the chance of human error. Rather than counting the hangers that customers take into the fitting rooms, the attendants scan each tag so the information on the items—including colour and size—is automatically captured on the touchscreen. The real advantage behind the Fitting Room Central solution is that it ultimately allows retailers to deliver better service, which in itself is a most effective loss prevention tactic.

Some Facts

- Companies that have used integrity tests to interview potential employees have seen inventory shrinkage drop to 1% of sales from 20% because of the weeding out of bad prospects.
- There is a direct correlation between employee satisfaction, loyalty, and theft. Employees often steal to right what they view as a wrong, such as being treated disrespectfully, which in their view, can mean receiving low pay or not being rewarded for putting in extra effort.
- In the last 10 years, employee theft has almost equalled customer losses as the greatest cause of shrinkage.
- Small retailers in Canada who have been a victim of employee theft, customer theft, or break-ins estimate they are losing an average of $1,005 per month.

What do You Think?

Suppose you own a number of camera shops selling mid-level, as well as expensive, cameras and camera equipment. You have been experiencing significant losses from theft at your stores. You suspect that it is a combination of both employee and customer theft. Assuming it would be cost-effective, would you install video cameras to monitor both employees and customers?

YES | Most employees and customers are honest. However, some will steal if they are given the opportunity. Management has a responsibility to employ reasonable, cost-effective approaches to safeguard company assets.

NO | The use of video technology to monitor employees and customers sends a message of distrust. You may alienate your employees. Cameras might also reduce the welcoming atmosphere for your customers, who might find the cameras offensive.

Sources:

Denise Deveau, "Out of the Fitting Rooms, Into the Profits," *Canadian Retailer*, September/October 2007, pp. 22–24.

Randy Ray, "Workplace Theft Takes Big Toll," *Globe and Mail*, August 4, 2004, C1.

Retail Council of Canada, "Eighty Seven Percent of Canada's Small and Medium Sized Retailers Victimized by Crime in the Past Year," News release, January 30, 2008.

The Navigator

Summary of Study Objectives

. Describe the steps in determining inventory quantities. The steps are (1) taking a physical inventory of goods on hand and (2) determining the ownership of goods in transit, on consignment, and in similar situations.

. Apply the methods of cost determination—specific identification, FIFO, and average—under a perpetual inventory system. Costs are allocated to the cost of goods sold account each time that a sale occurs in a perpetual inventory system. The cost is determined by specific identification or by one of two cost formulas—FIFO (first-in, first-out) and average.

Specific identification is used for goods that are not ordinarily interchangeable. This method tracks the actual physical flow of goods, allocating the exact cost of each merchandise item to cost of goods sold and ending inventory.

The FIFO cost formula assumes a first-in, first-out cost flow for sales. Cost of goods sold consists of the cost of the earliest goods purchased. Ending inventory is determined by allocating the cost of the most recent goods purchased to the units on hand.

The average cost formula is used for goods that are homogeneous or non-distinguishable. Under average, a new weighted (moving) average unit cost is calculated after each purchase and applied to the number of units sold and the number of units remaining in ending inventory.

. Explain the financial statement effects of the inventory cost determination methods and of inventory errors. Specific identification results in the best match of costs and revenues on the statement of earnings. When prices are rising, average results in a higher cost of goods sold and lower net earnings than FIFO. Average therefore results in a better match on the statement of earnings of more recent costs with current revenues than does FIFO. In the balance sheet, FIFO results in an ending inventory that is closest to current (replacement) value and the best balance sheet valuation. All three methods result in the same cash flow before income taxes.

An error in beginning inventory will have a reverse effect on net earnings in the current year (e.g., an overstatement of inventory results in an understatement of net earnings). An error in ending inventory will have a similar effect on net earnings (e.g., an overstatement of inventory results in an overstatement of net earnings). If ending inventory errors are not corrected in

the following fiscal year, their effect on net earnings for that year is reversed, and total net earnings for the two years will be correct. In the balance sheet, ending inventory errors will have the same effects on total assets and total shareholders' equity (e.g., an overstatement of inventory results in an overstatement of assets and shareholders' equity), and no effect on liabilities (ignoring income taxes).

4. Demonstrate the presentation and analysis of inventory. Inventory is valued at the lower of its cost and net realizable value, which results in the recording of an increase in cost of goods sold and reduction in inventory when the net realizable value is less than cost. This write-down is reversed if the net realizable value of the inventory increases, but the value of the inventory can never be recorded above the original cost.

Ending inventory is reported as a current asset on the balance sheet at the lower of cost and net realizable value. Cost of goods sold is reported as an operating expense on the statement of earnings. Additional disclosure includes the method of cost determination.

The inventory turnover ratio is a measure of liquidity. It is calculated by dividing the cost of goods sold by average inventory. It can be converted to days in inventory by dividing 365 days by the inventory turnover ratio.

5. Apply the inventory cost formulas—FIFO and average—under a periodic inventory system (Appendix 6A). Under FIFO, the cost of the oldest goods on hand is allocated to the cost of goods sold. The cost of the most recent goods purchased is allocated to ending inventory. Goods available for sale are used to calculate a weighted average cost per unit. This unit cost is then applied to the number of units sold to determine the cost of goods sold and to the number of units remaining to prove the ending inventory.

Each of these cost formulas is applied in the same cost flow order as in a perpetual inventory system. The main difference is that in a perpetual inventory system the cost formula is applied at the date of each sale to determine the cost of goods sold. In a periodic inventory system, the cost formula is applied only at the end of the period.

The Navigator

Glossary

Average cost formula   An inventory cost formula that assumes that the goods available for sale are homogeneous or nondistinguishable. The cost of goods sold and ending inventory are determined using an average cost, calculated by dividing the cost of the goods available for sale by the units available for sale. (p. 289)

Consigned goods   Goods shipped by a consignor, who retains ownership, to a party called the consignee, who holds the goods for sale. (p. 284)

Days in inventory   A liquidity measure of the average number of days that inventory is held. It is calculated as 365 days divided by the inventory turnover ratio. (p. 301)

First-in, first-out (FIFO) cost formula   An inventory cost formula that assumes that the costs of the earliest (oldest) goods acquired are the first to be recognized as the cost of goods sold. The costs of the latest goods acquired are assumed to remain in ending inventory. (p. 287)

Internal control   The methods and measures adopted within an organization to help it achieve reliable financial reporting, effective and efficient operations, and compliance with relevant laws and regulations. (p. 282)

Inventory turnover   A liquidity measure of the number of times, on average, that inventory is sold during the period. It is calculated by dividing the cost of goods sold by the average inventory. Average inventory is calculated by adding the beginning and ending inventory balances and dividing the result by two. (p. 301)

Lower of cost and net realizable value (LCNRV)   A basis for stating inventory at the lower of its original cost and its net realizable value at the end of the period. (p. 298)

Net realizable value (NRV)   The selling price of an inventory item, less any costs required to make the item saleable. (p. 298)

Specific identification method   An inventory costing method used when goods are distinguishable and not ordinarily interchangeable. It follows the actual physical flow of goods, and individual items are specifically costed to arrive at the cost of goods sold and cost of the ending inventory. (p. 285)

Weighted average unit cost   The average cost of inventory weighted by the number of units purchased at each unit cost. It is calculated as the cost of goods available for sale divided by the number of units available for sale. (p. 289)

Analysis Tools (Decision Toolkit Summaries)

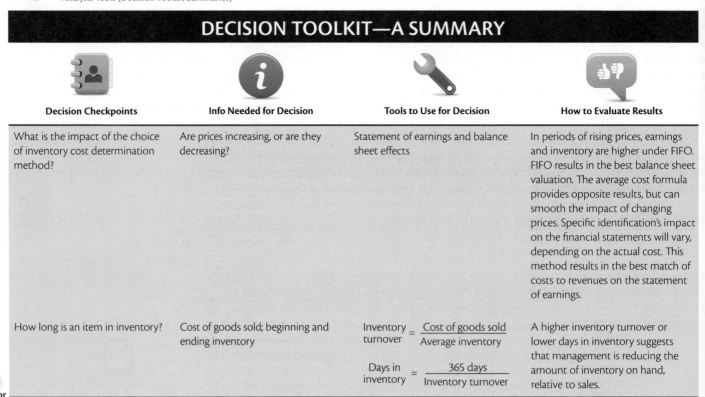

DECISION TOOLKIT—A SUMMARY

Decision Checkpoints	Info Needed for Decision	Tools to Use for Decision	How to Evaluate Results
What is the impact of the choice of inventory cost determination method?	Are prices increasing, or are they decreasing?	Statement of earnings and balance sheet effects	In periods of rising prices, earnings and inventory are higher under FIFO. FIFO results in the best balance sheet valuation. The average cost formula provides opposite results, but can smooth the impact of changing prices. Specific identification's impact on the financial statements will vary, depending on the actual cost. This method results in the best match of costs to revenues on the statement of earnings.
How long is an item in inventory?	Cost of goods sold; beginning and ending inventory	$\text{Inventory turnover} = \dfrac{\text{Cost of goods sold}}{\text{Average inventory}}$ $\text{Days in inventory} = \dfrac{365 \text{ days}}{\text{Inventory turnover}}$	A higher inventory turnover or lower days in inventory suggests that management is reducing the amount of inventory on hand, relative to sales.

The Navigator

Using the Decision Toolkit

CNH (Case New Holland) Global, headquartered in Amsterdam, is the No. 3 maker of construction equipment (trailing Caterpillar and Komatsu). Selected financial information for CNH's inventories follows:

	CNH GLOBAL N.V. Selected Financial Information December 31 (in USD millions)		
	2007	2006	2005
Inventories	$ 3,488	$ 2,735	$ 2,466
Net sales	14,971	12,115	11,806
Cost of goods sold	12,154	9,933	9,934
Net earnings	559	292	163

Selected industry data:

	2007	2006
Inventory turnover	4.5 times	5.0 times
Days in inventory	81 days	73 days
Gross profit margin	21.4%	25.5%
Profit margin	5.5%	7.8%

Instructions

(a) CNH uses the first-in, first-out inventory cost formula. Construction equipment prices have risen over the last two years in response to increased demand. If CNH had used average instead of FIFO, would its gross profit margin and profit margin have been higher or lower than currently reported?

(b) Do each of the following:
1. Calculate the inventory turnover and days in inventory for 2007 and 2006.
2. Calculate the gross profit margin and profit margin for each of 2007 and 2006.
3. Evaluate CNH's performance with inventories over the most recent two years and compare its performance to that of the industry.

Solution

(a) If CNH used the average cost formula rather than FIFO during a period of rising prices, its cost of goods sold would be higher and its gross profit and net earnings lower than currently reported. Because sales prices are not affected by the choice of cost formula, the gross profit margin and profit margin would also be lower.

(b) (in USD millions)

1.

	2007	2006
Inventory turnover	$\dfrac{\$12,154}{(\$3,488 + \$2,735) \div 2} = 3.9$ times	$\dfrac{\$9,933}{(\$2,735 + \$2,466) \div 2} = 3.8$ times
Days in inventory	$\dfrac{365 \text{ days}}{3.9} = 94$ days	$\dfrac{365 \text{ days}}{3.8} = 96$ days

2.

	2007	2006
Gross profit margin	$\dfrac{\$14,971 - \$12,154}{\$14,971} = 18.8\%$	$\dfrac{\$12,115 - \$9,933}{\$12,115} = 18.0\%$
Profit margin	$\dfrac{\$559}{\$14,971} = 3.7\%$	$\dfrac{\$292}{\$12,115} = 2.4\%$

3. CNH's inventory turnover and days in inventory ratios improved marginally in 2007, although they remain below the industry averages. This means that CNH has more inventory on hand and is not selling it as fast as its competitors. It narrowed the gap between its own results and those of its competitors in 2007, as the industry also experienced a decline in inventory turnover.

    CNH's profitability ratios increased in 2007, although the company is still performing below the industry average. In contrast, the industry averages declined in 2007. CNH noted that these were the best annual margins in its history. The company attributed this to its actions to "revitalize our brands, enhance our customer and quality focus, and leverage our global footprint."

The Navigator

Demonstration Problem 1
(Perpetual Inventory System)

Study Tools
(Demonstration Problems)

Englehart Ltd. uses a perpetual inventory system. The company has the following inventory data available for the month of March:

Date	Explanation	Units	Unit Cost	Total Cost
Mar. 1	Beginning inventory	200	$4.30	$ 860
10	Purchase	500	4.50	2,250
15	Sale	(500)		
20	Purchase	400	4.75	1,900
25	Sale	(400)		
30	Purchase	300	5.00	1,500
		500		$6,510

Instructions

Determine the cost of goods sold for March and the cost of the inventory on hand at March 31 under (a) FIFO and (b) average.

Action Plan

- Perpetual inventory records maintain running balances of the ending inventory on hand.

- For FIFO, allocate the first costs to the cost of goods sold at each sale date (the latest costs will be allocated to the ending inventory).

- For average, calculate the weighted average unit cost (the cost of goods available for sale ÷ the number of units available for sale) at each sale date. Multiply this cost by the number of units sold.

- Check that the cost of goods sold plus the ending inventory equals the cost of goods available for sale.

Solution to Demonstration Problem 1 (Perpetual Inventory System)
(a) FIFO

	Purchases			Cost of Goods Sold			Balance		
Date	Units	Cost	Total	Units	Cost	Total	Units	Cost	Total
Mar. 1							200	$4.30	$860
10	500	$4.50	$2,250				200 / 500	4.30 / 4.50	} 3,110
15				200 / 300	$4.30 / 4.50	} $2,210	200	4.50	900
20	400	4.75	1,900				200 / 400	4.50 / 4.75	} 2,800
25				200 / 200	4.50 / 4.75	} 1,850	200	4.75	950
30	300	5.00	1,500				200 / 300	4.75 / 5.00	} 2,450
	1,200		$5,650	900		$4,060			

Check: $4,060 + $2,450 = $6,510 ($860 + $5,650)

(b) Average

	Purchases			Cost of Goods Sold			Balance		
Date	Units	Cost	Total	Units	Cost	Total	Units	Cost	Total
Mar. 1							200	$4.30	$860
10	500	$4.50	$2,250				700	4.44	3,110
15				500	$4.44	$2,221	200	4.44	889
20	400	4.75	1,900				600	4.65	2,789
25				400	4.65	1,859	200	4.65	930
30	300	5.00	1,500				500	4.86	2,430
	1,200		$5,650	900		$4,080			

Check: $4,080 + $2,430 = $6,510 ($860 + $5,650)

Demonstration Problem 2
(Periodic Inventory System–Appendix 6A)

Englehart Ltd. uses a periodic inventory system. The company has the following inventory data available for the month of March:

Date	Explanation	Units	Unit Cost	Total Cost
Mar. 1	Beginning inventory	200	$4.30	$ 860
10	Purchase	500	4.50	2,250
20	Purchase	400	4.75	1,900
30	Purchase	300	5.00	1,500
		1,400		$6,510

The physical inventory count on March 31 shows 500 units on hand.

Instructions

Determine the cost of the inventory on hand at March 31 and the cost of goods sold for March under (a) FIFO and (b) average.

Solution to Demonstration Problem 2 (Periodic Inventory System—Appendix 6A)

(a) FIFO

	Units	Unit Cost	Total Cost
Ending inventory			
Mar. 30	300	$5.00	$1,500
20	200	4.75	950
	500		$2,450

Cost of goods sold: $6,510 – $2,450 = $4,060

Proof of cost of goods sold:

	Units	Unit Cost	Total Cost
Beginning inventory	200	$4.30	$ 860
Mar. 10	500	4.50	2,250
20	200	4.75	950
	900		$4,060

Check: $2,450 + $4,060 = $6,510

(b) Average

Weighted average unit cost: $6,510 ÷ 1,400 = $4.65
Ending inventory: 500 × $4.65 = $2,325
Cost of goods sold: $6,510 – $2,325 = $4,185
Proof of cost of goods sold: 900 × $4.65 = $4,185
Check: $2,325 + $4,185 = $6,510

Action Plan

- In a periodic inventory system, assume that everything happens at the end of the period.

- Allocate costs to ending inventory at the end of the period. Subtract ending inventory from the cost of goods available for sale to determine the cost of goods sold for each method.

- For FIFO, allocate the latest costs to the goods on hand (the first costs will be allocated to the cost of goods sold).

- For average, calculate the weighted average unit cost (the cost of goods available for sale ÷ the number of units available for sale). Multiply this cost by the number of units on hand.

- Prove the cost of goods sold separately and then check that ending inventory plus the cost of goods sold equals the cost of goods available for sale.

The Navigator

Note: All questions, exercises, and problems below with an asterisk (*) relate to material in Appendix 6A.

Self-Study Questions

Answers are at the end of the chapter.

www.wiley.com/canada/kimmel

Study Tools (Self-Assessment Quizzes)

(SO 1) 1. A physical inventory count is normally taken:
  (a) in a periodic inventory system.
  (b) in a perpetual inventory system.
  (c) at the end of the company's fiscal year.
  (d) All of the above

(SO 1) 2. Which of the following should *not* be included in the physical inventory of a company?
  (a) Goods held on consignment from another company
  (b) Goods shipped on consignment to another company
  (c) Goods in transit that have been sold to another company and shipped FOB destination
  (d) Goods in transit that have been purchased from another company and shipped FOB shipping point

(SO 2) 3. The specific identification method should only be used if the inventory consists of:
  (a) homogeneous, nondistinguishable goods.
  (b) non-interchangeable, distinguishable goods.
  (c) high-priced, low-volume goods.
  (d) low-priced, high-volume goods.

(SO 2) 4. Mayerthorpe Inc. uses a perpetual inventory system and has the following beginning inventory, purchases, and sales in March:

	Units	Unit Cost	Total Cost
Inventory, Mar. 1	10,000	$ 9	$ 90,000
Purchase, Mar. 9	12,000	10	120,000
Sale, Mar. 12	(20,000)	?	?
Purchase, Mar. 18	7,000	11	77,000

What is the cost of goods sold using FIFO for the month of March?
  (a) $95,000
  (b) $97,000
  (c) $190,000
  (d) $192,000

(SO 2) 5. Based on the data in question 4, what is the average cost per unit after the last purchase on March 18? Round the per unit cost to the nearest cent in all of your calculations.
  (a) $9.55
  (b) $9.90
  (c) $10.00
  (d) $10.67

(SO 3) 6. ☞ In periods of declining prices, the average cost formula will produce:
  (a) higher net earnings than FIFO.
  (b) the same net earnings as FIFO.
  (c) lower sales than FIFO.
  (d) lower net earnings than FIFO.

7. Lavigne Ltd.'s ending inventory is understated by $4,000. The effects of this error on the current year's cost of goods sold and net earnings, respectively, are:
  (a) an understatement and an overstatement.
  (b) an overstatement and an understatement.
  (c) an overstatement and an overstatement.
  (d) an understatement and an understatement.

8. Avonlea Corp. reported inventory at a cost of $5,000 and a lower of cost and net realizable value of $4,750 at the end of Year 1. At the end of Year 2, it reported inventory at a cost of $6,000 and a lower of cost and net realizable value of $6,500. The balances in the allowance account at the end of Year 1 and Year 2, respectively, are:
  (a) a $250 credit and $500 debit.
  (b) a $250 credit and $250 debit.
  (c) a $250 credit and nil.
  (d) nil and a $500 debit.

9. If a company's cost of goods sold is $120,000, its beginning inventory is $15,000, and its ending inventory is $25,000, what are its inventory turnover and days in inventory?
  (a) 0.2 times and 1,825 days
  (b) 4.8 times and 76 days
  (c) 6 times and 61 days
  (d) 8 times and 46 days

10. ☞ Which of these would cause the inventory turnover ratio to increase the most?
  (a) Increasing the amount of inventory on hand
  (b) Keeping the amount of inventory on hand constant but increasing sales
  (c) Keeping the amount of inventory on hand constant but decreasing sales
  (d) Decreasing the amount of inventory on hand and increasing sales

*11. Kam Ltd. has the following units and costs, and uses a periodic inventory system:

	Units	Unit Cost	Total Cost
Inventory, Jan. 1	8,000	$11	$ 88,000
Purchase, June 19	13,000	12	156,000
Purchase, Nov. 9	5,000	13	65,000
	26,000		$309,000

If 9,000 units are on hand at December 31, what is the cost of the ending inventory using the FIFO cost formula?
  (a) $100,000
  (b) $113,000
  (c) $196,000
  (d) $209,000

*12. Based on the data in question 11, what is the cost of goods sold (rounded to the nearest thousand dollars) using the average cost formula?

(a) $105,000

(b) $107,000

(c) $202,000

(d) $204,000

The Navigator

Questions

1. Your friend Tom Wetzel has been hired to help take the physical inventory in Kikujiro's Hardware Store. Explain to Tom how to do this job, giving him specific instructions for determining the inventory quantities that Kikujiro's has legal title over.

2. What is internal control? How does it apply to taking a physical inventory count?

3. Janine Ltd. ships merchandise to Fastrak Corporation on December 30. The merchandise reaches the buyer on January 5. Indicate the terms of sale (e.g., FOB shipping point or FOB destination) that will result in the goods being included in (a) Janine's December 31 inventory and (b) Fastrak's December 31 inventory.

4. What are consigned goods? Which company, the consignee or the consignor, should include consigned goods in its inventory balance? Explain why.

5. Dave Wier believes that the allocation of the cost of goods available for sale should be based on the actual physical flow of the goods. Explain to Dave why this may be both impractical and inappropriate.

6. Distinguish between the three methods of determining cost for inventories—specific identification, FIFO, and average. Include in your answer the advantages of each method.

7. Identify (a) in what circumstances the specific identification method should be used and (b) the advantages and disadvantages of using this method.

8. Why is specific identification used only in a perpetual inventory system and not in a periodic inventory system?

9. Which of the three inventory cost determination methods assumes that goods available for sale are identical? Assumes that the first goods purchased are the first to be sold? Matches the actual physical flow of merchandise?

10. Which inventory cost formula—FIFO or average—provides the best statement of earnings valuation? The best balance sheet valuation? Explain.

11. What factors should a company consider when it is choosing between the two inventory cost formulas—FIFO and average?

12. Compare the financial effects of using the FIFO and (SO 3) average inventory cost formulas during a period of declining prices on (a) cash (pre-tax), (b) ending inventory, (c) retained earnings, (d) cost of goods sold, and (e) net earnings.

13. If an error in ending inventory in one year will have the (SO 3) reverse effect in the following year, does this error need to be corrected when it is discovered?

14. Mila Ltd.'s ending inventory at December 31, 2009, was (SO 3) understated by $5,000. Assuming that this error is not detected, what effect will it have on (a) 2009 net earnings, (b) 2009 retained earnings, (c) 2010 net earnings, and (d) 2010 retained earnings?

15. A customer took merchandise home on approval before (SO 3) deciding whether or not to purchase it. The clerk recorded this as a sale on the cash register and this transaction was recorded by the accountant. Accounts Receivable was debited and Sales credited, and Cost of Goods Sold was debited and Merchandise Inventory was credited. What effect will this error have on the components of the accounting equation—assets, liabilities, and shareholders' equity—assuming (a) the customer decides to keep the merchandise, and (b) the customer decides to return the merchandise?

16. What is the cost principle of accounting? Why is it not (SO 4) followed when the net realizable value of inventory is less than its cost?

17. Why is the allowance method preferred over the direct method (SO 4) to record a loss from a decline in the net realizable value of inventory below its cost, or a subsequent reversal of this loss?

18. Canadian Tire Corporation, Limited reports merchandise (SO 4) inventory of $756.7 million on its December 29, 2007, balance sheet. What additional disclosures about inventory are you likely to find in the notes to Canadian Tire's financial statements?

19. What are the consequences for a company when its (SO 4) inventory turnover ratio is (a) too high and (b) too low?

20. Would an increase in the days in inventory ratio (SO 4) from one year to the next be viewed as an improvement or a deterioration in how efficiently a company manages its inventory?

(SO 5) *21. Your classmate does not understand the difference between the perpetual and periodic inventory systems. "The same cost formulas are used in both systems," he says, "and a physical inventory count is required in both systems—so what's the difference?" Explain to your confused classmate how the perpetual and periodic inventory systems differ.

(SO 5) *22. In a periodic inventory system, the ending inventory is counted and costed. This number is then used to calculate cost of goods sold. Emad asks, "Why can't you apply the cost formula to determine the cost of goods sold first instead of going through all of these steps?"

*23. Explain why, when a company uses the periodic inventory system, its results under the FIFO cost formula are the same as they would be in a perpetual inventory system.

*24. Explain why, when a company uses the periodic inventory system, its results under the average cost formula are *not* the same as they would be in a perpetual inventory system.

Brief Exercises

Identify items in inventory.
(SO 1)

BE6–1 Helgeson Inc. identifies the following items as possibly belonging in its physical inventory count. For each item, indicate whether or not it should be included in the inventory.

    (a) Goods shipped on consignment by Helgeson to another company

    (b) Goods held on consignment by Helgeson from another company

    (c) Goods sold to a customer, but being held for customer pickup

    (d) Goods in transit to Helgeson from a supplier, shipped FOB destination

    (e) Goods in transit to a customer, shipped FOB destination

Calculate inventory cost.
(SO 1)

BE6–2 The Village Hat Shop Limited counted the entire inventory in its store on August 31 and arrived at a total inventory cost of $65,000. The count included $5,000 of inventory held on consignment for a local designer; $500 of inventory that was being held for customers who were deciding if they actually wanted to purchase the merchandise; and $750 of inventory that had been sold to customers but was being held for alterations. There were two shipments of inventory received on September 1. The first shipment cost $6,000. It had been shipped on August 29, terms FOB destination, with freight charges of $240. The second shipment cost $3,750. It had been shipped on August 28, terms FOB shipping point, with freight charges of $150. Neither of these shipments was included in the August 31 count. Calculate the correct cost of the inventory on August 31.

Match businesses with inventory cost determination method.
(SO 2)

BE6–3 The following are the three inventory cost determination methods:
    1. Specific identification
    2. FIFO
    3. Average

Below is a list of different types of companies and their main inventory item. Beside each one, insert the number of the inventory cost determination method above that the company would most likely use.

        _____ (a) Grocery store (food)
        _____ (b) Brewing company (hops)
        _____ (c) Car dealership (automobiles)
        _____ (d) Gas station (fuel)
        _____ (e) Clothing store (clothing)

Apply specific identification.
(SO 2)

BE6–4 On January 3, Piano Corp. purchased three model EBS electronic pianos for $1,000 each. On January 20, it purchased two more model EBS electronic pianos for $1,200 each. During the month, it sold two pianos; one was purchased on January 3 and the other was purchased on January 20. (a) Calculate the cost of goods sold and ending inventory for the month under specific identification. (b) Explain how management could manipulate earnings, if it wished to, using this method.

Apply perpetual FIFO.
(SO 2)

BE6–5 Akshay Limited uses the FIFO cost formula in a perpetual inventory system. Fill in the missing amounts for items (a) through (k) in the following inventory schedule:

Purchases				Cost of Goods Sold			Balance		
Date	Units	Cost	Total	Units	Cost	Total	Units	Cost	Total
Apr. 1							10	$15	$150
6	15	$14	$210				(a)	(b)	(c)
9				20	(d)	(e)	(f)	(g)	(h)
14	15	13	195				(i)	(j)	(k)

BE6–6   Battory Limited uses the average cost formula in a perpetual inventory system. Fill in the missing amounts for items (a) through (k) in the following inventory schedule:

Apply perpetual average.
(SO 2)

Purchases				Cost of Goods Sold			Balance		
Date	Units	Cost	Total	Units	Cost	Total	Units	Cost	Total
Apr. 1							10	$15	$150
6	15	$14	$210				(a)	(b)	(c)
9				20	(d)	(e)	(f)	(g)	(h)
14	15	13	195				(i)	(j)	(k)

BE6–7   Interactive.com just started business and is trying to decide which inventory cost formula—FIFO or average—to use. Assuming prices are falling, as they often do in the information technology sector, answer the following questions for Interactive.com:

Identify inventory cost
formulas and factors.
(SO 3)

   (a) Which formula will result in the higher ending inventory? Explain.

   (b) Which formula will result in the higher cost of goods sold? Explain.

   (c) Which formula will result in the higher pre-tax cash flow? Explain.

   (d) What factors are important for Interactive.com to consider as it tries to select the most appropriate inventory cost formula?

BE6–8   DuPlessis Corporation incorrectly recorded $25,000 of goods held on consignment for another company as a purchase during the current year. This transaction was recorded by debiting Merchandise Inventory and crediting Accounts Payable. Assuming the company reported net earnings of $90,000 for the year ended December 31, 2009, what is the correct net earnings for 2009 (ignore income taxes)? What effect, if any, will this error have on total assets and shareholders' equity reported in the balance sheet at December 31, 2009?

Determine effect of inventory
error.
(SO 3)

BE6–9   In its year-end physical inventory count, Tire Track Corporation forgot to count tires it had stored outside its warehouse in a trailer. As a result, ending inventory was understated by $7,000. Assuming that this error was not subsequently discovered and corrected, what is the impact of this error on assets, liabilities, and shareholders' equity at the end of the current year? At the end of the next year?

Determine effect of inventory
error for two years.
(SO 3)

BE6–10   Hawkeye Video Centre Ltd. accumulates the following cost and net realizable value data at December 31:

Determine LCNRV valuation.
(SO 4)

Inventory Categories	Cost	NRV
Cameras	$12,000	$11,200
Camcorders	9,000	9,500
DVD players	14,000	12,800

Calculate the lower of cost and net realizable value for Hawkeye's inventory.

BE6–11   The cost of Piper Music Inc.'s inventory at December 31, 2009, is $54,700. Its net realizable value on the same date is $52,500. Prepare the adjusting journal entry required, if any, to record the decline in value of the inventory, assuming Piper Music uses a perpetual inventory system.

Record LCNRV valuation.
(SO 4)

BE6–12   ⚷ The following information (in USD thousands) is available for Limited Brands, Inc., the parent company of Victoria's Secret, La Senza, and Bath & Body Works, among other companies:

Calculate inventory turnover
and days in inventory.
(SO 4)

	2008	2007
Inventories	$ 1,250,625	$ 1,769,974
Net sales	10,134,205	10,670,599
Cost of goods sold	6,592,036	6,657,087

Calculate the inventory turnover and days in inventory ratios for 2008.

Apply periodic FIFO and
average.
(SO 5)

*BE6–13   In its first month of operations, Quilt Inc. made three purchases of merchandise in the following sequence: (1) 250 units @ $6 each, (2) 400 units @ $7 each, and (3) 350 units @ $8 each. A physical inventory count determined that there were 400 units on hand at the end of the month. Assuming Quilt uses a periodic inventory system, calculate the cost of the ending inventory and cost of goods sold under (a) FIFO and (b) average.

Apply periodic FIFO.
(SO 5)

*BE6–14 G-Mac Corporation reports the following inventory data for the month of January:

Date	Explanation	Units	Unit Cost	Total Cost
Jan. 1	Beginning inventory	9	$3.00	$ 27
15	Purchase	12	3.50	42
27	Purchase	14	4.00	56
		35		$125

A physical inventory count determined that there were 10 units on hand at the end of January. (a) Calculate the cost of the ending inventory and cost of goods sold under FIFO, assuming G-Mac uses a periodic inventory system. (b) Would your answers differ if G-Mac used a perpetual inventory system?

Record transactions under
perpetual and periodic FIFO.
(SO 5)

*BE6–15 At the beginning of the year, Seller Ltd. had 700 units with a cost of $3 per unit in its beginning inventory. The following inventory transactions occurred during the month of January:

Jan.   3   Sold 500 units on account for $5 each.
       9   Purchased 1,000 units on account for $4 per unit.
      15   Sold 800 units for cash at $8 each.

Prepare journal entries assuming that Seller Ltd. uses FIFO (a) under a perpetual inventory system and (b) under a periodic inventory system.

Exercises

Identify items in inventory.
(SO 1)

E6–1   Shippers Ltd. had the following inventory situations to consider at January 31, its year end:
1. Goods held on consignment for MailBoxes Etc. since December 22
2. Goods shipped on consignment to Rinehart Holdings Ltd. on January 5
3. Goods that are still in transit and were shipped to a customer FOB destination on January 29
4. Goods that are still in transit and were shipped to a customer FOB shipping point on January 29
5. Goods that are still in transit and were purchased FOB destination from a supplier on January 25
6. Goods that are still in transit and were purchased FOB shipping point from a supplier on January 25
7. Freight costs due on goods in transit from item 6 above
8. Office supplies on hand at January 31

Instructions
Identify which of the above items should be included in inventory. If the item should not be included in inventory, state where it should be recorded.

Determine correct inventory
amount.
(SO 1)

E6–2   Gatineau Bank is considering giving Novotna Corporation a loan. Before doing so, it decides that further discussions with Novotna's accountant may be desirable. One area of particular concern is the inventory account, which has a year-end balance of $281,000. Discussions with the accountant reveal the following:
1. Novotna sold goods costing $35,000 to India-based Moghul Company, FOB shipping point, on December 28. The goods are not expected to arrive in India until January 12. The goods were not included in the physical inventory, because they were not in the warehouse.
2. The physical count of the inventory did not include goods costing $95,000 that were shipped to Novotna, FOB destination, on December 27 and were still in transit at year end.
3. Novotna received goods costing $28,000 on January 2. The goods were shipped FOB shipping point on December 26 by Cellar Corp. The goods were not included in the physical count.
4. Novotna sold goods costing $49,000 to UK-based Sterling of Britain Ltd., FOB destination, on December 30. The goods were received by Sterling on January 8. They were not included in Novotna's physical inventory.

5. On December 31, Schiller Corporation had $30,500 of goods held on consignment for No-
    votna. The goods were not included in the ending inventory of $281,000.

Instructions

Determine the correct inventory amount on December 31.

E6–3   On December 1, Discount Electronics Ltd. has three home entertainment systems left in stock.   *Apply specific identification.*
The purchase dates, serial numbers, and cost of each of the three systems are as follows: *(SO 2)*

Date	Serial Number	Cost
Oct. 1	#1012	$1,500
Nov. 1	#1045	1,400
Nov. 30	#1056	1,300

All three systems are priced to sell at $1,800. At December 31, one system remained in inventory.

Instructions

(a) Explain how Discount Electronics would use specific identification to determine the cost of the
    ending inventory and the cost of goods sold.

(b) Explain how Discount Electronics could manipulate its earnings under specific identification by
    "selectively choosing" which home entertainment system to sell to the two customers in the
    month of December. What would Discount Electronics' cost of goods sold and gross profit be if
    the company wished to minimize earnings? To maximize earnings? Ignore income taxes.

(c) What are the advantages and disadvantages (other than possible manipulation of earnings) of
    using specific identification?

E6–4   Outdoor Experience Ltd. uses a perpetual inventory system and has a beginning inventory, as at   *Apply perpetual FIFO.*
June 1, of 200 tents. This consists of 50 tents at a cost of $200 and 150 tents at a cost of $225. During June,   *(SO 2)*
the company had the following purchases and sales of tents:

	Purchases		Sales	
Date	Units	Unit Cost	Units	Unit Price
June 9			120	$320
12	300	$205		
16			280	320
21	400	210		
24			350	330

Instructions

(a) Determine the cost of goods sold and the cost of the ending inventory using FIFO.

(b) Calculate Outdoor Experience's gross profit and gross profit margin for the month of June.

(c) Is the gross profit determined in part (b) higher or lower than it would be if Outdoor Experience
    had used the average cost formula? Why?

E6–5   Basis Furniture Ltd. uses a perpetual inventory system and has a beginning inventory, as at June 1,   *Apply perpetual average.*
of 500 bookcases at a cost of $125 each. During June, the company had the following purchases and sales   *(SO 2)*
of bookcases:

	Purchases		Sales	
Date	Units	Unit Cost	Units	Unit Price
June 6	1,500	$127		
10			1,000	$200
14	1,200	128		
16			1,600	205
26	1,100	129		

Instructions

(a) Determine the cost of goods sold and the cost of the ending inventory using average.

(b) Calculate Basis Furniture's gross profit and gross profit margin for the month of June.

(c) Is the gross profit determined in part (b) higher or lower than it would be if Basis Furniture had
    used the FIFO cost formula? Why?

Apply perpetual FIFO and
average and compare effects.
(SO 2)

E6–6   Lakshmi Ltd. uses the perpetual inventory system and reports the following inventory transactions for the month of June:

Date	Explanation	Units	Unit Cost	Total Cost
June 1	Inventory	150	$5	$ 750
12	Purchase	230	6	1,380
15	Sale	250		
16	Purchase	490	7	3,430
23	Purchase	175	8	1,400
27	Sale	570		

Instructions

(a) Calculate the cost of goods sold and the cost of the ending inventory under (1) FIFO and (2) average.

(b) Which cost formula results in the higher cost of goods sold? Why?

(c) Which cost formula results in the higher ending inventory? Why?

(d) Which cost formula results in the higher pre-tax cash flow? Why?

Determine effects of inventory
errors for two years.
(SO 3)

E6–7   Seles Hardware Limited reported the following amounts for its cost of goods sold and merchandise inventory:

	2009	2008
Cost of goods sold	$170,000	$175,000
Merchandise inventory	30,000	30,000

Seles made two errors: (1) ending inventory for 2008 was overstated by $3,000 and (2) ending inventory for 2009 was understated by $4,000.

Instructions

(a) Calculate the correct cost of goods sold and merchandise inventory amounts for each year.

(b) Describe the impact of the error on each account in total for the two years.

(c) What journal entry should Seles Hardware have made if it discovered the $3,000 error in inventory in 2008?

(d) Explain why it is important that Seles Hardware correct these errors as soon as they are discovered.

Correct partial statements of
earnings and comment.
(SO 3)

E6–8   Aruba Inc. reported the following partial statement of earnings data for the years ended December 31, 2009 and 2008:

	2009	2008
Sales	$265,000	$250,000
Cost of goods sold	205,000	194,000
Gross profit	60,000	56,000

Merchandise inventory was reported in the current assets section of the balance sheet at $44,000, $52,000, and $49,000 at the end of 2007, 2008, and 2009, respectively. The amounts for 2007 and 2009 are correct. However, the ending inventory at December 31, 2008, is overstated by $10,000.

Instructions

(a) Prepare correct statements of earnings for 2008 and 2009 through to gross profit.

(b) What is the cumulative effect of the inventory error on total gross profit for these two years?

(c) Calculate the gross profit margin for each of these two years, before and after the correction.

(d) In a letter to the president of Aruba, explain what has happened—that is, explain the nature of the error and its effect on the financial statements.

E6–9 Cody Camera Shop Ltd. reports the following cost and net realizable value information for its inventory at December 31:

Record LCNRV valuation.
(SO 4)

	Units	Unit Cost	Unit NRV
Cameras:			
Minolta	5	$175	$160
Canon	7	140	142
Light Meters:			
Vivitar	12	135	129
Kodak	10	115	120

Instructions

(a) Determine the lower of cost and net realizable value of the ending inventory.

(b) Prepare the adjusting journal entry required, if any, to record the lower of cost and net realizable value of the inventory assuming Cody Camera Shop uses a perpetual inventory system.

E6–10 Energy Savings Ltd. reported the following inventory information for the fiscal years ended December 31:

Determine LCNRV valuation for three years; show balance sheet presentation.
(SO 4)

Year	Cost	NRV
2007	$188,000	$176,000
2008	194,000	187,000
2009	173,000	175,000

Instructions

(a) Determine the balance in the allowance account at the end of 2007, 2008, and 2009.

(b) Determine the amount of the loss or gain in each of 2007, 2008, and 2009.

(c) Show how the inventory would be presented on the December 31, 2007, 2008, and 2009 balance sheets.

E6–11 ⚷ This information is available for **Danier Leather Inc.** for three recent years (in thousands):

Calculate inventory turnover, days in inventory, and gross profit margin.
(SO 4)

	2007	2006	2005
Inventory	$ 28,561	$ 32,348	$ 29,031
Net sales	158,099	148,351	166,350
Cost of goods sold	79,565	76,953	82,863

Instructions

Calculate the inventory turnover, days in inventory, and gross profit margin for 2006 and 2007. Comment on any trends.

E6–12 ⚷ The following is a list of unrelated errors or transactions:

Determine impact of transactions on inventory turnover.
(SO 3, 4)

1._____ The accounting clerk made an extension error in calculating inventory that resulted in an overstatement of ending inventory.

2._____ The cost of goods purchased was reduced by moving to a new, cheaper supplier.

3._____ During a time of rising prices, FIFO was misapplied in calculating ending inventory: the oldest costs rather than most recent costs were used in calculating the ending inventory value.

4._____ Goods in transit related to a purchase made FOB shipping point were not recorded in the Merchandise Inventory account, or included in the physical inventory count.

5._____ Operating expenses increased.

Instructions

Indicate whether each the above transactions would increase (+), decrease (−), or have no effect (NE) on the inventory turnover ratio.

*E6–13 Mawmey Inc. uses a periodic inventory system. Its records show the following for the month of May, with 25 units on hand at May 31:

Apply periodic FIFO and average.
(SO 5)

Date	Explanation	Units	Unit Cost	Total Cost
May 1	Inventory	30	$ 8	$240
15	Purchase	45	11	495
24	Purchase	15	12	180
	Total	90		$915

Instructions

Calculate the cost of the ending inventory and cost of goods sold using (a) FIFO and (b) average.

Apply periodic FIFO and average.
(SO 5)

*E6–14 Lakshmi Ltd. reports the following inventory transactions in a periodic inventory system for the month of June. A physical inventory count determined that 225 units were on hand at the end of the month.

Date	Explanation	Units	Unit Cost	Total Cost
June 1	Inventory	150	$5	$ 750
12	Purchase	230	6	1,380
16	Purchase	490	7	3,430
23	Purchase	175	8	1,400

Instructions

(a) Calculate the ending inventory and cost of goods sold under (1) FIFO and (2) average.

(b) For part 2 of instruction (a), explain why the average unit cost is not $6.50 [($5 + $6 + $7 + $8) ÷ 4].

(c) How do the results for instruction (a) differ from E6–6, where the same information was used in a perpetual inventory system?

Apply perpetual and periodic FIFO and average.
(SO 2, 5)

*E6–15 Powder, Inc. sells an Xpert snowboard that is popular with snowboard enthusiasts. The following information shows Powder's purchases and sales of Xpert snowboards during November:

Date	Transaction	Units	Unit Price	Total Sales	Total Cost
Nov. 1	Beginning inventory	25	$295		$ 7,375
5	Purchase	30	300		9,000
12	Sale	(42)	450	$18,900	
19	Purchase	35	305		10,675
22	Sale	(45)	460	20,700	
25	Purchase	20	310		6,200
		23		$39,600	$33,250

Instructions

(a) Calculate the cost of goods sold and ending inventory using FIFO and average, assuming Powder uses a perpetual inventory system.

(b) What would the cost of cost of goods sold and ending inventory be if Powder used FIFO and average in a periodic inventory system?

Record transactions in perpetual and periodic inventory systems.
(SO 2, 5)

*E6–16 Refer to the data provided for Powder in E6–15.

Instructions

(a) Prepare journal entries to record purchases and sales for Powder in a perpetual inventory system under (1) FIFO and (2) average.

(b) Prepare journal entries to record purchases and sales for Powder in a periodic inventory system under (1) FIFO and (2) average.

Problems: Set A

Identify items in inventory.
(SO 1)

P6–1A Banff Limited is trying to determine the value of its ending inventory as at February 28, the company's year end. The accountant counted everything that was in the warehouse, as at February 28, which resulted in an ending inventory valuation of $56,000. However, she did not know how to treat the following transactions, so she chose not to include them in the count, with the exception of item 8:

1. On February 20, Banff received $875 of inventory on consignment from Kananaskis Limited. By February 28, Banff had sold $365 of this inventory for Kananaskis.
2. On February 25, Banff ordered goods costing $750. The goods were shipped FOB shipping point on February 27. The receiving report indicates that Banff received them on March 2.
3. On February 26, Banff shipped goods costing $800 to a customer. The goods were shipped FOB shipping point. The receiving report indicates that the customer received the goods on March 2.
4. On February 26, Canmore Inc. shipped goods FOB destination to Banff. The invoice price was $350 plus $25 for freight. The receiving report indicates that the goods were received by Banff on March 2.
5. On February 27, Banff packaged goods and had them ready for shipping to a customer, FOB destination. The invoice price was $425 plus $20 for freight; the cost of the items was $360. The receiving report indicates that the goods were received by the customer on March 3.

6. Banff had $620 of inventory at a customer's warehouse "on approval." The customer was going to let Banff know whether it wanted the merchandise before March 6.
7. Banff had $570 of its own inventory on consignment at a Jasper craft shop.
8. Banff had damaged goods set aside in the warehouse because they were not saleable. These goods were included in the count at their original cost of $400.

Instructions

(a) For each of the above situations, specify whether the item should be included in ending inventory, and if so, at what amount. For each item that is not included in ending inventory, indicate who owns it and what account, if any, it should have been recorded in.

(b) How much is the revised ending inventory amount?

P6–2A Carolyn's Piano Sales Ltd. has provided you with the following information with respect to its piano inventory for the month of August. The company uses the specific identification method.

Apply specific identification.
(SO 2)

Date	Explanation	Supplier	Serial #	Cost/Unit or Sales Price/Unit
August 1	Inventory	Yamaha	YH6318	$1,500
		Suzuki	SZ5716	1,100
		Suzuki	SZ5824	1,700
		Suzuki	SZ5828	1,600
		Kawai	KG1239	900
		Kawai	KG1268	1,500
		Kawai	KG1520	600
		Steinway	ST0815	1,200
		Steinway	ST8411	2,600
		Steinway	ST0944	2,200
10	Sales	Suzuki	SZ5828	2,700
		Kawai	KG1520	1,400
15	Purchases	Yamaha	YH4418	1,300
		Yamaha	YH5632	1,600
18	Sales	Yamaha	YH4418	2,100
		Steinway	ST0944	3,700
		Kawai	KG1239	1,400
		Suzuki	SZ5824	2,850
22	Purchases	Suzuki	SZ6132	1,800
		Suzuki	SZ6148	1,600
26	Sales	Suzuki	SZ6132	2,900
		Steinway	ST0815	2,000
		Yamaha	YH6318	2,500
		Yamaha	YH5632	2,600

Instructions

(a) Determine the cost of goods sold and ending inventory for the month of August.

(b) Determine the gross profit for the month of August.

(c) Discuss why Carolyn's Piano Sales is likely using the specific identification method.

P6–3A BigFishTackle Co. Ltd. reports the following inventory transactions for its classic fly fishing rods for the month of April. The company uses a perpetual inventory system.

Apply perpetual FIFO and answer questions.
(SO 2, 3)

Date	Explanation	Units	Unit Cost	Total Cost
Apr. 1	Inventory	50	$325	$16,250
6	Purchase	25	350	8,750
9	Sale	45		
14	Purchase	20	355	7,100
20	Sale	30		
28	Purchase	20	360	7,200

Instructions

(a) Determine the cost of goods sold and cost of ending inventory using FIFO.

(b) Assume that BigFishTackle wants to change to the average cost formula. What factors must it consider before making this change?

(c) If the company does change to the average cost formula and prices continue to rise, would you expect the cost of goods sold and ending inventory amounts to be higher or lower than these amounts under FIFO?

Apply perpetual average and discuss errors.
(SO 2, 3)

P6–4A Information for BigFishTackle Co. Ltd. is presented in P6–3A. Assume the same inventory data and that the company uses the perpetual inventory system.

Instructions

(a) Determine the cost of goods sold and cost of ending inventory using average.

(b) When the company counted its inventory at the end of April, it counted only 35 rods on hand. What journal entry, if any, should the company make to record this shortage?

(c) If the company had not discovered this shortage, identify what accounts would be overstated or understated and by what amount. Ignore income taxes.

(d) Identify two things that the company might do to reduce or eliminate such shortages.

Apply perpetual FIFO and average, and compare effects.
(SO 2, 3)

P6–5A Family Appliance Mart Ltd. began operations on May 1 and uses a perpetual inventory system. During May, the company had the following purchases and sales for one of its products:

Date	Purchases		Sales	
	Units	Unit Cost	Units	Unit Price
May 1	100	$18		
6	150	20		
11			200	$35
14	80	22		
21			100	40
27	60	26		

Instructions

(a) Determine the cost of goods sold and cost of ending inventory using (1) FIFO and (2) average.

(b) What factors should Family Appliance Mart consider in choosing between the FIFO and average cost formulas?

(c) Which cost formula produces the higher gross profit and net earnings?

(d) Assume that the Family Appliance Mart chooses to use the cost formula that results in the higher net earnings amount. Can the company change cost formulas each year if the direction of prices change, so that it will always report the higher net earnings amount? Explain.

(e) Which cost formula produces the higher ending inventory valuation?

(f) Which cost formula produces the higher pre-tax cash flow?

Record transactions using perpetual FIFO; apply LCNRV.
(SO 2, 4)

P6–6A You are provided with the following information for G Inc., which purchases all items from Pataki Inc. and makes sales to a variety of customers. All transactions are settled on account. Returns are normally undamaged and are immediately restored to inventory for resale. Both companies use FIFO in a perpetual inventory system; and increased competition has recently reduced the price of the product.

Date	Description	Units	Unit Price
Oct. 1	Beginning inventory	60	$14
5	Purchase	110	13
8	Sale	140	20
10	Sales return	25	20
15	Purchase	35	12
16	Purchase return	5	12
20	Sale	70	16
26	Purchase	15	11

Instructions

    (a) Prepare all journal entries for the month of October for G, the buyer.

    (b) Prepare all journal entries for the month of October for Pataki, the seller.

    (c) Determine the ending inventory amount for G Inc.

    (d) By October 31, G Inc. learns that the product has a net realizable value of $10 per unit. What amount should ending inventory be valued at on the October 31 balance sheet?

P6–7A In its physical inventory count at March 31, 2008, Handspring Corporation excluded inventory that was being held on consignment for Handspring by another company. The goods were sold in the next year and the inventory was correctly stated at March 31, 2009.

Determine effects of inventory errors for two years.
(SO 3, 4)

Instructions

Indicate the effect of this error (overstated, understated, or no effect) on the following:

    (a) Cash at the end of 2008 and 2009

    (b) The cost of goods sold for each of 2008 and 2009

    (c) Net earnings for each of 2008 and 2009

    (d) Retained earnings at the end of 2008 and 2009

    (e) Ending inventory at the end of 2008 and 2009

    (f) The gross profit margin for each of 2008 and 2009

    (g) The days in inventory ratio for each of 2008 and 2009

P6–8A The records of Pelletier Inc. show the following data:

Determine effects of inventory errors for three years.
(SO 3, 4)

	2009	2008	2007
Statement of earnings:			
Sales	$300,000	$312,000	$300,000
Cost of goods sold	258,000	273,000	258,000
Operating expenses	50,000	52,000	50,000
Balance sheet:			
Merchandise inventory	17,000	29,000	17,000

After the company's July 31, 2009, year end, the controller discovers two errors:

    1. Ending inventory in 2007 was understated by $10,000.

    2. The cost of goods purchased recorded in the Merchandise Inventory account for 2008 included $25,000 of merchandise that should have been recorded as a purchase in 2009. The July 31, 2008, and 2009 inventories were correctly calculated.

Instructions

    (a) For each of the three years, prepare both the incorrect and corrected statements of earnings. The income tax rate is 25%.

    (b) What is the combined (total) impact of the errors on retained earnings for the three years before correction? After correction?

    (c) Calculate both the incorrect and corrected inventory turnover ratios for each of 2008 and 2009.

P6–9A Flin Flon Limited sells three products whose prices are sensitive to changes in value. The following inventory information is available for these products at March 31, 2009:

Determine and record LCNRV.
(SO 4)

Product	Units	Unit Cost	Net Realizable Value
A	20	$ 8	$8
B	40	6	7
C	60	10	9

Instructions

    (a) Calculate Flin Flon's inventory at the lower of cost and net realizable value.

    (b) Prepare any journal entry required to record the LCNRV, assuming that Flin Flon uses (1) a periodic inventory system, and (2) a perpetual inventory system.

    (c) What accounting convention and principle underlies the application of the lower of cost and NRV rule?

Record and present LCNRV
valuation for multiple periods.
(SO 4)

P6–10A You have been provided with the following information regarding R-Steel Inc.'s inventory for March, April, and May.

	Steel Inventory (in tonnes)	Cost/Tonne	NRV/Tonne
March 31	3,000	$705	$740
April 30	2,500	735	720
May 31	2,800	725	730

Instructions

(a) Calculate the cost and net realizable value of R-Steel's inventory at (1) March 31, (2) April 30, and (3) May 31.

(b) Prepare any journal entry required to record the LCNRV of the steel inventory at (1) March 31, (2) April 30, and (3) May 31. Assume that R-Steel uses a perpetual inventory system.

(c) Discuss why the journal entries made in part (b) are required under GAAP.

Calculate ratios; comment on
liquidity and effect of cost formulas on ratios.
(SO 3, 4)

P6–11A The following information is available for **PepsiCo, Inc.** (in USD millions):

	2007	2006	2005
Cost of goods sold	$18,038	$15,762	$14,176
Inventories	2,290	1,926	1,693
Current assets	10,151	9,130	10,454
Current liabilities	7,753	6,860	9,406

In the notes to its financial statements, PepsiCo disclosed that it used the FIFO and average cost formulas to determine the cost of 86 percent of its inventory in 2007, and another method to account for the remainder. It did not disclose the allocation of the 86 percent between FIFO and average.

The industry averages for the inventory turnover, days in inventory, and current ratios are as follows:

	2007	2006
Inventory turnover	6.8 times	7.0 times
Days in inventory	54 days	52 days
Current ratio	1.5:1	1.1:1

Instructions

(a) Calculate PepsiCo's inventory turnover, days in inventory, and current ratios for 2007 and 2006. Comment on the company's liquidity over the two years, and in comparison to the industry.

(b) What might be the reason that PepsiCo uses more than one method to determine the cost of its inventory?

(c) If PepsiCo used only the FIFO cost formula to account for its inventory in 2007, instead of FIFO and average, would you expect its inventory turnover ratio to increase or decrease if prices are rising? Explain.

*P6–12A Steward Inc. had a beginning inventory on January 1 of 200 units of Product MLN at a cost of $9 per unit. During the year, purchases were as follows:

	Units	Unit Cost	Total Cost
Feb. 20	600	$10	$6,000
May 5	500	11	5,500
Aug. 12	600	12	7,200
Dec. 8	200	13	2,600

Steward uses a periodic inventory system. At the end of the year, a physical inventory count determined that there were 400 units on hand.

Instructions

(a) Determine the cost of goods available for sale.

(b) Determine the cost of the ending inventory and the cost of goods sold using (1) FIFO and (2) average.

Prepare partial financial statements and assess effects.
(SO 5)

*P6–13A Data for Steward Inc. are presented in P6–12A. Assume that Steward sold product MLN for $20 per unit during the year.

Instructions

(a) Prepare a partial statement of earnings through to gross profit for each of the two cost formulas: (1) FIFO and (2) average.

(b) Show how inventory would be reported in the current assets section of the balance sheet for (1) FIFO and (2) average.

(c) Which cost formula results in the higher inventory amount for the balance sheet? The higher net earnings on the statement of earnings?

*P6–14A You are provided with the following information about Bear River Inc.'s inventory for the month of May:

Date		Description	Units	Unit Cost
May	1	Beginning inventory	15,000	$2.30
	6	Purchase	50,000	2.40
	11	Sale	40,000	
	14	Purchase	60,000	2.60
	21	Sale	75,000	
	27	Purchase	70,000	2.70

Apply perpetual and periodic FIFO. (SO 2, 5)

Instructions

(a) Calculate the ending inventory and cost of goods sold using FIFO in (1) a perpetual inventory system, and (2) a periodic inventory system.

(b) Compare your results for parts 1 and 2 of instruction (a), commenting specifically on any differences or similarities between the two inventory systems.

*P6–15A You are provided with the following information about Lahti Inc.'s inventory for the month of October. Returns are normally undamaged and are restored to inventory for resale.

Date		Description	Units	Unit Cost
Oct.	1	Beginning inventory	60	$24
	9	Purchase	125	26
	12	Purchase return	10	26
	15	Sale	150	
	16	Sales return	5	
	20	Purchase	70	27
	29	Sale	75	

Apply perpetual and periodic average. (SO 2, 5)

Instructions

(a) Calculate the cost of ending inventory and cost of goods sold using average in (1) a perpetual inventory system, and (2) a periodic inventory system.

(b) Compare your results for parts 1 and 2 of instruction (a), commenting specifically on any differences or similarities between the two inventory systems.

Problems: Set B

P6–1B Kananaskis Limited is trying to determine the amount of its ending inventory as at February 28, the company's year end. The accountant counted everything in the warehouse, which resulted in an ending inventory value of $65,000. However, the accountant was not sure how to treat the following transactions, so he did not record them. He has asked for your help in determining whether or not they should be included in inventory:

Identify items in inventory. (SO 1)

1. Kananaskis shipped $875 of inventory on consignment to Banff Corporation on February 20. By February 28, Banff had sold $365 of this inventory for Kananaskis.
2. Kananaskis was holding merchandise at a cost of $490 that had been sold to a customer for $880 on February 23. The merchandise needed some minor alterations before the customer would take possession. The customer paid for the goods on February 23 and will pick them up on March 2 after the alterations are complete.
3. On February 25, Kananaskis shipped goods FOB shipping point to a customer. The invoice price was $350 plus $25 for freight; the cost of the items sold was $280. The receiving report indicates that the goods were received by the customer on March 2.

4. On February 26, Custom Inc. shipped goods FOB shipping point to Kananaskis. The invoice price was $375 plus $30 for freight. The receiving report indicates that the goods were received by Kananaskis on March 2.

5. On February 26, Kananaskis purchased goods costing $750. The goods were shipped FOB destination. The receiving report indicates that Kananaskis received the goods on March 2.

6. On February 27, Kananaskis shipped goods costing $950 to a customer and charged the customer $1,300. The goods were shipped FOB destination. The receiving report indicates that the customer received the goods on March 3.

7. Kananaskis had $630 of inventory isolated in the warehouse. The inventory is designated for a customer who has requested that the goods be shipped on March 10.

8. Also in Kananaskis' warehouse is $400 of inventory that Craft Producers Ltd. shipped to Kananaskis on consignment.

Instructions

(a) For each of the above situations, specify whether the item should be included in ending inventory, and if so, at what amount. For each item that is not included in ending inventory, indicate who owns it and what account, if any, it should have been recorded in.

(b) How much is the revised ending inventory amount?

Apply specific identification.
(SO 2)

P6–2B Dean's Sales Ltd., a Ford dealership, has provided you with the following information with respect to its vehicle inventory for the month of April. The company uses the specific identification method.

Date		Explanation	Model	Serial #	Cost/Unit or Sales Price/Unit
April	1	Inventory	Focus	C63825	$14,000
			Focus	C81362	19,000
			Mustang	G62313	25,000
			Escape	E11396	23,000
			Flex	X3892	26,000
			F-150	F1883	21,000
			F-150	F1921	24,000
	8	Sales	Focus	C81362	21,000
			Mustang	G62313	27,000
	12	Purchases	Mustang	G71811	26,000
			Mustang	G71891	24,000
			Flex	X4212	27,000
			Flex	X4214	30,000
			Escape	E21202	25,000
	18	Sales	Mustang	G71891	26,000
			Flex	X3892	28,000
			F-150	F1921	26,000
			Escape	E21202	27,000
	23	Purchases	F-150	F2182	22,000
			Mustang	G72166	29,000
			Escape	E28268	25,000

Instructions

(a) Determine the cost of goods sold and ending inventory for the month of April.

(b) Determine the gross profit for the month of April.

(c) Discuss why Dean's Sales is likely using the specific identification method.

Apply perpetual FIFO and discuss errors.
(SO 2, 3)

P6–3B Sandoval Skateshop Ltd. reports the following inventory transactions for its Knife series skateboards for the month of April. The company uses a perpetual inventory system.

Date		Explanation	Units	Unit Cost	Total Cost
Apr.	1	Inventory	30	$100	$3,000
	6	Purchase	15	90	1,350
	9	Sale	35		
	14	Purchase	20	85	1,700
	20	Sale	25		
	28	Purchase	20	75	1,500

Instructions

(a) Determine the cost of goods sold and cost of ending inventory using FIFO.

(b) When the company counted its inventory at the end of April, it counted only 23 skateboards on hand. What journal entry, if any, should the company make to record this shortage?

(c) If the company had not discovered this shortage, identify what accounts would be overstated or understated and by what amount.

(d) Identify two things that the company might do to reduce or eliminate such shortages.

P6–4B   Information for Sandoval Skateshop Ltd. is presented in P6–3B. Assume the same inventory data and that the company uses the perpetual inventory system.

Apply perpetual average and answer questions. (SO 2, 3)

Instructions

(a) Determine the cost of goods sold and cost of ending inventory using average.

(b) Assume that the Sandoval wants to change to the FIFO cost formula. What factors must it consider before making this change?

(c) If the company does change to FIFO and prices continue to fall, would you expect the cost of goods sold and ending inventory amounts to be higher or lower than these amounts under average?

P6–5B   Save-Mart Centre Inc. began operations on July 1 and uses a perpetual inventory system. During July, the company had the following purchases and sales:

Apply perpetual FIFO and average, and compare effects. (SO 2, 3)

Date		Purchases		Sales	
	Units	Unit Cost		Units	Unit Price
July 1	4	$ 90			
3				2	$200
8	5	100			
13				4	225
15	3	105			
20				2	245
27				2	245

Instructions

(a) Determine the cost of goods sold and cost of ending inventory using (1) FIFO and (2) average.

(b) What factors should Save-Mart consider in choosing between the FIFO and average cost formulas?

(c) Which cost formula produces the higher gross profit and net earnings?

(d) Assume that Save-Mart chooses to use the cost formula that results in the lower net earnings amount. Can the company change cost formulas each year if the direction of prices changes, so that it will always report the lower net earnings amount? Explain.

(e) Which cost formula produces the higher ending inventory valuation?

(f) Which cost formula produces the higher pre-tax cash flow?

P6–6B   You are provided with the following information for Amelia Inc, which purchases all items from Karina Inc. and makes sales to a variety of customers. All transactions are settled in cash. Returns are usually undamaged and are immediately restored to inventory for resale. Both companies use average in a perpetual inventory system; and increased competition has recently reduced the price of the product.

Record transactions using perpetual average; apply LCNRV. (SO 2, 4)

Date	Description	Units	Unit Price
July 1	Beginning inventory	25	$10
6	Purchase	55	9
8	Sale	70	15
10	Sales return	15	15
15	Purchase	50	8
16	Purchase return	10	8
20	Sale	55	12
27	Purchase	10	7

Instructions

(a) Prepare all journal entries for the month of July for Amelia, the buyer.

(b) Prepare all journal entries for the month of July for Karina, the seller.

(c) Determine the ending inventory amount for Amelia.

(d) By July 31, Amelia learns that the product has a net realizable value of $8 per unit. What amount should ending inventory be valued at on the July 31 balance sheet?

Determine effects of inventory errors.
(SO 3, 4)

P6–7B In its physical inventory count at its February 28, 2008, year end, The Orange Sprocket Corporation included inventory that was being held for another company on consignment. The merchandise was sold in the next year and inventory was correctly stated at February 28, 2009.

Instructions

Indicate the effect of this error (overstated, understated, or no effect) on the following:

(a) Cash at the end of 2008 and 2009

(b) The cost of goods sold for each of 2008 and 2009

(c) Net earnings for each of 2008 and 2009

(d) Retained earnings at the end of 2008 and 2009

(e) Ending inventory at the end of 2008 and 2009

(f) The gross profit margin for each of 2008 and 2009

(g) The inventory turnover ratio for each of 2008 and 2009

Determine effects of inventory errors for three years.
(SO 3, 4)

P6–8B The records of Kmeta Inc. show the following data:

	2009	2008	2007
Statement of earnings:			
Sales	$330,000	$320,000	$300,000
Cost of goods sold	225,000	229,000	216,000
Operating expenses	66,000	64,000	64,000
Balance sheet:			
Merchandise inventory	40,000	35,000	24,000

After the company's July 31, 2009, year end, the accountant discovers two errors:

1. Ending inventory at the end of 2007 was actually $33,000, not $24,000.
2. The cost of goods purchased amount that was recorded in the Merchandise Inventory account for 2008 included $20,000 of merchandise that should have been recorded as a purchase in 2009. The July 31, 2008, inventory was correctly calculated.

Instructions

(a) For each of the three years, prepare both incorrect and corrected statements of earnings. The income tax rate is 25%.

(b) What is the combined (total) impact of these errors on retained earnings for the three years before correction? After correction?

(c) Calculate both the incorrect and corrected inventory turnover ratios for 2008 and 2009.

Determine and record LCNRV.
(SO 4)

P6–9B Tascon Corporation sells coffee beans, which are sensitive to price fluctuations. The following inventory information is available for this product at December 31, 2009:

Coffee Bean	Units	Unit Cost	Net Realizable Value
Coffea Arabica	13,000 bags	$5.30	$5.50
Coffea Robusta	5,000 bags	3.50	3.25

Instructions

(a) Calculate Tascon's inventory at the lower of cost and net realizable value.

(b) Prepare any journal entry required to record the LCNRV, assuming that Tascon uses (1) a periodic inventory system, and (2) a perpetual inventory system.

(c) What accounting convention and principle underlies the application of the lower of cost and NRV rule?

P6–10B You have been provided with the following information regarding Love's Paper Ltd.'s inventory for June, July, and August.

Record and present LCNRV valuation for multiple periods. (SO 4)

Paper Inventory (in tonnes)		Cost/Tonne	NRV/Tonne
June 30	5,000	$760	$850
July 31	6,700	880	815
August 31	5,500	825	820

Instructions

(a) Calculate the cost and net realizable value of Love Paper's paper inventory at (1) June 30, (2) July 31, and (3) August 31.

(b) Prepare any journal entry necessary to record the LCNRV of the paper inventory at (1) June 30, (2) July 31, and (3) August 31. Assume that Love Paper uses a perpetual inventory system.

(c) Discuss why the journal entries made in part (b) are required under GAAP.

P6–11B The following information is available for The Coca-Cola Company (in USD millions):

Calculate ratios; comment on liquidity and effect of cost formulas on ratios. (SO 3, 4)

	2007	2006	2005
Cost of goods sold	$10,406	$ 8,164	$ 8,195
Inventory	2,220	1,641	1,379
Current assets	12,105	8,441	10,205
Current liabilities	13,225	8,890	9,836

In the notes to its financial statements, Coca-Cola disclosed that it uses the FIFO and average cost formulas to determine the cost of its inventory.

The industry averages for the inventory turnover, days in inventory, and current ratios are as follows:

	2007	2006
Inventory turnover	6.8 times	7.0 times
Days in inventory	54 days	52 days
Current ratio	1.5:1	1.1:1

Instructions

(a) Calculate Coca-Cola's inventory turnover, days in inventory, and current ratios for 2007 and 2006. Comment on the company's liquidity over the two years, and in comparison to the industry.

(b) What might be the reason that Coca-Cola uses more than one method to determine the cost of its inventory?

(c) If Coca-Cola used only the average cost formula to account for its inventory in 2007, instead of FIFO and average, would you expect its inventory turnover ratio to increase or decrease if prices are rising? Explain.

*P6–12B Kane Ltd. had a beginning inventory on January 1 of 250 units of Product SXL at a cost of $16 per unit. During the year, purchases were as follows:

Apply periodic FIFO and average. (SO 5)

	Units	Unit Cost	Total Cost
Mar. 15	700	$15	$10,500
July 20	500	14	7,000
Sept. 4	450	13	5,850
Dec. 2	100	12	1,200

Kane uses a periodic inventory system. At the end of the year, a physical inventory count determined that there were 200 units on hand.

Instructions

(a) Determine the cost of goods available for sale.

(b) Determine the cost of the ending inventory and the cost of the goods sold using (1) FIFO and (2) average.

Prepare partial financial statements and assess effects.
(SO 5)

*P6–13B Data for Kane Ltd. are presented in P6–12B. Assume that Kane sold product SXL for $20 per unit during the year.

Instructions

(a) Prepare a partial statement of earnings through to gross profit for each of the two cost formulas: (1) FIFO and (2) average.

(b) Show how inventory would be reported in the current assets section of the balance sheet for (1) FIFO and (2) average.

(c) Which cost formula results in the lower inventory amount for the balance sheet? The lower net earnings for the statement of earnings?

Apply perpetual and periodic FIFO.
(SO 2, 5)

*P6–14B You are provided with the following information about Lynk Inc.'s inventory for the month of June:

Date	Description	Units	Unit Cost
June 1	Beginning inventory	25	$60
4	Purchase	85	64
10	Sale	80	
18	Purchase	35	68
19	Purchase return	10	68
25	Sale	50	
26	Sales return	5	
28	Purchase	20	72

Instructions

(a) Calculate the cost of ending inventory and cost of goods sold using FIFO in (1) a periodic inventory system, and (2) a perpetual inventory system.

(b) Compare your results for parts 1 and 2 of instruction (a), commenting particularly on any differences or similarities between the two inventory systems.

Apply perpetual and periodic average.
(SO 2, 5)

*P6–15B You are provided with the following information about Apple River Inc.'s inventory for the month of November:

Date	Description	Units	Unit Cost
Nov. 1	Beginning inventory	100	$20
4	Purchase	500	22
11	Sale	400	
16	Purchase	700	24
20	Sale	800	
27	Purchase	600	25

Instructions

(a) Calculate the ending inventory and cost of goods sold using average in (1) a perpetual inventory system, and (2) a periodic inventory system.

(b) Compare your results for parts 1 and 2 of instruction (a), commenting specifically on any differences or similarities between the two inventory systems.

BROADENING YOUR PERSPECTIVE

Financial Reporting and Analysis Cases

Financial Reporting: *Shoppers Drug Mart*

BYP6–1 The financial statements of Shoppers Drug Mart are presented in Appendix A at the end of this book.

Instructions

(a) What amounts did Shoppers Drug Mart report for inventories in its balance sheet at the end of fiscal 2007 and 2006?

www.wiley.com/canada/kimmel

Analysis Tools

(b) Calculate the change in the dollar amount of inventories between 2007 and 2006 and the percentage change. Next calculate inventory as a percentage of current assets for each of the two years. Comment on the results.

(c) Shoppers Drug Mart uses the FIFO cost formula. Do you think that using a different cost formula would change Shoppers' results significantly?

(d) What factors should Shoppers consider when choosing between the FIFO and average cost formulas?

Comparative Analysis: *Shoppers Drug Mart and Jean Coutu*

BYP6–2 The financial statements of Jean Coutu are presented in Appendix B following the financial statements for Shoppers Drug Mart in Appendix A.

Instructions

(a) Calculate the following ratios for Shoppers Drug Mart for the year ended December 29, 2007, and for Jean Coutu for the year ended March 1, 2008:

1. Current ratio

2. Sales to inventory (Note: Because Shoppers does not separately disclose its cost of goods sold, its inventory turnover cannot be calculated. However, dividing net sales by average inventory will give us a comparable substitute for this measure).

(b) The industry average for the current ratio is 1.1:1 and the sales to inventory number is 13.1 times. What conclusions about each company's liquidity can you draw based on your results in (a) and the industry averages?

Interpreting Financial Statements

BYP6–3 The following information was taken from the December 31, 2007, financial statements of MEGA Brands Inc., which states its inventories at the lower of FIFO and net realizable value (in USD thousands):

	2007	2006	2005
Inventories	$ 91,681	$140,630	$ 82,280
Cost of goods sold	403,358	328,822	214,668

Instructions

(a) Calculate the company's inventory turnover and days in inventory ratios for 2007 and 2006. Comment on whether MEGA Brands' management of its inventory improved or deteriorated from 2006 to 2007.

(b) Assume that MEGA Brands' net realizable value has declined below the cost of its inventory by U.S. $100,000. Prepare the journal entry to record this decline, assuming that the company uses a perpetual inventory system.

A Global Focus

BYP6–4 The following information is from the December 31 financial statements of Japan-based Canon Inc. (in millions of yen) and U.S.-based competitor Eastman Kodak (in USD millions):

	Canon (JPY millions)		Eastman Kodak (USD millions)	
	2007	2006	2007	2006
Inventories	¥ 563,474	¥ 539,057	$ 943	$1,001
Cost of goods sold	2,234,365	2,096,279	7,785	8,159

International Resources

Additional information comes from the notes to the financial statements:

CANON	EASTMAN KODAK
Note 1. Basis of presentation and significant accounting policies	*Note 1. Summary of significant accounting policies*
Inventories are stated at the lower of cost or net realizable value. Cost is determined principally by the average method for domestic inventories and the first-in, first-out method for overseas inventories.	Inventories are stated at the lower of cost or net realizable value. The cost of all the Company's inventories is determined by either the FIFO or average cost method, which approximates current cost.

Instructions

(a) What is the likely reason that Canon and Kodak use two different cost formulas to account for their inventories? In particular, what is the probable reason for Canon to be using different methods to account for its domestic and overseas inventories?

(b) Calculate the inventory turnover and days in inventory ratios of the two companies for 2007. Comment on your findings.

(c) What does the statement "stated at the lower of cost and net realizable value" in the notes to the financial statements mean?

Critical Thinking Cases and Activities

Collaborative Learning Activity

BYP6–5 BigBox Distributors Limited is reviewing its year-end inventory calculations. It uses the FIFO cost formula, with inventory valued at the end of each year.

The company had $3.8 million of inventory at the beginning of the year and $4.5 million at the end of the year. During the year, it purchased $40.7 million of inventory and sold $40 million. It uses the FIFO cost formula in a perpetual inventory system.

The following items are unresolved and have not yet been reflected in the figures above:

1. Shipping logs show $2 million of goods in transit to customers, shipped FOB shipping point.

2. Shipping logs show $1.5 million of goods in transit to customers, shipped FOB destination.

3. The showroom contains $200,000 of a supplier's customized products held on consignment.

4. The electronic equipment included in ending inventory is recorded at its cost of $300,000. The manufacturer has discontinued these models of equipment so their sales value has been greatly reduced. The net realizable value of this equipment is $50,000.

5. A new clerk in the wireless products department calculated FIFO incorrectly for some of the inventory. The ending inventory was determined to have a FIFO cost of $175,000 but should have been $135,000 instead.

Instructions

With the class divided into groups, do the following:

(a) Discuss each of the five unresolved items and determine the effect of each error on the reporting cost of goods sold amount of $40 million and ending inventory amount of $4.5 million.

(b) Compare your final inventory and cost of goods sold figures to those of another group. Reconcile any differences.

(c) The industry's average inventory turnover is 10 times per year. Calculate BigBox's inventory turnover using the corrected figures you determined in (a) to determine how it compares to the industry average.

(d) When you are reporting your results on inventory turnover to BigBox's management team, the VP Sales states, "I don't care about inventory turnover numbers. As long as I meet my sales targets, we'll be profitable." Evaluate this statement. What is the relationship between turnover and profit?

Communication Activity

BYP6–6 You are the controller of Kitchen Accessories Inc. and you are meeting with the sales manager to discuss the selling prices of the company's inventory. You have discovered that the current sales price list for the inventory is less than what the company paid for the inventory. The sales manager tells you that you must have recorded the incorrect cost of the inventory when it was purchased. You explain to the sales manager that the inventory was purchased some time ago from a wholesaler in the United States. Since the time of the purchase of the inventory, the value of the U.S. dollar has declined in comparison to the value of the Canadian dollar. New inventory can be purchased today at a lower cost than was possible in the past; and the company has had to reduce its selling prices. The result is that the company's inventory on hand has a cost that is greater than its selling price. The sales manager says, "Well, you have to be creative and do something with the cost of the inventory, because my sales people work on commission and need to earn a profit on the inventory sold."

Instructions

Write a memo to Joy Small, the president of Kitchen Accessories Inc., and explain what has happened and what should be done in regard to the value of the inventory. Include in your memo the names of accounts and financial statements that will be affected by any adjustments you may recommend.

Ethics Case

BYP6–7 You are provided with the following information for Discount Diamonds Ltd. Discount only carries one brand and size of diamond—all are identical. Each batch of diamonds purchased is carefully coded and marked with its purchase cost.

Mar.	1	Beginning inventory is 140 diamonds at a cost of $300 per diamond.
	3	Purchased 200 diamonds at a cost of $340 each.
	5	Sold 170 diamonds for $600 each.
	10	Purchased 340 diamonds at a cost of $370 each.
	25	Sold 500 diamonds for $650 each.

Instructions

(a) Assuming that Discount Diamonds uses the specific identification cost determination method, do the following:
   1. Show how Discount Diamonds could maximize its gross profit for the month by selecting which diamonds to sell on March 5 and March 25.
   2. Show how Discount Diamonds could minimize its gross profit for the month by selecting which diamonds to sell on March 5 and March 25.

(b) Assuming that Discount Diamonds uses a perpetual inventory system and the average cost formula, how much gross profit would Discount Diamonds report?

(c) Which method of cost determination—specific identification or average—should Discount Diamonds select? Explain.

(d) Who are the stakeholders in this situation? Is there anything unethical in choosing which diamonds to sell in a month?

"All About You" Activity

BYP6–8 In the "All About You" feature in this chapter, you learned about inventory theft. Suppose, after graduating, that you accept a job as a manager for a retail store that sells high-end leather goods.

Instructions

(a) Based on what you have learned about internal control in this chapter (we will learn more in the next chapter), identify any internal control measures that you think should be in place in your store to safeguard the inventory.

(b) Assume the store uses a perpetual inventory system. At year end, a physical inventory count determines that the physical count differs from the inventory account balance on your books. Identify any accounts that would be affected by an adjusting journal entry to update the inventory value.

(c) Given that the inventory in the store is leather goods of high value and inventory prices are rising, what method of cost determination would you recommend the store use? Why?

Serial Case

(*Note:* This is a continuation of the serial case from Chapters 1 through 5.)

BYP6–9 Natalie is busy establishing both divisions of Cookie Creations (cookie classes and mixer sales) and completing her business degree. She has decided to concentrate her efforts on mixers for the next while, and try to sell at least one mixer a month.

The cost of the deluxe European mixers is expected to increase. New terms have just been negotiated with Kzinski that include shipping costs in the negotiated purchase price (mixers will be shipped FOB destination). The invoice price will be in Canadian dollars and will depend on the foreign exchange rate when Kzinski prepares its invoices for Cookie Creations. (Kzinski sets its mixer price in Euros). Natalie has chosen to use the FIFO cost formula.

The following transactions occur between the months of May and August, 2009:

May	4	Two deluxe mixers are purchased on account from Kzinski Supply Corp. for $1,100 ($550 each), FOB destination, terms n/30.
	14	One deluxe mixer is sold for $1,050 cash.
	25	Amounts owing to Kzinski are paid.
June	2	One deluxe mixer is purchased on account from Kzinski for $567, FOB destination, terms n/30.
	29	Two deluxe mixers are sold for a total of $2,100 cash.
	30	Amounts owing to Kzinski are paid.
July	3	Two deluxe mixers are purchased on account from Kzinski for $1,122 ($561 each), FOB destination, terms n/30.
	13	Three deluxe mixers are sold on account for a total of $3,150 cash.
	28	Amounts owing to Kzinski are paid.
Aug.	4	Three deluxe mixers are purchased on account from Kzinski for $1,720 ($573.33 each), FOB destination, terms n/30.
	25	One deluxe mixer is sold for $1,050 cash.

Natalie is finding it tedious to track the inventory information using FIFO in a perpetual inventory system. She wonders whether using FIFO in a periodic inventory system would save her both time and effort.

Instructions

(a) Using FIFO in a perpetual inventory system, prepare a schedule to track the purchases and sales of mixers, and the balance of the mixers inventory account. Use the format from Illustration 6-6. Recall from Chapter 5 that at the end of April, Cookie Creations had three mixers on hand at a cost of $545 each.

(b) Address Natalie's concerns. What would be the likely difference in the results using a perpetual or periodic inventory system? What are the differences in information provided by each of these systems? Which inventory system—perpetual or periodic—would you recommend that Cookie Creations use and why?

Answers to Chapter Questions

Answer to Shoppers Drug Mart Review It Question 4

Shoppers Drug Mart uses the FIFO (first-in, first-out) method to determine the cost of its inventories.

Answers to Self-Study Questions

1. d   2. a   3. b   4. c   5. d   6. a   7. b   8. c   9. c   10. d   *11. b   *12. c

Remember to go back to the beginning of the chapter to check off your completed work!

←

Comprehensive Case: Chapter 6

Precision Drilling Products Inc. has started to stock a new product, #57ABX, as of June 1 of the current year. The product is an active RFID chip that can broadcast the status of the remote electronic equipment it is attached to. Because of the product's high copper and silicon content, its price is extremely vulnerable to volatility in the international commodities markets.

Precision uses a perpetual inventory system. The purchase and sales data for #57ABX for the month of June follow:

Purchase Data				Sales Data	
Date	Quantity	Unit Cost	Total Cost	Date	Quantity
June 2	500	$65.00	$ 32,500	June 4	200
5	300	70.00	21,000	15	750
15	450	85.00	38,250	21	800
20	1,000	82.00	82,000	26	600
25	350	90.00	31,500	28	500
27	300	91.50	27,450		2,850
30	1,000	87.50	87,500		
	3,900		$320,200		

Instructions

(a) Calculate the cost of ending inventory using the (1) FIFO and (2) average cost formulas. Round your answers to the nearest cent.

(b) Prepare all required journal entries for the June purchase and sale transactions using (1) FIFO and (2) average. Assume that the selling price was consistent throughout the month at $100 per unit. Assume that all purchases and sales are on account.

(c) Create a table comparing the gross profit for this product's sales for the month of June under each of the two formulas (1) FIFO and (2) average. Calculate the gross profit margin under each formula.

(d) What factors should Precision consider in choosing between the FIFO and average cost formulas?

CHAPTER 7
Internal Control and Cash

Counting Out the Money

On any given evening, students and the after-work crowd gather at the Granite Brewery and Ginger's Tavern, enjoying pub snacks and live entertainment, not to mention quality ale brewed by owner Kevin Keefe.

The brewery and pub, which employs 10 people, has become something of a Halifax institution since it first opened in 1987. Indeed it became popular so quickly that in 1991 Kevin's brother Ron opened a second location in Toronto, Ontario, and later, in 2008, another brew pub was added in Windsor, Nova Scotia.

The brewery and pub takes in approximately $500,000 in annual sales, all of which flows through the hands of the wait staff and bartenders. Office manager Denise Avery says there's a detailed system to track it all, with the pub's POS (point-of-sale) system tracking the orders, inventory, and money.

Depending on the day of the week and whether there is any entertainment that night—there usually is and it ranges from bands to comedy acts to poetry readings—one to four servers work each shift. "Each server has an employee number and they ring in the items they require," Ms. Avery explains. The order information is then passed to the bar or kitchen, where the bartender or kitchen staff receive a slip indicating the order. The servers pick up the orders when filled and collect the money from the patrons. At the end of each server's shift, the POS system provides an employee report that itemizes the credit card, debit card, and cash sales that the server owes.

As the bartenders are given a float of $200 at the beginning of their shift—unlike the servers, who must bring their own float—they are responsible for turning in that amount plus their total cash receipts at the end of the day.

Internal control is straightforward since the POS system also tracks the inventory. The register is preprogrammed with the cost of each item and staff simply press a labelled button, for example, "domestic beer" or "club sandwich," rather than punch in numbers. "That eliminates a lot of problems," Ms. Avery says, "since we know what items have been sold."

Two to four bartenders work at the pub's two bars each day on two separate shifts. "When they come in to work, the first thing they do is count the inventory in the fridge—bottles of beer, pop, juice, and wine—and read the meters on each ale," explains Ms. Avery. "At the end of the shift, they do another count with the next bartender, who in turn rings off at closing." Everything must correspond to the POS system. For example, if three beers are missing from the fridge, three beers should have been entered in the system. If they weren't, the bartender is responsible.

"With a good system, discrepancies just don't happen often," Ms. Avery says. "If ever there is one, it's usually pretty easy to find the problem."

While cash is an obvious concern for internal control, these days fewer customers actually pay with cash. Ms. Avery estimates that about 75 percent of sales are paid for by debit or credit card, so actual cash makes up about a quarter of a day's receipts. "At the end of the day–or more realistically, the next morning," laughs Ms. Avery, "I prepare the deposit and take the cash to the bank."

While there may be fewer cash transactions than in the past, cash control remains crucial to a business like the brewery and pub. Fortunately, with a carefully thought-out system and the help of the latest technology, cash can be controlled reliably and fairly easily. And as far as Ms. Avery is concerned, that's a good thing—Mr. Keefe doesn't like to be bothered with daily problems. With an effective system running things smoothly, he prefers to spend his time brewing great beer.

nite Brewery: granitebrewery.ca

UDY OBJECTIVES

er studying this chapter, you should be able to:

Explain the activities that help achieve internal control.

Apply control activities to cash receipts and payments.

Prepare a bank reconciliation.

Explain the reporting and management of cash.

Navigator

✓ THE NAVIGATOR

☐ Read *Feature Story*

☐ Scan *Study Objectives*

☐ Read *Chapter Preview*

☐ Read text and answer *Before You Go On*

☐ Read *All About You*

☐ Review *Summary of Study Objectives*

☐ Review *Using the Decision Toolkit—A Summary*

☐ Work *Using the Decision Toolkit*

☐ Work *Demonstration Problem*

☐ Answer *Self-Study Questions*

☐ Complete assignments

PREVIEW OF CHAPTER 7

Cash is the lifeblood of any company. Large and small companies alike must guard it carefully. Even companies that are successful in every other way can go bankrupt if they fail to manage their cash well. Managers must know both how to use cash efficiently and how to control it, as described in the feature story. In this chapter, we explain the essential features of an internal control system and describe how these controls apply to cash receipts and cash payments. We then explain how cash is reported in the financial statements, and describe ways to manage and monitor cash.

The chapter is organized as follows:

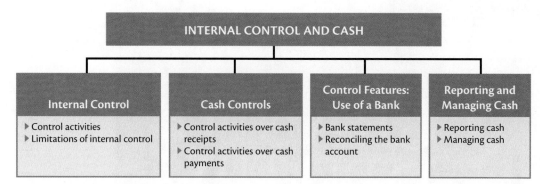

INTERNAL CONTROL AND CASH

Internal Control	Cash Controls	Control Features: Use of a Bank	Reporting and Managing Cash
▶ Control activities ▶ Limitations of internal control	▶ Control activities over cash receipts ▶ Control activities over cash payments	▶ Bank statements ▶ Reconciling the bank account	▶ Reporting cash ▶ Managing cash

The Navigator

Internal Control

study objective 1

Explain the activities that help achieve internal control.

According to research conducted recently by the Association of Certified Fraud Examiners, companies lose an estimated 5 percent of revenues annually due to fraudulent activities committed by their own employees. The association found that most of the fraud was committed by the accounting department or management. The next most commonly cited department was sales. Findings like these emphasize the need for a good system of internal control.

You were first introduced to the need for internal control in Chapter 6. As mentioned in that chapter, **internal control** consists of all the related methods and measures adopted within a company to help it achieve reliable financial reporting, effective and efficient operations, and compliance with relevant laws and regulations. Good internal control systems have the five primary components listed here:

- **Control environment**: It is the responsibility of management to make it clear that the organization values integrity, and that unethical activity will not be tolerated (often referred to as "setting the tone at the top").
- **Risk assessment**: Companies must identify and analyze the various factors that create risk for the business and determine how to manage these risks.
- **Control activities**: To reduce the occurrence of fraud, management must design policies and procedures to address the specific risks faced by the company.
- **Information and communication**: The system must capture and communicate all pertinent information both down and up the organization and communicate it to appropriate external parties.
- **Monitoring**: Internal control systems must be monitored periodically for their adequacy. Significant deficiencies need to be reported to management and/or the board of directors.

The importance of internal control to the efficient and effective operation of a company cannot be overestimated. All federally incorporated companies are required under the *Canada Business Corporations Act* to maintain an adequate system of internal control. In addition, the Canadian Securities Administrators require CEOs and CFOs of large publicly traded Canadian companies to evaluate the effectiveness of their internal control over financial reporting and discuss their conclusions in the company's annual management discussion and analysis (MD&A).

Control Activities

Each of the five components of an internal control system is important. However, we will now focus on one of these components in particular: the control activities. The reason? These activities are the backbone of a company's efforts to address the risks it faces.

The specific control activities that are used by a company will vary depending on management's assessment of these risks. This assessment is also heavily influenced by the size and nature of the company. Control activities that apply to most companies include the following:

- Authorization of transactions and activities
- Segregation of duties
- Documentation
- Physical controls
- Independent checks of performance
- Human resource controls

Each of these control activities is explained in the following sections.

Authorization of Transactions and Activities

An essential characteristic of internal control is the assignment of responsibility to specific employees. This control activity is most effective when **only one person is authorized to perform a specific task**.

To illustrate, assume that the cash on hand at the end of the day is $10 short of the cash rung up on the cash register. If only one person has operated the register, responsibility for the shortage can be attributed quickly. If two or more individuals have worked the same register, however, it may be impossible to determine who is responsible for the error unless each person is given a separate cash drawer or has their own employee report, as is done at the Granite Brewery and Ginger's Tavern described in the feature story.

Establishing responsibility is significantly easier when there is a system for proper authorization. For example, the automated systems that are used by companies typically require the use of identifying pass codes. These pass codes ensure that only authorized personnel may access the system. They also enable the company to establish responsibility by identifying the particular employee who carried out an activity. This is the case at the brewery and tavern, where each employee has their own employee number that they use to access the point-of-sale system.

Another example of assigning responsibility is the common practice of not allowing cashiers to reverse their own entry errors. A supervisor must insert a key or type a password to authorize the correction.

In addition, it is important that policies be established by the right individuals or departments. For example, the vice-president of finance should establish policies for making credit sales, not the vice-president of sales. The policies that are established also typically require written credit approval for sales transactions above a certain value. For example, sales on account amounting to more than $1,000 require written credit approval.

Segregation of Duties

Segregation of duties is essential in a system of internal control because the responsibility for related activities should be assigned to different individuals. **When the same individual is responsible for related activities, the potential for errors and irregularities is increased.** In general, the following categories of activities should be separated from one another: authorization of transactions and activities (which we discussed above), recording of transactions, and custody of assets.

As an example, consider what could happen if related purchasing activities were carried out by the same individual. These include ordering merchandise, receiving goods, and paying (or authorizing payment) for merchandise. In purchasing, orders could be placed with friends or with suppliers who give kickbacks. In addition, payment might be authorized without a careful review of the invoice or, even worse, fictitious invoices might be approved for payment. When the responsibilities for ordering, receiving, and paying are assigned to different individuals, the risk of such abuses is much lower.

Related sales activities, such as making a sale, shipping (or delivering) the goods to the customer, and billing the customer, should also be assigned to different individuals. Otherwise, a salesperson could make sales at unauthorized prices to increase sales commissions, a shipping clerk could ship goods to himself or herself, or a billing clerk could understate the amount billed for sales made to friends and relatives. These abuses are less likely to occur when the sales tasks are divided: salespersons make the sale, shipping department employees ship the goods based on the sales order, and billing department employees prepare the sales invoice after comparing the sales order with the report of goods shipped.

Because there are fewer people, it is harder to segregate duties in small businesses like the Granite Brewery and Ginger's Tavern in our feature story. Still, there are some examples of segregation of duties at the brewery and tavern. For example, the wait staff do not have access to bar or food inventory. Having more than one bartender with control of the bar inventory, however, does result in a weakness in segregation of duties as it becomes harder to assign responsibility for an irregularity. A compensating control is the point-of-sale system, where the sales prices are preprogrammed into the cash registers. This decreases the risk of an employee undercharging a friend on purpose. In addition, the office manager, Denise Avery, prepares the bank deposit and takes the cash to the bank rather than have this done by the cashiers or wait staff who receive the cash. In small businesses like the Granite Brewery and Ginger's Tavern, it is important that the owner and manager be actively involved in the business: they provide the oversight that is needed to ensure that controls are not violated.

In summary, segregation of duties means that responsibilities should be divided up so that one person cannot both commit a fraud and cover it up. In addition, the work of one employee should, without a duplication of effort, provide a reliable basis for evaluating the work of another employee as this helps ensure the accuracy of the accounting records.

Documentation

Documents provide evidence that transactions and events have occurred. At the Granite Brewery and Ginger's Tavern, the point-of-sale system and employee reports provide documentation for the sale and the amount of cash received. Similarly, in other businesses a shipping document indicates that goods have been shipped and a sales invoice indicates that the customer has been billed for the goods. By adding a signature (or initials) to a document, it also becomes possible to identify the individual who is responsible for the transaction or event.

Procedures should be established for documents. First, whenever possible, documents should be prenumbered and all documents should be accounted for. Prenumbering helps prevent a transaction from being recorded more than once or, conversely, from not being recorded at all. Second, documents that are source documents (the original receipts) for accounting entries should be promptly forwarded to the accounting department to help ensure timely recording of the transaction. This control contributes to the accuracy and reliability of the accounting records.

Physical Controls

It is essential to have controls that protect assets and records. If assets and records are not protected, they can be stolen, damaged, or lost. The most important protective measure for safeguarding assets and records, and enhancing the accuracy and reliability of the accounting records, is the use of physical controls. Physical controls include the controls shown in Illustration 7-1.

Illustration 7-1 ➡

Physical controls

Safes, vaults, and safety deposit boxes for cash and business papers

Locked warehouses and storage cabinets for inventories and records

Computer facilities with password or biometric access

Alarms to prevent break-ins

Television monitors and garment sensors to deter theft

Time clocks for recording time worked

Independent Checks of Performance

The four control activities that we just discussed—authorization of transactions and activities, segregation of duties, documentation, and physical controls—must be reviewed independently and frequently. Independent review is necessary because employees can forget or intentionally fail to follow internal controls, or they might become careless if there is no one to observe and evaluate their performance.

These reviews should take place internally and externally, as described below.

Internal Reviews. Independent internal reviews are especially useful in comparing accounting records with existing assets to ensure that nothing has been stolen. The inventory count at the end of each shift by the two bartenders in the feature story about the Granite Brewery and Ginger's Tavern is an example. Another example is the reconciliation by an independent person of the cash balance per books with the cash balance per bank. We will learn more about bank reconciliations later in this chapter.

For independent internal reviews to be beneficial, three measures are recommended:

1. The review should be done periodically on a surprise basis.
2. The review should be done by an employee who is independent of the personnel responsible for the information.
3. Discrepancies and exceptions should be reported to a management level that can take appropriate corrective action.

In large companies, control activities such as independent reviews are often monitored by internal auditors. Internal auditors are employees of the company who evaluate the effectiveness of the company's system of internal control. They periodically review the activities of departments and individuals to determine whether prescribed internal controls are being followed.

While it is management's responsibility to establish and maintain systems of internal control, management relies on internal auditors to assist with this responsibility. A copy of Shoppers Drug Mart's statement of management's responsibility for the financial statements is provided in Appendix A, and includes the following statement:

> These systems [of internal control] include controls to provide reasonable assurance that resources are safeguarded from material loss or inappropriate use, that transactions are authorized, recorded and reported properly and that financial records are reliable for preparing the consolidated financial statements. Internal auditors, who are employees of the Company, review and evaluate internal controls on management's behalf.

External Reviews. It is useful to contrast independent *internal* reviews with independent *external* reviews. An important type of external review is conducted by the external auditors. External auditors, in contrast to internal auditors, are independent of the company. They are professional accountants hired by a company to report on whether or not the company's financial statements fairly present its financial position and results of operations.

All public companies, including Shoppers Drug Mart, are required to have an external audit. A copy of Shoppers' auditors' report is included in Appendix A. As you will see in the report, external auditors plan and perform an audit to obtain reasonable assurance that the financial statements do not have any significant errors.

In addition, as part of the governance processes of the company, the independent audit committee of the board of directors is responsible for reviewing the company's internal control systems to ensure that they are adequate to result in fair, complete, and accurate financial reporting. You will note the following statement in Shoppers' statement of management's responsibility for the financial statements provided in Appendix A:

> The Board of Directors, acting through an Audit Committee which is comprised solely of directors who are not employees of the Company, is responsible for determining that management fulfils its responsibility for financial reporting and internal control. This responsibility is carried out through periodic meetings with senior officers, financial management, internal audit and the independent auditors to discuss audit activities, the adequacy of internal financial controls and financial reporting matters.

Human Resource Controls

Other control measures can include the following:

1. **Conduct thorough background checks.** Many believe that the most important and inexpensive measure any company can take to reduce employee theft and fraud is for the human resources department to conduct thorough background checks. Loblaw weeds out prospective employees with criminal records in an effort to reduce the number of items vanishing from its stores. Criminal record checks eliminated 7.5 percent of Loblaw's job applicants in 2008.

2. **Bonding of employees who handle cash.** Bonding means having insurance protection against theft of assets by dishonest employees. This is often referred to as "fidelity" insurance. Fidelity insurance contributes to the safeguarding of cash in two ways. First, the insurance company carefully screens all individuals before adding them to the policy and may reject risky applicants. Second, bonded employees know that the insurance company will vigorously prosecute all offenders. Common fidelity insurance claims arise from employee dishonesty, embezzlement, forgery, robbery, safe burglary, computer fraud, wire transfer fraud, counterfeiting, and other criminal acts.

3. **Rotating employees' duties and requiring employees to take vacations.** These measures are designed to deter employees from attempting any thefts, since they will not be able to permanently conceal their improper actions.. You would think that everyone would always take their vacation. However, an Ipsos-Reid vacation deprivation poll found that 29 percent of Canadians did not use all of their vacation entitlements in the past year. It is important for employers to require employees to take vacations, for personal health and wellness reasons as well as for internal control reasons. Many employee thefts have been discovered when the employee was on vacation or assigned to a new position.

⚖ ACCOUNTING MATTERS! | Ethics Perspective

The costliest fraud in history is alleged to have been committed by Jérôme Kerviel, a junior trader at French banking giant Société Générale. He has been accused of masterminding $7.2 billion of trading losses for no observable motive, other than to prove he could do it. He allegedly created fictitious accounts and moved money around constantly, eluding the company's 2,000-member internal control staff.

Should authorities have caught this earlier than they did? The answer is yes. Among other anomalies, Kerviel only took four days of vacation in 2007. This alone should have raised red flags with his superiors. As Kerviel himself said to French police investigators, "It's one of the elementary rules of internal control. A trader who doesn't take any days off is a trader who doesn't want to leave his book to another."

Source: Paul Waldie and Sinclair Stewart, "Massive Fraud Cripples French Bank," *The Globe and Mail*, January 26, 2008, A1.

Limitations of Internal Control

No matter how well it is designed and operated, a company's system of internal control can only provide **reasonable assurance** that assets are properly safeguarded and that the accounting records are reliable. The concept of reasonable assurance is based on the belief that the costs of establishing control activities should not be more than their expected benefit.

To illustrate, consider shoplifting losses in retail stores. Such losses could be completely eliminated by having a security guard stop and search customers as they leave the store. Store managers have concluded, however, that the negative effects of this procedure cannot be justified. Instead, stores have attempted to "control" shoplifting losses by using less costly procedures such as (1) posting signs saying, "We reserve the right to inspect all packages" and "All shoplifters will be prosecuted," (2) using hidden TV cameras and store detectives to monitor customer activity, and (3) using sensor equipment at exits.

The human element is an important factor in every system of internal control. A good system can become ineffective as a result of lack of training, employee fatigue, carelessness, or indifference. For example, a receiving clerk may not bother to count goods received or may just "fudge" the counts.

Occasionally, two or more individuals may work together to get around prescribed control activities. Such collusion can significantly lessen the effectiveness of internal control because it eliminates the protection expected from segregating the employees' duties. If a supervisor and a cashier collaborate to understate cash receipts, the system of internal control may be defeated (at least in the short run).

The size of the business may impose limitations on internal control. In a small company, for example, it may be difficult to apply segregation of duties and independent internal verification because of the small number of employees. In situations such as this, it is often necessary for management to assume responsibility for, or to oversee, incompatible functions. For example, at a small gas station, it is not unusual for a cashier to receive the cash and also prepare and make the night deposit at the bank. If the cash register tape is locked so that the cashier cannot access it, internal control is strengthened when the manager later reconciles the bank deposit to the cash register tape.

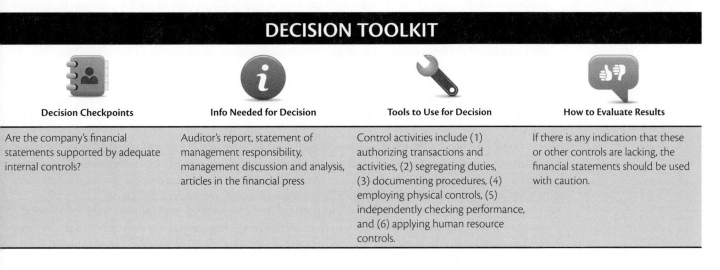

DECISION TOOLKIT

Decision Checkpoints	Info Needed for Decision	Tools to Use for Decision	How to Evaluate Results
Are the company's financial statements supported by adequate internal controls?	Auditor's report, statement of management responsibility, management discussion and analysis, articles in the financial press	Control activities include (1) authorizing transactions and activities, (2) segregating duties, (3) documenting procedures, (4) employing physical controls, (5) independently checking performance, and (6) applying human resource controls.	If there is any indication that these or other controls are lacking, the financial statements should be used with caution.

BEFORE YOU GO ON...

Review It

1. What is internal control?
2. What are the five primary components of a good internal control system?
3. Identify and describe control activities that help achieve internal control.
4. What are the limitations of internal control?

Do It

In each of the following situations, identify the appropriate control activity and state whether it has been supported or violated:

(a) The purchasing department orders, receives, and pays for merchandise.
(b) All cheques are prenumbered and accounted for.
(c) The internal auditor performs surprise cash counts.
(d) Extra cash is kept locked in a safe that can only be accessed by the head cashier.
(e) Each cashier has their own cash drawer.
(f) The company's controller received a plaque for distinguished service because he had not taken a vacation in five years.

Action Plan

• Understand each of the control activities: authorization of transactions and activities, segregation of duties, documentation, physical controls, independent checks of performance, and human resource controls.

Solution

(a) Violation of segregation of duties
(b) Support of documentation procedures
(c) Support of independent performance checks
(d) Support of physical controls
(e) Support of authorization of transactions and activities
(f) Violation of human resource controls (employees should take vacations)

The Navigator

Cash Controls

Just as cash is the beginning of a company's operating cycle, it is usually the starting point for a company's system of internal control. Cash is easily concealed and transported, lacks owner identification, and is much desired. Because of these characteristics, cash is highly susceptible to theft or misuse. In fact, the Association of Certified Fraud Examiners reports that cash is the asset targeted for theft 90 percent of the time. In addition, because of the large volume of cash transactions, errors may easily occur in executing and recording these transactions. To safeguard cash and to ensure the accuracy of the accounting records, effective control activities are essential.

Before we apply the control activities we learned in the last section to cash, let's first look at what cash is, and is not. Cash consists of coins, currency (paper money), cheques, money orders, and money on hand or on deposit in a bank or similar depository. The general rule is that if the bank will accept it for deposit, it is cash.

Debit card transactions and bank credit card receipts, such as VISA and MasterCard, are considered as cash but nonbank credit card receipts, such as Diner's Club, are not. In fact, debit and credit cards are used far more frequently than cash today, as Denise Avery mentioned in the chapter opening feature story. (We will learn more about accounting for debit and credit card transactions in Chapter 8.)

Cash does *not* include postdated cheques (cheques payable in the future), staledated cheques (cheques more than six months old), or returned cheques (cheques lacking sufficient funds). Because postage stamps or IOUs from employees are not the current medium of exchange or acceptable at face value on deposit, they are not considered cash either.

Control Activities over Cash Receipts

Cash receipts come from a variety of sources: cash sales; collections on account from customers; the receipt of interest, rents, and dividends; investments by shareholders; bank loans; and proceeds from the sale of assets. Generally, internal control over cash receipts is more effective when **cash receipts are deposited intact into the bank account on a daily basis or are made by electronic funds transfer**. Bank deposits should be made by an authorized employee, such as the head cashier or general manager.

Electronic funds transfer (EFT) is a way of transferring money electronically from one bank account directly to another without any paper money changing hands. Debit and credit card transactions, mentioned above, are examples of electronic funds transfers. Another example is when customers use on-line banking to pay their accounts. When a customer pays his or her account, the cash is instantly transferred from the customer's bank account to the company's bank account. Electronic funds transfers normally result in better internal control since no cash or cheques are handled by company employees. This does not mean that the opportunities for fraud are eliminated. For example, without proper authorization and segregation of duties, an employee might be able to redirect electronic collections into a personal bank account and conceal the theft with fraudulent accounting entries.

Illustration 7-2 shows how the control activities explained earlier apply to cash receipts.

Illustration 7-2 ⬇

Application of control activities to cash receipts

Control Activities over Cash Receipts

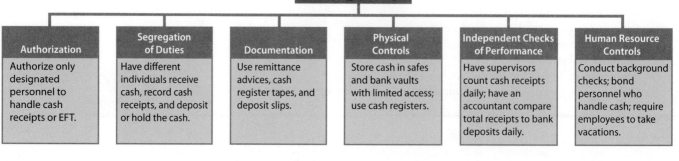

Authorization	Segregation of Duties	Documentation	Physical Controls	Independent Checks of Performance	Human Resource Controls
Authorize only designated personnel to handle cash receipts or EFT.	Have different individuals receive cash, record cash receipts, and deposit or hold the cash.	Use remittance advices, cash register tapes, and deposit slips.	Store cash in safes and bank vaults with limited access; use cash registers.	Have supervisors count cash receipts daily; have an accountant compare total receipts to bank deposits daily.	Conduct background checks; bond personnel who handle cash; require employees to take vacations.

Control Activities over Cash Payments

Cash is disbursed for a variety of reasons, such as to pay expenses and liabilities or to purchase assets. Generally, control activities over cash payments are more effective when **payments are made by cheque or by electronic funds transfer, rather than in cash**. Other control procedures (such as petty cash funds, which are not discussed here) are put in place for the few payments that cannot be made by cheque (e.g., for postage).

Good control for cheques includes the signing of cheques by an authorized person or persons (cheques often require two signatures). The cheque signer(s) should carefully review the supporting documentation for the payment before signing the cheque. There should be a clear segregation of duties between the cheque-signing function and the accounts payable function. Cheques should be prenumbered and all cheque numbers must be accounted for in the payment and recording process. Cheques should never be pre-signed and blank cheques should be safeguarded.

Today, the use of cheques is declining as more and more companies use electronic funds transfer systems to make payments to suppliers and employees. For example, when a company pays its employees' salaries using a direct deposit option, the cash is instantly transferred from the company's bank account to each employee's bank account. As we discussed in the cash receipts section, as long as there is proper authorization and segregation of duties, the use of EFT for cash payments will result in better internal control.

The control activities applied to cash payments are shown in Illustration 7-3.

⬇ **Illustration 7-3**

Application of control activities to cash payments

Control Activities over Cash Payments

Authorization	Segregation of Duties	Documentation	Physical Controls	Independent Checks of Performance	Human Resource Controls
Authorize only designated personnel to sign cheques or issue electronic payments.	Have different individuals approve and make payments; ensure cheque signers do not record cash payments.	Use prenumbered cheques and account for them in sequence; ensure each cheque has an approved invoice.	Store cash in safes and bank vaults with limited access; print cheque amounts electronically.	Compare cheques to invoices; reconcile the bank statement monthly.	Conduct background checks; bond personnel who handle cash; require employees to take vacations.

👥 ACCOUNTING MATTERS! | Management Perspective

According to the Canadian Payments Association, the increase in electronic payment options—debit cards, credit cards, on-line banking, telephone banking, automated banking machines—has resulted in a significant decline in customer payments by cheque. In 2007, 80 percent of personal payment items were electronic, compared to only 13 percent in 1990. Between 1990 and 2007, paper-based transactions decreased by 41 percent, while electronic transactions grew by approximately 1,454 percent.

BEFORE YOU GO ON...

Review It

1. How should the six control activities be applied to cash receipts?
2. How should the six control activities be applied to cash payments?

Do It

At The Coffee Cup Inc., two cash registers are shared by six employees working behind the counter. The owner says, "In an ideal situation, one person would be designated to ring in orders for each cash register, but when we get swamped, we all have to work together to keep things running smoothly." The prices of most items are preprogrammed into the cash register, and each register generates a sales report at the end of the day. One of the employees checks the day's cash receipts against the report to make sure they match.

Identify any violations of control activities over cash receipts at The Coffee Cup.

Action Plan

• Understand the application of each of the control activities to cash receipts: authorization of transactions and activities, segregation of duties, documentation, physical controls, independent checks of performance, and human resource controls.

Solution

Because more than one person can use the same cash register, the authorization of transactions and activities control has been violated. If there is a cash shortage in the register at the end of the day, it will not be possible to determine who is responsible for it.

In addition, segregation of duties has been violated. Staff members who ring up the sale on the cash register and have access to cash should not also check the cash receipts against the sales report. They could choose to not ring up a sale and pocket the cash instead.

The Navigator

Control Features: Use of a Bank

study objective 3

Prepare a bank reconciliation.

The use of a bank contributes significantly to good internal control over cash. A company can safeguard its cash by using a bank as a depository and clearing house for its cash, cheques received and written, and electronic funds received and paid. The use of a bank minimizes the amount of currency that must be kept on hand. In addition, control is strengthened because a double record is maintained of all bank transactions—one by the company and the other by the bank. The asset account Cash, maintained by the company (called the depositor), is the opposite of the bank's liability account for each depositor. It should be possible to **reconcile these accounts**—make them agree—at any time.

Bank Statements

Each month, the bank sends the company a bank statement showing the company's bank transactions and balances. For example, in Illustration 7-4, the statement for Laird Ltd. shows the following: (1) dates, (2) a description of each transaction, (3) the amounts deducted (debited) from the bank account (e.g., cheques and other payments), (4) the amounts added (credited) to the bank account (e.g., deposits and other receipts), and (5) the account balance after each transaction.

At first glance, it may appear that the debits and credits reported on the bank statement are backward. How can amounts deducted from your bank account, like a cheque, be a debit? And how can amounts added to your bank account, like a deposit, be a credit? Debits and credits are not really backward. To the company, Cash is an asset account. Assets are increased by debits (e.g., for cash receipts) and decreased by credits (e.g., for cash payments). To the bank, the cash in your bank account is a liability account—an amount it must repay to you upon request. Liabilities are increased by credits and decreased by debits. When you deposit money in your bank account, the bank's liability to you increases. That is why the bank shows deposits as credits. When you write a cheque on your account, the bank pays out this amount and decreases (debits) its liability to you.

Helpful Hint

Bank	Company
Credit	*Debit*
Debit	*Credit*

Amounts Deducted from a Bank Account (Debits)

Amounts deducted from your bank account include cheques and other payments. A cheque is a written order signed by the depositor that instructs the bank to pay a specific sum of money to a designated recipient. All paid cheques are listed on the bank statement along with the date the cheque was paid and its amount. As mentioned already, cheques generally are on the decline, but personal cheques in particular are now being used much less than they used to be. In fact, many retailers—including Loblaw, Sobeys, Wal-Mart, Sears, The Bay, and Zellers—no longer accept personal cheques. Although personal chequing is on the decline, cheques for businesses are still common. It is difficult to pay some corporate creditors any other way unless they are set up for on-line banking.

How do payments made by a company actually flow through the banking system? When cheques, debit cards, and pre-authorized or other payments occur, they may result in one financial institution

Everyday Banking

BMO ☸ Bank of Montreal

A member of BMO Financial Group

LAIRD LTD.
500 QUEEN STREET
FREDERICTON, NB E3B 5C2

Chequing Account# 0123 4567-890
-----------------------------LAIRD

Fredericton Main Office
505 King Street
FREDERICTON, NB E3B 1E7
Transit number: 0123

Your Everyday Banking statement

For the period ending April 30, 2009

Here's what happened in your account

Date	Description	Amounts deducted from account (debits)	Amounts added to account (credits)	Balance ($)
	Interest Chequing Account # 0123 4567-890			
Owner:				
	-----------------------LAIRD			
Apr 1	Opening balance			13,256.90
1	Cheque, No. 436	644.95		12,611.95
2	Deposit at BR. 0123		4,276.85	16,888.80
3	EFT, collection from Trask		2,137.50	19,026.30
6	Cheque, No. 438	776.65		18,249.65
6	Cheque, No. 437	1,185.79		17,063.86
7	Cheque, No. 439	3,260.00		13,803.86
7	Deposit at BR. 0123		1,350.47	15,154.33
8	Deposit at BR. 0249		982.46	16,136.79
9	Cheque, No. 440	1,487.90		14,648.89
10	EFT, payment of salaries	1,781.70		12,867.19
13	Cheque, No. 442	2,420.00		10,447.19
14	Deposit at BR. 0123		4,649.68	15,096.87
14	Cheque, No. 441	1,585.60		13,511.27
15	Deposit at BR. 0123		425.60	13,936.87
16	Cheque, No. 443	1,226.00		12,710.87
17	Deposit at BR. 0123		757.41	13,468.28
17	Deposit at BR. 0123		1,218.56	14,686.84
20	Deposit at BR. 0123		715.42	15,402.26
21	Returned cheque—NSF	425.60		14,976.66
21	NSF fee	40.00		14,936.66
22	Cheque, No. 444	3,437.11		11,499.55
23	Deposit at BR. 0249		1,578.90	13,078.45
24	EFT, collection from Gillco		1,350.55	14,429.00
24	EFT, payment of salaries	1,781.70		12,647.30
27	Deposit at BR. 0123		3,935.06	16,582.36
28	EFT, payment of insurance	659.91		15,922.45
30	SVC plan fee	15.00		15,907.45

owing money to another. For example, if a company (the payor) writes a cheque to a supplier (the payee), the payee deposits the cheque in its own bank account.

When the cheque is deposited, it is sent to a regional data centre for processing, usually the same day. When the cheque arrives at the centre, it is "presented" to the payor's financial institution, where it is determined whether the cheque will be honoured or returned (for example, for insufficient funds, which we will learn about shortly, or a stop payment order). This process is automated and happens very quickly. In most cases, the cheque will clear the company's bank account before the next day. **Clearing** is the term used when a cheque or deposit is accepted by the bank.

Other disbursements may appear on the bank statement, such as payments using electronic funds transfers. For example, pre-authorized payments, for things like loans and insurance paid on a recurring basis, are often made electronically. In Illustration 7-4, the notation "EFT, payment of insurance" tells us that on April 28 Laird paid its insurance using electronic funds transfer.

In addition, many companies pay their employees' salaries using a direct deposit option. Laird pays its salaries this way. You can see the notation "EFT, payment of salaries" on April 10 and April 24 in

Alternative Terminology
A *cleared* cheque is also called a *cancelled* cheque.

the bank statement in Illustration 7-4. When employee salaries are paid this way, the cash is instantly transferred from the company's bank account to each employee's bank account. No cheques are issued. Because the company initiated the transaction, it knows that the transaction is happening and it can therefore record it before it receives the bank statement. As we will learn later when we discuss deposits, this is not always the case when customers pay their account electronically.

Other deductions from a bank account can include service charges and fees assessed by the bank and other amounts that are deducted from the depositor's account. For example, the service (SVC) plan fee, $15, is deducted directly by the bank from Laird's account on April 30. Service charges vary widely depending on what kind of plan the company has with its bank. Note that banks do not bill companies for their fees. Rather, the bank deducts this amount directly from the company's bank account.

The bank statement is accompanied by a debit memorandum (DM) when additional detail is required about amounts that have been deducted by the bank that are not clear from reading the bank statement. For example, a debit memorandum is used by the bank when a previously deposited customer's cheque bounces (is not honoured) because of insufficient funds. When this occurs, the cheque is marked NSF (not sufficient funds) by the customer's bank, or **returned cheque**, and is returned to the depositor's bank. The bank then debits (decreases) the depositor's account, as shown by the notation "Returned cheque—NSF" on the bank statement in Illustration 7-4 in the amount of $425.60 on April 21.

Note that this cheque was previously deposited by the company on April 15. Because the deposit was credited (added) to the bank account on April 15 and the cheque was not honoured, it must be debited (deducted) by the bank (see April 21 transaction). The bank returns the NSF cheque and debit memorandum to the depositor as notification of the charge.

The company (depositor) will then advise the customer who wrote the NSF cheque that the payment was ineffective and that payment is still owed on the account. In addition, as the company's bank generally charges a service charge for processing a returned cheque, the company usually passes this on to the customer by adding the charged amount to the customer's account balance. You can see that the Bank of Montreal charged Laird a $40 NSF fee on April 21. In summary, the overall effect of an NSF cheque to the depositor is to create an account receivable and to reduce the cash in the depositor's bank account.

An account receivable is recorded on the assumption that the customer will honour the account due by replacing the bounced cheque with a valid cheque, or with cash. This happens in most cases. In the next chapter, we will discuss how to account for uncollectible accounts receivable when customers are unable to pay their accounts.

Amounts Added to a Bank Account (Credits)

Deposits to a company's bank account can be made by an authorized employee, and documented by a deposit slip. Deposits can also be made by direct deposit, through an automated banking machine, or through an electronic funds transfer if the company allows customers to pay their accounts on-line. For example, in Illustration 7-4 Laird electronically collected amounts from customers for $2,137.50 on April 3 and $1,350.55 on April 24 in payment of their accounts.

In cases of electronic collections from customers, the notification is on the bank statement and the company is unaware of the collection until it views its bank statement.

Why does a company not normally know that a customer has electronically submitted the cash in payment of their account? When a customer pays his or her account using on-line banking or other electronic means, the cash is instantly transferred from the customer's bank account to the company's bank account. The only evidence of these electronic cash receipts will be a line on the bank statement showing the amount, a reference number, and the name or account number of the person paying. Consequently, electronic receipts such as these are normally recorded directly from the bank statement.

In some cases, companies also earn interest on their bank account, although this is not usual for chequing accounts. No separate notification is given for these amounts either. Other deposits to the bank account sometimes include supporting documentation known as credit memoranda (CM). Credit memoranda are used to identify note collections, for example, and certain other amounts added to the depositor's account.

In summary, **debit memoranda result in debits on the bank's books and credits on the company's books. Credit memoranda result in credits on the bank's books and debits on the company's books.**

Reconciling the Bank Account

Because the bank and the company keep independent records of the company's chequing account, you might assume that the balances in both sets of records will always agree. In fact, the two balances are seldom the same at any specific time. It is therefore necessary to make the balance per books (the balance recorded in the company's general ledger Cash account) agree with the balance per bank (the balance recorded on the bank statement). This process is called reconciling the bank account.

The lack of agreement between the balances has two causes:

1. **Time lags** that prevent one of the parties from recording the transaction in the same period as the other party
2. **Errors** by either party in recording transactions

Except in electronic banking transactions, time lags occur often. For example, several days or longer will normally pass between the time a company mails a supplier a cheque and the date the supplier presents the cheque to the bank for payment. Cheques recorded by a company that have not yet cleared (been paid by) the bank are called outstanding cheques.

Similarly, when a company uses the bank's night depository to make its deposits, there will be a difference of one day (or more, if holidays intervene) between the time the receipts are recorded by the company and the time they are recorded by the bank. Deposits recorded by the company that have not yet been recorded by the bank are called deposits in transit.

Errors can also occur. How often errors occur depends on the effectiveness of the control activities employed by the company and the bank. Bank errors are infrequent. However, either party could accidentally record a $450 cheque as $45 or $540. In addition, the bank might mistakenly charge a cheque to the wrong account if the code is missing or if the cheque cannot be scanned. Direct deposits and electronic funds transfers also depend on the correct account being keyed into the system.

🧍 ACCOUNTING MATTERS! | Management Perspective

About two-thirds of payments made by the Government of Canada for things like Canada Pension Plan benefits or Old Age Security are made electronically by direct deposit rather than by cheque. Using direct deposit is a cheaper and greener way to pay. Each direct deposit costs the government 20 cents instead of 80 cents and, collectively, they save about 2,800 tonnes of paper that otherwise would be used to print cheques. But the downside is that if there's an error, millions of dollars can go astray. It happened 3,257 times for a total of $1.9 million in 2006–07.

How could this happen? "The payment information provided could be incorrect because of a clerical error or because the payee provided incorrect information," Lucie Brosseau, a spokesperson for the Receiver General, said. "The Receiver General does not have indications that fraudulent activities are prevalent in misdirected direct deposits."

Source: Dean Beeby, "$1.9 Million in Federal Cheques Directly Deposited to Wrong Accounts," *Globe and Mail*, March 3, 2008, A5.

Reconciliation Procedure

To get the most benefit from a bank reconciliation, it should be prepared by an employee who has no other responsibilities related to cash. When the control activity of segregation of duties is not followed in preparing the reconciliation, cash embezzlements may go unnoticed. For example, a cashier who prepares the reconciliation can steal cash and hide the theft by misstating the reconciliation. In this way, the bank account would appear to reconcile with the company records and the theft would not be detected.

In reconciling the bank account, it is customary to reconcile the balance per bank and the balance per books to their adjusted (correct) cash balances. Both the books and the bank balance will likely change as a result of the reconciliation process. The reconciliation is usually divided into two sections—one per the bank statement and one per the books. The starting point when preparing the reconciliation is to enter the balance per bank (found on the bank statement provided by the bank) and the balance per books (found in the Cash account in the general ledger) on the schedule. Adjustments are then made to each section, as shown in Illustration 7-5.

Illustration 7-5 ➡

Bank reconciliation
procedures

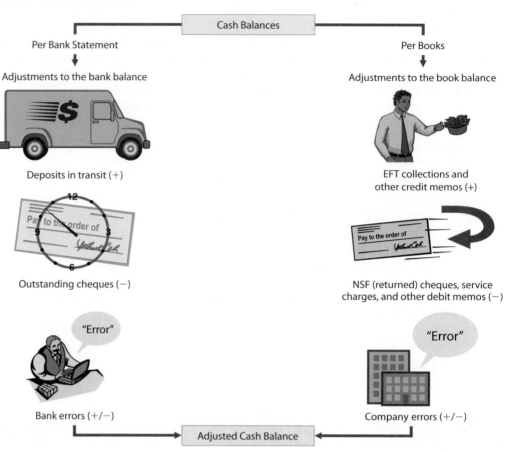

The following steps should reveal all the reconciling items that cause the difference between the two balances:

Reconciling Items per Bank. On the bank side of the reconciliation, the items to reconcile are deposits in transit (amounts added), outstanding cheques (amounts deducted), and bank errors (if any).

1. **Deposits in transit** (+). Compare the individual deposits on the bank statement with (1) the deposits in transit from the preceding bank reconciliation and (2) the deposits recorded in the books. Deposits in transit are already recorded on the company's books but have not yet been recorded by the bank because it does not know about them yet. Therefore, they must be added to the balance per bank in the reconciliation process.

   Before determining the deposits in transit for the current period, you must check whether all deposits in transit that are outstanding from a prior period have cleared. For example, assume that Laird Ltd. used a night deposit slot to deposit $2,201.40 on Thursday, April 30. The bank will not receive or record this deposit until Friday, May 1. This amount would be treated as a deposit in transit at the end of April and would be added to the balance per bank in the reconciliation process. However, this outstanding deposit will clear the bank in May and will therefore no longer be a deposit in transit at the end of May. As at the end of May, this amount will have been recorded by both the company and the bank.

2. **Outstanding cheques** (−)**.** Compare the paid cheques shown on the bank statement or returned with the bank statement with (a) cheques outstanding from the preceding bank reconciliation and (b) cheques issued by the company. Outstanding cheques are already recorded on the company's books but have not yet cleared the bank account. Therefore, they must be deducted from the balance per bank in the reconciliation process.

   Note that an outstanding cheque from a prior period means that the cheque was deducted from the books in the prior period, but not paid by the bank in the same period. If the cheque was paid by the bank in the current month, both sides (book and bank) are now reconciled, the cheque is no longer outstanding, and no further reconciling item is required. If the cheque has still not been presented to the bank for payment, it will continue to be outstanding.

3. **Bank errors** (+/−). Note any errors made by the bank that have been discovered in the previous steps. For example, if the bank processed a deposit of $1,693 as $1,639 in error, the difference of $54 ($1,693 − $1,639) is added to the balance per bank on the bank reconciliation.

   Errors can be made by either party—the company or the bank—and can be in any direction (increases or decreases). Make sure that you only include errors made by the bank as reconciling items in determining the adjusted cash balance per bank. Errors made by the company should be included as reconciling items per books, as we will discuss in the next section.

Reconciling Items per Books. Reconciling items on the book side include adjustments from credit memoranda and other deposits (amounts added), debit memoranda and other payments (amounts deducted), and company errors (if any).

1. **Credit memoranda and other deposits** (+). Compare the credit memoranda and other deposits on the bank statement with the company records. Any unrecorded amounts should be added to the balance per books. For example, if the bank statement shows electronic funds transfers from customers paying their accounts on-line, unless they had previously been recorded by the company, these amounts will be added to the balance per books on the bank reconciliation to make the company's records agree with the bank's records.

2. **Debit memoranda and other payments** (−). Similarly, any unrecorded debit memoranda or other payments should be deducted from the balance per books. For example, if the bank statement shows bank service charges, this amount is deducted from the balance per books on the bank reconciliation to make the company's records agree with the bank's records. Normally, electronic payments will already have been recorded by the company. However, if this has not been the case, then these payments must be deducted from the balance per books on the bank reconciliation to make the company's records agree with the bank's records.

3. **Book errors** (+/−). Note any errors made by the depositor that have been discovered in the previous steps. For example, if a paid cheque written by the company for $1,226 was mistakenly recorded by the company as $1,262, the error of $36 ($1,262 − $1,226) is added to the balance per books. The error of $36 is added to the balance per books because the company reduced the balance per books by $36 too much when it recorded the cheque as $1,262 instead of $1,226. Make sure that you only include errors made by the company as reconciling items in determining the adjusted cash balance per books.

Bank Reconciliation Illustrated

The bank statement for Laird Ltd. was shown in Illustration 7-4. It shows a balance per bank of $15,907.45 on April 30, 2009. On this date, the cash balance per books is $9,161.40.

From the steps described above, the following reconciling items for the bank can be determined:

1. **Deposits in transit** (+): After comparing the deposits recorded in the books with the deposits listed in the bank statement, it was determined that the April 30 deposit of $2,201.40 was not recorded by the bank until May 1. $2,201.40

2. **Outstanding cheques** (−): After comparing the cheques recorded in the books with the cheques listed in the bank statement, it was determined that three cheques were outstanding: No. 445, $3,000.00; No. 446, $1,401.30; and No. 447, $1,502.70.   5,904.00

3. **Bank errors** (+/−): None

Reconciling items per books are as follows:

1. **Credit memoranda and other deposits** (+): Unrecorded receipts on April 3 and 24 determined from the bank statement are as follows:
   Electronic receipts from customers on account: $2,137.50 + $1,350.55 $3,488.05

2. **Debit memoranda and other payments** (−): The electronic payments on April 10, 24 and 28 were previously recorded by the company when they were initiated. Unrecorded charges determined from the bank statement are as follows:

Returned cheque plus NSF fee on April 21 ($425.60 + $40)	465.60
Bank service charges on April 30	15.00

3. **Company errors (+):** Cheque No. 443 was correctly written by Laird for $1,226 and was correctly paid by the bank on April 16. However, it was recorded as $1,262 on Laird's books. | 36.00

The bank reconciliation follows:

LAIRD LTD. Bank Reconciliation April 30, 2009		
Cash balance per bank statement		$15,907.45
Add: Deposits in transit		2,201.40
		18,108.85
Less: Outstanding cheques		
No. 445	$3,000.00	
No. 446	1,401.30	
No. 447	1,502.70	5,904.00
Adjusted cash balance per bank		$12,204.85
Cash balance per books		$ 9,161.40
Add: Electronic payments by customers on account		
Trask	$2,137.50	
Gillco	1,350.55	
Error in recording cheque No. 443 ($1,262 − $1,226)	36.00	3,524.05
		12,685.45
Less: Returned (NSF) cheque plus service charge ($425.60 + $40)	$465.60	
Bank service charge	15.00	480.60
Adjusted cash balance per books		$12,204.85

Bank Reconciliation Journal Entries

The bank reconciliation shown above is only the first step in the reconciliation process. The reconciliation is not complete until the company books are adjusted to agree with the adjusted (correct) cash balance. Each reconciling item that arises from determining the adjusted cash balance per books must be recorded by the depositor. If these items are not journalized and posted, the Cash account will not show the correct balance.

The adjusting entries for Laird Ltd.'s bank reconciliation on April 30 are as follows:

Electronic Payments on Account. A payment of an account by a customer is recorded in the same way, whether the cash is received through the mail or electronically. The entry is:

A = L + SE		
+3,488.05		
−2,137.50		
−1,350.55		
⬆ Cash flows: +3,488.05		

Apr. 30	Cash	3,488.05	
	Accounts Receivable—Trask		2,137.50
	Accounts Receivable—Gillco		1,350.55
	(To record electronic collection of accounts)		

In some cases, the company will have already recorded these transactions. Some companies monitor their bank account on-line daily in order to track changes in their bank account. Other companies, such as Laird, wait until the bank statement is received to record transactions such as these.

Book Error. An examination of the general journal shows that the incorrectly recorded cheque, No. 443, was a payment on account to a supplier. The correcting entry is:

A = L + SE		
+36.00	+36.00	
⬆ Cash flows: +36.00		

Apr. 30	Cash	36.00	
	Accounts Payable		36.00
	(To correct error in recording cheque No. 443)		

NSF Cheque. As indicated earlier, a returned (NSF) cheque becomes an account receivable to the depositor. The entry is:

Apr. 30	Accounts Receivable ($425.60 + $40)	465.60	
	Cash		465.60
	(To re-establish accounts receivable for NSF cheque, and related		
	service charge)		

A = L + SE
+465.60
−465.60
↓ Cash flows: −465.60

Note that the $40 bank service charge has also been debited to Accounts Receivable rather than a Bank Charges Expense account. Because the bank service charge in this instance relates to processing the NSF cheque, this charge will be passed on to the customer by adding it to the customer's account balance.

Bank Service Charges. Bank service charges are normally debited to the expense account Bank Charges. Some companies use the account Interest Expense. The entry is:

Apr. 30	Bank Charges Expense	15.00	
	Cash		15.00
	(To record bank service plan fee)		

A = L + SE
+15.00
−15.00
↓ Cash flows: −15.00

All of the entries above could also be combined into one compound entry. Our presentation assumes that all adjustments are made at the end of the month. In practice, a company may also make journal entries during the month as it receives information from the bank regarding its account, or as the company checks its bank account balances on-line.

After the entries are posted, the Cash account will appear as in the T account which follows. The adjusted cash balance in the ledger should agree with the adjusted cash balance per books in the bank reconciliation shown on the previous page.

			Cash			
Apr.	30	Bal.	9,161.40	Apr. 30	465.60	
	30		3,488.05	30	15.00	
	30		36.00			
Apr.	30	Bal.	12,204.85			

What entries does the bank make? **The bank cannot correct your errors on its books and you cannot correct the bank's errors on your books.** If any bank errors are discovered in preparing the reconciliation, the bank should be notified so it can make the necessary corrections on its records. The bank does not make any entries for deposits in transit or outstanding cheques. Only when these items reach the bank will it record them.

BEFORE YOU GO ON...

Review It

1. How does a bank reconciliation strengthen internal control?
2. How are deposits in transit and outstanding cheques that arise in the current period treated in the reconciling process? That are still outstanding from a prior period?
3. How are electronic funds deposits and payments treated in the reconciliation process?
4. How are errors treated in the reconciliation process?

Do It

The Cash account of Zhizhi Corporation showed a balance of $16,333 on December 31. The bank statement as of that date showed a balance of $18,084. After comparing the bank statement with the company records, the following information was determined:

1. Deposits in transit as at December 31 amounted to $3,643.
2. Outstanding cheques for the month of December amounted to $3,000. Cheques still outstanding from the month of November totalled $280.
3. The bank made a mistake in recording a U.S. dollar payment, overcharging $28 of exchange in error.
4. Electronic receipts received from customers in payment of their accounts totalled $2,309. These receipts have not yet been recorded by the company.

5. The company made an error in recording a customer's deposit in payment of its account. The company recorded the collection of the account as $209, when it should have been $290. The bank correctly recorded the deposit as $290.

6. The bank returned an NSF cheque in the amount of $239 that Zhizhi had deposited on December 20. The cheque was a payment on a customer's account.

7. The bank debited Zhizhi's account for bank service charges of $65. Of this amount, $40 was for processing the NSF cheque (see item 6 above) and $25 was for the rental of a safety deposit box.

Prepare a bank reconciliation and any required journal entries for Zhizhi at December 31.

Action Plan

• Prepare the bank reconciliation in two sections: one for the bank and one for the company.
• Determine which reconciling items each side knows about and adjust the other side accordingly.
• Be careful when you determine the direction of an error correction.
• Prepare journal entries only for the book side, not the bank side.
• The adjusted cash balances must agree with each other when complete, and with the general ledger account after the journal entries are posted.

Solution

ZHIZHI CORPORATION			
Bank Reconciliation			
December 31			
Cash balance per bank statement			$18,084
Add: Deposits in transit			3,643
			21,727
Less: Outstanding cheques ($3,000 + $280)		$3,280	
Foreign exchange error correction		28	3,308
Adjusted cash balance per bank			$18,419
Cash balance per books			$16,333
Add: Electronic receipts from customers on account		$2,309	
Deposit error correction ($290 – $209)		81	2,390
			18,723
Less: NSF cheque ($239 + $40)		$ 279	
Bank service charges		25	304
Adjusted cash balance per books			$18,419

Dec. 31	Cash	2,309	
	Accounts Receivable		2,309
	(To record electronic receipts on account)		
31	Cash ($290 – $209)	81	
	Accounts Receivable		81
	(To correct deposit error)		
31	Accounts Receivable ($239 + $40)	279	
	Cash		279
	(To re-establish accounts receivable for NSF cheque and related service charge)		
31	Bank Charges Expense	25	
	Cash		25
	(To record bank service charges)		

Check:

			Cash				
Dec.	31	Bal.	16,333	Dec.	31		279
	31		2,309		31		25
	31		81				
Dec.	31	Bal.	18,419				

The Navigator

Reporting and Managing Cash

Corporate management must perform a difficult balancing act to properly manage cash. On one hand, it is critical to ensure that enough cash is available to pay bills as they come due, to buy goods, and to take advantage of opportunities as they present themselves. On the other hand, cash itself is an unproductive asset unless it is invested in other assets (e.g., investments, inventory, and property, plant, and equipment). Too much cash on hand may indicate that management is not maximizing its return on assets. So it is critical that management know at all times exactly how much cash there is, and to then manage it closely. In the next two sections, we will look at how cash is reported and will identify ways to manage and monitor cash.

study objective 4

Explain the reporting and management of cash.

Reporting Cash

Cash is reported in two different financial statements: the balance sheet and the cash flow statement. The balance sheet reports the amount of cash available at a specific point in time. The cash flow statement shows the sources and uses of cash during a period of time. These two statements are linked because the ending cash amount reported on the cash flow statement agrees with the cash amount reported on the balance sheet. The cash flow statement was introduced in Chapters 1 and 2 and will be discussed in detail in Chapter 13.

Because it is the most liquid asset owned by a company, cash is listed first in the current assets section of the balance sheet. Many companies combine cash with cash equivalents. Cash equivalents are short-term, highly liquid (easily sold) investments that are subject to an insignificant risk of changes in value. These investments include short-term deposits, short-term investments such as treasury bills and money-market funds, and short-term notes that normally have maturities of three months or less when purchased. All are typically purchased with cash that is not currently needed. Nearly 90 percent of Canadian public companies currently combine cash and cash equivalents for reporting purposes. However, as mentioned in Chapter 2, standard setters have recommended that cash equivalents not be combined with cash in the balance sheet in future, but rather reported with other short-term investments. While no decision has been reached to date on this issue, this is a change that we may very well see in the near future.

Some companies may be in a cash deficit or overdraft position at year end. Bank overdrafts occur when a cheque is written for more than the amount in the bank account. This, in effect, is a short-term loan from the bank. Most companies have overdraft protection up to a certain amount with their banks. In an overdraft situation, the cash account will show a credit balance in the general ledger and is reported as a current liability called bank indebtedness.

A company may have cash that is not available for general use because it is restricted for a special purpose. For example, landfill companies are often required to maintain a fund of restricted cash to ensure that they will have adequate resources to cover closing and cleanup costs at the end of a landfill site's useful life. Cash that has a restricted use should be reported separately on the balance sheet as restricted cash. If the restricted cash is expected to be used within the next year, the amount should be reported as a current asset. When this is not the case, the restricted funds should be reported as a noncurrent asset.

In making loans to depositors, banks commonly require borrowers to maintain minimum cash balances. These minimum balances, called a compensating balance, provide the bank with support for the loans. They are a form of restriction on the use of cash. Similar to other restricted cash, compensating balances are reported as a noncurrent asset.

Illustration 7-6 shows how Help the Aged (Canada), a not-for-profit corporation, reports both its cash and cash equivalents—called investments by Help the Aged (Canada)—and restricted cash.

HELP THE AGED (CANADA) Balance Sheet (partial) March 31, 2007	Help Aged Aidē Aînés CANADA
Current assets	
Cash and investments	$361,493
Accounts receivable	45,501
Prepaid expenses	19,597
	426,591
Restricted cash and investments	53,619

◂ Illustration 7-6

Presentation of cash

Managing Cash

Many companies struggle, not because they cannot generate sales, but because they cannot manage their cash. A real-life example of this is a clothing manufacturing company owned by Sharon McCollick. McCollick gave up a stable, high-paying marketing job to start her own company. Soon she had more clothing orders than she could fill. Yet she found herself on the brink of financial disaster, owing three mortgage payments on her house and $2,000 in income tax. Her company could generate sales, but it was not collecting cash fast enough to support its operations. The bottom line is that a business must have cash.

To understand cash management, consider the operating cycle of Sharon McCollick's clothing manufacturing company. First, it purchases cloth. Let's assume that it purchases the cloth on credit provided by the supplier, so the company owes its supplier money. Next, employees make the cloth into clothing. Now the company also owes its employees money. Then, it sells the clothing to retailers, on credit. McCollick's company will have no money to repay suppliers or employees until its customers pay.

Managing the often precarious balance created by the ebb and flow of cash during the operating cycle is one of a company's greatest challenges. Any company can improve its chances of having adequate cash by following basic principles of cash management:

1. **Increase the speed of collection on receivables.** Money owed to Sharon McCollick by her customers is money that she cannot use. The faster customers pay her, the faster she can use those funds. Thus, rather than have an average collection period of 30 days, she may want an average collection period of 20 days. However, any attempt to force her customers to pay earlier must be carefully weighed against the possibility that she may anger or alienate them. Perhaps her competitors are willing to provide a 30-day grace period. As noted in Chapter 5, a common way to encourage customers to pay more quickly is to offer cash discounts for early payments under such terms as 2/10, n/30.

2. **Keep inventory levels low.** Maintaining a large inventory of cloth and finished clothing is costly. It ties up large amounts of cash to carry the inventory, as well as warehouse space. In addition, inventory can quickly become obsolete if it is held for a long period. Many companies routinely use techniques to reduce their inventory on hand, thus conserving their cash. Of course, if Sharon McCollick has inadequate inventory, she will lose sales. The proper level of inventory is an important decision, as we learned in Chapter 6.

3. **Delay payment of liabilities.** By keeping track of when her bills are due, Sharon McCollick's company can avoid paying bills too early. Let's say her supplier allows 30 days for payment. If she pays in 10 days, she has lost the use of cash for 20 days. Therefore, she should use the full payment period, but she should not "stretch" payment past the point that could damage her credit rating (and future borrowing ability).

4. **Plan the timing of major expenditures.** To maintain operations or to grow, all companies must make major expenditures that normally require some form of outside financing. In order to increase the likelihood of obtaining outside financing, McCollick should carefully consider the timing of major expenditures in light of her company's operating cycle. If at all possible, the expenditure should be made when the firm normally has excess cash—usually during the off-season.

5. **Invest idle cash.** Cash on hand earns nothing. Excess cash should be invested, even if it is only overnight. Many businesses, such as Sharon McCollick's clothing company, are seasonal. During her slow season, if she has excess cash, she should invest it. To avoid a cash crisis, however, it is very important that these investments be liquid and risk-free. A liquid investment has a market in which someone is always willing to buy or sell the investment. A risk-free investment means there is no concern that the party will default on its promise to pay its principal and interest.

    For example, using excess cash to purchase shares in a small company because you heard that it was probably going to increase in value in the near term is inappropriate. First, the shares of small companies are often illiquid. Second, if the shares suddenly decrease in value, you might be forced to sell them at a loss in order to pay your bills as they come due. A common liquid, risk-free investment is treasury bills or money-market funds.

6. **Prepare a cash budget.** A cash budget is a critical tool, showing anticipated cash flows over a one- or two-year period. It can show when additional financing will be necessary well before the actual need arises. Conversely, it can indicate when excess cash will be available for the repayment of debts, for investments, or for other purposes. There is further discussion of cash budgets and budgets in general in managerial accounting courses.

Because cash is so vital to a company, applying these principles of cash management to plan the company's cash needs is essential for any business. The six principles of cash management are summarized in Illustration 7-7.

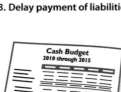

1. Increase collection of receivables   **2. Keep inventory low**   **3. Delay payment of liabilities**

◀ Illustration 7-7

Principles of cash management

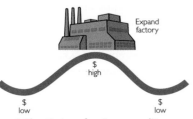

4. Plan timing of major expenditures   **5. Invest idle cash**   **6. Prepare a cash budget**

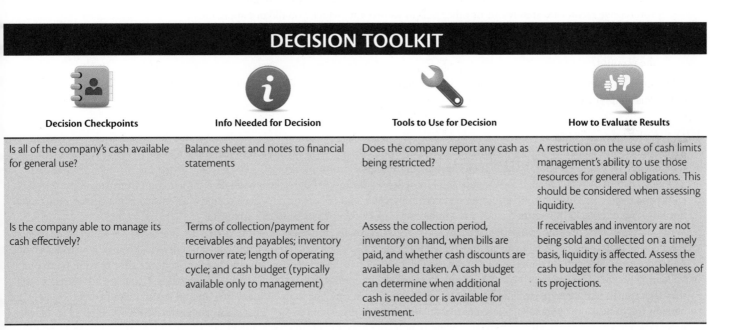

DECISION TOOLKIT

Decision Checkpoints	Info Needed for Decision	Tools to Use for Decision	How to Evaluate Results
Is all of the company's cash available for general use?	Balance sheet and notes to financial statements	Does the company report any cash as being restricted?	A restriction on the use of cash limits management's ability to use those resources for general obligations. This should be considered when assessing liquidity.
Is the company able to manage its cash effectively?	Terms of collection/payment for receivables and payables; inventory turnover rate; length of operating cycle; and cash budget (typically available only to management)	Assess the collection period, inventory on hand, when bills are paid, and whether cash discounts are available and taken. A cash budget can determine when additional cash is needed or is available for investment.	If receivables and inventory are not being sold and collected on a timely basis, liquidity is affected. Assess the cash budget for the reasonableness of its projections.

BEFORE YOU GO ON...

▶ **Review It**
1. Why is it that cash can sometimes be reported as a current asset, sometimes as a noncurrent asset, and sometimes as a current liability?
2. What was Shoppers Drug Mart's cash balance at December 29, 2007? Did the company report any restricted cash? The answers to these questions are provided at the end of this chapter.
3. Distinguish between restricted cash and compensating balances.
4. What are the six principles of cash management?

The Navigator

Protecting Yourself from Identity Theft

Chief executive officers and chief financial officers of publicly traded companies are required to evaluate the effectiveness of their internal control over financial reporting and to discuss their conclusions in the company's annual management discussion and analysis. For their part, management teams must establish and maintain systems of internal controls to help protect a company from both internal and external thieves.

With identity theft as one of the perils of life in the information age, what have you done lately to strengthen your own internal controls? Personal information such as your name, date of birth, address, credit card number, social insurance number and other identification can be used to steal money from your existing accounts, open other financial accounts, make purchases, or even obtain employment.

Are you a victim? The signs can be many, but typical indicators that your identity is being used include the following:

- A creditor informs you that an application for credit was received with your name and address, which you did not apply for.
- Telephone calls or letters state that you have been approved or denied by a creditor that you never applied to.
- You receive credit card statements or other bills in your name, which you did not apply for.
- You no longer receive credit card statements or you notice that not all of your mail is delivered.
- A collection agency informs you that it is collecting for a defaulted account established with your identity yet you never opened the account.

The identity thieves are not likely to go away, so what can you do to protect yourself? Many of the common-sense controls discussed in this chapter can be implemented in your personal life.

Some Facts

- Many Canadian companies and agencies have reported various sorts of privacy breaches, including Canadian Imperial Bank of Commerce, Club Monaco, Passport Canada, Bell Canada, and Rogers Communications.
- TJX Cos., parent of retailers such as Winners and HomeSense, disclosed that hackers had taken information from at least 45.7 million credit and debit cards after breaking into its system in July 2005, and collecting data back to 2003. The hackers continued undetected until the end of 2006. TJX recorded a U.S. $119-million charge to cover costs from the intrusion.
- While adults in their spending years are typically the targets, a growing number of victims are under the age of 18. Child identity theft is especially damaging because it can go undetected for years, unearthed when the victim goes for a driver's licence or a student loan, only to be turned down. By then the crime trail is cold, and the thief has likely long abandoned the accounts after maxing them out.
- Validating recent concerns over the incidence of fraud and debit/credit card theft in Canada, 17 percent of Canadian adults report that they themselves have been personally affected by debit/credit card fraud or theft. While conventional wisdom has been that older Canadians might be more likely to fall victim to fraudulent scams or deceitful operations, it is middle-aged Canadians, aged 35 to 54, who report the highest incidence rate (19 percent), while 16 percent of younger Canadians, aged 18 to 34, and 14 percent of older Canadians, aged 55 and above, have been personally affected by credit or debit card fraud or theft.

What Do You Think?

More and more personal business transactions are being completed by Internet, including bill payments, travel reservations, and on-line purchasing. Do you feel there are sufficient internal controls to protect any information you provide via the Internet from identity theft?

YES | There are additional security checks such as personal identification numbers built into these services.

NO | Even the best security system does not detect every kind of intruder.

The Navigator

Sources:

Janet McFarland, "Insurers Look to Cover Hacking Damage," *Globe and Mail*, March 13, 2008, B4.

"Identity Theft: Could It Happen to You?" Phonebusters, phonebusters.com/english/recognizeit_identitythe.html

Ipsos News Centre, "Two In Ten (17%) Canadians Report Being a Victim of Fraud or Credit Card Theft," Press Release, July 5, 2007.

Summary of Study Objectives

1. **Explain the activities that help achieve internal control.** Internal control systems have the following components: the control environment, risk assessment, control activities, information and communication, and monitoring. Control activities include the authorization of transactions and activities, segregation of duties, documentation, physical controls, independent performance checks, and human resource controls.

2. **Apply control activities to cash receipts and payments.** Control activities over cash receipts include (a) designating only personnel such as cashiers to handle cash; (b) assigning the duties of receiving cash, recording cash, and having custody of cash to different individuals; (c) obtaining remittance advices for mail receipts, cash register tapes for over-the-counter receipts, and deposit slips for bank deposits; (d) using company safes and bank vaults to store cash, with access limited to authorized personnel, and using cash registers in executing over-the-counter receipts; (e) depositing all cash intact daily in the bank account or using EFT; (f) making independent daily counts of register receipts and daily comparisons of total receipts with total deposits; and (g) conducting background checks, bonding personnel who handle cash, and requiring employees to take vacations.

Control activities over cash payments include (a) making all payments by cheque or by EFT; (b) having only specified individuals authorized to sign cheques; (c) assigning to different individuals the duties of approving items for payment, paying the items, and recording the payments; (d) using prenumbered cheques and accounting for all cheques; (e) storing each cheque in a safe or vault with access restricted to authorized personnel, and using electronic methods to print amounts on cheques; (f) comparing each cheque with the approved invoice before issuing the cheque, and making monthly reconciliations of bank and book balances; and (g) conducting background checks, bonding personnel who handle cash, and requiring employees to take vacations.

3. **Prepare a bank reconciliation.** In reconciling the bank account, it is customary to reconcile the balance per books and the balance per bank to their adjusted balances. Reconciling items for the bank include deposits in transit, outstanding cheques, and any errors made by the bank. Reconciling items for the books include unrecorded amounts added to or deducted from the bank account and any errors made by the company. Adjusting entries must be made for all items required to reconcile the balance per books to the adjusted cash balance.

4. **Explain the reporting and management of cash.** Cash is listed first in the current assets section of the balance sheet. Cash restricted for a special purpose is reported separately as a current asset or as a noncurrent asset, depending on when the cash is expected to be used. Compensating balances are a form of restriction on the use of cash and are reported as a noncurrent asset.

The six principles of cash management are to (a) accelerate the collection of receivables, (b) keep inventory levels low, (c) delay the payment of liabilities, (d) plan the timing of major expenditures, (e) invest idle cash, and (f) prepare a cash budget.

The Navigator

Glossary

Study Tools (Glossary)

Cash Resources that consist of coins, currency, cheques, money orders, and bank credit card slips that are acceptable at face value on deposit in a bank or similar institution. (p. 344)

Cash equivalents Short-term, highly liquid investments that can be easily sold. (p. 355)

Clearing The process of exchanging and settling payment items that results in a transfer of funds from one financial institution to another. (p. 347)

Compensating balance A minimum cash balance required by a bank in support of a bank loan. (p. 355)

Credit memoranda (CM) Supporting documentation for increases (additions) that appear on a bank statement, such as maturing loans. (p. 348)

Debit memoranda (DM) Supporting documentation for charges (deductions) that appear on a bank statement, such as NSF cheques. (p. 348)

Deposits in transit Amounts deposited and recorded by the depositor that have not yet been recorded by the bank. (p. 349)

Electronic funds transfer (EFT) The system of transferring money electronically from one bank account directly to another without any paper money changing hands. (p. 344)

External auditors Auditors who are independent of the organization. They examine internal control and report on whether or not the financial statements are reported fairly in accordance with generally accepted accounting principles. (p. 341)

Internal auditors Company employees who evaluate the effectiveness of the company's system of internal control. (p. 341)

NSF (not sufficient funds) A cheque that is not paid by a bank, because there are insufficient funds in the bank account of the customer who wrote the cheque. (p. 348)

Outstanding cheques Cheques issued and recorded by a company that have not yet been paid (cleared) by the bank. (p. 349)

Restricted cash Cash that is not available for general use, but instead is restricted for a particular purpose. (p. 355)

DECISION TOOLKIT—A SUMMARY

Decision Checkpoints	Info Needed for Decision	Tools to Use for Decision	How to Evaluate Results
Are the company's financial statements supported by adequate internal controls?	Auditor's report, statement of management responsibility, management discussion and analysis, articles in the financial press	Control activities include (1) authorizing transactions and activities, (2) segregating duties, (3) documenting procedures, (4) employing physical controls, (5) independently checking performance, and (6) applying human resource controls.	If there is any indication that these or other controls are lacking, the financial statements should be used with caution.
Is all of the company's cash available for general use?	Balance sheet and notes to financial statements	Does the company report any cash as being restricted?	A restriction on the use of cash limits management's ability to use those resources for general obligations. This should be considered when assessing liquidity.
Is the company able to manage its cash effectively?	Terms of collection/payment for receivables and payables; inventory turnover rate; length of operating cycle; and cash budget (typically available only to management)	Assess the collection period, inventory on hand, when bills are paid, and whether cash discounts are available and taken. A cash budget can determine when additional cash is needed or is available for investment.	If receivables and inventory are not being sold and collected on a timely basis, liquidity is affected. Assess the cash budget for the reasonableness of its projections.

Analysis Tools
(Decision Toolkit Summaries)

The Navigator

Using the Decision Toolkit

Sparks Basketball (SB) is a not-for-profit organization whose main purpose is to promote healthy living through sports activity. Its members are basketball associations throughout the province, for which SB provides a variety of services. These services include insurance coverage, the organization of provincial tournaments, and discounts from sponsor organizations. It is a volunteer organization with an independent board of directors, and one paid position—that of executive director. While the executive director was on parental leave, this position was filled by SB's vice-president of finance, John Stevens.

Unfortunately, some financial irregularities occurred while Mr. Stevens was acting as executive director. As the acting executive director, Mr. Stevens was responsible for paying invoices, making deposits, signing cheques along with SB's president, completing the bank reconciliation, and preparing financial statements for the annual general meeting.

One irregularity was that several cheques with the president's signature on them were actually forged. It was also discovered that Mr. Stevens handled all deposits and cash payments by himself for a national basketball tournament hosted by SB. He had promised to have an independent treasurer for the tournament but did not get one. He also coached a basketball team in a nearby city, and had full access to the team's bank account. During this time, to save on bank fees, Mr. Stevens had also stopped having the bank return SB's cancelled cheques.

A forensic accountant was brought in to investigate further. He discovered many problems. The financial records were a mess, and there was almost no "paper trail" for the many expenditures that were made. There were instances of "double dipping"—where one individual was reimbursed several times for the same expense claim. There were also several cheques made out to the team coached by Mr. Stevens. There was even a cheque where the payee's name had been scratched out and Mrs. Stevens' name was inserted.

Instructions

(a) Identify the main weakness in control activities at Sparks Basketball.

(b) Discuss what steps should be taken to ensure that this situation does not happen again.

(c) Discuss the trade-off between implementing an extensive internal control system and the cost of having such a system for a volunteer organization that has limited funds.

Solution

(a) The main control weakness at SB was the lack of segregation of duties. While the executive director was on parental leave, one person was responsible for all financial matters. There was also no review of Mr. Stevens' work, so he could make fraudulent transactions without anyone knowing about them.

(b) SB should require proper segregation of duties. Although it is often difficult to have proper segregation of duties in a not-for-profit organization such as this, at least two people should be involved in all financial transactions. SB should require monthly bank reconciliations to be prepared by someone other than the executive director. The cancelled cheques should be returned each month so that they can be reviewed as well. In addition, independent checks of performance could be done by having someone from the board of directors review transactions and financial statements regularly.

(c) Implementation of extensive control systems can be expensive. Not-for-profit organizations must carefully choose what control measures are most important for their specific needs. However, the value of some control activities, such as segregation of duties, often offsets the cost, as it would have for SB. In addition, the organization should use as many free controls as it can. Examples include proper screening of possible volunteers and employees, written policies for how transactions should be processed, and requiring employees and volunteers to sign a formal statement of ethical guidelines.

Demonstration Problem

The Navigator

Trillo Corporation reports the following condensed information from its general ledger Cash account and bank statement at June 30:

www.wiley.com/canada/kimmel

Study Tools
(Demonstration Problems)

Cash				
June 1	Bal.	17,040		
June deposits		17,000	June cheques written	19,760
June 30	Bal.	14,280		

TRILLO CORPORATION Bank Statement June 30			
	Amounts Deducted (Debits)	Amounts Added (Credits)	Balance
Opening balance, June 1			17,690
Deposits		15,248	32,938
Cheques cleared	18,100		14,838
EFT, insurance payment	500		14,338
NSF cheque ($135 + $40 service charge)	175		14,163
Service charge	12		14,151
EFT, collection from Zukata		35	14,186

Additional information:

1. There was a deposit in transit of $600 at May 30, the preceding month, that cleared the bank in June.

2. There were $750 of outstanding cheques at the end of May.

3. The EFT payment for insurance is a pre-authorized monthly payment, which has already been recorded.

4. The NSF cheque was for $135, from Massif Corp., a customer, in payment of its account. The bank charged a $40 processing fee.

5. The EFT collection of $35 was incorrectly deposited by the bank to Trillo's account. It should have been deposited to Trilo's account, a different company with a similar name.

Instructions

(a) Prepare a bank reconciliation at June 30.

(b) Prepare the entries required by the reconciliation.

Solution to Demonstration Problem

(a)

TRILLO CORPORATION	
Bank Reconciliation	
June 30	

Cash balance per bank statement		$14,186
Add: Deposits in transit [$17,000 − ($15,248 − $600)]		2,352
		16,538
Less: Outstanding cheques [$19,760 − ($18,100 − $750)]	$2,410	
Bank deposit error	35	2,445
Adjusted cash balance per bank		$14,093
Cash balance per books		$14,280
Less: NSF cheque ($135 + $40)	$175	
Bank service charge	12	187
Adjusted cash balance per books		$14,093

(b)

June 30	Accounts Receivable		175	
	Cash			175
	(To re-establish accounts receivable for Massif Corp. for NSF cheque and related service charge)			
30	Bank Charges Expense		12	
	Cash			12
	(To record bank service charges)			

Check:

Cash				
June 30	Bal.	14,280	June 30	175
			30	12
June 30	Bal.	14,093		

The Navigator

Self-Study Questions

Answers are at the end of the chapter.

1. Which of the following is not one of the five primary components of internal control?
   (a) Control environment
   (b) Size of business
   (c) Risk assessment
   (d) Control activities

2. Control activities do not include:
   (a) authorization of transactions and activities.
   (b) documentation.
   (c) cost-benefit constraints.
   (d) independent checks of performance.

3. Which of the following items in a cash drawer at November 30 is not cash?
   (a) Debit card slips from sales to customers
   (b) Unsubmitted bank credit card slips from sales to customers
   (c) A customer cheque dated December 1
   (a) A customer cheque dated November 28

4. Permitting only designated personnel, such as cashiers, to handle cash receipts is an application of which of the following control activities?
   (a) Segregation of duties
   (b) Authorization of transactions and activities
   (c) Independent checks of performance
   (d) Human resource controls

5. The use of prenumbered cheques in disbursing cash is an example of which of the following control activities?
   (a) Authorization of transactions and activities
   (b) Segregation of duties
   (c) Physical controls
   (d) Documentation

6. Davis Corporation had cheques outstanding totalling $5,400 on its June bank reconciliation. In July, Davis Corporation issued cheques totalling $38,900. The July bank statement shows that $26,300 in cheques cleared the bank in July. The amount of outstanding cheques on Davis's July bank reconciliation is:
   (a) $5,400.
   (b) $7,200.
   (c) $12,600.
   (d) $18,000.

7. Terriault Ltée reports an ending cash balance per books of $4,100 at the end of the month and $5,000 on its bank statement. Reconciling items include deposits in transit of $2,500, outstanding cheques of $3,500, and service charges of $100. What is the company's adjusted cash balance? (SO 3)
   (a) $3,900
   (b) $4,000
   (c) $4,100
   (d) $5,000

8. Which of the following items on a bank reconciliation would require an adjusting entry on the company's books? (SO 3)
   (a) An error by the bank
   (b) Outstanding cheques
   (c) A bank service charge
   (d) A deposit in transit

9. Which statement correctly describes the reporting of cash? (SO 4)
   (a) Cash is reported in the long-term assets section if the company doesn't expect to spend all of it in the next year.
   (b) Restricted cash funds may be combined with cash.
   (c) Cash is listed first in the current assets section.
   (d) Compensating balances are reported as a current asset.

10. The principles of cash management do not include: (SO 4)
    (a) accelerating the collection of receivables.
    (b) accelerating the payment of liabilities.
    (c) keeping inventory low.
    (d) investing idle cash.

The Navigator

Questions

1. Identify and describe the five primary components of a good internal control system.

2. Identify the six control activities that apply to most companies.

3. How do documentation procedures contribute to good internal control?

4. Matt Tau is questioning the need for independent checks of performance if the company also segregates duties. What do you think about this?

5. Faced with labour shortages and high staff turnover, most retail stores do not bother with criminal record checks when hiring employees. Explain what internal control activity is missing from this practice and what kind of problems this could result in. (SO 1)

6. Kim is trying to design internal control activities so that there is no possibility of errors or theft. Explain to Kim why this may be impractical, and even impossible. (SO 1)

(SO 2) 7. Explain how electronic funds transfers can result in better internal control.

(SO 2) 8. In the corner grocery store, all the clerks make change out of the same cash register drawer. Is this a violation of an internal control activity? Explain.

(SO 2) 9. Dent Department Stores Ltd. has just installed new electronic cash registers with scanners in its stores. How do these cash registers improve control activities over cash receipts?

(SO 2) 10. "To have maximum control over cash payments, all payments should be made by cheque." Is this true? Explain.

(SO 2) 11. Watch Central Ltd. is a small retail store. One of its employees, Wanda, is responsible for ordering the merchandise, receiving the goods, and paying for the goods. Describe the various ways Wanda could potentially commit a fraud with this arrangement.

(SO 2, 3) 12. Who should be responsible for preparing a bank reconciliation? Why?

(SO 3) 13. "The use of a bank contributes significantly to good internal control over cash." Is this true? Explain.

(SO 3) 14. Paul Pascal is confused about the lack of agreement between the cash balance per books and the balance per bank. Explain the possible causes for the lack of agreement to Paul, and give an example of each cause.

(SO 3) 15. Mary Mora asks for your help concerning an NSF cheque. Explain to Mary (a) what an NSF cheque is, (b) how it is treated in a bank reconciliation, and (c) whether it will require an adjusting entry.

16. The Diable Corporation wrote cheque #2375 for $1,325 on March 16. At March 31, the cheque had not cleared the company's bank account and was correctly listed as an outstanding cheque on the March 31 bank reconciliation. If the cheque has still not cleared the bank account on April 30, should it be included in the April bank reconciliation or not? Explain.

17. Explain why electronic payments appearing on a bank statement are often recorded by a company but electronic receipts are not.

18. Why do you think standard setters are considering not allowing cash equivalents to be combined with cash for reporting purposes?

19. The John Howard Society of Ottawa reported bank indebtedness on its March 31, 2007, balance sheet of $102,584. Would this amount be reported in the current assets or current liabilities section of the statement? Explain.

20. What is restricted cash? What are compensating balances? How should these items be reported on the balance sheet?

21. Describe the six principles of cash management.

22. ━━◖ Avery Dennison Corporation deliberately keeps little cash on hand—just one day's worth of operating expenses. Explain which principles of cash management are important to Avery Dennison in maintaining this strategy.

23. ━━◖ Talisman Energy Inc. reported an ending cash balance of $536 million at December 31, 2007, an increase of 520 percent from the prior year. What cash management problems might this cause for Talisman?

Brief Exercises

Identify control activities.
(SO 1)

BE7–1   Gina Milan is the new manager of Plenty Parking Ltd., a parking garage. She has heard about internal control but is not clear about its importance for the company. Explain to Gina the six control activities, and give her an example of an application of each control for Plenty Parking.

Match control activities.
(SO 1)

BE7–2   Match each of the following control activities with its appropriate description.

1. Authorization of transactions and activities   4. Physical controls
2. Segregation of duties   5. Independent checks of performance
3. Documentation   6. Human resource controls

(a) _____ All transactions should include original, detailed receipts.

(b) _____ Undeposited cash should be stored in the company safe.

(c) _____ Employees must take their full vacation allotment each year.

(d) _____ Surprise cash counts are performed.

(e) _____ Responsibility for related activities should be assigned to specific employees.

(f) _____ Cheque signers are not allowed to record cash transactions.

Identify control activities for cash receipts.
(SO 1, 2)

BE7–3   Tene Ltd. has the following internal controls over cash receipts. Identify the control activity that is applicable to each procedure.

1. All over-the-counter receipts are recorded on cash registers.
2. All cashiers are bonded.

3. Daily cash counts are made by the head cashier.

4. The duties of receiving cash, recording cash, and maintaining custody of cash are assigned to different individuals.

5. Only cashiers may operate cash registers.

6. All cash is deposited intact in the bank account every day.

BE7–4   Rolling Hills Ltd. has the following internal controls over cash payments. Identify the control activity that is applicable to each procedure.

1. Company cheques are prenumbered.

2. The bank statement is reconciled monthly by the assistant controller.

3. Blank cheques are stored in a safe in the controller's office.

4. Only the controller or assistant controller may sign cheques.

5. Cheque signers are not allowed to record cash payments.

6. All payments are made by cheque.

Identify control activities for cash payments.
(SO 1, 2)

BE7–5   West Inc. owns these assets at the balance sheet date:

Cash in bank—savings account	$ 6,000
Cash on hand	850
Income tax refund due from CRA	1,000
Cash in bank—chequing account	12,000
Bank credit card slips	2,500
Debit card slips	1,200
Postdated cheques	500

(a) What amount should be reported as cash in the balance sheet? (b) For any item not included in (a), identify where it should be reported.

Calculate cash.
(SO 2)

BE7–6   For each of the items in the following list, identify where it is included on a bank reconciliation. Next to each item write "bank +" for an increase in the bank balance; "bank –" for a decrease in the bank balance; "book +" for an increase in the book balance; "book –" for a decrease in the book balance; or "NA" for not applicable, to indicate that the item is not included in the bank reconciliation.

_____ 1. Bank service charges

_____ 2. An EFT collection on account

_____ 3. Outstanding cheques from the current month

_____ 4. Outstanding cheques from a prior month that are still outstanding

_____ 5. Outstanding cheques from a prior month that are no longer outstanding

_____ 6. A bank error in recording a company cheque made out for $200 as $290

_____ 7. A bank credit memorandum for interest earned on an investment

_____ 8. A company error in recording a $1,280 deposit as $1,680

_____ 9. A bank debit memorandum for an NSF cheque

_____ 10. A deposit in transit from the current month

_____ 11. A company error in recording a cheque made out for $630 as $360

_____ 12. A bank error in recording a $2,575 deposit as $2,755

Identify location of items in bank reconciliation.
(SO 3)

BE7–7   Using the data in BE7–6, indicate (a) the items that will result in an adjustment to the depositor's records and (b) why the other items do not require adjustment.

Identify entries required for bank reconciliation.
(SO 3)

BE7–8   For the months of January and February, Kahn Ltd. recorded cash deposits in its books of $2,500 and $2,800, respectively. For the same two months, the bank reported deposits totalling $2,000 and $2,300, respectively. Assuming that there were no outstanding deposits at the beginning of January, what was the amount of outstanding deposits at the end of January? At the end of February?

Analyze deposits in transit.
(SO 3)

BE7–9   In the month of November, its first month of operations, Jayasinghe Inc. wrote cheques in the amount of $12,600. In December, cheques in the amount of $9,500 were written. In November, $11,100 of these cheques were presented to the bank for payment and $9,900 in December. What is the amount of outstanding cheques at the end of November? At the end of December?

Analyze outstanding cheques.
(SO 3)

Analyze errors.
(SO 3)

BE7–10 Kashechewan Inc. mistakenly recorded a cheque as $68 that was written for $86. In addition, the company noticed the bank had mistakenly deducted a cheque for $125 from its bank account that was written by another company. (a) Explain how each of these errors should be treated on the bank reconciliation. (b) Identify any entries required on Kashechewan's books to correct these errors.

Prepare bank reconciliation.
(SO 3)

BE7–11 At July 31, Dana Limited had an unadjusted cash balance of $8,160. An examination of the July bank statement shows a balance of $7,920 on July 31; outstanding cheques $1,150; deposits in transit $2,150; EFT collections on account $980; NSF cheque $145; NSF fee $40; and bank services charges $35. Prepare a bank reconciliation at July 31.

Prepare entries for bank reconciliation.
(SO 3)
Report cash.
(SO 4)

BE7–12 Using the data in BE7–11, prepare the adjusting entries required on July 31 for Dana Limited.

BE7–13 Ouellette Ltée reports the following items: cash in bank $17,500; payroll bank account $6,000; cash register floats $500; short-term investments with maturity dates of less than 90 days $5,000; and cash restricted for plant expansion $25,000. Ouellette also maintains a $5,000 compensating bank balance in a separate bank account. Explain how each of these items should be reported on the balance sheet.

Identify cash management issues.
(SO 4)

BE7–14 ⬛ Identify and discuss the likely cash management issues faced by the following businesses:
  (a) Toronto Maple Leafs hockey team
  (b) WestJet Airlines Ltd.
  (c) Memorial University Bookstore
  (d) Tim Hortons
  (e) Pillar 'N Pine Christmas Tree Farm

Exercises

Identify control activities.
(SO 1)

E7–1 The following situations suggest either a strength or weakness in an internal control activity:

1. At Tingley's, Jill and John work alternate lunch hours. Normally, Jill works the cash register at the checkout counter, but during her lunch hour John takes her place. They both use the same cash drawer and jointly count cash at the end of the day.
2. The Do It Corporation accepts both cash and credit cards for its sales. Due to new privacy legislation, it shreds all credit card slips after they are processed.
3. The mail clerk of Mail Boxes prepares a daily list of all cash receipts. The cash receipts are forwarded to a staff accountant, who deposits the cash in the company's bank account. The list is sent to the accounts receivable clerk for recording.
4. The Candy Store can only afford a part-time bookkeeper. The bookkeeper's responsibilities include making the bank deposit, recording transactions, and reconciling the bank statement.
5. The Decorator Shoppe counts inventory at the end of each month. Two staff members count the inventory together. It is then priced and totalled by the accounting department and reconciled to the perpetual inventory records. Any variances are investigated.

Instructions

  (a) State whether each situation above is a control strength or weakness.

  (b) For each weakness, suggest an improvement.

Identify control activities for cash receipts.
(SO 1, 2)

E7–2 The following control activities are used in Tolan Ltd. for over-the-counter cash receipts:
1. Cashiers are experienced, so they are not bonded.
2. All over-the-counter receipts are received by one of three clerks. The clerks share a cash register with a single cash drawer.
3. To minimize the risk of robbery, cash in excess of $100 is stored in an unlocked strongbox in the stockroom until it is deposited in the bank.
4. At the end of each day, the total receipts are counted by the cashier on duty and reconciled to the cash register total.
5. The company accountant makes the bank deposit and then records the day's receipts.
6. If a customer has the exact change and does not want a receipt, the sale is not entered in the cash register. The money is kept in a loose change box.

Instructions

(a) For each of the above situations, explain the weakness and identify the control activity that is violated.

(b) For each weakness, suggest an improvement.

E7–3　The following control activities are used in Ann's Boutique Shoppe Ltd. for cash payments:

1. Blank cheques are stored in an unmarked envelope on a shelf behind the cash register.
2. The store manager personally approves all payments before cheques are signed or before an EFT payment is made.
3. When the store manager has to go away for an extended period of time, she pre-signs several cheques to be used in her absence.
4. The company cheques are not prenumbered.
5. The company accountant prepares the bank reconciliation and reports any discrepancies to the store manager.

Identify control activities for cash payments.
(SO 1, 2)

Instructions

(a) For each of the above situations, explain the weakness and identify the control activity that is violated.

(b) For each weakness, suggest an improvement.

E7–4　Complete the table shown below, identifying where each item should be included on a bank reconciliation prepared for the month of April. Insert a check mark (✓) in the appropriate column indicating whether the item should be added to, or deducted from, the bank or the books. If the item should not be included in the bank reconciliation, write "NA" for not applicable. Finally, indicate whether the item will require an adjusting entry on the company books by writing "yes" or "no" in the last column. The first one has been done for you as an example.

Indicate effect of items in bank reconciliation.
(SO 3)

Item	Bank		Books		Adjusting Entry
	Add (Credit)	Deduct (Debit)	Add (Debit)	Deduct (Credit)	
1.　Deposits in transit in April	✓				No
2.　Deposits in transit in April that cleared the bank in May					
3.　Outstanding cheques in April					
4.　Outstanding cheques in April that cleared the bank in May					
5.　Cheque written for $250 recorded in error as $520 on the books					
6.　Deposit of $400 made in error by the bank to the company's account					
7.　Bank service charges					
8.　EFT, collection on account					
9.　NSF cheque					
10.　Interest earned on bank account					

E7–5　The cash records of Lejeune Inc. show the following situations:

Calculate deposits in transit and outstanding cheques.
(SO 3)

Deposits in transit

1. The June 30 bank reconciliation indicated that deposits in transit total $2,000. During July, the general ledger account Cash shows deposits of $14,750, but the bank statement indicates that only $15,820 in deposits was received during the month.
2. In August, deposits per bank statement totalled $22,500 and deposits per books were $22,900.

Outstanding cheques

1. The June 30 bank reconciliation reported outstanding cheques of $570. During July, the Lejeune books show that $18,200 of cheques were issued. The bank statement showed that $17,200 of cheques cleared the bank in July.
2. In August, cash payments per books were $22,700 and cheques clearing the bank were $23,520.

Instructions

(a) What were the deposits in transit at July 31? At August 31?

(b) What were the outstanding cheques at July 31? At August 31?

Calculate deposits in transit.
(SO 3)

E7–6   On April 30, the bank reconciliation of Drofo Limited shows a deposit in transit of $1,437. A lis'
of cash deposits recorded by the bank and the company in the month of May follows:

DROFO LIMITED Bank Statement (partial) Amounts Added to Account (Credits)				DROFO LIMITED Cash Account (partial) Deposits Made (Debits)	
Date	Description	Amount		Date	Amount
May 1	Deposit	$1,437		May 7	$2,255
8	Deposit	2,255		14	3,218
15	Deposit	3,218		19	954
20	Deposit	954		28	1,531
25	EFT, collection from customer	1,298		31	1,892
29	Deposit	1,531			

Instructions

(a) List the deposits in transit at May 31.

(b) List any other items that must be included in the bank reconciliation. Describe the impact of each
item on the reconciliation.

Calculate outstanding cheques.
(SO 3)

E7–7   At April 30, the bank reconciliation of Drofo Limited shows three outstanding cheques: No. 254,
$560; No. 255, $800; and No. 257, $410. A list of cheques recorded by the bank and the company in the
month of May follows:

DROFO LIMITED Bank Statement (partial) Amounts Deducted from Account (Debits)				DROFO LIMITED Cash Account (partial) Cheques Written (Credits)		
Date	Cheque No.	Amount		Date	Cheque No.	Amount
May 2	254	$560		May 2	258	$159
4	257	410		5	259	275
12	258	159		10	260	500
17	259	275		15	261	867
20	260	500		22	262	750
29	263	840		24	263	440
30	262	750		29	264	650
31	Service charge	54				

Additional information:
1.   The bank did not make any errors.
2.   The company made one error.

Instructions

(a) List the outstanding cheques at May 31.

(b) List any other items that must be included in the bank reconciliation. Describe the impact of each
item on the reconciliation.

Prepare bank reconciliation and
adjusting entries.
(SO 3)

E7–8   Refer to the data presented in E7–6 and E7–7. On May 31, Drofo Limited had an unadjusted cash
balance of $5,109 in the general ledger. The bank statement showed a balance of $6,378 on May 31.

Instructions

(a) Prepare the bank reconciliation on May 31.

(b) Prepare any adjusting journal entries required from the reconciliation. Assume that the EFT
collection from a customer on May 25 shown in E7–6 has not yet been recorded.

Prepare bank reconciliation and
adjusting entries.
(SO 3)

E7–9   The following information is for Mohammed Ltd. in July:
1.   Cash balance per bank, July 31, $8,833
2.   Cash balance per books, July 31, $7,190
3.   Bank service charge, $24

4. Deposits in transit, $1,575
5. Electronic receipts from customers in payment of their accounts, $883
6. Outstanding cheques, $2,449
7. Cheque #373 was correctly written and recorded by the company as $672. The bank deducted $762 from the company's account in error. The cheque was written for the purchase of office supplies.

Instructions

(a) Prepare the bank reconciliation on July 31.

(b) Prepare any adjusting journal entries required from the reconciliation.

E7–10   The following information is for Sharaf Corporation.

Calculate amounts for bank reconciliation.
(SO 3)

SHARAF CORPORATION Bank Reconciliation August 31	
Cash balance per bank	$20,860
Add: Deposits in transit	3,370
	24,230
Less: Outstanding cheques	6,880
Adjusted cash balance per bank	$17,350

Additional information:

1. The September bank statement shows the following selected items:

Amounts Deducted from Account (Debits)		Amounts Added to Account (Credits)	
NSF cheque: J. Hower	$410	EFT collections	$1,825
Bank service charge, NSF cheque	40		
Bank service charge	25		
EFT payments	900		

2. In September, $66,787 of cheques cleared the bank.
3. In September, the company wrote and recorded cheques totalling $63,746.
4. In September, deposits per bank statement (excluding the EFT collections listed in point 1 of this list) were $62,789.
5. In September, the company recorded deposits totalling $64,329.

Instructions

(a) Calculate the unadjusted balance in the Cash account on September 30.

(b) Calculate the unadjusted balance in the bank account on September 30.

(c) Calculate the deposits in transit at September 30.

(d) Calculate the outstanding cheques at September 30.

(e) Calculate the adjusted cash balance per bank at September 30.

E7–11   A new accountant at La Maison Ltée is trying to identify which of the following amounts should be reported as the current asset cash in the year-end balance sheet, as at April 30:

Calculate cash balance.
(SO 4)

1. Currency and coin totalling $87 in a locked box used for incidental cash transactions
2. A $10,000 guaranteed investment certificate, due the next month, May 31
3. April-dated cheques worth $300 that La Maison has received from customers but not yet deposited
4. An $85 cheque received from a customer in payment of its April account, but postdated to May 1
5. A balance of $2,575 in the Royal Bank chequing account
6. A balance of $4,000 in the Royal Bank savings account
7. Prepaid postage of $75 in the postage meter
8. A $50 IOU from the company receptionist
9. Cash register floats of $250
10. Over-the-counter receipts for April 30 consisting of $550 of currency and coin, $185 of cheques from customers, $685 of debit card slips, and $755 of bank credit card slips. These amounts were processed by the bank on May 1.

Instructions

    (a) What amount should La Maison report as its cash balance at April 30?

    (b) In which financial statement(s) and in what account(s) should the items not included in (a) be reported?

Discuss cash management.
(SO 4)

E7–12 ▬ℂ Tory, Hachey, and Wedunn, three young lawyers who have joined together to open a law practice, are struggling to manage their cash flow. They have not yet built up enough clientele and revenues to support the cost of running their legal practice. Initial costs, such as advertising, renovations to the premises, and so on, all result in outgoing cash flow at a time when little is coming in! Tory, Hachey, and Wedunn have not had time to establish a billing system since most of their clients' cases have not yet reached the courts and the lawyers did not think it would be right to bill them until "results were achieved." Unfortunately, Tory, Hachey, and Wedunn's suppliers do not feel the same way. Their suppliers expect them to pay their accounts payable within a few weeks of receiving their bills. So far, there has not ever been enough money to pay the three lawyers, and they are not sure how long they can keep practising law without getting some money into their pockets!

Instructions

Provide suggestions for Tory, Hachey, and Wedunn to improve their cash management practices.

Problems: Set A

Identify control weaknesses over cash receipts.
(SO 1, 2)

P7–1A You are asked to join the board of trustees of a local church to help with the control activities for the offerings collection made at weekly services. At a meeting of the board of trustees, you learn the following:

    1.   The board of trustees has delegated responsibility for the financial management and audit of the financial records to the finance committee. This group prepares the annual budget and approves major payments but is not involved in collections or record keeping. No audit has been done in recent years, because the same trusted employee has kept church records and served as financial secretary for 15 years. The church does not carry any fidelity insurance.

    2.   The collection at the weekly service is taken by a team of ushers who volunteer to serve for one month. The ushers take the collection plates to a basement office at the back of the church. They hand their plates to the head usher and return to the church service. After all plates have been turned in, the head usher counts the cash collected in them. The head usher then places the cash in the church safe along with a note that includes the amount counted. The safe is unlocked because no one can remember the combination, and after all, it is in a church.

    3.   The morning after the service, the financial secretary goes to the safe and recounts the collection. The secretary withholds $200 to pay for cash purchases for the week, and deposits the remainder of the collection in the bank. To facilitate the deposit, church members who contribute by cheque are asked to make their cheques payable to "Cash."

    4.   Each month, the financial secretary reconciles the bank statement and submits a copy of the reconciliation to the board of trustees. The reconciliations have rarely revealed any bank errors and have never shown any errors per books.

Instructions

    (a) Identify the weaknesses in control activities in the handling of collections.

    (b) List the improvements in control activities that should be recommended for (1) the head usher, (2) the ushers, (3) the financial secretary, and (4) the finance committee.

Identify control activities over cash payments.
(SO 1, 2)

P7–2A Segal Office Supply Limited recently changed its control activities over cash payments. The new activities include the following features:

    1.   All cheques are prenumbered and written by an electronic cheque-writing system.

    2.   Before a cheque or electronic payment can be issued, each invoice must have the approval of Cindy Morris, the purchasing agent, and Ray Mills, the receiving department supervisor.

    3.   Cheques must be signed by either controller Frank Malone or assistant controller Mary Arno. Before signing a cheque, the signer is expected to compare the amount of the cheque with the amount on the invoice.

4. After signing a cheque, the signer stamps the invoice "Paid" and writes in the date, cheque number, and amount of the cheque. The paid invoice is then sent to the accounting department for recording.

5. Blank cheques are stored in a safe in the controller's office. The combination to the safe is known only to the controller and assistant controller.

6. Each month the bank statement is reconciled by a staff accountant.

Instructions

Identify the control activities and how they are applied to cash payments at Segal Office Supply.

P7–3A Each of the following independent situations has a control activity weakness:

Identify control weaknesses.
(SO 1, 2)

1. Rowena's Cleaning Service Inc. provides home cleaning services for a large number of clients who all pay cash. Rowena collects the cash and keeps it in the glove compartment of her car until the end of the week when she has time to count it and prepare a bank deposit.

2. Hornet's Convenience Store Limited sells a variety of items, including cigarettes, non-alcoholic beverages, and snack foods. A long-term employee is responsible for ordering all merchandise, checking all deliveries, and approving invoices for payment.

3. At Ye Olde Ice Cream Shoppe Ltd., there are three sales clerks on duty during busy times. All three of them use the same cash drawer.

4. Most customers at Better Used Car dealership use the option to pay for their vehicles in 24 equal payments over two years. These customers send the company cheques or cash each month. The office manager opens the mail each day, makes a bank deposit with the cash and cheques received in the mail that day, and prepares and posts a journal entry in the accounting records.

5. Jimmy's Truck Parts Ltd. employs sales staff who visit current and prospective customers. The sales staff keep product samples in their vehicles so they can demonstrate the product to the customers. If a customer has a large order, the order is e-mailed to the warehouse. The warehouse then ships the product to the customer on account. If a customer wishes to purchase one or two sample items, the salesperson can sell these for cash or on account. To obtain more inventory, the salespeople go to the warehouse and restock the vehicle themselves.

Instructions

(a) Identify the control weakness(es) in each of the above situations.

(b) Explain the problems that could occur as a result of these weaknesses.

(c) Make recommendations for correcting each situation.

P7–4A The president of a registered charity, the Helping Elderly Low-Income People Foundation (HELP), approaches you for help on a special project to set up the charity's accounting system. HELP is a relatively new organization, just established, and is regulated by both the federal and provincial governments. One requirement is that it maintain current financial records for the public to scrutinize. In other words, the records must be available to anyone who is interested in reviewing them. It is now the end of the company's first fiscal year, and HELP has come to you with a shoebox of receipts and bank statements. You notice that the bank statements are still in their envelopes—they have not been opened.

Identify control weaknesses over cash receipts and payments.
(SO 1, 2)

The charity's revenue is mostly from donations. A van driver takes volunteers around the city and they go door to door asking for donations. The volunteers give a donation receipt for amounts over $20. Since volunteering takes a lot of time, the charity has many short-term volunteers and anyone is welcome to be one.

Fortunately for HELP, two car companies generously donated vans to the organization. The van drivers are paid $50 a day, which they take from the donations. Drivers keep a summary of the total donations collected by the volunteers, and at the end of the day the drivers take the money to a bank and deposit it. Drivers also pay for their gas out of the donated funds.

HELP also held a fundraising dance last month. The president said he was disappointed with the project, though, because it did not bring in much money. On the plus side, it did raise public awareness. To keep costs down, the president made the dance tickets by photocopying tickets and cutting them up. He gave them out to volunteers to sell for $25 each. He estimates that he printed 500 tickets, but can only account for about $5,000 (200 tickets @ $25) of revenues given in by his volunteers.

Instructions

(a) Identify the weaknesses in control activities over cash receipts and payments.

(b) List the improvements in control activities that should be considered by HELP.

Prepare bank reconciliation and adjusting entries.
(SO 3)

P7–5A On May 31, Maloney Inc. had a cash balance per books of $6,700. The bank statement from Community Bank on that date showed a balance of $7,615. A comparison of the bank statement with the company's Cash account revealed the following:

1. The bank statement included a bank service charge of $40.
2. The bank statement included two electronic collections from customers on account: $2,055 received from C. Dicerni and $39 received from R. Doyle. These were not previously recorded.
3. Cash sales of $836 on May 12 were deposited in the bank. The journal entry and the deposit slip were incorrectly made out and recorded by Maloney for $856. The bank detected the error and credited Maloney for the correct amount.
4. Outstanding cheques at April 30 totalled $1,450. Of these, $1,120 cleared the bank in May. There were $946 of cheques written in May that were still outstanding on May 31.
5. On May 18, the company issued cheque #1181 for $685 to a creditor in payment of its account. The cheque, which cleared the bank in May, was incorrectly journalized and posted by Maloney as being for $568.
6. Included with the cancelled cheques was a cheque issued by Baloney Inc. for $600 that was incorrectly charged to Maloney by the bank.
7. On May 31, the bank statement showed a returned (NSF) cheque of $675 issued by a customer in payment of its account. In addition, the bank charged a $40 processing fee for this transaction.
8. The May 31 deposit of $963 was not included in the deposits on the May bank statement. The deposit had been placed in the bank's night deposit vault on May 31.

Instructions

(a) Prepare the bank reconciliation on May 31.

(b) Prepare any adjusting journal entries required from the reconciliation.

Prepare bank reconciliation and adjusting entries.
(SO 3)

P7–6A The bank portion of last month's bank reconciliation showed the following for River Adventures Ltd.:

RIVER ADVENTURES LTD. Bank Reconciliation April 30		
Cash balance per bank		$9,009
Add: Deposits in transit		846
		9,855
Less: Outstanding cheques		
#533	$279	
#541	363	
#555	79	721
Adjusted cash balance		$9,134

The adjusted cash balance per bank agreed with the cash balance per books at April 30. The May bank statement showed the following:

RIVER ADVENTURES LTD.
Bank Statement
May 31

Date		Description	Amounts Deducted from Account (Debits)	Amounts Added to Account (Credits)	Balance
Apr.	30	Opening balance			9,009
May	1	Deposit		846	9,855
	3	Cheque, No. 541	363		9,492
	4	Cheque, No. 533	279		9,213
	5	Cheque, No. 556	223		8,990
	6	Cheque, No. 557	1,800		7,190
	6	Deposit		1,250	8,440
	7	Cheque, No. 558	934		7,506
	8	Deposit		975	8,481
	10	Cheque, No. 559	1,650		6,831
	15	Deposit		426	7,257
	18	EFT, collection on account from A. Osborne		650	7,907
	19	Cheque, No. 561	799		7,108
	20	Cheque, No. 562	2,045		5,063
	21	EFT, collection on account from P. Lau		1,222	6,285
	23	Cheque, No. 563	2,487		3,798
	25	Deposit		980	4,778
	28	Deposit		1,771	6,549
	28	Returned cheque—NSF, R. Lajeunesse	440		6,109
	28	NSF fee	40		6,069
	30	EFT, insurance payment	578		5,491
	31	SVC plan fee	25		5,466

River Adventure's cash receipts and payments for the month of May showed the following:

Cash Receipts			Cash Payments		
Date		Amount	Date	Number	Amount
May	6	$1,250	May 4	556	$ 223
	8	975	5	557	1,800
	15	426	7	558	943
	25	890	7	559	1,650
	28	1,771	10	560	890
	31	1,286	15	561	799
		$6,598	17	562	2,045
			22	563	2,487
			31	564	950
					$11,787

Additional information:
1. The EFT collections were not previously recorded.
2. Because the EFT insurance payment occurred near the end of the month, it has not been recorded yet.
3. The bank made an error when processing cheque #558.
4. The company made an error in recording the May 25 deposit.

Instructions

(a) Calculate the unadjusted cash balance per books at May 31, prior to reconciliation.

(b) What is the amount of the deposits in transit at May 31?

(c) What is the amount of the outstanding cheques at May 31?

(d) Prepare a bank reconciliation on May 31.

(e) Prepare any adjusting journal entries required from the reconciliation.

Prepare bank reconciliation and adjusting entries.
(SO 3)

P7–7A The bank portion of the bank reconciliation for Racine Limited at November 30 is shown here:

RACINE LIMITED Bank Reconciliation November 30		
Cash balance per bank		$14,368
Add: Deposits in transit		2,530
		16,898
Less: Outstanding cheques		
#3451	$2,260	
#3471	845	
#3474	1,050	4,155
Adjusted cash balance		$12,743

The adjusted cash balance per bank agreed with the cash balance per books at November 30. The December bank statement showed the following:

RACINE LIMITED Bank Statement December 31				
Date	Description	Amounts Deducted from Account (Debits)	Amounts Added to Account (Credits)	Balance
Nov. 30	Opening balance			14,368
Dec. 1	Deposit		2,530	16,898
1	Cheque, No. 3451	2,260		14,638
2	Cheque, No. 3471	845		13,793
3	Deposit		1,212	15,005
4	Cheque, No. 3475	1,641		13,364
7	EFT, salaries	1,427		11,937
8	Cheque, No. 3476	1,300		10,637
10	Cheque, No. 3477	2,130		8,507
15	Cheque, No. 3479	3,080		5,427
15	EFT, collection on account, R. Nishimura		3,145	8,572
17	Deposit		2,945	11,517
21	EFT, salaries	1,427		10,090
24	Returned cheque—NSF, Hilo Holdings	987		9,103
24	NSF fee	40		9,063
27	Deposit		2,567	11,630
27	Cheque, No. 3480	600		11,030
29	Cheque, No. 3482	1,140		9,890
30	Deposit		1,025	10,915
30	Cheque, No. 3481	475		10,440
31	SVC plan fee	45		10,395

The cash records per books for December showed the following:

Cash Receipts	
Date	Amount
Dec. 1	$1,212
17	2,954
27	2,567
30	1,025
31	1,197
	$8,955

Cash Payments		
Date	Number	Amount
Dec. 1	3475	$ 1,641
2	3476	1,300
2	3477	2,130
4	3478	538
7	EFT, salaries	1,427
8	3479	3,080
10	3480	600
20	3481	475
21	EFT, salaries	1,427
22	3482	1,140
30	3483	1,390
		$15,148

Additional information:

1. The EFT collections were not previously recorded.
2. EFT payments are recorded when they occur.
3. The bank did not make any errors.
4. One error was made by the company. The correction of any errors in recording cheques should be made to Accounts Payable. The correction of any errors in recording cash receipts should be made to Accounts Receivable.

Instructions

(a) Calculate the unadjusted cash balance per books at December 31, prior to reconciliation.

(b) Prepare the bank reconciliation on December 31.

(c) Prepare any adjusting journal entries required from the reconciliation.

P7–8A   Giant Inc. is a profitable small business. It has not, however, given much consideration to internal control. For example, in an attempt to keep clerical and office expenses to a minimum, the company has combined the jobs of cashier and bookkeeper. As a result, Karen Kilgora handles all cash receipts, keeps the accounting records, and prepares the monthly bank reconciliations.

Prepare bank reconciliation and identify weaknesses in control activities.
(SO 1, 3)

The balance per bank statement on November 30, was $13,655. Outstanding cheques were #62 for $127, #83 for $180, #84 for $253, and #86 for $190. There was one deposit in transit for $4,040. Included in the bank statement was a notification about a $225 electronic collection on account from a customer.

The company's general ledger showed the Cash account with a balance of $17,341. The balance included undeposited cash on hand. Because of the lack of internal controls, Kilgora took all of the undeposited receipts for personal use. She then prepared the following bank reconciliation to hide her theft of cash:

GIANT INC. Bank Reconciliation November 30		
Cash balance per books		$17,341
Less: EFT, collection from customer		225
Adjusted cash balance per books		$17,116
Cash balance per bank statement		$13,655
Add: Deposit in transit		4,040
		17,695
Less: Outstanding cheques		
#62	$127	
#83	108	
#84	235	
#86	109	579
Adjusted cash balance per bank		$17,116

Instructions

    (a) Identify the errors in the above bank reconciliation.

    (b) Prepare a correct bank reconciliation.

    (c) Identify how much Kilgora stole for personal use. (*Hint*: The theft is the difference between the adjusted balance per books before the theft and adjusted balance per bank.)

    (d) Indicate the various ways that Kilgora tried to hide the theft and the dollar amount for each method.

    (e) What control activities were violated in this case?

Calculate cash balance.
(SO 4)

P7–9A   A new CGA student has been asked to determine the balance that should be reported as cash as at December 31 for one of the firm's clients. The following information is available:

1. Cash on hand in the cash registers on December 31 totals $1,600. Of this amount, $500 is kept on hand as a cash float.
2. At December 31, the company has debit card slips in the cash register totalling $500.
3. At December 31, the company has MasterCard credit card slips in the cash register totalling $975.
4. The balance in the bank chequing account at December 31 is $7,460.
5. Short-term investments include $5,000 in a money-market fund and an investment of $2,500 in a six-month term deposit.
6. The company sold $250 of merchandise to a customer late in the day on December 31. The customer had forgotten her wallet and promised to pay the amount on January 2.
7. The company has a U.S. dollar bank account. At December 31, its U.S. funds were worth the equivalent of $2,241 Canadian.
8. In order to hook up utilities, the company is required to deposit $1,000 in trust with Ontario Hydro. This amount must remain on deposit until a satisfactory credit history has been established. The company expects to have this deposit back within the year.

Instructions

    (a) Calculate the cash balance that should be reported on the year-end balance sheet.

    (b) Identify where any items that were not reported in (a) should be reported.

Discuss reporting of cash.
(SO 4)

P7–10A   Royal Roads University reports the following selected information in its March 31, 2008, financial statements:

	2008	2007
Cash and cash equivalents	$ 7,702,186	$ 9,592,893
Short-term investments	18,643,783	15,742,220
Restricted funds (net assets)	7,135,466	7,379,973
Cash provided by operating activities	3,086,735	2,587,071

Additional information:

1. Cash and cash equivalents comprise cash in the bank, cash on hand, and instruments with maturity dates of three months or less when acquired.
2. Short-term investments are all highly liquid marketable securities that have a term to maturity of 90 days to 1 year when acquired.
3. Restricted funds are for an infrastructure fund, a human resources strategy fund, and various research funds.

Instructions

    (a) Explain the difference between cash equivalents and short-term investments.

    (b) Royal Roads has $7,135,466 of restricted net assets (similar to restricted retained earnings) for a variety of funds. Is this the same as restricted cash? Explain.

    (c) How is it possible that Royal Roads has $7,702,186 of cash and cash equivalents at the end of 2008 but generated only $3,086,735 of cash from operating activities in the same year?

Recommend cash management improvements.
(SO 4)

P7–11A   Jackie Smith started a business, Jackie's Designs Inc., on the completion of her interior design courses eight months ago. Jackie has been fortunate in that the company has already completed six contracts and has four more signed contracts and meetings with prospective customers. A number of the prospective customers are referrals from the six contracts she has already completed.

Jackie is having difficulty understanding why her business has no cash in the bank since it has been so successful. You asked her to explain the terms of the contracts and her system for purchases.

A contract is signed once the customer and Jackie agree on the work to be done. There is no deposit on signing the contract. The contract price is a flat fee for Jackie's work and cost plus a percentage for all items purchased by the company. The fee for Jackie's work is due once the contract is completed. The amount for items purchased by the company is due three weeks after the items are delivered to the customer, in case the customer wants to return them. To date, an average contract takes four months to complete.

The company does not have a formalized system for purchases. If a customer agrees that they would like to purchase certain items, Jackie will purchase the items when she finds them. Generally, she uses cash to pay for the items at the time of purchase. The items are then delivered to the customer within a week.

Instructions

Identify ways the company can improve its cash management practices.

Problems: Set B

P7–1B   High Tech Inc. commenced operations recently. The company shares are jointly owned by two friends from university, John Street and Rehana Avenue. John and Rehana have developed a new software application to track shipping. The two friends spend most of their time on the development of new products and the marketing of the current product.

Identify control weaknesses over cash payments.
(SO 1, 2)

John and Rehana hired Fred Glass to be High Tech's controller. Fred has been given overall responsibility for the books and records of High Tech so that John and Rehana can spend their time on development and marketing.

Fred has one assistant, Janet. Both Fred and Janet have the authority to order goods for High Tech. Janet can approve invoices for payment up to $5,000. Fred has the authority to approve any invoice for payment. Fred, John, and Rehana are all signing officers on the company's bank account. Only one of the three signing officers needs to sign a cheque under $20,000. For cheques greater than $20,000, two signing officers must sign. Unsigned cheques are kept in the company safe. Fred is responsible for preparing the monthly bank reconciliations and making any necessary journal entries.

Instructions

(a) Identify the control weaknesses over the cash payments.

(b) List the improvements in control activities that should be considered by High Tech.

P7–2B   Red River Theatre has a cashier's booth located near the entrance to the theatre. There are two cashiers: one works from 1 p.m. to 5 p.m., the other from 5 p.m. to 9 p.m. Each cashier is bonded. The cashiers receive cash from customers and operate a machine that ejects serially numbered tickets. The rolls of tickets are inserted and locked into the machine by the theatre manager at the beginning of each cashier's shift.

Identify control activities over cash receipts.
(SO 1, 2)

After purchasing a ticket, which costs a different amount depending on the day of the week and the customer's age group, the customer takes the ticket to an usher stationed at the entrance to the theatre lobby, a few metres from the cashier's booth. The usher tears the ticket in half, admits the customer, and returns the ticket stub to the customer. The other half of the ticket is dropped into a locked box by the usher.

At the end of each cashier's shift, the theatre manager removes the ticket rolls from the machine and makes a cash count. The cash count sheet is initialled by the cashier. At the end of the day, the manager deposits the total receipts in a bank night deposit slot. In addition, the manager sends copies of the deposit slip and the initialled cash count sheets to the head cashier for verification and to the accounting department. Receipts from the first shift are stored in a safe located in the manager's office.

Instructions

(a) Identify the control activities and their application to cash receipts at the theatre.

(b) If the usher and cashier decided to collaborate to steal cash, what actions might they take?

P7–3B   Each of the following independent situations has one or more control activity weaknesses:

Identify control weaknesses.
(SO 1, 2)

1. Board Riders Ltd. is a small snowboarding club that offers specialized coaching for teenagers who want to improve their skills. Group lessons are offered every day. Members who want a lesson pay a $25 fee directly to the teacher at the start of the lesson that day. Most members pay cash. At the end of the lesson, the teacher reports the number of students and turns over the cash to the office manager.

2. Coloroso Agency Corp. offers parenting advice to young single mothers. Most of the agency's revenues are from government grants. The general manager is responsible for all of the accounting work, including approving invoices for payment, preparing and posting all entries into the accounting system, and preparing bank reconciliations.

3. At Nexus Corporation, each salesperson is responsible for deciding on the correct credit policies for his or her customers. For example, the salesperson decides if Nexus should sell to the customer on credit and how high the credit limit should be. Salespeople receive a commission based on their sales.

4. Algorithm Limited is a software company that employs many computer programmers. The company uses accounting software that was created by one of the employees. In order to be more flexible and share the workload, all of the programmers have access to the accounting software program in case changes are needed.

5. The warehouse manager at Orange Wing Distributors Ltd. is well known for running an efficient, cost-saving operation. He has eliminated the requirement for staff to create receiving reports and purchase orders because it was taking staff too long to prepare them.

Instructions

(a) Identify the control weakness(es) in each of the above situations.

(b) Explain the problems that could occur as a result of these weaknesses.

(c) Make recommendations for correcting each situation.

Identify control weaknesses over cash receipts and payments.
(SO 1, 2)

P7–4B Cedar Grove Middle School wants to raise money for a new sound system for its auditorium. The main fundraising event is a dance at which the famous disc jockey Obnoxious Al will play rap music. Roger DeMaster, the music teacher, has been given the responsibility for coordinating the fundraising efforts. This is Roger's first experience with fundraising. He decides to put the Student Representative Council (SRC) in charge of the event.

Roger had 500 unnumbered tickets printed for the dance. He left the tickets in a locked box on his desk and told the SRC students to take as many tickets as they thought they could sell for $20 each. To ensure that no extra tickets would be floating around, he told the students to get rid of any unsold tickets. When the students received payment for the tickets, they were to bring the cash back to Roger, and he would put it in the locked box on his desk.

Some of the students were responsible for decorating the gymnasium for the dance. Roger gave each of them a key to the locked box and told them that if they took money out to purchase materials, they should put a note in the box saying how much they took and what it was used for. After two weeks, the locked box appeared to be getting full, so Roger asked Steve Stevens to count the money, prepare a deposit slip, and deposit the money in a bank account Roger had opened.

The day of the dance, Roger wrote a cheque from the account to pay Obnoxious Al. Al, however, said that he accepted only cash and did not give receipts. Having no alternative, Roger took $500 out of the locked box and gave it to Al. At the dance, Roger had Sara Billings working at the entrance to the gymnasium, collecting tickets from students and selling tickets to those who had not prepurchased them. Roger estimated that 400 students attended the dance.

The following day, Roger closed out the bank account, which had $750 in it, and gave that amount plus the $1,800 in the locked box to Principal Skinner. Principal Skinner seemed surprised that, after generating roughly $8,000 (400 tickets @ $20) in sales, the dance netted only $2,550 in cash. Roger did not know how to respond.

Instructions

(a) Identify the weaknesses in control activities over cash receipts and payments.

(b) Suggest how each weakness could be addressed.

Prepare bank reconciliation and adjusting entries.
(SO 3)

P7–5B On July 31, Dubeau Ltd. had a cash balance per books of $7,393. The statement from the Caisse Populaire on that date showed a balance of $9,994. A comparison of the bank statement with the Cash account revealed the following:

1. The bank statement included a bank service charge of $50.

2. The bank statement included two electronic collections from customers on account: $2,031 from D. Hinton and $24 from A. Leonard. These were not previously recorded.

3. The July 31 cash receipts of $1,393 were not included in the bank deposits for July. These receipts were deposited by the company in a night deposit vault on July 31.

4. Company cheque #2480 for $585, issued to J. Brokaw, a creditor, cleared the bank in July and was incorrectly entered in the general journal on July 10 as $855.
5. A deposit of $900 made by another company was incorrectly added to Dubeau's account by the Caisse Populaire.
6. Salaries of $2,000 were paid electronically during the month. These have already been recorded by the company.
7. Cheques outstanding on June 30 totalled $922. Of these, $689 cleared the bank in July. There were $1,446 of cheques written in July that were still outstanding July 31.
8. On July 31, the bank statement showed a returned (NSF) cheque of $820 received by the company from a customer on account. In addition, the bank charged a $40 processing fee for this transaction.

Instructions

(a) Prepare the bank reconciliation on July 31.

(b) Prepare any adjusting journal entries required from the reconciliation.

P7–6B   The bank portion of last month's bank reconciliation for Yap Ltd. at February 28 was as follows:

Prepare bank reconciliation and adjusting entries.
(SO 3)

YAP LTD. Bank Reconciliation February 28		
Cash balance per bank		$14,368
Add: Deposits in transit		2,530
		16,898
Less: Outstanding cheques		
#3451	$2,260	
#3470	1,535	
#3471	845	4,640
Adjusted cash balance		$12,258

The adjusted cash balance per bank agreed with the cash balance per books at February 28. The March bank statement showed the following:

YAP LTD. Bank Statement March 31				
Date	Description	Amounts Deducted from Account (Debits)	Amounts Added to Account (Credits)	Balance
Feb. 28	Opening balance			14,368
Mar. 1	Cheque, No. 3451	2,260		12,108
1	Deposit		2,530	14,638
2	Cheque, No. 3471	845		13,793
4	Deposit		1,212	15,005
7	Deposit		550	15,555
9	Cheque, No. 3472	1,427		14,128
10	Returned cheque—NSF, R. Aubut	550		13,578
10	NSF fee	40		13,538
15	EFT, loan payment	1,062		12,476
19	Cheque, No. 3473	1,641		10,835
24	Cheque, No. 3474	2,130		8,705
26	Deposit		2,567	11,272
31	EFT, collection on account from M. Boudreault		230	11,502
31	SVC plan fee	49		11,453

Yap's cash receipts and payments for the month of March showed the following:

Cash Receipts		
Date		Amount
Mar. 4		$1,221
7		550
26		2,567
31		1,025
		$5,363

Cash Payments		
Date	Number	Amount
Mar. 7	3472	$1,427
15	3473	1,461
22	3474	2,130
29	3475	487
		$5,505

Additional information:

1. The EFT collections were not previously recorded.
2. The EFT loan payment should have been recorded by the company on March 15, but this entry was missed. The payment included $62 of interest and a $1,000 payment on the loan principal.
3. The bank made an error processing cheque #3473.
4. The company made an error in recording the March 4 deposit.

Instructions

(a) Calculate the unadjusted cash balance per books at March 31, prior to reconciliation.

(b) What is the amount of the deposits in transit at March 31?

(c) What is the amount of the outstanding cheques at March 31?

(d) Prepare a bank reconciliation at March 31.

(e) Prepare any adjusting journal entries required from the reconciliation.

Prepare bank reconciliation and adjusting entries.
(SO 3)

P7–7B   The bank portion of the bank reconciliation for London Inc. at October 31 is shown here:

LONDON INC. Bank Reconciliation October 31		
Cash balance per bank		$12,445
Add: Deposits in transit		1,530
		13,975
Less: Outstanding cheques		
#2472	$720	
#2473	845	
#2474	504	2,069
Adjusted cash balance		$11,906

The adjusted cash balance per bank agreed with the cash balance per books at October 31. The November bank statement showed the following:

LONDON INC. Bank Statement November 30				
Date	Description	Amounts Deducted from Account (Debits)	Amounts Added to Account(Credits)	Balance
Oct. 31				12,445
Nov. 1	Cheque, No. 2472	720		11,725
1	Deposit		1,530	13,255
2	Cheque, No. 2473	845		12,410
3	Deposit		1,212	13,622
4	Cheque, No. 2475	1,641		11,981
7	Deposit		990	12,971
8	Cheque, No. 2476	2,830		10,141
10	Cheque, No. 2477	600		9,541

14	Deposit			2,575	12,116
15	Cheque, No. 2478		1,750		10,366
15	EFT, salaries		3,200		7,166
20	Deposit			2,945	10,111
25	Returned cheque—NSF,				
	Giasson Developments		250		9,861
25	NSF fee		40		9,821
26	Cheque, No. 2479		695		9,126
27	Deposit			1,650	10,776
28	EFT, collection of note receivable				
	and interest			2,504	13,280
30	Cheque, No. 2481		576		12,704
30	EFT, salaries		3,200		9,504
30	SVC plan fee		25		9,479

The cash records per books for November showed the following:

Cash Receipts			Cash Payments		
Date		Amount	Date	Number	Amount
Nov. 3		$ 1,212	Nov. 1	2475	$ 1,641
7		990	2	2476	2,380
12		2,575	2	2477	600
20		2,954	8	2478	1,750
27		1,650	15	2479	695
30		1,338	15	EFT, salaries	3,200
		$10,719	18	2480	612
			20	2481	576
			29	2482	830
			30	EFT, salaries	3,200
					$15,484

Additional information:

1. The EFT collections were not previously recorded. The collection of the note was for $2,200, plus $304 interest. Interest was not previously accrued.
2. EFT payments are recorded when they occur.
3. The bank did not make any errors.
4. Two errors were made by the company—one in recording a cheque and one in recording a cash receipt. The correction of any errors in the recording of cheques should be made to Accounts Payable. The correction of any errors in the recording of cash receipts should be made to Accounts Receivable.

Instructions

(a) Calculate the unadjusted cash balance per books as at November 30, prior to reconciliation.

(b) Prepare a bank reconciliation at November 30.

(c) Prepare any adjusting journal entries required from the reconciliation.

P7–8B   Tarika Ltd. is a profitable small business. It has not, however, given much consideration to internal control. For example, in an attempt to keep clerical and office expenses to a minimum, the company has combined the jobs of cashier and bookkeeper. As a result, Rob Tang handles all cash receipts, keeps the accounting records, and prepares the monthly bank reconciliations.

Prepare bank reconciliation and identify weaknesses in control activities.
(SO 1, 3)

The balance per bank statement on October 31 was $19,460. Outstanding cheques were #782 for $114, #783 for $160, #784 for $267, #789 for $171, #791 for $325, and #792 for $173. There were no outstanding deposits in transit. Included with the bank statement was a $299 electronic collection on account from a customer.

The company's general ledger showed the Cash account with a balance of $19,640. The balance included undeposited cash on hand. Because of the lack of internal controls, Tang took all of the undeposited receipts for personal use. He then prepared the following bank reconciliation to hide his theft of cash:

TARIKA LTD.		
Bank Reconciliation		
October 31		

Cash balance per books		$19,640
Less: EFT, collection from customer		299
Adjusted cash balance per books		$19,341
Cash balance per bank statement		$19,460
Less: Outstanding cheques		
#782	$11	
#783	16	
#784	26	
#789	17	
#791	32	
#792	17	119
Adjusted cash balance per bank		$19,341

Instructions

(a) Identify the errors in the above bank reconciliation.

(b) Prepare a correct bank reconciliation.

(c) Identify how much Tang stole for personal use. (*Hint*: The theft is the difference between the adjusted balance per books before the theft and the adjusted balance per bank.)

(d) Indicate the various ways that Tang tried to hide the theft and the dollar amount for each method.

(e) What control activities were violated in this case?

Calculate cash balance.
(SO 4)

P7–9B   A first year co-op student is trying to determine the amount of cash that should be reported on a company's balance sheet. The following information was provided to the student at year end:

1.   Cash on hand in the cash registers totals $5,000.
2.   The balance in the commercial bank savings account is $100,000 and in the commercial bank chequing account, $25,000. The company also has a U.S. bank account, which contains the equivalent of $45,000 Canadian at year end.
3.   A special bank account holds $150,000 in cash that is restricted for equipment replacement.
4.   Amounts due from employees (travel advances) total $12,000.
5.   Short-term investments held by the company include $32,000 in a money-market fund; $75,000 in treasury bills; and $40,000 in shares of Shoppers Drug Mart.
6.   The company has a supply of unused postage stamps totalling $150.
7.   The company has $1,750 of NSF cheques from customers that were returned by the bank. NSF fees charged by the bank for processing these cheques totalled $80.
8.   The company keeps $5,000 as a compensating balance in a special account.

Instructions
(a) Calculate the cash balance that should be reported on the year-end balance sheet.
(b) Identify where any items that were not reported in the cash balance in (a) should be reported.

Discuss reporting of cash.
(SO 4)

P7–10B   ◯━◖ **Wilfrid Laurier University** reports the following selected information (in thousands) in its April 30, 2007, financial statements:

	2007	2006
Cash and short-term deposits	$39,095	$30,354
Restricted cash	850	1,350
Cash provided by operating activities	22,184	15,776

Additional information:
Cash was restricted for the funding of post-retirement benefits.

Instructions

(a) Explain the difference between cash and short-term deposits. Why are they combined for reporting purposes?

(b) In which section of the balance sheet would the restricted cash most likely be reported? Explain.

(c) How is it possible that Wilfrid Laurier University has $39,095 thousand of cash and short-term deposits at the end of fiscal 2007 but generated only $22,184 thousand of cash flow from operating activities in the same year?

P7–11B 🔑 Bev's Design Services Ltd. commenced operations approximately nine months ago. Bev, the sole shareholder and designer, organizes the hall and table decorations for a variety of functions. Bev has completed 15 contracts so far and, with wedding season coming up, has 20 more signed contracts. However, the company has no cash in its bank account and Bev has had to loan the business money from her personal funds.

Recommend cash management improvements. (SO 4)

For each signed contract, the company requires a $50 non-refundable deposit. The balance of the payment is due three weeks following the function. For the weddings Bev has serviced, payment has been made on average five weeks after the function. All the decorations must be purchased about two months before the function or once the contract has been signed, whichever is earlier. The company pays for the decorations at the time of purchase. Recently, the company has learned that it can apply for an account, which will permit it to pay 30 days after purchase.

Instructions

Identify ways the company can improve its cash management practices.

BROADENING YOUR PERSPECTIVE

Financial Reporting and Analysis Cases

Analysis Tools

Financial Reporting: *Shoppers Drug Mart*

BYP7–1 Two reports are attached to the Shoppers Drug Mart financial statements presented in Appendix A of this book: (1) Management's Responsibility for Financial Statements and (2) the Auditors' Report.

Instructions

(a) What comments, if any, about the company's system of internal control are included in the Management's Responsibility for Financial Statements report? In the Auditors' Report?

(b) What reference, if any, is made to internal and external auditors in each of the above reports?

(c) Explain how Shoppers Drug Mart can report both cash and bank indebtedness on its balance sheet at the same time.

Comparative Analysis: *Shoppers Drug Mart and Jean Coutu*

BYP7–2 The financial statements of Jean Coutu are presented in Appendix B, following the financial statements for Shoppers Drug Mart in Appendix A.

Instructions

(a) What is the balance in cash and cash equivalents reported by Jean Coutu and the cash balance reported by Shoppers Drug Mart at the end of the current fiscal year? How much cash was provided by operating activities for each company for the current year?

(b) What conclusions about each company's ability to generate cash and its cash management can be made from this comparison of their results?

Interpreting Financial Statements

BYP7–3 Selected account balances follow for Q9 Networks Inc., headquartered in Toronto:

Q9 NETWORKS INC. Balance Sheet (partial) October 31, 2007 (in thousands)		
	2007	2006
Assets		
Current assets		
Cash and cash equivalents	$ 5,956	$ 5,961
Short-term investments	36,922	61,448
Accounts receivable	4,552	4,330
Unbilled revenue	593	345
Other current assets	3,240	1,351
Total current assets	51,263	73,435
Restricted cash	50	230
Other assets	90,122	65,933
Total assets	$141,435	$139,598

Instructions

(a) What are cash equivalents?

(b) What is meant by restricted cash?

(c) What percentage of the 2007 total assets is represented by short-term investments?

(d) What would be the characteristics of short-term investments that are not grouped with cash equivalents?

A Global Focus

www.wiley.com/canada/kimmel

International Resources

BYP7–4 Selected information follows from Microsoft Corporation's balance sheet:

MICROSOFT CORPORATION Balance Sheet (partial) June 30, 2007 (in USD millions)		
	2007	2006
Current assets		
Cash and equivalents	$ 6,111	$ 6,714
Short-term investments	17,300	27,447
Other current assets	16,757	14,849
Total current assets	40,168	49,010
Total current liabilities	23,754	22,442

Instructions

(a) How do cash equivalents differ from other types of short-term investments?

(b) Calculate (1) the working capital and (2) the current ratio for each year. The industry average for the current ratio was 1.5:1 in 2007 and 1.9:1 in 2006. Comment on your results.

(c) What reason(s) might Microsoft have for holding such large balances of short-term investments?

(d) As an international company, Microsoft is affected by economic conditions in each of the countries in which it operates. For example, when the U.S. dollar devalues against other foreign currencies, as it did in 2007, Microsoft's financial results are affected. Explain how its financial results might be affected by changes in foreign currency.

Critical Thinking Cases and Activities

Collaborative Learning Activity

BYP7–5 Think of your past or current employment and personal experiences, and identify situations in which cash was received and disbursed.

Instructions

With the class divided into groups, do the following:

(a) Identify the strengths and weaknesses in internal control used for cash receipts in the situations you have chosen.

(b) Identify the strengths and weaknesses in internal control used for cash disbursements in the situations you have chosen.

Communication Activity

BYP7–6 Landry Corporation is a small family-owned company selling office supplies. Guylaine Lavoie has been with the company from the beginning, doing all the clerical work, including recording and depositing cash, paying the bills, and reconciling the bank account monthly. The company has grown in size from 3 employees to 20. Annual sales have increased from $200,000 to $7 million. Guylaine is still looking after the cash and says she does not need any help in completing her tasks.

Instructions

Write a letter to Lucette Landry, the president of Landry Corporation, explaining the weaknesses in control activities over cash and your recommendations for improving the system. In your letter, address the fact that the company used to be small but has now grown in both size and revenues.

Ethics Case

BYP7–7 Banks charge fees of up to $40 for bounced cheques—that is, NSF cheques that exceed the balance in the payor's account. It has been estimated that processing bounced cheques costs a bank less than $5 per cheque. Thus, the profit margin on bounced cheques is high. Recognizing this, banks process cheques from largest to smallest within the same date range. By doing this, they maximize the number of cheques that bounce if a customer overdraws an account.

Ethics in Accounting

Instructions

(a) Who are the stakeholders in this case?

(b) Freeman Corp. had a balance of $1,500 in its chequing account on a day when the bank received the following five cheques for processing against that account:

Cheque Number	Amount
3150	$ 35
3158	1,510
3162	400
3165	890
3169	180

Assuming a $40 fee is charged by the bank, how much fee revenue would the bank generate if it processed cheques (1) from largest to smallest, and (2) from smallest to largest?

(c) Do you think that processing cheques from largest to smallest is an ethical business practice?

(d) Besides ethical issues, what else must a bank consider in deciding whether to process cheques from largest to smallest?

(e) If you were managing a bank, what policy would you adopt on bounced cheques?

"All About You" Activity

BYP7–8 The "All About You" feature in this chapter indicates potential security risks that may arise.

Instructions

(a) Go to the website phonebusters.com. What does the term "phishing" mean? What are some of the tips on how to spot and avoid phishing scams?

(b) Go to the website privcom.gc.ca and click on "Information for Individuals" and then "Protecting Your Personal Information." What are some tips you should know on how to protect your personal information?

(c) Is it safe to pay bills on-line? What control activities can a company put in place to make a consumer feel safe in regard to paying bills on-line? Would companies pay bills on-line? If so, what safeguards would companies want in place to ensure the safety of their bill payments?

Serial Case

(*Note:* This is a continuation of the serial case from Chapters 1 through 6.)

BYP7–9 Natalie is struggling to keep up with the recording of the accounting transactions of Cookie Creations Ltd. She is spending a lot of time marketing and selling mixers and giving cookie-making classes. Her friend John is an accounting student who runs his own accounting service. He has asked Natalie if she would like to have him do the accounting for Cookie Creations.

John and Natalie meet and discuss the business. John suggests that he do the following for Natalie:
1. Hold onto cash until there is enough to be deposited. (He would keep Cookie Creations' cash locked up in his vehicle.) He would take all of the deposits to the bank at least twice a month.
2. Write and sign all of the cheques. He would review the invoices and send out cheques as soon as the invoices are received.
3. Record all of the deposits in the accounting records.
4. Record all of the cheques in the accounting records.
5. Prepare the monthly bank reconciliation.
6. Transfer all of Cookie Creations' accounting records to his computer accounting program. John maintains all of the accounting information that he keeps for his clients on his computer.
7. Prepare Cookie Creations' monthly financial statements for Natalie to review.
8. Write himself a cheque each month for the work he has done for Cookie Creations.

Instructions

(a) Identify the weaknesses in internal control that you see in the system that John is recommending. For each weakness identified, describe the control activity that is violated.

(b) For each weakness identified in (a), suggest an improvement.

Answers to Chapter Questions

Answer to Shoppers Drug Mart Review It Question 2

Shoppers Drug Mart reported $27,588 thousand of cash at December 29, 2007. It did not report any restricted cash.

Answers to Self-Study Questions

1. b   2. c   3. c   4. b   5. d   6. d   7. b   8. c   9. c   10. b

CHAPTER 8
Reporting and Analyzing Receivables

ACCOUNTING MATTERS!

Varying Degrees of Credit

Receivables are generally a company's third largest asset, after its property, plant, and equipment and inventory. For large retail operations like Canadian Tire, keeping tabs on the repayment of credit accounts that often total millions of dollars is essential.

"The major receivables would fall into three broad buckets," explains Canadian Tire Chief Financial Officer Huw Thomas. First, there is the Canadian Tire credit card, issued to some 4.6 million customers, 1.8 million of whom are actively using it in any given month. Second are the receivable accounts created by the 450 separate dealers across the country that buy merchandise from the company. The third category is vendor receivables, which would be money due from vendors in support of various programs like product launches or new store openings.

The company has also recently added a fourth bucket with the banking services it launched in 2006. Clients can apply for mortgages through Canadian Tire's virtual bank, by phone, or at small kiosks located in several test markets. "The total mortgage balances are only 35 to 40 million dollars right now but it will grow over time as we roll out the bank," says Mr. Thomas.

In contrast, Canadian Tire's credit card program represents about $4 billion in receivables. The criteria for issuing a card are similar to any credit card program, says Mr. Thomas. Customers apply for new accounts, usually through the hostess program, where someone in the store will invite you to apply. The company assesses applications, does a credit score, and decides whether to issue a card and at what credit limit. It then manages the account, updating the credit score and adjusting the limit when appropriate.

The credit card processing is outsourced to a Georgia-based company that handles a large number of North American credit card accounts. Canadian Tire also has a large call centre in Welland, Ontario, that deals with customer service and some collections—although certain collections are outsourced to collection agencies. The decision on when to send the account to the outside agency depends on the individual account, says Mr. Thomas. "You have a whole series of different strategies depending on how big the balance might be, what the past non-payment history has been, etc."

Still, despite efforts to secure repayment of its credit card accounts, Canadian Tire records about $200 million per year in bad debts, essentially as much as the credit card program actually earns. "The benefit is you still make $200 million," says Mr. Thomas. "Whenever you lend money to anybody, you're always into a risk-reward balance."

Fortunately, the company's other receivable buckets carry virtually no bad debt. Canadian Tire essentially acts as a wholesaler, where dealers acquire from Canadian Tire all the merchandise that they sell. "At any point in time, there are hundreds of millions of dollars outstanding based on monies that they owe to us for product that we've shipped to them," explains Mr. Thomas. Canadian Tire has a dedicated system that tracks shipments to each store, immediately recording the liability and billing the dealer for the amount owed. "It's very unusual for a dealer to go into a position where they can't repay the monies that are owed to us," says Mr. Thomas. "Similarly, it's very unusual not to collect amounts that would be due from vendors because we typically owe them money as well."

And, just as retail sales go through cycles of peaks and valleys, so too do the company's receivables. Dealer receivables peak around Christmas time and in the second quarter, which is an intense selling period; meanwhile, credit card accounts increase in the second and fourth quarters in response to the holiday season in December and the spring and summer selling season, says Mr. Thomas.

So, for a large retail operation like Canadian Tire, it pays to have its receivables in more than one bucket.

Canadian Tire: canadiantire.com

✔ THE NAVIGATOR

- ☐ Read *Feature Story*
- ☐ Scan *Study Objectives*
- ☐ Read *Chapter Preview*
- ☐ Read text and answer *Before You Go On*
- ☐ Read *All About You*
- ☐ Review *Summary of Study Objectives*
- ☐ Review *Using the Decision Toolkit—A Summary*
- ☐ Work *Using the Decision Toolkit*
- ☐ Work *Demonstration Problem*
- ☐ Answer *Self-Study Questions*
- ☐ Complete assignments

STUDY OBJECTIVES

After studying this chapter, you should be able to:

Explain how accounts receivable are recognized in the accounts.

Account for bad debts.

Explain how notes receivable are recognized and valued in the accounts.

Explain the statement presentation of receivables.

Apply the principles of sound accounts receivable management.

The Navigator

PREVIEW OF CHAPTER 8

As indicated in our feature story, the management of receivables is important for any company that sells on credit, as Canadian Tire does. In this chapter, we will learn how companies estimate, record, and then in some cases collect their uncollectible accounts. We will also discuss how receivables are reported on the financial statements and how they are managed.

The chapter is organized as follows:

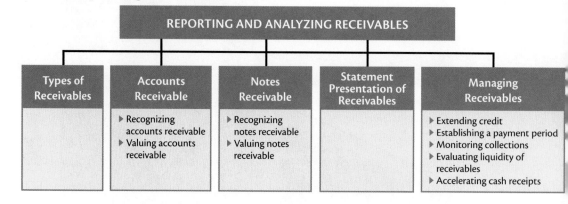

The Navigator

Types of Receivables

The term "receivables" refers to amounts that are due from individuals and other companies. Receivables are claims that are expected to be collected in cash, and they are frequently classified as (1) accounts receivable, (2) notes receivable, and (3) other receivables.

Accounts receivable are amounts owed by customers on account. They result from the sale of goods and services. These receivables are generally expected to be collected within 30 days or so, and are classified as current assets. They are usually the most significant type of claim held by a company.

Notes receivable are claims where formal instruments of credit—a written promise to repay—are issued as evidence of the debt. The credit instrument normally requires the debtor to pay interest and is for time periods of 30 days or longer. Notes receivable may be either current assets or noncurrent assets, depending on their due dates. Notes and accounts receivable that result from sales transactions are often called trade receivables.

Other receivables include credit card receivables, interest receivable, loans to company officers, advances to employees, and recoverable sales taxes and income taxes. As mentioned in our feature story, Canadian Tire also has dealer receivables, vendor receivables, and mortgage receivables. All of these different types of receivables are generally classified and reported as separate items in the current or noncurrent assets section of the balance sheet, according to their due dates.

Accounts Receivable

We will now examine two accounting problems for accounts receivable: (1) recognizing accounts receivable and (2) valuing accounts receivable. A third issue, accelerating cash receipts from receivables, is discussed later in the chapter.

Recognizing Accounts Receivable

study objective 1

Explain how accounts receivable are recognized in the accounts.

The first step in recognizing an account receivable is straightforward. For a service company, a receivable is recorded when a service is provided on account. For a merchandising company, a receivable is recorded at the point of sale of merchandise on account. Recall that we learned about the **revenue recognition principle** in Chapter 4. Revenue (and any related receivable) should be recognized when the sales effort is substantially complete. This normally occurs either when the service is performed or when the good is delivered at the point of sale. In addition, collection must be reasonably certain and measurable. This will be discussed in the next section.

Receivables are created by services or sales on account and reduced by sales discounts and sales returns. The seller may offer terms, such as providing a discount, that encourage early payment. If the buyer chooses to pay within the discount period, the seller's account receivable is reduced by the amount of the sales discount. Finally, the buyer might find some of the goods unacceptable and choose to return them. This also results in a reduction of the account receivable. For example, if $100 of merchandise purchased on account is returned, the seller reduces the account receivable by $100 when the returned merchandise is received. We learned about the entries required to record sales discounts and sales returns in Chapter 5. You may find it helpful to return to Chapter 5 and refresh your memory about these.

Accounts Receivable Subsidiary Ledger

In Chapter 3, we learned about the general ledger. Using the Accounts Receivable account in the general ledger works well for companies that do not have many customer accounts. Imagine what would happen, however, if a company like Canadian Tire recorded the account receivable for each of its customers in only one general ledger account. If it did, it would be very difficult to determine the balance owed by any one customer at a specific point in time.

Instead, companies like Canadian Tire use a subsidiary ledger in addition to the general ledger. A subsidiary ledger is a group of accounts that share a common characteristic (e.g., all receivable accounts). Unlike the general ledger, which has a single account for receivables, the subsidiary ledger has a receivable account for each customer. The total of all the customer accounts in the subsidiary ledger should equal the total in the general ledger receivable account. The subsidiary ledger provides supporting detail to the general ledger, freeing it from excessive detail. It is common to have subsidiary ledgers for accounts receivable (to track individual customer balances), inventory (to track inventory quantities and balances), accounts payable (to track individual creditor balances), and payroll (to track individual employee pay records).

In the case of an accounts receivable subsidiary ledger, it contains all the individual customer receivables accounts—for example, a separate one for Adert Limited, Bortz Corporation, Mr. B. Carl, and so on. The general ledger contains only one receivables account—Accounts Receivable—which acts as a control account to the subsidiary ledger. A control account is a general ledger account that summarizes the subsidiary ledger data. At all times, the control account balance must equal the total of all the individual customer receivable balances in the subsidiary ledger.

Under this system of control and subsidiary accounts, each journal entry that affects accounts receivable must therefore be posted twice—once to the subsidiary ledger account and once to the general ledger control account. Normally, entries to the subsidiary ledger are posted daily. Entries to the general ledger are normally summarized and posted monthly in a manual accounting system. In a computerized accounting system, the posting to both ledgers occurs simultaneously.

Interest Revenue

At the end of each month, the company can use the subsidiary ledger to easily determine the transactions in each customer's account and then send the customer a statement of transactions that occurred that month. If the customer does not pay in full within a specified period of time (usually 30 days), most retailers add an interest (financing) charge to the balance due.

When financing charges are added, the seller recognizes interest revenue and increases the account receivable amount owed by the customer. This can be a substantial amount for some service and merchandising companies.

BEFORE YOU GO ON...

▸ **Review It**

1. What types of receivables does Shoppers Drug Mart report on its balance sheet? The answer to this question is at the end of the chapter.
2. Explain the similarities and differences between a general ledger and a subsidiary ledger.
3. How is interest revenue on overdue accounts calculated and recorded?

➡ **Do It**

Information for Kinholm Corporation follows for its first month of operations:

Credit Sales			Cash Collections		
Jan. 5	Sych Ltd.	$12,000	Jan. 16	Sych Ltd.	$9,000
9	Downey Inc.	5,000	22	Downey Inc.	3,500
13	Pawlak Corp.	6,000	28	Pawlak Corp.	6,000

Calculate (a) the balances that appear in the accounts receivable subsidiary ledger for each customer, and (b) the accounts receivable balance that appears in the general ledger at the end of January.

Action Plan
- Create separate accounts for each customer and post their transactions to their accounts.
- Create one account for the Accounts Receivable control account.
- Post the total credit sales and the total cash collections to the general ledger.

Solution

Accounts Receivable Subsidiary Ledger

General Ledger

Sych Ltd.

Jan	5	12,000	Jan.	16	9,000
Bal.		3,000			

Accounts Receivable

Jan.	31	23,000ᵃ	Jan.	31	18,500ᵇ
Bal.		4,500			

Downey Inc.

Jan.	9	5,000	Jan.	22	3,500
Bal.		1,500			

ᵃ $12,000 + $5,000 + $6,000 = $23,000
ᵇ $9,000 + $3,500 + $6,000 = $18,500

Pawlak Corp.

Jan.	13	6,000	Jan.	28	6,000
Bal.		0			

The Navigator

Valuing Accounts Receivable

Once receivables are recorded in the accounts, the next question is at what amount these receivables should be reported in the financial statements. Although each customer must satisfy the seller's credit requirements before the credit sale is approved, inevitably some accounts receivable become uncollectible. For example, a corporate customer may not be able to pay because of a decline in sales due to a downturn in the economy. Similarly, individuals may be laid off from their jobs or faced with unexpected bills and find themselves unable to pay.

Credit losses are debited to an account called Bad Debts Expense. Note that a new account, Bad Debts Expense, is used instead of debiting a contra sales account as we did for sales returns and allowances. An expense account is used because the responsibilities for granting credit and collecting accounts are normally separated from sales and marketing. You will recall from Chapter 7 that establishing responsibility to authorize transactions and activities is an important feature of a good internal control system.

Credit losses are considered a normal and necessary risk of doing business. The key issue in valuing accounts receivable is when to recognize these credit losses. If the company waits until it knows for sure that the specific account will not be collected, it could end up recording the bad debts expense in a different period than when the revenue was recorded.

Consider the following example. In 2008, Quick Buck Computer Corporation decides it could increase its revenues by offering computers to students without requiring any money down, and with no credit approval process. It goes on campuses across the country and distributes one million computers with a selling price of $800 each. This increases Quick Buck Computer's receivables and revenues by $800 million. The promotion is a huge success! The 2008 balance sheet and statement of earnings look wonderful. Unfortunately, during 2009, nearly 40 percent of the student customers default on their accounts. This makes the 2009 balance sheet and statement of earnings look terrible. Illustration 8-1 shows that the promotion in 2008 was not such a great success after all.

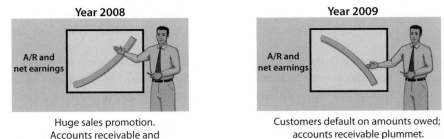

Year 2008

Huge sales promotion.
Accounts receivable and
sales increase dramatically.

Year 2009

Customers default on amounts owed;
accounts receivable plummet.
Bad debts expense increases dramatically.

If bad debt expenses are not recorded until they occur, no attempt is made to match this expense to sales revenues in the statement of earnings. Recall that the matching principle requires expenses to be reported in the same period as the sales they helped generate. Quick Buck Computer Corporation's statement of earnings is skewed in both 2008 and 2009 because of mismatched sales and bad debts expense.

In addition, accounts receivable in the balance sheet are not reported at the amount actually expected to be collected. Consequently, Quick Buck Computer's receivables are overstated in 2008, misrepresenting its balance sheet.

The allowance method offers a solution to this problem. The allowance method of accounting for bad debts estimates the uncollectible accounts at the end of each period and shows this estimate in Allowance for Doubtful Accounts. Allowance for Doubtful Accounts is a contra asset account that shows the receivables that are expected to become uncollectible in the future.

A contra account is used instead of a direct credit to Accounts Receivable for two reasons. First, we do not know which individual customers will not pay. If the company uses a subsidiary ledger, we are therefore unable to credit specific customer accounts. We are also unable to credit the control account itself: as mentioned above, the subsidiary ledger accounts must balance with the Accounts Receivable control account, and this would not happen if the control account were credited and the subsidiary ledger accounts were not. Second, the balance in Allowance for Doubtful Accounts is just an estimate. A contra account helps to separate estimates from actual amounts, such as those found in Accounts Receivable. You will recall that we used a similar contra asset account, called Allowance to Reduce Inventory to Net Realizable Value, in Chapter 6.

The Accounts Receivable balance less the Allowance for Doubtful Accounts equals the net realizable value or collectible portion of these accounts. The allowance has a credit balance and, when it is increased, the offsetting debit is recorded in bad debts expense. Because these adjustments are made at the end of the period, the bad debts expense is recorded in the same period as the related sales.

The allowance method is required for financial reporting purposes. It has three essential features:

1. **Recording estimated uncollectible accounts**: The amount of uncollectible accounts receivable is estimated by ensuring that the balance in Allowance for Doubtful Accounts is equal to the estimate of uncollectible accounts. Any adjustment to the allowance is also recorded in Bad Debts Expense so that it can be matched against revenue in the accounting period in which the revenue was earned.
2. **Recording the write-off of an uncollectible account**: Actual uncollectibles are written off at the time the specific account is determined to be uncollectible.
3. **Recording the recovery of an uncollectible account**: When an account that was previously written off is later collected, the original write-off is reversed and the collection is recorded. As neither the write-off nor the subsequent recovery affects the statement of earnings, matching is not distorted.

Tutorials
(Bad Debts)

1. Recording Estimated Uncollectible Accounts

To illustrate the allowance method, assume that Abrams Furniture Ltd. has net credit sales of $1.2 million in 2009. Of this amount, $200,000 remains uncollected at December 31. The credit manager estimates (using techniques we will discuss shortly) that bad debt expense is $10,000. The adjusting entry to record the bad debt expense for the year is:

Dec. 31	Bad Debts Expense	10,000	
	Allowance for Doubtful Accounts		10,000
	(To record estimate of uncollectible accounts)		

A	=	L	+	SE
−10,000				−10,000

Cash flows: no effect

▶ Reporting and Analyzing Receivables

Bad debts expense is reported in the statement of earnings as an operating expense. The estimated uncollectibles are matched with sales in 2009 because the expense is recorded in the same year that the sales are made. Canadian Tire records about $200 million each year in bad debts expense, as mentioned in our feature story.

The balance in Allowance for Doubtful Accounts is deducted from Accounts Receivable in the current assets section of the balance sheet. Assuming that Abrams Furniture Ltd. has an opening balance of $1,000 in Allowance for Doubtful Accounts, its ending balance of $11,000 ($1,000 + $10,000) would be reported as follows:

ABRAMS FURNITURE LTD.
Balance Sheet (partial)
December 31, 2009

Current assets		
Cash		$ 14,800
Accounts receivable	$200,000	
Less: Allowance for doubtful accounts	11,000	189,000
Merchandise inventory		310,000
Prepaid expenses		25,000
Total current assets		538,800

The $189,000 represents the expected net realizable value of the accounts receivable at the statement date. This can be represented by the formula shown in Illustration 8-2.

Illustration 8-2 ➡

Formula for calculating net realizable value

Accounts Receivable	−	Allowance for Doubtful Accounts	=	Net Realizable Value
$200,000	−	$11,000	=	$189,000

Estimating the Allowance. For Abrams Furniture above, we simply gave the amount of the expected uncollectibles for the current period ($10,000). In actual practice, however, companies do a calculation to estimate the amount of their likely uncollectible accounts. While there are several acceptable ways to estimate uncollectible accounts, most companies use a percentage of their outstanding receivables to determine the allowance for doubtful accounts.

Under the percentage of receivables basis, management estimates what percentage of receivables will result in losses from uncollectible accounts. This percentage can be assigned to receivables in total, or stratified (divided further) by the ages of the receivables. Stratifying the percentage classifies customer balances by the length of time they have been unpaid, which can improve the reliability of the estimate. Because of its emphasis on time, using stratification is called aging the accounts receivable.

After the accounts are classified by age, the expected allowance amount for bad debts is determined by applying percentages, based on past experience, to the totals of each category. The longer a receivable is past due, the less likely it is to be collected. As a result, the estimated percentage of uncollectible debts increases as the number of days past due increases. An aging schedule for Abrams Furniture is shown in Illustration 8-3. Note the increasing uncollectible percentages from 2% to 50%.

Illustration 8-3 ➡

Aging schedule

Customer	Total	Number of Days Outstanding				
		0–30	31–60	61–90	91–120	Over 120
Adert Limited	$ 6,800	$ 3,800	$ 3,000			
Bortz Corporation	12,200	8,700	3,500			
B. Carl	9,400	6,400	3,000			
Diker Furnishings Ltd.	36,600	22,400	8,600	$ 4,000	$1,600	
T. Ebbet	2,500					$2,500
Others	132,500	70,200	23,300	34,000	5,000	
	$200,000	$111,500	$41,400	$38,000	$6,600	$2,500
Estimated percentage uncollectible		2%	5%	10%	25%	50%
Total estimated bad debts	**$ 11,000**	$ 2,230	$ 2,070	$ 3,800	$1,650	$1,250

The $11,000 total is the amount of existing receivables that is expected to become uncollectible in the future. This amount is also the required balance in Allowance for Doubtful Accounts at the balance sheet date. Note that this is the amount of the balance in the account, and not the amount of the adjustment required. This is because the aging includes all receivables, including those still outstanding from prior years (if any) which have already been adjusted for expected bad debts. **The amount of the bad debt adjusting entry is the difference between the required balance and the existing balance in the Allowance account.** If the trial balance shows Allowance for Doubtful Accounts with a credit balance of $1,000, then, as we have seen, an adjusting entry for $10,000 ($11,000 – $1,000) is necessary, as follows:

Dec. 31	Bad Debts Expense	10,000	
	Allowance for Doubtful Accounts		10,000
	(To record estimate of uncollectible accounts)		

A	=	L	+	SE
−10,000				−10,000

Cash flows: no effect

After the adjusting entry is posted, the accounts of Abrams Furniture will show the following:

Bad Debts Expense			Allowance for Doubtful Accounts			
Dec. 31 Adj. 10,000			Jan. 1 Bal.	1,000
			Dec. 31 Adj.	10,000
			Dec. 31 Bal.	11,000

Occasionally, the allowance account will have a debit balance before the adjustment. This occurs when write-offs during the year exceed previous estimates for bad debts. (We will discuss write-offs in the next section.) If there is an opening debit balance, the debit balance is added to the required balance when the adjusting entry is made. That is, if there had been a $1,000 debit balance in Abrams Furniture's allowance account before adjustment, the adjusting entry would have been for $12,000 to arrive at a credit balance in the allowance account of $11,000.

An important aspect of accounts receivable management is simply keeping a close watch on the accounts. Studies have shown that accounts that are more than 60 days past due lose approximately 50 percent of their value if no payment activity occurs within the next 30 days. For each additional 30 days that pass, the collectible value halves once again. The majority of companies today use an aging schedule to closely monitor the collectibility of their accounts and to identify problem accounts.

ACCOUNTING MATTERS! | Management Perspective

At Mississauga-based Wyeth Consumer Healthcare, a Canadian subsidiary of global pharmaceutical company Wyeth, an aging schedule is used to assess the collectibility of its accounts receivable on a timely basis. Maria Cardoso, supervisor of credit and collections, comments: "We get an aging report every morning that shows exactly what each customer owes and what category the account falls into—current, 1–30 days, 31–60 days, 61–90, and over 90. Fortunately, our receivables are always at 95% current or better." When an account is overdue, there is usually an explanation. Ms. Cardoso tends to call as soon as a payment is late. "If the invoice has gone missing, for example, you want to find out right away," she says.

2. Recording the Write-Off of an Uncollectible Account

Companies use various methods of collecting past-due accounts, such as letters, phone calls, collection agencies, and legal action. In the feature story, Canadian Tire has a call centre that deals with some overdue accounts and it outsources other cases to a collection agency. When all ways of collecting a past-due account have been tried and collection appears unlikely, the account should be written off and removed from the allowance because there is no longer any doubt about its collection. Canadian Tire writes off any credit card receivables that are 180 days past due.

To prevent premature or unauthorized write-offs, each write-off should be formally approved in writing by authorized management personnel. To adhere to the appropriate internal control activity, authorization to write off accounts should not be given to someone who also has daily responsibilities related to cash or receivables.

To illustrate a receivables write-off, assume that on March 1, 2010, Abrams Furniture's vice-president of finance authorizes a write-off of the $2,500 balance owed by T. Ebbet, a customer. The entry to record the write-off is:

A	=	L	+	SE
+2,500				
−2,500				

Cash flows: no effect

Mar. 1	Allowance for Doubtful Accounts		2,500	
	Accounts Receivable—T. Ebbet			2,500
	(Write-off of T. Ebbet account)			

Bad Debts Expense is not increased (debited) when the write-off occurs. **Under the allowance method, every accounts receivable write-off entry is debited to the allowance account and not to Bad Debts Expense.** A debit to Bad Debts Expense would be incorrect because the expense was already recognized when the adjusting entry that estimated the allowance balance was recorded last year.

Instead, the entry to record the write-off of an uncollectible account reduces both Accounts Receivable and Allowance for Doubtful Accounts. After posting, using an assumed Accounts Receivable opening balance of $227,500, the general ledger accounts will appear as follows:

Accounts Receivable						Allowance for Doubtful Accounts					
Feb. 28	Bal.	227,500	Mar. 1		2,500	Mar.	1	2,500	Jan. 1	Bal.	11,000
Mar. 1	Bal.	225,000							Mar. 1	Bal.	8,500

A write-off affects only balance sheet accounts and reduces both Accounts Receivable and Allowance for Doubtful Accounts equally. Net realizable value on the balance sheet remains the same, as shown below:

	Before Write-Off	After Write-Off
Accounts receivable	$227,500	$225,000
Less: Allowance for doubtful accounts	11,000	8,500
Net realizable value	$216,500	$216,500

As mentioned earlier, the allowance account can sometimes end up with a debit balance after a write-off of an uncollectible account. This occurs if the write-offs during the period exceed the opening balance. This is only a temporary situation: it will be corrected when the adjusting entry for estimated uncollectible accounts is made at the end of the period.

3. Recording the Recovery of an Uncollectible Account

Occasionally, a company collects from a customer after the account has been written off as uncollectible. Two entries are required to record the recovery of a bad debt: (1) the entry made in writing off the account is reversed to reinstate the customer's account; and (2) the collection is recorded in the usual way.

To illustrate, assume that on July 1, T. Ebbet's fortunes have changed and he now wants to restore his credit with Abrams Furniture. In order to do so, he has to pay the $2,500 amount that had been written off on March 1. The entries are as follows:

A	=	L	+	SE
+2,500				
−2,500				

Cash flows: no effect

		(1)		
July 1	Accounts Receivable—T. Ebbet		2,500	
	Allowance for Doubtful Accounts			2,500
	(To reverse write-off of T. Ebbet account)			

A	=	L	+	SE
+2,500				
−2,500				

⬆Cash flows: +2,500

		(2)		
1	Cash		2,500	
	Accounts Receivable—T. Ebbet			2,500
	(To record collection from T. Ebbet)			

Note that the recovery of a bad debt, like the write-off of a bad debt, affects only balance sheet accounts. The net effect of the two entries is an increase (a debit) to Cash and an increase (a credit) to Allowance for Doubtful Accounts for $2,500. Accounts Receivable is debited and later credited in a second entry, as shown above, for two reasons. First, the company should reverse the write-off as soon as the receivable is considered collectible. Second, T. Ebbet did pay, and the accounts receivable account in the subsidiary (and general) ledger should show this collection as it will need to be considered for future credit purposes.

Summary of Allowance Method

In summary, there are three types of transactions when accounts receivable are valued using the allowance method:

1. Estimated uncollectible accounts receivable are recorded at the end of the period by debiting Bad Debts Expense and crediting Allowance for Doubtful Accounts. The amount to record can be determined by using a percentage of total receivables, or an aging schedule. This entry is an adjusting entry that is made at the end of the period.
2. Actual uncollectibles, or write-offs, are then debited to Allowance for Doubtful Accounts and credited to an accounts receivable account. This entry is not an adjusting entry and is recorded as soon as it can be determined that collection of an account is unlikely.
3. Later recoveries, if any, are recorded in two separate entries. The first reverses the write-off by debiting Accounts Receivable and crediting Allowance for Doubtful Accounts. The second records the normal collection of the account by debiting Cash and crediting Accounts Receivable.

These entries are summarized and illustrated in the following T accounts:

Accounts Receivable		Allowance for Doubtful Accounts	
Beginning balance	Collections	Write-offs	Beginning balance
Credit sales	Write-offs		Subsequent recoveries
Subsequent recoveries			Bad debt adjustment
Ending balance			Ending balance

DECISION TOOLKIT

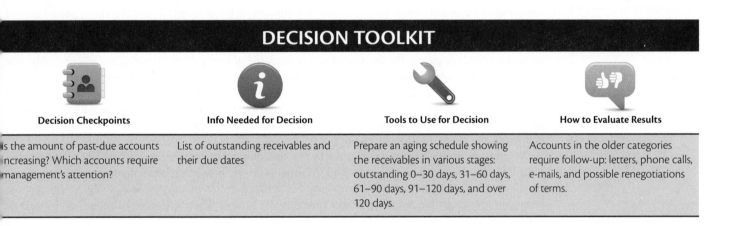

Decision Checkpoints	Info Needed for Decision	Tools to Use for Decision	How to Evaluate Results
Is the amount of past-due accounts increasing? Which accounts require management's attention?	List of outstanding receivables and their due dates	Prepare an aging schedule showing the receivables in various stages: outstanding 0–30 days, 31–60 days, 61–90 days, 91–120 days, and over 120 days.	Accounts in the older categories require follow-up: letters, phone calls, e-mails, and possible renegotiations of terms.

BEFORE YOU GO ON...

Review It

1. Explain how the allowance method better matches bad debts expense to its related revenue.
2. Distinguish between the journal entries that are required to record (a) estimated uncollectibles, (b) a write-off of an uncollectible account, and (c) a subsequent recovery of an uncollectible account.
3. To apply good internal control activities over receivables, who should authorize receivables write-offs?

Do It

A partially prepared aging schedule for Woo Wholesalers Corporation at its year end, December 31, follows:

	Number of Days Outstanding				
	Total	0–30	31–60	61–90	Over 90
Accounts receivable	$230,000	$100,000	$60,000	$50,000	$20,000
Estimated percentage uncollectible		2%	5%	10%	20%
Total estimated bad debts					

Complete the aging schedule and prepare the required journal entry to record the estimated bad debts expense at December 31. Assume that prior to performing the above calculations, Allowance for Doubtful Accounts has an opening credit balance of $4,000.

Action Plan

- Apply percentages to outstanding receivables in each age category to determine total estimated bad debts.
- The total estimated bad debts determined in the aging schedule is the ending balance required in the allowance account.
- Consider both the required ending balance and any existing balance in the allowance account to determine the adjustment amount.

Solution

Total estimated bad debts is $14,000 [($100,000 × 2%) + ($60,000 × 5%) + ($50,000 × 10%) + ($20,000 × 20%)]. The following entry should be made to adjust Allowance for Doubtful Accounts by $10,000 ($14,000 – $4,000) to reach the required ending balance of $14,000:

Dec. 31	Bad Debts Expense	10,000	
	Allowance for Doubtful Accounts		10,000
	(To record estimate of uncollectible accounts)		

The Navigator

Notes Receivable

study objective 3

Explain how notes receivable are recognized and valued in the accounts.

Credit may also be granted in exchange for a formal credit instrument known as a promissory note. A **promissory note** is a written promise to pay a specified amount of money on demand (i.e., as soon as the payee demands repayment) or at a definite time. Promissory notes may be used (1) when individuals and companies lend or borrow money, (2) when the amount of the transaction and the credit period exceed normal limits, and (3) in settlement of accounts receivable.

In a promissory note, the party making the promise to pay is called the maker; the party who will be paid is called the payee. For the maker of the note, the note would be classified as a note payable. For the payee of the note, the note would be classified as a note receivable. The promissory note details the names of the maker and the payee, the principal or face value of the loan, the loan period, the interest rate, and whether interest is payable monthly or at maturity (the note's due date) along with the principal amount. Other details might include whether any security is pledged as collateral for the loan and what happens if the maker defaults (does not pay).

A note receivable is a formal promise to pay an amount that bears interest from the time it is issued until it is due. An account receivable is an informal promise to pay that bears interest only after its due date. Because it is less formal, it does not have as strong a legal claim as a note receivable. Most accounts receivable are due within a short period of time, usually 30 days, whereas notes receivable can be due over a longer period.

There are also similarities between notes and accounts receivable. Both are credit instruments. Both can be sold to another party. And, as you will learn in the next section, both are valued at their net realizable value. The basic issues in accounting for notes receivable are the same as those for accounts receivable: (1) recognizing notes receivable and (2) valuing notes receivable.

Recognizing Notes Receivable

To illustrate the basic accounting for notes receivable, we will assume that on May 1, Tabusintac Inc. (the payee) accepts a note receivable in exchange for an account receivable from Raja Ltd. (the maker). The note is for $10,000, with 6-percent interest due in four months, on September 1.

We record this entry as follows for the receipt of the note by Tabusintac:

A	=	L	+	SE
+10,000				
−10,000				
Cash flows: no effect				

May 1	Notes Receivable—Raja	10,000	
	Accounts Receivable—Raja		10,000
	(To record acceptance of Raja note)		

If a note is exchanged for cash, the entry is a debit to Notes Receivable and a credit to Cash in the amount of the loan.

The note receivable is recorded at its principal value, the value shown on the face of the note. No interest revenue is reported when the note is accepted, because the revenue recognition principle does not allow us to recognize revenue until it is earned. As we learned in Chapter 4, interest is earned (accrued) as time passes, and it is calculated as follows:

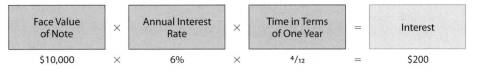

Face Value of Note	×	Annual Interest Rate	×	Time in Terms of One Year	=	Interest
$10,000	×	6%	×	4/12	=	$200

The interest rate specified on the note is an **annual** rate of interest. The time factor in the calculation represents the fraction of the year that the note is outstanding. As we did in past chapters, for simplicity we will continue to assume that interest is calculated in months, rather than days.

It is important to know that the calculation of interest as shown above applies only to short-term notes receivable with interest due at maturity. Notes that have a maturity date beyond one year from the balance sheet date would be classified as long-term. Long-term notes generally are repayable in instalments rather than at maturity. Although not as common, short-term notes can also be repaid in instalments rather than at maturity. The interest calculations for instalment notes use a method to determine interest revenue called the effective-interest method. This method will be introduced in Chapter 10.

Interest on the Raja note will total $50 ($10,000 × 6% × 1/12) a month, or $200 for the four-month period. This interest will be recorded as interest revenue for Tabusintac and interest expense for Raja. If Tabusintac's year end was May 31, the following adjusting journal entry would be required to accrue interest for the month of May:

May 31	Interest Receivable	50	
	Interest Revenue		50
	(To accrue interest on Raja note receivable)		

A	=	L	+	SE
+50				+50

Cash flows: no effect

Note that while interest on an overdue account receivable is debited to Accounts Receivable, interest on a note receivable is *not* debited to the Notes Receivable account. Instead, a separate account for the interest receivable is used. Since the note is a formal credit instrument, its recorded principal must remain unchanged. In addition, it is useful for a company to track how much interest it is earning from notes receivable.

Notes are normally held to their maturity date, at which time the principal plus accrued interest is due. This is known as honouring (collecting) the note. In some situations, the maker of the note defaults and an appropriate adjustment must be made. This is known as dishonouring (not collecting) the note.

Honouring of Notes Receivable

A note is said to be honoured when it is paid in full at its maturity date. If Raja pays its note when it is due on September 1, the maturity date, the entry by Tabusintac to record the collection is:

Sept. 1	Cash	10,200	
	Notes Receivable—Raja		10,000
	Interest Receivable		50
	Interest Revenue		150
	(To record collection of Raja note and interest)		

A	=	L	+	SE
+10,200				+150
−10,000				
−50				

Cash flows: +10,200

Recall that one month of interest, $50, was previously accrued on May 31. Consequently, only three months of interest revenue relating to June, July, and August, $150 ($10,000 × 6% × 3/12), is recorded in this period.

Dishonouring of Notes Receivable

A dishonoured note is a note that is not paid in full at maturity. A dishonoured note receivable is no longer negotiable. However, the payee still has a claim against the maker of the note for both the principal and any unpaid interest. Therefore, the Notes Receivable account balance and related interest is usually transferred to an account receivable by debiting Accounts Receivable for the total of the principal amount of the note and the interest due.

As shown below, the journal entry to record this is identical to the one above, except that the debit to Cash would instead be made to the Accounts Receivable account:

A	=	L	+	SE
+10,200				+150
−10,000				
−50				

Cash flows: no effect

Sept. 1	Accounts Receivable	10,200	
	Notes Receivable—Raja		10,000
	Interest Receivable		50
	Interest Revenue		150
	(To record dishonoured Raja note ; eventual collection expected)		

If there is no hope of collection, the principal and any accrued interest should be written off. No interest revenue would be recorded, because collection will not occur. The entry to write off the amount is:

A	=	L	+	SE
+10,050				
−10,000				
−50				

Cash flows: no effect

Sept. 1	Allowance for Doubtful Accounts (Notes)	10,050	
	Notes Receivable—Raja		10,000
	Interest Receivable		50
	(To write off dishonoured Raja note)		

ACCOUNTING MATTERS! | Management Perspective

Until recently, U.S. consumers were able to obtain subprime mortgage loans from banks. A subprime loan is a high-risk loan that is given to someone who does not have sufficient income to qualify for a conventional mortgage. Many banks and other financial institutions believed that the risk of lending to these individuals was lessened by the explosive growth in home prices and that, if these individuals could not pay down their mortgages, the collateral for the loans was at least safe and would grow in value.

When house prices in the U.S. began to fall in 2007 and individuals who had received the subprime loans were unable to pay down their loans, a credit crisis arose. Many U.S. banks were forced to write off loan receivable balances. The crisis also affected Canadian banks. By the spring of 2008, the CIBC had written off $6.7 billion worth of loans and the Royal Bank, $1.6 billion.

Valuing Notes Receivable

Like accounts receivable, notes receivable are reported at their **net realizable value**. Each note must be analyzed to determine its probability of collection. If circumstances suggest that eventual collection is in doubt, bad debts expense and an allowance for doubtful accounts (notes) must be recorded in the same way these are recorded for accounts receivable. Many companies use just the one account, Allowance for Doubtful Accounts, for all trade receivables: it thus includes both accounts receivable and notes receivable.

BEFORE YOU GO ON...

▶ **Review It**

1. Identify the similarities and differences between an account receivable and a note receivable.
2. How is interest recorded for a note receivable?
3. At what value are notes receivable reported on the balance sheet?
4. Explain the difference between honouring and dishonouring a note receivable.

▶ **Do It**

Gambit Stores Ltd. accepts from Leonard Corp. a three-month, 6%, $3,400 note dated May 10 in settlement of Leonard's overdue account. (a) What journal entries would be made by Gambit on May 10 and on August 10, the maturity date, assuming Leonard pays the note and interest in full at that time and no interest was previously accrued? (b) What entry would be made on August 10 if Leonard could not pay the note but the note is still expected to be collected in the future?

Action Plan

• Calculate the accrued interest. The formula is: face value × annual interest rate × time in terms of one year.
• If the note is honoured, record the collection of the note and any interest earned. Use separate accounts for the principal amount of the note and the interest.
• If the note is dishonoured, record the transfer of the note and any interest earned to an accounts receivable account if eventual collection is expected, or to an allowance account if collection is not expected.

Solution

(a) Note honoured:

May 10	Notes Receivable—Leonard	3,400	
	Accounts Receivable—Leonard		3,400
	(To replace account receivable with a 6% note		
	receivable, due August 10)		
Aug. 10	Cash	3,451	
	Notes Receivable—Leonard		3,400
	Interest Revenue ($3,400 × 6% × 3/12)		51
	(To record collection of Leonard note and interest)		

(b) Note dishonoured:

Aug. 10	Accounts Receivable—Leonard	3,451	
	Notes Receivable—Leonard		3,400
	Interest Revenue ($3,400 × 6% × 3/12)		51
	(To record transfer of dishonoured Leonard		
	note and interest to accounts receivable)		

The Navigator

Statement Presentation of Receivables

Each of the major types of receivables should be identified in the balance sheet or in the notes to the financial statements. Short-term receivables are reported in the current assets section of the balance sheet, following cash and short-term investments. Although only the net realizable value of receivables must be disclosed, it is helpful to report both the gross amount of receivables and the allowance for doubtful accounts either in the statement or in the notes to the financial statements.

Illustration 8-4 shows the presentation of receivables for Shaw Communications, which provides cable services to customers.

study objective 4

Explain the statement presentation of receivables.

◄— **Illustration 8-4**

Presentation of receivables

SHAW COMMUNICATIONS INC.
Notes to the Financial Statements (partial)
August 31, 2007
(in thousands)
SHAW

Note 3: Accounts Receivable

	2007	2006
Subscriber and trade receivables	$161,765	$155,583
Due from officers and employees	230	339
Due from related parties	841	1,318
Miscellaneous receivables	7,842	8,981
	170,678	166,221
Less: Allowance for doubtful accounts	(15,179)	(28,079)
	155,499	138,142

In note 3, Shaw discloses the components of its receivables. Notice how the Allowance for Doubtful Accounts decreased from approximately $28 million in 2006 to $15 million in 2007. The net realizable value of the accounts receivable of $155 million in 2007 and $138 million in 2006 was reported in the current assets section of Shaw's balance sheet.

Shaw also reported, on its statement of earnings, bad debts expense of $3 million. Using this information, along with the beginning and ending balances in the allowance account, we can determine that the receivables written off in 2007 must have been approximately $16 million ($28 million + $3 million – $15 million).

BEFORE YOU GO ON...

Review It

1. Explain where accounts and notes receivable are classified on the balance sheet.
2. Where are bad debts expense and interest revenue reported on the statement of earnings?

The Navigator

Managing Receivables

study objective 5

Apply the principles of sound accounts receivable management.

There are five steps in managing accounts receivable:

1. Determine who to extend credit to.
2. Establish a payment period.
3. Monitor collections.
4. Evaluate the liquidity of receivables.
5. Accelerate cash receipts from receivables when necessary.

Extending Credit

A critical part of managing receivables is determining who should receive credit and who should not. Many companies increase sales by being generous with their credit policy, but they may end up extending credit to risky customers who do not pay. If the credit policy is too tight, the company will lose sales. If it is too loose, it may sell to those who will pay either very late or not at all.

Certain steps can be taken to help minimize losses if credit standards are relaxed. Risky customers might be required to provide letters of credit or guarantees. Then, if the customer does not pay, the person or company that provided the guarantee will pay. Particularly risky customers might be required to pay a deposit in advance or cash on delivery.

In addition, companies should ask potential customers for references from banks and suppliers to determine their payment history. It is important to check these references on potential new customers, and to periodically check the financial health of existing customers. Many resources are available for investigating customers. For example, to aid in lending decisions, companies such as Equifax provide credit opinions on companies around the world.

Establishing a Payment Period

Companies that extend credit should determine a required payment period and inform their customers about it. Normally, this period would be similar to the period used by competitors. If the period is shorter than a competitor's, sales could be lost. If the period is longer, the slower receipt of cash from customers may require the company to carry higher levels of debt.

Monitoring Collections

An accounts receivable aging schedule should be prepared and reviewed often. Almost all accounting software programs can generate an aged listing at any time. In addition to its use in estimating the allowance for doubtful accounts, the aging schedule helps estimate the timing of future cash inflows when preparing a cash budget. It also provides information about the overall collection experience of the company, and it identifies problem accounts. As we learned in our feature story, Canadian Tire uses a variety of different strategies to deal with its problem accounts depending on how big the balance might be, what the payment history has been, and so on.

Credit risk increases during periods of economic downturn. Credit policies and collection experience must always be monitored not only in comparison to past experience, but also in light of current economic conditions. This is especially important when a company has a high level of receivables from few customers.

If a company sells services or products to only a few customers, it has a concentration of credit risk and it is required to discuss this risk in the notes to its financial statements because the financial health of the company could weaken. An excerpt from the credit risk note from the financial statements of Canadian Tire is shown in Illustration 8-5.

Illustration 8-5 ➡

Concentration of credit risk

CANADIAN TIRE LIMITED
Notes to the Financial Statements (partial)
December 29, 2007

Note 15: Financial Instruments
Credit risk   The Company's exposure to concentrations of credit risk is limited. Accounts receivable are primarily from dealers spread across Canada who individually, generally comprise less than one percent of the total balance outstanding. Similarly, loans receivable are generated by credit card, personal loan and mortgage customers, a large and geographically dispersed group.

As the note states, Canadian Tire does not believe it has any significant concentration of credit risk.

DECISION TOOLKIT

Decision Checkpoints	Info Needed for Decision	Tools to Use for Decision	How to Evaluate Results
Is the company's credit risk increasing?	Customer account balances and due dates	Accounts receivable aging schedule	Calculate and compare the percentage of receivables overdue in each age classification.
Does the company have significant concentrations of credit risk?	Note to the financial statements on concentrations of credit risk	If risky credit customers are identified, the financial health of those customers should be evaluated to gain an independent assessment of the potential for a material credit loss.	If a material loss appears likely, the potential negative impact of that loss on the company should be carefully evaluated, as well as the adequacy of the allowance for doubtful accounts.

Evaluating Liquidity of Receivables

Investors and managers keep a watchful eye on the relationship between sales, accounts receivable, and cash collections. If sales increase, then accounts receivable are also expected to increase. However, if accounts receivable rise faster than sales, this may be an indication of collection problems. Perhaps the company increased its sales by loosening its credit policy, and these receivables may be difficult or impossible to collect. Such receivables are considered less liquid. Recall that liquidity is measured by how quickly certain assets can be converted to cash.

The ratio that is used to assess the liquidity of receivables is the receivables turnover ratio. This ratio measures the number of times, on average, that receivables are collected during the year. The receivables turnover is calculated by dividing net credit sales by the average gross accounts receivable during the year.

Unfortunately, companies seldom report the amount of net credit sales in their financial statements. In such instances, net sales (including both cash and credit sales) can be used as a substitute. In addition, because some companies do not publicly report their gross accounts receivable, net accounts receivable must be used. As long as one consistently chooses the same components of a ratio, the resulting ratio will be useful for comparisons.

A popular variant of the receivables turnover is to convert it into an average collection period in terms of days. This is done by dividing 365 days by the receivables turnover. Alternatively, it can be calculated by dividing accounts receivable by the average amount of net credit sales per day. The average collection period is frequently used to assess the effectiveness of a company's credit and collection policies. The general rule is that the collection period should not greatly exceed the credit term period (i.e., the time allowed for payment).

Canadian Tire does not report its allowance account separately. So we will use the following data for Apple Inc. (in USD millions) to illustrate the calculation of the receivables turnover. We have assumed that all sales are credit sales for the purpose of this illustration.

	2007	2006	2005
Net sales	$24,006	$19,315	$13,931
Accounts receivable (gross)	1,684	1,304	941
Allowance for doubtful accounts	47	52	46

The receivables turnover and average collection period for Apple Inc. are shown in Illustration 8-6, along with comparative industry data.

Illustration 8-6 ➡

Receivables turnover

		RECEIVABLES TURNOVER = $\dfrac{\text{NET CREDIT SALES}}{\text{AVERAGE GROSS ACCOUNTS RECEIVABLE}}$	
		AVERAGE COLLECTION PERIOD = $\dfrac{365 \text{ DAYS}}{\text{RECEIVABLES TURNOVER}}$	

(in USD millions)	Ratio	2007	2006
Apple	Receivables turnover	$\dfrac{\$24,006}{(\$1,684 + \$1,304) \div 2} = 16.1$ times	$\dfrac{\$19,315}{(\$1,304 + \$941) \div 2} = 17.2$ times
	Average collection period	$\dfrac{365}{16.1} = 23$ days	$\dfrac{365}{17.2} = 21$ days
Industry Average	Receivables turnover	10.7 times	11.2 times
	Average collection period	34 days	33 days

Apple's receivables turnover was 16.1 times in 2007, with an average collection period of 23 days. This was a slight decrease from its 2006 collection period of 21 days and compares favourably with the industry average collection period. We must be careful, however, when comparing to the industry average because, compared to its competitors, Apple tends to sell more of its products directly to consumers who use bank credit cards and this reduces the average collection period for the company. We will learn more about credit cards in the next section.

The receivables turnover is an important component of a company's overall liquidity. Ideally, it should be analyzed along with other information about a company's liquidity, including the current ratio and inventory turnover. Recall from earlier chapters that the receivables turnover and inventory turnover can distort a company's current ratio. In general, the faster the turnover, the more reliable the current ratio is for assessing liquidity.

In some cases, receivables turnover may be misleading. Some companies, especially large retail chains, encourage credit and revolving charge sales. However, they deliberately slow down collections in order to earn a healthy return on the outstanding receivables in the form of interest at rates that can be as high as 28 percent.

DECISION TOOLKIT

Decision Checkpoints	Info Needed for Decision	Tools to Use for Decision	How to Evaluate Results
Are collections being made in a timely fashion?	Net credit sales and average accounts receivable balance	$\text{Receivables turnover} = \dfrac{\text{Net credit sales}}{\text{Average gross accounts receivable}}$ $\text{Average collection period} = \dfrac{365 \text{ days}}{\text{Receivables turnover}}$	The average collection period should be consistent with corporate credit policy. An increase may suggest a decline in the financial health of customers.

Accelerating Cash Receipts

Normally, receivables are simply collected in cash and then removed from the books. However, as credit sales and receivables grow in size and significance, waiting for receivables to be collected within the normal collection period can result in increased costs and delays in being able to use the cash that is awaited. Two typical ways to accelerate the receipt of cash from receivables are to use the receivables to secure a loan and to sell the receivables.

Loans Secured by Receivables

One of the most common ways to speed up cash flow from receivables is to go to a bank and borrow money using receivables as collateral. While this does have a cost (interest has to be paid to the bank on the loan), the cash is available for the company to use earlier and the loan can be repaid as the receivables are collected. Generally, banks are willing to provide financing for up to 75 percent of receivables that are less than 90 days old. Quite often, these arrangements occur through an **operating line of credit**. We will learn more about an operating line of credit in Chapter 10.

Sale of Receivables

Companies also frequently sell their receivables to another company for cash, thereby shortening the cash-to-cash operating cycle. There are three reasons for the sale of receivables:

1. Due to the size of the business, it may make sense to establish a financing subsidiary that buys the accounts receivable from the company. In this way, the company's balance sheet will appear more liquid due to the absence of the receivables.
2. Selling receivables provides a source of immediate cash flow for the company.
3. It allows the company to save costs relating to the monitoring and collection of receivables.

Securitization of Receivables. A common way to accelerate receivables collection is to transfer receivables to investors in return for cash through a process called securitization. In certain cases, this transfer is treated as a sale of receivables; in other cases, it is treated as a secured loan. Companies such as Canadian Tire regularly securitize some of their receivables to speed up collection. For the year ended December 29, 2007, Canadian Tire securitized $2.3 million of its credit cards receivable.

Another way to accelerate receivables collection is by sale to a factor. A factor is a finance company or bank that buys receivables from businesses for a fee. If the customer does not pay, normally the company is responsible for reimbursing the factor for the uncollected amounts.

The differences between securitization and factoring are that securitization involves many investors, the cost is lower, the receivables are of a higher quality, and the seller usually continues to have some involvement with (e.g., responsibility to collect) the receivables. In factoring, the sale is usually to only one company, the cost is higher, the receivables quality is lower, and the seller does not normally have any involvement with the receivables. These topics will be covered in more detail in an intermediate accounting course.

Credit Card Sales. Three parties are involved when credit cards are used in making retail sales: (1) the credit card issuer, who is independent of the retailer; (2) the retailer; and (3) the customer. A retailer's acceptance of a national credit card is another form of the retailer selling a receivable.

The issuer is responsible for performing the credit approval process. In addition, the issuer maintains and collects the customer accounts and absorbs any bad debts. The retailer receives cash more quickly from the credit card issuer than would have been the case in a normal credit situation. In exchange for these services, the retailer pays the credit card issuer a fee of 1 to 5 percent of the invoice price.

Sales resulting from the use of bank cards, such as VISA, MasterCard, and American Express are considered cash sales by the retailer. According to the Canadian Bankers Association, there were approximately 64 million bank credit cards in use in Canada in 2007. As soon as bank credit cards are electronically swiped, or when the bank that issued the card receives credit card sales slips from a retailer, the bank adds the amount to the seller's bank balance. These credit card sales slips are therefore recorded in the same way as cheques deposited from a cash sale, except for the additional service fee, which is normally deducted directly from the cash proceeds.

To illustrate, assume that MuchMusic Corp. sells $100 of DVDs to Anita Ferreri on January 19 and that Anita pays for this purchase with her Royal Bank VISA card. The service fee that Royal Bank charges MuchMusic is 3 percent. The entry by MuchMusic to record this transaction is:

Jan. 19	Cash ($100 − $3)	97	
	Credit Card Expense ($100 x 3%)	3	
	Sales		100
	(To record VISA credit card sale)		

A	=	L	+	SE
+97				−3
				+100

↑ Cash flows: +97

Nonbank cards, such as the Canadian Tire MasterCard and Petro-Canada Personal Credit Card, are reported as credit sales, not cash sales. Conversion into cash does not occur until the financing company remits the net amount to the seller.

Debit Card Sales. Canadians are the world's second most frequent users of debit cards, with only the inhabitants of Sweden using them more often. What is the difference between a debit card and a credit card? Debit cards allow customers to spend only what is in their bank account. Credit cards give a customer access to money made available by a bank or other financial institution, just like a loan. Credit cards are issued with the understanding that the amount charged will be repaid, with interest, if the account is not paid in full each month.

As we learned in Chapter 7, when a debit card sale occurs, the bank immediately deducts the cost of the purchase from the customer's bank account. This amount is electronically transferred into the retailer's bank account, less a service fee. The entries to record a debit card sale are identical to those shown earlier for bank credit card sales.

There is a wide variety of practices in reporting credit and debit card charges. Some companies report credit and debit card charges as part of net sales. Still other companies report these charges as cost of goods sold or as an operating expense.

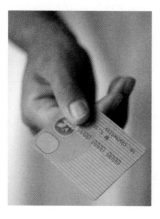

ACCOUNTING MATTERS! | Management Perspective

The average interest rate on a bank credit card in Canada is 19 percent. Nonbank cards, such as Canadian Tire's, can charge 26 percent or even higher. The Bank of Canada interest rate is currently 3 percent, and changes based on the supply and demand for money. Credit card rates, on the other hand, hardly budge at all. Why are credit card rates consistently so much higher than other interest rates?

The higher rate, according to the Canadian Bankers Association (CBA), is due to the risk involved. A bank loan such as a mortgage is a secured loan because the loan is backed up with a tangible asset: your house. Using a credit card is essentially taking out an unsecured loan because nothing physical is used as security for the lender. In addition, the CBA says, credit cards are much more susceptible to fraud, which necessitates an interest rate that remains consistently high.

Source: "Interest Rates: What You Need to Know about the Cost of Money," CBC News, April 22, 2008.

BEFORE YOU GO ON...

➡ **Review It**

1. What is meant by a concentration of credit risk?
2. What do the receivables turnover and the average collection period reveal?
3. Why do companies accelerate cash receipts from receivables?
4. What's the difference, if any, between a credit card sale and a debit card sale?

➡ **Do It**

Prepare journal entries to record the following selected debit and credit card transactions for the Bulk Department Store Ltd:

July 18   A customer used her debit card to pay for a $650 purchase. The company was charged a $2 service fee.

22   A customer paid for a $1,200 purchase with her Visa credit card. The bank charges a service fee of 3%.

25   A customer paid for a $500 purchase with his Bulk Department Store credit card.

Action Plan

• Debit cards are recorded as cash sales, less the service charge.
• Bank credit cards are recorded as cash sales, less the service charge.
• Nonbank credit cards, including company cards, are recorded as receivables. There is no service charge for a company credit card.

Solution

July 18	Cash		648	
	Debit Card Expense		2	
	Sales			650
	(To record debit card sale)			
22	Cash		1,164	
	Credit Card Expense ($1,200 × 3%)		36	
	Sales			1,200
	(To record Visa credit card sale)			
25	Accounts Receivable		500	
	Sales			500
	(To record company credit card sale)			

ALL ABOUT YOU

Should You Be Carrying Plastic?

Smart businesspeople carefully consider their use of credit. They evaluate who they lend to, and how they finance their own operations. They know that being overextended on credit can destroy their business.

Individuals need to evaluate their personal credit positions using the same thought processes as businesspeople. Some of you might consider the idea of not having a credit card ridiculous. The reality, however, is that the misuse of credit cards brings financial hardship to many Canadians each year. The best way to avoid credit problems is to be disciplined when using credit cards or not to have them at all. Reduce the number of credit cards you carry and do not accept all the tempting credit card offers that come to you via e-mail and regular mail.

Credit cards can make your life easier, as long as they are used properly. They certainly have advantages: (1) they provide interest-free loans on the purchase of goods as long as you pay your bill in full before the end of the grace period; and (2) monthly credit card statements provide detailed records of all transactions, payments, and returned merchandise. However, credit cards also have disadvantages: (1) if you do not pay your bill in full each month, expect to pay a very high interest rate on the unpaid balance; and (2) they are so easy to use that you might start buying items without really thinking about whether you really need them—and can afford them.

Credit scoring is a system used by lenders and others to assess the credit risk of prospective borrowers, and is used most often when an individual applies for a credit card, automobile loan, or, a home mortgage. Your credit score is a judgment about your financial health, at a specific point in time. It indicates the risk you represent for lenders, compared with other consumers. Lenders must decide on the lowest score you can have before they decide it is no longer wise to lend money to you. They can also use your score to set the interest rate you will pay.

One factor that lenders take into account in determining your credit score is your payment history. Do you carry over a balance on your credit card from month to month? Have you ever missed a payment on any of your debts?

Some Facts

A recent consumer poll showed some surprising facts about Canadians and credit:

- 80% of Canadians do not know their credit score and more than half do not know how a credit score is determined.
- 28% of Canadians have no idea what their credit card interest rates are.
- 40% of Canadians do not pay their full credit card balance each month.
- 30% of Canadians carry a total credit card balance each month greater than $1,000, on average.
- 25% of Canadians do not consider the consequences of rising interest rates when borrowing money.
- 90% of Canadians feel they have more debt today than they did five years ago.

What Do You Think?

Should you destroy your credit card?

YES | Credit cards encourage unnecessary, spontaneous expenditures. The interest rates on credit cards are very high, which causes debt problems to worsen.

NO | Credit cards are a necessity for transactions in today's economy. In fact, many transactions are difficult or impossible to carry out without a credit card. People should learn to use credit cards responsibly.

The Navigator

Sources:

Lawrence Gitman, Michael Joehnk, Leo Gallant, and Kenneth MacAulay, *Personal Financial Planning* (Toronto: Nelson Education Ltd., 2008), p. 223.

TransUnion, "Who's More in Debt: Canadians or Americans?" Sympatico-MSN finance, 2008, http://finance.sympatico.msn.ca/Banking/Credit/TransUnion/Article.aspx?cp-documentid=6369093.

Summary of Study Objectives

1. **Explain how accounts receivable are recognized in the accounts.** Accounts receivable are recorded at the invoice price. They are reduced by sales returns and allowances. Sales discounts also reduce the amount received on accounts receivable. When interest is charged on a past-due receivable, this interest is added to the accounts receivable balance and is recognized as interest revenue.

2. **Account for bad debts.** The allowance method, using a percentage of receivables, is used to match bad debts expense against sales, in the period in which the sales occurred. A percentage of total receivables, or an aging schedule applying percentages to different categories of receivables, is used to estimate the allowance for doubtful accounts. The allowance is deducted from the receivables balance to report accounts receivable at their net realizable value on the balance sheet.

3. **Explain how notes receivable are recognized and valued in the accounts.** Notes receivable are recorded at their principal or face value. Interest is earned from the date the note is issued until it matures and is recorded in a separate interest receivable account. Like accounts receivable, notes receivable are also reported at their net realizable value.

Notes can be held to maturity, at which time the principal plus any unpaid interest is due and the note is removed from the accounts. In some situations, the maker of the note dishonours the note (defaults). If eventual collection is expected, an account receivable replaces the note receivable and any unpaid interest. If the amount is not expected to be repaid, the note is written off.

4. **Explain the statement presentation of receivables.** Each major type of receivable should be identified in the balance sheet or in the notes to the financial statements. It is desirable to report the gross amount of receivables and allowance for doubtful accounts. Bad debts and service charge expenses are reported in the statement of earnings as operating expenses, and interest revenue is shown as other revenues in the non-operating section of the statement.

5. **Apply the principles of sound accounts receivable management.** To properly manage receivables, management must (a) determine who to extend credit to, (b) establish a payment period, (c) monitor collections, (d) evaluate the liquidity of receivables by calculating the receivables turnover and average collection period, and (e) accelerate cash receipts from receivables when necessary.

The Navigator

Glossary

Study Tools (Glossary)

Accounts receivable Amounts owed by customers on account. (p. 390)

Aging the accounts receivable The analysis of customer balances by the length of time they have been unpaid. (p. 394)

Allowance method A method of accounting for bad debts that involves estimating uncollectible accounts at the end of each period. (p. 393)

Average collection period The average amount of time that a receivable is outstanding. It is calculated by dividing 365 days by the receivables turnover. (p. 403)

Concentration of credit risk The threat of nonpayment from a single customer or class of customers that could hurt the financial health of the company. (p. 402)

Control account An account in the general ledger that summarizes the details for a subsidiary ledger and controls it. (p. 391)

Dishonoured note A note that is not paid in full at maturity. (p. 399)

Factor A finance company or bank that buys receivables from businesses for a fee. (p. 405)

Net realizable value The difference between gross receivables and the allowance for doubtful accounts. Net realizable value measures the net amount expected to be received in cash. (p. 393)

Notes receivable Claims that are backed up by formal instruments of credit that are issued as evidence of the debt. (p. 390)

Percentage of receivables basis A percentage relationship established by management between the amount of receivables and the expected losses from uncollectible accounts. (p. 394)

Promissory note A written promise to pay a specified amount of money on demand or at a definite time. (p. 398)

Receivables turnover A measure of the liquidity of receivables. It is calculated by dividing net credit sales by the average gross accounts receivable and is expressed as the number of times per year that the accounts receivable could be collected. (p. 403)

Securitization The transfer of assets such as receivables to a company that issues securities as collateral for the receivables. (p. 405)

Subsidiary ledger A group of accounts that provide details of a control account in the general ledger. (p. 391)

Trade receivables Notes and accounts receivable that result from sales transactions. (p. 390)

DECISION TOOLKIT—A SUMMARY

	Decision Checkpoints	Info Needed for Decision	Tools to Use for Decision	How to Evaluate Results
	Is the amount of past-due accounts increasing? Which accounts require management's attention?	List of outstanding receivables and their due dates	Prepare an aging schedule showing the receivables in various stages: outstanding 0–30 days, 31–60 days, 61–90 days, 91–120 days, and over 120 days.	Accounts in the older categories require follow-up: letters, phone calls, e-mails, and possible renegotiations of terms.
	Is the company's credit risk increasing?	Customer account balances and due dates	Accounts receivable aging schedule	Calculate and compare the percentage of receivables overdue in each age classification.
	Does the company have significant concentrations of credit risk?	Note to the financial statements on concentrations of credit risk	If risky credit customers are identified, the financial health of those customers should be evaluated to gain an independent assessment of the potential for a material credit loss.	If a material loss appears likely, the potential negative impact of that loss on the company should be carefully evaluated, as well as the adequacy of the allowance for doubtful accounts.
	Are collections being made in a timely fashion?	Net credit sales and average accounts receivable balance	$$\text{Receivables turnover} = \frac{\text{Net credit sales}}{\text{Average gross accounts receivable}}$$ $$\text{Average collection period} = \frac{365 \text{ days}}{\text{Receivables turnover}}$$	The average collection period should be consistent with corporate credit policy. An increase may suggest a decline in the financial health of customers.

The Navigator

www.wiley.com/canada/kimmel

Analysis Tools (Decision Toolkit Summaries)

Using the Decision Toolkit

Dell is one of Apple's top competitors. Selected financial information from Dell's financial statements follows (in USD millions):

	2007	2006
Net sales	$61,133	$57,420
Accounts receivable (gross)	6,064	4,748
Total current assets	19,880	19,939
Total current liabilities	18,526	17,791

Instructions

Calculate Dell's current ratio, receivables turnover, and average collection period for 2007. Comment on the company's accounts receivable management and liquidity compared to that of Apple and that of the industry. Apple's 2007 current ratio was 2.4:1; the industry average, 1.6:1 for 2007. Apple's receivables turnover and average collection period were calculated earlier in the chapter.

Solution

(in USD millions)	Dell	Apple	Industry
Current ratio	$\dfrac{\$19,880}{\$18,526} = 1.1{:}1$	2.4:1	1.9:1
Receivables turnover	$\dfrac{\$61,133}{(\$4,748 + \$6,064) \div 2} = 11.3 \text{ times}$	16.1 times	10.7 times
Average collection period	$\dfrac{365 \text{ days}}{11.3} = 32 \text{ days}$	23 days	34 days

Based on the above information, Apple has a higher receivables turnover and a shorter collection period than Dell and the industry. Apple also has a higher current ratio. When analyzing this ratio, it is important to remember that the current ratio can increase because the company has greater liquidity through higher cash balances, higher accounts receivable balances due to collection problems, or higher inventory balances due to obsolete or slow-moving products. In Apple's case, however, the higher current ratio is due to higher cash balances created by a surging demand for Apple products and its above-average collection of receivables.

The Navigator

www.wiley.com/canada/kimmel

Study Tools
(Demonstration Problems)

Demonstration Problem

Presented here are selected transactions for O'Reilly Corp.:

Mar.	1	Sold $20,000 of merchandise to Potter Corporation, terms 2/10, n/30.
	11	Received payment in full from Potter for balance due.
	12	Accepted Juno Ltd.'s four-month, 6%, $20,000 note for its balance due. Interest is payable at maturity.
	13	Made O'Reilly Corp. credit card sales for $13,200.
	15	Made VISA credit card sales totalling $6,700. A 3% service fee is charged by VISA.
Apr.	13	Received collections of $8,200 on O'Reilly credit card sales and added interest charges of 18% per annum (1.5% per month) to the remaining balances.
May	10	Wrote off as uncollectible $16,000 of accounts receivable.
June	30	The balance in Accounts Receivable is $200,000. Using an aging schedule, estimated uncollectible accounts are determined to be $20,000. At June 30, the credit balance in the allowance account before adjustment is $3,500.
July	12	Collected Juno note (see March 12 transaction).
	16	One of the accounts receivable written off in May paid the amount due, $4,000, in full.

Instructions

Record the above transactions.

Action Plan

• Record accounts receivable at the invoice price.

• Recognize that sales returns and allowances and cash discounts reduce the amount received on accounts receivable.

• Record a credit card expense when credit cards are used.

• Calculate interest by multiplying the interest rate by the face value, adjusting for the portion of the year that has passed.

• Consider any existing balance in the allowance account when making the adjustment for uncollectible accounts.

• Record write-offs of accounts receivable only in balance sheet accounts.

Solution to Demonstration Problem

Mar.	1	Accounts Receivable—Potter	20,000	
		Sales		20,000
		(To record sales on account)		
	11	Cash	19,600	
		Sales Discounts (2% × $20,000)	400	
		Accounts Receivable—Potter		20,000
		(To record collection of account receivable)		
	12	Notes Receivable—Juno	20,000	
		Accounts Receivable—Juno		20,000
		(To record acceptance of Juno note)		
	13	Accounts Receivable—O'Reilly	13,200	
		Sales		13,200
		(To record company credit card sales)		
	15	Cash	6,499	
		Credit Card Expense (3% × $6,700)	201	
		Sales		6,700
		(To record credit card sales)		

Apr. 13	Cash	8,200	
	Accounts Receivable—O'Reilly		8,200
	(To record collection of accounts receivable)		
	Accounts Receivable [($13,200 − $8,200) × 18% × $\frac{1}{12}$]	75	
	Interest Revenue		75
	(To record interest charges on overdue receivables)		
May 10	Allowance for Doubtful Accounts	16,000	
	Accounts Receivable		16,000
	(To record write-off of accounts receivable)		
June 30	Bad Debts Expense ($20,000 − $3,500)	16,500	
	Allowance for Doubtful Accounts		16,500
	(To record estimate of uncollectible accounts)		
July 12	Cash	20,400	
	Notes Receivable—Juno		20,000
	Interest Revenue ($20,000 × 6% × $\frac{4}{12}$)		400
	(To record collection of Juno note receivable)		
16	Accounts Receivable	4,000	
	Allowance for Doubtful Accounts		4,000
	(To reverse write-off of account receivable)		
	Cash	4,000	
	Accounts Receivable		4,000
	(To record collection of account receivable)		

The Navigator

Self-Study Questions

Answers are at the end of the chapter.

Study Tools (Self-Assessment Quizzes)

1. On June 15, Patel Ltd. sold merchandise on account to Bullock Corp. for $1,000, terms 2/10, n/30. On June 20, Bullock returned merchandise worth $300 to Patel. On June 24, payment was received from Bullock for the balance due. What was the amount of cash received?

   (a) $680
   (b) $686
   (c) $700
   (d) $1,000

2. Sanderson Corporation has a debit balance of $5,000 in its Allowance for Doubtful Accounts before any adjustments are made. Based on an aging of its accounts receivable at the end of the period, the company estimates that $60,000 of its receivables are uncollectible at the end of the period. The adjusting journal entry that would be recorded for bad debts expense at the end of this period would be:

(a)	Bad Debts Expense	55,000	
	Accounts Receivable		55,000
(b)	Bad Debts Expense	60,000	
	Accounts Receivable		60,000
(c)	Bad Debts Expense	65,000	
	Allowance for Doubtful Accounts		65,000
(d)	Bad Debts Expense	60,000	
	Allowance for Doubtful Accounts		60,000

3. On January 1, 2009, Allowance for Doubtful Accounts (SO 2) had a credit balance of $18,000. During 2009, $30,000 of uncollectible accounts receivable were written off. Aging indicates that uncollectible accounts are $20,000 at the end of 2009. What is the required adjustment in Bad Debts Expense at December 31, 2009?

   (a) $2,000
   (b) $8,000
   (c) $20,000
   (d) $32,000

4. On December 31, 2009, Allowance for Doubtful Accounts (SO 2) had a credit balance of $40,000, compared to a credit balance of $28,000 at the end of 2008. During 2009, $30,000 of uncollectible accounts receivable were written off. What was the bad debts expense recorded by the company for the year ended December 31, 2009?

   (a) $12,000
   (b) $30,000
   (c) $40,000
   (d) $42,000

(SO 3) 5. Sorenson Corp. accepts a three-month, 7%, $1,000 promissory note in settlement of Parton Ltd.'s account. The entry to record this transaction on Sorenson's books is:

(a) Notes Receivable 1,017
    Accounts Receivable 1,017

(b) Notes Receivable 1,000
    Accounts Receivable 1,000

(c) Notes Receivable 1,000
    Sales 1,000

(d) Notes Receivable 1,070
    Accounts Receivable 1,070

(SO 3) 6. Schlicht Corp. holds Osgrove Inc.'s four-month, 9%, $10,000 note. The entry made by Schlicht Corp. when the note is collected, assuming no interest has previously been recorded, is:

(a) Cash 10,300
    Notes Receivable 10,300

(b) Cash 10,000
    Notes Receivable 10,000

(c) Accounts Receivable 10,300
    Notes Receivable 10,000
    Interest Revenue 300

(d) Cash 10,300
    Notes Receivable 10,000
    Interest Revenue 300

7. Accounts and notes receivable are reported in the assets section of the balance sheet at:
(a) net realizable value.
(b) invoice cost.
(c) lower of cost and net realizable value.
(d) carrying amount.

8. The principles of sound accounts receivable management do not include:
(a) instituting a "cash only" policy.
(b) establishing a payment period.
(c) monitoring collections.
(d) evaluating the liquidity of receivables.

9. Moore Corporation had net credit sales during the year of $800,000 and cost of goods sold of $500,000. The balance in Accounts Receivable at the beginning of the year was $100,000, and at the end of the year it was $150,000. What were the receivables turnover and average collection period ratios, respectively?
(a) 4.0 and 91 days
(b) 5.3 and 69 days
(c) 6.4 and 57 days
(d) 8.0 and 46 days

10. New Millennium Retailers Corp. accepted $50,000 of VISA credit card charges for merchandise sold on July 1. If the service charge is 4%, the entry to record this transaction will include a credit to Sales of $50,000 and a debit (or debits) to:
(a) Cash $48,000 and Credit Card Expense $2,000.
(b) Accounts Receivable $48,000 and Credit Card Expense $2,000.
(c) Cash $50,000.
(d) Accounts Receivable $50,000.

The Navigator

Questions

(SO 1) 1. What are the three major types of receivables? Where is each type of receivable generally classified on a balance sheet?

(SO 1) 2. When should a receivable be recorded for a service company? For a merchandising company? Explain by referring to any relevant accounting principle(s).

(SO 1) 3. (a) What are the advantages of using an accounts receivable subsidiary ledger? (b) Describe the relationship between the general ledger control account and the subsidiary ledger.

(SO 1) 4. Under what circumstances is interest normally recorded for an account receivable?

(SO 2) 5. What are the essential features of the allowance method of accounting for bad debts? How does the allowance method respect the matching of revenues and expenses?

(SO 2) 6. Allowance for Doubtful Accounts is just one example of a contra account. (a) Name two other contra asset accounts

and their related asset accounts. (b) Name two contra revenue accounts and their related revenue accounts.

7. Why is the bad debts expense that is reported in the statement of earnings usually not the same amount as the allowance for doubtful accounts amount reported in the balance sheet?

8. Soo Eng cannot understand why the net realizable value does not change when an uncollectible account is written off under the allowance method. Clarify this for Soo Eng.

9. (a) What is the purpose of the account Allowance for Doubtful Accounts? (b) Although the normal balance of this account is a credit balance, it can sometimes have a debit balance. Explain how and when this can happen.

10. When an account receivable that was previously written off is later collected, two separate journal entries are usually made rather than one compound journal entry. Explain why.

11. (a) Explain how accounts receivable and notes receivable are alike. (b) Explain how they differ.

12. Danielle does not understand why a note receivable is not immediately recorded at its maturity value (principal plus interest), rather than its principal value. After all, you know you are going to collect both the principal and the interest and you know how much each will be. Explain to Danielle why notes are not recorded at their maturity value.

13. Explain how recording interest revenue differs for accounts receivable and notes receivable.

14. What is the difference between honouring a note receivable at maturity and dishonouring a note at maturity?

15. How would the entries differ if a note receivable were dishonoured and eventual collection was expected compared to eventual collection not being expected?

16. Saucier Ltd. has accounts receivable, notes receivable due in three months, notes receivable due in two years, an allowance for doubtful accounts, sales tax recoverable, and income tax receivable. How should the receivables be reported on the balance sheet?

17. Athabasca Ltd. has several dozen notes receivable. It expects approximately 10% of these notes to be uncollectible. How should these estimated notes be accounted for?

18. What are the five steps in good receivables management?

19. What is meant by a concentration of credit risk?

20. CanWest Global Communications Corp.'s receivables (SO 5) turnover was 5.8 times in 2007 and 6.3 times in 2006. Has CanWest's receivables management improved or worsened?

21. The president of Ho Inc. proudly announces that her (SO 5) company has improved its liquidity since its current ratio has increased substantially. Does an increase in the current ratio always indicate improved liquidity? What other ratio or ratios might you review to determine whether or not the increase in the current ratio indicates an improvement in financial health?

22. Why should a company not want to have a receivables (SO 5) turnover that is significantly higher than that of its competitors? Why would it not want a receivables turnover that is significantly lower than that of its competitors?

23. During the year ended December 31, 2007, Canadian Pacific (SO 5) Railway Limited transferred $120 million to an independent trust in a transaction known as securitization. Why might a company like Canadian Pacific Railway securitize its receivables?

24. Canadian Tire accepts its own company credit card, bank (SO 5) credit cards, and debit cards. What are the advantages of accepting each type of card? Explain how the accounting differs for sales of each type.

25. In July 2008, the University of Calgary, like many post- (SO 5) secondary institutions across Canada, stopped allowing students to pay their tuition with their credit cards. Despite significant student protest, the new policy was not overturned. Discuss the reasons why students would want to pay using credit cards and why the university would find paying in this way unacceptable.

Brief Exercises

BE8–1 Presented below are six receivables transactions. For each transaction, indicate whether the receivables should be reported as accounts receivable, notes receivable, or other receivables on a balance sheet.

Identify types of receivables.
(SO 1)

(a) Advanced $10,000 to an employee.

(b) Estimated $5,000 of income tax to be refunded.

(c) Received a promissory note of $5,000 for services performed.

(d) Sold merchandise on account to a customer for $6,000.

(e) GST of $2,500 is recoverable at the end of the quarter.

(f) Extended a customer's account for six months by accepting a note in exchange for the amount owed on the account.

BE8–2 Record the following transactions on the books of Essex Corp., which uses a perpetual inventory system:

Record receivables transactions.
(SO 1)

(a) On July 1, Essex Corp. sold merchandise on account to Cambridge Inc. for $42,000, terms 2/10, n/30. The cost of the merchandise sold was $30,000.

(b) On July 8, Cambridge returned merchandise worth $7,200 to Essex. Its original cost was $4,320. The merchandise was restored to inventory.

(c) On July 10, Cambridge paid for the merchandise.

(d) Assume now that Cambridge did not pay on July 10, as indicated in transaction (c). At the end of August, Essex added one month's interest to Cambridge's account for the overdue receivable. Essex charges 24% per year on overdue accounts.

Record bad debts
(SO 2)

BE8–3 At December 31, Massey Corp. estimates that 4% of total accounts receivable will become uncollectible. Accounts receivable are $300,000 at the end of the year. Allowance for Doubtful Accounts has a credit balance of $1,800 prior to recording any year-end adjusting entries.

(a) Prepare the adjusting journal entry to record bad debts expense at December 31.

(b) Assuming that Allowance for Doubtful Accounts had a debit balance of $2,000 instead of a credit balance of $1,800, determine the amount that would be reported for bad debts expense.

Complete aging schedule and record bad debts.
(SO 2)

BE8–4 Refer to BE8–3 and assume that Massey Corp. decides to refine its estimate of uncollectible accounts by preparing an aging schedule. Complete the following schedule and prepare the adjusting journal entry at December 31 to record bad debts expense, assuming that the allowance account has a credit balance of $1,800.

Number of Days Outstanding	Accounts Receivable	Estimated Percentage Uncollectible	Estimated Bad Debts
0–30 days	$184,000	1%	
31–60 days	60,000	4%	
61–90 days	36,000	10%	
Over 90 days	20,000	20%	
Total	$300,000		

Record write-off, and compare net realizable value.
(SO 2)

BE8–5 At the end of 2009, Searcy Corp. has accounts receivable of $600,000 and an allowance for doubtful accounts of $36,000. On January 24, 2010, Searcy learns that its $8,000 receivable from Hutley Inc. is not collectible. Management authorizes a write-off.

(a) Prepare the journal entry to record the write-off.

(b) What is the net realizable value of the accounts receivable (1) before the write-off and (2) after the write-off?

Record recovery of bad debt.
(SO 2)

BE8–6 Assume the same information as in BE8–5, but that on March 4, 2010, Searcy Corp. receives payment in full of $8,000 from Hutley Inc., after the write-off. Prepare the required journal entry (entries) to record this transaction.

Calculate interest.
(SO 3)

BE8–7 Data on three promissory notes follow. Determine the missing amounts.

Date of Note	Term in Months	Principal	Interest Rate	Total Interest	Interest Revenue to Record for Year Ended December 31
Apr. 1	3	$900,000	10%	(c)	$22,500
July 2	6	84,000	(b)	$ 3,360	(d)
Nov. 1	12	(a)	6%	12,600	(e)

Record receivables transactions.
(SO 3)

BE8–8 On January 10, 2009, Kyiv Corp. sold merchandise on account to R. Opal for $24,000, terms n/30. The merchandise originally cost $16,000. On February 1, R. Opal gave Kyiv a five-month, 7% promissory note in settlement of this account. On July 1, R. Opal paid the note and accrued interest. Prepare the journal entries for Kyiv to record the above transactions. Kyiv has an April 30 year end and adjusts its accounts annually.

Record note receivable transactions.
(SO 3)

BE8–9 Stratus Ltd. sells inventory on April 1, 2009, to Red River Enterprises for a 12-month, 9%, $10,000 note, with interest due at maturity. The company uses a perpetual inventory system and the cost of the inventory sold was $6,000. Stratus has a December 31 year end and adjusts its accounts annually. Prepare the journal entries that Stratus will record with regard to this note from April 1, 2009, until the note matures on March 31, 2010.

Record note payable transactions.
(SO 3)

BE8–10 Using the same information from BE8-9 above, prepare the journal entries that Red River Enterprises will record regarding the note. Red River, however, has a September 30 year end and adjusts its accounts annually.

BE8–11 Lee Corporation accepts a three-month, 7%, $27,000 note receivable in settlement of an account receivable on April 1, 2009. Interest is due at maturity.

Record note receivable transactions. (SO 3)

(a) Prepare the journal entries required by Lee Corporation to record the issue of the note on April 1, and the settlement of the note on July 1, assuming the note is honoured. No interest has previously been accrued. Round your answers to the nearest dollar.

(b) Repeat part (a) assuming that the note is dishonoured, but eventual collection is expected.

(c) Repeat part (a) assuming that the note is dishonoured, and eventual collection is not expected.

BE8–12 Prepare the current assets section of the balance sheet for Nias Corporation, which reported the following selected items at February 28, 2009:

Prepare current assets section. (SO 4)

Accounts payable	$938,000	Notes receivable—due November 1, 2009	$300,000
Accounts receivable	470,000	Notes receivable—due April 1, 2012	400,000
Allowance for doubtful accounts	30,000	Prepaid expenses	58,000
Bad debts expense	24,000	Recoverable sales taxes	38,000
Cash	150,000	Short-term investments	330,000
Inventory	380,000	Unearned revenue	5,000

BE8–13 The financial statements of Maple Leaf Foods Inc. report net sales of $5,209.6 million for the year ended December 31, 2007. Accounts receivable were $201.7 million at the beginning of the year, and $202.3 million at the end of the year. Calculate Maple Leaf's receivables turnover and average collection period.

Calculate ratios. (SO 5)

BE8–14 St. Pierre Restaurant, situated in a Starwood Hotel, accepted a VISA card in payment of a $100 lunch bill. The bank charges a 2.5% fee. What entry should St. Pierre make to record the sale? How would this entry be different if payment had been made with a Starwood Preferred Guest credit card instead of a VISA card? With a debit card instead of a VISA card? Assume that the same percentage fee applies for each type of card.

Record credit and debit card sales. (SO 5)

Exercises

E8–1 On January 6, Nicklaus Corp. sold merchandise on account to Singh Inc. for $12,000, terms 2/10, n/30. The merchandise originally cost Nicklaus $8,000. On January 15, Singh paid the amount due. Both Nicklaus and Singh use a perpetual inventory system.

Record receivables and payables transactions. (SO 1)

Instructions

(a) Prepare the entries on Nicklaus Corp.'s books to record the sale and related collection.

(b) Prepare the entries on Singh Inc.'s books to record the purchase and related payment.

E8–2 The transactions that follow were for Discovery Sports Ltd. with four of its customers during the company's first month of business:

Record receivables transactions; post to subsidiary and general ledger. (SO 1)

Feb. 2 Sold $1,140 of merchandise to Andrew Noren on account, terms n/30.
4 Andrew Noren returned for credit $140 of the merchandise purchased on February 2.
5 Sold $760 of merchandise to Dong Corporation on account, terms 2/10, n/30.
8 Sold $842 of merchandise to Michael Collis for cash.
14 Dong Corporation paid its account in full.
17 Andrew Noren purchased an additional $696 of merchandise on account, terms n/30.
22 Sold $1,738 of merchandise to Batstone Corporation, terms 2/10, n/30.
28 Andrew Noren paid $1,000 on account.

Instructions

(a) Prepare the journal entries to record each of the above transactions. Round your answers to the nearest dollar.

(b) Set up T accounts for the Accounts Receivable control account and for the Accounts Receivable subsidiary ledger accounts. Post the journal entries to these accounts.

(c) Prepare a list of customers and the balances of their accounts from the subsidiary ledger. Prove that the total of the subsidiary ledger balances is equal to the control account balance.

Record bad debts
(SO 2)

E8–3   Patillo Inc.'s general ledger reports a balance in Accounts Receivable of $180,000 at the end of December.

Instructions

(a) Assuming that Allowance for Doubtful Accounts has a credit balance of $2,200 and that uncollectible accounts are determined to be $18,000 by aging the accounts, record the adjusting entry at December 31.

(b) Assuming the same information as in (a) except that uncollectible accounts are expected to be 10% of the accounts receivable, record the adjusting entry at December 31.

(c) Assuming the same information as in (a) except that the Allowance for Doubtful Accounts has a debit balance of $1,200, record the adjusting entry at December 31.

Prepare aging schedule, record bad debts, and discuss implications.
(SO 2)

E8–4   ⚙ Grevina Ltd. has accounts receivable of $185,000 at March 31, 2009. An analysis of the accounts shows these amounts:

Month of Sale	2009	2008
March	$130,000	$150,000
February	25,200	16,000
January	17,000	4,800
October–December	12,800	2,200
	$185,000	$173,000

Credit terms are 2/10, n/30. At March 31, 2009, there is a $4,400 credit balance in the allowance account before adjustment. The company estimates its uncollectible accounts as follows:

Number of Days Outstanding	Estimated Percentage Uncollectible
0–30	2%
31–60	10%
61–90	30%
Over 90	50%

Instructions

(a) Prepare an aging schedule to determine the total estimated uncollectibles at March 31, 2009.

(b) Prepare the adjusting entry at March 31, 2009, to record bad debts expense.

(c) Discuss the implications of the changes in the age of receivables from 2008 to 2009.

Record bad debts transactions.
(SO 2)

E8–5   On December 31, 2009, when its Allowance for Doubtful Accounts had a debit balance of $2,000, Ceja Corp. estimated that $16,800 of its accounts receivable would become uncollectible, and it recorded the bad debts adjusting entry. On May 11, 2010, Ceja determined that Robert Worthy's account was uncollectible and wrote off $1,900. On November 12, 2010, Worthy paid the amount previously written off.

Instructions

Prepare the required journal entries to record each of the above transactions.

Record bad debts transactions and assess policy.
(SO 2)

E8–6   ⚙ During its first year of operations, which ended on December 31, 2009, Fort Nelson Resources Ltd. determined that customers owing the company $12,000 would not be able to pay and wrote off these accounts. By the end of the year, the company had $1.7 million of accounts receivable and estimated that 10% of these were doubtful of collection. In 2010, the company wrote off accounts receivable amounting to $14,000. By December 31, 2010, the company had accounts receivable of $2.1 million and estimated doubtful accounts at 10% of outstanding accounts receivable.

Instructions

(a) Prepare the journal entries that Fort Nelson Resources would record in 2009.

(b) Prepare the journal entries that Fort Nelson Resources would record in 2010.

(c) Assess whether the company's policy of estimating doubtful accounts at 10% of outstanding receivables is appropriate.

E8–7 Passara Supply Corp. has the following selected transactions for notes receivable:

Record notes receivable transactions. (SO 3)

Nov. 1 Loaned $48,000 cash to A. Bouchard on a one-year, 8% note.

Dec. 1 Sold goods to Wright, Inc., receiving a two-month, 6%, $8,400 note. The goods cost $5,000.

15 Received a six-month, 7%, $16,000 note on account from Barnes Corporation.

31 Accrued interest on all notes receivable at year end. Interest is due at maturity.

Feb. 1 Collected the amount owing on the Wright note.

Instructions

Record the above transactions for Passara Supply Corp. Round your answers to the nearest dollar.

E8–8 The following selected transactions for notes receivable are for Rather Corp.:

Record notes receivable transactions. (SO 3)

May 1 Received a six-month, 5%, $6,000 note on account from Jioux Company. Interest is due at maturity.

June 30 Accrued interest on the Jioux note on this date, which is Rather's year end.

July 31 Lent $5,000 cash to an employee, Noreen Wong, issuing a three-month, 7% note. Interest is due at at the end of each month.

Aug. 31 Received the interest due from Ms. Wong.

Sept. 30 Received the interest due from Ms. Wong.

Oct. 31 Received payment in full for the employee note from Ms. Wong.

Nov. 1 Wrote off the Jioux note as Jioux defaulted. Future payment is not expected.

Instructions

Record the above transactions for Rather Corp. Round your answers to the nearest dollar.

E8–9 Deere & Company had the following balances in its short-term receivable accounts at October 31, 2007 (in USD millions): Allowance for Doubtful Trade Receivables $64; Allowance for Doubtful Financing Receivables $172; Financing Receivables $17,920; Other Receivables $596; and Trade Accounts and Notes Receivable $3,119.

Show presentation of receivables. (SO 4)

Instructions

Show the presentation of Deere & Company's receivables in the current assets section of its balance sheet at October 31.

E8–10 ☞ Refer to E8–9. Deere & Company reports in the notes to its financial statements that its trade accounts and notes receivable have significant concentrations of credit risk in the agricultural, commercial and consumer, and construction and forestry sectors. However, it does not believe that it has a significant concentration of credit risk on a geographic basis.

Discuss concentration of credit risk. (SO 5)

Instructions

Should readers of Deere & Company's financial statements be concerned about its credit risk?

E8–11 ☞ The following information (in millions) was taken from the December 31 financial statements of Canadian National Railway Company (CN):

Calculate ratios and comment. (SO 5)

	2007	2006	2005
Accounts receivable, gross	$ 397	$ 711	$ 703
Allowance for doubtful accounts	27	19	80
Accounts receivable, net	370	692	623
Revenues	7,897	7,929	7,446
Total current assets	1,048	1,336	1,149
Total current liabilities	1,590	2,114	1,958

Instructions

(a) Calculate CN's current ratio, receivables turnover, and average collection period for each of 2007 and 2006.

(b) Comment on any improvement or deterioration in CN's liquidity and management of its accounts receivable.

Record credit and debit card sales and indicate statement presentation.
(SO 4, 5)

E8–12 Kasko Stores Ltd. accepts both its own credit cards and bank credit cards, in addition to debit cards. During the year, the following selected summary transactions occurred:

Jan. 15 Made Kasko credit card sales totalling $17,000.
     20 Made VISA credit card sales (credit card charge of 3%) totalling $4,500.
     30 Made debit card sales (debit card charge of 2%) totalling $1,000.
Feb. 10 Collected $12,000 on Kasko credit card sales.
     15 Added interest charges of 28.8% to outstanding Kasko credit card balances.

Instructions

(a) Record the transactions for Kasko Stores.

(b) Indicate the statement presentation of the interest and credit and debit card charges for Kasko Stores.

Problems: Set A

Record receivables and bad debts transactions; show balance sheet presentation.
(SO 1, 2)

P8–1A At January 1, 2009, Bordeaux Inc. reported the following information on its balance sheet:

Accounts receivable	$480,000
Allowance for doubtful accounts	35,000

During 2009, the company had the following summary transactions for receivables:

1. Sales on account, $1,600,000
2. Sales returns and allowances, $250,000
3. Collections of accounts receivable, $1,500,000
4. Interest added to overdue accounts, $125,000
5. Write-offs of accounts receivable deemed uncollectible, $45,000
6. Recovery of accounts previously written off as uncollectible, $10,500

Instructions

(a) Prepare the journal entries to record each of the summary transactions.

(b) Enter the January 1, 2009, balances in Accounts Receivable and Allowance for Doubtful Accounts, post the entries to the two accounts, and determine the balances.

(c) Prepare the journal entry to record bad debts expense at December 31, 2009, assuming that aging the accounts receivable indicates that the amount for estimated uncollectible accounts is $55,000.

(d) Determine the net realizable value of the accounts receivable as at December 31.

(e) Show the balance sheet presentation of the receivables as at December 31.

Record receivables and bad debts transactions; show balance sheet presentation.
(SO 1, 2)

P8–2A At the beginning of the current period, Huang Corp. had balances in Accounts Receivable of $100,000 and in Allowance for Doubtful Accounts of $7,000 (credit). During the period, it had net credit sales of $400,000 and collections of $361,500. It wrote off accounts receivable of $10,500. However, a $1,750 account written off as uncollectible was recovered before the end of the current period. Uncollectible accounts are estimated to total $8,000 at the end of the period.

Instructions

(a) Prepare the entries to record the sales and collections during the period.

(b) Prepare the entry to record the write-off of uncollectible accounts during the period.

(c) Prepare the entries to record the recovery of the uncollectible account during the period.

(d) Prepare the entry to record bad debts expense for the period.

(e) Determine the ending balances in Accounts Receivable and Allowance for Doubtful Accounts.

(f) Show the balance sheet presentation of the receivables at the end of the period.

P8–3A Yasukuni Corporation reported the following information in its general ledger at June 30:

Determine missing amounts.
(SO 1, 2)

Accounts Receivable		
Beg. bal.	(a)	
	22,500	23,000
End. bal.	2,250	

Sales	
	(d)

Allowance for Doubtful Accounts		
Beg. bal.		100
	25	(b)
End. bal.		(c)

Bad Debts Expense	
(e)	

All sales were on account. At the end of the year, uncollectible accounts were estimated to total $115 based on an aging schedule.

Instructions

Using your knowledge of receivables transactions, determine the missing amounts. (*Hint*: You may not be able to solve the above items in alphabetical order. In addition, you may find it helpful to reconstruct the journal entries.)

P8–4A Here is information for Volkov Ltd. for the year ended April 30, 2009:

Calculate bad debts amounts.
(SO 2)

Total credit sales	$1,000,000
Accounts receivable at April 30	400,000
Accounts receivable written off during year	17,500
Accounts receivable later recovered (after write-off but before year-end)	2,500

Instructions

(a) What amount of bad debts expense will Volkov report if it does *not* use the allowance method of accounting for bad debts?

(b) Assume that Volkov decides to estimate its uncollectible accounts using the allowance method and an aging schedule. Uncollectible accounts are estimated to be $30,000. What amount of bad debts expense will Volkov record if Allowance for Doubtful Accounts has an opening credit balance of $2,000 on May 1, 2008?

(c) Assume the same facts as in part (b) except that there is a $2,000 opening debit balance in Allowance for Doubtful Accounts. What amount of bad debts expense will Volkov record?

(d) What are the advantages of using the allowance method of reporting bad debts expense?

P8–5A Imagine Corporation produced the following aging schedule of its accounts receivable at year end:

Prepare aging schedule and record bad debts transactions.
(SO 2)

		Number of Days Outstanding			
	Total	0–30	31–60	61–90	Over 90
Accounts receivable	$192,500	$110,000	$50,000	$20,000	$12,500
Estimated percentage uncollectible		1%	5%	10%	20%
Estimated bad debts					

The unadjusted balance in Allowance for Doubtful Accounts is a debit of $5,000.

Instructions

(a) Complete the aging schedule and calculate the total estimated bad debts from the above information.

(b) Prepare the adjusting journal entry to record the bad debts using the information determined in (a).

(c) In the following year, $3,000 of the outstanding receivables is determined to be uncollectible. Prepare the journal entry to write off the uncollectible amount.

(d) The company subsequently collects $1,500 of the $3,000 that was determined to be uncollectible in (c). Prepare the journal entries to restore the account receivable and record the collection.

(e) Comment on how your answers in (a) to (d) would change if Imagine used a percentage of total accounts receivable of 4%, rather than aging the accounts.

(f) What are the advantages to the company of aging the accounts receivable rather than applying a percentage to total accounts receivable?

Prepare aging schedule, record bad debts transactions, and comment on policy.
(SO 2)

P8–6A ▬ An aging analysis of Toshiro Corporation's accounts receivable at December 31, 2009 and 2008, showed the following:

Number of Days Outstanding	Estimated Percentage Uncollectible	December 31 2009	December 31 2008
0–30 days	3%	$120,000	$110,000
31–60 days	6%	52,000	43,000
61–90 days	12%	31,000	26,000
Over 90 days	20%	17,000	11,000
Total		$220,000	$190,000

1. At December 31, 2008, the unadjusted balance in Allowance for Doubtful Accounts was a credit of $1,500.
2. In 2009, $14,000 of accounts were written off as uncollectible and $1,500 of accounts previously written off were recovered.

Instructions

(a) Prepare an aging schedule to calculate the estimated uncollectible accounts at December 31, 2008 and 2009. Comment on the results.

(b) Record the adjusting entry relating to bad debts on December 31, 2008.

(c) Record the write-off of uncollectible accounts in 2009.

(d) Record the collection of accounts previously written off in 2009.

(e) Prepare the adjusting entry relating to bad debts on December 31, 2009.

(f) Calculate the net realizable value of Toshiro's accounts receivable at December 31, 2008 and 2009.

(g) Do you think that Toshiro was conservative when estimating its bad debts expense? Explain.

Record receivables transactions.
(SO 1, 3)

P8–7A The following selected transactions are for Vu Ltd., which has a September 30 year end and adjusts its accounts annually:

Jan. 1 Loaned Emily Collis, an employee, $6,000 on a four-month, 8% note. Interest is due at maturity.
    5 Sold $8,000 of merchandise to Asiz Limited, terms n/15. The merchandise cost $4,800.
   20 Accepted Asiz Limited's two-month, 9%, $8,000 note for its balance due. Interest is due monthly. (See January 5 transaction.)

Feb. 18 Sold $4,000 of merchandise costing $2,400 to Swaim Corp. Accepted Swaim's six-month, 7% note in payment. Interest is due at maturity.
   20 Collected interest on the Asiz note. (See January 20 transaction.)

Mar. 20 Collected principal and interest for the month on the Asiz note. (See January 20 transaction.)

May 1 Received payment in full from Emily Collis. (See January 1 transaction.)
   25 Accepted Avery Inc.'s three-month, 8%, $3,000 note in settlement of a past-due balance on account. Interest is due at maturity.

Aug. 18 Received payment in full from Swaim Corp. on its note due. (See February 18 transaction.)
   25 The Avery note was dishonoured. Eventual payment is not expected. (See May 25 transaction.)

Sept. 30 Adjusted any accrued interest at year end.

Instructions
Record the transactions.

Record notes receivable transactions.
(SO 3)

P8–8A On August 1, 2009, a company accepted a two-month, 4%, $25,000 note from a customer in settlement of the customer's account. Interest is due on the first day of each month, starting September 1. The company's year end is August 31.

Instructions

(a) Prepare all journal entries for the company over the life of the note. Assume that the customer settles the note in full on the maturity date. Round your answers to the nearest dollar.

(b) Assume that instead of honouring the note at maturity, the customer dishonours it. Prepare the necessary journal entry at the maturity date, September 30, 2009, assuming that eventual collection of the note is (1) expected, and (2) not expected.

P8–9A   Sears Canada Inc. reports the following asset accounts (in millions) at February 2, 2008:

Accounts receivable (net)	$ 118.4	Income taxes recoverable	$ 0.4
Accumulated depreciation—buildings	691.6	Inventories	855.4
Accumulated depreciation—		Land	55.9
equipment and fixtures	1,040.1	Other current assets	30.6
Buildings	1,136.8	Other long-term assets	264.1
Cash and short-term investments	871.6	Prepaid expenses and other assets	115.4
Equipment and fixtures	1,281.0	Restricted cash (noncurrent)	5.2

Prepare assets section of balance sheet.
(SO 4)

Instructions

Prepare the assets section of Sears Canada's balance sheet.

P8–10A   During April, the following selected transactions occurred for Orient Retail Corporation:

Record receivables and credit and debit card transactions.
(SO 1, 5)

Apr.   1   Sold $7,600 of merchandise for cash. The cost of the goods sold was $4,600.

      7   Sold merchandise of $13,600 on Orient Retail credit cards. The cost of the goods sold was $8,000.

    12   Performed services for $3,400, paid for with MasterCard credit cards. The credit card charge was 3%.

    12   Sold merchandise for $4,400, paid for with American Express credit cards. The cost of goods sold was $2,640 and the credit card charge was 5%.

    18   Performed services for $4,000 on account, terms 1/10, n/30.

    20   Sold $5,600 of merchandise to customers, who paid with their debit cards. The cost of goods sold was $3,400 and the debit card charge was 2%.

    27   Collected amount owing from April 18 transaction.

    30   Added $300 of interest to overdue Orient Retail credit card account holders.

    30   Submitted Orient Retail credit card slips accumulated to date to the credit card division for payment.

Instructions

Record the transactions.

P8–11A   Presented here is selected information (in millions) from the 2007 financial statements of Rogers Communications Inc. and Shaw Communications Inc.:

Calculate and interpret ratios.
(SO 5)

	Rogers	Shaw
Net sales	$10,123	$2,774
Allowance for doubtful accounts, Jan. 1	151	28
Allowance for doubtful accounts, Dec. 31	114	15
Accounts receivable (gross), Jan. 1	1,191	166
Accounts receivable (gross), Dec. 31	1,396	170

Instructions

(a) Calculate the receivables turnover and average collection period for both companies, assuming all sales are credit sales. The industry average for the receivables turnover was 12.6 times and the average collection period was 29 days.

(b) Comment on the difference in the companies' collection experiences.

P8–12A   The following ratios are available for Tianjin Inc.:

Evaluate liquidity.
(SO 5)

	2009	2008	2007
Current ratio	1.5:1	1.5:1	1.5:1
Receivables turnover	8 times	7 times	6 times
Inventory turnover	6 times	7 times	8 times

Instructions

(a) Is Tianjin's short-term liquidity improving or worsening? Explain.

(b) Do changes in turnover ratios affect profitability? Explain.

(c) Identify any steps that the company may wish to consider in order to improve its management of its receivables and inventory.

Problems: Set B

Record receivables and bad debts transactions; show balance sheet presentation.
(SO 1, 2)

P8–1B   At January 1, 2009, Underwood Imports Inc. reported the following on its balance sheet:

Accounts receivable	$1,990,000
Allowance for doubtful accounts	124,000

During 2009, the company had the following summary transactions for receivables:

1. Sales on account, $5,200,000
2. Sales returns and allowances, $80,000
3. Collections of accounts receivable, $5,400,000
4. Interest added to overdue accounts, $400,000
5. Write-offs of accounts receivable deemed uncollectible, $150,000
6. Recovery of accounts previously written off as uncollectible, $60,000

Instructions

(a) Prepare the journal entries to record each of the summary transactions.

(b) Enter the January 1, 2009, balances in Accounts Receivable and Allowance for Doubtful Accounts, post the entries to the two accounts, and determine the balances.

(c) Prepare the journal entry to record bad debts expense at December 31, 2009, assuming that the aging of the accounts receivable indicates that the amount for estimated uncollectible accounts is $100,000.

(d) Determine the net realizable value of the accounts receivable as at December 31, 2009.

(e) Show the balance sheet presentation of the receivables as at December 31, 2009.

Record receivables and bad debts transactions; show balance sheet presentation.
(SO 1, 2)

P8–2B   At the beginning of the current period, Fassi Corp. had balances in Accounts Receivable of $800,000 and in Allowance for Doubtful Accounts of $44,000 (credit). During the period, it had net credit sales of $1,900,000 and collections of $2,042,000. It wrote off accounts receivable of $58,000. However, a $4,000 account written off as uncollectible was recovered before the end of the current period. Uncollectible accounts are estimated to total $36,000 at the end of the period.

Instructions

(a) Prepare the entries to record sales and collections during the period.

(b) Prepare the entry to record the write-off of uncollectible accounts during the period.

(c) Prepare the entries to record the recovery of the uncollectible account during the period.

(d) Prepare the entry to record bad debts expense for the period.

(e) Determine the ending balances in Accounts Receivable and Allowance for Doubtful Accounts.

(f) Show the balance sheet presentation of the receivables at the end of the period.

Determine missing amounts.
(SO 1, 2)

P8–3B   Wilton Corporation reported the following information in its general ledger at December 31:

Accounts Receivable				Sales	
Beg. bal.	18,000				60,000
	(a)	56,000			
End. bal.	(b)				

Allowance for Doubtful Accounts			Bad Debts Expense	
Beg. bal.		1,800	(e)	
	1,000	(c)		
End. bal.		(d)		

All sales were on account. At the end of the year, uncollectible accounts were estimated to total $2,000 based on an aging schedule.

Instructions

Using your knowledge of receivables transactions, determine the missing amounts. (*Hint*: You may not be able to solve the above items in alphabetical order. In addition, you may find it helpful to reconstruct the journal entries.)

P8–4B Here is information for Aris Ltd. for the 2009 calendar year:

Calculate bad debts amounts. (SO 2)

Total credit sales	$3,300,000
Accounts receivable at December 31	1,250,000
Accounts receivable written off during year	48,000
Accounts receivable later recovered (after write-off but before year-end)	8,000

Instructions

(a) What amount of bad debts expense will Aris report if it does *not* use the allowance method of accounting for bad debts?

(b) Assume that Aris decides to estimate its uncollectible accounts using the allowance method and an aging schedule. Uncollectible accounts are estimated to total $52,000. What amount of bad debts expense will Aris record if Allowance for Doubtful Accounts has an opening credit balance of $20,000 on January 1?

(c) Assume the same facts as in (b) except that there is a $2,000 opening debit balance in Allowance for Doubtful Accounts. What amount of bad debts expense will Aris record?

(d) What are the advantages of using the allowance method of reporting bad debts expense?

P8–5B The following selected information is from a company's aging schedule to estimate uncollectible accounts receivable at year end:

Prepare aging schedule and record bad debts transactions. (SO 2)

		Number of Days Outstanding			
	Total	0–30	31–60	61–90	Over 90
Accounts receivable	$520,000	$240,000	$120,000	$100,000	$60,000
Estimated percentage uncollectible		1%	5%	10%	25%
Estimated bad debts					

The unadjusted balance in Allowance for Doubtful Accounts is a credit of $20,000.

Instructions

(a) Complete the aging schedule and calculate the total estimated bad debts from the above information.

(b) Prepare the adjusting journal entry to record the bad debts using the information determined in (a).

(c) In the following year, $4,000 of the outstanding receivables is determined to be specifically uncollectible. Prepare the journal entry to write off the uncollectible amount.

(d) The company subsequently collects $1,700 of the $4,000 that was determined to be uncollectible in (c). Prepare the journal entries to restore the account receivable and record the collection.

(e) Explain how establishing an allowance satisfies the matching principle.

(f) What are the advantages to the company of aging the accounts receivable rather than applying a percentage to total accounts receivable?

P8–6B ⬤▬ An aging analysis of Hake Corporation's accounts receivable at December 31, 2009 and 2008, showed the following:

Prepare aging schedule, record bad debts transactions, and comment on policy. (SO 2)

Number of Days Outstanding	Estimated Percentage Uncollectible	December 31	
		2009	2008
0–30 days	3%	$150,000	$160,000
31–60 days	6%	32,000	57,000
61–90 days	12%	43,000	38,000
Over 90 days	24%	65,000	25,000
Total		$290,000	$280,000

1. At December 31, 2008, the unadjusted balance in Allowance for Doubtful Accounts was a credit of $4,500.

2. In 2009, $21,000 of accounts were written off as uncollectible and $1,500 of accounts previously written off were recovered.

Instructions

(a) Prepare an aging schedule to calculate the estimated uncollectible accounts at December 31, 2008 and 2009. Comment on the results.

(b) Record the adjusting entry relating to bad debts on December 31, 2008.

(c) Record the write-off of uncollectible accounts in 2009.

(d) Record the collection of accounts previously written off in 2009.

(e) Prepare the adjusting entry relating to bad debts on December 31, 2009.

(f) Calculate the net realizable value of Hake's accounts receivable at December 31, 2008 and 2009.

(g) Do you think that Hake was conservative when estimating bad debts expense? Explain.

Record receivables transactions.
(SO 1, 3)

P8–7B   The following selected transactions occurred for Bleumortier Corporation. The company has a March 31 year end and adjusts its accounts annually.

Jan.   5 Sold $18,000 of merchandise to Brooks Limited, terms n/30. The cost of goods sold was $12,000.

Feb.   2 Accepted a four-month, 6%, $18,000 promissory note from Brooks for the balance due. Interest is payable at maturity. (See January 5 transaction.)

12 Sold $13,400 of merchandise costing $8,800 to Gage Company and accepted Gage's two-month, 6% note in payment. Interest is payable at maturity.

26 Sold $8,000 of merchandise to Mathias Corp., terms n/30. The cost of the merchandise sold was $5,400.

Mar. 31 Accepted a two-month, 7%, $8,000 note from Mathias for the balance due. Interest is payable at maturity. (See February 26 transaction.)

31 Adjusted any accrued interest at year end.

Apr. 12 Collected the Gage note in full. (See February 12 transaction.)

May   31 Mathias note of March 31 is dishonoured. It is expected that Mathias will eventually pay the amount owed.

June   2 Collected the Brooks note in full. (See February 2 transaction.)

Instructions
Record the transactions. Round your answers to the nearest dollar.

Record notes receivable transactions.
(SO 3)

P8–8B   On November 1, 2009, a company accepted a three-month, 6%, $20,000 note from a customer in settlement of the customer's account. Interest is due on the first day of each month, starting December 1. The company's year end is December 31.

Instructions

(a) Prepare all journal entries for the company over the life of the note. Assume that the customer settles the note in full on the maturity date.

(b) Assume that instead of honouring the note at maturity, the customer dishonours it. Prepare the necessary journal entry at the maturity date, February 1, 2010, assuming that eventual collection of the note is (1) expected, and (2) not expected.

Prepare assets section of balance sheet.
(SO 4)

P8–9B   Canadian Tire Corporation, Limited reports the following asset accounts (in millions) at December 29, 2007:

Accounts receivable (net)	$ 707.1	Intangible assets	$ 52.4
Accumulated depreciation—buildings	733.5	Land	749.7
Accumulated depreciation—		Loans receivable (short-term)	1,486.1
furniture and equipment	416.7	Long-term receivables and other assets	231.2
Accumulated depreciation—other	437.2	Merchandise inventories	756.7
Buildings	2,230.3	Other current assets	77.7

Furniture and equipment	627.7	Other long-term investments	7.6
Goodwill	51.8	Other property, plant, and equipment	1,263.3
Income taxes recoverable	59.0	Prepaid expenses and deposits	29.5

Instructions

Prepare the assets section of Canadian Tire's balance sheet.

P8–10B During July, the following selected transactions occurred for Bon Ton Limited:

Record receivables and credit and debit card transactions.
(SO 1, 5)

July   1   Sold $5,600 of merchandise for cash. The cost of the goods sold was $3,400.

      5   Sold merchandise of $15,600 on Bon Ton credit cards. The cost of the goods sold was $9,400.

     14   Performed services for $1,400 on VISA credit cards. The credit card charge was 3%.

     15   Sold merchandise for $2,400 on American Express credit cards. The cost of goods sold was $1,400 and the credit card charge was 5%.

     17   Performed services for $2,000 on account, terms 2/10, n/30.

     20   Sold $3,600 of merchandise to customers who paid with their debit cards. The cost of goods sold was $2,000 and the debit card charge was 2%.

     26   Collected the amount owing from the July 17 transaction.

     31   Added $400 of interest to overdue Bon Ton credit card account holders.

     31   Submitted Bon Ton credit card slips accumulated to date to the credit card division for payment.

Instructions

Record the transactions.

P8–11B ⚿ Presented here is selected information from the 2007 financial statements of **Nike, Inc.** (in USD millions) and **Adidas AG** (in euro millions):

Calculate and interpret ratios.
(SO 5)

	Nike	Adidas
Net sales	$16,325.9	€10,299
Allowance for doubtful accounts, beginning of year	10.9	111
Allowance for doubtful accounts, end of year	12.4	112
Accounts receivable (gross), beginning of year	2,395.3	1,527
Accounts receivable (gross), end of year	2,505.6	1,570

Instructions

(a) Calculate the receivables turnover and average collection period for both companies, assuming all sales are credit sales. The industry average for the receivables turnover was 6.1 times and the average collection period was 60 days.

(b) Comment on the difference in the two companies' collection experiences.

P8–12B ⚿ The following selected ratios are available for Pampered Pets Inc. for the most recent three years:

Evaluate liquidity
(SO 5)

	2009	2008	2007
Current ratio	2.6:1	2.4:1	2.1:1
Receivables turnover	8.2 times	7.4 times	6.7 times
Inventory turnover	9.9 times	8.7 times	7.5 times

Instructions

(a) Is Pampered Pets' liquidity improving or worsening? Explain.

(b) Do changes in turnover ratios affect cash flow? Explain.

(c) Identify any steps that the company may wish to take in order to improve its management of receivables and inventory.

BROADENING YOUR PERSPECTIVE

Analysis Tools

Financial Reporting and Analysis Cases

Financial Reporting: *Shoppers Drug Mart*

BYP8–1   The financial statements of Shoppers Drug Mart are presented in Appendix A at the end of this book.

Instructions

(a) Assuming that all sales are credit sales, use net receivables instead of gross receivables to calculate the receivables turnover and average collection period for 2007.

(b) Is Shoppers likely concerned about any concentration of credit risk? Why or why not? (*Hint*: Review Note 15 to the financial statements.)

(c) What conclusions can you draw about Shoppers' management of its receivables from your answers to questions (a) and (b)?

Comparative Analysis: *Shoppers Drug Mart and Jean Coutu*

BYP8–2   The financial statements of Jean Coutu are presented in Appendix B after the financial statements for Shoppers Drug Mart in Appendix A.

Instructions

(a) What types of receivables does each company report in its balance sheet?

(b) Calculate the following for each company for its most recent fiscal year. The industry average is shown in parentheses.

   1. Current ratio (1.1:1)

   2. Receivables turnover (17.1 times) (Assume all sales were credit sales and use net receivables instead of gross receivables.)

   3. Average collection period (21 days)

(c) Given the nature of each company's accounts receivable, what conclusions about each company's liquidity and management of its accounts receivable can be drawn from your calculations in (b)?

Interpreting Financial Statements

BYP8–3   Suncor Energy Inc. reported the following information (in millions) in its financial statements:

	2007	2006	2005
Total current assets	$ 2,818	$ 2,302	$1,916
Total current liabilities	3,097	2,158	1,935
Operating revenues (assume all credit)	15,020	13,798	9,749
Accounts receivable (gross)	1,419	1,054	1,143
Allowance for doubtful accounts	3	4	4
Cost of goods sold	5,935	4,678	4,164
Inventory	608	589	523

Additional detail about Suncor's receivables includes the following:

The company has a securitization program in place to sell to a third party, on a revolving, fully serviced, and limited recourse basis, up to $170 million of accounts receivable having a maturity of 45 days or less. Proceeds received from new securitizations and proceeds from collections reinvested in securitizations on a revolving basis for the year ended December 31, 2007, were $170 million. The company recorded an after-tax loss of approximately $4 million on the securitization program in 2007 (and after-tax losses of $2 million in 2006 and $4 million in 2005).

Instructions

(a) Calculate the current ratio, receivables turnover, and inventory turnover for 2007 and 2006. Comment on Suncor's liquidity.

(b) In 2007, the dollar amount of Suncor's allowance for doubtful accounts was lower than it was in the previous year even though its accounts receivable were higher. Comment on the reasons why this could have occurred.

(c) Suncor regularly securitizes a portion of its accounts receivable. Comment on this practice as part of Suncor's management of its accounts receivable. Why would the company continue with this program if losses were incurred from its operations?

A Global Focus

BYP8–4 Potash Corporation of Saskatchewan Inc. is one of the world's largest potash producers. In its financial statements, all amounts are reported in U.S. dollars (in millions) because the company's stock is also listed on the New York stock exchange. The company reported the following receivables as at December 31:

International Resources

	2007	2006
Trade accounts		
Canpotex	$ 110.2	$ 84.1
Other	439.0	329.3
Non-trade accounts	52.9	33.6
	602.1	447.0
Less allowance for doubtful accounts	(5.9)	(4.7)
Net accounts receivable	596.2	442.3
Total current assets	1,811.3	1,310.2

Note 28 to the 2007 financial statements includes the following:

> The major concentration of credit risk arises from the company's receivables. A majority of its sales are in North America and are primarily for use in the agricultural industry. The company seeks to manage the credit risk relating to these sales through a credit management program. Internationally, the company's products are sold primarily through two export associations (one of which is Canpotex), whose accounts receivable are substantially insured or secured by letters of credit.

Instructions

(a) Is the receivable amount from Canpotex a significant component of the company's total accounts receivable? Of its total current assets?

(b) Evaluate Potash Corporation's credit risk.

(c) Potash Corporation had net accounts receivable in 2005 of U.S. $453.3 million. The company had sales of U.S. $5,234.2 million in 2007 and U.S. $3,766.7 million in 2006. Based on these amounts, did Potash Corporation improve its management of accounts receivable in 2007?

Critical Thinking Cases and Activities

Collaborative Learning Activity

BYP8–5 A small construction equipment rental and sales business has customers of two main types: retail consumers who rent equipment on a short-term basis and pay by cash or credit card, and business customers who may rent higher-valued equipment for longer periods of time. These longer-term contracts are more profitable because they minimize nonrental times for the equipment. The company offers sales on account to qualified business customers.

At a monthly management meeting, there are two agenda items that require a decision:

1. The average collection period of accounts receivable is increasing from about 45 days last year to over 60 days this year.

2. The company has the opportunity to bid on a municipal government equipment supply contract. This contract would increase its overall sales volume by 20%, but the collection period for contract payments could stretch to 120 days.

Instructions

After the class has been divided into groups and you have been assigned one of the two agenda items identified above, do the following:

(a) Discuss the effects on cash flow, the risks for the business, and suggestions to improve the company's financial operations for your assigned item.

(b) Identify any missing information that would be helpful in analyzing the situation.

Communication Activity

BYP8–6 Toys for Big Boys sells snowmobiles, personal watercraft, ATVs, and the like. Recently, the company's credit manager retired. The sales staff threw him a big retirement party—they were glad to see him go, because they felt his credit policies restricted their selling ability. The sales staff then convinced management that there was no need to replace the credit manager, since they could handle this responsibility in addition to their sales positions.

Management was thrilled at year end when sales doubled. However, gross accounts receivable also quadrupled and cash flow halved. The average collection period increased from 30 days to 90 days.

Instructions

In a memo to management, explain the internal control and financial impact of allowing the sales staff to manage the credit function. Has the business assumed any additional credit risk? What would you recommend the company do to better manage its increasing accounts receivable?

Ethics Case

www.wiley.com/canada/kimmel

Ethics in Accounting

BYP8–7 The controller of Proust Corporation has completed an aging schedule, using the following percentages to estimate the uncollectible accounts: 0–30 days, 5%; 31–60 days, 10%; 61–90 days, 30%; and over 90 days, 50%. The president of the company, Suzanne Bros, is nervous because the bank expects the company to sustain its current growth rate of at least 5% over the next two years—the remaining term of its bank loan. President Bros suggests that the controller increase the percentages, which will increase the amount of the required bad debts expense adjustment. The president thinks that the lower net earnings (because of the increased bad debts expense) will make it easier to show a better growth rate next year.

Instructions

(a) Who are the stakeholders in this case?

(b) Does the president's request pose an ethical dilemma for the controller?

(c) Should the controller be concerned with the company's growth rate in estimating the allowance? Explain.

"All About You" Activity

BYP8–8 As the "All About You" feature in this chapter indicates, credit card use in Canada is substantial. In order to finance their education, some students resort to borrowing on credit cards at high interest rates. Suppose you have one year left of university and you decide you may need to use one or more credit cards to fund the cash shortfall you expect to have in your final year.

Instructions

(a) The Financial Consumer Agency of Canada provides tables comparing the costs and benefits of credit cards available in Canada. Go to the agency's website (fcac-acfc.gc.ca/eng/publications/CreditCardsYou/CreditCardComparisonTables_e.asp) and create a personal list, from most important to least important, of the features that are important to you in selecting a credit card.

(b) Examine the features of your present credit card. If you do not have a credit card, select a likely one on-line for this exercise. Given your analysis above, what are the three major disadvantages of your present credit card?

Serial Case

(*Note:* This is a continuation of the serial case from Chapters 1 through 7.)

BYP8–9 Natalie has been approached by one of her friends, Curtis Lesperance. Curtis runs the coffee shop Curtis' Coffee Ltd., where he sells specialty coffees, and prepares and sells muffins and cookies. He is anxious to purchase a deluxe European mixer from Cookie Creations Ltd. in order to prepare larger batches of muffins and cookies. Curtis' Coffee, however, cannot afford to pay for the mixer for at least 30 days. Curtis has asked Natalie if Cookie Creations would be willing to sell his company the mixer on credit.

Natalie comes to you for advice and asks the following questions:

1. Curtis has provided me with the most recent financial statements of Curtis' Coffee. What calculations should I do with the data from these statements and what questions should I ask him after I have analyzed the financial statements? How will this information help me decide if I should extend credit to Curtis' Coffee?

2. Is there an alternative other than extending credit to Curtis' Coffee for 30 days?

3. I am seriously thinking about allowing Cookie Creations' customers to use credit cards. What are some of the advantages and disadvantages of allowing my customers to pay by credit card?

Natalie continues to record the transactions of Cookie Creations on her own as she eventually decided not to hire her friend John to perform the accounting functions. The following transactions occurred during the months of August through October 2009:

Aug. 5 A mixer is sold on credit to Curtis' Coffee for $1,025, n/30. The original cost of the mixer is $566.

6 A credit card account with a bank is established for Cookie Creations. In payment, the bank will deduct from Cookie Creations' bank account a monthly equipment rental fee of $25, in addition to 3% of each credit card sales transaction.

31 Natalie teaches 12 classes in August. Seven classes were paid for in cash, $875; the remaining five classes were paid for by credit card, $750.

31 Curtis calls Natalie. Curtis' Coffee is unable to pay the amount outstanding for another month. Curtis' Coffee converts its account receivable due to Cookie Creations into a note receivable, signing a one-month, 6.25% promissory note.

31 Natalie reconciles Cookie Creations' bank account. The bank account has been correctly charged for the rental of the credit card equipment, $25, and the 3% fee on all credit card transactions processed by the bank.

Sept.14 A mixer is sold to one of Curtis' friends for $1,025. The mixer is paid for by credit card. The cost of the mixer is $566.

30 Natalie teaches 15 classes in September. Eight classes are paid for in cash, $1,000; and seven classes are paid for by credit card, $1,050.

30 Natalie reconciles the bank account of Cookie Creations. The bank account has been correctly charged for the rental of the credit card equipment and the credit card sales.

30 Curtis calls Natalie. Curtis' Coffee is unable to pay its note receivable today but hopes to be able to pay by the end of the week. Natalie prepares the appropriate journal entry.

Oct. 8 Curtis calls again and promises that the outstanding account with Cookie Creations will be paid by the end of October, including interest for two months.

31 A cheque is received from Curtis' Coffee in payment of the balance owed, including interest.

Instructions

(a) Answer Natalie's questions.

(b) Record the transactions. Round your answers to the nearest dollar.

Answers to Chapter Questions

Answer to Shoppers Drug Mart Review It Question 1
Shoppers Drug Mart reports accounts receivable in the current assets section of its balance sheet.

Answers to Self-Study Questions
1. b   2. c   3.d   4. d   5. b
6. d   7. a   8. a   9. c   10. a

CHAPTER 9
Reporting and Analyzing Long-Lived Assets

ACCOUNTING MATTERS!

Rolling Stock

VIA Rail Canada, an independent Crown corporation established in 1978, operates trains in all regions of Canada over a network stretching from the Atlantic to the Pacific, and from the Great Lakes to Hudson Bay. This network includes 492 intercity trains serving more than 450 Canadian communities each week. A fleet of 75 locomotives pull 454 passenger cars carrying more than 4 million passengers a year over 12,500 kilometres of track. These are no small numbers, and neither are the numbers to allocate the cost of these trains.

Corporate Controller Patricia Jasmin says VIA Rail follows generally accepted accounting practices for depreciating its property, plant, and equipment, including the trains. Of the total property, plant, and equipment of $1,382.8 million, VIA Rail's trains, or "rolling stock," amounted to $777.2 million in 2007. Of that amount, $484.7 million has been depreciated to date, leaving a carrying amount of $292.5 million.

VIA Rail calculates the depreciation of its property, plant, and equipment on a "straight-line basis" at rates that allocate the cost of the assets, less their residual value, over their estimated useful economic lives. The corporation maintains detailed subsidiary records for each train's cost and accumulated depreciation. Depreciation is first charged in the month following the date when the trains are put into service, and depreciation is also charged in the month of disposal, Ms. Jasmin explains. The fleet's economic useful life is calculated in consultation with the engineering group and equipment manufacturers. For the current rolling stock, that figure varies from 12 to 30 years.

The trains' purchase price, refurbishment costs, and any other upgrading costs are capitalized if they were incurred to improve the trains' service value or extend their useful lives; otherwise, these costs are expensed.

The capitalization of costs will certainly apply to the significant investment VIA plans to make in refurbishing its fleet of locomotives. In 2007, the federal government announced a funding package for VIA Rail, totalling $691.9 million, to revitalize inter-city passenger rail services in Canada. This package included $516 million of capital funding over five years for infrastructure improvements and equipment refurbishments. The investment will be targeted toward a fleet renewal through the refurbishment of VIA's F-40 locomotives and light, rapid, and comfortable (LRC) passenger cars, as well as infrastructure improvements along the Quebec City–Windsor corridor, and station refurbishments. The equipment refurbishments are expected to help improve the company's environmental performance through increased fuel efficiency and reduced greenhouse gas emissions per passenger.

The rest of the funding—$175.9 million over five years—will go toward VIA Rail's operating costs, to sustain its national network until the capital program is completed.

VIA Rail has entered into a five-year contract valued at more than $100 million with CAD Railway Industries Ltd. (CAD) to rebuild all 54 of its F-40 locomotives. CAD will strip the 20-year-old locomotives down to their shells and rebuild them using the latest technology. The trains' new systems will meet today's environmental and safety standards, and VIA expects to see a reduction in greenhouse gas emissions of up to 12 percent once the work is done. The refurbishment will extend the service life of the locomotives by 15 to 20 years, and at less than half the cost of a new locomotive. The first rebuilt locomotive was to be ready by March 2009, and the project should be complete by 2012.

THE NAVIGATOR

- [ ] Read *Feature Story*
- [ ] Scan *Study Objectives*
- [ ] Read *Chapter Preview*
- [ ] Read text and answer *Before You Go On*
- [ ] Read *All About You*
- [ ] Review *Summary of Study Objectives*
- [ ] Review *Using the Decision Toolkit—A Summary*
- [ ] Work *Using the Decision Toolkit*
- [ ] Work *Demonstration Problem*
- [ ] Answer *Self-Study Questions*
- [ ] Complete assignments

6437

Canada

Rail: viarail.ca

STUDY OBJECTIVES

After studying this chapter, you should be able to:

Determine the cost of property, plant, and equipment.

Explain and calculate depreciation.

Describe other accounting issues related to depreciation.

Account for the disposal of property, plant, and equipment.

Identify the basic accounting issues for intangible assets and goodwill.

Illustrate how long-lived assets are reported in the financial statements.

Describe the methods for evaluating the use of assets.

Navigator

PREVIEW OF CHAPTER 9

For railways and many other companies, making the right decisions about long-lived assets is critical because these assets represent huge investments. Among others, these decisions include what assets to acquire and when, how to finance the acquisitions, how to account for the assets, and when to dispose of them.

In this chapter, we address these and other issues surrounding long-lived assets. Our discussion focuses on two types of long-lived assets: (1) property, plant, and equipment, and (2) intangible assets. Long-lived assets can also include natural resources, which we will leave for another accounting course.

The chapter is organized as follows:

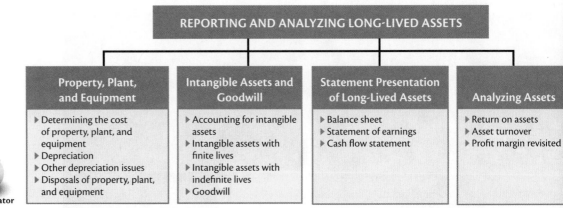

REPORTING AND ANALYZING LONG-LIVED ASSETS

Property, Plant, and Equipment	Intangible Assets and Goodwill	Statement Presentation of Long-Lived Assets	Analyzing Assets
▸ Determining the cost of property, plant, and equipment ▸ Depreciation ▸ Other depreciation issues ▸ Disposals of property, plant, and equipment	▸ Accounting for intangible assets ▸ Intangible assets with finite lives ▸ Intangible assets with indefinite lives ▸ Goodwill	▸ Balance sheet ▸ Statement of earnings ▸ Cash flow statement	▸ Return on assets ▸ Asset turnover ▸ Profit margin revisited

The Navigator

Property, Plant, and Equipment

Property, plant, and equipment are long-lived resources that the company owns that have physical substance (a definite size and shape), are used in the operations of a business, and are not intended for sale to customers. Unlike current assets, which are used or consumed in the current accounting period, property, plant, and equipment provide benefits over many years. Their benefits arise from their use for the production and sale of goods or services to customers, for rental to others, or for administrative purposes.

Property, plant, and equipment are critical to a company's success because they determine the company's production capacity and ability to satisfy customers. For example, with too few trains, VIA Rail would lose customers to its competitors. With too many trains, there would be a lot of empty seats. Management must constantly monitor its needs and adjust its assets accordingly. Not doing this can result in lost business opportunities or inefficient use of existing assets, and is a common reason for poor financial results.

Many companies have large investments in property, plant, and equipment. Illustration 9-1 shows the percentages of property, plant, and equipment (PPE) in relation to total assets in several companies.

Illustration 9-1 ➡

Property, plant, and equipment (PPE) as a percentage of total assets

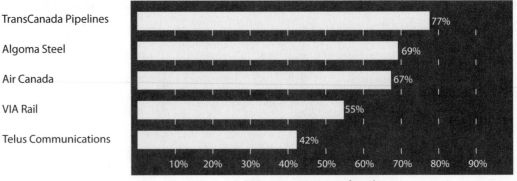

PPE as a percentage of total assets

Determining the Cost of Property, Plant, and Equipment

The **cost principle** requires that property, plant, and equipment be recognized (recorded) at cost, which includes the following:

> **study objective 1**
>
> Determine the cost of property, plant, and equipment.

1. The purchase price, less any discounts or rebates
2. The expenditures necessary to bring the asset to its required location and to make it ready for its intended use

These costs are **capitalized** (recorded as property, plant, and equipment), rather than expensed, if it is probable that the company will receive an economic benefit in the future from the asset. Determining which costs to include in a property, plant, and equipment or other long-lived asset account and which costs not to include is very important. In general, costs which benefit only the current period are expensed. Such costs are called operating expenditures. Costs that benefit future periods are included in a long-lived asset account. These are called capital expenditures.

For example, the cost to purchase an asset should be recorded as a capital expenditure, because the asset will benefit future periods. In addition, the insurance paid on the same asset as it is shipped to the company should also be capitalized because the insurance during transit benefits more than the current period; it will benefit the asset over its useful life. It is considered to be a necessary expenditure to get the asset to its required location and ready for use. Insurance paid to insure the asset against fire or theft after the asset is situated and in use would be expensed because these costs benefit only the current period and should be matched against the current period revenue.

Subsequent to acquisition, the same distinction exists between operating and capital expenditures. Operating expenditures normally benefit only the current period. They are required to maintain an asset in its normal operating condition and often recur, although not always annually. As the feature story explained, VIA Rail expenses all costs that are incurred for the ordinary servicing of its trains. Other examples include repainting a building or replacing the tires on a truck. These costs would be debited to an expense account, such as Maintenance Expense.

Capital expenditures after acquisition include costs that increase the life of an asset or its productivity or efficiency. These costs are normally larger than operating expenditures and occur less frequently. VIA Rail capitalizes all refurbishment and upgrading costs if they are incurred to improve the trains' service value or extend their useful lives. Other examples include the cost to replace the roof on a building or to overhaul an engine in a truck. These costs would be debited to an asset account, such as Buildings or Trucks.

Property, plant, and equipment are often subdivided into four classes:

1. **Land**, such as a building site
2. **Land improvements**, such as driveways, parking lots, fences, and underground sprinkler systems
3. **Buildings**, such as stores, offices, factories, and warehouses
4. **Equipment**, such as store checkout counters, cash registers, computers, office furniture, factory machinery, and delivery equipment

How to determine the cost of each of the major classes of property, plant, and equipment is explained in the following sections.

Land

All costs related to the purchase of land, including such costs as survey and legal fees for closing the deal, are added to the Land account. If additional work is required to prepare the land for its intended use, such as clearing, grading, and filling, these costs are also recorded as capital expenditures in the Land account. If the land has a building on it that must be removed to make the site suitable for construction of a new building, all demolition and removal costs, less any proceeds from salvaged materials, are added to the Land account. When land has been purchased to construct a building, all costs that are incurred up to the time of excavation for the new building are considered to be part of the costs that are necessary to prepare the land for its intended use.

To illustrate, assume that Brochu Corporation purchases real estate for $100,000 and that the property contains an old warehouse that is torn down at a net cost of $6,000 ($7,500 in costs less $1,500 in proceeds from salvaged materials). Additional expenditures of $1,000 are also incurred for legal fees. Put together, these factors make the cost of the land $107,000, calculated as follows:

Cash price of property	$100,000
Net cost of removing warehouse	6,000
Legal fees	1,000
Cost of land	$107,000

When the acquisition is recorded, Land is debited for $107,000 and Cash is credited for $107,000 (assuming the expenditures were paid in cash). Once the land is ready for its intended use, recurring costs, such as annual property taxes, are recorded as operating expenditures—in other words, these costs are matched against the revenues that the land helps generate.

You will recall from Chapter 4 that, because land has an unlimited useful life, the cost of land is not depreciated (allocated over its useful life).

Land Improvements

Land improvements are structural additions made to land, such as driveways, sidewalks, fences, and parking lots. Land improvements, unlike land, decline in service potential over time and require maintenance and replacement. Because of this, land improvements are recorded separately from land and are depreciated over their useful lives.

Many students confuse the cost to get land ready for its intended use with land improvements. They think, for example, that removing an old building or grading are "improving" the land, and thus incorrectly reason that these costs should be called land improvements. When classifying costs, it is important to remember that one-time costs that are required for getting the land ready to use are always charged to the Land account, not the Land Improvements account.

Buildings

The cost of a building includes all costs that are directly related to its purchase or construction. When a building is purchased, its cost includes the purchase price, the closing costs, and all costs to make the building ready for its intended use. This can include expenditures for remodelling rooms and offices, and for replacing or repairing the roof, floors, electrical wiring, and plumbing. All of these costs are capitalized (i.e., charged) to the Building account.

When a new building is constructed, its cost consists of the contract price plus payments made for architect fees, building permits, and excavation costs. In addition, interest costs that are incurred specifically to finance a construction project (i.e., interest that could not be avoided) are also included in the cost of the asset. In these circumstances, interest costs are considered as necessary as materials and labour. There are specific rules for determining the amount of interest costs to capitalize; these are not discussed here as they are normally taught in an intermediate accounting course.

Equipment

The "equipment" classification is a broad one that can include delivery equipment, office equipment, machinery, vehicles, furniture and fixtures, and other similar assets. As with land and buildings, the cost of equipment includes the purchase price and all costs that are necessary to get the equipment ready for its intended use. Thus, freight charges, insurance during transit that is paid by the purchaser, and expenditures that are required in assembling, installing, and testing the equipment are all charged to the Equipment account.

Because they are recurring expenditures that do not benefit future periods, annual costs such as licences and insurance are treated as operating expenditures when they are incurred. To illustrate, assume that Perfect Pizza Ltd. purchases a delivery van for $32,500. Related expenditures are $500 for painting and lettering, $80 for a motor vehicle licence, and a one-year accident insurance policy of $1,600. The cost of the delivery van is $33,000, calculated as follows:

Cash price	$32,500
Painting and lettering	500
Cost of delivery van	$33,000

The cost of a motor vehicle licence is treated as a current expense because it is an annual cost. For the same reasons, the cost of the insurance policy is considered a prepaid expense (a current asset). It will be allocated to Insurance Expense throughout the period. The cost of the van and the cost incurred for painting and lettering are capital expenditures because these costs benefit future periods.

The entry to record the purchase of the van and related expenditures, assuming all were paid in cash, is as follows:

Delivery Van ($32,500 + $500)	33,000	
Licence Expense	80	
Prepaid Insurance	1,600	
Cash ($33,000 + $80 + $1,600)		34,680
(To record purchase of delivery van and related expenditures)		

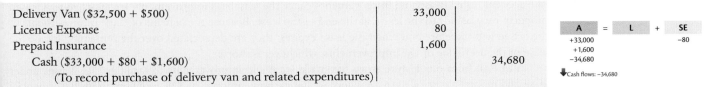

A	=	L	+	SE
+33,000				−80
+1,600				
−34,680				

↓Cash flows: −34,680

Asset Retirement Costs

The cost of property, plant, and equipment must also include an estimate of the cost of any obligation to dismantle, remove, or restore the long-lived asset when it is retired. For example, Petro-Canada has a natural gas processing plant on which it expects to incur environmental costs to clean up and restore the property at the end of its useful life.

Costs such as these must be estimated (using present-value concepts) and added to the asset account. The other side of the entry records a liability for the asset retirement obligation. These costs, and the liability, are recorded in the period when the legal obligation is created, which can be at the time the asset is acquired, or later when the asset is used.

While we will leave a more detailed discussion of asset retirement costs and their associated liabilities to a future accounting course, students should be aware that the cost of many property, plant, and equipment items includes the cost of retiring the asset. We will assume that asset retirement costs equal zero in the examples in this chapter.

To Buy or Lease?

In this chapter, we focus on assets that are purchased, but we would like to give you a brief look at an alternative to purchasing—leasing. In a lease, a party that owns an asset agrees to allow another party to use the asset for an agreed period of time at an agreed price. The party that is allowing its asset to be leased is known as the lessor, and the party that is paying to use the asset is known as the lessee.

Here are some advantages of leasing an asset versus purchasing it:

1. **Reduced risk of the negative impact of obsolescence.** Obsolescence is the process by which an asset becomes out of date before it physically wears out. Frequently, lease terms allow the party using the asset (the lessee) to exchange the asset for a more modern or technologically capable asset if it becomes outdated. This is much easier than trying to sell an obsolete asset.

2. **100-percent financing.** If a company borrows to purchase an asset, it is usually required to make a down payment of at least 20 percent. Leasing an asset does not require any money down, which helps to conserve cash. In addition, interest payments are often fixed for the term of the lease, unlike other financing which often has a floating interest rate.

3. **Income tax advantages.** When a company owns a depreciable asset, it can only deduct the depreciation expense (called capital cost allowance for income tax purposes) on its income tax return. (We will learn more about capital cost allowance in a later section of this chapter.) If the company has borrowed to purchase an asset, it can also deduct the interest expense. When a company leases an asset, it can deduct 100 percent of the lease payment on its income tax return.

4. **Off–balance sheet financing.** Many companies prefer to keep assets and, especially, liabilities off their books. A certain type of lease called an operating lease allows the lessee to account for the transaction as a rental and therefore not record an asset or liability on the company's books. This is known as off–balance sheet financing, which is discussed in Chapter 10.

Under another type of lease, a finance lease, both the asset and the liability are shown on the balance sheet. On the lessee's balance sheet, the leased item is shown as an asset and the obligation owed

Alternative Terminology
A *finance lease* is also known as a *capital lease*.

to the lessor is shown as a liability. In addition, the leased asset is depreciated by the lessee just as other long-lived assets are. In addition we should note that standard setters have commenced a project on lease accounting, which is likely to result in significant changes in the future. Distinguishing between, and accounting for, operating and finance leases can be complex. Further details on this subject can be found in an intermediate accounting course.

Companies often incur costs when they renovate leased property. These costs are charged to a separate account called Leasehold Improvements. Since the leasehold improvements are attached to a leased property, they belong to the lessor at the end of the lease. Because the benefits of these improvements to the lessee will therefore end when the lease expires, they are depreciated over the remaining life of the lease or the useful life of the improvements, whichever is shorter.

VIA Rail from our feature story has made leasehold improvements to facilities that it uses under lease and reports a cost of $116.4 million, with a carrying amount of $23.4 million, in its 2007 financial statements. In addition, VIA Rail has a number of operating leases for real estate, maintenance of railroad rights-of-way, and computer equipment. The notes to the financial statements show that the company has commitments to pay a total of $238.8 million for these operating leases over the remaining life of the leases, some of which last until 2049. VIA Rail did not report any finance leases in its statements for 2007.

ACCOUNTING MATTERS! | Management Perspective

In 1997, Canadian businesses and consumers had $50 billion of assets financed with leases. One decade later, by 2007, the value of assets financed with leases had more than doubled to $107 billion. Of this $107 billion, 40 percent was used to finance equipment purchases, 7 percent was used to finance business vehicle purchases, and 53 percent was used to finance consumer vehicle purchases. In 2008, the percentage of vehicles financed using leases dropped sharply as automobile companies stopped subsidizing lease rates in response to credit market pressures and declining values for vehicles.

Source: Canadian Finance & Leasing Association, *Annual Report, 2006–2007*, p. 6.

BEFORE YOU GO ON...

▸ **Review It**

1. What are long-lived assets? What are the major classes of property, plant, and equipment?
2. What types of costs are included in each major class of property, plant, and equipment?
3. Explain the difference between operating expenditures and capital expenditures.
4. What are the main advantages of leasing?

▸ **Do It**

Assume that $50,000 of factory machinery is purchased on February 4. A $20,000 down payment is made and a note payable is issued for the balance. Cash expenditures that relate to this purchase include insurance during shipping, $100; an annual insurance policy, $750; and installation and testing costs, $500. (a) What is the cost of the machinery? (b) Record these expenditures.

Action Plan

- Capitalize expenditures that are made to get the machinery ready for its intended use.
- Expense operating costs that benefit only the current period, or which are recurring expenditures.

Solution

(a) The cost of the machinery is $50,600 ($50,000 + $100 + $500).

(b)

Feb. 4	Factory Machinery	50,600	
	Prepaid Insurance	750	
	Cash ($20,000 + $100 + $750 + $500)		21,350
	Note Payable ($50,000 – $20,000)		30,000
	(To record purchase of factory machinery and related expenditures)		

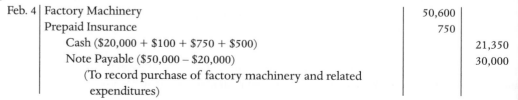

The Navigator

Depreciation

Under international financial reporting standards, companies will have two models they can choose between to account for their property, plant, and equipment: the cost model and the revaluation model. The cost model is much more commonly used, and is the method Canadian companies used before IFRS. We will cover the cost model in the following sections of the chapter and refer briefly to the revaluation method in a later section.

The cost model records property, plant, and equipment at cost at acquisition. Subsequent to acquisition, depreciation is recorded each period and the assets are carried at cost less the accumulated depreciation.

As we learned in Chapter 4, **depreciation is the systematic allocation of the cost of property, plant, and equipment (and certain other long-lived assets) over the asset's useful life.** The cost is allocated to expense over the asset's useful life so that expenses are properly matched with the expected use of the asset's future economic benefits.

You will recall that depreciation is recorded in an adjusting journal entry which debits Depreciation Expense and credits Accumulated Depreciation. Depreciation Expense is a statement of earnings account; Accumulated Depreciation appears on the balance sheet as a contra asset account to the relevant property, plant, or equipment account. This contra asset account is similar in purpose to the one used in Chapter 8 for the allowance for doubtful accounts. Both contra accounts reduce assets to their carrying amounts. The carrying amount of a depreciable asset was defined in Chapter 4 as its cost less accumulated depreciation.

Tutorials
(Depreciation)

It is important to understand that **depreciation is the process of cost allocation, not a process of determining an asset's fair value.** Under the cost model, an increase in the asset's current fair value is not considered relevant, because property, plant, and equipment are not held for resale. (Fair values are only relevant if an impairment loss has occurred, which we will discuss later in this chapter.) As a result, the carrying amount of property, plant, and equipment may be very different from its fair value. In fact, if an asset is fully depreciated, it can have a carrying amount of zero but still have a large fair value.

Alternative Terminology
An asset's *carrying amount* is also called its *carrying value, book value,* or *net book value.*

It is also important to understand that **depreciation does not provide cash to replace the asset.** The balance in Accumulated Depreciation only represents the total amount of the asset's cost that has been allocated to expense to date: it is not a cash fund. Cash is neither increased nor decreased by the adjusting entry to record depreciation.

During a depreciable asset's useful life, its revenue-producing ability declines because of physical factors, such as wear and tear, and economic factors, such as obsolescence. For example, a company may replace a truck because it has physically worn out. Or a company may choose to replace its computers long before they physically wear out, because improvements in hardware and software have made the old computers obsolete.

You will recall from Chapter 4 that we can expect to see companies using a variety of terms as we make the transition to international financial reporting standards. Getting used to different terminology is not new for Canadians. For example, the term "depreciation" was used for property, plant, and equipment and the term "amortization" was used for intangible assets until 2001. Then, accounting standards changed and the term "amortization" was recommended for all long-lived assets, although both terms were still acceptable. Consequently, many companies continued to use "depreciation" for the allocation of the cost of property, plant, and equipment. Now, however, with Canadian standards being changed to be consistent with international financial accounting standards, the term "depreciation" should be used for property, plant, and equipment and, as we will learn in a later section of this chapter, "amortization" is used for intangible assets. In addition, "carrying amount" will replace "book value." It will not be unusual in the next few years to find a considerable mix of the terms "depreciation" and "amortization," and "carrying amount" and "book value."

International Resources

Factors in Calculating Depreciation

In Chapter 4, we learned that depreciation expense is calculated by dividing the cost of the depreciable asset by its useful life. At that time, however, we were assuming that the residual value of the asset was zero. In this chapter, we will now include an actual residual value when calculating depreciation. Thus, there are now three factors that affect the calculation of depreciation:

1. **Cost.** Factors that affect the cost of a depreciable asset were explained earlier in this chapter. Remember that the cost of property, plant, and equipment includes the purchase price plus all costs necessary to get the asset ready for use. Cost also includes retirement costs, if there are any.

2. **Useful life.** Useful life is (a) the period of time over which an asset is expected to be available for use or (b) the number of units of production (such as machine hours) or units of output that

are expected to be obtained from an asset. Useful life is an estimate based on such factors as the intended use of the asset, repair and maintenance policies, and how vulnerable the asset is to wearing out or becoming obsolete. The company's past experience with similar assets is often helpful in estimating a particular asset's useful life.

3. **Residual value.** Residual value is an estimate of the amount that a company would obtain from the disposal of the asset if the asset were already as old as it will be and in the condition it is expected to be in at the end of its useful life. Residual value is not depreciated, since the amount is expected to be recovered at the end of the asset's useful life.

Alternative Terminology
Residual value is sometimes called *salvage value*.

These three factors are summarized in Illustration 9-2.

Illustration 9-2 ➡

Three factors in calculating depreciation

Cost: the purchase price plus all necessary costs to make the asset ready for its intended use

Useful life: an estimate of the period over which an asset is expected to be available for use

Residual value: an estimate of the amount that will be received upon disposal of the asset

Alternative Terminology
Depreciable amount is sometimes called *amortizable cost*.

The difference between a depreciable asset's cost and its residual value is called the depreciable amount, which is the total amount to be depreciated.

Depreciation Methods

Depreciation is generally calculated using one of these three methods:

1. Straight-line
2. Diminishing-balance
3. Units-of-production

While all three methods are used, *Financial Reporting in Canada* reported that 87 percent of Canadian publicly traded companies used the straight-line method of depreciation, 3 percent used diminishing-balance, and 10 percent used units-of-production in a recent year. We saw in our feature story that VIA Rail uses straight-line depreciation.

How do companies choose which method to use? Management must choose the depreciation method that it believes will best reflect the pattern in which the asset's future economic benefits are expected to be consumed. The depreciation method must be reviewed at least once a year. If the expected pattern of consumption of the future economic benefits has changed, the depreciation method must be changed. However, as changing methods makes it more difficult to compare the company's results of from one year to another, the change must be justifiable. We will discuss how to account for a changes in depreciation methods later in the chapter.

In the sections that now follow, the application of each of these depreciation methods is illustrated using the following data for a delivery van purchased by Perfect Pizzas Ltd. on January 1, 2009:

Cost	$33,000
Estimated residual value	$3,000
Estimated useful life (in years)	5
Estimated useful life (in kilometres)	100,000

Straight-Line. The straight-line method of depreciation was originally defined in Chapter 4. We will re-define it again here, this time including the impact of the residual amount on this method. The straight-line method of calculating depreciation has two steps. First, the depreciable amount is determined by deducting the residual value from the cost of the asset. Second, the depreciable amount is divided by the asset's useful life to calculate the annual depreciation expense.

The depreciation expense will be the same for each year of the asset's useful life if the cost, the useful life, and the residual value do not change. The calculation of depreciation expense in the first year for Perfect Pizzas' delivery van is shown in Illustration 9-3.

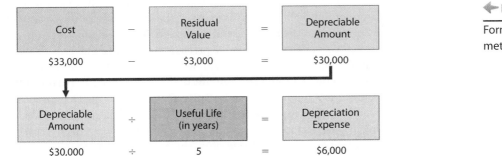

◄ Illustration 9-3

Formula for straight-line method

Alternatively, we can calculate a percentage rate to use when determining the delivery van's straight-line annual depreciation expense. First, the depreciation rate is calculated by dividing 100% by the useful life in years. In Perfect Pizza's case, the depreciation rate is 20% (100% ÷ 5 years). Second, the depreciation expense is calculated by multiplying the asset's depreciable amount by the depreciation rate, as shown in the depreciation schedule in Illustration 9-4.

| | | | | | End of Year | |
Year	Depreciable Amount	×	Depreciation Rate	=	Depreciation Expense	Accumulated Depreciation	Carrying Amount
							$33,000
2009	$30,000		20%		$ 6,000	$6,000	27,000
2010	30,000		20%		6,000	12,000	21,000
2011	30,000		20%		6,000	18,000	15,000
2012	30,000		20%		6,000	24,000	9,000
2013	30,000		20%		6,000	30,000	3,000
					$30,000		

PERFECT PIZZAS LTD.
Straight-Line Depreciation Schedule

◄ Illustration 9-4

Straight-line depreciation schedule

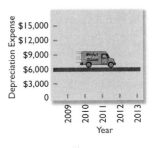

Note that the depreciation expense of $6,000 is the same each year, and that the carrying amount at the end of the useful life is equal to the estimated $3,000 residual value.

What happens when an asset is purchased during the year, rather than on January 1 as in our example? In such cases, it is necessary **to prorate the annual depreciation for the part of the year when the asset is available for use.** If Perfect Pizzas' delivery van was ready to be used on April 1, 2009, the van would be used for nine months in 2009 (April through December). The depreciation for 2009 would be $4,500 ($30,000 × 20% × 9/12). Note that depreciation is normally rounded to the nearest month. Since depreciation is only an estimate, calculating it to the nearest day gives a false sense of accuracy.

To keep things simple, some companies use a convention for partial-period depreciation rather than calculating depreciation monthly. Companies may choose to allocate a full year's depreciation in the year of acquisition and none in the year of disposal. Other companies record a half year's depreciation in the year of acquisition, and a half year's depreciation in the year of disposal. VIA Rail follows the practice of not recording any depreciation in the month the asset is acquired and recording a full month's depreciation in the month in which the asset is disposed. Whatever company policy is used for partial-year depreciation, the impact is not significant in the long run if the policy is used consistently.

Recall that the depreciation method that is used must be consistent with the pattern in which the economic benefits from owning the asset are expected to be consumed. It is therefore appropriate to use the straight-line method when the asset is used quite uniformly throughout its useful life. Examples of assets that deliver their benefit primarily as a function of time (and therefore uniformly) include office furniture and fixtures, buildings, warehouses, and garages for motor vehicles.

Diminishing-Balance. The diminishing-balance method produces a decreasing annual depreciation expense over the useful life of the asset. It is called the "diminishing-balance" method because the periodic

Alternative Terminology
The *diminishing-balance* method is also sometimes called the *declining-balance* method.

‣ Reporting and Analyzing Long-Lived Assets

depreciation is calculated using the asset's carrying amount, which diminishes each year because accumulated depreciation increases. Annual depreciation expense is calculated by multiplying the carrying amount at the beginning of the year by the depreciation rate. The depreciation rate remains constant from year to year, but the carrying amount that the rate is applied to declines each year.

The carrying amount for the first year is the cost of the asset, because the balance in Accumulated Depreciation at the beginning of the asset's useful life is zero. In subsequent years, the carrying amount is the difference between cost and accumulated depreciation at the beginning of the year. Unlike other depreciation methods, the diminishing-balance method does not use the depreciable amount. **Thus, residual value is not used in determining the amount that the diminishing-balance rate is applied to.** Residual value does, however, limit the total depreciation that can be taken. Depreciation stops when the asset's carrying amount equals its expected residual value.

The diminishing-balance method can be applied using different rates, which result in varying speeds of depreciation. You will find rates such as one time (single), two times (double), and even three times (triple) the straight-line rate of depreciation. A depreciation rate that is often used is double the straight-line rate. This method is referred to as the **double diminishing-balance method**.

If Perfect Pizzas uses double the straight-line rate, the depreciation rate is 40% (2 multiplied by the straight-line rate of 20%). Illustration 9-5 presents the formula and calculation of the first year's depreciation on the delivery van.

Helpful Hint The straight-line rate is determined by dividing 100% by the estimated useful life. In Perfect Pizza's case, it is 100% ÷ 5 = 20%.

Illustration 9-5 ➡

Formula for diminishing-balance method

Carrying Amount at Beginning of Year	×	Depreciation Rate (Straight-Line Rate × Multiplier)	=	Depreciation Expense
$33,000	×	20% × 2	=	$13,200

The depreciation schedule under this method is given in Illustration 9-6.

Illustration 9-6 ➡

Diminishing-balance depreciation schedule

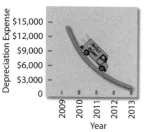

PERFECT PIZZAS LTD.
Diminishing-Balance Depreciation Schedule

| | | | | | End of Year | |
Year	Carrying Amount Beginning of Year	× Depreciation Rate	= Depreciation Expense		Accumulated Depreciation	Carrying Amount
						$33,000
2009	$33,000	40%	$13,200		$13,200	19,800
2010	19,800	40%	7,920		21,120	11,880
2011	11,880	40%	4,752		25,872	7,128
2012	7,128	40%	2,851		28,723	4,277
2013	4,277	40%	1,277[a]		30,000	3,000
			$30,000			

[a] The calculation of $1,711 ($4,277 × 40%) is adjusted to $1,277 so that the carrying amount will equal the residual value.

When an asset is purchased during the year, it is necessary to prorate the diminishing-balance depreciation in the first year, based on time. For example, if Perfect Pizzas had purchased the delivery equipment on April 1, 2009, depreciation for 2009 would be $9,900 ($33,000 × 40% × ⁹⁄₁₂) if depreciation is calculated monthly. The carrying amount for calculating depreciation in 2010 then becomes $23,100 ($33,000 − $9,900), and the 2010 depreciation is $9,240 ($23,100 × 40%). Future calculations would follow from these amounts until the carrying amount equalled the residual value.

Returning to Illustration 9-6, which assumes that the asset was purchased at the beginning of the year, you can see that the delivery equipment is 64-percent depreciated ($21,120 ÷ $33,000) at the end of the second year. Under the straight-line method, it would be depreciated 36 percent ($12,000 ÷ $33,000) at that time.

Regardless of the method that is used, the total amount of depreciation over the life of the delivery van is $30,000—the depreciable amount. In the early years, however, the diminishing-balance depreciation expense will be higher than the straight-line depreciation expense, and in later years it will be less than the straight-line expense. Methods such as the diminishing-balance method that produce higher depreciation expense in the early years than in the later years are known as *accelerated* depreciation methods.

Managers must choose the diminishing-balance, or another accelerated method, if the company receives more economic benefit in the early years of the asset's useful life than in the later years. That s, this method is used if the asset has higher revenue-producing ability in its early years, or if the asset is expected to become less useful over time.

Units-of-Production. As indicated earlier, useful life can be expressed in ways other than a time period. In the **units-of-production method**, useful life is either the estimated total units of production or total use expected from the asset, not the number of years that the asset is expected to be used. The units-of-production method works well for factory machinery where production can be measured in terms of units produced or machine hours used in operating the machinery. It is also possible to use the method for such items as motor vehicles (kilometres driven) and airplanes (hours in use). The units-of-production method is generally not suitable for such assets as buildings or furniture, because activity levels are difficult to measure for these types of assets.

To use this method, the units of production in total for the entire useful life are estimated. This amount is divided into the depreciable amount (cost less residual value) to determine the depreciable amount per unit. The depreciable amount per unit is then multiplied by the units of production during the year and the result is the depreciation expense.

To illustrate, assume that Perfect Pizzas' delivery van is driven 15,000 kilometres in the first year of a total estimated useful life of 100,000 kilometres. Using this distance, Illustration 9-7 presents the formula and calculation of depreciation expense in the first year.

◀ Illustration 9-7

Formula for units-of-production method

Cost	−	Residual Value	=	Depreciable Amount
$33,000	−	$3,000	=	$30,000

Depreciable Amount	÷	Estimated Total Units of Activity	=	Depreciable Amount per Unit
$30,000	÷	100,000 kilometres	=	$0.30

Depreciable Amount per Unit	×	Units of Activity During the Year	=	Depreciation Expense
$0.30	×	15,000 kilometres	=	$4,500

Illustration 9-8 shows the units-of-production depreciation schedule, using assumed distance data for the later years.

◀ Illustration 9-8

Units-of-production depreciation schedule

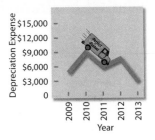

PERFECT PIZZAS LTD.
Units-of-Production Depreciation Schedule

Year	Units of Production	Depreciable Amount/Unit	Depreciation Expense	End of Year Accumulated Depreciation	End of Year Carrying Amount
					$33,000
2009	15,000	$0.30	$ 4,500	$ 4,500	28,500
2010	30,000	0.30	9,000	13,500	19,500
2011	20,000	0.30	6,000	19,500	13,500
2012	25,000	0.30	7,500	27,000	6,000
2013	10,000	0.30	3,000	30,000	3,000
	100,000		$30,000		

This method is easy to apply when assets are purchased during the year. In such cases, the productivity of the asset for the partial year is used in calculating the depreciation. The units-of-production method, therefore, does not require adjustments for partial periods as the calculation already reflects how much the asset was used during the specific period.

Even though it is often difficult to make a reasonable estimate of total activity, about 10 percent of Canadian companies use this method for assets whose productivity varies significantly from one period to another. In this situation, the units-of-production method results in depreciation amounts that match the benefits consumed as the asset is used.

Alternative Terminology
The *units-of-production* method is also sometimes called the *units-of-activity* method.

Comparison of Methods. The following schedule presents a comparison of annual and total depreciation expense for Perfect Pizzas under the three depreciation methods. In addition, if we assume that net earnings, before deducting depreciation expense, were $45,000 for each of the five years, we can clearly see the impact of each method on net earnings.

Year	Straight-Line Depreciation Expense	Straight-Line Net Earnings	Diminishing-Balance Depreciation Expense	Diminishing-Balance Net Earnings	Units-of-Production Depreciation Expense	Units-of-Production Net Earnings
2009	$ 6,000	$ 39,000	$13,200	$ 31,800	$ 4,500	$ 40,500
2010	6,000	39,000	7,920	37,080	9,000	36,000
2011	6,000	39,000	4,752	40,248	6,000	39,000
2012	6,000	39,000	2,851	42,149	7,500	37,500
2013	6,000	39,000	1,277	43,723	3,000	42,000
	$30,000	$195,000	$30,000	$195,000	$30,000	$195,000

As discussed earlier, straight-line depreciation results in the same amount of expense, and therefore earnings, each year on the statement of earnings. Diminishing-balance results in higher expenses, and therefore lower earnings, in the early years. It also results in lower expenses and higher earnings in later years. Results for the units-of-production method vary, depending on the actual usage each year. While periodic depreciation and net earnings vary each year under the different methods, total depreciation and total net earnings are the same for the five-year period. All three methods have the same income tax expense so there are no additional differences because of taxes. In the next section, we will learn about the depreciation method used for income tax purposes.

The balance sheet is also affected because accumulated depreciation is increased by depreciation expense and shareholders' equity is increased by net earnings. Of course, the choice of depreciation method has no impact on cash flow, or the cash flow statement.

As explained earlier, management should choose the method that best matches the estimated pattern in which the benefits of the asset are expected to be consumed. If the economic benefit of owning an asset is fairly consistent over time, the straight-line method is appropriate. The diminishing-balance method is appropriate if the company receives more economic benefit in the early years of the asset's useful life than in the later years. The units-of-production method is appropriate for assets whose usage varies over time. Because companies have more than one type of asset, they often use more than one depreciation method. About 50 percent of the companies that report using more than one depreciation method use both the straight-line and units-of-production methods. Forty percent use the straight-line and diminishing-balance methods, and 10 percent use a combination of other methods.

DECISION TOOLKIT

Decision Checkpoints	Info Needed for Decision	Tools to Use for Decision	How to Evaluate Results
What is the impact of the choice of depreciation method?	Depreciation policy	Statement of earnings, balance sheet, and accounting policy note to the statements	In the early years, straight-line depreciation results in a lower amount of depreciation expense and higher net earnings than the diminishing-balance method on the statement of earnings. It also results in higher total assets and higher shareholders' equity on the balance sheet. The opposite is true of the later years. There is no impact on cash flow and both methods give the same total results over their useful lives.

BEFORE YOU GO ON...

Review It

1. What relationship, if any, is there between depreciation and (a) cost allocation, (b) asset valuation, and (c) cash accumulation?
2. Explain the factors that affect the calculation of depreciation.
3. What range does Shoppers Drug Mart use as its estimated useful life for buildings? For its equipment and fixtures? For its computer software and equipment? For its leasehold improvements? The answers to these questions are at the end of the chapter.
4. What are the differences in depreciation and net earnings each year, and in total, over the useful life of an asset under each of the three depreciation methods?

Do It

On October 1, 2009, Iron Mountain Ski Corporation purchases a new snow grooming machine for $52,000. The machine is estimated to have a five-year useful life and a $4,000 residual value. It is also estimated to have a total useful life of 6,000 hours. It is used 1,000 hours in the year ended December 31, 2009, and 1,300 hours in the year ended December 31, 2010. How much depreciation expense should Iron Mountain Ski record in each of 2009 and 2010 under each depreciation method: (a) straight-line, (b) diminishing-balance using twice the straight-line rate, and (c) units-of-production?

Action Plan

- Under straight-line depreciation, annual depreciation expense is equal to the depreciable amount (cost less residual value) divided by the estimated useful life.
- Under diminishing-balance depreciation, annual depreciation expense is equal to twice the straight-line rate of depreciation times the carrying amount of the asset at the beginning of the year. Residual values are ignored in this method.
- Under the straight-line and diminishing-balance methods, the annual depreciation expense must be pro-rated if the asset is purchased during the year.
- Under units-of-production depreciation, the depreciable amount per unit is equal to the total depreciable amount divided by the total estimated units of production. The annual depreciation expense is equal to the depreciable amount per unit times the actual usage in each year.

Solution

	2009	2010
Straight-line	$2,400	$ 9,600
Diminishing-balance	5,200	18,720
Units-of-production	8,000	10,400

(a) Straight-line: ($52,000 − $4,000) ÷ 5 years = $9,600 per year; for the partial period in 2009:
$9,600 × ³⁄₁₂ = $2,400

(b) Diminishing-balance: 100% ÷ 5 years = 20% straight-line rate
      20% × 2 = 40% depreciation rate
    2009: $52,000 × 40% × ³⁄₁₂ = $5,200
    2010:   ($52,000 − $5,200) × 40% = $18,720

(c) Units-of-production: ($52,000 − $4,000) ÷ 6,000 hours = $8 per hour
    2009:   1,000 × $8 = $8,000
    2010:   1,300 × $8 = $10,400

The Navigator

Other Depreciation Issues

There are several other issues related to depreciation that we will briefly introduce here. These include how certain assets are separated into their significant components for depreciation purposes, how assets are depreciated for income tax purposes, how the impairment of assets is recorded when the fair value declines, and under what circumstances depreciation is revised.

study objective 3

Describe other accounting issues related to depreciation.

Significant Components

When an item of property, plant, and equipment includes individual components for which different depreciation methods or rates are appropriate, the cost should be allocated to the asset's significant components and each component should be depreciated separately. For example, an aircraft and its engines may need to be treated as separate depreciable assets if they have different useful lives. The SAS Group, an airline in Europe, depreciates its aircraft over an estimated useful life of 20 years and its engine components over an estimated useful life of 8 years. It comments upon this practice in the notes to its financial statements: "For aircraft, a number of essential components have been identified. The useful life of the various components has been determined and all components apart from engine components have the same useful life. In accordance with official requirements, aircraft engines must be maintained and significant engine components changed after a specific number of takeoffs and landings and flight hours. This maintenance occurs on average every eighth year depending on type of aircraft."

Further discussion of calculating depreciation for the different parts of an asset will be left to a later accounting course. For simplicity, we will assume in this text that all of the components of the depreciable asset have the same useful life and we will therefore depreciate each asset as a whole.

Depreciation and Income Taxes

Helpful Hint Depreciation for accounting purposes is usually different from depreciation for income tax purposes.

The Canada Revenue Agency (CRA) allows companies to deduct a specified amount of depreciation expense when they calculate their taxable income. As we have just learned, however, for accounting purposes (e.g., financial statements) a company must choose the depreciation method that best reflects the pattern in which the asset's future economic benefits are consumed. In contrast, income tax regulations require the taxpayer to use a specific depreciation method—single diminishing-balance—on the income tax return, regardless of which method is used in preparing financial statements.

In addition, the CRA does not permit companies to estimate the useful lives, or depreciation rates, of assets. Assets are grouped into various classes—depreciation for income tax purposes is calculated on a class (group) basis—and the maximum depreciation rates for each asset class are specified. Depreciation for income tax purposes is called capital cost allowance (CCA), not depreciation expense. Capital cost allowance is an optional deduction from taxable income, but depreciation expense is not optional for calculating net earnings. Consequently, you may see some businesses deducting depreciation expense for accounting purposes, which is required by GAAP, while deducting no CCA for income tax purposes.

Impairments

As noted earlier in the chapter, under the cost model, the carrying amount of property, plant, and equipment is the asset's cost less any accumulated depreciation since its acquisition. And as already discussed, the carrying amount of property, plant, and equipment is rarely the same as its fair value. Remember that the fair value is normally not relevant since property, plant, and equipment are not purchased for resale, but rather for use in operations over the long term.

While it is accepted that long-lived assets such as property, plant, and equipment may be undervalued on the balance sheet, it is not appropriate if property, plant, and equipment are overvalued. Property, plant, and equipment are considered impaired if the carrying amount of the asset exceeds its recoverable amount (the higher of the asset's fair value less costs to sell, or its value in use). If this is the case, an impairment loss must be recorded. An impairment loss is the amount by which the carrying amount of an asset exceeds its recoverable amount.

Companies are required to review their assets regularly for possible impairment and to do so whenever a change in circumstances affects an asset's recoverable amount. For example, if a machine has become obsolete, or if the market for a product made by a machine has dried up or has become very competitive, there is strong possibility that an impairment loss exists. Management is then required to estimate the machine's recoverable amount.

To illustrate the write-down of a long-lived asset, assume that Piniwa Corporation reviews its equipment for possible impairment. It owns equipment with a cost of $800,000 and accumulated depreciation of $200,000. The equipment's recoverable amount is currently $550,000. The amount of the impairment loss is determined by comparing the asset's carrying amount to its recoverable amount as follows:

Carrying amount ($800,000 − $200,000)	$600,000
Recoverable amount	550,000
Impairment loss	$ 50,000

The journal entry to record the impairment is:

A = L + SE
−50,000   −50,000
Cash flows: no effect

Impairment Loss	50,000	
Accumulated Depreciation—Equipment		50,000
(To record impairment loss on equipment)		

Assuming that the asset will continue to be used in operations, the impairment loss is reported on the statement of earnings as part of income from continuing operations and not as an "other expense." Often the loss is combined and reported with depreciation expense on the statement of earnings. An accumulated depreciation account is credited for the impairment loss, rather than an asset account, in order to preserve the asset's original cost.

We had previously defined an asset's carrying amount as its cost less accumulated depreciation. This is still the case, but the Accumulated Depreciation account can now include more than just the depreciation recorded on the asset to date. It will also include impairment losses, if there have been any.

International financial reporting standards allow the reversal of a previously recorded impairment loss. Traditionally, Canadian standards have not permitted companies to do this. Under IFRS, at each year end the company must determine whether or not an impairment loss still exists by measuring the asset's recoverable amount. If this recoverable amount exceeds the current carrying amount, then a reversal is recorded. The reversal for an asset is limited to the amount required to increase the asset's carrying amount to what it would have been if the impairment loss had not been recorded.

International Resources

Cost Model versus the Revaluation Model

As previously mentioned, under international financial reporting standards, companies can choose to account for their property, plant, and equipment under either the cost model or the revaluation model. We have been describing the cost model in this chapter because it is used by almost all companies. Only about 3 percent of companies reporting under IFRS use the revaluation model. The revaluation model is allowed under IFRS mainly because it is particularly useful in countries that experience high rates of inflation and for companies in certain industries, such as real estate, where fair values are more relevant than cost.

Under the revaluation model, the carrying amount of property, plant, and equipment is the fair value less any subsequent accumulated depreciation less any subsequent impairment losses. This model can be applied only to assets whose fair value can be reliably measured, and revaluations must be carried out often enough that the carrying amount is not materially different from the asset's fair value at the balance sheet date. As application of the revaluation model is relatively complex, and because so few companies will use this model, we will leave further discussion of it to a later accounting course.

ACCOUNTING MATTERS! | International Perspective

There are several reasons why a company might choose to use the revaluation model rather than the cost model to account for its assets. A study published in the *Journal of Business Finance & Accounting* examined companies in 35 countries that permit asset revaluations. It found that companies that have low cash reserves, borrowing constraints, and high growth potential are more likely to revalue their assets than others, although the results differed by country depending on the specific economic and legal environment. It also examined the impact of the revaluation on a number of ratios, and determined that revaluations did not necessarily lead to improved future performance, as might be expected.

Source: Benzion Barlev, Dov Fried, Joshua Haddad, and Joshua Livnat, "Reevaluation of Revaluations: A Cross-Country Examination of the Motives and Effects on Future Performance," *Journal of Business Finance & Accounting*, September/October 2007, pp. 1025–1050.

DECISION TOOLKIT

Decision Checkpoints	Info Needed for Decision	Tools to Use for Decision	How to Evaluate Results
Are the company's long-lived assets over- or undervalued?	Impairment loss; carrying amount of long-lived assets	Compare the carrying and recoverable amounts in light of current business conditions and company performance.	If assets have been adjusted for impairment, expect improved results in the subsequent period. If assets are substantially undervalued on the balance sheet, be cautious when interpreting ratios that use carrying amounts, as these ratios will not show the company's potential.

Revising Periodic Depreciation

There are several reasons why periodic depreciation may need to be revised during an asset's useful life. These include:

1. **Capital expenditures during the asset's useful life.** After purchasing an asset, the company will incur costs as it continues to use the asset. To determine which of these costs are capital expenditures and which are operating expenditures, companies apply the same rules during an asset's useful life as when the asset was first purchased.

   As explained earlier in the chapter, if a cost, such as ordinary repairs and maintenance, benefits the company only in the current period, the cost is an operating expenditure and is recorded as an expense in the statement of earnings. If the cost, such as a replacement of a major part or an addition to a building, will benefit future periods, then it is a capital expenditure and is added to the cost of the asset in the balance sheet. As capital expenditures during the asset's useful life increase the cost of a long-lived asset, the depreciation calculations will have to be revised.

2. **Impairment losses.** As described in the previous section, an impairment loss will result in the reduction of the asset's carrying amount. Since the carrying value is reduced, the depreciation calculations will also need to be revised.

3. **Changes in the estimated useful life or residual value.** Management should regularly review its estimates of useful life and residual value. For example, wear and tear or obsolescence might indicate that annual depreciation is either not enough or too much. Capital expenditures may increase the useful life of the asset and/or its residual value. Impairment losses might signal a reduction in useful life and/or residual value. Regardless of the reason for the change, a change in estimated useful life or residual value will cause a revision to the depreciation calculations.

4. **Changes in the pattern in which the economic benefits of the asset are consumed.** As discussed earlier, management must review the choice of depreciation method for a long-lived asset at least annually. If the pattern in which the future benefits will be consumed is expected to change, the depreciation method must change as well. A change in methods will obviously result in a revision to depreciation calculations.

Revising depreciation is known as a change in estimate. **Changes in estimates are made in current and future years but not to prior periods.** Thus, when a change in depreciation is made, (1) there is no correction of previously recorded depreciation expense, and (2) depreciation expense for current and future years is revised. The rationale for this treatment is that the original calculations were based on information known at the time when the asset was purchased. The revision is based on new information which should only affect future periods. In addition, regular restatements of prior periods would make users feel less confident about financial statements.

A significant change in an estimate must be disclosed in the notes to the financial statements so that financial statement users are aware of the financial impact. For example, extending an asset's useful life will reduce depreciation expense and increase the current period net earnings. Remember that changes in depreciation result in periodic effects only: total net earnings over the life of an asset will not be affected by any change in depreciation.

While we will leave the detailed calculation of a change in the depreciation estimate for another accounting course, you should know that many companies need to make revisions to their depreciation. For example, we learned in our feature story that VIA Rail capitalizes its trains' refurbishment costs and any other upgrading costs if they were incurred to improve the trains' service value or extend their useful lives. We also learned that VIA Rail is receiving $516 million from the federal government for a major refurbishment of its locomotives and passenger cars. This will result in extensive revisions to VIA Rail's depreciation calculations.

BEFORE YOU GO ON...

Review It

1. How does depreciation for accounting purposes differ from depreciation for income tax purposes?
2. What is an impairment loss? How is it calculated?
3. Distinguish between the cost and revaluation models.
4. Under what circumstances will depreciation need to be revised?
5. Are revisions of periodic depreciation made to prior periods, future periods, or both? Explain.

Do It

Millennium Satellite Inc. tested its property, plant, and equipment for impairment. The company determined that the recoverable amount of a particular machine was $275,000. The machine cost $400,000 and had accumulated depreciation of $50,000. (a) Record the impairment loss, if any. (b) Calculate the carrying amount of the machine, after any impairment has been determined in (a).

Action Plan

• Calculate carrying amount (cost less accumulated depreciation).
• If the recoverable amount is less than the carrying amount, the asset has been impaired.

Solution

(a)

Carrying amount ($400,000 − $50,000)		$350,000
Recoverable amount		275,000
Impairment loss		$ 75,000
Impairment Loss	75,000	
Accumulated Depreciation—Machinery		75,000
(To record impairment loss on machinery)		

(b) Carrying amount: $400,000 − $50,000 − $75,000 = $275,000

The Navigator

Disposals of Property, Plant, and Equipment

Companies dispose of property, plant, and equipment that is no longer useful to them. Illustration 9-9 shows three methods of disposal.

Sale
Equipment is sold

Retirement
Equipment is scrapped or discarded

Exchange
Existing equipment is traded for new equipment

◄ **Illustration 9-9**

Methods of property, plant, and equipment disposal

Whatever the disposal method, the company must perform the following four steps to record the sale, retirement, or exchange of the property, plant, or equipment:

Step 1: Update depreciation. Depreciation must be recorded over the entire period of time that an asset is available for use. If the disposal occurs in the middle of an accounting period, depreciation must therefore be updated for the fraction of the year that has passed since the last time adjusting entries were recorded up to the date of disposal. Note that the update period will never exceed one year, since adjusting entries are made at least annually. Depreciation is recorded even if the asset is not in use, but not if the asset is already fully depreciated.

Step 2: Calculate the carrying amount. Calculate the carrying amount at the time of disposal after updating the accumulated depreciation for any partial-year depreciation recorded in Step 1:

study objective 4

Account for the disposal of property, plant, and equipment.

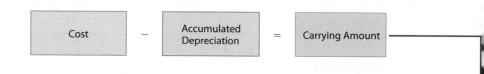

Step 3: Calculate the gain or loss. Determine the amount of the gain or loss on disposal, if any, by comparing the carrying amount to the proceeds received on disposal:

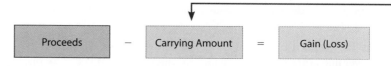

If the proceeds of the sale are more than the carrying amount of the property, plant, or equipment, there is a gain on disposal. If the proceeds of the sale are less than the carrying amount of the asset, there is a loss on disposal.

Step 4: Record the disposal. Record the disposal, removing the cost of the asset and the accumulated depreciation from each affected account. The Accumulated Depreciation account is decreased by the balance in the account, which is the total amount of depreciation and any impairment losses that have been recorded for the asset up to its disposal date. This is the same amount that was used to calculate the carrying amount in Step 2. Record the proceeds (if any) and record the gain or loss on disposal (if any) by crediting a gain account or debiting a loss account.

Sale of Property, Plant, and Equipment

In the following sections, we will illustrate the recording of a sale of office furniture, using the straight-line depreciation method, at both a gain and a loss.

Gain on Disposal. Assume that on July 1, 2009, Wright Ltd. sells office furniture for $25,000 cash. The office furniture was purchased January 1, 2006, at a cost of $60,000. At that time, it was estimated that the office furniture would have a residual value of $5,000 and a useful life of five years.

The first step is to update any unrecorded depreciation. Annual depreciation using the straight-line method is $11,000 [($60,000 − $5,000) ÷ 5]. The entry to record depreciation expense and update the accumulated depreciation for the first six months of 2009 is as follows:

July 1	Depreciation Expense ($11,000 × $^{6}/_{12}$)	5,500	
	Accumulated Depreciation—Office Furniture		5,500
	(To record depreciation expense for the		
	first six months of 2009)		

The second step is to calculate the carrying amount on July 1, 2009. As at December 31, 2008, Wright's year end, the office furniture had accumulated depreciation of $33,000 ($11,000 × 3). After the accumulated depreciation balance is updated on July 1, 2009, to $38,500 ($33,000 + $5,500), the carrying amount is $21,500 (cost of $60,000 – accumulated depreciation of $38,500).

The third step is to calculate the gain or loss on disposal. A $3,500 gain is calculated as follows:

Proceeds from sale	$25,000
Less: Carrying amount at date of disposal	21,500
Gain on disposal	$ 3,500

The fourth step is the entry to record the sale of the office furniture, as follows:

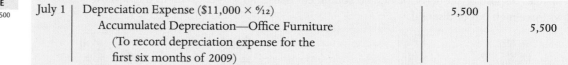

July 1	Cash	25,000	
	Accumulated Depreciation—Office Furniture	38,500	
	Office Furniture		60,000
	Gain on Disposal		3,500
	(To record sale of office furniture at a gain)		

A gain on disposal is reported in the "Other revenues" section of the statement of earnings.

Loss on Disposal. Assume that instead of selling the office furniture for $25,000, Wright sells it for $20,000. In this case, a loss of $1,500 is calculated:

Proceeds from sale	$20,000
Less: Carrying amount at date of disposal	21,500
Loss on disposal	$(1,500)

The entry to record the sale of the office furniture is:

July 1	Cash	20,000	
	Accumulated Depreciation—Office Furniture	38,500	
	Loss on Disposal	1,500	
	Office Furniture		60,000
	(To record sale of office furniture at a loss)		

A	=	L	+	SE
+20,000				−1,500
+38,500				
−60,000				

⬆ Cash flows: +20,000

A loss on disposal is reported in the "Other expenses" section of the statement of earnings.

Retirement of Property, Plant, and Equipment

Instead of being sold, some assets are simply retired by a company at the end of their useful lives. For example, some productive assets may have very specific uses and consequently have no ready market when the company no longer needs them. In this case, the asset is simply retired.

Retirement of an asset is recorded as a special case of a sale, one where no cash is received. As illustrated earlier, depreciation is first updated for any partial period up to the date of retirement. The carrying amount is then calculated. If the asset is retired before it is fully depreciated, there is a loss on disposal that is equal to the asset's carrying amount at the date of retirement. Since no proceeds are received in a retirement, a gain will never occur.

Quite often the carrying amount will equal zero; however, a journal entry is still required to remove all accounts related to the retired asset from the books. The Accumulated Depreciation account is decreased (debited) for the balance in the account related to the retired asset. The retired asset account is reduced (credited) for its balance. Any loss on disposal is recorded as a debit.

What happens if a company is still using a fully depreciated asset? In this case, the asset and its accumulated depreciation continue to be reported on the balance sheet, without further depreciation, until the asset is retired. Reporting the asset and related depreciation on the balance sheet informs the reader of the financial statements that the asset is still being used by the company. Once an asset is fully depreciated, even if it is still being used, no additional depreciation should be taken. Accumulated depreciation on a piece of property, plant, and equipment can never be more than the asset's cost less residual value.

Exchanges of Property, Plant, and Equipment

In an exchange of assets, a new asset is typically purchased by trading in an old asset, and a **trade-in allowance** is given toward the purchase price of the new asset. An additional cash payment is usually also required for the difference between the trade-in allowance and the purchase price of the new asset.

Instead of being sold for cash, therefore, the old asset is sold for a trade-in allowance on the purchase of the new asset. The new asset is seen as being purchased for cash plus the value of the old asset. Accounting for exchange transactions is complex and further discussion of exchanges is left for future accounting courses.

BEFORE YOU GO ON...

▸ **Review It**

1. What are the steps in accounting for the sale of property, plant, and equipment?
2. What is the formula for calculating a gain or loss on disposal?
3. How does the retirement of an asset differ from a sale?

▸ **Do It**

Overland Trucking Ltd. has a truck that it purchased on January 1, 2005, for $30,000. The truck has been depreciated on a straight-line basis with an estimated residual value of $3,000 and a useful life of six years.

Overland has a December 31 fiscal year end. Assume two different situations: (a) the company sells the truck on October 1, 2009, for $10,000 cash, and (b) the truck is determined to be worthless on January 1, 2010, so the company simply retires it. What entry should Overland use to record each scenario?

Action Plan
- Update any unrecorded depreciation for partial periods.
- Calculate the carrying amount.
- Compare the proceeds to the carrying amount to determine whether any gain or loss has occurred.
- Record any proceeds that are received and any gain or loss.
- Recall that a gain is not possible in a retirement of assets and that all accounts related to the retired asset must be removed.

Solution

(a) Sale of the truck for cash:

Annual depreciation expense: ($30,000 – $3,000) ÷ 6 years = $4,500
Accumulated depreciation recorded from Jan. 1, 2005, to Dec. 31, 2008 (the last time adjusting entries were recorded): $4,500 × 4 years = $18,000

Oct 1, 2009	Depreciation Expense ($4,500 × 9/12)	3,375	
	Accumulated Depreciation—Truck		3,375
	(To record depreciation for nine months)		
	Cash	10,000	
	Accumulated Depreciation—Truck ($18,000 + $3,375)	21,375	
	Gain on Disposal [$10,000 – ($30,000 – $21,375)]		1,375
	Truck		30,000
	(To record sale of truck at a gain)		

(b) Retirement of the truck:

Jan 1, 2010	Accumulated Depreciation—Truck ($4,500 × 5 years)	22,500	
	Loss on Disposal [$0 – ($30,000 – $22,500)]	7,500	
	Truck		30,000
	(To record retirement of truck at a loss)		

The Navigator

Intangible Assets and Goodwill

study objective 5

Identify the basic accounting issues for intangible assets and goodwill.

Property, plant, and equipment and intangible assets are similar in that both are long-lived resources that are used in the operations of a business, and are not intended for sale to customers. Both provide economic benefits in future periods. Intangible assets differ from property, plant, and equipment in that they do not have physical substance; in other words, they are not physical things. The future economic benefits flowing from an intangible asset may include revenue from the sale of products or services, cost savings, or other benefits resulting from the use of the asset by the company.

Intangible assets involve rights, privileges, and/or competitive advantages. For example, the use of intellectual property in a production process may reduce future production costs and allow the company to sell the product at a lower price. Many companies' most valuable assets are intangible. Some widely known intangibles are Alexander Graham Bell's patent on the telephone, the franchises of Tim Hortons, the trade name of President's Choice, and the trademark CBC.

An intangible asset must be identifiable, which means it must meet one of the two following criteria: (1) it can be separated from the company and sold whether or not the company intends to do so, or (2) it is based on contractual or legal rights, regardless of whether or not it can be separated from the company. Since goodwill cannot be separated from a company and sold, there are differences in the accounting for goodwill versus other intangible assets.

As you will learn in this section, although financial statements do report many intangibles, many other significant intangibles are not reported. To give an example, according to its 2008 financial statements, Research In Motion had a carrying amount of U.S. $3.9 billion. But its *fair value*—the total market price of all its shares on that same date—was U.S. $56.3 billion. Thus, its actual fair value was more than 14 times greater than what its balance sheet said the company was worth at that time. It is not uncommon for a company's reported carrying amount to differ from its fair value because balance sheets are reported at historical cost. But an extreme difference like that for Research In Motion seriously lessens the usefulness of the balance sheet to decision-makers. In the case of Research In Motion, the difference is primarily due to unrecorded intangibles. For many high-tech or intellectual property companies, most of their value is from intangibles such as knowledge assets, and many of these are not reported under current accounting practices.

Accounting for Intangible Assets

Similar to property, plant, and equipment, **intangible assets are recorded at cost**. Cost includes all the costs of acquisition and other costs that are needed to make the intangible asset ready for its intended use, including legal fees and similar charges.

As with property, plant, and equipment, companies have a choice of following the cost model or revaluation model when accounting for an intangible asset subsequent to acquisition. The majority of companies use the cost model for both types of long-lived assets. So we will leave further study of the revaluation model, as it applies to intangible assets, for a later accounting course.

Under the cost model, if an intangible asset has a **finite (limited) life** its cost must be systematically allocated over its useful life. We called this *depreciation* when discussing property, plant, and equipment. With intangible assets, we will use the term amortization.

For an intangible asset with a finite life, its amortizable amount (its cost less its residual value) should be allocated over the shorter of (1) the estimated useful life and (2) the legal life. Intangible assets, by their nature, rarely have any residual value, so the amortizable amount is normally equal to the cost. In addition, the useful life of an intangible asset is usually shorter than its legal life, so useful life is most often used as the amortization period.

When a company estimates the useful life of an intangible asset, it must consider factors such as how long the company expects to use the asset, obsolescence, inadequacy, demand, and other factors that can make the intangible ineffective at helping earn revenue. For example, suppose a computer hardware manufacturer obtains a patent on a new computer chip that it has developed (we will discuss patents in the next section). The legal life of the patent is 20 years. From experience, we know that the useful life of a computer chip is not more than four to five years—and often less—because new, superior chips are developed so rapidly that existing chips quickly become obsolete. Consequently, we would question the amortization expense of a company if it amortized its patent on a computer chip for longer than five years. Amortizing an intangible over a period that is too long will understate amortization expense, overstate the company's net earnings, and overstate its assets.

Amortization begins when the intangible asset is ready to be used as intended by management. Similar to depreciation, the company must use the amortization method that best matches the pattern in which the asset's future economic benefits are expected to be consumed. If that pattern cannot be reliably determined, the straight-line method should be used. The amortization expense is recognized on the statement of earnings as an operating expense. Companies often combine depreciation and amortization expense for reporting purposes.

Just as land is considered to have an indefinite life, there are also intangible assets with an indefinite life. An intangible asset is considered to have an **indefinite (unlimited) life** when, based on an analysis of all of the relevant factors, there is no foreseeable limit to the period over which the intangible asset is expected to generate net cash inflows for the company. If an intangible asset has an indefinite life, it is not amortized.

As with property, plant, and equipment, all intangible assets must be reviewed and tested for impairment whenever circumstances make this appropriate. Intangible assets with indefinite lives are tested more frequently for impairment than are intangible assets with finite lives. Indefinite-life assets should be tested for impairment at least annually.

Recall from earlier in this chapter that an asset is impaired if its recoverable amount falls below its carrying amount. If any impairment is evident, the asset must be written down to its recoverable amount and an impairment loss must be recorded in the statement of earnings. Under international financial reporting standards, an impairment loss cannot be reversed for goodwill, but it can for other intangible assets, just as it can for property, plant, and equipment.

Similar to property, plant, and equipment, the amortization is revised if there is a change in cost or useful life, or an impairment loss, and the revision is treated as a change in estimate.

At disposal, just as with property, plant, and equipment, the carrying amount of the intangible asset is eliminated, and a gain or loss, if any, is recorded.

In the next two sections, we will look at the accounting for intangibles with finite lives and those with indefinite lives in more detail.

Intangible Assets with Finite Lives

Examples of intangible assets with finite lives include patents and copyrights. We also include research and development costs in this section because these costs often lead to the creation of patents and copyrights.

Patents

A **patent** is an exclusive right issued by the Canadian Intellectual Property Office of Industry Canada that allows the patent holder to manufacture, sell, or otherwise control an invention for a period of 20 years from the date of the application. A patent cannot be renewed. But the legal life of a patent can be extended if the patent holder obtains new patents for improvements or other changes in the basic design.

The initial cost of a patent is the price paid to acquire the patent. Subsequent to acquisition, legal costs are often incurred. The saying "A patent is only as good as the money you're prepared to spend defending it" is very true. In 2006 and 2007, Microsoft was sued 43 times, Verizon 29, Dell 28, and Hewlett-Packard 24 for patent infringement. About 80 percent of patent suits are against large technology and financial companies.

Legal costs to successfully defend a patent in an infringement suit are considered necessary to prove the patent's validity. They are added to the patent account and amortized over the remaining life of the patent.

The cost of a patent should be amortized over its 20-year legal life or its useful life, whichever is shorter. As mentioned earlier, the useful life should be carefully assessed by considering whether the patent is likely to become ineffective at contributing to revenue before the end of its legal life.

Copyrights

A **copyright** is granted by the Canadian Intellectual Property Office, giving the owner the exclusive right to reproduce and sell an artistic or published work. Copyrights extend for the life of the creator plus 50 years. Generally, the useful life of a copyright is significantly shorter than its legal life, and the copyright is therefore amortized over its useful life.

The cost of the copyright consists of the cost of acquiring and defending it. The cost may be only the fee paid, or it may amount to a great deal more if a copyright infringement suit is involved.

⚖ ACCOUNTING MATTERS! | Ethics Perspective

If Canada's new copyright bill becomes law, can you expect the police to be knocking on your door for downloading the latest song? The amendments to the *Copyright Act* tabled in June 2008, would allow record companies to sue any person who downloads unauthorized songs worth more than $500—down from the previous level of $20,000 under an existing but never enforced section of law. The amendments will also allow people to videotape television for only a short time. These changes bring several questions to mind. Could technology eventually make it easier to monitor consumers? And if so, what privacy issues will this raise? And how long is a short time?

The primary target of the new legislation is people who download illegal copies of DVDs or songs. Legal downloads in the United States totalled $1.2 billion last year, while in Canada, where unauthorized downloading is still flourishing, sales totalled $40 million.

Source: Steve Lambert, "Canada's Copyright Crackdown," *The Daily Gleaner,* July 10, 2008, p. C7.

Research and Development Costs

Research and development (R&D) costs are not intangible assets per se. But they may lead to patents, copyrights, new processes, and new products. Many companies spend very large sums of money on research and development in an ongoing effort to develop new products or processes. For example, nineteen Canadian companies spent more than $100 million on research and development in 2007. Nortel Networks headed this list, with R&D costs of close to $2 billion in 2007.

Research and development costs present two accounting problems: (1) It is sometimes difficult to determine the costs related to a specific project. (2) It is also hard to know the extent and timing of future benefits. As a result, accounting distinguishes between research costs and development costs.

Research is original planned investigation that is done to gain new knowledge and understanding. **All research costs should be expensed when incurred.**

Development is the use of research findings and knowledge for a plan or design before the start of commercial production. **Development costs with probable future benefits should be capitalized.** In addition, all of the following conditions must be met for development costs to be capitalized: Management must have the technical feasibility, intention, and ability to complete the intangible asset and use or sell it; a future market must be defined; adequate resources must exist to complete the project; and management must be able to measure the costs related to the development of the intangible asset. If any of these conditions is not met, the development costs must be expensed.

← Illustration 9-10

Distinction between research and development

Research

Development

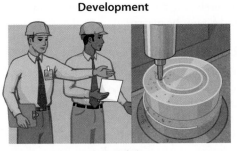

Examples
- Laboratory research aimed at the discovery of new knowledge
- Searching for ways to use new research findings or other knowledge
- Forming concepts and designs of possible product or process alternatives

Examples
- Testing in search or evaluation of product or process alternatives
- Design, construction, and testing of pre-production prototypes and models
- Design of tools, jigs, moulds, and dies involving new technology

DECISION TOOLKIT

Decision Checkpoints	Info Needed for Decision	Tools to Use for Decision	How to Evaluate Results
Is the company's amortization of intangibles reasonable?	The estimated useful life of intangibles with finite lives from notes to the financial statements of both the company and its competitors	If the company's estimated useful life is significantly higher than that of its competitors, or does not seem reasonable in light of the circumstances, the reason for the difference should be investigated.	Too high an estimated useful life will result in understating amortization expense and overstating net earnings.

Intangible Assets with Indefinite Lives

An intangible asset is considered to have an indefinite life when there is no foreseeable limit to the length of time over which the asset is expected to generate net cash inflows for the company. Examples of intangible assets with indefinite lives include trademarks and trade names, franchises and licences, and goodwill. Intangible assets do not always fit perfectly in a specific category. Sometimes trademarks, trade names, franchises, or licences do have limited lives. In such cases, they would be amortized over the shorter of their legal life and useful life. It is more usual, however, for these intangible assets, along with goodwill, to have indefinite lives.

Trademarks, Trade Names, and Brands

A trademark (trade name) or brand is a word, phrase, jingle, or symbol that distinguishes or identifies a particular business or product. Trade names like Blue Jays, Big Mac, Nike, Calgary Stampede, and TSN create immediate brand recognition and generally help the sale of the product or service. Each year, Interbrand ranks the world's best brands. In 2008, it ranked Coca-Cola as the most successful brand in the world. There are only two Canadian companies included in the list of the most successful global brands: Thomson Reuters, ranked 44th, and Blackberry, ranked 73rd.

The creator or original user may obtain the exclusive legal right to the trademark or trade name by registering it with the Canadian Intellectual Property Office. This registration provides continuous protection and may be renewed every 15 years as long as the trademark or trade name is in use. In most cases, companies continuously renew their trademarks or trade names. In such cases, as long as the trademark or trade name continues to be marketable, it will have an indefinite useful life.

If the trademark or trade name is purchased, the cost is the purchase price. If it is developed internally rather than purchased, it cannot be recognized as an intangible asset on the balance sheet. The reason is that expenditures on internally developed trademarks or brands cannot be distinguished from the cost of developing the business as a whole. In other words, the cost of an internally developed trademark or brand cannot be measured.

Franchises and Licences

When you purchase a Civic from a Honda dealer, fill up your tank at the corner Irving station, or order a double-double at Tim Hortons, you are dealing with franchises. A franchise is a contractual arrangement under which the franchisor grants the franchisee the right to sell certain products, to provide specific services, or to use certain trademarks or trade names, usually within a designated geographic area.

Another type of franchise, granted by a government body, permits the company to use public property in performing its services. Examples are the use of city streets for a bus line or taxi service; the use of public land for telephone, power, and cable television lines; and the use of airwaves for wireless devices, radio, or TV broadcasting. Such operating rights are referred to as licences.

When costs can be identified with the acquisition of the franchise or licence, an intangible asset should be recognized. These rights have indefinite lives and are not amortized.

Annual payments, which are often in proportion to the franchise's total sales, are sometimes required under a franchise agreement. These are called royalties and are recorded as operating expenses in the period in which they are incurred.

Goodwill

Goodwill represents the value of all favourable attributes that relate to a company. These include exceptional management, a desirable location, good customer relations, skilled employees, high-quality products, fair pricing policies, and harmonious relations with labour unions. Unlike other assets, which can be sold *individually* in the marketplace—such as investments or property, plant, and equipment—goodwill can be identified only with the business *as a whole*. This is also what differentiates goodwill from other intangible assets. It cannot be separated from the company, nor is it based on legal rights.

If goodwill can only be identified with the business as a whole, how can it be determined? Certainly, a number of businesses have many of the factors cited above (exceptional management, a desirable location, and so on). However, to determine the cost of these items would be difficult and very subjective—and subjective valuations do not contribute to the reliability of financial statements. For this reason, internally generated goodwill is not recognized as an asset.

Goodwill is recorded only when there is a purchase of an entire business, at which time an independent valuation can be determined. The cost of the goodwill is measured by comparing the cost paid to acquire the business to the fair value of its net identifiable assets (assets less liabilities). If the cost is greater than the net identifiable assets, then the purchaser has paid for something that is not identifiable. The purchaser has paid for something that cannot be separated and sold—goodwill. In this situation, because a transaction has occurred, the cost of the purchased goodwill can be measured and therefore recorded as an asset.

Because goodwill has an indefinite life, just as the company has an indefinite life, it is not amortized. Since goodwill is measured using the fair value of a company—a value which can easily change—it must be tested annually for impairment. Both goodwill and indefinite life intangible assets must be tested for impairment annually regardless of whether there is any indication of impairment. This is different from finite life intangible assets. Finite life intangible assets are assessed for indications of impairment at the end of each year, and are tested only if the assessment shows that an impairment may exist.

Impairment losses on goodwill are never reversed, even if the value of the company increases after the impairment loss has been recorded. On the other hand, under international standards, impairment losses can be reversed for both finite life and other infinite life intangible assets if their value increases in the future, just as for property, plant, and equipment.

BEFORE YOU GO ON...

Review It

1. What are the similarities and differences between accounting for intangible assets and for property, plant, and equipment?
2. Give some examples of intangible assets in your everyday surroundings.
3. Distinguish between the amortization policy for intangible assets with finite lives and the policy for those with indefinite lives.
4. Distinguish between the treatment of impairment losses for intangible assets (a) with finite lives, (b) with indefinite lives, and (c) goodwill.

Do It

The Dummies R' Us Corporation purchased a copyright on a new book series for $15,000 cash on August 1, 2009. The books are anticipated to have a saleable life of three years. One year later, the company incurs $6,000 of legal costs (paid in cash) to successfully defend this copyright in court. The company's year end is July 31. Record the purchase of the copyright on August 1, 2009; the year-end amortization at July 31, 2010; and the legal costs incurred at August 1, 2010.

Action Plan

- Amortize intangible assets with limited lives over the shorter of their useful life and legal life (the legal life of a copyright is the life of the author plus 50 years).
- Treat costs to successfully defend an intangible asset as capital expenditures because they benefit future periods.

Solution

Aug. 1, 2009	Copyright	15,000	
	Cash		15,000
	(To record purchase of copyright)		
July 31, 2010	Amortization Expense ($15,000 ÷ 3)	5,000	
	Accumulated Amortization—Copyright		5,000
	(To record amortization expense)		
Aug. 1, 2010	Copyright	6,000	
	Cash		6,000
	(To record costs incurred to defend copyright)		

The Navigator

Statement Presentation of Long-Lived Assets

study objective 6

Illustrate how long-lived assets are reported in the financial statements.

Long-lived assets have a major impact on three financial statements: the balance sheet, statement of earnings, and cash flow statement.

Balance Sheet

Long-lived assets are normally reported in the balance sheet under the headings "Property, Plant, and Equipment" and "Intangible Assets." Goodwill must be separately disclosed; other intangibles can be grouped together for reporting purposes. Sometimes intangible assets are listed separately without a heading after property, plant, and equipment. Some companies combine property, plant, and equipment and intangible assets, other than goodwill, under a single heading, such as "Capital Assets."

▸ Reporting and Analyzing Long-Lived Assets

Either on the balance sheet or in the notes, the cost of each of the major classes of assets should be disclosed, as well as the accumulated depreciation for assets that are depreciated and accumulated amortization for intangible assets that are amortized. In addition, the company must specify which depreciation and amortization methods it uses and the useful lives or rates in the notes to its financial statements.

Under international financial reporting standards, companies will also have to disclose if they are using the cost or the revaluation model for each class of assets, and include a reconciliation of the carrying amount at the beginning and end of the period for each class of long-lived assets in the notes to the financial statements. This means they must show all of the following for each class of long-lived assets: (1) additions, (2) disposals, (3) depreciation or amortization, (4) impairment losses, and (5) reversals of impairment losses. If a company uses the revaluation model, it must also disclose any increases or decreases from revaluations, as well as other information about the revaluation.

Illustration 9-11 is an excerpt from the notes to VIA Rail's balance sheet. Property, plant, and equipment are summarized in the balance sheet and detailed in the notes.

International Resources

Illustration 9-11 ➡

Note disclosure of property, plant, and equipment

VIA RAIL CANADA Notes to Financial Statements (partial) December 31, 2007 (in millions)			

Note 5. Property, plant, and equipment

	Cost	Accumulated Depreciation	Net
Land	$ 5.7	$ 0.0	$ 5.7
Rolling stock	777.2	484.7	292.5
Maintenance buildings	181.8	141.5	40.3
Stations and facilities	45.3	30.4	14.9
Infrastructure improvements	148.5	57.9	90.6
Leasehold improvements	116.4	93.0	23.4
Machinery and equipment	36.3	30.3	6.0
Information systems	51.1	45.9	5.2
Other property, plant, and equipment	20.5	19.6	0.9
	1,382.8	903.3	479.5
Projects in progress			8.1
Retired property, plant, and equipment			0.3
	$1,382.8	$903.3	$487.9

The cost and accumulated depreciation amounts are not separately shown for projects in progress or for retired property, plant, and equipment. Only the net amount is reported for these two items.

At December 31, 2007, VIA Rail did not have any intangible assets. The accounting policy note to the financial statements reports that the company uses straight-line depreciation and indicates the estimated useful lives for each category of property, plant, and equipment.

Statement of Earnings

Depreciation expense and impairment losses are presented in the operating section of the statement of earnings. VIA Rail reported $55,396 thousand for "depreciation and losses on write-down and disposal of property, plant, and equipment" in the operating expenses section of its statement of earnings for the year ended December 31, 2007. Companies must disclose their impairment policy in the notes to the financial statements. VIA Rail states in the notes to its financial statements that "retired property, plant, and equipment are written down to their net realizable value." Unlike in VIA Rail's statement of earnings, gains and losses on disposal are normally segregated and presented as "Other revenues/expenses."

Cash Flow Statement

The cash flows from the purchase and sale of long-lived assets are reported in the investing activities section of the cash flow statement. Illustration 9-12 shows the investing activities section of VIA Rail's cash flow statement.

	VIA RAIL CANADA Cash Flow Statement (partial) Year Ended December 31, 2007 (in thousands)	

Investing activities	
Acquisition of property, plant, and equipment	$(12,438)
Proceeds from disposal of property, plant, and equipment	1,918

◀ Illustration 9-12

Cash flow statement presentation of property, plant, and equipment

In the Management Discussion and Analysis section of VIA's annual report, we are told that three-quarters of these capital expenditures were devoted to equipment, station upgrading, and information technology projects. It is a good idea to also examine the financing activities section of the cash flow statement to determine how a company finances its capital expenditures. VIA Rail, a Crown corporation, received $12,138 thousand in capital funding from the Canadian government; in contrast, privately owned companies typically have to borrow or sell shares to finance their acquisitions.

BEFORE YOU GO ON...

Review It

1. How are long-lived assets presented on the balance sheet? The statement of earnings? The cash flow statement?
2. What information about long-lived assets is disclosed in the notes to the financial statements?

The Navigator

Analyzing Assets

The presentation of financial statement information about long-lived assets allows decision-makers to analyze a company's use of its total assets. We will use two ratios to analyze assets: the return on assets and asset turnover.

Return on Assets

The return on assets ratio measures overall profitability. This ratio is calculated by dividing net earnings by average total assets. The return on assets ratio indicates the amount of net earnings generated by each dollar invested in assets. The higher the return on assets, the more profitable the company.

The following data are provided for VIA Rail (in CAD thousands) for the fiscal years 2007 and 2006:

	2007	2006
Net sales	$268,959	$266,609
Net earnings (loss)	43,540	33,732
Total assets	893,966	880,430

> **study objective 7**
>
> Describe the methods for evaluating the use of assets.

Since VIA Rail provides a service, as opposed to selling goods, we have used passenger and commuter revenue as net sales for this ratio calculation. Total assets at the end of 2005 were $894,660 thousand.

The return on assets for VIA Rail is shown in Illustration 9-13. This illustration also shows this ratio for Amtrak, one of VIA's competitors, as well as the industry average.

RETURN ON ASSETS =	$\dfrac{\text{NET EARNINGS}}{\text{AVERAGE TOTAL ASSETS}}$	
(in thousands)	**2007**	**2006**
VIA Rail	$\dfrac{\$43,540}{(\$893,966 + \$880,430) \div 2} = 4.9\%$	$\dfrac{\$33,732}{(\$880,430 + \$894,660) \div 2} = 3.8\%$
Amtrak	(11.2%)	(10.9%)
Industry average	5.0%	5.2%

◀ Illustration 9-13

Return on assets

▸ Reporting and Analyzing Long-Lived Assets

As the illustration shows, VIA Rail's return on assets improved in 2007 compared with 2006. In both years, it was less than the industry average, but in 2007 VIA was very close to the industry average. Amtrak appears to be much less successful as it had a negative return on assets both years. There is an explanation for this.

The passenger rail industry in the United States and Canada requires substantial federal subsidies to operate the national passenger rail system and maintain the underlying infrastructure. But the accounting treatment of these subsidies is different in Canada than it is in the United States. In Canada, operating funding from the Government of Canada is included in calculating net income. In the United States, federal operating funding is not. VIA Rail had operating losses of $204,465 in 2007, and $190,657 in 2006, before including funding from the Government of Canada and income taxes. If VIA's return on assets is calculated using these numbers, the results are negative 23% in 2007, and negative 21.5% in 2006. From this perspective, VIA did much worse than Amtrak and the industry averages. This is a perfect illustration of the difficulty that can arise when trying to compare companies in different countries and the need to understand differing accounting practices when working with their data.

Asset Turnover

The **asset turnover** ratio indicates how efficiently a company uses its assets—that is, how many dollars of sales are generated by each dollar invested in assets. It is calculated by dividing net sales by average total assets. When we compare two companies in the same industry, the one with the higher asset turnover ratio is operating more efficiently. It is generating more sales for every dollar invested in assets.

The asset turnover ratios of VIA Rail, Amtrak, and their industry for 2007 and 2006 are presented in Illustration 9-14.

Illustration 9-14 ➡

Asset turnover

	ASSET TURNOVER = $\dfrac{\text{NET SALES}}{\text{AVERAGE TOTAL ASSETS}}$	
(in thousands)	**2007**	**2006**
VIA Rail	$\dfrac{\$268,959}{(\$893,966 + \$880,430) \div 2} = 0.3$ times	$\dfrac{\$266,609}{(\$880,430 + \$894,660) \div 2} = 0.3$ times
Amtrak	0.2 times	0.2 times
Industry average	0.4 times	0.4 times

The asset turnover ratios in the illustration indicate that for each dollar invested in assets in 2007, VIA Rail generated sales of $0.30 and Amtrak $0.20. While VIA Rail's return on assets improved in 2007, its asset turnover remained the same. The main reason for this is that VIA received more government operating funding in 2007 than in 2006. This increased VIA's return on assets, but had no impact on its asset turnover result.

Note that the difference in the accounting treatment of government funding between VIA Rail and Amtrak does not impact asset turnover, as it did the return on assets. While VIA Rail's asset turnover in 2007 and 2006 is higher than Amtrak's, the difference is not as great as it was for the return on assets calculation. VIA Rail's load factor (the percentage of available seats that it filled), at 55 percent, was better than Amtrak's 46 percent in 2007, which may partially explain the differing asset turnover ratios.

Asset turnover ratios vary considerably across industries. The average asset turnover for utility companies is 0.4 times, and the drug store industry has an average asset turnover of 1.7 times. Asset turnover ratios, therefore, should only be compared within an industry, not between different industries.

Profit Margin Revisited

For a complete picture of the sales-generating ability of assets, it is also important to look at a company's profit margin ratio. In Chapter 5, you learned about profit margin. Profit margin is calculated by dividing net earnings by net sales. It tells how effective a company is in turning its sales into earnings—that is, how much earnings are generated by each dollar of sales.

Together, the profit margin and asset turnover explain the return on assets ratio. Illustration 9-15 shows how return on assets can be calculated from the profit margin and asset turnover ratios for VIA Rail in 2007.

PROFIT MARGIN	×	ASSET TURNOVER	=	RETURN ON ASSETS
$\dfrac{\text{Net Earnings}}{\text{Net Sales}}$	×	$\dfrac{\text{Net Sales}}{\text{Average Total Assets}}$	=	$\dfrac{\text{Net Earnings}}{\text{Average Total Assets}}$
$\dfrac{\$43,540}{\$268,959} = 16.2\%$		$\dfrac{\$268,959}{(\$893,966 + \$880,430) \div 2} = 0.3 \text{ times}$		$\dfrac{\$43,540}{(\$893,966 + \$880,430) \div 2} = 4.9\%$

◄ Illustration 9-15

Composition of VIA Rail's 2007 return on assets (in thousands)

This relationship has important implications for management. From Illustration 9-15, we can see that if a company wants to increase its return on assets, it can do so either by increasing the margin it generates from each dollar of goods that it sells (profit margin), or by trying to increase the volume of goods that it sells (asset turnover).

Let's evaluate VIA Rail's return on assets for 2007 again, but this time by evaluating the ratio's components—the profit margin and asset turnover ratios. VIA Rail has a profit margin of 16.2 percent. Compared to the industry average of 11.6 percent, this might indicate that VIA Rail has better control of its costs than most of its industry competitors. However, because VIA Rail's asset turnover is lower than the industry's asset turnover, this offsets VIA's higher profit margin and results in its return on assets being very similar to the industry average.

DECISION TOOLKIT

Decision Checkpoints	Info Needed for Decision	Tools to Use for Decision	How to Evaluate Results
How efficient is the company at generating earnings from its assets?	Net earnings and average total assets	$\text{Return on assets} = \dfrac{\text{Net earnings}}{\text{Average total assets}}$	Indicates the net earnings generated per dollar of assets. A high value suggests that the company is efficient in using its resources to generate earnings.
How efficient is the company at generating sales from its assets?	Net sales and average total assets	$\text{Asset turnover} = \dfrac{\text{Net sales}}{\text{Average total assets}}$	Indicates the sales dollars generated per dollar of assets. A high value suggests that the company is efficient in using its resources to generate sales.

BEFORE YOU GO ON...

Review It

1. What is the purpose of the return on assets? Of the asset turnover? How are these ratios calculated?
2. How can the profit margin and asset turnover be used to explain the return on assets ratio?

The Navigator

Are You Sure You Need a Car?

Rent-A-Wreck is the registered trademark held by Practicar Systems Inc., a wholly owned subsidiary of Franchise Services of North America, Inc. Rent-A-Wreck, Canada's No. 1 used car rental franchise, has determined that it can maximize its profitability by buying and renting used cars instead of new cars.

Having decided that you need a car, could you maximize your economic well-being by buying a used car rather than a new one? Perhaps you might consider leasing a car instead of buying one. Buying a vehicle is a fairly straightforward process if you purchase a new car. You borrow money from a lending institution, pay the dealership for the car, and then make monthly payments on the loan until it is paid in full. As you pay off the loan, you gain equity in the vehicle until it is eventually all yours. You can keep the vehicle as long as you like and do whatever you want to it.

On the surface, leasing appears even simpler. You pay the leasing company a monthly payment that's lower than the loan payment when buying a car. Then, after enjoying the most trouble-free two or three years of the vehicle's life, you simply bring it back to the dealership and lease another new one, or walk away.

Benefits to leasing include:
- There's often no down payment required when leasing, or only a low one.
- You're always driving a late-model vehicle that's usually covered by the manufacturer's warranty.

Disadvantages to leasing include:
- You have a limited number of kilometres in your contract and will have to pay extra if you go over.
- You must maintain the vehicle in good condition. If you don't, you'll have to pay penalties for excess wear and tear when you turn it in.
- At the end of the lease, you have no equity in the vehicle to put toward a new car.

In addition, arranging a lease can be a confusing, complicated process that can easily leave you paying more than you should. The graph presented below indicates that, after five years, buying a car—whether new or used—is more economical than leasing one. However, some people might point out that, yes, driving a used car costs less, but the pleasure of driving an older car is lower, too.

Some Facts

- On average, drivers paid $31,723 for a new vehicle in 2007.
- Forty-three percent of the passenger and light vehicles sold in Canada were financed by leases.
- Vehicle sales rose 3.6 percent in 2007 to $87.4 billion, mostly on the strength of a 7.4 percent increase in sales of used vehicles.
- Statistics Canada noted that the used car industry said the rise in sales of used automotive vehicles in 2007 may have been influenced by a surge in imports of second-hand vehicles from the United States, pushing down prices.
- For every $100 consumers spent in retail stores in 2007, $18.70 went to new car dealers. This was the lowest proportion since 1993, when the figure was $17.90.
- A car loses between 15 and 20 percent of its value each year.

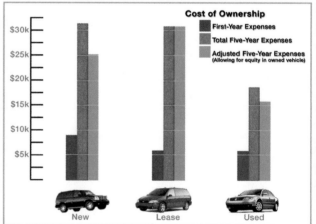

Source: www.edmunds.com

What Do You Think?

Should you buy a new car?

YES | I do not want to worry about my car breaking down and, if it does break down, I want it to be covered by a warranty.

NO | I am a university student and I want to keep my costs down. Used cars are more dependable than they used to be.

The Navigator

Sources:

Philip Reed, "Compare the Costs: Buying vs. Leasing vs. Buying a Used Car," edmunds.com/advice/buying/articles/47079/article.html

Joseph Patrick Dunlavy, "New Motor Vehicle Sales: 2007 in Review," Statistics Canada, April 23, 2008, statcan.ca/english/research/11-621-MIE/11-621-MIE2008069.htm

"2008 Canadian Retail Sales Unlikely to Beat 2007, Retail Council Says," CEP News, April 9, 2008, economicnews.ca/cepnews/wire/article/69773

Summary of Study Objectives

1. Determine the cost of property, plant, and equipment. The cost of property, plant, and equipment includes all expenditures that are necessary to acquire these assets and make them ready for their intended use. When applicable, cost also includes asset retirement costs.

2. Explain and calculate depreciation. Depreciation is the process of allocating the cost of a long-lived asset over the asset's useful (service) life in a systematic way. Depreciation is not a process of valuation, and it does not result in an accumulation of cash.

There are three depreciation methods: straight-line, diminishing-balance, and units-of-production.

Method	Annual Depreciation Pattern	Calculation
Straight-line	Constant amount	(Cost – residual value) ÷ estimated useful life (in years)
Diminishing-balance	Diminishing amount	Carrying amount at beginning of year × diminishing-balance rate
Units-of-production	Varying amount	(Cost – residual value) ÷ total estimated units of production × actual production during the year

Each method results in the same amount of total depreciation over the useful life of the asset.

3. Describe other accounting issues related to depreciation. When an item of property, plant, and equipment includes individual components for which different depreciation methods or rates are appropriate, the cost should be allocated to the asset's significant components and each component should be depreciated separately.

Depreciation expense for income tax purposes is called capital cost allowance (CCA). The Canada Revenue Agency requires companies to use the single diminishing-balance method and prescribes the CCA rates.

Property, plant, and equipment are tested for impairment whenever circumstances indicate that an asset might be impaired. If the asset is impaired, an impairment loss, equal to the difference between the asset's carrying amount and recoverable amount, is recorded. The asset is then tested annually to determine if the recoverable amount has increased or continued decreasing. A previously recorded loss will be able to be reversed under IFRS.

When circumstances change the cost, residual value, or useful life of an asset, or the pattern in which the future benefits are consumed, a revision of depreciation is required. Revisions are also necessary if an impairment loss has been recorded or reversed. Revisions are treated as changes in estimates and are adjusted in the present and future periods, not retroactively.

Under international financial reporting standards, companies must choose between the cost and revaluation models. Most companies are expected to continue to use the cost model, where property, plant, and equipment are carried at cost less accumulated depreciation.

4. Account for the disposal of property, plant, and equipment. The procedure for accounting for the disposal of property, plant, and equipment through sale or retirement is:

Step 1: Update any unrecorded depreciation.

Step 2: Calculate the carrying amount.

Step 3: Calculate any gain (proceeds less carrying amount) or loss (carrying amount less proceeds) on disposal.

Step 4: Remove the asset and accumulated depreciation accounts related to the sold or retired asset. Record the proceeds received and the gain or loss (if any).

5. Identify the basic accounting issues for intangible assets and goodwill. The accounting for property, plant, and equipment and intangible assets is much the same. Intangible assets are reported at cost, which includes all expenditures that are necessary to prepare the asset for its intended use. An intangible asset with a finite life is amortized over the shorter of its useful life or legal life, and must be assessed for impairment annually. Both goodwill and an intangible asset with an indefinite life are not amortized and are tested at least annually for impairment.

6. Illustrate how long-lived assets are reported in the financial statements. In the balance sheet, land, land improvements, buildings, and equipment are usually combined and shown under the heading "Property, Plant, and Equipment." Intangible assets with finite and indefinite lives are sometimes combined under the heading "Intangible Assets" or are listed separately. Goodwill must be presented separately. Either on the balance sheet or in the notes, the cost of the major classes of long-lived assets is presented. The accumulated depreciation and amortization, and carrying amount by major classes, or in total, are also disclosed. The depreciation and amortization methods and rates must also be indicated. Finally, the company's impairment policy and any impairment losses should be described and reported.

Depreciation expense and any impairment losses are reported as operating expenses in the statement of earnings. Any gain or loss on disposal is reported in the "Other revenues / expenses" section of the statement of earnings.

In the cash flow statement, any cash flows from the purchase or sale of long-lived assets are reported as investing activities.

7. Describe the methods for evaluating the use of assets. The use of assets may be analyzed using the return on assets and asset turnover ratios. Return on assets (net earnings ÷ average total assets) indicates how profitably assets are used to generate earnings. Asset turnover (net sales ÷ average total assets) indicates how efficiently assets are used to generate revenue. The components of the return on assets ratio can be further analyzed by multiplying the asset turnover and the profit margin.

The Navigator

Glossary

Amortizable amount The cost of a finite life intangible asset less its residual value. (p. 451)

Amortization The systematic allocation of the amortizable cost of a finite life intangible asset over the asset's useful life. (p. 451)

Asset turnover A measure of how efficiently a company uses its total assets to generate sales. It is calculated by dividing net sales by average total assets. (p. 458)

Capital expenditures Expenditures that benefit future periods. They are recorded as long-lived assets. (p. 433)

Copyright An exclusive right granted by the federal government allowing the owner to reproduce and sell an artistic or published work. (p. 452)

Cost model A model for accounting for a long-lived asset that carries the asset at its cost less accumulated depreciation or amortization, which includes any impairment losses. (p. 437)

Depreciable amount The cost of a depreciable asset (e.g., property, plant, and equipment) less its residual value. (p. 438)

Diminishing-balance method A depreciation method that applies a constant rate (the straight-line rate, which is 100% divided by the useful life) to the carrying amount of an asset. This method produces a decreasing annual depreciation expense over the useful life of the asset. (p. 439)

Finance lease A long-term agreement allowing one party (the lessee) to use the asset of another party (the lessor). The arrangement is accounted for as a purchase. (p. 435)

Franchise A contractual arrangement under which the franchisor grants the franchisee the right to sell certain products, to render specific services, or to use certain trademarks or trade names, usually within a designated geographic area. (p. 454)

Goodwill The amount paid to acquire another company that exceeds the fair value of the company's net identifiable assets. (p. 454)

Impairment loss The amount by which the carrying amount of an asset exceeds its recoverable amount. (p. 444)

Lessee A party that has made contractual arrangements to pay for the use of another party's asset. (p. 435)

Lessor A party that has agreed contractually to let another party use its asset. (p. 435)

Licences Operating rights to use property that are granted by a government agency to a company. (p. 454)

Operating expenditures Expenditures that benefit only the current period. They are immediately matched against revenues as an expense. (p. 433)

Operating lease An arrangement allowing one party (the lessee) to use the asset of another party (the lessor). The arrangement is accounted for as a rental. (p. 435)

Patent An exclusive right issued by the federal government that enables the recipient to manufacture, sell, or otherwise control an invention for a period of 20 years from the date of the application. (p. 452)

Recoverable amount The higher of the asset's fair value, less costs to sell, and its value in use. (p. 444)

Research and development (R&D) costs Expenditures that may lead to patents, copyrights, new processes, and new products. (p. 452)

Residual value An estimate of the amount that a company would obtain from the disposal of an asset if the asset were already as old as it will be and in the condition it is expected to be in at the end of its useful life. (p. 438)

Return on assets A profitability measure that indicates the amount of net earnings generated by each dollar invested in assets. It is calculated as net earnings divided by average total assets. (p. 457)

Revaluation model A model for accounting for a long-lived asset that carries the asset at its fair value less accumulated depreciation or amortization, which includes any impairment losses. (p. 445)

Straight-line method A depreciation method in which the depreciable amount of an asset is divided by its estimated useful life. This method produces the same depreciation expense for each year of the asset's useful life. (p. 438)

Trademark (trade name) A word, phrase, jingle, or symbol that distinguishes or identifies a particular business or product. (p. 453)

Units-of-production method A depreciation method in which the useful life is expressed in terms of the total units of production or total use expected from the asset. Depreciation expense is calculated by multiplying the depreciable amount by actual activity during the year divided by the estimated total activity. The method will produce an expense that will vary each period depending on the amount of activity. (p. 441)

DECISION TOOLKIT—A SUMMARY

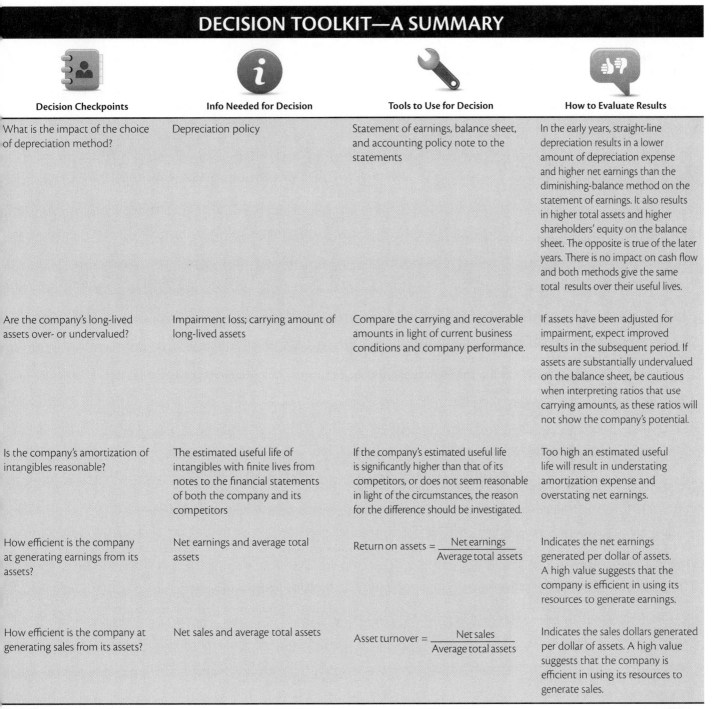

Decision Checkpoints	Info Needed for Decision	Tools to Use for Decision	How to Evaluate Results
What is the impact of the choice of depreciation method?	Depreciation policy	Statement of earnings, balance sheet, and accounting policy note to the statements	In the early years, straight-line depreciation results in a lower amount of depreciation expense and higher net earnings than the diminishing-balance method on the statement of earnings. It also results in higher total assets and higher shareholders' equity on the balance sheet. The opposite is true of the later years. There is no impact on cash flow and both methods give the same total results over their useful lives.
Are the company's long-lived assets over- or undervalued?	Impairment loss; carrying amount of long-lived assets	Compare the carrying and recoverable amounts in light of current business conditions and company performance.	If assets have been adjusted for impairment, expect improved results in the subsequent period. If assets are substantially undervalued on the balance sheet, be cautious when interpreting ratios that use carrying amounts, as these ratios will not show the company's potential.
Is the company's amortization of intangibles reasonable?	The estimated useful life of intangibles with finite lives from notes to the financial statements of both the company and its competitors	If the company's estimated useful life is significantly higher than that of its competitors, or does not seem reasonable in light of the circumstances, the reason for the difference should be investigated.	Too high an estimated useful life will result in understating amortization expense and overstating net earnings.
How efficient is the company at generating earnings from its assets?	Net earnings and average total assets	$\text{Return on assets} = \dfrac{\text{Net earnings}}{\text{Average total assets}}$	Indicates the net earnings generated per dollar of assets. A high value suggests that the company is efficient in using its resources to generate earnings.
How efficient is the company at generating sales from its assets?	Net sales and average total assets	$\text{Asset turnover} = \dfrac{\text{Net sales}}{\text{Average total assets}}$	Indicates the sales dollars generated per dollar of assets. A high value suggests that the company is efficient in using its resources to generate sales.

Using the Decision Toolkit

Research In Motion (RIM) Limited, headquartered in Waterloo, Ontario, manufactures and markets innovative wireless products (including the popular BlackBerry) for the worldwide mobile communications market.

Many stock analysts have recommended purchasing RIM's shares. A friend of yours, Rafik Khan, has an interest in buying RIM's shares and has asked you some questions about its financial statements. Excerpts from RIM's financial statements follow:

RESEARCH IN MOTION LIMITED Balance Sheet (partial) March 1, 2008 (in USD thousands)	*RIM*

Assets

Capital assets	$705,955
Intangible assets	469,988
Goodwill	114,455

RESEARCH IN MOTION LIMITED Notes to the Consolidated Financial Statements March 1, 2008 (in USD thousands)	*RIM*

2. Summary of Significant Accounting Policies

(k) Capital assets

Capital assets are stated at cost less accumulated amortization ... Amortization is provided using the following rates and methods:

Buildings, leaseholds and other	Straight-line over terms between 5 and 40 years
BlackBerry operations and other information technology	Straight-line over terms between 3 and 5 years
Manufacturing equipment, research and development equipment, and tooling	Straight-line over terms between 2 and 8 years
Furniture and fixtures	20% per annum diminishing balance

(l) Intangible assets

Intangible assets are stated at cost less accumulated amortization ... Intangible assets are amortized as follows:

Acquired technology	Straight-line over 2 to 5 years
Licences	Lesser of 5 years or on a per unit basis based upon the anticipated number of units sold during the terms of the licence agreements
Patents	Straight-line over 17 years or over estimated useful life

(n) Goodwill

Goodwill is not amortized, but is tested for impairment annually.

Instructions

Answer the following questions asked by Rafik:

1. Why does RIM report its intangible assets and goodwill separately on its balance sheet?
2. Why does RIM likely use a different amortization method for its furniture and fixtures than it uses for its buildings and leaseholds?
3. Why does RIM not amortize its goodwill?
4. Rafik has determined that on the March 1, 2008, balance sheet, RIM's shareholders' equity was U.S. $3.9 billion. He also knows on that on March 1, 2008, the company's shares had a fair value of approximately U.S. $100 each and that the company had 563 million shares. He wonders if this information can be used when testing to see if goodwill has been impaired. Explain to Rafik what the information shows.

5. Rafik was able to get the following information related to RIM:

	RIM	Industry Average
Profit margin	21.5%	8.2%
Return on assets	23.5%	8.8%

Rafik knows that the profit margin and return on assets are somehow related to the asset turnover ratio. He expects that RIM will have a much higher asset turnover than the industry average because RIM's profit margin and return on assets are so much higher than the industry average. Explain to Rafik why this is not so.

Solution

1. RIM's intangible assets consist of acquired technology, licences, and patents. These assets have a limited life and are amortized, whereas goodwill has an indefinite life and is not amortized.
2. RIM likely uses a different amortization method (diminishing balance) for its furniture and fixtures because they produce a different economic benefit pattern than its buildings and leaseholds. In the case of buildings, time is normally the main factor affecting usage and therefore the straight-line method of amortization is often the most appropriate. In the case of furniture and fixtures, it may be that these are anticipated to be more productive in their early years than in their later years, and so the diminishing-balance method would be the most appropriate.
3. Goodwill is not amortized because it has an indefinite life.
4. Rafik can use his information to calculate the total fair value of RIM on March 1, 2008, as U.S. $100 per share multiplied by 563 million shares, or $56.3 billion. This is significantly higher than the U.S. $3.9 billion of shareholders' equity on the balance sheet, which is an indication that goodwill had not been impaired at March 1, 2008.
5. Rafik is correct that profit margin and return on assets are related to the asset turnover ratio. Asset turnover × profit margin = return on assets. Therefore, asset turnover = return on assets ÷ profit margin. Using this formula to calculate the asset turnover, we find that Rafik was incorrect in thinking that RIM's asset turnover will be much higher than the industry average asset turnover. RIM's asset turnover of 1.1 times (23.5% ÷ 21.5%) is the same as the industry average asset turnover of 1.1 times (8.8% ÷ 8.2%).

The Navigator

Demonstration Problem

DuPage Ltd. purchased a factory machine at a cost of $17,500 on June 1, 2009. The machine was expected to have a residual value of $1,500 at the end of its four-year useful life. DuPage has a December 31 year end.

During its useful life, the machine was expected to be used 10,000 hours. Actual annual hourly use was as follows: 1,300 hours in 2009; 2,800 hours in 2010; 3,300 hours in 2011; 1,900 hours in 2012; and 700 hours in 2013.

Instructions

Prepare depreciation schedules using the following methods: (a) straight-line, (b) diminishing-balance using double the straight-line rate, and (c) units-of-production.

Solution to Demonstration Problem

(a)

					End of Year	
Year	Depreciable Amount	×	Depreciation Rate	= Depreciation Expense	Accumulated Depreciation	Carrying Amount
						$17,500
2009	$16,000[a]		25%[b] × 7/12	$2,333	$ 2,333	15,167
2010	16,000		25%	4,000	6,333	11,167
2011	16,000		25%	4,000	10,333	7,167
2012	16,000		25%	4,000	14,333	3,167
2013	16,000		25% × 5/12	1,667	16,000	1,500

DUPAGE LTD.
Straight-Line Depreciation Schedule

a $17,500 − $1,500 = $16,000
b 100% ÷ 4 years = 25%

Action Plan

- Deduct the residual value in the straight-line and units-of-production methods, but not the diminishing-balance method.

- In the diminishing-balance method, the depreciation rate is applied to the carrying amount. The residual value is not used in the calculations except to make sure the carrying amount is not reduced below the expected residual value.

- When the asset is purchased during the year, the first year's depreciation for the straight-line and diminishing-balance methods must be adjusted for the part of the year that the asset is owned. No adjustment is required for the units-of-production method. In the straight-line method, the final year must also be adjusted.

			DUPAGE LTD. Diminishing-Balance Depreciation Schedule				
						End of Year	
Year	Carrying Amount Beginning of Year	×	Depreciation Rate	=	Depreciation Expense	Accumulated Depreciation	Carrying Amount
							$17,500
2009	$17,500		50%ᵃ × 7/12		$5,104	$ 5,104	12,396
2010	12,396		50%		6,198	11,302	6,198
2011	6,198		50%		3,099	14,401	3,099
2012	3,099		50%		1,549	15,951	1,549
2013	1,549		50%		49ᵇ	16,000	1,500

a 25% × 2
b Adjusted to $49 because the ending carrying amount should not be less than the expected residual value.

			DUPAGE LTD. Units-of-Production Depreciation Schedule				
						End of Year	
Year	Units of Activity	×	Depreciable Cost/Unit	=	Depreciation Expense	Accumulated Depreciation	Carrying Amount
							$17,500
2009	1,300		$1.60ᵃ		$2,080	$ 2,080	15,420
2010	2,800		1.60		4,480	6,560	10,940
2011	3,300		1.60		5,280	11,840	5,660
2012	1,900		1.60		3,040	14,880	2,620
2013	700		1.60		1,120	16,000	1,500

a $17,500 − $1,500 = $16,000 ÷ 10,000 total units = $1.60/unit

The Navigator

Self-Study Questions

Answers are at the end of the chapter.

www.wiley.com/canada/kimmel

Study Tools (Self-Assessment Quizzes)

(SO 1) 1. Corrieten Ltd. purchased equipment and incurred these costs:

Invoice price	$24,000
Freight—FOB shipping point	1,000
Insurance during transit	200
Annual licence fee	350
Installation and testing	400
Total costs	$25,950

What amount should be recorded as the cost of the equipment?
(a) $24,000
(b) $24,200
(c) $25,600
(d) $25,950

(SO 2) 2. Cuso Ltd. purchased equipment on January 1, 2008, at a total invoice cost of $400,000. The equipment has an estimated residual value of $10,000 and an estimated useful life of five years. Assuming the straight-line method of depreciation is used, what is the amount of accumulated depreciation at December 31, 2009, the second year of the asset's useful life?
(a) $78,000
(b) $80,000
(c) $156,000
(d) $160,000

3. Kant Enterprises Ltd. purchased a truck for $32,000 on July 1, 2009. The truck has an estimated residual value of $2,000, an estimated useful life of five years, and an estimated total mileage of 300,000 kilometres. If 50,000 kilometres are driven in 2009, what amount of depreciation expense would Kant record at December 31, 2009, assuming it uses the units-of-production method?
(a) $2,500
(b) $3,000
(c) $5,000
(d) $5,333

4. Refer to the data provided for Kant Enterprises in question 3. If Kant uses the double diminishing-balance method of depreciation, what amount of depreciation expense would be recorded at December 31, 2009?
(a) $6,000
(b) $6,400
(c) $12,000
(d) $12,800

5. Which depreciation method would result in the highest net earnings in the first year of an asset's life, if the asset's output was relatively high in its first year of operations?

(a) Straight-line
(b) Double diminishing-balance
(c) Units-of-production
(d) Capital cost allowance

6. A piece of equipment has an original cost of $125,000, accumulated depreciation of $25,000, and a recoverable amount of $80,000. The impairment loss is:

(a) $0.
(b) $20,000.
(c) $45,000.
(d) $55,000.

7. Oviatt Ltd. sold equipment for $10,000 cash. At the time of disposal, the equipment had a cost of $45,000 and accumulated depreciation of $30,000. Oviatt should record a:

(a) $5,000 loss on disposal.
(b) $5,000 gain on disposal.
(c) $15,000 loss on disposal.
(d) $15,000 gain on disposal.

8. Pierce Inc. incurred $150,000 of research costs in its laboratory to develop a new product. On January 2, 2009, it spent $20,000 in legal fees for a patent related to the new product. On July 31, 2009, Pierce paid $15,000 for legal fees in a successful defence of the patent. What is the total amount that should be debited to the Patents account through July 31, 2009?

(a) $15,000
(b) $20,000
(c) $35,000
(d) $185,000

9. Which of the following statements is true? (SO 6)

(a) Since intangible assets lack physical substance, they need to be disclosed only in the notes to the financial statements.
(b) Goodwill should be combined and reported with other intangible assets on the balance sheet.
(c) Intangible assets are typically combined with property, plant, and equipment and reported in the "Property, Plant, and Equipment" section of the balance sheet.
(d) Property, plant, and equipment, goodwill, and intangible assets should be separately reported on the balance sheet.

10. Which of the following ratios helps determine how (SO 7) efficiently a company uses its assets?

(a) Current ratio
(b) Profit margin
(c) Debt to total assets
(d) Asset turnover

The Navigator

Questions

1. Susan Leung is uncertain about how to determine the cost of property, plant, and equipment. Explain this for her.

2. Deer Fern Inc. purchases equipment and incurs a number of expenditures before it is ready to use the equipment. Give two examples of operating expenditures and two examples of capital expenditures and explain how these expenditures on new equipment would be recorded and why.

3. What are land improvements? Should the cost of clearing and grading land be recorded as a land improvement or not? Why or why not?

4. Explain the difference between an operating lease and a finance lease.

5. In a recent press release, the president of Anwar Inc. stated that something has to be done about depreciation. The president said, "Depreciation does not come close to accumulating the cash needed to replace the asset at the end of its useful life." What is your response to the president?

6. Contrast the effects of the three depreciation methods on (1) depreciation expense, (2) net earnings, (3) accumulated depreciation, and (4) carrying amount in each of the following: (a) the early years of an asset's life, and (b) over the total life of the asset.

7. Why is the depreciable amount (the asset's cost less residual (SO 2) value) used in the straight-line and units-of-production methods but not in the diminishing-balance method?

8. Why must the calculation of depreciation be adjusted for any (SO 2) fraction of a year since purchase when the straight-line and diminishing-balance methods are used, but no adjustment is needed when the units-of-production method is used?

9. What factors should a company consider when choosing a (SO 2, 3) depreciation method? When revising a depreciation method?

10. Lucien Corporation uses straight-line depreciation for (SO 3) financial reporting purposes but CCA (the single diminishing-balance method) for income tax purposes. Is it acceptable to use different methods for these two purposes? Why is Lucien likely doing this?

11. What factors could contribute to an impairment loss? In what (SO 3) circumstances, if any, is a company allowed to write up its property, plant, and equipment?

12. How do impairment losses and capital expenditures during a (SO 3) depreciable asset's useful life affect the factors that are used in annual depreciation calculations? What impact might this have on the annual depreciation expense?

(SO 4) 13. If equipment is sold in the middle of a fiscal year, why does depreciation have to be updated for the partial period? Doesn't the journal entry to record the sale subsequently remove the accumulated depreciation from the books anyway?

(SO 4) 14. How is a gain or loss on the sale of property, plant, or equipment calculated? Is the calculation the same for the retirement of property, plant, or equipment?

(SO 4) 15. Rashid Corporation owns a machine that is fully depreciated but is still being used. How should Rashid account for this asset and report it in the financial statements?

(SO 5) 16. 🔧 Heflin Corporation has been amortizing its finite life intangible assets over their legal life. The company's accountant argues that this is appropriate because an intangible asset's legal life is known with certainty, but the useful life of an intangible asset is subjective. Why is this not correct, and what impact might it have on the company's financial statements?

(SO 5) 17. Two years ago, Pesowski Corp. purchased a patent for $5 million that allows the company to produce and sell a special video game controller. During the year, the company determined that Sucha Ltd. was producing and selling an identical game controller. Pesowski spent $500,000 on legal fees to successfully enforce its rights under the patent. How should Pesowski account for the legal fees and why?

(SO 5) 18. Why are intangible assets with a finite life amortized, but intangible assets with an indefinite life are not?

19. Bob Leno, a business student, is working on a case for one of his classes. The company in the case needs to raise cash to market a new product it has developed. Saul Cain, an engineering student, takes one look at the company's balance sheet and says, "This company has an awful lot of goodwill. Why don't you recommend that they sell some of it to raise cash?" How should Bob respond to Saul?

20. Explain how long-lived assets should be reported on (a) the balance sheet, (b) the statement of earnings, and (c) the cash flow statement.

21. What information about long-lived assets should be disclosed in the notes to the financial statements?

22. 🔧 Give an example of an industry that would be characterized by (a) a high asset turnover and low profit margin, and (b) a low asset turnover and high profit margin.

23. Explain how the profit margin and asset turnover ratios can be used to help explain the return on assets.

24. 🔧 In 2007, Tim Hortons reported net sales of U.S. $1,248.6 million, and average total assets of U.S. $1,771.1 million. In 2006, its net sales were U.S. $1,072.4 million and average total assets, U.S. $1,670.9 million. How effective has the company been at generating sales from its assets over these two years?

Brief Exercises

Determine cost of land.
(SO 1)

BE9–1   These expenditures were incurred by Shumway Ltd. in purchasing land: cash price $50,000; legal fees $2,500; clearing and grading $3,500; installation of fence $3,000. What is the cost of the land?

Determine cost of truck.
(SO 1)

BE9–2   Basler Ltd. incurs these expenditures in purchasing a truck: invoice price $42,000; installation of a trailer hitch $1,000; one-year accident insurance policy $2,000; motor vehicle licence $150; painting and lettering $750. What is the cost of the truck?

Identify operating and capital expenditures.
(SO 1)

BE9–3   Indicate whether each of the following items is an operating expenditure (O) or a capital expenditure (C). If the expenditure is neither, write NA for "not applicable" in the space provided.

(a) ___ Repaired building roof, $1,500
(b) ___ Replaced building roof, $27,500
(c) ___ Purchased building, $480,000
(d) ___ Purchased supplies, $350
(e) ___ Purchased truck, $55,000
(f) ___ Purchased oil and gas for truck, $155
(g) ___ Replaced tires on truck, $500
(h) ___ Anticipated retirement costs for plant, $5,000,000
(i) ___ Added new wing to building, $250,000
(j) ___ Painted interior of building, $1,500
(k) ___ Rebuilt engine on truck, $7,500
(l) ___ Upgrade air conditioning system, $10,000

Calculate straight-line depreciation.
(SO 2)

BE9–4   Cunningham Ltd. purchases a delivery truck on January 2, 2009, at a cost of $43,000. The truck is expected to have a residual value of $3,000 at the end of its four-year useful life. Cunningham has a December 31 year end. Calculate the depreciation using the straight-line method (a) for each year of the truck's life, and (b) in total over the truck's life.

BE9–5 Depreciation information for Cunningham Ltd. is given in BE9–4. Assuming the delivery truck was purchased on April 3, 2009, calculate the depreciation expense using the straight-line method for 2009, 2010, and 2013.

Calculate partial-year straight-line depreciation.
(SO 2)

BE9–6 Depreciation information for Cunningham Ltd. is given in BE9–4. Using the diminishing-balance method and assuming the depreciation rate is equal to one time the straight-line rate, calculate the depreciation (a) for 2009 and 2010, and (b) in total over the truck's life.

Calculate diminishing-balance depreciation.
(SO 2)

BE9–7 Depreciation information for Cunningham Ltd. is given in BE9–4. Assuming the delivery truck was purchased on April 3, 2009, calculate the depreciation expense using the diminishing-balance method for 2009 and 2010. Assume the depreciation rate is equal to one time the straight-line rate.

Calculate partial-year diminishing-balance depreciation.
(SO 2)

BE9–8 Speedy Taxi Service uses the units-of-production method to calculate depreciation on its taxicabs. Each cab is expected to be driven 325,000 kilometres. Taxi 10 was purchased on March 1, 2009, for $33,000 and is expected to have a residual value of $500. Taxi 10 was driven 125,000 kilometres in 2009 and 105,000 kilometres in 2010. Speedy Taxi Service has a December 31 year end. Calculate the depreciation expense on Taxi 10 for each year.

Calculate units-of-production depreciation.
(SO 2)

BE9–9 Fortune Cookie Corporation owns machinery that cost $90,000 and has accumulated depreciation of $54,000. The machinery's recoverable amount is $30,000. Prepare the journal entry to record the impairment loss.

Record impairment loss.
(SO 3)

BE9–10 Tibble Corporation recently determined that the recoverable value of one of its milling machines is less than its current carrying amount. In addition, the useful life of the machine is now expected to be three years less than what the company had originally estimated. Explain how the impairment loss and the reduction in useful life will affect the company's annual depreciation expense calculation for (a) previous years, (b) the current year, and (c) future years.

Explain depreciation revision and impairment.
(SO 3)

BE9–11 Wiley Inc. sells office equipment on September 30, 2009, for $21,000 cash. The office equipment originally cost $72,000 when purchased on January 1, 2006. It has an estimated residual value of $2,000 and a useful life of five years. Depreciation was last recorded on December 31, 2008, the company's year end. Prepare the journal entries to (a) update depreciation to September 30, 2009, and (b) record the sale of the equipment.

Record sale of equipment.
(SO 4)

BE9–12 Ruiz Ltd. retires delivery equipment which cost $42,000. Prepare journal entries to record the transaction if accumulated depreciation is (a) $42,000, and (b) $40,000.

Record retirement of equipment.
(SO 4)

BE9–13 In its unadjusted trial balance, Sprint Nextel Corporation had goodwill of U.S. $30,664 million at December 31, 2007. At year end, it was determined that goodwill was impaired by approximately U.S. $29,729 million. At what value should goodwill be reported on Sprint's balance sheet at December 31, 2007? Explain why.

Determine value to report for goodwill.
(SO 5)

BE9–14 Surkis Corporation purchased a patent for $180,000 cash on January 2, 2009. Its legal life is 20 years and its estimated useful life is 10 years. (a) Prepare the journal entry to record the (1) purchase of the patent on January 2, 2009, and (2) amortization for the first year ended December 31, 2009. (b) Show how the patent would be reported on the balance sheet at December 31.

Record patent transactions; show balance sheet presentation.
(SO 5, 6)

BE9–15 Indicate whether each of the following items should be recorded as property, plant, and equipment (PPE) or an intangible asset (I) on the balance sheet. If the asset does not fit either of these categories, write NA for "not applicable" in the space provided.

Classify long-lived assets.
(SO 6)

(a) ____ Building	(h) ____ Cash
(b) ____ Franchise	(i) ____ Goodwill
(c) ____ Inventory	(j) ____ Machinery
(d) ____ Common shares	(k) ____ Parking lot
(e) ____ Land	(l) ____ Patent
(f) ____ Land held for sale	(m) ____ Research costs
(g) ____ Licence right	(n) ____ Trademark

Prepare partial balance sheet.
(SO 6)

BE9–16 Canadian Tire Corporation, Limited reported the following selected information about long-lived assets at December 29, 2007 (in millions):

Accumulated amortization—asset under finance lease	$ 4.8
Accumulated amortization—buildings	733.5
Accumulated amortization—fixtures and equipment	416.7
Accumulated amortization—leasehold improvements	123.9
Asset under finance lease	33.7
Buildings	2,230.3
Construction in progress	400.1
Fixtures and equipment	627.7
Goodwill	51.8
Land	749.7
Leasehold improvements	402.4
Mark's Work Wearhouse store brands and banners	50.4
Mark's Work Wearhouse franchise agreements	2.0

Mark's Work Wearhouse store brands, banners, and franchises are considered to have indefinite lives. Prepare a partial balance sheet for Canadian Tire.

Calculate ratios.
(SO 7)

BE9–17 Magna International Inc. reported the following in its 2007 financial statements (in USD millions): net sales $26,067; net earnings $663; total assets at December 31, 2007, $15,343; and total assets at December 31, 2006, $13,154. Calculate Magna's return on assets and asset turnover for 2007.

Exercises

Classify expenditures.
(SO 1)

E9–1   The following expenditures relating to property, plant, and equipment were made by Kosinki Ltd.:

1. Paid $45,000 for a new delivery truck.
2. Paid $250 to have the company name and advertising slogan painted on the new truck.
3. Paid a $75 motor vehicle licence fee on the new truck.
4. Paid $900 for a one-year accident insurance policy on the new truck.
5. Paid $300,000 for a plant site.
6. Paid $4,000 of legal fees on the purchase of the plant site.
7. Paid $16,500 to demolish an old building on the plant site; residual materials were sold for $2,500.
8. Paid $17,500 for paving the parking lot on the plant site.
9. Paid $18,800 in architect fees for the design of the new plant.
10. Promised to pay $25,000 in restoration costs when the company is finished using the plant site.

Instructions

(a) Explain what types of expenditures should be included in determining the cost of property, plant, and equipment.

(b) List the numbers of the preceding transactions, and beside each number write the account title that the expenditure should be debited to.

Calculate cost and straight-line depreciation.
(SO 1, 2)

E9–2   Hohnberger Enterprises purchased machinery on March 15, 2009, for $75,000. The company also paid the following amounts: $1,000 for delivery charges; $200 for insurance while the machine was in transit; $1,800 for a one-year insurance policy; and $2,800 for testing and installation. The machine was ready for use on April 1, 2009, but the company did not start using it until May 1, 2009.

Hohnberger has estimated the machinery will have a 10-year useful life with no residual value. It expects to consume the machinery's future economic benefits evenly over the useful life. The company has a December 31 year end.

Instructions

(a) Calculate the cost of the machinery.

(b) When should the company begin depreciating the machinery: March 15, April 1, or May 1? Why?

(c) Which depreciation method should the company use? Why?

(d) Calculate the depreciation on the machinery for 2009.

E9–3   Intercity Bus Lines Inc. purchased a bus on January 1, 2008, at a cost of $410,000. The company estimated that the bus will have a residual value of $10,000. The bus is expected to be driven 500,000 kilometres during its 10-year life. The company has a December 31 year end.

Calculate and compare depreciation under different methods.
(SO 2)

Instructions

(a) Calculate the depreciation expense under the straight-line method for 2008 and 2009.

(b) Calculate the depreciation expense under the diminishing-balance method, using double the straight-line rate, for 2008 and 2009.

(c) Calculate the depreciation expense under the units-of-production method, assuming the actual distance driven was 44,800 kilometres for 2008, and 60,300 kilometres for 2009.

(d) Based on this information, which depreciation method should Intercity Bus Lines use?

E9–4   ◙▬◙ Sitrus Corporation purchased a new machine on October 4, 2008, at a cost of $86,000. The company estimated that the machine will have a residual value of $8,000. The machine is expected to be used for 10,000 working hours during its four-year life. Actual machine usage was 500 hours in 2008; 2,800 hours in 2009; 2,900 hours in 2010; 2,600 hours in 2011; and 1,200 hours in 2012. Sitrus Corporation has a December 31 year end.

Calculate and compare depreciation under different methods.
(SO 2)

Instructions

(a) Calculate depreciation for the machine under each of the following methods: (1) straight-line, (2) diminishing-balance using double the straight-line rate, and (3) units-of-production.

(b) Which method results in the highest depreciation expense over the life of the asset?

(c) Which method results in the highest cash flow over the life of the asset?

E9–5   ◙▬▬▶ TransAlta Corporation changed its depreciation policy for its Ottawa, Mississauga, Windsor-Essex, Fort Saskatchewan, and Meridian power generating plants because of uncertainty about the plants' operations beyond the terms of the current sales contracts. Previously, these plants were depreciated using the units-of-production method. TransAlta determined that it was more reasonable to allocate the remaining carrying amount of the plants on a straight-line basis over the remaining term of each contract.

Discuss implication of changing depreciation methods.
(SO 2)

Instructions

Write a short memo to your client that explains the implications of this change for the analysis of Trans-Alta's results. Include in your memo a discussion of whether this change in depreciation method looks reasonable.

E9–6   At the beginning of 2009, Lindy Weink, the new controller of Lafrenière Inc., reviewed the expected useful life and residual value of two of the company's machines and proposed changes as follows:

Calculate straight-line depreciation; discuss revision of estimate.
(SO 2, 3)

		Useful Life (in years)		Residual Value	
Date Acquired	Cost	Original	Proposed	Original	Proposed
Jan. 1, 1999	$800,000	20	25	$40,000	$62,000
Jan. 1, 2007	$120,000	5	4	$5,000	$3,600

Instructions

(a) Calculate the annual depreciation for each asset using the straight-line method and the original useful life and residual value.

(b) Calculate the accumulated depreciation and carrying amount of each asset on December 31, 2008.

(c) If the company accepts Lindy's proposed changes in useful life and residual value, will depreciation expense for each asset in 2009 be higher or lower than depreciation expense in 2008?

E9–7   Penang Corporation purchased a piece of equipment on January 1, 2007, for $850,000. It had an estimated useful life of eight years and a $50,000 residual value. Penang uses straight-line depreciation and has a December 31 year end. At December 31, 2009, management tested the asset for impairment. The equipment's recoverable amount was $320,000.

Record impairment loss; discuss presentation.
(SO 3)

Instructions

(a) Calculate the equipment's carrying amount at December 31, 2009.

(b) Record the impairment loss.

(c) How should the impairment loss be reported in the financial statements?

Record disposal of equipment.
(SO 4)

E9–8   Presented here are selected transactions for Beck Corporation for 2009. Beck uses straight-line depreciation.

Jan.   1   Retired a piece of machinery that was purchased on January 1, 2000. The machine cost $75,000 and had a useful life of 10 years with no residual value.

Sept. 1   Sold a computer that was purchased on January 1, 2007. The computer cost $5,490 and had a useful life of three years with no residual value. The computer was sold for $750 cash.

Dec. 30   Sold a delivery truck for $9,000 cash. The truck cost $31,000 when it was purchased on January 1, 2007, and was depreciated based on a four-year useful life with a $3,000 residual value.

Instructions
Record the above transactions.

Determine effect of depreciation method over life of asset.
(SO 2, 4)

E9–9   Rahim Corporation purchased a boardroom table for $5,000. The company planned to keep it for four years, after which it was expected to be sold for $500.

Instructions

(a) Calculate the depreciation expense for each of the first three years under (1) the straight-line method, and (2) the double diminishing-balance method.

(b) Assuming Rahim sold the table for $1,225 at the end of the third year, calculate the gain or loss on disposal under each depreciation method.

(c) Determine the impact on earnings (total depreciation of the table plus any loss on disposal or less any gain on disposal) of each method over the entire three-year period.

Record intangible asset transactions; show balance sheet presentation.
(SO 5, 6)

E9–10   Collins Ltd. has these transactions related to intangible assets in 2009, its first year of operations:

Jan.   2   Purchased a patent with an estimated useful life of five years and a legal life of 20 years for $40,000.

Apr.   1   Acquired another company and recorded goodwill of $300,000 as part of the purchase.

July   1   Acquired a franchise for $250,000. The franchise agreement expires on July 1, 2016.

Sept. 1   Incurred research costs of $150,000.

      30   Incurred development costs of $50,000. No marketable product has been identified as yet.

Dec. 31   Recorded annual amortization.

      31   Tested the intangible assets for impairment. Recoverable amounts exceeded carrying amounts in all cases.

Instructions

(a) Prepare the entries to record the above transactions. Assume all costs incurred were for cash.

(b) Show the balance sheet presentation of the intangible assets at December 31, 2009.

Apply accounting concepts.
(SO 1, 2, 5)

E9–11   A co-op student, Toni Johnston, encountered the following situations at Chin Chin Corporation:

1. Toni learned that Chin Chin is depreciating its buildings and equipment, but not its land. She could not understand why land was omitted, so she prepared journal entries to depreciate all the company's property, plant, and equipment for the current year end.

2. Toni determined that Chin Chin's amortization policy on its intangible assets was wrong. The company was amortizing its patents but not its goodwill. She fixed that for the current year end by adding goodwill to her adjusting entry for amortization. She told a fellow student that she felt she had improved the consistency of the company's accounting policies by making these changes.

3. Chin Chin has a building still in use that has a zero carrying amount but a substantial fair value. Toni felt that this practice did not benefit the company's users—especially the bank—and wrote the building up to its fair value. After all, she reasoned, you can write down assets if fair values are lower. Writing them up if fair value is higher is yet another example of the improved consistency that her employment has brought to the company's accounting practices.

Instructions

Explain whether or not the accounting treatment in each of the above situations follows generally accepted accounting principles. If an accounting principle or assumption has been violated, explain what the appropriate accounting treatment should be.

E9–12   **ACE Aviation Holdings Inc.** reported the following selected information as at December 31, 2007 (in millions):

Classify long-lived accounts; show balance sheet presentation.
(SO 6)

Account	Amount
Accumulated depreciation—assets under finance leases	$ 438
Accumulated depreciation—buildings, including leasehold improvements	118
Accumulated depreciation—flight equipment, including spare engines	685
Accumulated depreciation—ground and other equipment	35
Accumulated amortization—other finite life intangible assets	138
Accumulated amortization—Star Alliance membership	27
Additions to capital assets	2,622
Air Canada and other trade names	189
Assets under finance leases	1,899
Buildings, including leasehold improvements	609
Depreciation, amortization and obsolescence expense	582
Flight equipment, including spare engines	5,433
Gain on disposal of assets	1.366
Ground and other equipment	136
International route rights and slots	192
Other finite life intangible assets	339
Purchase deposits	1,124
Star Alliance membership	92

ACE Aviation's other finite-life intangible assets include technology and customer-based intangible assets.

Instructions

(a) Identify in which financial statement (balance sheet, statement of earnings, or cash flow statement) and which section (e.g., property, plant, and equipment) each of the above items should be reported.

(b) Prepare the property, plant, and equipment and intangible assets sections of the balance sheet as at December 31, 2007.

E9–13   ◼—C **Empire Company Limited** reported the following information (in millions) at May 3, 2008: net sales $14,065; net earnings $315.8; total assets at May 3, 2008, $5,706.9; and total assets at May 5, 2007, $5,224.9.

Calculate ratios.
(SO 7)

Instructions

(a) Calculate the following ratios for the year: (1) return on assets, (2) asset turnover, and (3) profit margin.

(b) By showing the appropriate calculation, prove mathematically how the profit margin and asset turnover work together to explain the return on assets.

(c) Empire Company owns Sobeys, Empire Theatres, and Lawton Drugstores. It also has an ownership interest in Wajax and oil and gas properties, and manages commercial real estate, among other activities. Does this diversity of activities affect your ability to interpret the ratios you calculated in (a)? Explain.

Problems: Set A

P9–1A   In 2009, Kadlec Inc. incurred the following transactions related to the purchase of a property. Assume all transactions are for cash unless otherwise stated.

Analyze and record property transactions.
(SO 1)

Jan.   22   Purchased real estate for a future plant site for $220,000, paying $55,000 cash and signing a note payable for the balance. There was an old building on the site. The fair values of the land and building were $170,000 and $50,000, respectively.

24 Paid $4,500 for legal fees on the real estate purchase.

31 Paid $25,000 to demolish the old building to make room for the new plant.

Feb. 13 Graded and filled the land at a cost of $8,000 in preparation for the construction.

28 Received $7,500 for residual materials from the demolished building.

Mar. 14 Paid $34,000 in architect fees for the building plans.

31 Paid the local municipality $5,000 for building permits and $10,000 for the 2009 property taxes.

Apr. 22 Excavation costs for the new building were $17,000.

June 15 Received a bill from the building contractor for half of the cost of the new building, $300,000. Paid $75,000 in cash and signed a note payable for the balance.

Sept. 14 Received a bill for the remaining $300,000 owed to the building contractor for the construction of the new building. Paid $100,000 cash and signed a note payable for the balance.

Oct. 12 Paved the parking lots, driveways, and sidewalks for $42,000.

20 Installed a fence for $8,000.

Instructions

(a) Record the transactions.

(b) Determine the cost of the land, land improvements, and building that will appear on Kadlec's December 31, 2009, balance sheet.

Classify operating and capital expenditures.
(SO 1)

P9–2A The following expenditures are for a forklift:

1. Rebuilding of the diesel engine, $10,000

2. New tires, $4,000

3. New safety cab, $5,000

4. Replacement of the windshield, $800

5. Training a new operator, $1,600

6. New paint job after the company changed its logo and colours, $2,000

7. One-year accident insurance policy, $1,110

8. To increase efficiency, paid an operator $2,400 to reorganize where items were stored in the warehouse.

Instructions

For each of the transactions listed above, indicate the title of the account that you think should be debited in recording the transaction. Briefly explain your reasoning.

Determine cost; calculate depreciation under different methods.
(SO 1, 2)

P9–3A The Moussaoui Corporation purchased a machine on September 3, 2009, at a cash price of $93,900. On September 4, it paid $600 for delivery of the machine. A one-year, $975 insurance policy on the machine was purchased on September 6. On September 20, Moussaoui paid $3,500 for installation and testing of the machine. The machine was ready for use on September 30.

Moussaoui estimates the useful life of the machine will be four years, or 40,000 units, with no residual value. Assume the equipment produces the following number of units each year: 2,500 units in 2009; 10,300 units in 2010; 9,900 units in 2011; 8,800 units in 2012; and 8,500 units in 2013. Moussaoui has a December 31 year end.

Instructions

(a) Determine the cost of the machine.

(b) Calculate the annual depreciation and the total depreciation over the asset's life using (1) straight-line depreciation, and (2) units-of-production depreciation.

(c) Assume instead that when Moussaoui Corporation purchased the machine, the company had a legal obligation to ensure that the machine would be recycled at the end of its useful life and that the cost of this recycling would be significant. Would this have an impact on the answers to (a) and (b) above? Explain.

Calculate and compare
depreciation under different
methods.
(SO 2)

P9–4A Piper Corporation purchased machinery on January 1, 2009, at a cost of $280,000. The estimated useful life of the machinery is five years, with a residual value of $10,000. The company is considering which depreciation method to use for financial reporting purposes.

Instructions

(a) Prepare separate depreciation schedules for the life of the machinery using the straight-line and double diminishing-balance methods.

(b) Which method would result in the higher net earnings for 2009? In the higher total net earnings over the five-year period?

(c) Which method would result in the higher carrying amount at the end of 2009? In the higher carrying amount at the end of the five-year period?

(d) Which method would result in the higher cash flow for 2009? In the higher total cash flow over the five-year period?

(e) What factors should management consider when deciding on the appropriate depreciation method?

Calculate and compare
depreciation under different
methods.
(SO 2)

P9–5A Rapid Transportation Ltd. purchased a new bus on October 3, 2009, at a cost of $130,000. Management is contemplating the merits of using the diminishing-balance or units-of-production methods of depreciation instead of the straight-line method, which it currently uses for other buses. The new bus has an estimated residual value of $10,000, and an estimated useful life of either three years or 300,000 kilometres. Assume the bus is driven as follows: 15,000 kilometres in 2009; 130,000 kilometres in 2010; 65,000 kilometres in 2011; and 90,000 kilometres in 2012. Rapid Transportation has a December 31 year end.

Instructions

(a) Prepare separate depreciation schedules for the life of the bus using the straight-line method, the diminishing-balance method using double the straight-line rate, and the units-of-production method.

(b) Compare the total depreciation expense and accumulated depreciation under each of the three methods over the life of the bus.

(c) Which method do you recommend? Why?

Calculate and compare
depreciation and gains or
losses on disposal under
different depreciation
methods.
(SO 2, 4)

P9–6A PEI Productions Ltd. purchased equipment on December 31, 2009, for $50,000. The company estimated the equipment would have a useful life of three years, or 10,000 units, with a residual value of $10,000. During 2010, the equipment produced 4,000 units. On October 31, 2011, the machine was sold for $12,000; it had produced 5,000 units in 2011.

Instructions

(a) Record all the necessary entries for the years ended December 31, 2010 and 2011 for the following depreciation methods: (1) straight-line, (2) single diminishing-balance, and (3) units-of-production.

(b) Prepare a schedule to show the overall impact of the total depreciation expense, combined with the gain or loss on sale for the two-year period, under each method of depreciation (consider the total effect on net earnings over the two-year period). Comment on your results.

Record property, plant, and
equipment transactions;
prepare partial balance sheet.
(SO 2, 4, 6)

P9–7A At January 1, 2009, Yount Corporation reported the following property, plant, and equipment accounts:

Accumulated depreciation—buildings	$12,100,000
Accumulated depreciation—equipment	15,000,000
Buildings	28,500,000
Equipment	48,000,000
Land	4,000,000

Yount uses straight-line depreciation for buildings and equipment, and its fiscal year end is December 31. The buildings are estimated to have a 50-year life and no residual value; the equipment is estimated to have a 10-year useful life and no residual value. Interest on all notes is payable or collectible at maturity on the anniversary date of the issue.

During 2009, the following selected transactions occurred:

Apr.   1 Purchased land for $1.9 million. Paid $475,000 cash and issued a 10-year, 6% note for the balance.

May   1 Sold equipment for $350,000 cash. The equipment cost $750,000 when it was originally purchased on January 1, 2005.

June   1 Sold land for $1.2 million. Received $380,000 cash and accepted a 6% note for the balance. The land cost $300,000 when purchased on June 1, 1993.

July   1 Purchased equipment for $1 million on account, terms n/60.

Aug. 30   Paid amount owing on account for purchase of equipment on July 1.

Dec. 31   Retired equipment that cost $470,000 when purchased on December 31, 1999.

Instructions

(a) Record the above transactions.

(b) Record any adjusting entries required at December 31.

(c) Prepare the property, plant, and equipment section of Yount's balance sheet at December 31, 2009.

Calculate depreciation; discuss revision of estimate.
(SO 2, 3)

P9–8A   On January 1, 2007, Bérubé Ltée acquired equipment costing $60,000. It was estimated at that time that this equipment would have a useful life of five years and a residual value of $4,500. The straight-line method of depreciation is used by Bérubé for its equipment, and its fiscal year end is December 31.

At the beginning of 2009 (the beginning of the third year of the equipment's life), the company's engineers reconsidered their expectations. They estimated that the equipment's useful life would more likely be seven years in total, instead of the previously estimated five years.

Instructions

(a) Calculate the accumulated depreciation and carrying amount of the equipment at the beginning of 2009, immediately before the change in useful life.

(b) Would you expect Bérubé's depreciation expense to increase or decrease in 2009 after the change in useful life? Explain why.

(c) Should Bérubé treat the change in the useful life retroactively or only for current and future periods? Explain.

(d) If Bérubé had *not* revised the equipment's remaining useful life at the beginning of 2009, what would its total depreciation expense have been over the equipment's life? What would have been the accumulated depreciation and carrying amount at the end of the equipment's useful life?

(e) Would you expect Bérubé's total depreciation expense to change after the useful life has been revised? Would there be changes to the accumulated depreciation and carrying amount at the end of the equipment's useful life?

Record acquisition, depreciation, and disposal of equipment.
(SO 2, 4)

P9–9A   Walker Corp. purchased office furniture on February 1, 2007, for $85,000 on account. At that time, the furniture was estimated to have a useful life of five years and a $1,000 residual value. The furniture was disposed of on June 2, 2009, when the company relocated to new premises. Walker uses the straight-line method of depreciation and has a September 30 year end.

Instructions

(a) Record the acquisition of the office furniture on February 1, 2007.

(b) Record the depreciation at September 30, 2007 and 2008.

(c) Record the disposal of the office furniture on June 2, 2009, under each of the following independent assumptions:
   1. It was sold for $50,000.
   2. It was sold for $40,000.
   3. It was retired.

Record acquisition, depreciation, impairment, and disposal of equipment.
(SO 2, 3, 4)

P9–10A   Arnison Corp. purchased land and a building on May 1, 2008, for $385,000. The company paid $115,000 in cash and signed a 5% note payable for the balance. At that time, it estimated that the land was worth $150,000 and the building $235,000. The building was estimated to have a 25-year useful life with a

$35,000 residual value. The company has a December 31 year end and uses the single diminishing-balance depreciation method for buildings. The following are related transactions and adjustments during the next three years:

2008

Dec. 31   Recorded the annual depreciation.

     31   Paid the interest owing on the note payable.

2009

Feb. 17   Paid $225 to have the furnace cleaned and serviced.

Dec. 31   Recorded the annual depreciation.

     31   Paid the interest owing on the note payable.

     31   The land and building were tested for impairment. The land had a recoverable amount of $120,000 and the building $240,000.

2010

Jan. 31   Sold the land and building for $320,000 cash—$110,000 for the land and $210,000 for the building.

Feb. 1   Paid the note payable and interest owing.

Instructions

(a) Record the above transactions and adjustments.

(b) What factors may have been responsible for the impairment?

(c) Assume instead that the company sold the land and building on January 31, 2010, for $400,000 cash—$160,000 for the land and $240,000 for the building. Record the journal entry (or entries) to record the sale.

P9–11A Due to rapid employee turnover in the accounting department, the following transactions involving intangible assets were recorded in a questionable way by Baiji Ltd. in the year ended December 31, 2009:

Correct errors in recording intangible asset transactions. (SO 5)

1. Baiji developed an electronic monitoring device for running shoes. It incurred research costs of $70,000 and development costs with probable future benefits of $45,000. It recorded all of these costs in the Patent account.

2. The company registered the patent for the "cyber shoe" device developed in transaction 1. Legal fees and registration costs totalled $21,000. These costs were recorded in the Legal Fees Expense account.

3. The company successfully fought off a competitor in court to defend its patent, incurring $38,000 of legal fees. These costs were debited to the Legal Fees Expense account.

4. The company recorded $5,750 of annual amortization for the patent over its legal life of 20 years [$70,000 + $45,000 = $115,000 ÷ 20 years]. The expected useful life of the patent is five years. In calculating the amortization, assume that all costs occurred at the beginning of the year.

5. Baiji tested the patent for impairment and found that its recoverable amount of $110,000 exceeded its carrying amount of $109,250 ($115,000 – $5,750). Since Baiji follows the cost model, it did not record an adjustment.

Instructions

Prepare the necessary journal entries to correct any errors made in recording the above transactions.

P9–12A The intangible assets reported by Ip Corp. at December 31, 2008, follow:

Record intangible asset transactions; prepare partial balance sheet. (SO 5, 6)

Patent #1	$70,000	
Less: Accumulated amortization	14,000	$ 56,000
Copyright #1	$48,000	
Less: Accumulated amortization	28,800	19,200
Goodwill		210,000
Total		$285,200

▸ Reporting and Analyzing Long-Lived Assets

Patent #1 was acquired in January 2007 and has a useful life of 10 years. Copyright #1 was acquired in January 2004 and also has a useful life of 10 years. The following cash transactions may have affected intangible assets during 2009:

Jan. 2 Paid $22,500 in legal costs to successfully defend patent #1 against infringement by another company. Determined that the revised annual amortization for this patent will be $9,812.

July 1 Developed a new product, incurring $220,000 in research costs and $60,000 in development costs. Patent #2 was granted for the product on July 1, and its useful life is equal to its legal life of 20 years.

Sept. 1 Paid $11,000 to an Olympic rower to appear in commercials advertising the company's products. The commercials will air in September.

Oct. 1 Acquired a second copyright for $16,000. Copyright #2 has a useful life of five years.

Dec. 31 Determined the recoverable amount of the goodwill to be $175,000. There was no indication that the patents and copyrights were impaired.

Instructions

(a) Prepare the journal entries to record the above transactions.

(b) Prepare any adjusting journal entries required at December 31, the company's year end.

(c) Prepare the intangible assets section of the balance sheet at December 31, 2009.

Calculate and evaluate ratios.
(SO 7)

P9–13A ◖◗ Sapporo Breweries Ltd. (the parent company of Canada's Sleeman Breweries) and Asahi Breweries, Ltd. are two leading beer companies in Japan. They reported the following information at December 31, 2007 (in millions of yen):

	Sapporo	Asahi
Total assets, Dec. 31, 2007	¥561,859	¥1,324,392
Total assets, Dec. 31, 2006	589,597	1,288,501
Net sales	449,011	1,464,072
Net earnings	5,509	44,798

Industry averages are as follows: profit margin, 1.7%; return on assets, 1.1%; and asset turnover, 0.7 times.

Instructions

(a) For each company, calculate the profit margin, return on assets, and asset turnover ratios for 2007.

(b) Based on your calculations in part (a), comment on how effectively each company is using its assets to generate sales and produce net earnings.

(c) What, if anything, complicates your ability to compare the two companies in (b)?

Evaluate ratios.
(SO 7)

P9–14A ◖◗ The following ratios are available for a company operating in the computer industry:

	Company	Industry Average
Return on assets	7.5%	8.9%
Profit margin	8.5%	17.9%
Asset turnover	0.9 times	0.5 times

Instructions

(a) The company's return on assets and profit margin are lower than the industry averages, yet its asset turnover is higher than the industry average. Explain whether margin (profit margin) or volume (asset turnover) is the main factor that is driving the company's return on assets compared to that of the industry.

(b) Speculate on this company's strategy for computer sales compared to that of its competitors in the industry.

Problems: Set B

P9–1B   In 2009, Weisman Ltd. had the following transactions related to the purchase of property. Assume all transactions are for cash unless otherwise stated.

Analyze and record property transactions.
(SO 1)

Feb.   7   Purchased real estate for $275,000, paying $75,000 cash and signing a note payable for the balance. The site had an old building on it and the fair values of the land and building were $250,000 and $25,000, respectively. Weisman intends to construct an apartment building on the site.

       9   Paid legal fees of $5,500 on the real estate purchase of February 7.

      15   Paid $15,000 to demolish the old building and make the land ready for the construction of the apartment building.

      17   Received $4,000 from the sale of material from the demolished building.

Mar.   2   Architect fees on the apartment building were $18,000.

July   5   The full cost for construction of the apartment building was $650,000. Paid $170,000 cash and signed a note payable for the balance.

Aug. 22   Paid $12,000 for sidewalks and a parking lot for the building.

Sept. 1   Purchased a one-year insurance policy on the finished building for $2,500.

Instructions

(a) Record the transactions.

(b) Determine the cost of the land, land improvements, and building that will appear on Weisman's December 31, 2009, balance sheet.

P9–2B   The transactions that follow are expenditures related to property, plant, and equipment:

Classify operating and capital expenditures.
(SO 1)

1. Operator controls on equipment were replaced for $7,000, because the original control devices were not adequate.

2. A total of $4,600 was spent for decorative landscaping (planting flowers and shrubs, etc.).

3. A new air conditioning system for the factory office was purchased for $16,000.

4. Windows broken in a labour dispute were replaced for $2,400.

5. A fee of $1,500 was paid for adjusting and testing new machinery before its use.

6. Machinery damaged by a forklift was repaired for $5,000.

7. The transmission in a delivery truck was repaired for $2,500.

8. Expenditures totalling $3,000 were incurred to repaint the exterior of the factory.

Instructions

For each of the transactions listed above, indicate the title of the account that you think should be debited in recording the transaction. Briefly explain your reasoning.

P9–3B   Mazlish Corporation purchased a machine on account on April 6, 2009, at an invoice price of $180,000. On April 7, it paid $1,000 for delivery of the machine. A one-year, $2,000 insurance policy on the machine was purchased on April 9. On April 22, Mazlish paid $4,000 for installation and testing of the machine. The machine was ready for use on April 30.

Determine cost; calculate depreciation under different methods.
(SO 1, 2)

Mazlish estimates the useful life of the machine will be five years with a residual value of $40,000. Mazlish has a December 31 year end.

Instructions

(a) Determine the cost of the machine.

(b) Calculate the annual depreciation and total depreciation over the asset's life using (1) straight-line depreciation, and (2) single diminishing-balance depreciation.

(c) Assume instead that when Mazlish Corporation purchased the machine, there was no residual value and the company had a legal obligation to ensure that the machine would be recycled at the end of its useful life. The cost of the recycling will be significant. Would this have an impact on the answers to (a) and (b) above? Explain.

Calculate and compare
depreciation under different
methods.
(SO 2)

P9–4B   ◔◖ Whitley Corporation purchased machinery on January 1, 2009, at a cost of $450,000. The estimated useful life of the machinery is four years or 350,000 units, with a residual value of $12,500. The machine actually produces 115,000 units in 2009; 95,000 units in 2010; 75,000 units in 2011; and 65,000 units in 2012. The company is considering which depreciation method should be used for financial reporting purposes.

Instructions

(a) Prepare separate depreciation schedules for the life of the machinery using the straight-line and units-of-production methods.

(b) Which method would result in the lower net earnings for 2009? In the lower total net earnings over the four-year period?

(c) Which method would result in the lower carrying amount at the end of 2009? In the lower carrying amount at the end of the four-year period?

(d) Which method would result in the lower cash flow for 2009? In the lower total cash flow over the four-year period?

(e) What factors should management consider when deciding on the appropriate depreciation method?

Calculate and compare
depreciation under different
methods.
(SO 2)

P9–5B   Quai d'Valmy Inc. purchased a piece of high-tech equipment on March 27, 2009, at a cost of $61,000. Management is contemplating the merits of using the diminishing-balance or units-of-production method of depreciation instead of the straight-line method, which it currently uses for other equipment. The new equipment has an estimated residual value of $1,000 and an estimated useful life of either three years or 30,000 units. Assume the equipment produces the following number of units each year: 7,400 units in 2009; 10,200 units in 2010; 9,900 units in 2011; and 2,500 units in 2012. Quai d'Valmy Inc. has a December 31 year end.

Instructions

(a) Prepare separate depreciation schedules for the life of the equipment using the straight-line method, the diminishing-balance method using double the straight-line rate, and the units-of-production method.

(b) Compare the total depreciation expense and accumulated depreciation under each of the three methods over the life of the equipment

(c) Which method do you recommend? Why?

Calculate and compare
depreciation and gains or
losses on disposal under
different depreciation
methods.
(SO 2, 4)

P9–6B   Yukon Productions Corp. purchased equipment on December 31, 2009, for $70,000. The company estimated the equipment would have a useful life of three years, or 12,000 units, with a residual value of $10,000. During 2010, the equipment produced 4,900 units. On November 30, 2011, the machine was sold for $18,000 and had produced 5,600 units that year.

Instructions

(a) Record all the necessary entries for the years ended December 31, 2010 and 2011 using the following depreciation methods: (1) straight-line, (2) single diminishing-balance, and (3) units-of-production.

(b) Prepare a schedule to show the overall impact of the total depreciation expense, combined with the gain or loss on sale for the two-year period, under each method of depreciation (consider the total effect on net earnings over the two-year period). Comment on your results.

Record property, plant, and
equipment transactions;
prepare partial balance sheet.
(SO 2, 4, 6)

P9–7B   At January 1, 2009, Hamsmith Corporation reported the following property, plant, and equipment accounts:

Accumulated depreciation—buildings	$31,100,000
Accumulated depreciation—equipment	27,000,000
Buildings	48,700,000
Equipment	75,000,000
Land	10,000,000

Hamsmith uses straight-line depreciation for buildings and equipment, and its fiscal year end is December 31. The buildings are estimated to have a 50-year useful life and no residual value; the equipment is estimated to have a 10-year useful life and no residual value. Interest on the notes (described below) is due annually on the anniversary date of the issue.

During 2009, the following selected transactions occurred:

Apr.   1   Purchased land for $2.2 million. Paid $550,000 cash and issued a three-year, 6% note for the balance.

May   1   Sold equipment for $150,000 cash. The equipment cost $1,400,000 when originally purchased on January 1, 2001.

June 1   Sold land for $1.8 million. Received $450,000 cash and accepted a three-year, 5% note for the balance. The land cost $700,000 when purchased on June 1, 2003.

July   1   Purchased equipment for $1.1 million cash.

Dec. 31   Retired equipment that cost $500,000 when purchased on December 31, 1999.

Instructions

(a) Record the above transactions.

(b) Record any adjusting entries required at December 31.

(c) Prepare the property, plant, and equipment section of Hamsmith's balance sheet at December 31, 2009.

P9–8B   On January 1, 2007, Penaji Corporation acquired equipment costing $65,000. It was estimated at that time that this equipment would have a useful life of eight years and a residual value of $3,000. The straight-line method of depreciation is used by Penaji for its equipment, and its fiscal year end is December 31.

Calculate depreciation; discuss revision of estimate.
(SO 2, 3)

At the beginning of 2009 (the beginning of the third year of the equipment's life), the company's engineers reconsidered their expectations. They estimated that the equipment's useful life would more likely be six years in total, instead of the previously estimated eight years.

Instructions

(a) Calculate the accumulated depreciation and carrying amount of the equipment at the beginning of 2009 immediately before the change in useful life.

(b) Would you expect Penaji's depreciation expense to increase or decrease in 2009 after the change in useful life? Explain why.

(c) Should Penaji treat the change in useful life retroactively or only for current and future periods? Explain.

(d) If Penaji had *not* revised the equipment's remaining useful life at the beginning of 2009, what would its total depreciation expense have been over the equipment's life? What would have been the accumulated depreciation and carrying amount at the end of the equipment's useful life?

(e) Would you expect Penaji's total depreciation expense to change after the useful life has been revised? Would there be changes to the accumulated depreciation and carrying amount at the end of the equipment's useful life?

P9–9B   Express Corp. purchased delivery equipment on March 1, 2007, for $65,000 cash. At that time, the equipment was estimated to have a useful life of five years and a residual value of $5,000. The equipment was disposed of on September 30, 2009. Express uses the straight-line method of depreciation and has an August 31 year end.

Record acquisition, depreciation, and disposal of equipment.
(SO 2, 4)

Instructions

(a) Record the acquisition of equipment on March 1, 2007.

(b) Record depreciation at August 31, 2007, 2008, and 2009.

(c) Record the disposal of the equipment on September 30, 2009, under each of the following independent assumptions:
   1. It was sold for $30,000.
   2. It was sold for $40,000.
   3. It was retired.

P9–10B Sugden Limited purchased land and a building on August 1, 2008, for $595,000. The company paid $200,000 in cash and signed a 5% note payable for the balance. At that time, it estimated that the land was worth $340,000 and the building $255,000. The building was estimated to have a 40-year useful life with a $15,000 residual value. The company has a December 31 year end and uses the straight-line depreciation method for buildings. The following are related transactions and adjustments during the next three years:

2008
Dec. 31   Recorded the annual depreciation.
     31   Paid the interest owing on the note payable.

2009
May 21   Paid $2,000 for repairs to the roof.
Dec. 31   Recorded the annual depreciation.
     31   Paid the interest owing on the note payable.
     31   The land and building were tested for impairment. The land had a recoverable amount of $280,000 and the building $249,000.

2010
Mar. 31   Sold the land and building for $480,000 cash—$250,000 for the land and $230,000 for the building.
Apr. 1   Paid the note payable and interest owing.

Instructions

(a) Record the above transactions and adjustments.

(b) What factors may have been responsible for the impairment?

(c) Assume instead that the company sold the land and building on March 31, 2010, for $650,000 cash—$390,000 for the land and $260,000 for the building. Record the journal entry (or entries) to record the sale.

P9–11B Due to rapid employee turnover in the accounting department, the following transactions involving intangible assets were recorded in a questionable way by Riley Corporation in the year ended December 31, 2009:

1. Riley developed a new manufacturing process at the beginning of the year, incurring research costs of $160,000. Of this amount, 45% was considered to be development costs that could be capitalized. Riley recorded the entire $160,000 in the Patents account and amortized it over a 15-year useful life.

2. On July 1, 2009, Riley purchased a small company and recorded goodwill of $400,000 as part of the transaction. Riley recorded a half year's amortization for the goodwill in 2009, based on an estimated 40-year life.

3. The company purchased a trademark for $47,500. Shortly thereafter, it was sued for trademark infringement. At the end of the year, Riley determined that the recoverable amount of the trademark was $35,000. Riley did not record an impairment loss, because Riley is hopeful that the recoverable amount will rebound next year after the conclusion of the legal case defending the company's right to use this trademark.

4. The company made a $6,000 charitable donation on December 31, 2009, which it debited to goodwill.

Instructions
Prepare the necessary journal entries to correct any errors made in recording the above transactions.

P9–12B The intangible assets section of Ghani Corporation's balance sheet at December 31, 2008, follows:

Copyright #1	$36,000	
Less: Accumulated amortization	24,000	$ 12,000
Trademark		54,000
Goodwill		125,000
Total		$191,000

The copyright was acquired on January 1, 2007, and has a useful life of three years. The trademark was acquired on January 1, 2005, and is expected to have an indefinite life. The company has a December 31 year end.

The following cash transactions may have affected intangible assets during 2009:

Jan.   5   Paid $7,000 in legal costs to successfully defend the trademark against infringement by another company.

July   1   Developed a new product, incurring $210,000 in research and $50,000 in development costs. A patent was granted for the product on July 1, and its useful life is equal to its legal life of 20 years.

Sept. 1   Paid $60,000 to a popular hockey player to appear in commercials advertising the company's products. The commercials will air in September and October.

Oct.   1   Acquired another copyright for $180,000. The new copyright has a useful life of three years.

Dec. 31   Determined the recoverable amount of the trademark and goodwill to be $65,000 and $90,000, respectively. There was no indication that any of the patents or copyrights were impaired.

Instructions

(a) Prepare journal entries to record the transactions.

(b) Prepare any adjusting journal entries required at December 31.

(c) Prepare the intangible assets section of the balance sheet at December 31, 2009.

P9–13B ◼◻ Green Mountain Coffee Roasters, Inc. and Starbucks Corporation reported the following information in 2007 (in USD millions):

Calculate and evaluate ratios. (SO 7)

	Green Mountain	Starbucks
Total assets, 2007	$264.5	$5,343.9
Total assets, 2006	234.0	4,429.9
Net sales	341.7	9,411.5
Net earnings	12.8	672.6

Industry averages are as follows: profit margin, 3.5%; return on assets, 5.2%; and asset turnover, 1.5 times.

Instructions

(a) For each company, calculate the profit margin, return on assets, and asset turnover ratios for 2007.

(b) Based on your calculations in part (a), comment on how effectively each company is using its assets to generate sales and produce net earnings.

(c) What, if anything, complicates your ability to compare the two companies in (b)?

P9–14B ◼◻ The following ratios are available for a company operating in the restaurant industry:

Evaluate ratios. (SO 7)

	Company	Industry Average
Return on assets	8.2%	7.0%
Profit margin	12.0%	6.4%
Asset turnover	0.7 times	1.2 times

Instructions

(a) The company's return on assets and profit margin are higher than that of the industry, yet its asset turnover is lower than the industry average. Explain whether margin (profit margin) or volume (asset turnover) is the main factor that is driving the company's return on assets compared to that of the industry.

(b) Explain how the company might be able to improve its asset turnover ratio and what impact this might have on the profit margin and return on assets.

BROADENING YOUR PERSPECTIVE

Analysis Tools

Financial Reporting and Analysis Cases

Financial Reporting: *Shoppers Drug Mart*

BYP9–1 The financial statements of Shoppers Drug Mart Corporation are presented in Appendix A at the end of this textbook.

Instructions

(a) What amortization method is used by Shoppers Drug Mart? (Note that Shoppers uses the term amortization rather than depreciation.)

(b) Identify the following amounts for the company's property and equipment at the end of fiscal 2007 and 2006: (1) cost, (2) accumulated amortization, and (3) carrying amount.

(c) What was the amount of amortization expense reported in the statement of earnings for fiscal 2007? What is the difference between the accumulated amortization reported at the end of fiscal 2007 and 2006 (see Note 6)? Why is this difference not the same as the amortization expense reported in 2007?

(d) Using the cash flow statement, determine what amount of cash was received from property and equipment sales and what amount of cash was spent for property and equipment purchases in 2007.

(e) What type of intangible assets does Shoppers Drug Mart have?

(f) Did Shoppers Drug Mart report any impairment losses in 2007?

Comparative Analysis: *Shoppers Drug Mart and Jean Coutu*

BYP9–2 The financial statements of Jean Coutu are presented in Appendix B following the financial statements for Shoppers Drug Mart in Appendix A.

Instructions

(a) Based on the information in these financial statements, calculate the following values for each company for its most recent fiscal year:
   1. Profit margin
   2. Return on assets
   3. Asset turnover

(b) Industry averages for the above three ratios are as follows: profit margin, (1.1)%; return on assets, 2.0%; and asset turnover, 1.7 times. What conclusions about the management of assets can be drawn from your results in (a) and these data?

Interpreting Financial Statements

BYP9–3 Potash Corporation of Saskatchewan Inc. (PotashCorp) is an integrated producer of fertilizer and industrial products, as well as animal feed products. In New Brunswick, PotashCorp is investing $1.7 billion in both a new 2-million-tonne mine and a 1.2-million-tonne enhancement to an existing facility in the province. The expansion is expected to be completed in 2011.

Instructions

(a) Identify and discuss the advantages and disadvantages of each depreciation method—straight-line, diminishing-balance, and units-of-production. Which method would you recommend PotashCorp use to depreciate its property, plant, and equipment at its new mine? Explain why you chose this method.

(b) How should PotashCorp account for the cost of the 1.2-million-tonne enhancement to the existing facility? Discuss whether the costs in regard to the enhancement should be treated as operating expenditures or capital expenditures, and the impact on future depreciation, if any.

A Global Focus

BYP9–4 Headquartered in France, Vivendi S.A. is a world leader in entertainment. The following discussion of asset impairment was taken from the notes to the company's 2007 financial statements:

> **VIVENDI S.A.**
> **Notes to the Financial Statements**
> **December 31, 2007**   
>
> **1.3.5.6. Asset impairment**
>
> Each time events or changes in the economic environment indicate a current risk of impairment of goodwill, other intangible assets, property, plant and equipment and assets in progress, Vivendi re-examines the value of these assets. In addition, goodwill, other indefinite life intangible assets as well as assets in progress are subject to an annual impairment test during the fourth quarter of each fiscal year. This test is performed in order to compare the carrying amount of each group's operating units to the carrying amount of the corresponding assets (including goodwill) … The impairment losses recognized in respect of property, plant and equipment and intangible assets (other than goodwill) may be reversed in a later period if the recoverable amount becomes greater than the carrying amount, within the limit of impairment losses previously recognized. Impairment losses recognized in respect of goodwill cannot be reversed.
>
> Total impairment losses recorded in 2007 amounted to €34 million and were recognized as a deduction from goodwill (€6 million) and other intangible assets (€28 million).

Instructions

(a) Vivendi follows international accounting principles. How does the company's treatment of the impairment losses compare with accounting practices currently in use in Canada?

(b) Reproduce the journal entry that Vivendi would have made to record the impairment loss in 2007.

(c) How will this write-down affect Vivendi's balance sheet and statement of earnings in future years?

Critical Thinking Cases and Activities

Collaborative Learning Activity

BYP9–5 The reporting of long-lived assets in the financial statements is often described as the area that is most dependent on management judgement and estimates. The result is that companies with similar performance in their day-to-day operations may report significantly different earnings.

Areas affecting financial reporting include:

1. The decision to lease or purchase long-lived assets
2. Depreciation of buildings and equipment
3. Determining the impairment of assets
4. Treatment of research and development costs

Instructions

After the class has been divided into groups and you have been assigned one of the four areas listed above, do the following:

(a) Identify where management makes judgements that will affect the reported financial results for your chosen area.

(b) Identify the effect of the judgements you identified in (a) on key financial statement totals and ratios.

Communication Activity

BYP9–6 John Bull, the chief financial officer of a real estate company, has been asked to review International Accounting Standard (IAS) 16 to see how it would apply to the company. IAS 16 permits two accounting models for the treatment of property, plant, and equipment:

- Cost Model: Assets are carried at their cost less accumulated depreciation and impairment.

- Revaluation Model: Assets are carried at a revalued amount, which is the asset's fair value at the date of revaluation less subsequent depreciation and impairment, and provided that the fair value can be measured reliably.

Under the revaluation model, revaluations should be done regularly so that the carrying amount of an asset does not differ materially from its fair value at the balance sheet date.

If a revaluation results in an increase in value, it should be credited to equity under the heading "Revaluation surplus," with one exception: if the increase is actually a reversal of a revaluation decrease for the same asset that was previously recognized as an expense, the increase should instead be recognized as income.

Instructions

Write a letter to John that outlines the advantages and disadvantages of increasing the value of property, plant, and equipment in a real estate company. You should discuss in your letter the depreciable amount, the subsequent disposal of a revalued asset, and any other points that you wish to raise.

Ethics Case

Ethics in Accounting

BYP9–7 Imporia Container Ltd. is suffering from declining sales of its main product, nonbiodegradable plastic cartons. The president, Benny Benson, instructs his controller, Yeoh Siew Hoon, to lengthen asset lives to reduce their depreciation expense.

A processing line of automated plastic extruding equipment, purchased for $3 million in January 2007, was originally estimated to have a useful life of five years and a residual value of $200,000. Depreciation has been recorded for two years on that basis. Benny wants the estimated useful life changed to a total of seven years. Yeoh Siew is hesitant to make the change, believing it inappropriate to "manage earnings" in this way. Benny says, "Hey, the useful life is only an estimate, and I've heard that our competition uses a seven-year life on their production equipment."

Instructions

(a) Who are the stakeholders in this situation?

(b) Will Benny Benson's proposed change in useful life increase or decrease net earnings in 2009?

(c) Discuss whether the proposed change in useful life is unethical or simply a good business practice by an astute president.

"All About You" Activity

BYP9–8 The "All About You" feature in this chapter discusses the advantages of buying or leasing a vehicle. You probably have a vehicle in mind that you would like to purchase some day and may have explored everything from the colour, to the options, to the engine. Now it's time to explore the facts about leasing and buying.

Instructions

(a) Go to Canada's Office of Consumer Affairs Lease or Buy website at ic.gc.ca/epic/site/oca-bc.nsf/en/ca01851e.html to determine how much leasing or buying will cost in the case of a car. The calculator will give you a comparison of three ownership options over an eight-year time period. Before you use the calculator, you should read "What the calculator can do for you" and "How to use the calculator." Why would an eight-year time period be used in the calculation?

(b) Go to the calculator and see the completed calculation for the purchase of a vehicle in Ontario. What is the amount of interest to be paid? Enter another province and calculate the interest. Is the interest the same as the Ontario calculation? Why or why not?

(c) Click on the radio button beside leasing option 1 and click on Submit twice. How much interest would be charged on this option? What is the total outlay including maintenance costs for the purchase of the vehicle? For the lease?

(d) Click on the radio button beside leasing option 2 and click on Submit twice. How much interest would be charged on this option? What is the total outlay including maintenance costs for this option?

(e) Which of the three options would you prefer and why?

Serial Case

(*Note:* This is a continuation of the serial case from Chapters 1 through 8.)

BYP9–9 Cookie Creations is thinking about purchasing a van on August 17, 2009, and having it ready for use on September 1. The cost of the van is estimated to be $34,500. An additional $2,500 would be spent to have the van painted. The back seat of the van would also be removed to make more room for transporting the mixer inventory and baking supplies. The cost of taking out the back seat and installing shelving units is estimated at $1,500. It is expected that the estimated useful life of the van will be five years or 200,000 kilometres. It is estimated that the van will be driven as follows: 15,000 km in 2009; 45,000 km in 2010; 50,000 km in 2011; 45,000 in 2012; 35,000 in 2013; and 10,000 km in 2014. The annual cost of vehicle insurance will be $2,400. At the end of its useful life, it is expected that the van will sell for $6,500.

Natalie is concerned about the impact of the van's cost on Cookie Creations' statement of earnings and balance sheet. She has come to you for advice on how the purchase of the van will affect her company's financial position.

Natalie is also concerned about how Cookie Creations will finance the purchase of the van. She has come to you with questions about leasing rather than buying the van.

Instructions

(a) Determine the cost of the van.

(b) Prepare schedules for each method of depreciation: (1) straight-line, (2) double diminishing-balance, and (3) units-of-production. Recall that Cookie Creations has a December 31 year end.

(c) What impact will each method of depreciation have on Cookie Creations' balance sheet at December 31, 2009? What impact will each method have on Cookie Creations' statement of earnings for the year ended December 31, 2009?

(d) What impact will each method of depreciation have on Cookie Creations' statement of earnings in total over the van's five-year useful life?

(e) What impact will each method of depreciation have on Cookie Creations' cash flow in total over the van's five-year useful life?

(f) Which method of depreciation would you recommend Cookie Creations use? Explain.

(g) What are some of the advantages and disadvantages of leasing the van instead of buying it?

Answers to Chapter Questions

Answer to Shoppers Drug Mart Review It Question 3
Shoppers Drug Mart depreciates its buildings over 20 years, its equipment and fixtures over a period of 3 to 10 years, and its computer software and equipment over a period of 2 to 10 years. Leasehold improvements are depreciated over the lesser of the term of the lease and the asset's useful life. Note that Shoppers uses the term "amortization" instead of "depreciation" in its financial statements.

Remember to go back to the beginning of the chapter to check off your completed work!

←

Answers to Self-Study Questions

1. c	2. c	3. c	4. b	5. a
6. b	7. a	8. c	9. d	10. d

Comprehensive Case: Chapter 9

Digital Images Ltd. has been in operation for several years. It purchases, customizes, and sells studio sets for its clients. The company's post-closing trial balance at July 31, 2009, the end of its fiscal year, is presented below:

DIGITAL IMAGES LTD. Post-Closing Trial Balance July 31, 2009		
	Debit	Credit
Cash	$ 83,667	
Accounts receivable	1,350,000	
Allowance for doubtful accounts		$ 150,000
Interest receivable	1,333	
Notes receivable	100,000	
Inventory	250,000	
Office equipment	22,000	
Accumulated depreciation—office equipment		9,625
Computer equipment	75,000	
Accumulated depreciation—computer equipment		24,750
Delivery vehicles	130,000	
Accumulated depreciation—delivery vehicles		16,500
Accounts payable		504,500
Bank loan payable		175,000
Common shares		150,000
Retained earnings		981,625
	$2,012,000	$2,012,000

The company had a limited amount of business activity in August 2009 because of holidays for both the company and its major customers. You have been hired on a temporary basis to update the company's records for August. The August transactions and adjustments are presented below:

Aug. 1   Sale on account to Hugo Ltd. for $250,000, terms 2/10, n/30. Cost of goods sold, $95,000. Digital Images uses a perpetual inventory system.

1   Purchase of computer equipment (a digital imaging machine) for $25,000 cash, plus freight and installation, $5,000 cash.

15   All of the old office equipment was sold to a used furniture dealer for $1,000. The original cost of the equipment was $22,000; accumulated depreciation to the date of disposal was $9,625.

15   Determined that an account receivable from Betz Ltd. of $35,000 is uncollectible.

18   Accepted a 6-month, 8% note in exchange for Choi Enterprises' overdue account receivable of $50,000.

31   Purchased new office equipment on account, $12,000. No depreciation is recorded on long-lived assets acquired during the last half of the month.

31   Collected note receivable and interest from Dukakis Ltd. at maturity. The note was originally issued for $100,000 on May 31st of the current year at an 8% interest rate. Interest was due at maturity, and not previously collected.

31   Recorded credit card sales from sales of digital library images for the month, $37,500. Credit card charges are 1.5%. The cost of goods sold is $7,500.

31   Paid $10,000 for the monthly income tax instalment.

31 Recorded depreciation on the new computer equipment acquired August 1. Useful life estimated to be three years with no residual value. The diminishing-balance method of depreciation is used at one times the straight-line rate.

31 Recorded depreciation for the month on the original computer equipment. Original cost $75,000; useful life, 3 years; no estimated residual value. The diminishing-balance method of depreciation is used at one times the straight-line rate.

31 Recorded depreciation for the month on the delivery vehicles. Original cost, $130,000; useful life, 5 years. Estimated kilometres expected to be driven over the 5-year period, 1,000,000. Estimated residual value, $20,000. The units-of-production method of depreciation is used. Actual kilometres driven during August, 8,000.

31 Reviewed outstanding accounts receivable. Determined, through an aging of accounts, that doubtful accounts totalled $175,000 at month-end.

31 Paid invoices for the following: office expenses, $10,000; and rent expense, $18,000.

31 Paid salaries for the month of $50,000.

31 The monthly bank statement revealed the following unrecorded items: interest on bank loan, $750, and bank charges, $65.

Instructions

(a) Record the August transactions and adjustments.

(b) Set up T accounts, enter the July 31 balances, and post the journal entries from (a) to the accounts.

(c) Prepare a trial balance at August 31.

(d) Prepare a multiple-step statement of earnings, statement of retained earnings, and balance sheet at August 31.

CHAPTER 10
Reporting and Analyzing Liabilities

Borrowing Money to Make Money

"You've got to spend money to make money" has become a cliché in the business world. However, for many businesses, you could say "You've got to *borrow* money to make money." For Plazacorp Retail Properties Ltd. in Fredericton, New Brunswick, the revision of this cliché is certainly true.

Plazacorp is owner of shopping malls and strip plazas throughout Atlantic Canada, Quebec, and Ontario. Its assets include 90 properties comprising more than four million square feet of retail real estate, with the Village Mall in St. John's, Newfoundland, and Exhibition Plaza in Saint John, New Brunswick, among them. For all its real estate investments, Plazacorp has used debt financing.

After finding a suitable site in which to invest, Plazacorp buys the land and develops it for either a small strip mall or a stand-alone big box store like Staples or Shoppers Drug Mart. This process involves various types of financing vehicles, including short-term loans, lines of credit, mortgage bonds, and long-term mortgage financing.

"If we were looking to develop a parcel of land, we might buy the land without financing pre-conditions," explains Peter Sheehan, Plazacorp's chief financial officer. "Mortgage bonds are used to fund our purchase price of the land. After closing, we would then seek conventional interim or construction financing for the property and replace the mortgage bonds."

Plazacorp has raised $20.5 million to date in a series of mortgage bond offerings. "The bonds allow Plazacorp to finance new retail developments quickly and efficiently and also provide Plazacorp with the ability to complete and maximize long-term financing for new development properties at the most appropriate time," said President and CEO Michael Zakuta in a news release. In fact mortgage bond offerings helped fund a portion of the 14 development projects Plazacorp undertook in 2007.

Plazacorp's typical approach is to enter into a long-term lease arrangement with a tenant and then begin construction. Construction costs are covered by two development lines of credit that can provide Plazacorp with a combined total of $50 million.

"Once the tenant is paying rent, we seek financing in the long-term mortgage market," says Mr. Sheehan. That could be from any of a number of sources: life insurance companies, banks, pension funds, and conduit or securitized debt lenders. Then, once long-term financing is secured, Plazacorp would look to "recycle" funds for another investment site.

Why continue this cycle of borrowing and investing? Mr. Sheehan explains, using a simplified example: Let's say you invest in land and build a building for a total investment of $3 million, and then rent it for $270,000. If you had done your job well, that building might be worth, say, $3,850,000. You could borrow 75 percent of the building's value, or approximately $2.9 million, with a conventional mortgage. With interest rates at 6.5 percent on a 25-year amortization, the resulting annual mortgage payment is $233,000. So you'll be netting $37,000 ($270,000 – $233,000) on a $100,000 ($3 million – $2.9 million) investment, essentially making a 37-percent return. "Of the $3 million invested initially, we leave $100,000 invested in that property and have recycled $2.9 million to use on other investments. Now that's an extreme example," he stresses. "In the real estate business, you'd be looking to enhance your yield from, say, 9 percent to somewhere between 14 and 20 percent. That's how a developer uses debt to effectively enhance the return."

So why not simply develop the site and sell it at a profit? Mr. Sheehan describes two types of developers: those who buy, build, and flip for an immediate profit; and those who build to hold, using long-term financing to enhance the return. Once the property has reached its absolute income potential, the company might investigate selling it. However, "as long as the debt equation is working, you are not inclined to do so," he says.

acorp Retail Properties: plaza.ca

THE NAVIGATOR

- [ ] Read *Feature Story*
- [ ] Scan *Study Objectives*
- [ ] Read *Chapter Preview*
- [ ] Read text and answer B*efore You Go On*
- [ ] Read *All About You*
- [ ] Review *Summary of Study Objectives*
- [ ] Review *Using the Decision Toolkit— A Summary*
- [ ] Work *Using the Decision Toolkit*
- [ ] Work *Demonstration Problem*
- [ ] Answer *Self-Study Questions*
- [ ] Complete assignments

ЈDY OBJECTIVES

er studying this chapter, you should be able to:

Account for current liabilities.

Account for long-term notes payable.

Account for bonds payable.

Identify the requirements for the financial statement presentation and analysis of liabilities.

PREVIEW OF CHAPTER 10

The feature story indicates that Plazacorp uses debt to finance its growth. It is unlikely that it could have grown from 35 properties to 90 properties over the last five years without debt, but at times debt can also threaten a company's very existence. Given this risk, why do companies borrow money? Why do they sometimes borrow for the short term and other times long term? Aside from bank borrowings, what other kinds of debt might a company incur? In this chapter, we answer these questions.

This chapter is organized as follows:

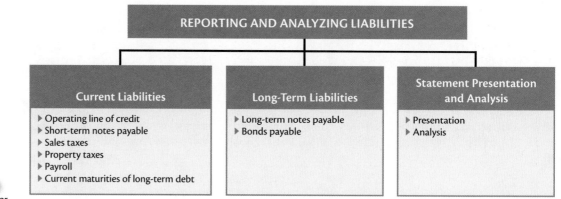

The Navigator

Current Liabilities

In Chapter 2, we defined liabilities as obligations that result from past transactions. These obligations (debts) must be paid some time in the future by the transfer of assets or services. This future payment date (the maturity date) is the reason for the two basic classifications of liabilities: (1) current liabilities, and (2) long-term liabilities.

A **current liability** is a debt that will be paid within one year and from existing current assets or through the creation of other current liabilities. Most companies pay current liabilities out of current assets (e.g., cash) rather than by creating other liabilities (e.g., paying an account payable by issuing a note payable). Debts that do not meet both criteria are classified as **long-term liabilities**.

Financial statement users want to know whether a company's obligations are current or long-term. This is important since a company that has more current liabilities than current assets often lacks liquidity—i.e., short-term debt-paying ability. Users must also look at total (short- and long-term) liabilities in order to assess a company's solvency—its ability to pay its interest and debt when due. Finally, users want to know the types of liabilities a company has.

The different types of current liabilities include bank indebtedness arising from operating lines of credit; notes payable; accounts payable; unearned revenue; accrued liabilities such as taxes, salaries and wages, and interest; and the current portion of long-term debt. Entries for many of these liabilities, including accounts payable and unearned revenue, have been explained in previous chapters. In this section, we discuss operating lines of credit, notes payable, sales taxes, property taxes, payroll, and current maturities of long-term debt in more detail.

Operating Line of Credit

Current assets (such as accounts receivable) do not always turn into cash at the exact time that current liabilities (such as accounts payable) must be paid. Consequently, most companies have an operating line of credit at their bank to help them manage temporary cash shortfalls. This means that the company has been pre-authorized by the bank to borrow money, up to a pre-set limit, when it is needed. Interest is usually charged at a floating interest rate on any amounts used from the line of credit. A floating (or variable) interest rate changes as market rates change and is usually based on the prime borrowing rate. The prime rate is the interest rate that banks charge their best customers. This rate is usually increased by a specified percentage that matches the risk profile of the company.

Security, called collateral, is often required by banks as protection against a possible default on the loan by the borrower. Collateral normally includes some, or all, of the company's current assets (e.g., accounts receivable or inventories), investments, or property, plant, and equipment.

Line of credit borrowings are normally on a short-term basis, and are repayable immediately upon request—that is, on demand—by the bank. In reality, repayment is rarely demanded without notice. A line of credit makes it very easy for a company to borrow money. It does not have to call or visit its bank to actually arrange the transaction. The bank simply covers any cheques written in excess of the bank account balance, up to the approved credit limit.

Amounts drawn on an operating line of credit result in a negative, or overdrawn, cash balance at year end. No special entry is required to record the overdrawn amount. The normal credits to Cash will simply accumulate and are reported as **bank indebtedness** in the current liability section of the balance sheet and with a suitable note disclosure.

Plazacorp has an $8.4-million operating line of credit, which it describes in the notes to its 2007 financial statements. It has drawn $3.568 million of this amount and reports it as bank indebtedness in the current liabilities section of its December 31, 2007, balance sheet. It is important to look not only at any amounts drawn on the operating line of credit, but also at any unused capacity. Amounts available to be drawn in the future from an operating line of credit add to a company's liquidity.

Short-Term Notes Payable

The operating line of credit described above is similar to a note payable. Obligations in the form of written notes are recorded as notes payable. Notes payable are often used instead of accounts payable because they give the lender written documentation of the obligation, which helps if legal action is needed to collect the debt. Notes payable are also frequently issued to meet short-term financing needs.

Notes are issued for varying periods. Notes that are due for payment within one year of the balance sheet date are classified as current liabilities. Most notes are interest-bearing, with interest due monthly or at maturity. While short-term notes can have floating interest rates, similar to that described earlier for an operating line of credit, it is more usual for them to have a fixed interest rate. A fixed interest rate is a constant rate for the entire term of the note.

Students often find it difficult to understand the difference between a note payable and an account payable. There are differences, however. An account payable is an informal promise to pay, while a note payable is a written promise to pay that gives the payee a stronger legal claim. An account payable arises only from credit purchases (amounts owed to suppliers), while a note payable can be used for credit purchases, extending an account payable beyond normal amounts or due dates, or to borrow money. An account payable is usually due within a short period of time (e.g., 30 days), while a note payable can extend for longer periods (e.g., 30 days to several years). Finally, an account payable does not incur interest unless the account is overdue, while a note payable usually bears interest for the entire period of its duration.

To illustrate the accounting for notes payable, assume that HSBC Bank lends $100,000 to Williams Ltd. on March 1, 2009. Williams signs a four-month, 6%, $100,000 note payable. The note matures on July 1 and interest, along with the principal of the note, is payable at maturity.

Williams makes the following journal entry when it receives the $100,000:

Mar. 1	Cash	100,000	
	Notes Payable		100,000
	(To record issue of four-month, 6% note to HSBC Bank)		

A	=	L	+	SE
+100,000		+100,000		

↑ Cash flows: +100,000

Interest accrues over the life of the note and must be recorded periodically. If Williams has a March 31 year end, an adjusting entry is required to recognize the interest expense and interest payable of $500 ($100,000 × 6% × $\frac{1}{12}$) at March 31. Recall from Chapter 4 that interest is calculated for short-term notes by multiplying the principal amount by the annual interest rate by the fraction of the year. That is, the 6% is an annual interest rate and must be adjusted for the monthly time period. Interest rates are always expressed as an annual (one-year) rate, regardless of the term of the note.

The adjusting entry is:

Mar. 31	Interest Expense	500	
	Interest Payable		500
	(To accrue interest for one month on HSBC Bank note)		

A	=	L	+	SE
		+500		−500

Cash flows: no effect

In the March 31 financial statements, the current liabilities section of the balance sheet will show notes payable of $100,000, and interest payable of $500. In addition, interest expense of $500 will be reported as an "other expense" in the statement of earnings.

At maturity (July 1), Williams Ltd. must pay the principal of the note ($100,000) plus $2,000 interest ($100,000 × 6% × ⁴⁄₁₂). One month, $500 for the month of March, of this interest has already been accrued. Interest must also be updated for $1,500 ($100,000 × 6% × ³⁄₁₂) for the three additional months—April through June—since interest was last recorded. This can be done in two separate entries as shown below, or in one compound entry to record the interest and payment of the note.

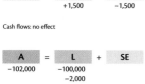

A = L + SE
      +1,500   −1,500

Cash flows: no effect

July	1	Interest Expense	1,500	
		Interest Payable		1,500
		(To accrue interest for April, May, and June)		

A = L + SE
−102,000   −100,000
           −2,000

⬇ Cash flows: −102,000

	1	Note Payable	100,000	
		Interest Payable ($500 + $1,500)	2,000	
		Cash ($100,000 + $2,000)		102,000
		(To record payment of HSBC note and interest at maturity)		

Sales Taxes

As consumers, we are well aware that many of the products and services we purchase are subject to sales taxes. The taxes are expressed as a percentage of the sales price. Sales taxes may take the form of the Goods and Services Tax (GST), Provincial Sales Tax (PST), or Harmonized Sales Tax (HST). In Quebec, the PST is known as the Quebec Sales Tax (QST). In many provinces, sales taxes are collectively known as retail sales tax (RST).

In 2008, the federal GST was assessed at a rate of 5% across Canada. Note that this rate is subject to change. It was 6% in 2007 and 7% before that. At the time of writing this textbook, it is expected that the GST rate will remain at 5% for the foreseeable future.

Provincial sales tax rates vary from 0% to 10% across Canada. In Newfoundland and Labrador, Nova Scotia, and New Brunswick, the PST and GST have been combined into one 13% Harmonized Sales Tax.

As we discussed in Chapter 5, the retailer collects the sales tax from the customer when the sale occurs, and periodically (normally monthly) remits (sends) the sales tax collected to the designated federal and provincial collecting authorities. In the case of GST and HST, collections may be offset against payments (i.e., sales tax payments made by the company on its own eligible purchases). Only the net amount owing or recoverable will be paid or refunded.

The amount of the sale and the amount of the sales tax collected are usually rung up separately on the cash register. The cash register readings are then used to credit the two accounts Sales and Sales Taxes Payable. For example, assuming that the March 25 cash register readings for the Setthawiwat Corporation show sales of $10,000, federal sales taxes of $500 (GST rate of 5%), and provincial sales taxes of $800 (PST rate of 8%), the entry is:

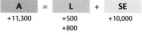

A = L + SE
+11,300   +500   +10,000
          +800

⬆ Cash flows: +11,300

Mar. 25	Cash	11,300	
	Sales		10,000
	GST Payable ($10,000 × 5%)		500
	PST Payable ($10,000 × 8%)		800
	(To record sales and sales taxes)		

When the sales taxes are remitted, GST and PST (or HST) Payable are debited and Cash is credited. The company does not report sales taxes as an expense; it simply forwards the amount paid by the customer to the respective government. Thus, Setthawiwat Corporation is really only a collection agent for the governments.

In all but two provinces, GST is charged on the selling price of the item before PST is applied, thus avoiding GST being charged on PST. In Quebec and Prince Edward Island, PST is charged on GST. For example, in Quebec a $100 sale would result in $5 of GST (5%) and $7.88 of QST [($100 + $5) × 7.5%]. The increased sales tax rate is 12.9% [($5 + $7.88) ÷ $100] rather than 12.5% (5% GST + 7.5% QST). Because of the varying rate combinations that are used, it is important to be careful when recording sales tax amounts.

Property Taxes

Businesses that own property pay property taxes each year. These taxes are charged by the municipal and provincial governments, and are calculated at a specified rate for every $100 of the assessed value of the property (i.e., land and building). Property taxes are generally for a calendar year, although bills are not usually issued until the spring of each year.

To illustrate, assume that Tantramar Management Ltd. owns land and a building in the city of Regina. Tantramar's year end is December 31 and it makes adjusting entries annually. Tantramar receives its property tax bill of $6,000 for the calendar year on March 1, payable on May 31.

In March, when Tantramar receives the property tax bill, two months have passed in the year. The company records the property tax expense for the months of January and February and the liability owed at that point in time as follows:

Mar. 1	Property Tax Expense [($6,000 × 2/12]	1,000	
	Property Tax Payable		1,000
	(To record property tax expense for January and February)		

Cash flows: no effect

In May, when Tantramar records the payment of the liability recorded on March 1, it also records the expense incurred to date for the months of March, April, and May. As at May 31, five months have passed and should be recorded as property tax expense. The remaining seven months of the year are recorded as a prepayment, as shown in the following entry:

May 31	Property Tax Payable	1,000	
	Property Tax Expense ($6,000 × 3/12)	1,500	
	Prepaid Property Tax ($6,000 × 7/12)	3,500	
	Cash		6,000
	(To record payment of property tax expense for March through May, and amount prepaid for June through December)		

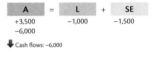

After the payment of the property tax, Tantramar has a zero balance in its liability account but still has a prepayment. Since Tantramar only makes adjusting entries annually, it would not adjust the prepaid property tax account until year end, December 31. At that time, it would make the following entry:

Dec. 31	Property Tax Expense	3,500	
	Prepaid Property Tax		3,500
	(To record property tax expense for June through December)		

Cash flows: no effect

There are other acceptable ways to record and adjust property taxes. Some companies would debit Prepaid Property Tax for $6,000 on March 1 and wait until adjusting entries are prepared to record any expense. Other companies would debit Property Tax Expense initially when the bill is recorded on March 1 to save a later adjusting entry. In addition, companies may prepare monthly or quarterly adjusting entries. Regardless, at year end, whatever way is used, the company should have the same ending balances. In this case, the accounts Prepaid Property Tax and Property Tax Payable should each have a zero balance and Property Tax Expense should have a balance of $6,000.

Payroll

Every employer incurs three types of liabilities related to employees' salaries or wages: (1) the net pay owed to employees, (2) employee payroll deductions, and (3) employer payroll deductions.

The first type of liability is the amount of salary or wages owed to employees. Management personnel are generally paid salaries, which are expressed as a specific amount per week, per month, or per year. Part-time employees or employees paid on an hourly basis or by the work produced (an amount per unit of product) are normally paid wages. The total amount of salaries or wages earned by the employee is called gross pay, or gross earnings.

Note that salaries and wages do not include payments made for services of professionals such as accountants, lawyers, and architects. Such professionals are independent contractors rather than salaried employees. Payments to them are called fees, rather than salaries or wages. This distinction is important, because government regulations for the payment and reporting of payroll apply only to employees.

The second type of liability is the amount of payroll deductions required by law to be withheld from employees' gross, or total, pay. Assume that Linfang Wang works 40 hours this week for Pepitone Inc., earning $10 per hour. Will Linfang receive a cheque for $400 (40 × $10) at the end of the week?

Definitely not. The reason: Pepitone has to withhold amounts known as payroll deductions from Lin-fang's wages, and pay these amounts to various other parties. Mandatory payroll deductions include amounts withheld for federal and provincial income taxes, Canada Pension Plan (CPP) contributions, and employment insurance (EI) premiums. Companies might also withhold voluntary deductions for charitable, union, pension, insurance, and other purposes.

An employee's gross pay, or total earnings, less any employee payroll deductions withheld from the employee's earnings is known as **net pay**. This is the amount that the company (the employer) must pay to the employee. Illustration 10-1 summarizes the types of payroll deductions that most companies normally have and that are responsible for the difference between gross and net pay.

Illustration 10-1

Payroll deductions

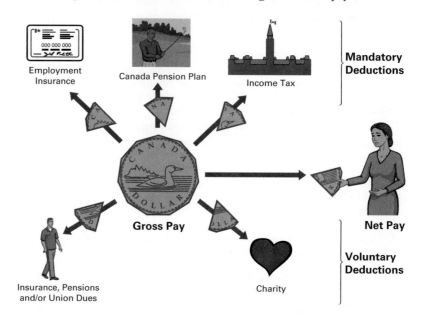

In addition to the liabilities incurred as a result of employee payroll deductions, employers also incur another liability related to these deductions. The employer is expected to pay various payroll costs that are charged on certain payroll deductions, such as the employer's share of CPP and EI. In addition, the provincial governments require employer funding of a Workplace Health, Safety, and Compensation Plan. All of these contributions, plus items such as paid vacations and employer-sponsored pensions, are referred to together as **employee benefits**. The employer's share of these costs is recorded as an employee benefits expense.

In summary, companies must collect payroll deductions from themselves and their employees on behalf of the government and other third parties. Until these payroll deductions and costs are remitted to the third parties that they are collected for, they are reported as a current liability in the balance sheet.

To illustrate the recording of payroll, we will continue to use Pepitone as our example. The accrual of a $100,000 weekly payroll for Pepitone is illustrated in the following journal entry, using assumed amounts:

A	=	L	+	SE
		+4,950		−100,000
		+2,100		
		+20,427		
		+2,445		
		+667		
		+69,411		

Cash flows: no effect

Mar. 7	Wages Expense	100,000	
	CPP Payable		4,950
	EI Payable		2,100
	Income Taxes Payable		20,427
	United Way Payable		2,445
	Union Dues Payable		667
	Wages Payable		69,411
	(To record payroll and employee deductions for the week ending March 7)		

In the above journal entry, Pepitone records $100,000—the gross pay amount—as wages expense. The net pay of $69,411 that is owed to employees is recorded as wages payable. In addition, Pepitone records as separate liabilities amounts it owes for its employee payroll deductions withheld on behalf of others, such as the government, United Way, and the union.

Note that while the employee payroll deductions are part of wages expense, employer payroll costs are not. Employer payroll costs are debited to a separate expense account called Employee Benefits Expense. Based on the $100,000 payroll in our Pepitone example, the following entry would be made to record the employer's expense and liability for its share of the payroll costs, or employee benefits:

Mar. 7	Employee Benefits Expense	12,465	
	CPP Payable		4,950
	EI Payable		2,940
	Workers' Compensation Payable		575
	Vacation Pay Payable		4,000
	(To record employer's payroll costs on March 7 payroll)		

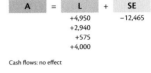

A	=	L	+	SE
		+4,950		−12,465
		+2,940		
		+575		
		+4,000		

Cash flows: no effect

On the same day, or on a later day, Pepitone must also pay its employees. The following entry records the payment of the weekly payroll on March 7:

Mar. 7	Wages Payable	69,411	
	Cash		69,411
	(To record payment of the March 7 payroll)		

A	=	L	+	SE
−69,411		−69,411		

⬇ Cash flows: −69,411

Note that Pepitone is only paying its employees in this entry and not its payroll deductions. Employee and employer deductions will be remitted later in the month when they are due to government authorities or other third parties. Normally payroll deductions must be remitted no later than the 15th day of the month following the monthly pay period. Depending on the size of the payroll deductions, however, the employer's payment deadline could be different.

ACCOUNTING MATTERS! | Management Perspective

The battle over employee benefits has grown as increases in the cost of benefits outpace increases in salaries and wages. Benefit costs represent between 7 and 12 percent of payroll and are increasing by an average of 7 percent per year. Limiting benefit costs is a priority for most companies. Many have started to look at the impact of sharing benefit-costs with employees. "One of the things that's probably happening in almost every country is cost shifting from the employer more to the employees," says Ron Hoskins, an assistant vice-president with Manulife Financial. But while cutting benefits may be the obvious solution, it is not always the best strategy—especially in a competitive labour market. Consequently, companies are moving slowly in order to measure this shift's effect on employee relations.

Source: Andrea Davis, "2008 Group Insurance Report," *Benefits Canada*, April 1, 2008.

Current Maturities of Long-Term Debt

Companies often have a portion of long-term debt that is due in the current year. As an example, assume that Cudini Construction issues a five-year, interest-bearing, $25,000 note on January 1, 2009. This note specifies that each January 1, starting January 1, 2010, $5,000 of the note will be repaid. When financial statements are prepared on December 31, 2009, $5,000 should be reported as a current liability and $20,000 as a long-term liability.

It is not necessary to prepare an adjusting entry to recognize the current maturity of long-term debt. The proper statement classification of each balance sheet account is recognized when the balance sheet is prepared.

BEFORE YOU GO ON...

Review It

1. What are the two criteria for classifying a debt as a current liability?
2. What are some examples of current liabilities?
3. Why is sales tax not revenue to the company that collects it?
4. Distinguish (1) between gross pay and net pay and (2) between employee payroll deductions and employer payroll costs.
5. Identify the liabilities that Shoppers Drug Mart classifies as current. The answer to this question is at the end of the chapter.

▶ Do It

Prepare the journal entries to record the following transactions:

1. Accrue interest on December 31 (the company's year end) for a three-month, 6%, $10,000 note payable issued November 1. Interest is payable on the first of each month.
2. Pre-tax sales on April 2 totalled $256,000. The GST tax rate is 5% and the PST is 8%. Record the sales and sales taxes.
3. A property tax bill for the calendar year of $12,000 is received on May 1 and is due June 30. Record the entries on May 1 and June 30, assuming the company has a calendar year end.
4. A company's gross wages amount to $10,000 for the week ended July 11. Amounts deducted from the employees' wages are CPP of $492, EI of $173, income tax of $3,965, and health insurance of $950. The employer's portion of CPP is $492 and of EI, $242. Record the weekly payroll on July 11, assuming cash is paid to the employees but the payroll amounts withheld are still due.

Action Plan

• Remember the formula for interest: principal (face) value × annual interest rate × time.
• Record sales separately from sales taxes. Recall that sales taxes are a liability until they are remitted.
• Record the property tax expense and the property tax payable for the amounts incurred to date. Record the prepaid property tax at the time of payment for any amounts paid in advance.
• Record both the employees' portion of the payroll and the benefits owed by the employer. Employee deductions are not an expense for the employer.

Solution

1. Dec. 31	Interest Expense ($10,000 × 6% × ¹⁄₁₂)		50	
	Interest Payable			50
	(To accrue interest for the month of December on note payable)			
2. Apr. 2	Cash ($256,000 + $12,800 + $20,480)		289,280	
	Sales			256,000
	GST Payable ($256,000 × 5%)			12,800
	PST Payable ($256,000 × 8%)			20,480
	(To record sales and sales taxes)			
3. May 1	Property Tax Expense ($12,000 × ⁴⁄₁₂)		4,000	
	Property Tax Payable			4,000
	(To record property tax expense for January–April and amount owing)			
June 30	Property Tax Expense ($12,000 × ²⁄₁₂)		2,000	
	Property Tax Payable		4,000	
	Prepaid Property Tax ($12,000 × ⁶⁄₁₂)		6,000	
	Cash			12,000
	(To record payment of property tax expense for May and June, and amount prepaid for July through December)			
4. July 11	Wages Expense		10,000	
	CPP Payable			492
	EI Payable			173
	Income Tax Payable			3,965
	Health Insurance Payable			950
	Wages Payable			4,420
	(To record payroll and employee deductions)			
11	Employee Benefits Expense		734	
	CPP Payable			492
	EI Payable			242
	(To record employee benefits)			

The Navigator

Long-Term Liabilities

A **long-term liability** is an obligation that is expected to be paid after one year or longer. In this section, we explain the accounting for the main types of obligations that are reported in the long-term liability section of the balance sheet. These obligations are often in the form of long-term notes or bonds, which are a form of financial instrument—more specifically a financial liability. Notes payable are explained in the next section, followed by bonds.

study objective 2

Account for long-term notes payable.

Long-Term Notes Payable

Using long-term notes payable in debt financing is common. Long-term notes payable are similar to short-term notes payable except that the terms of the notes are for more than one year. Long-term notes may have fixed or floating interest rates. In periods of unstable interest rates, it is common for notes to have a floating interest rate that changes as the prime rate changes. Plazacorp, introduced in our feature story, pays interest of prime plus 1 percent on its long-term notes payable.

A long-term note may be secured or unsecured. A secured note pledges title (gives ownership) to specific assets as collateral or security for the loan. Plazacorp had $187,449 thousand of secured notes payable at the end of 2007. Secured notes are also known as mortgages. A mortgage note payable is widely used by individuals to purchase homes. It is also used by many companies to acquire property, plant, and equipment.

Unsecured notes are issued against the general credit of the borrower. There are no assets used as collateral. Unsecured notes are also called debentures, and are used by large corporations with good credit ratings. Plazacorp reported $11,704 thousand of debentures at the end of 2007.

Sometimes notes or other forms of long-term debt have a special feature that allows them to be converted into shares. These are called convertible debt. Convertible debt has features that are attractive to both debt holders and issuers. The conversion often gives the holder an opportunity to benefit if the price of the borrower's common shares increases. Until conversion, though, the debt holder receives interest on the debt. For the issuer, the debt normally pays a lower rate of interest than comparable debt securities that have no conversion option. For example, Plazacorp reported one series of convertible debentures in 2007, with an interest rate of 7 percent. Similar notes without the conversion feature that were issued at about the same time were paying an interest rate of 8 percent.

Convertible debt has two basic aspects. First, it is a liability because of the agreement to repay the principal upon maturity. Second, it is equity, since the debt holder has the right to convert the debt into shares. These two aspects—liability and equity—must be recorded and presented separately on the balance sheet. Accounting for financial instruments such as these is complex and is discussed in more advanced accounting courses.

While short-term notes are normally repayable in full at maturity, most long-term notes are repayable in a series of periodic payments. These payments are known as **instalments** and are paid monthly, quarterly, semi-annually, or at another defined period. Each instalment payment consists of a mix of (1) interest on the unpaid balance of the loan, and (2) a reduction of the loan principal. The actual instalment payments generally take one of two forms: (1) fixed principal payments plus interest, or (2) blended principal and interest payments. Let's look at each of these payment patterns in more detail.

Fixed Principal Payments

Instalment notes with fixed principal payments are repayable in **equal periodic amounts, plus interest**. As mentioned earlier, interest may be either fixed or floating. For simplicity, we will assume a fixed interest rate. To illustrate, assume that on January 1, 2009, Belanger Ltée issues a five-year, 7%, $120,000 note payable to obtain financing for a new research laboratory. The entry to record the issue of the note payable is as follows:

Jan.	1	Cash	120,000	
		Notes Payable		120,000
		(To record five-year, 7% note payable)		

A	=	L	+	SE
+120,000		+120,000		

↑ Cash flows: +120,000

The terms of the note provide for equal monthly instalment payments of $2,000 ($120,000 ÷ 60 monthly periods) on the first of each month, plus interest of 7% on the outstanding principal balance.

Monthly interest expense is calculated by multiplying the outstanding principal balance by the interest rate. Because a portion of the principal balance is repaid each month, the outstanding principal balance will change (decrease) each month. This is different from what we observed in the calculation of interest on short-term notes payable, because the principal balance does not change throughout the term of a short-term note.

For Belanger's the first payment date—February 1—interest expense is $700 ($120,000 × 7% × 1/12). Similar to short-term notes, the 7% is an annual interest rate and must be adjusted for the monthly time period. The cash payment of $2,700 for the month of February is the total of the instalment payment of $2,000, which is applied against the principal, plus the interest of $700.

The entry to record the first instalment payment on February 1 is as follows:

A	=	L	+	SE
−2,700		−2,000		−700

⬇ Cash flows: −2,700

Feb.	1	Interest Expense ($120,000 × 7% × 1/12)	700	
		Note Payable	2,000	
		Cash ($2,000 + $700)		2,700
		(To record monthly payment on note)		

An instalment payment schedule is a useful tool to help organize this information and to provide information that helps prepare journal entries. A partial instalment payment schedule for the first few months for Belanger Ltée, rounded to the nearest dollar, is shown in Illustration 10-2.

Illustration 10-2 ➡

Instalment payment schedule—fixed principal payments

	BELANGER LTÉE		
	Instalment Payment Schedule—Fixed Principal Payments		
Interest Period	(A) Cash Payment (B+C)	(B) Interest Expense (D × 7% × 1/12)	(C) Reduction of Principal ($120,000 ÷ 60)	(D) Principal Balance (D − C)
---	---	---	---	---
Jan. 1				$120,000
Feb. 1	$2,700	$700	$2,000	118,000
Mar. 1	2,688	688	2,000	116,000
Apr. 1	2,677	677	2,000	114,000

Column A, the cash payment, is the total of the instalment payment, $2,000, plus the interest. The cash payment changes each period because the interest changes. Column B determines the interest expense, which decreases each period because the principal balance, on which interest is calculated, decreases. Column C is the instalment payment of $2,000, which is applied against the principal. The instalment payment is constant each period in a "fixed principal payment plus interest" pattern. Column D is the principal balance, which decreases each period by the amount of the instalment payment.

In summary, with fixed principal payments, the interest decreases each period (as the principal decreases). The portion applied to the reduction of the loan principal stays constant, but because of the decreasing interest, the total payment decreases.

Blended Principal and Interest Payments

Instalment notes with blended principal and interest payments are repayable in **equal periodic amounts, including interest**. Blended principal and interest payments result in changing amounts of interest and principal applied to the loan. As with fixed principal payments, the interest decreases each period (as the principal decreases). In contrast to fixed principal payments, the portion applied to the loan principal increases each period. Most consumer and mortgage loans use a blend of principal and interest payments rather than fixed principal payments.

To illustrate this option, assume that instead of fixed principal payments, Belanger Ltée repays its note in equal monthly instalments of $2,376. As with the fixed principal payments illustrated above, monthly interest expense is calculated by multiplying the outstanding principal balance by the interest rate. For the first payment date—February 1—interest expense is $700 ($120,000 × 7% × 1/12). The instalment payment of $2,376 is fixed for each month, and includes interest and principal amounts which will vary. In February, the principal balance will be reduced by $1,676, which is the difference between the instalment payment of $2,376 and the interest amount of $700.

The entry to record the issue of the note payable is the same as in the previous section. The entry to record the instalment payment uses the same accounts but different amounts. The first instalment payment on February 1 is recorded as follows:

Feb. 1	Interest Expense ($120,000 × 7% × $\frac{1}{12}$)	700	
	Note Payable ($2,376 − $700)	1,676	
	Cash		2,376
	(To record monthly payment on note)		

A = L + SE
−2,376 −1,676 −700

Cash flows: −2,376

An instalment payment schedule can also be prepared for blended principal and interest payments. Illustration 10-3 shows a partial instalment payment schedule for the first few months for Belanger Ltée, rounded to the nearest dollar.

BELANGER LTÉE
Instalment Payment Schedule—Blended Payments

Interest Period	(A) Cash Payment (B+C)	(B) Interest Expense (D × 7% × $\frac{1}{12}$)	(C) Reduction of Principal (A − B)	(D) Principal Balance (D − C)
Jan. 1				$120,000
Feb. 1	$2,376	$700	$1,676	118,324
Mar. 1	2,376	690	1,686	116,638
Apr. 1	2,376	680	1,696	114,942

◀ Illustration 10-3

Instalment payment schedule—blended principal and interest payments

Column A, the cash payment, is specified and is the same for each period. The amount of this cash payment can actually be calculated mathematically. It can also be determined using present value techniques, which are discussed later in the chapter, and in the Study Tools section of the Toolkit website that accompanies this textbook.

Column B determines the interest expense, which decreases each period because the principal balance that the interest is calculated on decreases. Column C is how much the principal is reduced by. This is the difference between the cash payment of $2,376 and the interest for the period. Consequently, this amount will increase each period. Column D is the principal balance, which decreases each period by a varying amount, that is, by the reduction of the principal amount from Column C.

With both types of instalment note payable, as with any other long-term note payable, the reduction in principal for the next year must be reported as a current liability. The remaining unpaid principal is classified as a long-term liability. For example, consider the following fixed principal annual instalment payment schedule:

Interest Period	Cash Payment	Interest Expense	Reduction of Principal	Principal Balance
Issue Date				$50,000
2008	$13,500	$3,500	$10,000	40,000
2009	12,800	2,800	10,000	30,000
2010	12,100	2,100	10,000	20,000
2011	11,400	1,400	10,000	10,000
2012	10,700	700	10,000	0

If financial statements were being prepared at the end of 2009, the company would report $30,000 as its total liability on the note, as shown in the principal balance column. Of this, $10,000 ($30,000 − $20,000)—the amount to be repaid within the next year—would be reported as a current liability. The company would report $20,000—the amount to be repaid beyond next year—as a long-term liability. Note that, when the current portion ($10,000) and the long-term portion ($20,000) are added, together, the amount should agree with the total amount owing at the end of 2009, $30,000.

BEFORE YOU GO ON...

Review It

1. Distinguish between short-term and long-term notes payable.
2. Explain the accounting for long-term notes payable.
3. How does the reduction in principal differ in a note with fixed principal payments compared to a note with blended principal and interest payments?

Do It

On December 31, 2009, Tian Inc. issued a 15-year, 8%, $500,000 mortgage note payable. The terms provide for semi-annual blended instalment payments of $28,915 (principal and interest) on June 30 and

December 31. (a) Prepare an instalment payment schedule for the first two years of the note through to December 31, 2011. (b) Prepare the journal entries required to record the issue of the note on December 31, 2009, and the first two instalment payments on June 30, 2010, and December 31, 2010. (c) Show the presentation of the liability on the balance sheet at December 31, 2010.

Action Plan

• Prepare an instalment payment schedule. Multiply the semi-annual interest rate by the principal balance at the beginning of the period to determine the interest expense. The reduction of principal is the difference between the cash payment and the interest expense.
• Record the mortgage payments, recognizing that each payment consists of (1) interest on the unpaid loan balance, and (2) a reduction of the loan principal.
• Remember to separate the current and long-term portions of the note in the balance sheet.

Solution

(a)

Interest Period	Cash Payment	Interest Expense	Reduction of Principal	Principal Balance
Dec. 31, 2009				$500,000
June 30, 2010	$28,915	$20,000	$ 8,915	491,085
Dec. 31, 2010	28,915	19,643	9,272	481,813
June 30, 2011	28,915	19,273	9,642	472,171
Dec. 31, 2011	28,915	18,887	10,028	462,143

(b)

Dec. 31, 2009	Cash	500,000	
	Mortgage Note Payable		500,000
	(To record issue of 15-year, 8% mortgage note payable)		
June 30, 2010	Interest Expense ($500,000 × 8% × $\frac{6}{12}$)	20,000	
	Mortgage Note Payable ($28,915 – $20,000)	8,915	
	Cash		28,915
	(To record semi-annual mortgage payment)		
Dec. 31, 2010	Interest Expense [($500,000 – $8,915) × 8% × $\frac{6}{12}$)]	19,643	
	Mortgage Note Payable ($28,915 – $19,643)	9,272	
	Cash		28,915
	(To record semi-annual mortgage payment)		

(c)

TIAN INC.
December 31, 2010
Balance Sheet (partial)

Current liabilities	
Current portion of mortgage note payable ($9,642 + $10,028)	$ 19,670
Long-term liabilities	
Mortgage note payable	462,143
Total liabilities	481,813

The Navigator

Bonds Payable

study objective 3

Account for bonds payable.

A **bond** is a form of interest-bearing note payable. Accounting for notes and bonds is quite similar. Both have a fixed maturity date and pay interest. However, whereas notes can have a fixed or floating interest rate, bonds only have a fixed interest rate. This rate, which determines the amount of interest to pay to bondholders, is known as the contractual interest rate. Usually, the contractual rate is stated as an annual rate and bond interest is paid semi-annually. For notes, the interest rate is also stated as an annual rate, but interest is paid either monthly or at maturity, depending on the term of the note.

Bonds can have many different features, similar to notes. They may be **unsecured** or **secured**. As mentioned in our feature story, Plazacorp has issued $20.5 million of secured mortgage bonds. Bonds may also be **convertible** into shares. Both notes and bonds can be payable at maturity or in instalments. Bonds that mature (are due for payment) on a single specified future date are known as **term bonds**. The amount of principal due at maturity is usually called the **face value**. Bonds that mature in instalments are known as **serial bonds**, although these are not a common type of bonds. In contrast to most long-term notes, which are repayable in a series of periodic instalment payments, bonds are normally repayable in full at maturity.

www.wiley.com/canada/kimmel

Tutorials
(Bonds)

ACCOUNTING MATTERS! | Management Perspective

Bonds are increasingly being issued by universities. In the last decade, six Canadian universities issued bonds totalling nearly $1 billion. The bond issues range in size from $125 million (University of British Columbia) to $225 million (Concordia University). Faced with decreasing financial resources from provincial governments, universities find bonds an attractive option to help finance the construction of new facilities and the repair of badly dated ones. By issuing bonds, universities pay less interest than they would have to pay with a bank loan. And, unlike bank loans, which usually have to be renegotiated every few years, the interest rate for a bond offering is locked in for the duration of the term, which makes future budgets more stable.

Bond Trading

A significant difference between notes and bonds is that bonds are often traded on a stock exchange in the same way as shares are. Notes are seldom traded on the stock exchange. Small and large corporations issue notes, whereas only large corporations issue bonds. Bonds enable a company to borrow when the amount of financing needed is too large for one lender. To attract many investors, bonds are thus typically sold in small denominations (usually $1,000 or multiples of $1,000).

As Plazacorp's bonds do not trade on any stock exchange, we have chosen to illustrate a sample listing for Bell Canada bonds from the daily financial press:

Issuer	Coupon	Maturity Date	Price	Yield
Bell CDA	8.88	2026-Apr-17	88.42	10.30

This bond listing for Bell Canada (CDA) bonds indicates that these bonds have a contractual (coupon) interest rate of 8.88% per year. However, as is the norm, interest is paid semi-annually at a rate of 4.44 percent (8.88% × ⁶⁄₁₂). The bonds mature on April 17, 2026.

Bond prices are quoted as a percentage of the face value of the bonds, which is usually $1,000. For example, if the bond price is stated as 100, this means that the bonds will sell at 100 percent of the face value. If the face value is $1,000, then the bonds will sell for $1,000 ($1,000 × 100%). You can assume that bonds are issued in $1,000 denominations unless you are told otherwise. With respect to the Bell Canada bonds described in the above listing, the price of 88.42 means that $884.20 ($1,000 × 88.42%) was the selling price of each $1,000 bond on the date of the above listing. The yield, or market interest rate, on the bonds was 10.3%. The market interest rate is the rate investors demand for lending their money. This rate is also commonly known as the effective interest rate.

As is the case with share transactions, transactions between a bondholder and other investors are not journalized by the issuing corporation. If Vinod Thakkar sells his Bell Canada bonds to Julie Tarrel, the issuing corporation, Bell Canada, does not record the transaction. While the issuer (or its trustee) does keep records of the names of bondholders, a corporation makes journal entries only when it issues bonds, makes an interest payment, or buys back bonds.

Determining the Issue Price of Bonds

If you were an investor interested in purchasing a bond, how would you decide how much to pay? To be more specific, assume that Candlestick Inc. issues a zero-interest bond (a bond that pays no interest) with a face value of $1 million due in five years. For this bond, the only cash you receive is $1 million at the end of five years. Would you pay $1 million for this bond? We hope not, because $1 million received five years from now is not the same as $1 million received today.

You should not pay $1 million because of what is called the **time value of money**. If you had $1 million today, you would invest it and earn interest so that after five years your investment could be worth much more than $1 million. Thus, if someone is going to pay you $1 million five years from now, you

Alternative Terminology
The *issue price* is also called the *selling price, fair value,* or *market value* of the bonds.

would want to find its equivalent today. That amount—how much must be invested today at current interest rates to have $1 million in five years—is called the present value.

The present value of a bond is the amount at which it sells in the marketplace. The issue price (present value), therefore, depends on three factors: (1) the dollar amounts to be received, (2) the length of time until the amounts are received, and (3) the market rate of interest. The process of finding the present value is referred to as discounting the future amounts.

To illustrate, assume that on January 1, 2009, Candlestick Inc. issues $1 million of 5% bonds, due in five years, with interest payable semi-annually. The purchaser of the bonds would receive the following two cash inflows: (1) the face or principal amount of $1 million to be paid at maturity, and (2) ten $25,000 interest payments ($1,000,000 × 5% × $\%_{12}$ months) over the term of the bonds. A time diagram for both cash flows is shown in Illustration 10-4.

Illustration 10-4 ➡

Time diagram of cash flows

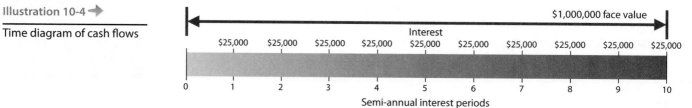

The fair value, or issue price, of a bond is equal to the present value of all the future cash payments promised by the bond. The present values of these amounts are as follows:

Helpful Hint Bond prices vary inversely with changes in the market interest rate. As market interest rates decline, bond prices increase. When a bond is issued, if the market interest rate is below the contractual interest rate, the issue price will be higher than the face value.

Present value of $1,000,000 received in 10 periods	
$1,000,000 × 0.78120 ($n = 10$, $i = 2.5\%$)	$ 781,200
Present value of $25,000 received for each of 10 periods	
$25,000 × 8.75206 ($n = 10$, $i = 2.5\%$)	218,800
Present value (issue price) of bonds	$1,000,000
Where n = number of interest periods and i = interest rate	

Present value tables are included as Appendix 10A in this chapter. Table 1 in Appendix 10A provides the present value factor used to calculate the present value of the principal in the above calculation (0.78120). This is known as the present value of $1, which is a single sum received at the end of the bond term. Table 2 in Appendix 10A provides the present value factor used to calculate the present value of the interest, which is received each interest period, in the above calculation (8.75206). This is known as the present value of an annuity of $1.

Alternatively, these amounts can also be determined mathematically using a financial calculator or spreadsheet program. Additional discussion of concepts and time value of money calculations is available on the website accompanying this book.

www.wiley.com/canada/kimmel

Analysis Tools
(Present Value Concepts)

Discount or Premium on Bonds

The present value illustration above assumed that the contractual interest rate and the market interest rate were the same. The present value (issue price) will always equal the face value when the two rates are the same, as was assumed in this case. However, market interest rates change daily. They are influenced by the type of bond issued, the state of the economy, current industry conditions, and the company's individual performance. As a result, the contractual and market interest rates often differ, and bonds therefore sell below or above their face value.

To illustrate, suppose that investors have one of two options: (1) purchase bonds that have just been issued with a contractual interest rate of 6 percent, or (2) purchase bonds issued at an earlier date with a lower contractual interest rate of 5 percent. If the bonds are of equal risk, investors will choose the 6-percent investment. To make the investments equal, and the option 2 bonds worth purchasing, investors would need a higher rate of interest for option 2 than the 5-percent contractual interest. But investors cannot change the contractual interest rate. What they can do instead is pay less than the face value for the bonds. By paying less for the bonds, investors can effectively obtain the market interest rate of 6 percent. When the market interest rate is higher than the contractual interest rate, the bonds are said to sell at a discount.

The Bell Canada bonds shown in the bond trading section earlier in this chapter were issued at a discount. In that particular case, the market interest rate (10.3%) was higher than the contractual interest rate (8.88%).

On the other hand, the market interest rate may be lower than the contractual interest rate. In that case, investors will pay more than face value for the bonds. That is, if the market interest rate is 4 percent but the contractual interest rate on the bonds is 5 percent, everyone will want to buy the bonds and the price will rise above the bonds' face value. In these cases, the bonds are said to sell at a **premium**.

These relationships are shown in Illustration 10-5.

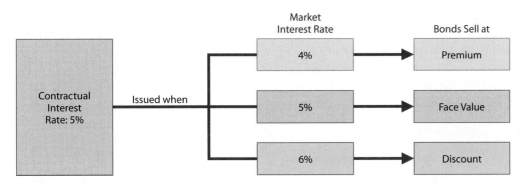

◀ Illustration 10-5

Interest rates and bond prices

Issuing bonds at an amount different from face value is quite common. By the time a company prints the bond certificates (which provide the legal documentation for the bonds) and markets the bonds, it will be a coincidence if the market rate and the contractual rate are the same. Thus, the issue of bonds at a discount does not mean there is doubt about the financial strength of the issuer. Conversely, the sale of bonds at a premium does not indicate that the financial strength of the issuer is exceptional.

Once the bonds are issued, the interest on bonds payable is calculated using the effective-interest method. The effective-interest method is an amortization method used to allocate a bond discount or premium to interest expense over the life of the bond. This method results in a periodic interest expense that equals a constant percentage (the market or effective interest rate) of the carrying amount of the bond. The **carrying amount** of a bond is its face value plus any unamortized premium, or less any unamortized discount. At the date of issue, the carrying amount equals the bond's issue price.

The calculation of amortization using the effective-interest method is shown in Illustration 10-6.

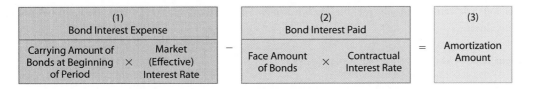

◀ Illustration 10-6

Calculation of amortization using effective-interest method

As shown in Illustration 10-6, the following steps are required under the effective-interest method of amortization:

1. Calculate the **bond interest expense**: Multiply the carrying amount of the bonds at the beginning of the interest period by the market (effective) interest rate for the semi-annual (or appropriate) period.

2. Calculate the **bond interest paid** (or accrued): Multiply the face value of the bonds by the contractual interest rate for the semi-annual (or appropriate) period.

3. Calculate the **amortization amount**: Determine the difference between the amounts calculated in steps (1) and (2).

Note that this is similar to the calculation of interest for long-term notes payable, where interest expense was calculated using the carrying amount multiplied by the interest rate. In the case of the note, there was no "effective" interest rate as there is for bonds. In addition, we did not have to worry about amortizing any discount or premium with the notes, although there are circumstances where non–interest bearing notes can also be issued with a discount or premium.

▸ Reporting and Analyzing Liabilities

Accounting for Bond Issues

Bonds may be issued at face value, below face value (discount), or above face value (premium).

Issuing Bonds at Face Value.   To illustrate the accounting for bonds issued at face value, let's continue the example discussed in the last section where Candlestick Inc. issues five-year, 5%, $1-million bonds on January 1, 2009, for $1 million (100% of face value). The entry to record the sale is:

Jan.	1	Cash	1,000,000	
		Bonds Payable		1,000,000
		(To record sale of bonds at face value)		

Because these bonds were issued at face value, the interest expense and interest paid are the same. Interest expense and interest paid are calculated by multiplying $1,000,000 × 5% × %12, which equals $25,000. Interest is payable semi-annually on January 1 and July 1, so the following entry must be made on July 1 to record the interest expense and interest paid:

July	1	Bond Interest Expense	25,000	
		Cash		25,000
		(To record payment of bond interest)		

At December 31, Candlestick's year end, an adjusting entry is required to recognize the $25,000 of interest expense incurred since July 1 that is due to be paid on January 1. The entry is:

Dec. 31	Bond Interest Expense	25,000	
	Bond Interest Payable		25,000
	(To accrue bond interest)		

Bond interest payable is classified as a current liability at December 31, 2009, because it is scheduled for payment within the next year. The bonds payable are reported in the long-term liability section of the balance sheet because the maturity date is January 1, 2014 (more than one year away). When the interest is paid on January 1, 2010, Bond Interest Payable is decreased (debited) and Cash is also decreased (credited) for $25,000.

Issuing Bonds at a Discount.   To illustrate the issue of bonds at a discount, assume that Candlestick sells its bonds to yield a market (effective) interest rate of 6 percent rather than 5 percent (100% of face value) as we assumed above.

Using time value of money techniques, we determine that the bonds will sell for $957,345 (95.7345% of face value):

Present value of $1,000,000 received in 10 periods	
$1,000,000 × 0.74409 ($n = 10, i = 3\%$)	$744,090
Present value of $25,000 received for each of 10 periods	
$25,000 × 8.53020 ($n = 10, i = 3\%$)	213,255
Present value (issue price) of bonds	$957,345
Where n = number of interest periods and i = interest rate	

The issue price of $957,345 results in a bond discount of $42,655 ($1,000,000 − $957,345). The entry to record the sale is:

Jan.	1	Cash	957,345	
		Bonds Payable		957,345
		(To record sale of bonds at a discount)		

Rather than crediting the Bonds Payable account for the issue price of $957,345, some companies use a separate contra liability account to keep track of the bond discount. That is, they would record bonds payable as a credit of $1,000,000 and record the bond discount in a separate account as a debit of $42,655. For reporting purposes, however, current accounting standards—both Canadian and international—require the presentation of bonds net of any discounts (or premiums, as we will learn in the next section). Consequently, many companies record their journal entries on a net basis as well. Although both ways of *recording* bond transactions are acceptable, we will illustrate the recording of bond journal entries net of any discount or premium in this text, which is what is required for *reporting* purposes.

The issue of bonds at a discount (below face value) will result in a total cost of borrowing that is higher than the bond interest paid. That is, the issuing corporation must pay not only the contractual interest rate over the term of the bonds but also the face value (rather than the issue price) at maturity. Therefore, the difference between the issue price ($957,345) and the face value ($1 million) of the bonds—the discount ($42,655)—is an **additional cost of borrowing**. That is, Candlestick must repay $1 million at maturity even though it received only $957,345 from the sale of the bonds.

To follow the matching principle, the bond discount should be allocated to expense over the life of the bonds. The $25,000 interest payment is recorded as interest expense every semi-annual period for five years (10 semi-annual periods). The bond discount is also allocated to interest expense over the 10 periods—this allocation is referred to as **amortizing the discount**. Consequently, the amortization of the discount increases the amount of interest expense that is reported each period, in addition to increasing the carrying amount in the liability account.

For the first interest period, the bond interest expense is $28,720, calculated by multiplying the carrying amount of the bonds by the market interest rate ($957,345 × 6% × %12). The interest payment, $25,000, is the same whether the bonds are issued at face value, at a discount, or at a premium. It is calculated by multiplying the face value of the bonds by the contractual interest rate ($1,000,000 × 5% × %12). The amortization is the difference between the interest expense and the interest paid ($28,720 − $25,000 = $3,720).

At July 1, the entry to record the payment of interest and amortization of bond discount by Candlestick is as follows:

July 1	Bond Interest Expense	28,720	
	Bonds Payable		3,720
	Cash		25,000
	(To record payment of bond interest and amortization of bond discount)		

A	=	L	+	SE
−25,000		+3,720		−28,720

⬇ Cash flows: −25,000

At the second interest period, the carrying amount of the bonds is now $961,065 ($957,345 + $3,720). The carrying amount will continue to increase by the amount of the discount amortization until, at maturity, the carrying amount of the bonds equals their face value.

To calculate the interest expense for the second interest period, we multiply the carrying amount of the bonds by the market interest rate to arrive at $28,832 ($961,065 × 6% × %12). The interest payment is unchanged at $25,000. As before, the amortization is the difference between the interest expense and the interest paid ($28,832 − $25,000 = $3,832).

At December 31, Candlestick's year end, the following adjusting entry is made to record interest for the second interest period:

Dec. 31	Bond Interest Expense	28,832	
	Bonds Payable		3,832
	Bond Interest Payable		25,000
	(To record accrued bond interest and amortization of bond discount)		

A	=	L	+	SE
		+3,832		−28,832
		+25,000		

Cash flows: no effect

A bond discount amortization schedule is useful to organize and track the interest expense, discount amortization, and interest payable amounts, similar to the instalment payment schedules shown earlier in the chapter for notes payable. Such a schedule is especially useful when the amortization of the bond discount is recorded directly in the Bonds Payable account as we have done above, rather than recorded in a separate contra liability account. A partial bond amortization schedule for the first two interest periods is shown in Illustration 10-7.

Illustration 10-7 ⬇

Bond discount amortization schedule

	(A)	(B)	(C)	(D)	(E)
	CANDLESTICK INC.				
	Bond Discount Amortization Schedule				
Semi-Annual Interest Period	Interest Payment ($1,000,000 × 5% × %12)	Interest Expense (Preceding Bond Carrying Amount × 6% × %12)	Discount Amortization (B − A)	Unamortized Discount (D − C)	Bond Carrying Amount ($1,000,000 − D)
Issue date (Jan. 1, 2009)				$42,655	$957,345
1 (July 1, 2009)	$25,000	$28,720	$3,720	38,935	961,065
2 (Jan. 1, 2010)	25,000	28,832	3,832	35,103	964,897

Column A, the interest payment, is calculated by multiplying the face value of the bonds by the semi-annual contractual interest rate. This amount remains constant for each period. Column B determines the interest expense, which increases each period because the carrying amount that the interest is calculated on increases. It is calculated by multiplying the carrying amount by the semi-annual market interest rate.

Column C is the amount of the discount amortization. It is the difference between the interest expense (Column B) and the interest payment (Column A) for each period. Just as the interest expense increases each period, so does the discount amortization. Column D is the amortized discount. It is reduced each period by the discount amortization (Column C) until it reaches zero at maturity.

Column E is the carrying amount of the bond. The face value, $1,000,000 in this case, is decreased each period by the amount of the unamortized discount (Column D). Because the unamortized discount amount will be fully amortized and decline to a zero balance at maturity, the bond carrying amount will increase each period until it finally reaches the face value at maturity.

A complete bond discount amortization schedule for the entire five-year period of the bond issue is shown in Appendix 10B to this chapter.

Issuing Bonds at a Premium. The issue of bonds at a premium can be illustrated by assuming that the Candlestick bonds described above are instead sold to yield a market (effective) interest rate of 4 percent rather than 5 percent (at face value) or 6 percent (at a discount), as we illustrated above.

Using time value of money techniques, we determine that the bonds will sell for $1,044,915 (104.4915% of face value).

Present value of $1,000,000 received in 10 periods	
$1,000,000 × 0.82035 ($n = 10, i = 2$)	$ 820,350
Present value of $25,000 received for each of 10 periods	
$25,000 × 8.98259 ($n = 10, i = 2$)	224,565
Present value (issue price) of bonds	$1,044,915
Where n = number of interest periods and i = interest rate	

This issue price of $1,044,915 results in a premium of $44,915 ($1,044,915 − $1,000,000). The entry to record the sale of the bonds is:

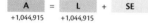

Jan.	1	Cash	1,044,915	
		Bonds Payable		1,044,915
		(To record sale of bonds at a premium)		

Rather than crediting the Bonds Payable account for the issue price of $1,044,915, some companies use a separate adjunct account to keep track of the bond premium. An **adjunct account** is the opposite of a contra account. A contra account reduces a related account while an adjunct account increases, or is added to, a related account. If an adjunct account was used, Bonds Payable would be credited for $1,000,000 and the bond premium would be recorded in a separate account as a credit of $44,915.

As we explained in the Issuing Bonds at a Discount section, both Canadian and international accounting standards require the presentation of bonds net of any premiums (or discounts, as we learned in the previous section). We have chosen to illustrate the recording of bond journal entries net of any premium or discount in this text.

The issue of bonds at a premium (above face value) results in the total cost of borrowing being less than the bond interest paid because the borrower is not required to pay the bond premium at the maturity date of the bonds. That is, Candlestick received $1,044,915 from the sale of the bonds but is only required to repay the maturity value, $1 million. Thus, the bond premium, $44,915 in this case, is considered to be **a reduction in the cost of borrowing** that reduces bond interest expense over the life of the bonds.

To follow the matching principle, the bond premium should be allocated to expense over the life of the bonds. The $25,000 interest payment is recorded as interest expense every semi-annual period for five years (10 semi-annual periods). The bond premium is also allocated so that it reduces the interest expense over the 10 periods—this allocation is called **amortizing the premium**.

For the first interest period, the bond interest expense is $20,898, calculated by multiplying the carrying amount of the bonds by the market interest rate ($1,044,915 × 4% × %₁₂). The interest payment is unchanged at $25,000. It is calculated by multiplying the face value of the bonds by the contractual interest rate ($1,000,000 × 5% × %₁₂). The amortization is the difference between the interest paid and the interest expense ($25,000 − $20,898 = $4,102).

At July 1, the entry to record the payment of interest and amortization of the bond premium by Candlestick is as follows:

July 1	Bond Interest Expense	20,898	
	Bonds Payable	4,102	
	Cash		25,000
	(To record payment of bond interest and amortization of bond premium)		

A = L + SE
−25,000 −4,102 −20,898

↓ Cash flows: −25,000

In the above entry, the interest expense account is effectively increased (debited) for the interest payment ($25,000) and decreased (credited) for the bond premium amortization ($4,102). The overall effect is that the amortization of the premium decreases the amount of interest expense that is reported each period, in addition to decreasing the carrying amount in the liability account.

At the second interest period, the carrying amount of the bonds is now $1,040,813 (1,044,915 − $4,102). The carrying amount will continue to decrease until, at maturity, the carrying amount of the bonds equals their face value.

To calculate the interest expense for the second interest period, we multiply the carrying amount of the bonds by the market interest rate to arrive at $20,816 ($1,040,813 × 4% × %12). The interest payment is unchanged at $25,000. As before, the amortization is the difference between the interest paid and the interest expense ($25,000 − $20,816 = $4,184).

At December 31, Candlestick's year end, the following adjusting entry is made to record interest for the second interest period:

Dec. 31	Bond Interest Expense	20,816	
	Bonds Payable	4,184	
	Bond Interest Payable		25,000
	(To record accrued bond interest and amortization of bond premium)		

A = L + SE
−4,184 −20,816
+25,000

Cash flows: no effect

A bond premium amortization schedule is useful to organize and track the interest expense, premium amortization, and interest payable amounts, similar to the schedule shown above for the amortization of a bond discount. A partial bond amortization schedule for the first two interest periods of our current example is shown in Illustration 10-8.

⬇ **Illustration 10-8**

Bond premium amortization schedule

CANDLESTICK INC. Bond Premium Amortization Schedule					
Semi-Annual Interest Period	(A) Interest Payment ($1,000,000 × 5% × %12)	(B) Interest Expense (Preceding Bond Carrying Amount × 4% × %12)	(C) Premium Amortization (A − B)	(D) Unamortized Premium (D − C)	(E) Bond Carrying Amount ($1,000,000 + D)
Issue date (Jan. 1, 2009)				$44,915	$1,044,915
1 (July 1, 2009)	$ 25,000	$ 20,898	$ 4,102	40,813	1,040,813
2 (Jan. 1, 2010)	25,000	20,816	4,184	36,629	1,036,629

Column A, the interest payment, is calculated by multiplying the face value of the bonds by the semi-annual contractual interest rate. This amount remains constant for each period. Column B determines the interest expense, which decreases each period because the carrying amount that the interest is calculated on decreases. It is calculated by multiplying the carrying amount by the semi-annual market interest rate.

Column C is the amount of the premium amortization. It is the difference between the interest payment (Column A) and the interest expense (Column B) for each period. Because the interest expense decreases each period while the interest payment remains constant, the premium amortization increases each period. Column D is the amortized premium. It is reduced each period by the premium amortization (Column C) until it reaches zero at maturity.

Column E is the carrying amount of the bond. The face value, $1,000,000 in this case, is increased each period by the amounts of the unamortized premium (Column D). Because the unamortized premium amount will be fully amortized and decline to a zero balance at maturity, the bond carrying amount will decrease each period until it finally reaches the face value at maturity.

A complete bond premium amortization schedule for the entire five-year period of the bond issue is shown in Appendix 10B to this chapter.

Accounting for Bond Retirements

Bonds are retired either (1) when they mature, or (2) when the issuing corporation purchases them on the open market before they mature. Some bonds have special redemption provisions that allow them to be retired before they mature. Bonds that can be retired at a stated dollar amount before maturity at the option of the company (the issuer) are known as redeemable (callable) bonds. To make the bonds more attractive to investors, the redemption or call price is usually a few percentage points above the face value.

Why would a company want to have the option to retire its bonds early? If interest rates drop, it can be financially advantageous to retire the bond issue and replace it with a new bond issue at a lower interest rate. Or a company may become financially able to repay its debt earlier than expected. Before a company does this, it should do an in-depth financial analysis to be sure it has enough cash resources to retire its bonds early. You will learn more about this type of analysis in a finance course.

Let's look now at the required entries for redeeming bonds at maturity and before maturity.

Redeeming Bonds at Maturity. Regardless of the issue price of bonds, the carrying amount of the bonds at maturity will equal their face value. By the time the bonds mature, any discount or premium will be fully amortized and will have a zero balance.

Assuming that the interest for the last interest payment period is recorded, the entry to record the redemption of the Candlestick bonds at maturity, on January 1, 2014, is:

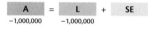

Jan.	1	Bonds Payable	1,000,000	
		Cash		1,000,000
		(To record redemption of bonds at maturity)		

Since no proceeds are received, there is no gain or loss when bonds are retired at maturity.

Redeeming Bonds Before Maturity. Redeeming bonds early is similar to disposing of property, plant, and equipment. To record a redemption of bonds, it is necessary to (1) update any unrecorded interest and amortization, (2) eliminate the carrying amount of the bonds at the redemption date, (3) record the cash paid, and (4) recognize the gain or loss on redemption.

For the first step, interest must be updated if the bonds are redeemed between semi-annual interest payment dates. For the second step, the Bonds Payable account must be removed from the books. For the third and fourth steps, the cash paid to repurchase the bonds is recorded. A gain on redemption results when the cash paid is less than the carrying amount of the bonds. A loss on redemption results when the cash paid is more than the carrying amount of the bonds.

To illustrate, assume that Candlestick sells its bonds at a premium as described in the last section. It redeems the bonds at 101 at the end of the fourth year (eighth period), after paying the semi-annual interest. Assume that the carrying amount of the bonds at the redemption date is $1,009,709. That is, the face value of the bonds is $1 million and the unamortized premium is $9,709. The entry to record the redemption on January 1, 2013 (end of the eighth period), is:

Jan.	1	Bonds Payable	1,009,709	
		Loss on Bond Redemption ($1,010,000 − $1,009,709)	291	
		Cash ($1,000,000 × 101%)		1,010,000
		(To record redemption of bonds at 101)		

The loss of $291 is the difference between the cash paid of $1,010,000 and the carrying amount of the bonds of $1,009,709. Calculating a loss or a gain on the redemption of bonds is similar to the calculation of a loss or gain on the sale of property, plant, and equipment. In both cases, the proceeds (cash) are compared to the carrying amount. However, the determination of whether there is a loss or a gain is, of course, different. For example, when you sell an asset (such as property, plant, and equipment), you gain when the cash received is greater than the carrying amount. When you retire a liability (such as bonds), you gain when the cash paid is less than the carrying amount.

Losses and gains on bond redemption are reported in the statement of earnings as other expenses or revenues. Unlike the sale of property, plant, and equipment, which is considered part of earnings from operations, the redemption of bonds usually results in large and infrequent amounts which, because they are unusual, are reported separately.

BEFORE YOU GO ON...

Review It

1. How is the issue price of bonds determined?
2. Why do bonds sell at face value? At a discount? At a premium?
3. Explain why bond discounts and premiums are amortized.
4. Explain the accounting for the redemption of bonds at maturity and before maturity.

Do It

On January 1, 2006, R & B Inc. issued $500,000 of 10-year, 4% bonds to yield a market interest rate of 5%, which resulted in an issue price of 92.2. Interest is paid semi-annually on January 1 and July 1. On July 1, 2010, before maturity and after the interest payment had been made, the carrying amount of the bonds was $476,214. The company redeems the bonds at 95 on this date. (a) Using present value factors, prove the issue price of the bonds of 92.2. (b) Prepare the entries to record (1) the issue of the bonds on January 1, 2006, (2) the payment of interest and amortization of any bond discount or premium on July 1, 2006, and (3) the redemption of the bonds on July 1, 2010. Round all calculations to the nearest dollar.

Action Plan

• To calculate the present value (issue price), use Table 1 (the present value of $1) in Appendix 10A to determine the factor to use to calculate the present value of the principal, which is a single sum. Use Table 2 (the present value of an annuity of $1) in Appendix 10A to calculate the present value of the interest, which recurs periodically (as an annuity). Remember to double the number of periods and halve the annual interest rate when the interest is paid semi-annually.
• Apply the issue price as a percentage (e.g., 92.2%) to the face value of the bonds to determine the proceeds received. Prove this number to the present value (issue price) that is calculated.
• Recall that the amortization of a bond discount results in a debit to interest expense and a credit to bonds payable, while the amortization of a bond premium results in the reverse.
• To record the redemption, eliminate the carrying amount of the bonds and record the cash paid. Calculate and record the gain or loss (the difference between the cash paid and the carrying amount).

Solution

(a)

Present value of $500,000 received in 20 periods	
$500,000 × 0.61027 (n = 20, i = 2.5)	$305,135
Present value of $10,000 received for each of 20 periods	
$10,000 × 15.58916 (n = 20, i = 2.5)	155,892
Present value (issue price) of bonds	$461,027

Issue price = $461,027 ÷ $500,000 = 92.2%

(b)

(1) Jan. 1, 2006	Cash ($500,000 × 92.2%)	461,027	
	Bonds Payable		461,027
	(To record issue of bonds at 92.2)		
(2) July 1, 2006	Interest Expense ($461,027 × 5% × ⁶⁄₁₂)	11,526	
	Bonds Payable ($11,526 – $10,000)		1,526
	Cash ($500,000 × 4% × ⁶⁄₁₂)		10,000
	(To record payment of interest and amortization of discount)		
(3) July 1, 2010	Bonds Payable	476,214	
	Gain on Bond Redemption ($476,214 – $475,000)		1,214
	Cash ($500,000 × 95%)		475,000
	(To record redemption of bonds at 95)		

The Navigator

Statement Presentation and Analysis

study objective 4

Identify the requirements for the financial statement presentation and analysis of liabilities.

Liabilities add up to a significant amount on the financial statements of almost all companies and must be disclosed in detail so they can be properly understood by creditors and investors. These and other users are very interested in assessing a company's liquidity and solvency in regard to its liabilities. We will look at the presentation and analysis of liabilities in the next sections.

Presentation

The presentation of liabilities affects three financial statements: the statement of earnings, balance sheet, and cash flow statement. In the statement of earnings, gains on bond redemptions are reported as "other revenues" and losses on bond redemptions and interest expense are reported as "other expenses." The balance sheet and cash flow statement presentations are a bit more involved, so we will look at each of these in more detail.

Balance Sheet Presentation

Current liabilities are reported as the first category in the liabilities section of the balance sheet. Each of the main types of current liabilities is listed separately within this category.

Similar to current assets, current liabilities are generally listed in their order of maturity. However, this is not always possible, because of the varying maturity dates that may exist for specific obligations such as notes payable. Long-term liabilities are usually reported separately, immediately following current liabilities.

Plazacorp follows a reverse order of liquidity when presenting its liabilities. This is common to real estate companies, which predominantly have long-term liabilities. Use of this reverse order is also common to many international companies. In contrast to what is done internationally, however, real estate companies do not separately identify their long-term and current liabilities. Plazacorp's presentation of its liabilities is shown in Illustration 10-9.

Illustration 10-9 ➡

Plazacorp liabilities

PLAZACORP RETAIL PROPERTIES INC. Balance Sheet (partial) December 31, 2007 (in thousands)		PLAZA PLAZACORP RETAIL PROPERTIES LTD.
Liabilities		
Mortgages payable (Note 12)		$187,449
Mortgage bonds payable (Note 13)		20,356
Debentures payable (Note 14)		11,704
Notes payable (Note 15)		2,657
Bank indebtedness (Note 16)		3,568
Accounts payable and accrued liabilities		5,688
Income taxes payable		186
Future income tax liability (Note 17)		9,403
Other liabilities (Note 18)		674
Total liabilities		241,685

See if you can identify which of the liabilities in the illustration are current and which are likely long-term. The long-term liabilities start with Mortgages Payable and include the next three lines (Mortgage Bonds Payable, Debentures Payable, and Notes Payable) and the last two lines (Future Income Tax Liabilities and Other Liabilities). The remaining liabilities that are shown are current liabilities.

Full disclosure of debt is very important. Summary data are usually presented in the balance sheet and detailed data (such as interest rates, maturity dates, conversion privileges, and assets pledged as collateral) are shown in the notes to the financial statements. Plazacorp's disclosure about its debt fills five pages in the notes to its financial statements.

Cash Flow Statement Presentation

The balance sheet presents the balances of a company's debt at a point in time. Information on cash inflows and outflows during the year that resulted from the principal portion of debt transactions is reported in the financing activities section of the cash flow statement. Interest expense is reported in the operating activities section even though it resulted from debt transactions.

Illustration 10-10 presents selected debt items from the financing activities section of Plazacorp's cash flow statement.

◀ **Illustration 10-10**

Plazacorp financing activities

PLAZACORP RETAIL PROPERTIES INC. Cash Flow Statement (partial) Year Ended December 31, 2007 (in thousands)	
Financing activities	
Decrease in notes payable	$ (665)
Net proceeds from mortgage bonds	2,947
Net proceeds from mortgage financing	71,331
Mortgage repayments	(25,223)

From Plazacorp's cash flow statement, we learn that the company repaid $665 thousand of notes payable and $25,223 thousand of mortgages. It increased its borrowing using mortgage bonds and mortgage financing by $2,947 thousand and $71,331 thousand, respectively. It borrowed more than it repaid in 2007, so it has increased its reliance on debt. We will check on the company's ability to handle this additional debt when we analyze its solvency in the next section.

Analysis

A careful examination of debt obligations makes it easier to assess a company's ability to pay its current obligations. It also helps determine whether a company can obtain long-term financing in order to grow.

Liquidity

Liquidity ratios measure the short-term ability of a company to pay its maturing obligations and to meet unexpected needs for cash. You will recall that we learned about the current ratio (current assets ÷ current liabilities) in Chapter 2. You will also recall that the current ratio can sometimes be misleading. For example, the current ratio's numerator can include some items in current assets that are not very liquid. When a company is having a difficult time selling its merchandise, its inventory and current ratio increase even though its liquidity has actually declined. Similarly, slow-moving accounts receivable increase current assets but are not always collectible. Consequently, the analysis of the current ratio should be supplemented by other ratios, such as the inventory turnover (cost of goods sold ÷ average inventory), which we learned about in Chapter 6, and the receivables turnover (net sales ÷ average receivables), which we learned about in Chapter 7. We will not illustrate these ratios again here.

In recent years, many companies have intentionally reduced their liquid assets (such as accounts receivable and inventory) because these assets cost too much to hold. Companies that keep fewer liquid assets on hand must rely on other sources of liquidity. One such source is an **operating line of credit**, as discussed earlier in this chapter. If a low amount of liquid assets causes a cash shortfall, a company can borrow money on its available short-term lines of credit as necessary.

You may recall that we discussed Plazacorp's operating line of credit earlier in the chapter. It has an $8.4-million operating line of credit, of which it has drawn $3.6 million. It still has $4.8 million of unused capacity to draw upon should it need it.

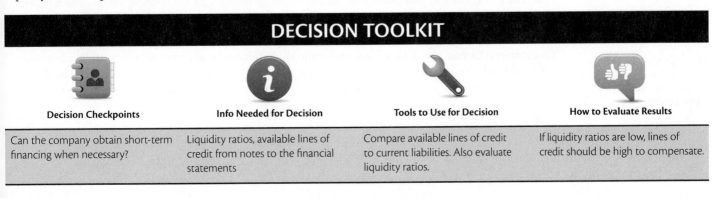

DECISION TOOLKIT

Decision Checkpoints	Info Needed for Decision	Tools to Use for Decision	How to Evaluate Results
Can the company obtain short-term financing when necessary?	Liquidity ratios, available lines of credit from notes to the financial statements	Compare available lines of credit to current liabilities. Also evaluate liquidity ratios.	If liquidity ratios are low, lines of credit should be high to compensate.

Solvency

Solvency ratios, such as the debt to total assets and times interest earned ratios, measure the ability of a company to repay its long-term debt and survive over a long period of time. As the feature story about Plazacorp shows, going into debt is often necessary in order to grow a business. However, debt must be carefully monitored to ensure that it does not hurt a company's solvency. We will review the debt to total assets ratio next, and then introduce a related ratio, the times interest earned ratio.

Debt to Total Assets. In Chapter 2, you learned that one measure of a company's solvency is **debt to total assets**. It is calculated by dividing total liabilities by total assets. This ratio indicates how much of a company's debt could be repaid by liquidating the company's assets.

Using the following selected information (in thousands) from Plazacorp's balance sheet, the company's debt to total assets ratios for 2007 and 2006 are calculated in Illustration 10-11. The illustration also shows industry averages and these ratios for Crombie REIT, one of Plazacorp's competitors in Atlantic Canada.

	2007	2006
Total assets	$269,888	$229,888
Total liabilities	241,685	205,545

Illustration 10-11 ➡

Debt to total assets

DEBT TO TOTAL ASSETS = $\dfrac{\text{TOTAL LIABILITIES}}{\text{TOTAL ASSETS}}$		
(in thousands)	**2007**	**2006**
Plazacorp	$\dfrac{\$241,685}{\$269,888} = 89.6\%$	$\dfrac{\$205,545}{\$229,888} = 89.4\%$
Crombie REIT	63.6%	59.7%
Industry average	74.4%	66.8%

Plazacorp's debt to total assets ratio weakened marginally in 2007. Recall that with debt ratios such as debt to total assets, the higher the value, the worse the solvency. However, keep in mind from our earlier discussion about the cash flow statement that Plazacorp had borrowed more than it repaid in 2007, so it is notable that it was able to maintain its solvency position despite its increased debt.

Nonetheless, Plazacorp's debt to total assets ratio is higher (worse) than Crombie REIT's and the industry average, both of which also weakened in 2007. Note that it is important to be careful when interpreting debt to total assets ratios in the real estate industry. The above numbers use the carrying amount (cost less accumulated depreciation), which is less relevant to this industry than the assets' fair value. For this reason, fair value is more often used as a measure of solvency in the real estate industry. In fact, the real estate industry does not normally use a debt to total assets ratio, but instead calculates a debt to market capitalization ratio, which has more relevance to this industry. Unfortunately, we do not have access to this information for the purpose of our analysis of Plazacorp.

Debt to total assets varies across industries because different financing options are appropriate for different industries. For example, the average debt to total assets ratio for the retail industry was 16 percent in 2007. The average debt to total assets ratio for the real estate industry for the same period was much higher, at 74 percent. The real estate industry is heavily financed because it uses debt to increase its return, as discussed in our feature story.

Alternative Terminology
The *times interest earned* ratio is also known as the *interest coverage ratio.*

Times Interest Earned. The debt to total assets ratio should always be interpreted in light of the company's ability to handle its debt. That is, a company might have a high debt to total assets ratio, but still be able to easily cover its interest payments. Alternatively, a company may have a low debt to total assets ratio and struggle to cover its interest payments.

The **times interest earned** ratio gives an indication of a company's ability to meet interest payments as they come due. It is calculated by dividing the sum of net earnings, interest expense, and income tax expense, by interest expense. It uses earnings before interest and taxes (often abbreviated as **EBIT**) because this number best represents the amount that is available to cover interest. EBIT can be found directly on the statement of earnings or calculated by adding interest expense and income tax expense to net earnings. These are amounts that were originally deducted to determine net earnings. They are added back now to *remove* them from net earnings, and give the amount of earnings before interest and taxes.

Illustration 10-12 uses the following selected information (in thousands) from Plazacorp's statement of earnings to calculate its times interest earned ratios for 2007 and 2006. The illustration also shows these ratios for Crombie REIT and industry averages.

	2007	2006
Interest expense	$12,469	$11,870
Income tax expense	1,165	1,209
Net earnings	3,605	3,019

◂ Illustration 10-12

Times interest earned

$$\text{TIMES INTEREST EARNED} = \frac{\text{EBIT}}{\text{INTEREST EXPENSE}}$$

(in thousands)	2007	2006
Plazacorp	$\dfrac{(\$3,605 + \$1,165 + \$12,469)}{\$12,469}$ = 1.4 times	$\dfrac{(\$3,019 + \$1,209 + \$11,870)}{\$11,870}$ = 1.4 times
Crombie REIT	1.5 times	1.5 times
Industry average	1.4 times	1.5 times

Plazacorp's times interest earned ratio is relatively constant, and similar to that of the industry in 2007. It was slightly lower than Crombie REIT's in both years.

It is interesting to note that although Crombie REIT's debt to total assets ratio was significantly better than that of Plazacorp, their times interest earned ratios are relatively close. This means that Plazacorp is able to handle its high level of debt as well as Crombie REIT, which has a much lower level of debt. As mentioned earlier, this is why it is important to review both the debt to total assets and interest earned ratios together.

ACCOUNTING MATTERS! | Investor Perspective

Credit-rating agencies, such as the DBRS, provide opinions about a company's ability to make timely payments (of principal and interest) on its short- and long-term debt. Short-term debt is rated using an "R" scale, with R-1 being the highest credit quality. Within this scale, the rating is further divided as R-1 (high), R-1 (middle), and R-1 (low) to further distinguish between high, superior, and satisfactory credit quality. Short-term debt rated as R-4 or higher is considered to be speculative.

Long-term debt is rated using a different letter scale than short-term debt. The highest-quality long-term debt is rated as AAA, superior quality as AA, and good quality as A. The credit scale descends to the D, or default, category. Generally, long-term debt rated below BBB is referred to as speculative and non-investment grade, with a higher risk of default.

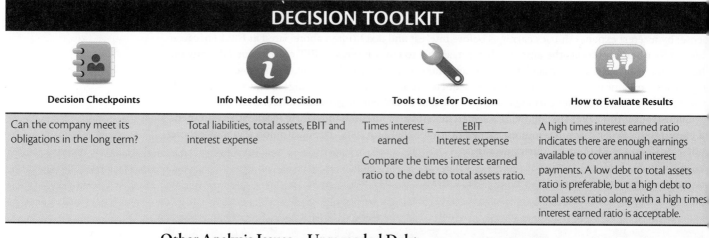

DECISION TOOLKIT

Decision Checkpoints	Info Needed for Decision	Tools to Use for Decision	How to Evaluate Results
Can the company meet its obligations in the long term?	Total liabilities, total assets, EBIT and interest expense	$\dfrac{\text{Times interest}}{\text{earned}} = \dfrac{\text{EBIT}}{\text{Interest expense}}$ Compare the times interest earned ratio to the debt to total assets ratio.	A high times interest earned ratio indicates there are enough earnings available to cover annual interest payments. A low debt to total assets ratio is preferable, but a high debt to total assets ratio along with a high times interest earned ratio is acceptable.

Other Analysis Issues—Unrecorded Debt

One concern for analysts when they evaluate a company's liquidity and solvency is whether the company has properly recorded all of its obligations. Two examples are discussed here—contingencies and off–balance sheet financing.

Contingencies. Sometimes a company's balance sheet does not fully disclose its actual obligations. One reason for this is that potential obligations which may result from contingencies are not always recorded. Contingencies are events with uncertain outcomes. A common type of contingency is a lawsuit. Suppose, for example, that you were analyzing the financial statements of a cigarette manufacturer and did not consider the possible negative implications of major unsettled lawsuits. Your analysis of the company's financial position could be misleading if the company were to lose these suits. Other common types of contingencies are guarantees, product warranties, and environmental cleanup obligations.

Although contingent assets exist (and are recognized if virtually certain to occur), contingent liabilities (which are the focus of this chapter) are far more common. Accounting rules require that a contingent liability (and related contingent loss) be either accrued or disclosed in the notes to the financial statements, unless it is unlikely to occur. If the company can determine a **reasonable estimate** of the expected loss, and if it is **likely** to occur, then the company should accrue the potential loss and liability. If *both* of these conditions are not met, then the company must disclose the contingent loss in the notes to its financial statements.

In its contingency note, Plazacorp discloses guarantees that it has provided on debt assumed by purchasers and co-venturers. It also discloses a guarantee it has provided for environmental matters and litigation that it is involved in. In the note, management also states that in its opinion none of these will have a "significant adverse effect on these financial statements."

The IASB and FASB are currently reviewing the accounting for contingencies and are expected to release a revised standard in 2009. Amongst other items under consideration is the deletion of the terms "contingent asset" and "contingent liability."

Off–Balance Sheet Financing. A second reason that a company's balance sheet might understate its actual obligations is that the company might have "off–balance sheet financing." Off–balance sheet financing refers to a situation where liabilities are not recorded on the balance sheet. This situation can occur when a company is able to obtain financing under certain terms that allow it to avoid recording the obligation. One common type of off–balance sheet financing results from leasing transactions, which you will recall were discussed in Chapter 9.

Critics of off–balance sheet financing argue that many operating leases are actually unavoidable obligations that meet the definition of a liability, and that they should therefore be reported as liabilities on the balance sheet. To reduce these concerns, companies are required to report their operating lease obligations in a note to the financial statements. Plazacorp reports a total of $151,329 thousand for its operating land leases. This allows analysts and other financial statement users to adjust a company's ratios for unrecorded debt if they feel that the inclusion of this debt would have a significant effect on the interpretation of a company's solvency.

The inclusion of land leases for Plazacorp could have a significant effect on an analysis of its financial status. Its land lease commitments comprise more than half (56 percent) of its total assets and 63 percent of its total liabilities. As the adjustments required to remove the effects of these leases from solvency ratios are complex, they are left to a financial statement analysis course.

DECISION TOOLKIT

Decision Checkpoints	Info Needed for Decision	Tools to Use for Decision	How to Evaluate Results
Does the company have any contingent liabilities?	Knowledge of events with uncertain but possibly negative outcomes	Financial statements and notes to the financial statements	If negative outcomes are possible, determine the likelihood and amount of the loss, and the potential impact on the financial statements.
Does the company have significant off–balance sheet financing, such as unrecorded lease obligations?	Information on unrecorded obligations, such as operating lease payments disclosed in the notes to the financial statements	Compare liquidity and solvency ratios with and without unrecorded obligations included.	If ratios differ significantly after including unrecorded obligations, these obligations should not be ignored in analysis.

BEFORE YOU GO ON...

Review It

1. How are liability transactions presented on the statement of earnings, balance sheet, and cash flow statement?
2. Distinguish between liquidity and solvency.
3. How does the times interest earned ratio help with the interpretation of the debt to total assets ratio?
4. What is off–balance sheet financing? Give some examples.

The Navigator

APPENDIX 10A—PRESENT VALUE TABLES

Standard tables to determine the present value factors that are used to calculate the fair value or issue price of bonds are reproduced below.

TABLE 1: PRESENT VALUE OF $1													
(n) Periods	1%	1.5%	2%	2.5%	3%	3.5%	4%	4.5%	5%	6%	7%	8%	9%	10%
1	0.99010	0.98522	0.98039	0.97561	0.97087	0.96618	0.96154	0.95694	0.95238	0.94340	0.93458	0.92593	0.91743	0.90909
2	0.98030	0.97066	0.96117	0.95181	0.94260	0.93351	0.92456	0.91573	0.90703	0.89000	0.87344	0.85734	0.84168	0.82645
3	0.97059	0.95632	0.94232	0.92860	0.91514	0.90194	0.88900	0.87630	0.86384	0.83962	0.81630	0.79383	0.77218	0.75131
4	0.96098	0.94218	0.92385	0.90595	0.88849	0.87144	0.85480	0.83856	0.82270	0.79209	0.76290	0.73503	0.70843	0.68301
5	0.95147	0.92826	0.90573	0.88385	0.86261	0.84197	0.82193	0.80245	0.78353	0.74726	0.71299	0.68058	0.64993	0.62092
6	0.94205	0.91454	0.88797	0.86230	0.83748	0.81350	0.79031	0.76790	0.74622	0.70496	0.66634	0.63017	0.59627	0.56447
7	0.93272	0.90103	0.87056	0.84127	0.81309	0.78599	0.75992	0.73483	0.71068	0.66506	0.62275	0.58349	0.54703	0.51316
8	0.92348	0.88771	0.85349	0.82075	0.78941	0.75941	0.73069	0.70319	0.67684	0.62741	0.58201	0.54027	0.50187	0.46651
9	0.91434	0.87459	0.83676	0.80073	0.76642	0.73373	0.70259	0.67290	0.64461	0.59190	0.54393	0.50025	0.46043	0.42410
10	0.90529	0.86167	0.82035	0.78120	0.74409	0.70892	0.67556	0.64393	0.61391	0.55839	0.50835	0.46319	0.42241	0.38554
11	0.89632	0.84893	0.80426	0.76214	0.72242	0.68495	0.64958	0.61620	0.58468	0.52679	0.47509	0.42888	0.38753	0.35049
12	0.88745	0.83639	0.78849	0.74356	0.70138	0.66178	0.62460	0.58966	0.55684	0.49697	0.44401	0.39711	0.35553	0.31863
13	0.87866	0.82403	0.77303	0.72542	0.68095	0.63940	0.60057	0.56427	0.53032	0.46884	0.41496	0.36770	0.32618	0.28966
14	0.86996	0.81185	0.75788	0.70773	0.66112	0.61778	0.57748	0.53997	0.50507	0.44230	0.38782	0.34046	0.29925	0.26333
15	0.86135	0.79985	0.74301	0.69047	0.64186	0.59689	0.55526	0.51672	0.48102	0.41727	0.36245	0.31524	0.27454	0.23939
16	0.85282	0.78803	0.72845	0.67362	0.62317	0.57671	0.53391	0.49447	0.45811	0.39365	0.33873	0.29189	0.25187	0.21763
17	0.84438	0.77639	0.71416	0.65720	0.60502	0.55720	0.51337	0.47318	0.43630	0.37136	0.31657	0.27027	0.23107	0.19784
18	0.83602	0.76491	0.70016	0.64117	0.58739	0.53836	0.49363	0.45280	0.41552	0.35034	0.29586	0.25025	0.21199	0.17986
19	0.82774	0.75361	0.68643	0.62553	0.57029	0.52016	0.47464	0.43330	0.39573	0.33051	0.27651	0.23171	0.19449	0.16351
20	0.81954	0.74247	0.67297	0.61027	0.55368	0.50257	0.45639	0.41464	0.37689	0.31180	0.25842	0.21455	0.17843	0.14864

| TABLE 2: PRESENT VALUE OF AN ANNUITY OF $1 | | | | | | | | | | | | | |

(n) Periods	1%	1.5%	2%	2.5%	3%	3.5%	4%	4.5%	5%	6%	7%	8%	9%	10%
1	0.99010	0.98522	0.98039	0.97561	0.97087	0.96618	0.96154	0.95694	0.95238	0.94340	0.93458	0.92593	0.91743	0.90909
2	1.97040	1.95588	1.94156	1.92742	1.91347	1.89969	1.88609	1.87267	1.85941	1.83339	1.80802	1.78326	1.75911	1.73554
3	2.94099	2.91220	2.88388	2.85602	2.82861	2.80164	2.77509	2.74896	2.72325	2.67301	2.62432	2.57710	2.53129	2.48685
4	3.90197	3.85438	3.80773	3.76197	3.71710	3.67308	3.62990	3.58753	3.54595	3.46511	3.38721	3.31213	3.23972	3.16987
5	4.85343	4.78264	4.71346	4.64583	4.57971	4.51505	4.45182	4.38998	4.32948	4.21236	4.10020	3.99271	3.88965	3.79079
6	5.79548	5.69719	5.60143	5.50813	5.41719	5.32855	5.24214	5.15787	5.07569	4.91732	4.76654	4.62288	4.48592	4.35526
7	6.72819	6.59821	6.47199	6.34939	6.23028	6.11454	6.00205	5.89270	5.78637	5.58238	5.38929	5.20637	5.03295	4.86842
8	7.65168	7.48593	7.32548	7.17014	7.01969	6.87396	6.73274	6.59589	6.46321	6.20979	5.97130	5.74664	5.53482	5.33493
9	8.56602	8.36052	8.16224	7.97087	7.78611	7.60769	7.43533	7.26879	7.10782	6.80169	6.51523	6.24689	5.99525	5.75902
10	9.47130	9.22218	8.98259	8.75206	8.53020	8.31661	8.11090	7.91272	7.72173	7.36009	7.02358	6.71008	6.41766	6.14457
11	10.36763	10.07112	9.78685	9.51421	9.25262	9.00155	8.76048	8.52892	8.30641	7.88687	7.49867	7.13896	6.80519	6.49506
12	11.25508	10.90751	10.57534	10.25776	9.95400	9.66333	9.38507	9.11858	8.86325	8.38384	7.94269	7.53608	7.16073	6.81369
13	12.13374	11.73153	11.34837	10.98318	10.63496	10.30274	9.98565	9.68285	9.39357	8.85268	8.35765	7.90378	7.48690	7.10336
14	13.00370	12.54338	12.10625	11.69091	11.29607	10.92052	10.56312	10.22283	9.89864	9.29498	8.74547	8.24424	7.78615	7.36669
15	13.86505	13.34323	12.84926	12.38138	11.93794	11.51741	11.11839	10.73955	10.37966	9.71225	9.10791	8.55948	8.06069	7.60608
16	14.71787	14.13126	13.57771	13.05500	12.56110	12.09412	11.65230	11.23402	10.83777	10.10590	9.44665	8.85137	8.31256	7.82371
17	15.56225	14.90765	14.29187	13.71220	13.16612	12.65132	12.16567	11.70719	11.27407	10.47726	9.76322	9.12164	8.54363	8.02155
18	16.39827	15.67256	14.99203	14.35336	13.75351	13.18968	12.65930	12.15999	11.68959	10.82760	10.05909	9.37189	8.75563	8.20141
19	17.22601	16.42617	15.67846	14.97889	14.32380	13.70984	13.13394	12.59329	12.08532	11.15812	10.33560	9.60360	8.95011	8.36492
20	18.04555	17.16864	16.35143	15.58916	14.87747	14.21240	13.59033	13.00794	12.46221	11.46992	10.59401	9.81815	9.12855	8.51356

Follow these brief instructions to help you use the tables:

1. Use Table 1 (the present value of $1) to determine the right factor to use to calculate the present value of the principal, which is a single sum.
2. Use Table 2 (the present value of an annuity of $1) to calculate the present value of the interest, which recurs periodically (as an annuity).
3. To find the right factor in each table, locate the factor at the intersection of the number of periods and the interest rate. When interest is paid semi-annually, remember to double the number of periods and halve the annual interest rate. For example, in our Candlestick example used in the chapter, the five-year term of the bonds means that there are 10 semi-annual interest periods. In addition, the market interest rate of 6 percent when bonds are sold at a discount becomes 3 percent (6% × 6/12). When bonds are sold at a premium, the market interest rate of 4 percent becomes 2 percent (4% × 6/12) when adjusted for the semi-annual period.
4. The face value of the bonds and the contractual interest rate are used to calculate the interest payment. Note that while the contractual interest rate is used to determine the interest payment, the market interest rate is what is used to determine the present value.

APPENDIX 10B—AMORTIZATION SCHEDULES

As shown in the chapter, bond amortization schedules make it easier to calculate and record the interest expense and the amortization on bond issues.

Using our Candlestick Inc. example from the chapter, a bond discount amortization schedule for the entire five years (10 semi-annual interest periods) is shown below in Illustration 10B-1. For simplicity, amounts have been rounded to the nearest dollar in this schedule.

	CANDLESTICK INC.				
	Bond Discount Amortization Schedule				
Semi-Annual Interest Period	(A) Interest Payment ($1,000,000 × 5% × %₁₂)	(B) Interest Expense (Preceding Bond Carrying Amount × 6% × %₁₂)	(C) Discount Amortization (B – A)	(D) Unamortized Discount (D – C)	(E) Bond Carrying Amount ($1,000,000 – D)
Issue date				$42,655	$ 957,345
1	$ 25,000	$ 28,720	$ 3,720	38,935	961,065
2	25,000	28,832	3,832	35,103	964,897
3	25,000	28,947	3,947	31,156	968,844
4	25,000	29,065	4,065	27,091	972,909
5	25,000	29,187	4,187	22,904	977,096
6	25,000	29,313	4,313	18,591	981,409
7	25,000	29,442	4,442	14,149	985,851
8	25,000	29,576	4,576	9,573	990,427
9	25,000	29,713	4,713	4,860	995,140
10	25,000	29,860*	4,860	0	1,000,000
	$250,000	$292,655	$42,655		

*Adjusted for rounding differences.

Column (A) remains constant because the face value of the bonds ($1,000,000) is multiplied by the semi-annual contractual interest rate each period.

Column (B) is the bond carrying amount at the end of the preceding period multiplied by the semi-annual market interest rate.

Column (C) indicates the discount amortization each period.

Column (D) decreases each period by the amortization amount until it reaches zero at maturity.

Column (E) increases each period by the amortization amount until it equals the face value at maturity.

⬆ Illustration 10-B1

Bond discount amortization schedule

A bond premium amortization schedule is shown in Illustration 10B-2. Figures have been rounded to the nearest dollar for simplicity.

	CANDLESTICK INC.				
	Bond Premium Amortization Schedule				
Semi-Annual Interest Period	(A) Interest Payment ($1,000,000 × 5% × %₁₂)	(B) Interest Expense (Preceding Bond Carrying Amount × 4% × %₁₂)	(C) Premium Amortization (A – B)	(D) Unamortized Premium (D – C)	(E) Bond Carrying Amount ($1,000,000 + D)
Issue date				$44,915	$1,044,915
1	$ 25,000	$ 20,898	$ 4,102	40,813	1,040,813
2	25,000	20,816	4,184	36,629	1,036,629
3	25,000	20,733	4,267	32,362	1,032,362
4	25,000	20,647	4,353	28,009	1,028,009
5	25,000	20,560	4,440	23,569	1,023,569
6	25,000	20,471	4,529	19,040	1,019,040
7	25,000	20,381	4,619	14,421	1,014,421
8	25,000	20,288	4,712	9,709	1,009,709
9	25,000	20,194	4,806	4,903	1,004,903
10	25,000	20,097*	4,903	0	1,000,000
	$250,000	$205,085	$44,915		

*Adjusted for rounding differences.

Column (A) remains constant because the face value of the bonds ($1,000,000) is multiplied by the semi-annual contractual interest rate each period.

Column (B) is the bond carrying amount at the end of the preceding period multiplied by the semi-annual market interest rate.

Column (C) indicates the premium amortization each period.

Column (D) decreases each period by the amortization amount until it reaches zero at maturity.

Column (E) decreases each period by the amortization amount until it equals the face value at maturity.

⬆ Illustration 10-B2

Bond premium amortization schedule

Managing Personal Financial Reporting

When companies need money for operations, they go to creditors or investors. When you, a student, need money for school, you must rely on contributions from parents and other relatives, money from summer or part-time jobs, plus grants, bursaries, and scholarships. If these sources do not cover the cost of post-secondary education, you can also look into student loans. Federal, provincial, and territorial governments offer student loan programs. Private institutions such as banks, trust companies, and credit unions may also offer loan options if you do not qualify for a government student loan.

Student loans are just one option to consider when you are deciding how to pay for your education. It is important to understand your obligations and responsibilities as a borrower because a student loan is a loan, and you are required to pay it back. The amount of your student loan is determined based on an assessment of your financial need, which is different for each student. First, your allowable costs (which may include education, living, and transportation costs) and your resources are calculated. The difference between the two is your assessed financial need. For this purpose, and for future personal financial planning, maintenance of your personal financial records is critical. These personal financial records include such records as your income tax return, payroll documents, and other invoices and payments. It is also imperative that you keep your personal financial statements up to date, such as your balance sheet discussed in the Chapter 2 "All About You."

Some Facts

- Canada Student Grants funding is budgeted to increase by $80 million by 2012–2013, to $430 million.
- Canadian full-time undergraduate students paid an average of $4,524 in tuition fees for the 2007–2008 academic year, up from $4,400 the year before.
- Full-time students owe more in federal student loans than ever before, according to new statistics released by the Canada Student Loan Program. The latest annual report reported that full-time students received an average annual federal loan of $5,631.
- In a recent survey, 42 percent of students anticipated having student loan debt at the end of their program and 50 percent of these students anticipate it will take between three and seven years to repay the debt.

What Do You Think?

Suppose you own a car, but your parents use their car to drop you off at university and pick you up later on their way home. You decide to add your parents' car expenses to your list of expenses when applying for a student loan because you know the more expenses you have, the more likely you are to obtain financial aid. To increase your chances of receiving aid, should you overstate your expenses?

YES | You are playing within the rules as you do own a car and how would the government know that you were not commuting to university in your own car?

NO | Random audits are conducted each year and, if it were found out that you lied about your expenses, you would never be able to apply for another Government Student Loan.

The Navigator

Sources:

Statistics Canada, "University Tuition Fees," October 18, 2007, statcan.ca/Daily/English/071018/d071018b.htm

Erin Millar, "Deeper in Debt," Maclean's on Campus, April 11, 2008, oncampus.macleans.ca/education/2008/04/11/students-borrowed-17-per-cent-more-in-federal-student-loans-in-2005-06-than-2004-06

R.A. Malatest & Associates Ltd., "Survey of Canadian Career College Students, Phase II: In-School Student Survey," March 2008, millenniumscholarships.ca/images/Publications/080331_SCCCS_EN.pdf

Summary of Study Objectives

1. Account for current liabilities. A current liability is a debt that will be paid (1) from existing current assets or through the creation of other current liabilities, and (2) within one year. An example of a current liability is an operating line of credit that results in bank indebtedness. Current liabilities also include sales taxes, payroll deductions, and employee benefits, all of which the company collects on behalf of third parties. Other examples include property taxes and interest on notes payable, which must be accrued until paid. The portion of long-term debt that is due within the next year must be deducted from the long-term liability and reported as a current liability.

2. Account for long-term notes payable. Long-term notes payable are repayable in a series of payments. Each payment consists of (1) interest on the unpaid balance of the note, and (2) a reduction in the principal balance. These payments can be either (1) fixed principal payments or (2) blended principal and interest payments. With fixed principal payments, the reduction in principal is constant but the cash payment and interest decrease each period (as the principal decreases). Blended principal and interest payments result in a constant cash payment but changing amounts of interest and principal.

3. Account for bonds payable. Bonds are issued at their present (fair) value. When they are issued, the Cash account is debited and the Bonds Payable account is credited for the issue price of the bonds.

Bond discounts and bond premiums are amortized to interest expense over the life of the bond using the effective-interest method of amortization. Amortization is calculated as the difference between the interest paid and the interest expense. Interest paid is calculated by multiplying the face value of the bonds by the contractual interest rate. Interest expense is calculated by multiplying the carrying amount of the bonds at the beginning of the interest period by the market interest rate. The amortization of a bond discount increases interest expense and the carrying amount of the bond. The amortization of a bond premium decreases interest expense and the carrying amount of the bond.

When bonds are retired at maturity, Bonds Payable is debited and Cash is credited. There is no gain or loss at retirement. When bonds are redeemed before maturity, it is necessary to (a) update any unrecorded interest and amortization, (b) eliminate the carrying amount of the bonds at the redemption date, (c) record the cash paid, and (d) recognize any gain or loss on redemption.

4. Identify the requirements for the financial statement presentation and analysis of liabilities. Interest expense and any gain or loss on the redemption of bonds are reported as "other expenses" or "other revenues" in the statement of earnings. In the balance sheet, current liabilities are reported first, followed by long-term liabilities. Inflows and outflows of cash related to the principal portion of long-term debt are reported in the financing activities section of the cash flow statement. The nature of each liability should be described in the notes accompanying the financial statements.

The liquidity of a company may be analyzed by calculating the current ratio, in addition to the receivables and inventory turnover ratios. The solvency of a company may be analyzed by calculating the debt to total assets and times interest earned ratios. Other factors to consider are unrecorded debt, such as contingent liabilities and operating lease obligations.

The Navigator

Glossary

Study Tools (Glossary)

Bond A form of interest-bearing note payable issued by large corporations, universities, and governments. (p. 502)

Collateral Assets pledged as security for the payment of a debt (e.g., land, buildings, and equipment in the case of a mortgage; accounts receivable or inventory in the case of a bank loan). (p. 493)

Contingencies Events with uncertain outcomes, such as a potential liability that may become an actual liability sometime in the future. (p. 516)

Contractual interest rate The rate used to determine the amount of interest the borrower pays and the investor receives. (p. 502)

Convertible debt Debt such as notes or bonds that has the option of being converted into (exchanged for) common shares. (p. 499)

Debentures Unsecured debt issued against the general credit of the borrower. (p. 499)

Discount The difference between the face value of a bond and its issue price when a bond is sold for less than its face value. This occurs when the market interest rate is higher than the contractual interest rate. (p. 504)

EBIT Earnings before interest expense and income tax expense. (p. 515)

Effective-interest method A method of amortizing a bond discount or premium that results in a periodic interest expense that equals a constant percentage (the market or effective interest rate) of the carrying amount of the bond. Amortization is calculated as the difference between the interest expense and the interest paid. (p. 505)

Employee benefits Payments made by an employer to give pension, insurance, medical, or other benefits to its employees. (p. 496)

Fixed interest rate An interest rate that is constant (unchanged) over the term of the debt. (p. 493)

Floating (variable) interest rate An interest rate that changes over the term of the debt with fluctuating market rates. (p. 492)

Gross pay The total compensation earned by an employee. Also known as gross earnings. (p. 495)

Market interest rate The rate that investors demand for loaning funds to a corporation. Also known as the effective interest rate. (p. 503)

Mortgage note payable A long-term note secured by a mortgage that pledges title to property as collateral for the loan. (p. 499)

Net pay Gross pay less payroll deductions. (p. 496)

Notes payable Obligations in the form of written notes. (p. 493)

Operating line of credit A pre-arranged agreement to borrow money at a bank, up to an agreed-upon amount. (p. 492)

Payroll deductions Deductions from gross pay to determine the amount of a paycheque. (p. 495)

Premium The difference between the issue price and the face value of a bond when a bond is sold for more than its face value. This occurs when the market interest rate is less than the contractual interest rate. (p. 505)

Redeemable (callable) bonds Bonds that are subject to retirement at a stated dollar amount before maturity at the option of the issuer. (p. 510)

Secured Describes debt, such as notes or bonds, for which specific assets of the issuer have been pledged as collateral. (p. 499)

Times interest earned A measure of a company's solvency, calculated by dividing earnings before interest expense and income tax expense (EBIT) by interest expense. (p. 515)

Unsecured Describes debt, such as notes or bonds, that has been issued against the general credit of the borrower; also called debentures. (p. 499)

The Navigator

DECISION TOOLKIT—A SUMMARY

Decision Checkpoints	Info Needed for Decision	Tools to Use for Decision	How to Evaluate Results
Can the company obtain short-term financing when necessary?	Liquidity ratios, available lines of credit from notes to the financial statements	Compare available lines of credit to current liabilities. Also evaluate liquidity ratios.	If liquidity ratios are low, lines of credit should be high to compensate.
Can the company meet its obligations in the long term?	Total liabilities, total assets, EBIT and interest expense	$$\text{Times interest earned} = \frac{\text{EBIT}}{\text{Interest expense}}$$ Compare the times interest earned ratio to the debt to total assets ratio.	A high times interest earned ratio indicates there are enough earnings available to cover annual interest payments. A low debt to total assets ratio is preferable, but a high debt to total assets ratio along with a high times interest earned ratio is acceptable.
Does the company have any contingent liabilities?	Knowledge of events with uncertain but possibly negative outcomes	Financial statements and notes to the financial statements	If negative outcomes are possible, determine the likelihood and amount of the loss, and the potential impact on the financial statements.
Does the company have significant off–balance sheet financing, such as unrecorded lease obligations?	Information on unrecorded obligations, such as operating lease payments disclosed in the notes to the financial statements	Compare liquidity and solvency ratios with and without unrecorded obligations included.	If ratios differ significantly after including unrecorded obligations, these obligations should not be ignored in analysis.

Analysis Tools (Decision Toolkit Summaries)

The Navigator

Using the Decision Toolkit

First Capital Realty Inc. is a real estate development company headquartered in Toronto. It is one of Plazacorp's competitors, although where Plazacorp operates only in Atlantic Canada, Quebec, and Ontario, First Capital Realty is much larger and operates across Canada. Selected financial information for First Capital Realty follows:

FIRST CAPITAL REALTY INC. Selected Financial Information December 31, 2007 (in thousands)	FIRST CAPITAL ®

Balance sheet	
Current assets	$ 46,459
Total assets	3,409,409
Current liabilities	110,006
Total liabilities	2,458,078
Statement of earnings	
Interest expense	116,043
Income tax expense	12,602
Net earnings	30,353

Additional information:
1. The company has an undrawn operating line of credit of $128 million at December 31, 2007.
2. The fair value of the company's total assets is $4,141,409 thousand.

Instructions

(a) Plazacorp's current ratio is 1.3:1. Calculate First Capital Realty's current ratio, and compare its liquidity to that of Plazacorp.

(b) Calculate First Capital Realty's debt to total assets and times interest earned ratios, and compare its solvency to that of Plazacorp and the industry averages.

(c) Recalculate First Capital Realty's debt to total assets ratio using the fair value of the assets, rather than their recorded cost.

Solution

(a) Liquidity:

	First Capital Realty	Plazacorp	Industry Average
Current ratio	$\dfrac{\$46,459}{\$110,006} = 0.4:1$	1.3:1	n/a

First Capital Realty's current ratio is 0.4:1, which means that it has $0.40 of current assets for every $1 of current liabilities. Although its available line of credit improves its liquidity, the latter is still not good and is significantly below that of Plazacorp. Neither company has inventory nor many receivables, but if they did, these ratios should also be calculated for both companies before reaching a conclusion about the adequacy of their liquidity.

(b) Solvency:

	First Capital Realty	Plazacorp	Industry Average
Debt to total assets	$\dfrac{\$2,458,078}{\$3,409,409} = 72.1\%$	89.6%	74.4%
Times interest earned	$\dfrac{\$30,353 + \$12,602 + \$116,043}{\$116,043} = 1.4 \text{ times}$	1.4 times	1.4 times

First Capital Realty's debt to total assets ratio of 72.1% is better than that of Plazacorp, and slightly better than that of the industry. Despite this improved debt to total assets position, First Capital Realty's times interest earned ratio of 1.4 times is the same as that of Plazacorp and the industry average.

(c) The debt to total assets ratio, using cost and fair values, follows:

	Debt to Total Assets (Fair Value)	Debt to Total Assets (Cost)
Debt to total assets	$\dfrac{\$2,458,078}{\$4,141,409} = 59.4\%$	$\dfrac{\$2,458,078}{\$3,409,409} = 72.1\%$

First Capital Realty's debt to total assets ratio improves from 72.1% to 59.4% when fair value is used for total assets rather than cost.

The Navigator

Study Tools
(Demonstration Problems)

Demonstration Problem

Snyder Software Inc. successfully developed a new computer program. To produce and market the program, the company needed to raise $500,000. On December 31, 2008, Snyder issued a 15-year, 6%, $500,000 mortgage note payable. The terms provide for semi-annual blended instalment payments of $25,510 (principal and interest) on June 30 and December 31.

Instructions
(a) Prepare a payment schedule for the first four instalment payments.
(b) Record the issue of the note on December 31, 2008.
(c) Record the first instalment payment on June 30, 2009.
(d) Indicate the current, noncurrent, and total amounts that would be presented in the balance sheet for the mortgage note payable at December 31, 2009.

Action Plan

- Determine the interest expense for the mortgage by multiplying the semi-annual interest rate by the principal balance at the beginning of the period. The reduction of principal is the difference between the cash payment and the interest expense amounts.

- Recognize that, as the principal amount decreases, so does the interest expense.

- Record mortgage payments, recognizing that each payment consists of (1) interest on the unpaid loan balance, and (2) a reduction of the loan principal.

Solution to Demonstration Problem

(a)

Semi-Annual Interest Period	Cash Payment	Interest Expense	Reduction of Principal	Principal Balance
Issue date (Dec. 31, 2008)				$500,000
1 (June 30, 2009)	$25,510	$15,000[a]	$10,510[b]	489,490[c]
2 (Dec. 31, 2009)	25,510	14,685	10,825	478,665
3 (June 30, 2010)	25,510	14,360	11,150	467,515
4 (Dec. 31, 2010)	25,510	14,025	11,485	456,030

[a] $500,000 × 6% × 6/12 = $15,000
[b] $25,510 − $15,000 = $10,510
[c] $500,000 − $10,510 = $489,490

(b)

Dec. 31, 2008	Cash	500,000	
	Mortgage Note Payable		500,000
	(To record issue of 15-year, 6% mortgage note payable)		

(c)

June 30, 2009	Interest Expense	15,000	
	Mortgage Note Payable	10,510	
	Cash		25,510
	(To record interest and instalment payment on mortgage note payable)		

(d) The current liability is $22,635 ($11,150 + $11,485).
The long-term liability is $456,030.
The total liability is the balance of $478,665 at the end of the second period, December 31, 2009.

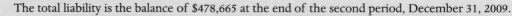

The Navigator

Self-Study Questions

Answers are at the end of the chapter.

1. Restouche Ltd. has $4,515 of pre-tax sales. If Restouche collects 13% HST with each sale, what is the amount to be credited to Sales?
    (a) $587
    (b) $3,996
    (c) $4,515
    (d) $5,102

2. On March 1, Swift Current Limited received its property tax assessment in the amount of $12,000 for the calendar year. The property tax bill is due May 1. If Swift Current prepares quarterly financial statements, how much prepaid property tax should the company report at May 1?
    (a) $2,000
    (b) $4000
    (c) $8,000
    (d) $12,000

3. Severin works for the Blue Door Corporation at a salary of $550 per week. Canada Pension Plan contributions are $23.89 for the employee and the same for the employer. Income taxes are $79.15. Employment insurance premiums are $9.51 for the employee and $13.31 for the employer. How much is Severin's weekly net pay (i.e., take-home pay)?
    (a) $400.25
    (b) $437.45
    (c) $512.80
    (d) $550.00

4. Zhang Inc. issues a three-year, 7%, $497,000 instalment note payable on January 1. The note will be paid in three annual blended instalment payments of $189,383 that are payable at the end of each year. What is the amount of interest expense that should be recognized by Zhang in the second year?
    (a) $17,395
    (b) $23,193
    (c) $23,968
    (d) $34,790

5. Boudreault Ltée issues a three-year, 7%, $497,000 instalment note payable on January 1. The note will be paid with fixed principal instalment payments of $165,667 that are payable at the end of each year. What is the amount of interest expense that should be recognized by Boudreault in the second year?
    (a) $17,395
    (b) $23,193
    (c) $23,968
    (d) $34,790

6. On January 1, Scissors Corp. issues $200,000 of five-year, 7% (SO 3) bonds at 97. The entry to record the issue of the bonds would include a:
    (a) debit to Cash for $200,000.
    (b) credit to Bonds Payable for $200,000.
    (c) debit to Investment in Bonds for $194,000.
    (d) credit to Bonds Payable for $194,000.

7. On January 1, Daigle Corporation issued $2 million of five- (SO 3) year, 7% bonds with interest payable on January 1 and July 1. The bonds sold for $1,918,880 to yield a market interest rate of 8%. The debit entry to the Bond Interest Expense account (rounded to the nearest dollar) on July 1 is for:
    (a) $67,161.
    (b) $70,000.
    (c) $76,755.
    (d) $80,000.

8. Gester Corporation redeems its $100,000 of face value bonds (SO 3) at 105 on January 1. The carrying amount of the bonds at the redemption date is $103,745. The entry to record the redemption will include a:
    (a) debit of $1,255 to Loss on Bond Redemption.
    (b) credit of $1,255 to Gain on Bond Redemption.
    (c) credit of $103,745 to Bonds Payable.
    (d) debit of $105,000 to Cash.

9. Which of the following ratio combinations indicates (SO 4) that a company's solvency is improving?
    (a) Debt to total assets ratios of 55% in year 2 and 45% in year 1
    (b) Times interest earned ratios of 7 times in year 2 and 10 times in year 1
    (c) Debt to total assets ratios of 55% in year 2 and 45% in year 1 and times interest earned ratios of 7 times in year 2 and 10 times in year 1
    (d) Debt to total assets ratios of 45% in year 2 and 55% in year 1 and times interest earned ratios of 10 times in year 2 and 7 times in year 1

10. In a recent year, K-Dough Corporation had net earnings (SO 4) of $150,000, interest expense of $30,000, and income tax expense of $20,000. What was K-Dough's times interest earned ratio?
    (a) 5.0 times
    (b) 5.7 times
    (c) 6.0 times
    (d) 6.7 times

The Navigator

Questions

(SO 1) 1. Identify the similarities and differences between accounts payable and notes payable.

(SO 1) 2. What is the difference between an operating line of credit and a note payable?

(SO 1) 3. Your roommate says, "Sales taxes are part of the cost of doing business and should be reported as a deduction from sales in the sales revenue section of the statement of earnings." Do you agree? Explain.

(SO 1) 4. Explain how recording property taxes can result in an expense (property tax expense), a liability (property tax payable), and an asset (prepaid property tax).

(SO 1) 5. What is the difference (a) between gross and net pay, and (b) between employee payroll deductions and employee benefits?

(SO 1, 2) 6. Explain how to properly present the current portion of long-term debt in the liabilities section of the balance sheet.

(SO 2) 7. Identify the similarities and differences between short-term and long-term notes payable.

(SO 2) 8. Distinguish between instalment notes payable with fixed principal payments and those with blended principal and interest payments.

(SO 2) 9. When students borrow money for their post-secondary education under the Canada Student Loans Program, they sign an instalment note payable. It must be repaid, starting six months are graduation, in equal monthly amounts including principal and interest. Is this a fixed or blended payment pattern?

(SO 2) 10. Canada Student Loans charge interest at prime plus an added percentage, such as 2.5 percent. Is this a fixed or floating rate?

(SO 2) 11. Doug Bareak, a friend of yours, has recently purchased a home for $200,000. He paid $20,000 down and financed the remainder with a 20-year, 5% mortgage that is payable in blended payments of principal and interest of $1,290 per month. At the end of the first month, Doug received a statement from the bank indicating that only $540 of the principal was paid during the month. At this rate, he calculated that it would take over 28 years to pay off the mortgage. Explain why Doug is incorrect.

12. Identify the similarities and differences between long-term notes payable and bonds payable.

13. La Mi and Jack Dalton are discussing how the issue price of a bond is determined. La believes that the issue price depends only on the amount of the principal payment at the end of the term of a bond. Is she right? Discuss.

14. Stoney Inc. sold bonds with a face value of $100,000 for $104,000. Was the market interest rate equal to, less than, or greater than the bonds' contractual interest rate? Explain.

15. Explain how amortization is calculated when bonds are issued (a) at a discount, and (b) at a premium.

16. How will the total cost of borrowing be affected if a bond is sold (a) at a discount and (b) at a premium? Explain when this cost of borrowing should be recorded and identify the relevant generally accepted accounting principle.

17. Why is there no gain or loss when bonds are redeemed at maturity, but there usually is a gain or loss when bonds are redeemed before maturity?

18. In general, what are the requirements for the financial statement presentation of (a) current liabilities, and (b) long-term liabilities?

19. ◼️◖ Distinguish between liquidity and solvency. Provide an example of two ratios that are used to measure each.

20. ◼️◖ Explain how an operating line of credit can help improve a company's liquidity.

21. ◼️◖ Explain why the debt to total assets ratio should never be interpreted without referring to the times interest earned ratio.

22. ◼️◖ What is a contingency? Why do investors need to know about something that might not even happen?

23. ◼️◖ Explain why it is important to know if a company has significant operating lease commitments.

Brief Exercises

Record short-term note.
(SO 1)

BE10–1 Romez Limited borrowed $55,000 from the bank on July 1 by signing a three-month, 5% note payable. Interest is payable the first of each month, starting August 1. Romez's year end is August 31 Prepare journal entries to record (a) the issue of the note on July 1, (b) (1) the payment of interest on August 1, (2) the accrual of interest on August 31, (3) the payment of interest on September 1, and (4) the payment of interest on October 1, and (c) repayment of the note at maturity on October 1. Round your answers to the nearest dollar.

BE10–2 Centennial Sales Ltd. reports cash sales of $6,500 on October 1. (a) Record the sales assuming they occurred in Ontario and are subject to 5% GST and 8% PST (charged on selling price only). (b) Record the sales assuming they occurred in Quebec and are subject to 5% GST and 7.5% QST (charged on selling price plus GST).

Record sales taxes.
(SO 1)

BE10–3 Pierce Corp. has a December 31 year end. It received its property tax assessment of $25,200 on April 30 for the calendar year. The property tax bill is payable on July 15. Prepare the journal entries to record the property tax on (a) April 30, (b) July 15, and (c) December 31.

Record property tax.
(SO 1)

BE10–4 Zerbe Consulting Inc.'s gross salaries for the bi-weekly period ended August 22 were $15,000. Deductions included $736 for CPP, $260 for EI, and $6,258 for income taxes. The company's payroll costs were $736 for CPP and $364 for EI. Prepare journal entries to record (a) the payment of salaries on August 22, and (b) the employer payroll costs on August 22, assuming they will not be remitted to the government until September.

Record payroll.
(SO 1)

BE10–5 Assume that you qualify for a $15,000 loan from the Canada Student Loans Program to help finance your education. Once you graduate, you start repaying this 7% note payable with a monthly cash payment of $174, principal and interest, for 120 payments (10 years). Prepare an instalment payment schedule for the first three payments.

Prepare instalment payment schedule.
(SO 2)

BE10–6 Eyre Inc. issues a 10-year, 7%, $300,000 mortgage note payable on November 30, 2009, to obtain financing for a new building. The terms provide for monthly payments. Prepare the entries to record the mortgage loan on November 30, 2009, and the first two payments on December 31, 2009, and January 31, 2010, assuming the payment is (a) a fixed principal payment of $2,500, and (b) a blended principal and interest payment of $3,483.

Record mortgage note payable.
(SO 2)

BE10–7 Assad Inc. issued a five-year, 7% note payable, with fixed principal payments of $10,000 due annually. The following instalment payment schedule is partially completed:

Complete instalment payment schedule; identify current and long-term portions of debt.
(SO 2)

Interest Period	Cash Payment	Interest Expense	Reduction of Principal	Principal Balance
Issue date				$50,000
1	$13,500	(1)	$10,000	40,000
2	12,800	$2,800	(2)	30,000
3	(3)	2,100	10,000	(4)
4	11,400	1,400	10,000	10,000
5	10,700	700	10,000	(5)

(a) Fill in the missing amounts for items (1) through (5).

(b) What are the long-term and current portions of the note at the end of period 2?

BE10–8 Carvel Corp. issued $500,000 of five-year, 6% bonds, with interest payable semi-annually. How much did Carvel receive from the sale of these bonds if the market interest rate was (a) 5%, (b) 6%, and (c) 7%?

Calculate present value of bond.
(SO 3)

BE10–9 Keyser Corporation issued $100,000 of five-year, 5% bonds dated May 1, 2009. (a) Prepare the journal entry to record the sale of these bonds on May 1, 2009, assuming that the bonds were issued at (1) 99, (2) 100, and (3) 101. (b) What will the carrying amount be at maturity, May 1, 2014, under each of the three different issue price scenarios?

Record bond issue.
(SO 3)

BE10–10 Keystone Corporation issued $1 million of five-year, 6% bonds dated March 1, 2009, at 100. Interest is payable semi-annually on September 1 and March 1. Keystone has a December 31 year end. (a) Record the issue of these bonds on March 1, 2009. (b) Record the first interest payment on September 1, 2009. (c) Record the adjusting journal entry on December 31, 2009, to accrue the interest. (d) Prepare the journal entry to record the second interest payment on March 1, 2010.

Record bond transactions.
(SO 3)

BE10–11 A partial bond discount amortization schedule for Chiasson Corp. follows:

Complete bond amortization schedule; answer questions..
(SO 3)

Semi-Annual Interest Period	Interest Payment	Interest Expense	Discount Amortization	Unamortized Discount	Bond Carrying Amount
Issue Date				$62,311	$937,689
1 (Apr. 30)	$45,000	(1)	$1,884	(2)	939,573
2 (Oct. 31)	45,000	$46,979	(3)	58,448	(4)

▸ Reporting and Analyzing Liabilities

(a) Fill in the missing amounts for items (1) through (4).

(b) What is the face value of the bonds?

(c) What is the contractual interest rate on the bonds? The market interest rate?

(d) Explain why interest expense is greater than interest paid.

(e) Prepare the journal entry to record the payments of interest on April 30 and October 31.

Calculate present value; record bond transactions.
(SO 3)

BE10–12 On May 1, 2009, Jianhua Corporation issued $200,000 of five-year, 8% bonds, with interest payable semi-annually on November 1 and May 1. The bonds were issued to yield a market interest rate of 6%. (a) Calculate the present value (issue price) of the bonds on May 1. (b) Record the issue of the bonds on May 1. (c) Prepare the journal entry to record the first and second interest payments on November 1 2009, and May 1, 2010.

Record bond redemption.
(SO 3)

BE10–13 Hathaway Ltd.'s general ledger reported a balance in its Bonds Payable account of $940,000 at November 30, 2009. The bonds had a face value of $1,000,000, and were redeemed on November 30 Prepare the journal entry to record the redemption, assuming the bonds are redeemed at (a) 99, and (b) 101.

Identify current liabilities.
(SO 4)

BE10–14 Identify which of the following transactions would be classified as a current liability. For those that are not current liabilities, identify where they should be classified.

1. A note payable due in two years
2. Cash received in advance by WestJet Airlines for airline tickets
3. GST collected on sales
4. Bank indebtedness
5. Interest owing on an overdue account payable
6. Interest due on an overdue account receivable
7. A nuisance lawsuit pending against the company
8. Amounts withheld from the employees' weekly pay
9. Prepaid property tax
10. A $75,000 mortgage payable, of which $5,000 is due in the next year

Prepare liabilities section of balance sheet.
(SO 4)

BE10–15 Presented here are liability items for Warner Ltd. at December 31, 2009. Prepare the liabilities section of Warner's balance sheet.

Accounts payable	$ 35,000	Mortgage note payable, due 2025	$400,000
Bank indebtedness	10,000	Notes payable, due 2010	80,000
Bonds payable, due 2016	495,000	Property tax payable	5,500
Current portion of long-term debt	40,000	Salaries payable	135,000
Employee benefits payable	7,800	Sales taxes payable	1,400
Income tax payable	25,000	Unearned revenue	2,500
Interest payable	40,000		

Calculate liquidity and solvency ratios.
(SO 4)

BE10–16 Molson Coors' 2007 financial statements contain the following selected data (in USD millions):

Income tax expense	$ 4.2	Total current assets	$1,776.8
Interest expense	126.5	Total current liabilities	1,735.6
Net earnings	497.2	Total liabilities	6,258.4
Total assets	13,451.6		

Calculate Molson Coors' (a) current ratio, (b) debt to total assets ratio, and (c) times interest earned ratio.

Analyze solvency.
(SO 4)

BE10–17 The following solvency ratios are available for Hinton Corporation:

	2009	2008
Debt to total assets	50%	45%
Times interest earned	10 times	8 times

Did the company's solvency improve or deteriorate in 2009?

Exercises

E10–1   Dougald Construction Ltd. borrowed $250,000 from TD Bank on October 1, 2009, signing a nine-month, 5% note payable. Interest is payable at maturity. Both companies have a December 31 year end.

Record short-term notes.
(SO 1)

Instructions

(a) Record the receipt of the proceeds of the note on October 1, and the accrual of interest on December 31 for Dougald Construction.

(b) Record the issue of the note on October 1, and the accrual of interest on December 31 for TD Bank. (*Hint:* You might find it helpful to review accounting for notes receivable in Chapter 8.)

E10–2   Jintao Ltd. incurred the following transactions related to current liabilities:

Record current liabilities.
(SO 1)

1. Jintao's cash register showed the following totals at the end of the day on April 10: pre-tax sales $25,000; GST $1,250; and PST $2,000.

2. Jintao received its property tax bill for the calendar year for $26,400 on May 1, payable July 1.

3. Jintao's gross payroll for the week of August 15 was $40,500. The company deducted $1,715 for CPP, $700 for EI, $3,200 for pension, and $8,010 for income taxes from the employees' earnings. Jintao's payroll costs for the week were $1,715 for CPP and $980 for EI.

4. On November 1, Jintao borrowed $50,000 from First Bank on a six-month, 8%, $50,000 note. Interest is payable the first of each month.

Instructions

(a) Record the above transactions.

(b) Assuming that Jintao's year end is December 31 and that it makes adjusting entries annually, prepare any adjusting entries required for the property tax in transaction 2 and the interest in transaction 4.

E10–3   A list of transactions follows:

Determine impact of current liability transactions.
(SO 1)

1. Purchased inventory (perpetual system) on account.

2. Extended payment terms of the account payable in item 1 by issuing a nine-month, 5% note payable.

3. Recorded accrued interest on the note payable from item 2.

4. Recorded payment of the note and accrued interest from items 2 and 3.

5. Recorded cash sales, plus HST.

6. Recorded wage expense, employee payroll deductions, and paid employees.

7. Recorded employer's share of employee benefits.

8. Recorded property tax expense and property tax payable when bill was received.

9. Recorded a receipt of cash for services that will be performed in the future.

10. Recorded the performance of services for item 9.

Instructions

Set up a table using the format that follows. Indicate the effect of each of the above transactions on the financial statement categories in the table: use "+" for increase, "–" for decrease, and "NE" for no effect. The first one has been done for you as an example.

	Assets	Liabilities	Shareholders' Equity	Revenues	Expenses	Net Earnings
1.	+	+	NE	NE	NE	NE

E10–4   Ste. Anne Corp. issued a 10-year, 6%, $150,000 mortgage note payable to finance the construction of a building at December 31, 2009. The terms provide for semi-annual instalment payments on June 30 and December 31.

Record mortgage note payable.
(SO 2)

▸ Reporting and Analyzing Liabilities

Instructions

(a) Record the issue of the mortgage note payable on December 31, 2009.

(b) Record the first two instalment payments on June 30, 2010, and December 31, 2010, assuming the payment is (1) a fixed principal payment of $7,500, and (2) a blended principal and interest payment of $10,082.

Record instalment note payable.
(SO 2)

E10–5 On January 1, 2009, Wolstenholme Corp. borrowed $10,000 by signing a four-year, 7% note payable. The note is repayable in three annual blended principal and interest instalments of $2,952.28 at the end of each year, December 31.

Instructions

(a) Prepare an instalment payment schedule for the term of the note.

(b) Record (1) the issue of the note on January 1, and (2) the first instalment payment on December 31.

(c) What amounts would be reported as current and long-term in the liabilities section of Wolstenholme's balance sheet on December 31, 2009?

Analyze instalment payment schedule.
(SO 2)

E10–6 The following instalment payment schedule is for a long-term instalment note payable:

Interest Period	Cash Payment	Interest Expense	Reduction of Principal	Principal Balance
Issue date				$100,000.00
1	$23,097.48	$5,000.00	$18,097.48	81,902.52
2	23,097.48	4,095.13	19,002.35	62,900.17
3	23,097.48	3,145.01	19,952.47	42,947.70
4	23,097.48	2,147.38	20,950.10	21,997.60
5	23,097.48	1,099.88	21,997.60	0.00

Instructions

(a) Is the above schedule a fixed principal or blended principal and interest payment schedule?

(b) Assuming payments are made annually, what is the interest rate on the note?

(c) Prepare the journal entry to record the first instalment payment.

(d) What are the long-term and current portions of the note at the end of period 2?

(e) Assume the instalment note payable is also a convertible note. What circumstances would result in the note holders, converting their notes into common shares?

Analyze and record bond issue.
(SO 3)

E10–7 The following information about two independent bond issues was reported in the financial press:

1. George Weston Ltd. 7.1% bonds, maturing February 5, 2032, were issued at a price of 85.45 to yield a market interest rate of 8.54%.

2. Greater Toronto Airport Authority (GTAA) 7.1% bonds, maturing June 4, 2031, were issued at a price of 120.75 to yield a market interest rate of 5.5%.

Instructions

(a) Were the George Weston bonds issued at a premium or a discount?

(b) Were the GTAA bonds issued at a premium or a discount?

(c) Explain how bonds, both paying the same contractual interest rate (7.1%), could be issued at different prices.

(d) Record the issue of $100,000 of each of these two bonds.

Record bond transactions; show balance sheet presentation.
(SO 3, 4)

E10–8 On September 1, 2009, Mooney Corporation issued $400,000 of 10-year, 5% bonds at 100. Interest is payable semi-annually on September 1 and March 1. Mooney's year end is December 31.

Instructions

(a) Prepare journal entries to record the following:

1. The issue of the bonds on September 1, 2009

2. The accrual of interest on December 31, 2009

3. The payment of interest on March 1, 2010

(b) Show how the bonds and interest would be presented in the liabilities section of Mooney's balance sheet at December 31, 2009.

E10–9   A partial bond amortization schedule follows for Chiasson Corporation:

Complete amortization schedule; answer questions. (SO 3)

Semi-Annual Interest Period	Interest Payment	Interest Expense	Discount/Premium Amortization	Unamortized Discount/Premium	Bond Carrying Amount
Issue date				$74,387	$925,613
1 (Apr. 30)	$25,000	(1)	$2,768	(2)	928,381
2 (Oct. 31)	25,000	$27,851	(3)	68,768	(4)
3 (Apr. 30)	(5)	27,937	(6)	(7)	934,169

Instructions

(a) Fill in the missing amounts for items (1) through (7).

(b) What is the face value of the bonds?

(c) What is the contractual interest rate on the bonds? The market interest rate?

(d) Explain why interest expense is greater than interest paid.

(e) Explain why interest expense will increase each period.

(f) What will be the carrying amount of the bonds on their maturity date?

E10–10   Tagawa Corporation issued $500,000 of 10-year, 7% bonds on January 1, 2009, at a price to yield a market interest rate of 6%. Interest is payable semi-annually on July 1 and January 1. Tagawa has a December 31 year end.

Calculate present value; record bond transactions. (SO 3)

Instructions

(a) Calculate the present value (issue price) of the bonds on January 1.

(b) Record the issue of the bonds on January 1.

(c) Record the payment of interest on July 1.

(d) Record the accrual of interest on December 31.

E10–11   The following independent situations occurred on June 30, 2009:

Record bond redemption. (SO 3)

1. Ernst Corporation redeemed $120,000 of 7% bonds at 101. The carrying amount of the bonds at the redemption date was $115,133.

2. Takase Corporation redeemed $150,000 of 8% bonds at 99. The carrying amount of the bonds at the redemption date was $156,237.

3. Young, Inc. redeemed $150,000 of 6% bonds at their maturity date, June 30, 2009.

Instructions

Record the transaction for each of the above situations.

E10–12   **Bombardier Inc.** reported the following liabilities (in USD millions) in its January 31, 2008, financial statements:

Prepare liabilities section of balance sheet. (SO 4)

Accrued pension benefit liabilities	$1,066	Notes payable—long-term	$4,057
Accrued liabilities	1,251	Operating leases	720
Advances and unearned revenues	4,790	Other current liabilities	2,803
Bonds payable, due 2026	150	Other long-term liabilities	451
Current portion of long-term debt	11	Payroll-related liabilities	496
Income and other taxes payable	213	Trade accounts payable	2,079
Interest payable	77	Unused operating line of credit	893

Instructions

(a) Identify which of the above liabilities are likely current and which are likely long-term. Say if an item fits in neither category. Explain the reasoning for your selections.

(b) Prepare the liabilities section of Bombardier's balance sheet.

E10–13 🔗 The following selected information (in thousands) was taken from Fruition Collections Ltd.'s December 31 balance sheet:

	2009	2008
Cash	$ 1,634	$ 1,544
Total current assets	8,075	8,330
Bank indebtedness	4,482	4,467
Accounts payable and accrued liabilities	6,025	7,675
Total current liabilities	16,086	17,676

Instructions

(a) Calculate the current ratio for each of the two years. (1) Based only on this information, would you say that the company's liquidity is strong or weak? (2) What additional information should you request to complete your assessment of liquidity?

(b) Suppose that Fruition Collections paid off $500,000 of its bank indebtedness. Would this transaction change the current ratio?

(c) At December 31, 2009, Fruition Collections had an unused operating line of credit of $38 million. Does this information affect the assessment of the company's short-term liquidity that you made in (a) above?

E10–14 🔗 Maple Leaf Foods Inc.'s financial statements contain the following selected data (in thousands):

	2007	2006
Total assets	$2,997,844	$3,275,726
Total liabilities	1,756,863	2,191,047
Net earnings	207,144	4,525
Income tax expense	801	35,799
Interest expense	94,122	90,204

Instructions

(a) Calculate the debt to total assets and times interest earned ratios for 2007 and 2006. Did Maple Leaf's solvency improve or deteriorate in 2007?

(b) The notes to Maple Leaf Foods' financial statements show that the company has future operating lease commitments totalling $280,671 thousand. Discuss how these unrecorded obligations affect the analysis of Maple Leaf Foods' solvency.

Problems: Set A

P10–1A On January 1, 2010, Burlington Inc.'s general ledger contained these opening balances for its liability accounts:

Accounts payable	$52,000
CPP payable	1,905
EI payable	1,058
GST payable	7,500
Income tax payable	4,640
PST payable	10,500
Unearned service revenue	16,000

The following selected transactions occurred during the month:

Jan. 5 Sold merchandise for cash totalling $15,000, plus 5% GST and 7% PST. The cost of goods sold was $9,000. Burlington uses a perpetual inventory system.

13 Paid $7,500 GST to the Receiver General and $10,500 PST to the provincial Minister of Finance for sales taxes collected in December.

14 Paid $7,603 to the Receiver General for amounts owing from the December payroll for CPP, EI, and income tax ($1,905 + $1,058 + $4,640).

15 Borrowed $18,000 from HSBC Bank on a three-month, 6% note. Interest is payable monthly on the 15th of each month.

19   Provided services for customers who had made advance payments of $7,000.

22   Paid $12,000 to trade creditors on account.

28   Received assessment of property taxes of $4,000 for the calendar year. They are payable on March 1.

29   Paid monthly payroll. Gross salaries totalled $22,500 and payroll deductions include CPP of $1,110; EI of $389; and income tax of $9,474. Employee benefits included CPP of $1,110 and EI of $545.

Instructions

(a) Record the above transactions.

(b) Record any required adjusting entries at January 31.

(c) Prepare the current liabilities section of the balance sheet at January 31.

P10–2A MileHi Mountain Bikes Ltd. markets mountain-bike tours to clients vacationing in various locations in the mountains of British Columbia. On March 1, 2009, the company had a balance of $15,000 in Notes Payable—Eifert Corp. and $1,500 in Interest Payable. In preparation for the upcoming summer biking season, MileHi incurred the following transactions related to notes payable:

Record short-term notes; show balance sheet presentation. (SO 1, 4)

Mar. 2   Purchased Mongoose bikes for use as rentals by issuing a three-month, 7%, $8,000 note payable. Interest is payable at maturity.

31   Paid the $15,000 note payable to Eifert Corp. (see opening balance), plus the $1,500 of interest payable (see opening balance) and $750 of interest for the month of March.

Apr. 1   Issued a nine-month, 6%, $25,000 note to Mountain Real Estate for the purchase of mountain property on which to build bike trails. Interest is payable at the first of each month.

May 1   Paid interest on the Mountain Real Estate note (see April 1 transaction).

2   Borrowed $18,000 from Western Bank on a four-month, 5% note. The funds will be used for working capital for the beginning of the season. Interest is payable at maturity.

June 1   Paid interest on the Mountain Real Estate note (see April 1 transaction).

2   Paid principal and interest on the Mongoose note (see March 2 transaction).

30   Recorded accrued interest for the Mountain Real Estate and Western Bank notes at MileHi's year end.

Instructions

(a) Record the above transactions.

(b) Show the balance sheet presentation of the notes payable and interest payable at June 30.

P10–3A On July 31, 2009, Myron Corporation purchased a piece of equipment for $750,000. The equipment was purchased with a $50,000 down payment and through the issue of a four-year, 6%, $700,000 mortgage note payable for the balance. The terms provide for the mortgage to be repaid with monthly blended principal and interest instalment payments of $16,440 starting on August 31. Myron has a September 30 year end.

Record instalment note. (SO 2)

Instructions

(a) Record the purchase of equipment and issue of the note payable on July 31.

(b) Record the first two instalment payments, on August 31 and September 30. Round all calculations to the nearest dollar.

(c) Repeat part (b) assuming that the terms provide for monthly fixed principal payments of $14,583, rather than blended payments of $16,440.

P10–4A Kinyae Electronics Limited issued a 10-year, 8%, $500,000 mortgage note on December 31, 2009, to help finance a plant expansion. The terms of the note provide for fixed principal payments of $25,000, plus interest. Payments are due on June 30 and December 31.

Prepare instalment payment schedule; record instalment note; show balance sheet presentation. (SO 2, 4)

Instructions

(a) Prepare an instalment payment schedule for the first two years. Round all calculations to the nearest dollar.

(b) Record the issue of the mortgage note payable on December 31, 2009.

(c) Show the balance sheet presentation of the mortgage payable at December 31, 2009.

(d) Record the first two instalment payments, on June 30, 2010 and December 31, 2010.

(e) Show the balance sheet presentation of the mortgage payable on December 31, 2010.

Prepare instalment payment schedule; record instalment note; show balance sheet presentation.
(SO 2, 4)

P10–5A A local ski hill has just approached a venture capitalist for financing for its new business venture, the development of another local ski hill. On April 1, 2009, the venture capitalist loaned the company $100,000 at an interest rate of 10%. The loan is repayable over four years in annual blended principal and interest instalments of $31,547.08, due each March 31. The first payment is due March 31, 2010. The ski hill's year end is March 31.

Instructions

(a) Prepare an instalment payment schedule for the loan period.

(b) Record the issue of the note payable on April 1, 2009.

(c) Record the first two instalment payments, on March 31, 2010, and March 31, 2011.

(d) Show the balance sheet presentation of the note payable as at March 31, 2011.

(e) Explain how the interest expense and reduction of the note payable would change in (c) if the note had been repayable in fixed principal payments of $25,000, rather than in blended principal and interest payments.

Record bond transactions.
(SO 3)

P10–6A On May 1, 2009, MEM Corp. issued $800,000 of five-year, 6% bonds at 100. The bonds pay interest semi-annually on November 1 and May 1. MEM's year end is December 31.

Instructions

(a) Record the issue of the bonds on May 1, 2009.

(b) Record the first interest payment on November 1, 2009.

(c) Prepare the adjusting entry to record the accrual of interest on December 31, 2009.

(d) Record the second interest payment on May 1, 2010.

(e) Assume that on May 1, 2010, immediately after paying the semi-annual interest, MEM redeems all of the bonds at 98. Record the redemption of the bonds.

Record bond transactions.
(SO 3)

P10–7A The following is from Disch Corp.'s balance sheet at December 31, 2009:

DISCH CORP Balance Sheet (partial) December 31, 2009	
Current liabilities	
Bond interest payable	$ 45,000
Long-term liabilities	
Bonds payable, 6%, due January 1, 2018	1,607,650

The bonds have a face value of $1,500,000 and were issued one year ago at a price to yield a market interest rate of 5%. Interest is payable semi-annually on January 1 and July 1.

Instructions

(a) Record the payment of bond interest on January 1, 2010, assuming the accrued interest expense is $40,309 and the interest payable is $45,000 at December 31.

(b) Assume that on January 1, 2010, after paying interest, Disch redeems bonds having a face value of $500,000 at 104. Record the redemption of the bonds.

(c) Record the payment of bond interest on July 1, 2010, on the remaining bonds.

(d) Prepare the adjusting entry on December 31, 2010, to accrue the interest on the remaining bonds.

Calculate present value; prepare amortization schedule; record bond transactions; show balance sheet presentation.
(SO 3, 4)

P10–8A On July 1, 2009, Ponasis Corporation issued $1.5 million of 10-year, 6% bonds at a price to yield a market interest rate of 7%. The bonds pay semi-annual interest on July 1 and January 1. Ponasis has a December 31 year end.

Instructions

(a) Calculate the present value (issue price) of the bonds on July 1.

(b) Record the issue of the bonds on July 1.

(c) Prepare an amortization table through December 31, 2010 (three interest periods) for this bond issue. Round all calculations to the nearest dollar.

(d) Show the balance sheet presentation of the liabilities at December 31, 2010.

Classify liabilities.
(SO 4)

P10–9A The following transactions are for Iqaluit Ltd., which has an April 30 fiscal year end:

1. Received property taxes assessment of $12,000 on March 1 for the calendar year. They are payable by May 1.

2. Purchased equipment for $35,000 on April 1 by making a $5,000 down payment and issuing a six-month, 8% note for the balance. Interest is payable on the first of each month.

3. Purchased merchandise for $7,000 on April 27 on account, terms 2/10, n/30.

4. Sold merchandise on April 28 for $12,000, plus 5% GST (there is no PST in Iqaluit, where Iqaluit Ltd. is based). The cost of the goods sold was $7,500. The company uses a perpetual inventory system.

5. Received $25,000 from customers on April 29 for services to be performed in May.

6. Weekly salaries of $10,000 are paid every Friday for a five-day work week (Monday to Friday). This year, April 30 is a Thursday. Payroll deductions for the four days include CPP of $394, EI of $168, and income tax of $3,710. Employee benefits include CPP of $394 and EI of $235.

7. Iqaluit was named in a lawsuit alleging negligence for an oil spill that leaked into the neighbouring company's water system. Iqaluit's legal counsel estimates that the company will likely lose the suit but the costs cannot be determined as yet.

8. Iqaluit paid income tax instalments of $60,000 throughout the year. After the preparation of its year-end corporate income tax return, it was determined that the total income tax payable for the year was $65,000.

9. Iqaluit reported long-term debt of $150,000 at April 30, of which $15,000 was due within the next year.

Instructions

(a) Identify which of the above transactions should be presented in the current liabilities section and which should be recorded in the long-term liabilities section of Iqaluit Ltd.'s balance sheet on April 30. Identify the account title(s) and amount(s) for each reported liability.

(b) Indicate any information that should be disclosed in the notes to Iqaluit Ltd.'s financial statements.

Analyze liquidity and solvency.
(SO 4)

P10–10A ⊙▬C The following selected information was taken from Barrick Gold Corporation's financial statements (in USD millions):

	2007	2006	2005
Balance sheet			
Accounts receivable	$ 256	$ 234	$ 54
Inventory	1,118	931	402
Total current assets	4,288	4,796	1,748
Total assets	21,951	21,510	6,862
Current liabilities	1,296	1,852	560
Total liabilities	6,613	7,255	3,012

Statement of earnings			
Net sales	6,332	5,630	2,348
Cost of goods sold	3,184	2,741	1,198
Interest expense	113	126	3
Income tax expense	341	348	60
Net earnings	1,119	1,506	401

Instructions

(a) Calculate each of the following ratios for 2007 and 2006. Industry ratios are shown in parentheses.

1. Current ratio (2007, 3.8:1; 2006, 3.2:1)

2. Receivables turnover (2007, 29.2 times; 2006, 31.3 times)

3. Inventory turnover (2007, 4.0 times; 2006, 5.0 times)

4. Debt to total assets (2007, 18.0%; 2006, 13.0%)

5. Times interest earned (2007, 15.5 times; 2006, 27.4 times)

(b) Comment on Barrick Gold's liquidity and solvency.

(c) Barrick Gold has two full pages of disclosure in the notes to its statements about pending litigation. Discuss the implications of this information for your analysis.

Analyze liquidity and solvency.
(SO 4)

P10–11A 🔑 The following selected liquidity and solvency ratios are available for two companies operating in the fast food industry:

Ratio	Grab 'N Gab	Chick 'N Lick	Industry Average
Current ratio	0.8:1	0.7:1	0.9:1
Receivables turnover	46 times	38 times	34 times
Inventory turnover	39 times	45 times	31 times
Debt to total assets	49%	40%	39%
Times interest earned	10 times	5 times	7 times

Instructions

Assume that you are the credit manager of the local bank. Answer the following questions, using relevant ratios to justify your answer:

(a) Both Grab 'N Gab and Chick 'N Lick have applied for a short-term loan from your bank. Which of the two companies is more liquid and should get more consideration for a short-term loan? Explain.

(b) Both Grab 'N Gab and Chick 'N Lick have applied for a long-term loan from your bank. Are you concerned about the solvency of either company? Explain why or why not.

Problems: Set B

Record current liabilities; show balance sheet presentation.
(SO 1, 4)

P10–1B On February 28, 2009, Molega Ltd.'s general ledger contained the following liability accounts:

Accounts payable	$42,500
CPP payable	1,340
EI payable	756
GST payable	5,800
Income tax payable	2,515
PST payable	9,280
Unearned service revenue	15,000

The following selected transactions occurred during the month:

Mar. 2   Issued a three-month, 7% note payable in exchange for an account payable in the amount of $10,000. Interest is due at maturity.

5   Sold merchandise for cash totalling $40,000, plus 5% GST and 8% PST. The cost of goods sold was $24,000. Molega uses a perpetual inventory system.

9   Received the property tax bill of $18,000 for the calendar year. It is payable on May 1.

12   Provided services for customers who had made advance payments of $7,500.

13   Paid $5,800 GST to the Receiver General and $9,280 PST to the provincial Minister of Finance for sales taxes collected in February.

16   Paid $4,611 to the Receiver General for amounts owing from the February payroll for CPP, EI, and income tax ($1,340 + $756 + $2,515).

27   Paid $30,000 to trade creditors on account.

31   Paid monthly payroll. Gross salaries totalled $16,000 and payroll deductions included CPP of $778; EI of $277; and income tax of $5,870. Employee benefits included CPP of $778 and EI of $388.

Instructions

(a) Record the above transactions.

(b) Record any required adjusting entries at March 31.

(c) Prepare the current liabilities section of the balance sheet at March 31.

P10–2B Cling-on Ltd. sells rock-climbing products and also operates an indoor climbing facility for climbing enthusiasts. On September 1, 2009, the company had a balance of $12,000 in Notes Payable—Seiffert Inc. and $1,680 in Interest Payable. During the next four months, Cling-on incurred the following transactions related to notes payable:

Record short-term notes; show balance sheet presentation.
(SO 1, 4)

Sept. 1   Purchased inventory on account for $15,000 from Black Diamond, terms n/30. The company uses a perpetual inventory system.

30   Paid the $12,000 note payable to Seiffert Inc. (see opening balance), plus the $1,680 of interest payable (see opening balance) and $840 of interest for the month of September.

Oct. 1   Issued a three-month, 9%, $15,000 note to Black Diamond in exchange for the account payable (see Sept. 1 transaction). Interest is payable at maturity.

2   Issued a 12-month, 8%, $25,000 note to Montpelier Bank to finance the building of a new climbing area for advanced climbers (use the asset account Climbing Wall). Interest is payable monthly on the first of each month.

Nov. 1   Paid interest on the Montpelier Bank note.

2   Purchased a vehicle for $28,000 from Auto Dealer Ltd. to transport clients to nearby climbing sites. Paid $8,000 as a down payment and issued a one-month, 7% note payable for the remaining balance. Interest is payable at maturity.

Dec. 1   Paid interest on the Montpelier Bank note.

2   Paid principal and interest on the Auto Dealer note (see Nov. 2 transaction).

31   Recorded accrued interest for the Black Diamond and Montpelier Bank notes at the company's year end.

Instructions

(a) Record the above transactions.

(b) Show the balance sheet presentation of notes payable and interest payable at December 31.

P10–3B On September 30, 2009, Atwater Corporation purchased a piece of equipment for $550,000. The equipment was purchased with a $50,000 down payment and the issue of a three-year, 8%, $500,000 mortgage note payable for the balance. The terms provide for repayment of the mortgage with quarterly fixed principal payments of $41,667 starting on December 31. Atwater has a December 31 year end.

Record instalment note.
(SO 2)

Instructions

(a) Record the purchase of equipment and issue of the note on September 30, 2009.

(b) Record the first two instalment payments, on December 31, 2009, and March 31, 2010. Round all calculations to the nearest dollar.

(c) Repeat part (b) assuming that the terms provide for quarterly blended principal and interest payments of $47,280, rather than fixed principal payments of $41,667.

P10–4B   Elite Electronics issued a 10-year, 6.5%, $350,000 mortgage note on June 30, 2009, to help finance a new research laboratory. The terms of the note provide for blended principal and interest payments of $24,073. Payments are due on December 31 and June 30. The company's year end is June 30.

Instructions

(a) Prepare an instalment payment schedule for the first two years. Round all calculations to the nearest dollar.

(b) Record the issue of the mortgage note payable on June 30, 2009.

(c) Show the balance sheet presentation of the mortgage note payable at June 30, 2009.

(d) Record the first two instalment payments, on December 31, 2009, and June 30, 2010.

(e) Show the balance sheet presentation of the mortgage payable at June 30, 2010.

P10–5B   Peter Furlong has just approached a venture capitalist for financing for his sailing school. The lender is willing to loan Peter $50,000 at a high-risk interest rate of 12%. The loan is payable over three years in fixed principal payments each quarter of $4,166.67. Peter receives the loan on April 30, 2009, and makes the first payment on July 31. The company's year end is October 31.

Instructions

(a) Prepare an instalment payment schedule for the loan period.

(b) Record the issue of the note payable on April 30.

(c) Record the first two instalment payments, on July 31 and October 31.

(d) Show the balance sheet presentation of the note payable at October 31, 2009.

(e) Explain how the interest expense and reduction of the note payable would change in (c) if the note had been repayable in blended principal and interest payments of $5,023.10, rather than fixed principal payments.

P10–6B   On October 1, 2009, PFQ Corp. issued $600,000 of 10-year, 7% bonds at 100. The bonds pay interest semi-annually on April 1 and October 1. PFQ's year end is December 31.

Instructions

(a) Record the issue of the bonds on October 1, 2009.

(b) Prepare the adjusting entry to record the accrual of interest on December 31, 2009.

(c) Record the first interest payment on April 1, 2010.

(d) Record the second interest payment on October 1, 2010.

(e) Assume that on October 1, 2010, immediately after paying the semi-annual interest, PFQ redeems all of the bonds at 102. Record the redemption of the bonds.

P10–7B   The following is from Peppermint Patty Ltd.'s balance sheet at December 31, 2009:

PEPPERMINT PATTY LTD. Balance Sheet (partial) December 31, 2009	
Current liabilities	
Bond interest payable	$ 7,000
Long-term liabilities	
Bonds payable, 7%, due January 1, 2019	187,341

The bonds have a face value of $200,000 and were issued one year ago at a price to yield a market interest rate of 8%. Interest is payable semi-annually on January 1 and July 1.

Instructions

(a) Record the payment of bond interest on January 1, 2010, assuming the accrued interest expense is $7,475 and interest payable is $7,000 at December 31.

(b) Assume that on January 1, 2010, after paying interest, Peppermint Patty redeems bonds having a face value of $50,000 at 94. Record the redemption of the bonds.

(c) Record the payment of bond interest on July 1, 2010, on the remaining bonds.

(d) Prepare the adjusting entry on December 31, 2010, to accrue the interest on the remaining bonds.

P10–8B On July 1, 2009, Global Satellites Corporation issued $1.2 million of 10-year, 7% bonds to yield a market interest rate of 6%. The bonds pay semi-annual interest on July 1 and January 1. Global has a December 31 year end.

Calculate present value; prepare amortization schedule; record bond transactions; show balance sheet presentation.
(SO 3, 4)

Instructions

(a) Calculate the present value (issue price) of the bonds on July 1.

(b) Record the issue of the bonds on July 1.

(c) Prepare an amortization table through December 31, 2010 (three interest periods) for this bond issue. Round all calculations to the nearest dollar.

(d) Show the balance sheet presentation of the liabilities at December 31, 2010.

P10–9B The following transactions occurred in Wendell Corporation, which has a December 31 year end:

Classify liabilities.
(SO 4)

1. Property taxes of $40,000 were assessed on March 1 for the calendar year. They are payable by May 1.

2. Wendell received $10,000 from customers on May 28 for services to be performed in June.

3. Wendell signed a 6%, $250,000 note payable on July 1. The note requires fixed principal instalment payments of $50,000 annually on each June 30 for the next five years. Interest is also payable annually, each June 30.

4. Wendell purchased merchandise for $120,000 on December 23 on account, terms n/30.

5. On December 31, Wendell sold merchandise for $8,000, plus 13% HST. The cost of goods sold was $5,000. The company uses a perpetual inventory system.

6. Weekly salaries of $6,000 are paid every Friday for a five-day work week (Monday to Friday). This year, December 31 is a Wednesday. Payroll deductions for the three days include CPP of $178, EI of $75, and income tax of $1,300. Employee benefits include CPP of $178 and EI of $105.

7. Wendell is the defendant in a negligence suit. Wendell's legal counsel estimates that Wendell may suffer a $75,000 loss if it loses the suit. In legal counsel's opinion, it is not possible at this time to determine whether or not the case will be lost.

8. Wendell made income tax instalments of $60,000 throughout the year. After the preparation of its corporate income tax return at year end, it was determined that total income tax payable for the year was $50,000.

9. Wendell reported long-term debt of $250,000 at December 31, of which $30,000 was due within the next year.

Instructions

(a) Identify which of the above transactions should be presented in the current liabilities section and which should be recorded in the long-term liabilities section of Wendell's balance sheet on December 31. Identify the account title(s) and amount(s) for each reported liability.

(b) Indicate any information that should be disclosed in the notes to Wendell's financial statements.

Analyze liquidity and solvency.
(SO 4)

P10–10B ◉ You have been presented with the following selected information taken from the financial statements of Magna International Inc. (in USD millions):

	2007	2006	2005
Balance sheet			
Accounts receivable	$ 3,981	$ 3,629	$ 3,436
Inventory	1,681	1,437	1,388
Total current assets	8,770	7,060	6,603
Total assets	15,343	13,154	12,321
Current liabilities	5,658	4,783	4,388
Total liabilities	6,701	5,997	5,756
Statement of earnings			
Net sales	26,067	24,180	22,811
Cost of goods sold	22,599	21,211	19,831
Interest expense	52	50	60
Income tax expense	489	264	292
Net earnings	663	528	639

Instructions

(a) Calculate each of the following ratios for 2007 and 2006. Industry ratios are shown in parentheses.

    1. Current ratio (2007, 3.2:1; 2006, 3.1:1)

    2. Receivables turnover (2007, 5.8 times; 2006, 5.7 times)

    3. Inventory turnover (2007, 11 times; 2006, 9.9 times)

    4. Debt to total assets (2007, 10.7%; 2006, 10.7%)

    5. Times interest earned (2007, 8.4 times; 2006, 10.7 times)

(b) Comment on Magna's liquidity and solvency.

(c) Magna had operating lease commitments totalling $2,228 million in 2007 and $1,766 million in 2006. Discuss the implications of this information for your analysis.

Analyze liquidity and solvency.
(SO 4)

P10–11B ◉ The following selected liquidity and solvency ratios are available for two companies operating in the petroleum industry:

Ratio	Petro-Zoom	Sun-Oil	Industry Average
Current ratio	1.3:1	1.2:1	1.4:1
Receivables turnover	12 times	13 times	11 times
Inventory turnover	16 times	10 times	19 times
Debt to total assets	41%	39%	34%
Times interest earned	21 times	24 times	26 times

Instructions

Assume that you are the credit manager of the local bank. Answer the following questions, using relevant ratios to justify your answer:

(a) Both Petro-Zoom and Sun-Oil have applied for a short-term loan from your bank. Which of the two companies is more liquid and should get more consideration for a short-term loan? Explain.

(b) Both Petro-Zoom and Sun-Oil have applied for a long-term loan from your bank. Are you concerned about the solvency of either company? Explain why or why not.

BROADENING YOUR PERSPECTIVE

Financial Reporting and Analysis Cases

Analysis Tools

Financial Reporting: *Shoppers Drug Mart*

BYP10–1 The financial statements of Shoppers Drug Mart are presented in Appendix A at the end of the book.

Instructions

(a) What current and long-term liabilities were reported in Shoppers Drug Mart's balance sheet at the end of fiscal 2007?

(b) What items related to liabilities were reported in Shoppers Drug Mart's statement of earnings for fiscal 2007?

(c) What financing activities related to liabilities were reported in Shoppers Drug Mart's cash flow statement for fiscal 2007?

(d) Does Shoppers Drug Mart disclose any off–balance sheet financing that could have an impact on its financial position?

Comparative Analysis: *Shoppers Drug Mart and Jean Coutu*

BYP10–2 The financial statements of Jean Coutu are presented in Appendix B following the financial statements for Shoppers Drug Mart in Appendix A.

Instructions

(a) Based on the information contained in the financial statements, calculate the following ratios for each company for its most recent fiscal year. Industry ratios are shown in parentheses.

1. Current ratio (1.1:1)
2. Receivables turnover (25.8 times)
3. Debt to total assets (24.8%)
4. Times interest earned (8.5 times)

(b) What conclusions about the companies' liquidity and solvency can be drawn from the ratios calculated in (a)?

Interpreting Financial Statements

BYP10–3 Reitmans (Canada) Limited and Le Château Inc. are two specialty clothing merchandisers. Here are financial data for both companies at January 31, 2008 (in thousands):

	Reitmans	Le Château
Balance sheet data		
Beginning accounts receivable	$ 3,439	$ 4,457
Ending accounts receivable	3,546	6,307
Total current assets	324,960	119,513
Beginning total assets	600,411	185,709
Ending total assets	620,960	203,979
Total current liabilities	87,642	47,099
Total liabilities	125,841	72,344

Statement of earnings data		
Net sales	1,057,720	336,070
Interest expense	990	1,429
Income tax expense	44,314	18,400
Net earnings	114,902	33,604
Cash flow statement data		
Cash provided by operating activities	133,178	54,117
Capital expenditures	73,402	24,091
Dividends paid	46,930	30,363
Notes to the financial statements		
Operating lease commitments	443,315	232,807

Instructions

(a) Calculate the current ratio and receivables turnover for each company. Discuss their relative liquidity.

(b) Calculate the debt to total assets, times interest earned, and free cash flow for each company. Discuss their relative solvency.

(c) The notes to the financial statements indicate that many of the retail stores' furniture, fixtures, and similar items are leased using operating leases. Discuss the implications of these operating leases for each company's solvency.

(d) Calculate the profit margin, return on assets, and asset turnover for each company. Discuss their relative profitability.

A Global Focus

International Resources

BYP10–4 Swedish Match AB reports the following selected information about contingencies in the notes to its financial statements:

SWEDISH MATCH AB Notes to the Financial Statements (partial) December 31, 2007 (in SEK millions)		
Note 30: Contingent liabilities	2007	2006
Guarantees to subsidiaries	343	256
Guarantees to external companies	12	26
Other guarantees and contingent liabilities	164	85
Total contingent liabilities	519	367

Legal disputes
The Company is involved in a number of legal proceedings of a routine character. Although the outcome of these proceedings cannot be predicted with any certainty, and accordingly no guarantees can be made, management is of the opinion that obligations attributable to these disputes, if any, should not have any significant impact on the results of operations or the financial position of Swedish Match.

Instructions

(a) Why are guarantees considered to be contingent liabilities?

(b) Swedish Match is the defendant in more than 1,200 cases against tobacco companies. Management holds the view that there are good defences against all the claims and states that it will defend each case vigorously. In light of this statement, does it make sense to you that Swedish Match only discloses information about its legal disputes rather than accruing the amounts of the lawsuits as liabilities? Explain.

(c) Swedish Match's debt to total assets ratio is 95.6% and its times interest earned is 9 times. What implications do the contingent liabilities reported in Note 30 of Swedish Match's financial statements have for an analysis of its solvency?

Critical Thinking Cases and Activities

Collaborative Learning Activity

BYP10–5 Every major airline has a frequent-flyer program to encourage passenger loyalty. Various types of awards are available for points accumulated under the program, including the right to free travel. There is great debate about how airlines should record the cost of the "free" seat when frequent-flyer points are redeemed.

Some airlines believe that frequent-flyer liabilities should be disclosed as contingent liabilities, arguing that the probability of the air miles being redeemed is not quantifiable.

Others believe that the liability should be estimated and accrued, but have different views on how the amount to be recorded should be determined. Some argue that only the increased or incremental cost of rewarding frequent-flyer members should be recorded. These costs would include food, drink, and ticket delivery costs. Other costs, such as fuel for the airplane and labour to staff it, are going to be incurred whether frequent flyers travel or not.

The other point of view is that the cost to be recorded should be a percentage of the ticket price originally eligible for point accumulation. This usually results in a cost allocation for each seat redeemed using frequent-flyer points that is roughly equivalent to a discounted or seat-sale price. Full fare is not usually a consideration, because it is unlikely that full-fare passengers will be displaced by passengers using free travel awards.

Instructions

With the class divided into groups, assign a debate position for the following issues:

(a) Recording the liability: One group should provide the arguments for disclosing the liability as a contingent liability, rather than recording it. Another group should provide the arguments for estimating and accruing the liability.

(b) Determining the amount of the liability: One group should provide the arguments in support of using incremental costs. Another group should provide the arguments for using a seat-sale fare. A third group should provide arguments for other cost allocations that should also be considered.

Communication Activity

BYP10–6 Financial statement users often use ratio analysis to determine whether a company is liquid and solvent. A friend of yours has inherited some money and is looking at investing in some companies. Your friend has never used ratio analysis before and would like you to help him interpret some ratios as he is confused as to whether the ratio value should be high or low.

Instructions

Write a memorandum to your friend listing all of the liquidity and solvency ratios that you have learned about so far in this textbook. Explain in your memo which ratios would be considered to be improving and which ratios would be considered to be deteriorating if the value of the ratio has increased from one period to another. Also identify any important considerations in interpreting these ratios that your friend should be aware of.

Ethics Case

BYP10–7 Would you like a mortgage that lends you more than the value of your house? Would you like the mortgage structured so that your first payments are extra low? Do you have a poor credit history? Do you think housing prices will continue to rise? If you answered yes to these questions, you are a target for a subprime mortgage lender.

Ethics in Accounting

"Subprime" refers to the risk associated with a borrower, not to the interest rate being charged on the mortgage. Typically, subprime mortgages are offered at interest rates above prime, to customers with below-average credit ratings. Subprime mortgage lenders often target lower-income people, the elderly, new immigrants, people with a proven record of not paying their debts on time—just about anyone who would have trouble getting a mortgage from a conventional lender. Hence, these people are willing to pay a premium, in the form of a higher interest rate and likely higher fees, for their mortgages.

Obviously, lending to this group of borrowers has its upside: higher interest rates mean greater profits to the lending institutions, especially if they can borrow at low interest rates, as the spread becomes huge. But this phenomenon should not be the gateway to exploitation, as the subprime business has become.

Instructions

(a) Who are the stakeholders in this situation?

(b) Explain how a drop in housing prices and an increase in interest rates could pose problems for (1) borrowers and (2) lenders.

(c) Do you think that investing in subprime lending companies is worth the risk? Explain.

"All About You" Activity

BYP10–8   As indicated in the "All About You" feature in this chapter, a student loan is a loan that must be repaid. With most government student loan programs, you have at least six months after your post-secondary studies before you have to start paying back your loan. This is called a grace period. It's meant to give you enough time to find a job and start making money. But be aware that most programs start charging you interest as soon as you finish school. You can either choose to:

• start making those interest payments right away,
• pay the six months of interest as a lump sum before you start making your regular payments, or
• have your loan providers add the interest amount to your loan total after the 6-month grace period.

Instructions

Assume your total debt from post-secondary education is $20,000. Go to the Loan Repayment Calculator at http://tools.canlearn.ca/cslgs-scpse/cln-cln/40/lrc-crp/calculate.do to estimate your loan repayment. Use the interest rates that are suggested in this website.

(a) Interest on loans may be a fixed interest rate or a floating interest rate. What is the difference between the two interest rates? Are there any advantages of having one over the other if interest rates rise over your payment period?

(b) Under option 1 in the Loan Repayment Calculator, enter the loan amount of $20,000 and assume a fixed interest rate and 114 months of repayment.

1. What is the amount of each monthly payment?
2. How much interest is payable over the 114 months?
3. How much in total is payable over the 114 months?

(c) Under option 2 in the Loan Repayment Calculator, enter the loan amount of $20,000 and assume a floating interest rate and 114 months of repayment.

1. What is the amount of each monthly payment?
2. How much interest is payable over the 114 months?
3. How much in total is payable over the 114 months?

Serial Case

(*Note:* This is a continuation of the serial case from Chapters 1 through 9.)

BYP10–9 Recall that Cookie Creations Ltd. borrowed $2,000 on February 18, 2009, from Natalie's grandmother. Interest on the note is 6% per annum and the note plus interest was to be repaid in 12 months. Monthly adjusting journal entries were prepared for the months of February 2009 (half month), March 2009, and April 2009.

Instructions

(a) Calculate the interest payable that was accrued and recorded from February 18, 2009, through April 30, 2009.

(b) Calculate the total interest expense from February 18, 2009, through August 31, 2009. Prepare the adjusting journal entry required at August 31, 2009, to update the interest.

(c) Cookie Creations repaid Natalie's grandmother on September 17, 2009, seven months after the loan was extended. Prepare the journal entry to record the loan repayment.

Answers to Chapter Questions

Answer to Shoppers Drug Mart Review It Question 5

Shoppers Drug Mart has the following current liabilities, totalling $2,159,045 thousand at December 29, 2007: bank indebtedness, commercial paper, accounts payable and accrued liabilities, income taxes, dividends, and the current portion of long-term debt.

Answers to Self-Study Questions

1. c   2. c   3. b   4. c   5. b   6. d   7. c   8. a   9. d   10. d

Remember to go back to the beginning of the chapter to check off your completed work!

CHAPTER 11
Reporting and Analyzing Shareholders' Equity

ACCOUNTING MATTERS!

lululemon Stretches to Success

lululemon athletica inc. (note that the company does not use any capital letters in the spelling of its name) sells not only fashionable yoga-inspired athletic apparel, but also the philosophy of living a longer and healthier life that is more fun as well. And the idea has certainly caught on. A simple step inside a yoga or fitness class anywhere across the country will provide evidence of the company's success—its logo will no doubt be on the backs and hips of a good number of those in attendance.

In less than 10 years, the company has grown from a combined design studio and retail outlet sharing space with a Vancouver yoga studio to one of the fastest growing athletic apparel companies in the world. For the fiscal year ended February 3, 2008, it had nearly 2,700 employees working in 81 locations, including Canada, the United States, and Australia.

Company founder Chip Wilson took his first yoga lesson in 1998 and inspiration came because he didn't like the cotton clothing worn for strenuous power yoga classes. Using his 20 years of experience in the surf-skate, and snowboard business, he designed clothing made from technical athletic fabrics and opened his first design studio, which also served as a yoga studio at night. He asked the yoga instructors to wear the products and provide feedback.

lululemon's first real store opened in November 2000 in Vancouver's hip beach area of Kitsilano. Although there was no official plan to open more locations, the store's popularity called for expansion. At the end of 2005, with 33 stores in operation, Mr. Wilson sold a 48-percent interest in the company for U.S. $100 million to a group of investors led by the private equity firm Advent International Corp. and venture capital company Highland Capital Partners, both based in Boston.

In July 2007, the company went public with an initial public offering (IPO) of 27 percent of its stock, or 18.2 million common shares. Of those shares, 2.3 million were offered by lululemon itself for sale at U.S. $18 per share. The remaining 15.9 million were offered by current shareholders. During the next few months, the stock went on a roller-coaster ride as the company faced bad press about its seaweed-infused clothing. Canada's Competition Bureau forced lululemon to remove all claims alleging health benefits from its VitaSea line.

Then, five months after its IPO, in January 2008, the company faced another financial fitness test when the 180-day lock-up period for insider investors following the IPO ended. This meant a significant number of shares could have been open to the public, raising concern that the share price might fall. It didn't. In fact, lululemon's shares sold for as much as $58 in 2008. As one analyst pointed out, big shareholders weren't likely to sell their shares since spending money on expensive yoga gear didn't look like it was going out of fashion any time soon. Indeed, lululemon's focus on the high-end recreational clothing market might even shelter it from an economic downturn.

Christine Day, former president of Starbucks' Asia Pacific group, was hired in January 2008 as lululemon's new president to oversee the company's future growth plans. lululemon plans to have a total of 250 stores worldwide by 2012. Ms Day comments: "lululemon has an extraordinary brand with a loyal and growing following around the globe who have embraced our yoga-inspired apparel and unique store experience. I am excited to be taking on this important role in shaping lululemon's future."

Ms. Day doesn't seem overly concerned about the new store timetable. After all, she opened upwards of 350 stores a year for Starbucks. Even the faltering U.S. economy doesn't worry her. She sees it as an opportunity to lease real estate in shopping centres that would otherwise be full. "Looking ahead, we are excited by our continued sales momentum and the tremendous opportunity for the lululemon brand as we expand our store base."

lululemon athletica inc.: lululemon.com

STUDY OBJECTIVES

After studying this chapter, you should be able to:

Identify and discuss the major characteristics of a corporation.

Record share transactions.

Prepare the entries for cash dividends, stock dividends, and stock splits, and understand their financial impact.

Indicate how shareholders' equity is presented in the financial statements.

Evaluate dividend and earnings performance.

THE NAVIGATOR

- [ ] Read *Feature Story*
- [ ] Scan *Study Objectives*
- [ ] Read *Chapter Preview*
- [ ] Read text and answer *Before You Go On*
- [ ] Read *All About You*
- [ ] Review *Summary of Study Objectives*
- [ ] Review *Using the Decision Toolkit— A Summary*
- [ ] Work *Using the Decision Toolkit*
- [ ] Work *Demonstration Problem*
- [ ] Answer *Self-Study Questions*
- [ ] Complete assignments

PREVIEW OF CHAPTER 11

Many companies start out small and grow into large corporations, just as lululemon in our feature story has. It should not be surprising, then, that corporations are the dominant form of business organization. In this chapter, we look at the essential features of a corporation. The accounting for, and reporting of, shareholders' equity is explained. We conclude by reviewing dividend and earnings measures of performance.

The chapter is organized as follows:

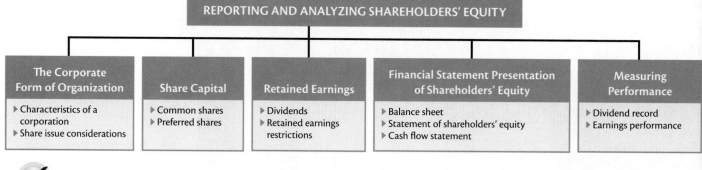

The Navigator

The Corporate Form of Organization

A **corporation** is a legal entity that is separate and distinct from its owners, who are known as shareholders. As a legal entity, a corporation has most of the rights and privileges of a person. It must respect laws and it must pay income tax. The major exceptions are privileges that only a living person can exercise, such as the right to vote or to hold public office.

Corporations may be classified in a variety of ways. Two common classifications are by purpose and by ownership. A corporation may be organized for the purpose of making a **profit** (such as lululemon), or it may be **not-for-profit** (such as the Canadian Cancer Society).

In classification by ownership, there is also a distinction between public and private corporations. A **public corporation** may have thousands of shareholders, and its shares are regularly traded on a securities market, such as the Toronto Stock Exchange. Most of the largest Canadian companies are publicly held. Examples are the Royal Bank, George Weston Ltd., Magna International Inc., and Imperial Oil Ltd., as well as our textbook feature companies Shoppers Drug Mart Corporation and The Jean Coutu Group Inc.

In contrast, a **private corporation**—often called a closely held corporation—usually has only a few shareholders. It does not offer its shares for sale to the general public. Private companies are generally much smaller than public companies, although there are some big exceptions, such as McCain Foods, The Jim Pattison Group, and the Irving companies. lululemon, in our feature story, was a privately held corporation until it offered its shares for sale to the public in 2007, after which it became a publicly traded company.

There are other more specialized forms of corporations in Canada. A common example is an income trust. An **income trust** is a special or limited purpose company that is set up specifically to invest in income-producing assets. Its "trust units" are traded on organized securities exchanges, just like shares. The trust pays out most of its earnings to investors, called unitholders. For certain kinds of income trusts, such as real estate income trusts (REIT) and mutual fund investment trusts, there is no income tax payable for the trust itself. Instead, the unitholders pay income tax on the cash they receive. The largest real estate income trust in Canada is the RioCan REIT.

The only significant differences in accounting for income trusts compared to other types of corporations involves their distribution of earnings and equity structure. These exceptions aside, they are accounted for in the same way.

Characteristics of a Corporation

study objective 1

Identify and discuss the major characteristics of a corporation.

Many characteristics distinguish corporations from proprietorships and partnerships. Recall from Chapter 1 that a proprietorship is a business owned by one person, and a partnership is owned by two or more people who are associated as partners. A corporation has the following distinguishing characteristics:

Separate Legal Existence

As an entity that is separate and distinct from its owners, the corporation acts under its own name rather than in the name of its shareholders. lululemon, for example, may buy, own, and sell property, borrow money, and enter into legally binding contracts in its own name. It may also sue or be sued. And it pays income taxes as a separate entity.

In contrast to a proprietorship or partnership, where the owners' actions bind the proprietorship or partnership, the acts of a corporation's owners (shareholders) do not bind the corporation unless these owners are also agents of the corporation. For example, if you owned lululemon shares, you would not have the right to purchase a new production facility for the company unless you were designated as an agent of the corporation.

Limited Liability of Shareholders

The liability of shareholders is limited to their investment in the corporation, and ownership is represented by the number of shares that the individual shareholder owns. This means that creditors only have access to corporate assets to satisfy their claims: in other words, shareholders cannot be made to pay for the company's liabilities out of their personal assets.

Limited liability is a significant advantage for the corporate form of organization. However, in certain situations, creditors may demand a personal guarantee from a controlling shareholder. This has the effect of making the controlling shareholder's personal assets available, if required, to satisfy the creditor's claim—which, of course, eliminates or reduces the advantage of limited liability.

Transferable Ownership Rights

Ownership of a corporation is held in shares of capital, which are transferable units. Shareholders can dispose of part or all of their interest in a corporation simply by selling their shares. The transfer of shares is entirely up to the shareholder. It does not require the approval of either the corporation or other shareholders.

In addition, the transfer of ownership rights among shareholders has no effect on the operating activities of the corporation. Nor does it affect the corporation's assets, liabilities, or shareholders' equity. The transfer of ownership rights is a transaction between individual shareholders. The corporation does not participate in the transfer of these ownership rights; it is only involved in the original sale of the share capital. For example, when 15.9 million shares were sold by lululemon shareholders in 2007, no journal entry was made by the company. Each sale of shares was a personal transaction between the former shareholder and the new shareholder who purchased the shares.

Ability to Acquire Capital

It is fairly easy for a corporation to obtain capital by issuing shares. Buying shares in a corporation is often attractive to an investor because a shareholder has limited liability and shares are readily transferable. Also, because only small amounts of money need to be invested, many individuals can become shareholders. The ability of a successful corporation to obtain capital is almost unlimited.

Note that the "almost unlimited" ability to acquire capital is only true for large, publicly traded corporations. Small, or closely held, corporations can have as much difficulty in acquiring capital as do proprietorships or partnerships.

Continuous Life

Corporations have an unlimited life. Since a corporation is a separate legal entity, its continuance as a going concern is not affected by the withdrawal, death, or incapacity of a shareholder, employee, or officer. As a result, a successful corporation can have a continuous and indefinite life. For example, Hudson's Bay Company, the oldest commercial corporation in North America, was founded in 1670 and is still going strong. Its ownership has changed over the years from a publicly traded corporation to a private corporation, but the corporation itself still continues. In contrast, proprietorships end if anything happens to the proprietor and partnerships normally re-form if anything happens to one of the partners.

Corporation Management

Shareholders can invest in a corporation without having to manage it personally. Although shareholders legally own the corporation, they manage it indirectly through a board of directors they elect. The board, in turn, sets the broad strategic objectives for the company. The board also selects officers, such as a president and one or more vice-presidents, to execute policy and to perform daily management functions. Dennis (Chip) Wilson is the chair of lululemon's board of directors. Christine Day is lululemon's president and chief executive officer. She and the chief financial officer also sit on lululemon's board of directors, as do seven independent (outside) directors.

Government Regulations

Canadian companies may be incorporated federally, under the terms of the *Canada Business Corporations Act*, or provincially, under the terms of a provincial business corporations act. Federal and provincial laws usually state the requirements for issuing and reacquiring shares and distributing earnings. Similarly, the regulations of provincial securities commissions control the sale of share capital to the general public. When a corporation's shares are listed and traded on foreign securities markets, the corporation must also respect the reporting requirements of these exchanges. For example, lululemon's shares are listed on both the Toronto Stock Exchange in Canada and the NASDAQ Stock Market in the U.S. Complying with federal, provincial, and securities regulations in multiple jurisdictions increases the cost and complexity of the corporate form of organization.

Income Taxes

Proprietorships, partnerships, and certain kinds of income trusts do not pay income tax as separate entities. Instead, each owner's (or partner's or unitholder's) share of earnings from these organizations is reported on his or her personal income tax return. Income tax is then paid on this amount by the individual.

Corporations, on the other hand, must pay income taxes as separate legal entities (with the exception of real estate income trusts and mutual fund investment trusts). These taxes can be substantial and can amount to as much as 35 percent of taxable income. There are, however, income tax rate reductions available to some corporations. With eligible reductions, or other corporate tax incentives, a corporation's tax rate may be reduced to between 13 and 20 percent on certain kinds of active small business income. This rate is much lower than the tax rate for the same amount of income earned by an individual.

In some circumstances, an advantage of incorporation is being able to delay personal income tax. The shareholders of a corporation do not pay tax on the corporate earnings until the earnings are distributed to them as dividends. Many people argue that corporate earnings are taxed twice (double taxation), once at the corporate level and again at the individual level. This is not exactly true, however, as individuals receive a dividend tax credit to reduce some of this tax burden.

It is wise to get expert advice to determine whether incorporating will result in more or less income tax than operating as a proprietorship or partnership. Income tax laws are complex, and careful tax planning is essential for any business venture.

⊕ ACCOUNTING MATTERS! | International Perspective

Corporations in North America and China, amongst others, are identified by "Ltd.," "Inc.," "Corp.," or in some cases, "Co." following their names. These abbreviations can also be spelled out. In Brazil and France, the letters used are "SA" (Sôciedade Anonima, Société Anonyme); in Japan, "KK" (Kabushiki Kaisha); in Egypt, "SAE" (Société Anonyme Égyptienne), in the Netherlands, "NV" (Naamloze Vennootschap); in Italy, "SpA" (Società per Azioni); and in Sweden, "AB" (Aktiebolag).

In the UK, public corporations are identified by "Plc" (Public limited company), while private corporations are denoted by "Ltd." The same designations in Germany are "AG" (Aktiengesellschaft) for public corporations and "GmbH" (Gesellschaft mit beschränkter Haftung) for private corporations.

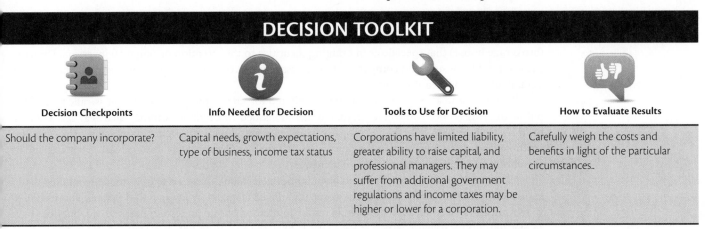

DECISION TOOLKIT

Decision Checkpoints	Info Needed for Decision	Tools to Use for Decision	How to Evaluate Results
Should the company incorporate?	Capital needs, growth expectations, type of business, income tax status	Corporations have limited liability, greater ability to raise capital, and professional managers. They may suffer from additional government regulations and income taxes may be higher or lower for a corporation.	Carefully weigh the costs and benefits in light of the particular circumstances..

Share Issue Considerations

After incorporation, a corporation sells ownership rights as shares. The shares of the company are divided into different classes, such as Class A, Class B, and so on. The rights and privileges for each class of shares are stated in articles of incorporation, which form the "constitution" of the company. The different classes are usually identified by the generic terms *common shares* and *preferred shares*. When a corporation has only one class of shares, that class has the rights and privileges of common shares. lululemon has common shares, in addition to another class of shares called "special voting stock."

Each common share gives the shareholder the ownership rights shown in Illustration 11-1.

Vote Shareholders have the right to vote on certain matters, such as the election of the board of directors and appointment of external auditors. Each shareholder normally has one vote for each common share owned.

◄ Illustration 11-1

Ownership rights of shareholders

Dividends Shareholders share in the distribution of the corporate income through dividends, in proportion to the number of shares owned.

Liquidation Shareholders share in any assets that remain after liquidation, in proportion to the number of shares owned. This is known as a residual claim because shareholders are paid only if any cash remains after all the assets have been sold and all liabilities paid.

When lululemon issued common shares in 2007, it had to make several decisions. How many shares should be authorized for sale? At what price should the shares be issued? What value should be assigned to the shares? These questions are discussed in the following sections.

Authorized Share Capital

The amount of share capital that a corporation is authorized to sell is indicated in its articles of incorporation. It may be specified as either an unlimited amount or a specific number (e.g., 500,000 shares authorized). Most companies in Canada have an unlimited amount of authorized shares. If a number is specified, the amount of authorized shares normally anticipates a company's initial and later capital needs.

lululemon has an authorized number of shares specified. It has 5 million preferred shares and 200 million common shares authorized. The authorization of share capital does not result in a formal accounting entry, because the event has no immediate effect on either corporate assets or shareholders' equity. However, the number of shares authorized must be disclosed in the shareholders' equity section of the balance sheet.

Issue of Shares

A corporation can issue common shares directly to investors or indirectly through an investment dealer (brokerage house) that specializes in bringing securities to the attention of potential investors. Direct issue is typical in closely held companies. Indirect issue is customary for a publicly held corporation, such as lululemon in our feature story.

The first time a corporation's shares are offered for sale to the public, the offer is called an initial public offering (IPO). You will recall that lululemon issued 18.2 million common shares at U.S. $18 each in an IPO in July 2007. Whether a company issues its shares directly or indirectly, it receives the cash (less any financing or issue fees) from the sale of the IPO shares. The company's assets (cash) increase, and its shareholders' equity (share capital) also increases.

Whereas a journal entry is not made for authorized share capital, an entry is made whenever shares are issued by the company because the company's financial position changes as described above. Issued shares are authorized shares that have been sold. lululemon has no preferred shares issued, but does have 46,684,700 common shares issued at February 3, 2008, the end of its 2007 fiscal year. It also has 20,935,041 of special voting shares, which are also common shares.

Once the shares have been issued and sold, they then trade on the secondary market. That is, investors buy and sell shares from each other rather than from the company, using a stock exchange such as the Toronto Stock Exchange. When shares are sold among investors, there is no impact on the company's financial position. The company receives no additional assets, and it issues no additional shares. The only change in the company records is the name of the shareholder, not the number of shares issued.

Fair Value of Shares

After the initial issue of new shares, the share price changes according to the interaction between buyers and sellers. In general, the price follows the trend of a company's earnings and dividends. Factors that are beyond a company's control (such as an embargo on oil, an economic recession, changes in interest rates, the outcome of an election, and war) also influence market prices.

For each listed security, the financial press reports the highest and lowest prices that the share sold at for the year, the annual dividend rate, the high and low prices for the day, and the net change over the previous day. The total volume of shares traded on a particular day, the dividend yield, and the price-earnings ratio are also reported. A recent listing for lululemon's common shares on the Toronto Stock Exchange follows:

365-day		stock	sym	div	high	low	close	chg	vol (000)	yld	p/e ratio
high	low										
58.77	21.20	lululemon athletica	LLL	0.00	29.93	28.44	29.70	+0.83	68,919	0.00	123.80

lululemon's shares have traded as high as $58.77 and as low as $21.20 during the past year. The stock's ticker symbol is "LLL." lululemon does not pay an annual dividend, which is indicated by the "0.00" amount in the "div" column. The high and low prices for the date shown were $29.93 and $28.44 per share, respectively. The closing share price was $29.70, an increase of $0.83 from the previous day. The trading volume was 68,919,000 shares.

Since lululemon does not pay dividends, there is no dividend yield ("yld"). The dividend yield reports the rate of return an investor earned from dividends, calculated by dividing the dividend by the share price. We will learn more about this ratio later in the chapter. lululemon's shares are currently trading at a price-earnings ("p/e") ratio (share price divided by earnings per share) of 123.80 times earnings. The dividend yield and price-earnings ratios are often interpreted together to determine how much investors favour a company.

One commonly reported measure of the fair value of a company's total equity is its market capitalization. The market capitalization of a company is calculated by multiplying the number of shares issued by the share price at any given date. lululemon's market capitalization was $2 billion at the time of writing. The largest market capitalization for any company in Canada is that of Research In Motion Ltd., whose market capitalization at September 30, 2008, was $55 billion.

Legal Capital

When shares are issued, they form the share capital of the corporation. You will recall that the shareholders' equity section of a corporation's balance sheet includes both share capital and retained earnings. The distinction between retained earnings and share capital is important from both a legal and an economic point of view. Retained earnings can be distributed to shareholders as dividends or retained in the company for operating needs. On the other hand, share capital is legal capital that cannot be distributed to shareholders. It must remain invested in the company for the protection of corporate creditors.

Some countries, notably the US, assign a par or stated value to shares to predetermine the amount of legal capital. lululemon was originally incorporated in Delaware, and its common shares have a $0.01 par value. The use of par values for shares is rare in Canada, with less than 3 percent of publicly traded companies reporting par value shares. In fact, companies that are incorporated federally and companies incorporated in some provinces are not allowed to issue shares with par values.

Instead, no par value shares or shares that have not been assigned a predetermined value are issued. When no par value shares are issued, all of the proceeds received are considered to be legal capital. Whenever shares are issued in this chapter, you can assume that they are no par value shares.

BEFORE YOU GO ON...

Review It

1. What are the advantages and disadvantages of a corporation compared to a proprietorship or a partnership?
2. To a corporation, what is the significance of the amount of authorized shares? Of the amount of issued shares?
3. How does the sale of shares affect a company in an initial public offering? And afterwards when they are sold in the secondary market?
4. How is the legal capital of shares determined when no par value shares are issued?

The Navigator

Share Capital

Contributed capital is the amount shareholders paid, or contributed, to the corporation in exchange for shares of ownership. This includes share capital, in addition to other sources of capital affected by share transactions. Recall that share capital can consist of both common shares and preferred shares. We will look at common shares in this section and preferred shares in the next. We will also learn more about other sources of contributed capital.

study objective 2
Record share transactions.

Common Shares

Common shares may be issued (sold) to investors, who then become shareholders of the corporation. Common shares can also be reacquired from shareholders. We will look at each of these types of transactions in more detail.

Issue of Shares

To illustrate the issue of common shares, assume that Hydro-Slide, Inc. is authorized to issue an unlimited number of no par value common shares and that it issues 1,000 of these shares for $6 per share on January 12.

As mentioned earlier, when no par value common shares are issued, the entire proceeds from the sale become legal capital. That means that the proceeds are credited to the Common Shares account. The entry to record this transaction is:

Jan. 12	Cash	6,000	
	Common Shares		6,000
	(To record issue of 1,000 common shares)		

A	=	L	+	SE
+6,000				+6,000

⬆ Cash flows: +6,000

Common shares are most commonly issued in exchange for cash. However, they may also be issued for other considerations than cash, such as services (e.g., compensation to lawyers or consultants) or noncash assets (e.g., land, buildings, or equipment). When shares are issued for a noncash consideration, they should be recorded at their **cash equivalent price**. The cash equivalent price is the fair value of the consideration (common shares) given up. If the common shares do not have a ready market (i.e., their value cannot be easily determined), the cash equivalent price is instead the fair value of the consideration that is received (i.e., the service, land, building, and so on).

Reacquisition of Shares

Companies can purchase their own shares on the open market. A corporation may acquire its own shares to meet any of the following objectives:

1. To increase trading of the company's shares in the securities market in the hope of enhancing the company's value. If a company feels that the shares are trading at a price that is less than what they are worth, it may buy back the shares. When the number of shares available for sale in the stock market decreases, the share price should increase.
2. To reduce the number of shares issued. By reducing the number of shares issued and reducing shareholders' equity, earnings per share and return on equity will increase.
3. To eliminate hostile shareholders by buying them out
4. To have additional shares available for issue to employees under bonus and stock compensation plans, or for use in acquiring other companies

For federally incorporated companies, and most provincially incorporated companies, the repurchased shares must be retired and cancelled. This effectively restores the shares to the status of authorized but unissued shares. In some Canadian provinces, in the U.S., and internationally, reacquired shares can also be held in for subsequent reissue. If they are not retired and cancelled, these shares are referred to as treasury shares. Only 4 percent of Canadian companies reported having treasury shares in a recent year. Because treasury shares are relatively uncommon in Canada, they are not discussed here.

The reacquisition of shares is a common practice and the financial press often contains announcements of "normal course issuer bids," which inform the public that a company plans to repurchase its shares. Shoppers Drug Mart has a normal course issuer bid that allows it to repurchase for cancellation up to 5,400,000 (2.5 percent) of its common shares.

To record a reacquisition of common (or preferred) shares, the following steps are required (note that we illustrate them below):

1. **Remove the cost of the shares from the share capital account:** Recall that when a long-lived asset is retired, the cost of the asset must be deleted (credited) from the appropriate asset account. Similarly, the cost of the common shares that are reacquired and retired must be determined and this amount is then deleted (debited) from the Common Shares account.

   In order to determine the cost of the common shares reacquired, it is necessary to calculate an **average cost per share**. It is impractical, and often impossible, to determine the cost of each individual common share that is reacquired. An average cost per common share is therefore calculated by dividing the balance in the Common Shares account by the number of shares issued at the transaction date.

2. **Record the cash paid:** The Cash account is credited for the amount paid to reacquire the shares. Note that a company has little choice in *what* it has to pay to reacquire the shares. It must purchase the shares on the secondary market by paying whatever the current share price is on the date of purchase. It can only decide *when* to make the reacquisition.

3. **Record the "gain" or loss" on reacquisition:** The difference between the price paid to reacquire the shares and their original cost is basically a "gain" or "loss" on reacquisition. However, because companies cannot realize a gain or suffer a loss from share transactions with their own shareholders, these amounts are not reported on the statement of earnings. They are seen instead as an excess or deficiency that belongs to the original shareholders. As a result, the amount is reported as an increase or decrease in a separate contributed capital account in the shareholders' equity section of the balance sheet.

The accounting for the reacquisition of shares is different depending on whether the shares are reacquired by paying less than average cost or more than average cost. We will examine each situation in the next two sections.

Reacquisition below Average Cost

To illustrate the reacquisition of common shares at a price less than their average cost, assume that Hydro-Slide, Inc. now has a total of 25,000 common shares issued and a balance in its Common Shares account of $50,000. The average cost of Hydro-Slide's common shares, immediately before the reacquisition, is $2 per share ($50,000 ÷ 25,000).

On September 23, Hydro-Slide reacquired 5,000 of its common shares at a price of $1.50 per share. Since the average cost of the shares was $2 per share, a $0.50 ($2.00 − $1.50) addition to contributed capital results, as shown below:

Sept. 23	Common Shares (5,000 × $2)	10,000	
	Contributed Capital—Reacquisition of Common Shares		2,500
	Cash (5,000 × $1.50)		7,500
	(To record reacquisition and retirement of 5,000 common shares)		

A = L + SE
−7,500   −10,000
                +2,500

Cash flows: −7,500

After this entry, Hydro-Slide still has an unlimited number of shares authorized, but only 20,000 (25,000 − 5,000) shares issued, and a balance of $40,000 ($50,000 − $10,000) in its Common Shares account. The difference between the average cost of the shares and the amount paid to repurchase them is credited to a new account, one that is specifically for the contributed capital realized from the reacquisition of shares. The cash in the entry was paid to the shareholders from whom the shares were repurchased.

Reacquisition above Average Cost

If Hydro-Slide had paid $2.50 per share to reacquire 5,000 of its common shares, rather than the $1.50 per share assumed above, it would result in a debit for the difference between the price paid to reacquire the shares and their average cost. If there is any balance in the contributed capital account from previous reacquisitions, this amount would first be reduced (debited). However, contributed capital cannot be reduced beyond any existing balance. In other words, contributed capital can never have a negative, or debit, balance. Instead, any excess deficiency amount would be debited to Retained Earnings.

The journal entry to record the reacquisition and retirement of Hydro-Slide's common shares at a price of $2.50 per share is as follows:

Sept. 23	Common Shares (5,000 × $2)	10,000	
	Retained Earnings	2,500	
	Cash (5,000 × $2.50)		12,500
	(To record reacquisition and retirement of 5,000 common shares)		

A = L + SE
−12,500   −10,000
                 −2,500

Cash flows: −12,500

In this entry, Hydro-Slide is assumed to have no previous balance in the contributed capital account. After this entry, Hydro-Slide still has 20,000 (25,000 − 5,000) shares issued and a balance of $40,000 ($50,000 − $10,000) in its Common Shares account.

In summary, the only difference in the accounting for reacquisitions at prices below or above the average cost has to do with recording the difference between the amount paid to repurchase the shares and their average cost. If the shares are reacquired at a price below their average cost, the difference is credited to a contributed capital account. If the shares are reacquired at a price above the average cost, the difference is debited first to the contributed capital account used in prior reacquisitions, and second, to the Retained Earnings account if there is no credit balance remaining in the contributed capital account.

Preferred Shares

A corporation may issue preferred shares in addition to common shares. Like common shares, preferred shares may be issued for cash or for noncash considerations. They can also be reacquired. The entries for these transactions are similar to the entries for common shares, so they are not repeated here. When a company has more than one class of shares, separate account titles should be used (e.g., Preferred Shares, Common Shares).

Preferred shares have contractual provisions that give them a preference, or priority, over common shares in certain areas. Typically, preferred shareholders have priority over the payment of dividends and, in the event of liquidation, over the distribution of assets. However, they do not usually have the voting rights that the common shares have. A recent survey indicated that about 20 percent of Canadian companies have preferred shares.

Dividend Preference

As indicated above, **preferred shareholders have the right to share in the distribution of dividends before common shareholders do**. For example, if the annual dividend rate on preferred shares is $5 per share, common shareholders will not receive any dividends in the current year until preferred shareholders have received $5 per share. Preferred shares such as these would be called "$5 preferred"—the $5 indicates the dividend rate which, similar to interest rates, is always stated as an annual rate.

Note that, even if preferred shareholders have a first claim on dividends, this does not guarantee that there will actually be dividends. Dividends depend on many factors, such as adequate retained earnings and the availability of cash. In addition, all dividends must be formally approved by the board of directors.

Preferred shares may contain a cumulative dividend feature. This right means that preferred shareholders must be paid both current-year dividends and any unpaid prior-year dividends before common shareholders receive dividends. Preferred shares without this feature are called noncumulative. A dividend that is not declared on noncumulative preferred shares in any particular year is lost forever.

When preferred shares are cumulative, preferred dividends that are not declared in a period are called dividends in arrears. No distribution can be made to common shareholders until this entire cumulative preferred dividend is paid. In other words, dividends cannot be paid to common shareholders while any preferred share dividends are in arrears. It is unusual for a company to have any dividends in arrears. At the time of writing, no Canadian company reported dividends in arrears for its most recent fiscal year.

It is important to understand that if a company does have dividends in arrears, they would not be considered a liability. No obligation exists until a dividend is declared by the board of directors. However, the amount of dividends in arrears should be disclosed in the notes to the financial statements. This allows investors to evaluate the potential impact of this commitment on the corporation's financial position.

Even though there is no requirement to pay an annual dividend, companies that are unable to meet their dividend obligations—whether cumulative or noncumulative—are not looked upon favourably by the investment community. As a financial officer noted in discussing one company's failure to pay its preferred dividend for a period of time, "Not meeting your obligations on something like that is a major black mark on your record."

Liquidation Preference

In addition to having a priority claim over common shares on any distribution of dividends, preferred shares also have a priority claim on corporate assets if the corporation fails. This means that if the company is bankrupt, preferred shareholders will get money back before common shareholders do. The preference on assets may be for the legal value of the shares or for a specified liquidating value. So, while creditors still rank above all shareholders in terms of preference in liquidations, preferred shareholders rank above common shareholders. This is important as the money usually runs out before everyone gets paid.

Because of these two preferential rights—the right to dividends and the right to assets—preferred shareholders generally do not mind that they do not have the voting right that common shareholders have.

Other Preferences

The attractiveness of preferred shares as an investment is sometimes increased by adding a conversion privilege. Convertible preferred shares allow the exchange of preferred shares for common shares at a specified ratio, at the shareholder's option. Nearly half of the companies in Canada that have preferred shares also have this conversion privilege. Convertible preferred shares are purchased by investors who want the greater security of preferred shares, but who also desire the added option of conversion if the value of the common shares increases significantly.

Most preferred shares are also issued with a redemption or call feature. Redeemable (or callable) preferred shares give the issuing corporation the right to purchase the shares from shareholders at specified future dates and prices. The redemption feature offers some flexibility to a corporation by enabling it to eliminate this type of equity security when it is advantageous to do so.

Retractable preferred shares are similar to redeemable or callable preferred shares, except that it is at the *shareholder's* option, rather than the corporation's option, that the shares are redeemed. This usually occurs at an arranged price and date. When preferred shares are redeemable or retractable, the distinction between equity and debt is less clear. Redeemable and retractable preferred shares are similar in some ways to debt. They both offer a rate of return to the investor, and with the redemption of the shares, they both offer a repayment of the principal investment.

Contractual arrangements of this sort are known as financial instruments—a broad category that includes, but is not limited to, debt and equity investments. A **financial instrument** is a contract that creates a financial asset for one company and a financial liability or equity instrument for another company. Convertible debt, as we discussed in Chapter 10, is an example of a financial instrument. Redeemable and retractable preferred shares are another example.

Financial instruments must be presented in accordance with their economic substance rather than their form. That is, redeemable and retractable preferred shares are usually presented in the *liabilities* section of the balance sheet rather than in the equity section. This is because they often have more of the features of debt than of equity.

Companies are issuing an increasing number of shares with innovative preferences. Some have the attributes of both debt and equity; others have the attributes of both common and preferred shares. Accounting for such financial instruments presents unique challenges for accountants. Further detail is left for an intermediate accounting course.

BEFORE YOU GO ON...

Review It

1. Explain the accounting for the issue of shares.
2. Distinguish between the accounting for a repurchase of shares at a price less than average cost and more than average cost.
3. Did Shoppers Drug Mart repurchase and cancel any of its own common shares in fiscal 2007? The answer to this question is at the end of the chapter.
4. Compare the normal rights and privileges of common and preferred shares.

Do It

On March 1, Assiniboia Corporation had 100,000 common shares issued, with a balance in the Common Shares account of $1,200,000 and a balance in the Contributed Capital—Reacquisition of Shares account of $25,000. On March 15, Assiniboia issued an additional 20,000 common shares at $15 per share. On June 1, it repurchased 10,000 of its own common shares at $16 per share. On September 1, the company issued 25,000 preferred shares at $50 per share. Record the share transactions.

Action Plan

• Credit the appropriate share capital account for the proceeds received in a share issue.
• Calculate the average cost per share by dividing the balance in the shares account by the number of shares issued.
• Debit the shares account for the average cost of the reacquired shares. If the reacquisition cost is below the average cost, credit the difference to a contributed capital account. If the reacquisition cost is above the average cost, debit the difference to Retained Earnings unless there is already a balance in a contributed capital account from previous reacquisitions and retirements.

Solution

Mar. 15	Cash (20,000 × $15)	300,000	
	Common Shares		300,000
	(To record issue of 20,000 common shares at $15 per share)		

Mar. 15: Balance in Common Shares account: $1,200,000 + $300,000 = $1,500,000
Number of common shares issued: 100,000 + 20,000 = 120,000
Average cost: $1,500,000 ÷ 120,000 = $12.50

June 1	Common Shares (10,000 × $12.50)	125,000	
	Contributed Capital—Reacquisition of Shares	25,000	
	Retained Earnings	10,000	
	Cash (10,000 × $16)		160,000
	(To record reacquisition and retirement of 10,000 common shares at an average cost of $12.50)		

June 1: Balance in Common Shares account: $1,200,000 + $300,000 − $125,000 = $1,375,000
Number of common shares issued: 100,000 + 20,000 − 10,000 = 110,000
Average cost: $1,375,000 ÷ 110,000 = $12.50

Sept. 1	Cash (25,000 × $50)	1,250,000	
	Preferred Shares		1,250,000
	(To record issue of 25,000 preferred shares at $50 per share)		

The Navigator

Retained Earnings

As we have learned in past chapters, retained earnings are the cumulative net earnings since incorporation that have been retained in the company (i.e., that have not been distributed to shareholders). Each year, net earnings are added to (or a net loss is deducted from) the opening Retained Earnings account balance and dividends are then deducted from this balance: the result is the ending retained earnings amount. We have looked at the components of net earnings in prior chapters. We will focus on the impact of dividends on retained earnings in this section.

Dividends

A **dividend** is a pro rata (equal) distribution of a portion of a corporation's retained earnings to its shareholders. "Pro rata" means that if you own, say, 10 percent of the common shares, you will receive 10 percent of the dividend.

Many high-growth companies, such as lululemon in our feature story, do not pay dividends. Their policy is to retain all of their earnings to make it easier for the company to grow. Investors purchase shares in companies like lululemon with the hope that the share price will increase in value and they will realize a profit when they sell their shares. Other investors purchase shares of established companies with the hope of earning dividend revenue (and maybe also of profiting from some share price appreciation when they sell their shares). The Bank of Montreal has the longest unbroken dividend record in Canadian history, having begun paying dividends in 1829.

As mentioned earlier, **dividends are reported as an annual dollar amount per share**, even though it is usual to pay dividends quarterly. For example, in 2007, Shoppers Drug Mart had an annual dividend rate of $0.64 on its common shares. This dividend is paid quarterly at a rate of $0.16 ($0.64 ÷ 4) per share.

Cash dividends are the most common in practice but stock dividends are also declared fairly often. We will look at each of these types of dividends in the next two sections.

Cash Dividends

A **cash dividend** is a distribution of cash to shareholders. Cash dividends can be paid to preferred or common shareholders. If dividends are paid to both the preferred and common shareholders, remember that the preferred shareholders have to be paid first.

For a corporation to pay a cash dividend, it must have the following:

1. **Enough retained earnings.** Dividends are distributed from (reduce) retained earnings, so a company must have enough retained earnings in order to pay a dividend. Although the laws for cash dividends differ depending on the jurisdiction, in general, a deficit cannot be created by the declaration of a dividend. Recall from Chapter 2 that a deficit is a negative, or debit, balance in retained earnings.

   Companies seldom pay out dividends equal to their retained earnings, however. They must retain a certain portion of retained earnings to finance their operations. In addition, some level of retained earnings must be maintained to provide a cushion or buffer against possible future losses.

2. **Enough cash.** The fact that a company has enough retained earnings does not necessarily mean that it has enough cash to pay the dividend. There is no direct relationship between the balance in the Retained Earnings account and the balance in the Cash account at any point in time. So, in addition to having enough retained earnings, a company must also have enough cash before it can pay a dividend.

   Shoppers Drug Mart had $1,580,888 thousand of retained earnings and $27,588 thousand of cash remaining at the end of its 2007 fiscal year, after declaring and paying dividends. It obviously had enough retained earnings and enough cash to pay a dividend.

   How much cash is enough? That is hard to say but a company must keep enough cash on hand to pay for its ongoing operations and to pay its bills as they come due. Under the *Canada Business Corporations Act*, a corporation cannot pay a dividend if the payment will make the company unable to pay its liabilities. Before paying a cash dividend, a company's board of directors must carefully consider current and future demands on the company's cash resources. In some cases, current (or planned future) liabilities may make a cash dividend inappropriate.

3. **A declaration of dividends.** A company does not pay dividends unless its board of directors decides to do so, at which point the board "declares" (i.e., officially states) the dividend to be payable.

The board of directors has full authority to determine the amount of retained earnings to be distributed in the form of dividends and the amount to be retained in the company. Dividends do not accrue like interest on a note payable, and they are not a liability until they are declared. Moreover, as explained previously in the chapter, even if the preferred shares are cumulative, dividends in arrears are not a liability until they are declared.

In order to remain in business, companies *must* honour their interest payments to creditors, bankers, and debt holders. But the payment of dividends to shareholders is discretionary (i.e., a choice). Consequently, investors must keep an eye on the company's dividend policy and understand what it may mean. For most companies, for example, regular increases in the amount of dividends paid when the company has irregular earnings can be a warning signal. Companies with high dividends and rising debt may be borrowing money to pay shareholders.

On the other hand, low dividends may not be a negative sign. This could mean that higher returns will be earned through share price appreciation rather than through the receipt of dividends. Presumably, investors for whom regular dividends are important tend to buy shares in companies that pay periodic dividends, and those for whom growth in the share price is more important tend to buy shares in companies that retain earnings.

ACCOUNTING MATTERS! | Investor Perspective

For years, you could always count on the banks to pay ever-increasing dividends. The Royal Bank of Canada, the largest of the Canadian banks, raised its dividend by 20 percent annually over each of the past five years. Other Canadian banks also raised their dividends annually.

In 2008, however, all of the banks, except for the TD Bank, which declared a token 2-percent increase, left their dividend rates unchanged. This is because, with the credit crisis and declining economy, there is less wealth to share. By not making dividend increases, "banks are giving you a message that things are not as good, and that paying out a higher dividend is not the best use of their money right now," said Norman Levine, the managing director of Portfolio Management Corp.

Source: John Heinzl, "Don't Bank on More Payout Hikes Soon," *The Globe and Mail*, March 5, 2008, p. B14.

Entries for Cash Dividends. Three dates are important in connection with dividends: (1) the declaration date, (2) the record date, and (3) the payment date. Normally, there are several weeks between each date and the next one. For example, on November 6, 2007 (the declaration date), Shoppers Drug Mart declared a quarterly dividend of $0.16 per share payable to its common shareholders. These dividends were paid on January 15, 2008 (the payment date), to the shareholders of record at the close of business on December 31, 2007 (the record date). Accounting entries are required on two of the dates—the declaration date and the payment date.

On the **declaration date**, the board of directors formally authorizes the cash dividend and announces it to shareholders. The declaration of a cash dividend commits the corporation to a binding legal obligation. An entry is therefore required to recognize the increase in Cash Dividends (which results in a decrease in retained earnings) and the increase in the liability Dividends Payable.

To illustrate a cash dividend to preferred shareholders, assume that on December 1, 2009, the directors of IBR Inc. declare a $0.50 per share cash dividend on the company's 100,000 preferred shares, payable on January 20 to shareholders of record on December 22. The dividend is $50,000 (100,000 × $0.50), and the entry to record the declaration is:

Declaration Date		
Dec. 1	Cash Dividends	50,000	
	Dividends Payable		50,000
	(To record declaration of cash dividend)		

A = L + SE
+50,000   −50,000

Cash flows no effect

The Cash Dividends account will be closed into, and reduce, the Retained Earnings account at the end of the year. Dividends Payable is a current liability: it will normally be paid within the next month or so.

On the **record date**, ownership of the shares is determined so that the company knows who to pay the dividend to. The shareholder records give this information. In the interval between the declaration date and the record date, the company updates its share ownership record. For IBR, the record date is December 22. No entry is required on the record date, because the corporation's liability that was recog-

Helpful Hint Between the declaration date and the record date, the number of shares remains the same. The purpose of the record date is to identify the persons or companies that will receive the dividend, not to determine the total amount of the dividend liability.

nized on the declaration date is unchanged.

On the **payment date**, dividend cheques are mailed to the shareholders and the payment of the dividend is recorded. The entry on January 20, the payment date, is:

A = L + SE
−50,000   −50,000

⬇ Cash flows: −50,000

Payment Date

Jan. 20	Dividends Payable	50,000	
	Cash		50,000
	(To record payment of cash dividend)		

Note that the declaration of a cash dividend increases liabilities and reduces shareholders' equity. The payment of a dividend reduces both assets and liabilities, but it has no effect on shareholders' equity. The cumulative effect of the declaration and payment of a cash dividend on a company's financial statements is to decrease both assets (through cash) and shareholders' equity (through retained earnings).

Stock Dividends

A **stock dividend** is a distribution of the corporation's own shares to shareholders. Whereas a cash dividend is paid in cash, a stock dividend is distributed (paid) in shares. And, while a cash dividend decreases assets and shareholders' equity, a stock dividend does not change either assets, liabilities, or total shareholders' equity. No cash has been paid, and no liabilities have been assumed. Two accounts in shareholders' equity are affected, but the changes offset each other. A stock dividend results in a decrease in retained earnings and an increase in share capital but it does not change *total* shareholders' equity.

What, then, are the purposes and benefits of a stock dividend? A corporation generally issues a stock dividend for one or more of the following reasons:

1. To satisfy shareholders' dividend expectations while conserving cash
2. To increase the marketability of the shares. When the number of shares increases, the price per share decreases on the stock market. Decreasing the market price of the shares makes it easier for investors to purchase them.
3. To emphasize that a portion of shareholders' equity has been permanently reinvested in the legal capital of the business and is unavailable for cash dividends

Similar to a cash dividend, there is a declaration date, record date, and distribution (payment) date for a stock dividend. The size of the stock dividend and the value to be assigned to each dividend share are determined by the board of directors when the dividend is declared. The *Canada Business Corporations Act* requires that stock dividends be recorded at **fair value** (market price per share) at the declaration date because this is what the corporation would have received if the shares had been issued for cash rather than as a stock dividend.

Entries for Stock Dividends. To illustrate the accounting for stock dividends, assume that IBR Inc. has 50,000 common shares with a balance of $500,000 in Common Shares and $300,000 in Retained Earnings. On June 30, it declares a 10-percent stock dividend to shareholders of record at July 20, to be distributed to shareholders on August 5. The share price on June 30 is $15 per share.

The number of shares to be issued is 5,000 (50,000 × 10%). The total amount to be debited to the Stock Dividends account is $75,000 (5,000 × $15). Note that it is the fair value at the declaration date that is relevant for this transaction, and not the fair value on the record date or distribution date.

The entry to record the declaration of the stock dividend is as follows:

A = L + SE
    −75,000
    +75,000

Cash flows: no effect

June 30	Stock Dividends—Common	75,000	
	Common Stock Dividends Distributable		75,000
	(To record declaration of 10% stock dividend)		

Similar to cash dividends, there is no entry at the record date. At the declaration date, the Stock Dividends account is increased by the fair value of the shares to be issued, and Common Stock Dividends Distributable is increased by the same amount. Common Stock Dividends Distributable is a shareholders' equity account. It is not a liability, because assets will not be used to pay the dividend. Instead, it will be "paid" with common shares. If a balance sheet is prepared before the dividend shares are issued, the distributable account is reported as share capital in the shareholders' equity section of the balance sheet. As was the case with cash dividends, the Stock Dividends account will be closed into, and reduce, the Retained Earnings account at the end of the year.

When the dividend shares are issued on August 5, the account Common Stock Dividends Distributable is decreased (debited) and the account Common Shares is increased (credited), as follows:

Helpful Hint Note that the dividend account title uses the word "Distributable," not "Payable."

Aug. 5	Common Stock Dividends Distributable	75,000	
	Common Shares		75,000
	(To record issue of 5,000 common shares in a 10% stock dividend)		

A	=	L	+	SE
				−75,000
				+75,000

Cash flows: no effect

Note that neither of the above entries changes shareholders' equity in total. However, the composition of shareholders' equity changes because a portion of retained earnings is transferred to the common shares account. These effects are shown below for IBR Inc.:

	Before Stock Dividend	After Stock Dividend
Shareholders' equity		
Common shares	$500,000	$575,000
Retained earnings	300,000	225,000
Total shareholders' equity	$800,000	$800,000
Number of shares	50,000	55,000

In this example, the Common Shares account increased by $75,000 and Retained Earnings decreased by the same amount. Note also that total shareholders' equity remains unchanged at $800,000, the total both before and after the stock dividend.

Stock Splits

We discuss stock splits in this section because of their similarities to stock dividends. A **stock split**, like a stock dividend, involves the issue of additional shares to shareholders according to their percentage ownership. However, a stock split is usually much larger than a stock dividend. For example, a stock dividend might result in an additional 10% of common shares issued, whereas a stock split could result in 100% more common shares issued. This is because the main purpose of a stock split is to increase the marketability of the shares by lowering the price per share. A lower stock market price increases investors' interest in a company and makes it easier for the corporation to issue additional shares.

The effect of a stock split on the share price is generally inversely proportional to the size of the split—i.e., the larger the split, the lower the price per share. Sometimes, due to increased investor interest, the share price then rises more rapidly beyond its original split value.

lululemon split its stock in 2007 as it reorganized its shares for its initial public offering. At that time, common shareholders received an additional 1.38267841 shares for every share they owned. Although Shoppers Drug Mart has never split its stock, Jean Coutu has split its stock two-for-one three different times to date, once in 1992, again in 2000, and again in 2002. Jean Coutu said that the purpose of their stock splits was to keep the value of the company's shares low and increase the liquidity of the shares.

In a stock split, the number of shares is increased by a specified proportion. For example, in a two-for-one split, a company that has 100,000 shares issued before the split will issue an additional 100,000 shares and have a total of 200,000 shares (100,000 × 2) issued after the split. Jean Coutu had 50,858,940 Class A common shares before its latest two-for-one stock split, and 101,717,880 after (50,858,940 × 2). A stock split does not have any effect on total share capital, retained earnings, or total shareholders' equity. Only the number of shares increases.

These effects are shown below for IBR Inc., assuming that instead of issuing a 10-percent stock dividend, it split its 50,000 common shares on a two-for-one basis:

	Before Stock Split	After Stock Split
Shareholders' equity		
Common shares	$500,000	$500,000
Retained earnings	300,000	300,000
Total shareholders' equity	$800,000	$800,000
Number of shares	50,000	100,000

Because a stock split does not affect the balances in any shareholders' equity accounts, **it is not necessary to journalize a stock split**. Only a memo entry explaining the effect of the split (e.g., the change in the number of shares) is needed.

ACCOUNTING MATTERS! | Investor Perspective

Google Inc., which operates the world's most powerful on-line search engine, has no interest in splitting its stock. The stock split is a widely used market manoeuvre designed to make shares more affordable. In fact, stock splits have become so commonplace that investors almost automatically expect them whenever a company's share price approaches $100. However, despite Google's share price nearing U.S. $600 per share in January 2008, its management continues to defy stock market convention and show no interest in a stock split.

Comparison of Effects

A cash dividend, stock dividend, and stock split have different impacts on both a company and its shareholders.

Corporate Effects. Significant differences between the effects of cash dividends, stock dividends, and stock splits for a company are shown in Illustration 11-2. In the illustration, "+" means increase, "–" means decrease, and "NE" means "no effect."

Illustration 11-2 ➡

Corporate effects of cash dividends, stock dividends, and stock splits

	Assets	Liabilities	Shareholders' Equity Share Capital	Retained Earnings	Number of Shares
Cash dividend	–	NE	NE	–	NE
Stock dividend	NE	NE	+	–	+
Stock split	NE	NE	NE	NE	+

Cash dividends reduce assets (the Cash account) and retained earnings (the Cash Dividends account). Stock dividends increase share capital (the Common or Preferred Shares accounts) and decrease retained earnings (the Stock Dividends account). Stock splits do not affect any of the accounts. However, both a stock dividend and stock split increase the number of shares issued.

Individual Effects. Illustration 11-2 describes how dividends and splits affect a company. But how do they affect an individual shareholder (investor)? A cash dividend is relatively simple—the shareholder simply receives cash. The share price may drop marginally after the declaration of a cash dividend because the company is distributing some of its earnings to shareholders. However, the price normally recovers fairly rapidly.

A stock dividend is slightly more complicated. Since a stock dividend neither increases nor decreases the assets in the company, shareholders are not receiving anything they did not already own. In a sense, it is like ordering a piece of pie and cutting it into smaller pieces. You are no better or worse off, as you have the same amount of pie.

To illustrate a stock dividend for an individual shareholder, assume that you, a shareholder, have a 2% ownership interest in IBR Inc. You own 1,000 of its 50,000 common shares. If IBR declares a 10% stock dividend, 5,000 (50,000 × 10%) additional shares would be issued. You would receive 100 (5,000 × 2%) new common shares. Would your ownership interest change? No, it would remain at 2% (1,100 ÷ 55,000). You now own more shares, but your ownership interest has not changed.

Illustration 11-3 shows the effect of a stock dividend for shareholders:

Illustration 11-3 ➡

Effect of stock dividend for shareholder

Before Stock Dividend

After Stock Dividend

1,000 of 50,000 shares = 2% ownership   1,100 of 55,000 shares = 2% ownership

In addition, because there are more shares issued, if the market is efficient, the share price should decline proportionately to the size of the dividend. That is, if the share price was $15 before a 10% stock dividend, the share price should be $13.64 ($15 ÷ 110%) after the stock dividend. But stock markets do not always react this way. In fact, because the number of shares issued in a stock dividend is relatively small, the impact on share price is usually minimal. Sometimes the stock dividend makes the shares more attractive to investors, and the share price even rises. For simplicity, in this chapter we will assume that the share price in a stock dividend always declines proportionately to the size of the dividend.

In a stock split, a shareholder receives additional shares. For example, in a two-for-one stock split, an individual shareholder who owns 1,000 common shares before the split will receive an additional 1,000 shares and own 2,000 shares after the split. In addition, the share price is expected to drop proportionately (again assuming the market is efficient). The share price will decline in a stock split simply because of the number of additional shares now for sale in the marketplace. For example, if IBR's common shares were trading for $15 before a two-for-one split, the share price should be $7.50 ($15 ÷ 2) after the split. Quite often, as mentioned above, the share price will initially decline and then the price will start to climb more rapidly than previously.

To illustrate the effects of a cash dividend, stock dividend, and stock split for an individual shareholder, assume that Patsy Spencer, a shareholder in IBR Inc., owns 300 preferred shares and 1,000 common shares. Illustration 11-4 shows the effects of each option. In the illustration, "+" means increase, "–" means decrease, and "NE" means "no effect."

	Cash	Fair Value	Number of Shares
Cash dividend	+	NE	NE
Stock dividend	NE	NE	+
Stock split	NE	NE	+

◀ Illustration 11-4

Individual effects of cash dividends, stock dividends, and stock splits

You will recall that IBR declared a $0.50 cash dividend, so Patsy would receive $1,500 (300 × $0.50) on payment of this dividend. With the 10% stock dividend, Patsy would receive 100 (1,000 × 10%) additional common shares. The price of the common shares at the time of the stock dividend was $15, so the value of the stock dividend was $1,500 for Patsy (100 × $15). The fair value of her stock portfolio was $15,000 (1,000 × $15) before the stock dividend and unchanged at $15,000 (1,100 × $13.64) after the stock dividend.

In a stock split, Patsy would receive an additional 1,000 common shares, giving her 2,000 shares in total. They were previously worth $15 each and are now assumed to be worth $7.50 each. The value of Patsy's common share investment in IBR is unchanged at $15,000 (2,000 × $7.50). Of course, in both cases, Patsy now has additional shares that may earn future dividends and be profitable to resell.

Retained Earnings Restrictions

The balance in Retained Earnings is generally available for dividend declarations. In some cases, however, there may be retained earnings restrictions. These make a portion of the balance unavailable for dividends. Restrictions result from one or more of the following causes:

1. **Contractual restrictions**. Long-term debt contracts may restrict retained earnings as a condition for the loan. These restrictions are known as **debt covenants**, which, among other things, can limit the use of corporate assets for the payment of dividends. Such restrictions make it more likely that a corporation will be able to meet its required loan payments.
2. **Voluntary restrictions**. The board of directors may voluntarily create retained earnings restrictions for specific purposes. For example, the board may authorize a restriction because of a future plant expansion. By reducing the amount of retained earnings available for dividends, the company makes more cash available for the planned expansion.

No journal entry is necessary to record a retained earnings restriction, but they are disclosed in the notes to the financial statements. In a recent year, only about 3 percent of Canadian companies reported retained earnings restrictions.

Remember that retained earnings are part of the shareholders' claim on the corporation's total assets. The balance in Retained Earnings does not, however, represent a claim on any one specific asset. For example, restricting $100,000 of retained earnings does not necessarily mean that there will be $100,000 of cash set aside. All that a restriction does is to inform users that a portion of retained earnings is not available for dividend payments.

Alternative Terminology
Restrictions are sometimes called *reserves*.

BEFORE YOU GO ON...

▸ Review It

1. What entries are made for (a) cash dividends, (b) stock dividends, and (c) stock splits?
2. Distinguish between stock dividends and stock splits.
3. Contrast the effects of a stock dividend and a stock split on (a) assets, (b) liabilities, (c) shareholders' equity, and (d) the number of shares.
4. Describe the effects of a cash dividend, stock dividend, and stock split on an individual shareholder.
5. What is a retained earnings restriction?

▸ Do It

Sing CD Corporation has had five years of record earnings. Due to this success, the price of its 500,000 common shares tripled from $15 per share to $45. During this period, the Common Shares account remained the same at $2 million. Retained Earnings increased from $1.5 million to $10 million. President Bill McGrath is considering either (1) a 10-percent stock dividend or (2) a two-for-one stock split. He asks you to show the before-and-after effects of each option on the corporation's shareholders' equity and on the number of shares.

Action Plan

• Calculate the stock dividend effects on retained earnings by multiplying the stock dividend percentage by the number of existing shares to determine the number of new shares to be issued. Multiply the number of new shares by the price (fair value) of each share.

• A stock dividend increases the number of shares and affects both Common Shares and Retained Earnings.

• A stock split increases the number of shares but does not affect Common Shares or Retained Earnings.

Solution:

1. With a 10% stock dividend, the stock dividend amount is $2,250,000 [(500,000 × 10%) × $45]. The new balance in Common Shares is $4,250,000 ($2,000,000 + $2,250,000) and Retained Earnings is now $7,750,000 ($10,000,000 − $2,250,000).

2. With a stock split, the account balances in Common Shares and Retained Earnings after the stock split are the same as they were before: $2 million and $10 million, respectively.

The effects on the shareholders' equity accounts of each option are as follows:

	Original Balances	After Stock Dividend	After Stock Split
Common shares	$ 2,000,000	$ 4,250,000	$ 2,000,000
Retained earnings	10,000,000	7,750,000	10,000,000
Total shareholders' equity	$12,000,000	$12,000,000	$12,000,000
Number of shares	500,000	550,000	1,000,000

The Navigator

Financial Statement Presentation of Shareholders' Equity

Shareholders' equity transactions are reported in the balance sheet, statement of shareholders' equity, and cash flow statement. Equity transactions are not reported in the statement of earnings, although the statement of earnings is linked to shareholders' equity through retained earnings.

Balance Sheet

In the shareholders' equity section of the balance sheet, the following are reported: (1) contributed capital, (2) retained earnings, and (3) accumulated other comprehensive income. We have already learned about the first two categories and will review them briefly here. Accumulated other comprehensive income is a new concept that we are introducing in this chapter and will discuss in more detail in the next one.

Contributed Capital

Within contributed capital, two classifications are recognized:

1. **Share capital.** This category consists of preferred and common shares. Because of the additional rights they give, preferred shares are shown before common shares. Information about the legal capital, number of shares authorized, number of shares issued, and any particular share preferences (e.g., a dividend rate) is reported for each class of shares either directly in the shareholders' equity section of the balance sheet or in a note to the financial statements. Note also that any stock dividends distributable that exist at year end are also reported under share capital.

2. **Additional contributed capital.** This category includes amounts contributed from reacquiring and retiring shares. If shares have been issued with a par value, then amounts paid for the shares in excess of par value are recorded as additional contributed capital. Other situations not discussed in this textbook can also result in additional contributed capital. If a company has a variety of sources of additional contributed capital, it is important to distinguish each one by source. For many companies, however, there is no additional contributed capital. The caption "share capital" is therefore used more often than "contributed capital."

Retained Earnings

Retained earnings are the cumulative net earnings (or loss) since incorporation that has been retained in the company (i.e., not distributed to shareholders). Each year, net earnings are added (or a net loss is deducted) and dividends declared are deducted from the opening retained earnings balance to determine the ending retained earnings amount. Other additions or deductions from retained earnings can also occur, most notably from changes in accounting principles. We will learn more about this type of adjustment to retained earnings in Chapter 14. Recall that it is only the end-of-period balance of retained earnings that is presented in the shareholders' equity section of the balance sheet, not the detailed changes that are presented in the statement of shareholders' equity.

Retained Earnings is a shareholders' equity account whose normal balance is a credit. If a deficit (debit balance) exists, it is reported as a deduction from shareholders' equity, rather than as the usual addition. Notes to the financial statements are required to explain any restricted retained earnings and any dividends that may be in arrears.

Accumulated Other Comprehensive Income

Most revenues, expenses, gains, and losses are included in net earnings. However, certain gains and losses bypass net earnings and are recorded as direct adjustments to shareholders' equity. Comprehensive income includes all changes in shareholders' equity during a period except for changes that result from the sale or repurchase of shares or from the payment of dividends. This means that it includes (1) the revenues, expenses, gains, and losses included in net earnings, *and* (2) the gains and losses that bypass net earnings but affect shareholders' equity. This latter category is referred to as "other comprehensive income."

Reporting other comprehensive income separately from net earnings and retained earnings is done for two important reasons: (1) it protects earnings from sudden changes that would simply be caused by fluctuations in fair value, and (2) it informs the financial statement user of the gain or loss that would have occurred if the securities had actually been sold at year end.

There are several examples of other comprehensive income. One example, which we will learn about in more detail in the next chapter, is unrealized gains and losses on certain types of investments. If a company has debt or equity securities available for sale, they must be adjusted up or down to their fair value at the end of each accounting period. This results in an unrealized gain or loss. We say "unrealized" to distinguish it from the "realized" gains and losses that occur when the investment is actually sold. Other examples of comprehensive income include certain translation gains and losses on foreign currency, unrealized gains and losses from cash flow hedges, and unrealized pension cost from a minimum pension liability adjustment. These are all topics for more advanced accounting courses.

As mentioned above, comprehensive income includes both net earnings and other comprehensive income. Just as net earnings is included in retained earnings on the balance sheet, other comprehensive income is included in accumulated other comprehensive income. Accumulated other comprehensive income is the *cumulative* change in shareholders' equity that results from the gains and losses that bypass net earnings but affect shareholders' equity. Similar to retained earnings, which is the cumulative total of earnings retained in the business, accumulated other comprehensive income is the cumulative total of all past credits and charges to other comprehensive income. In other words, it starts with the balance at the beginning of the period and is increased by other comprehensive income and decreased by other comprehensive losses during the period, to arrive at the ending balance. It is this ending balance that is reported in the shareholders' equity section of the balance sheet.

Of course, not all companies will have examples of other comprehensive income. However, if they do, they must report comprehensive income separately in a statement of comprehensive income, and accumulated other comprehensive income as a separate component of shareholders' equity. We will learn about the preparation of the statement of comprehensive income in the next chapter when we discuss the sources of comprehensive income more fully.

Presentation

lululemon reports common shares, retained earnings, and accumulated other comprehensive income in the shareholders' equity section of its balance sheet, as shown in Illustration 11-5. Note that the current year end is February 3, 2008; this is known as its 2007 fiscal year. Last year's fiscal year—2006—ended on January 31, 2007.

Illustration 11-5 ➡

lululemon balance sheet— shareholders' equity section

LULULEMON ATHLETICA INC.
Balance Sheet (partial)
February 3, 2008
(in USD)

lululemon ⟳ athletica

	2007	2006
Shareholders' equity		
Contributed capital		
Special voting stock, $0.00001 par value, 30,000,000 shares authorized and 20,935,041 shares issued in 2007 (20,935,041 in 2006)	$ 209	$ 209
Common shares, $0.01 par value, 200,000,000 shares authorized and 46,684,700 shares issued in 2007 (44,290,778 in 2006)	466,847	442,908
Additional paid-in capital	136,004,955	98,669,641
Total contributed capital	136,472,011	99,112,758
Retained earnings (deficit)	(29,834,956)	(60,677,395)
Accumulated other comprehensive income (loss)	5,396,954	(1,056,565)
	$112,034,009	$37,378,798

lululemon has 30,000,000 special voting shares authorized, with 20,935,041 shares issued at the end of both fiscal years. It also has 200,000,000 common shares authorized, with 46,684,700 issued at February 3, 2008 (44,290,778 as at January 31, 2007). It also has a significant amount of paid-in capital. This is an additional contributed capital account that arises because of the low legal capital (par) value of lululemon's shares. If the shares had been of no par value, which is the norm in Canada, this entire amount would have been credited directly to a share capital account (e.g., common shares) rather than to an additional contributed capital account. lululemon's total contributed capital is U.S. $136,472,011 at February 3, 2008 (U.S. $99,112,758 at January 31, 2007).

lululemon reported a deficit in both years, which is deducted from shareholders' equity as indicated earlier in this section. The company also reported accumulated other comprehensive income of U.S. $5,396.954 at the end of fiscal 2007, whereas it reported an accumulated other comprehensive loss of U.S. $1,056,565 at the end of fiscal 2006. Note that comprehensive income is identified as *accumulated* other comprehensive income because it is a balance sheet account that builds on prior period balances, just as other balance sheet accounts do. lululemon's total shareholders' equity is U.S. $112,034,009 at February 3, 2008, a significant increase over U.S. $37,378,798 at January 31, 2007.

Alternative Terminology
The *statement of shareholders' equity* is also known as the *statement of changes in equity.*

Statement of Shareholders' Equity

In Canada, until recently, the financial statements included a statement of retained earnings, with detail about changes in other equity accounts disclosed in the notes to the statements. An alternative, and preferred, approach is to disclose changes affecting each shareholders' equity account in a statement of shareholders' equity. Although new to Canada, the statement of shareholders' equity has been used for many years in the United States and internationally. This statement discloses changes in total shareholders' equity for the period, as well as changes in each shareholders' equity account, including contributed capital, retained earnings, and accumulated other comprehensive income.

For simplicity, until now in this textbook we have focused only on the statement of retained earnings. When a statement of shareholders' equity is prepared, it explains any changes in retained earnings, which makes a statement of retained earnings unnecessary. In this, and subsequent, chapters, we will include the statement of shareholders' equity in our list of required financial statements. Our financial statement package now includes the statement of earnings, statement of comprehensive income (illustrated in Chapter 12), statement of shareholders' equity, balance sheet, and cash flow statement. All of these statements, except the balance sheet, cover the fiscal year. The balance sheet reports the company's financial position at the end of the fiscal year.

lululemon's statement of shareholders' equity is shown in Illustration 11-6. lululemon has prepared its statement in tabular form, but other formats are also acceptable.

▼ Illustration 11-6

lululemon statement of shareholders' equity

LULULEMON ATHLETICA INC.
Statement of Shareholders' Equity (partial)
Year Ended February 3, 2008
(in USD)

lululemon Ω athletica

| | Special Voting Shares | | Common Shares | | | | Accumulated Other Comprehensive | |
	Number of Shares	Legal Capital	Number of Shares	Legal Capital	Additional Paid-In Capital	Deficit	Income (Loss)	Total
Bal., Jan. 31, 2007	20,935,041	$209	44,290,778	$442,908	$ 98,669,641	$(60,677,395)	$(1,056,565)	$ 37,378,798
Comprehensive income								
Net earnings						30,842,439		30,842,439
Foreign currency translation adjustment							6,453,519	6,453,519
Stock-based compensation					5,947,097			5,947,097
Common shares, net of financing costs			2,290,909	22,909	31,334,598			31,357,507
Restricted shares			10,458	105	(105)			
Stock option exercises			92,555	925	53,724			54,649
Bal., Feb. 3, 2008	20,935,041	$209	46,684,700	$466,847	$136,004,955	$(29,834,956)	$5,396,954	$112,034,009

lululemon details the changes in its equity accounts starting with the account balances at the beginning of the fiscal year (January 31, 2007) and ending with the account balances at the end of the fiscal year (February 3, 2008). While we have included the changes for only one year in Illustration 11-6, lululemon actually includes the changes for the last three fiscal years in its published statement.

In the above statement, you can see both the number of shares issued and the dollar amount of the changes in the year in the legal capital (par value, in lululemon's case) and additional contributed (paid-in) capital received for the shares. You can also see how net earnings reduces its deficit. The net earnings were separately determined on lululemon's statement of earnings (not shown here). Finally, the accumulated other comprehensive loss is reduced by a foreign currency translation adjustment, which results in an accumulated other comprehensive income amount at the end of the year.

Note that all of the balances as at February 3, 2008, that are shown in the above illustration were reported on lululemon's balance sheet shown in Illustration 11-5. We recommend that you now trace these opening and ending balances, and the total shareholders' equity amounts, to those shown in Illustration 11-5.

Cash Flow Statement

The balance sheet presents the balances of a company's shareholders' equity accounts at a point in time. Information about cash inflows and outflows during the year that result from equity transactions is reported in the financing activities section of the cash flow statement. Illustration 11-7 presents information about cash flows related to equity transactions from lululemon's cash flow statement.

Illustration 11-7 ➡

lululemon cash flow statement

LULULEMON ATHLETICA INC. Cash Flow Statement (partial) Year Ended February 3, 2008 (in USD)		
	2007	2006
Cash flows from financing activities		
Cash received on exercise of stock options	$ 54,649	
Issue of common shares	38,349,817	$446,419
Payment of public offering costs	(6,992,309)	

From the equity-related information presented in the financing activities section of the cash flow statement, we learn that the company issued a significant amount of new shares in 2007. As mentioned in the feature story, lululemon issued 18.2 million common shares in an IPO in July 2007. It received U.S. $38,349,817 from the sale of these shares. Note that there were financing costs of U.S. $6,992,309 related to this share issue.

lululemon also issued shares through its stock option program: these are special rights to purchase shares that are discussed in intermediate accounting courses. Note that, as discussed earlier in the chapter, no dividends were paid.

BEFORE YOU GO ON...

➤ **Review It**

1. Why is accumulated other comprehensive income reported separately from retained earnings?
2. Where are shareholders' equity transactions reported in the cash flow statement?
3. Explain how the statement of shareholders' equity relates to the balance sheet.

➤ **Do It**

Grand Lake Corporation had the following shareholders' equity balances at January 1, 2009:

Common shares, unlimited number authorized, no par value, 500,000 issued	$1,000,000
Retained earnings	600,000
Accumulated other comprehensive income	100,000

The following selected information is available for the year ended December 31, 2009:

1. Issued 100,000 common shares for $300,000.
2. Declared dividends of $50,000.
3. Reported net earnings of $360,000.
4. Reported an unrealized gain (other comprehensive income) of $25,000.

Prepare a statement of shareholders' equity.

Action Plan

• The statement of shareholders' equity covers a period of time, starting with the opening balances and ending with the ending balances for the period.
• Explain the changes in each shareholders' equity account, as well as total shareholders' equity.
• Recall that comprehensive income consists of both net earnings and any other comprehensive income.

Solution

GRAND LAKE CORPORATION Statement of Shareholders' Equity Year Ended December 31, 2009					
	Common Shares			Accumulated Other	
	Number of Shares	Legal Capital	Retained Earnings	Comprehensive Income	Total
Bal., Jan. 1, 2009	500,000	$1,000,000	$600,000	$100,000	$1,700,000
Issued common shares	100,000	300,000			300,000
Declared dividends			(50,000)		(50,000)
Comprehensive income					
Net earnings			360,000		360,000
Unrealized gain				25,000	25,000
Bal., Dec. 31, 2009	600,000	$1,300,000	$910,000	$125,000	$2,335,000

The Navigator

Measuring Performance

Investors are interested in both a company's dividend record and its earnings performance. Although they are often parallel, sometimes they are not. Each item should therefore be investigated separately.

study objective 5

Evaluate dividend and earnings performance.

Dividend Record

One way that companies reward investors for their investment is to pay them dividends. The payout ratio measures the percentage of earnings distributed as cash dividends. It is calculated by dividing the cash dividends by net earnings.

We are unable to calculate a payout ratio for lululemon because it does not pay dividends. To illustrate the calculation of the payout ratio, we will use Canadian National (CN) Railway Company. We will look at the payout ratios for its common shares for the years ended December 31, 2007 and 2006. The following selected information (in millions, except for per share information) is used in the calculation of the payout ratio shown in Illustration 11-8:

	2007	2006
Net earnings	$2,158	$2,087
Dividends	418	340
Dividends per common share	$0.84	$0.65
Common share price	$46.25	$48.87

$$\text{PAYOUT RATIO} = \frac{\text{CASH DIVIDENDS}}{\text{NET EARNINGS}}$$

(in millions)	2007	2006
Payout ratio	$\frac{\$418}{\$2,158} = 19.4\%$	$\frac{\$340}{\$2,087} = 16.3\%$
Industry average	2.4%	n/a

Illustration 11-8

CN Railway payout ratio

In 2007, CN paid 19.4 percent of its earnings back to its common shareholders, an increase from 2006 when it paid 16.3 percent. Its payout ratio was much higher than that of the industry in 2007. It is actually difficult to compare a specific company's payout ratio to industry averages because so many factors affect a company's dividend policy, not to mention the variability within the earnings..

Another dividend measure that interests shareholders is the dividend yield. You may recall that earlier in the chapter the dividend yield was mentioned when we looked at stock market information presented for lululemon. The dividend yield is calculated by dividing the dividend per share by the market price per share, as shown in Illustration 11-9.

$$\text{DIVIDEND YIELD} = \frac{\text{DIVIDEND PER SHARE}}{\text{MARKET PRICE PER SHARE}}$$

	2007	2006
Dividend yield	$\frac{\$0.84}{\$46.25} = 1.8\%$	$\frac{\$0.65}{\$48.87} = 1.3\%$
Industry average	0.5%	0.5%

Illustration 11-9

CN Railway dividend yield

The dividend yield is a measure of the earnings generated for the shareholder by each share, and is based on the market price of the shares. CN's dividend yield was 1.8 percent at the end of 2007 and 1.3 percent at the end of 2006. Both amounts are higher than the industry average, which is also notable because the industry average was unchanged over the two years while the company's dividend yield increased.

The dividend yield is, in essence, a measure of a shareholder's return on his or her investment (using the current market price). In CN's case, an investor who purchased common shares at the end of 2007 would have paid $46.25 to purchase each share. Based on the annual dividend of $0.84 per share, the investor is earning a return of 1.8 percent on this investment. Of course, dividend income is only one part of an investor's return on an investment in shares. Investors hope to also earn a return from increases in the market price of their shares when they are ready to sell them. In general, however, investors tend to buy shares with high payout ratios and dividend yields if they are looking to earn a regular income (dividend). They tend to buy shares with low payout ratios and dividend yields if they are looking for more capital appreciation (growth) from their shares.

Illustration 11-10 shows the payout ratios and dividend yields of selected companies in 2007.

Illustration 11-10

Payout ratios and dividend yields

	Payout Ratio (%)	Dividend Yield (%)
Bank of Montreal	64.8	4.3
Great West Life	46.1	3.0
Homburg Investment	80.8	9.5
Loblaw Companies	70.0	2.5
Reitmans	41.0	3.9
Rothmans	81.6	5.8

Earnings Performance

The earnings performance, or profitability, of a company is measured in several different ways. In an earlier chapter, we learned about the earnings per share ratio. In this section, we will revisit the calculation of this ratio and introduce a new profitability ratio, the return on common shareholders' equity.

Earnings per Share

You will recall that we learned how to calculate earnings per share in Chapter 2. In that chapter, the formula for earnings per share was presented as shown in Illustration 11-11. At that time, we gave the information for you to calculate the earnings per share and said that you would learn how to calculate the numerator (net earnings available to common shareholders) and the denominator (weighted average number of common shares) in Chapter 11.

Illustration 11-11

lululemon earnings per share

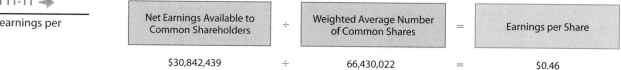

Net Earnings Available to Common Shareholders	÷	Weighted Average Number of Common Shares	=	Earnings per Share
$30,842,439	÷	66,430,022	=	$0.46

To further what we learned in Chapter 2, we have added to the above illustration the information that is needed for calculating earnings per share for lululemon. The numerator, **net earnings available to common shareholders**, is calculated by subtracting any preferred dividends from net earnings. This is because preferred shareholders have preferential rights to receive these dividends before the common shareholders can share in any remaining amounts. In lululemon's case, no preferred shares have been issued so its net earnings available to common shareholders is the same as its net earnings.

For the denominator of the earnings per share calculation, the weighted average number of shares is used. Note that lululemon's weighted average number of common shares, 66,430,022, is not the same as the ending balance of its two classes of common shares, 67,619,741 (46,684,700 common shares + 20,935,041 special voting shares), that was reported earlier in Illustration 11-6. You will recall that whenever we calculate a ratio with a period figure (e.g., net earnings) and an end-of-period figure (e.g., the number of common shares), we always average the end-of-period figure so that the numerator and denominator in the calculation are for the same period of time. However, we do not use a straight average in the calculation of the number of common shares as we do in some other ratio calculations. For example, we do not take the beginning and ending balances of the number of common shares, add them together, and divide the result by two.

Instead, we use a **weighted average number of common shares** as this considers the impact of shares issued at different times throughout the year. This is done because the issue of shares changes the amount of assets on which earnings can be generated. Consequently, shares issued or purchased during ach current period must be weighted by the fraction of the year (or period) that they have been issued. If there is no change in the number of common shares issued during the year, the weighted average number of shares will be the same as the ending balance. If new shares are issued throughout the year, then these shares are adjusted for the fraction of the year they are outstanding to determine the weighted average number of shares.

To illustrate the calculation of the weighted average number of common shares, assume that a company had 100,000 common shares on January 1, and issued an additional 10,000 shares on October 1. The weighted average number of shares for the year would be calculated as follows:

Date	Actual Number		Weighted Average
Jan. 1	100,000	× 12/12 =	100,000
Oct. 1	10,000	× 3/12 =	2,500
	110,000		102,500

As illustrated, 110,000 shares were actually issued by the end of the year. Of these, 100,000 were outstanding for the full year and are allocated a full weight, or 12 months of 12 months. The other 10,000 shares have only been outstanding for three months (from October 1 to December 31) and are weighted for 3/12 of the year, to result in 2,500 weighted shares. In total, the company's weighted average number of shares is 102,500 for the year. In the next calendar year, the 110,000 shares would receive full weight (unless some of these shares are repurchased) because all 110,000 shares would be outstanding for the entire year.

Complex Capital Structure. When a corporation has securities that may be converted into common shares, it has what is called a complex capital structure. One example of a convertible security is convertible preferred shares. When the preferred shares are converted into common shares, the additional common shares will result in a reduced, or diluted, earnings per share figure.

Two earnings per share figures are calculated when a corporation has a complex capital structure. The first earnings per share figure is called **basic earnings per share**. The earnings per share amount we calculated in Illustration 11-11, $0.46, is known as basic earnings per share, which is what lululemon reported on its statement of earnings for fiscal 2007.

The second earnings per share figure is called **fully diluted earnings per share**. This figure calculates *hypothetical* earnings per share as though *all* securities that can be converted into, or exchanged for, common shares have actually been converted or exchanged (even though they really have not). lululemon, which has other securities that can be converted into common shares (stock options, in this case) is considered to have a complex capital structure. It reports fully diluted earnings per share of $0.45 for fiscal 2007. Note that fully diluted earnings per share will never be higher than basic earnings per share.

The calculation of fully diluted earnings per share is complex. In addition, the determination of the weighted average number of shares for both basic and fully diluted earnings per share becomes more complicated when there are stock dividends and stock splits during the year. Further discussion of these and other earnings per share complexities is left to an intermediate accounting course.

Return on Equity

A widely used ratio that measures profitability from the common shareholders' viewpoint is the return on common shareholders' equity. This ratio shows how many dollars were earned for each dollar invested by common shareholders. It is calculated by dividing net earnings available to common shareholders by average common shareholders' equity. You will recall that the net earnings available to common shareholders is net earnings less any preferred dividends. Common shareholders' equity is total shareholders' equity less the legal capital of any preferred shares. Recall that everything else belongs to the common, or residual, shareholders.

We can calculate a return on common shareholders' equity for lululemon using the information presented below. In lululemon's particular case, its common shareholders' equity is the same as its total shareholders' equity since it does not have any preferred shares.

(in USD)	2007	2006	2005
Net earnings	$ 30,842,439	$ 7,666,331	$ 1,394,104
Shareholders' equity	112,034,009	37,378,798	28,052,000

▶ Reporting and Analyzing Shareholders' Equity

lululemon's return on common shareholders' equity ratios are calculated for 2007 and 2006 in Illustration 11-12.

Illustration 11-12 ➡

lululemon return on
common shareholders'
equity

	RETURN ON COMMON SHAREHOLDERS' EQUITY	=	NET EARNINGS − PREFERRED DIVIDENDS / AVERAGE COMMON SHAREHOLDERS' EQUITY
(in USD)	2007		2006
Return on common shareholders' equity	$\dfrac{\$30{,}842{,}439 - \$0}{(\$112{,}034{,}009 + \$37{,}378{,}798) \div 2} = 41.3\%$		$\dfrac{\$7{,}666{,}331 - \$0}{(\$37{,}378{,}798 + \$28{,}052{,}000) \div 2} = 23.4\%$
Industry average	14.4%		17.1%

In 2007, lululemon's return on common shareholders' equity was a very high 41.3 percent, much higher than the industry average. Its return increased significantly over 2006, which was notable because the industry's return was declining at the same time. This increase in return is not surprising, because lululemon nearly doubled the number of its stores in fiscal 2007, from 41 at the end of 2006 to 71 at the end of 2007.

Return on equity is a widely published figure. Recently, the highest return on equity among Canada's top 500 corporations, 113.7 percent, was reported by Pelangio Mines Inc., a junior gold mining company headquartered in Milton, Ontario.

BEFORE YOU GO ON...

➡ **Review It**

1. What measures can be used to evaluate a company's dividend record, and how are they calculated?
2. Why are net earnings available to common shareholders not always the same as net earnings?
3. How is the weighted average number of common shares calculated?
4. Distinguish between basic and fully diluted earnings per share.
5. How is the return on common shareholders' equity calculated?

➡ **Do It**

The Shoten Corporation reported net earnings of $249,750 for the year ended October 31, 2009. The shareholders' equity section of its balance sheet reported 3,000 $2 cumulative preferred shares and 50,000 common shares issued. Of the common shares, 40,000 had been outstanding since the beginning of the year, 15,000 shares were issued on March 1, and 5,000 shares were repurchased on August 1. Calculate Shoten's earnings per share.

Action Plan

- Subtract any preferred dividends from net earnings to determine the earnings available for common shareholders.
- Adjust the shares for the fraction of the year outstanding to determine the weighted average number of common shares.
- Divide the earnings available for common shareholders by the weighted average number of common shares to calculate earnings per share.

Solution

Preferred dividends: 3,000 × $2 = $6,000
Weighted average number of common shares

Date	Actual Number		Weighted Average
Nov. 1	40,000	× 12/12 =	40,000
Mar. 1	15,000	× 8/12 =	10,000
Aug. 1	(5,000)	× 3/12 =	(1,250)
	50,000		48,750

Earnings per share $\dfrac{\$249{,}750 - \$6{,}000}{48{,}750} = \$5$

The Navigator

DECISION TOOLKIT

Decision Checkpoints	Info Needed for Decision	Tools to Use for Decision	How to Evaluate Results
What portion of its earnings does the company pay out in dividends?	Net earnings and total cash dividends	Payout ratio = $\dfrac{\text{Cash dividends}}{\text{Net earnings}}$	A low ratio suggests that the company is retaining its earnings for investment in future growth.
What percentage of the share price is the company paying in dividends?	Dividends and share price	Dividend yield = $\dfrac{\text{Dividend per share}}{\text{Market price per share}}$	A high dividend yield is considered desirable for investors. It also means that the company is paying out its earnings rather than retaining them.
What is the company's return on its common shareholders' investment?	Earnings available to common shareholders and average common shareholders' equity	$\dfrac{\text{Return on common shareholders' equity}}{} = \dfrac{\text{Net earnings} - \text{Preferred dividends}}{\text{Average common shareholders' equity}}$	A high measure suggests a strong earnings performance from the common shareholders' perspective.

Summary of Study Objectives

1. **Identify and discuss the major characteristics of a corporation.** The major characteristics of a corporation are separate legal existence, limited liability of shareholders, transferable ownership rights, the ability to acquire capital, continuous life, corporation management, government regulations, and corporate income taxes.

Companies issue shares for sale to the public. After the initial share offering, the shares trade among investors and do not affect the company's financial position. A company can also reacquire its own shares from investors, but it must then cancel the shares.

2. **Record share transactions.** When no par value shares are issued for cash, the entire proceeds from the issue become legal capital and are credited to the Preferred Shares or Common Shares account, depending on what class of shares is issued. Preferred shares have contractual provisions that give them priority over common shares in certain areas. Typically, preferred shareholders have a preference over (a) dividends and (b) assets in the event of liquidation. However, only common shares have voting rights.

When shares are reacquired, the average cost is debited to the shares account. If the shares are reacquired at a price below the average cost, the difference is credited to a contributed capital account created from prior reacquisitions. If the shares are reacquired at a price above the average cost, the difference is debited first to a contributed capital account if it has a balance, and secondly to the Retained Earnings account.

3. **Prepare the entries for cash dividends, stock dividends, and stock splits, and understand their financial impact.** Entries for both cash and stock dividends are required at the declaration date and the payment or distribution date. There is no entry (other than a memo entry) for a stock split. Cash dividends reduce assets (cash) and shareholders' equity (retained earnings). Stock dividends increase common shares and decrease retained earn-

ings but do not affect assets, liabilities, or shareholders' equity in total. Stock splits also have no impact on assets, liabilities, or shareholders' equity. The number of shares increases with both stock dividends and stock splits.

For an individual, a cash dividend increases cash, while stock dividends and stock splits increase the number of shares. Share prices decline in a stock dividend and stock split so that the fair value of the total investment is initially unchanged.

4. **Indicate how shareholders' equity is presented in the financial statements.** In the shareholders' equity section of the balance sheet, share capital, retained earnings, and accumulated other comprehensive income are reported separately. If additional contributed capital exists, then the caption "Contributed capital" is used for share capital (preferred and common shares) and additional contributed capital that may have been created from the reacquisition of shares or from other sources. A statement of shareholders' equity explains the changes in each shareholders' equity account, and in total, for the reporting period. Cash inflows and outflows for the issue or reacquisition of shares, or a payment of dividends, are reported in the financing activities section of the cash flow statement. Notes to the financial statements explain restrictions on retained earnings and dividends in arrears, if there are any.

5. **Evaluate dividend and earnings performance.** A company's dividend record can be evaluated by looking at what percentage of net earnings it chooses to pay out in dividends, as measured by the dividend payout ratio (dividends divided by net earnings) and the dividend yield (dividends per share divided by the share price). One profitability ratio to measure earnings performance is the return on common shareholders' equity ratio (earnings available to common shareholders divided by average common shareholders' equity).

ALL ABOUT YOU

Should I Play the Market?

When companies need additional financing, they raise this money by equity financing or debt financing. Equity financing is the act of raising money for company activities by selling common or preferred shares to individual or institutional investors. In return for the money paid, shareholders receive ownership interests in the corporation. The other way to raise money is through debt financing, which occurs when the company borrows money, as discussed in Chapter 10.

Suppose you have some extra cash and would like to buy some shares (equity) in a public company. An equity investment carries neither a promise that your investment will be returned to you nor a guarantee that your investment will earn income. Buying common shares rather than preferred shares of a company represents a decision to take a greater risk because of the potential for a greater return. The share's real value is its fair value: the price of a share in the secondary securities market.

This share price is a result of the interaction of buyers and sellers. It can be influenced by both objective factors such as a company's profits and subjective factors such as future expectations, including unverified information or rumours. Nevertheless, if a company prospers, its common shares typically rise in value more than its preferred shares do. And, if a company doesn't prosper, or if external factors such as the economy, the price of the dollar, and the like are negative or expected to be negative, the share price will decline.

If you plan to invest in shares, you need to consider the following:

- How will you decide what shares to purchase? Do you plan to purchase shares for dividend income or for growth (share price appreciation)?
- Do you want to purchase Canadian shares, U.S. shares, or international shares?
- How will you manage your investment portfolio? What is your time frame, how will you evaluate performance, and how will you determine the right time to sell and the right time to buy?

Some Facts

- The number of listed companies with the TSX Group in 2007 was 3,951, comprising 3,881 domestic companies and 70 foreign companies as compared to 3,842 companies comprising 3,790 domestic companies and 52 foreign companies in 2006.
- Canadian markets are pretty small compared to the number of listed companies in the world. In 2007, there were 46,509 listed companies worldwide (45,211 in 2006).
- The TSX Group is third in North America and seventh in the world by total listed market capitalization ($2.2 trillion).
- A recent survey by Digital Look, an investment website, found that women investors were more successful than men. The average woman's share portfolio grew by 17 percent, while the average man's rose by just 11 percent. Women tend to build a balanced share portfolio and take a more considered view while men tend to take more risks.

What Do You Think?

Rachel Bull has a good salary with excellent potential for advancement in the newly listed public company where she works. She has accumulated $10,000 in savings, which is sitting in a bank savings account earning very little interest. She has decided to withdraw $8,000 from her savings account and buy some of her employer's common shares. Should Rachel make this investment?

YES | She has a good income, and this is a good opportunity for her to earn a higher return on her savings.

NO | There is more risk with a stock investment. She may make more money if the share price increases but she may also lose her savings if the share price decreases and she has to sell her shares before the price recovers.

The Navigator

Sources:

Naomi Caine, "Are Women Better Investors than Men?" uk.biz.yahoo.com/09112005/389/women-better-investors-men.html

World Federation of Stock Exchanges, "Statistics: Number of Listed Companies," world-exchanges.org/publications/EQUITY307.pdf

Glossary

Study Tools (Glossary)

Accumulated other comprehensive income The cumulative change in shareholders' equity that result from the gains and losses that bypass net earnings but affect shareholders' equity. (p. 565)

Authorized shares The amount of share capital that a corporation is authorized to sell. The amount may be unlimited or specified. (p. 551)

Cash dividend A pro rata (proportional) distribution of cash to shareholders. (p. 558)

Comprehensive income All changes in shareholders' equity during a period except those changes resulting from the sale or repurchase of shares, or from the payment of dividends. Comprehensive income includes (1) the revenues, expenses, gains, and losses included in net earnings, *and* (2) the gains and losses that bypass net earnings but affect shareholders' equity. (p. 565)

Contributed capital The total amount contributed by shareholders, or reacquired from them, in exchange for shares of ownership. It consists of share capital and additional contributed capital, if any. (p. 553)

Convertible preferred shares Preferred shares that the shareholder can convert into common shares at a specified ratio. (p. 556)

Corporation A company organized as a separate legal entity, with most of the rights and privileges of a person. Shares are evidence of ownership. (p. 548)

Cumulative A feature of preferred shares that entitles the shareholder to receive current- and unpaid prior-year dividends before common shareholders receive any dividends. (p. 556)

Declaration date The date the board of directors formally declares (approves) a dividend and announces it to shareholders. (p. 559)

Dividend A distribution of cash or shares by a corporation to its shareholders on a pro rata (proportional) basis. (p. 558)

Dividends in arrears Preferred dividends that were not declared during a period. (p. 556)

Dividend yield A measure of the percentage of the share price that is paid in dividends. It is calculated by dividing dividends per share by the share price. (p. 569)

Initial public offering (IPO) The initial offering of a corporation's shares to the public. (p. 552)

Issued shares The portion of authorized shares that has been sold. (p. 552)

Legal capital The amount per share that must be retained in the business for the protection of corporate creditors. (p. 553)

Market capitalization A measure of the value of a company's equity. It is calculated by multiplying the number of shares by the share price at any given date. (p. 552)

Net earnings available to common shareholders Net earnings less the annual preferred dividend. (p. 570)

Noncumulative Preferred shares that are entitled to the current dividend, but not to any unpaid amounts from prior years. (p. 556)

No par value shares Share capital that has not been pre-assigned a legal capital value. The total proceeds from the sale of no par value shares becomes the legal capital. (p. 553)

Payment date The date dividend cheques are mailed to shareholders. (p. 560)

Payout ratio A measure of the percentage of earnings distributed in the form of cash dividends to common shareholders. It is calculated by dividing cash dividends by net earnings. (p. 569)

Preferred shares Share capital that has contractual preferences over common shares in certain areas. (p. 555)

Record date The date when ownership of shares is determined for dividend purposes. (p. 559)

Redeemable (or callable) preferred shares Preferred shares that grant the issuer the right to purchase the shares from shareholders at specified future dates and prices. (p. 556)

Retained earnings restrictions Circumstances that make a portion of retained earnings currently unavailable for dividends. (p. 563)

Retractable preferred shares Preferred shares that grant the shareholder the right to redeem the shares at specified future dates and prices. (p. 556)

Return on common shareholders' equity A measure of profitability from the shareholders' point of view. It is calculated by dividing net earnings minus preferred dividends by average common shareholders' equity. (p. 571)

Share capital The amount paid, or contributed, to the corporation by shareholders in exchange for shares of ownership. It can consist of preferred and common shares. (p. 553)

Statement of shareholders' equity A statement which summarizes the changes in each shareholders' equity account, and to total shareholders' equity, during the period. Also known as the statement of changes in equity. (p. 566-567)

Stock dividend A pro rata (proportional) distribution of the corporation's own shares to shareholders. (p. 560)

Stock split The issue of additional shares to shareholders accompanied by a reduction in the legal capital per share. (p. 561)

Treasury shares A corporation's own shares that have been reacquired and not retired and cancelled. They are held in the "treasury" for later reissue. (p. 554)

Weighted average number of common shares A weighted average of the number of common shares outstanding during the year. Shares issued or purchased during the year are weighted by the fraction of the year for which they have been outstanding. (p. 570)

DECISION TOOLKIT—A SUMMARY

Decision Checkpoints	Info Needed for Decision	Tools to Use for Decision	How to Evaluate Results
Should the company incorporate?	Capital needs, growth expectations, type of business, income tax status	Corporations have limited liability, greater ability to raise capital, and professional managers. They may suffer from additional government regulations and income taxes may be higher or lower for a corporation.	Carefully weigh the costs and benefits in light of the particular circumstances.
What portion of its earnings does the company pay out in dividends?	Net earnings and total cash dividends	$\text{Payout ratio} = \dfrac{\text{Cash dividends}}{\text{Net earnings}}$	A low ratio suggests that the company is retaining its earnings for investment in future growth.
What percentage of the share price is the company paying in dividends?	Dividends and share price	$\text{Dividend yield} = \dfrac{\text{Dividend per share}}{\text{Market price per share}}$	A high dividend yield is considered desirable for investors. It also means that the company is paying out its earnings rather than retaining them.
What is the company's return on its common shareholders' investment?	Earnings available to common shareholders and average common shareholders' equity	$\dfrac{\text{Return on common shareholders' equity}}{} = \dfrac{\text{Net earnings} - \text{Preferred dividends}}{\text{Average common shareholders' equity}}$	A high measure suggests a strong earnings performance from the common shareholders' perspective.

The Navigator

www.wiley.com/canada/kimmel

Analysis Tools (Decision ToolKit Summaries)

Using the Decision Toolkit

Many companies, including La Senza and Victoria's Secret, have added high-performance yoga clothing in an attempt to compete with lululemon. The following selected information (in USD millions, except per share information) is available for Limited Brands, Inc., parent company to La Senza and Victoria's Secret. Note that Limited Brands has no preferred shares.

	2007	2006
Net earnings	$718	$676
Cash dividends	$227	$238
Dividends per share	$0.60	$0.60
Shareholders' equity	$2,219	$2,955
Weighted average number of common shares	375	396
Share price	$18.76	$26.78

Instructions

Calculate the (a) payout ratio, (b) dividend yield, (c) earnings per share, (d) price-earnings ratio, and (e) return on common shareholders' equity for Limited Brands for 2007. Contrast the company's earnings performance, where available, with that of lululemon and the industry, which is given in the chapter and below. lululemon's price-earnings ratio was 86.6 times in 2007. Industry averages were 23.7% for the payout ratio; 1.5% for the dividend yield; and 14.0 times for the price-earnings ratio. There is no industry average available for earnings per share.

Solution

(in USD millions, except per share information)	Limited Brands	lululemon	Industry
(a) Payout ratio	$\dfrac{\$227}{\$718}$ = 31.6%	n/a	23.7%
(b) Dividend yield	$\dfrac{\$0.60}{\$18.76}$ = 3.2%	n/a	1.5%
(c) Earnings per share	$\dfrac{\$718}{375}$ = $1.91	$0.46	n/a
(d) Price-earnings ratio	$\dfrac{\$18.76}{\$1.91}$ = 9.8 times	86.6 times	14.0 times
(e) Return on common shareholders' equity	$\dfrac{\$718 - \$0}{(\$2,219 + \$2,955) \div 2}$ = 27.8%	41.3%	14.4%

You will recall that lululemon paid no dividends in 2007, so it has no payout ratio or dividend yield. Limited Brands' payout ratio and dividend yield are both higher than those of its competitors in the industry.

It is not possible to compare earnings per share between companies, because of the differing capital structures. However, it is possible to compare the price-earnings ratios. Investors appear to favour lululemon much more than Limited Brands. This could be because of lululemon's rapid growth, or anticipated future performance. Limited Brands' price-earnings ratio is also below that of the industry, so it is not as well favoured by investors as other companies. This is interesting because Limited Brands' payout ratio and dividend yield are both above that of the industry. Investors may be showing their concerns about Limited Brands' future potential in light of declining economic conditions.

Both companies have a return on common shareholders' equity in excess of that of the industry. lululemon's return is significantly above that of both Limited Brands and the industry, which may be one of the factors driving its high price-earnings ratio.

The Navigator

Demonstration Problem

Rolman Corporation is authorized to issue an unlimited number of no par value common shares and 100,000 no par value $6-cumulative preferred shares. At January 1, 2009, it had the following selected opening balances: Preferred shares, nil; Common Shares, 300,000 issued, $1,800,000; Contributed Capital—Reacquisition of Shares, nil; Retained Earnings, $1,150,000; and Accumulated Other Comprehensive Income, $50,000.

During the year ended December 31, 2009, the company had the following share transactions:

Jan. 10   Issued 100,000 common shares at $8 per share.
July   1   Issued 20,000 preferred shares at $50 per share.
Sept. 1   Declared a 5% stock dividend to common shareholders of record on September 15, distributable September 30. The price of the common shares on this date was $10 per share.
Nov.   1   Reacquired 5,000 preferred shares at $40 per share.
Dec. 24   Declared a semi-annual preferred cash dividend to shareholders of record on January 15, payable January 31.

In addition, it reported net earnings of $392,000 and other comprehensive income of $5,000 for the year.

Instructions

(a) Record the above transactions.
(b) Prepare the statement of shareholders' equity and the shareholders' equity section of the balance sheet.

Action Plan

- Keep a running total of the number of shares issued to date.

- Apply the stock dividend percentage to the number of common shares issued. Multiply the new shares to be issued by the fair value of the shares.

- Record the reacquisition of shares at the average cost. Calculate the average cost per share by dividing the balance in the share account by the number of shares issued.

- Note that the preferred dividend rate is an annual rate. Adjust for any partial periods.

- Recall that the statement of shareholders' equity explains the changes for the period in the beginning and ending balances of each shareholders' equity account.

- The balance sheet reports shareholders' equity at the end of the period. Disclose the share details in the shareholders' equity section of the balance sheet.

Solution to Demonstration Problem

(a)

Jan. 10	Cash (100,000 × $8)		800,000	
	Common Shares			800,000
	(To record issue of 100,000 common shares)			
July 1	Cash (20,000 × $50)		1,000,000	
	Preferred Shares			1,000,000
	(To record issue of 20,000 preferred shares)			
Sept. 1	Stock Dividends (300,000 + 100,000 = 400,000			
	× 5% = 20,000 × $10)		200,000	
	Stock Dividends Distributable			200,000
	(To record declaration of 5% stock dividend)			
Sept. 15	Record date—no entry required			
Sept. 30	Stock Dividends Distributable		200,000	
	Common Shares			200,000
	(To record issue of 20,000 common shares in a 5% stock dividend)			
Nov. 1	Preferred Shares (5,000 × $50)		250,000	
	Cash (5,000 × $40)			200,000
	Contributed Capital—Reacquisition of Preferred Shares			50,000
	(To record reacquisition of 5,000 preferred shares at an average cost of $50 [$1,000,000 ÷ 20,000] per share)			
Dec. 24	Cash Dividends—Preferred			
	(20,000 − 5,000 = 15,000 × $6 × 6/12)		45,000	
	Dividends Payable			45,000
	(To record declaration of semi-annual preferred cash dividend)			

(b)

ROLMAN CORPORATION
Statement of Shareholders' Equity
Year Ended December 31, 2009

	Preferred Shares Number of Shares	Preferred Shares Legal Capital	Common Shares Number of Shares	Common Shares Legal Capital	Additional Contributed Capital	Retained Earnings	Accumulated Other Comprehensive Income	Total
Bal., Jan. 1, 2009			300,000	$1,800,000		$1,150,000	$50,000	$3,000,000
Issued common shares			100,000	800,000				800,000
Issued preferred shares	20,000	$1,000,000						1,000,000
Declared and issued stock dividend			20,000	200,000		(200,000)		0
Reacquired preferred shares	(5,000)	(250,000)			$50,000			(200,000)
Declared dividends						(45,000)		(45,000)
Comprehensive income								
Net earnings						392,000		392,000
Other comprehensive income							5,000	5,000
Bal., Dec. 31, 2009	15,000	$ 750,000	420,000	$2,800,000	$50,000	$1,297,000	$55,000	$4,952,000

ROLMAN CORPORATION
Balance Sheet (partial)
December 31, 2009

Shareholders' equity
    Contributed capital
        Share capital
            Preferred shares, 100,000 no par value $6-cumulative
            authorized, 15,000 shares issued $ 750,000
            Common shares, unlimited number of no par value
            shares authorized, 420,000 shares issued   2,800,000 $3,550,000
        Additional contributed capital
            Contributed capital—reacquisition of preferred shares   50,000
        Total contributed capital   3,600,000
    Retained earnings   1,297,000
    Accumulated other comprehensive income   55,000
Total shareholders' equity $4,952,000

The Navigator

Self-Study Questions

Answers are at the end of the chapter.

Study Tools (Self-Assessment Quizzes)

1. Which of these is *not* a major advantage of a corporation?
    (a) Separate legal existence
    (b) Continuous life
    (c) Government regulations
    (d) Transferable ownership rights

2. Saint Simeon Corporation has 100,000 common shares authorized and 75,000 common shares issued. How many more common shares can Saint Simeon sell?
    (a) 0
    (b) 25,000
    (c) 75,000
    (d) 100,000

3. ABC Corporation issues 1,000 preferred shares at $12 per share. In recording the transaction, a credit of $12,000 is made to:
    (a) Investment in ABC Corporation
    (b) Preferred Shares
    (c) Accumulated Other Comprehensive Income
    (d) Contributed Capital

4. A company will buy back its own shares:
    (a) to force the share price up.
    (b) to force the share price down.
    (c) to increase the number of shares available for dividends.
    (d) to save cash.

5. Entries for cash dividends are required on the:
    (a) declaration date and record date.
    (b) record date and payment date.
    (c) declaration date, record date, and payment date.
    (d) declaration date and payment date.

6. Which of the following statements about stock dividends and stock splits is true? (SO 3)
    (a) A stock dividend and stock split increase total shareholders' equity.
    (b) A stock dividend and stock split decrease total shareholders' equity.
    (c) A stock dividend and stock split have no effect on total shareholders' equity.
    (d) A stock dividend and stock split have no effect on the number of common shares.

7. Which of the following is *not* reported in a statement of shareholders' equity? (SO 4)
    (a) Legal capital of common shares
    (b) Fair value of common shares
    (c) Dividends
    (d) Accumulated other comprehensive income

8. The cash received on issuing shares would be reported in what section of the cash flow statement? (SO 4)
    (a) Operating activities
    (b) Investing activities
    (c) Financing activities
    (d) It is not reported in the cash flow statement.

9. If a company's net earnings are $50,000, its total assets $1,000,000, (SO 5) its average common shareholders' equity $500,000, and its net sales $800,000, its return on common shareholders' equity is:
    (a) 3.3%
    (b) 5%.
    (c) 6.25%.
    (d) 10%.

(SO 5) 10. For the year ended June 30, 2010, Dupuis Inc. reported net earnings of $90,000. It had 5,000 common shares outstanding since the beginning of the year, July 1, 2009, and 2,000 shares issued on January 1, 2010. In addition, it paid dividends of $3 per common share at the end of the year (it had no preferred shares) and had a share price of $60. It had no preferred shares. What were its earnings per share and dividend yield?

    (a) $12.86 and 5%
    (b) $12.86 and 23%
    (c) $15 and 5%
    (d) $15 and 20%

Questions

(SO 1) 1. Pat Kabza, a student, asks for your help in understanding the different corporation characteristics. Explain the following characteristics to Pat and identify whether they are an advantage or a disadvantage of the corporate form of organization: (a) separate legal existence, (b) limited liability of shareholders, (c) transferable ownership rights, (d) ability to acquire capital, (e) continuous life, (f) separation of management and ownership, (g) government regulations, and (h) income taxation.

(SO 1) 2. Explain why some of the advantages of the corporate form of organization may not apply to small, privately held corporations.

(SO 1) 3. Richard Boudreault purchased 100 lululemon athletica common shares for $18 a share from the company's initial public offering. A later year, Richard purchased 200 more lululemon shares for $30 each on the Toronto Stock Exchange. Explain the impact of each of these transactions on lululemon's (a) assets, (b) liabilities, and (c) shareholders' equity.

(SO 1) 4. What is legal capital? How is the value of the legal capital determined? Why is legal capital reported separately from retained earnings in the shareholders' equity section of the balance sheet?

(SO 1) 5. What is market capitalization? Explain how it relates, or does not relate, to the legal capital of a company.

(SO 1, 2) 6. What are the basic ownership rights of common shareholders? Of preferred shareholders?

(SO 1, 2) 7. Letson Corporation is authorized to issue 100,000 common shares. During its first two years of operation, Letson issued 60,000 shares and reacquired and cancelled 7,000 of these shares. (a) After these transactions, how many shares are authorized and issued? (b) Are both authorized and issued shares recorded in the general journal?

(SO 2) 8. Why would a company repurchase some of its own shares? Under what circumstances are the repurchased shares held as treasury shares?

(SO 2) 9. Explain how the accounting for the reacquisition of shares changes depending on whether the reacquisition price is greater or lower than average cost.

10. Ciana Chiasson is confused. She says, "I don't understand why sometimes, when the price paid to reacquire shares is greater than their average cost, the 'loss on reacquisition' is debited to a contributed capital account. But at other times, it is debited to the Retained Earnings account. And sometimes it is even debited to both!" Help Ciana understand.

11. What is the difference between cumulative and noncumulative preferred shares? Between redeemable and retractable preferred shares?

12. What three conditions must be met before a cash dividend is paid?

13. Contrast the effects of a cash dividend, stock dividend, and stock split on a company's (a) assets, (b) liabilities, (c) share capital, (d) retained earnings, (e) total shareholders' equity, and (f) number of shares.

14. George Karygiannis has heard that a company in which he owns shares is thinking of declaring either a cash dividend or a stock dividend. He is hoping that the company decides to pay a cash dividend, since he has heard that a stock dividend does not change anything. Is George right in thinking that it is better for shareholders to receive a cash dividend than a stock dividend?

15. Bella Corporation has 500,000 common shares authorized and 10,000 common shares issued when it announces a two-for-one split. Before the split, the shares were trading for $140 per share. (a) After the split, how many shares will be authorized and issued? (b) What will be the approximate share price? (c) What will be the impact on the total value of an individual shareholder's investment portfolio?

16. Why are stock dividends recorded in the general journal but stock splits are not?

17. What is the purpose of a retained earnings restriction? How are retained earnings restrictions reported in the financial statements?

18. Indicate how each of the following should be reported in the shareholders' equity section of the balance sheet: (a) common shares, (b) preferred shares, (c) stock dividends distributable, (d) contributed capital—reacquisition of shares, (e) retained earnings, and (f) accumulated other comprehensive income.

19. Explain how the statement of shareholders' equity is interrelated with other financial statements.

20. Why is a statement of retained earnings not required if a statement of shareholders' equity is prepared?

21. What is comprehensive income? Why is comprehensive income reported separately from net earnings?

22. Explain where equity transactions are reported in (a) the balance sheet, (b) the statement of shareholders' equity, and (c) the cash flow statement.

23. ⚲ Indicate whether each of the following is generally considered favourable or unfavourable by a potential investor:

(a) A decrease in the payout ratio
(b) An increase in the dividend yield
(c) A decrease in the return on common shareholders' equity
(d) An increase in earnings per share

24. ⚲ Coca-Cola recently reported dividends per share of U.S. $1.44 and a dividend yield of 2.9%. Pepsi reported

dividends per share of U.S. $0.59 and a dividend yield of 2.2% for the same period. Which company had the higher share price?

25. In the calculation of earnings per share, why is the weighted average number of common shares used instead of the number of common shares at the end of the year? (SO 5)

26. Why do the earnings per share and return on common shareholders' equity ratios use net earnings available to common shareholders in their numerator rather than net earnings? (SO 5)

27. Distinguish between basic earnings per share and fully diluted earnings per share. (SO 5)

28. ⚲ Company A has a price-earnings ratio of 12 times and a payout ratio of 3.5%. Company B has a price-earnings ratio of 62 times and a payout ratio of 0%. (a) Which company's shares would be of more interest to an investor interested in a steady dividend income? (b) Which company's shares would be of more interest to an investor interested in selling her shares for a profit? (SO 5)

Brief Exercises

BE11–1 The share price of BCE Inc. rose by $1.98, or 5.7 percent, to close at $36.58 on June 24, 2008, after the Supreme Court of Canada approved a plan to sell the country's largest telephone company. What was the impact of this increase in share price on (a) BCE's financial position and (b) its shareholders' financial position?

Evaluate share price impact.
(SO 1)

BE11–2 On May 10, Armada Corporation issued 1,000 common shares for $15 per share. On June 15, Armada issued an additional 500 shares for $17 per share. On November 1, Armada issued 100 preferred shares for $35 per share. (a) Record the share transactions. (b) What is the average cost of the common and preferred shares?

Record issue of shares.
(SO 2)

BE11–3 On June 12, Dieppe Corporation commenced operations and issued 60,000 common shares for $300,000. On July 11, it issued an additional 15,000 common shares for $90,000. On November 28, it repurchased 25,000 shares. Record the share transactions assuming the company paid (a) $120,000 to reacquire the shares, and (b) $135,000 to reacquire the shares.

Record issue and reacquisition of shares.
(SO 2)

BE11–4 Cascades Inc. repurchased 492,700 of its own common shares in 2007 and cancelled them. The share reacquisition resulted in a debit of $2 million to the Common Shares account and a debit of $3 million to the Retained Earnings account. (a) How much did Cascades pay, on average, to reacquire its shares? (b) What was the initial issue price of the shares, on average? (c) What are some of the likely reasons that Cascades reacquired some of its own shares?

Discuss share reacquisition.
(SO 2)

BE11–5 The Seabee Corporation has 10,000 $2-noncumulative preferred shares. It declares a quarterly cash dividend on November 1 to shareholders of record on December 1. The dividend is paid on December 31. Prepare the entries on the appropriate dates to record the cash dividend.

Record cash dividend.
(SO 3)

BE11–6 Satina Corporation has 100,000 common shares. It declares a 5% stock dividend on December 1, when the price of the shares is $15, to shareholders of record on December 20. The shares are issued on January 10. Prepare the entries on the appropriate dates to record the stock dividend.

Record stock dividend.
(SO 3)

BE11–7 The shareholders' equity section of Chew Corporation's balance sheet consists of 100,000 common shares for $1 million, and retained earnings of $500,000. A 10% stock dividend is declared when the share price is $10. Show the before-and-after effects of the dividend on (a) share capital, (b) retained earnings, (c) total shareholders' equity, and (d) the number of shares.

Analyze impact of stock dividend for corporation.
(SO 3)

BE11–8 Refer to the data given in BE11–7 for Chew Corporation. What is the impact of the stock dividend on an individual shareholder who owns 100 common shares before the dividend is declared?

BE11–9 In June 2008, Southern Copper Corporation, one of the world's largest copper producers, announced a three-for-one stock split. Immediately before the split, Southern Copper had 294,865,362 common shares trading at U.S. $99 per share. (a) How many shares did it have after the stock split? (b) What was the most likely price of the shares after the stock split? (c) How would Southern Copper record this stock split?

BE11–10 Indicate whether each of the following transactions would increase (+), decrease (–), or have no effect (NE) on total assets, total liabilities, total shareholders' equity, and the number of shares:

	Assets	Liabilities	Shareholders' Equity	Number of Shares
(a) Declared and paid cash dividend.				
(b) Declared and distributed stock dividend.				
(c) Split stock two-for-one.				

BE11–11 Canning Corporation reported the following statement of shareholders' equity accounts for the year ended December 31, 2009.

CANNING CORPORATION
Statement of Shareholders' Equity
Year Ended December 31, 2009

	Common Shares		Additional			Accumulated Other	
	Number of Shares	Legal Capital	Contributed Capital	Retained Earnings		Comprehensive Income	Total
Bal., Jan. 1, 2009	500,000	$1,500,000		$3,500,000		$100,000	$5,100,000
Issued common shares	100,000	(b)					400,000
Declared and issued stock dividend	20,000	100,000		(e)			0
Reacquired common shares	(a)	(258,000)	$(c)				(220,000)
Declared dividends				(135,000)			(135,000)
Comprehensive income							
Net earnings				750,000			(g)
Other comprehensive income						(f)	25,000
Bal., Dec. 31, 2009	540,000	$1,742,000	$(d)	$4,015,000		$125,000	$5,920,000

Determine the missing amounts.

BE11–12 Refer to the data given in BE11–11 for Canning Corporation. Canning had an unlimited number of no par value common shares authorized. Prepare the shareholders' equity section of its balance sheet at December 31, 2009.

BE11–13 Paul Schwartz, president of Schwartz Corporation, believes that it is good practice to maintain a constant payout of dividends relative to earnings. Last year, net earnings were $600,000, and the corporation paid $60,000 in dividends. This year, due to some unusual circumstances, the corporation had net earnings of $2 million. Paul expects next year's net earnings to be about $700,000. What was Schwartz Corporation's payout ratio last year? If it is to maintain the same payout ratio, what amount of dividends would it pay this year? Is this a good idea? In other words, what are the pros and cons of maintaining a constant payout ratio?

BE11–14 Messier Inc. has 40,000 common shares on January 1, 2009. On April 1, 8,000 shares were repurchased. On August 31 and November 30, 12,000 and 6,000 shares were issued, respectively. Calculate (a) the number of common shares issued at December 31, 2009, and (b) the weighted average number of common shares for 2009.

BE11–15 Refer to the data for Messier Inc. given in BE11–14. Messier reported net earnings of $370,000. Messier also had 10,000 $2-cumulative preferred shares, on which the dividend for the current year was declared and paid. Calculate the earnings per share.

BE11–16 Sleeman Ltd. reported the following selected information for the year ended January 31, 2010: net earnings, $14,000; beginning shareholders' equity, $104,000; and ending shareholders' equity, $122,000. Sleeman has no preferred shares. (a) Calculate the return on common shareholders' equity. (b) Explain how your calculation in (a) would change if Sleeman had preferred shares.

Calculate return on equity.
(SO 5)

Exercises

E11–1   The following is a recent stock market listing for **Bombardier Inc.** Class A (common) shares:

Interpret stock market listing.
(SO 1)

| 365-day | | | | | | | | | | |
high	low	stock	sym	div	high	low	close	chg	vol (000)	yld	p/e ratio
9.00	4.10	Bombardier	BBD.A	0.10	7.67	7.28	7.28	+0.10	101,130	1.40	2.80

Instructions

(a) What is the highest price Bombardier's shares traded for during the year? The lowest?

(b) What is the annual per share dividend paid on these shares?

(c) If you had purchased 1,000 common shares at Bombardier's closing price of the day in the above listing, what would be the total cost of your share purchase?

(d) What was the closing price of Bombardier's common shares on the previous day?

(e) How many Bombardier common shares were sold on the trading day of the listing?

(f) What would be your likely motivation for purchasing these shares—future dividend income or future price increase? Explain.

E11–2   Santiago Corp. had the following share transactions during the year:

Record issue of shares.
(SO 2)

June 12   Issued 50,000 common shares for $5 per share.
July 11   Issued 1,000 preferred shares for $25 per share.
Oct.   1   Issued 10,000 common shares in exchange for land. The common shares were trading for $6 per share on that date. The fair value of the land was estimated to be $65,000.
Nov. 15   Issued 1,500 preferred shares for $30 per share.

Instructions

(a) Record the above transactions.

(b) Calculate the average cost for each of the common and preferred shares.

E11–3   Enviro Corporation reported having 35,000 common shares issued for a total share capital of $140,000 on its December 31, 2009, balance sheet. On February 15, 2010, it reacquired 5,000 of these shares. This is the first time Enviro has reacquired any of its shares.

Record reacquisition of shares.
(SO 2)

Instructions

(a) Record the reacquisition of the shares, assuming the company paid $17,500 to reacquire them.

(b) Repeat part (a), assuming instead that the company paid $22,500 to reacquire the shares.

E11–4   Moosonee Ltd. was incorporated on January 5, 2009, and is authorized to issue an unlimited number of common and preferred shares. The company had the following share transactions in its first month of operations:

Record issue and reacquisition
of shares.
(SO 2)

Jan. 6   Issued 200,000 common shares for $1.50 per share.
12   Issued 50,000 common shares for $1.75 per share.
17   Issued 1,000 preferred shares for $10 per share.
18   Issued 500,000 common shares for $2 per share.
24   Reacquired 200,000 common shares for $1.90 per share.
30   Reacquired 150,000 common shares for $1.80 per share.

Instructions

(a) Record the above transactions.

(b) What is the number of common shares remaining, and their average cost, at the end of January?

E11–5 On January 1, Tarow Corporation had 75,000 common shares, recorded at $600,000. During the year, the following transactions occurred:

Apr. 1 Issued 5,000 common shares at $10 per share.

June 15 Declared a cash dividend of $0.50 per share to common shareholders of record on June 30, payable on July 10.

July 10 Paid the $0.50 cash dividend.

Aug. 21 Declared a 5% stock dividend to shareholders of record on September 5, distributable on September 20. The shares were trading for $12 a share at this time.

Nov. 1 Issued 3,000 common shares at $12 per share.

Dec. 20 Repurchased 10,000 common shares for $11 per share. This was the first time Tarow had repurchased its own shares.

Instructions

(a) Record the above transactions.

(b) Explain where each of the accounts recorded in (a) would be reported in the December 31 financial statements. Be specific in your answer. For example, cash would be reported as a current asset in the balance sheet.

E11–6 Laine Inc. is considering one of three following courses of action: (1) paying a $0.50 cash dividend, (2) distributing a 5% stock dividend, or (3) effecting a two-for-one stock split. The current share price is $14 per share.

Instructions

Help Laine make its decision by completing the following chart (treat each possibility independently):

	Before Action	After Cash Dividend	After Stock Dividend	After Stock Split
Total assets	$1,250,000			
Total liabilities	$ 50,000			
Common shares	800,000			
Retained earnings	400,000			
Total shareholders' equity	1,200,000			
Total liabilities and shareholders' equity	$1,250,000			
Number of common shares	80,000			

E11–7 Refer to the data given in E11–6 for Laine Inc. Suppose a shareholder owns 800 common shares. Explain the impact of each of the proposed courses of action—(1) receipt of a $0.50 cash dividend; (2) receipt of a 5% stock dividend; and (3) a two-for-one stock split—on the shareholder's (a) cash, (b) investment portfolio fair value, and (c) number of shares.

E11–8 Before preparing financial statements for the current year, the auditors for Koo Ltd. discovered the following errors in the accounts:

1. Koo has 10,000 $5-noncumulative preferred shares issued. It paid the preferred shareholders the quarterly dividend, which was recorded as a debit to Dividends Expense and a credit to Cash.

2. A 5% common stock dividend (1,000 shares) was declared when the shares were trading for $5. To record the declaration, the account Investment in Equity Securities was debited and Dividends Payable was credited. The shares have not yet been distributed.

3. A three-for-one stock split involving the issue of 200,000 new common shares (for a total of 300,000 common shares) was recorded as a debit to Retained Earnings and a credit to Common Shares for the fair value of the shares. The shares were trading for $5 on the date of the split.

Instructions

Prepare any correcting entries that are required.

E11–9 The general ledger of Val d'Or Corporation contains the following selected accounts and information:

1. Cash
2. Common shares
3. Unrealized gain on available-for-sale investments
4. Patents
5. Preferred shares

6. Retained earnings
7. Contributed capital—reacquisition of common shares
8. Cash dividend
9. Stock dividend
10. Cash paid for dividends

Instructions

Using the table headings below, indicate whether or not each of the above accounts should be reported in the statement of shareholders' equity. If yes, indicate whether the account should be reported in the share capital, additional contributed capital, retained earnings, or accumulated other comprehensive income section of the statement. If not, indicate in which financial statement (balance sheet, statement of earnings, or cash flow statement) and in which section the account should be reported. The first account has been done for you as an example.

		Statement of Shareholders' Equity				
Account	Share Capital	Additional Contributed Capital	Retained Earnings	Accumulated Other Comprehensive Income	Financial Statement	Classification
1. Cash					Balance Sheet	Current assets

E11–10 The following accounts appear in the ledger of Ozabal Inc. after the books are closed at December 31, 2009:

Prepare shareholders' equity section.
(SO 4)

Accumulated other comprehensive loss	$ 50,000
Common shares (no par value, unlimited number of shares authorized, 300,000 shares issued)	300,000
Common stock dividends distributable	75,000
Contributed capital—reacquisition of common shares	25,000
Preferred shares ($4-noncumulative, no par value, 100,000 shares authorized, 30,000 shares issued)	150,000
Retained earnings	900,000

Instructions

Prepare the shareholders' equity section of Ozabal's balance sheet, assuming $100,000 of retained earnings is restricted for a plant expansion.

E11–11 The Blue Canoe Limited reported the following changes to its shareholders' equity accounts for the year ended December 31, 2009.

Prepare statement of shareholders' equity and shareholders' equity section.
(SO 4)

Accumulated other comprehensive income:	
Balance, Jan. 1	$ 40,000
Balance, Dec. 31	65,000
Unrealized gain on available-for-sale-investments	25,000
Other contributed capital:	
Balance, Jan. 1	540,000
Balance, Dec. 31	120,000
Repurchase of shares	(420,000)
Retained earnings:	
Balance, Jan. 1	1,500,000
Balance, Dec. 31	1,830,000
Net earnings	400,000
Dividends	(70,000)
Share capital:	
Balance, Jan. 1 (32,000)	800,000
Balance, Dec. 31 (33,000)	807,000
Repurchase of shares (1,000)	(23,000)
Shares issued (2,000)	30,000

(a) Prepare a statement of shareholders' equity for the year.

(b) Prepare the shareholders' equity section of the balance sheet at December 31.

E11–12 🔑 The following selected information is available for two competitors, Nike, Inc. and Adidas AG:

	Nike (in USD)	Adidas (in EUR)
Share price	$55.81	€36.20
Dividends per share	0.88	0.50
Earnings per share	3.49	2.70

Instructions

(a) Calculate the payout, dividend yield, and price-earnings ratios for each company.

(b) Which company would investors favour for income purposes? For growth purposes?

E11–13 Chinook Corporation reported net earnings of $350,000 for its November 30, 2009, year end. During the year, cash dividends of $45,000 were paid on the common shares and $75,000 on the preferred shares. Chinook started the year with 60,000 common shares. The following changes in share capital occurred during the year:

Feb. 28 Issued 15,000 common shares for $200,000.
May 31 Reacquired 5,000 shares for $90,000.
Nov. 1 Issued 10,000 preferred shares for $500,000.

Instructions

(a) Calculate the earnings available for the common shareholders.

(b) Calculate the weighted average number of common shares for the year.

(c) Calculate the earnings per share for the year.

(d) Why is it necessary to calculate a weighted average number of shares? Why not use the number of shares at the end of the year?

E11–14 🔑 Selected financial information (in millions, except per share information) is available for CIBC at October 31:

	2007	2006	2005
Total dividends paid to common shareholders	$1,044	$924	$902
Dividends per common shares	$3.11	$2.76	$2.66
Total dividends paid to preferred shareholders	$170	$163	$177
Net earnings (loss)	$3,296	$2,646	$(32)
Weighted average number of common shares	336	335	339
Common shareholders' equity	$11,158	$9,941	$8,350
Price per common share	$102.00	$87.60	$72.20

Instructions
Calculate the dividend yield, payout, earnings per share, and return on common shareholders' equity ratios for the common shareholders for 2007 and 2006. Comment on your findings.

Problems: Set A

P11–1A Wetland Corporation was organized on June 1, 2009. It is authorized to issue an unlimited number of no par value $4-cumulative preferred shares and an unlimited number of no par value common shares. The following share transactions were completed during the company's first year of operations:

June 5 Issued 80,000 common shares for $4 per share.
Aug. 21 Issued 5,000 preferred shares for $55 per share.
Sept. 15 Issued 22,000 common shares in exchange for land. The asking price of the land was $100,000. The common shares were trading for $4.25 per share on this date.
Nov. 20 Issued 78,000 common shares for $4.50 per share.
Jan. 12 Repurchased 80,000 common shares for $4 per share.
Mar. 9 Issued 10,000 common shares for $5 per share.
Apr. 16 Issued 2,000 preferred shares for $60 per share.
May 15 Declared the annual preferred dividend to the preferred shareholders, to shareholders of record on May 30, payable on June 10.
31 Reported net earnings of $500,000 for the year.

Instructions

(a) Record the above transactions.

(b) Open T accounts and post to the shareholders' equity accounts.

(c) Prepare the shareholders' equity section of the balance sheet at May 31, 2010.

P11–2A The following shareholders' equity accounts are reported by Branch Inc. on January 1, 2009:

Show impact of transactions on accounts.
(SO 2, 3, 4)

Common shares (150,000 issued)	$2,400,000
Preferred shares ($4-noncumulative, 5,000 issued)	350,000
Contributed capital—reacquisition of common shares	50,000
Retained earnings	1,276,000
Accumulated other comprehensive income	15,000

The following selected transactions occurred during the year:

1. Issued 10,000 common shares for $18 per share.
2. Issued 100 preferred shares for $75 per share.
3. Reacquired 25,000 common shares for $20 per share.
4. Issued 1,000 common shares in exchange for land. The fair value of the shares was $25 per share; of the land, $23,500.
5. Declared and paid the preferred shareholders a $2 per share dividend.
6. Determined that the company had an unrealized gain on its investments of $5,000.

Instructions

For each of the above transactions, indicate its impact on the items in the table below. Indicate if the item will increase (+) or decrease (–), and by how much, or if it will not be affected (n/a). The first transaction has been done for you as an example.

					Shareholders' Equity		
	Assets	Liabilities	Preferred Shares	Common Shares	Other Contributed Capital	Retained Earnings	Accumulated Other Comprehensive Income
1.	+$180,000	n/a	n/a	+$180,000	n/a	n/a	n/a

P11–3A Cattrall Corporation is authorized to issue an unlimited number of no par value $5-noncumulative preferred shares and an unlimited number of no par value common shares. On February 1, 2009, the general ledger contained the following shareholders' equity accounts:

Record and post equity transactions; prepare statements.
(SO 2, 3, 4)

Preferred shares (8,000 shares issued)	$ 440,000
Common shares (70,000 shares issued)	1,050,000
Contributed capital—reacquisition of common shares	75,000
Retained earnings	1,000,000
Accumulated other comprehensive income	65,000

The following equity transactions occurred during the year ended January 31, 2010:

Feb.	28	Issued 2,400 preferred shares for $150,000.
Apr.	12	Issued 200,000 common shares for $3,200,000.
May	25	Issued 5,000 common shares in exchange for land. At the time of the exchange, the land was valued at $75,000 and the common shares at $80,000.
Sept.	12	Repurchased 75,000 common shares for $1,275,000.
Dec.	29	Declared a $2.50 per share dividend to the preferred shareholders of record at January 15, payable February 1.
Jan.	31	A net loss of $5,000 was incurred for the year.

Instructions

(a) Record the above transactions.

(b) Open T accounts and post to the shareholders' equity accounts.

(c) Prepare the statement of shareholders' equity for the year.

(d) Prepare the shareholders' equity section of the balance sheet at January 31, 2010.

Record and post equity
transactions; prepare
statements.
(SO 2, 3, 4)

P11–4A On January 1, 2009, Schipper Ltd. had the following shareholders' equity accounts:

Preferred shares, $4-noncumulative, no par value, unlimited number authorized, none issued	
Common shares, no par value, unlimited number authorized, 1,000,000 issued	$1,500,000
Retained earnings	1,800,000
Accumulated other comprehensive income (loss)	(25,000)

The following selected transactions occurred during 2009:

Jan.	2	Issued 100,000 preferred shares for $50 per share.
Mar.	10	Declared the quarterly cash dividend to preferred shareholders of record on March 22, payable April 1.
June	10	Declared the quarterly cash dividend to preferred shareholders of record on June 22, payable July 1.
Aug.	12	Issued 100,000 common shares for $1.70 per share.
Oct.	1	Declared the quarterly cash dividend to preferred shareholders of record on October 22, payable November 1. Also declared a $0.25 cash dividend per share to the common shareholders of record on October 22, payable November 1.
Dec.	10	Due to a temporary shortfall of cash, was unable to declare or pay the quarterly cash dividend to preferred shareholders.
	31	Net loss for the year was $100,000.

Instructions

(a) Record the above transactions.

(b) Open T accounts and post to the shareholders' equity accounts.

(c) Prepare a statement of shareholders' equity for the year.

(d) Prepare the shareholders' equity section of the balance sheet at December 31.

(e) Prepare the financing activities section of the cash flow statement for the year.

Reproduce equity accounts;
prepare shareholders' equity
section.
(SO 3, 4)

P11–5A The general ledger of Maggio Corporation contained the following shareholders' equity accounts in 2009:

	Jan. 1	Dec. 31
Preferred shares (15,000 issued at both dates)	$ 750,000	$ 750,000
Common shares (255,000 issued at Jan. 1, and 291,500 issued at Dec. 31)	3,210,000	3,850,000
Contributed capital—reacquisition of common shares	200,000	200,000
Retained earnings	980,000	1,310,000

A review of the accounting records for the year ended December 31, 2009, reveals the following information:

1. On March 1, 20,000 no par value common shares were sold for $15.50 per share. An unlimited number are authorized.

2. On August 18, a 6% common stock dividend was declared for 16,500 shares when the share price was $20. The stock dividend was distributed on September 25.

3. The preferred shares are $6-cumulative no par value. An unlimited number of preferred shares is authorized. The quarterly preferred shareholders' dividend was declared and paid in 2009 for each quarter.

4. Net earnings for the year were $750,000.

5. On December 31, the directors authorized a $200,000 restriction on retained earnings in accordance with a debt covenant.

Instructions

(a) Reproduce the Preferred Shares, Common Shares, Contributed Capital, and Retained Earnings general ledger accounts for the year.

(b) Prepare the shareholders' equity section of the balance sheet at December 31, including any required note disclosure.

P11–6A The condensed balance sheet of Erickson Corporation reports the following amounts:

Compare impact of cash dividend, stock dividend, and stock split.
(SO 3)

ERICKSON CORPORATION Balance Sheet (partial) January 31, 2010		
Total assets		$9,000,000
Total liabilities		$2,500,000
Shareholders' equity		
Common shares, unlimited number		
authorized, 500,000 issued	$3,000,000	
Retained earnings	3,500,000	6,500,000
Total liabilities and shareholders' equity		$9,000,000

The common shares are currently trading for $20 per share. Erickson wants to assess the impact of three possible alternatives on the corporation and its shareholders:

1. Payment of a $1.50 per share cash dividend
2. Distribution of a 5% stock dividend
3. A two-for-one stock split

Instructions

(a) Determine the impact of each alternative on (1) assets, (2) liabilities, (3) common shares, (4) retained earnings, (5) total shareholders' equity, and (6) the number of shares.

(b) Assume an Erickson shareholder currently owns 2,000 common shares for which he paid $35,000. What is the impact of each alternative for the shareholder?

P11–7A On January 1, 2009, Stengel Corporation had these shareholders' equity accounts:

Record and post dividend transactions, prepare statements, and calculate ratios.
(SO 3, 4, 5)

Common shares (no par value, unlimited number of shares authorized, 75,000 issued)	$1,700,000
Retained earnings	900,000

During the year, the following transactions occurred:

Feb.   1   Declared a $1 per share cash dividend to shareholders of record on February 15, payable March 1.

Apr.   1   Effected a three-for-one stock split. On April 1, the share price was $36.

July   1   Declared a 5% stock dividend to shareholders of record on July 15, distributable July 31. On July 1, the share price was $15.

Dec. 31   Determined that net earnings for the year were $400,000.

      31   The share price was $20 on this date.

Instructions

(a) Record the above transactions.

(b) Open T accounts as required and post to the shareholders' equity accounts.

(c) Prepare a statement of shareholders' equity for the year.

(d) Prepare the shareholders' equity section of the balance sheet at December 31.

(e) Calculate the dividend payout, dividend yield, and return on common shareholders' equity ratios.

P11–8A Tim Hortons Inc. reported the following changes to its shareholders' equity accounts (in thousands) for the year ended December 31, 2007.

Prepare statement of shareholders' equity and shareholders' equity section of balance sheet.
(SO 4)

Accumulated other comprehensive income (loss):	
Balance, Jan. 1	$ (74,766)
Balance, Dec. 31	(138,465)
Other comprehensive loss	(63,699)

Other contributed capital (in excess of par value):

Balance, Jan. 1	$853,072
Balance, Dec. 31	695,929
Repurchase of shares	(170,604)
Issue of shares	4,345
Other	9,116

Retained earnings:

Balance, Jan. 1	248,980
Balance, Dec. 31	458,958
Net earnings	269,551
Dividends	(52,865)
Other	(6,708)

Share capital:

Balance, Jan. 1 (191,107)	289
Balance, Dec. 31 (186,132)	289
Repurchase of shares (5,039)	0
Shares issued (64)	0

(a) Prepare a statement of shareholders' equity for the year.

(b) Prepare the shareholders' equity section of the balance sheet. Tim Hortons has 1 billion U.S. $0.001 par value common shares authorized. The number of shares issued is shown in parentheses in the share capital section of the above table.

Calculate earnings per share.
(SO 5)

P11–9A Blue Bay Logistics Ltd.'s shareholders' equity accounts were as follows at the beginning of the current fiscal year, April 1, 2009:

$6-cumulative preferred shares (20,000 shares issued)	$1,800,000
Common shares (500,000 shares issued)	3,750,000
Contributed capital—reacquisition of common shares	50,000
Retained earnings	1,500,000
Total shareholders' equity	$7,100,000

During the year, the following selected transactions occurred:

June 1 Reacquired 12,000 common shares for $9 per share.
July 1 Issued 50,000 common shares for $10 per share.
Feb. 28 Declared the annual preferred dividend to shareholders of record on March 12, payable on April 1.
Mar. 31 Net earnings for the year ended March 31, 2009, were $1,016,750.

Instructions

(a) Calculate the weighted average number of common shares for the year.

(b) Calculate the earnings per share.

(c) Why is it important to use net earnings available to common shareholders in the calculation of earnings per share? Why not just use net earnings?

Evaluate corporate
performance.
(SO 5)

P11–10A The following summary of the earnings per share, price-earnings (P-E), payout, and dividend yield ratios is available for the five years ended December 31 for TransAlta Corporation:

	Earnings per Share	P-E Ratio	Payout Ratio	Dividend Yield
2003	$1.26	14.7 times	79.0%	5.4%
2004	0.88	21.7	120.0	5.5
2005	1.01	26.7	113.0	3.9
2006	0.22	121.1	447.7	3.8
2007	1.53	21.8	65.6	3.0

Instructions

(a) What are some possible reasons that TransAlta's price-earnings and dividend payout ratios jumped to 121.1 times and 447.7%, respectively, in 2006? What does this mean?

(b) Why do you think TransAlta's price-earnings ratio declined to 21.8 times while its earnings per share improved to $1.53 in 2007?

(c) What are some possible reasons that TransAlta's payout and price-earnings ratios increased in 2006 at a time when its earnings per share decreased substantially?

(d) If you were an investor looking for dividend income, would you be happy with TransAlta's dividend policy? Explain.

P11–11A ⚬━ The following selected information (in millions, except for per share information) is available for **ScotiaBank** for the year ended October 31:

Evaluate corporate performance.
(SO 5)

	2007	2006
Weighted average number of common shares	989	988
Net earnings	$4,045	$3,579
Total common cash dividends (per share)	$1,720 ($1.74)	$1,483 ($1.50)
Total preferred cash dividends	$51	$30
Average common shareholders' equity	$17,058	$16,214
Price per common share	$53.48	$49.30

Industry averages were as follows:

Payout ratio	12.2%	n/a
Dividend yield	3.2%	3.1%
Earnings per share	n/a	n/a
Price-earnings ratio	13.8 times	12.6 times
Return on common shareholders' equity	19.0%	19.9%

Instructions

(a) Calculate the following ratios for the common shareholders for each fiscal year:
   1. Payout ratio
   2. Dividend yield
   3. Earnings per share
   4. Price-earnings ratio
   5. Return on common shareholders' equity

(b) Comment on the above ratios for 2007 in comparison to the prior year and in comparison to the industry.

P11–12A ⚬━ Selected ratios for two retailers follow, along with the industry averages:

Evaluate corporate performance.
(SO 5)

Ratio	Bargain Hunters	Discount Paradise	Industry Average
Profit margin	6.8%	3.5%	3.7%
Return on common shareholders' equity	24.9%	22.4%	20.8%
Return on assets	10.4%	8.6%	8.7%
Asset turnover	1.5 times	2.5 times	2.5 times
Earnings per share	$3.30	$2.49	$2.33
Price-earnings ratio	12.3 times	17.0 times	16.3 times
Payout ratio	9.4%	25.0%	19.3%
Dividend yield	0.8%	1.5%	1.2%

Instructions

(a) Compare the profitability of Bargain Hunters to that of Discount Paradise and to the industry. Which company is more profitable? Explain.

(b) You would like to invest in the shares of one of the two companies. Your goal is to have regular income from your investment that will help pay your tuition fees for the next few years. Which of the two companies is a better choice for you? Explain.

(c) Assume that instead of looking for regular income, you are looking for growth in the share value so that you can resell the shares at a gain in the future. Now which of the two companies is better for you? Explain.

Problems: Set B

Record and post equity transactions; prepare shareholders' equity section. (SO 2, 4)

P11–1B Remmers Corporation was organized on January 1, 2009. It is authorized to issue an unlimited number of no par value $3-noncumulative preferred shares and an unlimited number of no par value common shares. The following share transactions were completed during the company's first year of operations:

Jan. 10 Issued 100,000 common shares for $2 per share.
Mar. 1 Issued 10,000 preferred shares for $32 per share.
May 1 Issued 75,000 common shares for $3 per share.
July 24 Issued 16,800 common shares for $60,000 cash and used equipment. The equipment originally cost $15,000. It now has a carrying amount of $7,500 and a fair value of $8,000. The common shares were trading for $4 per share on this date.
Sept. 1 Issued 5,000 common shares for $5 per share.
Nov. 1 Issued 2,000 preferred shares for $35 per share.
Dec. 15 Declared a $36,000 dividend to the preferred shareholders, to shareholders of record on December 31, payable on January 10.
31 Reported net earnings of $650,000 for the year.

Instructions

(a) Record the above transactions.

(b) Open T accounts and post to the shareholders' equity accounts.

(c) Prepare the shareholders' equity section of the balance sheet at December 31.

Show impact of transactions on accounts. (SO 2, 3, 4)

P11–2B The following shareholders' equity accounts are reported by Talty Inc. on January 1, 2009:

Common shares (500,000 issued)	$4,000,000
Preferred shares ($6-cumulative, 4,000 issued)	600,000
Contributed capital—reacquisition of preferred shares	2,000
Retained earnings	1,958,000
Accumulated other comprehensive income	25,000

The following selected transactions occurred during the year:

1. Issued 10,000 common shares for $10 per share.
2. Issued 500 common shares in exchange for equipment. The fair value of the shares was $11 per share; of the equipment, $6,000.
3. Issued 1,000 preferred shares for $60 per share.
4. Reacquired 500 preferred shares for $50 each.
5. The annual preferred share dividend was declared and paid during the year.
6. Determined that the company had an unrealized loss on its investments of $5,000.

Instructions

For each of the above transactions, indicate its impact on the items in the table that follows. Indicate if the item will increase (+) or decrease (–), and by how much, or if it will not be affected (n/a). The first transaction has been done for you as an example.

					Shareholders' Equity		
	Assets	Liabilities	Preferred Shares	Common Shares	Other Contributed Capital	Retained Earnings	Accumulated Other Comprehensive Income
1.	+$100,000	n/a	n/a	+$100,000	n/a	n/a	n/a

Record and post equity transactions; prepare statements. (SO 2, 3, 4)

P11–3B Largent Corporation is authorized to issue 200,000 no par value $4-cumulative preferred shares and an unlimited number of no par value common shares. On January 1, 2009, the general ledger contained the following shareholders' equity accounts:

Preferred shares (8,000 shares issued)	$ 440,000
Common shares (70,000 shares issued)	1,050,000
Contributed capital—reacquisition of preferred shares	25,000
Retained earnings	800,000
Accumulated other comprehensive income	10,000

The following equity transactions occurred in 2009:

Jan. 10 Repurchased 20,000 common shares for $240,000.

Feb.   6 Issued 10,000 preferred shares for $600,000.

Apr. 14 Issued 40,000 common shares for $560,000.

May 29 Declared a semi-annual dividend to the preferred shareholders of record at June 12, payable July 1.

Aug. 22 Issued 10,000 common shares in exchange for a building. At the time of the exchange, the building was valued at $165,000 and the common shares at $150,000.

Nov. 29 Declared a semi-annual dividend to the preferred shareholders of record at December 12, payable January 1.

Dec. 31 Net earnings for the year were $582,000.

Instructions

(a) Record the above transactions.

(b) Open T accounts and post to the shareholders' equity accounts.

(c) Prepare the statement of shareholders' equity for the year.

(d) Prepare the shareholders' equity section of the balance sheet at December 31.

P11–4B On January 1, 2009, Conway Ltd. had the following shareholders' equity accounts:

Record and post equity transactions; prepare statements. (SO 2, 3, 4)

Preferred shares, $6-noncumulative, no par value, unlimited number authorized, none issued	
Common shares, no par value, unlimited number authorized, 1.5 million issued	$16,500,000
Retained earnings	1,900,000
Accumulated other comprehensive income	25,000

The following selected transactions occurred during 2009:

Jan.   2 Issued 100,000 preferred shares at $66 per share.

Mar.   5 Declared the quarterly cash dividend to preferred shareholders of record on March 20, payable April 1.

Apr. 18 Issued 250,000 common shares at $13 per share.

June   5 Declared the quarterly cash dividend to preferred shareholders of record on June 20, payable July 1.

Sept.   5 Declared the quarterly cash dividend to preferred shareholders of record on September 20, payable October 1.

Dec. 15 Declared the quarterly cash dividend to preferred shareholders of record on December 20, payable January 1.

       31 Net earnings for the year were $3.6 million.

Instructions

(a) Record the above transactions.

(b) Open T accounts and post to the shareholders' equity accounts.

(c) Prepare a statement of shareholders' equity for the year.

(d) Prepare the shareholders' equity section of the balance sheet at December 31.

(e) Prepare the financing activities section of the cash flow statement for the year.

P11–5B The general ledger of Robichaud Corporation contained the following shareholders' equity accounts in 2009:

Reproduce equity accounts; prepare shareholders' equity section. (SO 3, 4)

	Jan. 1	Dec. 31
Preferred shares (10,000 and 20,000 shares issued, respectively)	$ 500,000	$1,000,000
Common shares (320,000 and 420,000 shares issued, respectively)	2,700,000	3,700,000
Common stock dividends distributable	0	252,000
Retained earnings	2,980,000	3,500,000

A review of the accounting records for the year ended December 31, 2009, reveals the following information:

1. On January 1, 10,000 no par value $5-noncumulative preferred shares were issued for $50 each. An unlimited number are authorized.

2. On October 1, 100,000 no par value common shares were sold for cash at $10 per share. An unlimited number are authorized.
3. The preferred shareholders' dividend was declared and paid in cash in 2009. No dividends were paid to preferred shareholders in 2008.
4. On December 31, a 5% common stock dividend was declared on common shares when the share price was $12. The stock dividend is distributable on January 20.
5. Net earnings for the year were $872,000.
6. On December 31, the board of directors authorized a $250,000 restriction on retained earnings for a plant expansion.

Instructions

(a) Reproduce the Preferred Shares, Common Shares, Common Stock Dividends Distributable, and Retained Earnings general ledger accounts for the year.

(b) Prepare the shareholders' equity section of the balance sheet at December 31, including any required note disclosure.

Compare impact of cash dividend, stock dividend, and stock split.
(SO 3)

P11–6B The condensed balance sheet of Laporte Corporation reports the following amounts:

LAPORTE CORPORATION Balance Sheet (partial) June 30, 2009		
Total assets		$16,000,000
Total liabilities		$ 6,000,000
Shareholders' equity		
Common shares, unlimited number authorized, 400,000 issued	$2,000,000	
Retained earnings	8,000,000	10,000,000
Total liabilities and shareholders' equity		$16,000,000

The common shares are currently trading for $30 per share. Laporte wants to assess the impact of three possible alternatives on the corporation and its shareholders:

1. Payment of a $1.50 per share cash dividend
2. Distribution of a 5% stock dividend
3. A three-for-two stock split

Instructions

(a) Determine the impact of each alternative on (1) assets, (2) liabilities, (3) common shares, (4) retained earnings, (5) total shareholders' equity, and (6) the number of shares.

(b) Assume a Laporte shareholder currently owns 1,000 common shares for which she paid $28,000. What is the impact of each alternative for the shareholder, assuming the share price changes proportionately with the alternative?

Record and post dividend transactions, prepare statements, and calculate ratios.
(SO 3, 4, 5)

P11–7B On January 1, 2009, Wirth Corporation had these shareholders' equity accounts:

Common shares (no par value, unlimited number of shares authorized, 110,000 shares issued)	$1,100,000
Retained earnings	540,000

During the year, the following transactions occurred:

Jan.	15	Declared a $1 per share cash dividend to shareholders of record on January 31, payable February 15.
Apr.	15	Declared a 10% stock dividend to shareholders of record on April 30, distributable May 15. On April 15, the share price was $15.
July	1	Effected a two-for-one stock split. On July 1, the share price was $20.
Dec.	31	Determined that net earnings for the year were $350,000.
	31	The share price was $11 on this date.

Instructions

(a) Record the above transactions.

(b) Open T accounts as required and post to the shareholders' equity accounts.

(c) Prepare a statement of shareholders' equity for the year.

(d) Prepare the shareholders' equity section of the balance sheet at December 31.

(e) Calculate the dividend payout, dividend yield, and return on common shareholders' equity ratios.

P11–8B Cameco Corporation reported the following changes to its shareholders' equity accounts (in thousands) for the year ended December 31, 2007:

Prepare statement of shareholders' equity and shareholders' equity section of balance sheet.
(SO 4)

Accumulated other comprehensive income (loss):	
Balance, Jan. 1	$ (39,766)
Balance, Dec. 31	25,433
Other comprehensive income	65,199
Other contributed capital:	
Balance, Jan. 1	540,173
Balance, Dec. 31	119,531
Repurchase of shares	(406,577)
Other	(14,065)
Retained earnings:	
Balance, Jan. 1	1,428,206
Balance, Dec. 31	1,779,629
Net earnings	416,112
Dividends	(70,032)
Other	5,343
Share capital:	
Balance, Jan. 1 (352,292,632)	812,769
Balance, Dec. 31 (344,398,698)	819,268
Repurchase of shares (9,575,300)	(22,750)
Shares issued (1,681,366)	29,249

Instructions

(a) Prepare a statement of shareholders' equity for the year.

(b) Prepare the shareholders' equity section of the balance sheet. Cameco has an unlimited number of common shares authorized. The number of shares issued is shown in parentheses in the share capital section of the above table.

P11–9B Gualtieri Inc.'s shareholders' equity accounts were as follows at the beginning of the current fiscal year, August 1, 2009:

Calculate earnings per share.
(SO 5)

$5-noncumulative preferred shares (25,000 shares issued)	$2,500,000
Common shares (350,000 shares issued)	3,750,000
Retained earnings	2,250,000
Total shareholders' equity	$8,500,000

During the year, the following selected transactions occurred:

Dec. 1 Issued 60,000 common shares for $12 per share.

Feb. 1 Reacquired 10,000 common shares for $10 per share.

June 20 Declared the annual preferred dividend to shareholders of record on July 10, payable on July 31.

July 31 Net earnings for the year ended July 31, 2010, were $1,280,000.

Instructions

(a) Calculate the weighted average number of common shares for the year.

(b) Calculate the earnings per share.

(c) Why is it important to use a weighted average number of shares in the calculation of earnings per share? Why not just use the number of shares issued at year end?

Evaluate corporate
performance.
(SO 5)

P11–10B The following summary of the earnings per share (in USD), price-earnings (P-E), payout, and dividend yield ratios is available for the five years ended December 31 for **Barrick Gold Corporation**:

	Earnings per Share	P-E Ratio	Payout Ratio	Dividend Yield
2003	$0.27	67.8 times	81%	1.2%
2004	(0.19)	n/a	n/a	1.0
2005	0.74	34.4	30	0.9
2006	1.44	21.2	15	0.7
2007	1.28	26.8	23	0.9

Note that the price-earnings and payout ratios could not be calculated for 2004 because share prices and dividends cannot be meaningfully compared to a loss.

Instructions

(a) What are some possible reasons that Barrick Gold's dividend payout ratio improved to 30% in 2005 while its dividend yield ratio dropped to 0.9% in the same year?

(b) Why do you think Barrick Gold's price-earnings ratio was higher in 2005 than in 2007 even though its earnings per share was lower and its dividend yield was the same?

(c) If you were an investor looking for dividend income, would you be happy with Barrick Gold's dividend policy? Explain.

(d) If you were one of Barrick Gold's creditors, what would you think about the company continuing to pay dividends regardless of whether it reports net earnings or a net loss? Explain.

Evaluate corporate
performance.
(SO 5)

P11–11B The following selected information (in millions, except for per share information) is available for the **National Bank of Canada** for the year ended October 31:

	2007	2006
Weighted average number of common shares	160	163
Net earnings	$541	$871
Total common cash dividends (per share)	$364 ($2.28)	$320 ($1.96)
Total preferred cash dividends	$21	$21
Average common shareholders' equity	$4,312	$4,292
Price per common share	$54.65	$61.25

Industry averages were as follows:

Payout ratio	12.2%	n/a
Dividend yield	3.2%	3.1%
Earnings per share	n/a	n/a
Price-earnings ratio	13.8 times	12.6 times
Return on common shareholders' equity	19.0%	19.9%

Instructions

(a) Calculate the following ratios for the common shareholders for each fiscal year:
   1. Payout ratio
   2. Dividend yield
   3. Earnings per share
   4. Price-earnings ratio
   5. Return on common shareholders' equity

(b) Comment on the above ratios for 2007 in comparison to the prior year, and in comparison to the industry.

Evaluate corporate
performance.
(SO 5)

P11–12B Selected ratios for two companies operating in the petroleum industry follow, along with the industry averages:

Ratio	Petro-Boost	World Oil	Industry Average
Profit margin	10.0%	8.4%	5.7%
Return on common shareholders' equity	15.1%	29.6%	18.1%
Return on assets	9.0%	13.4%	6.1%
Asset turnover	1.1 times	1.5 times	1.1 times
Earnings per share	$4.06	$4.38	n/a
Price-earnings ratio	14.2 times	17.1 times	11.8 times
Payout ratio	12.3%	9.9%	17.0%
Dividend yield	0.9%	0.7%	n/a

Instructions

(a) Compare the profitability of Petro-Boost to that of World Oil, and to the industry average. Which company is more profitable? Explain.

(b) You would like to invest in the shares of one of the two companies. Your goal is to have regular income from your investment that will help pay your tuition fees for the next few years. Which of the companies is a better choice for you? Explain.

(c) Assume that instead of looking for regular income, you are looking for growth in the share value so that you can resell the shares at a gain in the future. Now which of the two companies is better for you? Explain.

BROADENING YOUR PERSPECTIVE

Financial Reporting and Analysis Cases

Financial Reporting: *Shoppers Drug Mart*

Analysis Tools

BYP11–1 The financial statements of Shoppers Drug Mart are presented in Appendix A at the end of this book.

Instructions

(a) How many common shares and preferred shares has Shoppers Drug Mart authorized? How many common shares were issued at the end of the 2007 and 2006 fiscal years? What was the weighted average of the number of common shares for each fiscal year?

(b) Did Shoppers Drug Mart repurchase any shares in 2007 and 2006? If so, how much cash did it spend on this activity in each year?

(c) Using the statement of retained earnings, determine the dividends declared by Shoppers Drug Mart in each of 2007 and 2006?

(d) Calculate the payout and return on common shareholders' equity ratios for 2007 and 2006. Shoppers Drug Mart's shareholders' equity was $2,386,508 thousand at the end of 2005.

Comparative Analysis: *Shoppers Drug Mart and Jean Coutu*

BYP11–2 The financial statements of Jean Coutu are presented in Appendix B, after the financial statements for Shoppers Drug Mart in Appendix A.

Instructions

(a) Calculate the payout ratios for each company for the most recent fiscal year. Which company pays out a higher percentage of its earnings to shareholders?

(b) Calculate or find the earnings per share and return on common shareholders' equity ratios for each company for the most recent fiscal year. Based on these measures, which company is more profitable?

Interpreting Financial Statements

BYP11–3 The authorized share capital of Talisman Energy Inc. includes an unlimited number of common shares. During the 2007 fiscal year, Talisman repurchased 45,994,100 common shares for a total of $951 million. During 2006, Talisman effected a three-for-one common stock split.

The following additional information is available for the year ended December 31 (in millions of dollars, except per share data):

	2007	2006
Net earnings	$2,078	$2,005
Common dividends	$180	$163
Cash dividend per common share	$0.175	$0.15
Weighted average number of common shares	1,032	1,092
Average common shareholders' equity	$7,635	$6,518
Price per common share	$18.39	$19.80

Instructions

    (a) What are some of the reasons that a company repurchases its own shares?

    (b) Talisman debited Retained Earnings for $838 million and debited Contributed Surplus for $3 million when it repurchased 45,994,100 common shares in 2007. Did the company repurchase its shares at more than or less than average cost?

    (c) Why did Talisman likely split its shares in 2006?

    (d) Calculate the dividend payout, dividend yield, earnings per share, price-earnings, and return on common shareholders' ratios for 2007 and 2006. Discuss the implications of your findings for investors.

A Global Focus

International Resources

BYP11–4 Germany-based sportswear retailer PUMA AG Rudolf Dassler Sport reported the following selected information (in EUR millions, except per share data) for fiscal 2007 and 2006:

	2007	2006
Net sales	€2,373.5	€2,369.2
Average total assets	€1,788.9	€1,517.9
Average shareholders' equity	€1,101.9	€962.2
Total dividends	€43.7	€39.9
Net earnings	€269.0	€263.2
Weighted average number of shares	16.018	16.054
Cash dividend per share	€2.75	€2.50
Price per share	€273.00	€295.67

PUMA has no preferred shares.

Instructions

    (a) Calculate the asset turnover, return on assets, and return on common shareholders' equity ratios for each fiscal year. Evaluate PUMA's change in profitability.

    (b) Calculate the earnings per share, price-earnings, dividend payout, and dividend yield ratios for each fiscal year. Discuss the implications of your findings for investors.

Critical Thinking Cases and Activities

Collaborative Learning Activity

BYP11–5 The senior management of Rodart Corporation Ltd. has just returned from a series of meetings with the investment dealers who cover their industry for the investing public. The analysts expressed concern about the company's growing percentage of debt in relation to shareholders' equity. Rodart needs to raise funds in the next year and is investigating what steps it should take next.

    The following alternatives have been identified:

1. Issue new shares (preferred or common).

2. Increase Rodart's dividend above the industry average, in the hope that the market will respond to the improved dividend yield by increasing the market price of the shares.

Instructions

After the class has been divided into groups and you have been assigned one of the two alternatives for analysis, do the following:

    (a) Identify the risks and benefits of the alternative. Identify the measurements (ratios, share prices, and so on) that will be used to determine the success or failure of your option if it is implemented.

    (b) Present your analysis to a group that has been assigned the other alternative.

    (c) In the combined group, vote on a course of action.

Communication Activity

BYP11–6 Earnings per share is the most commonly cited financial ratio. Indeed, share prices rise and fall in reaction to a company's earnings per share. The price-earnings ratio is also published in many newspapers' stock market listings.

Instructions

Write a memo explaining why earnings per share and the price-earnings ratio are so important to investors. Explain how both ratios are calculated and how they relate to each other. Include in your memo an explanation of how to interpret a high or low price-earnings ratio.

Ethics Case

BYP11–7   Flambeau Corporation has paid 60 consecutive quarterly cash dividends (15 years' worth). The last six months have been a real cash drain on the company, however, as profit margins have been greatly narrowed by increasing competition. With a cash balance that is only enough to meet day-to-day operating needs, the president, Vince Ramsey, has decided that a stock dividend instead of a cash dividend should be declared. He tells Flambeau's financial vice-president, Janice Rahn, to issue a press release stating that the company is extending its consecutive dividend record with the declaration of a 5% stock dividend. "Write the press release convincing the shareholders that the stock dividend is just as good as a cash dividend," he orders. "Just watch our share price rise when we announce the stock dividend; it must be a good thing if that happens."

Ethics in Accounting

Instructions

    (a) Who are the stakeholders in this situation?

    (b) Will the share price rise if a stock dividend is declared as the president expects?

    (c) Is there anything unethical about President Ramsey's intentions or actions?

    (d) What is the effect of a stock dividend on a corporation's shareholders' equity accounts? As a shareholder, would you prefer to receive a cash dividend or a stock dividend? Why?

"All About You" Activity

BYP11–8 In this chapter, you learned about equity financing and in Chapter 10 you learned about debt financing.

Instructions

Distinguish among investments in common shares, preferred shares, and bonds in terms of their risk and return to an investor.

Serial Case

(Note: This is a continuation of the serial case from Chapters 1 through 10.)

BYP11–9 Natalie's friend Curtis Lesperance has operated a coffee shop for the past two years as a sole proprietorship. He buys coffee, muffins, and cookies from a local supplier. He now meets with Natalie to discuss the possibility of combining her business, Cookie Creations, with his. As you know, Natalie's business consists of giving cookie-making classes and selling fine European mixers. The plan is for Natalie to use the premises Curtis currently rents as a place to give her cookie-making classes and demonstrations of the mixers that she sells. Natalie will also hire, train, and supervise staff hired to bake cookies and muffins sold in the coffee shop. By offering her classes on the premises, Natalie will save on travel time going from place to place. The coffee shop will also provide one central location for selling the mixers.

    Because Natalie has been so successful with Cookie Creations and Curtis has been just as successful with his coffee shop, they both conclude that they could benefit from each other's business expertise. Curtis will transfer two of his assets (inventory and equipment) into Cookie Creations in exchange for common shares of Cookie Creations.

    On January 1, 2010, Curtis transfers his assets to Cookie Creations at their current fair values as follows: merchandise inventory $400, and equipment $2,500. In exchange, Curtis receives 1,450 Cookie Creations common shares.

The share capital and retained earnings of Cookie Creations at January 1, 2010, after the transfer takes place, are as follows:

Share capital	
$6 cumulative preferred shares, no par value, 10,000 shares authorized, none issued	
Common shares, no par value, unlimited number of shares authorized, 3,250 shares issued	$ 4,700
Retained earnings	12,500

Natalie and Curtis are very excited about combining their two companies. They come to you with the following questions:

1. Curtis's dad and Natalie's grandmother are interested in investing $5,000 each in Cookie Creations. We are considering issuing preferred shares to them. What would be the advantage of issuing the preferred shares instead of common shares?

2. Our lawyer has sent us a bill for $750. When we discussed the bill with her, she said that she would be willing to receive common shares in our corporation instead of cash. We would be happy to issue shares to her, but we are a bit worried about accounting for this transaction. Can we do this? If so, how do we determine how many shares to give her?

Instructions

(a) Answer Natalie and Curtis's questions.

(b) Assume that Cookie Creations issues 1,000 $6 cumulative preferred shares to Curtis's dad and the same number to Natalie's grandmother for $5,000 each on January 2, 2010. Also assume that Cookie Creations issues 375 common shares to its lawyer on the same date. Prepare the journal entries required to record each of these transactions , as well as the transfer of assets from Curtis.

(c) Prepare the shareholders' equity section for Cookie Creations balance sheet as at January 2, 2010, after the transactions are recorded in (b) above.

(d) For the year ended December 31, 2009, Cookie Creations' earnings per share was $11.75. Explain whether you expect Cookie Creations' earnings per share to increase, decrease, or not change in the upcoming year because of the transactions that occurred on January 2, 2010.

Answers to Chapter Questions

Answer to Shoppers Drug Mart Review It Question 3

Shoppers did not repurchase any common shares in 2007 (see Note 11).

Answers to Self-Study Questions

1. c   2. b   3. b   4. a   5. d   6. c   7. b   8. c   9. d   10. c

Remember to go back to the beginning of the chapter to check off your completed work!

←

Comprehensive Case: Chapter 11

QFR Inc. is a fast-growing real estate company owned 100 percent by Flip Roberts. Flip sees significant opportunities to acquire properties, fix them up, and sell them for a profit. There is just one problem: he is not sure how he should raise the money to buy these properties as the banks and mortgage companies are not interested in financing real estate at this time.

Flip has identified properties with great potential for resale that can be bought for $25 million. He is confident that he will be able to resell them within two to three years for $35 million. Flip has identified two possible financing options for QFR to consider: (1) Issue 10% bonds for $25 million or, (2) Issue 500,000 additional common shares for $50 each (for a total of $25 million).

Flip believes the properties will generate an additional $3.75 million of rental revenue with additional expenses of $1 million for depreciation, $375,000 for repairs and maintenance, and $125,000 for other expenses. The income tax rate will remain at 30 percent. The company will have to pay additional interest of $2.5 million if bonds are issued, whereas Flip will have to give up 50 percent of his equity ownership if common shares are issued.

The company's balance sheet and statement of earnings follow:

QFR INC. Balance Sheet December 31, 2009					
Assets			**Liabilities and Shareholders' Equity**		
Current assets			Current liabilities		
Cash		$ 1,000,000	Payables and accruals	$ 80,000	
Accounts receivable		100,000	Current portion of long-term debt	1,420,000	$ 1,500,000
		1,100,000	Long-term liabilities		38,500,000
Property, plant, and equipment			Shareholders' equity		
(net of accumulated depreciation)		48,900,000	Common shares, unlimited number		
Total assets		$50,000,000	authorized, 500,000 issued	$5,000,000	
			Retained earnings	5,000,000	10,000,000
			Total liabilities and shareholders' equity		$50,000,000

QFR INC. Statement of Earnings Year Ended December 31, 2009		
Rental revenue		$7,500,000
Expenses		
Interest	$3,000,000	
Depreciation	2,000,000	
Repairs and maintenance	1,125,000	
Other expenses	375,000	6,500,000
Earnings before income tax		1,000,000
Income tax expense		300,000
Net earnings		$ 700,000
Earnings per share		$1.40

Instructions

(a) Record the purchase of the property for $25 million, assuming the purchase is completed on January 1, 2010, under each of the two financing options identified above.

(b) For option 1 (issue of bonds), record the accrual of 10% interest on the bonds on December 31, 2010, assuming interest is paid annually each January 1.

(c) Prepare the 2010 statement of earnings under each option, using both the amounts recorded in (a) and (b) and the additional revenue and expense information provided above.

(d) Calculate earnings per share and return on common shareholders' equity (using ending equity rather than average equity) before and after each of the two financing options.

(e) Which financing option would you recommend? Explain.

CHAPTER 12

Reporting and Analyzing Investments

ACCOUNTING MATTERS!

Microsoft and Facebook Are Now Friends

Late in 2007, Microsoft Corporation spent a lot of money for just a small part of a much smaller company, leaving many analysts to wonder what was in it for the computer software giant. Since the smaller company is Facebook—one of the fastest-growing websites on the Internet—you can assume the investment involved some kind of strategy.

Microsoft's U.S. $240-million investment in a 1.6-percent stake in Facebook was part of a strategic alliance that the two companies created. It gives Microsoft the exclusive right to sell advertising on Facebook internationally, as well as in the United States. This deal expands on the alliance the companies formed in 2006, naming Microsoft as the exclusive provider of standard banner advertising on Facebook in the United States. And it's not exactly a bad deal when you consider that Facebook is one of the busiest websites on the Internet, and that more than 60 percent of its users are outside the United States.

"The opportunity to further collaborate as advertising partners is a big reason we have decided to take an equity stake," said Kevin Johnson, president of Microsoft's Platforms and Services Division.

It was reported that Yahoo offered Mark Zuckerberg, Facebook's twenty-something founder, U.S. $1 billion for control of the company in 2006, an offer that was declined. A little more than a year later, Microsoft's investment effectively gave the site a market value of U.S. $15 billion.

Microsoft's move could be viewed simply as a good investment. After all, Facebook, which was founded in 2004, is the fastest growing social networking site in the world. Based in Palo Alto, California, Facebook boasts 61 million active users, that is, people who return to the website within 30 days. More than half of these active users return to the site daily, spending on average 20 minutes browsing the site. The number of active users has been doubling every six months, and there has been an average of 250,000 new registrations each day since January 2007.

Still, the investment was much more likely a strategic move in a larger plan to become a major player in the world of Internet advertising. Consider the fact that Microsoft's largest acquisition to date was the U.S. $6-billion purchase of the on-line ad brokering firm aQuantive in May 2007. Joe Doran, the general manager of Microsoft's digital advertising solutions unit, said that Microsoft realized some time ago that much of the future revenue companies will generate from the Internet will come from advertising. "Microsoft is clearly making a bet on on-line services and on advertising and we're clearly saying this is one of the growth revenue streams for us in the future," he noted.

Microsoft's deal with Facebook also nudged out a competitor. Analysts believed Google was considering an investment in Facebook as a way to extend its presence in the search-related advertising market. This would have given the Web-search company the opportunity to add a potentially lucrative part of the on-line ad business to its services.

So Microsoft likely invested in Facebook not only to get its own teeth into this piece of the Internet ad revenue pie, but also to prevent Google from getting a taste as well. Since Microsoft already generates about a quarter million dollars in profit each week, its U.S. $240-million investment in Facebook doesn't appear to be too difficult to swallow.

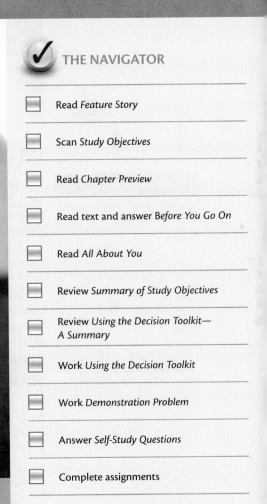

✓ THE NAVIGATOR

▢ Read *Feature Story*

▢ Scan *Study Objectives*

▢ Read *Chapter Preview*

▢ Read text and answer *Before You Go On*

▢ Read *All About You*

▢ Review *Summary of Study Objectives*

▢ Review *Using the Decision Toolkit—A Summary*

▢ Work *Using the Decision Toolkit*

▢ Work *Demonstration Problem*

▢ Answer *Self-Study Questions*

▢ Complete assignments

cebook: facebook.com

STUDY OBJECTIVES

After studying this chapter, you should be able to:

1. Identify reasons to invest, and classify investments.

2. Account for passive investments.

3. Account for strategic investments.

4. Indicate how investments are reported in the financial statements.

5. Compare the accounting for a bond investment and a bond payable (Appendix 12A).

The Navigator

PREVIEW OF CHAPTER 12

Investments can be made by purchasing debt and equity (shares) securities of other companies. Investments can be either passive, where the goal is to generate investment income, or strategic, as was the case with Microsoft's purchase of 1.6 percent of Facebook's shares. As you will see in the chapter, the way in which a company accounts for each of its investments is determined by several factors, including whether the investment is passive or strategic.

The chapter is organized as follows:

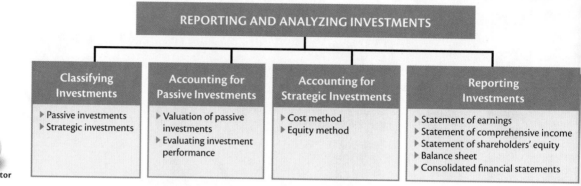

REPORTING AND ANALYZING INVESTMENTS

Classifying Investments	Accounting for Passive Investments	Accounting for Strategic Investments	Reporting Investments
▶ Passive investments ▶ Strategic investments	▶ Valuation of passive investments ▶ Evaluating investment performance	▶ Cost method ▶ Equity method	▶ Statement of earnings ▶ Statement of comprehensive income ▶ Statement of shareholders' equity ▶ Balance sheet ▶ Consolidated financial statements

The Navigator

Classifying Investments

It is common practice for corporations to purchase investments in debt securities and equity securities. **Debt investments** include investments in money-market instruments, as well as investments in bonds, commercial paper, and a large variety of other debt securities available for purchase. **Equity investments** are investments in the share capital—common and/or preferred—of other corporations.

These investments may be made for one of two reasons: as a **passive investment** to generate investment income or as a **strategic investment** to influence or control the operations of another company in some way. While either debt or equity securities can be purchased as a passive investment, equity securities (normally common shares) are what a company purchases for strategic purposes. This is because only common shareholders have voting rights and therefore have influence or control. Preferred shareholders generally do not have voting rights and therefore have no influence or control. These reasons are shown in Illustration 12-1.

Illustration 12-1 ➡

Why corporations invest

Reason	Purpose	Type of Investment
I need 1,000 treasury bills by tonight. Passive investment	To generate investment income	Debt securities (money-market instruments, bonds, commercial paper) and equity securities (preferred and common shares)
Strategic investment	To influence or control another company	Equity securities (common shares)

Passive Investments

There are several reasons for a company to purchase debt or equity securities of another company as a passive investment. A corporation may have **excess cash** that it does not immediately need. For example, many companies have seasonal fluctuations in their sales levels, which can lead to idle cash until purchases are made for the next busy season. Until the cash is needed, the excess funds may be invested to earn a greater return than would be realized by just holding the funds in the company's chequing account.

When investing excess cash for short periods of time, corporations generally invest in debt securities, usually money-market instruments that are low-risk and high liquidity. Examples include money-market funds, bankers' acceptances, term deposits, and treasury bills. It is usually not wise to invest short-term excess cash in equity securities. If the price of the shares drops just before the company needs the cash again, it will be forced to sell its investment at a loss. Money-market instruments do not change in value. Their value arises from the interest they generate.

Excess cash may also be invested for the longer term to **generate investment revenue**. Companies generate interest revenue from debt securities and dividend revenue from some equity securities. Recall from Chapter 11 that there is no obligation for a company to pay dividends on its shares. Most companies buy preferred shares of companies that have a stable dividend policy if they are trying to generate dividend revenue.

A company can also invest in debt and equity securities with the hope of later selling at a higher price than it originally paid for them. The company speculates that the investment will increase in value and result in a gain when sold.

Passive investments can be further classified as either held-for-trading, available-for-sale, or held-to-maturity investments. They can be a **short-term investment**, classified as a current asset on the balance sheet, or a **long-term investment**. Illustration 12-2 summarizes these classifications.

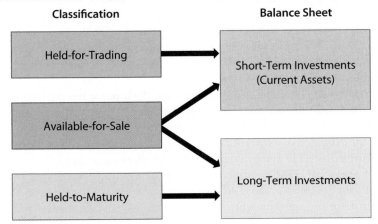

Classification	Balance Sheet
Held-for-Trading	Short-Term Investments (Current Assets)
Available-for-Sale	
Held-to-Maturity	Long-Term Investments

◀ Illustration 12-2

Classification of passive investments

As we will learn in the next few sections, held-for-trading securities are always short-term and held-to-maturity securities are always long-term (unless they mature within the next year). The determination of whether an available-for-sale security is short- or long-term depends on management's intent or purpose, whether the investment can be promptly liquidated, and whether a value for the investment can be reliably determined.

We will discuss the classification of passive investments in the following sections. Strategic investments will be discussed in a later section.

Held-for-Trading (HFT) Securities

Held-for-trading (HFT) securities are debt or equity securities that are purchased with the objective of generating a profit from short-term price fluctuations. Trading securities are always classified as current assets. Interestingly, management intent is not a factor in classifying these securities. An investment can still be classified as HFT even if the company does not *intend* to sell it within a year, which is our normal definition of a current asset (i.e., intending to sell it within a year). The key for their classification instead is that the securities in this category are part of a strategy of active and frequent buying and selling. Trading securities are often found in financial institutions, such as banks, which actively manage an investment portfolio as part of their normal business operations.

Any debt or equity security can be designated by management as a held-for-trading security when purchased (as long as it meets the above criteria). Once an initial classification is made, securities cannot be transferred into or out of the HFT category.

Throughout this chapter, we will illustrate the reporting of investments by Clarke Inc., a diversified investment company based in Halifax, Nova Scotia. Included among Clarke's HFT investments are certain marketable securities acquired principally for the purpose of generating a profit in the near (i.e., short) term.

Alternative Terminology
Held-for-trading securities are also called *marketable securities* or *temporary investments*.

Available-for-Sale (AFS) Securities

The definition of available-for-sale (AFS) securities is expressed by what they are not. Thus, the category includes those investments that are not classified as held-for-trading or held-to-maturity (which will be discussed in the next section). The name of the category "available-for-sale" can be a little misleading as AFS investments can include investments that the investor does not intend to sell in the near term. While held-for-trading securities are always considered to be short-term investments, available-for-sale securities can be either short- or long-term, depending on whether they can be promptly liquidated and on management's intent.

Clarke Inc. reports its AFS investments in both the current and long-term categories. It reports marketable securities as current assets, which include investment funds and share and trust units. Other AFS investments—investment funds—are included with Clarke's long-term investments. Later in this chapter, we will see detailed illustrations of how Clarke reports these on its balance sheet.

These three types of investments—held-for-trading, available-for-sale, and held-to-maturity—are known as financial instruments. You will recall that financial instruments were first introduced in Chapters 10 and 11. Financial instruments are contracts that result in, or create, a financial asset of one company and a financial liability or equity instrument of another company. Financial instruments make up a broad category that includes, but is not limited to, debt and equity investments. In the case of investments, the contract establishes financial rights to receive cash or another financial asset. They are marketable or tradeable, and relatively easy to measure. While we do discuss debt and equity investments here, discussion of other types of financial assets and investments is left for an intermediate accounting course.

Held-to-Maturity (HTM) Securities

Held-to-maturity (HTM) securities are debt securities that the investor has the intention and ability to hold to maturity. Held-to-maturity securities are always classified as long-term investments, except when they are less than one year from maturity. When long-term investments are expected to come due within a year, they then fit the definition of a current asset and are therefore classified as a short-term investment. Shares cannot be classified as HTM as they do not have a maturity or due date.

An example of a personal HTM investment would be the mortgage you or your parents owe on the family home. From your perspective, the mortgage is debt or a liability. To the financial institution that leant you the money, this mortgage represents an asset. This long-term asset may be classified as a held-to-maturity investment or as a loan receivable.

Strategic Investments

Although both debt and equity securities can be purchased as passive investments, only equity securities (normally common shares) can be purchased for the strategic purpose of influencing relationships between companies. For example, a company may acquire common shares of another company in order to use the shares' voting rights to exercise some influence or control. In the case of Facebook, described in our feature story, Microsoft invested in its shares in order to influence the development of a strategic advertising alliance.

The degree of influence determines how a strategic investment is classified. We will learn more about the degree of influence and how it affects the classification of an investment later in this chapter. Note also that while passive investments can be either short- or long-term, strategic investments can only be long-term.

ACCOUNTING MATTERS! | Management Perspective

Acquisitions of Canadian companies set a new record in 2007 with 1,941 strategic investments totalling $270 billion during the year. Of these, 1,083 were domestic—Canadian companies buying Canadian companies. The biggest investment that year was Rio Tinto's $40-billion acquisition of Alcan, creating the world's largest aluminum company. "While growing concerns about the economic outlook together with the ongoing credit crunch are certainly hurting the [mergers and acquisition] market, overall activity levels have remained respectable by historical standards," said Ian Macdonell, managing director of Crosbie & Company.

Source: Canadian M&A Activity, Crosbie & Company Inc. news release, February 21, 2008

BEFORE YOU GO ON...

Review It

1. What are the reasons that corporations invest in debt and equity securities?
2. Distinguish between passive and strategic investments.
3. What is necessary in order for an investment to be classified as held-for-trading? Held-to-maturity?
4. How do you determine if an available-for-sale investment is a current or a long-term asset?

Do It

Match each of the investments described below with one of the three types of passive investments.

_____ (a) Investment in treasury bills, purchased for interest income
_____ (b) Investment in Microsoft common shares, intended to be sold when the price rises 10 percent above cost
_____ (c) Investment in Bombardier 20-year bonds, intended to be held for 20 years
_____ (d) Investment in Loblaw common shares, intended to be sold next year

1. Held-for-trading securities
2. Available-for-sale securities
3. Held-to-maturity securities

Action Plan

• Recall the definitions of HFT, AFS, and HTM securities:
  ○ HFT securities are debt and equity securities held mainly for sale in the near term to generate a profit on short-term price fluctuations.
  ○ AFS securities are debt and equity securities that are not classified as HFT or HTM.
  ○ HTM securities are debt securities that are intended to be held until they mature.

Solution

(a) 2   (b) 1   (c) 3   (d) 2

The Navigator

Accounting for Passive Investments

At acquisition, debt and equity investments are recorded at their purchase cost. Transaction costs, such as brokerage fees, are sometimes incurred when investments are purchased. Companies can choose to either expense or capitalize transaction costs on available-for-sale or held-to-maturity securities, but they must expense transaction costs on held-for-trading securities. For simplicity, we will ignore the accounting for transaction costs in this textbook and leave it to an intermediate accounting course.

Although purchase cost is the same as fair value at the date of acquisition, this value may rise and fall greatly during the time debt and equity investments are held. Bond and share prices may jump dramatically with favourable economic events and drop drastically with unfavourable conditions. For example, in the 52 weeks ended in early April 2008, Clarke's share price ranged in value from a low of $5.55 per share to a high of more than twice that amount. This was during a time when the investment market had weakened in response to, among other things, changes in commodity prices and foreign exchange rates. If prices can change so much, an important question arises: How should passive investments be valued at the balance sheet date—at fair value or at cost?

study objective 2
Account for passive investments.

Valuation of Passive Investments

Whether fair value or cost should be used to value debt or equity securities that are held as passive investments depends on the classification of the security. You will recall that we learned earlier in the chapter that there are three categories of securities:

1. **Held-for-trading securities** are securities held mainly to generate profits on short-term price fluctuations.
2. **Available-for-sale securities** are securities that are not classified as held-to-maturity investments or held-for-trading investments.
3. **Held-to-maturity securities** are debt securities that the investor has the intention and ability to hold to maturity.

Their valuation, and the reasoning behind it, are as follows. Held-for-trading and available-for-sale securities are valued at fair value, while held-to-maturity securities are valued at cost. Because held-for-trading and available-for-sale securities are purchased for the purpose of resale, it makes sense to value them at the amount of cash that is expected to be received from selling them (their fair value). The advantage of doing this is that it allows users to better assess the impact of changing prices on a company's liquidity and solvency. In addition, the value of these types of investments can be easily obtained. This does not mean that the prices will not change again; rather, it simply means that at any specific point in time, fair value can be objectively determined from market quotes.

Illustration 12-3 shows these valuation guidelines.

Illustration 12-3

Recognition and measurement criteria

Note that the above guidelines apply to all debt investments. The held-for-trading and available-for-sale classifications apply to passive equity investments. The available-for-sale classification also applies to strategic equity investments where there is no significant influence or control. When there is significant influence or control, the accounting for strategic equity investments differs, as we will learn later in this chapter.

Held-for-Trading Securities

Since held-for-trading securities are purchased with the intention of selling them to make a profit on short-term price changes, it is not surprising that they are valued at fair value, as shown in Illustration 12-3. This valuation approach is also referred to as mark-to-market accounting.

When investments are valued at their fair value (whether they are held for trading or are available for sale, as we will see in the next section), any increase or decrease in the market prices changes the asset value reported on the balance sheet, with a corresponding gain or loss. The difference between cost (or carrying amount) and fair value while an investment is held is called an unrealized gain or loss. This is distinguished from a realized gain or loss, which is the real gain or loss that results when the investment is actually sold.

To illustrate the valuation of held-for-trading securities, assume that on December 31, 2009, Plano Corporation has the following costs and fair values for its held-for-trading securities:

HFT Securities	Cost	Fair Value	Unrealized Gain (Loss)
Bell Canada bonds	$ 50,000	$ 48,000	$(2,000)
Norbord shares	90,000	95,000	5,000
Total	$140,000	$143,000	$3,000

Plano has an overall unrealized gain of $3,000 because the total fair value ($143,000) is $3,000 greater than the total cost ($140,000). Its held-for-trading securities would be reported at $143,000 at December 31 in the current assets section of the balance sheet. In addition, Plano would report an unrealized gain of $3,000 as other revenue in its statement of earnings. **Note that unrealized gains and losses for held-for-trading securities are reported in exactly the same way as realized gains and losses.**

The adjustment of the HFT securities to fair value and the recognition of any unrealized gain or loss is usually done through an adjusting journal entry at year end. The adjusting entry for Plano is:

A	=	L	+	SE
+3,000				+3,000

Cash flows: no effect

Dec. 31	HFT Investments	3,000	
	Unrealized Gain—HFT		3,000
	(To record unrealized gain on held-for-trading securities)		

Note that this entry assumes that it is the entire portfolio of securities that is adjusted—not individual securities. It would be equally correct to prepare separate entries for each of the two HFT securities listed on the previous page.

If, early in January, Plano sells its Bell Canada bonds for $48,000, the following journal entry would be recorded:

Jan. 5	Cash	48,000	
	HFT Investments—Bell Canada Bonds		48,000
	(To record sale of HFT Bell Canada bonds)		

A = L + SE
+48,000
−48,000
⬆ Cash flows +48,000

Although the Bell Canada bonds originally cost $50,000, because they were written down to their fair value of $48,000 on December 31, the new cost base is $48,000. Consequently, the investment account is credited for that amount.

If the bonds had been sold for $47,000 instead of $48,000, then a realized loss of $1,000 ($48,000 − $47,000) would have also been recorded. In other words, a loss of $2,000 ($50,000 − $48,000) would have been recorded in the last period when that loss occurred. A further loss of $1,000 would then be recorded in this period, again in the same period as when the loss occurs.

Available-for-Sale Securities

As indicated earlier, available-for-sale securities are also valued at fair value at year end. The procedure for determining and recording any change in value and resulting unrealized gain or loss on these securities is the same as for held-for-trading securities.

To illustrate, assume that Plano also has available-for-sale securities as follows:

AFS Securities	Cost	Fair Value	Unrealized Gain (Loss)
Bombardier shares	$ 80,000	$ 64,000	$(16,000)
Bank of Montreal shares	150,000	146,000	(4,000)
Total	$230,000	$210,000	$(20,000)

Plano has an unrealized loss in its AFS investment portfolio of $20,000 because the total fair value ($210,000) is $20,000 less than the total cost ($230,000). The adjusting entry to record this loss for Plano would be as follows:

Dec. 31	Unrealized Loss—AFS (OCI)	20,000	
	AFS Investments		20,000
	(To record unrealized loss on available-for-sale securities)		

A = L + SE
−20,000
−20,000
Cash flows: no effect

Plano's available-for-sale securities would be reported at $210,000 at December 31 in the balance sheet. Recall that AFS securities can be classified as either current or long-term assets, depending on management's intent and whether or not the securities can be liquidated promptly. In this particular case, management has classified these securities as long-term investments.

In addition to the above, Plano would report its unrealized loss of $20,000 as other comprehensive income (commonly abbreviated as OCI). While the valuation of HFT and AFS securities is similar, the reporting of an unrealized gain or loss is different. There is a reporting difference because, while held-for-trading securities will likely be sold in the near term, available-for-sale securities may or may not be sold in the near term. Thus, before the actual sale of AFS securities, it is more likely that changes in value may reverse any unrealized gain or loss at a specific point in time. Consequently, an unrealized gain or loss on AFS securities is not reported as part of net earnings, contrary to the practice for HFT securities. Instead, unrealized gains and losses on AFS securities are separately reported as other comprehensive income.

As we learned in Chapter 11, **comprehensive income** includes all changes to shareholders' equity during a period, except changes resulting from investments by shareholders and dividends. Net earnings is a major component of comprehensive income, with other comprehensive income (such as unrealized gains and losses for AFS securities and other items) making up the remainder.

The statement of comprehensive income reports net earnings for the period in addition to other comprehensive income. Illustration 12-4 presents a sample statement of comprehensive income for Plano Corporation, using assumed data.

Illustration 12-4 ➡

Statement of comprehensive income

PLANO CORPORATION Statement of Comprehensive Income Year Ended December 31, 2009	
Net earnings	$651,000
Other comprehensive income (loss)	
Unrealized loss on available-for-sale securities	(20,000)
Comprehensive income	$631,000

As was just shown, unrealized gains and losses on AFS securities are first recorded as increases or decreases to other comprehensive income. When an AFS security that changed OCI is later sold, the total of its changes to OCI must be reversed from OCI, and the AFS account adjusted for any previously recorded unrealized gains and losses. To be able to make such reversals, it is essential to know the original cost, and any adjustments, for the specific security. It is therefore important to keep individual subsidiary records that track each security's original cost and any adjustments.

These individual subsidiary records are maintained as follows. At each year end, the carrying amount of each individual AFS security is compared to its fair value. Adjustments are then made to revalue the security at that year end. Later, when the security is sold, any unrealized gains or losses must first be reversed from OCI before the actual realized gain or loss can be calculated and recorded.

To illustrate, assume that in 2010, Plano sells its Bank of Montreal shares for $149,000. Recall that the shares originally cost $150,000 but had been written down to their fair value of $146,000 at the end of 2009, as shown in the following T account:

AFS Investment—Bank of Montreal			
Bal. Jan. 1, 2009	150,000	Adj. Dec. 31, 2009	4,000
Bal. Dec. 31, 2009	146,000		

The $4,000 unrealized loss that was recorded in 2009 must now be removed from other comprehensive income, and the realized loss, which is actually $1,000 ($150,000 cost – $149,000 selling price), must be recorded. The following journal entry is therefore necessary on the date of sale:

A	=	L	+	SE
+149,000				−1,000
−146,000				+4,000

⬆ Cash flows: +149,000

Feb. 2	Cash	149,000	
	Realized Loss—AFS	1,000	
	Unrealized Loss—AFS (OCI)		4,000
	AFS Investments—Bank of Montreal Shares		146,000
	(To record sale of AFS Bank of Montreal shares)		

The realized loss would then be reported on the statement of earnings as other expense. The unrealized loss would be reported as an adjustment to other comprehensive income on the statement of comprehensive income.

Held-to-Maturity Securities

Only debt securities are classified as held-to-maturity; equity securities have no maturity date. A debt security is classified as held-to-maturity if the investor has the intention and ability to hold the investment until it matures. If the company intends to hold the security until it matures and has no plans to sell it, then fair values are irrelevant. Consequently, these investments are valued at cost, and their values are not adjusted for changes in fair value.

We usually say that held-to-maturity investments are valued at their *amortized* cost, because any premiums or discounts included in the investment account must be amortized. You will recall that we learned about premiums (when bonds are purchased above face value) and discounts (when bonds are purchased below face value) in Chapter 10. We also learned about using the effective-interest method to amortize these premiums and discounts. Further information about accounting for investments in bonds with premiums and discounts is detailed in Appendix 12A and compared to the accounting for bonds payable.

You will recall that we learned about impairment losses in Chapter 9. Like many other long-term assets, HTM investments are evaluated at year-end to determine if they are impaired. If the fair value falls below cost and the decline is considered permanent, then (and only then) will a held-to-maturity debt security be adjusted to its fair value. This value becomes the debt investment's new amortized cost base. Any write-down to fair value results in a debit to an impairment loss account and a credit to the investment (or contra allowance) account. International accounting standards allow the reversal of such a write-down in certain circumstances, although this rarely occurs.

The following summarizes the valuation and reporting of passive investments discussed in this section. Held-for-trading and available-for-sale investments are carried at fair value. Held-to-maturity investments are carried at amortized cost. Realized gains and losses are reported on the statement of earnings as other revenue for all types of securities. Unrealized gains and losses are reported as other revenue (expense) on the statement of earnings for held-for-trading securities and as other comprehensive income on the statement of comprehensive income for available-for-sale securities.

Illustration 12-5 summarizes the valuation and reporting of these investments after acquisition.

Passive Investment	Valuation Subsequent to Acquisition	Reporting of Unrealized Gains and Losses
Held-for-trading	Fair value	Other revenue (expense) (statement of earnings)
Available-for-sale	Fair value	Other comprehensive income (statement of comprehensive income)
Held-to-maturity	Amortized cost (unless permanent decline in value below cost)	Not applicable

◀ Illustration 12-5

Valuation of passive investments after acquisition

In some instances, for the year-end valuation of securities, it may not be possible to obtain a reliable value. This is true for investments in the shares of a private company. The requirement in such cases is that the investment be reported as available for sale. A note to the financial statements would explain that these AFS securities were being reported at cost due to the absence of a quoted price in an active stock market.

Evaluating Investment Performance

We have learned that whether fair value or cost is used to value investments depends on the classification of the security—as held-for-trading, available-for-sale, or held-to-maturity—and that companies can choose which category to use for each investment. Choosing the original classification of a security requires a substantial amount of management judgement. In addition, as held-for-trading and available-for-sale securities are recorded at fair value, changing values can have a significant impact on the financial position and performance of the company.

The statement on which realized and unrealized gains and losses are recorded can also affect the evaluation of a company's performance. Realized and unrealized gains and losses on held-for-trading securities are reported in the statement of earnings, while only realized gains and losses are reported in this statement for available-for-sale and held-to-maturity securities. You may wonder why it matters whether a gain or loss is reported in the statement of earnings or as other comprehensive income in the statement of comprehensive income. After all, both affect shareholders' equity—whether realized or unrealized—and the information is fully reported and disclosed. Investors do not usually pay as much attention to comprehensive income as to net earnings. In addition, ratio analyses, such as the ones that we have learned so far in this textbook, use net earnings rather than comprehensive income in their formulas.

Although it may be tempting to think about how one could manage earnings by reclassifying investments from one category to another (since HFT securities affect net earnings and AFS securities do not), if companies could move securities from one classification to another at a whim, the credibility of financial reporting would be greatly reduced. It is not surprising, therefore, that there are specified restrictions to minimize this possibility. Companies are generally prohibited from reclassifying held-for-trading and held-to-maturity securities except in rare circumstances.

In the fall of 2008, at a time when financial markets around the world were experiencing record declines in value, companies were permitted to reclassify certain investments in specified circumstances. This allowed companies to delay write-downs to fair value unless or until the investments were determined to be permanently impaired.

Whether an available-for-sale security is classified as short- or long-term will also impact the presentation of a company's results. As this decision depends primarily on management intent, it too is a subjective determination. In addition, economic circumstances can change for a company, which may require management to change the intended timing of the sale of an investment. Consequently, companies are required at least annually to reassess their intent for an investment and their ability to hold it.

▶ Reporting and Analyzing Investments

Because of all the judgement required with respect to the classification and valuation of investments, it is important to recognize that the potential for earnings management exists. Companies can easily "window dress" their reported earnings results—that is, make net earnings look better or worse than they really are—if they want to do so. For example, if a company wanted to increase its reported earnings, it could simply sell its available-for-sale securities that have unrealized gains and not sell its available-for-sale securities that have unrealized losses. By doing this, the company would realize its gains and report them in the statement of earnings, thus increasing net earnings. It would report its unrealized losses in the statement of comprehensive income, thus deferring the recognition of the losses until a later period.

Sometimes unrealized losses on available-for-sale securities can be significant. For example, for the year ended December 31, 2007, Clarke Inc. reported net earnings of $64 million. It also reported $22.5 million in unrealized losses on its available-for-sale securities as a reduction to other comprehensive income. If these securities had been sold before year end, net earnings would have declined by $22.5 million, or 35 percent. Clearly, when the performance of a company's investment portfolio is being evaluated, it is important to consider the impact of both actual and potential gains and losses on current and future earnings.

ACCOUNTING MATTERS! | Investor Perspective

In early 2008, the stock market was at its most volatile in 60 years. The credit crunch, fears of a recession, subprime investment write-downs, and other market uncertainties caused big swings in share prices, both up and down. This caused great difficulties for companies reporting investments at fair value, resulting in extremely volatile earnings.

Mark Carney, governor of the Bank of Canada, commented on the potential for earnings management in such conditions: "By reflecting market moves, fair value accounting certainly increases the volatility of reported earnings. Whether it contributes pro-cyclically to market volatility depends on the behaviour of management. Management's incentive to realize mark-to-market losses depends not only on their expectations of future market moves but also, importantly, on the extent to which investors reward them for capping downside risk or penalize them for higher book leverage caused by unrealized losses."

Source: Mark Carney, "Addressing Financial Market Turbulence," speech given to the Toronto Board of Trade, Toronto, March 13, 2008

DECISION TOOLKIT

Decision Checkpoints	Info Needed for Decision	Tools to Use for Decision	How to Evaluate Results
Is the company window dressing its results by manipulating its investment portfolio?	Balance of unrealized gains and losses; classification of AFS investments	A company can window dress by selling AFS winners and holding AFS losers to increase reported earnings, or doing the opposite to reduce reported earnings. Misclassification of investments as available-for-sale allows companies to "time" (advance or defer) the recognition of losses.	Window dressing and misclassification are not easy to spot: it is difficult for an outsider to determine why companies choose to sell or hold securities, or classify them as they do. A user should evaluate a company's earnings as reported, including any unrealized gains and losses, to see the total valuation.

BEFORE YOU GO ON...

➡ **Review It**

1. What is the proper valuation for (a) held-for-trading securities, (b) available-for-sale securities, and (c) held-to-maturity securities?
2. Distinguish between the journal entries that are made to record realized gains and losses and unrealized gains and losses for (a) held-for-trading securities, (b) available-for-sale securities, and (c) held-to-maturity securities.

3. Distinguish between the reporting of unrealized gains and losses for held-for-trading securities and available-for-sale securities.
4. How might a company window dress its reported earnings using its available-for-sale securities?

Do It

Wang Corporation had the following transactions:

Jan.	2	Purchased an investment in Hillary Corp. bonds for $30,400 as a held-for-trading investment.
July	1	Received semi-annual interest on the Hillary bonds, $750.
	2	Sold half of the investment in Hillary bonds for $14,250.
Dec.	31	The remaining Hillary bonds are worth $15,000 on this date.

(a) Record the above transactions.
(b) Prepare the adjusting entry for the valuation of the investment on December 31, Wang's year end.
(c) Identify where each account would be reported and on what financial statement.

Action Plan

• Record the held-for-trading investment initially at cost.
• When the investment is sold, record any difference between the cost of the bonds and the proceeds as a realized gain or loss: Gain = proceeds > cost. Loss = proceeds < cost.
• When the investment is adjusted for any change in value, record any difference between the cost of the bonds and the fair value as an unrealized gain or loss.
• Report interest revenue and both realized and unrealized gains (losses) as other revenue (expense) on the statement of earnings.

Solution

(a)

Jan.	2	HFT Investment—Hillary Bonds	30,400	
		Cash		30,400
		(To record purchase of Hillary Corp. bonds)		
July	1	Cash	750	
		Interest Revenue		750
		(To record receipt of semi-annual interest on Hillary bonds)		
	2	Cash	14,250	
		Realized Loss—HFT	950	
		HFT Investment—Hillary Bonds ($30,400 × ½)		15,200
		(To record sale of half of Hillary bonds)		

(b)

Dec.	31	Unrealized Loss—HFT ($15,200 – $15,000)	200	
		HFT Investment—Hillary Bonds		200
		(To record unrealized loss on held-for-trading securities)		

(c) Cash and the HFT Investment accounts would be reported as current assets on the balance sheet. Interest Revenue, Realized Loss, and Unrealized Loss would be reported as other revenue (expense) on the statement of earnings.

The Navigator

Accounting for Strategic Investments

An investor who owns common shares has the potential to strategically influence the investee. The **investor** is the company that purchases (owns) the securities. The **investee** is the company that issues (sells) the securities. The accounting for equity investments in common shares is based on how much influence the investor has over the operating, investing, and financial affairs of the investee.

Illustration 12-6 presents the guidelines for the levels of influence.

Illustration 12-6 ➡

Accounting guidelines for
equity investments

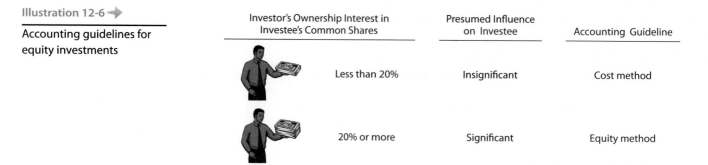

Investor's Ownership Interest in Investee's Common Shares	Presumed Influence on Investee	Accounting Guideline
Less than 20%	Insignificant	Cost method
20% or more	Significant	Equity method

As we will soon see, the cost method refers to how income is reported, not how the investment is valued on the balance sheet. As noted in Illustration 12-6, if the investor owns less than 20% of the investee's common shares, it uses the cost method to account for any investment income.

When an investor owns 20 percent or more of the common shares of another company, the investor is generally presumed to have a significant influence over the decisions of the investee company. The presumed influence may be cancelled by other circumstances, however. For example, a company that acquires a 25-percent interest in another company in a "hostile" takeover may not have any significant influence over the investee.

Among the questions that should be considered in determining an investor's influence are (1) whether the investor has representation on the investee's board of directors, (2) whether the investor participates in the investee's policy-making process, (3) whether there are material transactions between the investor and the investee, and (4) whether the common shares held by other shareholders are concentrated or dispersed. Companies are required to use judgement instead of blindly following the guidelines. We will now learn about and show the application of each guideline.

Cost Method

The **cost method** is used to account for equity investments where there is no significant influence (normally holdings of less than 20 percent). Under this method, the investment is recorded at its original purchase cost on the acquisition date. As explained earlier in the chapter, "cost" is the same as fair value at acquisition.

Under the cost method, the investor records investment income when the investee decides to pay dividends on the common shares. The equity investment in common shares is reported on the balance sheet at the fair value of those shares. This value is reviewed and adjusted, as required, at each reporting date.

The accounting for equity investments using the cost method is identical regardless of whether the investment is short-term or long-term. Strategic equity investments that have no significant influence are normally classified as available-for-sale investments. While the possibility exists for these investments to be classified as held-for-trading, it would be an unlikely classification for a strategic investment. Microsoft's acquisition of 1.6 percent of Facebook's shares would be classified as a long-term, available-for-sale equity investment.

Recording Acquisitions of Shares

At acquisition, the cost of the investment is the price paid to acquire the equity securities. Assume, for example, that on July 1, 2009, Passera Corporation (the investor) acquires 1,000 common shares of Beal Corporation (the investee) at $40 per share. If Beal has a total of 10,000 common shares, then Passera has a 10-percent (1,000 ÷ 10,000) ownership interest in Beal. Assume also that Passera plans to hold these securities as an available-for-sale investment. This investment would thus be recorded using the cost method, since it is unlikely that there is significant influence.

The entry to record the acquisition of the Beal shares is as follows:

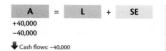

July 1	AFS Investment—Beal Common	40,000	
	Cash		40,000
	(To record purchase of 1,000 common shares of Beal)		

This investment would be reported as a current asset on the balance sheet if it is capable of prompt liquidation and management intends to sell it in the near term. This is unlikely in the case of a strategic investment. More often, it would be classified as a long-term investment on the balance sheet.

While the investor, Passera Corporation, must make an entry to record this acquisition, no entry is required by Beal Corporation. Recall that, after shares have been issued, they are only traded among investors. In other words, Passera did not purchase these shares directly from Beal. It purchased them from investors on organized stock exchanges, such as the TMX Group (TSX).

Recording Dividend Revenue

During the time the shares are held, entries are required for any cash dividends that are received. If a $2-per-share dividend is received by Passera Corporation on October 1, the entry is:

Oct. 1	Cash (1,000 × $2)	2,000	
	Dividend Revenue		2,000
	(To record receipt of cash dividend)		

Dividend revenue is reported as other revenue in the statement of earnings.

Recording Sales of Shares

When shares are sold, the difference between the net proceeds from the sale and the cost of the shares is recognized as a realized gain or loss. Assume that Passera Corporation receives net proceeds of $39,000 on the sale of its Beal Corporation shares on December 10. Because the shares cost $40,000, a loss of $1,000 has been realized. The entry to record the sale is:

Dec. 10	Cash	39,000	
	Realized Loss—AFS	1,000	
	AFS Investment—Beal Common		40,000
	(To record sale of Beal common shares)		

The loss is reported as other expenses in the statement of earnings. A gain on sale would have been reported as other revenues.

If the shares had not been sold on December 10, the cost (or carrying amount) would have been adjusted to the fair value at year end. Any difference between the fair value and the carrying amount would be recorded as an unrealized gain or loss. You will recall that unrealized gains and losses on available-for-sale securities are reported as other comprehensive income in the statement of comprehensive income.

Because this investment was actually sold on December 10, in the same year it was purchased, there was no previously recorded unrealized gain or loss. If this investment had been sold subsequent to year end, in addition to recording the realized loss as shown above, any previously recorded OCI would also have to be reversed as shown earlier in the chapter.

Equity Method

When an investor owns only a small portion of the common shares of another company, the investor cannot control the investee in any way. But when an investor owns at least 20 percent of the common shares of a corporation, it is presumed that the investor has significant influence over the investee's financial and operating activities and plans to hold this investment for the long term. The investor also probably has a representative on the investee's board of directors and begins to exercise some control over the investee through that representative. The investee company, to some extent, becomes part of the investor company.

Of course, when an investor owns more than 50 percent of the common shares of a corporation, it has more than significant influence—it has control. Either way, when an investor owns 20 percent or more of the common shares of another company, unless there is other evidence to the contrary, it will be able to exercise significant influence or total control over the investee. In these circumstances, the equity method is used to account for the investment. Consequently, if an investment is for strategic purposes and the investor has significant influence or control, you will never find it classified as AFS and recorded at fair value. It will be recorded using the equity method. On the other hand, if the investment results in no control or influence but is still for strategic purposes, as was the case with Microsoft's acquisition of 1.6 percent of Facebook in our feature story, then the investment would normally be recorded as an available-for-sale investment and carried at fair value, as shown in Illustration 12-7.

Illustration 12-7 ➡

Accounting for strategic investments

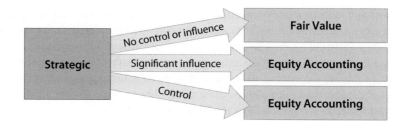

At December 31, 2007, Clarke Inc. used the equity method to account for its investment in Midlake Oil and Gas Limited, over which it had significant influence. Under the equity method, the investment is initially recorded at cost. After that, the investment account is adjusted annually to show the investor's equity in the investee. That is, the investor records its share of the net earnings of the investee in the year the earnings occur. Each year therefore, Clarke reports its share of Midlake Oil and Gas Limited's net earnings. An alternative might be to delay recognizing the investor's share of net earnings until a cash dividend is received or declared. But that approach would ignore the fact that the investor and investee are, in some sense, one company, and that the investor therefore benefits from, and can influence the timing of, the distribution of the investee's earnings.

To keep its records up to date, each year the investor adjusts the investment account to:

> **Helpful Hint**
> Under the equity method, revenue is recognized on the accrual basis—i.e., when it is earned by the investee.

1. **Record its share of the investee's net earnings (loss):** This is done by increasing (debiting) the investment account and increasing (crediting) revenue for the investor's share of the investee's net earnings. Conversely, when the investee has a net loss, the investor increases (debits) a loss account and decreases (credits) the investment account for its share of the investee's net loss.
2. **Record the dividends received:** This is done by decreasing (crediting) the investment account for the amount of any dividends received. The investment account is reduced for dividends received because the net assets of the investee are decreased when a dividend is paid.

We will now illustrate the equity method, using two fictitious companies, Milar Corporation and Beck Inc.

Recording Acquisitions of Shares

Beck Inc. has 10,000 common shares issued in total. Assume that on January 1, 2009, Milar Corporation (the investor) acquires 30 percent, or 3,000 common shares, of Beck (the investee) for $120,000 cash or $40 per share. Milar is assumed to have significant influence over Beck and will use the equity method to account for this transaction. The entry to record this investment is:

A	=	L	+	SE
+120,000				
−120,000				

⬇ Cash flows: −120,000

Jan. 1	Equity Investment—Beck Common	120,000	
	Cash		120,000
	(To record purchase of Beck common shares)		

Recording Investment Revenue

Now assume that for the year ended December 31, 2009, Beck reports net earnings of $100,000 and declares and pays a $40,000 cash dividend. At December 31, 2009, Beck's common shares were trading at $42 each. Milar is required to record (1) its share of Beck's earnings, $30,000 (30% × $100,000), and (2) the reduction in the investment account for the dividends received, $12,000 ($40,000 × 30%). The entries are as follows:

A	=	L	+	SE
+30,000				+30,000

Cash flows: no effect

		(1)		
Dec. 31	Equity Investment—Beck Common		30,000	
	Revenue from Investment in Beck			30,000
	(To record 30% equity in Beck's net earnings)			

A	=	L	+	SE
+12,000				
−12,000				

⬆ Cash flows: +12,000

		(2)		
Dec. 31	Cash		12,000	
	Equity Investment—Beck Common			12,000
	(To record dividends received)			

No entry is required under the equity method for the increase in the fair value of the shares (from $40 to $42 per share). After the above transactions are posted, the investment and revenue accounts show the following:

Equity Investment—Beck Common				
Jan. 1	120,000	Dec. 31	12,000	
Dec. 31	30,000			
Bal. Dec. 31	138,000			

Revenue from Equity Investment in Beck		
	Dec. 31	30,000

During the year, the investment account has increased by $18,000 ($30,000 – $12,000). This $18,000 is Milar's 30-percent equity in the $60,000 increase in Beck's retained earnings ($100,000 – $40,000). In addition, Milar will report $30,000 of revenue from its investment, which is 30 percent of Beck's net earnings of $100,000.

The difference between reported earnings under the cost method and under the equity method can be significant. Illustration 12-8 compares the journal entries used to record these investment transactions under the cost and equity methods. On the left-hand side of the illustration, we assume that Milar had no significant influence over Beck and used the cost method. On the right-hand side of the illustration, we assume that Milar did have significant influence over Beck and used the equity method (as we just illustrated in this section).

Cost Method			Equity Method		
Acquisition			*Acquisition*		
AFS Investment—Beck Common	120,000		Equity Investment—Beck Common	120,000	
Cash		120,000	Cash		120,000
Investee reports net earnings			*Investee reports net earnings*		
No entry			Equity Investment—Beck Common	30,000	
			Revenue from Equity Investment in Beck		30,000
Investee pays dividends			*Investee pays dividends*		
Cash	12,000		Cash	12,000	
Dividend Revenue		12,000	Equity Investment—Beck Common		12,000
Adjustment to fair value			*Adjustment to fair value*		
AFS Investment—Beck Common	6,000		No entry		
Unrealized Gain—AFS (OCI)		6,000			

Using the cost method, the investment is reported as a long-term available-for-sale investment of $120,000. Revenue of $12,000 is recognized in the statement of earnings and an unrealized gain of $6,000 (3,000 shares × $2 [$42 fair value less $40 purchase price] per share) is recognized in the statement of comprehensive income.

Using the equity method of accounting, the investment account is reported as $138,000 and revenue of $30,000 is recognized on the statement of earnings.

⬆ **Illustration 12-8**

Comparison of cost and equity methods

Impairment Losses

Similar to held-to-maturity investments, equity investments must be assessed for impairment annually and written down if necessary. As discussed earlier in the chapter, the write-down results in a debit to an impairment loss account and a credit to the equity investment account. Clarke Inc. reported impairment write-downs of $4,838 thousand on its significantly influenced investments during 2007.

BEFORE YOU GO ON...

Review It

1. Compare the accounting for equity investments in common shares with ownership of (a) less than 20 percent with no significant influence, and (b) more than 20 percent with significant or total influence.
2. If the cost method is used to account for an equity investment, are the shares reported on the year-end balance sheet at their original cost or their fair value?
3. If the equity method is used to account for an equity investment, are the shares reported on the year-end balance sheet at their original cost or their fair value?

▸ **Do It**

CJW Inc. purchased 20 percent of North Sails Ltd.'s 60,000 common shares for $10 per share on January 2, 2009. On April 15, North Sails paid a cash dividend of $45,000. On December 31, North Sails reported net earnings of $120,000 for the year and had a share value of $10.25. Prepare all necessary journal entries assuming (a) there is no significant influence and the investment is classified as an available-for-sale investment and (b) there is significant influence and the investment is classified as an equity investment.

Action Plan
- Cost Method
  - Use the cost method when there is no significant influence (normally less than 20 percent ownership of the common shares of another corporation).
  - Under the cost method, recognize investment revenue when dividends are declared.
  - Under the cost method, the AFS investment is marked to market at year end.
- Equity Method
  - Use the equity method when there is significant influence (normally 20 percent or more ownership of the common shares of another corporation).
  - Under the equity method, recognize investment revenue when the investee declares net earnings. The distribution of dividends is not revenue; rather, it reduces the equity investment.

Solution
(a) Cost Method

Date		Account	Debit	Credit
Jan.	1	AFS Investment—North Sails Common		
		(20% × 60,000 × $10)	120,000	
		Cash		120,000
		(To record purchase of 12,000		
		[20% × 60,000] North Sails shares)		
Apr.	15	Cash	9,000	
		Dividend Revenue (20% × $45,000)		9,000
		(To record receipt of cash dividend)		
Dec.	31	AFS Investment—North Sails Common	3,000	
		Unrealized Gain—AFS (OCI)		3,000
		(12,000 × $0.25 [$10.25 - $10])		
		(To record unrealized gain on		
		available-for-sale securities)		

(b) Equity Method

Date		Account	Debit	Credit
Jan.	1	Equity Investment—North Sails Common		
		(20% × 60,000 × $10)	120,000	
		Cash		120,000
		(To record purchase of 12,000		
		[20% × 60,000] North Sails shares)		
Apr.	15	Cash	9,000	
		Equity Investment—North Sails Common		
		(20% × $45,000)		9,000
		(To record receipt of cash dividend)		
Dec.	31	Equity Investment—North Sails Common		
		(20% × $120,000)	24,000	
		Revenue from Investment in North Sails		24,000
		(To record 20% equity in North Sails'		
		net earnings)		

The Navigator

---

study objective 4

Indicate how investments
are reported in the financial
statements.

Reporting Investments

In this section, we will review the presentation of investments in the statement of earnings, statement of comprehensive income, statement of shareholders' equity, and balance sheet. We will also learn how equity investments are reported when one company controls another company.

Statement of Earnings

Gains and losses on investments, whether they are realized or unrealized, must be presented in the financial statements. Realized gains and losses are presented in the statement of earnings. Unrealized gains and losses from held-for-trading securities are also presented in the statement of earnings. These gains (losses), as well as other investment-related accounts such as those for interest and dividend revenue, are reported as other revenue (expense) in the non-operating section of the statement of earnings.

Clarke Inc. reported realized securities gains of $84,889 thousand and investment and other income of $15,208 thousand in its statement of earnings for the year ended December 31, 2007.

Statement of Comprehensive Income

We learned in Chapter 11 that the statement of comprehensive income includes not only net earnings reported on the traditional statement of earnings but also "comprehensive income" transactions. Recall that comprehensive income is created when, among other things, unrealized gains and losses are recorded on available-for-sale securities. Other sources of comprehensive income include certain translation gains and losses on foreign currency, unrealized gains and losses from ineffective cash flow hedges, and unrealized pension cost from a minimum pension liability adjustment. These are all topics for more advanced accounting courses.

Clarke reports comprehensive income of $40,260 thousand, as Illustration 12-9 shows.

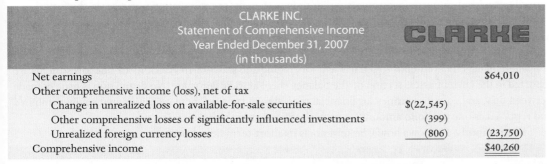

CLARKE INC.
Statement of Comprehensive Income
Year Ended December 31, 2007
(in thousands)

Net earnings		$64,010
Other comprehensive income (loss), net of tax		
Change in unrealized loss on available-for-sale securities	$(22,545)	
Other comprehensive losses of significantly influenced investments	(399)	
Unrealized foreign currency losses	(806)	(23,750)
Comprehensive income		$40,260

◀ **Illustration 12-9**

Statement of comprehensive income

Its net earnings of $64,010 thousand were reduced by the other comprehensive loss of $23,750 thousand, resulting in overall comprehensive income of $40,260 thousand. Note that adjustments to comprehensive income are reported net of income tax. For simplicity, we are ignoring the income tax implications of comprehensive income in this chapter.

Statement of Shareholders' Equity

As we learned in Chapter 11, the statement of shareholders' equity presents the changes in shareholders' equity each period. This includes changes in share capital, retained earnings, accumulated other comprehensive income (loss), and any other equity items that a company might report. While net earnings increase retained earnings, other comprehensive income (loss) increases (decreases) accumulated other comprehensive income.

Clarke reports an accumulated other comprehensive loss of $16,689 thousand at December 31, 2007. An extract from Clark's statement of shareholders' equity, detailing the determination of this amount, is shown below in Illustration 12-10. Note that detailed calculations of the changes in share capital, contributed surplus, and retained earnings have been omitted in the following illustration for simplicity.

CLARKE INC.
Statement of Shareholders' Equity (partial)
Year Ended December 31, 2007
(in thousands)

Share capital		$ 53,312
Contributed surplus		17,951
Retained earnings		144,142
Accumulated other comprehensive loss		
Balance at beginning of year	$ (406)	
Change in accounting policy	7,467	
Other comprehensive income (loss)	(23,750)	
Balance at end of year		(16,689)
Total shareholders' equity		$198,716

◀ **Illustration 12-10**

Statement of shareholders' equity

It is important to understand that the other comprehensive loss of $23,750 thousand shown in Illustration 12-10 is not the same amount reported as the ending comprehensive income (loss) amount on Clarke's statement of comprehensive income, $40,260 thousand. This is because the $40,260 thousand of comprehensive income shown in Illustration 12-9 comprises both net earnings ($64,010 thousand) and the other comprehensive loss ($23,750 thousand). Similar to how ending retained earnings is determined, the current period's other comprehensive loss of $23,750 thousand is deducted from the opening OCI balance as one of the determinants of the ending balance. This results in an ending accumulated other comprehensive loss of $16,689 thousand, as shown above. It is this amount that is reported in the shareholders' equity section of the balance sheet.

Balance Sheet

In the balance sheet presentation, investments are classified as short- or long-term. As discussed earlier, passive investments must be further categorized as held-for-trading, available-for-sale, or held-to-maturity.

Short-Term Investments

Cash, the most liquid asset, is listed first in the current assets section of the balance sheet. Clarke also views its highly liquid investments that are near maturity (usually less than three months) as cash equivalents. You will recall that we mentioned in Chapter 2 that consideration is currently being given to combining cash equivalents with short-term investments rather than with cash for presentation purposes in the future.

Other short-term investments rank next in order of liquidity. As we learned earlier, held-for-trading investments are always classified as current assets, whereas available-for-sale investments may be either current or long-term, depending on whether the investment is capable of reasonably prompt liquidation and when management intends to sell it. Held-for-trading and short-term available-for-sale investments are reported in the current assets section of the balance sheet at their fair value. No distinction is usually made between debt and equity securities for financial reporting purposes. These securities are usually combined and reported as one portfolio amount for each classification in the balance sheet.

Illustration 12-11 shows how Clarke reports its short-term investments.

Illustration 12-11 ➡

Presentation of short-term investments

CLARKE INC. Balance Sheet (partial) December 31, 2007 (in thousands)	CLARKE
Assets	
Current assets	
Cash and cash equivalents	$ 43,968
Marketable securities (notes 2 and 3)	218,627

In notes 2 and 3 of its statements, Clarke details its mix of held-for-trading, available-for-sale, and other types of securities. It also provides information about the total cost and fair value of the securities in each category.

Long-Term Investments

Available-for-sale securities are debt and equity securities reported on the balance sheet at their fair value. Held-to-maturity securities are debt securities that are classified as long-term investments until they are about to mature. Any portion that is expected to mature within the year is classified as a current asset. Held-to-maturity securities are reported at their amortized cost.

Certain equity securities that are purchased to have significant influence or control are also classified as long-term investments, and supporting details are given in the notes to the financial statements. Microsoft reports its 1.6-percent equity investment in Facebook discussed in the feature story as a long-term investment on its balance sheet.

Clarke reports its long-term investments as in Illustration 12-12.

Illustration 12-12 ➡

Presentation of long-term investments

CLARKE INC. Balance Sheet (partial) December 31, 2007 (in thousands)	CLARKE
Assets	
Long-term investments (note 7)	$15,795

n Note 7, Clarke reports that its long-term investments consist of available-for-sale equity securities, an quity investment in Midlake Oil and Gas subject to significant influence, and an equity investment in a rivate company.

Illustration 12-13 summarizes the reporting and valuation requirements of both short- and long-erm investments on the balance sheet.

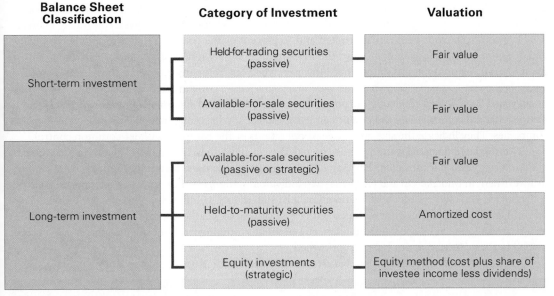

◄ Illustration 12-13

Reporting and valuation of short- and long-term investments

Accumulated Other Comprehensive Income (Loss)

Accumulated other comprehensive income (or loss) is presented in the shareholders' equity section of the balance sheet. Clarke reports an accumulated other comprehensive loss of $16,689 thousand as shown earlier in Illustration 12-10.

Illustration 12-14 reviews the interrelationships between the statement of earnings, statement of comprehensive income, statement of shareholders' equity, and balance sheet. Note that changes in share capital have not been detailed in the illustration shown below but the statement of shareholders' equity would include this information as well as changes in retained earnings, accumulated other comprehensive income, and any other equity items.

Illustration 12-14 ▼

Financial statement interrelationships

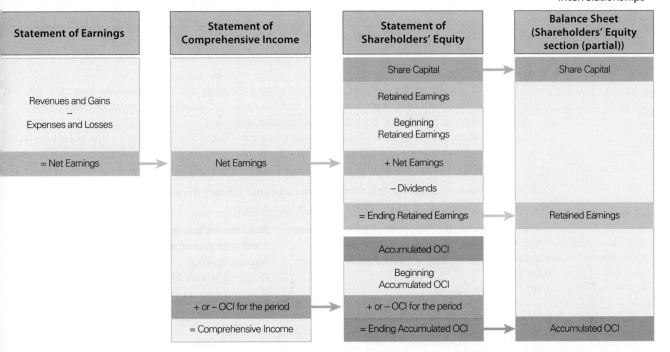

Although we have chosen not to illustrate the cash flow statement here, you will recall from earlier chapters that the purchase and sale of investments is reported in the investing activities section of the cash flow statement. We will learn more about this in the next chapter.

Consolidated Financial Statements

Earlier in the chapter, we learned that when a company has significant influence over another company it uses the equity method of accounting. This is true whether a company owns 20 percent or 100 percent of another company. A reporting distinction is to be made, however, when a company has a controlling interest.

If a company owns between 20 percent and 50 percent of the common shares of another company, and does not have a controlling interest, the investment is simply reported as a long-term equity investment in the investor's financial statements. However, when one company (known as the **parent company**) controls another company (known as the **subsidiary company**), **consolidated financial statements** must be prepared for financial reporting purposes. Consolidated financial statements present the assets and liabilities that are controlled by the parent company and the total revenues and expenses of the subsidiary companies. They indicate the size and scope of operations of the companies under common control.

Consolidated financial statements are prepared as an addition to the financial statements for the parent company and each subsidiary company. For example, Clarke uses the equity method to account for its investment in Midlake Oil and Gas in its own individual statements. But, for external reporting, Clarke consolidates Midlake's results with its own financial statements. Under this approach, the individual assets and liabilities of Midlake are included with those of Clarke. Clarke also has other subsidiaries whose results are included in its consolidated financial statements, ranging from subsidiaries that are 48 percent owned to subsidiaries that are 100 percent owned.

Consolidation is a complex topic which is usually dealt with in advanced accounting courses.

ACCOUNTING MATTERS! | Management Perspective

The top five subsidiary companies in Canada, ranked by revenue, are listed below. In all cases, the major shareholder (parent) controls the subsidiary's shares.

Rank	Subsidiary	Parent
1	General Motors of Canada	General Motors Corporation
2	Chrysler Canada	Chrysler LLC
3	Bell Canada	BCE Inc.
4	Shell Canada	Royal Dutch Shell plc
5	Honda Canada	Honda Motor Co., Ltd.

BEFORE YOU GO ON...

▸ **Review It**

1. What investment accounts or investment-related accounts are reported on the statement of earnings? Statement of comprehensive income? Statement of shareholders' equity? Balance sheet?
2. What is the purpose of consolidated financial statements?
3. Are Shoppers Drug Mart's financial statements consolidated? The answer to this question is at the end of the chapter.

▸ **Do It**

Zaboschuk Corporation has the following selected accounts. Identify the financial statement on which each account would be reported and its classification in the statement.

Accumulated other comprehensive income	Held-for-trading securities
Available-for-sale securities (long-term)	Held-to-maturity securities
Available-for-sale securities (short-term)	Interest revenue
Cash	Realized loss on AFS securities
Common shares	Realized gain on HTM securities
Dividend revenue	Unrealized gain on AFS securities
Dividends	Unrealized gain on HFT securities
Equity investments, at equity	

Action Plan

• Determine whether each account belongs on the statement of earnings, statement of comprehensive income, statement of shareholders' equity, and/or balance sheet.

• Organize each account into its proper classification on each statement.

Solution

Account	Financial Statement	Classification
Accumulated other comprehensive income	Statement of shareholders' equity; balance sheet	Accumulated OCI; shareholders' equity
Available-for-sale securities (long-term)	Balance sheet	Long-term investments
Available-for-sale securities (short-term)	Balance sheet	Current assets
Cash	Balance sheet	Current assets
Common shares	Statement of shareholders' equity; balance sheet	Share capital; shareholders' equity
Dividend revenue	Statement of earnings	Other revenue
Dividends	Statement of shareholders' equity	Retained earnings
Equity investments, at equity	Balance sheet	Long-term investments
Held-for-trading securities	Balance sheet	Current assets
Held-to-maturity securities	Balance sheet	Long-term investments
Interest revenue	Statement of earnings	Other revenue
Realized loss on AFS securities	Statement of earnings	Other expense
Realized gain on HTM securities	Statement of earnings	Other revenue
Unrealized gain on AFS securities	Statement of comprehensive income	Other comprehensive income
Unrealized gain on HFT securities	Statement of earnings	Other revenue

The Navigator

APPENDIX 12A—INVESTMENTS IN BONDS

We learned about bonds in Chapter 10 from the liability side—i.e., from the issuer's perspective. Corporations, governments, and universities issue bonds, which are purchased by investors. The issuer of the bonds is known as the investee. The purchaser of the bonds, or the bondholder, is known as the investor. Short-term investments in bonds can be classified as held-for-trading securities or available-for-sale securities. Long-term investments in bonds are classified as available-for-sale or held-to-maturity.

study objective 5

Compare the accounting for a bond investment and a bond payable.

The recording of investments in bonds is similar to the recording of a bond liability. Bond premiums (when the bond is purchased above its face value) and discounts (when a bond is purchased below its face value) are not recorded in a separate account for bond investments (or bond liabilities). Instead, the investment account is simply debited for the purchase cost of the bond (that is, for the face value net of any premium or discount).

You will recall from Chapter 10 that premiums or discounts on long-term bonds payable must be amortized using the effective-interest method of amortization. Similarly, premiums or discounts on bond investments must be amortized using the effective-interest method.

This is true for all bond investments except those that are held for trading. Because HFT bond investments are expected to be held only for a short time, there is no requirement to amortize any premium or discount. Any misstatement of interest that might result would not be significant. In contrast, for bond investments classified as available-for-sale (whether short- or long-term) and as held-to-maturity, any premium or discount must be amortized using the effective-interest method.

While the amortization for bonds payable was recorded in an Interest Expense account, the amortization of a bond investment is recorded in an Interest Revenue account. If there is a bond premium on a long-term bond investment, the Interest Revenue account and carrying amount of the investment is *reduced* by the amortization amount. If there is a bond discount, the Interest Revenue account and carrying amount of the investment is *increased* by the amortization amount.

Recording a Bond Investment for the Investor

We will now illustrate the recording of a bond investment using an example for Kuhl Corporation (the bond purchaser). We will then compare Kuhl's recording to Doan Inc.'s (the bond issuer's) recording of its bond liability. Assume that Kuhl Corporation acquires $50,000 of Doan 10-year, 6-percent bonds on January 1, 2009, for $49,000. This means that the bonds sold at a discount of $1,000 ($50,000 − $49,000). The price of $49,000 was based on a market, or effective, rate of interest of approximately 6.272%. The bonds pay interest semi-annually, on July 1 and January 1. Assuming that Kuhl is holding these bonds as an AFS security, the entry to record the investment is as follows:

Jan.	1	AFS Investment—Doan Bonds	49,000	
		Cash		49,000
		(To record purchase of Doan bonds)		

With the preceding entry, the bonds are thus recorded at their acquisition cost of $49,000. Note that the $1,000 discount on the bonds is not separately recorded but rather is netted with the cost in the investment account.

Interest to be received is calculated by multiplying the face value of the bond investment by the contractual or stated interest rate per semi-annual period. Kuhl will collect interest of $1,500 ($50,000 × 6% × 6/12) semi-annually on July 1 and January 1.

Interest revenue is calculated by multiplying the carrying amount of the bond investment by the market (effective) rate of interest per semi-annual interest period. Kuhl's interest revenue is $1,537 ($49,000 × 6.272% × 6/12) for the first interest period. Interest revenue is then compared to the interest received to determine the amount by which to amortize the discount (i.e., the portion of the $1,000 discount that is amortized in this six-month period). The amortization is $37 ($1,537 − $1,500), in this case, and is debited to the bond investment account.

The entry to record the receipt of interest on July 1 is:

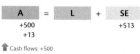

July	1	Cash ($50,000 × 6% × 6/12)	1,500	
		AFS Investment—Doan Bonds	37	
		Interest Revenue ($49,000 × 6.272% × 6/12)		1,537
		(To record receipt of interest on Doan bonds)		

After amortization, the carrying amount of the investment will increase to $49,037, as the following T account shows:

AFS Investment—Doan Bonds			
Jan.	1	49,000	
July	1	37	
Bal. July 1		49,037	

If the bonds are later sold before their maturity date, it is necessary to (1) update any unrecorded interest, (2) debit Cash for the proceeds received, (3) credit the investment account for the cost of the bonds, and (4) record any gain or loss realized on the sale. Any difference between the proceeds from the sale and their original cost is recorded as a realized gain or loss.

Assume, for example, that Kuhl receives proceeds of $50,500 plus accrued interest on the sale of the Doan bonds on September 1, 2009. First, we will record the interest entry for the two months from July 1 to September 1.

Sept.	1	Cash ($50,000 × 6% × 2/12)	500	
		AFS Investment—Doan Bonds	13	
		Interest Revenue ($49,037 × 6.272% × 2/12)		513
		(To record receipt of interest on Doan bonds)		

The difference between the cash, $500, and the interest revenue, $513, is the amortization of the discount, $13 ($513 − $500). The carrying amount of the investment is now $49,050, as shown here:

AFS Investment—Doan Bonds			
Jan.	1	49,000	
July	1	37	
Sept.	1	13	
Bal. Sept. 1		49,050	

Since the investment has been sold for $50,500, a gain of $1,450 has been realized ($50,500 − $49,050). The entry to record the sale is:

Sept. 1	Cash	50,500	
	AFS Investment—Doan Bonds		49,050
	Realized Gain—AFS		1,450
	(To record sale of Doan bonds)		

A	=	L	+	SE
+50,500				+1,450
−49,050				

↑ Cash flows: +50,500

Note that a gain on the sale of debt investments is reported as other revenue in the statement of earnings.

Similar to what was illustrated in the chapter for other AFS securities, if the bonds had not been sold, their carrying amount would have been compared to their fair value at year end. An adjustment to fair value would then have been required for this available-for-sale investment. If the fair value exceeded the carrying amount, the investment account would be debited and an unrealized gain account credited. If the fair value was less than the carrying amount, an unrealized loss account would be debited and the investment account credited. Although not illustrated here, a new market interest rate would have to be calculated for the next amortization period after revaluation to equate interest and principal payments for the remaining periods to the revised fair value. If the bonds were instead being held to maturity, no revaluation would have occurred.

Recording a Bond for Investor and Investee

With a few exceptions, recording a debt investment in bonds (an asset) for an investor is essentially the opposite of recording bonds payable (a liability) for an investee, which was discussed in Chapter 10. Using the Kuhl Corporation example, Illustration 12A-1 compares the recording of the bonds as an investment for Kuhl and as a liability for Doan.

Illustration 12-A1 ↓

Comparison of an AFS bond investment and liability

Kuhl Corporation (Investor)				Doan Inc. (Investee)			
Acquisition of bonds				*Issue of bonds*			
Jan. 1	AFS Investment—Doan Bonds	49,000		Cash	49,000		
	Cash		49,000	Bonds Payable			49,000
	Receipt of interest and amortization of discount			*Payment of interest and amortization of discount*			
July 1	Cash	1,500		Interest Expense	1,537		
	AFS Investment—Doan Bonds	37		Bonds Payable			37
	Interest Revenue		1,537	Cash			1,500
	Sale of investment						
Sept. 1	Cash	500		No entry			
	AFS Investment—Doan Bonds	13					
	Interest Revenue		513				
1	Cash	50,500					
	AFS Investment—Doan Bonds		49,050				
	Realized Gain—AFS		1,450				

Recording an investment in bonds (an asset) for an investor differs from the recording of bonds payable (a liability) for an investee in the following two ways. First, any premium or discount is not amortized by the investor as it is for the investee if the bonds are held for trading. Similar to bonds payable, premiums and discounts are amortized if the investment in bonds is classified as available-for-sale or held-to-maturity. Second, assuming that Kuhl sold its bonds on the open market, the issuer, Doan, is not affected by this transaction. It would only be affected if the bonds were redeemed before maturity or repaid at maturity.

ALL ABOUT YOU

A Good Day to Start Saving

Savings are an essential part of personal financial planning. Without savings, you cannot invest nor can you deal with emergencies when they unexpectedly occur. Also, if you have no savings, it may be difficult for you to buy a car or a house or to have a carefree retirement in the future.

Some people may be good savers but have little idea of how to invest. There are two basic ways to invest: (1) by lending money or (2) by acquiring ownership. Lenders become creditors by purchasing debt investments. As you learned from Chapter 10, the borrower promises to repay the principal with interest at some specified time. You become a creditor when investing in Canada Savings Bonds and guaranteed investment certificates. Both are considered safe and risk-free.

You acquire equity when you own investments such as shares in publicly traded companies. This equity investment does not guarantee you any gain or income and often an equity investment is riskier than a debt investment. Investors should realize that moderate inflation isn't necessarily a bad thing, which is why the Bank of Canada's target is an annual rate of two percent (give or take one percentage point). Inflation is supposed to be beneficial to the stock market for the very simple reason that it has a tendency to push prices higher.

The three key rules for becoming a successful saver are: (1) have a purpose or goal for which you are saving, (2) make a plan for accomplishing your goal, and (3) save regularly. There is always a reason not to start saving but today is as good as any day to take the first step.

Some Facts

- A Mackenzie Investments poll recently discovered that more than half of Canadians under the age of 50 either are over-spenders or demonstrate over-spending tendencies. This is supported by other statistics that show that 90 percent of Canadians have more debt today than they did five years ago.
- In recent years, the amount of money Canadians have invested in Canada Savings Bonds has steadily dropped. Canadians held $15.3 billion in bonds as at March 31, 2007. That was a drop of $2.2 billion from the previous year and less than half of the total in 1992. The current low interest rate environment may explain part of the drop. A recent issue of Canada Savings Bonds paid 3.25 per cent in the first year.
- Two-thirds of Canadians say the first investment they ever owned was a Canada Savings Bond.
- The seasonally adjusted annual rate for personal savings in the first quarter of 2008 was 2.8%.

What Do You Think?

You are entering the first year of university and have recently inherited $30,000. This $30,000 will help you fund your education. Your parents want you to invest the money in Canada Savings Bonds but you know you could get a greater return by purchasing shares in a public company.

YES | You should invest your inheritance in Canada Savings Bonds as they are a safe investment.

NO | Canada Savings Bonds pay a low interest rate and you can earn a higher return by buying shares in a public company.

Sources:

Elliot J. Currie et al., *Personal Finance for Canadians,* 9th edition, (Toronto: Pearson Prentice Hall, 2008), p. 226.

Talbot Boggs, *"When to Retire?"* July 8, 2008, cbc.ca/cp/Money/080708/J070802AU.html#skip300x250.

"Canada Savings Bonds, An Old Standby Faces New Challenges," October 3, 2007, cbc.ca/news/background/canada-savings-bonds/.

Statistics Canada "Economic Indicators, by Province and Territory," July 25, 2008, www40.statcan.ca/l01/cst01/indi02a.htm.

The Navigator

Summary of Study Objectives

1. Identify reasons to invest, and classify investments. Corporations generally purchase investments in debt and equity securities for one of two reasons. The investment may be purchased as a passive investment to generate investment income. Or, it might be purchased as a strategic investment to influence or control the operations of another company in some way.

Passive investments in debt and equity securities are classified as held-for-trading (HFT), available-for-sale (AFS), or held-to-maturity (HTM) investments. HFT investments are always classified as current assets; HTM as long-term investments; and AFS may be either short- or long-term investments, depending on how long management intends to hold these securities. Strategic investments in common shares are classified as long-term investments.

2. Account for passive investments. Held-for-trading securities are reported at fair value. Unrealized gains and losses that result from adjusting cost to fair value for HFT securities are reported as other revenue (expense) in the statement of earnings. Available-for-sale securities are reported at fair value. Unrealized gains and losses that result from adjusting cost to fair value for AFS securities are reported as other comprehensive income (loss) in the statement of comprehensive income. Held-to-maturity securities are reported at amortized cost. Care must be taken to classify securities appropriately and evaluate the impact of both realized and unrealized gains and losses on current and future earnings.

3. Account for strategic investments. When the investor company is not able to exert significant influence over the investee company, the cost method should be used. The cost method records investment revenue when dividends are received. The investment would normally be classified as a long-term available-for-sale investment on the balance sheet, with the investment adjusted to fair value at each balance sheet date.

When significant influence exists (share ownership usually 20 percent or more), the equity method should be used. The equity method records investment revenue when net earnings are reported, and dividends reduce the value of the investment account. These investments are not adjusted to fair value unless there is a permanent decline in value below cost.

4. Indicate how investments are reported in the financial statements. Held-for-trading securities are presented in the current assets section of the balance sheet. Available-for-sale securities may be classified as short-term or long-term, depending on management's intention. Held-to-maturity securities and strategic equity investments are classified as long-term investments. Accumulated other comprehensive income, which includes unrealized gains or losses from available-for-sale securities, is presented in the shareholders' equity section of the balance sheet.

Realized gains and losses are presented as other revenue and other expenses in the statement of earnings. Unrealized gains and losses on held-for-trading securities are presented as other revenue (expense) in the statement of earnings, while unrealized gains and losses on available-for-sale securities are presented as other comprehensive income (loss) in the statement of comprehensive income.

Changes in share capital, retained earnings, and accumulated comprehensive income are shown in the statement of shareholders' equity. The purchase and sale of investments are reported in the investing activities section of the cash flow statement.

When a company controls the common shares of another company (ownership usually greater than 50 percent), consolidated financial statements that detail the financial position of the combined entity must also be prepared.

5. Compare the accounting for a bond investment and a bond payable (Appendix 12A). The accounting for a bond investment is similar to that of a bond payable in that any premium or discount is amortized using the effective-interest method of amortization. There is one exception: premiums and discounts are not amortized for held-for-trading investments. Held-for-trading and available-for-sale investments in bonds are revalued at year end. Held-to-maturity investments are not revalued; nor are liabilities.

The Navigator

Glossary  Study Tools (Glossary)

Available-for-sale (AFS) securities Debt or equity securities that are not classified as held-to-maturity or held-for-trading investments. Reported at fair value on the balance sheet. (p. 606)

Consolidated financial statements Financial statements that present the assets and liabilities controlled by the parent company and the total profitability of the combined companies (the parent company and the subsidiary companies). (p. 622)

Cost method An accounting method in which the equity investment is recorded at cost as an AFS investment, and adjusted for changes in fair value. Investment revenue is recognized only when cash dividends are received. (p. 614)

Debt investments Investments in money-market instruments, bonds, commercial paper, or similar items. (p. 604)

Equity investments Investments in the share capital (common and/or preferred shares) of other corporations. (p. 604)

Equity method An accounting method in which the investment in common shares is initially recorded at cost. The investment account is then adjusted (increased for the investor's share of the investee's net earnings and decreased for dividends received) to show the investor's equity in the investee. (p. 616)

Held-for-trading (HFT) securities   Debt or equity securities that are bought to generate profits from short-term price fluctuations. Reported at fair value on the balance sheet. (p. 605)

Held-to-maturity (HTM) securities   Debt securities that the investor has the intention and ability to hold to their maturity date. Reported at amortized cost on the balance sheet. (p. 606)

Investee   The corporation that issues (sells) the debt or equity securities. (p. 613)

Investor   The corporation that buys (owns) the debt or equity securities. (p. 613)

Parent company   A company that controls (owns) more than 50 percent of the common shares of another company. (p. 622)

Passive investment   An investment that is purchased mainly to generate investment income. (p. 604)

Realized gain or loss   The difference between fair value and cost (carrying amount) when an investment is actually sold. (p. 608)

Statement of comprehensive income   A financial statement that presents the net earnings (loss) and other comprehensive income (loss) for a specific period of time. Other comprehensive items, such as unrealized gains and losses from available-for-sale securities, are not reported on the statement of earnings because they have not been realized but are included in comprehensive income. (p. 609)

Strategic investment   An investment that is purchased to influence or control another company. (p. 604)

Subsidiary company   A company whose common shares are controlled (more than 50 percent of the common shares are owned) by another company. (p. 622)

Unrealized gain or loss   The difference between the fair value and cost (carrying amount) of an investment still held (owned) by the investor. (p. 608)

The Navigator

DECISION TOOLKIT—A SUMMARY

Decision Checkpoints	Info Needed for Decision	Tools to Use for Decision	How to Evaluate Results
Is the company window dressing its results by manipulating its investment portfolio?	Balance of unrealized gains and losses; classification of AFS investments	A company can window dress by selling AFS winners and holding AFS losers to increase reported earnings, or doing the opposite to reduce reported earnings. Misclassification of investments as available-for-sale allows companies to "time" (advance or defer) the recognition of losses.	Window dressing and misclassification are not easy to spot: it is difficult for an outsider to determine why companies choose to sell or hold securities, or classify them as they do. A user should evaluate a company's earnings as reported, including any unrealized gains and losses, to see the total valuation.

www.wiley.com/canada/kimmel

Analysis Tools (Decision Toolkit Summaries)

The Navigator

Using the Decision Toolkit

The Royal Bank of Canada reports the following selected information related to its investments for its first quarter ended January 31, 2008:

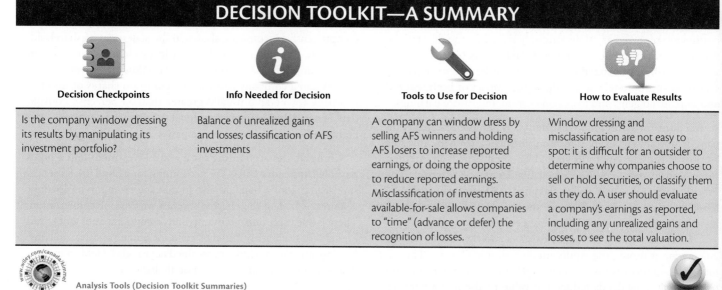

ROYAL BANK OF CANADA Consolidated Balance Sheet (partial) January 31, 2008 (in millions)		
	2008	2007
Held-for-trading securities	$151,230	$169,030
Available-for-sale securities	33,118	27,821
	$184,348	$196,851
Accumulated other comprehensive income (loss)	$ (3,193)	$ (1,760)

Additional information:

1. Held-for-trading and available-for-sale securities include both debt and equity securities. The maturity dates of the debt securities vary from within three months to more than 10 years in each category.
2. A net realized and unrealized gain of $366 million was reported for held-for-trading securities for the three months ended January 31, 2008.
3. A net realized loss of $20 million and a net unrealized gain of $10 million were reported for available-for-sale securities for the three months ended January 31, 2008.

Instructions

(a) What reason does the Royal Bank likely have for purchasing investments rather than only making loans? Why does it purchase investments that vary in terms of both their maturities and their type (debt and equity)?

(b) In what section of a classified balance sheet do you think the Royal Bank reports its held-for-trading securities, available-for-sale securities, and accumulated other comprehensive loss? At what value are held-for-trading and available-for-sale securities reported in the balance sheet?

(c) Where would the Royal Bank report the net realized and unrealized gain of $366 million for its held-for-trading securities, the net realized loss of $20 million for its available-for-sale securities, and the net unrealized gain of $10 million reported for its available-for-sale securities?

Solution

(a) Although banks are mainly in the business of lending money, they need to balance their portfolios through investments. For example, a bank may have cash on hand from depositors that it has not yet loaned and wants to invest in short-term liquid assets. A bank may also believe that it can earn a higher rate of interest by buying certain investments than by making new loans. In addition, banks also purchase investments for speculation because they believe these investments will increase in value. Banks purchase a variety of investments with a variety of terms to match the duration of their loans.

(b) Held-for-trading securities are reported at fair value in the current assets section. Even though there are varying terms within the held-for-trading securities category, it is management's intention to sell these securities if the need for cash arises, and they are therefore classified as short-term investments. Available-for-sale securities are reported at fair value as a short- or long-term investment, depending on management's intention. Accumulated other comprehensive loss is reported in the shareholders' equity section.

(c) The net realized and unrealized gain for held-for-trading securities is presented in the other revenue section of the statement of earnings. The net realized loss for available-for-sale securities is also presented in the other revenue section of the statement of earnings. The net unrealized gain for available-for-sale securities is presented as other comprehensive income in the statement of comprehensive income.

Demonstration Problem

In 2009, its first year of operations, Northstar Finance Corporation had the following transactions in held-for-trading securities:

Study Tools
(Demonstration Problems)

June	1	Purchased 600 Sanburg common shares for $24.50 per share.
July	1	Purchased 800 Cey common shares for $33.75 per share.
Sept.	1	Received a $1-per-share cash dividend from Cey Corporation.
Nov.	1	Sold 200 Sanburg common shares for $26.25 per share.
Dec.	15	Received a $0.50-per-share cash dividend on Sanburg common shares.
	31	On this date, the market values per share were $25 for Sanburg and $30 for Cey.

Instructions

(a) Record the above transactions.

(b) Prepare the adjusting entry required to report the securities at their fair value.

(c) Show the presentation of the held-for-trading securities, and related investment accounts, in the balance sheet and statement of earnings.

Action Plan

- Keep a running balance of the number of shares purchased and sold for each company.

- Calculate the gain or loss by subtracting the cost of the securities from the proceeds.

- Determine the adjustment to fair value based on the difference between the total cost and total fair value of the securities.

Solution to Demonstration Problem

(a)

June 1	HFT Investments—Sanburg Common		14,700	
	Cash (600 × $24.50)			14,700
	(To record purchase of 600 Sanburg common shares)			
July 1	HFT Investments—Cey Common		27,000	
	Cash (800 × $33.75)			27,000
	(To record purchase of 800 Cey common shares)			
Sept. 1	Cash (800 × $1)		800	
	Dividend Revenue			800
	(To record receipt of $1-per-share cash dividend from Cey)			
Nov. 1	Cash (200 × $26.25)		5,250	
	HFT Investments—Sanburg Common (200 × $ 24.50)			4,900
	Realized Gain—HFT			350
	(To record sale of 200 Sanburg common shares)			
Dec. 15	Cash [(600 – 200) × $0.50]		200	
	Dividend Revenue			200
	(To record receipt of $0.50-per-share dividend from Sanburg)			

(b)

Dec. 31	Unrealized Loss—HFT		2,800	
	HFT Investments			2,800
	(To record unrealized loss on held-for-trading securities)			

HFT Securities	Cost	Fair Value	Unrealized Gain (Loss)
Sanburg common shares (400)	$ 9,800[1]	$10,000[2]	$ 200
Cey common shares (800)	27,000	24,000[3]	(3,000)
Total	$36,800	$34,000	$(2,800)

[1] $14,700 – $4,900 = $9,800   [2] 400 × $25 = $10,000   [3] 800 × $30 = $24,000

(c)

NORTHSTAR FINANCE CORPORATION
Balance Sheet (partial)
December 31, 2009

Assets	
Current assets	
Held-for-trading securities	34,000

Note: Details of the adjustment from cost to fair value would be disclosed in the notes to the financial statements.

NORTHSTAR FINANCE CORPORATION
Statement of Earnings (partial)
Year Ended December 31, 2009

Other revenue	
Realized gain on held-for-trading securities	$ 350
Dividend revenue ($800 + $200)	1,000
Other expenses	
Unrealized loss on held-for-trading securities	2,800

The Navigator

Note: All questions, exercises, and problems below with an asterisk (*) relate to material in Appendix 12A.

Self-Study Questions

Answers are at the end of the chapter.

www.wiley.com/canada/kimmel

Study Tools (Self-Assessment Quizzes)

1. Which of the following is *not* a reason that corporations purchase debt or equity securities as a passive investment?
   (a) They want to exert influence over the decisions of the investee company.
   (b) They want to invest excess cash for short periods of time to earn a greater return than would be earned if the funds were simply held in the company's chequing account.
   (c) They want to invest excess cash for the long term to generate investment income.
   (d) They speculate that the investment will increase in value and result in a gain when sold.

2. Which of the following is *not* an appropriate classification for a passive investment in equity securities?
   (a) Long-term available-for-sale investment
   (b) Held-to-maturity investment
   (c) Short-term available-for-sale investment
   (d) Held-for-trading investment

3. Which statement does *not* apply to held-to-maturity securities?
   (a) The company speculates that the debt securities will increase in value and it will therefore be able to sell them at a gain.
   (b) The company intends to hold the investment to maturity.
   (c) The company has the ability to hold the investment to maturity.
   (d) Held-to-maturity investments are classified as long-term except when they are within one year of maturity.

4. Which statement is *incorrect* with respect to the valuation of passive investments on the balance sheet?
   (a) HTM securities are valued at amortized cost.
   (b) AFS debt securities are valued at amortized cost.
   (c) HFT securities are valued at fair value.
   (d) AFS equity securities are valued at fair value.

5. Boisclair Ltée sells HFT securities costing $28,000 for $26,000 in the same year as they were purchased. The entry to record this sale would include a:
   (a) debit to a realized loss account of $2,000.
   (b) debit to an unrealized loss account of $2,000.
   (c) debit to OCI of $2,000.
   (d) debit to a HFT investment account of $26,000.

6. If a company wants to increase its earnings by manipulating its investment accounts, what should it do?
   (a) Sell its "winner" held-for-trading securities and hold its "loser" held-for-trading securities.
   (b) Hold its "winner" held-for-trading securities and sell its "loser" held-for-trading securities.

   (c) Sell its "winner" available-for-sale securities and hold its "loser" available-for-sale securities.
   (d) Hold its "winner" available-for-sale securities and sell its "loser" available-for-sale securities.

7. The equity method of accounting for strategic long-term (SO 3) equity investments should be used when the investor owns:
   (a) more than zero percent of the investee's common shares
   (b) less than 20 percent of the investee's common shares.
   (c) 20 percent or more of the investee's common shares.
   (d) more than 20 percent but less than 50 percent of the investee's common shares.

8. Big K Ranch owns 20 percent of Little L Ranch. Little L (SO 3) Ranch reported net earnings of $150,000 and paid dividends of $40,000 this year. How much investment revenue would Big K Ranch report if it used the equity method to account for this investment?
   (a) $8,000
   (b) $22,000
   (c) $30,000
   (d) $110,000

9. Unrealized gains and losses on available-for-sale securities (SO 4) would be reported as follows:
   (a) in the statement of earnings under other revenue or expenses.
   (b) in the investing activities section of the cash flow statement.
   (c) in the statement of comprehensive income (loss).
   (d) in the balance sheet.

10. Accumulated other comprehensive income is reported on (SO 4) which of the following statements?
    (a) Statement of earnings
    (b) Balance sheet
    (c) Statement of shareholders' equity
    (d) Both (b) and (c)

*11. Which of the following statements is *incorrect* with regard to (SO 5) recording bonds?
    (a) Any premium or discount is not amortized by the investor if a bond investment is classified as HFT.
    (b) Any premium or discount is not amortized by the investor if a bond investment is classified as HTM.
    (c) Premiums and discounts are not recorded separately for the investor or the investee.
    (d) The investor records the bonds initially at acquisition cost and the investee records the bonds at the amount that the bonds were issued at.

(SO 5) *12. Bonds with a face value of $100,000 were issued for $90,000. The investor classified the bonds as HTM. The following entries would be made by the investor and investee when the investee paid the semi-annual interest (assuming no previous accrual of interest):

    (a) Investor: DR Cash, CR Interest Revenue. Investee: DR Interest Expense, CR Cash

    (b) Investor: DR Interest Expense, CR Bonds Payable, CR Cash. Investee: DR Cash, CR Interest Revenue

    (c) Investor: DR Cash, DR HTM Investment, CR Interest Revenue. Investee: DR Interest Expense, CR Bonds Payable, CR Cash

    (d) Investor: DR Interest Expense, CR Bonds Payable, CR Cash. Investee: DR Cash, DR HTM Investment, CR Interest Revenue.

The Navigator

Questions

(SO 1) 1. What are the reasons that corporations invest in debt and equity securities?

(SO 1) 2. Distinguish between passive and strategic investments.

(SO 1) 3. Distinguish between held-for-trading securities, available-for-sale securities, and held-to maturity securities.

(SO 1, 4) 4. Cumby Corporation is a golf equipment retailer that owns common shares in EnCana Corporation. It intends to sell these shares if it needs cash. (a) Should the investment in EnCana be classified as a held-for-trading, available-for-sale, or held-to-maturity security? Explain your reasoning. (b) Would the investment be classified as a current asset or a long-term asset on Cumby's balance sheet?

(SO 2) 5. At what amount—cost or fair value—are each of the following reported on a balance sheet: (a) held-for-trading securities, (b) available-for-sale securities, and (c) held-to-maturity securities?

(SO 2) 6. What is the difference between realized gains/losses and unrealized gains/losses?

(SO 2) 7. Communications Inc. reported available-for-sale securities at their fair value of $255 million on its year-end balance sheet. These securities were purchased earlier in the year at a cost of $245 million. (a) How should the difference between these two amounts be recorded and reported? (b) Would your answer differ if these securities were classified as held-for-trading securities?

(SO 2) 8. Time Ltd. purchased $1 million of 10-year bonds at face value (100) in 2009. The bonds were trading at 105 on December 31, 2009. (a) At what amount would the bonds be reported in the December 31, 2009, balance sheet if they are classified as a held-to-maturity investment? (b) How would your answer differ if they were classified as (1) held-for-trading, or (2) available-for-sale? Explain why the investment is reported differently depending on its classification.

(SO 2) 9. Indicate when it is appropriate to adjust a held-to-maturity debt security to its fair value.

(SO 2) 10. Music Makers Ltd. reported an available-for-sale investment with an original cost of $115,000 and a fair value of $130,000 at December 31, 2008. It also reported an unrealized gain (other comprehensive income) of $15,000 relating to the investment.

During 2009, the investment was sold for $125,000. Describe how the sale of the investment would be recorded and reported in the 2009 financial statements, including the treatment of the other comprehensive income.

11. Identify ways a company might be able to "manage its earnings" with respect to its investment portfolio.

12. What constitutes "significant influence"? Is it safe to conclude that there is significant influence when a company owns 20 percent of the common shares of another company?

13. When should a strategic equity investment be accounted for using (a) the cost method and (b) the equity method?

14. Identify what is included in the carrying amount of a strategic equity investment using (a) the cost method and (b) the equity method.

15. Explain how, and why, the investment revenue differs when a strategic long-term equity investment is accounted for using (a) the cost method and (b) the equity method.

16. Indicate how (a) held-for-trading, (b) available-for-sale, and (c) held-to-maturity investments are classified on the balance sheet.

17. Identify the proper statement presentation of the following accounts: (a) Unrealized Gain on Held-for-Trading Securities, (b) Realized Loss on Held-for-Trading Securities, (c) Unrealized Gain on Available-for-Sale Securities, and (d) Realized Loss on Available-for-Sale Securities.

18. Distinguish between other comprehensive income and accumulated other comprehensive income. Indicate how each is reported in the financial statements.

19. Explain how the statement of earnings, statement of comprehensive income, statement of shareholders' equity, and balance sheet are interrelated.

20. Onex Corporation owns 100 percent of the common shares of Cineplex-Galaxy. (a) What method should Onex use to account for this investment? (b) Which company is the parent? The subsidiary? (c) What kind of financial statements should Onex prepare to properly present this investment?

*21. Compare the accounting for a debt investment in bonds to the accounting for a bond liability.

*22. Explain why premiums and discounts must be amortized for available-for-sale or held-to-maturity bond investments, but not for those that are held for trading.

*23. When bonds mature, a journal entry is recorded on the books of both the investor and the investee (issuer). However, when bonds are sold prior to maturity on the open market, the sale of the bond investment results in a journal entry on the books of the investor, but not on the books of the investee (issuer). Explain why.

Brief Exercises

BE12–1   The following terms were introduced in this chapter:

Match type of investment.
(SO 1)

1. Strategic investments
2. Passive investments
3. Held-for-trading securities
4. Available-for-sale securities
5. Held-to-maturity securities

Match each term with the appropriate definition:

(a) _____   Debt or equity securities that are not held-for-trading securities and that are not held-to-maturity securities

(b) _____   Equity investments that are purchased to influence or control another company

(c) _____   Debt or equity securities that are bought and held for sale in the near term at a profit

(d) _____   Debt securities that the investor has the intent and ability to hold until they mature

(e) _____   Equity investments that are purchased mainly to generate investment income

BE12–2   Identify whether each of the following is most likely (a) a passive or strategic investment, (b) a short-term (current asset) or long-term investment, and (c) a held-for-trading, available-for-sale, held-to-maturity security, or equity investment. The first one has been done for you as an example.

Classify investments.
(SO 1)

		(a) Passive or Strategic?	(b) Short-Term or Long-Term?	(c) Type of Security?
1.	120-day treasury bill	Passive	Short-term	Available-for-sale
2.	Common shares purchased by a bank for resale in the near future at a profit			
3.	Common shares purchased by a manufacturing company for resale if cash is needed			
4.	Common shares purchased to control another company			
5.	Common shares purchased to influence another company			
6.	Five-year bonds intended to be held for the entire term of the bonds			

BE12–3   On January 1, 2009, Seniors R Us Ltd. purchased $100,000 of 10%, 10-year bonds at face value (100). Interest is received semi-annually on July 1 and January 1. Seniors R Us has classified the bonds as a held-to-maturity investment. At December 31, 2009, Seniors R Us' fiscal year end, the bonds were trading in the market at 97. Prepare the journal entries to record (a) the purchase of the bonds on January 1, (b) the receipt of the interest on July 1, and (c) any adjusting entries required at December 31.

Record HTM investment.
(SO 2)

BE12–4   Using the data presented in BE12–3, assume that Seniors R Us Ltd. classified the bonds as available-for-sale rather than held-to-maturity. Prepare the journal entries to record (a) the purchase of the bonds on January 1, (b) the receipt of the interest on July 1, and (c) any adjusting entries required at December 31.

Record AFS investment.
(SO 2)

BE12–5 On January 2, 2010, Seniors R Us Ltd. sold bonds for $97,000. The bonds were originally purchased for $100,000 at face value on January 1, 2009, and were classified as available-for-sale. Interest is received semi-annually on the bonds on July 1 and January 1. At December 31, 2009, the bonds were reported at $97,000 on the balance sheet. Record the sale of the bonds on January 2, 2010.

BE12–6 On August 1, 2009, McLellan Ltd. purchased 1,000 Datawave common shares for $45,000 cash. McLellan classified the investment as held-for-trading. On December 31, 2009, McLellan's year end, the market value of the shares was $49,000. Prepare the journal entry to record (a) the purchase of this investment on August 1 and (b) any adjusting journal entry required at December 31.

BE12–7 Using the data presented in BE12–6, assume that the shares were sold for $47,000 on February 1, 2010. Record the sale.

BE12–8 On August 1, 2009, McLellan Ltd. purchased 1,000 Datawave common shares for $45,000 cash. The investment was classified as available-for-sale. On December 31, 2009, McLellan's year end, the market value of the shares was $49,000. On February 1, 2010, McLellan sold the shares for $47,000. Prepare the journal entries to record (a) the purchase of this investment on August 1, 2009, (b) any necessary adjusting journal entry at December 31, 2009, and (c) the sale of the shares on February 1, 2010.

BE12–9 On January 1, Crook Corporation purchased 25% of Hook Ltd. common shares for $200,000. At December 31, Hook paid a $16,000 dividend and reported net earnings of $400,000. The market value of the shares at December 31 was $210,000. Record each of these transactions, assuming Crook has significant influence over Hook. How much revenue would be reported by Crook because of its share of Hook?

BE12–10 Using the data presented in BE12–9, assume that Crook Corporation does not have significant influence over Hook Ltd. Record each of the transactions and any necessary adjusting journal entries under this assumption. How much revenue would be reported by Crook in this situation? Explain why this differs from the answer in BE12–9.

BE12–11 Chan Inc. purchased 20% of Dong Ltd.'s common shares for $225,000 on January 1. During the year, Dong reported net earnings of $350,000 and paid a dividend of $40,000. The fair value of the investment at December 31 was $275,000. (a) Assuming there is significant influence, indicate the balance in the investment account at the end of the year and where it would be reported in the balance sheet. (b) Assuming Chan does not have significant influence, indicate the balance in the investment account at the end of the year and where it would be reported in the balance sheet.

BE12–12 Indicate whether each of the following transactions would increase, decrease, or have no effect on (1) net earnings and (2) other comprehensive income:

  (a) Classification of available-for-sale securities as short-term rather than long-term
  (b) Classification of short-term investments as available-for-sale rather than held-for-trading at a time when the fair value was lower than cost
  (c) Sale of an available-for-sale security with a fair value greater than cost at the time of sale, and where the fair value was also greater than cost at the balance sheet date prior to the sale
  (d) Sale of an available-for-sale security with a fair value greater than cost at the time of sale, and where the fair value was lower than cost at the balance sheet date prior to the sale

BE12–13 Cost and fair value for the held-for-trading securities of Deal.com Ltd. at December 31, 2009, are $56,000 and $59,000, respectively. (a) Prepare the adjusting entry to record the securities at fair value. (b) Show the financial statement presentation of the held-for-trading securities and any related accounts.

BE12–14 Cost and fair value for the available-for-sale securities of Leaf Blower Ltd. at December 31, 2009, are $84,000 and $87,000, respectively. It is not management's intent to sell the securities in the short term even if the need for cash arises. (a) Prepare the adjusting entry to record the securities at fair value. (b) Show the financial statement presentation of the available-for-sale securities and any related accounts.

BE12–15 Indicate on which financial statement (i.e., the balance sheet, statement of earnings, or statement of comprehensive income) each of the following accounts would be reported. Also give the appropriate financial statement classification (e.g., current assets, long-term investments, other revenue, etc.).

	Financial Statement	Classification
Available-for-sale securities (short-term investment)	_____	_____
Dividend revenue	_____	_____
Equity investment, equity method	_____	_____
Held-for-trading securities	_____	_____
Held-to-maturity securities	_____	_____
Realized gain on available-for-sale securities	_____	_____
Unrealized gain on held-for-trading securities	_____	_____
Unrealized loss on available-for-sale securities	_____	_____

BE12–16 Atwater Corporation reported net earnings of $625,000 and an unrealized loss of $28,000 on its available-for-sale securities for the year ended April 30, 2009. Net earnings included an unrealized gain of $40,000 on held-for-trading securities, and a realized loss of $24,000 on available-for-sale securities. The accountant wasn't absolutely sure if these should have been included in net earnings or in other comprehensive income. Prepare a statement of comprehensive income.

Prepare statement of comprehensive income.
(SO 4)

BE12–17 Sabre Corporation has the following investments at November 30, 2009:

1. Held-for-trading securities: common shares of National Bank, cost $25,000, fair value $29,000
2. Available-for-sale securities (short-term): common shares of Sword Corp., cost $110,000, fair value $105,000
3. Equity investment: common shares of Epee Inc. (30% ownership), cost $210,000, equity $275,000
4. Held-to-maturity securities: bonds of Ghoti Ltd., amortized cost $160,000, fair value $172,000

Prepare a partial balance sheet for Sabre Corporation at November 30, 2009.

Prepare investments section of balance sheet.
(SO 4)

BE12–18 BCE Inc. reported net earnings of $4,057 million and an unrealized gain of $49 million on its available-for-sale securities for the year ended December 31, 2007. It also reported accumulated other comprehensive income of $68 million as at December 31, 2007. Explain how each of these amounts should be reported in BCE's financial statements.

Indicate statement presentation.
(SO 4)

*BE12–19 On June 30, $150,000 of five-year, 10% Plaza bonds are issued at $138,960 to yield a market interest rate of 12%. Interest is payable semi-annually each June 30 and December 31. (a) Record the purchase of these bonds as a held-to-maturity investment on June 30 and the receipt of the first interest payment on December 31 on the books of the investor. (b) Record the issue of the bonds on June 30 and the first interest payment on December 31 on the books of the investee (issuer).

Record bonds for investor and investee.
(SO 5)

Exercises

E12–1 Gleason Telecommunications Ltd. has several investments in debt and equity securities of other companies:

1. 15% of the common shares of Morrison Telecommunications Inc., with the intent of purchasing at least 10% more of the common shares and requesting a seat on Morrison's board of directors
2. 100% of the 15-year bonds issued by Li Internet Ltd., intended to be held for 15 years
3. 95% of the common shares of Barlow Internet Services Inc.
4. 120-day treasury bills, purchased for interest income
5. 10% of the common shares of Talk to Us Ltd., to be sold if the share price increases

Distinguish between passive and strategic investments.
(SO 1)

Instructions
Indicate whether each of the above investments is a passive or strategic investment.

E12–2 Kroshka Holdings Corporation has several investments in debt and equity securities of other companies:

1. 10-year BCE bonds, intended to be held for the duration of the bonds
2. 10-year GE bonds, intended to be sold if interest rates go down
3. 5-year Government of Canada bonds, intended to be sold if cash is needed
4. a 180-day treasury bill
5. Bank of Montreal preferred shares, purchased for the dividend income
6. TMX common shares, purchased to sell in the near term at a profit. These shares are part of an investment portfolio that is actively traded.

Classify investments.
(SO 1)

Instructions

(a) Indicate whether each of the above investments is a passive or strategic investment.

(b) Indicate whether each of the above investments would be classified as a short-term (current asset) or long-term investment on Kroshka Holdings' balance sheet.

(c) For each investment that you classified as passive in (a), indicate whether it is a held-for-trading, available-for-sale, or held-to-maturity security.

Record HTM investment.
(SO 2)

E12–3   Riley Ltd. purchased $500,000 of 10-year, 10% bonds on July 1, 2009, at 106.5. The purchase price was based on a market interest rate of 9%. Interest is received semi-annually on January 1 and July 1. The bonds were trading at 107 at December 31, 2009. Riley intends to hold the bonds until they mature on June 30, 2019.

Instructions

(a) Record the purchase of the bonds.

(b) Record any required adjusting journal entries at December 31, 2009.

(c) How would your answers in (a) and (b) change if Riley classified the bonds as available-for-sale instead of held-to-maturity?

Record AFS investment.
(SO 2)

E12–4   During the year ended December 31, 2009, McCormick Inc. had the following transactions for its available-for-sale securities:

Jan.	1	Purchased 2,000 Starr Corporation $5, preferred shares for $210,000 cash.
Apr.	1	Received quarterly cash dividend.
July	1	Received quarterly cash dividend.
	2	Sold 500 Starr shares for $57,000 cash.
Oct.	1	Received quarterly cash dividend.
Nov.	22	Starr declared the quarterly dividend on November 22, to preferred shareholders of record on December 15, payable on January 1.
Dec.	31	Starr's shares were trading at $115 per share.

Instructions

(a) Record the above transactions.

(b) Prepare any required adjusting entries at December 31. If no adjusting entries are required, explain why.

(c) On February 15, 2010, McCormick sold 500 Starr shares for $117 per share. Record the sale of the shares.

Adjust AFS investment for multiple years; indicate statement presentation.
(SO 4)

E12–5   Kouchibouguac Inc. reports the following cost and fair values for its investment portfolio of available-for-sale securities at June 30:

	2007	2008	2009
Cost	$269,000	$269,000	$269,000
Fair value	260,500	275,400	281,200

Instructions

(a) Prepare the required adjusting entry to report the investment portfolio at its fair value at June 30 of each year.

(b) Provide the balance in the Accumulated Other Comprehensive Income (Loss) account at June 30 of each year, assuming the opening balance at July 1, 2006, was nil.

(c) Indicate where accumulated other comprehensive income is reported in the financial statements.

Record HFT investment; indicate statement presentation.
(SO 2, 4)

E12–6   At December 31, 2009, the held-for-trading securities for Yanik Inc. are as follows:

Security	Cost	Fair Value
A	$18,500	$21,000
B	12,500	14,000
C	21,000	19,000
Totals	$52,000	$54,000

Instructions

(a) Prepare the adjusting entry at December 31 to report the investment portfolio at fair value.

(b) Show the financial statement presentation of the held-for-trading securities and any related accounts at December 31, 2009.

(c) On March 22, 2010, Yanik sold security A for $22,000 cash. Record the sale of the security.

E12–7 Visage Cosmetics Ltd. acquired 40% of Diner Corporation's 30,000 common shares for $8 per share on January 1, 2009. On June 15, Diner paid a cash dividend of $35,000. On December 31, Diner reported net earnings of $75,000 for the year. At December 31, Diner's shares were trading at $10 per share.

Visage Cosmetics also acquired 15% of the 200,000 common shares of Bell Fashion Ltd. for $14 per share on March 18, 2009. On June 30, Bell paid a $75,000 dividend. On December 31, Bell reported net earnings of $160,000 for the year. At December 31, Bell's shares were trading at $13 per share. Visage intends to hold onto the Bell shares as a long-term investment for the dividend income.

Record strategic equity investment, using cost and equity methods.
(SO 3)

Instructions

Record the above transactions for the year ended December 31, 2009.

E12–8 Cameco Corp., the world's largest producer of uranium concentrates, has several long-term investments, including 53% of Centerra Gold Inc., 21.365% of UEX Corporation and 20% of Unor Inc.

Identify method of accounting for strategic equity investments.
(SO 3, 4)

Instructions

(a) Indicate whether each of the above investments should be accounted for using the cost method or the equity method, and explain why.

(b) Which of the above investments, if any, should be consolidated with Cameco's operations?

E12–9 Lowe Corporation reported earnings from operations of $425,000 for the year ended December 31, 2009. The following data apply to Lowe's investments at December 31, 2008:

Account for HFT and AFS investments; calculate net earnings and comprehensive income.
(SO 2, 4)

Type of Investment	Cost	Fair Value
Held-for-trading portfolio	$125,000	$137,000
Available-for-sale portfolio	213,000	208,000

The following investment activities occurred during the year ended December 31, 2009:

1. Lowe sold for $31,000 a security in its held-for-trading portfolio that had a cost of $18,000 and a fair value of $22,500 at December 31, 2008.
2. Lowe purchased a security for its held-for-trading portfolio for $30,000.
3. Lowe sold for $52,000 a security from its available-for-sale portfolio that had a cost of $48,000 and a fair value of $45,000 at December 31, 2008.
4. The fair values of the investment portfolios at December 31, 2009, were $142,000 (held-for-trading) and $170,000 (available-for-sale).

Instructions

(a) Calculate net earnings for the year ended December 31, 2009. Ignore income taxes.

(b) Calculate comprehensive income for the year ended December 31, 2009.

(c) Assuming AOCI was $7,000 at December 31, 2008, calculate accumulated other comprehensive income at December 31, 2009.

E12–10 Royal Bank of Canada reported the following selected information related to investments in its financial statements for the year ended October 31, 2007 (in millions):

Indicate statement presentation.
(SO 4)

Account	Amount	Financial Statement
Securities—held-for-trading	$148,246	_____
Accumulated other comprehensive income (loss)	(3,206)	_____
Gain on sale of available-for-sale securities	63	_____
Securities—available-for-sale	30,009	_____
Unrealized losses on available-for-sale securities	(93)	_____
Proceeds from sale of available-for-sale securities	7,565	_____

Instructions

Indicate on which financial statement (i.e., the balance sheet, statement of earnings, statement of comprehensive income, statement of shareholders' equity, or cash flow statement) each of the above accounts would be reported.

*E12–11   On June 30, 2009, Imperial Inc. purchased $500,000 of Acme Corp. 5% bonds at a price to yield a market interest rate of 6%. The bonds pay interest semi-annually on June 30 and December 31, and mature June 30, 2019. Imperial plans to hold this investment until it matures. At December 31, 2009, the year end for both companies, the bonds were trading at 93.

Instructions

(a) Calculate the present value (issue price) of the bonds on June 30, 2009.

(b) For Imperial, the investor, record (1) the purchase of the bonds on June 30, 2009, (2) the receipt of interest on December 31, 2009, and (3) the receipt of interest on June 30, 2010.

(c) For Acme, the investee (issuer), record (1) the issue of the bonds on June 30, 2009, (2) the payment of interest on December 31, 2009, and (3) the payment of interest on June 30, 2010.

(d) Explain how your responses to (a) and (b) would differ if Imperial classified the bond investment as available-for-sale instead of held-to-maturity.

Problems: Set A

P12–1A   The following Liu Corporation transactions are for bonds purchased as a short-term available-for-sale security during the year ended December 31, 2009:

Jan.	1	Purchased $100,000 of RAM Corporation 8% bonds at 96. The purchase price was based on a market interest rate of 9%. Interest is received semi-annually on July 1 and January 1. The bonds mature January 1, 2014.
July	1	Received interest on the RAM bonds.
	2	Sold $25,000 of RAM bonds at 100.
Dec.	31	Accrued interest on the remaining bonds.
	31	The fair value of the remaining bonds was $76,000 on this date.

Instructions

(a) Record the above transactions, including any required adjusting entries.

(b) Show the financial statement presentation of the bonds and any related accounts at December 31.

P12–2A   On January 1, 2009, Morrison Inc. purchased $400,000 of 10-year, 6% bonds for $385,460. The purchase price was based on a market interest rate of 6.5%. Interest is received semi-annually on July 1 and January 1. Morrison's year end is October 31. Morrison intends to hold the bonds until January 1, 2019, the date the bonds mature. The fair value of the bonds on October 31, 2009, was $395,000.

Instructions

(a) Record the purchase of the bonds on January 1, 2009.

(b) Prepare a bond amortization schedule for the term of the bonds.

(c) Prepare the entry to record the receipt of interest on July 1, 2009.

(d) Prepare any adjusting entries required at October 31, 2009.

(e) Prepare the entry to record the repayment of the bonds on January 1, 2019.

(f) Show the financial statement presentation of the bonds at October 31, 2009.

(g) How would your answer to (d) change if the bonds were classified as available-for-sale?

P12–3A   During 2009, Money Mart Ltd. had the following held-for-trading investment transactions:

Feb.	1	Purchased 1,000 IBF common shares for $30,000.
Mar.	1	Purchased 500 RST common shares for $29,000.
Apr.	1	Purchased 6% CRT bonds at face value, for $90,000. Interest is received semi-annually on April 1 and October 1.
July	1	Received a cash dividend of $2 per share on the IBF common shares.
Aug.	1	Sold 350 IBF common shares at $33 per share.
Sept.	1	Received a cash dividend of $1.50 per share on the RST common shares.
Oct.	1	Received the semi-annual interest on the CRT bonds.
	1	Sold the CRT bonds for $86,000.
Dec.	31	The market prices of the IBF and RST common shares were $28 and $62 per share, respectively.

Instructions

(a) Record the above transactions, including required adjusting entries (if any).

(b) Show the balance sheet presentation of the held-for-trading securities at December 31, 2009.

(c) Identify the statement of earnings accounts that are involved in the above transactions and give the statement classification of each account.

P12–4A Data for Money Mart's held-for-trading investment transactions in 2009 are presented in P12–3A. Money Mart had the following held-for-trading investment transactions in 2010:

Record HFT investments; show statement presentation. (SO 2, 4)

Mar.	1	Sold 650 IBF common shares for $22,100.
Jun.	1	Purchased 2,000 DEF common shares for $18,000.
Sept.	1	Received a cash dividend of $1.50 per share on the RST common shares.
Oct.	1	Sold 250 RST common shares for $14,250.
Dec.	31	The market prices of the RST and DEF common shares were $56 and $12 per share, respectively.

Instructions

(a) Record the above transactions, including required adjusting entries (if any).

(b) Show the balance sheet presentation of the held-for-trading securities at December 31, 2010.

P12–5A On December 31, 2008, Hi-Tech Limited's portfolio of short-term available-for-sale investments was as follows:

Record AFS investments; show statement presentation. (SO 2, 4)

	Quantity	Cost	Fair Value
Awixa common shares	500	$28,000	$28,000
HAL common shares	700	49,000	49,000
Renda preferred shares	400	18,000	18,000
		$95,000	$95,000

The following transactions occurred in 2009:

Jan.	7	Sold all of the Awixa common shares at $59 per share.
	10	Purchased 200 Mintor Corporation common shares at $65 per share.
	26	Received a cash dividend of $1.20 per share on the HAL common shares.
Feb.	2	Received a cash dividend of $1 per share on the Renda preferred shares.
	10	Sold all of the Renda preferred shares at $42 per share.
Apr.	30	Received 700 additional HAL common shares as a result of a two-for-one stock split.
July	1	Received a cash dividend of $0.60 per share on the HAL common shares.
Aug.	23	Received 20 Mintor common shares as a result of a 10% stock dividend when the price was $62 per share.
Sept.	1	Purchased an additional 400 Mintor common shares at $62 per share.
Dec.	31	The market price of HAL's common shares was $37 per share and the market price of Mintor's common shares was $43 per share.

Instructions

(a) Record the above transactions, including any required adjusting entries (if any).

(b) Show the financial statement presentation of the investments and any related accounts at December 31.

(c) How would your answer in (b) change if the investment portfolio was classified as held-for-trading securities rather than as available-for-sale securities?

P12–6A Data for Hi Tech's available-for-sale investment transactions in 2009 are presented in P12–5A. The following data relate to Hi Tech's available-for-sale investments during 2010:

Record AFS investments; prepare statement of comprehensive income. (SO 2, 4)

1. Sold all of the HAL common shares for $39 a share.

2. The market price of the Mintor common shares at December 31, 2010, was $41 per share.

3. Hi Tech reported net earnings of $415,000.

Instructions

(a) Record the sale of the HAL common shares.

(b) Prepare the adjusting entry at December 31 to adjust the available-for-sale securities to fair value.

(c) Prepare the statement of comprehensive income for the year ended December 31, 2010.

(d) Provide the balance in Hi Tech's accumulated other comprehensive income account at December 31, 2010, assuming the account had a credit balance on December 31, 2009, of $2,500.

Determine valuation of
investments.
(SO 2, 4)

P12–7A On January 1, 2009, Sturge Enterprises Inc. held the following equity investments:

Security	Quantity	Cost Per Share
X	1,500	$12
Y	2,000	7

During the year, Sturge made the following purchases:

Security	Quantity	Cost Per Share
X	1,200	$11
X	1,000	9
X	1,000	10
Y	500	8
Z	3,000	14

There were no differences between cost and fair value at January 1, 2009. The market prices of the various securities at year end, December 31, 2009, were as follows: X $6; Y $9; and Z $15.

Instructions

(a) Calculate the cost and fair value of Sturge Enterprises' equity investment portfolio at December 31.

(b) If Sturge Enterprises considers its entire portfolio to be held-for-trading securities, at what value should the equity investments be reported on the balance sheet at December 31? At what amount, and where, should any unrealized gains or losses be reported?

(c) If Sturge Enterprises considers its entire portfolio to be available-for-sale securities, at what value should the equity investments be reported on the balance sheet at December 31? At what amount, and where, should any unrealized gains or losses be reported?

(d) If Sturge Enterprises decides to classify the X shares as available-for-sale securities and the Y and Z shares as held-for-trading securities, what would be the impact on the statement of earnings? On the statement of comprehensive income? On the balance sheet?

(e) Any debt or equity security can be designated by management as a held-for-trading security when purchased. However, once an initial classification is made for a security, it cannot be transferred into or out of the held-for-trading category. Why is management precluded by GAAP from moving securities into or out of the held-for-trading category?

Identify impact of investment
transactions.
(SO 2, 3, 4)

P12–8A Olsztyn Inc. had the following investment transactions:

1. Purchased Arichat Corporation common shares as a held-for-trading security.
2. Received a cash dividend on Arichat common shares.
3. Purchased Bombardier bonds as an available-for-sale security.
4. Received interest on Bombardier bonds.
5. Sold half of the Bombardier bonds at a price greater than originally paid.
6. Purchased 40% of LaHave Ltd.'s common shares.
7. Received LaHave's financial statements, which reported net earnings for the year.
8. Received a cash dividend from LaHave.
9. The fair value of Arichat's common shares was higher than cost at year end.
10. The fair value of Bombardier's bonds was lower than their amortized cost at year end.

Instructions

Using the following table format, indicate whether each of the above transactions would result in an increase (+), a decrease (−), or no effect (NE) on the specific element on the statement. (Note that OCI stands for Other Comprehensive Income.) The first one has been done for you as an example.

	Balance Sheet			Statement of Earnings			Statement of Comprehensive Income
	Assets	Liabilities	Shareholders' Equity	Revenues	Expenses	Net Earnings	OCI
1.	(+/−) NE	NE	NE	NE	NE	NE	NE

P12–9A Cardinal Concrete Corp. acquired 20% of Edra Inc.'s common shares on January 1, 2009, by paying $1.5 million for 50,000 shares. Edra paid a $0.50-per-share cash dividend on June 30 and again on December 31. Edra reported net earnings of $840,000 for the year. At December 31, the market price of the Edra shares was $31 per share.

Record strategic equity investment, using cost and equity methods; prepare memo.
(SO 3)

Instructions

(a) Prepare the journal entries for Cardinal Concrete for 2009, assuming Cardinal cannot exercise significant influence over Edra.

(b) Prepare the journal entries for Cardinal Concrete for 2009, assuming Cardinal can exercise significant influence over Edra.

(c) The board of directors of Cardinal Concrete is confused about the differences between the cost and equity methods. Write a memo to the board that (1) explains each method, and (2) shows the investment, revenue, and other comprehensive income (loss) account balances at December 31, 2009, under each method of accounting for strategic equity investments.

P12–10A Sub Corporation has a total of 500,000 common shares issued. On January 10, 2009, Par Inc. purchased a block of these shares in the open market at $10 per share to hold as a long-term equity investment. Par intends to hold as an AFS investment any investment for which it uses the cost method. At the end of 2009, Sub Corporation reported net earnings of $350,000 and paid a $0.50-per-share dividend. Sub Corporation's shares were trading at $12 per share at December 31, 2009.

Record strategic equity investment, using cost and equity methods; show statement presentation.
(SO 3, 4)

This problem assumes three independent situations related to the accounting for this investment by Par:

Situation 1: Par purchased 60,000 Sub common shares.
Situation 2: Par purchased 125,000 Sub common shares.
Situation 3: Par purchased 500,000 Sub common shares.

Instructions

(a) For each situation, identify whether Par should use the cost or equity method to account for its investment in Sub.

(b) For each situation, record in Par's books all transactions related to the investment for the year ended December 31, 2009.

(c) Compare the balances for each account under the three situations that would be reported at December 31 in Par's nonconsolidated balance sheet, statement of earnings, and statement of comprehensive income.

(d) In situation 3, what kind of financial statements should be prepared to report the combined operations of Par and Sub? Whose name will be on the financial statements?

P12–11A On January 2, 2009, Haidey Inc. purchased shares of Jordan Cycles Corp. for $10 per share. Haidey intends to hold these shares as a long-term investment. During 2009, Jordan Cycles reported net earnings of $500,000 and paid cash dividends of $100,000. The fair value of the investment at December 31, 2009, was $425,000.

Analyze strategic equity investment.
(SO 3)

Haidey's accountant prepared a trial balance as at December 31, 2009, under the assumption that Haidey could exercise significant influence over Jordan Cycles. Under this assumption, the trial balance included the following accounts and amounts:

Equity investment—Jordan Cycles	$480,000
Investment revenue—Jordan Cycles	100,000

Instructions

(a) What percentage of the Jordan Cycles' shares does Haidey own?

(b) How many shares of Jordan Cycles did Haidey purchase on January 2?

(c) What was the amount of the cash dividend that Haidey received from Jordan Cycles during 2009?

(d) What questions need to be asked to determine if Haidey has significant influence over Jordan Cycles?

(e) Assume that, after closely examining the situation, Haidey's auditors determine that Haidey does not have significant influence over Jordan Cycles and should report the investment as an available-for-sale investment. What amount should be reported on Haidey's balance sheet at December 31 for its investment in Jordan Cycles? What will be reported on Haidey's statement of earnings for 2009? What will be reported on Haidey's statement of comprehensive income?

Prepare financial statements.
(SO 4)

P12–12A The following is the adjusted trial balance of Stinson Corporation at December 31, 2009:

STINSON CORPORATION Adjusted Trial Balance December 31, 2009		
	Dr.	Cr.
Cash	$ 125,000	
Available-for-sale securities (short-term)	345,000	
Accounts receivable	80,000	
Allowance for doubtful accounts		$ 6,000
Merchandise inventory, at average cost	170,000	
Long-term equity investment	370,000	
Held-to-maturity securities, at amortized cost	600,000	
Land	500,000	
Buildings	900,000	
Equipment	275,000	
Accumulated depreciation—buildings		180,000
Accumulated depreciation—equipment		76,000
Goodwill	200,000	
Accounts payable		285,000
Interest payable		12,000
Income tax payable		50,000
Salaries payable		5,000
Dividends payable		70,000
Bonds payable (6%, due 2012)		375,000
Note payable (due 2015)		80,000
Common shares (no par value, unlimited authorized, 300,000 issued)		1,000,000
Accumulated other comprehensive income		35,000
Dividends	70,000	
Retained earnings		1,153,300
Sales		900,000
Cost of goods sold	325,000	
Sales salaries	65,000	
Office expenses	45,000	
Depreciation expense	75,000	
Interest expense	29,800	
Interest revenue		36,000
Dividend revenue		5,000
Equity investment revenue		25,000
Income tax expense	110,000	
Realized loss on available-for-sale securities	16,000	
Unrealized gain on available-for-sale securities		7,500
	$4,300,800	$4,300,800

Instructions

Prepare a statement of earnings, statement of comprehensive income, statement of shareholders' equity, and balance sheet at December 31, 2009. There was no change in the company's share capital during the year.

Record bonds for investor and
investee.
(SO 5)

*P12–13A On January 1, 2009, CASB Incorporated issued $1 million of 10-year, 8% bonds at face value. The bonds pay interest semi-annually on June 30 and December 31. On July 1, Densmore Consulting Ltd. purchased $200,000 of CASB bonds at 101 as a held-for-trading security. On December 31, after receiving the bond interest, Densmore Consulting sold its CASB bonds at 102. Both companies have a December 31 year end.

Instructions

(a) Prepare all required entries for Densmore Consulting, the investor, to record the above transactions.
(b) Prepare all required entries for CASB, the investee, to record the above transactions.
(c) Comment on the differences in recording that you observe between the investor and the investee.

Problems: Set B

P12–1B The following Givarz Corporation transactions are for bonds purchased as a long-term available-for-sale security during the year ended December 31, 2009:

Record AFS investment; show statement presentation. (SO 2, 4)

Feb. 1   Purchased $100,000 of Leslye Corporation 9% bonds at 104. The purchase price was based on a market interest rate of 8%. Interest is received semi-annually on August 1 and February 1. The bonds mature February 1, 2014.

Aug. 1   Received interest on Leslye bonds.

    2   Sold $40,000 of the Leslye bonds at 102.

Dec.31   Accrued interest on the remaining bonds.

   31   The fair value of the remaining bonds was $60,000 on this date.

Instructions

(a) Record the above transactions, including any required adjusting entries.

(b) Show the financial statement presentation of the bonds and any related accounts at December 31.

P12–2B On January 1, 2009, Leonard Corp. purchased $800,000 of 10-year, 7% bonds for $829,079. The purchase price was based on a market interest rate of 6.5%. Interest is received semi-annually on July 1 and January 1. Leonard's year end is September 30. Leonard intends to hold the bonds until January 1, 2019, the date the bonds mature. The bonds' trading value was $830,000 on September 30, 2009.

Record HTM investment; show statement presentation. (SO 2, 4)

Instructions

(a) Record the purchase of the bonds on January 1, 2009.

(b) Prepare a bond amortization schedule for the term of the bonds.

(c) Prepare the entry to record the receipt of interest on July 1, 2009.

(d) Prepare any adjusting entries required at September 30, 2009.

(e) Prepare the entry to record the repayment of the bonds on January 1, 2019.

(f) Show the financial statement presentation of the bonds at September 30, 2009.

(g) How would your answer for (d) change if the bonds were classified as available-for-sale?

P12–3B During 2009, Kakisa Financial Corporation had the following held-for-trading investment transactions:

Record HFT investments; show statement presentation. (SO 2, 4)

Feb. 1   Purchased 600 CBF common shares for $36,000.

Mar. 1   Purchased 800 RSD common shares for $24,000.

Apr. 1   Purchased 7% MRT bonds at face value, for $60,000. Interest is received semi-annually on April 1 and October 1.

Jul. 1   Received a cash dividend of $3 per share on the CBF common shares.

Aug. 1   Sold 200 CBF common shares at $58 per share.

Sept. 1   Received a cash dividend of $1.50 per share on the RSD common shares.

Oct. 1   Received the semi-annual interest on the MRT bonds.

   1   Sold the MRT bonds for $62,000.

Dec.31   The market prices of the CBF and RSD common shares were $55 and $31 per share, respectively.

Instructions

(a) Record the above transactions, including required adjusting entries (if any).

(b) Show the balance sheet presentation of the held-for-trading securities at December 31, 2009.

(c) Identify the statement of earnings accounts that are involved and give the statement classification of each account.

P12–4B Data for Kakisa Financial Corporation's held-for-trading investment transactions in 2009 are presented in P12–3B. Kakisa had the following held-for-trading investment transactions in 2010:

Record HFT investments; show statement presentation. (SO 2, 4)

Mar. 1   Sold 400 CBF common shares for $23,600.

Jun. 1   Purchased 2,000 KEF common shares for $28,000.

Sept. 1   Received a cash dividend of $1.50 per share on the RSD common shares.

Oct. 1   Sold 400 RSD common shares for $12,500.

Dec.31   The market prices of the RSD and KEF common shares were $33 and $11 per share, respectively.

Instructions

(a) Record the above transactions, including required adjusting entries (if any).

(b) Show the balance sheet presentation of the held-for-trading securities at December 31, 2010.

P12–5B On December 31, 2008, Head Financial Corporation's portfolio of short-term available-for-sale investments was as follows:

	Quantity	Cost	Fair Value
Aglar common shares	500	$25,000	$25,000
BAL common shares	700	49,000	49,000
Hicks preferred shares	400	16,000	16,000
		$90,000	$90,000

The following transactions occurred in 2009:

Jan.	7	Sold all of the Aglar common shares at $48 per share.
	10	Purchased 400 Miley Corporation common shares at $90 per share.
Feb.	2	Received a cash dividend of $2.50 per share on the Hicks preferred shares.
	10	Sold all the Hicks preferred shares at $35 per share.
Mar.	15	Received 70 BAL common shares as a result of a 10% stock dividend when the price was $66 per share.
Jun.	23	Received 800 additional Miley common shares as a result of a three-for-one stock split.
Sept.	1	Purchased an additional 300 Miley common shares at $28 per share.
Dec.	15	Received a cash dividend of $0.50 per share on the Miley common shares.
	31	The market prices of the BAL and Miley common shares were $60 per share and $32 per share, respectively.

Instructions

(a) Record the above transactions, including required adjusting entries (if any).
(b) Show the financial statement presentation of the investments and any related accounts at December 31.
(c) How would your answer to (b) change if the investment portfolio was classified as held-for-trading securities rather than as available-for-sale securities?

P12–6B Data for Head Financial's available-for-sale investment transactions in 2009 presented in P12–5B. The following data relate to Head Financial's available-for-sale investments during 2010:

1. Sold all of the BAL common shares for $58 per share.
2. The market price of the Miley common shares at December 31, 2010, was $34 per share.
3. Head Financial reported net earnings of $565,000.

Instructions

(a) Record the sale of the BAL common shares.
(b) Prepare the adjusting entry at December 31 to adjust the available-for-sale securities to fair value.
(c) Prepare the statement of comprehensive income for the year ended December 31, 2010.
(d) Provide the balance in Head Financial's accumulated other comprehensive income at December 31, 2010, assuming the account had a credit balance on December 31, 2009, of $10,800.

P12–7B On December 31, 2009, Val d'Or Ltée held the following debt and equity investments:

	Quantity	Cost Per Unit	Fair Value Per Unit
Debt Securities			
CIBC bonds	2,000	$ 97	$100
Government of Canada bonds	1,000	100	135
Equity Securities			
Bank of Montreal	1,000	30	55
Bombardier	5,000	14	3
Nortel Networks	5,000	55	2

Instructions

(a) Calculate the cost and fair value of Val d'Or's investment portfolio at December 31.
(b) If Val d'Or considers its entire portfolio to be held-for-trading securities, at what value should the investments be reported on the balance sheet at December 31? At what amount, and where, should any unrealized gains or losses be reported?

(c) If Val d'Or considers its entire portfolio to be available-for-sale securities, at what value should the investments be reported on the balance sheet at December 31? At what amount, and where, should any unrealized gains or losses be reported?

(d) If Val d'Or decides to classify the Bombardier and Nortel shares as available-for-sale securities and the Bank of Montreal and debt securities as held-for-trading securities, what would be the impact on the statement of earnings? On the statement of comprehensive income? On the balance sheet?

(e) Any debt or equity security can be designated by management as a held-for-trading security when purchased. However, once an initial classification is made for a security, it cannot be transferred into or out of the held-for-trading category. Why is management precluded by GAAP from moving securities into or out of the held-for trading category?

P12–8B Lai Inc. had the following investment transactions:

1. Purchased Chang Corporation preferred shares as an available-for-sale security.
2. Received a stock dividend on the Chang preferred shares.
3. Purchased Government of Canada bonds for cash as a held-for-trading security.
4. Accrued interest on the Government of Canada bonds.
5. Sold half of the Chang preferred shares at a price less than originally paid.
6. Purchased 25% of Xing Ltd.'s common shares as a long-term equity investment.
7. Received Xing's financial statements, which reported a net loss for the year.
8. Received a cash dividend from Xing.
9. The fair value of Chang's preferred shares was lower than cost at year end.
10. The fair value of the Government of Canada bonds was higher than cost at year end.

Identify impact of investment transactions.
(SO 2, 3, 4)

Instructions

Using the following table format, indicate whether each of the above transactions would result in an increase (+), a decrease (−), or no effect (NE) on the specific element in the statement. (Note that OCI stands for Other Comprehensive Income). The first one has been done for you as an example.

Balance Sheet			Statement of Earnings			Statement of Comprehensive Income
Assets	Liabilities	Shareholders' Equity	Revenues	Expenses	Net Earnings	OCI
1. (+/−) NE	NE	NE	NE	NE	NE	NE

P12–9B DFM Services Ltd. acquired 25% of the common shares of BNA Ltd. on January 1, 2009, by paying $900,000 for 50,000 shares. BNA paid a $0.50-per-share cash dividend on each of March 15, June 15, September 15, and December 15. BNA reported net earnings of $550,000 for the year. At December 31, the market price of the BNA shares was $17 per share.

Record strategic equity investment, using cost and equity methods; compare balances.
(SO 3)

Instructions

(a) Prepare the journal entries for DFM Services for 2009, assuming DFM cannot exercise significant influence over BNA.

(b) Prepare the journal entries for DFM Services for 2009, assuming DFM can exercise significant influence over BNA.

(c) Compare the investment, revenue, and other comprehensive income (loss) account balances at December 31, 2009, under each method of accounting for strategic equity investments.

(d) What factors help determine whether a company has significant influence over another company?

P12–10B Hat Limited has a total of 200,000 common shares issued. On October 1, 2008, Cat Inc. purchased a block of these shares in the open market at $50 per share to hold as a long-term equity investment. Cat intends to hold as an AFS investment any investment for which it uses the cost method. Hat reported net earnings of $575,000 for the year ended September 30, 2009, and paid a $0.25-per-share dividend. Hat's shares were trading at $53 per share at September 30, 2009.

Record strategic equity investment, using cost and equity methods; show statement presentation.
(SO 3, 4)

This problem assumes three independent situations related to the accounting for this investment by Cat:

Situation 1: Cat purchased 25,000 Hat common shares.
Situation 2: Cat purchased 70,000 Hat common shares.
Situation 3: Cat purchased 200,000 Hat common shares.

Instructions

(a) For each situation, identify whether Cat should use the cost or equity method to account for its investment in Hat.

(b) For each situation, record in Cat's books all transactions related to the investment for the year ended September 30, 2009.

(c) Compare the balances for each account under the three situations that would be reported at September 30 in Cat's nonconsolidated balance sheet, statement of earnings, and statement of comprehensive income.

(d) In situation 3, what kind of financial statements should be prepared to report the combined operations of Cat and Hat? Whose name will be on the financial statements?

Analyze strategic equity investment.
(SO 3)

P12–11B Khalil Travel Agency Ltd. has 400,000 common shares authorized and 120,000 shares issued on December 31, 2008. On January 2, 2009, Stewart Inc. purchased shares of Khalil Travel Agency for $20 per share. Stewart intends to hold these shares as a long-term investment.

Stewart's accountant prepared a trial balance as at December 31, 2009, under the assumption that Stewart could not exercise significant influence over Khalil Travel Agency. Under this assumption, the trial balance included the following accounts and amounts related to the Khalil investment:

AFS investment—Khalil	$660,000
Dividend revenue	45,000
Unrealized gain—AFS (OCI)	60,000

Instructions

(a) How many shares of Khalil Travel Agency did Stewart purchase on January 2? (*Hint*: Remove unrealized gain from the AFS investment account.)

(b) What percentage of Khalil Travel Agency's shares does Stewart own?

(c) What was the amount of the cash dividend per share that Stewart received from Khalil Travel Agency in 2009?

(d) What was the market price per share of the Khalil Travel Agency shares at December 31, 2009?

(e) Assume that, after closely examining the situation, Stewart's auditors determine that Stewart does have significant influence over Khalil Travel Agency. Accordingly, the investment account balance was adjusted to $700,000 at December 31, 2009. What were the net earnings reported by Khalil Travel Agency for the year ended December 31, 2009?

(f) Assuming that Stewart does have significant influence over Khalil Travel Agency, what amount will Stewart report on its statement of earnings for 2009 for this investment?

Prepare financial statements.
(SO 4)

P12–12B The following is the adjusted trial balance of Yeung Finance Corporation at December 31, 2009:

YEUNG FINANCE CORPORATION
Adjusted Trial Balance
December 31, 2009

	Dr.	Cr.
Cash	$ 225,000	
Available-for-sale securities (short-term)	245,000	
Accounts receivable	90,000	
Allowance for doubtful accounts		$ 16,000
Merchandise inventory, at average cost	270,000	
Long-term equity investment	270,000	
Held-to-maturity securities, at amortized cost	700,000	
Land	400,000	
Buildings	1,000,000	
Equipment	375,000	
Accumulated depreciation—buildings		280,000
Accumulated depreciation—equipment		176,000
Goodwill	175,000	
Accounts payable		260,000
Interest payable		15,000
Income tax payable		47,000

Salaries payable		5,000
Dividends payable		80,000
Bonds payable (6%, due 2012)		475,000
Note payable (due 2015)		80,000
Common shares (no par value, unlimited authorized, 300,000 issued)		900,000
Accumulated other comprehensive income		45,000
Dividends	80,000	
Retained earnings		1,153,300
Sales		890,000
Cost of goods sold	325,000	
Sales salaries expense	75,000	
Office expenses	35,000	
Depreciation expense	75,000	
Interest expense	34,800	
Interest revenue		26,000
Dividend revenue		6,000
Equity investment revenue		22,000
Income tax expense	110,000	
Realized gain on available-for-sale securities		16,000
Unrealized loss on available-for-sale securities	7,500	
	$4,492,300	$4,492,300

Instructions

Prepare a statement of earnings, statement of comprehensive income, statement of shareholders' equity, and balance sheet at December 31, 2009. There was no change in the company's share capital during the year.

*P12–13B The following bond transactions occurred during 2009 for the University of Higher Learning (UHL) and Otutye Ltd.:

Record bonds for investor and investee.
(SO 5)

Feb.	1	UHL issued $10 million of five-year, 8% bonds at face value which pay interest semi-annually on August 1 and February 1.
	1	Otutye Ltd. purchased $3 million of UHL's bonds at 98 as a short-term AFS investment. The purchase price was based on a market interest rate of 8.5%.
Aug.	1	The semi-annual interest on the bonds was paid.
	1	After paying the semi-annual interest on the bonds on this date, UHL decided to repurchase $3 million of its bonds and retire them. UHL repurchased all $3 million of the bonds from Otutye at 99.

Instructions

(a) Prepare all required journal entries for Otutye Ltd., the investor, to record the above transactions.
(b) Prepare all required entries for UHL, the investee, to record the above transactions.
(c) Comment on the differences in recording that you observe between the investor and the investee.

BROADENING YOUR PERSPECTIVE

Financial Reporting and Analysis Cases

Financial Reporting: *Shoppers Drug Mart*

BYP12–1 The financial statements of Shoppers Drug Mart are presented in Appendix A at the end of the book.

Analysis Tools

Instructions

(a) What information about investments is reported in the consolidated balance sheet?
(b) Note 1 to the financial statements describes Shoppers Drug Mart's business. What other companies or entities are included in Shoppers' consolidated financial statements?

(c) Shoppers presented consolidated statements of comprehensive income and accumulated other comprehensive income. Explain what is included in these statements and how they interrelate.

(d) Judging from the cash flow statement, did Shoppers acquire any new businesses in 2007? If yes, identify the new businesses it acquired.

Comparative Analysis: *Shoppers Drug Mart and Jean Coutu*

BYP12–2 The financial statements of Jean Coutu are presented in Appendix B, following the financial statements for Shoppers Drug Mart in Appendix A. The notes to the statements can be found in the Student Toolkit section of the textbook website.

Instructions

(a) Compare the investment transactions reported in the investing activities sections of the cash flow statements of the two companies for the two most recent fiscal years.

(b) Indicate what company was acquired by Jean Coutu during fiscal 2008. (*Hint*: See Note 11.)

(c) Jean Coutu's Note 9 "Investments" describes its long-term investments. Included in investments is an investment in Rite Aid. What is Jean Coutu's percentage ownership of Rite Aid? (*Hint*: See Note 1 (a).) What income or loss did Jean Coutu report for its investments that are subject to significant influence?

(d) Note 9 also reports an investment in "third party asset-backed commercial paper." Is this investment classified as held-for-trading or available-for-sale? Did Jean Coutu report any unrealized gain or loss with respect to this investment? If it did, where is the unrealized gain or loss reported? Why did Jean Coutu classify this investment as long-term?

Interpreting Financial Statements

BYP12–3 Agrium Inc. is a leading global producer and supplier of agriculture products and services in North and South America. During the second quarter of 2007, Agrium acquired approximately 20% of Hanfeng Evergreen Inc.'s common shares for $63 million. Hanfeng is a Chinese specialty fertilizer company. The investment in Hanfeng provides Agrium with a platform for future growth in the Chinese fertilizer and agriculture market.

Instructions

(a) Assuming cash was paid for this investment, prepare the journal entry that Agrium made to record the acquisition of Hanfeng.

(b) What method—cost or equity—should Agrium use to account for its investment in Hanfeng? Explain.

(c) At December 31, 2007, Agrium reported its investment in Hanfeng at $78 million on its balance sheet. Explain why the recorded value of the investment likely changed from $63 million to $78 million.

(d) Would Agrium prepare consolidated financial statements for its investment in Hanfeng?

(e) In April 2008, Agrium announced that it had entered an agreement to acquire 70% of Common Market Fertilizers S.A. The acquisition is a key step in Agrium's global wholesale distribution strategy. What method will Agrium use to record this investment in its accounting records? How will Agrium's investment in Common Market Fertilizers be reported in its financial statements?

A Global Focus

International Resources

BYP12–4 American Express Company is the world's No. 1 travel company, with operations in more than 130 countries. The company reported the following selected information for its investment portfolio for the year ended December 31, 2007 (in USD millions):

	2007	2006
Held-for-trading securities	$ 2,650	
Available-for-sale securities	13,214	$17,954
	$15,864	$17,954

The following additional information was available for the company's available-for-sale investment portfolio (in USD millions):

	Cost	Unrealized Gains	Unrealized Losses	Fair Value
2007	$13,173	$182	$141	$13,214
2006	17,861	214	124	17,954

Instructions

(a) Why does American Express most likely have an investment portfolio consisting of two different types of securities?

(b) In relation to its total investment portfolio, American Express has a significant amount invested in available-for-sale securities. Why do you suppose it has such a high percentage of its portfolio invested in AFS securities?

(c) American Express's net earnings were U.S. $4,012 million in 2007. How much, and by what percentage, could the company have increased its net earnings in 2007 by selling its "winners" while holding its "losers"?

(d) Why should a company not engage in earnings management as described in question (c)?

Critical Thinking Cases and Activities

Collaborative Learning Activity

BYP12–5 Martino Ltd. owns and manages commercial and construction projects. Martino needs advice on the correct classification of two investments on its December 31, 2009, financial statements:

Investment #1: A $2.5-million investment in a REIT (real estate investment trust), purchased during the year, with a current fair value of $3 million. Martino's senior management has noted the recent, rapid increase in fair value but does not expect the same rate of increase in value to continue. The managers are considering cashing in the investment to realize the gain but have agreed to wait three months to reconsider their decision.

Investment #2: A $5-million investment in 10-year bonds, purchased four years ago, with a current fair value of $4.5 million. These bonds are classified as held-to-maturity securities. Martino will be facing a significant income tax liability next year as a major construction project comes to a profitable close. Selling these bonds in the open market would reduce this tax liability. Management's view is that these bonds are of exceptional quality, and that the company should consider repurchasing them in the new year.

Instructions

After the class has been divided into groups and you have been assigned one of the two investments for analysis, do the following:

(a) Identify the classification options (short- or long-term; trading, available-for-sale, or held-to-maturity) that are available for the investment you are analyzing. Discuss the appropriateness of each option and recommend the best classification.

(b) Based on your recommendation in (a), prepare the financial statement presentation of the investment at December 31, 2009.

(c) Assuming your investment is sold in 2010, identify the impact of this sale on the financial statements.

Communication Activity

BYP12–6 Comprehensive income is a recently introduced concept in Canada, although it has been used in the United States and internationally for many years. Unrealized gains and losses on available-for-sale securities are reported separately as other comprehensive income in the statement of comprehensive income rather than in the statement of earnings.

Instructions

Write a memo explaining why we record unrealized gains and losses on available-for-sale securities and why they are reported separately from net earnings.

Ethics Case

Ethics in Accounting

BYP12–7 Kreiter Financial Services Ltd. recently purchased a portfolio of debt and equity securities. Financial vice-president Vicki Lemke and controller Ula Greenwood are in the process of classifying the securities in the portfolio.

Lemke suggests classifying the securities that they expect to increase in value during the year as held-for-trading in order to increase net earnings. She wants to classify the securities that they expect to decrease in value as available-for-sale so that the decreases in value will not affect the current period's net earnings.

Greenwood disagrees. She recommends classifying the securities that are expected to decrease in value during the year as held-for-trading and those that are expected to increase in value as available-for-sale. Greenwood argues that the company is expected to have a good earnings year and that recognizing the losses in the current period will help to smooth earnings for this year. Moreover, for future years, when the company may not be as profitable, the company will have built-in gains "held in reserve."

Instructions

(a) Will classifying the investments as Lemke and Greenwood suggest actually affect earnings as each says it will, assuming they are correct in their expectations as to which securities will increase in value and which will decrease in value?

(b) Is there anything unethical in what Lemke and Greenwood propose? Who are the stakeholders that would be affected by their proposals?

(c) Assume that Lemke and Greenwood classify the portfolio properly. Now, at year end, Greenwood proposes to sell the securities that will decrease net earnings on the year-end date. Is this unethical?

"All About You" Activity

BYP12–8 In this chapter you learned that saving was an important part of personal financial planning and that without savings you cannot make investments. One way to invest your savings is to purchase Canada Savings Bonds. You would earn interest on the investment and be repaid the principal at some specified time.

Instructions

Go to the Government of Canada website at csb.gc.ca/eng/ and answer the following questions:

(a) What are the Canada Savings Bond and Canada Premium Bond?

(b) When and where can these bonds be purchased?

(c) What is the interest rate on a year one bond?

(d) One way to purchase a bond is through the Payroll Savings Plan. Click on "Payroll Savings" and use the calculator to determine an approximate value of your savings over ten years. Insert the purchase amount of $25, biweekly at an annual interest rate of 2.45%. How much principal will you contribute and how much interest will you earn over the ten year period?

Serial Case

(*Note:* This is a continuation of the serial case from Chapters 1 through 11.)

BYP12–9 Natalie and Curtis have been approached by Ken Thornton, a shareholder of The Beanery Coffee Ltd. Ken wants to retire and would like to sell his 1,000 shares in The Beanery, which represent 20 percent of all common shares issued. The Beanery is currently operated by Ken's twin daughters, who each own 40 percent of the common shares. The Beanery not only operates a coffee shop but also roasts and sells beans to retailers, under the name "Rocky Mountain Beanery."

The business has been operating for approximately five years, and in the last two years Ken has lost interest and left the day-to-day operations to his daughters. Both daughters at times find work at the coffee shop overwhelming. They would like to have a third shareholder to take over some of the responsibilities of running a small business. Both feel that Natalie and Curtis are entrepreneurial in spirit and that their expertise would be a welcome addition to the business operation. The twins have also said that they plan to operate this business for another ten years and then retire.

Ken has met with Curtis and Natalie to discuss the operations of The Beanery. All have concluded that there would be many advantages if Cookie Creations acquired an interest in The Beanery. One of the advantages would be volume discounts for purchases of coffee bean inventory.

Despite the apparent advantages, Natalie and Curtis are still not convinced that Cookie Creations should participate in this business venture. They come to you with the following questions:

1. We view this investment as strategic; however, we are a little concerned about how much influence we would have in the decision-making process for The Beanery. Would the amount of influence we have affect how we would account for this investment in the accounting records of Cookie Creations?
2. Can you think of other advantages of going ahead with the purchase of this investment?
3. Can you think of other disadvantages of going ahead with the purchase of this investment?

Instructions

(a) Answer the three questions posed above.
(b) Assume that Ken wants to sell his 1,000 shares of The Beanery for $12,500. Prepare the journal entry that Cookie Creations would record if it buys Ken's shares.
(c) Assume that Cookie Creations buys the shares, and in the following year The Beanery earns $50,000 and pays $40,000 in dividends. Also assume that the fair value of Cookie Creations' investment in The Beanery shares has increased from $12,500 to $15,000 at year end. Prepare the journal entries required under both the cost method and the equity method of accounting for this investment.
(d) Identify where the investment in (c) and any related accounts would be classified on the financial statements of Cookie Creations using (1) the cost method, and (2) the equity method of accounting for this investment.

Answers to Chapter Questions

Answer to Shoppers Drug Mart Review It Question 3
Shoppers Drug Mart's financial statements are consolidated, as is indicated on the title of each statement. Note 1 outlines the basis of consolidation.

Answers to Self-Study Questions

1. a   2. b   3. a   4. b   5. a   6. c   7. c   8. c   9. c   10. d.
*11. b   *12. c

Remember to go back to the beginning of the chapter to check off your completed work!

←

CHAPTER 13
Cash Flow Statement

ACCOUNTING MATTERS!

Rock-Solid Cash Flow Benefits

Metal prices were riding high on the stock markets in the early to mid-2000's, creating a swell of cash for mining companies. Teck Cominco Limited, headquartered in Vancouver, is a world leader in the production of zinc and metallurgical coal, as well as a significant producer of copper, gold, and specialty metals. The recent performance of these resources has produced an extremely healthy cash flow for Teck, forcing the company to consider how best to spend its money.

Cominco started in 1906 as The Consolidated Mining and Smelting Company of Canada; it changed its name to Cominco in 1966. The company's core Sullivan mine began production in 1909 and operated for more than 90 years until its ore reserves were exhausted in 2001. Teck began in 1913 as Teck-Hughes Gold Mines Limited. The Teck-Hughes gold mine was in production for 50 years until 1965. In 1969, the company purchased the Beaverdell silver mine, which was first explored in 1898 and was in production until 1991. Teck and Cominco began their association in 1986 and the two companies merged in 2001.

Teck Cominco's financial position at the end of 2006 was, in the words of president and CEO, Don Lindsay, "rock solid." The company's earnings were over $2.4 billion, and its year-end cash balance was $5 billion. It had no debt due in the next five years; more than half of the $1.5-billion debt the company did have wouldn't mature for 29 years. In fact, the company generated more than $2 billion in free cash flow.

So the next question would obviously be—what should Teck Cominco do with all that extra cash? "Clearly one of our key challenges is how to best deploy this financial capacity," Mr. Lindsay said in Teck Cominco's 2006 Annual Report. "It is not easy; good opportunities are scarce, valuations are often quite high and our competition is also well funded. But there's no rush. These are, by their very nature, long-term decisions."

Teck Cominco took part in a bidding war to purchase Inco Ltd. in 2006; however, Brazil-based Vale (Companhia Vale do Rio Doce), a much larger competitor, won control of Inco with its all-cash offer of $19.4 billion. "We could not put our shareholders at risk by offering over $20 billion in cash and taking on an extremely high level of debt," said Mr. Lindsay.

Clearly, Teck Cominco is a company that enjoys its financial comfort. Its objectives for 2007 included investing a significant amount of the excess cash in productive assets or high-quality resources, which it did with the purchase of Aur Resources Inc. It offered a combination of cash and Class B voting shares, for a total of $4 billion, in the friendly takeover of Aur, which owned interests in three operating mines, the Quebrada Blanca and Andacollo copper mines located in Chile, and the Duck Pond copper-zinc mine in Newfoundland.

With the greater volatility of the commodities market in 2007, however, there was a drop in the company's financial results. Its net earnings were $1.6 billion, compared with the $2.4 billion earned in 2006. And its cash balance was $1.4 billion compared with $5 billion in 2006. At the same time, however, the drop in cash was due in large part to the investment in Aur Resources and the earnings numbers still represented "the second best earnings year in our history," Mr. Lindsay reported in the 2007 Annual Report.

And Teck Cominco continues to find more ways to spend its money. In March 2008, it received approval to purchase 40 million, or 9.23 percent, of its Class B voting shares. In July 2008, it increased its ownership of Fording Canadian Coal Trust from 20 percent to 100 percent for $14.1 billion of cash and Class B voting shares.

In October 2008, Teck Cominco announced that it would change its name to Teck Resources, otherwise known as Teck. Says Don Lindsay, President and CEO, "Seven years ago when Teck Cominco was formed, two strong Canadian companies with a tradition of excellence in mining and metal refining were brought together. Since then, we've grown stronger through the acquisition and development of a diversified range of commodities ... Today, under one simplified name (Teck) and a new strategic business unit structure, Teck is well positioned to build on our strength as a diversified resource leader."

k Resources: teck.com

THE NAVIGATOR

☐ Read *Feature Story*

☐ Scan *Study Objectives*

☐ Read *Chapter Preview*

☐ Read text and answer *Before You Go On*

☐ Read *All About You*

☐ Review *Summary of Study Objectives*

☐ Review *Using the Decision Toolkit— A Summary*

☐ Work *Using the Decision Toolkit*

☐ Work *Demonstration Problem*

☐ Answer *Self-Study Questions*

☐ Complete assignments

UDY OBJECTIVES

er studying this chapter, you should be able to:

Describe the purpose and content of the cash flow statement.

Prepare a cash flow statement using one of two approaches: (a) the indirect method or (b) the direct method.

Use the cash flow statement to evaluate a company's liquidity and solvency.

e Navigator

PREVIEW OF CHAPTER 13

The balance sheet, statement of earnings, statement of comprehensive income, and statement of shareholders' equity (or retained earnings) do not show the whole picture of the financial condition of a company. In fact, looking at the financial statements of some well-known companies, a thoughtful investor might ask questions like these: How did Global Energy Services purchase equipment in a year when it had no cash but only bank indebtedness? Why did the Wilfrid Laurier University Students' Union spend $632,000 of cash in a year in which it earned only $345,000? Where did Vale get $19.4 billion of cash to purchase Inco? This chapter presents the cash flow statement, which answers these and similar questions.

The chapter is organized as follows:

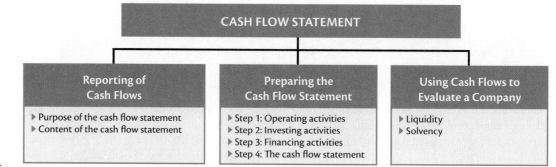

The Navigator

Reporting of Cash Flows

The financial statements that we have studied so far present only partial information about a company's cash flows (cash receipts and cash payments). For example, comparative balance sheets show the increase in property, plant, and equipment during the year, but they do not show how the additions were financed or paid for. The statement of earnings shows net earnings, but it does not indicate the amount of cash generated or used by operating activities. The statement of comprehensive income reports the changes in fair values of available-for-sale investments, but not the cash generated from an investment once it is actually sold. The statement of shareholders' equity shows cash dividends declared, but not the cash dividends paid during the year.

Purpose of the Cash Flow Statement

The main purpose of the cash flow statement is to provide information that enables its users to assess a company's ability to generate cash, and the needs of the company in using these cash flows. The information reported in the cash flow statement includes the cash receipts, cash payments, and net change in cash that result from the operating, investing, and financing activities of a company during a specific period. Reporting the causes of changes in cash is useful because investors, creditors, and other interested parties want to know what is happening to a company's most liquid resource—its cash. As the feature story about Teck demonstrates, it is essential to understand a company's cash flows in order to determine its financial capabilities and options to wisely use (or obtain) cash.

The information in a cash flow statement should help investors, creditors, and others assess the following aspects of a company's financial position:

1. **The reasons for the difference between net earnings and cash provided (used) by operating activities.** Net earnings provide information on the success or failure of a business. However, some people are critical of accrual-based net earnings because these earnings require estimates, allocations, and assumptions. As a result, the reliability of net earnings is sometimes doubted. Cash, in contrast, is often thought of as being different. If readers of the cash flow statement understand the reasons for the difference between net earnings and net cash provided or used by operating activities, they can then decide for themselves how reliable the net earnings amount is.

2. **The investing and financing transactions during the period.** By examining a company's investing and financing activities, a financial statement reader can better understand why assets and liabilities increased or decreased during the period.

3. **The company's ability to generate future cash flows.** Investors and others examine the relationships between items in the cash flow statement. From these, they can better predict the amounts, timing, and uncertainty of future cash flows than they can from accrual-based data.

ACCOUNTING MATTERS! | Investor Perspective

Analysts often use cash-based measures, such as cash provided by operating activities, instead of, or in addition to, net earnings. The reason is their belief that cash-based measures are more reliable than accrual-based measures. Sadly, even cash flow is not always what it seems to be.

Take, for example, Loews Corporation. In 2006, the company announced that it would have to restate its cash flow statements for 2003, 2004, and 2005 because of "classification errors." The company said the restatements were required because of the "lack of an effectively designed control process to ensure correct classification of cash flow activity in its cash flow statements."

While total cash was not affected, cash provided by operating activities was understated while cash provided or used by investing and financing activities was overstated. Consequently, any cash-based measures using cash provided by operating activities were also understated for this three-year period.

Loews is not the only example. Hewlett-Packard, Blockbuster, CAN Financial, and Atari join the list of companies that have had to restate their cash flow statement in recent years. The moral of this story is that errors can be made in calculating not only net earnings, but also cash flow.

Source: Stephen Taub, "Loews, CNA Restate Cash Flows Again," CFO.com, March 9, 2006.

Content of the Cash Flow Statement

Before we can start preparing the cash flow statement, we must first understand what it includes and why. We will begin by reviewing the definition of cash used in the cash flow statement and then discuss how cash receipts and payments are classified within the statement.

Definition of Cash

The cash flow statement is often prepared using **cash and cash equivalents** as its basis rather than just cash. You will recall from Chapter 7 that cash equivalents are short-term, highly liquid investments that are readily convertible to cash within a very short period of time. Generally, only money-market instruments due within three months qualify by this definition. Sometimes short-term or demand loans are also deducted from this amount. Because of the varying definitions of "cash" that can be used in this statement, companies must clearly define *cash equivalents* when they are included.

The International Accounting Standards Board and the Financial Accounting Standards Board are currently working on a project to improve the presentation of information in certain financial statements, including the cash flow statement, which is more commonly referred to as the statement of cash flows internationally. While this project is still in its early stages, preliminary views have been issued and discussed. One of the recommendations is to exclude "cash equivalents" from the definition of cash. In other words, the cash flow statement would present information about the changes in cash only, and not cash and cash equivalents. We have also chosen to present the cash flow statement in this chapter using cash only, although you will see different companies using different definitions over the next few years until this recommendation is finalized.

International Resources

Classification and Reporting of Cash Flows

The cash flow statement classifies cash receipts and cash payments into three types of activities: (1) operating, (2) investing, and (3) financing. The transactions that are found within each type of activity include the following:

1. **Operating activities** include the cash effects of transactions that create revenues and expenses. They affect net earnings.

2. **Investing activities** include (a) purchasing and disposing of investments and long-lived assets and (b) lending money and collecting the loans. Investing activities affect short-term investment and long-term asset accounts.

3. **Financing activities** include (a) obtaining cash from issuing debt and repaying the amounts borrowed and (b) obtaining cash from shareholders and paying them dividends. Financing activities affect short-term notes payable and long-term liability and shareholders' equity accounts.

Illustration 13-1 lists typical cash receipts and cash payments in each of the three activities.

Illustration 13-1 ➡

Cash receipts and payments classified by activity

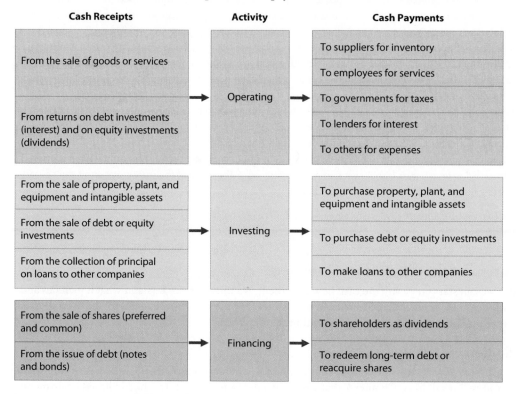

As you can see, some cash flows relating to investing or financing activities are classified as operating activities. For example, receipts of investment revenue (interest and dividends) are classified as operating activities. So are payments of interest to lenders. Why are these considered operating activities? Because these items are reported in the statement of earnings, where results of operations are shown.

Internationally, companies currently have a choice as to whether to classify interest and dividends received (and paid) as either an operating, investing, or financing activity. Once the choice is made, it must be applied consistently. Most companies follow the same practice mandated in Canada. That is, interest and dividends received are classified as operating activities and interest and dividends paid are classified as financing activities. However, as the financial statement presentation project currently under way is looking at the definitions of each of these activities to better link them to the other financial statements, there may be further changes in the future. Another change currently under review involves the presentation of operating and investing activities, which might be combined in a section titled "business activities" in future.

In terms of today's presentation requirements, we report cash flows in three separate sections: operating, investing, and financing. The section that reports cash flows from operating activities always appears first. It is followed by the investing activities section and then the financing activities section. Note also that the individual inflows and outflows from investing and financing activities are reported separately. Thus, the cash outflow for the purchase of equipment is reported separately from the cash inflow from the sale of equipment. Similarly, the cash inflow from the issue of debt securities is reported separately from the cash outflow for the retirement of debt. If a company did not report the inflows and outflows separately, some of the investing and financing activities would be hidden. This would make it more difficult for the user to assess future cash flows.

www.wiley.com/canada/kimmel

International Resources

Significant Noncash Activities

In addition, it is important to recognize that not all of a company's significant activities involve cash. The following are examples of noncash activities:

1. Issue of debt to purchase assets
2. Issue of shares to purchase assets
3. Conversion of debt into equity
4. Exchange of property, plant, and equipment

Significant investing and financing activities that do not affect cash are not reported in the body of the cash flow statement. However, these activities are reported in a note to the financial statements. The reporting of these activities in a note satisfies the **full disclosure principle**.

Note that this disclosure requirement also includes the noncash portion of a partial cash transaction, as the following example shows. Assume that a building is purchased for $10 million. A $1-million down payment was made and the remainder was financed with a mortgage note payable. Transactions such as these should not be netted. The acquisition of the building (a $10-million investing activity) by a mortgage note payable (a $9-million financing activity) would be disclosed in the notes and cross-referenced to the $1-million cash outflow reported in the investing activities section of the cash flow statement.

Teck reported a significant noncash activity in the notes to its financial statements. You will recall from our feature story that the company purchased Aur Resources for $4 billion, which it paid in cash and shares. The acquisition was reported in the investing activities section, in the amount of $3 billion. The issue of shares for this acquisition was reported as a noncash finance activity, in the amount of $1 billion.

BEFORE YOU GO ON...

Review It

1. How does the cash flow statement help users understand a company's financial position?
2. What are the three types of activities reported in the cash flow statement? Give an example of each.
3. What amounts does Shoppers Drug Mart report in its 2007 cash flow statement for (a) operating activities, (b) investing activities, and (c) financing activities? The answers to these questions are provided at the end of this chapter.
4. Where are significant noncash activities reported? Give an example.

Do It

Plano Moulding Corp. had the following cash transactions:

(a) Issued common shares.
(b) Sold an available-for-sale security.
(c) Purchased a tractor-trailer truck. Made a cash down payment and financed the remainder with a mortgage note payable.
(d) Paid interest on the mortgage note payable.
(e) Collected cash for services provided.

Classify each of these transactions by type of cash flow activity. Indicate whether the transaction would be reported as a cash inflow or cash outflow, or as a noncash activity.

Action Plan

- Report as operating activities the cash effects of transactions that create revenues and expenses and are used to determine net earnings.
- Report as investing activities the transactions that (a) acquire and dispose of investments and long-lived assets, and (b) lend money and collect loans.
- Report as financing activities the transactions that (a) obtain cash by issuing debt or repay the amounts borrowed, and (b) obtain cash from shareholders or pay them dividends.

Solution

(a) Financing activity, cash inflow
(b) Investing activity, cash inflow
(c) Investing activity, cash outflow for down payment. The remainder is a noncash investing (tractor-trailer truck) and financing (mortgage note payable) activity.
(d) Operating activity, cash outflow
(e) Operating activity, cash inflow

The Navigator

Preparing the Cash Flow Statement

Alternative Terminology
The *cash flow statement* is also commonly known as the *statement of cash flows* and the *statement of changes in financial position*.

Tutorials
(Cash Flow Statement)

We first introduced the cash flow statement in Chapter 1. You may recall that it covers the same period of time as the statements of earnings, comprehensive income, and shareholders' equity (e.g., for the year ended). As mentioned in the previous section, cash flows from operating activities are shown first, followed by the investing activities section and then the financing activities section. The reported operating, investing, and financing activities result in net cash either provided or used by each activity. The amounts of net cash provided or used by each activity are then totalled. The result is the net increase or decrease in cash for the period. This amount is then added to or subtracted from the beginning-of-period cash balance to obtain the end-of-period cash balance. The end-of-period cash balance should agree with the cash balance reported on the balance sheet.

When we illustrated the cash flow statement in Chapter 1, and in subsequent chapters, we did so without explaining how to prepare it. Let's return to basics now and learn how to prepare the cash flow statement. Where do we find the information to prepare this statement? There are no specific accounts in the general ledger for the types of operating activities, investing activities, or financing activities shown in Illustration 13-1. This is because the cash flow statement is prepared differently from the other financial statements.

First, it is not prepared from an adjusted trial balance. The statement requires detailed information about the changes in account balances that occurred between two periods of time. An adjusted trial balance will not provide the necessary data. Second, the cash flow statement deals with cash receipts and payments. Accordingly, the accrual concept is not used in the preparation of a cash flow statement.

The information to prepare this statement usually comes from three sources:

1. The **comparative balance** sheet indicates the amounts of the changes in assets, liabilities, and shareholders' equity from the beginning of the period to its end.

2. The **statement of earnings** helps the reader determine the amount of cash provided or used by operating activities during the period.

3. **Additional information** includes transaction data that are needed to determine how cash was provided or used during the period. We will also use selected information from the statement of comprehensive income and statement of shareholders' equity to help us complete the cash flow statement and the notes to the financial statements.

There are four steps to prepare the cash flow statement from these data sources, as shown in Illustration 13-2:

Illustration 13-2 ➡

Steps in preparing the cash flow statement

Step 1: Prepare operating activities section.
Determine the net cash provided (used) by operating activities by converting net earnings from an accrual basis to a cash basis. To do this, analyze the current year's statement of earnings, relevant current asset and current liability accounts from the comparative balance sheet, and selected information.

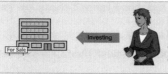
Step 2: Prepare investing activities section.
Determine the net cash provided (used) by investing activities by analyzing changes in short-term investment and long-term asset accounts from the comparative balance sheet, and selected information.

Step 3: Prepare financing activities section.
Determine the net cash provided (used) by financing activities by analyzing changes in short-term notes payable and long-term liability and equity accounts from the comparative balance sheet, and selected information.

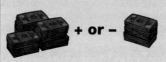
Step 4: Complete the cash flow statement.
Determine the net increase (decrease) in cash. Compare the net change in cash reported on the cash flow statement with the change in cash reported on the balance sheet to make sure the amounts agree.

To explain and illustrate the preparation of a cash flow statement, we will use financial information from Computer Services Corporation. Illustration 13-3 presents Computer Services' current- and previous-year balance sheet, its current-year statement of earnings, and related financial information.

◄ Illustration 13-3

Computer Services' financial information

COMPUTER SERVICES CORPORATION
Balance Sheet
December 31

	2009	2008	Increase (Decrease)
Assets			
Current assets			
Cash	$ 55,000	$ 33,000	$ 22,000
Accounts receivable	20,000	30,000	(10,000)
Inventory	15,000	10,000	5,000
Prepaid expenses	5,000	1,000	4,000
Property, plant, and equipment			
Land	130,000	20,000	110,000
Building	160,000	40,000	120,000
Accumulated depreciation	(11,000)	(5,000)	6,000
Equipment	27,000	10,000	17,000
Accumulated depreciation	(3,000)	(1,000)	2,000
Total assets	$398,000	$138,000	
Liabilities and Shareholders' Equity			
Liabilities			
Current liabilities			
Accounts payable	$ 28,000	$ 12,000	16,000
Income tax payable	6,000	8,000	(2,000)
Long-term liabilities			
Bonds payable	130,000	20,000	110,000
Shareholders' equity			
Common shares	70,000	50,000	20,000
Retained earnings	164,000	48,000	116,000
Total liabilities and shareholders' equity	$398,000	$138,000	

COMPUTER SERVICES CORPORATION
Statement of Earnings
Year Ended December 31, 2009

Sales revenue		$507,000
Cost of goods sold		150,000
Gross profit		357,000
Operating expenses (excluding depreciation)	$111,000	
Depreciation expense	9,000	120,000
Earnings from operations		237,000
Other expenses		
Loss on sale of equipment	$ 3,000	
Interest expense	42,000	45,000
Earnings before income tax		192,000
Income tax expense		47,000
Net earnings		$145,000

Additional information for 2009:

1. The company acquired land by issuing $110,000 of long-term bonds.
2. Equipment costing $25,000 was purchased for cash.

3. The company sold equipment with a carrying amount of $7,000 (cost of $8,000, less accumulated depreciation of $1,000) for $4,000 cash.
4. Depreciation expense consists of $6,000 for the building and $3,000 for equipment.
5. The company paid a $29,000 cash dividend.

We will now apply the four steps shown in Illustration 13-2 using the above information for Computer Services Corporation.

STEP 1: OPERATING ACTIVITIES

Determine the Net Cash Provided (Used) by Operating Activities by Converting Net Earnings from an Accrual Basis to a Cash Basis

In order to perform step 1 and determine the cash provided (used) by operating activities, net earnings must be converted from an accrual basis to a cash basis. Why is this necessary? Under generally accepted accounting principles, companies use the accrual basis of accounting. As you have learned, this basis requires that revenue be recorded when it is earned and that expenses be matched against the revenue that they helped generate. Earned revenues may include credit sales that have not been collected in cash. Expenses incurred, such as depreciation, may not have been paid in cash. Thus, under the accrual basis of accounting, net earnings is not the same as net cash provided (used) by operating activities.

Net earnings can be converted to net cash provided (used) by operating activities by one of two methods: (1) the indirect method or (2) the direct method. The **indirect method** converts total net earnings from an accrual basis to a cash basis. The **direct method** converts each individual revenue and expense account from an accrual basis to a cash basis, identifying specific cash receipts and payments. **Both methods arrive at the same total amount** for "Net cash provided (used) by operating activities." The only difference is which items they disclose.

While both the indirect and direct methods are acceptable choices to determine cash flows from operating activities, the direct method is preferred by standard setters. It is considered to be more informative to users and is easier to compare to other financial statements. Despite this preference, most companies use the indirect method. All but one company in Canada use the indirect method, and 92 percent of international companies use the indirect method. Teck, introduced in our feature story, uses the indirect method as do Shoppers Drug Mart and Jean Coutu, our textbook feature companies. Companies prefer to use the indirect method because it is easier to prepare and reveals less company information to competitors.

ACCOUNTING MATTERS! | Investor Perspective

The cash flow statement should be one of the most important tools for any user across the organization, whether internal or external. But, all too often, this statement adds little insight in to a company's operations. Take, for example, Sears Canada. Sears' business is pretty simple. It buys clothes, housewares, and other products, puts them in its stores, and sells them.

When you look at the operating activities section of Sears' cash flow statement, prepared using the indirect method, you find references to noncash items such as depreciation and changes in noncash working capital balances. Nowhere does it tell you how much cash Sears received from shoppers or how much it paid its suppliers.

The authors of *Financial Reporting in Canada* note: "We continue to be surprised by the failure to use the direct method for presenting [the operating activities]. It is difficult to believe that investors would not find information on various functional cash flows (e.g., payments to employees) more useful than the information on the adjustments required under the indirect method to reconcile net income into cash flows from operating activities (e.g., depreciation expense). However, [we note that] the AcSB concluded that the indirect method also provides worthwhile information and the additional expense and effort involved in the direct method presentation may not always be justified."

Source: Nadi Chlala, Diane Paul, Louise Martel, and Andrée Lavigne, *Financial Reporting in Canada*, CICA, 32nd Edition, 2007, p. 147.

On the following pages, in two separate sections, we describe the use of the two methods. Section 1 explains the indirect method. Section 2 explains the direct method. These sections are independent of each other. When you have finished the section(s) assigned by your instructor, turn to the next topic after these sections, "Step 2: Investing Activities."

Section 1: Indirect Method

To determine the net cash provided (used) by operating activities under the indirect method, net earnings is adjusted for items that did not affect cash. Illustration 13-4 shows three types of adjustments that are made to adjust net earnings for items that affect accrual-based net earnings but do not affect cash. The first two types of adjustments are found on the statement of earnings. The last type of adjustment—changes (increases or decreases) in current asset and current liability accounts—is found on the balance sheet.

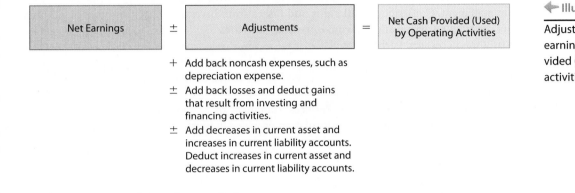

+ Add back noncash expenses, such as depreciation expense.
± Add back losses and deduct gains that result from investing and financing activities.
± Add decreases in current asset and increases in current liability accounts. Deduct increases in current asset and decreases in current liability accounts.

◀ **Illustration 13-4**

Adjustments to convert net earnings to net cash provided (used) by operating activities

The next three sections explain each type of adjustment.

Noncash Expenses

The statement of earnings includes expenses that do not use cash, such as depreciation expense. Computer Services' statement of earnings reports depreciation expense of $9,000. Although depreciation expense reduces net earnings, it does not reduce cash. Recall that the entry to record depreciation is:

Depreciation Expense	9,000	
Accumulated Depreciation—Building		6,000
Accumulated Depreciation—Equipment		3,000

A	=	L	+	SE
−6,000				−9,000
−3,000				

Cash flows: no effect

This entry has no effect on cash, so depreciation expense is added back to net earnings in order to arrive at net cash provided (used) by operating activities. It is important to understand that depreciation expense is not added to operating activities as if it were a source of cash. As shown in the journal entry above, depreciation does not involve cash. It is added to cancel the deduction that was created by the depreciation expense when net earnings was determined.

The following is a partial operating activities section of the cash flow statement for Computer Services. The addition of the noncash expense to net earnings is highlighted in red.

Operating activities	
Net earnings	$145,000
Adjustments to reconcile net earnings to net cash	
provided (used) by operating activities:	
Depreciation expense	9,000

Similar to depreciation expense, amortization expense for intangible assets is also added to net earnings to arrive at net cash provided (used) by operating activities. Another example of a noncash expense is the amortization of bond discounts and premiums. The amortization of a bond discount increases interest expense but does not use cash. Recall from Chapter 10 that the journal entry to amortize a bond discount results in a debit to the Interest Expense account and a credit to the Bonds Payable account. So any portion of interest expense that is related to the amortization of a bond discount must be added to net earnings to determine the net cash provided (used) by operating activities.

The amortization of a bond premium reduces interest expense but does not reduce cash. The journal entry to amortize a bond premium results in a debit to the Bonds Payable account and a credit to the Interest Expense account. So any portion of interest expense that is related to the amortization of a bond premium must be deducted from net earnings to determine the net cash provided (used) by operating activities.

▸ Cash Flow Statement

Just as a bond issuer can incur amortization for a bond discount or premium, so can a bond investor who is holding the bonds as a held-to-maturity security. You will recall that we learned about amortizing bond discounts and premiums for investors in Chapter 12. Adjusting net earnings for the effects of the amortization on bond discounts and premiums for investors is similar except that amortization of a bond discount increases interest revenue and the amortization of a bond premium decreases interest revenue.

Gains and Losses

Helpful Hint
Gains are deducted from, and losses are added to, net earnings in the indirect method.

Cash received from the sale of long-lived assets should be reported in the investing activities section of the cash flow statement. Consequently, **all gains and losses from investing activities must be eliminated from net earnings to arrive at cash from operating activities**.

Why is this necessary? Perhaps it will help if we review the accounting for the sale of property, plant, and equipment. The sale of property, plant, and equipment is recorded by (1) recognizing the cash proceeds that are received, (2) removing the asset and accumulated depreciation accounts from the books, and (3) recognizing any gain or loss on the sale.

To illustrate, recall that Computer Services' statement of earnings reported a $3,000 loss on the sale of equipment. With the additional information provided in Illustration 13-3, we can reconstruct the journal entry to record the sale of equipment:

A	= L +	SE
+4,000		–3,000
+1,000		
–8,000		

⬆ Cash flows +4,000

Cash	4,000	
Accumulated Depreciation	1,000	
Loss on Sale of Equipment	3,000	
Equipment		8,000

The cash proceeds that are received are not considered part of operating activities; rather, they are part of investing activities. Selling equipment is not part of a company's primary activities. **There is therefore no cash inflow (or outflow) from operating activities.** Logically, then, to calculate the net cash provided (used) by operating activities, we have to eliminate the gain or loss on the sale of an asset from net earnings.

To eliminate the $3,000 loss on the sale of the equipment, we have to add the loss back to net earnings to arrive at net cash provided (used) by operating activities as shown in the following partial cash flow statement for Computer Services:

Operating activities	
Net earnings	$145,000
Adjustments to reconcile net earnings to net cash	
provided (used) by operating activities:	
Depreciation expense	9,000
Loss on sale of equipment	3,000

If a gain on sale occurs, the gain is deducted from net earnings in order to determine net cash provided (used) by operating activities. For both a gain and a loss, the actual amount of cash received from the sale is reported as a source of cash in the investing activities section of the cash flow statement.

Gains and losses are also possible in other circumstances, such as when debt is retired. The same adjustment guidelines apply as described for gains and losses on the sale of assets, except that the other side of the transaction is reported in financing activities, rather than investing activities.

Changes in Current Asset and Current Liability Accounts

Another type of adjustment in converting net earnings to net cash provided (used) by operating activities involves changes (increases or decreases) in noncash current asset and current liability accounts. You will recall that **current assets and current liabilities are also known as working capital accounts**.

Most current asset and current liability accounts include transactions that result in revenues or expenses. For example, the Accounts Receivable account includes credit sales accrued as revenue before the cash has actually been received. Prepaid expenses include assets that have been paid in advance, but which have not yet expired or been used up, and have therefore not yet been recorded as an expense. An example is Prepaid Insurance, which is only recorded as Insurance Expense after it expires. Similarly, Income Tax Payable includes income tax expense that a company has incurred but not yet paid.

You will recall from Chapter 4 that accruals affect a noncash current asset and a revenue account or a current liability and an expense account. Prepayments affect a noncash current asset and an expense account or a current liability and a revenue account. Because accruals and prepayments affect revenue and expense accounts in the statement of earnings but do not involve cash, we need to adjust net earnings to determine the net cash provided (used) by operating activities. We do this by analyzing the change in each current asset and current liability account to determine each change's impact on net earnings and cash.

There are situations when current asset and current liability accounts do not result from operating activities. Short-term investments, such as trading and available-for-sale securities, are examples of current assets that do not relate to operating activities. The purchase and sale of investments are shown in the investing activities section of the cash flow statement. Short-term notes payable are an example of a current liability that does not relate to operating activities. The issue and repayment of notes payable are shown instead in the financing section of the cash flow statement.

Changes in Current Assets

The adjustments that are required for changes in noncash current asset accounts are as follows: increases in current asset accounts are deducted from net earnings, and decreases in current asset accounts are added to net earnings, to arrive at net cash provided (used) by operating activities.

We will look at these relationships by analyzing Computer Services' current asset accounts.

Decrease in Accounts Receivable. When accounts receivable decrease during the year, revenues on an accrual basis are lower than revenues on a cash basis. In other words, more cash was collected during the period than was recorded as revenue. Computer Services' accounts receivable decreased by $10,000 (from $30,000 to $20,000) during the year. For Computer Services, this means that cash receipts were $10,000 higher than revenues.

Illustration 13-3 shows that Computer Services had $507,000 in sales revenue reported on its statement of earnings. To determine how much cash was collected in connection with this revenue, it is useful to analyze the Accounts Receivable account:

Accounts Receivable				
Jan.	1	Balance	30,000	
		Sales on account	507,000	Receipts from customers	517,000
Dec.	31	Balance	20,000	

$10,000 net decrease

If sales revenue (assumed to be sales on account) recorded during the period was $507,000 (Dr. Accounts Receivable; Cr. Sales Revenue), and the change in Accounts Receivable during the period was a decrease of $10,000, then cash receipts from customers must have been $517,000 (Dr. Cash; Cr. Accounts Receivable).

Consequently, revenues reported on the accrual-based statement of earnings were $10,000 lower than cash collections. To convert net earnings to net cash provided (used) by operating activities, the $10,000 decrease in accounts receivable must be added to net earnings because $10,000 more cash was collected than was reported as accrual-based revenue in the statement of earnings.

When the Accounts Receivable balance increases during the year, revenues on an accrual basis are higher than cash receipts. Therefore, the amount of the increase in accounts receivable is deducted from net earnings to arrive at net cash provided (used) by operating activities.

Increase in Inventory. Assuming a perpetual inventory system is being used, the Merchandise Inventory account is increased by the cost of goods purchased. It is decreased by the cost of goods sold. When inventory increases during the year, the cost of goods purchased is greater than the cost of goods sold expense recorded in the statement of earnings. Any increase in the Inventory account must be deducted from net earnings, in a manner similar to the increase in the Accounts Receivable account explained above.

Inventory increased by $5,000 for Computer Services Corporation. Because the Inventory account is increased by the purchase of goods (Dr. Inventory; Cr. Accounts Payable) and is decreased by the cost of goods sold (Dr. Cost of Goods Sold; Cr. Inventory), Computer Services must have purchased $5,000 more inventory than it sold. Therefore, because the cost of goods sold reported on the statement of earnings is $150,000, purchases of merchandise during the year must have been $155,000:

Inventory				
Jan.	1	Balance	10,000	
		Purchases	155,000	Cost of goods sold	150,000
Dec.	31	Balance	15,000	

$5,000 net increase

Helpful Hint

Increases in current assets are deducted from, and decreases in current assets are added to, net earnings.

−
↑
Current assets
↓
+

To convert net earnings to net cash provided (used) by operating activities, the $5,000 increase in inventory must be deducted from net earnings. The increase in inventory means that the cash-based expense must be increased, which has the effect of reducing net earnings.

This deduction does not completely convert an accrual-based figure to a cash-based figure. It does not tell us how much cash was paid for the goods purchased. It just converts the cost of goods sold to the cost of goods purchased during the year. The analysis of accounts payable—shown later—completes this analysis by converting the cost of goods purchased from an accrual basis to a cash basis.

Increase in Prepaid Expenses. Prepaid expenses increased during the period by $4,000. This means that the cash paid for expenses is higher than the expenses reported on the accrual basis. In other words, cash payments were made in the current period, but expenses have been deferred to future periods. To determine how much cash was paid relative to the operating expenses, it is useful to analyze the Prepaid Expenses account. Operating expenses, as reported on the statement of earnings, are $111,000. Accordingly, payments for expenses must have been $115,000:

Prepaid Expenses				
Jan.	1	Balance	1,000	
		Payments for expenses	115,000	Operating expenses　111,000
Dec.	31	Balance	5,000	

$4,000 net increase

To adjust net earnings to net cash provided (used) by operating activities, the $4,000 increase in prepaid expenses must be deducted from net earnings to determine the cash paid for expenses. If prepaid expenses decrease, reported expenses are higher than the expenses paid. Therefore, the decrease in prepaid expenses is added to net earnings to arrive at net cash provided (used) by operating activities.

These adjustments may not completely convert accrual-based expenses to cash-based expenses. For example, Computer Services reported depreciation expense separately from its operating expenses on its statement of earnings in Illustration 13-3. Sometimes, depreciation expense is combined and reported in the operating expenses category rather than reported separately. If Computer Services had combined depreciation expense with operating expenses for reporting purposes, operating expenses would also have to be reduced by the amount of the depreciation expense included. Other charges that do not require the use of cash, such as the amortization of intangible assets, are treated in the same way as the depreciation of property, plant, and equipment.

In addition, if Computer Services Corporation had any accrued expenses payable, these would also have to be considered before we could completely determine the amount of cash paid for operating expenses.

Changes in Current Liabilities

The adjustments that are required for changes in current liability accounts are as follows: increases in current liability accounts are added to net earnings, and decreases in current liability accounts are deducted from net earnings, to arrive at net cash provided (used) by operating activities.

We will look at these relationships by analyzing two of Computer Services' current liability accounts: Accounts Payable and Income Tax Payable.

Increase in Accounts Payable. In some companies, the Accounts Payable account is used only to record purchases of merchandise on account. An accrued expenses payable account is used to record other credit purchases. In other companies, the Accounts Payable account is used to record all credit purchases. For simplicity, in this chapter we have assumed that Accounts Payable is used only to record purchases of merchandise on account.

Computer Services' Accounts Payable account is therefore increased by purchases of merchandise (Dr. Inventory; Cr. Accounts Payable) and decreased by payments to suppliers (Dr. Accounts Payable; Cr. Cash). We determined the amount of purchases made by Computer Services in the analysis of the Inventory account earlier: $155,000. Using this figure, we can now determine that payments to suppliers must have been $139,000:

Helpful Hint
Increases in current liabilities are added to, and decreases in current liabilities are deducted from, net earnings.

+
↑
Current liabilities
↓
−

	Accounts Payable				
		Jan.	1	Balance	12,000
Payments to suppliers	139,000			Purchases	155,000
		Dec.	31	Balance	28,000

$16,000 net increase

To convert net earnings to net cash provided (used) by operating activities, the $16,000 increase in accounts payable must be added to net earnings. The increase in accounts payable means that less cash was paid for the purchases than was deducted in the accrual-based expenses section of the statement of earnings. The addition of $16,000 completes the adjustment required to convert the cost of goods purchased to the cash paid for these goods.

In summary, the conversion of the cost of goods sold on the accrual-based statement of earnings to the cash paid for goods purchased involves two steps: (1) The change in the Inventory account adjusts the cost of goods sold to the accrual-based cost of goods purchased. (2) The change in the Accounts Payable account adjusts the accrual-based cost of goods purchased to the cash-based payments to suppliers. These changes for Computer Services are summarized here:

Cost of goods sold	$150,000
Add: Increase in inventory	5,000
Cost of goods purchased	155,000
Less: Increase in accounts payable	16,000
Cash payments to suppliers	139,000

Remember that adjustments to accrual-based expense accounts result in an adjustment in the opposite direction to net earnings. That is, when an expense account such as Cost of Goods Sold is increased because of an increase in inventory, this amount must be *deducted* from net earnings. This is because expenses reduce net earnings. Likewise, when Cost of Goods Sold is decreased because of an increase in accounts payable, this amount must be *added* to net earnings.

If a periodic inventory system was in use, the accounts for purchases and related expenses, rather than cost of goods sold, would be adjusted in a similar way for any change in accounts payable. There would be no change in the Inventory account throughout the period in a periodic inventory system.

Decrease in Income Tax Payable. When a company incurs income tax expense but has not yet paid its taxes, it records income tax payable. A change in the Income Tax Payable account reflects the difference between the income tax expense incurred and the income tax actually paid during the year.

Computer Services' Income Tax Payable account decreased by $2,000. This means that the $47,000 of income tax expense reported on the statement of earnings was $2,000 less than the $49,000 of taxes paid during the period, as shown in the following T account:

	Income Tax Payable				
		Jan.	1	Balance	8,000
Payments for income tax	49,000			Income tax expense	47,000
		Dec.	31	Balance	6,000

$2,000 net decrease

To adjust net earnings to net cash provided (used) by operating activities, the $2,000 decrease in income tax payable must be deducted from net earnings. If the amount of income tax payable had increased during the year, the increase would be added to net earnings to reflect the fact that income tax expense deducted on the accrual-based statement of earnings was higher than the cash paid during the period.

If Computer Services had any accrued expenses payable, they would be treated just as income tax payable was. Income tax payable is actually an example of an accrued expense payable; however, it is dealt with separately because income tax expense is reported by itself on the statement of earnings.

The partial cash flow statement that follows shows the impact on operating activities of the changes in the current asset and current liability accounts (the changes are highlighted in red). It also shows the adjustments that were described earlier for noncash expenses and gains and losses. The operating activities section of the cash flow statement is now complete.

Helpful Hint
Whether the indirect or direct method (Section 2) is used, net cash provided (used) by operating activities will be the same.

COMPUTER SERVICES CORPORATION
Cash Flow Statement—Indirect Method (partial)
Year Ended December 31, 2009

Operating activities		
Net earnings		$145,000
Adjustments to reconcile net earnings to net cash provided (used) by		
operating activities:		
Depreciation expense	$ 9,000	
Loss on sale of equipment	3,000	
Decrease in accounts receivable	10,000	
Increase in inventory	(5,000)	
Increase in prepaid expenses	(4,000)	
Increase in accounts payable	16,000	
Decrease in income tax payable	(2,000)	27,000
Net cash provided by operating activities		172,000

In summary, the operating activities section of Computer Services' cash flow statement shows that the accrual-based net earnings of $145,000 resulted in net cash provided by operating activities of $172,000, after adjustments for noncash items.

Summary of Conversion to Net Cash Provided (Used) by Operating Activities—Indirect Method

As shown in the previous pages, the cash flow statement prepared by the indirect method starts with net earnings. It then adds or deducts items from net earnings to arrive at net cash provided (used) by operating activities. The adjustments generally take one of three forms: (1) noncash expenses, (2) gains and losses, and (3) changes in noncash current asset and current liability accounts. The required adjustments to net earnings to determine cash provided (used) by operating activities are summarized here:

Noncash expenses	Depreciation expense	Add
	Amortization expense (intangible assets)	Add
	Amortization expense (bond discount)	Add
	Amortization expense (bond premium)	Deduct
Gains and losses	Gain on sale of asset	Deduct
	Loss on sale of asset	Add
Changes in noncash current asset and current liability accounts	Increase in current asset account	Deduct
	Decrease in current asset account	Add
	Increase in current liability account	Add
	Decrease in current liability account	Deduct

BEFORE YOU GO ON...

➡ **Review It**

1. What is the format of the operating activities section of the cash flow statement when the indirect method is used?
2. Why are depreciation expense and losses added to net earnings in the operating activities section when the indirect method is used?
3. Explain why increases in noncash current asset account balances are deducted from net earnings and increases in noncash current liability account balances are added to net earnings when preparing the operating activities section using the indirect method.

➡ **Do It**

Selected financial information follows for Reynolds Ltd. at December 31. Prepare the operating activities section of the cash flow statement using the indirect method.

	2009	2008	Increase (Decrease)
Current assets			
Cash	$29,000	$37,000	$(8,000)
Accounts receivable	68,000	26,000	42,000
Inventories	54,000	10,000	44,000
Prepaid expenses	4,000	6,000	(2,000)
Current liabilities			
Accounts payable	23,000	50,000	(27,000)
Accrued expenses payable	10,000	0	10,000

REYNOLDS LTD.
Statement of Earnings
Year Ended December 31, 2009

Sales revenue		$890,000
Cost of goods sold		465,000
Gross profit		425,000
Operating expenses	$188,000	
Depreciation expense	33,000	221,000
Earnings from operations		204,000
Other expenses		
Loss on sale of equipment	$ 2,000	
Interest expense	12,000	14,000
Earnings before income tax		190,000
Income tax expense		65,000
Net earnings		$125,000

Action Plan
- Start with net earnings to determine the net cash provided (used) by operating activities.
- Look at the statement of earnings: Add noncash expenses and losses and deduct noncash revenues and gains.
- Look at the current portion of the balance sheet: Add decreases in noncash current asset accounts and increases in noncash current liability accounts. Deduct increases in noncash current asset accounts and decreases in noncash current liability accounts.

Solution

REYNOLDS LTD.
Cash Flow Statement (partial)
Year Ended December 31, 2009

Operating activities		
Net earnings		$125,000
Adjustments to reconcile net earnings to net cash		
provided (used) by operating activities:		
Depreciation expense	$ 33,000	
Loss on sale of equipment	2,000	
Increase in accounts receivable	(42,000)	
Increase in inventories	(44,000)	
Decrease in prepaid expenses	2,000	
Decrease in accounts payable	(27,000)	
Increase in accrued expenses payable	10,000	(66,000)
Net cash provided by operating activities		59,000

The Navigator

▶ Cash Flow Statement

Section 2: Direct Method

As we mentioned earlier in the chapter, the direct method is preferred by standard setters. Nonetheless, at the time of writing, very few companies actually use the direct method. Why is this the case? Mostly because of the additional effort and expense involved in gathering data for the operating activities section under this method. The International Accounting Standards Board is currently working on a joint project with the FASB which may require the use of the direct method in the future. Let's learn how to prepare a cash flow statement under the direct method and see whether you think the benefits justify the additional cost.

Under the direct method, net cash provided (used) by operating activities is calculated by adjusting each individual revenue and expense item in the statement of earnings from the accrual basis to the cash basis. To simplify and condense the operating activities section, only major classes of operating cash receipts and cash payments are reported. The difference between the cash receipts and cash payments for these major classes is the net cash provided (used) by operating activities. These relationships are shown in Illustration 13-6.

Illustration 13-6 ➡

Major classes of cash receipts and payments

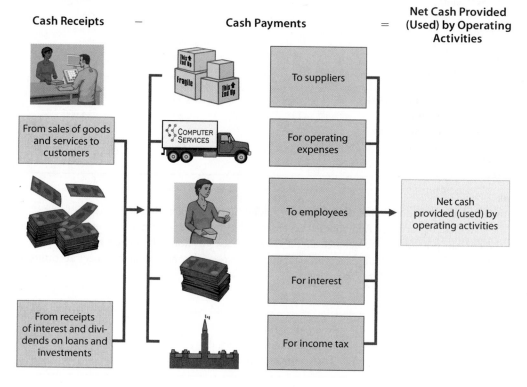

An efficient way to apply the direct method is to analyze the items reported in the statement of earnings in the order in which they are listed. The cash receipts and cash payments that relate to these revenues and expenses are then determined by adjusting for changes (increases or decreases) in the related current asset and current liability accounts.

Most current asset and current liability accounts include transactions that result in revenues or expenses. For example, the Accounts Receivable account records credit sales accrued as revenue before the cash has actually been received. Prepaid expenses record assets that have been paid in advance, but which have not yet expired or been used up, and have therefore not yet been recorded as an expense. An example is Prepaid Insurance, which is only recorded as Insurance Expense after it expires. Similarly, Income Tax Payable includes income tax expense that a company has incurred but not yet paid.

You will recall from Chapter 4 that accruals affect a noncash current asset and a revenue account or a current liability and an expense account. Prepayments affect a noncash current asset and an expense account or a current liability and a revenue account. Because accruals and prepayments affect revenue and expense accounts in the statement of earnings but do not involve cash, we need to examine each account to convert accrual-based statement of earnings amounts to cash-based amounts.

The adjustments that are required to convert revenues and expenses from an accrual system to a cash system are summarized here:

	Revenues	Expenses
Current assets		
Increase in account balance	Deduct (−)	Add (+)
Decrease in account balance	Add (+)	Deduct (−)
Current liabilities		
Increase in account balance	Add (+)	Deduct (−)
Decrease in account balance	Deduct (−)	Add (+)

We explain the reasoning behind these adjustments for Computer Services Corporation, first for cash receipts and then for cash payments, in the following sections.

Cash Receipts

Computer Services has only one source of cash receipts—its customers.

Cash Receipts from Customers

The statement of earnings for Computer Services reported sales revenue from customers of $507,000. How much of that was received in cash? To answer that, it is necessary to look at the change in accounts receivable during the year.

When accounts receivable decrease during the year, revenues on an accrual basis are lower than revenues on a cash basis. In other words, more cash was collected during the period than was recorded as revenue. Computer Services' accounts receivable decreased by $10,000 (from $30,000 to $20,000) during the year. This means that cash receipts were $10,000 higher than revenues. To determine the amount of cash receipts, the decrease in accounts receivable is added to sales revenue.

Thus, cash receipts from customers were $517,000, calculated as in Illustration 13-7.

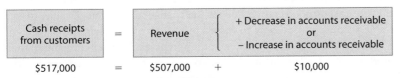

$$\text{Cash receipts from customers} = \text{Revenue} \begin{cases} + \text{ Decrease in accounts receivable} \\ \text{or} \\ - \text{ Increase in accounts receivable} \end{cases}$$

| $517,000 | = | $507,000 | + | $10,000 |

◀ Illustration 13-7

Formula to calculate cash receipts from customers

Alternatively, when the Accounts Receivable account balance increases during the year, revenues on an accrual basis are higher than cash receipts. In other words, revenues have increased, but not all of these revenues resulted in cash receipts. Therefore, the amount of the increase in accounts receivable is deducted from sales revenues to arrive at cash receipts from customers.

Cash receipts from customers can also be determined by analyzing the Accounts Receivable account as follows:

		Accounts Receivable			
Jan.	1	Balance	30,000		
		Sales on account	507,000	Receipts from customers	517,000
Dec.	31	Balance	20,000		

$10,000 net decrease

Cash Receipts from Interest and Dividends

Computer Services does not have cash receipts from any source other than customers. If a statement of earnings details other revenue, such as interest revenue, these amounts must be adjusted for any receivable amounts to determine the actual cash receipts.

Interest is the most common source of other revenue. Similar to the adjustments shown in Illustration 13-7, increases in interest receivable would be deducted from interest revenue. Decreases in interest receivable would be added to interest revenue.

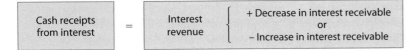

$$\text{Cash receipts from interest} = \text{Interest revenue} \begin{cases} + \text{ Decrease in interest receivable} \\ \text{or} \\ - \text{ Increase in interest receivable} \end{cases}$$

◀ Illustration 13-8

Formula to calculate cash receipts from interest

Sometimes interest revenue may include noncash amounts for the amortization of discounts and premiums on long-term available-for-sale and held-to-maturity investments in bonds. Recall from Chapter 12 that the amortization of a bond discount for an investee increases interest revenue but does not affect cash. The journal entry debits the Investment account and credits the Interest Revenue account. The amortization of a bond premium reduces interest revenue but does not affect cash. The journal entry debits the Interest Revenue account and credits the Investment account. So any portion of interest revenue that is related to the amortization of a bond discount or premium must also be removed from interest revenue to determine cash receipts from interest.

Dividends are not normally accrued, so determining cash receipts from dividends earned on investments seldom requires any adjustment.

Cash Payments

Computer Services has many sources of cash payments—suppliers, operating expenses, interest, and income taxes. We will analyze each of these in the next sections.

Cash Payments to Suppliers

Using the perpetual inventory system, Computer Services reported a cost of goods sold of $150,000 on its statement of earnings. How much of that was paid in cash to suppliers? To answer that, it is necessary to find the cost of goods purchased for the year. To find purchases, the cost of goods sold is adjusted for the change in inventory. When the Inventory account increases during the year, the cost of goods purchased is higher than the cost of goods sold. To determine the cost of goods purchased, the increase in inventory is added to the cost of goods sold. Any decrease in inventory would be deducted from the cost of goods sold. Computer Services' inventory increased by $5,000 so its cost of goods purchased is $155,000 ($150,000 + $5,000).

After the cost of goods purchased is calculated, cash payments to suppliers can be determined. This is done by adjusting the cost of goods purchased for the change in accounts payable. In some companies, the Accounts Payable account is used only to record purchases of merchandise on account. An accrued expenses payable account is used to record other credit purchases. In other companies, the Accounts Payable account is used to record all credit purchases. For simplicity, we have assumed in this chapter that Accounts Payable is only used to record purchases of merchandise on account.

Consequently, when accounts payable increase during the year, purchases on an accrual basis are higher than they are on a cash basis. To determine cash payments to suppliers, an increase in accounts payable is deducted from the cost of goods purchased. On the other hand, there may be a decrease in accounts payable. That would occur if cash payments to suppliers amounted to more than the purchases. In that case, the decrease in accounts payable is added to the cost of goods purchased.

For Computer Services, cash payments to suppliers were $139,000 ($150,000 + $5,000 = $155,000 − $16,000), as calculated in Illustration 13-9.

Illustration 13-9 ➡

Formula to calculate cash payments to suppliers

Cash payments to suppliers	=	Cost of goods sold	{ + Increase in inventory or − Decrease in inventory }	{ + Decrease in accounts payable or − Increase in accounts payable }
$139,000	=	$150,000	+ $5,000	− $16,000

Cash payments to suppliers (also known as creditors) can also be determined from an analysis of the Inventory and Accounts Payable accounts as follows:

Inventory					
Jan.	1	Balance	10,000		
		Purchases	155,000	Cost of goods sold	150,000
Dec.	31	Balance	15,000		

$5,000 net increase

Accounts Payable					
		Jan.	1	Balance	12,000
Payments to suppliers	139,000			Purchases	155,000
		Dec.	31	Balance	28,000

$16,000 net increase

Cash Payments for Operating Expenses

Computer Services' statement of earnings includes $111,000 of operating expenses. To determine the cash paid for operating expenses, we need to adjust this amount for any changes in prepaid expenses and accrued liabilities.

If prepaid expenses increase during the year, the cash paid for operating expenses will be higher than the operating expenses reported on the statement of earnings. To adjust operating expenses to cash payments for services, any increase in prepaid expenses must be added to operating expenses. On the other hand, if prepaid expenses decrease during the year, the decrease must be deducted from operating expenses.

Operating expenses must also be adjusted for changes in accrued liability accounts (e.g., accrued expenses payable). While for simplicity we have assumed in this chapter that accrued liabilities are recorded separately from accounts payable, some companies do combine them with accounts payable. This is one reason that using the direct method can be difficult in real life. If accrued liabilities and accounts payable are combined and recorded in one account, you have to figure out what proportion of accounts payable relate to purchases of merchandise, and what relates to other payables, in order to determine the cash payments to suppliers and cash payments for operating expenses.

At this point in time, Computer Services does not have any accrued expenses payable related to its operating expenses. If it did, any changes in the Accrued Expenses Payable account would affect operating expenses as follows: When accrued expenses payable increase during the year, operating expenses on an accrual basis are higher than they are on a cash basis. To determine cash payments for operating expenses, an increase in accrued expenses payable is deducted from operating expenses. On the other hand, a decrease in accrued expenses payable is added to operating expenses because the cash payments are greater than the operating expenses.

Computer Services' cash payments for operating expenses were $115,000, calculated as in Illustration 13-10.

$$\begin{array}{ccccccc}
\boxed{\begin{array}{c}\text{Cash payments}\\\text{for operating}\\\text{expenses}\end{array}} & = & \boxed{\begin{array}{c}\text{Operating}\\\text{expenses}\end{array}} & + & \left\{\begin{array}{c}\text{+ Increase in}\\\text{prepaid expenses}\\\text{or}\\\text{– Decrease in}\\\text{prepaid expenses}\end{array}\right. & + & \left\{\begin{array}{c}\text{+ Decrease in accrued}\\\text{expenses payable}\\\text{or}\\\text{– Increase in accrued}\\\text{expenses payable}\end{array}\right.
\end{array}$$

| $115,000 | = | $111,000 | + | $4,000 | + | $0 |

◄— **Illustration 13-10**

Formula to calculate cash payments for operating expenses

Cash payments for operating expenses can also be determined by analyzing the prepaid expenses account as follows:

Prepaid Expenses					
Jan.	1	Balance	1,000		
		Payments for expenses	115,000	Operating expenses	111,000
Dec.	31	Balance	5,000		

$4,000 net increase

Computer Services reported depreciation expense separately from its operating expenses on its statement of earnings in Illustration 13-3. Sometimes, noncash expenses are combined and reported in the operating expenses category rather than reported separately. If it had combined depreciation expense with operating expenses for reporting purposes, operating expenses would also have to be reduced by the amount of any noncash expenses such as depreciation. Other charges that do not require the use of cash, such as the amortization of intangible assets, are treated in the same way as depreciation.

Cash Payments to Employees

Some companies report payments to employees separately, removing these payments from their operating expenses. To determine payments to employees, you would have to know the salary expense amount on the statement of earnings and any salaries payable on the comparative balance sheets. Cash payments to employees would equal the salary expense plus any decrease (or less any increase) during the period in the amount of salaries payable.

Other companies condense their statement of earnings in such a way that cash payments to suppliers and employees cannot be separated from cash payments for operating expenses (i.e., they do not disclose their salary expense separately). Although the disclosure will not be as informative, for reporting purposes it is acceptable to combine these sources of cash payments.

Cash Payments for Interest

Computer Services reports $42,000 of interest expense on its statement of earnings in Illustration 13-3. This amount equals the cash paid, since the comparative balance sheet indicated no interest payable at the beginning or end of the year. The relationship among cash payments for interest, interest expense, and changes in interest payable (if any) is shown in Illustration 13-11.

Illustration 13-11 ➡

Formula to calculate cash payments for interest

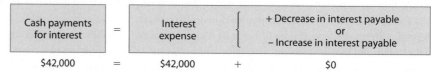

Sometimes interest expense may include a noncash expense amount, such as the amortization of bond discounts and premiums. The amortization of a bond discount increases interest expense but does not use cash. Recall from Chapter 10 that the journal entry to amortize a bond discount results in a debit to the Interest Expense account and a credit to the Bonds Payable account. The amortization of a bond premium reduces interest expense but does not reduce cash. The journal entry to amortize a bond premium results in a debit to the Bonds Payable account and a credit to the Interest Expense account. So any portion of interest expense that is related to the amortization of a bond discount or premium must also be removed from interest expense to determine cash payments for interest.

Cash Payments for Income Tax

The statement of earnings for Computer Services shows an income tax expense of $47,000 and the balance sheet shows a decrease in income tax payable of $2,000. When a company incurs income tax expense but has not yet paid its taxes, it records income tax payable. A change in the Income Tax Payable account is due to the difference between the income tax expense that was incurred and the income tax that was actually paid during the year.

The relationship among cash payments for income tax, income tax expense, and changes in income tax payable is shown in Illustration 13-12.

Illustration 13-12 ➡

Formula to calculate cash payments for income tax

Computer Services' Income Tax Payable account decreased by $2,000. This means that the $47,000 of income tax expense reported on the statement of earnings was $2,000 less than the $49,000 of taxes paid during the period, as detailed in the following T account:

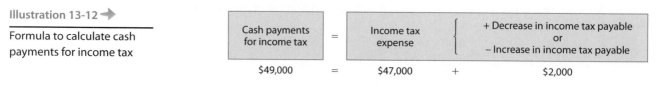

Income Tax Payable				
		Jan.	1	Balance	8,000
Payments for income tax	49,000			Income tax expense	47,000
		Dec.	31	Balance	6,000

$2,000 net decrease

All of the revenues and expenses in Computer Services' statement of earnings have now been adjusted to a cash basis. The operating activities section of the cash flow statement is shown in Illustration

13-13. Note that positive numbers in this illustration indicate cash inflows (receipts) and negative numbers, shown in parentheses, indicate cash outflows (payments).

← Illustration 13-13

Net cash provided by operating activities—direct method

COMPUTER SERVICES CORPORATION Cash Flow Statement (partial) Year Ended December 31, 2009		
Operating activities		
Cash receipts from customers		$517,000
Cash payments		
To suppliers	$(139,000)	
For operating expenses	(115,000)	
For interest	(42,000)	
For income tax	(49,000)	(345,000)
Net cash provided by operating activities		172,000

Helpful Hint
Whether the direct or indirect method (Section 1) is used, net cash provided (used) by operating activities will be the same.

BEFORE YOU GO ON...

Review It

1. What is the format of the operating activities section of the cash flow statement for the direct method?
2. Give the formulas to calculate cash receipts from customers, cash receipts from interest, cash payments to suppliers, cash payments for operating expenses, cash payments for interest expense, and cash payments for income tax expense.
3. If both the indirect and direct methods arrive at the same net cash provided (used) by operating activities, why does it matter which method is used?

Do It

Selected financial information follows for Reynolds Ltd. at December 31. Prepare the operating activities section of the cash statement using the direct method.

	2009	2008	Increase (Decrease)
Current assets			
Cash	$ 29,000	$ 37,000	$(8,000)
Accounts receivable	68,000	26,000	42,000
Inventories	54,000	10,000	44,000
Prepaid expenses	4,000	6,000	(2,000)
Current liabilities			
Accounts payable	23,000	50,000	(27,000)
Accrued expenses payable	10,000	0	10,000

REYNOLDS LTD. Statement of Earnings Year Ended December 31, 2009		
Sales revenue		$890,000
Cost of goods sold		465,000
Gross profit		425,000
Operating expenses	$188,000	
Depreciation expense	33,000	221,000
Earnings from operations		204,000
Other expenses		
Loss on sale of equipment	$ 2,000	
Interest expense	12,000	14,000
Earnings before income tax		190,000
Income tax expense		65,000
Net earnings		$125,000

Action Plan

- Determine the net cash provided (used) by operating activities by adjusting each individual revenue and expense item for changes in the related current asset and current liability account.
- Report cash receipts and cash payments by major sources and uses: cash receipts from customers, and cash payments to suppliers, for operating expenses, to employees, for interest, and for income taxes.

Solution

REYNOLDS LTD. Cash Flow Statement (partial) Year Ended December 31, 2009			
Operating activities			
Cash receipts from customers			$848,000[a]
Cash payments			
To suppliers		$(536,000)[b]	
For operating expenses		(176,000)[c]	
For interest		(12,000)	
For income tax		(65,000)	(789,000)
Net cash provided by operating activities			59,000

Calculations:
[a] Cash receipts from customers: $890,000 − $42,000 = $848,000
[b] Payments to suppliers: $465,000 + $44,000 + $27,000 = $536,000
[c] Payments for operating expenses: $188,000 − $2,000 − $10,000 = $176,000

The Navigator

STEP 2: INVESTING ACTIVITIES

Determine the Net Cash Provided (Used) by Investing Activities by Analyzing Changes in Short-Term Investment and Long-Term Asset Accounts

Regardless of whether the indirect or direct method is used to calculate operating activities, investing and financing activities are measured and reported in the same way. We will look first at investing activities in this section, and financing activities in the next.

Investing activities affect long-term asset accounts, such as property, plant, and equipment, and intangible assets. Short-term investments (for example, trading or available-for-sale securities) are also reported as investing activities. There are other less common examples of investing activities that can be found outside of long-term asset accounts, such as short-term notes receivable issued for loans rather than for trade transactions. As a result, one must be careful about applying general guidelines too widely.

As indicated in Illustration 13-1, typical cash flows from investing activities include:

Cash Inflows	Cash Outflows
• Sale of property, plant, and equipment or intangible assets	• Purchase of property, plant, and equipment or intangible assets
• Sale of debt or equity investments	• Purchase of debt or equity investments
• Collection of principal on loans to other companies	• Loans to other companies

The difference between these cash inflows and outflows is the net cash provided (used) by investing activities.

We will use the balance sheet and additional information provided in Illustration 13-3 to determine what effect, if any, the change in each long-term asset account (and any other affected short-term asset accounts) had on cash. Computer Services has three long-term asset accounts that must be analyzed: Land, Building, and Equipment.

Land

Land increased by $110,000 during the year, as reported in Computer Services' balance sheet. The additional information states that this land was purchased by issuing long-term bonds. Issuing bonds for land has no effect on cash, but it is a significant noncash investing activity that must be disclosed in a note to the statement.

Building

The Building account increased by $120,000 during the year. What caused this increase? No additional information has been provided regarding this change. Whenever unexplained differences in noncurrent accounts occur, we assume the transaction was for cash. That is, we would assume in this case that a building was acquired, or expanded, for $120,000 cash.

Accumulated Depreciation—Building

Accumulated Depreciation increased by $6,000 during the year. As explained in the additional information, this increase resulted from the depreciation expense reported on the statement of earnings for the building:

Accumulated Depreciation—Building				
	Jan.	1	Balance	5,000
			Depreciation expense	6,000
	Dec.	31	Balance	11,000

$6,000 net increase

Depreciation expense is a noncash charge and does not affect the cash flow statement.

Equipment

Computer Services' Equipment account increased by $17,000. The additional information explains that this was a net increase resulting from two different transactions: (1) a purchase of equipment for $25,000 cash, and (2) a sale of equipment that cost $8,000 for $4,000 cash. The following entries show the details of the equipment transactions:

Equipment	25,000	
Cash		25,000

A = L + SE
+25,000
−25,000
⬇ Cash flows −25,000

Cash	4,000	
Accumulated Depreciation	1,000	
Loss on Sale of Equipment	3,000	
Equipment		8,000

A = L + SE
+4,000   −3,000
+1,000
−8,000
⬆ Cash flows +4,000

The T account that follows summarizes the changes in this account during the year:

Equipment					
Jan.	1	Balance	10,000		
		Purchase of equipment	25,000	Cost of equipment sold	8,000
Dec.	31	Balance	27,000		

$17,000 net increase

In the above example, you were given information about both the purchase and the sale of equipment. Often, in analyzing accounts, you will be given just one piece of information and will have to figure out the information that is missing. For example, if you knew the beginning and ending balances of the Equipment account as well as the fact that the cost of the equipment sold was $8,000, you could determine that the cost of the equipment purchased must have been $25,000.

Each transaction should be reported separately on the cash flow statement. When a net change in a noncurrent balance sheet account has occurred during the year, the individual items that caused the net change should be reported separately. In this particular case, the purchase of equipment should be reported as a $25,000 outflow of cash. The sale of equipment should be reported as a $4,000 inflow of cash. Note that it is the cash proceeds that are reported on the cash flow statement, not the cost of the equipment sold.

Accumulated Depreciation—Equipment

The accumulated depreciation for equipment increased by $2,000. This change does not represent the overall depreciation expense for the year. The additional information in Illustration 13-3 helps us determine the details of this change.

	Accumulated Depreciation—Equipment				
	Sale of equipment	1,000	Jan.	1	Balance	1,000
					Depreciation expense	3,000
			Dec.	31	Balance	3,000

$2,000 net increase

This account was decreased (debited $1,000) as a result of the sale of equipment, as described earlier. The account was also increased by $3,000 of depreciation expense for the current period.

As we have seen, the sale of the equipment affected a number of accounts: one account on Computer Services' statement of earnings (Loss on Sale of Equipment) and three accounts on its balance sheet (Cash, Equipment, and Accumulated Depreciation). In the cash flow statement, it is important to combine the effects of this sale in one place—in the investing activities section. The overall result, then, is that the loss on the sale of the equipment is removed from the operating activities section of the cash flow statement and the cash proceeds received from the sale of the equipment are shown in their entirety in the investing activities section.

Investments

Although Computer Services has no investment accounts, it is important to remember to remove any noncash transactions when analyzing changes in any investment accounts, as we discussed earlier. These include the amortization of any bond discounts or premiums for investments in bonds, and any adjustments to fair value.

The investing activities section of Computer Services' cash flow statement is shown in Illustration 13-14. It reports the changes in the accounts Land, Building, and Equipment. Note that positive numbers in this illustration indicate cash inflows (receipts) and negative numbers, shown in parentheses, indicate cash outflows (payments).

Illustration 13-14 ➡

Net cash used by investing activities

COMPUTER SERVICES CORPORATION
Cash Flow Statement (partial)
Year Ended December 31, 2009

Investing activities		
Purchase of building	$(120,000)	
Purchase of equipment	(25,000)	
Sale of equipment	4,000	
Net cash used by investing activities		$(141,000)
Note x: Significant noncash investing and financing activities		
Issue of bonds to purchase land		$110,000

BEFORE YOU GO ON...

➡ **Review It**

1. What are some examples of items reported in the investing activities section of the cash flow statement?
2. Since trading securities are a current asset, why are they reported in the investing activities section of the cash flow statement instead of the operating activities section?
3. Why are gains or losses on the sale of equipment not reported in the operating activities section, and why is the carrying amount of equipment sold not reported in the investing activities section of the cash flow statement?
4. What are some significant noncash investing activities that are shown in a cash flow statement? Give an example.

Do It

Umiujaq Corporation reported an opening balance of $146,000 and an ending balance of $135,000 in its Equipment account; and an opening balance of $47,000 and an ending balance of $62,000 in its Accumulated Depreciation—Equipment account. During the year, it sold equipment for cash with a cost of $21,000, a carrying amount of $5,000, and a gain on the sale of $1,000. It also purchased equipment for cash. And it recorded depreciation expense of $31,000. Calculate the cash received from the sale of equipment and the cash paid for equipment.

Action Plan

• Use journal entries and T accounts to reconstruct the transactions affecting the Equipment and Accumulated Depreciation accounts.

Solution

Cash received from sale of equipment = $6,000

Cash	6,000	
Accumulated Depreciation ($21,000 – $5,000)	16,000	
Gain on Sale of Equipment		1,000
Equipment		21,000

Cash paid for equipment = $10,000

Equipment	10,000	
Cash		10,000

Equipment

Opening balance	146,000		
Purchase of equipment	10,000	Sale of equipment	21,000
Ending balance	135,000		

Accumulated Depreciation—Equipment

		Opening balance	47,000
Sale of equipment	16,000	Depreciation expense	31,000
		Ending balance	62,000

The Navigator

STEP 3: FINANCING ACTIVITIES

Determine the Net Cash Provided (Used) by Financing Activities by Analyzing Changes in Short-Term Notes Payable and Long-Term Liability and Equity Accounts

The third step is to analyze the changes in long-term liability and equity accounts, including changes involving short-term notes payable. As indicated in Illustration 13-1, typical cash flows from financing activities include:

<u>Cash Inflows</u>	<u>Cash Outflows</u>
• Issue of shares	• Reacquisition of shares
• Issue of debt	• Repayment of debt
	• Payment of dividends

The difference between these cash inflows and outflows is the net cash provided (used) by financing activities.

    To determine the financing activities, we need to examine the short-term notes payable, long-term liability, and shareholders' equity accounts on the balance sheet or statement of shareholders' equity, and any additional information. Computer Services has one long-term liability account (Bonds Payable) and two shareholders' equity accounts (Common Shares and Retained Earnings) that are affected, as shown in Illustration 13-3.

Bonds Payable

Bonds Payable increased by $110,000. As indicated earlier, land was acquired by issuing these bonds. This non-cash transaction is reported as a note to the cash flow statement because it is a significant financing activity.

Common Shares

Computer Services' Common Shares account increased by $20,000. Since no additional information is provided about any reacquisition of shares, we assume that this change relates solely to the issue of additional common shares for cash. This cash inflow is reported in the financing activities section of the cash flow statement.

Retained Earnings

What caused the net increase of $116,000 in Retained Earnings? This increase can be explained by two factors. First, net earnings increased retained earnings by $145,000. Second, the additional information provided in Illustration 13-3 indicates that a cash dividend of $29,000 was paid. This information could also have been determined by analyzing the T account:

		Retained Earnings			
		Jan.	1	Balance	48,000
Cash dividend	29,000			Net earnings	145,000
		Dec.	31	Balance	164,000

$116,000 net increase

As noted earlier, these two changes must be reported separately. The net earnings is therefore reported in the operating activities section of the cash flow statement (after the revenue and expense components have been adjusted to a cash basis using either the indirect or direct method).

The cash dividend paid is reported as a cash outflow in the financing activities section of the statement. Note that the Retained Earnings account above only reports the dividend declared. This amount must be adjusted to determine the dividend paid, if there is any balance in the Dividends Payable account reported in the current liabilities section of the balance sheet. Computer Services did not have any dividends payable.

The financing activities section of Computer Services' cash flow statement is shown below and reports the issue of common shares and payment of a dividend:

Illustration 13-15 ➡

Net cash used by financing activities

COMPUTER SERVICES CORPORATION		
Cash Flow Statement (partial)		
Year Ended December 31, 2009		
Financing activities		
Issue of common shares	$20,000	
Payment of cash dividend	(29,000)	
Net cash used by financing activities		$(9,000)
Note x: Significant noncash investing and financing activities		
Issue of bonds to purchase land		$110,000

BEFORE YOU GO ON...

➡ **Review It**

1. What are some examples of items reported in the financing activities section of the cash flow statement?
2. Since short-term notes payable are a current liability, why are they reported in the financing activities section of the cash flow statement instead of the operating activities section?
3. If you know the opening and ending Retained Earnings balances and the amount of net earnings, explain how you can figure out the amount of dividends paid to report in the financing activities section of the cash flow statement.
4. What are some significant noncash financing activities that are shown in a cash flow statement? Give an example.

Do It

La Tuque Corporation reported an opening balance of $80,000 and an ending balance of $95,000 in its Common Shares account and an opening balance of $15,000 and an ending balance of $20,000 in its Contributed Capital—Reacquisition of Common Shares account. During the year, it issued $50,000 of common shares for cash and reacquired common shares for cash. Calculate the cash paid to reacquire the shares.

Action Plan

• Use journal entries and T accounts to reconstruct the transactions affecting the Common Shares and Contributed Capital accounts.

Solution

Cash paid to reacquire shares = $30,000

Common Shares	35,000	
Contributed Capital—Reacquisition of Common Shares		5,000
Cash		30,000

Common Shares

Reacquisition of shares	35,000	Opening balance	80,000
		Issue of shares	50,000
		Ending balance	95,000

Contributed Capital—Reacquisition of Common Shares

	Opening balance	15,000
	Reacquisition of shares	5,000
	Ending balance	20,000

The Navigator

STEP 4: THE CASH FLOW STATEMENT

Complete the Cash Flow Statement and Determine the Net Increase (Decrease) in Cash

Using the partial information shown in Illustration 13-13 for operating activities, in Illustration 13-14 for investing activities, and in Illustration 13-15 for financing activities, we can now combine the sections and present a complete cash flow statement for Computer Services Corporation, as shown in Illustration 13-16.

◄ **Illustration 13-16**

Cash flow statement—direct method

COMPUTER SERVICES CORPORATION
Cash Flow Statement—Direct Method
Year Ended December 31, 2009

Operating activities		
Cash receipts from customers		$517,000
Cash payments		
To suppliers	$(139,000)	
For operating expenses	(115,000)	
For interest	(42,000)	
For income tax	(49,000)	(345,000)
Net cash provided by operating activities		172,000
Investing activities		
Purchase of building	$(120,000)	
Purchase of equipment	(25,000)	
Sale of equipment	4,000	
Net cash used by investing activities		(141,000)
Financing activities		
Issue of common shares	$ 20,000	
Payment of cash dividend	(29,000)	
Net cash used by financing activities		(9,000)
Net increase in cash		22,000
Cash, January 1		33,000
Cash, December 31		$ 55,000
Note x: Significant noncash investing and financing activities		
Issue of bonds to purchase land		$110,000

▶ Cash Flow Statement

The cash flow statement shown in Illustration 13-16 covers the same time period as the other period statements: the statement of earnings, statement of comprehensive income, and statement of shareholders' equity. The statement starts with the operating activities section. Because it is preferred by standard setters, we have chosen to illustrate the direct method of preparing the operating activities section in Illustration 13-16. The operating activities section prepared using the indirect method was shown in Illustration 13-5, and could be substituted in this illustration if desired. Both methods report cash provided by operating activities of $172,000. As mentioned earlier in the chapter, while the operating activities sections differ between the indirect and direct methods, the investing and financing activities sections are exactly the same.

The statement continues with investing activities, reporting that investing activities used $141,000 of cash. Financing activities follow, and used $9,000 of cash. The statement concludes with the net change in cash, reconciled to the beginning- and end-of-period cash balances. The comparative balance sheets in Illustration 13-3 indicate that the net change in cash during the period was an increase of $22,000. The $22,000 net increase in cash reported in the cash flow statement above agrees with this change.

Notice how the cash flow statement links the different statements with the beginning and ending balance sheet amounts. For example, the revenues and expenses that are reported on the statement of earnings and the changes in the balance sheet accounts are explained on the cash flow statement in terms of their impact on cash. Another example can be seen in information about the issue and reacquisition of shares or payment of dividends obtained from the statement of shareholders' equity or from additional information that is provided, as in Illustration 13-3. These changes lead to the end-of-period cash balances on the balance sheet and on the cash flow statement.

Additional disclosures are required to complete the cash flow statement. As we previously discussed, significant noncash investing and financing activities must be reported in the notes to the financial statements. In addition, if a company has combined cash equivalents with its cash, it must disclose the components of its cash equivalents along with a reconciliation of the amounts reported on the cash flow statement with those reported on the balance sheet. Currently, 88 percent of Canadian companies combine cash with cash equivalents on the cash flow statement, however, this practice is expected to stop with the movement to international financial reporting standards. There are other disclosures required, but we will leave discussion of these to a future accounting course.

You will recall that we mentioned earlier in the chapter that the International Accounting Standards Board and the Financial Accounting Standards Board are working on a project to improve the presentation of information in the cash flow statement, among other statements. One of the tentative decisions they have made is to require a reconciliation of the information in the cash flow statement to the statement of comprehensive income. This reconciliation would separate earnings into its cash and accrual components, including accruals that are due to changes in fair value. The IASB believes that investors need to analyze these components separately because the components can differ in how well they predict future profitability.

International Resources

BEFORE YOU GO ON...

➡ **Review It**

1. How do you determine the net increase or decrease in cash?
2. Explain how the statement of earnings, statement of shareholders' equity, statement of comprehensive income, and balance sheet are interrelated with the cash flow statement.
3. What disclosures are required in the notes to the financial statements about the cash flow statement?

➡ **Do It**

Selected information follows for Reynolds Ltd. at December 31:

	2009	2008	Increase (Decrease)
Cash	$29,000	$37,000	$ (8,000)
Property, plant, and equipment			
Land	45,000	70,000	(25,000)
Buildings	200,000	200,000	0
Accumulated depreciation—buildings	(21,000)	(11,000)	10,000
Equipment	193,000	68,000	125,000
Accumulated depreciation—equipment	(28,000)	(10,000)	18,000

Liabilities and shareholders' equity

Bonds payable	50,000	150,000	(100,000)
Common shares	220,000	60,000	160,000
Retained earnings	241,000	136,000	105,000

Additional information:

1. Cash provided by operating activities was $59,000 for the year.
2. Equipment was purchased for cash. Equipment with a cost of $41,000 and a carrying amount of $36,000 was sold at a loss of $2,000.
3. Bonds of $100,000 were redeemed at their face value for cash.
4. Net earnings were $125,000.
5. A cash dividend was paid.

Prepare a cash flow statement, excluding the detail normally required for the operating activities section.

Action Plan

• Begin with the operating activities section.
• Determine the net cash provided (used) by investing activities. Investing activities generally relate to changes in short-term investment and long-term asset accounts.
• Determine the net cash provided (used) by financing activities. Financing activities generally relate to changes in short-term notes payable, long-term liabilities, and shareholders' equity accounts.
• Determine the net increase (decrease) in cash. Reconcile to the end-of-period cash balance reported on the balance sheet.

Solution

REYNOLDS LTD.
Cash Flow Statement
Year Ended December 31, 2009

Operating activities		
Net cash provided by operating activities		$ 59,000
Investing activities		
Sale of land	$ 25,000	
Sale of equipment	34,000ᵃ	
Purchase of equipment	(166,000)ᵇ	
Net cash used by investing activities		(107,000)
Financing activities		
Redemption of bonds	$(100,000)	
Issue of common shares	160,000	
Payment of dividends	(20,000)ᶜ	
Net cash provided by financing activities		40,000
Net decrease in cash		(8,000)
Cash, January 1		37,000
Cash, December 31		$ 29,000

ᵃ Sale of equipment: $36,000 – $2,000 = $34,000
ᵇ Purchase of equipment: $68,000 – $41,000 – $193,000 = $166,000
ᶜ Payment of dividends: $136,000 + $125,000 – $241,000 = $20,000

The Navigator

Using Cash Flows to Evaluate a Company

Previous chapters have presented ratios that are used to analyze a company's liquidity and solvency. Most of those ratios used accrual-based numbers from the statement of earnings and balance sheet. Analysts often have doubts about accrual-based numbers because they feel that the adjustment process allows management too much discretion. These analysts like to supplement accrual-based analysis with measures that use information from the cash flow statement.

In this section, we will use the following selected information (in millions) for Teck to introduce liquidity and solvency ratios that are *cash-based* rather than accrual-based:

study objective 3

Use the cash flow statement to evaluate a company's liquidity and solvency.

	2007	2006
Cash provided by operating activities	$1,719	$2,905
Current liabilities	1,350	1,688
Total liabilities	4,504	3,210

Liquidity

Liquidity is the ability of a company to meet its immediate obligations. In Chapter 2, you learned that one measure of liquidity is the current ratio (current assets divided by current liabilities). One disadvantage of the current ratio is that it uses year-end balances of current asset and current liability accounts. These year-end balances may not be representative of the company's position during most of the year. Another disadvantage is that current assets and current liabilities include accrual-based numbers.

A ratio that partially corrects this problem is the cash current debt coverage ratio. It is calculated by dividing cash provided by operating activities by average current liabilities. We say "partially corrects this problem" because, even though the numerator uses cash-based numbers, the denominator, current liabilities, does not.

The cash current debt coverage ratio for Teck is shown in Illustration 13-17, along with comparative information given for Freeport-McMoRan Copper & Gold Inc. Freeport-McMoRan, a key competitor to Teck, is an international mining company headquartered in Arizona. We have also provided each company's current ratio. Unfortunately, although there are industry averages for the more commonly used accrual-based measures, no averages are available for cash-based measures.

Illustration 13-17 ➡

Cash current debt coverage ratio

CASH CURRENT DEBT COVERAGE =	$\dfrac{\text{CASH PROVIDED BY OPERATING ACTIVITIES}}{\text{AVERAGE CURRENT LIABILITIES}}$	
(in millions)	Cash Current Debt Coverage Ratio	Current Ratio
Teck	$\dfrac{\$1,719}{(\$1,350 + \$1,688) \div 2} = 1.1$ times	2.2:1
Freeport-McMoRan	2.6 times	1.5:1

Teck's cash provided by operating activities is marginally more than its average current liabilities. Its cash current debt coverage ratio of 1.1 times means that $1.10 of cash flow from operating activities has been generated to cover each dollar of current liabilities. The higher the cash current debt coverage ratio is, the better a company's liquidity is.

Teck's current ratio is much stronger than its cash current debt coverage ratio. However, with the amount of the difference between the two measures, it is likely that Teck's current assets include a large amount of accruals (e.g., from revenue billed but not yet collected, from merchandise purchased on account, prepayments, etc.). This is not a problem, however, as long as the receivables are collectable and the inventory is saleable.

Teck's cash current debt coverage ratio is significantly lower than that of Freeport-McMoRan, even though its current ratio is higher. As we have learned in previous chapters, additional ratios such as receivables turnover and inventory turnover must be calculated in order to properly assess a company's liquidity.

DECISION TOOLKIT

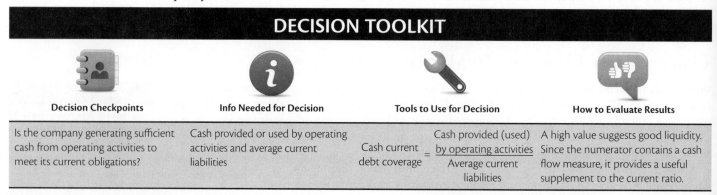

Decision Checkpoints	Info Needed for Decision	Tools to Use for Decision	How to Evaluate Results
Is the company generating sufficient cash from operating activities to meet its current obligations?	Cash provided or used by operating activities and average current liabilities	$\text{Cash current debt coverage} = \dfrac{\text{Cash provided (used) by operating activities}}{\text{Average current liabilities}}$	A high value suggests good liquidity. Since the numerator contains a cash flow measure, it provides a useful supplement to the current ratio.

Solvency

Solvency is the ability of a company to survive over the long term. In Chapter 2, you learned about one cash-based measure of solvency, free cash flow. **Free cash flow** describes the cash remaining from operating activities after adjusting for capital expenditures and dividends. As indicated in our feature story, Teck generated more than $2 billion of free cash flow in 2006. In 2007, it generated only $722 million in free cash flow. In 2007, its net earnings were down substantially because of changes in commodities prices. Consequently, its cash from operating activities also declined and, correspondingly, its free cash flow.

Another cash-based measure of solvency is the cash total debt coverage ratio. It is similar to the cash current debt coverage ratio except that it uses total liabilities instead of current liabilities. The cash total debt coverage ratio is calculated by dividing cash provided by operating activities by average total liabilities. The higher the cash total debt coverage ratio is, the more solvent a company is.

The cash total debt coverage ratios for Teck and Freeport-McMoRan are given in Illustration 13-18. For comparative purposes, the accrual-based counterpart, the debt to total assets ratio, is also provided for each company. You will recall from Chapter 2 that the debt to total assets ratio is calculated by dividing total liabilities by total assets.

$$\text{CASH TOTAL DEBT COVERAGE} = \frac{\text{CASH PROVIDED (USED) BY OPERATING ACTIVITIES}}{\text{AVERAGE TOTAL LIABILITIES}}$$

(in millions)	Cash Total Debt Coverage Ratio	Debt to Total Assets
Teck	$\dfrac{\$1,719}{(\$4,504 + \$3,210) \div 2} = 0.4 \text{ times}$	33.2%
Freeport-McMoRan	0.5 times	55.2%

◀ Illustration 13-18
Cash total debt coverage ratio

The two companies have relatively close cash total debt coverage ratios, although Freeport-McMoRan's coverage is slightly better than that of Teck. Teck's cash total debt coverage ratio of 0.4 times means that it is generating $0.40 to cover each dollar of total liabilities. This ratio is significantly less than its cash current debt coverage ratio of 1.1 times, so we know that Teck has a considerable amount of long-term liabilities.

Although the two cash total debt coverage ratios are relatively close, Teck's debt to total assets is much better than that of Freeport-McMoRan. Recall that the *higher* the cash total debt coverage ratio, the better the result, while the *lower* the debt to total assets ratio, the better the result. Since both ratios are moving in different directions (i.e., the cash total debt coverage ratio is worse while the debt to total assets ratio is better), we can conclude that there is likely some difference between the cash and accrual measures for the two companies.

It is difficult to reach a conclusion about either company's solvency position without also knowing more about each company's ability to handle its debt (e.g., its times interest earned ratio). However, a low cash total debt coverage ratio could signal a long-term solvency problem if the company is not able to generate enough cash internally to repay its debt. Because Teck has significantly less debt than Freeport-McMoRan, this would be less of a concern in its case.

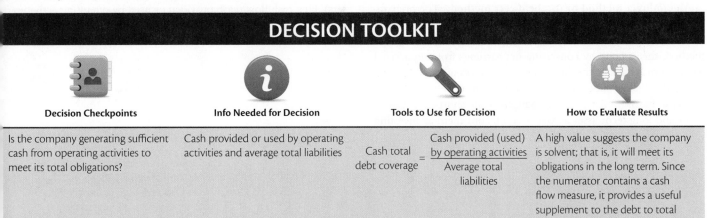

DECISION TOOLKIT

Decision Checkpoints	Info Needed for Decision	Tools to Use for Decision	How to Evaluate Results
Is the company generating sufficient cash from operating activities to meet its total obligations?	Cash provided or used by operating activities and average total liabilities	$\text{Cash total debt coverage} = \dfrac{\text{Cash provided (used) by operating activities}}{\text{Average total liabilities}}$	A high value suggests the company is solvent; that is, it will meet its obligations in the long term. Since the numerator contains a cash flow measure, it provides a useful supplement to the debt to total assets ratio.

ACCOUNTING MATTERS! | Investor Perspective

Another commonly used cash-based measure is EBITDA. It is an abbreviation for "earnings before interest, tax, depreciation, and amortization." EBITDA is frequently cited in annual reports and in the financial press as a cash-based measure of earnings. Freeport-McMoRan's EBITDA is more than three times that of Teck. Banks and other creditors prefer EBITDA over net earnings because it eliminates the effects of many accounting and financing decisions. Still, one must be cautious in interpreting EBITDA because there is no standard definition for this measure and different companies often calculate it in different ways.

BEFORE YOU GO ON...

Review It

1. Why might an analyst want to supplement accrual-based ratios with cash-based ratios?
2. What are some cash-based ratios to measure liquidity and solvency?
3. What accrual-based ratio does the cash current debt coverage ratio compare to?
4. What accrual-based ratio does the cash total debt coverage ratio compare to?

The Navigator

Summary of Study Objectives

1. Describe the purpose and content of the cash flow statement. The cash flow statement provides information about the cash receipts and cash payments resulting from the operating, investing, and financing activities of a company during a specific period.

In general, operating activities include the cash effects of transactions that are used in the determination of net earnings. Operating activities are affected by noncash items in the statement of earnings and changes in noncash current asset and current liability accounts in the balance sheet. Investing activities involve cash flows resulting from changes in short-term investment and long-term asset items. Financing activities involve cash flows resulting from changes in short-term notes payable, long-term liabilities, and shareholders' equity items.

2. Prepare a cash flow statement using one of two approaches: (a) the indirect method or (b) the direct method. The preparation of a cash flow statement involves four steps: (1) Determine the net cash provided (used) by operating activities. In the indirect method, this is done by converting net earnings from an accrual basis to a cash basis. In the direct method, this is done by converting each individual revenue and expense account from an accrual basis to a cash basis. (2) Analyze the changes in the short-term investment and long-term asset accounts and record them as investing

activities, or as significant noncash transactions. (3) Analyze the changes in the short-term notes payable, long-term liability, and equity accounts and record them as financing activities, or as significant noncash transactions. (4) Complete the cash flow statement and determine the net increase or decrease in cash.

3. Use the cash flow statement to evaluate a company's liquidity and solvency. Liquidity can be measured by the cash-based cash current debt coverage ratio (cash provided or used by operating activities divided by average current liabilities) and compared to the accrual-based current ratio (current assets divided by current liabilities). Solvency can be measured by the cash-based cash total debt coverage ratio (cash provided or used by operating activities divided by average total liabilities) and compared to the accrual-based debt to total assets ratio (total liabilities divided by total assets). Free cash flow (cash provided or used by operating activities minus capital expenditures minus dividends) is another measure of solvency.

The Navigator

ALL ABOUT YOU

Where Does the Money Go?

Because cash is so vital to a company, planning the company's cash needs is a key business activity. It enables the company to plan ahead to cover possible cash shortfalls and to invest idle funds. When a company's cash flow from operating activities does not cover its cash needs, it must find additional cash. In the short-term that is fine, but in the long-term it can spell disaster. Sooner or later, the company needs to increase its cash from operating activities or cut back on its expenditures, or it will go broke. A company should always have a cash budget that shows anticipated cash flows, usually over a one- to two-year period. You should too.

Where do you spend your cash? A personal cash flow statement can help you track the relationship between your cash inflows and cash outflows over a period of time. Most of us know how much we spend on rent and car payments as well as university tuition. Do you know how much you spend each month on coffee, cell phone service, and music downloads? Suppose you spend on average $5 per day on unneeded incidentals. That is $35 a week or $1,820 per year. And, instead of buying forty $5 lottery tickets a year, invest the $200 in true investments at the end of each year at 8 percent. If you start at age 18, you will have $106,068 by the time you reach 67. With lottery tickets, chances are you will have nothing.

Some Facts

- On average, each Canadian household spent $48,770 on goods and services in 2006, up 4.6% from 2005.
- Household spending on cell phone and other wireless services was up more than 18% from 2005 to an average of $470 in 2006. At the same time, spending for conventional land-line telephone service continued to fall, dropping 3% to $650.
- Households spent 38% more in 2006 on new audio equipment, such as digital music players, and 16% more on new video equipment, including big-screen TVs. For the first time, more households reported owning a DVD player (83%) than a VCR (82%).
- Ten percent of household income went toward food in 2006, the lowest-ever proportion of total spending on food. In the 1960s, food represented the largest proportion of household spending, at 19 percent.

What Do You Think?

You live on campus and own a car. You use the car for pleasure and to drive to a job that is five miles away. Suppose your personal cash flow statement includes the following items for the current year:

Cash inflows of $18,000

Cash outflows of tuition, board, and books $14,000; vehicle costs $3,000; vacation $2,000; cell phone service $600; and snacks and beverages $500.

Should you get rid of your car and cell phone, stop eating snacks, and give up the idea of a vacation?

YES | Because the cash outflows ($14,000 + $3,000 + $2,000 + $600 + $500 = $20,100) are greater than the cash inflows ($18,000), you will accumulate debt that you will have to pay back when you finish university.

NO | A person has to have a bit of fun. Life would be boring if I couldn't drink my Tim Hortons coffee while driving along the highway.

The Navigator

Sources:

Statistics Canada, "Survey of Household Spending," February 26, 2008, statcan.ca/Daily/English/080226/d080226a.htm

Lawrence J. Gitman, et al., *Personal Financial Planning*, 1st Canadian ed. (Toronto: Thomson Nelson, 2008), p. 70

Glossary    Study Tools (Glossary)

Cash current debt coverage A cash-based ratio used to evaluate liquidity. It is calculated by dividing cash provided (used) by operating activities by average current liabilities. (p. 682)

Cash total debt coverage A cash-based ratio used to evaluate solvency. It is calculated by dividing cash provided (used) by operating activities by average total liabilities. (p. 683)

Direct method A method of determining net cash provided (used) by operating activities by adjusting each item in the statement of earnings from the accrual basis to the cash basis. (p. 660)

Financing activities Cash flow activities from short-term notes payable, long-term liability, and equity items. These include (a) obtaining cash by issuing debt and repaying the amounts borrowed and (b) obtaining cash from shareholders and providing them with a return on their investment. (p. 656)

Indirect method A method of determining net cash provided (used) by operating activities in which net earnings is adjusted for items that do not affect cash. (p. 660)

Investing activities Cash flow activities from short-term investments and long-term assets. These include (a) purchasing and disposing of investments and long-lived assets and (b) lending money and collecting on those loans. (p. 656)

Operating activities Cash flow activities from transactions which create revenues and expenses and therefore are included in the determination of net earnings. They are affected by noncash items in the statement of earnings and changes (increases or decreases) in noncash current asset and liability accounts in the balance sheet. (p. 656)

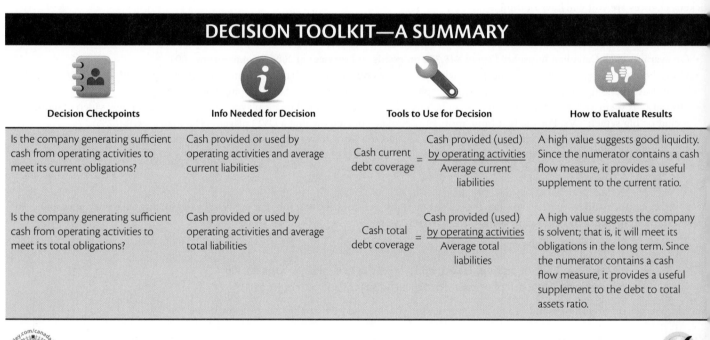

DECISION TOOLKIT—A SUMMARY

Decision Checkpoints	Info Needed for Decision	Tools to Use for Decision	How to Evaluate Results
Is the company generating sufficient cash from operating activities to meet its current obligations?	Cash provided or used by operating activities and average current liabilities	$\text{Cash current debt coverage} = \dfrac{\text{Cash provided (used) by operating activities}}{\text{Average current liabilities}}$	A high value suggests good liquidity. Since the numerator contains a cash flow measure, it provides a useful supplement to the current ratio.
Is the company generating sufficient cash from operating activities to meet its total obligations?	Cash provided or used by operating activities and average total liabilities	$\text{Cash total debt coverage} = \dfrac{\text{Cash provided (used) by operating activities}}{\text{Average total liabilities}}$	A high value suggests the company is solvent; that is, it will meet its obligations in the long term. Since the numerator contains a cash flow measure, it provides a useful supplement to the debt to total assets ratio.

   Analysis Tools (Decision Toolkit Summaries)

The Navigator

Using the Decision Toolkit

Stantec Inc., headquartered in Edmonton, is a design and consulting services company with more than 9,000 employees in 125 locations throughout North America. Stantec's cash flow statement for the most recent three years follows:

STANTEC INC.
Cash Flow Statement
Years Ended December 31
(in thousands)

	2007	2006	2005
Operating activities			
Cash receipts from clients	$940,085	$816,846	$637,391
Cash paid to suppliers	(259,493)	(221,056)	(200,445)
Cash paid to employees	(565,803)	(467,766)	(355,621)
Dividends received	450	450	550
Interest received	6,496	6,292	6,531
Interest paid	(4,271)	(7,665)	(6,551)
Income taxes paid	(33,656)	(37,588)	(28,882)
Income taxes recovered	3,691	3,876	4,341
Net cash provided by operating activities	87,499	93,389	57,314
Investing activities			
Business acquisitions	(104,280)	7,612	(91,383)
Increase in investments	(3,786)	(4,355)	(7,295)
Proceeds on disposition of investments	51	9	522
Collection of notes receivable			406
Purchase of property and equipment	(27,291)	(18,920)	(17,005)
Proceeds on disposition of property and equipment	134	104	155
Net cash used by investing activities	(135,172)	(15,550)	(114,600)
Financing activities			
Repayment of long-term debt	(78,514)	(85,612)	(46,875)
Proceeds from long-term borrowings	117,049	9,142	95,929
Repayment of bank indebtedness	(6,282)	(1,787)	
Repurchase of shares for cancellation	(294)	(1,016)	(195)
Proceeds from issue of share capital	1,920	1,865	(1,008)
Net cash provided (used) by financing activities	33,879	(77,408)	47,851
Other (foreign exchange loss)	(394)	(211)	(312)
Net increase (decrease) in cash and cash equivalents	(14,188)	220	(9,747)
Cash and cash equivalents, beginning of the year	28,363	28,143	37,890
Cash and cash equivalents, end of the year	$ 14,175	$ 28,363	$ 28,143

Additional information:
1. Current liabilities were $232,697 thousand, $159,695 thousand, and $157,814 thousand at the end of 2007, 2006, and 2005, respectively.
2. Total liabilities were $370,863 thousand, $223,575 thousand, and $280,726 thousand at the end of 2007, 2006, and 2005 respectively.
3. Net earnings were $69,279 thousand, $60,182 thousand, and $40,522 thousand in 2007, 2006, and 2005 respectively.

Instructions
(a) Does Stantec use the indirect or direct method to prepare its operating activities section?
(b) Calculate Stantec's cash current debt coverage and cash total debt coverage ratios for 2007 and 2006.
(c) Comment on any significant changes in Stantec's cash flows over the last three years.

Solution

(a) Stantec uses the direct method to prepare the operating activities section of its cash flow statement.

(b) (in thousands)

	2007		2006	
Cash current debt coverage	$\dfrac{\$87,499}{(\$232,697 + \$159,695) \div 2}$ = 0.4 times		$\dfrac{\$93,389}{(\$159,695 + \$157,814) \div 2}$ = 0.6 times	
Cash total debt coverage	$\dfrac{\$87,499}{(\$370,863 + \$223,575) \div 2}$ = 0.3 times		$\dfrac{\$93,389}{(\$223,575 + \$280,726) \div 2}$ = 0.4 times	

(c) Cash provided by operating activities increased substantially in 2006 and declined slightly in 2007 for Stantec despite increases in its net earnings year over year. In 2006, its cash receipts increased faster than did its payments to suppliers and employees, which are its most significant cash outflows. In 2007, Stantec's cash receipts increased again, but its cash paid to suppliers and employees increased much faster. Its cash current debt coverage and cash total debt coverage ratios also declined during this same period.

During the past three years, Stantec spent considerable cash on business acquisitions. In 2007, it spent $104,280 thousand for acquisitions and in 2005, it spent $91,383 thousand. In 2006, it did sell off some of the other companies it owned, realizing cash of $7,612 thousand. These business acquisitions and divestitures account for the major swings in cash flow from investing activities during the past three years.

Stantec has obtained significant new long-term financing over the last three years. These borrowings and the cash from operating activities have been used to finance the business acquisitions and to repay some of the long-term debt.

Overall, Stantec has seen a decrease in its cash position. At the beginning of 2005, it had $37,890 thousand in cash and cash equivalents. At the end of 2005 and 2006, it's cash and cash equivalents remained relatively unchanged, but declined to $14,175 thousand at the end of 2007.

The Navigator

Demonstration Problem

www.wiley.com/canada/kimmel

Study Tools
(Demonstration Problems)

The statement of earnings for Kosinski Manufacturing Inc. contains the following condensed information:

KOSINSKI MANUFACTURING INC. Statement of Earnings Year Ended December 31, 2009	
Sales	$6,583,000
Cost of goods sold	3,427,000
Gross profit	3,156,000
Operating expenses	2,349,000
Earnings from operations	807,000
Other expenses	
Loss on sale of machinery	24,000
Earnings before income taxes	783,000
Income tax expense	353,000
Net earnings	$ 430,000

The following selected current asset and current liability balances are reported on Kosinski's comparative balance sheet at December 31:

	2009	2008	Increase (Decrease)
Cash	$252,000	$130,000	$122,000
Accounts receivable	775,000	610,000	165,000
Inventories	834,000	867,000	(33,000)
Accounts payable	521,000	501,000	20,000

Additional information:

1. Operating expenses include depreciation expense of $200,000 and amortization expense of $80,000.
2. Machinery was sold for $270,000, at a loss of $24,000.
3. New machinery was purchased during the year for $1,250,000. It was partially financed by a mortgage payable issued for $500,000.
4. Dividends paid in 2009 totalled $20,000.

Instructions

(a) Prepare the cash flow statement using the indirect method.
(b) Prepare the cash flow statement using the direct method.
(c) Identify the similarities and differences between your answers in (a) and (b).

Solution to Demonstration Problem

(a)

KOSINSKI MANUFACTURING INC.
Cash Flow Statement—Indirect Method
Year Ended December 31, 2009

Operating activities		
Net earnings		$ 430,000
Adjustments to reconcile net earnings to net cash		
provided by operating activities		
Depreciation expense	$ 200,000	
Amortization expense	80,000	
Loss on sale of machinery	24,000	
Increase in accounts receivable	(165,000)	
Decrease in inventories	33,000	
Increase in accounts payable	20,000	192,000
Net cash provided by operating activities		622,000
Investing activities		
Sale of machinery	$ 270,000	
Purchase of machinery (see Note x)	(750,000)	
Net cash used by investing activities		(480,000)
Financing activities		
Payment of cash dividends	$ (20,000)	
Net cash used by financing activities		(20,000)
Net increase in cash		122,000
Cash, January 1		130,000
Cash, December 31		$ 252,000

Note x: Machinery was purchased for $1,250,000 and partially financed by the issue of a $500,000 mortgage note payable.

(b)

KOSINSKI MANUFACTURING INC.
Cash Flow Statement—Direct Method
Year Ended December 31, 2009

Operating activities	
Cash receipts from customers	$ 6,418,000[a]
Cash payments to suppliers	(3,374,000)[b]
Cash payments for operating expenses	(2,069,000)[c]
Cash payment for income taxes	(353,000)
Net cash provided by operating activities	622,000

Action Plan

- Determine the net cash provided (used) by operating activities. Operating activities generally relate to revenues and expenses shown on the statement of earnings, which are affected by noncash items in the statement of earnings and changes in noncash current assets and current liabilities in the balance sheet.

- Determine the net cash provided (used) by investing activities. Investing activities generally relate to changes in short-term investments and long-term assets.

- Determine the net cash provided (used) by financing activities. Financing activities generally relate to changes in notes payable, long-term liability, and shareholders' equity accounts.

- Determine the net increase (decrease) in cash. Verify that this amount agrees with the end-of-period cash balance reported on the balance sheet.

Investing activities		
Sale of machinery	$ 270,000	
Purchase of machinery (see Note x)	(750,000)	
Net cash used by investing activities		(480,000)
Financing activities		
Payment of cash dividends	$ (20,000)	
Net cash used by financing activities		(20,000)
Net increase in cash		122,000
Cash, January 1		130,000
Cash, December 31		$ 252,000

Note x: Machinery was purchased for $1,250,000 and partially financed by the issue of a $500,000 mortgage note payable.

Calculations
[a] Cash receipts from customers: $6,583,000 – $165,000 = $6,418,000
[b] Cash payments to suppliers: $3,427,000 – $33,000 – $20,000 = $3,374,000
[c] Cash payments for operating expenses: $2,349,000 – $200,000 – $80,000 = $2,069,000

(c) Both the indirect and direct methods report the same net cash provided by operating activities, but they report different detail within each section. Both methods report the same totals and detail for the investing and financing activities section. Both methods arrive at the same change in cash for the period.

The Navigator

Self-Study Questions

Answers are at the end of the chapter.

Study Tools (Self-Assessment Quizzes)

(SO 1) 1. Which is an example of a cash flow from an operating activity?

(a) A payment of cash to lenders for interest
(b) A receipt of cash from the sale of common shares
(c) A payment of cash dividends to shareholders
(d) A receipt of cash from the issue of a short-term note payable

(SO 1) 2. Which is an example of a cash flow from an investing activity?

(a) A receipt of cash from the issue of bonds payable
(b) A payment of cash to repurchase common shares
(c) A receipt of cash from the sale of equipment
(d) A payment of cash to suppliers of inventory

(SO 1) 3. Which is an example of a cash flow from a financing activity?

(a) A receipt of cash from the sale of land
(b) A payment of dividends
(c) A purchase of inventory on credit
(d) A receipt of cash for interest on an investment

(SO 2) 4. Net earnings are $132,000. During the year, accounts payable increased by $10,000, inventory decreased by $6,000, and accounts receivable increased by $12,000. Under the indirect method, what is net cash provided (used) by operating activities?

(a) $102,000
(b) $112,000

(c) $124,000
(d) $136,000

5. In determining cash provided (used) by operating activities under the indirect method, noncash items that are added back to net earnings do *not* include:

(a) depreciation expense.
(b) a decrease in inventory.
(c) a gain on the sale of equipment.
(d) a loss on the sale of equipment.

6. The beginning balance in Accounts Receivable is $44,000. The ending balance is $42,000. Sales on account during the period are $129,000. What are the cash receipts from customers?

(a) $127,000
(b) $129,000
(c) $131,000
(d) $141,000

7. Which of the following items is reported in the operating activities section of a cash flow statement prepared by the direct method?

(a) A loss on the sale of a building
(b) An increase in accounts receivable
(c) Depreciation expense
(d) Cash payments to suppliers

8. ⚷ Which of the following statements is *not* true?
   (a) The higher the cash current debt coverage ratio, the better.
   (b) The higher the cash total debt coverage ratio, the better.
   (c) The higher the debt to total assets ratio, the better.
   (d) The higher the free cash flow, the better.

9. ⚷ The cash current debt coverage ratio is a cash-based counterpart to the accrual-based:
   (a) current ratio.
   (b) receivables turnover.

(c) debt to total assets.
(d) free cash flow.

10. ⚷ Which of the following is not a measure of solvency?   (SO 3)
    (a) Free cash flow
    (b) Cash current debt coverage
    (c) Cash total debt coverage
    (d) Debt to total assets

Questions

1. What is a cash flow statement and why is it useful?

2. Denis says, "I understand that operating activities are affected by changes in current asset and current liability accounts. I also know that short-term investments are current assets. What I don't understand is why short-term investments are not classified as operating activities?" Help Denis understand the classification of short-term investments.

3. What are "cash and cash equivalents?" What is the likely reason that international standard setters might not allow this definition to be used in the preparation of the cash flow statement in the future?

4. Explain the differences between the three categories of activities reported in the cash flow statement.

5. Darren and Adriana were discussing where they should report significant noncash transactions in Rock Candy Corp.'s cash flow statement. Give two examples of noncash transactions and describe where they should be reported.

6. Explain how each of the following statements is used in the preparation of a cash flow statement: (a) the comparative balance sheet, (b) the statement of earnings, (c) the statement of comprehensive income, and (d) the statement of shareholders' equity.

7. Contrast the advantages and disadvantages of the indirect and direct methods of preparing the cash flow statement. Are both methods acceptable? Which method is preferred by standard setters? Which method is more popular? Why?

8. Goh Corporation changed its method of reporting operating activities from the indirect method to the direct method in order to make its cash flow statement more informative to its readers. Will this change increase, decrease, or not affect the net cash provided by operating activities?

9. In 2007, The Brick Group, one of Canada's largest retailers of household furniture, reported $5 million of net earnings. Yet, during the same period of time, its cash provided by operating activities was $70 million. Explain how this could occur.

10. Describe the indirect method for determining net cash provided (used) by operating activities.

11. Identify at least four adjustments that are required under the (SO 2a) indirect method to convert net earnings to net cash provided (used) by operating activities.

12. Why and how is depreciation and amortization expense reported (SO 2a) in a cash flow statement prepared using the indirect method?

13. Explain how the sale of equipment at a gain is reported on a (SO 2a) cash flow statement using the indirect method.

14. Describe the direct method for determining net cash provided (SO 2b) (used) by operating activities.

15. Give the formulas under the direct method for calculating (a) (SO 2b) cash receipts from customers, (b) cash payments to suppliers, and (c) cash payments for operating expenses.

16. Under the direct method, why is depreciation and amortization (SO 2b) expense not reported in the operating activities section?

17. Explain how the sale of equipment at a gain is reported on a (SO 2b) cash flow statement using the direct method.

18. Give examples of cash- and accrual-based ratios that measure (SO 3) (a) liquidity, and (b) solvency.

19. ⚷ In 2007, Leon's Furniture Limited reported a current (SO 3) ratio of 2:1 and a cash current debt coverage ratio of 0.5 times. Explain why Leon's cash current debt coverage is likely so much lower than its current ratio.

20. ⚷ In 2007, Rogers Communications Inc. reported a debt (SO 3) to total assets ratio of 70% and a cash total debt coverage ratio of 0.3 times. Its competitor, Shaw Communications Inc., reported a debt to total assets ratio of 76% and a cash total debt coverage ratio of 0.2 times in the same year. Based only on this information, which company is more solvent?

21. ⚷ A company's cash total debt coverage ratio and free cash (SO 3) flow have been declining steadily over the last five years. What does this decline likely mean to creditors and investors?

22. ⚷ How is it possible for a company to report positive net cash (SO 3) from operating activities but have a negative free cash flow?

Brief Exercises

Classify activities.
(SO 1)

BE13–1   **Mega Brands Inc.** reported the following items on its cash flow statement:

(a) _____   Repayment of long-term debt

(b) _____   Income taxes paid

(c) _____   Acquisition of property, plant, and equipment

(d) _____   Issue of common shares

(e) _____   Proceeds from disposal of property, plant, and equipment

(f) _____   Interest paid

Indicate where each of the above items was reported in Mega Brand's cash flow statement—as an operating activity (O), investing activity (I), financing activity (F), or noncash investing and financing activity (NC).

Indicate impact of transactions on cash.
(SO 1)

BE13–2   For each of the following transactions, indicate whether it will result in an increase (+), decrease (−), or have no effect (NE) on cash flows:

(a) _____   Repayment of short-term notes payable   (f) _____   Collection of accounts receivable

(b) _____   Sale of land for cash   (g) _____   Payment of a cash dividend

(c) _____   Distribution of a stock dividend   (h) _____   Amortization of a bond premium

(d) _____   Purchase of a trading security   (i) _____   Purchase of inventory

(e) _____   Issue of preferred shares   (j) _____   Recording of depreciation expense

Classify transactions.
(SO 1)

BE13–3   Classify each of the transactions listed in BE13–2 as an operating (O), investing (I), or financing (F) activity. If a transaction does not belong in any of these classifications, explain why.

Indicate impact on operating activities—indirect method.
(SO 2a)

BE13–4   Indicate whether each of the following transactions would be added to (+) or subtracted from (−) net earnings in calculating cash provided (used) by operating activities using the indirect method. If a transaction is not an operating activity, indicate that it is NA (not applicable).

(a) _____   Depreciation expense   (g) _____   Realized loss on sale of an available-for-sale security

(b) _____   Increase in accounts receivable

(c) _____   Decrease in inventory   (h) _____   Unrealized loss on an available-for-sale security

(d) _____   Increase in accounts payable   (i) _____   Amortization of a discount on a bond investment

(e) _____   Decrease in income tax payable

(f) _____   Gain on sale of equipment   (j) _____   Impairment loss for goodwill

Calculate cash from operating activities—indirect method.
(SO 2a)

BE13–5   Crystal, Inc. reported net earnings of $775,000 for the year ended November 30. During that same year, depreciation expense was $200,000, amortization expense was $60,000, accounts receivable decreased by $350,000, prepaid expenses increased by $95,000, accounts payable decreased by $280,000, and the company incurred a $10,000 gain on the sale of equipment. Calculate cash provided (used) by operating activities using the indirect method.

Calculate cash from operating activities—indirect method.
(SO 2a)

BE13–6   The comparative balance sheet for Dupigne Corporation shows the following noncash current asset and liability accounts at March 31:

	2010	2009
Accounts receivable	$60,000	$40,000
Merchandise inventory	64,000	70,000
Prepaid expenses	6,000	4,000
Accounts payable	35,000	40,000
Interest payable	7,500	5,000
Income tax payable	17,000	12,000

Dupigne's statement of earnings reported the following selected information for the year ended March 31, 2010: net earnings were $275,000 and depreciation expense was $60,000. Calculate net cash provided (used) by operating activities using the indirect method.

BE13–7   Idol Corporation has accounts receivable of $14,000 at January 1, and of $24,000 at December 31. Sales revenues were $170,000 for the year. What amount of cash was received from customers?

Calculate cash receipts from customers—direct method.
(SO 2b)

BE13–8   Columbia Sportswear Company reported cost of goods sold of U.S. $776.3 million on its 2007 statement of earnings. It also reported an increase in inventory of U.S. $53.6 million and an increase in accounts payable of U.S. $7.3 million. What amount of cash was paid to suppliers, assuming accounts payable relate only to merchandise creditors?

Calculate cash payments to suppliers—direct method.
(SO 2b)

BE13–9   Excel Corporation reports operating expenses of $100,000, including depreciation expense of $15,000 and amortization expense of $2,500 for the current year. During this same time period, prepaid expenses increased by $6,600 and accrued expenses payable decreased by $2,400. Calculate the cash payments for operating expenses.

Calculate cash payments for operating expenses—direct method.
(SO 2b)

BE13–10   Linux Corporation reports salary expense of $189,000 on its statement of earnings for the year ended August 31, 2009. It also reported salaries payable of $2,500 at September 1, 2008, and of $3,000 at August 31, 2009. Calculate the cash payments to employees.

Calculate cash payments to employees—direct method.
(SO 2b)

BE13–11   Home Grocery Limited reported income tax expense of $90,000 for the year. (a) Calculate the cash payments for income tax assuming income tax payable increased by $1,000 during the year. (b) Repeat part (a), assuming income tax payable decreased by $1,000 during the year.

Calculate cash payments for income tax—direct method.
(SO 2b)

BE13–12   The T accounts for equipment and accumulated depreciation for Trevis Ltd. are shown here:

Calculate cash received from sale of equipment.
(SO 2)

Equipment					Accumulated Depreciation—Equipment			
Beg. Bal.	80,000	Disposals	22,000		Disposals	5,500	Beg. Bal.	44,500
Acquisitions	41,600						Depreciation	12,000
End Bal.	99,600						End Bal.	51,000

In addition, Trevis' statement of earnings reported a $1,500 loss on the sale of equipment. (a) What amount was reported on the cash flow statement as "cash provided by sale of equipment"? (b) In what section of the cash flow statement would this transaction be reported?

BE13–13   Canadian Tire Corporation, Limited reported net earnings of $417.6 million for the year ended December 29, 2007. Its retained earnings were $2,083.7 million at the beginning of the year and $2,440.9 million at the end of the year. What amount of dividends did Canadian Tire pay during the year?

Calculate dividends paid.
(SO 2)

BE13–14   The following information is available for Baker Corporation for the year ended April 30, 2010:

Prepare cash flow statement.
(SO 2)

Cash, May 1, 2009	$ 7,000
Cash provided by operating activities	52,000
Cash receipts	
Sale of equipment	6,000
Issue of note payable	20,000
Issue of $75,000 mortgage note payable to partially	
finance purchase of land for $100,000	75,000
Cash payments	
Dividends	25,000
Reacquisition of common shares	19,000
Purchase of land for $100,000, partially	
financed by issuing a $75,000 mortgage note payable	100,000

Prepare a cash flow statement for the year, including any required note disclosure.

BE13–15   Jain Corporation reported cash provided by operating activities of $325,000, cash used by investing activities of $250,000, and cash provided by financing activities of $70,000. In addition, cash spent for capital expenditures during the period was $200,000 and $25,000 of dividends were paid. Average current liabilities were $215,000 and average total liabilities were $360,000. Calculate these values: (a) free cash flow, (b) cash current debt coverage, and (c) cash total debt coverage.

Calculate cash-based ratios.
(SO 3)

Evaluate liquidity.
(SO 3)

BE13–16 ◖▬◗ The L'Oréal Group reported the following selected liquidity ratios:

	2007	2006
Current ratio	1.1:1	0.8:1
Cash current debt coverage	0.4 times	0.4 times

How is it possible that L'Oréal's current ratio improved in 2007 but its cash current debt coverage ratio remained unchanged? What does this mean?

Evaluate solvency.
(SO 3)

BE13–17 ◖▬◗ Costco Wholesale Corporation reported the following selected solvency ratios:

	2007	2006
Debt to total assets	55.7%	47.4%
Cash total debt coverage	0.2 times	0.2 times

Based on the above, has Costco's solvency improved or deteriorated? Explain.

Exercises

Classify transactions.
(SO 1)

E13–1   A list of cash transactions follows:

Transaction	(a)	(b)	(c)
1. Provided services.	+ Cash	Service Revenue	Operating
2. Repaid a note payable.			
3. Purchased equipment.			
4. Collected accounts receivable.			
5. Paid employees.			
6. Paid a dividend.			
7. Issued common shares.			
8. Sold merchandise.			
9. Purchased land.			
10. Sold a trading security.			

Instructions
Complete the above table indicating for each transaction (a) whether it increases (+) or decreases (–) cash, (b) what other account is affected in the transaction besides cash, and (c) where the transaction should be classified on a cash flow statement. The first one has been done for you as an example.

Classify transactions.
(SO 1)

E13–2   Eng Corporation had the following transactions:

Transaction	(a) Classification	(b) Cash Flow
1. Issued common shares for $50,000.	F	+$50,000
2. Purchased a machine for $30,000. Made a $5,000 down payment and issued a long-term note for the remainder.		
3. Collected $16,000 of accounts receivable.		
4. Paid a $25,000 cash dividend.		
5. Sold a trading security with a carrying amount of $15,000 for $10,000.		
6. Sold inventory for $1,000.		
7. Paid $18,000 on accounts payable.		
8. Purchased a held-to-maturity security for $100,000.		
9. Purchased merchandise inventory for $28,000 on account.		
10. Collected $1,000 in advance from customers.		

Instructions
Complete the above table indicating whether each transaction (a) should be classified as an operating activity (O), investing activity (I), financing activity (F), or noncash transaction (NC); and (b) represents a cash inflow (+), cash outflow (–), or has no effect (NE) on cash. If the transaction results in a cash inflow or outflow, state the amount. The first one has been done for you as an example.

E13–3 He Corporation had the following transactions:

Indicate impact of transactions on net earnings and operating activities.
(SO 2)

Transaction	(a) Net Earnings	(b) Cash Provided (Used) by Operating Activities
1. Sold merchandise inventory for cash at a higher price than cost.	+	+
2. Sold merchandise inventory on account at a price less than cost.		
3. Purchased merchandise inventory on account.		
4. Paid a cash dividend.		
5. Paid salaries.		
6. Accrued salaries payable.		
7. Accrued interest receivable.		
8. Recorded depreciation expense.		
9. Paid an amount owing on account to a supplier.		
10. Collected an amount owing from a customer.		

Instructions

Complete the above table indicating whether each transaction will increase (+), decrease (−), or have no effect (NE) on (a) net earnings and (b) cash provided (used) by operating activities. The first one has been done for you as an example.

E13–4 **Clearly Canadian Beverage Corporation** reports the following selected information in the notes to its cash flow statement:

Discuss noncash items.
(SO 2)

> Note 16 (a) Supplementary cash flow information:
> Items not involving cash:
> 1. Property, plant and equipment written down
> 2. Amortization of property, plant, and equipment and intangibles
> 3. Gain on sale of investment
> 4. Loss on settlement of lawsuit
> 5. Investment written down

Instructions

Explain why each of the above items does not involve cash and is not included on the cash flow statement.

Classify transactions—indirect method.
(SO 2a)

E13–5 The following is a list of transactions that occurred during the year.

Transaction	Operating Activities	Investing Activities	Financing Activities	Noncash Investing and Financing Activities
1. Purchased inventory for cash.	−	NE	NE	NE
2. Sold inventory on account.				
3. Sold equipment for cash at a loss.				
4. Recorded depreciation on equipment.				
5. Paid a cash dividend.				
6. Revalued an available-for-sale security downward to fair market value.				
7. Collected an account from a customer.				
8. Issued bonds payable at a discount.				
9. Reacquired common shares at a price less than the average cost.				
10. Purchased land by issuing common shares.				

Instructions

Complete the above table indicating in which category each transaction would appear in a cash flow statement prepared using the indirect method, and whether the transaction should be added (+), deducted (−), or has no effect (NE) on the category you have chosen. The first one has been done for you as an example.

▶ Cash Flow Statement

Identify increases and
decreases—indirect method.
(SO 2a)

E13–6   Clearly Canadian Beverage Corporation reported the following selected information in the operating activities section of its cash flow statement for the year ended December 31, 2007:

CLEARLY CANADIAN BEVERAGE CORPORATION		
Cash Flow Statement (partial)		
Year Ended December 31, 2007		
(in USD thousands)		
Operating activities		
Net loss		$(12,796)
Changes in noncash working capital balances		
Accounts receivable	$ 518	
Inventories	(355)	
Prepaid expenses and other current assets	(946)	
Prepaid contracts	3,007	
Accounts payable and accrued liabilities	1,245	3,469

Instructions

Identify whether each of the current asset and current liability accounts listed above increased or decreased during the year.

Prepare operating activities
section—indirect method.
(SO 2a)

E13–7   Pesci Ltd. reported net earnings of $200,000 for the year ended July 31, 2010. Pesci also reported depreciation expense of $25,000 and a loss of $5,000 on the sale of equipment on its statement of earnings. The comparative balance sheet shows an increase in accounts receivable of $15,000, an increase in accounts payable of $10,000, an increase in prepaid expenses of $4,000, and an increase in accrued liabilities of $3,500 for the year.

Instructions

Prepare the operating activities section of the cash flow statement, using the indirect method.

Indicate impact of transactions
on operating activities—direct
method.
(SO 2b)

E13–8   The following is a list of transactions that must be converted from the accrual basis to the cash basis in order to calculate cash provided (used) by operating activities using the direct method:

Transaction	(a) Related Statement of Earnings Account	(b) Add to (+) or Deduct from (−) Statement of Earnings Account	(c) Related Cash Receipt or Payment
1. Increase in accounts receivable	Sales revenue	−	Cash receipts from customers
2. Decrease in accounts receivable			
3. Increase in interest receivable due on a loan			
4. Increase in prepaid insurance			
5. Increase in inventory			
6. Increase in accounts payable			
7. Decrease in accounts payable			
8. Increase in income tax payable			
9. Increase in interest payable			
10. Increase in salaries payable			

Instructions

Complete the above table, indicating (a) the related statement of earnings account; (b) if the transaction should be added to (+) or deducted from (−) the statement of earnings account that you identified in (a) in order to convert the accrual-based number to a cash-based number; and (c) the title of the resulting cash receipt or payment on the cash flow statement. The first one has been done for you as an example.

Calculate operating cash
flows—direct method.
(SO 2b)

E13–9   The following selected information is available:

Sales:	Revenue from sales	$190,000
	Accounts receivable, Jan. 1	12,000
	Accounts receivable, Dec. 31	7,000

Inventory:	Cost of goods sold	114,000
	Inventory, Jan. 1	4,500
	Inventory, Dec. 31	5,900
	Accounts payable, Jan. 1	2,500
	Accounts payable, Dec. 31	3,750
Operating expenses:	Operating expenses	60,000
	Depreciation expense	11,000
	Prepaid expenses, Jan. 1	2,500
	Prepaid expenses, Dec. 31	3,000
	Accrued expenses payable, Jan. 1	4,500
	Accrued expenses payable, Dec. 31	5,500

Instructions

Using the direct method, calculate (a) cash receipts from customers, (b) cash payments to suppliers, and (c) cash payments for operating expenses.

E13–10 McGillis Ltd. completed its first year of operations on December 31, 2009. Its statement of earnings showed revenues of $170,000, operating expenses of $70,000, and income tax expense of $21,000. Accounts receivable, accounts payable, and income tax payable at year end were $42,000, $33,000, and $2,500, respectively. Assume that accounts payable related to operating expenses.

Prepare operating activities section—direct method. (SO 2b)

Instructions

Prepare the operating activities section of the cash flow statement, using the direct method.

E13–11 The following selected accounts are from Dupré Corp.'s general ledger:

Calculate investing and financing activities. (SO 2)

Equipment

Jan.	1	Bal.	160,000				
July	31		70,000				
Sept.	2		53,000	Nov.	10		39,000
Dec.	31	Bal.	244,000				

Accumulated Depreciation—Equipment

				Jan.	1	Bal.	71,000
Nov.	10		30,000	Dec.	31		28,000
				Dec.	31	Bal.	69,000

Notes Payable

				Jan.	1	Bal.	0
				Sept.	2		43,000
				Dec.	31	Bal.	43,000

Retained Earnings

				Jan.	1	Bal.	105,000
Aug.	23		4,000	Dec.	31		70,000
				Dec.	31	Bal.	171,000

Additional information:

July	31	Equipment was purchased for cash.
Sept.	2	Equipment was purchased and partially financed through the issue of a note.
Aug.	23	A cash dividend was paid.
Nov.	10	A loss of $3,000 was incurred on the sale of equipment.
Dec.	31	Depreciation expense was recorded for the year.
	31	Net earnings for the year were $70,000.

Instructions

From the postings in the above accounts and additional information provided, indicate what information would be reported in the investing and/or financing activities sections of, and notes to, the cash flow statement.

Prepare cash flow statement—
indirect and direct methods.
(SO 2a, 2b)

▸ Cash Flow Statement

E13–12 The comparative balance sheet for Puffy Ltd. follows:

PUFFY LTD.		
Balance Sheet		
December 31		
	2009	**2008**
Assets		
Cash	$ 53,000	$ 22,000
Accounts receivable	80,000	76,000
Inventories	185,000	189,000
Land	70,000	100,000
Equipment	265,000	200,000
Accumulated depreciation	(66,000)	(32,000)
Total assets	$587,000	$555,000
Liabilities and Shareholders' Equity		
Accounts payable	$ 39,000	$ 47,000
Bonds payable	150,000	200,000
Common shares	199,000	174,000
Retained earnings	199,000	134,000
Total liabilities and shareholders' equity	$587,000	$555,000

Additional information:

1. Net earnings were $115,000.
2. Sales were $978,000.
3. Cost of goods sold was $751,000.
4. Operating expenses were $43,000, not including depreciation expense.
5. Income tax expense was $40,000.
6. Land was sold at a gain of $5,000.
7. No equipment was sold during the year.
8. Bonds payable amounting to $50,000 were retired at maturity.
9. Common shares were issued for $25,000.

Instructions

Prepare a cash flow statement using (a) the indirect method, or (b) the direct method, as assigned by your instructor.

Compare cash flows for three
companies.
(SO 3)

E13–13 🔑 Condensed earnings and cash flow information follow for three companies operating in the same industry:

	Company A	Company B	Company C
Net earnings	$75,000	$25,000	$(50,000)
Cash provided (used) by operating activities	$100,000	$(25,000)	$(25,000)
Cash provided (used) by investing activities	(50,000)	(25,000)	35,000
Cash provided (used) by financing activities	(25,000)	75,000	15,000
Net increase in cash	$ 25,000	$ 25,000	$ 25,000

Instructions

Which company is in better financial condition? Explain the reasoning behind your decision.

Calculate and assess cash-
based ratios.
(SO 3)

E13–14 🔑 Information for two companies in the same industry, Ria Corporation and Les Corporation, is presented here:

	Ria Corporation	Les Corporation
Cash provided by operating activities	$200,000	$200,000
Average current liabilities	50,000	100,000
Average total liabilities	200,000	250,000
Capital expenditures	20,000	35,000
Dividends paid	14,000	18,000

Instructions

(a) Calculate the cash current debt coverage ratio, cash total debt coverage ratio, and free cash flow for each company.

(b) Compare the liquidity and solvency of the two companies.

E13–15 ◐▬ Presented here are selected ratios for PepsiCo, Inc. and The Coca-Cola Company:

Evaluate liquidity and solvency.
(SO 3)

	PepsiCo	Coca-Cola
Current ratio	1.3:1	0.9:1
Cash current debt coverage	0.9 times	0.6 times
Debt to total assets	50.2%	49.7%
Cash total debt coverage	0.4 times	0.4 times
Free cash flow (in USD millions)	$2,300	$2,353

Instructions

Evaluate the liquidity and solvency of the two companies.

Problems: Set A

P13–1A The following is a list of transactions that took place during the year:

Classify transactions; indicate impact on cash flow and net earnings.
(SO 1, 2)

Transaction	(a) Classification	(b) Cash Flow	(c) Net Earnings
1. Collected an account receivable.	O	+	NE
2. Sold equipment for cash, at a loss.			
3. Revalued a trading security upward to fair market value.			
4. Acquired land by issuing common shares.			
5. Reacquired common shares at a price in excess of average cost.			
6. Paid dividends to preferred shareholders.			
7. Recorded depreciation expense.			
8. Issued preferred shares for cash.			
9. Purchased inventory for cash. The company uses a perpetual inventory system.			
10. Provided services on account.			

Instructions

(a) Classify each of the above transactions as an operating activity (O), investing activity (I), financing activity (F), or noncash transaction (NC). The first one has been done for you as an example.

(b) Specify if the transaction will result in a cash inflow (+), cash outflow (−), or have no effect on cash (NE).

(c) Indicate if the transaction will increase (+), decrease (−), or have no effect (NE) on net earnings.

P13–2A The statement of earnings for Gum San Ltd. is presented here:

Prepare operating activities section—indirect and direct methods.
(SO 2a, 2b)

GUM SAN LTD. Statement of Earnings Year Ended December 31, 2009		
Sales		$4,500,000
Cost of goods sold		2,390,000
Gross profit		2,110,000
Operating expenses	$920,000	
Depreciation expense	150,000	1,070,000
Earnings before income taxes		1,040,000
Other revenues		
Gain on sale of equipment		12,000
Earnings before income tax		1,052,000
Income tax expense		260,000
Net earnings		$ 792,000

▸ Cash Flow Statement

Additional information:
1. Accounts receivable increased by $500,000.
2. Inventory decreased by $220,000.
3. Prepaid expenses increased by $170,000.
4. Accounts payable to suppliers increased by $50,000.
5. Accrued expenses payable decreased by $165,000.
6. Income taxes payable decreased by $16,000.

Instructions

Prepare the operating activities section of the cash flow statement, using either (a) the indirect method or (b) the direct method, as assigned by your instructor.

Prepare operating activities section—indirect and direct methods.
(SO 2a, 2b)

P13–3A The statement of earnings for Hanalei International Inc. is presented here:

HANALEI INTERNATIONAL INC.		
Statement of Earnings		
Year Ended December 31, 2009		
Fee revenue		$565,000
Operating expenses		390,000
Earnings from operations		175,000
Other revenue and expenses		
Gain on sale of equipment	$ 25,000	
Interest expense	(10,000)	15,000
Earnings before income taxes		190,000
Income tax expense		47,500
Net earnings		$142,500

Hanalei's balance sheet contained these comparative data at December 31:

	2009	2008
Accounts receivable	$50,000	$60,000
Prepaid insurance	8,000	5,000
Accounts payable	30,000	41,000
Unearned revenue	10,000	14,000
Interest payable	2,000	750
Income tax payable	4,000	3,500

Additional information:
1. Operating expenses include $45,000 of depreciation expense and $5,000 of amortization expense.
2. Interest expense includes $500 related to the amortization of a bond discount on bonds payable.
3. Accounts payable relate to operating expenses.

Instructions

Prepare the operating activities section of the cash flow statement, using either (a) the indirect method or (b) the direct method, as assigned by your instructor.

Calculate and classify cash flows for property, plant, and equipment.
(SO 2)

P13–4A The following selected account balances relate to the property, plant, and equipment accounts of Bird Corp.:

	2009	2008
Accumulated depreciation—buildings	$ 675,000	$ 600,000
Accumulated depreciation—equipment	288,000	192,000
Depreciation expense—buildings	75,000	75,000
Depreciation expense—equipment	128,000	96,000
Land	250,000	200,000
Buildings	1,250,000	1,250,000
Equipment	500,000	480,000
Loss on sale of equipment	5,000	0

Additional information:
1. Purchased land for $50,000, making a $15,000 down payment and financing the remainder with a mortgage note payable.
2. Equipment was purchased for $80,000 cash. Equipment was also sold during the year.

Instructions

(a) Calculate any cash inflows or outflows related to the property, plant, and equipment accounts in 2009.

(b) Indicate where each of the cash inflows or outflows identified in (a) would be classified on the cash flow statement.

P13–5A The following selected account balances relate to the shareholders' equity accounts of Mathur Corp. at year end:

Calculate and classify cash flows for shareholders' equity. (SO 2)

	2009	2008
Preferred shares, 5,000 shares	$125,000	$125,000
Common shares, 9,000 shares in 2009, 10,000 in 2008	122,000	136,000
Contributed capital—reacquired common shares	1,500	0
Cash dividends—preferred	6,250	6,250
Stock dividends—common	14,000	0

Additional information:

1. The company reacquired 2,000 common shares in 2009, with an average cost of $28,000.
2. During the year, 1,000 common shares were issued as a stock dividend.

Instructions

(a) Determine the amounts of any cash inflows or outflows related to the share capital and dividend accounts in 2009.

(b) Indicate where each of the cash inflows or outflows identified in (a) would be classified on the cash flow statement.

P13–6A Bombardier Inc.'s statement of shareholders' equity reported the following information for the year ended January 31, 2008:

Determine cash flows from statement of shareholders' equity. (SO 2)

BOMBARDIER INC. Statement of Shareholders' Equity Year Ended January 31, 2008 (in USD millions)		
	Number (in thousands)	Amount
Share capital		
Preferred shares		
Balance, beg. and end of year	21,400	$ 347
Common shares		
Class A shares		
Balance, beg. of year	317,044	29
Converted to Class B	(82)	0
Balance, end of year	316,962	29
Class B shares		
Balance, beg. of year	1,433,423	1,448
Issue of shares	1,469	5
Converted from Class A	82	0
Repurchased shares	(21,273)	(55)
Balance, end of year	1,413,701	1,398
Total common shares	1,730,663	1,427
Total share capital		$1,774
Retained earnings		
Balance, beg. of year		$ 765
Net earnings		317
Dividends on preferred shares		(30)
Balance, end of year		$1,052
Accumulated other comprehensive income		
Balance, beg. of year		$ 178
Other comprehensive income		126
Balance, end of year		$ 304

Instructions

(a) Determine the amounts of any cash inflows or outflows related to the shareholders' equity accounts for fiscal 2008.

(b) Indicate where each of the cash inflows and outflows identified in (a) would be classified on the cash flow statement.

(c) For those items on the statement of shareholders' equity that you did not include in (a), explain why you believe these items do not affect cash.

Prepare cash flow statement—
indirect and direct methods.
(SO 2a, 2b)

P13–7A Financial statements for Nackawic Inc. follow:

NACKAWIC INC.
Balance Sheet
December 31

	2009	2008
Assets		
Cash	$102,700	$ 47,250
Accounts receivable	80,800	37,000
Inventories	111,900	102,650
Available-for-sale securities	94,500	107,000
Property, plant, and equipment	290,000	205,000
Accumulated depreciation	(49,500)	(40,000)
Total assets	$630,400	$458,900
Liabilities and Shareholders' Equity		
Accounts payable	$ 62,700	$ 48,280
Accrued expenses payable	12,100	18,830
Notes payable	140,000	70,000
Common shares	240,000	200,000
Retained earnings	175,600	121,790
Total liabilities and shareholders' equity	$630,400	$458,900

NACKAWIC INC.
Statement of Earnings
Year Ended December 31, 2009

Sales		$307,500
Cost of goods sold		99,460
Gross profit		208,040
Operating expenses		
Depreciation expense	$58,700	
Other operating expenses	24,670	83,370
Earnings from operations		124,670
Other revenues and expenses		
Gain on sale of equipment	($8,750)	
Interest expense	2,940	
Realized loss on sale of available-for-sale security	7,500	1,690
Earnings before income taxes		122,980
Income tax expense		32,670
Net earnings		$ 90,310

Additional information:

1. Available-for-sale securities were sold for $5,000, resulting in a loss of $7,500.
2. New equipment costing $141,000 was purchased for $71,000 cash and a $70,000 note payable.
3. Equipment costing $56,000 was sold for $15,550, resulting in a gain of $8,750.
4. Accounts payable relate only to merchandise creditors.

Instructions

Prepare the cash flow statement, using either (a) the indirect method or (b) the direct method, as assigned by your instructor.

P13–8A The financial statements of Wetaskiwin Limited are presented here:

Prepare cash flow statement—indirect and direct methods.
(SO 2a, 2b)

WETASKIWIN LIMITED Balance Sheet December 31		
	2009	**2008**
Assets		
Cash	$ 9,000	$ 10,000
Available-for-sale securities	14,000	23,000
Accounts receivable	28,000	14,000
Merchandise inventory	29,000	25,000
Property, plant, and equipment	73,000	78,000
Accumulated depreciation	(30,000)	(24,000)
Total assets	$123,000	$126,000
Liabilities and Shareholders' Equity		
Accounts payable	$ 25,000	$ 43,000
Income tax payable	3,000	20,000
Notes payable	15,000	10,000
Common shares	25,000	25,000
Retained earnings	64,000	28,000
Accumulated other comprehensive loss	(9,000)	0
Total liabilities and shareholders' equity	$123,000	$126,000

WETASKIWIN LIMITED Statement of Earnings Year Ended December 31, 2009		
Sales		$286,000
Cost of goods sold		194,000
Gross profit		92,000
Operating expenses		34,000
Earnings from operations		58,000
Other expenses		
Loss on sale of equipment	$2,000	
Interest expense	5,000	7,000
Earnings before income taxes		51,000
Income tax expense		15,000
Net earnings		$ 36,000

Additional information:

1. The available-for-sale securities were revalued to their fair value of $14,000 at the end of 2009.
2. Equipment was sold during the year for $8,000 cash. This equipment originally cost $15,000 and had a carrying amount of $10,000 at the time of sale.
3. Equipment costing $10,000 was purchased in exchange for $5,000 cash and a note payable for the balance.
4. Depreciation expense of $11,000 is included in operating expenses.
5. Accounts payable relate only to merchandise creditors.

Instructions

Prepare the cash flow statement, using either (a) the indirect method or (b) the direct method, as assigned by your instructor.

P13–9A 🔑 Selected information (in USD millions) for Google Inc. and Yahoo! Inc. for 2007 follows:

Calculate and assess cash-based ratios.
(SO 3)

	Google	Yahoo!
Cash provided by operating activities	$5,775	$1,919
Average current liabilities	1,670	1,887
Average total liabilities	2,040	2,525
Capital expenditures	2,403	602
Dividends	0	0

Instructions

(a) Calculate the cash current debt coverage ratio, cash total debt coverage ratio, and free cash flow for each company.

(b) Using the ratios calculated in (a), compare the liquidity and solvency of the two companies.

Evaluate liquidity and solvency. (SO 3)

P13–10A ⚫━C Selected ratios for two companies are as follows:

	Burrard	Pender
Current ratio	1:1	0.8:1
Receivables turnover	6 times	4 times
Inventory turnover	5 times	4 times
Cash current debt coverage	0.5 times	0.4 times
Debt to total assets	75%	50%
Times interest earned	6 times	2 times
Cash total debt coverage	0.4 times	0.3 times

Instructions

(a) Which company is more liquid? Explain.

(b) Which company is more solvent? Explain.

Discuss cash position. (SO 3)

P13–11A ⚫━C **Ontario Power Generation (OPG) Inc.**'s cash flow statement reported cash provided by operating activities of $407 million in 2007, an increase over the $397 million reported in 2006. It reported net earnings of $528 million in 2007, an increase over net earnings of $490 million reported in 2006. Cash and cash equivalents reported on the balance sheet also increased, but much more significantly from $6 million in 2006 to $110 million in 2007.

Instructions

(a) How is it possible that OPG can have $528 of net earnings in 2007 but generate only $407 million of cash provided by operating activities in the same year?

(b) Explain how OPG increased its net earnings by $38 million ($528 million – $490 million) from 2006 to 2007, while its cash provided by operating activities increased by only $10 million ($407 million – $397 million) over the same period.

(c) Explain how OPG can have an increase in its cash and cash equivalents of $104 million ($110 million − $6 million) from 2006 to 2007, but experience an increase of only $10 million ($407 million − $397 million) in its cash provided by operating activities over the same period.

Problems: Set B

Classify transactions; indicate impact on cash flow and net earnings. (SO 1, 2)

P13–1B The following is a list of transactions that took place during the year:

Transaction	(a) Classification	(b) Cash Flow	(c) Net Earnings
1. Paid wages to employees.	O	–	–
2. Revalued an available-for-sale security downward to fair market value.			
3. Sold land for cash, at a gain.			
4. Purchased a building by paying 10% in cash and signing a mortgage payable for the balance.			
5. Made principal repayment on the mortgage.			
6. Paid interest on the mortgage.			
7. Issued common shares for cash.			
8. Purchased shares of another company to be held as an available-for-sale investment.			
9. Paid dividends to common shareholders.			
10. Sold inventory on account, at a price greater than cost.			

Instructions

(a) Classify each of the above transactions as an operating activity (O), investing activity (I), financing activity (F), or noncash transaction (NC). The first one has been done for you as an example.

(b) Specify if the transaction will result in a cash inflow (+), cash outflow (−), or have no effect on cash (NE).

(c) Indicate if the transaction will increase (+), decrease (−), or have no effect (NE) on net earnings.

P13–2B The statement of earnings for Breckenridge Ltd. is presented here:

Prepare operating activities section—indirect and direct methods.
(SO 2a, 2b)

BRECKENRIDGE LTD. Statement of Earnings Year Ended November 30, 2009		
Sales		$8,000,000
Cost of goods sold		5,000,000
Gross profit		3,000,000
Operating expenses	$1,925,000	
Depreciation expense	75,000	2,000,000
Earnings from operations		1,000,000
Other expenses		
Impairment loss on goodwill		100,000
Earnings before income taxes		900,000
Income tax expense		300,000
Net earnings		$ 600,000

Additional information:

1. Accounts receivable increased by $190,000.
2. Inventory decreased by $50,000.
3. Prepaid expenses increased by $140,000.
4. Accounts payable to suppliers of merchandise decreased by $280,000.
5. Accrued expenses payable decreased by $90,000.
6. Income tax payable increased by $20,000.

Instructions

Prepare the operating activities section of the cash flow statement, using either (a) the indirect method or (b) the direct method, as assigned by your instructor.

P13–3B The statement of earnings for Vail Limited is presented here:

Prepare operating activities section—indirect and direct methods.
(SO 2a, 2b)

VAIL LIMITED Statement of Earnings Year Ended December 31, 2009		
Revenues		$925,000
Operating expenses		675,000
Earnings from operations		250,000
Other expenses		
Interest expense	$75,000	
Loss on sale of equipment	26,000	101,000
Earnings before income taxes		149,000
Income tax expense		37,250
Net earnings		$111,750

Vail's balance sheet contained these comparative data at December 31:

	2009	2008
Accounts receivable	$ 47,000	$57,000
Prepaid expenses	15,000	12,000
Accounts payable	41,000	36,000
Unearned revenue	12,000	9,000
Interest payable	6,250	5,000
Income tax payable	4,000	9,250

▸ Cash Flow Statement

Additional information:

1. Operating expenses include $50,000 of depreciation expense and $15,000 of amortization expense.
2. Interest expense includes $10,000 related to the amortization of a bond premium on bonds payable.
3. Accounts payable relate to operating expenses.

Instructions

Prepare the operating activities section of the cash flow statement, using either (a) the indirect method or (b) the direct method, as assigned by your instructor.

Calculate and classify cash flows for property, plant, and equipment.
(SO 2)

P13–4B The following selected account balances relate to the property, plant, and equipment accounts of Trudeau Inc.:

	2009	2008
Accumulated depreciation—buildings	$337,500	$300,000
Accumulated depreciation—equipment	144,000	96,000
Depreciation expense—buildings	37,500	37,500
Depreciation expense—equipment	60,000	48,000
Land	90,000	60,000
Buildings	750,000	750,000
Equipment	300,000	240,000
Gain on sale of equipment	10,000	0

Additional information:

1. Purchased $30,000 of land for cash.
2. Purchased $75,000 of equipment for $10,000 cash, issuing a note payable for the remainder. Equipment was also sold during the year.

Instructions

(a) Calculate any cash inflows or outflows related to the property, plant, and equipment accounts in 2009.

(b) Indicate where each of the cash inflows or outflows identified in (a) would be classified on the cash flow statement.

Calculate and classify cash flows for shareholders' equity.
(SO 2)

P13–5B The following selected account balances relate to the shareholder's equity accounts of Valerio Corp.:

	2009	2008
Preferred shares, 2,250 shares in 2009; 2,750 in 2008	$225,000	$275,000
Common shares, 55,000 shares in 2009; 40,000 in 2008	575,000	410,000
Contributed capital—reacquired preferred shares	35,000	50,000
Cash dividends—preferred	10,750	13,750
Dividends payable	2,687	3,437

Additional information:

1. The company reacquired 500 preferred shares in 2009, with an average cost of $50,000.
2. During the year, 15,000 common shares were issued. No common shares were repurchased.

Instructions

(a) Determine the amounts of any cash inflows or outflows related to the share capital and dividend accounts in 2009.

(b) Indicate where each of the cash inflows or outflows identified in (a) would be classified on the cash flow statement.

Determine cash flows from statement of shareholders' equity.
(SO 2)

P13–6B Loblaw Companies Limited's statement of shareholders' equity reported the following information for the year ended December 29, 2007:

	2007	2006
LOBLAW COMPANIES LIMITED		
Statement of Shareholders' Equity		
Year Ended December 29		
(in millions)		
Common share capital, beg. and end of year	$1,196	$1,196
Retained earnings, beginning of year	4,245	4,694
Cumulative impact of new accounting standards	(15)	
Net earnings (loss)	330	(219)
Dividends on common shares	(230)	(230)
Retained earnings, end of year	4,330	4,245
Accumulated other comprehensive income, beginning of year	0	
Cumulative impact of new accounting standards	16	
Other comprehensive income	3	
Accumulated other comprehensive income, end of year	19	
Total shareholders' equity	$5,545	$5,441

Note: There is no cash impact for the change to new accounting standards so you can ignore it for this assignment. We will learn more about changes in standards in the next chapter.

Instructions

(a) Determine the amounts of any cash inflows or outflows related to the shareholders' equity accounts for 2007.

(b) Indicate where each of the cash inflows and outflows identified in (a) would be classified on the cash flow statement.

(c) For those items on the statement of shareholders' equity that you did not include in (a), explain why you believe these items do not affect cash.

P13–7B Financial statements for E-Perform, Inc. follow:

Prepare cash flow statement—
indirect and direct methods.
(SO 2a, 2b)

	2009	2008
E-PERFORM, INC		
Balance Sheet		
December 31		
Assets		
Cash	$ 97,800	$ 48,400
Accounts receivable	75,800	43,000
Inventories	122,500	92,850
Prepaid expenses	38,400	26,000
Available-for-sale securities	128,000	114,000
Property, plant, and equipment	270,000	242,500
Accumulated depreciation	(50,000)	(52,000)
Total assets	$682,500	$514,750
Liabilities and Shareholders' Equity		
Accounts payable	$ 93,000	$ 77,300
Accrued expenses payable	11,500	7,000
Notes payable	110,000	150,000
Common shares	220,000	175,000
Retained earnings	234,000	105,450
Accumulated other comprehensive income	14,000	0
Total liabilities and shareholders' equity	$682,500	$514,750

E-PERFORM, INC
Statement of Earnings
Year Ended December 31, 2009

Sales		$492,780
Cost of goods sold		185,460
Gross profit		307,320
Operating expenses		
Other operating expenses	$62,410	
Depreciation expense	46,500	108,910
Earnings from operations		198,410
Other expenses		
Interest expense	$4,730	
Loss on sale of equipment	7,500	12,230
Earnings before income tax		186,180
Income tax expense		45,000
Net earnings		$141,180

Additional information:

1. The available-for-sale securities were revalued to their fair value of $128,000 at the end of 2009.
2. New equipment costing $85,000 was purchased for $25,000 cash and a $60,000 note payable.
3. Old equipment having an original cost of $57,500 was sold for $1,500.
4. Accounts payable relate only to merchandise creditors.
5. Notes payable were repaid during the year.

Instructions

Prepare the cash flow statement, using either (a) the indirect method or (b) the direct method, as assigned by your instructor.

Prepare cash flow statement—indirect and direct methods.
(SO 2a, 2b)

P13–8B   The financial statements of Resolute Inc. are presented here:

RESOLUTE INC.
Balance Sheet
December 31

	2009	2008
Assets		
Cash	$ 13,000	$ 5,000
Accounts receivable	38,000	24,000
Merchandise inventory	27,000	20,000
Property, plant, and equipment	80,000	78,000
Accumulated depreciation	(30,000)	(24,000)
Goodwill	5,000	16,000
Total assets	$133,000	$119,000
Liabilities and Shareholders' Equity		
Accounts payable	$ 17,000	$ 15,000
Income tax payable	1,000	4,000
Notes payable	36,000	52,750
Common shares	18,000	14,000
Retained earnings	61,000	33,250
Total liabilities and shareholders' equity	$133,000	$119,000

RESOLUTE INC.
Statement of Earnings
Year Ended December 31, 2009

Sales	$256,000
Cost of goods sold	140,000
Gross profit	116,000
Operating expenses	64,000
Earnings from operations	52,000

Other expenses		
Impairment loss on goodwill	$11,000	
Interest expense	4,000	15,000
Earnings before income taxes		37,000
Income tax expense		9,250
Net earnings		$ 27,750

Additional information:

1. Equipment was sold during the year for $8,500 cash. The equipment originally cost $12,000 and had a carrying amount of $8,500 at the time of sale.
2. Equipment costing $14,000 was purchased in exchange for $4,000 cash and a $10,000 note payable.
3. Accounts payable relate only to merchandise creditors.
4. Notes payable were also repaid during the year.
5. Depreciation expense of $9,500 is included in the operating expenses.

Instructions

Prepare the cash flow statement, using either (a) the indirect method or (b) the direct method, as assigned by your instructor.

P13–9B ⚙ Selected information (in thousands) for Reitmans (Canada) Limited and Le Château Inc. for fiscal 2008 follows:

Calculate and assess cash-based ratios.
(SO 3)

	Reitmans	Le Château
Cash provided by operating activities	$133,178	$54,117
Average current liabilities	107,286	54,118
Average total liabilities	145,066	74,940
Capital expenditures	73,402	24,091
Dividends paid	46,930	30,363

Instructions

(a) Calculate the cash current debt coverage ratio, cash total debt coverage ratio, and free cash flow for each company.

(b) Using the ratios calculated in (a), compare the liquidity and solvency of the two companies.

P13–10B ⚙ Selected ratios for two companies are as follows:

Evaluate liquidity and solvency.
(SO 3)

	Grenville	Robson
Current ratio	1.7:1	1.2:1
Receivables turnover	10 times	20 times
Inventory turnover	4 times	2 times
Cash current debt coverage	0.4 times	0.3 times
Debt to total assets	60%	20%
Times interest earned	5 times	20 times
Cash total debt coverage	0.2 times	0.1 times

Instructions

(a) Which company is more liquid? Explain.

(b) Which company is more solvent? Explain.

P13–11B ⚙ The TJX Companies, Inc., parent company of Winners and HomeSense, among other companies, reported cash provided by operating activities of $1,361,107 thousand for the year ended January 26, 2008, an increase of $166,074 thousand over the $1,195,033 thousand reported for 2007. The company also reported net earnings of $771,750 thousand, an increase over net earnings of $738,039 thousand reported for 2007. Its cash and cash equivalents declined during fiscal 2008, from $856,669 thousand to $732,612 thousand.

Discuss cash position.
(SO 3)

Instructions

(a) How is it possible that TJX can generate $1,361,107 thousand of cash provided by operating activities in fiscal 2008 but earn only $771,750 thousand of net earnings in the same year?

▸ Cash Flow Statement

(b) Explain how TJX increased its cash provided by operating activities by $166,074 thousand in 2008 while net earnings increased by only $33,711 thousand ($771,750 thousand − $738,039 thousand) over the same period.

(c) Explain how TJX can have an increase of $166,074 thousand in its cash provided by operating activities but a decline of $124,057 thousand ($856,669 thousand − $732,612 thousand) in its cash and cash equivalents over the same period.

BROADENING YOUR PERSPECTIVE

Financial Reporting and Analysis Cases

Financial Reporting: *Shoppers Drug Mart*

www.wiley.com/canada/kimmel

Analysis Tools

BYP13–1 The financial statements of Shoppers Drug Mart are presented in Appendix A at the end of this book.

Instructions

(a) What amount was reported as the increase or decrease in cash on the statement of cash flows for fiscal 2007? For fiscal 2006?

(b) What was the amount of cash flows from operating activities for 2007? For 2006?

(c) Does Shoppers Drug Mart use the indirect or direct method of calculating operating activities?

(d) From your analysis of the 2007 statement of cash flows, what were the most significant investing activities? Financing activities?

(e) Did Shoppers Drug Mart report any significant noncash investing and financing activities?

Comparative Analysis: *Shoppers Drug Mart and Jean Coutu*

BYP13–2 The financial statements of Jean Coutu are presented in Appendix B, following the financial statements for Shoppers Drug Mart in Appendix A.

Instructions

(a) Based on the information in the financial statements, calculate the following ratios for Shoppers Drug Mart for the year ended December 31, 2007, and Jean Coutu for the year ended March 1, 2008:

1. Cash current debt coverage

2. Current ratio

3. Cash total debt coverage

4. Debt to total assets

5. Times interest earned

(b) What conclusions about the liquidity and solvency of each company can be drawn from the ratios calculated in (a)?

Interpreting Financial Statements

BYP13–3 The following information is available from WestJet Airlines Ltd.'s financial statements (in thousands):

	2007	2006	2005
Total current assets	$ 717,788	$ 456,066	$ 319,576
Total assets	2,984,222	2,726,527	2,213,092
Total current liabilities	590,606	464,484	376,897
Total liabilities	2,034,314	1,920,500	1,542,939
Cash provided by operating activities	541,065	338,272	247,324
Capital expenditures	200,282	477,063	300,439
Dividends paid	0	0	0

Instructions

(a) Calculate the current and cash current debt coverage ratios for WestJet for 2007 and 2006 and discuss the airline's liquidity.

(b) Calculate the debt to total assets and cash total debt coverage ratios for WestJet for 2007 and 2006 and discuss the airline's solvency.

(c) Calculate the free cash flow for WestJet for 2007 and 2006 and discuss the airline's ability to finance expansion from internally generated cash.

A Global Focus

BYP13–4 PaperlinX Limited, an Australian paper manufacturer, reported the following in the operating activities section of its cash flow statement:

International Resources

PAPERLINX LIMITED Cash Flow Statement (partial) Year Ended June 30 (in AUD millions)		
	2008	2007
Cash flows from operating activities		
Receipts		
Receipts from customers	$7,526.1	$7,803.6
Dividends received	0.6	0.5
Interest received	5.4	6.3
Other income received	11.7	10.1
	7,543.8	7,820.5
Payments		
Payments to suppliers and employees	(7,304.9)	(7,578.7)
Interest paid	(87.1)	(82.6)
Income taxes paid	(38.8)	(16.3)
	(7,430.8)	(7,677.6)
Net cash provided by operating activities	113.0	142.9

Additional information:

	2008	2007
Net capital expenditures	$ 270.7	$ 153.4
Dividends paid	23.8	33.8
Average total liabilities	2,540.2	2,659.5

Instructions

(a) Is PaperlinX using the direct or indirect method when preparing its cash flow statement?

(b) If PaperlinX used the other method of preparing the operating activities section of the cash flow statement, what similarities and differences would you see between a cash flow statement prepared under this other method and the cash flow statement presented above?

(c) Calculate PaperlinX's free cash flow and cash total debt coverage for 2008 and 2007. Comment on the company's solvency.

Critical Thinking Cases and Activities

Collaborative Learning Activity

BYP13–5   You are completing a course on being a financial advisor and have been given the financial statements of two companies to analyze their solvency. You have summarized financial data for these two companies that are from very different industries:

	Auto Sales & Leasing Corp.		Steel Inc.	
	2009	2008	2009	2008
Cash provided by operating activities	$ 17,500	$ 9,500	$ 17,000	$ 24,000
Current assets	15,000	16,000	320,000	330,000
Total assets	125,000	160,000	500,000	510,000
Current liabilities	12,000	12,500	75,000	95,000
Total liabilities	85,000	100,000	225,000	228,000

Instructions

After the class has been divided into groups, assign half your group members to one company and the remaining group members to the other company. Then do the following:

(a) Calculate the following ratios for 2009: (1) cash current debt coverage, (2) current ratio, (3) cash total debt coverage, and (4) debt to total assets.

(b) Assess the company's current and long-term solvency position, including the answers to the following questions in your analysis:

1. Does your company face a risk of not being able to pay its current obligations?

2. Could your company raise funds by issuing more long-term debt?

3. If you are missing key pieces of information, identify them and any assumptions you have made.

(c) As a group, compare the results of your analysis for each company.

Communication Activity

BYP13–6   Cash provided (used) by operating activities is the result of the conversion of net earnings to a cash basis from an accrual basis. This conversion may be done by either the indirect or direct method.

Instructions

Write a brief memo explaining why you believe most companies prefer using the indirect method over the direct method. In your answer, explain the differences in data used in preparing the cash provided (used) by operating activities section of the cash flow statements under the two methods.

Ethics Case

Ethics in Accounting

BYP13–7   Onwards and Upwards Corporation has paid cash dividends to its shareholders for eight consecutive years. The board of directors' policy requires that in order for a dividend to be declared, cash provided by operating activities as reported in the current year's cash flow statement must exceed $1 million. The job of president Phil Monat is secure so long as Phil produces annual operating cash flows to support the usual dividend.

At the end of the current year, controller Leland Yee informs president Monat of some disappointing news. The cash provided by operating activities is only $970,000. The president says to Leland, "We must get that amount above $1 million. Isn't there some way to increase cash from operating activities by another $30,000?" Leland answers, "These figures were prepared by my assistant. I'll go back to my office and see what I can do." The president replies, "I know you won't let me down, Leland."

Upon close scrutiny of the cash flow statement, Leland concludes that he can get cash from operating activities above $1 million by reclassifying a one-year, $60,000 note payable listed in the financing activities section as "Proceeds from bank loan—$60,000." Leland will prepare the operating activities section of the cash flow statement using the indirect method and report the note as an adjustment to net earnings called "Increase in payables—$60,000." He returns to the president, exclaims, "You can tell the board to declare their usual dividend. Our cash flow provided by operating activities is $1,030,000." Excited, the president exclaims, "Good man, Leland! I knew I could count on you."

Instructions

(a) Who are the stakeholders in this situation?

(b) Was there anything unethical about the president's actions? Was there anything unethical about the controller's actions?

(c) Are the board members or anyone else likely to discover the misclassification?

"All About You" Activity

BYP13–8 In this chapter, you learned about cash flow and the important decisions that must be made when cash inflow does not cover cash outflow.

Instructions

Go to your university or college website and search for a budget calculator. Complete the budget calculator exercise. Is your cash outflow greater than your cash inflow? Are there any discretionary expenses that you can live without?

Serial Case

(*Note:* This is a continuation of the serial problem from Chapters 1 through 12.)

BYP13–9 Natalie has prepared the balance sheet and statement of earnings of Cookie Creations for the year ended December 31, 2011, but she does not understand how to prepare the cash flow statement. The balance sheet and the statement of earnings follow:

COOKIE CREATIONS LTD. Balance Sheet December 31		
	2011	2010
Assets		
Cash	$ 16,344	$ 3,050
Accounts receivable	3,250	1,710
Inventory	7,897	5,450
Prepaid expenses	6,300	3,050
Furniture and fixtures	12,500	5,000
Accumulated depreciation—furniture and fixtures	(2,000)	(1,000)
Computer equipment	4,000	4,500
Accumulated depreciation—computer equipment	(600)	(1,500)
Kitchen equipment	80,000	66,000
Accumulated depreciation—kitchen equipment	(22,600)	(6,600)
Total assets	$105,091	$79,660
Liabilities and Shareholders' Equity		
Accounts payable	$ 3,650	$ 6,930
Income taxes payable	10,251	11,200
Dividends payable	28,000	25,000
Salaries payable	2,250	1,280
Interest payable	188	0
Note payable—current portion	3,000	0
Note payable—long-term portion	4,500	0
Preferred shares ($6 cumulative, 3,000 in 2011 and 2,500 in 2010)	15,000	10,000
Common shares (3,625 shares issued)	5,450	5,450
Retained earnings	32,802	19,800
Total liabilities and shareholders' equity	$105,091	$79,660

COOKIE CREATIONS LTD.
Statement of Earnings
Year Ended December 31, 2011

Sales		$485,625
Cost of goods sold		222,694
Gross profit		262,931
Operating expenses		
Depreciation expense	$ 17,600	
Salaries and wage expense	147,979	
Other operating expenses	43,186	208,765
Earnings from operations		54,166
Other expenses		
Interest expense	$ 413	
Loss on sale of computer equipment	2,500	2,913
Earnings before income tax		51,253
Income tax expense		10,251
Net earnings		$ 41,002

Additional information:

1. All of the computer equipment was sold at the beginning of the year for $500 cash. New computer equipment was then bought for $4,000 cash.

2. Additional kitchen equipment was bought for $14,000 on January 1, 2011. A $9,000 note payable was signed. The terms provide for equal semi-annual instalment payments of $1,500 on July 1 and January 1 of each year, plus interest of 5% on the outstanding principal balance.

3. Additional furniture was bought for $7,500 cash.

4. Dividends were declared to the preferred and common shareholders on December 15, 2010, to be paid January 15, 2011.

5. Accounts payable relate only to merchandise creditors.

6. Prepaid expenses relate only to other operating expenses.

Instructions

(a) Prepare a cash flow statement, using the indirect method or the direct method, as required by your instructor.

(b) Calculate total current assets, total current liabilities, and total liabilities for each of 2011 and 2010.

(c) Calculate and compare the cash current debt coverage ratio to the current ratio, and the cash total debt coverage ratio to the debt to total assets ratio for 2011.

Answers to Chapter Questions

Answer to Shoppers Drug Mart Review It Question 3

For the year ended December 29, 2007, Shoppers Drug Mart reported (a) $565,058 thousand provided by operating activities, (b) $612,747 thousand used by investing activities, and (c) $12,412 thousand provided by financing activities.

Answers to Self-Study Questions

1. a   2. c   3. b   4. d   5. c   6. c   7. d   8. c   9. a   10. b

Remember to go back to the beginning of the chapter to check off your completed work! ←

CHAPTER 14

Performance Measurement

ACCOUNTING MATTERS!

Corporate Reporting Proves to Be Fertile Ground

With the global population increasing, demands on the world's food and agricultural resources also keep increasing. And as the world's largest producer of primary plant nutrients—nitrogen, phosphate, and potassium—as well as fertilizers, animal feed supplements, and industrial products, Potash Corporation of Saskatchewan Inc. (PotashCorp) is helping to address these demands.

Launched as a Crown corporation by the Province of Saskatchewan in 1975, PotashCorp became a publicly traded company in 1989. Today, its products come from seven potash operations in Canada, seven phosphate operations in the United States and one in Brazil, and three nitrogen plants in the United States and one in Trinidad.

PotashCorp takes the transparency and accountability that come with being a public company very seriously. And it has been rewarded for its efforts. In 2008, in the mining industry sector and for the sixth consecutive year, the Saskatoon-based company took home the Canadian Institute of Chartered Accountants' Corporate Reporting Award for its 2007 annual report. In addition to the award for the mining industry sector, PotashCorp received awards of excellence in electronic disclosure and sustainable development reporting.

"Stakeholders are looking for a company they can trust, to invest in, to partner with, or to be employed by, and the role transparency has in building that trust cannot be underestimated," said Wayne Brownlee, executive vice president and chief financial officer at PotashCorp.

CICA judges described PotashCorp as "an industry leader in financial reporting." Like all annual reports, the company's document presents the financial results, a message from the president and CEO, a management discussion and analysis (MD&A), and information on the company's directors. In addition, the report describes what the company's goals for the current year were and how well it met them, and lists targets for the following year.

The judges were also impressed by the report's supplemental reporting in areas such as product markets, market growth, and operating segments, as well as the electronic disclosure on the company's website. "The company's electronic disclosure is very much a benchmark in terms of the depth of content and overall functionality," the judges said.

The annual report is the most important document a company produces. It is a crucial tool for investors, creditors, and regulators to gather the information they require to make important decisions about a company. To this end, PotashCorp's financial statements provide a 10-year review of its financial performance, as well as an explanation of risks and how the company manages them.

PotashCorp also addresses head-on two of the huge performance issues of today—corporate governance and sustainable development. The judges said, "PotashCorp exhibits strong commitment to good corporate governance, which is evident in the quality of the disclosure in the proxy and in the Governance section of the website. Compliance checklist and core governance documents are tailored and specific, with an innovative approach to transparency in this area."

PotashCorp became the first publicly traded fertilizer company in North America to produce a separate sustainability report in 2003, documenting its economic impact, social involvement, and progress in safety, health, and the environment. "PotashCorp consistently produces exceptional sustainability reports and is clearly among the leaders in sustainability reporting," the judges said, adding, "It is clear from the content and effort that has gone into this report that sustainability is a priority for Potash."

In taking care to communicate effectively with its shareholders and other parties, PotashCorp demonstrates its commitment to keeping investors and other stakeholders informed—one of the most important issues in corporate governance today.

ash: potashcorp.com

THE NAVIGATOR

☐ Read *Feature Story*

☐ Scan *Study Objectives*

☐ Read *Chapter Preview*

☐ Read text and answer *Before You Go On*

☐ Read *All About You*

☐ Review *Summary of Study Objectives*

☐ Review *Using the Decision Toolkit—A Summary*

☐ Work *Using the Decision Toolkit*

☐ Work *Demonstration Problem*

☐ Answer *Self-Study Questions*

☐ Complete assignments

UDY OBJECTIVES

er studying this chapter, you should be able to:

Understand the concept of sustainable earnings and indicate how irregular items are presented.

Explain and apply horizontal analysis.

Explain and apply vertical analysis.

Identify and calculate ratios that are used to analyze liquidity, solvency, and profitability.

Understand the limitations of financial analysis.

e Navigator

PREVIEW OF CHAPTER 14

An important lesson can be learned from PotashCorp's annual report, described in our feature story. Effective communication is the key to understanding. The purpose of this chapter is to give you a comprehensive review of financial statements—a company's most important means of communication. We will examine the impact of certain irregular items on financial results and analyses. We will also review all of the decision tools presented in this text and use them to analyze PotashCorp's financial statements. In addition, we will identify factors that can impose limits on the analysis of financial information.

The chapter is organized as follows:

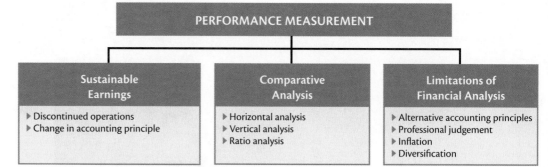

PERFORMANCE MEASUREMENT

Sustainable Earnings	Comparative Analysis	Limitations of Financial Analysis
▶ Discontinued operations ▶ Change in accounting principle	▶ Horizontal analysis ▶ Vertical analysis ▶ Ratio analysis	▶ Alternative accounting principles ▶ Professional judgement ▶ Inflation ▶ Diversification

The Navigator

Sustainable Earnings

Sustainable earnings are the level of earnings that is most likely to be obtained in the future. They differ from actual net earnings by the amount of irregular (i.e., non-typical) revenues, expenses, gains, and losses that are included in net earnings. Users are interested in sustainable earnings because the amount helps them estimate future earnings without the "noise" of irregular items. For example, suppose Rye Corporation reports that this year's net earnings are $500,000, but this amount includes a once-in-a-lifetime gain of $400,000. In estimating next year's net earnings for Rye Corporation, we would likely ignore this $400,000 gain and estimate that next year's net earnings will be in the neighbourhood of $100,000, plus or minus any expected changes. That is, based on this year's results, the company's sustainable earnings are roughly $100,000.

To help determine sustainable earnings, irregular items are reported separately on the financial statements. We will discuss two types of irregular items in this chapter—discontinued operations and changes in accounting principle. There is a third type of irregular item, known as an extraordinary item, that is often reported on the statement of earnings in the US. However, extraordinary items are rarely reported in Canada as the criteria for recognizing such items in Canada are far more restrictive. In addition, international standards have eliminated the concept of "extraordinary items." Consequently, we do not cover extraordinary items in this textbook.

Discontinued Operations

The term **discontinued operations** refers to the disposal, or availability for sale, of an identifiable operating segment of a business. An **operating segment** can be a subsidiary company or an operating division within the company, as long as it is a separate business unit with its own financial elements (e.g., revenues, expenses, and cash flows) that can be clearly distinguished from the rest of the company.

Whether an operating segment has been disposed of (by sale, abandonment, or spin-off), or is classified as held for sale, it is expected that:

1. the operations and cash flows have been (or will be) eliminated from the ongoing operations of the company as a result of the disposal transaction, and

2. the company will have no continuing involvement after the disposal transaction.

International standard setters are currently in the process of revising the definition of a discontinued operation. A revised standard is expected to be issued in 2009.

International Resources

Balance Sheet

Assets (net of any related liabilities) that are held for sale as discontinued operations are valued and reported on the balance sheet at the lower of their carrying amount and fair value (less any anticipated costs of selling). They retain their original classification as assets or liabilities, and are reported as current or noncurrent. Once an asset has been classified as held for sale, no additional depreciation is recognized. Of course, assets that have already been disposed of are no longer recorded or reported on the balance sheet.

PotashCorp did not report any discontinued operations in 2007. However, Tembec Inc., a Quebec-based integrated forest products company and a global leader in sustainable forest management practices, ceased operations in 2007 at its Louisiana coated paper facility and was actively seeking to sell the site. Illustration 14-1 shows the information about these operations that Tembec reported on its balance sheet at year end.

◀ Illustration 14-1

Presentation of discontinued operations on balance sheet

TEMBEC INC.
Balance Sheet (partial)
September 29, 2007
(in millions)

Current assets of discontinued operations	$18
Current liabilities related to discontinued operations	6
Noncurrent liabilities related to discontinued operations	25

In the notes to its financial statements, Tembec explains the details of this decision and presents financial information about each of the specific assets and liabilities that were affected.

Statement of Earnings

When a company disposes of one of its operating segments, the disposal is reported separately on the statement of earnings as an irregular item called discontinued operations. The discontinued operations item consists of two parts: the earnings (loss) from the discontinued operations and the gain (loss) on the disposal of the segment. Of course, if the segment has not yet been disposed of and is being held for sale, only the first part (the earnings or loss from the discontinued operations) will be segregated and reported on the statement until the actual disposal occurs.

Like all irregular items, discontinued operations are reported net of income tax. That is, the applicable income tax expense or tax savings is shown for earnings before income tax and for each component that is reported for discontinued operations. The general concept is "Let the tax follow the earnings or loss." We will leave the detailed calculation of discontinued operations and their income tax impact for an intermediate accounting course and illustrate only the presentation of this information in this textbook.

Illustration 14-2 shows the information that Tembec reported on its statement of earnings regarding the planned discontinuation of its Louisiana coated paper facility.

◀ Illustration 14-2

Presentation of discontinued operations on statement of earnings

TEMBEC INC.
Statement of Earnings (partial)
Year Ended September 29, 2007
(in millions, except per share data)

Earnings from continuing operations	$150
Earnings (loss) from discontinued operations	(199)
Net earnings (loss)	$(49)
Earnings per share from continuing operations	$1.75
Earnings (loss) per share from discontinued operations	$(2.33)

Tembec's statement of earnings presents the company's continuing operations in the usual manner. Expenses are deducted from revenues to calculate earnings from continuing operations, although it is not detailed in the above illustration. Note that the caption "earnings from continuing operations" is used and "discontinued operations" are separately reported. Within this section, both the operating loss and the loss on disposal (if Tembec had one) are reported net of applicable income taxes. Tembec provides further information about its operating loss in the notes to its financial statements.

In addition, on its statement of earnings, earnings per share are reported separately for continuing operations and for discontinued operations so that investors can clearly see the impact of this decision on the company. The impact of the discontinued operations on cash flow must also be reported separately on the cash flow statement, although we have not illustrated it here.

Discontinued operations are not uncommon. In a recent year, nearly 20 percent of the companies surveyed by *Financial Reporting in Canada* reported assets either disposed of, or held for sale, as discontinued operations. Discontinued operations can have a significant impact on a company's financial position and net earnings. In general, in evaluating a company it makes sense to eliminate irregular items such as discontinued operations from the analysis.

Change in Accounting Principle

Another type of irregular item, one that affects earnings of prior periods, is a change in accounting principle. A **change in accounting principle** occurs when the principle used in the current year is different from the one used in the preceding year. To ensure the comparability of financial statements from year to year, accounting principles should be applied consistently from period to period. This does not mean, however, that changes can never be made. When a change is made, it is classified as either voluntary or mandatory.

A voluntary change in accounting principle is allowed when management can show that the new accounting principle results in a more reliable and relevant presentation of events or transactions in the financial statements. Examples of voluntary changes in accounting principle include a change in inventory cost formula (e.g., from average cost to FIFO) or a change in depreciation method (e.g., from diminishing-balance to straight-line).

A mandatory change in accounting principle is one that is required by standard-setters. We can expect to see more of these in the next few years as Canadian standards move closer to international financial reporting standards. PotashCorp reported three changes in accounting principles in its 2007 financial statements—all mandated by the CICA. In 2007, the company adopted new accounting principles for comprehensive income, financial instruments, and hedges.

Changes in accounting principles affect financial reporting in four ways:

1. The cumulative effect of the change in accounting principle should be reported (net of income tax) as an adjustment to opening retained earnings. Since prior-period earnings are affected, a change in accounting principle must be reported in the retained earnings section of the statement of shareholders' equity (or in the statement of retained earnings), rather than in the current period's statement of earnings.

2. The new principle should be used for reporting the results of operations in the current year.

3. All prior-period financial statements should be restated to make comparisons easier.

4. The effects of the change should be detailed and disclosed in a note.

Ideally, all accounting changes are applied retrospectively. This means that a financial statement from any prior year that is presented for comparative purposes must be restated as if the new accounting principle had been used in the past. At times, especially with accounting changes that are mandated, it is impractical to do this and the change is only reported prospectively—that is, for the current and future years.

In PotashCorp's case, the three accounting changes resulted in a $200,000 increase in PotashCorp's opening retained earnings, after tax. They were reported in detail in the notes to the company's financial statements, and were also presented as an adjustment in the statement of retained earnings. Rather than present a statement of shareholders' equity in 2007, the company presented a statement of retained earnings, as shown in Illustration 14-3.

Illustration 14-3 ➡

Presentation of change in accounting principle

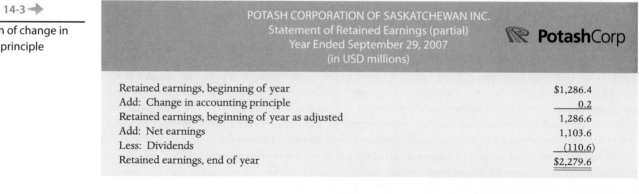

POTASH CORPORATION OF SASKATCHEWAN INC. Statement of Retained Earnings (partial) Year Ended September 29, 2007 (in USD millions)	
Retained earnings, beginning of year	$1,286.4
Add: Change in accounting principle	0.2
Retained earnings, beginning of year as adjusted	1,286.6
Add: Net earnings	1,103.6
Less: Dividends	(110.6)
Retained earnings, end of year	$2,279.6

⊕ ACCOUNTING MATTERS! | International Insight

One of the most daunting accounting changes that public companies will face in the near future is the adoption of International Financial Reporting Standards (IFRS). Companies are required to prepare and present an opening balance sheet at the date of transition to IFRS. For Canadian companies with December 31 year ends that are adopting IFRS on January 1, 2011, the date of the opening balance sheet for the transition date will be January 1, 2010. This will allow for one comparative period to be presented in the financial statements.

Similar to other accounting changes, the application of IFRS will require companies to restate opening balances to comply with many of the new standards. Fortunately, the standard-setters are aware of the practical difficulties of applying these standards retrospectively, and they have therefore provided some exemptions. The exemptions are for specific standards where the cost was considered to outweigh the benefits of applying the standard. In such cases, the change will only require prospective application.

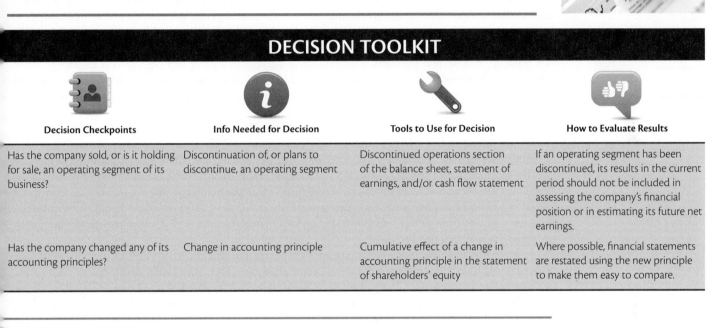

DECISION TOOLKIT

Decision Checkpoints	Info Needed for Decision	Tools to Use for Decision	How to Evaluate Results
Has the company sold, or is it holding for sale, an operating segment of its business?	Discontinuation of, or plans to discontinue, an operating segment	Discontinued operations section of the balance sheet, statement of earnings, and/or cash flow statement	If an operating segment has been discontinued, its results in the current period should not be included in assessing the company's financial position or in estimating its future net earnings.
Has the company changed any of its accounting principles?	Change in accounting principle	Cumulative effect of a change in accounting principle in the statement of shareholders' equity	Where possible, financial statements are restated using the new principle to make them easy to compare.

BEFORE YOU GO ON...

Review It

1. What are sustainable earnings?
2. Identify two irregular items, and indicate which financial statement(s) they affect and how.
3. What effect do irregular items have on estimating future earnings?
4. Did Shoppers Drug Mart report any irregular items in 2007? The answer to this question is at the end of this chapter.

The Navigator

Comparative Analysis

As mentioned earlier, in assessing financial performance, investors and creditors are interested in the sustainable earnings of a company. In addition to this, they are also interested in making comparisons from period to period. Throughout this book, we have relied on three types of comparisons to improve the usefulness of financial information for decision-making:

1. **Intracompany basis.** This basis compares an item or financial relationship inside a company within the current year or with one or more prior years. Comparisons within a company are often useful to detect changes in financial relationships and significant trends. For example, a comparison of PotashCorp's year-end cash amount with the amount of its total assets at year end shows the proportion of total assets that is cash. Likewise, a comparison of PotashCorp's current-year cash amount with its prior-year cash amount will show either an increase or a decrease.

2. **Intercompany basis.** This basis compares an item or financial relationship of one company with the same item or relationship in one or more competing companies. Comparisons with other companies give insight into a company's competitive position. For example, PotashCorp's net sales for the year can be compared with the net sales of Agrium Inc., one of its competitors in the fertilizer industry.

3. **Industry averages.** This basis compares an item or financial relationship of a company with that of the industry. Comparisons with industry averages give information about a company's relative position within the industry. For example, PotashCorp's financial data can be compared with the averages for its industry that are calculated by financial ratings organizations such as Dun & Bradstreet, the *Financial Post*, and Statistics Canada.

In assessing a company's financial performance, we usually start with the financial statements. It is important, however, to also review other financial and non-financial information included in the company's annual report. Other financial information includes a management discussion and analysis (MD&A) of the company's financial position and a summary of historical key financial figures and ratios.

Non-financial information includes a discussion of the company's mission, goals and objectives, market position, people, and products. Understanding a company's goals and objectives is important when interpreting financial performance. As mentioned in our feature story, PotashCorp's annual report not only presents the company's goals but also compares those goals to the company's actual performance and identifies targets for the upcoming year.

We must also consider the economic circumstances that a company is operating in. Economic measures such as the rate of interest, inflation, unemployment, and changes in demand and supply can have a significant impact on a company's performance. For example, in the fall of 2008, it became evident that North America, and in particular the U.S., was in the midst of the worst financial and economic crisis since the 1920s. Shares in fertilizer companies such as PotashCorp suffered enormous losses on fears that a slowdown in the economy would affect every sector, including agriculture. It would be difficult to properly interpret PotashCorp's performance without understanding the effects of demand and supply on potash prices in the period under analysis.

Other non-financial information includes corporate governance, customer satisfaction, employee satisfaction, product reputation, innovation, knowledge resources, sustainable development, and so on. As mentioned in our feature story, the judges were impressed by PotashCorp's supplemental reporting in areas such as product markets, market growth, and sustainable development. It was the first fertilizer producer in North America to include a sustainable development report documenting the company's economic impact, social involvement, and progress in safety, health, and care for the environment.

Various tools are used to evaluate the significance of financial data for a company. Three commonly used tools follow:

1. **Horizontal analysis.** This tool evaluates a series of financial statement data over time, expressing changes between periods as either an amount or a percentage.

2. **Vertical analysis.** This tool evaluates financial statement data by expressing each item in a financial statement as a percentage of a base amount for the same period of time.

3. **Ratio analysis.** This tool expresses relationships among selected items of financial statement data.

Horizontal analysis is used in intracompany comparisons. Vertical analysis is used in both intracompany and intercompany comparisons. Ratio analysis is used in all three types of comparisons (intracompany, intercompany, and industry averages). In the following sections, we will explain and illustrate each of the three types of analysis.

Horizontal Analysis

study objective 2

Explain and apply horizontal analysis.

Horizontal analysis, also called **trend analysis**, is a technique for evaluating a series of financial statement data over a period of time. Two features in annual reports make this type of comparison easier. First, each of the financial statements is presented on a comparative basis for one or more previous years. Second, a summary of selected financial data is presented for a series of 5 to 10 years or more.

The purpose of horizontal analysis is to determine the increase or decrease that has taken place, and this can be expressed as either an amount or a percentage. For example, net sales for the last five years for PotashCorp are shown on the following page in dollars and percentages:

	2007	2006	2005	2004	2003
Net sales	$5,234.2	$3,766.7	$3,847.2	$2,901.4	$2,465.8
% of base-period amount	212.3%	152.8%	156.0%	117.7%	100.0%
% change for year	39.0%	(2.1%)	32.6%	17.7%	—

In the second line of the above analysis, we have assumed that 2003 is the base year, and we have expressed net sales in each year as a percentage of the base-period amount (i.e., as a percentage of the amount from 2003). This is done by dividing the amount for the specific year we are analyzing by the base-year amount from 2003. This means that all amounts in 2003 are set at 100 percent, as they are base-year amounts. For example, net sales of U.S. $2,465.8 million in 2003 are divided by U.S. $2,465.8 million to equal 100 percent.

We can use horizontal analysis to determine that net sales in 2007 are 212.3 percent of net sales in 2003 by dividing U.S. $5,234.2 million by U.S. $2,465.8 million. In other words, net sales in 2007 are 112.3 percent greater than sales five years earlier in 2003. From this horizontal analysis, we can easily see PotashCorp's sales trend. Net sales have increased significantly over the five years, with 2006 as the only year that saw a decline in net sales.

We can also use horizontal analysis to measure the percentage change for any one specific period. This is done by dividing the dollar amount of the change between the specific year and the base year by the base-year amount. For example, if we set each prior year as our base year, we can see that net sales increased by U.S. $1,467.5 million ($5,234.2 − $3,766.7) between 2007 and 2006. This increase can then be expressed as a percentage by dividing the amount of the change between the two years, U.S. $1,467.5 million, by the amount in 2006, U.S. $3,766.7 million. Thus, in 2007 net sales increased by 39 percent compared to 2006. The percentage change in net sales for each year is presented in the last row of the above table.

Balance Sheet

To further illustrate horizontal analysis, we will use PotashCorp's financial statements. Condensed balance sheets for 2007 and 2006, showing dollar and percentage changes for the two-year period, are shown in Illustration 14-4.

Helpful Hint Percentage of base-period amount = Analysis-period amount ÷ Base-period amount

Helpful Hint Percentage change for period = Dollar amount of change since base period ÷ Base-period amount

◂ Illustration 14-4

Horizontal analysis of balance sheet (% change for period)

POTASH CORPORATION OF SASKATCHEWAN INC.
Balance Sheet
December 31
(in USD millions)   ℞ **Potash**Corp

			Increase (Decrease)	
	2007	2006	Amount	Percentage
Assets				
Current assets				
Cash and cash equivalents	$ 719.5	$ 325.7	$ 393.8	120.9%
Accounts receivable	596.2	442.3	153.9	34.8%
Inventories	428.1	501.3	(73.2)	(14.6%)
Prepaid expenses and other current assets	67.5	40.9	26.6	65.0%
Total current assets	1,811.3	1,310.2	501.1	38.2%
Property, plant, and equipment	3,887.4	3,525.8	361.6	10.3%
Investments	3,581.5	1,148.9	2,432.6	211.7%
Intangible assets	24.5	29.3	(4.8)	(16.4%)
Goodwill	97.0	97.0	0.0	0.0%
Other assets	314.9	105.8	209.1	197.6%
Total assets	$9,716.6	$6,217.0	$3,499.6	56.3%
Liabilities and Shareholders' Equity				
Liabilities				
Current liabilities	$1,001.9	$1,103.5	$ (101.6)	(9.2%)
Long-term liabilities	2,696.0	2,333.2	362.8	15.5%
Total liabilities	3,697.9	3,436.7	261.2	7.6%
Shareholders' equity	6,018.7	2,780.3	3,238.4	116.5%
Total liabilities and shareholders' equity	$9,716.6	$6,217.0	$3,499.6	56.3%

▶ Performance Measurement

Note that in a horizontal analysis, while the amount column of the increase or decrease is additive (the total change is an increase of U.S. $3,499.6 million), the percentage column is not additive (56.3 percent is *not* a total).

The horizontal analysis of PotashCorp's comparative balance sheet shows that several changes occurred between 2006 and 2007. In the current assets section, cash and cash equivalents increased by 120.9 percent. It is helpful to look at the cash flow statement to determine the cause of key changes in cash during the year. After reviewing this statement, we can see that the increase in cash is primarily because of increased sales and reduced expenses.

The analysis also shows that accounts receivable increased by U.S. $153.9 million, or 34.8 percent. We will look at the statement of earnings in the next section to determine if sales increased proportionately to the receivables increase. If not, this may be an indicator of slow-moving receivables. Inventories actually decreased by U.S. $73.2 million, or 14.6 percent, likely indicating a high demand for products. Prepaid expenses and other current assets increased by U.S. $26.6 million, or 65 percent.

In the long-term assets section, the most significant change was an increase in investments of U.S. $2,432.6 million, or 211.7 percent. The notes to PotashCorp's financial statements explain that this increase was primarily due to the purchase of additional shares in offshore potash companies Sinofert, in China, and ICL, in Israel. As Illustration 14-4 shows, other long-term asset accounts also changed by various amounts.

PotashCorp's current liabilities decreased by U.S. $101.6 million, or 9.2 percent. Details in the notes to the financial statements show that the company's current portion of long-term debt decreased significantly in 2007. The total long-term liabilities increased by U.S. $362.8 million, or 15.5 percent, primarily because of an increase in a future income tax liability.

In the shareholders' equity section, increased earnings and the accumulated other comprehensive income accounted for most of the U.S. $3,238.4-million increase. We can see that PotashCorp had a very successful year and is financing its business by retaining earnings, rather than by assuming additional long-term debt.

Statement of Earnings

Illustration 14-5 presents a horizontal analysis of PotashCorp's condensed statement of earnings for the years 2007 and 2006.

Illustration 14-5 ➡

Horizontal analysis of statement of earnings (% change for period)

POTASH CORPORATION OF SASKATCHEWAN INC. Statement of Earnings Year Ended December 31 (in USD millions) ℝ PotashCorp				
			Increase (Decrease)	
	2007	2006	Amount	Percentage
Net sales	$5,234.2	$3,766.7	$1,467.5	39.0%
Cost of goods sold	3,353.0	2,764.7	588.3	21.3%
Gross profit	1,881.2	1,002.0	879.2	87.7%
Selling and administrative expenses	212.6	158.4	54.2	34.2%
Other operating expenses	205.6	62.1	143.5	231.1%
Earnings from operations	1,463.0	781.5	681.5	87.2%
Interest expense	68.7	85.6	(16.9)	(19.7%)
Other revenue	125.5	94.0	31.5	33.5%
Earnings before income tax	1,519.8	789.9	729.9	92.4%
Income taxes	416.2	158.1	258.1	163.3%
Net earnings	$1,103.6	$ 631.8	$ 471.8	74.7%

A horizontal analysis of the statement of earnings shows that net sales increased by U.S. $1,467.5 million, or 39 percent. This appears to be reasonably consistent with the 34.8-percent increase in accounts receivable we noted in the balance sheet. That is, if sales increase, it is not surprising to also have an increase in receivables. The fact that the increase in accounts receivables is less than the increase in sales reassures us about how collectible the receivables are. Interestingly, while net sales increased by 39 percent, cost of goods sold increased by only 21.3 percent. PotashCorp has been very good at controlling its costs. Taken together, increasing sales and decreasing costs have resulted in an increase in gross profit of 87.7 percent.

PotashCorp's selling and administrative expenses increased by U.S. $54.2 million, or 34.2 percent, which is slightly less than net sales. However, its other operating expenses increased by U.S. $143.5 million, or 231.1 percent. This was due mainly to provincial mining taxes and foreign exchange losses in 2007. Interest expense was down by U.S. $16.9 million, or 19.7 percent, and other revenue increased by U.S. $31.5 million, or 33.5 percent. PotashCorp did not report any irregular items in 2007 or 2006. If it had, these items should be excluded from our comparisons.

The measurement of changes from period to period in percentages is fairly straightforward and quite useful. However, the calculations can be affected by complications. For example, if an item has a small value in a base year and a large value in the next year, the percentage change may not be meaningful. In addition, if an item has no value in a base year and a value in the next year, no percentage change can be determined. Finally, if a negative amount appears in the base year and a positive amount in the following year, or vice versa, no percentage change can be calculated.

We have not done a horizontal analysis of PotashCorp's statement of comprehensive income, statement of retained earnings (PotashCorp does not present a separate statement of shareholders' equity), and cash flow statement as analyses of these statements are not as useful as horizontal analyses done on the balance sheet and statement of earnings. The amounts presented in these other statements already give details of the changes between two periods (the opening and ending balance sheet dates).

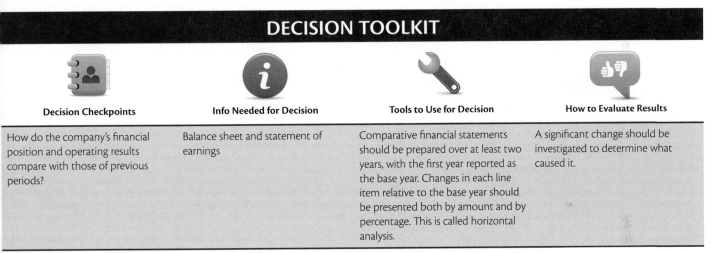

DECISION TOOLKIT

Decision Checkpoints	Info Needed for Decision	Tools to Use for Decision	How to Evaluate Results
How do the company's financial position and operating results compare with those of previous periods?	Balance sheet and statement of earnings	Comparative financial statements should be prepared over at least two years, with the first year reported as the base year. Changes in each line item relative to the base year should be presented both by amount and by percentage. This is called horizontal analysis.	A significant change should be investigated to determine what caused it.

BEFORE YOU GO ON...

Review It

1. Distinguish between intracompany, intercompany, and industry comparisons.
2. What are the different tools that are used to compare financial information?
3. How is a percentage change from a base period calculated? How is a percentage change for a period calculated?

Do It

Selected condensed information (in thousands) from Bonora Ltd.'s statements of earnings for four years ended June 30 follows:

	2010	2009	2008	2007
Revenues	$5,035	$6,294	$9,468	$8,646
Gross profit	936	1,077	2,146	1,900
Net earnings	251	110	546	428

(a) Calculate the percentage of the base-year amount for each year, assuming that 2007 is the base year.

(b) Calculate the percentage change between the following years: 2007 and 2008; 2008 and 2009; and 2009 and 2010.

▶ Performance Measurement

Action Plan

- Set the base-year (2007) dollar amounts at 100%. Express each later year's amount as a percentage of the base period.
- To find the percentage of the base-year amount, divide the dollar amount for the year under analysis by the base-year amount.
- To find the percentage change between two periods, divide the dollar amount of the change between the prior and current years by the prior-year amount.

Solution

(a) Percentage of the base-year amount

	2010	2009	2008	2007
Revenues	58.2%	72.8%	109.5%	100%
Gross profit	49.3%	56.7%	112.9%	100%
Net earnings	58.6%	25.7%	127.6%	100%

(b) Percentage change for each year

	2010	2009	2008
Revenues	(20.0%)	(33.5%)	9.5%
Gross profit	(13.1%)	(49.8%)	12.9%
Net earnings	128.2%	(80.0%)	27.6%

The Navigator

Vertical Analysis

study objective 3

Explain and apply vertical analysis.

Vertical analysis, also called **common size analysis**, is a technique for evaluating financial statement data that expresses each item in a financial statement as a percentage of a base amount in the same financial statement. For example, on a balance sheet we might say that current assets are 18.6 percent of total assets (total assets being the base amount). Or, on a statement of earnings we might say that cost of goods sold is 64.1 percent of net sales (net sales being the base amount).

Balance Sheet

Illustration 14-6 presents a vertical analysis of PotashCorp's comparative balance sheet. The base for the asset items is *total assets*, and the base for the liability and shareholders' equity items is *total liabilities and shareholders' equity*, which equals total assets.

Illustration 14-6 ➡️

Vertical analysis of balance sheet

Helpful Hint

$\% = \dfrac{\text{Each item on balance sheet}}{\text{Total assets}}$

POTASH CORPORATION OF SASKATCHEWAN INC. Balance Sheet December 31 (in USD millions)				
	2007		**2006**	
	Amount	Percentage	Amount	Percentage
Assets				
Current assets				
Cash and cash equivalents	$ 719.5	7.4%	$ 325.7	5.2%
Accounts receivable	596.2	6.1%	442.3	7.1%
Inventories	428.1	4.4%	501.3	8.1%
Prepaid expenses and other current assets	67.5	0.7%	40.9	0.7%
Total current assets	1,811.3	18.6%	1,310.2	21.1%
Property, plant, and equipment	3,887.4	40.0%	3,525.8	56.7%
Investments	3,581.5	36.9%	1,148.9	18.5%
Intangible assets	24.5	0.3%	29.3	0.5%
Goodwill	97.0	1.0%	97.0	1.5%
Other assets	314.9	3.2%	105.8	1.7%
Total assets	$9,716.6	100.0%	$6,217.0	100.0%
Liabilities and Shareholders' Equity				
Liabilities				
Current liabilities	$1,001.9	10.3%	$1,103.5	17.8%
Long-term liabilities	2,696.0	27.8%	2,333.2	37.5%
Total liabilities	3,697.9	38.1%	3,436.7	55.3%
Shareholders' equity	6,018.7	61.9%	2,780.3	44.7%
Total liabilities and shareholders' equity	$9,716.6	100.0%	$6,217.0	100.0%

Vertical analysis shows the relative size of each item in the balance sheet compared to a base amount. It can be prepared for one or more years, as we've shown in Illustration 14-6. It is also useful to compare vertically prepared information for multiple periods to similar information provided earlier in our horizontal analysis. For example, we can see that even though accounts receivable increased by 34.8 percent from 2006 to 2007 in our horizontal analysis in Illustration 14-4, they actually declined slightly as a percentage of total assets at 7.1 percent in 2006 and 6.1 percent in 2007, as shown in Illustration 14-6.

Property, plant, and equipment increased by 10.3 percent between 2006 and 2007 according to our horizontal analysis in Illustration 14-4. However, it decreased as a percentage of total assets, from 56.7 percent in 2006 to 40 percent in 2007. Investments increased by 211.7 percent in our horizontal analysis, but they only changed as a percentage of total assets from 18.5 percent in 2006 to 36.9 percent in 2007. Recall our earlier words of caution about interpreting a percentage change of a smaller base amount.

Current liabilities decreased from 17.8 percent to 10.3 percent as a percentage of total liabilities and shareholders' equity from 2006 to 2007, compared to showing a 9.2-percent horizontal decrease in Illustration 14-4. Long-term liabilities actually decreased from 37.5 percent in 2006 to 27.8 percent in 2007 as a percentage of total liabilities and shareholders' equity. Shareholders' equity increased from 44.7 percent in 2006 to 61.9 percent in 2007 as a percentage of total liabilities and shareholders' equity. This reinforces our earlier observation that PotashCorp is financing its growth by retaining earnings, rather than by assuming additional long-term debt.

Statement of Earnings

Illustration 14-7 presents a vertical analysis of PotashCorp's comparative statement of earnings. The base for this analysis is *net sales*.

POTASH CORPORATION OF SASKATCHEWAN INC.
Statement of Earnings
Year Ended December 31
(in USD millions)

	2007 Amount	2007 Percentage	2006 Amount	2006 Percentage
Net sales	$5,234.2	100.0%	$3,766.7	100.0%
Cost of goods sold	3,353.0	64.1%	2,764.7	73.4%
Gross profit	1,881.2	35.9%	1,002.0	26.6%
Selling and administrative expenses	212.6	4.0%	158.4	4.2%
Other operating expenses	205.6	3.9%	62.1	1.6%
Earnings from operations	1,463.0	28.0%	781.5	20.8%
Interest expense	68.7	1.3%	85.6	2.3%
Other revenue	125.5	2.4%	94.0	2.5%
Earnings before income tax	1,519.8	29.1%	789.9	21.0%
Income tax expense	416.2	8.0%	158.1	4.2%
Net earnings	$1,103.6	21.1%	$ 631.8	16.8%

◀ **Illustration 14-7**

Vertical analysis of statement of earnings

Helpful Hint

$\% = \dfrac{\text{Each item on statement of earnings}}{\text{Net sales}}$

Although cost of goods sold increased by 21.3 percent in 2007 in our horizontal analysis in Illustration 14-5, it actually declined as a percentage of sales from 73.4 percent in 2006 to 64.1 percent in 2007, as shown in Illustration 14-7. In our horizontal analysis, we also found that selling and administrative expenses increased, as did other operating expenses. However, in the vertical analysis they changed relatively little when expressed as a percentage of sales. And, of course, net earnings increased to 21.1 percent of sales in 2007, compared to net earnings of 16.8 percent reported in 2006.

Although vertical analysis can also be performed on the other period statements—comprehensive income, shareholders' equity, and cash flow—this is seldom done. As mentioned earlier, the value of these statements comes from the analysis of the changes during the year, and not from percentage comparisons of these changes against a base amount.

Intercompany Comparisons

Vertical analysis also makes it easier to compare different companies. For example, one of PotashCorp's main competitors is Agrium Inc. Using vertical analysis, we can make a more meaningful comparison of the condensed statements of earnings of PotashCorp and Agrium, as shown in Illustration 14-8.

Illustration 14-8 ➡

Intercompany comparison by vertical analysis

	PotashCorp		Agrium	
	Amount	Percentage	Amount	Percentage
Net sales	$5,234.2	100.0%	$5,270	100.0%
Cost of goods sold	3,353.0	64.1%	3,672	69.7%
Gross profit	1,881.2	35.9%	1,598	30.3%
Selling and administrative expenses	212.6	4.0%	471	8.9%
Other operating expenses	205.6	3.9%	412	7.8%
Earnings from operations	1,463.0	28.0%	715	13.6%
Interest expense	68.7	1.3%	70	1.3%
Other revenue	125.5	2.4%	0	0.0%
Earnings before income tax	1,519.8	29.1%	645	12.3%
Income taxes	416.2	8.0%	204	3.9%
Net earnings	$1,103.6	21.1%	$ 441	8.4%

POTASHCORP AND AGRIUM
Statement of Earnings
Year Ended December 31, 2007
(in USD millions)

PotashCorp's cost of goods sold is a lower percentage of net sales at 64.1 percent than Agrium's at 69.7 percent. It is interesting to note that PotashCorp's selling and administrative and other operating expenses are significantly lower than Agrium's. PotashCorp's net earnings are higher at 21.1 percent of net sales compared to Agrium's at 8.4 percent of net sales.

PotashCorp and Agrium are roughly the same size, and vertical analysis clearly shows the differences between the two companies. Vertical analysis is also useful in comparing companies of different sizes as it reduces each financial statement item to a percentage that can be compared more easily than large differences in dollar amounts. Vertical analysis can also be used to compare two companies' balance sheets, although we have not done so here.

DECISION TOOLKIT

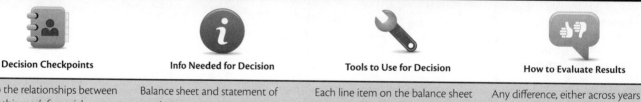

Decision Checkpoints	Info Needed for Decision	Tools to Use for Decision	How to Evaluate Results
How do the relationships between items in this year's financial statements compare with last year's relationships or those of competitors?	Balance sheet and statement of earnings	Each line item on the balance sheet should be presented as a percentage of total assets (total liabilities and shareholders' equity). Each line item on the statement of earnings should be presented as a percentage of net sales. This is called vertical analysis.	Any difference, either across years or between companies, should be investigated to determine the cause.

BEFORE YOU GO ON...

➡ **Review It**

1. What is vertical analysis?
2. How does vertical analysis differ from horizontal analysis?
3. What base is used to calculate the percentage size of an amount that is reported in a balance sheet? In a statement of earnings?
4. How can vertical analysis be used to compare two companies of differing sizes?

➡ **Do It**

Summary financial information for Grey Wolf Ltd. follows:

	2010	2009
Current assets	$234,000	$180,000
Property, plant, and equipment	756,000	420,000
Total assets	$990,000	$600,000

Calculate the percentage sizes of each category for each year, using vertical analysis.

Action Plan
- The base amount is total assets in a balance sheet.
- To find the relative percentage, divide the specific asset amount by the base amount for each year.

Solution

	2010 Amount	2010 Percentage	2009 Amount	2009 Percentage
Current assets	$234,000	23.6%	$180,000	30%
Property, plant, and equipment	756,000	76.4%	420,000	70%
Total assets	$990,000	100.0%	$600,000	100%

The Navigator

Ratio Analysis

Ratio analysis expresses the relationship between selected financial statement items. Ratios are generally classified into three types:

1. **Liquidity ratios.** These measure the short-term ability of the company to pay its maturing obligations and to meet unexpected needs for cash.
2. **Solvency ratios.** These measure the ability of the company to survive over a long period of time.
3. **Profitability ratios.** These measure the earnings or operating success of a company for a specific period of time.

In previous chapters, we presented liquidity, solvency, and profitability ratios to evaluate the financial position and performance of a company. In this section, we provide a summary listing of these ratios. Chapter and page references to earlier discussions are included so you can review any individual ratio.

In addition, in the appendix to this chapter, there is an example of a comprehensive financial analysis using these ratios. This analysis uses three categories of comparisons: (1) **intracompany**, comparing two years of data for PotashCorp; (2) **intercompany**, comparing PotashCorp and Agrium; and (3) **industry**, comparing both companies to industry averages for the fertilizer industry.

Liquidity Ratios

Liquidity ratios measure the short-term ability of a company to pay its maturing obligations and to meet unexpected needs for cash. Short-term creditors, such as bankers and suppliers, are particularly interested in assessing liquidity. Illustration 14-9 lists the liquidity ratios we have seen in this textbook. It is important to remember that these are only examples of commonly used liquidity ratios. You will find more examples as you learn more about financial analysis.

◀ Illustration 14-9

Liquidity ratios

Ratio	Formula	Purpose	Discussion
Working capital	Current assets – Current liabilities	Measures short-term debt-paying ability	Ch. 2, p. 69
Current ratio	$\dfrac{\text{Current assets}}{\text{Current liabilities}}$	Measures short-term debt-paying ability	Ch. 2, p. 69
Inventory turnover	$\dfrac{\text{Cost of goods sold}}{\text{Average inventory}}$	Measures liquidity of inventory	Ch. 6, p. 302
Days in inventory	$\dfrac{365 \text{ days}}{\text{Inventory turnover}}$	Measures number of days inventory is on hand	Ch. 6, p. 302
Receivables turnover	$\dfrac{\text{Net credit sales}}{\text{Average gross accounts receivable}}$	Measures liquidity of receivables	Ch. 8, p. 404
Average collection period	$\dfrac{365 \text{ days}}{\text{Receivables turnover}}$	Measures number of days receivables are outstanding	Ch. 8, p. 404
Cash current debt coverage	$\dfrac{\text{Cash provided (used) by operating activities}}{\text{Average current liabilities}}$	Measures short-term debt-paying ability (cash basis)	Ch. 13, p. 682

▶ Performance Measurement

Solvency Ratios

Solvency ratios measure the ability of a company to survive over a long period of time. Long-term creditors and shareholders are interested in a company's long-run solvency, particularly its ability to pay interest as it comes due and to repay the face value of debt at maturity. Illustration 14-10 lists the solvency ratios we have seen in this textbook.

Illustration 14-10 ➡

Solvency ratios

Ratio	Formula	Purpose	Discussion
Debt to total assets	$\dfrac{\text{Total liabilities}}{\text{Total assets}}$	Measures percentage of total assets provided by creditors	Ch. 2, p. 70; Ch. 10, p. 514
Free cash flow	Cash provided (used) by operating activities − Net capital expenditures − Dividends paid	Measures cash available from operating activities for discretionary purposes	Ch. 2, p. 72
Times interest earned	$\dfrac{\text{Net earnings + Interest expense + Income tax expense (EBIT)}}{\text{Interest expense}}$	Measures ability to meet interest payments	Ch. 10, p. 515
Cash total debt coverage	$\dfrac{\text{Cash provided (used) by operating activities}}{\text{Average total liabilities}}$	Measures long-term debt-paying ability (cash basis)	Ch. 13, p. 683

Profitability Ratios

Profitability ratios measure the earnings or operating success of a company for a specific period of time. A company's earnings, or lack of them, affect its ability to obtain debt and equity financing, its liquidity position, and its growth. As a result, both creditors and investors are interested in evaluating profitability. Profitability is frequently used as the ultimate test of management's operating effectiveness. Illustration 14-11 lists the profitability ratios we have seen in this textbook.

Illustration 14-11 ➡

Profitability ratios

Ratio	Formula	Purpose	Discussion
Corporate measures:			
Gross profit margin	$\dfrac{\text{Gross profit}}{\text{Net sales}}$	Measures margin between selling price and cost of goods sold	Ch. 5, p. 238
Profit margin	$\dfrac{\text{Net earnings}}{\text{Net sales}}$	Measures net earnings generated by each dollar of sales	Ch. 5, p. 239
Return on assets	$\dfrac{\text{Net earnings}}{\text{Average total assets}}$	Measures overall profitability of assets	Ch. 9, p. 457
Asset turnover	$\dfrac{\text{Net sales}}{\text{Average total assets}}$	Measures how efficiently assets are used to generate sales	Ch. 9, p. 458
Return on common shareholders' equity	$\dfrac{\text{Net earnings − Preferred dividends}}{\text{Average common shareholders' equity}}$	Measures profitability of shareholders' investment	Ch. 11, p. 572
Investor measures:			
Earnings per share	$\dfrac{\text{Net earnings − Preferred dividends}}{\text{Weighted average number of common shares}}$	Measures net earnings earned on each common share	Ch. 2, p. 66; Ch. 11, p. 570
Price-earnings ratio	$\dfrac{\text{Market price per share}}{\text{Earnings per share}}$	Measures relationship between market price per share and earnings per share	Ch. 2, p. 67
Payout ratio	$\dfrac{\text{Cash dividends}}{\text{Net earnings}}$	Measures percentage of earnings distributed as cash dividends	Ch. 11, p. 569
Dividend yield	$\dfrac{\text{Dividend per share}}{\text{Market price per share}}$	Measures earnings generated for the shareholder by each share, based on the market price per share	Ch. 11, p. 569

We have subdivided the profitability ratios on the previous page into two sections: ratios that are measures of the company's profitability and ratios that relate more to investors. The five profitability ratios that are shown for a corporation relate to the company's past profitability. Recall that financial statements are based on past information and are often issued as much as three to six months after the year end.

The earnings per share, price-earnings ratio, payout ratio, and dividend yield are not specific measures of a company's profitability. Rather, these are measures that investors use to determine whether to purchase a company's shares for growth or income. Of course, investors should look at all ratios before deciding to invest in a company, but these four ratios relate more to the needs of investors than corporations.

In conclusion, the ratios shown in Illustrations 14-9, 14-10, and 14-11 are some of the more common ratios that are used to evaluate a company's liquidity, solvency, and profitability. However, as mentioned earlier, there are many different and additional ratios and groupings that financial analysts use. Users should therefore determine which ratios best suit the decisions they need to make.

In addition, it is important to note that, except for earnings per share, there is no standard calculation for each ratio. Consequently, before using ratios that have been calculated by others, it is important to understand what components were used in the calculation.

Ratios can give clues about underlying conditions that may not be seen from an inspection of the individual components of a particular ratio. But a single ratio by itself is not very meaningful. Accordingly, ratios must be interpreted alongside information that has been gained from a detailed review of the financial information, including horizontal and vertical analyses, and the non-financial information that we described earlier in the chapter.

▮▮ ACCOUNTING MATTERS! | Investor Perspective

One must be careful in relying solely on financial information to assess what investors might think about a company's performance. Otherwise, you might be scratching your head wondering why the shares of Aeroplan are down more than 34 percent in a year when the company has very strong cash flow.

Investors are increasingly concerned about the health of the Canadian economy and Aeroplan is seen as a weather vane for the economy. Why is this? Aeroplan earns its revenue from air miles accumulated by its four million members through its partners in the retail and other sectors. When fewer air miles are being collected—by shoppers with fewer dollars to spend—the company's growth is expected to slow.

Source: David Berman, "A Weakening Economy Scars a Likeable Business Model," *The Globe and Mail*, August 23, 2008, p. B4

BEFORE YOU GO ON...

▶ **Review It**

1. What are liquidity ratios? Explain working capital, the current ratio, inventory turnover, days in inventory, receivables turnover, average collection period, and cash current debt coverage.
2. What are solvency ratios? Explain debt to total assets, free cash flow, times interest earned, and cash total debt coverage.
3. What are profitability ratios? Explain gross profit margin, profit margin, return on assets, asset turnover, and return on common shareholders' equity.
4. Distinguish between profitability ratios that are used to assess corporate profitability and those that are used more for investment purposes.

The Navigator

Limitations of Financial Analysis

Before relying on the information you have gathered through your horizontal, vertical, and ratio analyses, you must understand the limitations of these tools and of the financial statements they are based on. Some of the factors that can limit the usefulness of your analysis include alternative accounting principles, professional judgement, inflation, and diversification.

study objective 5

Understand the limitations of financial analysis.

Alternative Accounting Principles

Variations among companies in their use of generally accepted accounting principles may lessen the comparability of their statements. Companies may choose from a large number of acceptable accounting principles, such as different inventory cost formulas (FIFO or average) or depreciation methods (straight-line, diminishing-balance, or units-of-production). Different choices result in differing financial positions, which again affects how easily their results can be compared.

For example, PotashCorp uses two depreciation methods to allocate the cost of different components of its property, plant, and equipment: straight-line and units-of-production. Agrium, one of PotashCorp's competitors, uses the straight-line method for all of its property, plant, and equipment. You can therefore expect to have variations in the carrying amounts of property, plant, and equipment on the balance sheet and in depreciation expense and net earnings on the statement of earnings just because of these differing choices. That is, they result in ratio numbers whose comparative increase or decrease may be attributable solely to an accounting principle choice. Note that although depreciation may be different because of the choice of accounting principle, this is really just an "artificial," or timing, difference. Although there may be differences year by year, in total, over the life of the asset, there is no difference.

In more and more industries, competition is global and this too presents a challenge. To evaluate a company's standing, an investor must make comparisons to companies from other countries. For example, although both PotashCorp and Agrium are Canadian, other competitors include Yara International of Norway and the Mosaic Company in the United States. Although differences in accounting principles might be detectable from reading the notes to the financial statements, adjusting the financial data to compensate for the different principles is difficult, if not impossible, in some cases, both nationally and internationally. The movement to international accounting principles will help eliminate some of these differences in the future.

Professional Judgement

We must accept that management has to use professional judgement in choosing the most appropriate accounting principle for the circumstances. Because judgement is required, management's choices may be biased in favour of a presentation that furthers certain company objectives. In addition, many estimates are required in preparing financial information. Estimates are used, for example, in determining the allowance for uncollectible receivables, estimated useful lives and residual values for depreciation, and fair values of trading and available-for-sale securities. To the extent that these estimates are inaccurate or biased, ratios and percentages that are based on such information will also be inaccurate or biased.

To help reduce bias and inaccuracy and ensure that the quality of information is as high as possible, the chief executive officer and chief financial officer of publicly traded companies must ensure, and personally declare, that the reported financial information is accurate, relevant, and understandable. In addition, audit committees are also held responsible for quizzing management on the degree of aggressiveness or conservatism that has been applied and on the quality of underlying accounting principles, key estimates, and judgements.

A strong corporate governance process, including an active board of directors and audit committee, is essential to ensure that the quality of information is high. As mentioned in our feature story, PotashCorp would seem to have met this objective, as the judges of its annual report found that "PotashCorp exhibits strong commitment to good corporate governance, which is evident in the quality of the disclosure in the proxy and the Governance section of the website."

Inflation

Our accounting information system does not adjust data for price-level changes. For example, a five-year comparison of PotashCorp's net sales shows growth of 212.3 percent. But this growth trend would be misleading if the general price-level had increased or decreased greatly during the same period. In actuality, inflation was 11.4 percent during this same period, so while PotashCorp's sales have indeed increased, they have not increased as much as it first appears. Still, our comparisons are relevant because data that have not been adjusted for inflation are being used consistently for both revenues and expenses, and for each period.

In Canada, inflation is not very significant right now. In the 1990s and in the early 2000s, Canada's inflation rate was quite low, generally in the range of 1 to 3 percent. In the early 1980s, by comparison, the inflation rate exceeded 10 percent. Today, the Bank of Canada tries to maintain an inflation rate within the 1 to 3 percent range.

Some countries experience "hyper," or extremely rapid, inflation. Hyperinflation refers to situations where the cumulative inflation rate over a three-year period reaches or exceeds 100 percent. One such example is Zimbabwe, where inflation is currently 516 quintillion percent (that's 516 followed by 18 zeros) a year—the highest in the world. In countries where hyperinflation exists, financial statements are adjusted for the effects of inflation in order to make the financial information more meaningful for decision-making.

Diversification

Diversification in Canadian industry also can limit the usefulness of financial analysis. Many firms today are so diversified that they cannot be classified by industry. Canadian Tire, for example, sells selected grocery, home, car, clothing, sports, and leisure products. In addition, it is the country's largest independent gasoline retailer. Consequently, deciding what industry a company is in can actually be one of the main challenges to an effective evaluation of its results.

Other companies may appear to be comparable but are not. McCain Foods and Irving-owned Cavendish Farms compete in the frozen potato product field. Yet McCain produces other food products besides french fries, and Irving has many other interests, including oil, newspapers, tissue products, transportation, and shipbuilding.

Because of this diversification, analysts must be careful in interpreting consolidated financial statements. You will recall that we learned about consolidated financial statements in Chapter 12. Consolidated statements include financial information about the parent company and each of its subsidiaries. The parent company may have a strong debt to total assets ratio, and the subsidiary a weak one. However, because these statements are consolidated, the combined results may show that the debt to total assets ratio is close to the industry average. The fact that the subsidiary may have solvency problems is hidden from the general public because of the consolidated reporting of the financial information. Of course, such a situation would not be hidden from management as it has access to the individual statements of each subsidiary company even though the general public does not.

When companies have significant operations in different lines of business, they are required to report additional disclosures in a segmented information note to their financial statements. You will recall that we introduced operating segments earlier in the discontinued operations section of this chapter. There are specific revenue, earnings, and assets tests to determine if a company is required to report segmented information or not (you will learn more about this in an intermediate accounting course). If a company has reportable segments, it must disclose relevant information about revenues, operating income, and/or identifiable assets by products and services, by geographic area, and by major customer. Internationally, segmented information is not reported geographically (by country) as it currently is in Canada.

Many analysts say that segmented information is the most important data in the financial statements, especially when comparing diversified companies. PotashCorp has three reportable operating segments: potash, nitrogen, and phosphate. It reports this information by segment and by country (Canada, the United States, and Trinidad). In our feature story, the judges praised PotashCorp for reporting its operations by segment in its MD&A.

ACCOUNTING MATTERS! | Investor Perspective

Al and Mark Rosen recommend the following five steps in analyzing a company: (1) read the company's quarterly and annual financial statements, including all the notes and the management discussion and analysis; (2) watch for too-good-to-be-true situations; (3) be careful about who you trust; (4) watch for specific accounting games and poor financial statement disclosures; and (5) look out for executive compensation schemes that base management performance bonuses on slippery accounting figures.

Source: Al Rosen and Mark Rosen, "Dig Deeper," *Canadian Business,* January 17, 2005, p. 27

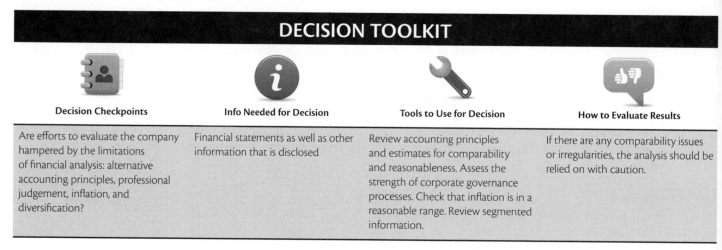

DECISION TOOLKIT

Decision Checkpoints	Info Needed for Decision	Tools to Use for Decision	How to Evaluate Results
Are efforts to evaluate the company hampered by the limitations of financial analysis: alternative accounting principles, professional judgement, inflation, and diversification?	Financial statements as well as other information that is disclosed	Review accounting principles and estimates for comparability and reasonableness. Assess the strength of corporate governance processes. Check that inflation is in a reasonable range. Review segmented information.	If there are any comparability issues or irregularities, the analysis should be relied on with caution.

BEFORE YOU GO ON...

➔ Review It

1. What are some of the limitations of financial analysis?
2. Explain how alternative accounting principles can affect the comparability and quality of information.
3. What are the audit committee's responsibilities to ensure that management's professional judgement is not overly aggressive or conservative?
4. Why is it useful to have financial information reported by operating segment?

The Navigator

APPENDIX 14A—COMPREHENSIVE ILLUSTRATION OF RATIO ANALYSIS

In previous chapters, we calculated many ratios that are used to evaluate the financial health and performance of a company. In this appendix, we review these ratios and discuss some important relationships among them. In this review, we use the following comparisons:

1. **Intracompany comparisons** covering two years (2006 and 2007) for the Potash Corporation of Saskatchewan Inc. (PotashCorp)
2. **Intercompany comparisons** for 2007 for Agrium Inc., one of PotashCorp's competitors
3. **Industry average comparisons** for 2007 for the fertilizer industry. For some of the ratios that we use, industry comparisons are not available. These are marked "n/a."

You will recall that PotashCorp's balance sheet was presented earlier in the chapter in Illustration 14-4 and its statement of earnings in Illustration 14-5. We will use the information in these two financial statements, in addition to the following data, to calculate PotashCorp's ratios:

(in USD millions, except for per share information)	2007	2006
Cash provided by operating activities	$1,688.9	$696.8
Net capital expenditures	607.2	508.6
Total dividends paid	93.6	60.9
Weighted average number of shares	315.4	312.6
Dividends per share	0.35	0.20
Market price per share	143.49	167.00

Although the calculations are not shown below, you can use the above data and the balance sheet and statement of earnings data to calculate each ratio yourself to make sure you understand where the numbers came from. Detailed financial data are not shown for either Agrium or the industry.

Liquidity Ratios

Liquidity ratios measure the ability of a company to pay its current liabilities. Consequently, liquidity ratios focus mainly on the relationships between current assets and current liabilities reported on the balance sheet and related accounts on the statement of earnings. Cash provided by operating activities, reported on the cash flow statement, is also useful in assessing liquidity. Liquidity ratios include working capital, the current ratio, cash current debt coverage, receivables turnover, average collection period, inventory turnover, and days in inventory.

Working Capital

Working capital is the difference between current assets and current liabilities. It is one measure of liquidity. However, as we learned in Chapter 2, the current ratio—which expresses current assets and current liabilities as a ratio rather than as an amount—is a more useful indicator of liquidity. Consequently, we will not illustrate working capital again here, and will focus instead on the current ratio.

Current Ratio

The current ratio expresses the relationship of current assets to current liabilities, and is calculated by dividing current assets by current liabilities. It is widely used for evaluating a company's liquidity and short-term debt-paying ability. The 2007 and 2006 current ratios for PotashCorp and comparative data are shown in Illustration 14-A1.

			PotashCorp		Agrium	Industry
Ratio	Formula	Indicates	2007	2006	2007	2007
Current ratio	Current assets / Current liabilities	Short-term debt-paying ability	1.8:1	1.2:1	2.8:1	2.2:1

► Illustration 14-A1

Current ratio

What does the ratio actually mean? The 2007 ratio of 1.8:1 means that for every dollar of current liabilities, PotashCorp has $1.80 of current assets. PotashCorp's current ratio increased between 2007 and 2006, mainly because of a significant increase in its cash and cash equivalents. Recall from Illustration 14-4 that current assets increased by 38.2 percent, while current liabilities decreased by 9.2 percent. During the year under analysis, potash prices were at an all-time high because of increased demand during a period of tight supply. Consequently, cash increased substantially because more sales were made at a higher price.

PotashCorp's current ratio is significantly less than Agrium's and somewhat less than that of the industry. However, it is too early in our analysis to draw any conclusions about PotashCorp's liquidity, because the current ratio is only one measure of liquidity. It does not take into account the composition of the current assets. For example, an "apparently satisfactory" current ratio could hide the fact that a portion of current assets may be tied up in uncollectible accounts receivable or slow-moving inventory.

Cash Current Debt Coverage

One disadvantage of the current ratio is that it uses year-end balances of current asset and current liability accounts. These year-end balances may not reflect the company's position during most of the year. A ratio that partially corrects this problem is the cash current debt coverage ratio. Because it uses cash provided by operating activities, which covers a period of time, rather than current assets, which represent a balance at a point in time, it may be a better indicator of liquidity.

PotashCorp's cash current debt coverage ratio is shown in Illustration 14-A2.

▼ Illustration 14-A2

Cash current debt coverage

			PotashCorp		Agrium	Industry
Ratio	Formula	Indicates	2007	2006	2007	2007
Cash current debt coverage	Cash provided (used) by operating activities / Average current liabilities	Short-term debt-paying ability (cash basis)	1.6 times	0.6 times	0.4 times	n/a

PotashCorp's cash provided by operating activities increased from U.S. $696.8 million in 2006 to U.S. $1,688.9 million in 2007. This represents an increase of 242 percent! Remember, its current liabilities decreased by 9.2 percent during the same period. Consequently, the cash current debt coverage increased in 2007 to 1.6 times from 0.6 times in 2006. This is not surprising given that its cash and cash equivalents increased by 120.9 percent during the same period, as we saw earlier in Illustration 14-4.

PotashCorp's cash current debt coverage is significantly higher than Agrium's. Industry averages are not available for cash-based ratios.

Receivables Turnover

We mentioned earlier that a high current ratio is not always a good indication of liquidity. The high result could be because of increased receivables resulting from uncollectible accounts. The ratio that is used to assess the liquidity of the receivables is the receivables turnover. It measures the number of times, on average, that receivables are collected during the period. The receivables turnover is calculated by dividing net credit sales (sales on account less sales returns and allowances and discounts) by average gross accounts receivable (before the allowance for doubtful accounts is deducted) during the year.

The receivables turnover ratio for PotashCorp is shown in Illustration 14-A3.

Illustration 14-A3 ⬇

Receivables turnover

Ratio	Formula	Indicates	PotashCorp 2007	PotashCorp 2006	Agrium 2007	Industry 2007
Receivables turnover	$\dfrac{\text{Net credit sales}}{\text{Average gross accounts receivable}}$	Liquidity of receivables	10.1 times	8.4 times	7.9 times	9.1 times

Since companies do not normally disclose the proportion of their sales that were made for cash and for credit, we normally assume that all sales are credit sales. In addition, not all companies report gross and net accounts receivable separately. In such cases, it is appropriate to use net accounts receivable. The important thing is to be consistent in your input data to ensure that the resulting ratios are comparable.

PotashCorp's receivables turnover increased in 2007. PotashCorp states in its annual report that its goal is to become "the supplier of choice to high-volume, high margin customers with the lowest credit risk." Its receivables turnover is also higher than Agrium's and the industry average for 2007.

Average Collection Period

A popular variant of the receivables turnover is calculated by converting it into a collection period stated in days. This is done by dividing 365 days by the receivables turnover.

The average collection period for PotashCorp is shown in Illustration 14-A4.

Illustration 14-A4 ⬇

Average collection period

Ratio	Formula	Indicates	PotashCorp 2007	PotashCorp 2006	Agrium 2007	Industry 2007
Average collection period	$\dfrac{\text{365 days}}{\text{Receivables turnover}}$	Number of days receivables are outstanding	36 days	43 days	46 days	40 days

PotashCorp's 2007 receivables turnover of 10.1 times is divided into 365 days to obtain an average collection period of 36 days. Analysts frequently use the average collection period to assess the effectiveness of a company's credit and collection policies. The general rule is that the collection period should not greatly exceed the credit period (i.e., the time allowed for payment). PotashCorp appears to have been better at collecting its accounts receivable in 2007 than in 2006.

PotashCorp's collection period is also better than that of Agrium and the industry. The company's receivables management appears to be in good shape, which makes the increased current ratio look more reliable.

Inventory Turnover

Slow-moving inventory can also distort the current ratio. The liquidity of a company's inventory is measured by the inventory turnover ratio. This ratio measures the number of times on average that the inventory is sold during the period, and is calculated by dividing the cost of goods sold by the average inventory. Unless seasonal factors are significant, average inventory can be calculated from the beginning and ending inventory balances.

Illustration 14-A5 ⬇

Inventory turnover

PotashCorp's inventory turnover is shown in Illustration 14-A5.

Ratio	Formula	Indicates	PotashCorp 2007	PotashCorp 2006	Agrium 2007	Industry 2007
Inventory turnover	$\dfrac{\text{Cost of goods sold}}{\text{Average inventory}}$	Liquidity of inventory	7.2 times	5.4 times	4.3 times	3.1 times

PotashCorp's inventory turnover increased (improved) in 2007. PotashCorp's strategy is to match supply to demand to minimize excess inventory. Its inventory turnover is significantly better than both Agrium's and the industry average.

Days in Inventory

A variant of the inventory turnover ratio is days in inventory, which measures the average number of days it takes to sell the inventory. It is calculated by dividing 365 days by the inventory turnover.

The days in inventory for PotashCorp is shown in Illustration 14-A6.

▼ Illustration 14-A6

Days in inventory

Ratio	Formula	Indicates	PotashCorp 2007	PotashCorp 2006	Agrium 2007	Industry 2007
Days in inventory	$\dfrac{365\ days}{Inventory\ turnover}$	Number of days inventory is on hand	51 days	68 days	85 days	118 days

PotashCorp's 2007 inventory turnover of 7.2 times is divided into 365 days to obtain 51 days in inventory. This means that, on average, it takes PotashCorp 51 days to sell its inventory. This average is much better than that of Agrium and the industry. Generally, the faster inventory is sold, the less cash there is tied up in inventory and the less chance there is of inventory becoming obsolete.

It is now safe to conclude that the increase in Potash Corp's current ratio indicates improved liquidity, since we have learned nothing to the contrary in our analysis of the receivables and inventory turnover ratios. It is worth noting here that the above interpretations are based not only on the financial data, but also on the knowledge gained from an understanding of PotashCorp and Agrium, their businesses, and their activities over the last year. As mentioned in the chapter, non-financial information is important in interpreting the financial results.

Liquidity Conclusion

In an intracompany comparison, all of PotashCorp's liquidity ratios improved from 2006 to 2007. In an intercompany and industry comparison, PotashCorp's current ratio was lower than both Agrium's and the industry average. However, all of its other liquidity ratios were better than both Agrium's and the industry average. Agrium's current ratio and the industry average were likely inflated because of slower-moving receivables and inventory. In addition, PotashCorp also has access to an operating line of credit, which gives it a source of additional liquidity if needed.

Solvency Ratios

While liquidity ratios measure the ability of a company to pay its current liabilities, solvency ratios measure the ability of a company to pay its total liabilities. The debt to total assets, times interest earned, and cash total debt coverage ratios give information about debt-paying ability. In addition, free cash flow gives information about the company's discretionary cash flow that is available to expand operations, go after new opportunities, or pay additional dividends, among other alternatives.

Debt to Total Assets

The debt to total assets ratio measures the percentage of the total assets that is provided by creditors. It is calculated by dividing total liabilities (both current and long-term) by total assets. This ratio indicates the company's reliance on debt. The higher the percentage of debt to total assets, the greater the risk that the company may be unable to meet its maturing obligations. The lower the ratio, the more equity "buffer" there is for creditors if the company becomes insolvent. So, from the creditors' point of view, a low ratio of debt to total assets is good.

PotashCorp's debt to total assets is shown in Illustration 14-A7.

▼ Illustration 14-A7

Debt to total assets

Ratio	Formula	Indicates	PotashCorp 2007	PotashCorp 2006	Agrium 2007	Industry 2007
Debt to total assets	$\dfrac{Total\ liabilities}{Total\ assets}$	Percentage of total assets provided by creditors	38.1%	55.3%	47.0%	30.1%

PotashCorp's debt to total assets ratio of 38.1 percent means that creditors have provided financing to cover 38.1 percent of the company's total assets. The inverse means that shareholders have provided financing to cover 61.9 percent (100% – 38.1%) of the company's total assets.

PotashCorp's solvency, as measured by the debt to total assets ratio, improved during the year, from 55.3 percent to 38.1 percent. According to Illustration 14-4, presented earlier in the chapter, total assets increased by 56.3 percent in 2007 and total liabilities increased by 7.6 percent. It appears that PotashCorp is financing additional assets by using equity rather than by adding additional debt. PotashCorp's debt to total assets ratio is better than Agrium's 47 percent but worse than the industry average of 30.1 percent.

Another ratio with a similar meaning is the **debt to equity ratio**. It shows the use of borrowed funds relative to the investments by shareholders. The debt to equity ratio is calculated by dividing total liabilities by total shareholders' equity. When the debt to total assets ratio equals 50 percent, the debt to equity ratio is 100 percent (because total liabilities plus shareholders' equity equals total assets).

Using this definition, PotashCorp's debt to equity ratio for 2007 is 61.4 percent (U.S. $3,697.9 million ÷ U.S. $6,018.7 million). This means that PotashCorp has financed its operations with .614 times as much debt as equity.

Times Interest Earned

While the debt level of a company is important, its ability to service the debt—that is, pay the interest—is of equal or greater importance. The times interest earned ratio (also called interest coverage) indicates the company's ability to meet interest payments as they come due. It is calculated by dividing earnings before interest expense and income taxes by interest expense. This is often abbreviated as EBIT, which stands for earnings before interest and taxes. EBIT represents the amount that is available to cover interest.

PotashCorp's times interest earned ratio is shown in Illustration 14-A8.

Illustration 14-A8 ⬇

Times interest earned

Ratio	Formula	Indicates	PotashCorp 2007	PotashCorp 2006	Agrium 2007	Industry 2007
Times interest earned	Earnings before interest and income tax expense (EBIT) / Interest expense	Ability to meet interest payments	23.1 times	10.2 times	10.2 times	15.2 times

PotashCorp's 2007 times interest earned number was 23.1 times. That is, earnings before interest and taxes were 23.1 times the amount needed for interest expense. PotashCorp's times interest earned ratio more than doubled from 2006 to 2007. It is now much more than the industry average of 15.2 times, and than Agrium's ratio of 10.2 times.

Times interest earned should always be interpreted along with the debt to total assets ratio. Since PotashCorp's debt to total assets improved in 2007, as did its times interest earned ratio, its solvency is in good shape.

Cash Total Debt Coverage

A cash-based equivalent to the debt to total assets ratio is the cash total debt coverage ratio. This ratio indicates a company's ability to repay its liabilities from cash provided by operating activities, without having to liquidate the assets used in its operations. It is calculated by dividing cash provided (or used) by operating activities (from the cash flow statement) by average total liabilities.

Illustration 14-A9 shows PotashCorp's cash total debt coverage.

Illustration 14-A9 ⬇

Cash total debt coverage

Ratio	Formula	Indicates	PotashCorp 2007	PotashCorp 2006	Agrium 2007	Industry 2007
Cash total debt coverage	Cash provided (used) by operating activities / Average total liabilities	Long-term debt-paying ability (cash basis)	0.5 times	0.2 times	0.2 times	n/a

An industry ratio for this measure is not available, but PotashCorp's cash total debt coverage ratio increased from 0.2 times in 2006 to 0.5 times in 2007. One way of interpreting the cash total debt coverage ratio is to say that cash provided from PotashCorp's 2007 operating activities would be enough to pay off 50 percent of its total liabilities. If 50 percent of liabilities were retired each year, it would take approximately two more years to retire all debt. PotashCorp's cash total debt coverage ratio was higher than Agrium's 0.2 times.

This ratio improved, similar to the debt to total assets ratio. Both are moving in the same direction, which lessens concerns about cash- and accrual-based accounting differences.

Free Cash Flow

Another indication of a company's solvency is the amount of excess cash that it generates after investing to maintain its current productive capacity and after paying current dividends. This amount is referred to as free cash flow.

PotashCorp's free cash flow is shown in Illustration 14-A10 (in USD millions):

⬇ Illustration 14-A10

Free cash flow

Ratio	Formula	Indicates	PotashCorp 2007	PotashCorp 2006	Agrium 2007	Industry 2007
Free cash flow	Cash provided (used) by operating activities – Net capital expenditures – Dividends paid	Cash available from operating activities for discretionary purposes	$988.1	$127.3	$25.0	n/a

PotashCorp's free cash flow improved considerably from 2006 to 2007. Cash provided by operating activities increased in 2007 by U.S. $992.1 million, which was the primary reason that free cash flow increased by U.S. $860.8 ($988.1 – $127.3) million. This huge increase, as discussed in the management discussion and analysis section of the company's annual report, was attributed mostly to the strengthening of the Canadian dollar against the U.S. dollar and higher product pricing.

PotashCorp's free cash flow was significantly higher than Agrium's U.S. $25 million. There is no amount available for the industry.

Solvency Conclusion

In an intracompany comparison, all of PotashCorp's solvency ratios improved in 2007. Intercompany and industry comparisons show that PotashCorp's solvency was better than Agrium's and the industry's, except for its debt to total assets ratio being slightly higher than that of the industry in 2007.

Profitability Ratios

For a company to be successful, assets must be used to efficiently generate revenue and expenses must be effectively controlled. Consequently, profitability ratios focus mainly on the relationships between statement of earnings items and balance sheet items. Understanding these relationships can help management determine where to focus efforts on improving profitability.

Illustration 14-A11 diagrams these relationships and will guide our discussion of PotashCorp's profitability. Profitability ratios include the return on common shareholders' equity, return on assets, profit margin, asset turnover, and gross profit margin ratios, as shown in Illustration 14-A11.

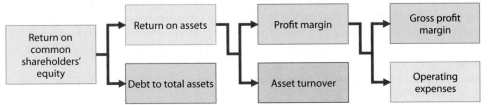

⬅ Illustration 14-A11

Relationship among profitability measures

As shown in the above illustration, the return on common shareholders' equity ratio is affected by the return on assets and debt to total assets ratios. If a company wants to increase its return on common shareholders' equity, it can either increase its return on assets or increase its reliance on debt financing. In fact, as long as the return on assets is higher than the interest rate paid on debt, the return on common shareholders' equity will always be increased by the use of debt.

The return on assets ratio is affected by the profit margin and asset turnover. If a company wants to increase its return on assets, it can do this by either increasing its operating efficiency (profit margin), or trying to increase its asset utilization (asset turnover).

And, of course, the profit margin is affected by the gross profit margin and the amount, or percentage, of operating expenses (assuming there are no other revenues or other expenses). If a company wants to increase its profit margin, it can increase its gross profit margin by either raising selling prices, reducing its cost of goods sold, or reducing its operating expenses.

We will now look at each of these ratios in turn and examine their relationships. In addition, we will review four other commonly used profitability measures that are of specific interest to investors—earnings per share, price-earnings ratio, payout ratio, and dividend yield.

Return on Common Shareholders' Equity

A widely used measure of profitability from the common shareholders' viewpoint is the return on common shareholders' equity. This ratio shows how many dollars of net earnings were earned for each dollar invested by the shareholders. It is calculated by dividing net earnings available to common shareholders (net earnings - preferred dividends) by average common shareholders' equity (total shareholders' equity - preferred shares).

The return on common shareholders' equity for PotashCorp is shown in Illustration 14-A12.

Illustration 14-A12 ⬇

Return on common shareholders' equity

Ratio	Formula	Indicates	PotashCorp 2007	PotashCorp 2006	Agrium 2007	Industry 2007
Return on common shareholders' equity	Net earnings available to common shareholders / Average common shareholders' equity	Profitability of shareholders' investment	25.1%	25.7%	20.4%	22.4%

PotashCorp's return on shareholders' equity declined marginally in 2007. It is slightly better than Agrium's and the industry average.

Return on Assets

The return on common shareholders' equity is affected by two factors: the return on assets ratio and the debt to total assets ratio. We looked earlier in this appendix at PotashCorp's debt to total assets ratio and noted a significant improvement. We will now look at its return on assets.

Return on assets measures the overall profitability of assets in terms of how much is earned on each dollar invested in assets. It is calculated by dividing net earnings by average total assets. PotashCorp's return on assets is shown in Illustration 14-A13.

Illustration 14-A13 ⬇

Return on assets

Ratio	Formula	Indicates	PotashCorp 2007	PotashCorp 2006	Agrium 2007	Industry 2007
Return on assets	Net earnings / Average total assets	Overall profitability of assets	13.9%	10.9%	9.7%	11.7%

PotashCorp's return on assets of 13.9 percent in 2007 is higher than its return of 10.9 percent in 2006. This change is once again influenced by the increase in net earnings. Its return on assets is higher than both Agrium's and the industry average.

Note that PotashCorp's rate of return on common shareholders' equity (25.1 percent) is much higher than its rate of return on assets (13.9 percent). The reason is that PotashCorp has made effective use of leverage. **Leveraging** or **trading on the equity** means that the company has borrowed money at a lower rate of interest than the rate of return it earns on the assets it purchased with the borrowed funds. Leverage enables management to use money supplied by non-shareholders (non-owners) to increase the return to shareholders.

PotashCorp's return on shareholders' equity is higher than its return on assets because of the positive benefit of leverage. Recall from our earlier discussion that PotashCorp's percentage of debt financing as measured by the ratio of debt to total assets was 38.1 percent in 2007 (see Illustration 14-A7). In contrast, Agrium had a higher (worse) debt to total assets ratio of 47 percent.

Profit Margin

The profit margin is one of two factors that affects the return on assets. The profit margin measures the percentage of net earnings that each dollar of sales produces. It is calculated by dividing net earnings by net sales for the period.

Illustration 14-A14 ⬇

Profit margin

PotashCorp's profit margin is shown in Illustration 14-A14.

Ratio	Formula	Indicates	PotashCorp 2007	PotashCorp 2006	Agrium 2007	Industry 2007
Profit margin	Net earnings / Net sales	Net earnings generated by each dollar of sales	21.1%	16.8%	8.4%	11.5%

PotashCorp reported a 21.1-percent profit margin in 2007. This profit margin was of course greater than that of 2006, given the change in earnings between the two years. It also exceeded Agrium's and the industry average by a considerable amount.

Asset Turnover

The other factor that affects the return on assets ratio is asset turnover. The asset turnover ratio measures how efficiently a company uses its assets to generate sales. It is calculated by dividing net sales by average total assets for the period. The resulting number shows the dollars of sales produced by each dollar invested in assets.

Illustration 14-A15 shows the asset turnover for PotashCorp.

▼ Illustration 14-A15

Asset turnover

Ratio	Formula	Indicates	PotashCorp 2007	PotashCorp 2006	Agrium 2007	Industry 2007
Asset turnover	Net sales / Average total assets	How efficiently assets are used to generate sales	0.7 times	0.7 times	1.2 times	0.9 times

The asset turnover ratio shows that PotashCorp generated $0.70 of sales in 2007 for each dollar it had invested in assets. Although the asset turnover was unchanged from 2006, it is lower than Agrium's and that of the industry.

Gross Profit Margin

We saw in Illustration 14-A14 that the profit margin increased in 2007 from 16.8 percent to 21.1 percent. Two factors influence the profit margin: one is the gross profit margin, the other is the company's ability to control its operating expenses.

The gross profit margin is calculated by dividing gross profit (net sales less cost of goods sold) by net sales. This ratio indicates a company's ability to maintain an adequate selling price above its cost of goods sold. Illustration 14-A16 shows PotashCorp's gross profit margin.

▼ Illustration 14-A16

Gross profit margin

Ratio	Formula	Indicates	PotashCorp 2007	PotashCorp 2006	Agrium 2007	Industry 2007
Gross profit margin	Gross profit / Net sales	Margin between selling price and cost of goods sold	35.9%	26.6%	30.3%	28.7%

PotashCorp's gross profit margin increased from 26.6 percent in 2006 to 35.9 percent in 2007. This gross profit margin is higher than Agrium's 30.3 percent and the industry average of 28.7 percent.

There were several reasons for the increased gross profit in 2007 for PotashCorp. First, there was a significant increase in sales revenue both in price and volume. Secondly, the cost of goods sold stayed relatively constant on a dollar basis and any increases related mainly to additional production. Overall the increase in gross profit margin over 2006 was mainly because of high demand and limited supply of its products.

PotashCorp's increase in its gross profit margin was a significant factor that contributed to the increase in its profit margin. The other factor affecting the profit margin is operating expenses. In 2007, PotashCorp had 35.9 percent of each dollar of sales remaining to cover its operating expenses and generate a profit.

The company was not quite as effective in controlling its operating expenses in 2007 as it was in controlling its cost of goods sold. As shown in Illustration 14-5, selling and administrative expenses increased by 34.2 percent, which was almost as much as the percentage increase in sales. However the company's other operating expenses increased significantly, by 231.1 percent, which resulted in an overall net increase in operating expenses. You will recall these were mainly due to increased mining taxes and losses on foreign exchange.

The ratios we just reviewed—return on common shareholders' equity, return on assets, profit margin, asset turnover, and gross profit margin—focus more on the company's profitability, based on past results. The next four ratios—earnings per share, price-earnings, payout ratio, and dividend yield—are of specific interest to investors, Two of these—the price-earnings and dividend yield—use market-based information and focus more on the current value, rather than the accounting (past) value, of the company.

Earnings per Share

Earnings per share is a measure of the net earnings realized on each common share. It is calculated by dividing net earnings available to common shareholders by the weighted average number of common shares. Shareholders usually think in terms of the number of shares they own or plan to buy or sell. Expressing net earnings on a per share basis provides a useful perspective for determining profitability. This measure is widely used and reported. Because of the ratio's importance, there are specific requirements for its calculation and companies are required to present it directly on their statement of earnings. It is the only ratio for which there is a standardized and audited calculation.

▶ Performance Measurement

Illustration 14-A17 ⬇

PotashCorp's earnings per share is shown in Illustration 14-A17.

Ratio	Formula	Indicates	PotashCorp 2007	PotashCorp 2006	Agrium 2007	Industry 2007
Earnings per share	Net earnings – Preferred dividends / Weighted average number of common shares	Net earnings earned on each common share	$3.50	$2.02	$3.28	n/a

Note that no industry average is presented in Illustration 14A-17. Comparisons to the industry average, or to Agrium's earnings per share, are not meaningful, because of the different financing structures (e.g., debt or equity) used by different companies, as well as the wide variations in numbers of shares issued by companies. The only meaningful earnings per share comparison is an intracompany one. PotashCorp's earnings per share increased significantly from $2.02 in 2006 to $3.50 in 2007.

Price-Earnings Ratio

The price-earnings ratio is an often-quoted statistic that measures the ratio of the market price of each common share to the earnings per share. The price-earnings ratio reflects investors' assessments of a company's future earnings. It is calculated by dividing the market price per share by earnings per share. PotashCorp's price-earnings ratio is shown in Illustration 14-A18.

Illustration 14-A18 ⬇

Price-earnings ratio

Ratio	Formula	Indicates	PotashCorp 2007	PotashCorp 2006	Agrium 2007	Industry 2007
Price-earnings ratio	Market price per share / Earnings per share	Relationship between market price per share and earnings per share	41.0 times	82.7 times	21.8 times	21.5 times

In 2007, each PotashCorp common share sold for 41 times the amount that was earned on each share. In 2006, each share sold for 82.7 times earnings. In general, a higher price-earnings ratio means that investors favour the company. They are willing to pay more for the shares because they believe the company has prospects for growth and earnings in the future.

Why did PotashCorp's price-earnings ratio drop so significantly in 2007? Recall that its earnings per share nearly doubled in 2007. This alone, with a constant share price, would cause the price-earnings ratio to drop by nearly half. In PotashCorp's case, its share price declined about 14 percent while its earnings per share increased about 73 percent. These combined to result in a large drop in the price-earnings ratio. Note that PotashCorp's price-earnings ratio is still much higher than both Agrium's and the industry average.

Some investors carefully study price-earnings ratios over time to help them determine when to buy or sell shares. If the highs and lows of a particular share's price-earnings ratio remain constant over several operating cycles, then these highs and lows can indicate selling and buying points for the shares. They could also mean other things, however, including that the share is over- or under-priced. Investors should be very cautious in interpreting price-earnings ratios.

Payout Ratio

The payout ratio measures the percentage of earnings that is distributed as cash dividends. It is calculated by dividing cash dividends by net earnings. Companies that have high growth rates usually have low payout ratios because they reinvest most of their net earnings back into the company.

Illustration 14-A19 ⬇

Payout ratio

The payout ratio for PotashCorp is shown in Illustration 14-A19.

Ratio	Formula	Indicates	PotashCorp 2007	PotashCorp 2006	Agrium 2007	Industry 2007
Payout ratio	Cash dividends / Net earnings	Percentage of earnings distributed as cash dividends	8.5%	9.6%	3.4%	9.8%

In 2007, PotashCorp's payout ratio was significantly higher than Agrium's, and less than the industry average. Corporate directors have control over the amount of dividends paid each year, and are generally reluctant to reduce a dividend below the amount paid in a previous year. Therefore, the payout ratio will actually decrease if a company's net earnings increase but the company keeps its total dividend payment the same or more. PotashCorp has historically paid quarterly dividends, and these dividends have increased as net earnings increased.

Dividend Yield

The dividend yield supplements the payout ratio. The dividend yield reports the rate of return a shareholder earned from dividends during the year. It is calculated by dividing the dividend per share by the market price per share, as shown in Illustration 14-A20.

↓ Illustration 14-A20

Dividend yield

Ratio	Formula	Indicates	PotashCorp 2007	PotashCorp 2006	Agrium 2007	Industry 2007
Dividend yield	$\dfrac{\text{Dividend per share}}{\text{Market price per share}}$	Earnings generated for the shareholder by each share, based on the market price per share	0.2%	0.1%	0.1%	n/a

PotashCorp's dividend yield increased in 2007 compared to 2006. Share prices declined slightly and the dividend paid per share increased, creating an increase in the dividend yield. PotashCorp's dividend yield is slightly higher than Agrium's. A dividend yield is not available for the industry as share prices are not comparable. As with the payout ratio, companies that are expanding rapidly can be expected to have lower dividend yields as shareholders are often looking for growth in the share value.

Profitability Conclusion

In an intracompany comparison, PotashCorp's corporate profitability measures have either remained stable or improved from 2006 to 2007, except for a slight decline in return on common shareholders' equity. In addition, its price-earnings, payout, and dividend yields have all declined. High earnings and share prices have the effect of reducing these ratios.

In an intercompany comparison, except for asset turnover, PotashCorp's profitability ratios are above Agrium's. Investors appear to be favouring PotashCorp over Agrium, likely because of its improved profitability and anticipated future growth. Both companies would likely be purchased by investors for capital appreciation (future profitable resale as the share price increases) rather than for the dividend income.

PotashCorp exceeded all the industry ratios except for the asset turnover and payout ratios. Agrium generally was lower than the industry in all ratios except for its asset turnover, gross profit margin, and price-earnings ratios.

This ends our comprehensive analysis illustration using PotashCorp. What can be practically covered in a textbook gives you only the tip of the iceberg when it comes to the types of financial information available and the ratios that are used by various industries. The availability of information is not a problem. The real trick is to be discriminating enough to do relevant analyses and choose pertinent data for comparisons.

Summary of Study Objectives

1. **Understand the concept of sustainable earnings and indicate how irregular items are presented.** Sustainable earnings are the level of earnings likely to be obtained in the future. They exclude irregular revenues and expenses that may be included in net earnings.

Irregular items are presented separately from continuing operations to highlight their infrequent nature. Discontinued operations are reported separately on the balance sheet, statement of earnings, and cash flow statement, net of income tax. The cumulative effect on prior-period earnings of a change in accounting principle is presented on the statement of shareholders' equity (or retained earnings), net of tax, as an adjustment to opening retained earnings. For comparability, all prior-period financial statements that are presented should be restated, if possible, using the new principle.

2. **Explain and apply horizontal analysis.** Horizontal analysis is a technique for evaluating a series of data over a period of time to determine the increase or decrease that has taken place, expressed as either an amount or a percentage. It is calculated by dividing the amount in a specific period (or the change between periods) by a base-period amount.

3. **Explain and apply vertical analysis.** Vertical analysis is a technique that expresses each item in a financial statement as a percentage of a relevant total (base amount) in that same financial statement. For example, each item on the statement of earnings may be expressed as a percentage of net sales or each item on the balance sheet may be expressed as a percentage of total assets.

4. **Identify and calculate ratios that are used to analyze liquidity, solvency, and profitability.** The formula and purpose of each ratio are presented in Illustration 14-9 (liquidity), Illustration 14-10 (solvency), and Illustration 14-11 (profitability).

5. **Understand the limitations of financial analysis.** The usefulness of financial analysis can be limited by (1) the use of alternative accounting principles, (2) professional judgement affecting the quality of the information, (3) inflation, and (4) diversification.

The Navigator

ALL ABOUT YOU

Why Invest in Common Shares?

As you have seen throughout this textbook, both individuals and companies use ratios to help them make decisions on investing in common shares. Some of the ratios they use to make decisions include the earnings per share, price-earnings, payout, and dividend yield ratios. The motive for investing can be either to have a steady source of income through dividends or to have the possibility of the investment appreciating in value over time as the share price rises.

An accumulation of capital or wealth is an important goal for individuals and companies that have long-term investment horizons. Some investors use growth shares to increase their wealth while other investors use shares as a source of dividend income. Investors looking for growth would view the price-earnings ratio as important because the higher the price-earnings ratio, the more investors believe the company has prospects for growth and earnings in the future. Investors looking for dividend income would look toward the dividend yield and payout ratios as indicators of companies that distribute cash dividends. Companies that distribute cash dividends do not reinvest all their earnings back into the company.

Some Facts

- Plunging share prices are to be expected once September begins.
- October is usually a solid month and, more importantly, it is a lead-in to much better returns on average in November, December, and January.
- In the fall of 2008, contrary to expectations, the world's stock markets experienced their largest decline in history.
- There are two ways for a company to return capital to shareholders: dividends and share buybacks.
- "True yield" measures the dividend yield, adjusting it for any growth or shrinkage in the number of shares issued. A company that buys back a lot of shares will have a higher true yield, while one that issues more shares and dilutes the number of its shares will have a lower true yield, all other things being equal.

What Do You Think?

Your grandparents have given you $40,000 to put towards your final years of post-secondary education and to help you get started with life after school by buying such things as furnishings for an apartment and a wardrobe for the workplace. You have just entered your first year of university and have earned enough money to pay for the first two years. You would like to invest the $40,000 in a company with a high payout ratio and dividend yield because you would like a regular dividend income to help with the "extras" you may need during your terms at school. Is choosing a company with a high payout ratio and dividend yield a good idea?

YES | The high payout and dividend yield ratio guarantee me a good quarterly dividend. Even if the share price goes down, I will still make money because of the dividends.

NO | Just because a company declared dividends in the past, that does not guarantee dividends will be declared in the future. You should also look at the price-earnings of the company and see what other investors think of it.

The Navigator

Sources:

Rob Carrick, "Seasonal Disorder: It's Time to Avoid the Markets," *Globe and Mail*, September 6, 2008, p. B13

John Heinzl, "There's More to the Story Than Dividend Yield," *Globe and Mail*, August 27, 2008, p. B12

Glossary

Study Tools (Glossary)

Change in accounting principle Use of a different accounting principle in the current year compared to what was used in the preceding year. (p. 720)

Discontinued operations The disposal, or availability for sale, of an identifiable operating segment of the business. (p. 718)

Horizontal analysis A technique for evaluating a series of financial statement data over a period of time to determine the increase (decrease) that has taken place. This increase (decrease) is expressed as either an amount or a percentage. Also known as trend analysis. (p. 722)

Sustainable earnings The most likely level of earnings to be obtained in the future, determined by adjusting net earnings for irregular items. (p. 718)

Vertical analysis A technique for evaluating financial statement data that expresses each item in a financial statement as a percentage of a base amount. Also known as common size analysis. (p. 726)

DECISION TOOLKIT—A SUMMARY

Decision Checkpoints	Info Needed for Decision	Tools to Use for Decision	How to Evaluate Results
Has the company sold, or is it holding for sale, an operating segment of its business?	Discontinuation of, or plans to discontinue, an operating segment	Discontinued operations section of the balance sheet, statement of earnings, and/or cash flow statement	If an operating segment has been discontinued, its results in the current period should not be included in assessing the company's financial position or in estimating its future net earnings.
Has the company changed any of its accounting principles?	Change in accounting principle	Cumulative effect of a change in accounting principle in the statement of shareholders' equity	Where possible, financial statements are restated using the new principle to make them easy to compare.
How do the company's financial position and operating results compare with those of previous periods?	Balance sheet and statement of earnings	Comparative financial statements should be prepared over at least two years, with the first year reported as the base year. Changes in each line item relative to the base year should be presented both by amount and by percentage. This is called horizontal analysis.	A significant change should be investigated to determine what caused it.
How do the relationships between items in this year's financial statements compare with last year's relationships or those of competitors?	Balance sheet and statement of earnings	Each line item on the balance sheet should be presented as a percentage of total assets (total liabilities and shareholders' equity). Each line item on the statement of earnings should be presented as a percentage of net sales. This is called vertical analysis.	Any difference, either across years or between companies, should be investigated to determine the cause.
Are efforts to evaluate the company hampered by the limitations of financial analysis: alternative accounting principles, professional judgement, inflation, and diversification?	Financial statements as well as other information that is disclosed	Review accounting principles and estimates for comparability and reasonableness. Assess the strength of corporate governance processes. Check that inflation is in a reasonable range. Review segmented information.	If there are any comparability issues or irregularities, the analysis should be relied on with caution.

Using the Decision Toolkit

Goldcorp Incorporated and Yamana Gold Incorporated are two competitors in the gold industry. Selected liquidity, solvency, and profitability ratios follow for the two companies and their industry for a recent year:

	Goldcorp	Yamana Gold	Industry
Liquidity			
Current ratio	1.9:1	1.4:1	2.9:1
Days in inventory	15 days	10 days	8 days
Average collection period	24 days	13 days	16 days
Solvency			
Debt to total assets	6.5%	9.1%	20.0%
Times interest earned	14.4 times	11.1 times	24.9 times
Profitability			
Gross profit margin	56.1%	65.2%	33.2%
Profit margin	26.0%	21.3%	(17.0%)
Return on assets	4.3%	2.9%	(4.0%)
Asset turnover	0.1 times	0.1 times	0.3 times
Return on common shareholders' equity	5.3%	4.1%	(19.3%)

Instructions

(a)   Which company is more liquid? Explain.

(b)   Which company is more solvent? Explain.

(c)   Which company is more profitable? Explain.

Solution

(a)   Yamana Gold is more liquid than Goldcorp. Although Goldcorp appears to have a stronger current ratio than Yamana Gold, it is slower at selling its inventory and collecting its receivables. The higher inventory and receivables may be artificially increasing Goldcorp's current ratio, making it appear better than it really is. Both companies are generally weaker than the industry, except that Yamana Gold is better at collecting its receivables.

(b)   Goldcorp is more solvent than Yamana Gold. It has a better debt to total assets ratio and times interest earned ratio than Yamana Gold. While both companies have better debt to total assets ratios than the industry, neither has as strong a times interest earned ratio.

(c)   Goldcorp is more profitable than Yamana Gold. Its profit margin is higher than that of Yamana Gold and the industry. This is interesting because Yamana Gold's gross profit margin is higher than that of Goldcorp and the industry. This indicates that Yamana Gold is able to keep its cost of goods sold lower, as the selling price of gold would generally be the same for both companies. Goldcorp's return on assets and return on common shareholders' equity are also higher than Yamana Gold's and its asset turnover is the same. Both companies outperformed the industry on all profitability measures, except for asset turnover.

The Navigator

Demonstration Problem

A vertical analysis of the condensed financial statements of Mukhin Inc. for the years 2007 to 2010 follows:

MUKHIN INC.
Percentage Balance Sheet
May 31

	2010	2009	2008	2007
Assets				
Current assets	11.1%	11.1%	13.9%	11.4%
Current assets of discontinued operations	0.2%	2.1%	0.6%	4.2%
Noncurrent assets	88.0%	77.0%	84.8%	81.2%
Noncurrent assets of discontinued operations	0.7%	9.8%	0.7%	3.2%
Total assets	100.0%	100.0%	100.0%	100.0%
Liabilities and Shareholders' Equity				
Current liabilities	19.3%	17.5%	19.0%	15.0%
Current liabilities of discontinued operations	0.0%	1.4%	0.2%	4.1%
Noncurrent liabilities	52.4%	52.1%	46.0%	45.3%
Noncurrent liabilities of discontinued operations	2.3%	4.8%	1.8%	3.4%
Total liabilities	74.0%	75.8%	67.0%	67.8%
Shareholders' equity	26.0%	24.2%	33.0%	32.2%
Total liabilities and shareholders' equity	100.0%	100.0%	100.0%	100.0%

MUKHIN INC.
Percentage Income Statement
Year Ended May 31

	2010	2009	2008	2007
Revenues	100.0%	100.0%	100.0%	100.0%
Expenses	87.8%	89.5%	104.0%	96.0%
Earnings (loss) before income taxes	12.2%	10.5%	(4.0%)	4.0%
Income tax expense (recovery)	3.8%	3.1%	(0.3%)	2.3%
Earnings (loss) from continuing operations	8.4%	7.4%	(3.7%)	1.7%
Earnings (loss) from discontinued operations	0.0%	(0.2%)	1.4%	9.0%
Net earnings (loss)	8.4%	7.2%	(2.3%)	10.7%

Instructions

Discuss the significant changes between 2007 and 2010 for the company.

Solution to Demonstration Problem

Current assets increased in 2008, declined in 2009, and remained stable in 2010. Mukhin's current liabilities are a higher percentage of total assets than are its current assets. Current liabilities have generally been increasing, except for in 2009. Except for during that same year, 2009, Mukhin's noncurrent assets have also been increasing as a percentage of total assets. Noncurrent liabilities have been increasing steadily. The company likely increased its long-term liabilities to help finance increasing purchases of noncurrent assets.

Mukhin's liquidity and solvency appear to be declining over recent years, with increasing percentages of liabilities (exclusive of discontinued operations). We would have to perform further analyses (e.g., ratio analysis) to determine the reasons for this decline.

In terms of profitability, Mukhin appears to be controlling its expenses, which have declined, except in 2008. Except for this same year, its profitability (earnings from continuing operations) also appears to be on the increase.

It is interesting to note the impact that discontinued operations have on Mukhin's financial position. These should be excluded from our comparative analysis. However, except in 2007, the discontinued operations have not significantly affected Mukhin's profitability.

Action Plan

- Exclude the impact of irregular items in your analysis.

- Look at the percentage comparisons both vertically (within the year) and horizontally (across the years).

Self-Study Questions

Answers are at the end of the chapter.

🔧 **All self-study questions in this section use decision tools.**

Study Tools (Self-Assessment Quizzes)

(SO 1) **1.** On which of the following financial statements can discontinued operations be reported?
 (a) Balance sheet
 (b) Statement of shareholders' equity
 (c) Cash flow statement
 (d) All of the above

(SO 1) **2.** On which of the following financial statements is a change in accounting principle reported?
 (a) Balance sheet
 (b) Statement of shareholders' equity
 (c) Cash flow statement
 (d) All of the above

(SO 2) **3.** In a horizontal analysis, each item is expressed as a percentage of the:
 (a) net sales amount.
 (b) net earnings amount.
 (c) total assets amount.
 (d) base-year amount.

(SO 2) **4.** Rankin Inlet Corporation reported net earnings of $300,000, $330,000, and $360,000 in the years 2008, 2009, and 2010, respectively. Net sales for 2010 were $1 million. If 2008 is the base year, what is the horizontal percentage of net earnings for 2010?
 (a) 36%
 (b) 100%
 (c) 110%
 (d) 120%

(SO 3) **5.** In a vertical analysis, the base amount for accumulated depreciation is generally:
 (a) net sales.
 (b) accumulated depreciation in a previous year.
 (c) total assets.
 (d) total property, plant, and equipment.

(SO 3) **6.** The following schedule shows what type of analysis?

	Amount	Percentage
Current assets	$200,000	25%
Noncurrent assets	600,000	75%
Total assets	$800,000	100%

 (a) Horizontal analysis
 (b) Differential analysis
 (c) Vertical analysis
 (d) Ratio analysis

7. Which of the following situations would be the most likely indicator that Wang Corporation might have a solvency problem?
 (a) Increasing debt to total assets and times interest earned ratios
 (b) Increasing debt to total assets and decreasing times interest earned ratios
 (c) Decreasing debt to total assets and times interest earned ratios
 (d) Decreasing debt to total assets and increasing times interest earned ratios

8. Which of the following situations is the most likely indicator of corporate profitability?
 (a) Increasing price-earnings ratio
 (b) Increasing return on assets, asset turnover, and profit margin ratios
 (c) Decreasing return on common shareholders' equity and increasing asset turnover
 (d) Decreasing gross profit margin and increasing profit margin

9. Torstar Corporation has two operating segments of significance: a newspaper and digital division and a book publishing division. Which of the following statements is true?
 (a) Torstar must report segmented information in the notes to its financial statements.
 (b) The reporting of segmented information is optional.
 (c) Torstar must report its primary operations from its newspapers and digital division in its financial statements, and report financial information about its book publishing division in the notes to its financial statements.
 (d) Torstar should report its financial results in individual subsidiary financial statements for each division, rather than in consolidated financial statements.

10. Which situation might indicate that a financial analysis should be used with caution?
 (a) Different accounting principles are being used by the different companies.
 (b) The quality of the financial information is high.
 (c) The company has no operating segments.
 (d) Inflation is low.

Questions

All of the questions in this section use decision tools.

1. Explain the concept of sustainable earnings.

2. Identify two irregular items and indicate which financial statement(s) they affect and how.

3. (a) What are discontinued operations? (b) Why is it important to report the results of discontinued operations separately from those of continuing operations?

4. What is a change in accounting principle? Distinguish between voluntary and mandatory changes.

5. Changes in accounting principles can affect financial reporting in four ways. Identify each way.

6. (a) Distinguish among the following bases of comparison: intracompany, intercompany, and industry average. (b) Explain whether these three bases of comparison should be used individually or together.

7. Explain how the percentage increase or decrease from a base-period amount is calculated in horizontal analysis.

8. Explain how a horizontal analysis is affected if an account (a) has no value in a base year and a value in the next year, or (b) has a negative value in the base year and a positive value in the next year.

9. The Forzani Group Limited had net earnings of $35 million for the year ended January 28, 2007. It experienced a 35% increase in net earnings for fiscal 2008. What are its net earnings for the year ended February 3, 2008?

10. Two methods of financial statement analysis are horizontal analysis and vertical analysis. Explain the difference between these two methods.

11. What items are usually assigned a 100% value in a vertical analysis of (a) the balance sheet and (b) the statement of earnings?

12. Can vertical analysis be used to compare two companies of different sizes and using different currencies, such as InBev, the world's largest brewer, headquartered in Belgium, and SABMiller, the second largest brewer, headquartered in the UK? Explain.

13. Tim Hortons reported U.S. $12.5 million of sales in 2007. If its cost of goods sold is 88% in a vertical analysis, what is the dollar amount of its cost of goods sold?

14. What does each of the following types of ratios measure: (a) liquidity, (b) solvency, and (c) profitability?

15. Is a high current ratio always a good indicator of a company's (SO 4) liquidity? Describe two situations in which a high current ratio might be hiding liquidity problems.

16. Starbucks Corporation reported a debt to total assets ratio (SO 4) of 32% in 2007. The industry average is 37%. Is Starbucks' solvency better or worse than that of the industry?

17. CIBC's return on assets is 1%. During the same year, CIBC (SO 4) reported a return on common shareholders' equity of 30%. Has CIBC made effective use of leverage? Explain.

18. In 2008, Lai Inc. reported a profit margin of 5% before (SO 1, 4) discontinued operations and a profit margin of 8% after discontinued operations. In 2009, the company had no discontinued operations and reported a profit margin of 6.5%. Has Lai's profit margin improved or weakened? Explain.

19. Distinguish between profitability ratios that are measures (SO 4) of corporate profitability and those that are used more by investors.

20. (a) If you were an investor interested in buying the shares (SO 4) of a company with growth potential, what ratios would you look at to help you make your decision? (b) How would your answer change if you were interested in buying shares with an income potential?

21. Which ratios should be used to help answer each of these (SO 4) questions?
    (a) How efficient is the company in using its assets to produce sales?
    (b) How near to sale is the inventory on hand?
    (c) How many dollars were earned for each dollar invested by shareholders?
    (d) How able is the company to pay interest charges as they come due?
    (e) How able is the company to repay a short-term loan?

22. Identify and explain the factors that can limit the usefulness (SO 5) of financial analysis.

23. Explain how changing from one generally accepted (SO 5) accounting principle to another can affect financial analysis.

24. Explain how management must use professional judgement in (SO 5) financial reporting and how this can affect financial analysis.

25. Why are the effects of inflation not reported in financial (SO 5) statements?

26. Why is reporting segmented information useful for analysts? (SO 5)

Brief Exercises

🔑 **All of the brief exercises in this section use decision tools.**

BE14–1 Avondale Inc. reported the following information from its statement of earnings for the current year:

Earnings from operations	$1,040,000
Interest expense	125,000
Gain on sale of equipment	175,000
Income tax expense	240,000
Loss on operations of discontinued chemical division, net of $60,000 income tax savings	140,000
Loss on disposal of chemical division, net of $30,000 income tax savings	70,000

Based on the above information, what are Avondale's sustainable earnings?

BE14–2 A list of statement of earnings classifications for a merchandising company follows. Write the number of the appropriate classification beside each item in the lettered list below to show in what section the item would be reported:

1. Gross profit section
2. Operating expenses section
3. Other revenues section
4. Other expenses section
5. Discontinued operations section
6. Not reported on statement of earnings

_____ (a) A realized gain on the sale of available-for-sale securities
_____ (b) Sales revenue
_____ (c) A change in accounting principle
_____ (d) Salaries expense
_____ (e) Cost of goods sold
_____ (f) Investment revenue
_____ (g) A loss from operations of a discontinued wholesale business
_____ (h) Interest expense
_____ (i) A write-down of obsolete inventory
_____ (j) A gain on the sale of assets of a discontinued wholesale business

BE14–3 Using the following selected data from the comparative balance sheet of Rioux Ltd., prepare a horizontal analysis, assuming 2007 is the base year:

	2009	2008	2007
Cash	$ 150,000	$ 175,000	$ 75,000
Accounts receivable	600,000	400,000	450,000
Inventory	780,000	600,000	700,000
Property, plant, and equipment	3,130,000	2,800,000	2,850,000
Intangible assets	90,000	100,000	0
Total assets	$4,750,000	$4,075,000	$4,075,000

BE14–4 The following information is available for Le Château Inc. (in thousands):

	2008	2007	2006	2005	2004
Sales	$336,070	$303,879	$279,064	$241,131	$226,766
Net earnings	33,604	24,751	23,513	24,336	17,123

(a) Calculate the percentage of the base-period amount for sales and net earnings, assuming 2004 is the base period. (b) Which grew faster, sales or net earnings?

BE14–5   Horizontal analysis percentages from Coastal Ltd.'s statement of earnings are listed here:

	2009	2008	2007
Sales	101%	110%	100%
Cost of goods sold	100%	111%	100%
Operating expenses	99%	112%	100%
Income tax expense	106%	105%	100%

Use horizontal analysis to determine change in net earnings. (SO 2)

Assuming that Coastal did not have any non-operating or irregular items, did its net earnings increase, decrease, or remain unchanged over the three-year period? Explain.

BE14–6   Prepare a vertical analysis using the following data (in thousands) from the comparative statement of earnings of JTI Inc. for the year ended May 31:

Prepare vertical analysis. (SO 3)

	2009	2008
Net sales	$1,914	$2,073
Cost of goods sold	1,612	1,674
Gross profit	302	399
Operating expenses	218	210
Earnings before income tax	84	189
Income tax expense	30	68
Net earnings	$ 54	$ 121

BE14–7   Vertical analysis percentages from Waubon Corp.'s statement of earnings are listed here:

Use vertical analysis to determine change in net earnings. (SO 3)

	2009	2008	2007
Sales	100.0%	100.0%	100.0%
Cost of goods sold	59.4%	60.5%	60.0%
Operating expenses	19.6%	20.4%	20.0%
Income tax expense	5.2%	4.8%	5.0%

Assuming that Waubon did not have any non-operating or irregular items, did its net earnings as a percentage of sales increase, decrease, or remain unchanged over the three-year period? Explain.

BE14–8   The following selected vertical percentages are available for three companies: a department store, a restaurant, and an accounting firm.

Use vertical analysis to identify company. (SO 3)

	Company		
	1	2	3
Balance sheet			
Cash	10%	10%	10%
Accounts receivable	5%	40%	5%
Inventory	25%	40%	45%
Property, plant, and equipment	60%	10%	40%
Statement of earnings			
Gross profit	60%	40%	50%
Net earnings	20%	30%	10%

Determine which company—the department store, restaurant, or accounting firm—is most likely company 1, 2, and 3 based on the information provided. Explain your choices.

Interpret changes in ratios. (SO 3)

BE14–9   For each of the following independent situations, indicate whether the change would be viewed as an improvement or deterioration:

(a) An increase in the profit margin

(b) A decrease in inventory turnover

(c) An increase in the current ratio

(d) A decrease in free cash flow

(e) An increase in cash current debt coverage

(f) An increase in debt to total assets

(g) A decrease in times interest earned

(h) A decrease in the asset turnover

Evaluate liquidity.
(SO 4)

BE14–10 Holysh Inc. reported a current ratio of 1.5:1 in the current fiscal year, which is higher than its current ratio last year of 1.2:1. It also reported a receivables turnover of 9 times, which is less than last year's receivables turnover of 12 times, and an inventory turnover of 6 times, which is less than last year's inventory turnover of 9 times. Is Holysh's liquidity improving or deteriorating? Explain.

Evaluate solvency.
(SO 4)

BE14–11 **Manulife Financial Corporation** reported the following measures for 2007 and 2006:

	2007	2006
Debt to total assets	84.4%	84.1%
Times interest earned	6.4 times	6.7 times
Cash total debt coverage	0.05 times	0.04 times
Free cash flow (in millions)	$6,100	$5,514

Is Manulife's solvency improving or deteriorating? Explain.

Evaluate corporate profitability.
(SO 4)

BE14–12 **Barrick Gold Corporation** reported the following ratios for 2007 and 2006:

	2007	2006
Asset turnover	0.3 times	0.3 times
Return on assets	5.5%	9.2%
Return on shareholders' equity	7.5%	13.4%
Profit margin	17.3%	21.4%

Is Barrick's profitability improving or deteriorating? Explain.

Evaluate investor profitability.
(SO 4)

BE14–13 Recently, the price-earnings ratio of **Shoppers Drug Mart** was 22.1 times, and the price-earnings ratio of **Bank of Montreal** was 13.1 times. The dividend yield of each company was 1.62% and 5.9% respectively. Which company's shares would you purchase for growth? For income? Explain.

Exercises

All of the exercises in this section use decision tools.

Indicate reporting of regular
and irregular items.
(SO 1)

E14–1   The following independent events occurred at Ike Inc. during the year:

(a) A realized gain on the sale of held-for-trading securities

(b) A loss caused by a labour strike

(c) A change from using straight-line to diminishing-balance depreciation

(d) Current assets of a discontinued operating segment being held for immediate and probable sale

(e) An operating loss from a discontinued operating segment, held for immediate and probable sale

(f) An impairment loss on goodwill

(g) An unrealized loss from the revaluation of available-for-sale securities

Instructions

(a) Identify which of the above items are sustainable (regular) items and which are irregular items.

(b) Indicate on which financial statement each of the above items would be reported, and where.

Identify reporting of discontinued operations and effect
on sustainable earnings.
(SO 1)

E14–2   On July 20, 2007, **Maple Leaf Foods Inc.** discontinued and sold its animal nutrition business. For the year ended December 31, 2007, it reported earnings from these discontinued operations of $10,994 thousand and a gain of $219,382 thousand on the sale of this business. For the same year, Maple Leaf reported a net loss from continuing operations of $23,232 thousand. All amounts are net of income tax.

Instructions

(a) Indicate where, and how, the earnings from the discontinued operations and gain on the sale of the animal nutrition business would be reported on Maple Leaf's financial statements.

(b) Based on the information provided above, what are Maple Leaf's sustainable earnings?

Identify reporting of change
in accounting principle
and effect on sustainable
earnings.
(SO 1)

E14–3   **Canada Post** reported a $1-million charge for the year ended December 31, 2007, after adopting new accounting principles related to financial instruments required by the Canadian Institute of Chartered Accountants. For the same year, Canada Post reported $54 million in net earnings. All amounts are net of income tax.

Instructions

(a) Indicate where, and how, this $1-million charge would be reported on Canada Post's financial statements.

(b) Based on the information provided above, what are Canada Post's sustainable earnings?

E14–4   Condensed data from the comparative balance sheets of Dressaire Inc. follow:

Prepare horizontal analysis. (SO 2)

	2009	2008	2007
Current assets	$120,000	$ 80,000	$100,000
Noncurrent assets	400,000	350,000	300,000
Current liabilities	90,000	70,000	65,000
Long-term liabilities	145,000	125,000	150,000
Common shares	150,000	115,000	100,000
Retained earnings	135,000	120,000	85,000

Instructions

(a) Prepare a horizontal analysis, calculating the percentage change since the base year (2007).

(b) Calculate the percentage changes between each year.

E14–5   Condensed data from the statement of earnings for Fleetwood Corporation follow:

Prepare vertical analysis. (SO 3)

	2009	2008
Sales	$800,000	$600,000
Cost of goods sold	550,000	375,000
Gross profit	250,000	225,000
Operating expenses	175,000	125,000
Earnings before income tax	75,000	100,000
Income tax expense	18,750	25,000
Net earnings	$ 56,250	$ 75,000

Instructions

Prepare a vertical analysis for each year.

E14–6   The statement of earnings for Gap Inc. follows:

Prepare horizontal and vertical analyses of statement of earnings. (SO 1, 2, 3)

GAP INC. Statement of Earnings Year Ended February 2 (in USD millions)			
	2008	2007	2006
Net sales	$15,763	$15,923	$16,019
Cost of goods sold	10,071	10,266	10,145
Gross profit	5,692	5,657	5,874
Operating expenses	4,377	4,432	4,099
Earnings from operations	1,315	1,225	1,775
Interest expense	26	41	45
Interest revenue	117	131	93
Earnings before income taxes	1,406	1,315	1,823
Income tax expense	539	506	692
Earnings from continuing operations	867	809	1,131
Loss from discontinued operations, net of income tax	34	31	18
Net earnings	$ 833	$ 778	$ 1,113

Instructions

(a) Prepare a horizontal analysis, assuming 2006 is the base year.

(b) Prepare a vertical analysis for each year.

(c) Identify any significant changes from 2006 to 2008, including the impact of discontinued operations on your analysis.

Prepare horizontal and vertical analyses of balance sheet.
(SO 2, 3)

E14–7   The condensed comparative balance sheet for **Mountain Equipment Co-operative** follows:

MOUNTAIN EQUIPMENT CO-OPERATIVE Balance Sheet December 31 (in thousands)		
	2007	2006
Assets		
Current assets	$ 61,747	$ 70,781
Property, plant, and equipment	83,782	56,597
Future income taxes	690	
Total assets	$146,219	$127,378
Liabilities and Members' Equity		
Liabilities		
Current liabilities	$ 29,167	$ 23,163
Long-term liabilities	1,684	867
Total liabilities	30,851	24,030
Members' equity		
Members' shares	116,849	103,318
Retained earnings	30	30
Accumulated other comprehensive loss	(1,511)	
Total members' equity	115,368	103,348
Total liabilities and members' equity	$146,219	$127,378

Instructions

(a) Prepare a horizontal analysis, calculating the percentage change between 2006 and 2007.

(b) Prepare a vertical analysis for each year.

(c) Identify any significant changes from 2006 to 2007.

Classify ratios.
(SO 4)

E14–8   The following is a list of the ratios and values we have calculated in this text:

_____ Asset turnover

_____ Average collection period

_____ Cash current debt coverage

_____ Cash total debt coverage

_____ Current ratio

_____ Days in inventory

_____ Debt to total assets

_____ Dividend yield

_____ Earnings per share

_____ Free cash flow

_____ Gross profit margin

_____ Inventory turnover

_____ Payout ratio

_____ Price-earnings ratio

_____ Profit margin

_____ Receivables turnover

_____ Return on assets

_____ Return on common shareholders' equity

_____ Times interest earned

_____ Working capital

Instructions

(a) Classify each of the above ratios as a liquidity (L), solvency (S), or profitability (P) ratio.

(b) Further classify each of the profitability ratios as corporate measures (C) or investor measures (I).

Evaluate liquidity.
(SO 4)

E14–9   The following selected ratios are available for Pampered Pets Inc. for the three most recent years:

	2009	2008	2007
Current ratio	2.7:1	2.4:1	2.1:1
Receivables turnover	6.7 times	7.4 times	8.2 times
Inventory turnover	7.7 times	8.6 times	9.9 times

Instructions

(a) Has the company's collection of its receivables improved or deteriorated over the last three years?

(b) Is the company selling its inventory faster or slower than in past years?

(c) Overall, has the company's liquidity improved or deteriorated over the last three years? Explain.

E14–10 The following selected ratios are available for Ice-T Inc. for the three most recent years:

Evaluate solvency.
(SO 4)

	2009	2008	2007
Debt to total assets	50.0%	45.5%	40.3%
Times interest earned	1.8 times	1.4 times	1.0 times
Cash total debt coverage	0.7 times	0.5 times	0.3 times

Instructions

(a) Has the company's solvency improved or deteriorated over the last three years? Explain.

(b) How should you interpret accrual- and cash-based ratios that move in opposite directions? For example, what does it mean when an accrual-based solvency ratio, such as debt to total assets, indicates a deterioration of solvency and a cash-based solvency ratio, such as cash total debt coverage, indicates an improvement of solvency?

E14–11 The following selected profitability ratios are available for two companies, Pop Corporation and Top Corporation, for a recent fiscal year:

Evaluate profitability.
(SO 4)

	Pop	Top	Industry
Gross profit margin	37.5%	48.2%	37.9%
Profit margin	5.2%	4.9%	4.8%
Return on common shareholders' equity	18.3%	12.4%	12.0%
Return on assets	5.6%	5.2%	4.8%
Asset turnover	1.1 times	1.1 times	1.0 times

Instructions

Which company is more profitable? Explain, making sure to refer to the industry ratios where appropriate.

E14–12 Selected information for Teck Resources (formerly Teck Cominco) for the most recent three years is as follows:

Identify drivers of profitability.
(SO 4)

	2007	2006	2005
Asset turnover	0.5 times	0.6 times	0.5 times
Debt to total assets	16.0%	18.7%	27.0%
Profit margin	26.8%	37.1%	30.8%
Return on assets	13.4%	22.3%	15.4%
Return on common shareholders' equity	23.3%	42.8%	33.2%

Instructions

(a) What is the main driver of the company's return on assets over the last three years? Explain.

(b) What is the main driver of the company's return on shareholders' equity over the last three years? Explain.

E14–13 Imperial Oil and Petro-Canada reported the following investor-related information recently:

Evaluate profitability for investors.
(SO 4)

	Imperial Oil	Petro-Canada
Earnings per share	$3.64	$7.44
Price-earnings ratio	12.1 times	5.3 times
Payout ratio	9.2%	6.5%
Dividend yield	0.8%	1.9%

Instructions

(a) Based on the above information, can you tell which company is more profitable?

(b) Which company do investors favour?

(c) Would investors purchase shares in these companies mainly for growth or for dividend income?

E14–14 Live Ltd. reported the following comparative balance sheet data:

LIVE LTD. Balance Sheet December 31		
	2009	**2008**
Assets		
Cash	$ 15,000	$ 30,000
Accounts receivable (net)	70,000	60,000
Inventories	80,000	65,000
Property, plant, and equipment (net)	180,000	165,000
Total assets	$345,000	$320,000
Liabilities and Shareholders' Equity		
Accounts payable	$ 70,000	$ 75,000
Mortgage payable	120,000	125,000
Common shares	100,000	80,000
Retained earnings	55,000	40,000
Total liabilities and shareholders' equity	$345,000	$320,000

Additional information for 2009:

1. Net earnings were $21,000.

2. Gross sales on account were $420,000. Sales returns and allowances on account amounted to $20,000.

3. Cost of goods sold was $198,000.

4. The allowance for doubtful accounts was $8,500 at the end of 2009, and $8,000 at the end of 2008.

5. Cash provided by operating activities was $41,000.

Instructions

(a) Calculate the following ratios for 2009:

1. Current ratio	6. Cash current debt coverage
2. Receivables turnover	7. Cash total debt coverage
3. Average collection period	8. Debt to total assets
4. Inventory turnover	9. Return on common shareholders' equity
5. Days in inventory	10. Return on assets

(b) Indicate whether each of the above ratios is a measure of liquidity (L), solvency (S), or profitability (P).

E14–15 The following selected ratios are available for a recent year for Rogers Communications Inc. and TELUS Corporation:

	Rogers	TELUS	Industry Average
Liquidity			
Current ratio	0.8:1	0.5:1	0.8:1
Receivables turnover	8.7 times	12.8 times	10.2 times
Solvency			
Debt to total assets	56.9%	39.8%	44.8%
Times interest earned	2.5 times	4.2 times	5.1 times
Profitability			
Profit margin	6.3%	13.9%	13.2%
Return on assets	7.2%	9.9%	9.4%
Return on common shareholders' equity	14.4%	18.2%	18.3%

Instructions

(a) Which company is more liquid? Explain.

(b) Which company is more solvent? Explain.

(c) Which company is more profitable? Explain.

Problems: Set A

🔧 **All of the problems in this section use decision tools.**

P14–1A   In 2006, CanWest Global Communications Corp. decided to sell its Canadian radio stations as they were not core operating assets. These were reported as "held for sale" in 2006 and sold in 2007. The company also sold its interest in CanWest Media Works Limited in 2007. Both of these transactions were reported as discontinued operations in CanWest's financial statements as follows, with supporting details provided in the notes to the financial statements:

Discuss impact of discontinued operations on analysis. (SO 1)

CANWEST GLOBAL COMMUNICATIONS CORP. Balance Sheet (partial) August 31 (in thousands)		
	2007	2006
Current assets of discontinued operations	-	$ 58,623
Long-term assets of discontinued operations	-	176,753
Current liabilities of discontinued operations	-	22,059
Noncurrent liabilities of discontinued operations	-	135,916

CANWEST GLOBAL COMMUNICATIONS CORP. Statement of Earnings (partial) Year Ended August 31 (in thousands)		
	2007	2006
Earnings (loss) from continuing operations	$ 16,578	$ (8,793)
Gain on sale of discontinued operations	251,998	163,547
Earnings from discontinued operations	10,751	23,918
Net earnings	$279,327	$178,672
Earnings (loss) per share from continuing operations	$0.09	$(0.05)
Total earnings per share	1.56	1.01

CANWEST GLOBAL COMMUNICATIONS CORP. Cash Flow Statement (partial) Year Ended August 31 (in thousands)		
	2007	2006
Operating activities		
Cash flows from operating activities of continuing operations	$ 230,064	$ 74,317
Cash flows from operating activities of discontinued operations	39,159	38,944
Investing activities		
Investing activities of continuing operations	(1,724,685)	538,727
Investing activities of discontinued operations	(6,448)	(13,089)
Financing activities		
Financing activities of continuing operations	1,323,189	(372,641)
Financing activities of discontinued operations	(13,363)	(13,691)

Instructions

Explain how these discontinued operations would affect your analysis of CanWest's financial position and performance in 2006 and 2007.

P14–2A lululemon athletica inc. has seen a significant amount of growth over the last three years. The following selected information is available:

LULULEMON ATHLETICA INC. Balance Sheet January 31 (in USD thousands)			
	2008	2007	2006
Assets			
Current assets	$ 97,906	$48,493	$27,217
Noncurrent assets	57,186	23,800	14,697
Total assets	$155,092	$72,293	$41,914
Liabilities and Shareholders' Equity			
Liabilities			
Current liabilities	$ 35,822	$31,939	$12,242
Long-term liabilities	7,236	2,975	1,620
Total liabilities	43,058	34,914	13,862
Shareholders' equity	112,034	37,379	28,052
Total liabilities and shareholders' equity	$155,092	$72,293	$41,914

LULULEMON ATHLETICA INC. Statement of Earnings Year Ended January 31 (in USD thousands)			
	2008	2007	2006
Net revenue	$274,713	$148,885	$84,129
Cost of goods sold	128,411	72,903	41,177
Gross profit	146,302	75,982	42,952
Operating expenses	96,177	59,769	39,225
Earnings from operations	50,125	16,213	3,727
Interest revenue	1,188	206	3
Earnings before income taxes	51,313	16,419	3,730
Income tax expense	20,471	8,753	2,336
Net earnings	$ 30,842	$ 7,666	$ 1,394

Instructions

(a) Prepare a horizontal analysis of the balance sheet and statement of earnings, assuming 2006 is the base year.

(b) Identify the key components in lululemon's balance sheet and statement of earnings that are primarily responsible for the change in the company's financial position and performance over the three-year period.

P14–3A The following condensed information is available for Yellow Pages Income Fund, Canada's largest telephone directories publisher:

YELLOW PAGES INCOME FUND Balance Sheet December 31 (in thousands)			
	2007	2006	2005
Assets			
Current assets	$ 478,619	$ 391,024	$ 297,926
Capital assets	175,492	134,743	89,267
Intangible assets	2,016,444	2,018,214	1,641,421
Goodwill	6,570,746	6,394,780	5,281,404
Other assets	24,211	64,486	63,581
Total assets	$9,265,512	$9,003,247	$7,373,599

Liabilities and Unitholders' Equity			
Liabilities			
Current liabilities	$ 364,724	$ 347,750	$ 264,527
Long-term liabilities	3,114,608	2,823,953	2,113,428
Total liabilities	3,479,332	3,171,703	2,377,955
Unitholders' equity	5,786,180	5,831,544	4,995,644
Total liabilities and unitholders' equity	$9,265,512	$9,003,247	$7,373,599

YELLOW PAGES INCOME FUND
Statement of Earnings
Year Ended December 31
(in thousands)

	2007	2006	2005
Revenues	$1,624,424	$1,384,956	$922,945
Operating expenses	975,848	810,441	610,400
Impairment of intangible assets		8,000	
Earnings from operations	648,576	566,515	312,545
Other expenses	153,975	134,306	108,647
Earnings before income taxes	494,601	432,209	203,898
Income tax expense (recovery)	(33,108)	276	(37,935)
Net earnings	$ 527,709	$ 431,933	$241,833

Additional information:
The intangible assets include trademarks, customer contracts, logos, and domain names.

Instructions

(a) Prepare a vertical analysis of the balance sheet and statement of earnings for each year.

(b) Identify the key components in Yellow Pages' balance sheet and statement of earnings that are primarily responsible for the change in the company's financial position and performance over the three-year period.

(c) How has Yellow Pages primarily financed its asset growth—through debt or equity—over this period of time?

P14–4A   The Home Depot Inc. reported the following selected information for the last five years (in USD millions, except earnings per share):

Calculate and evaluate profitability ratios with discontinued operations.
(SO 1, 4)

	2008	2007	2006	2005	2004
Net sales	$77,349	$79,022	$77,019	$71,100	$63,660
Average common shareholders' equity	21,372	25,970	25,534	23,282	21,104
Average total assets	48,294	48,334	41,712	36,728	32,224
Earnings from continuing operations	4,210	5,266	5,641	5,001	4,304
Discontinued operations	185	495	197	0	0
Net earnings	4,395	5,761	5,838	5,001	4,304
Earnings per share from continuing operations	2.28	2.56	2.64	2.27	1.88
Total earnings per share	2.38	2.80	2.73	2.27	1.88

Instructions

(a) Calculate Home Depot's profit margin, return on common shareholders' equity (for this calculation, note that the company has no preferred shares), and return on assets ratios before and after discontinued operations for each of the last five years.

(b) Evaluate Home Depot's profitability over the last five years before and after discontinued operations.

(c) Which analysis above is more relevant to investors? Explain.

Calculate and evaluate ratios.
(SO 4)

P14–5A Condensed balance sheet and statement of earnings data for Colinas Corporation follow:

COLINAS CORPORATION Balance Sheet December 31			
	2009	2008	2007
Assets			
Cash	$ 30,000	$ 24,000	$ 10,000
Accounts receivable (net)	70,000	50,000	53,000
Inventory	75,000	45,000	50,000
Other current assets	90,000	75,000	62,000
Held-to-maturity securities	100,000	76,000	50,000
Property, plant, and equipment (net)	595,000	345,000	315,000
Total assets	$960,000	$615,000	$540,000
Liabilities and Shareholders' Equity			
Liabilities			
Current liabilities	$ 63,500	$ 51,000	$ 65,000
Long-term liabilities	245,000	65,000	70,000
Total liabilities	308,500	116,000	135,000
Shareholders' equity			
Common shares	416,500	319,000	275,000
Retained earnings	185,000	140,000	105,000
Accumulated other comprehensive income	50,000	40,000	25,000
Total shareholders' equity	651,500	499,000	405,000
Total liabilities and shareholders' equity	$960,000	$615,000	$540,000

COLINAS CORPORATION Statement of Earnings Year Ended December 31		
	2009	2008
Sales	$950,000	$850,000
Less: Sales returns and allowances	60,000	50,000
Net sales	890,000	800,000
Cost of goods sold	500,000	450,000
Gross profit	390,000	350,000
Operating expenses	266,000	260,000
Earnings from operations	124,000	90,000
Interest expense	17,750	8,750
Earnings before income taxes	106,250	81,250
Income tax expense	21,250	16,250
Net earnings	$ 85,000	$ 65,000

Additional information:

1. The allowance for doubtful accounts was $3,650 in 2009, $2,750 in 2008, and $2,400 in 2007.
2. All sales were credit sales.
3. The market prices of Colinas' common shares were $14 and $12 for 2009 and 2008, respectively.
4. All dividends were paid in cash. (*Hint:* Analyze retained earnings to determine dividends.)
5. On July 1, 2008, 4,000 common shares were issued, and on July 1, 2009, 7,500 shares were issued. At the end of 2009, 50,000 shares have been issued in total.
6. Cash provided by operating activities was $51,800 in 2009 and $29,000 in 2008.

Instructions

(a) Calculate the following ratios for 2008 and 2009:

1. Current ratio	6. Cash total debt coverage
2. Receivables turnover	7. Gross profit margin
3. Inventory turnover	8. Profit margin
4. Debt to total assets	9. Return on assets
5. Times interest earned	10. Asset turnover

(b) Based on the ratios calculated, discuss the improvement or lack of improvement in the financial position and operating results from 2008 to 2009.

P14–6A   Condensed balance sheet and statement of earnings data for Star Track Ltd. follow:

Calculate and evaluate ratios.
(SO 4)

STAR TRACK LTD. Balance Sheet December 31		
	2009	**2008**
Assets		
Cash and cash equivalents	$ 50,000	$ 42,000
Accounts receivable (net)	120,000	87,000
Inventories	380,000	300,000
Prepaid expenses	25,000	31,000
Available-for-sale securities (long-term)	80,000	50,000
Land	125,000	75,000
Buildings and equipment (net)	560,000	400,000
Total assets	$1,340,000	$985,000
Liabilities and Shareholders' Equity		
Liabilities		
Notes payable	$ 135,000	$ 50,000
Accounts payable	260,000	190,000
Current portion of mortgage payable	48,750	25,000
Mortgage payable, due 2012	200,000	125,000
Total liabilities	643,750	390,000
Shareholders' equity		
Common shares (100,000 shares issued)	400,000	400,000
Retained earnings	292,250	195,000
Accumulated other comprehensive income	4,000	
Total shareholders' equity	696,250	595,000
Total liabilities and shareholders' equity	$1,340,000	$985,000

STAR TRACK LTD. Statement of Earnings Year Ended December 31		
	2009	**2008**
Sales	$1,050,000	$950,000
Cost of goods sold	650,000	635,000
Gross profit	400,000	315,000
Operating expenses	240,000	215,000
Earnings from operations	160,000	100,000
Interest expense	25,000	10,000
Earnings before income taxes	135,000	90,000
Income tax expense	33,750	22,500
Net earnings	$ 101,250	$ 67,500

Additional information:
1. The allowance for doubtful accounts was $5,000 in 2008 and $10,000 in 2009.
2. Accounts receivable at the beginning of 2008 were $80,000, net of an allowance for doubtful accounts of $3,000.
3. Inventories at the beginning of 2008 were $320,000.
4. Total assets at the beginning of 2008 were $1,075,000.
5. Current liabilities at the beginning of 2008 were $250,000.
6. Total liabilities at the beginning of 2008 were $543,500.
7. Total shareholders' equity at the beginning of 2008 was $531,500.
8. All sales were on account.
9. Cash provided by operating activities was $64,250 in 2009, and $65,000 in 2008.
10. Net capital expenditures were $92,000 in 2009 and $50,000 in 2008.
11. In each of 2008 and 2009, $4,000 of dividends were paid to the common shareholders.

▸ Performance Measurement

Instructions

(a) Calculate all possible liquidity, solvency, and profitability ratios for 2008 and 2009.

(b) Discuss the changes in Star Track's liquidity, solvency, and profitability from 2008 to 2009 by referring to the relevant ratios calculated in (a).

Evaluate ratios.
(SO 4)

P14–7A Selected ratios for the current year for two companies in the beverage industry, Refresh Corp. and Flavour Limited, follow:

	Refresh	Flavour	Industry Average
Asset turnover	1.0 times	1.0 times	0.9 times
Cash total debt coverage	30%	20%	n/a
Current ratio	0.7:1	1.1:1	0.8:1
Debt to total assets	56%	72%	81%
Earnings per share	$0.98	$1.37	$1.08
Gross profit margin	74%	60%	58%
Inventory turnover	6.8 times	7.9 times	8.3 times
Price-earnings ratio	50.3 times	24.3 times	32.2 times
Profit margin	14%	11%	8%
Receivables turnover	11.4 times	9.8 times	9.3 times
Return on assets	12%	9%	7%
Return on common shareholders' equity	30%	26%	26%
Times interest earned	15.3 times	7.9 times	5.3 times

Instructions

(a) Both companies offer their customers credit terms of net 30 days. Indicate which ratio(s) should be used to assess how well the accounts receivable are managed. Comment on how successful each company appears to be at managing its accounts receivable.

(b) How well does each company appear to be managing its inventory? Indicate the ratio(s) used to assess inventory management.

(c) Which company, Refresh or Flavour, is more solvent? Identify the ratio(s) used to determine this, and defend your choice.

(d) To your surprise, you notice that Refresh's gross profit margin is much higher than both Flavour's and the industry average. Identify two possible reasons for this.

(e) What is mostly responsible for Refresh's higher return on assets: its profit margin or asset turnover? Explain.

(f) What is the market price per share of each company's common shares?

(g) Which company, Refresh or Flavour, do investors appear to believe has greater prospects for growing its earnings and dividends? Indicate the ratio(s) you used to reach this conclusion, and explain your reasoning.

Evaluate liquidity, solvency, and profitability.
(SO 4)

P14–8A The following ratios are available for tool-makers **Black & Decker Corporation** and **Snap-On Incorporated**, and their industry, for a recent year:

	Black & Decker	Snap-On	Industry Average
Liquidity			
Current ratio	1.6:1	1.9:1	1.8:1
Receivables turnover	5.2 times	4.9 times	1.5 times
Inventory turnover	3.8 times	4.6 times	2.5 times
Solvency			
Debt to total assets	54.2%	27.0%	52.1%
Times interest earned	8.4 times	9.0 times	7.0 times
Profitability			
Gross profit margin	33.2%	44.9%	37.1%
Profit margin	7.1%	7.8%	5.8 %
Asset turnover	1.2 times	1.0 times	0.8 times
Return on assets	8.3%	8.1%	6.9%

Return on common shareholders' equity	32.8%	17.4%	20.4%
Price-earnings ratio	9.2 times	15.2 times	3.4 times
Dividend yield	2.5%	2.1%	1.9%
Payout ratio	22.7%	30.3%	3.5%

Instructions

(a) Which company is more liquid? Explain.

(b) Which company is more solvent? Explain.

(c) Which company is more profitable? Explain.

(d) Which company do investors favour? Is your answer consistent with your findings in (a) to (c)? Explain.

P14–9A The following ratios and measures are available for Hubei Corporation:

Determine effect of transactions on ratios.
(SO 4)

Receivables turnover	10 times
Profit margin	10%
Earnings per share	$2
Debt to total assets	40%
Free cash flow	$25,000

Instructions

(a) Indicate whether each of the above would increase, decrease, or remain unchanged by each of the following independent transactions:

1. Hubei issues common shares.

2. Hubei collects an account receivable.

3. Hubei issues a mortgage note payable.

4. Hubei sells equipment at a loss.

5. Hubei's share price increases from $10 to $12.

(b) Would your answers to any of the above change if the profit margin were negative and the earnings per share were a loss per share?

P14–10A Presented here are an incomplete balance sheet and statement of earnings for Vienna Corporation:

Calculate missing information using ratios.
(SO 4)

VIENNA CORPORATION		
Balance Sheet		
December 31, 2009		
Assets		
Current assets		
Cash	$	(a)
Accounts receivable (gross)		(b)
Inventory		(c)
Total current assets		(d)
Available-for-sale securities		430,000
Property, plant, and equipment		4,420,000
Total assets	$	(e)
Liabilities and Shareholders' Equity		
Liabilities		
Current liabilities	$	(f)
Long-term liabilities		(g)
Total liabilities		(h)
Shareholders' equity		
Common shares		1,500,000
Retained earnings		1,900,000
Total shareholders' equity		3,400,000
Total liabilities and shareholders' equity	$	(i)

VIENNA CORPORATION Statement of Earnings Year ended December 31, 2009	
Sales	$11,000,000
Cost of goods sold	(j)
Gross profit	(k)
Operating expenses	1,600,000
Earnings from operations	(l)
Interest expense	(m)
Earnings before income taxes	(n)
Income tax expense	707,000
Net earnings	$ (o)

Additional information:

1. The receivables turnover is 10 times.
2. All sales are on account.
3. The gross profit margin is 40%.
4. The profit margin is 15%.
5. The return on assets is 22%.
6. The current ratio is 2:1.
7. The inventory turnover is 8 times.

Instructions

Calculate the missing information using the ratios. Use ending balances instead of average balances if an average is needed for the ratio calculation. (*Hint:* Start with one ratio and get as much information as possible from it before trying another ratio. You will not be able to calculate the missing amounts in the same sequence as they are presented.)

P14–11A You are in the process of analyzing two similar companies in the same industry. You learn that they have different accounting practices and policies as follows:

1. Company A, which has the same type of equipment as Company B, uses the straight-line method of depreciation while Company B uses diminishing-balance. This is the first year of operations for both companies.

2. Company A invests its excess cash in available-for-sale securities, while Company B invests its excess cash in held-to-maturity securities. Prices have been generally rising for these investments.

Instructions

(a) Considering only the impact of the choice of depreciation method, determine which company will report a higher (1) current ratio, (2) debt to total assets ratio, and (3) profit margin ratio, or if the depreciation method will have no impact.

(b) Considering only the impact of the classification of securities, determine which company will report a higher (1) current ratio, (2) debt to total assets ratio, and (3) profit margin ratio, or if the classification will have no impact.

(c) Will the use of different accounting practices and policies affect your analysis? Explain.

(d) Identify two other limitations of financial analysis that an analyst should watch for when analyzing financial statements.

Problems: Set B

All of the problems in this section use decision tools.

P14–1B **Canadian Tire Corporation, Limited** adopted new accounting policies for financial instruments, hedges, comprehensive income, and equity in 2007. These were mandated changes in accounting policy, which, except for changes to foreign currency, were applied without restatement of prior periods.

The changes were reported as follows in the company's statement of shareholders' equity, with additional detail provided in the supporting notes to the statements:

CANADIAN TIRE CORPORATION, LIMITED
Statement of Changes in Shareholders' Equity (partial)
Year Ended December 29, 2007
(in millions)

Retained earnings	
Balance, beginning of year as previously reported	$2,088.1
Transitional adjustment on adoption of new accounting policies	(4.4)
Balance, beginning of year as restated	2,083.7
Net earnings	417.6
Dividends	(60.4)
Balance, end of year	$2,440.9

Canadian Tire also reported gross operating revenue and total assets, in addition to other selected information, for four reportable operating segments—Canadian Tire retail (CTR), financial services, petroleum, and Mark's Work Wearhouse—in the notes to its 2007 financial statements:

(in millions)	CTR	Financial Services	Petroleum	Mark's
Gross operating revenue	$5,485.1	$ 769.1	$1,666.5	$825.3
Total assets	5,498.4	1,852.0	573.4	454.2

Instructions

Explain how (a) the changes in accounting policy and (b) the segmented information would affect your analysis of Canadian Tire's financial position and performance in 2007.

P14–2B **ClubLink Corporation** is Canada's largest golf course and resort owner. The following selected information is available:

Prepare horizontal analysis.
(SO 2)

CLUBLINK CORPORATION
Balance Sheet
December 31
(in thousands)

	2007	2006	2005
Assets			
Current assets	$ 11,087	$ 19,999	$ 9,831
Noncurrent assets	552,072	542,864	539,062
Total assets	$563,159	$562,863	$548,893
Liabilities and Shareholders' Equity			
Liabilities			
Current liabilities	$ 38,188	$ 31,279	$ 32,606
Long-term liabilities	355,482	363,416	343,478
Total liabilities	393,670	394,695	376,084
Shareholders' equity	169,489	168,168	172,809
Total liabilities and shareholders' equity	$563,159	$562,863	$548,893

CLUBLINK CORPORATION
Statement of Earnings
Year Ended December 31
(in thousands)

	2007	2006	2005
Revenue	$166,192	$149,118	$138,562
Operating expenses	118,773	106,192	101,125
Earnings from operations	47,419	42,926	37,437
Other revenues	1,766	2,934	1,364
Other expenses	42,623	45,239	40,067
Earnings (loss) before income taxes	6,562	621	(1,266)
Income tax expense	1,685	205	435
Net earnings (loss)	$ 4,877	$ 416	$ (1,701)

ClubLink had 16,219, 14,502, and 14,100 golf club members as at December 31, 2007, 2006, and 2005, respectively.

Instructions

(a) Prepare a horizontal analysis of the balance sheet and statement of earnings, assuming 2005 is the base year.

(b) Identify the key components in ClubLink's balance sheet and statement of earnings that are primarily responsible for the change in the company's financial position and performance over the three-year period.

Prepare vertical analysis.
(SO 3)

P14–3B   The following condensed information is available for Big Rock Brewery, Canada's largest craft brewer:

BIG ROCK BREWERY INCOME TRUST
Balance Sheet
December 31
(in thousands)

	2007	2006	2005
Assets			
Current assets	$ 5,598	$11,554	$12,770
Noncurrent assets	30,263	30,617	29,016
Total assets	$35,861	$42,171	$41,786
Liabilities and Unitholders' Equity			
Liabilities			
Current liabilities	$ 5,511	$ 4,377	$ 3,896
Long-term liabilities	3,202	7,427	8,060
Total liabilities	8,713	11,804	11,956
Unitholders' equity	27,148	30,367	29,830
Total liabilities and unitholders' equity	$35,861	$42,171	$41,786

BIG ROCK BREWERY INCOME TRUST
Statement of Earnings
December 31
(in thousands)

	2007	2006	2005
Net sales	$36,451	$38,701	$40,563
Cost of sales	14,192	13,773	15,255
Gross profit	22,259	24,928	25,308
Operating expenses	16,960	16,183	17,561
Earnings before income taxes	5,299	8,745	7,747
Income tax expense (recovery)	(169)	365	1,127
Net earnings	$ 5,468	$ 8,380	$ 6,620

Instructions

(a) Prepare a vertical analysis of the balance sheet and statement of earnings for each year.

(b) Identify the key components in Big Rock's balance sheet and statement of earnings that are primarily responsible for the change in the company's financial position and performance over the three-year period.

(c) How has Big Rock primarily financed its assets—through debt or equity—over this period of time?

Calculate and evaluate profitability ratios with discontinued operations.
(SO 1, 4)

P14–4B   Nexen Inc. reported the following selected information for the last five years (in millions, except earnings per share):

	2007	2006	2005	2004	2003
Net sales	$ 5,583	$ 3,936	$3,932	$ 2,944	$2,632
Average common shareholders' equity	5,123	4,316	3,432	2,471	1,832
Average total assets	17,616	15,873	7,914	10,050	7,138
Earnings from continuing operations	1,086	601	688	780	550
Earnings from discontinued operations			452	13	28
Net earnings	1,086	601	1,140	793	578
Earnings per share from continuing operations	2.06	$1.15	1.32	6.07	4.45
Total earnings per share	2.06	1.15	2.19	6.17	4.67

Instructions

(a) Calculate Nexen's profit margin, return on common shareholders' equity (for this calculation, note that the company has no preferred shares), and return on assets ratios before and after discontinued operations for each of the last five years.

(b) Evaluate Nexen's profitability over the last five years before and after discontinued operations.

(c) Which analysis is more relevant to investors? Explain.

P14–5B Condensed balance sheet and statement of earnings data for Pitka Corporation follow:

Calculate and evaluate ratios. (SO 4)

PITKA CORPORATION
Balance Sheet
December 31

	2009	2008	2007
Assets			
Cash	$ 40,000	$ 20,000	$ 18,000
Accounts receivable (net)	50,000	45,000	48,000
Available-for-sale securities	55,000	70,000	45,000
Inventory	90,000	85,000	64,000
Property, plant, and equipment (net)	500,000	370,000	258,000
Total assets	$ 735,000	$590,000	$433,000
Liabilities and Shareholders' Equity			
Liabilities			
Current liabilities	$ 85,000	$ 80,000	$ 30,000
Long-term liabilities	165,000	85,000	20,000
Total liabilities	250,000	165,000	50,000
Shareholders' equity			
Common shares	330,000	300,000	300,000
Retained earnings	140,000	115,000	78,000
Accumulated comprehensive income	15,000	10,000	5,000
Total shareholders' equity	485,000	425,000	383,000
Total liabilities and shareholders' equity	$ 735,000	$590,000	$433,000

PITKA CORPORATION
Statement of Earnings
Year Ended December 31

	2009	2008
Sales	$640,000	$500,000
Less: Sales returns and allowances	40,000	50,000
Net sales	600,000	450,000
Cost of goods sold	425,000	300,000
Gross profit	175,000	150,000
Operating expenses	113,000	84,000
Earnings from operations	62,000	66,000
Interest expense	8,000	4,000
Earnings before income taxes	54,000	62,000
Income tax expense	10,800	12,400
Net earnings	$ 43,200	$ 49,600

Additional information:

1. The allowance for doubtful accounts was $5,000 in 2009, $4,500 in 2008, and $4,800 in 2007.

2. All sales were credit sales.

3. The market prices of Pitka's common shares were $16 at the end of 2009 and $15 at the end of 2008.

4. All dividends were paid in cash. (*Hint*: Analyze retained earnings to determine dividends.)

5. On July 1, 2009, 2,000 common shares were issued, bringing the total number of shares to 32,000.

6. Cash provided by operating activities was $38,200 in 2009 and $81,600 in 2008.

Instructions

(a) Calculate the following ratios for 2008 and 2009:

1. Current ratio	6. Cash total debt coverage
2. Receivables turnover	7. Gross profit margin
3. Inventory turnover	8. Profit margin
4. Debt to total assets	9. Return on assets
5. Times interest earned	10. Asset turnover

(b) Based on the ratios calculated, discuss the improvement or lack of improvement in the financial position and operating results from 2008 to 2009.

Calculate and evaluate ratios. (SO 4)

P14–6B Condensed balance sheet and statement of earnings data for Click and Clack Ltd. follow:

CLICK AND CLACK LTD.
Balance Sheet
December 31

	2009	2008
Assets		
Cash	$ 70,000	$ 65,000
Accounts receivable (net)	94,000	90,000
Inventories	130,000	125,000
Prepaid expenses	25,000	23,000
Available-for-sale securities (long-term)	45,000	40,000
Property, plant, and equipment (net)	390,000	305,000
Total assets	$754,000	$648,000
Liabilities and Shareholders' Equity		
Liabilities		
Notes payable	$110,000	$100,000
Accounts payable	45,000	42,000
Accrued liabilities	30,000	40,000
Bonds payable, due 2012	200,000	150,000
Total liabilities	385,000	332,000
Shareholders' equity		
Common shares (20,000 shares issued)	200,000	200,000
Retained earnings	172,000	116,000
Accumulated other comprehensive loss	(3,000)	
Total shareholders' equity	369,000	316,000
Total liabilities and shareholders' equity	$754,000	$648,000

CLICK AND CLACK LTD.
Statement of Earnings
Year Ended December 31

	2009	2008
Sales	$900,000	$840,000
Cost of goods sold	620,000	575,000
Gross profit	280,000	265,000
Operating expenses	164,000	160,000
Earnings from operations	116,000	105,000
Interest expense	30,000	20,000
Earnings before income taxes	86,000	85,000
Income tax expense	22,000	20,000
Net earnings	$ 64,000	$ 65,000

Additional information:

1. The allowance for doubtful accounts was $4,000 in 2008 and $5,000 in 2009.

2. Accounts receivable at the beginning of 2008 were $88,000, net of an allowance for doubtful accounts of $3,000.

3. Inventories at the beginning of 2008 were $115,000.

4. Total assets at the beginning of 2008 were $630,000.

5. Total current liabilities at the beginning of 2008 were $180,000.

6. Total liabilities at the beginning of 2008 were $361,000.

7. Shareholders' equity at the beginning of 2008 was $269,000.

8. Seventy-five percent of the sales were on account.

9. Cash provided by operating activities was $68,000 in 2009 and $60,000 in 2008.

10. Net capital expenditures were $120,000 in 2009 and $50,000 in 2008.

11. In each of 2008 and 2009, $8,000 of dividends were paid to the common shareholders.

Instructions

(a) Calculate all possible liquidity, solvency, and profitability ratios for 2008 and 2009.

(b) Discuss the changes in Click and Clack's liquidity, solvency, and profitability from 2008 to 2009 by referring to the relevant ratios calculated in (a).

P14–7B   Selected ratios for the current year for two companies in the office supplies industry, Paperclip Inc. and Stapler Ltd., follow:

Evaluate ratios.
(SO 4)

	Paperclip	Stapler	Industry Average
Asset turnover	2.6 times	2.2 times	2.5 times
Average collection period	31 days	35 days	36 days
Cash current debt coverage	0.3 times	0.1 times	0.2 times
Current ratio	1.7:1	3.0:1	1.6:1
Debt to total assets	50%	30%	50%
Earnings per share	$3.50	$0.40	n/a
Gross profit margin	23%	40%	27%
Inventory turnover	6 times	3 times	5 times
Payout ratio	8%	22%	10%
Price-earnings ratio	29 times	45 times	38 times
Profit margin	5%	4%	4%
Return on assets	12%	8%	10%
Return on common shareholders' equity	25%	13%	16%
Times interest earned	4.2 times	8.6 times	7.1 times

Instructions

(a) Both companies offer their customers credit terms of net 30 days. Indicate which ratio(s) should be used to assess how well the accounts receivable are managed. Comment on how successful each company appears to be at managing its accounts receivable.

(b) How well does each company appear to be managing its inventory? Indicate the ratio(s) used to assess inventory management.

(c) Which company, Paperclip or Stapler, is more solvent? Identify the ratio(s) used to determine this, and defend your choice.

(d) To your surprise, you notice that Paperclip's gross profit margin is less than both Stapler's and the industry average. Identify two possible reasons for this.

(e) What is mostly responsible for Paperclip's higher return on common shareholders' equity: return on assets or use of debt? Explain.

(f) Paperclip's payout ratio is lower than Stapler's and the industry average. Indicate one possible reason for this.

(g) What is the market price per share of Paperclip's common shares?

(h) Which company, Paperclip or Stapler, do investors appear to believe has greater prospects for growing its earnings and dividends? Indicate the ratio(s) you used to reach this conclusion, and explain your reasoning.

Evaluate liquidity, solvency, and profitability.
(SO 4)

P14–8B The following ratios are available for fast-food competitors McDonald's Corporation and Wendy's International, Inc., and their industry, for a recent year:

	McDonald's	Wendy's	Industry Average
Liquidity			
Current ratio	1.3:1	1.3:1	0.8:1
Receivables turnover	25.7 times	31.2 times	42.1 times
Inventory turnover	127.2 times	62.5 times	51.9 times
Solvency			
Debt to total assets	43.1%	39.9%	36.7%
Times interest earned	10.9 times	19.0 times	6.5 times
Profitability			
Gross profit margin	35.9%	19.9%	26.6%
Profit margin	18.9%	2.7%	3.5%
Return on common shareholders' equity	29.7%	8.4%	9.7%
Return on assets	14.8%	3.7%	5.1%
Asset turnover	0.8 times	1.4 times	1.5 times
Dividend yield	2.4%	2.2%	1.0%
Price-earnings ratio	16.9 times	30.5 times	16.9 times

Instructions

(a) Which company is more liquid? Explain.

(b) Which company is more solvent? Explain.

(c) Which company is more profitable? Explain.

(d) Which company do investors favour? Is your answer consistent with your findings in (a) to (c)?

Determine effect of transactions on ratios.
(SO 4)

P14–9B The following ratios are available for Yami Corporation:

Current ratio	1.5:1
Inventory turnover	10 times
Debt to total assets	40%
Asset turnover	2 times
Profit margin	10%

Instructions

(a) Indicate whether each of the above ratios would increase, decrease, or remain unchanged as a result of each of the following independent transactions:

1. Yami pays an account payable.

2. Yami collects an account receivable.

3. Yami purchases a held-to-maturity investment.

4. Yami sells merchandise for cash at a profit.

5. Yami buys equipment for cash.

(b) Would your answers to any of the above change if the current ratio were 0.5:1 instead of 1.5:1?

Calculate missing information using ratios.
(SO 4)

P14–10B Presented here are an incomplete statement of earnings and balance sheet for Schwenke Corporation:

SCHWENKE CORPORATION Statement of Earnings Year Ended December 31, 2009	
Sales	$ (a)
Cost of goods sold	(b)
Gross profit	(c)
Operating expenses	333,750
Earnings from operations	(d)
Interest expense	10,500
Earnings before income taxes	(e)
Income tax expense	(f)
Net earnings	$125,000

SCHWENKE CORPORATION
Balance Sheet
December 31, 2009

Assets

Current assets
Cash $ 7,500
Accounts receivable   (g)
Inventory   (h)
    Total current assets   (i)
Property, plant, and equipment   (j)
Total assets $ (k)

Liabilities and Shareholders' Equity

Liabilities
Current liabilities $ (l)
Long-term liabilities   120,000
    Total liabilities   (m)
Shareholders' equity
Common shares   250,000
Retained earnings   (n)
    Total shareholders' equity   650,000
Total liabilities and shareholders' equity $ (o)

Additional information:

1. The profit margin is 10%.

2. The gross profit margin is 40%.

3. The income tax rate is 20%.

4. The asset turnover is 1.5 times.

5. The current ratio is 3:1.

6. The inventory turnover is 8 times.

Instructions

Calculate the missing information using the ratios. Use ending balances instead of average balances if an average is needed for the ratio calculation. (*Hint:* Start with one ratio and get as much information as possible from it before trying another ratio. You will not be able to calculate the missing amounts in the same sequence as they are presented.)

P14–11B You are in the process of analyzing two similar companies in the same industry. You learn that they have different accounting practices and policies as follows:

1. Company A, which has the same type of inventory as Company B, uses the FIFO cost formula while Company B uses average. Prices have been generally rising in this industry.

2. Company A uses operating leases for most of its buildings, while Company B uses finance leases for its buildings.

Discuss impact of accounting principles on financial analysis.
(SO 5)

Instructions

(a) Considering only the impact of the choice of inventory cost formula, determine which company will report a higher (1) current ratio, (2) debt to total assets ratio, and (3) profit margin ratio, or if the choice of cost formula will have no impact.

(b) Considering only the impact of the choice of lease accounting, determine which company will report a higher (1) current ratio, (2) debt to total assets ratio, and (3) profit margin ratio, or if the choice of lease will have no impact.

(c) Will the use of different accounting practices and policies affect your analysis? Explain.

(d) Identify two other limitations of financial analysis that an analyst should watch for when analyzing financial statements.

BROADENING YOUR PERSPECTIVE

Analysis Tools

Financial Reporting and Analysis Cases

Financial Reporting: *Shoppers Drug Mart*

BYP14–1 The financial statements of Shoppers Drug Mart are presented in Appendix A at the end of this book.

Instructions

(a) Prepare a horizontal analysis of the statement of earnings for 2007 and 2006, calculating the percentage change between the two years.

(b) Prepare a vertical analysis of the statement of earnings for 2007 and 2006.

(c) Comment on any significant changes you observe from your calculations in (a) and (b).

Comparative Analysis: *Shoppers Drug Mart and Jean Coutu*

BYP14–2 The financial statements of Jean Coutu are presented in Appendix B following the financial statements for Shoppers Drug Mart in Appendix A.

Instructions

(a) Calculate or find liquidity ratios that you believe are relevant for each company. Which company is more liquid?

(b) Calculate or find solvency ratios that you believe are relevant for each company. Which company is more solvent?

(c) Calculate or find profitability ratios that you believe are relevant for each company. For the return on common shareholders' equity ratio, note that neither company has any preferred shares. Which company is more profitable?

(d) In 2008, Jean Coutu had a nine-month fiscal year as it changed to a new year-end, March 1. How does the shorter year end for Jean Coutu affect your analysis, if at all?

(e) What information that is not included in the financial statements might also be useful for comparing Jean Coutu and Shoppers Drug Mart?

Interpreting Financial Statements

BYP14–3 Selected ratios for Coca-Cola Company, PepsiCo, Inc., and their industry are presented here for a recent year:

	Coca-Cola	PepsiCo	Industry
Liquidity			
Current ratio	0.9:1	1.3:1	1.5:1
Receivables turnover	9.8 times	9.7 times	9.6 times
Inventory turnover	5.4 times	8.6 times	6.8 times
Solvency			
Debt to total assets	49.8%	50.0%	37.1%
Times interest earned	18.3 times	35.1 times	5.5 times
Profitability			
Gross profit margin	64.0%	54.3%	30.9%
Profit margin	20.7%	14.3%	3.5%
Return on common shareholders' equity	30.9%	34.6%	12.7%
Return on assets	16.3%	17.5%	4.3%
Asset turnover	0.8 times	1.2 times	1.1 times
Price-earnings ratio	23.7 times	19.8 times	19.6 times

Instructions

(a) Comment on the relative liquidity of the two companies.

(b) Comment on the relative solvency of the two companies.

(c) Comment on the relative profitability of the two companies.

(d) Which company do investors favour?

A Global Focus

BYP14–4 The following data were taken from the financial statements of tire manufacturers Compagnie Générale des Établissements Michelin (Michelin) and The Goodyear Tire & Rubber Company:

International Resources

	Michelin (in millions of Euros)		Goodyear (in USD millions)	
	2007	2006	2007	2006
Cash and cash equivalents	€ 330	€ 680	$ 3,463	$ 3,862
Accounts receivable (gross)	2,993	3,237	3,103	2,800
Total current assets	7,284	7,882	10,172	10,179
Total assets	16,449	16,874	17,191	17,029
Total current liabilities	4,711	5,844	4,664	4,666
Total liabilities	11,159	12,186	14,341	17,787
Total shareholders' equity	5,290	4,688	2,850	(758)
Net sales	16,867	16,384	19,644	18,751
Operating expenses	3,405	3,393	2,762	2,546
Interest expense	294	315	450	447
Income tax expense	299	369	255	60
Net earnings	772	573	602	(330)
Cash provided by operating activities	1,862	1,191	105	560
Net capital expenditures	1,484	1,379	739	637
Dividends	208	193	100	69

Instructions

Where available, industry averages are shown in parentheses next to each ratio below.

(a) Calculate the following liquidity ratios for 2007 and discuss the relative liquidity of the two companies and the tire manufacturing industry:

1. Current ratio (1.8:1)

2. Cash current debt coverage (n/a)

3. Receivables turnover (6.9 times)

(b) Calculate the following solvency ratios for 2007 and discuss the relative solvency of the two companies and of the tire manufacturing industry:

1. Debt to total assets (41.9%)

2. Times interest earned (4.8 times)

3. Cash total debt coverage (n/a)

4. Free cash flow (n/a)

(c) Calculate the following profitability ratios for 2007 and discuss the relative profitability of the two companies and the tire manufacturing industry:

1. Asset turnover (1.2 times)

2. Profit margin (3.5%)

3. Return on assets (4.0%)

4. Return on common shareholders' equity (16.7%). (Note that neither company has any preferred shares.)

(d) Identify the key differences between each company and their industry. What factors might be causing the differences you found?

Critical Thinking Cases and Activities

Collaborative Learning Activity

BYP14–5 As a General Manager of Operations for the Western Region plant of a construction materials manufacturing facility, you are seeking ways to make your operation more efficient, while constantly aware of how your operation is evaluated by Head Office.

Key ratios reported to head office in the last fiscal period included:

Current ratio	2.2:1
Receivables turnover	10 times
Inventory turnover	8 times
Gross profit margin	25%
Profit margin	10%
Return on assets	8%

The management team is reviewing a proposal to develop an Internet-based electronic marketplace. With an investment in internal IT infrastructure modification and connective technology, your operation could expect benefits in:

1. Materials sourcing and purchasing, resulting in lower product costs and lower levels of in-stock inventory requirements

2. Shipping and logistics planning, resulting in faster order-to-delivery cycles for customers, more efficient billing, and faster collection of customer accounts

3. Market intelligence data, resulting in the identification and pursuit of new customers and markets.

While all of these benefits are desirable, they must weighed against the significant expenditure over the next three years on IT infrastructure, business process redesign, and staff training. As General Manager, you expect to work at this plant for only another two to three years. After that, you hope to be promoted to a larger plant or a senior position at Head Office.

Instructions

With the class divided into groups, do the following:

(a) Considering the expected benefits described above, state whether you would expect each of the key ratios to improve or deteriorate in the short-term, if an Internet-based electronic marketplace is developed. Justify your answer.

(b) The VP of Sales is very enthusiastic about developing an electronic marketplace because she is confident that customers will reward the better service with loyalty to the company. If this is true, what could be the long-term effect on the key ratios given above?

(c) Could the two- to three-year time horizon of the General Manager affect the General Manager's decision on this project? Explain.

Communication Activity

BYP14–6 You are a new member of the board of directors of Shifty Inc. You are preparing for your first meeting of the audit committee and want to reassure yourself about the professional judgement used by management in preparing financial information and the quality of this information.

Instructions

Write a memo to yourself, listing questions that you should raise at the audit committee meeting to satisfy any concerns you may have about the professional judgement used by Shifty's management in preparing its financial information.

Ethics Case

BYP14–7 Vern Fairly, president of Flex Industries Inc., wants to issue a press release to boost the company's image and its share price, which has been gradually falling. As controller, you have been asked to provide a list of financial ratios and other operating statistics for Flex Industries' first-quarter operations.

Two days after you provide the ratios and data requested, you are asked by Anne Saint-Onge, Flex's public relations director, to review the accuracy of the financial and operating data contained in the press release written by the president and edited by Anne. In the news release, the president highlights the sales increase of 25% over last year's first quarter and the positive change in the current ratio from 1.5:1 last year to 3:1 this year. He also emphasizes that production was up 50% over last year's first quarter.

You note that the release contains only positive or improved ratios and none of the negative or worsening ratios. For instance, there is no mention of the fact that the debt to total assets ratio has increased from 35% to 55%, or that inventories are up 89%.

Instructions

    (a) Who are the stakeholders in this situation?

    (b) Is there anything unethical in President Fairly's actions?

    (c) As controller, should you remain silent? Does Anne have any responsibility?

"All About You" Activity

BYP14–8 A company's price-earnings ratio is one of the most widely used means for comparing and understanding the value of its shares. It is highly effective in relating the price that you pay for each share to the earnings that you can currently expect to receive.

Instructions

    (a) Does a price-earnings ratio reflect past or future performance expectations of a company, or both? Explain.

    (b) When you purchase a company's shares, should you look for shares with a high or low price-earnings ratio? Explain.

    (c) What other factors besides the price-earnings ratio should you consider in making your share purchase decision?

Serial Case

(*Note:* This is a continuation of the serial case from Chapters 1 through 13.)

BYP14–9 Cookie Creations' comparative balance sheets and statements of earnings for the years ended December 31, 2011 and 2010, follow:

COOKIE CREATIONS LTD. Balance Sheet December 31		
	2011	**2010**
<u>Assets</u>		
Cash	$ 16,344	$ 3,050
Accounts receivable	3,250	1,710
Inventory	7,897	5,450
Prepaid expenses	6,300	3,050
Furniture and fixtures	12,500	5,000
Accumulated depreciation—furniture and fixtures	(2,000)	(1,000)
Computer equipment	4,000	4,500
Accumulated depreciation—computer equipment	(600)	(1,500)
Kitchen equipment	80,000	66,000
Accumulated depreciation—kitchen equipment	(22,600)	(6,600)
Total assets	$105,091	$79,660

Liabilities and Shareholders' Equity		
Accounts payable	$ 3,650	$ 6,930
Income taxes payable	10,251	11,200
Dividends payable	28,000	25,000
Salaries payable	2,250	1,280
Interest payable	188	0
Note payable—current portion	3,000	0
Note payable—long-term portion	4,500	0
Preferred shares ($6 cumulative, 3,000 issued in 2011 and 2,000 issued in 2010)	15,000	10,000
Common shares (3,625 shares issued)	5,450	5,450
Retained earnings	32,802	19,800
Total liabilities and shareholders' equity	$105,091	$79,660

COOKIE CREATIONS LTD.
Statement of Earnings
Year Ended December 31

	2011	2010
Sales	$485,625	$462,500
Cost of goods sold	222,694	208,125
Gross profit	262,931	254,375
Operating expenses		
Depreciation expense	17,600	9,100
Salaries and wages expense	147,979	146,350
Other operating expenses	43,186	42,925
Total operating expenses	208,765	198,375
Earnings from operations	54,166	56,000
Other expenses		
Interest expense	413	0
Loss on sale of computer equipment	2,500	0
Total other expenses	2,913	0
Earnings before income tax	51,253	56,000
Income tax expense	10,251	11,200
Net earnings	$ 41,002	$ 44,800

Instructions

(a) Calculate the following ratios for 2010 and 2011:
1. Current ratio
2. Debt to total assets
3. Gross profit margin
4. Profit margin
5. Return on assets (Total assets at the beginning of 2010 were $33,180.)
6. Return on common shareholders' equity (Total common shareholders' equity at the beginning of 2010 was $17,200.)
7. Payout ratio (In 2011, $18,000 of dividends were paid to the preferred shareholders and $10,000 to the common shareholders. In 2010, $15,000 of dividends were paid to the preferred shareholders and $10,000 to the common shareholders.)

(b) Prepare a horizontal analysis of the statement of earnings, calculating the percentage change between 2010 and 2011.

(c) Prepare a vertical analysis of the statement of earnings for 2011 and 2010.

(d) Comment on your findings from parts (a) to (c).

Answers to Chapter Questions

Answer to Shoppers Drug Mart Review It Question 4

Shoppers Drug Mart reported a $66,000 increase to opening retained earnings as the impact of the adoption of three new accounting principles: financial instruments, hedges, and comprehensive income.

Answers to Self-Study Questions

1. d   2. b   3. d   4. d   5. c   6. c   7. b   8. b   9. a   10. a

Remember to go back to the beginning of the chapter to check off your completed work!

←

Comprehensive Case: Chapter 14

Manutech Ltd.'s industrial product sales were down in 2008. Fortunately, after investing in a customer relationship management system, it was able to turn its operations around considerably. The vice-president of Manutech has asked for an analysis of the 2009 financial results that will show how the company is performing in relation to the industry.

Selected financial statement data follow, with some 2007 balance sheet information for comparison:

MANUTECH LTD. Statement of Earnings Year Ended December 31		
	2009	2008
Sales	$1,470,000	$1,100,000
Cost of goods sold	735,000	655,000
Gross profit	735,000	445,000
Operating expenses	313,500	270,000
Earnings from operations	421,500	175,000
Interest expense	115,000	92,500
Earnings before income taxes	306,500	82,500
Income tax expense	76,625	20,625
Net earnings	$ 229,875	$ 61,875

MANUTECH LTD. Balance Sheet December 31			
	2009	2008	2007
Assets			
Current assets			
Cash	$ 94,000	$ 49,500	
Available-for-sale securities	25,000	50,000	
Accounts receivable (gross)	95,000	105,000	$ 85,000
Inventories	78,000	70,000	63,500
Total current assets	292,000	274,500	
Property, plant, and equipment (net)	1,100,000	965,000	
Intangible assets	120,000	120,000	
Total assets	$1,512,000	$1,359,500	1,425,000
Liabilities and Shareholders' Equity			
Liabilities			
Current liabilities			
Accounts payable	$ 65,000	$ 72,500	
Accrued liabilities	15,000	20,000	
Total current liabilities	80,000	92,500	
Long-term liabilities			
Bank loan payable	150,000	0	
Bonds payable	650,000	670,000	
Total long-term liabilities	800,000	670,000	
Total liabilities	880,000	762,500	
Shareholders' equity			
Common shares, 10,000 shares issued	100,000	100,000	
Retained earnings	532,000	497,000	
Total shareholders' equity	632,000	597,000	
Total liabilities and shareholders' equity	$1,512,000	$1,359,500	

Additional information for 2009:

1.   Assume all sales were credit sales.

2.   Manutech has no bad debts and no allowance for doubtful accounts.

3.   Property, plant, and equipment increased in 2009 by the $300,000 cost of a new customer relationship management system and decreased by additional accumulated depreciation for the year of $165,000.

4.   Cash dividends paid during the year amounted to $194,875.

Instructions

(a) Prepare a vertical analysis for the statements of earnings for 2009 and 2008. Use the results to answer the following question from management: "We know that sales volume has increased, but we don't know if the gross profit margin is also increasing. If the gross profit margin is increasing, what are some of the likely reasons for this increase?"

(b) Calculate the following liquidity ratios for 2009 and compare the company's results to the industry average:

	Industry Average
Current ratio	3:1
Average collection period	28 days
Days in inventory	30 days

(c) Calculate the following solvency ratios for 2009 and compare the company's results to the industry average:

	Industry Average
Debt to total assets	50%
Times interest earned	3.0 times

(d) Calculate the following profitability ratios for 2009 and compare the company's results to the industry average:

	Industry Average
Gross profit margin	44%
Profit margin	10%
Return on assets	15%
Asset turnover	0.8 times

(e) After a review of the financial statements, the vice-president is surprised that the cash balance reported on the balance sheet at year end is not higher even though financial performance improved and cash provided by operating activities was determined to be $384,375. Prepare the investing and financing activities sections of the cash flow statement for 2009 to explain where the cash has been used.

Specimen Financial Statements: Shoppers Drug Mart Corporation

SHOPPERS DRUG MART   **PHARMAPRIX**

In this appendix, and the next, we illustrate current financial reporting with two different sets of corporate financial statements that are prepared in accordance with Canadian generally accepted accounting principles. We are grateful for permission to use the actual financial statements of Shoppers Drug Mart Corporation in Appendix A and The Jean Coutu Group (PJC) Inc. in Appendix B.

The financial statement package for Shoppers Drug Mart includes the statements of earnings, statements of retained earnings, statements of comprehensive income and accumulated other comprehensive income, balance sheets, cash flow statements, and notes to the financial statements. The financial statements are preceded by two reports: management's responsibility for the financial statements and the auditors' report on these statements.

We encourage students to use these financial statements in conjunction with relevant material in the textbook. As well, these statements can be used to solve the Review It questions in the Before You Go On section of each chapter and the Financial Reporting and Comparative Analysis cases in the Broadening Your Perspective section of the end of chapter material.

The complete annual report for Shoppers Drug Mart can be found on the companion website to this textbook in the Annual Reports section. In addition, material about working with annual reports, including the financial statements, is included in the Analysis Tools section of the website.

www.wiley.com/canada/kimmel

Tutorials
(Annual Report Walkthrough)

Management's Report

Management's Responsibility for Financial Statements

Management is responsible for the preparation and presentation of the accompanying consolidated financial statements and all other information in the Annual Report. This responsibility includes the selection and consistent application of appropriate accounting principles and methods in addition to making the estimates, judgements and assumptions necessary to prepare the consolidated financial statements in accordance with Canadian generally accepted accounting principles. It also includes ensuring that the financial information presented elsewhere in the Annual Report is consistent with the consolidated financial statements.

In fulfilling its responsibilities, management has established and maintains systems of internal controls. Although no cost-effective system of internal controls will prevent or detect all errors and irregularities, these systems are designed to provide reasonable assurance regarding the reliability of the Company's financial reporting and preparation of the financial statements in accordance with Canadian generally accepted accounting principles. These systems include controls to provide reasonable assurance that resources are safeguarded from material loss or inappropriate use, that transactions are authorized, recorded and reported properly and that financial records are reliable for preparing the consolidated financial statements. Internal auditors, who are employees of the Company, review and evaluate internal controls on management's behalf. The consolidated financial statements have been audited by the independent auditors, Deloitte & Touche LLP, in accordance with generally accepted auditing standards. Their report follows.

The Board of Directors, acting through an Audit Committee which is comprised solely of directors who are not employees of the Company, is responsible for determining that management fulfils its responsibility for financial reporting and internal control. This responsibility is carried out through periodic meetings with senior officers, financial management, internal audit and the independent auditors to discuss audit activities, the adequacy of internal financial controls and financial reporting matters. The Audit Committee has reviewed these consolidated financial statements and the Management's Discussion and Analysis and has recommended their approval by the Board of Directors prior to their inclusion in this Annual Report.

Jürgen Schreiber
PRESIDENT AND CHIEF EXECUTIVE OFFICER

George Halatsis
EXECUTIVE VICE-PRESIDENT AND CHIEF FINANCIAL OFFICER

Auditors' Report

To the Shareholders of Shoppers Drug Mart Corporation

We have audited the consolidated balance sheets of Shoppers Drug Mart Corporation as at December 29, 2007 and December 30, 2006 and the consolidated statements of earnings, retained earnings, comprehensive income and accumulated other comprehensive income and cash flows for the 52 week periods then ended. These financial statements are the responsibility of the Company's management. Our responsibility is to express an opinion on these financial statements based on our audits.

We conducted our audits in accordance with Canadian generally accepted auditing standards. Those standards require that we plan and perform an audit to obtain reasonable assurance whether the financial statements are free of material misstatement. An audit includes examining, on a test basis, evidence supporting the amounts and disclosures in the financial statements. An audit also includes assessing the accounting principles used and significant estimates made by management, as well as evaluating the overall financial statement presentation.

In our opinion, these consolidated financial statements present fairly, in all material respects, the financial position of Shoppers Drug Mart Corporation as at December 29, 2007 and December 30, 2006 and the results of its operations and its cash flows for the 52 week periods then ended in accordance with Canadian generally accepted accounting principles.

Chartered Accountants,
Licensed Public Accountants

TORONTO, ONTARIO
FEBRUARY 5, 2008

Consolidated Statements of Earnings

52 weeks ended December 29, 2007 and December 30, 2006 (in thousands of dollars, except per share amounts)	2007	2006
Sales	**$ 8,478,382** $	7,786,436
Operating expenses		
Cost of goods sold and other operating expenses	**7,516,291**	6,958,361
Amortization	**172,075**	144,549
Operating income	**790,016**	683,526
Interest expense (Note 4)	**52,873**	49,872
Earnings before income taxes	**737,143**	633,654
Income taxes (Note 5)		
Current	**249,948**	220,398
Future	**(6,433)**	(9,235)
	243,515	211,163
Net earnings	**$ 493,628** $	422,491
Net earnings per common share (Note 11)		
Basic	**$ 2.28** $	1.97
Diluted	**$ 2.27** $	1.95

The accompanying notes are an integral part of these consolidated financial statements.

Consolidated Statements of Retained Earnings

52 weeks ended December 29, 2007 and December 30, 2006 (in thousands of dollars)	2007	2006
Retained earnings, beginning of period	**$ 1,225,616** $	941,672
Impact of the adoption of new accounting standards, Handbook Sections 3855, Financial Instruments – Recognition and Measurement; 3865, Hedges; and 1530, Comprehensive Income (Note 2)	**66**	–
Net earnings	**493,628**	422,491
Dividends	**(138,398)**	(102,952)
Premium on share capital purchased for cancellation (Note 11)	**(24)**	(35,595)
Retained earnings, end of period	**$ 1,580,888** $	1,225,616

The accompanying notes are an integral part of these consolidated financial statements.

Consolidated Statements of Comprehensive Income and
Accumulated Other Comprehensive Income

52 weeks ended December 29, 2007 and December 30, 2006
(in thousands of dollars)

	2007	2006
Net earnings	$ 493,628 $	–
Other comprehensive income, net of tax		
Change in unrealized gain on interest rate derivatives (net of tax of $65)	24	–
Change in unrealized gain on equity forward derivatives (net of tax of $12)	(23)	–
Amount of previously unrealized gain on equity forward derivatives recognized in earnings during the period (net of tax of $82)	(160)	–
Other comprehensive loss	(159)	–
Comprehensive income	$ 493,469 $	–
Accumulated other comprehensive income, upon adoption of new accounting standards (Note 2)	$ 406 $	–
Other comprehensive loss (net of tax of $29)	(159)	–
Accumulated other comprehensive income, end of period	$ 247 $	–

The accompanying notes are an integral part of these consolidated financial statements.

Consolidated Balance Sheets

As at December 29, 2007 and December 30, 2006
(in thousands of dollars)

	2007	2006
Assets		
Current		
Cash	$ 27,588 $	62,865
Accounts receivable	372,306	307,779
Inventory	1,577,524	1,372,124
Future income taxes (Note 5)	60,089	46,407
Prepaid expenses and deposits (Note 3)	134,692	32,248
	2,172,199	1,821,423
Property and equipment (Note 6)	1,126,513	907,728
Deferred costs (Note 7)	32,966	25,936
Goodwill	2,245,441	2,122,162
Other intangible assets (Note 8)	57,930	45,249
Other assets	8,990	6,516
Total assets	$ 5,644,039 $	4,929,014
Liabilities		
Current		
Bank indebtedness	$ 225,152 $	134,487
Commercial paper (Notes 4 and 14)	543,847	503,550
Accounts payable and accrued liabilities	990,545	843,278
Income taxes payable	65,825	70,672
Dividends payable	34,686	25,797
Current portion of long-term debt (Note 9)	298,990	–
	2,159,045	1,577,784
Long-term debt (Note 9)	–	300,000
Other long-term liabilities (Note 10)	244,657	188,938
Future income taxes (Note 5)	30,171	21,689
	2,433,873	2,088,411
Associate interest	113,119	116,649
Shareholders' equity		
Share capital (Note 11)	1,506,020	1,491,264
Contributed surplus (Note 12)	9,892	7,074
Accumulated other comprehensive income	247	–
Retained earnings	1,580,888	1,225,616
	1,581,135	1,225,616
	3,097,047	2,723,954
Total liabilities and shareholders' equity	$ 5,644,039 $	4,929,014

The accompanying notes are an integral part of these consolidated financial statements.

On behalf of the Board of Directors:

Jürgen Schreiber
DIRECTOR

David M. Williams
DIRECTOR

Consolidated Statements of Cash Flows

52 weeks ended December 29, 2007 and December 30, 2006
(in thousands of dollars)

	2007	2006
Operating activities		
Net earnings	$ **493,628** $	422,491
Items not affecting cash		
Amortization	**181,418**	150,088
Future income taxes	**(6,433)**	(9,235)
Loss on disposal of property and equipment	**4,165**	7,185
Stock-based compensation (Note 12)	**3,544**	3,492
	676,322	574,021
Net change in non-cash working capital balances (Note 13)	**(137,697)**	(26,551)
Increase in other long-term liabilities	**48,464**	38,990
Store opening costs	**(22,031)**	(16,644)
Cash flows from operating activities	**565,058**	569,816
Investing activities		
Purchase of property and equipment	**(395,526)**	(287,216)
Proceeds from disposition of property and equipment	**18,014**	3,269
Business acquisitions (Note 3)	**(139,833)**	(93,866)
Deposits (Note 3)	**(93,688)**	–
Other assets	**(1,714)**	(3,570)
Cash flows used in investing activities	**(612,747)**	(381,383)
Financing activities		
Bank indebtedness, net	**90,665**	(29,359)
Commercial paper, net	**40,800**	33,700
Repayment of long-term debt (Note 9)	**–**	(27,025)
Deferred financing costs	**(20)**	(454)
Associate interest	**(3,530)**	148
Proceeds from shares issued for stock options exercised	**13,710**	10,898
Repayment of share purchase loans	**325**	2,287
Repurchase of share capital	**(29)**	(41,789)
Dividends paid	**(129,509)**	(98,498)
Cash flows from (used in) financing activities	**12,412**	(150,092)
(Decrease) increase in cash	**(35,277)**	38,341
Cash, beginning of period	**62,865**	24,524
Cash, end of period	$ **27,588** $	62,865
Supplemental cash flow information		
Interest paid	$ **50,596** $	48,075
Income taxes paid	$ **280,393** $	188,270

The accompanying notes are an integral part of these consolidated financial statements.

Notes to the Consolidated Financial Statements

December 29, 2007 and December 30, 2006 (in thousands of dollars, except per share data)

1. Significant Accounting Policies

These financial statements have been prepared in accordance with Canadian generally accepted accounting principles.

Description of the Business

Shoppers Drug Mart Corporation (the "Company") is a licensor of approximately 1,057 Shoppers Drug Mart/Pharmaprix full-service retail drug stores across Canada. The Shoppers Drug Mart/Pharmaprix stores are licensed to Associate-owners ("Associates"). In addition, the Company owns and operates 64 Shoppers Home Health Care® stores. Under the Canadian Institute of Chartered Accountants' ("CICA") Accounting Guideline 15, "Consolidation of Variable Interest Entities", the Company consolidates the Associate-owned stores and an independent trust.

The individual Associate-owned stores that comprise the Company's store network are variable interest entities ("VIE") and the Company is the primary beneficiary. As such, the Associate-owned stores are subject to consolidation by the Company. The Associate-owned stores remain separate legal entities and consolidation of the Associate-owned stores has no impact on the underlying risks facing the Company.

The Company has an arrangement with an independent trust (the "Trust") to provide loans to Associates to facilitate their purchase of inventory and fund their working capital requirements. The Trust's activities are financed through the issuance of short-term, asset-backed notes to third-party investors. The Trust is a VIE and the Company is the primary beneficiary. As such, the Trust is subject to consolidation by the Company.

Fiscal Year

The fiscal year of the Company consists of a 52 or 53 week period ending on the Saturday closest to December 31. The Company's 2007 and 2006 fiscal years consisted of 52 week periods.

Basis of Consolidation

The consolidated financial statements include the accounts of Shoppers Drug Mart Corporation, its subsidiaries, the Associate-owned stores that comprise the Company's store network and the Trust. All intercompany balances and transactions are eliminated on consolidation.

Estimates

The preparation of the consolidated financial statements in conformity with Canadian generally accepted accounting principles requires management to make estimates and assumptions that affect the reported amounts of assets and liabilities and disclosure of contingent assets and liabilities at the date of the consolidated financial statements and the reported amounts of revenues and expenses during the reporting period. Estimates are used when accounting for items such as inventory provisions, Shoppers Optimum™ loyalty card program costs, assumptions underlying the actuarial determination of employee future benefits, income and other taxes and when testing goodwill, other intangible assets and long-lived assets for impairment. Actual results could differ from these estimates.

Comparative Amounts

Certain comparative amounts have been reclassified to conform with the current period's financial statement presentation.

Revenue Recognition

The Company recognizes revenue at the time goods are sold, net of returns.

Notes to the Consolidated Financial Statements (continued)
December 29, 2007 and December 30, 2006 (in thousands of dollars, except per share data)

1. Significant Accounting Policies (continued)

Bank Indebtedness

Bank indebtedness is comprised of corporate bank overdraft balances and bank lines of credit used by the Associate-owned stores to meet their operating needs and outstanding cheques.

Inventory

Inventory is valued at the lower of cost and estimated net realizable value, with cost being determined on the first-in, first-out basis.

Property and Equipment

Property and equipment are recorded at cost. Amortization is recorded on a straight-line basis over the estimated useful lives of the assets at the rates indicated below.

Buildings	20 years
Equipment and fixtures	3 to 10 years
Computer software and equipment	2 to 10 years
Leasehold improvements	Lesser of term of the lease and useful life

Long-lived assets are tested for impairment when events or circumstances indicate their carrying value exceeds the sum of the undiscounted cash flows expected from their use and eventual disposal. An impairment loss is measured as the amount by which the long-lived assets' carrying value exceeds the fair value. The Company reviews long-lived assets for impairment annually.

Deferred Costs

Store Opening Costs

Certain costs associated with the opening of new and relocated stores are deferred and amortized into cost of goods sold and other operating expenses on a straight-line basis over a period of three years.

Goodwill and Other Intangible Assets

The Company records as goodwill the excess amount of the purchase price of an acquired business over the fair value of the underlying net assets, including intangible assets, at the date of acquisition. Goodwill is not amortized but is tested for impairment on an annual basis. In the event of an impairment, the excess of the carrying amount over the fair value of goodwill would be charged to earnings.

Intangible assets are amortized on a straight-line basis over the estimated useful lives of the assets at the rates indicated below. Intangible assets are tested for impairment when an indication of impairment exists. In the event of an impairment, the excess of the carrying amount over the fair value of intangible assets would be charged to earnings.

Prescription files	7 years
Developed technology	3 years
Customer relationships	5 to 25 years
Other	Indefinite

Leases

The Company leases most of its store locations and office space. Terms vary in length and typically permit renewal for additional periods. Minimum rent, including scheduled escalations, is expensed on a straight-line basis over the term of the lease, including any rent-free periods. Landlord inducements are deferred and amortized as reductions to rent expense on a straight-line basis over the same period. The Company capitalizes rent expense during a store's fixturing period to leasehold improvements.

1. Significant Accounting Policies (continued)

Leases may include additional payments for real estate taxes, maintenance and insurance. These amounts are expensed in the period to which they relate.

Shoppers Optimum™ Loyalty Program

The Shoppers Optimum™ loyalty card program (the "Program") allows members to earn points on their purchases in Shoppers Drug Mart®, Pharmaprix® and Shoppers Home Health Care® stores at a rate of 10 points for each dollar spent on eligible products and services, plus any applicable bonus points. Members can then redeem points, in accordance with the Program rewards schedule or other offers, for discounts on front store merchandise at the time of a future purchase transaction. When points are earned by Program members, the Company records an expense and establishes a liability for future redemptions by multiplying the number of points issued by the estimated cost per point. The Program liability is included in accounts payable and accrued liabilities on the Company's consolidated balance sheets. The actual cost of Program redemptions is charged against the liability account.

The estimated cost per point is determined based on many factors, including the historical behaviour of Program members, expected future redemption patterns and associated costs. The Company monitors, on an ongoing basis, trends in redemption rates (points redeemed as a percentage of points issued) and net cost per point redeemed and adjusts the estimated cost per point based upon expected future activity. To the extent that estimates differ from actual experience, the Program costs could be higher or lower.

Employee Future Benefits

The Company maintains registered defined benefit pension plans under which benefits are available to certain employee groups. The Company also makes supplementary retirement benefits available to certain employees under a non-registered defined benefit pension plan.

The Company accrues its obligations for employee benefit plans under the following policies:
- The cost of pensions and other retirement benefits earned by employees is actuarially determined using the projected benefit method pro-rated on service and management's best estimate of expected plan investment performance, salary escalation, retirement ages of employees and expected health care costs.
- For the purpose of calculating the expected return on plan assets, those assets are valued at fair value.
- The excess of the net actuarial gain (loss) over 10% of the greater of the benefit obligation and the fair value of plan assets is amortized over the average remaining service period of active employees. The average remaining service period of the active employees covered by the pension plans and other retirement benefit plan is 14 and 10 years, respectively.

Stock-based Compensation

The Company has stock option compensation plans which are described in Note 12. Compensation expense is recognized for these plans for stock options granted to employees and directors after December 28, 2002 using the fair value method. Any consideration paid by employees and directors on exercise of stock options is credited to share capital.

Income Taxes

The Company accounts for income taxes using the liability method of accounting. Under the liability method, future income tax assets and liabilities are determined based on differences between the carrying amounts of balance sheet items and their corresponding tax values. The liability method requires the computation of future income taxes using the substantively enacted corporate income tax rates for the years in which the differences are expected to reverse.

1. Significant Accounting Policies (continued)

Derivative Financial Instruments

The Company uses interest rate derivatives to manage its exposure to fluctuations in interest rates related to the Company's commercial paper and long-term debt. The income or expense arising from the use of these instruments is included in interest expense for the year.

The Company uses cash-settled equity forward agreements to limit its exposure to future price changes in the Company's share price for share unit awards under the Company's long-term incentive plan ("LTIP"). The income and expense arising from the use of these instruments are included in cost of goods sold and other operating expenses for the year. See Note 12 for further discussion of the LTIP.

The Company formally identifies, designates and documents all relationships between hedging instruments and hedged items, as well as its risk assessment objective and strategy for undertaking various hedge transactions. The Company assesses, both at the hedge's inception and on an ongoing basis, whether the derivatives that are used in hedging transactions are highly effective in offsetting changes in fair values or cash flows of hedged items. When such derivative instruments cease to exist or be effective as hedges, or when designation of a hedging relationship is terminated, any associated deferred gains or losses are recognized in net earnings in the same period as the corresponding gains or losses associated with the hedged item. When a hedged item ceases to exist, any associated deferred gains or losses are recognized in net earnings in the period the hedged item ceases to exist.

Associate Interest

Associate interest reflects the investment the Associates have in the net assets of their corporations.

2. Changes in Accounting Policies

Financial Instruments

In 2006, the CICA issued new accounting standards concerning financial instruments: Financial Instruments – Recognition and Measurement ("Section 3855"); Financial Instruments – Disclosure and Presentation ("Section 3861"), Hedges ("Section 3865"); and Comprehensive Income ("Section 1530"). The standards require prospective application and were effective for the Company's first quarter of fiscal 2007. The Company applied the new accounting standards at the beginning of its current fiscal year.

Financial Assets and Liabilities

Section 3855 establishes standards for recognizing and measuring financial instruments. Under the new standards, all financial instruments are classified into one of the following five categories: held for trading, held-to-maturity investments, loans and receivables, available-for-sale financial assets or other financial liabilities.

The Company's financial assets and financial liabilities are classified and measured as follows:

Asset/Liability	Category	Measurement
Cash	Held for trading	Fair value
Accounts receivable	Loans and receivables	Amortized cost
Long-term receivables*	Loans and receivables	Amortized cost
Bank indebtedness	Held for trading	Fair value
Commercial paper	Other financial liabilities	Amortized cost
Accounts payable	Other financial liabilities	Amortized cost
Long-term debt	Other financial liabilities	Amortized cost
Other long-term liabilities	Other financial liabilities	Amortized cost

*Included in other assets in the consolidated balance sheets.

2. Changes in Accounting Policies (continued)

Derivative and Hedge Accounting

The Company's interest rate derivatives have been designated as cash flow hedges and reported at fair value, in accordance with the new standards, as a component of other assets. A percentage of the equity forward derivatives, related to unearned units under the LTIP, have been designated as a hedge. The fair value of the percentage of the equity derivatives designated as a hedge has been reflected in the opening balance of accumulated other comprehensive income, net of tax.

The following table summarizes the impact on the Company's opening balance sheet for fiscal 2007 as a result of the adjustments relating to interest rate and equity forward derivatives:

	December 30, 2006 Balance, as Reported	Interest Rate Derivatives	Long-term Incentive Plan and Equity Forward Derivatives	December 31, 2006 Opening Balance
Other assets	$ 6,516 $	338 $	610 $	7,464
Other long-term liabilities	$ 188,938 $	– $	234 $	189,172
Future income taxes (within liabilities)	$ 21,689 $	115 $	128 $	21,932
Retained earnings	$ 1,225,616 $	– $	66 $	1,225,682
Accumulated other comprehensive income	$ – $	223 $	183 $	406

In addition to the above adjustments, the Company has adopted the policy of adding transaction costs to financial assets and liabilities classified as other than "held for trading". As a result, the Company's deferred financing costs were reclassified to the debt balances to which they relate. As at December 31, 2006, the commercial paper balance was reduced by $707 of deferred financing costs and the long-term debt balance was reduced by $1,518 of deferred financing costs. As at December 29, 2007, the commercial paper balance was reduced by $503 of deferred financing costs and the long-term debt balance was reduced by $1,010 of deferred financing costs.

The Company does not have any significant embedded features in contractual arrangements that required separate presentation from the related host contract.

As a result of the implementation of these standards, the Consolidated Financial Statements include Consolidated Statements of Comprehensive Income and Accumulated Other Comprehensive Income, with the cumulative amount of other comprehensive income presented as a new category of shareholders' equity in the Consolidated Balance Sheets.

The components of accumulated other comprehensive income as at December 29, 2007 are comprised as follows:

Accumulated other comprehensive income	
Unrealized gain on interest rate derivatives (net of tax of $180)	$ 247
Unrealized gain on equity forward derivatives (net of tax of $nil)	–
Accumulated other comprehensive income	$ 247

Equity

As a result of the issuance of guidance on financial instruments accounting, the CICA issued an amended accounting standard regarding Equity ("Section 3251"), which replaces Section 3250, Equity. The standard requires companies to disclose the impact of the new financial instruments accounting standards on equity within the Consolidated Balance Sheets and the Consolidated Statements of Retained Earnings. The standard requires prospective application and was effective for the Company's first quarter of fiscal 2007. The Company applied the new accounting standard at the beginning of its current fiscal year.

Notes to the Consolidated Financial Statements (continued)
December 29, 2007 and December 30, 2006 (in thousands of dollars, except per share data)

2. Changes in Accounting Policies (continued)

Future Accounting Standards

Capital Disclosures

In 2006, the CICA issued a new accounting standard concerning Capital Disclosures ("Section 1535"), which requires the disclosure of both quantitative and qualitative information that enables users of financial statements to evaluate the entity's objectives, policies and processes for managing capital. The standard also requires an entity to disclose if it has complied with any capital requirements, and, if it has not complied, the consequences of such non-compliance. The standard is effective for interim and annual financial statements for fiscal years beginning on or after October 1, 2007. The Company will apply the new accounting standard at the beginning of its 2008 fiscal year with the impact being limited to the Company's disclosures, with no impact on the Company's results of operations or financial position.

Financial Instruments – Disclosure and Presentation

The Company will be required to adopt two new accounting standards concerning financial instruments: "Financial Instruments – Disclosures" ("Section 3862") and "Financial Instruments – Presentation" ("Section 3863"). These standards were issued in December 2006 and will replace Section 3861, "Financial Instruments, Disclosure and Presentation". The new disclosure standard increases the emphasis on the risk associated with financial instruments and how those risks are managed. The new presentation standard carries forward the former presentation requirements under the existing Section 3861. The standards are effective for interim and annual financial statements for fiscal years beginning on or after October 1, 2007. The Company will apply the new accounting standards at the beginning of its 2008 fiscal year with the impact being limited to the Company's disclosures, with no impact on the Company's results of operations or financial position.

Inventories

The CICA issued a new accounting standard concerning Inventories ("Section 3031"), in June 2007, which is based on the International Accounting Standards Board's International Accounting Standard 2. The new section replaced the existing guidance on inventories. The new section provides additional guidance on measuring the cost of inventory and the measurement and presentation of cost of goods sold as well as requiring additional associated disclosures. The new standard also allows for the reversal of any write-downs previously recognized. The standard is effective for interim and annual financial statements for fiscal years beginning on or after January 1, 2008. The Company will apply the new accounting standard at the beginning of its 2008 fiscal year. The Company is currently assessing the impact of the new standard on the Company's results of operations, financial position and disclosures.

Going Concern

In June 2007, the CICA issued amendments to Section 1400, "General Standards of Financial Statement Presentation" to include requirements to assess and disclose an entity's ability to continue as a going concern. The amendments are effective for interim and annual financial statements beginning on or after January 1, 2008. The Company will apply the new amendments at the beginning of its 2008 fiscal year and does not expect the implementation to have a significant impact on the Company's results of operations, financial position or disclosures.

3. Acquisitions

Centre d'Escomptes Racine

On September 25, 2007, the Company purchased the assets of the seven stores of Centre d'Escomptes Racine, a pharmacy chain in Québec. The total cost of the acquisition, including costs incurred in connection with the acquisition, was $77,077 and will be allocated among inventory, other assets, goodwill and other intangible assets. The purchase price allocation has not been completed and the full purchase price has been recorded in goodwill.

Notes to the Consolidated Financial Statements (continued)
December 29, 2007 and December 30, 2006 (in thousands of dollars, except per share data)

3. Acquisitions (continued)

The operations of the acquired stores have been included in the Company's results of operations from the date of acquisition.

Other Business Acquisitions

During the year, the Company acquired the assets or shares of a number of pharmacies, each of which is individually immaterial to the Company's total acquisitions. The total cost of the acquisitions of $62,756, including costs incurred in connection with the acquisitions, is allocated primarily to goodwill and other intangible assets based on their fair values. The operations of the acquired pharmacies have been included in the Company's results of operations from the date of acquisition.

Funds Held in Escrow

The Company had amounts held in escrow of $93,688 (2006 – $nil) with respect to a number of offers to acquire certain pharmacies. These amounts are included in the balance of prepaid expenses and deposits as at December 29, 2007.

4. Interest Expense

The significant components of the Company's interest expense are as follows:

	2007	2006
Interest on bank indebtedness	$ 10,887	$ 7,629
Interest on commercial paper	27,593	24,902
Interest on long-term debt	13,679	15,719
Amortization of deferred financing costs	714	1,622
	$ 52,873	$ 49,872

Commercial paper is issued with maturities from overnight to 90 days at floating interest rates based on Bankers' Acceptance rates. In December 2005, the Company entered into interest rate derivative agreements converting an aggregate notional principal amount of $250,000 of floating rate commercial paper debt issued by the Trust into fixed rate debt. The fixed rates payable by the Company under these agreements range from 4.03% to 4.18%. See Note 15 for further discussion of the derivative agreements.

5. Income Taxes

The effective income tax rate is comprised of the following:

	2007	2006
Combined Canadian federal and provincial statutory tax rate	33.0%	33.1%
Adjusted for:		
Future income tax benefit resulting from the recognition of net capital loss carryforwards	–	(1.1%)
Increase (decrease) in future income taxes resulting from statutory tax rate changes	0.3%	(0.2%)
Non-deductible charges and other	(0.3%)	1.5%
Effective income tax rate	33.0%	33.3%

5. Income Taxes (continued)

The components of the Company's future income tax assets and liabilities are as follows:

	2007	2006
Current		
Deferred income	$ 46,183 $	36,449
Accrued liabilities	14,053	11,132
Other	(147)	(1,174)
	$ 60,089 $	46,407
Long-term		
Depreciable assets	$ (60,803) $	(51,719)
Other long-term liabilities	33,854	31,894
Deferred costs	(7,916)	(6,323)
Net capital loss carryforwards	6,696	6,974
Other	(2,002)	(2,515)
	$ (30,171) $	(21,689)

6. Property and Equipment

		2007			2006	
	Cost	Accumulated Amortization	Net Book Value	Cost	Accumulated Amortization	Net Book Value
Properties held for development	$ 38,155 $	– $	38,155 $	10,386 $	– $	10,386
Properties under development	26,218	–	26,218	14,525	–	14,525
Land	34,778	–	34,778	32,686	–	32,686
Buildings	118,064	25,731	92,333	94,939	23,708	71,231
Equipment, fixtures, computer software and equipment	863,636	433,127	430,509	728,078	355,931	372,147
Leasehold improvements	691,460	186,940	504,520	554,780	148,027	406,753
	$ 1,772,311 $	645,798 $	1,126,513 $	1,435,394 $	527,666 $	907,728

The Company amortized $161,584 (2006 – $133,845) of property and equipment into amortization during the year.

7. Deferred Costs

		2007			2006	
	Cost	Accumulated Amortization	Net Book Value	Cost	Accumulated Amortization	Net Book Value
Financing costs	$ – $	– $	– $	15,041 $	12,816 $	2,225
Store opening costs	81,416	48,450	32,966	58,653	34,942	23,711
	$ 81,416 $	48,450 $	32,966 $	73,694 $	47,758 $	25,936

The Company amortized $13,508 (2006 – $11,102) of store opening costs into cost of goods sold and other operating expenses during the year.

In conjunction with the adoption of Section 3855, the Company adopted the policy of adding transaction costs to the financial assets and liabilities classified as other than "held for trading". As a result, the Company's deferred financing costs were reclassified to the debt balances to which they relate.

December 29, 2007 and December 30, 2006 (in thousands of dollars, except per share data)

8. Other Intangible Assets

		2007			2006	
	Cost	Accumulated Amortization	Net Book Value	Cost	Accumulated Amortization	Net Book Value
Prescription files	$ 40,529 $	11,472 $	29,057 $	26,703 $	7,192 $	19,511
Developed technology	1,486	516	970	1,305	95	1,210
Customer relationships	29,600	1,897	27,703	24,600	272	24,328
Other	200	–	200	200	–	200
	$ 71,815 $	13,885 $	57,930 $	52,808 $	7,559 $	45,249

The Company amortized $4,280 (2006 – $3,152) of prescription files, $421 (2006 – $95) of developed technology and $1,625 (2006 – $272) of customer relationships into amortization during the year.

9. Long-term Debt

	Maturity	2007	2006
Series 1 notes – 4.97%	October 2008 $	298,990 $	300,000
Less: current portion		298,990	–
	$	– $	300,000
$550,000 Revolving term facility	June 2011	–	–
Long-term debt	$	– $	300,000

As at December 29, 2007, $61,212 (2006 – $50,931) of the $550,000 revolving term facility was utilized, all in respect of letters of credit and trade finance guarantees, of which $50,000 (2006 – $45,500) relates to a letter of credit for the benefit of the Trust (Note 14).

In conjunction with the adoption of Section 3855, the Company adopted the policy of adding transaction costs to the financial assets and liabilities classified as other than "held for trading". As a result, the Company's deferred financing costs were reclassified to the debt balances to which they relate.

Minimum Repayments

Future minimum required repayments of long-term debt are as follows:

Series 1 notes		
2008	$	300,000

10. Other Long-term Liabilities

Other long-term liabilities are comprised as follows:

		2007	2006
Deferred rent obligation	$	206,611 $	163,532
Employee future benefits		15,247	13,648
Long-term incentive plan (Note 12)		6,742	3,592
Other		16,057	8,166
	$	244,657 $	188,938

10. Other Long-term Liabilities (continued)

Deferred Rent Obligation

The deferred rent obligation represents the difference between rent expense and cash rent payments and the deferral of landlord inducements.

Employee Future Benefits

The Company maintains registered defined benefit pension plans under which benefits are available to certain employee groups. The Company also makes supplementary retirement benefits available to certain employees under a non-registered defined benefit pension plan.

The pension plans are funded through contributions based on actuarial cost methods as permitted by pension regulatory bodies as applicable. Earnings are charged with the cost of benefits earned by employees as services are rendered. Benefits under these plans are based on the employee's years of service and final average earnings.

The most recent actuarial valuations of the registered plans for funding purposes were performed as at December 31, 2006 and the next valuations will be required as at December 31, 2009. The most recent actuarial valuation of the non-registered plan for funding purposes was as at December 31, 2007 and the next valuation will be required as at December 31, 2008.

The Company also maintains post-retirement benefit plans, other than pensions, covering benefits such as health and life insurance benefits for retirees. The cost of these plans is charged to earnings as benefits are earned by employees on the basis of service rendered.

Information about the Company's pension and other post-retirement benefit plans, measured at November 30, 2007 and 2006, respectively, is as follows:

	2007		2006	
	Pension Plans	Other Benefit Plans	Pension Plans	Other Benefit Plans
Fair value of plan assets				
Fair value of plan assets, beginning of period	$ 75,825 $	– $	67,718 $	–
Actual return on plan assets	3,164	–	7,043	–
Company contribution	4,735	491	4,237	344
Participant contributions	1,042	–	958	–
Benefits paid	(4,256)	(491)	(4,131)	(344)
Fair value of plan assets, end of period	$ 80,510 $	– $	75,825 $	–
Accrued benefit obligation				
Benefit obligation, beginning of period	$ 101,024 $	4,595 $	94,393 $	4,302
Service cost	6,230	415	5,967	392
Interest cost	4,198	256	3,722	245
Participant contributions	1,042	–	958	–
Plan amendments	(248)	–	–	–
Actuarial (gain) loss	(7,366)	–	115	–
Benefits paid	(4,256)	(491)	(4,131)	(344)
Accrued benefit obligation, end of period	$ 100,624 $	4,775 $	101,024 $	4,595
Funded status – plan deficit	$ (20,114) $	(4,775) $	(25,199) $	(4,595)
Unrecognized plan amendments	(1,507)	–	(1,708)	–
Unrecognized losses	11,149	–	17,854	–
Accrued benefit liability	$ (10,472) $	(4,775) $	(9,053) $	(4,595)

December 29, 2007 and December 30, 2006 (in thousands of dollars, except per share data)

10. Other Long-term Liabilities (continued)

The significant actuarial assumptions adopted are as follows:

	2007			2006		
	Registered Pension Plans	Non-registered Pension Plan	Other Benefit Plans	Registered Pension Plans	Non-registered Pension Plan	Other Benefit Plans
Accrued benefit obligation, end of period						
Discount rate	5.25%	2.63%	5.25%	5.00%	2.50%	5.00%
Compensation increase	4.00%	4.00%	4.00%	4.00%	4.00%	4.00%
Benefit expense for the period						
Discount rate	5.00%	2.50%	5.00%	5.00%	2.50%	5.00%
Expected return on assets	7.50%	3.75%	N/A	7.50%	3.75%	N/A
Compensation increase	4.00%	4.00%	4.00%	4.00%	4.00%	4.00%

The health care cost trend rates used were 5.5% for 2007 and 2006, with 5.5% being the ultimate trend rate for later years. A 1% change in the assumed health care cost trend rate would not have a significant effect on the amounts reported for other benefit plans.

The components of the Company's pension and other post-retirement benefit plans expense are as follows:

	2007		2006	
	Pension Plans	Other Benefit Plans	Pension Plans	Other Benefit Plans
Service costs	$ 6,230	$ 415	$ 5,967	$ 392
Interest cost	4,198	256	3,722	245
Actual return on plan assets	(3,164)	–	(7,043)	–
Actuarial (gain) loss	(7,366)	–	115	–
Plan amendments	(248)	–	–	–
Costs arising from events of the period	(350)	671	2,761	637
Difference between:				
Actual and expected return on plan assets	(1,225)	–	3,295	–
Actuarial gain or loss recognized for the year and actual actuarial gain or loss on accrued benefit obligation	7,930	–	749	–
Amortization of plan amendment and actual plan amendments	(201)	–	(201)	–
Net expense	$ 6,154	$ 671	$ 6,604	$ 637

Total cash payments for employee future benefits consist of the Company's contributions to the pension plans and cash payments made directly to beneficiaries of the other benefit plans and totalled $5,226 (2006 – $4,581).

The assets of the registered pension plans consist of cash, contributions receivable and a proportionate share of a Master Trust. The assets held by the Master Trust are invested in a limited number of pooled funds, based on market values as at November 30, 2007 and 2006, respectively, as follows:

	2007	2006
Equity	58%	59%
Fixed income	41%	40%
Cash and cash equivalents	1%	1%

The assets of the non-registered plan consist of cash and investments. The investments are in pooled funds with an allocation of 60% equities and 40% bonds based on market values as at November 30, 2007 and 2006, respectively.

11. Share Capital

Authorized

Unlimited number of common shares

Unlimited number of preferred shares, issuable in series without nominal or par value

Outstanding

	2007		2006	
	Number of Common Shares	Stated Value	Number of Common Shares	Stated Value
Beginning balance	214,975,945 $	1,491,264	213,430,744 $	1,441,254
Shares issued	1,813,199	13,710	2,459,012	53,915
Shares repurchased	(682)	(5)	(913,811)	(6,192)
Repayment of share purchase loans	–	325	–	2,287
Exercised options	–	726	–	–
Ending balance	216,788,462 $	1,506,020	214,975,945 $	1,491,264

Weighted Average Shares Outstanding

December 29, 2007

Basic	216,062,811
Diluted	217,220,846

December 30, 2006

Basic	213,931,722
Diluted	216,668,141

The common shares that may be issued under the Company's stock option plans, including contingently returnable shares issued as part of those plans, have a dilutive impact on the weighted average number of shares of 1,158,035 (2006 – 2,736,420).

Individual shareholder agreements address matters related to the transfer of certain shares issued to the Company's management and Associates, including shares issued under options granted to management. In particular, each provides, subject to certain exceptions, for a general prohibition on any transfer of a member of management's or Associate's shares for a period of five years from the date that the individual entered into the shareholder agreement.

The Company has issued loans to certain key employees under a stock purchase plan to acquire common shares of the Company. The share purchase loans receivable are non-interest bearing, mature in 2008 to 2010, are subject to certain terms of repayment pursuant to a shareholders' agreement and are secured by the shares to which the loans relate. Share purchase loans are presented as a reduction in share capital and the related shares are deducted in the determination of the weighted average shares outstanding for purposes of the basic net earnings per common share calculation.

Notes to the Consolidated Financial Statements (continued)

December 29, 2007 and December 30, 2006 (in thousands of dollars, except per share data)

11. Share Capital (continued)

Normal Course Issuer Bid

During 2007, the Company did not repurchase any common shares for cancellation under its normal course issuer bid. In 2006, the Company repurchased 913,600 common shares at a cost of $41,780. Repurchases were made at market prices through the Toronto Stock Exchange.

The Company's current normal course issuer bid, which became effective September 10, 2007 and expires September 9, 2008, allows for the repurchase for cancellation of up to 5,400,000 common shares, representing 2.5% of the Company's outstanding common shares. No common shares have been repurchased under the current normal course issuer bid.

12. Stock-based Compensation

The Company established stock option plans for certain employees and its Board of Directors as described below and has reserved 20,000,000 common shares for issuance under the plans. Effective February 2007, directors are no longer eligible to participate in the stock option plan. The Company established a deferred share unit plan for non-employee directors, which plan is also described below.

In 2003, the Company adopted the guidance of accounting standard 3870, "Stock-based Compensation and Other Stock-based Payments" on a prospective basis. The guidance requires the use of the fair value method to account for stock options issued under employee and director stock option programs. The Company expensed $3,544 in 2007 (2006 – $3,492) associated with stock options issued under the employee and director plans.

If compensation expense under the fair value method of accounting had been recognized on stock options issued in 2002, the Company's net earnings for the periods ended December 29, 2007 and December 30, 2006 would have been reduced by $176 and $582, respectively. Basic and diluted earnings per share would have been unchanged for both periods.

The fair value of each option was estimated on the date of the grant using the Black-Scholes option-pricing model.

Employee Stock Option Plan

Options issued to certain employees have an exercise price per share of no less than the fair market value on the date of the option grant. These options include awards for shares that vest based on the passage of time, performance criteria, or both. Time-based options are exercisable 20% per year on the anniversary of the grant date in each of the five subsequent years. Performance-based options are exercisable 20% per year on the anniversary of the grant date in each of the five subsequent years provided that the Company achieves specified earnings-based performance targets. Performance targets not achieved are considered to be met if the performance is achieved on a cumulative basis in subsequent years. The performance-based options become fully exercisable on the ninth anniversary of the date of grant, provided that they have not otherwise been terminated, whether or not the performance targets are achieved.

Upon the termination of an optionee's employment, all unexercisable options expire immediately and exercisable options expire within 180 days of the date of termination. The plan provides that the Company may pay, in cash, certain terminated option holders the appreciated value of the options to cancel exercisable options.

Subject to certain prior events of expiry, such as the termination of the employee's employment for cause, all exercisable options expire on the tenth anniversary of the date of grant.

Notes to the Consolidated Financial Statements (continued)

December 29, 2007 and December 30, 2006 (in thousands of dollars, except per share data)

12. Stock-based Compensation (continued)

A summary of the status of the employee stock option plan and changes during the period is presented below:

	2007		2006	
	Options on Common Shares	Weighted Average Exercise Price Per Share	Options on Common Shares	Weighted Average Exercise Price Per Share
Outstanding, beginning of period	2,916,450 $	15.30	4,015,825 $	9.65
Granted	–	–	350,000	46.32
Exercised	(1,773,199)	7.82	(1,412,277)	6.71
Forfeited/Cancelled including repurchased	(14,191)	29.64	(37,098)	22.83
Outstanding, end of period	1,129,060 $	26.88	2,916,450 $	15.30
Options exercisable, end of period	753,125 $	19.25	2,206,468 $	9.37

	2007 Outstanding Options			2007 Exercisable Options	
Range of Exercise Price	Number of Options Outstanding	Weighted Average Contractual Life (Years)	Weighted Average Exercise Price Per Share	Number of Exercisable Options	Weighted Average Exercise Price Per Share
$ 5.00 – $ 5.60	298,900	3.6 $	5.44	298,900 $	5.44
$17.13 – $24.84	253,600	4.4	22.17	240,885	22.09
$25.86 – $26.57	59,334	5.7	26.04	44,501	26.04
$29.30 – $36.41	167,226	6.4	31.90	98,839	31.87
$46.32	350,000	8.7	46.32	70,000	46.32
	1,129,060	5.9 $	26.88	753,125 $	19.25

Director Stock Option Plan

Prior to February 2007, under the Company's director stock option plan, participating directors were issued time-based options to purchase 60,000 common shares. The options have an exercise price per share at fair market value on the date of the option grant, which is normally the date the optionee becomes a director. One-third of the options become exercisable in each of the following three years on the anniversary of the date of grant. Unexercisable options expire upon the optionee ceasing to be a director. Exercisable options expire on the earlier of 180 days of the optionee ceasing to be a director or the expiry date of the options, which is on the tenth anniversary of the date of grant.

A summary of the status of the director stock option plan and changes during the period is presented below:

	2007		2006	
	Options on Common Shares	Weighted Average Exercise Price Per Share	Options on Common Shares	Weighted Average Exercise Price Per Share
Outstanding, beginning of period	460,000 $	37.66	420,000 $	29.93
Granted	–	–	180,000	44.02
Exercised	(40,000)	34.14	(120,000)	20.74
Cancelled	–	–	(20,000)	34.14
Outstanding, end of period	420,000 $	37.99	460,000 $	37.66
Options exercisable, end of period	260,000 $	34.63	200,000 $	30.28

12. Stock-based Compensation (continued)

| | 2007 Outstanding Options | | | 2007 Exercisable Options | |
Range of Exercise Price	Number of Options Outstanding	Weighted Average Contractual Life (Years)	Weighted Average Exercise Price Per Share	Number of Exercisable Options	Weighted Average Exercise Price Per Share
$23.35 – $26.95	120,000	5.2 $	25.15	120,000 $	25.15
$41.80	120,000	7.6	41.80	80,000	41.80
$44.02	180,000	8.1	44.02	60,000	44.02
	420,000	7.1 $	37.99	260,000 $	34.63

Deferred Share Unit Plan for Non-employee Directors

The Company maintains a deferred share unit ("DSU") plan to provide directors with the option to elect to receive DSUs in lieu of cash payment for all or a portion of their director fees. When such an election is made, the Company credits to the account of each director a number of DSUs (each equivalent in value to a common share) equal to the amount of fees divided by the fair market value of the common shares. The directors' accounts shall be credited with dividend equivalents in the form of additional DSUs if and when the Company pays dividends on the common shares. Upon the director ceasing to be a member of the Board of Directors, the director shall receive a cash amount equal to the number of DSUs in his or her account multiplied by the fair market value of the common shares on the date the director ceases to be a member of the Board of Directors or on a later date selected by the director, which shall in any event be a date prior to the end of the following calendar year. During 2007, the Company issued an aggregate of 15,635 DSUs (2006 – 9,689) and recorded $788 (2006 – $464) in director fee compensation.

Long-term Incentive Plan

The Company maintains a long-term incentive plan ("LTIP") for certain employees, which was initiated in 2006. Under the LTIP, the employees are eligible to receive an award of share units equivalent in value to common shares of the Company.

During 2007, the Company awarded 100,172 share units (2006 – 147,403), cumulatively totalling 247,575 share units, which vest one-third each year. 194,837 units were outstanding as at December 29, 2007 and 138,564 units were outstanding at December 30, 2006; the difference between share units awarded and outstanding was due to forfeitures of units by employees leaving the program before share units were vested. During 2007, the Company recognized compensation expense of $3,669 (2006 – $3,308) associated with the share units.

The liability associated with the share units earned by the employees under the LTIP is recorded in other long-term liabilities and is carried at the market value of the Company's shares at the end of the period.

The Company has entered into cash-settled equity forward agreements to limit its exposure to future price changes in the Company's share price for share unit awards. These agreements mature in December 2008 and December 2009. A percentage of the equity forward derivatives, related to unearned units under the LTIP, have been designated as a hedge.

13. Net Change in Non-cash Working Capital Balances

	2007	2006
Accounts receivable	$ (64,527) $	(38,227)
Inventory	(205,400)	(146,515)
Prepaid expenses	(8,756)	(2,904)
Accounts payable and accrued liabilities	147,267	130,795
Income taxes payable	(6,281)	30,300
	$ (137,697) $	(26,551)

14. Contingencies, Commitments and Guarantees

Obligations under Operating Leases

The minimum lease payments on a calendar year basis under long-term leases for store locations and office space are as follows:

	2008	2009	2010	2011	2012	Thereafter
Total lease obligations	$ 273,762	$ 288,797	$ 282,250	$ 262,046	$ 245,254	$ 1,823,171

Distribution Services

The Company has entered into an agreement with a third party to provide distribution services to the Company's locations to December 31, 2009. Under the terms of this agreement, the third party will charge the Company specified costs incurred to provide the distribution services, plus an annual management fee.

Information Services

During 2004 the Company entered into a five-year agreement to outsource certain information services activities to a third party. The Company has committed to average annual payments of approximately $7,000 over the term of the agreement.

Financing Trust

The Company has an arrangement for its Associates to obtain additional financing from an independent trust (the "Trust"). This arrangement was created to provide loans to facilitate the Associates' purchase of inventory and fund their working capital requirements. The Trust's activities are financed through the issuance of short-term, asset-backed notes to third-party investors.

The Company has arranged for a standby letter of credit for the benefit of the Trust from a syndicate of banks that is equal to approximately 10% of the aggregate principal amount of the loans, or $50,000, as a form of credit enhancement which, in turn, enables the Trust to provide favourable financing terms to the Company's Associates.

If at any time the Trust's cost of borrowing and applicable fees are greater than the interest rate charged to Associates on their loans, the Trust has the right to request payment from the Company for any shortfall. In the opinion of the Company's management, the Company is unlikely to have to make any such payment as it is involved in setting the rate that Associates are charged on their loans. In the event that an Associate defaults on a loan from the Trust, the Company has the right to purchase the Associate's loan from the Trust, at which time the Company is assigned the Associate's debt instrument and related security documentation provided to the Trust. The assignment of this documentation would provide the Company with first-priority security over the Associate's inventory, subject to certain prior-ranking statutory claims. The Company expects that the net proceeds from secured assets would cover any payments made to purchase a defaulted loan from the Trust, including any related expenses, as it is involved in setting the amount borrowed from the Trust by its Associates. In the event that the Company does not elect to purchase a defaulted loan from the Trust, the Trust may draw upon the standby letter of credit or realize on its security. If the Trust draws against the standby letter of credit, the Company has agreed to reimburse the issuing syndicate of banks for the amount so drawn.

The Company has determined that the Trust is a VIE and the Company is the primary beneficiary. As such, the Trust is subject to consolidation by the Company. The impact of consolidating the Trust is the reclassification of Associate loans payable to the Trust to commercial paper issued by the Trust to third parties. As at December 29, 2007, $499,350 (2006 – $453,550) of the consolidated commercial paper balance is commercial paper issued by the Trust.

Litigation

The Company has indemnified Imperial Tobacco Canada Limited for all legal claims against the Company for the period prior to February 4, 2000. In addition, the Company is involved in certain legal claims arising in the normal course of business.

14. Contingencies, Commitments and Guarantees (continued)

In the opinion of the Company's management, the eventual settlement of such claims will not have a significant effect on the Company's financial position or results of operations. Management has recorded a provision for these claims based on its best estimate of the final settlements.

Other

In the normal course of business, the Company enters into significant commitments for the purchase of goods and services, such as the purchase of inventory or capital assets, most of which are short-term in nature and are settled under normal trade terms.

The Company is involved in and potentially subject to various claims by third parties arising out of its business including, but not limited to, product liability, labour and employment, regulatory and environmental claims. In addition, the Company is subject to regular audits from federal and provincial tax authorities relating to income, capital and commodity taxes and as a result of these audits, may receive reassessments. While income, capital and commodity tax filings are subject to audits and reassessments, management believes that adequate provisions have been made for all income and other tax obligations. However, changes in the interpretations or judgements may result in an increase or decrease in the Company's income, capital, or commodity tax provisions in the future. The amount of any such increase or decrease cannot be reasonably estimated.

15. Financial Instruments

Interest Rate Derivatives

In December 2005, the Company entered into interest rate derivative agreements converting an aggregate notional principal amount of $250,000 of floating rate commercial paper debt issued by the Trust into fixed rate debt. The fixed rates payable by the Company under these agreements range from 4.03% to 4.18%. These agreements mature as follows: $150,000 in December 2008, $50,000 in December 2009 and $50,000 in December 2010, with reset terms from one to three months.

Based on market values at December 29, 2007, the Company has recognized an asset of $428 in other assets related to the interest rate derivative agreements. During the year ended December 29, 2007, the Company assessed that the interest rate derivatives were an effective hedge for the floating interest rates on the associated commercial paper debt. Market values were determined based on information received from the Company's counterparties to these agreements.

Equity Forward Derivatives

The Company uses cash-settled equity forward agreements to limit its exposure to future price changes in the Company's share price for share unit awards under the Company's LTIP. The income and expense arising from the use of these instruments are included in cost of goods sold and other operating expenses for the year.

Based on market values at December 29, 2007, the Company has recognized an asset of $332 in other assets related to the equity forward agreements. During the year ended December 29, 2007, the Company assessed that the percentage of the equity forward derivatives related to unearned units under the LTIP were an effective hedge for the common share price of the unearned units. Market values were determined based on information received from the Company's counterparties to these agreements.

Interest Rate Risk

Changes in underlying interest rates will result in market gains and losses associated with the Company's interest rate derivative agreements.

15. Financial Instruments (continued)

Counterparty Risk

The Company may be exposed to losses should any counterparty to its derivative agreements fail to fulfill its obligations. The Company has sought to minimize counterparty risk by transacting with counterparties that are large international financial institutions. The maximum exposure at December 29, 2007 was equal to the carrying value of the derivative agreements of $760.

Credit Risk

The Company has credit risk associated with accounts receivable. The risk of collection is mitigated since these balances have been billed primarily to governments and third-party drug plans. There is no concentration of balances with debtors in the remaining accounts receivable.

Liquidity Risk

The Company has the following sources of liquidity: (i) cash provided by operating activities; (ii) cash available from a committed $550,000 revolving bank credit facility maturing June 6, 2011, less what is currently drawn and/or being utilized to support commercial paper issued and outstanding; and (iii) up to $300,000 in availability under its commercial paper program, less what is currently issued.

The Company believes that its current credit facilities, commercial paper program and financing programs available to its Associates, together with cash generated from operating activities, will be sufficient to fund its operations, including the operations of its Associate-owned store network, investing activities and commitments for the foreseeable future. The Company does not foresee any difficulty in obtaining long-term financing given its current credit ratings and past experiences in the capital markets.

Fair Value of Financial Instruments

The fair value of a financial instrument is the estimated amount that the Company would receive or pay to settle the financial assets and financial liabilities as at the reporting date.

The fair values of cash, accounts receivable, bank indebtedness, commercial paper, accounts payable and dividends payable approximate their carrying values given their short-term maturities. The fair values of long-term receivables, long-term liabilities and long-term debt approximate their carrying values given the current market rates associated with these instruments.

The fair value of the interest rate and equity forward derivatives, as noted above, is determined based on current market rates and on information received from the Company's counterparties to these agreements.

Specimen Financial Statements: The Jean Coutu Group (PJC) Inc.

The
Jean Coutu
Group (PJC) Inc.

In this appendix, we illustrate current financial reporting using the financial statements of Jean Coutu, one of Canada's leading drugstore chains.

The financial statement package includes the auditors' report shown below in addition to statements of earnings, statements of comprehensive income, statements of changes in shareholders' equity, balance sheets, and cash flow statements. The notes to the financial statements are not included in this appendix, but can be found in Jean Coutu's annual report in the Annual Reports section of the Kimmel website.

We encourage students to use these financial statements in conjunction with relevant material in the textbook, and to solve the Comparative Analysis cases in the Broadening Your Perspective section of the end of chapter material.

Tutorials
(Annual Report Walkthrough)

Auditors' Report

To the Shareholders of
The Jean Coutu Group (PJC) Inc.

We have audited the consolidated balance sheets of The Jean Coutu Group (PJC) Inc. (the "Company") as at March 1st, 2008 and June 4, 2007 and the consolidated statements of earnings, retained earnings, comprehensive income and cash flows for the years then ended. These financial statements are the responsibility of the Company's management. Our responsibility is to express an opinion on these financial statements based on our audits.

We conducted our audits in accordance with Canadian generally accepted auditing standards. Those standards require that we plan and perform an audit to obtain reasonable assurance whether the financial statements are free of material misstatement. An audit includes examining, on a test basis, evidence supporting the amounts and disclosures in the financial statements. An audit also includes assessing the accounting principles used and significant estimates made by management, as well as evaluating the overall financial statement presentation.

In our opinion, these consolidated financial statements present fairly, in all material respects, the financial position of the Company as at March 1st, 2008 and June 4, 2007 and the results of its operations and its cash flows for the years then ended in accordance with Canadian generally accepted accounting principles.

/s/ Deloitte & Touche, L.L.P.

Chartered Accountants

April 28, 2008

THE JEAN COUTU GROUP (PJC) INC.

Consolidated statements of earnings

For the fiscal years ended March 1, 2008 and June 4, 2007	2008	2007
(in millions of Canadian dollars, unless otherwise noted)	$	$
	(Note 1b)	(Note 1b)
Sales	**1,507.6**	13,031.7
Other revenues (Note 3)	**168.7**	233.7
	1,676.3	13,265.4
Operating expenses		
Cost of goods sold	**1,370.0**	10,040.5
General and operating expenses	**139.6**	2,622.3
Restructuring charges (Note 4)	**-**	61.6
Amortization (Note 5)	**11.7**	75.4
	1,521.3	12,799.8
Operating income	**155.0**	465.6
Financing expenses (Note 6)	**5.1**	243.3
Adjustment to gain (gain) on sale of the retail sales segment (Note 4)	**4.2**	(144.1)
Loss on early debt retirement (Note 13)	**-**	178.9
Earnings before the following items	**145.7**	187.5
Share of loss from investments subject to significant influence	**393.3**	-
Income taxes (Note 7)	**3.8**	25.0
Net earnings (loss)	**(251.4)**	162.5
Earnings (loss) per share, in dollars (Note 8)		
Basic	**(0.98)**	0.62
Diluted	**(0.98)**	0.62

Consolidated statements of comprehensive income

For the fiscal years ended March 1, 2008 and June 4, 2007	2008	2007
(in millions of Canadian dollars)	$	$
	(Note 1b)	(Note 1b)
Net earnings (loss)	**(251.4)**	162.5
Other comprehensive income (loss)		
Foreign currency translation adjustments	**(97.9)**	148.3
Income taxes on the above item	**15.7**	0.6
	(82.2)	148.9
Comprehensive income (loss)	**(333.6)**	311.4

The segmented information and the accompanying notes are an integral part of these consolidated financial statements.

THE JEAN COUTU GROUP (PJC) INC.

Consolidated statements of changes in shareholders' equity

For the fiscal years ended March 1, 2008 and June 4, 2007	2008	2007
(in millions of Canadian dollars)	$	$
	(Note 1b)	(Note 1b)
Capital stock, beginning of year	**789.6**	787.5
Redemption of stock	**(74.7)**	-
Options exercised	**0.5**	2.1
Capital stock, end of year	**715.4**	789.6
Contributed surplus, beginning of year	**4.8**	2.9
Stock-based compensation cost	**2.2**	1.9
Stock-based compensation from investment subject to significant influence - Rite Aid	**9.7**	-
Contributed surplus, end of year	**16.7**	4.8
Retained earnings, beginning of year	**1,319.7**	1,188.6
Impact of the adoption of new accounting standards (Note 2b)	**(4.5)**	-
Net earnings (loss)	**(251.4)**	162.5
	1,063.8	1,351.1
Dividends	**(30.7)**	(31.4)
Excess of purchase price over carrying value of Class A subordinate voting shares acquired	**(102.3)**	-
Retained earnings, end of year	**930.8**	1,319.7
Accumulated other comprehensive income (loss), beginning of year (Note 2b)	**(96.6)**	(245.5)
Foreign currency translation adjustments, net of income taxes	**(82.2)**	148.9
Accumulated other comprehensive income (loss), end of year	**(178.8)**	(96.6)
Total shareholders' equity	**1,484.1**	2,017.5

The segmented information and the accompanying notes are an integral part of these consolidated financial statements.

THE JEAN COUTU GROUP (PJC) INC.

Consolidated balance sheets

(in millions of Canadian dollars)	As at March 1, 2008 $ (Note 1b)	As at June 4, 2007 $ (Note 1b)
Assets		
Current assets		
Cash and cash equivalents	-	40.7
Accounts receivable	167.5	162.6
Income taxes receivable	0.4	0.4
Inventories	154.7	138.0
Prepaid expenses	5.2	7.6
	327.8	349.3
Investments (Note 9)	1,143.2	1,597.8
Capital assets (Note 10)	329.3	319.4
Goodwill (Note 11)	35.3	20.0
Other long-term assets (Note 12)	113.7	50.2
	1,949.3	2,336.7
Liabilities		
Current liabilities		
Accounts payable and accrued liabilities	201.7	259.1
Income taxes payable	62.9	22.8
Current portion of long-term debt (Note 13)	2.0	0.6
	266.6	282.5
Long-term debt (Note 13)	169.5	7.4
Other long-term liabilities (Note 14)	29.1	29.3
	465.2	319.2
Shareholders' equity		
Capital stock (Note 15)	715.4	789.6
Contributed surplus	16.7	4.8
Retained earnings	930.8	1,319.7
Accumulated other comprehensive income (loss) (Note 16)	(178.8)	(96.6)
	752.0	1,223.1
	1,484.1	2,017.5
	1,949.3	2,336.7

Guarantees, contingencies and commitments (Notes 18 and 19).

The segmented information and the accompanying notes are an integral part of these consolidated financial statements.

Approved by the Board

/s/ François J. Coutu

/s/ L. Denis Desautels

François J. Coutu
Director

L. Denis Desautels
Director

THE JEAN COUTU GROUP (PJC) INC.

Consolidated statements of cash flows

For the fiscal years ended March 1, 2008 and June 4, 2007	2008	2007
(in millions of Canadian dollars)	$ (Note 1b)	$ (Note 1b)
Operating activities		
Net earnings (loss)	**(251.4)**	162.5
Items not affecting cash		
Amortization	**14.6**	94.7
Adjustment to gain (gain) on sale of the retail sales segment (Note 4)	**4.2**	(144.1)
Write-off of deferred financing fees (Note 13)	**-**	67.9
Change in fair value of third party asset-backed commercial paper	**7.1**	-
Share of loss from investments subject to significant influence	**393.3**	-
Future income taxes	**(29.2)**	(37.8)
Other	**(3.1)**	1.7
	135.5	144.9
Net changes in non-cash asset and liability items (Note 23)	**10.9**	47.4
Cash flow provided by operating activities	**146.4**	192.3
Investing activities		
Proceeds (adjustment to proceeds) from disposal of the retail sales segment (Note 4)	**(46.1)**	2,450.1
Investments and business acquisition	**(65.8)**	(2.2)
Purchase of capital assets	**(23.0)**	(154.1)
Proceeds from disposal of capital assets	**1.3**	9.3
Purchase of intangible assets	**-**	(2.3)
Proceeds from disposal of intangible assets	**-**	1.2
Other long-term assets	**(9.5)**	(2.4)
Cash flow provided (used) by investing activities	**(143.1)**	2,299.6
Financing activities		
Issuance of long-term debt, net of expenses	**163.9**	5.3
Repayment of long-term debt (Note 13)	**(0.6)**	(2,541.3)
Issuance of capital stock	**0.5**	2.1
Redemption of capital stock	**(177.0)**	-
Dividends	**(30.7)**	(31.4)
Cash flow used in financing activities	**(43.9)**	(2,565.3)
Effect of foreign exchange rate changes on cash and cash equivalents	**(0.1)**	(36.3)
Decrease in cash and cash equivalents	**(40.7)**	(109.7)
Cash and cash equivalents, beginning of year	**40.7**	150.4
Cash and cash equivalents, end of year	**-**	40.7

The segmented information and the accompanying notes are an integral part of these consolidated financial statements. See supplemental cash flow information in Note 23.

Photo Credits

Company Index

Subject Index *Boldface indicates key terms and definitions.*